THE MOST TRUSTED NAME IN TRAVEL

Frommer's®

JAPAN

12th Edition

By David McElhinney

FrommerMedia LLC

Frommer's Japan, 12th Edition

Published by:

FrommerMedia LLC

ISBN 978-1-62887-653-6 (paper), 978-1-62887-650-5 (ebk)

Editorial Director: Pauline Frommer
Editor: Holly Hughes
Production Editor: Heather Wilcox
Compositor: Lissa Auciello-Brogan
Cartographer: Andy Dolan
Photo Editor: Alyssa Mattei
Indexer: Kelly Henthorne
Cover Designer: Dave Riedy

Front cover photo: Woman wearing a kimono at Tsumago-juku in Nagano, Japan © Guitar photographer / Shutterstock.com

Back cover photo: Billboards in Shinjuku's Kabuki-cho district in Tokyo. The area is a nightlife district known as Sleepless Town © Luciano Mortula - LGM / Shutterstock.com

For information on our other products or services, see www.frommers.com.

FrommerMedia LLC also publishes its books in a variety of electronic formats. Some content that appears in print may not be available in electronic formats.

Manufactured in Malaysia

5 4 3 2 1

HOW TO CONTACT US

In researching this book, we discovered many wonderful places—hotels, restaurants, shops, and more. We're sure you'll find others. Please tell us about them, so we can share the information with your fellow travelers in upcoming editions. If you were disappointed with a recommendation, we'd love to know that, too. Please write to: Support@FrommerMedia.com

FROMMER'S RATINGS SYSTEM

Every hotel, restaurant and attraction listed in this guide has been ranked for quality and value. Here's what the hearts mean:

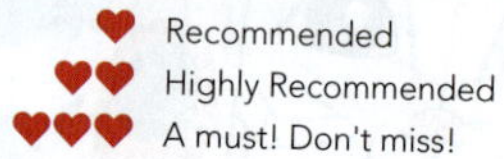

AN IMPORTANT NOTE

The world is a dynamic place. Hotels change ownership, restaurants hike their prices, museums alter their opening hours, and buses and trains change their routings. And all of this can occur in the several months after our authors have visited, inspected, and written about these hotels, restaurants, museums, and transportation services. Though we have made valiant efforts to keep all our information fresh and up-to-date, some few changes can inevitably occur in the periods before a revised edition of this guidebook is published. So please bear with us if a tiny number of the details in this book have changed. Please also note that we have no responsibility or liability for any inaccuracy or errors or omissions, or for inconvenience, loss, damage, or expenses suffered by anyone as a result of assertions in this guide.

CONTENTS

LIST OF MAPS

ABOUT THE AUTHOR

David McElhinney is a Northern Irish freelance writer, journalist, author, and editor who spent most of his 20s living in and writing about Japan. Since arriving in Tokyo in 2018, he has found Japan to be a continuous source of inspiration, which (he hopes) is reflected in the pages that follow. His travel writing and journalism have been published in *Tokyo Weekender*, the *Japan Times*, CNN, *Lonely Planet*, Al Jazeera, the *Belfast Telegraph*, and other publications. *Frommer's Japan* is his second book, and although it was a gargantuan undertaking, there were moments when it felt like a labor of love. He would like to extend special thanks to anyone who reads these words and for the small role they are playing in keeping print media alive.

ABOUT THE FROMMER TRAVEL GUIDES

For most of the past 65 years, Frommer's has been the leading series of travel guides in North America, accounting for as many as 24% of all guidebooks sold. I think I know why.

Though we hope our books are entertaining, we nevertheless deal with travel in a serious fashion. Our guidebooks have never looked on such journeys as a mere recreation, but as a far more important human function, a time of learning and introspection, an essential part of a civilized life. We stress the culture, lifestyle, history, and beliefs of the destinations we cover, and urge our readers to seek out people and new ideas as the chief rewards of travel.

We have never shied from controversy. We have, from the beginning, encouraged our authors to be intensely judgmental, critical—both pro and con—in their comments, and wholly independent. Our only clients are our readers, and we have triggered the ire of countless prominent sorts, from a tourist newspaper we called "practically worthless" (it unsuccessfully sued us) to the many rip-offs we've condemned.

And because we believe that travel should be available to everyone regardless of their incomes, we have always been cost-conscious at every level of expenditure. Though we have broadened our recommendations beyond the budget category, we insist that every lodging we include be sensibly priced. We use every form of media to assist our readers and are particularly proud of our feisty daily website, the award-winning Frommers.com.

I have high hopes for the future of Frommer's. May these guidebooks, in all the years ahead, continue to reflect the joy of travel and the freedom that travel represents. May they always pursue a cost-conscious path, so that people of all incomes can enjoy the rewards of travel. And may they create, for both the traveler and the persons among whom we travel, a community of friends, where all human beings live in harmony and peace.

Arthur Frommer
(1929–2024)

1 THE BEST OF JAPAN

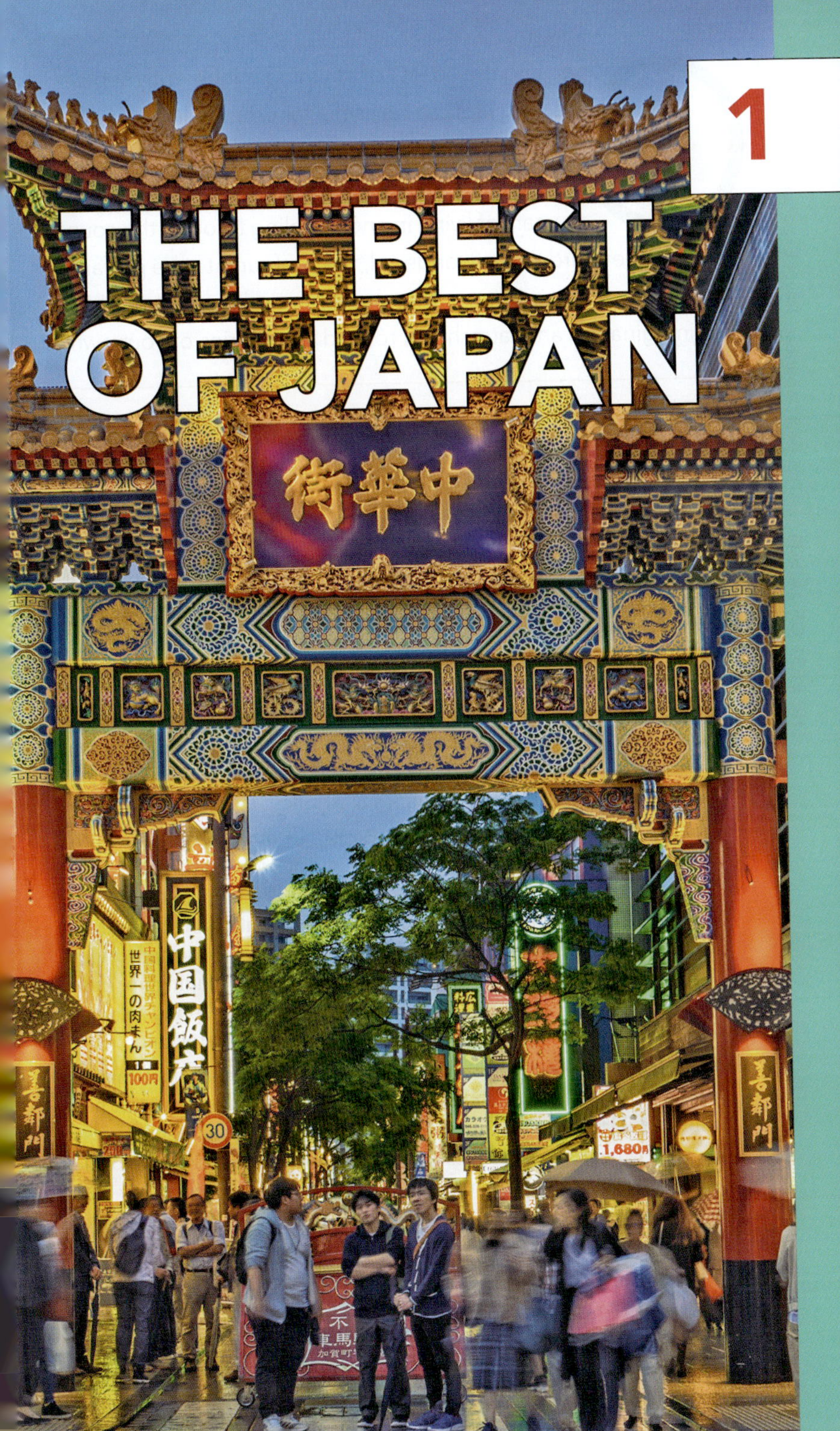

Choosing the "best" of anything is inherently subjective. Still, lists can be useful for establishing priorities. To help you get the most out of your stay, I've compiled this list of the best Japan has to offer based on years of living in and traveling through the country. From the weird to the wonderful, the profound to the profane, the obvious to the obscure, these recommendations should fire your imagination and launch you toward discoveries of your own.

THE best JAPANESE TRAVEL EXPERIENCES

- **Making a Pilgrimage to a Temple or Shrine:** From mountaintop shrines to neighborhood temples, Japan's religious structures rank among the nation's most popular attractions. Usually devoted to a particular deity or deities, they're visited for specific reasons: Shopkeepers call on Fushimi-Inari Shrine outside Kyoto, dedicated to the goddess of rice and therefore prosperity, while couples wishing for a happy marriage head to Kyoto's Jishu Shrine, a shrine to the deity of love. Shrines are connected to the Shinto faith and temples are presided over by Buddhist priests, but often they exist within the same complex, showing how Japan's two most prevalent religions are intertwined. See "The Best Temples & Shrines" below for more.
- **Taking a Communal Hot-Spring Bath:** No other people on earth bathe as enthusiastically, as frequently, and at such length as the Japanese. Their many hot-spring baths, known as *onsen,* are thought to cure all sorts of ailments as well as simply make you feel good. Whether at elegant, Zen-like facilities or rustic outdoor baths with countryside views, you'll soon warm to the ritual of soaping up, rinsing off, and then soaking in near-scalding waters. Hot-spring spas are located almost everywhere in Japan, from Kyushu to Hokkaido.
- **Celebrating a Festival:** With Shintoism and Buddhism as its major religions, and temples and shrines virtually everywhere, Japan has multiple festivals every week. Celebrations range from huge processions of wheeled floats to those featuring horseback archery and ladder-top acrobatics, and are usually lots of fun. To plan your trip around one (and book early for a hotel), see the "Japan Calendar of Events," p. 57, for a list of some of the most popular festivals.
- **Viewing the Cherry Blossoms:** Nothing symbolizes the approach of spring so vividly to Japanese as the appearance of the *sakura,* or

 PREVIOUS PAGE: Yokohama's vibrant Chinatown.

blossoms—and nothing so delights visitors as the way Japanese gather under the blossoms to celebrate the season with food, drink, and dance. This is also the busiest, and therefore most expensive, tourism period, so consider cherry blossom viewing locations outside the major cities. See the "Japan Calendar of Events," p. 57, for cherry blossom details.

A relaxing soak in the outdoor hot-spring baths at Suginoi Palace in Beppu.

- **Riding the Shinkansen Bullet Train:** The bullet train whips you across the countryside at more than 320km (199 miles) an hour as you relax, see glimpses of rural Japan, and dine on boxed meals filled with local specialties. See "Getting Around," in chapter 15, p. 686.
- **Trying Regional Foods:** There's more to Japanese cuisine than sushi, and part of what makes travel here so fascinating is the variety of dishes. Every prefecture, it seems, has its own style of noodles, its favorite vegetables, its preferred meats and seafood, and even special sweets known as *wagashi.* Thanks to the influence of Buddhism, some corners of Japan also have a deep tradition of refined vegetarian food. See "The Best Culinary Experiences," p. 57, for more on Japanese food.
- **Visiting a Local Market:** Tokyo's **Tsukiji** (p. 168) and **Toyosu Fish Markets** (p. 127) are Japan's largest, but there are local seafood and produce markets virtually everywhere, and you'd be hard pushed to

Ice sculptures dazzle the crowds at the annual Snow Festival in Sapporo.

Demons are stock characters in a traditional *kagura* performance, rooted in ancient Shinto ritual.

find one that wasn't fascinating to browse through. Among my favorites are the markets in **Kanazawa** (p. 395), **Kochi** (p. 524), **Okinawa** (p. 599), and **Hakodate** (p. 642).

- **Attending a Traditional Theater Performance:** Based on universal themes and designed to appeal to the masses, *kabuki* plays are extravaganzas of theatrical displays, costumes, and scenes—but mostly they're just plain fun. Try a performance at Tokyo's **Kabukiza Theatre** (p. 199). *Kagura,* an ancient style of theatrical dance borne out of Shinto ritual is less common, but it's one of the most enlivening (not to mention approachable) Japanese theater arts, as you'll discover at the **Tatsugozen** shrine in Yunotsu Onsen (p. 427).
- **Seeing Mount Fuji:** It may not seem like much of an accomplishment to see Japan's most famous and tallest mountain, visible from about 150km (100 miles) away. But the truth is, it's hardly ever visible, except during the winter months and rare occasions when the air is clear. Catching your first glimpse of the giant peak is truly breathtaking, whether you see it from aboard the Shinkansen, a Tokyo skyscraper, or a nearby national park. If you want to climb it (recommended only in July–Aug), be prepared for a group experience—up to 400,000 people climb Mount Fuji every summer. To ease congestion, the most popular **Yoshida Trail** now has a cap of 4,000 climbers per day and a ¥2,000 entry fee. See p. 234.

THE best OF OLD JAPAN

- **Splurging on a Night in a Ryokan:** Japan's legendary service, known as *omotenashi,* reigns supreme in a top-class *ryokan,* a traditional Japanese inn. You'll be pampered in a manner befitting an emperor; many of the nation's oldest ryokan were created to serve members of the imperial court and feudal lords as they traveled Japan's highways. Hallmarks of today's ryokans include multi-course *kaiseki* meals, bathing in a Japanese tub or hot-spring bath, and handsome *tatami* rooms with views of miniature landscaped gardens. See "Tips on Accommodations" in chapter 2 and the "Where to Stay" sections in chapters 4–14 for ryokan recommendations.
- **Attending a Sumo Match:** There's nothing quite like watching two massive sumo wrestlers square off, bluff, and grapple as they attempt to throw each other on the ground or out of the ring. Matches are true cultural events, but even if you can't attend one, you can watch them on TV during one of six annual 15-day tournaments (p. 32) or go to a performance at Tokyo's **Asakusa Sumo Club** (p. 109).
- **Admiring a Japanese Garden:** Most of Japan's famous gardens are relics of the Edo period, when the shogun, *daimyo* (feudal lords), imperial family, and even samurai and Buddhist priests developed private gardens for their own viewing pleasure. Smaller gardens in Zen temples, constructed with stones, moss and pine trees, are among Japan's most profound artistic creations, designed for viewing rather strolling through. See "The Best Gardens," p. 10, for more.

Professional sumo wrestlers square off in a match in Oshu City, in northwestern Honshu.

- **Attending a Traditional Tea Ceremony:** Developed in the 16th century as a means to achieve inner harmony with nature, the highly ritualized ceremony is carried out in teahouses throughout the country, including those set in Japan's many parks and gardens. Several Tokyo hotels, such as the **Hoshinoya Tokyo** (p. 144), the **Prince Gallery Tokyo Kioicho** (p. 155), and the **Shiba Park Hotel** (p. 160), offer English-language instruction in the tea ceremony. You can also experience the art of preparing tea in Kyoto's **Gion Corner** (p. 341) or in Kanazawa's **Higashi Chaya** district (p. 388).
- **Relaxing at a Hot-Spring Resort:** Japan has almost 30,000 hot springs, more than any other country on the planet, and hot-spring spas are beloved vacation getaways, featuring everything from hot-sand baths to open-air baths. Try to include a stop at one on your trip, whether it's the enormous **Hakone Kowaki-en Yunessun** (p. 240) in Hakone, near Mount Fuji; the charming old-world **Yunotsu Onsen** (p. 425) in western Honshu; Kyushu's **Unzen** (p. 559) or **Beppu** (p. 582), with their steaming pools known as "the Hells"; or lakeside **Akanko Onsen** (p. 669) on Hokkaido, with its Ainu village.
- **Exploring Kyoto's Higashiyama-ku District:** Kyoto's eastern sector is a lovely combination of wooded hills, temples, shrines, museums, shops, and traditional restaurants. It's one of the most touristed areas of the country, so to avoid the crowds, consider the more serene temples and shrines like the sub-temples of **Nanzenji** (p. 305) and the gardens of **Heian Shrine** (p. 301).
- **Walking to Kobo Daishi's Mausoleum on Mount Koya:** Since the 9th century, when Buddhist leader Kobo Daishi was laid to rest at Okunoin on Mount Koya, his faithful followers have followed him to their graves—and now tomb after tomb lines a 1.5km (1-mile) pathway to Daishi's mausoleum. Cypress trees, moss-covered stone lanterns, and thousands upon thousands of tombs make this the most impressive graveyard stroll in Japan, especially at night. See p. 397.
- **Wandering the Forests of Yakushima:** Yakushima is the closest thing you'll find to Japan before civilization and

Kyoto's Higashiyama district is like a window into the past, with its narrow winding streets lined with traditional wooden buildings.

rampant industrialization. A UNESCO-protected moss forest engulfs this island adrift in the Pacific, full of ancient *yakusugi* trees (Japanese cedar, also known as *cryptomeria japonica*) and rich in folklore and mythology. See p. 572.

THE best OF MODERN JAPAN

- **Viewing Tokyo from Above:** On the 45th floor of the **Tokyo Metropolitan Government Office** (p. 116), designed by legendary architect Tange Kenzo, an observatory offers a bird's-eye view of Shinjuku's cluster of skyscrapers, the never-ending metropolis, and, on fine winter days, Mount Fuji. Best of all, it's free. Alternatively, you can buy a ticket to ascend the world's tallest free-standing tower, **Tokyo SkyTree** (p. 126) to see the capital sprawling near-endlessly across the Kanto Plain.

Tokyo's immersive art installation *Borderless* is just one of several mind-blowing teamLab projects around Japan.

- **Visiting a Modern Art Museum:** Japan's modern art museums land on a wide spectrum. Some embody minimalism and Zen principles (the **D.T. Suzuki Museum** in Kanazawa, p. 387), some celebrate Japan's artistic pioneers (the **Yayoi Kusama Museum,** p. 115, or **Studio Ghibli,** p. 121, in Tokyo), and others focus on immersion and interactivity (**teamLab** museums throughout Japan—see pp. 119 and 124). Some even were launched to reinvigorate aging regions, like the stellar **Art Islands of Shikoku** (p. 497), or the **Towada Art Center** in Aomori (p. 625). Pencil at least one of these onto your itinerary.
- **Spending an Evening in an Entertainment District:** A spin through one of Japan's famous nightlife districts, such as **Shinjuku** (p. 203) or **Shibuya** (p. 202) in Tokyo, **Dotonbori** or **Shinsekai** in Osaka (p. 478), **Susukino** in Sapporo (p. 659), or **Shianbashi** in Nagasaki (p. 562) is a colorful way to rub elbows with the natives as you explore narrow streets with their whirls of neon, tiny hole-in-the-wall bars and restaurants, and all-night amusement spots.
- **Shopping for Pop-Culture Merchandise:** Pop culture, in particular video games, *manga* (comics), and anime is the engine of Japan's relentless soft power juggernaut. Visit districts like **Akihabara** in

Tokyo (p. 133) or **Den Den Town** in Osaka (p. 476) to hunt for retro games, forgotten consoles, obscure manga titles, and toys and figurines depicting your favorite characters.

- **Living History in a Jazz Kissa:** Visiting a jazz café, also known as a *kissa,* is like stepping back in time to around 1965, when records where the go-to medium for entertainment and John Coltrane was all the rage. You'll find jazz kissa scattered throughout **Tokyo** (p. 207), but **Mokuba** in Kochi (p. 525) and **Bird/56** in Osaka (p. 478) are also legendary spots. Whichever you visit, grab a seat at the counter (if available), order a whiskey, and let all your troubles melt away.
- **Roadtripping in Japan:** Because the transport system is so efficient (especially on Honshu, Japan's main island), few travelers on the main tourist trail consider renting a car. But if you travel to Tohoku, Hokkaido, Shikoku, or the small islands in the south, driving is much more convenient and adds texture, freedom, and spontaneity to your journey.

THE best TEMPLES & SHRINES

- **Meiji Jingu Shrine (Tokyo):** Tokyo's most venerable and refined Shinto shrine honors Emperor Meiji and his empress with simple yet dignified architecture surrounded by a dense forest. This is a great refuge in the heart of the city. See p. 117.
- **Sensoji Temple (Tokyo):** The capital's oldest temple is also its liveliest. Throngs of visitors and stalls selling both traditional and kitschy items lend it a festival-like atmosphere. This is the most important temple to see in Tokyo. See p. 110.
- **Kotokuin Temple (Kamakura):** At this temple, you can gaze upon the Great Buddha, Japan's second-largest bronze image, sitting outdoors against a magnificent wooded backdrop. Cast in the 13th century, the Buddha's face has a wonderful expression of contentment, serenity, and compassion. See p. 222.
- **Hase Kannon Temple (Kamakura):** Although this temple is famous for its 9m-tall (30-ft.) Kannon of Mercy, the largest wooden image in Japan, it's most memorable for its thousands of small statues of Jizo, the guardian deity of children, donated by parents of miscarried, stillborn, or aborted children. It's a rather haunting vision. See p. 223.
- **Toshogu Shrine (Nikko):** Dedicated to Japan's most powerful shogun, Tokugawa Ieyasu, this World Heritage Site is the nation's most elaborate and opulent shrine, made with 2.4 million sheets of gold leaf. It's set in a forest of cedar in a national park. See p. 229.
- **Kiyomizu Temple (Kyoto):** One of Japan's best-known (and most imitated) temples, Kiyomizu commands an exalted spot on a steep hill with a view over Kyoto. The pathway leading to the shrine is

In the vast main hall of Nara's Todaiji Temple, awed visitors encounter a giant bronze Buddha flanked by two attendant bodhisattva statues.

lined with pottery and souvenir shops—and, these days, hordes of tourists. Go early to avoid the crush. See p. 302.

- **Sanjusangendo Hall (Kyoto):** Japan's longest wooden building contains the spectacular sight of more than 1,000 life-size wood-carved statues, row upon row, of the thousand-handed Kannon of Mercy. See p. 306.
- **Todaiji Temple (Nara):** Japan's largest bronze Buddha sits in what was once the largest wooden structure in the world, making it the top attraction in this former capital. While not as impressive as the Great Buddha's dramatic outdoor stage in Kamakura (see above), the sheer size of Todaiji Temple and its Buddha make this a sight not to be missed if you're in the Kansai area. See p. 355.
- **Ise Grand Shrines (Ise):** Although there's not much to see, these are the most venerated Shinto shrines in all of Japan; pilgrims have been flocking here for centuries. Amazingly, the Inner Shrine, which contains the Sacred Mirror, is razed and reconstructed on a new site every 20 years in accordance with Shinto beliefs. See p. 374.
- **Itsukushima Shrine (Miyajima):** The huge red *torii* (the traditional entry gate of a shrine), standing in the waters of the Seto Inland Sea, is one of the most photographed landmarks in Japan. Built over tidal flats on a gem of an island called Miyajima, the shrine is one of Japan's most scenic spots. See p. 445.
- **Izumo Shrine (Izumo):** This sprawling shrine complex in Izumo is one of Japan's oldest shrines; it was likely founded more than 2,000

years ago. The main deity enshrined here, Okuninushi no Okami, played an instrumental role in Japan's origin story and is considered the first ruler of the known earth. All the Shinto deities are said to gather here during the 10th month on the lunar calendar; known as *Kamiarizuki,* "Month with the Gods," in Izumo, and *Kannazuki,* "Month without the Gods," elsewhere in Japan. See p. 421.

- **Zuiganji Temple (Matsushima):** Founded in the 9th century and remodeled at the behest of powerful samurai Date Masamune in 1604, this is probably the finest temple in northeastern Honshu. Most impressive are the grottoes dug out by long-ago priests for practicing *zazen* meditation, the ornate interior's gold-plated *fusuma* (sliding doors), and a room dedicated to the samurai who were laid to rest here. See p. 611.

THE best GARDENS

- **Rikugien Garden (Tokyo):** It's not as centrally located as Tokyo's other gardens, but Rikugien stands out not only for its quintessentially Japanese setting but also because its vistas are (mostly) unmarred by surrounding skyscrapers. Created in 1702 and later donated to the city by the founder of Mitsubishi, it has a strolling path around a pond complete with islets, teahouses, and arched bridges. See p. 124.
- **Sankeien Garden (Yokohama):** Historic villas, tea arbors, a farmhouse, a pagoda, and thatched-roof buildings make this century-old landscaped refuge one of the most picturesque gardens near the capital. See p. 251.
- **Ryoanji Temple (Kyoto):** Japan's most famous Zen rock garden, laid out at the end of the 15th century, consists of moss-covered boulders and raked pebbles enclosed by an earthen wall. It is said that it's impossible to see all 15 rocks from any vantage point; see if you can. Come early in the morning to beat the crowds. See p. 308.
- **Kongobuji Temple (Koyasan):** In Koyasan, the spiritual home of esoteric Buddhism, Kongobuji Temple has the country's largest *karensansui* (dry rock garden). Known as the Garden of the Guardian Dragons, it looks like twin dragons soaring through cloudy skies and is particularly ethereal during the rainy season. See p. 400.
- **Kenrokuen Garden (Kanazawa):** Considered by some to be Japan's grandest landscape garden, Kenrokuen is also one of the largest. The garden took 150 years to complete and consists of ponds, streams, rocks, mounds, trees, grassy expanses, and footpaths. Best of all, no tall buildings detract from the views. See p. 384.
- **Adachi Museum (Yasugi):** Voted the most beautiful garden in Japan for more than 20 years in a row by *Sukiya Living* (aka *The Journal of Japanese Gardening*), this garden is a perfect example of the *shakkei*

The ethereal Garden of the Guardian Dragons at Kongobuji Temple in Koyasan is Japan's largest dry rock garden.

technique, whereby surrounding scenery is "borrowed" and used in the composition of the garden. Viewed through apertures in the museum, the garden appears as a seamless extension of the hills in the background, and changes faces throughout the seasons as though it were a living painting. See p. 420.

- **Ritsurin Garden (Takamatsu):** Dating from the 17th century, this former private retreat of the ruling Matsudaira clan is an exquisite strolling garden that incorporates Mount Shiun in its landscaping and boasts 1,400 pine trees and 350 cherry trees. See p. 490.
- **Sengan-en (Kagoshima):** Laid out more than 300 years ago by the Shimadzu clan, this summer retreat with a 25-room villa was known for its poem-composing parties, held beside a rivulet that still exists. After touring the garden and villa, be sure to visit the nearby museum with relics belonging to the Shimadzu family. See p. 567.

THE best CASTLES & VILLAS

- **Tamozawa Imperial Villa (Nikko):** Comprised of a 1632 villa and an 1899 expansion, this 106-room villa was the home of a prince who later became emperor. You can learn about traditional Japanese architecture and lifestyles of the aristocracy. Unlike Japan's other imperial villas, it does not require a reservation. See p. 231.
- **Matsumoto Castle (Matsumoto):** Popularly known as the Crow Castle due to its black color, this small castle boasts the oldest *tenshu* (keep) in Japan (more than 400 years old) and a moon-viewing room added in 1635. Exhibited inside the castle is a superb collection of Japanese matchlocks and samurai armor dating from the mid–16th century through the Edo Period. Volunteer guides stand ready for personal tours. See p. 262.

Perhaps Japan's most beautiful feudal castle, 400-year-old Himeji Castle seems to float over the town of Himeji in western Honshu.

- **Nijo Castle (Kyoto):** One of the few castles built by the mighty Tokugawa shogunate as a residence rather than for defense, Nijo Castle is famous for its nightingale (creaking) floorboards that warned of enemy intruders. The castle is considered the quintessence of Momoyama architecture. See p. 298.
- **Kyoto Imperial Palace (Kyoto):** Home to Japan's imperial family from the 14th to the 19th centuries, this palace is praised for its Heian design and graceful garden. See p. 295.
- **Himeji Castle (Himeji):** Said to resemble a white heron poised in flight over the plains, this is quite simply Japan's most beautiful castle. With its extensive gates, moats, turrets, and maze of passageways, this UNESCO World Heritage Site has survived virtually intact since feudal times. If you see only one castle in Japan, make this the one. See p. 407.
- **Matsue Castle (Matsue):** This 17th-century castle features a five-story donjon with samurai gear and artifacts belonging to the ruling Matsudaira clan, with many Edo-era attractions just outside its moat. The surrounding park is filled with herons, one of the most spiritually significant avian creatures in Japanese folklore. See p. 416.
- **Matsuyama Castle (Matsuyama):** Occupying a hill above the city, this 400-year-old fortress offers lovely views over Matsuyama from its three-story donjon as well as a collection of armor and swords of the Matsudaira clan. See p. 512.
- **Shuri Castle (Okinawa Island):** One of nine historic structures in Okinawa that collectively make up a World Heritage Site, this castle with Chinese and Japanese influences was the center of the Ryukyu Kingdom, which thrived for about 500 years. The castle was set ablaze by an electrical fault in 2019 but is set to be faithfully restored by fall 2026. See p. 593.

THE best MUSEUMS

- **Tokyo National Museum (Tokyo):** Even professed museumphobes will enjoy visiting the National Museum, the world's largest repository of Japanese arts. Lacquerware, china, kimono, samurai armor, swords, woodblock prints, religious art, and more are on display. See p. 113.
- **Hakone Open-Air Museum (Chokoku-no-Mori, Hakone):** Beautifully landscaped grounds and spectacular scenery showcase approximately 400 20th-century sculptures, from Giacomo and Rodin to Henry Moore. Here, too, is the Picasso Pavilion, housing 200 of the artist's works. See p. 241.
- **Museum Meiji Mura (Nagoya):** This open-air architectural museum is an absolute treasure, with more than 60 original Meiji Period buildings and structures situated on 100 handsomely landscaped hectares (250 acres). Western-style homes, churches, a kabuki theater, a bathhouse, a prison, a brewery, and much more are fully furnished and open for viewing. Mail a postcard from an authentic post office, buy sweets at an old candy store, and drink tea in the lobby of the original Imperial Hotel, which was designed by Frank Lloyd Wright. See p. 368.
- **D.T. Suzuki Museum (Kanazawa):** Honoring the eponymous Zen scholar and prolific essayist, who helped introduce eastern spirituality to the West, this museum is simple yet deeply profound. It's not only the best museum in Kanazawa, it's one of the most contemplative museum spaces in the country. See p. 387.
- **Ohara Museum of Art (Kurashiki):** Founded in 1930, this museum just keeps getting bigger and better, with works by both Western and Japanese greats spread throughout several buildings. Its location in the picturesque Kurashiki historic district is a bonus. See p. 411.

The Zen simplicity of the D.T. Suzuki Museum in Kanazawa pays appropriate tribute to the spiritual scholar it honors.

- **Peace Memorial Museum (Hiroshima):** Japan's most thought-provoking museum examines Hiroshima's militaristic past, the events leading up to the explosion of the world's first atomic bomb, the city's terrible destruction, and its active antinuclear movement. See p. 435.

The highland valley of Kamikochi is one of many stunning mountain areas in the Japan Alps National Park.

- **Benesse Art Site Naoshima (Takamatsu):** This island in the Seto Inland Sea is devoted to cutting-edge art, with museums designed by Japan's "King of Concrete" Tadao Ando and interactive art installations in traditional Japanese buildings. There's no other place in Japan quite like this. See p. 499.
- **teamLab Museums (Tokyo):** Digital art collective teamLab are a self-proclaimed group of "ultratechnologists," whose immersive artworks have taken the contemporary Japanese art scene by storm. Their two flagship Tokyo museums are **Borderless** (p. 119), a "museum without a map" that blurs the boundaries between the viewer and the artwork, and **Planets** (p. 124), an exploration of how we influence the composite parts of our environment. Both are quite unlike any other art spaces in Japan.
- **Dejima (Nagasaki):** Located off the coast of northern Kyushu, the manmade islet of Dejima hosted Dutch traders during the Edo period, when Japan was otherwise closed off to the outside world. Re-created on its original location—now inland due to land reclamations—Dejima today is an open-air museum illuminating this fascinating era of Japanese history. See p. 544.
- **Ghibli Museum (Tokyo):** Studio Ghibli is a household name in Japan and probably the country's best-known animation studio abroad, with award-winning films like *Spirited Away, My Neighbor Totoro, Princess Mononoke,* and *The Boy and the Heron.* Count yourself lucky if you can nab tickets (a notoriously difficult feat) to this immersive museum celebrating the studio's works and visionary creatives. See p. 121.

THE best NATIONAL PARKS

- **Nikko National Park:** This 80,000-hectare (200,000-acre) national park centers on the sumptuous Toshogu Shrine with its mausoleum for Tokugawa Ieyasu, majestic cedars, and lakeside resorts. See p. 225.

- **Fuji-Hakone-Izu National Park:** With magnificent Mount Fuji at its core, this popular weekend getaway beckons Tokyoites with its many hot-spring spas, stunning close-up views of the mountain, sparkling lakes, historic attractions (relating to the famous Tokaido Hwy.), and coastal vistas. One of the best ways to see Hakone is via a circular route that involves travel on a two-car mountain streetcar, a cable car, a ropeway, and a boat. See p. 234.
- **Japan Alps (Chubu Sangaku) National Park:** Encompassing Honshu's most impressive mountain ranges and the site of the 1998 Winter Olympics, this national park offers skiing and hiking as well as unique villages worth a visit in their own rights. See p. 274.
- **Ise-Shima National Park:** The birthplace of cultivated pearls, this park is famous for its bays dotted with oyster rafts, its female divers, a pearl museum, and some of Japan's most venerable shrines. See p. 372.
- **Seto-Naikai (Inland Sea) National Park:** Covering 650 sq. km (251 sq. miles) of water, islands, islets, and coastline, this sea park is studded with numerous islands of all sizes, the most famous of which is Miyajima, home of Itsukushima Shrine. Cruises ply the waters of the Seto Inland Sea, as do regular ferries sailing between Honshu, Shikoku, and Kyushu. The adventuresome can even cycle across the Seto Inland Sea via the Shimanami Kaido route linking Honshu with Shikoku. See p. 443.
- **Unzen-Amakusa National Park:** At western Kyushu's high-altitude national park, you can climb Mount Fugen (1,360m/4,462 ft. above sea level), relax in a hot-spring bath, and take a walk through the Hells, the park's extra-steamy sulfur springs. See p. 557.
- **Towada-Hachimantai National Park:** Tohoku's most popular park offers scenic lakes, rustic hot-spring spas, hiking, and skiing. As winter approaches, the night sky is studded with stars, appearing so close you could be convinced you're standing in a planetarium. See p. 616.
- **Akan-Mashu National Park:** Popular for hiking, skiing, canoeing, and fishing, Akan National Park in Hokkaido is characterized by dense forests of subarctic primeval trees and caldera lakes, the most famous of which are Kussharo, one of Japan's largest mountain lakes, and Mashu, considered one of Japan's least-spoiled lakes and one of the world's clearest. See p. 669.
- **Shiretoko National Park:** On a blade-shaped peninsula piercing the Sea of Okhotsk, this park is the end of Japan's world. Despite its harsh winters, Shiretoko has incredible biodiversity. Adventurous types, trekking on foot or by boat, come here to see sea eagles, Ussuri brown bears, Hokkaido sika deer, Ezo red foxes, and cetacean species like whales and dolphins in their natural habitats. See p. 676.

THE best OUTDOOR ADVENTURES

- **Climbing Mount Fuji:** Okay, so climbing Japan's tallest—3,766m-high (12,355 ft.)—and most famous mountain is not the solitary, athletic pursuit you may have envisioned. But it can still be a great, culturally enriching group activity. Climbing through the night to watch the sunrise at the top is no longer allowed, unless you book a bed in a mountain hut in advance. See p. 233.
- **Skiing in Honshu & Hokkaido:** A great destination for skiing, Japan has hosted two winter Olympics—the 1972 Games in **Sapporo** (p. 652) and the 1998 Games in **Nagano.** The Japan Alps in central Honshu (chapter 6) and the mountains of Tohoku (chapter 13) and Hokkaido (chapter 14) are popular destinations for Japan's most popular winter sport.
- **Walking the Kumano Kodo:** Walking the Kumano Kodo, a series of trails webbing the Kii Peninsula in Wakayama, was for centuries a primarily spiritual pursuit, designed to connect three grand shrines—known as the Kumano Sanzan—with Koyasan, the home of Shingon Buddhism. It still attracts pilgrims and the devout today, as well as hikers who want to see a less developed corner of Japan. See p. 403.
- **Scuba Diving & Snorkeling:** Okinawa, an archipelago of 160 subtropical islands, is blessed with coral reefs, schools of manta rays, and operators offering excursions for all levels, not to mention some of the best dive spots in the world. See chapter 12.
- **Trekking the Michinoku Coastal Trail:** The Michinoku Coastal Trail runs almost the entire length of eastern Tohoku, making it one of Japan's longest trekking routes at 1,025km (637 miles). From wildlife-filled forests and thunderous seascapes to knotted coastal features and villages lost to time, this is the Japan less traveled. See p. 628.

Swimming with manta rays in the coral reefs of the Okinawa archipelago.

THE best CULINARY EXPERIENCES

- **Experiencing a Kaiseki Feast:** Consisting of a variety of exquisitely prepared and arranged dishes, a kaiseki meal is a multicourse event to be savored slowly. Both the ingredients and the dishes they comprise are chosen with great care to complement the season. For an unforgettable meal, try **Saryo Ichimatsu** in Tokyo (p. 169), **Hyotei** in Kyoto (p. 333), or **Juppo** in Osaka (p. 471)—or spend the night at any of the **traditional ryokan** recommended in this book that offer kaiseki as part of their guest package.

Wherever you travel in Japan, you'll find delicious local ramen variations.

- **Spending an Evening in a Robatayaki:** Harking back to the olden days when Japanese cooked over an open fireplace, a *robatayaki* is a convivial place for a protein-centric meal and alcoholic drinks. They're especially prevalent in Hokkaido—see chapter 14 for suggestions.
- **Slurping Noodles in a Noodle Shop:** You're supposed to slurp *audibly* when eating Japanese noodles, which are prepared in almost as many different ways as there are regions. Compare the ramen in **Tokyo Station's ramen alley** (p. 166) to the Hakata-style ramen shops in **Fukuoka** (p. 540), the Menbaka Fire ramen in **Kyoto** (p. 331), or the miso ramen in **Sapporo's ramen alley** (p. 656). And Yokohama even has not one but two museums devoted to ramen, the **Cup Noodles Museum** (p. 252) and the **Shin-Yokohama Ramen Museum** (p. 255).
- **Dining on Michelin-Starred Fare:** You'd be forgiven for thinking Michelin-starred cuisine refers only to exclusive sushi haunts with years-long waiting lists or boutique-y restaurants where every solid item has been whipped into a puree or turned into foam. But Japan typically has several hundred restaurants holding at least one Michelin star—the number changes every year—including affordable grilled chicken joints and tempura shops that prove deep-frying can also be an artform. Some of my favorites: **DEN** (p. 180) and **Florilège** (p. 177) in Tokyo, and **Hyotei** (p. 333) in Kyoto.

- **Taking a Cooking Class:** With Japanese food now arguably at the center of the global culinary world, English-language cooking classes on how to prepare everything from sushi and ramen to *sukiyaki* hot-pots and *teishoku* (meals with side dishes) are popping up all over the place. My advice: Cook something with ingredients you can replicate back home.
- **Sampling the Fare in a Fish Market:** Fish markets are the pulsing heart of many town centers each morning, and they're great places to try the local seafood. Tokyo's **Tsukiji** (p. 168) and **Toyosu** (p. 127) markets are legendary, but don't stop there—check out Omicho Market in **Kanazawa** (p. 393), the seafood markets in **Naha** on Okinawa Island (p. 601), or the Hakodate Morning Market in **Hakodate** on Hokkaido (p. 642). From snow crabs in Hokkaido to *umi budo* ("sea grapes") in Okinawa, you'll find a lot more than just salmon, prawns, and tuna.

THE best SHOPPING DESTINATIONS

- **For Everything:** Japanese department stores are microcosms of practically everything Japan produces, from the food halls in the basement to the departments selling clothing, accessories, office supplies, souvenirs, pottery, household goods, and cameras, to rooftop garden centers. Service is great and purchases are beautifully wrapped—you'll be spoiled for life. In Tokyo, **Mitsukoshi** (p. 188) and **Parco** (p. 189) are not to be missed, but don't overlook the biggest of them all, Osaka's **Kintetsu Abeno Harukas** (p. 475).
- **For Designer Fashions:** Tokyo's **Shibuya** (p. 194) has the most designer boutiques in town, while **Aoyama** (p. 185) and **Omotesando** (p. 184) host main shops for all the big-name designers, including Issey Miyake, Comme des Garçons, Louis Vuitton, Fendi, and Prada. Osaka's **Amemura** neighborhood (p. 475) is full of trendy clothing shops selling Japanese and Korean streetwear. Department stores also carry big-name designers; their annual summer sales are mob scenes.
- **For Souvenirs:** Japanese are avid souvenir shoppers when they travel, so souvenirs are sold literally everywhere, even near shrines and temples. **Nakamise Dor** (p. 191), a pedestrian lane leading to Tokyo's Sensoji Temple, is one of Japan's most colorful places to shop for paper umbrellas, toys, and other souvenirs. The two best places for one-stop memento shopping are **Ichibangai** (p. 166), a basement shopping street in Tokyo Station, and the **Kyoto Handicraft Center** (p. 338).

- **For Traditional Crafts:** Japan treasures its artisans so highly that it designates the best as National Living Treasures. Top spots include **Japan Traditional Crafts Aoyoma Square** in Tokyo (p. 192), the **Kyoto Handicraft Center** in Kyoto (p. 338), and the **Ishikawa Prefectural Products Center** in Kanazawa (p. 395), which offer varied inventories of everything from knives and baskets to lacquerware and pottery. Department stores also offer an excellent collection of traditional crafts.
- **For Antiques & Curios:** At Japan's flea markets you'll see everything from used kimono to Edo-era teapots for sale. Japan's largest market is held the 21st of each month at **Toji Temple** in Kyoto (p. 339). **Tokyo** also has great weekend markets.

For electronics or pop culture collectibles, head for Tokyo's Akihibara district or Osaka's Den Den Town.

- **For Electronics & Pop-Culture Merchandise:** Looking for that perfect digital camera, MP3 player, rice cooker, video game, or anime figure? Then join everyone else in the country by going to one of the nation's two largest electronics and electrical-appliance districts. In Tokyo's Akihabara district, where open-fronted shops beckon up to 50,000 weekday shoppers with whirring fans, blaring radios, and sales pitches, **Yodobashi Akiba** (p. 194) is by many estimations the largest store of its kind in the world. In Osaka, just north of Den Den Town, you'll find a huge branch of **Bic Camera** (p. 193). Be sure to comparison-shop and bargain!

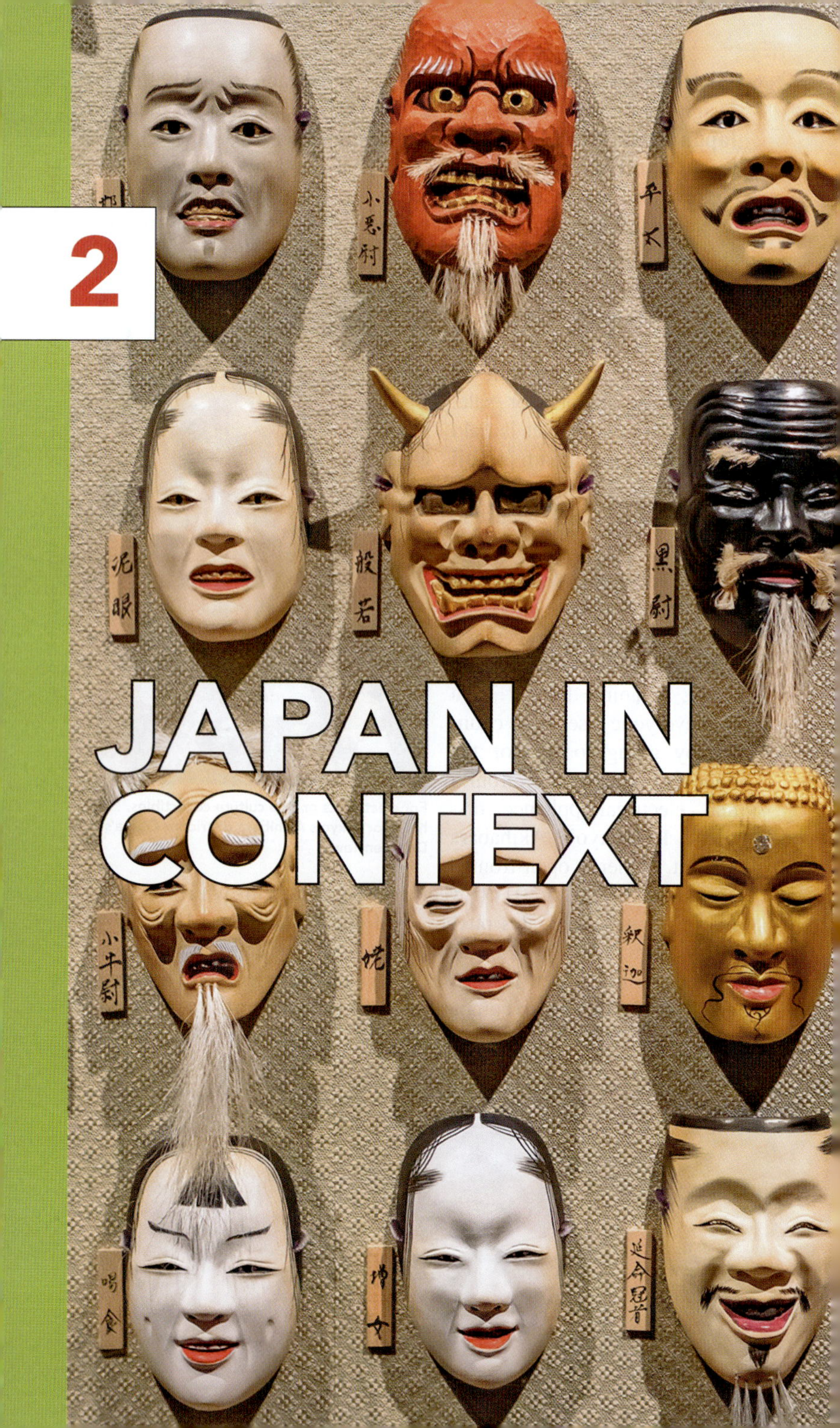

2

JAPAN IN CONTEXT

Hardly a day goes by when you don't hear something new about Japan, whether the subject is travel and overtourism, traditional Japanese cuisine (placed on UNESCO's Intangible Cultural Heritage list since 2013), the contemporary arts scene, the booming popularity of manga and *anime,* or a yen that's plummeted like a bird diving for prey. Yet this dynamic Asian nation remains something of an enigma to people in the Western world. What best encapsulates Japan? Is it the land of cutting-edge cars and customer service robots? Or is it the land of geisha and bonsai, the punctilious tea ceremony, and the delicate art of flower arranging? Has it become, in its outlook and pop culture, a country more Western than Asian? Or has it retained its ancient traditions and inherently Japanese sensibilities, while carving out its own space in the post-industrialized world?

Japan eludes easy definition. Its cities may look Westernized—often disappointingly so—but once you move beyond first impressions, very little about this Asian nation could lull you into thinking you're in the West. In fact, Japan has long adopted the best of the West (and the East, for that matter) and then adapted it to its own needs. That modern high-rise may look Western, but inside you might find a rustic-looking restaurant with open charcoal grills, corporate offices, a pachinko parlor, a cocktail bar with surreal city views, a McDonald's, an acupuncture clinic, a computer showroom, and a rooftop shrine. This unique synthesis of East and West has produced a culture that is distinctly Japanese.

Japan also differs greatly from its Asian neighbors, mostly because the island remained steadfastly isolated from the rest of the world throughout much of its history, usually deliberately so.

Discovering Japan today is like peeling an onion—you uncover one layer only to find more layers underneath. Thus, no matter how long you stay in Japan, you never stop learning something new—and that constant discovery is one of the most fascinating aspects of being here.

JAPAN TODAY

It was already happening before the pandemic, when Japan's draconian border controls brought inbound travel to a halt. But it's impossible to argue now: Japan's tourism boom has become a double-edged sword. In

FACING PAGE: **A display of Noh theater masks by contemporary artist Hidetomo Kimura.**

2024, almost 37 million people traveled to Japan, breaking the record for the highest number of inbound visitors in a calendar year, and resuming a trend that had steadily risen from 2012 to 2019. After cars, tourism is now Japan's second largest export, contributing trillions of yen to the economy each year. Rural destinations fortunate enough to have attracted some of the business, like Shirakawa-go, Kyotango, and Yakushima, are experiencing renaissances despite their aging populations, low productivity, and brain drain to the major cities.

Travel in Japan is also easier now than ever before, with more information in English and other foreign languages, from bus schedules to signage. The services and infrastructure to accommodate visitors have greatly improved, too, including more frequent runs of rural buses, more inexpensive guesthouses, longer hours for tourist information offices, and an emphasis on employing English-speaking staff in hotels and at attractions. That said, spoken English-language proficiency in Japan is still poor by both Asian and developed-country standards.

The flip side of the travel boom: Tourists, despite pleas and protestations from within Japan's travel industry, still flock to the most popular destinations and sites. This has caused bottlenecks in Kyoto, some historic quarters of Tokyo, and even in national parks like Fuji-Hakone-Izu, which are difficult for local authorities to manage. It's also been coupled with increased reports of "bad behavior," like camera-wielding tourists chasing geisha through the streets of Kyoto or brainless individuals defiling the walls of ancient temples. "Overtourism" stories get a lot of media attention and stir up anti-foreign sentiment in some quarters of Japan. At the extreme end, tourism has rendered some places almost unrecognizable, like once quiet ski villages in Nagano and Hokkaido that are now overrun with foreign money. Transportation and accommodations in the

One effect of Japan's tourism boom: Crowds often overwhelm the most popular sights, such as Sensoji Temple (p. 110) in central Tokyo.

cities are more crowded than I've ever seen them, especially during peak seasons like cherry-blossom time in spring and autumn leaf-viewing, always huge tourism draws. In Kyoto, this has generated controversy as visitors clog up commuter bus routes and are generally viewed as disturbers of the peace.

All of this has been spurred by the weak yen, which, at the time of writing, is at a 40-year-low against the dollar and languishing similarly against other major Western currencies. This means Japan, once considered an expensive, luxury travel destination, is surprisingly cheap. But this might not last. Recent reports claim that Japanese hotel rates have hit an all-time high, capitalizing on high demand and improved tourist purchasing power. Restaurants and tourist sites throughout the country are considering two-tiered pricing systems, where non-residents pay a hefty tax on food or for entrance to a castle or museum. Though the rationale for such systems is usually to cover the costs of hiring English-speaking staff or to help with heritage conservation, it will be interesting to see if such taxes actually encourage travelers to explore further afield. This could greatly benefit many rural destinations that are not yet on the wider tourism radar, who need to attract more foreign visitors for their own economic survival.

That is the crux of the issue: Japan is not overtouristed country-wide. France, Italy, and Spain (all of a similar size) receive two or three times as many annual visitors as Japan does. But certain towns and cities are suffering from the endless conveyor belt of crowds and are beginning to push back. So I would encourage you to keep in mind the enriching towns, mountain villages, and untrodden hinterlands of Japan mentioned in this book. They're the places that need you.

THE HISTORY OF JAPAN

ANCIENT HISTORY (CA. 30,000 B.C.–A.D. 710) Although the exact origin of Japanese people is unknown, evidence suggests the territory of Japan was occupied as early as 30,000 B.C. According to mythology, however, Japan's history began when the sun goddess, Amaterasu, sent one of her descendants down to the island of Kyushu to unify the people of Japan. Unification, however, was not realized until a few generations later when Jimmu, the great-grandson of the goddess's emissary, succeeded in bringing all of the country under his rule. Because of his divine descent, Jimmu became emperor in 660 B.C. (the date is mythical), thus establishing the line from which all of Japan's emperors are said to derive. However mysterious the origin of this imperial dynasty, it is acknowledged as the longest-reigning such family in the world.

Legend begins to give way to fact only in the A.D. 4th century, when a family by the name of Yamato succeeded in expanding its kingdom throughout much of the country and set up court in what is now Nara Prefecture. At the core of unification was the Shinto religion. Indigenous to

Japan, Shintoism is marked by the worship of natural things (like rivers and foxes) and of the spirits of ancestors, as well as the belief in the emperor's divinity.

Eventually, Yamato (present-day Japan) also began pointing cultural feelers toward its great neighbor to the west, China. In the 6th century, Buddhism, which originated in India, was brought to Japan via China and Korea, followed by the importation of Chinese cultural and scholarly knowledge—including art, architecture, and the use of Chinese written characters. In 604, the prince regent Shotoku, greatly influenced by the teachings of Buddhism and Confucianism, drafted a document calling for political reforms and a constitutional government. By 607, he was sending Japanese scholars to China to study Buddhism, and he started building Buddhist temples, including **Shitennoji Temple** (p. 459) in what is now Osaka and **Horyuji Temple** (p. 357) near Nara, the latter said to be the oldest existing wooden structure in the world. Even today, both Buddhism and Shintoism are driving influences in Japanese life.

THE NARA PERIOD (710–84) Before the 700s, the site of Japan's capital changed every time a new emperor came to the throne. In 710, however, a permanent capital was established at Nara. Although it remained the

SHRINES & TEMPLES: religion IN JAPAN

The main religions in Japan are Shintoism and Buddhism, and many Japanese consider themselves believers in both. Most Japanese, for example, will marry in a Shinto ceremony, but when they die, they'll have a Buddhist funeral. Increasingly, though, they get married in the Western style, leading to the maxim, a Japanese person is "born Shinto, weds Christian, dies Buddhist."

A native religion of Japan, **Shintoism** is the worship of ancestors and national heroes, as well as of all natural things—mountains, trees, stars, seas, fire, animals, even vegetables—as the embodiment of *kami* (gods). There are no scriptures in Shintoism, nor any ordained code of morals or ethics. The place of worship in Shintoism is called a *jinja*, or shrine. The most obvious sign of a shrine is its *torii*, an entrance gate, usually of wood and sometimes painted vermillion, consisting of two tall poles topped with either one or two crossbeams. Another feature common to shrines is a water trough with communal cups, where the Japanese will wash their hands and sometimes rinse out their mouths. Purification and cleanliness are important in Shintoism because they show respect to the gods. At the shrine, worshipers will throw a few coins into a money box, clap their hands twice to get the gods' attention, and then bow their heads and pray for whatever they wish—good health, the safe delivery of a child, or a prosperous year.

Founded in India in the 6th to 5th centuries B.C., **Buddhism** came to Japan in the A.D. 6th century, bringing with it the concept of eternal life. Whereas Shintoists have shrines, Buddhists have temples, called *otera*. Instead of *torii*, temples will often have an entrance gate with a raised doorsill and heavy doors. Temples may also have a cemetery on their grounds (which Shinto shrines never have) as well as a pagoda.

capital for only 74 years, seven successive emperors ruled from Nara. The period was graced with the expansion of Buddhism and flourishing temple construction throughout the country. Buddhism also inspired the arts, including Buddhist sculpture, metal casting, painting, and lacquerware. It was during this time that Emperor Shomu, the most devout Buddhist among the Nara emperors, ordered the casting of a huge bronze statue of Buddha to be erected in Nara. Known as the **Daibutsu** (p. 355), it remains Nara's biggest attraction.

THE HEIAN PERIOD (794–1192) In 794, the capital was moved to Heiankyo (present-day Kyoto), and, following the example of cities in China, Kyoto was laid out in a grid pattern with broad roads and canals. Heiankyo means "capital of peace and tranquility," and the Heian period was a glorious time for aristocratic families, a period of prosperous luxury during which court life reached new artistic heights. Moon viewing became popular. Chinese characters were blended with a new Japanese writing system, allowing for the first time the flowering of Japanese literature and poetry. The life of the times was captured in works by two women: Sei Shonagon, who wrote a collection of impressions of her life at court known as the *Pillow Book;* and Murasaki Shikibu, who wrote the world's first major novel, *The Tale of Genji.*

A statue of Minamoto Yoritomo, Japan's first shogun, in Kamakura (p. 218), where he established his capital.

Completely engrossed in their luxurious lifestyles, however, the court nobles failed to notice the growth of military clans in the provinces. The two most powerful warrior clans were the Taira (also called Heike) and the Minamoto (also called Genji), whose fierce civil wars tore the nation apart until a young warrior, Minamoto Yoritomo, established supremacy.

THE KAMAKURA PERIOD (1192–1333) Wishing to set up rule far away from Kyoto, Minamoto Yoritomo established his capital in a remote and easily defended fishing village called **Kamakura** (p. 218), not far from today's Tokyo. In becoming the nation's first shogun, or military dictator, Minamoto Yoritomo laid the groundwork for 700 years of military governments, in which the power of the country passed from the aristocratic court into the hands of the warrior class.

The Kamakura period is perhaps best known for the unrivaled ascendancy of the warrior caste, or **samurai.** Ruled by a rigid honor code, samurai were bound in loyalty to their feudal lord (*daimyo*), and they became the only caste allowed to carry two swords. They were expected to give up their lives for their lord without hesitation, and if they failed in their duty, they could regain their honor only by committing ritualistic suicide, or *seppuku.* Spurning the soft life led by court nobles, samurai embraced a spartan lifestyle. When **Zen Buddhism,** with its tenets of mental and physical discipline, was introduced into Japan from China in the 1190s, it appealed greatly to the samurai. Weapons and armor achieved new heights in artistry, while *Bushido,* the way of the warrior, contributed to the spirit of national unity.

Saved by a Divine Wind

In 1274, Mongolian forces under Kublai Khan made an unsuccessful attempt to invade Japan. They returned in 1281 with a larger fleet, but a typhoon destroyed it. Regarding the cyclone as a gift from the gods, Japanese called it *kamikaze,* meaning "divine wind," which took on a different significance at the end of World War II when Japanese pilots flew suicide missions in an attempt to turn the tide of war.

THE AGE OF THE WARRING STATES (1336–1603) After the fall of the Kamakura shogunate, a new feudal government was set up at Muromachi in Kyoto. The next 200 years, however, were marred by bloody civil wars as *daimyo* staked out their fiefdoms. Similar to the barons of Europe, each *daimyo* owned tracts of land, had complete rule over the people who lived on them, and had an army of retainers, the samurai, who fought his enemies. This period of civil wars is called *Sengoku-Jidai,* or Age of the Warring States. Yet these centuries of strife also saw a blossoming of art and culture. Kyoto witnessed the construction of the extravagant **Golden Pavilion** (p. 307) and **Silver Pavilion** (p. 301) as well as the artistic arrangement of the famous rock garden at **Ryoanji Temple** (p. 308). *Noh* drama, the tea ceremony, flower arranging, and landscape gardening became passions of the upper class. At the end of the 16th century, many mountaintop castles were built to demonstrate the strength of the *daimyo,* guard their fiefdoms, and defend themselves against the firearms introduced by the Portuguese.

THE EDO PERIOD (1603–1867) In 1600, power was seized by Tokugawa Ieyasu, a statesman so shrewd and skillful in eliminating enemies that his heirs would continue to rule Japan for the next 250 years. After defeating his greatest rival in the famous battle of Sekigahara, Tokugawa set up a shogunate government in 1603 in Edo (present-day Tokyo), leaving the emperor intact but virtually powerless in Kyoto.

In 1639, fearing the expansionist policies of European nations and the spread of Christianity, the Tokugawa shogunate adopted a policy of total isolation. Thus began an amazing 215-year period in Japanese history during which Japan was closed to the rest of the world. It was a time of political stability at the expense of personal freedom, as all aspects of

The great Edo Period shogun, Tokugawa Ieyesu, is honored with a statue at Nikko's splendid Toshogu Shrine (p. 225), his final resting place.

life were strictly controlled by the Tokugawa government.

Japanese society was divided into four distinct classes: samurai, farmers, craftspeople, and merchants. Class determined everything in daily life, from where a person could live to what he was allowed to wear or eat. Samurai led the most exalted social position, and it was probably during the Tokugawa reign that the samurai class reached the zenith of its glory. At the bottom of the social ladder were the merchants, but as they prospered under the peaceful regime, new forms of entertainment arose to occupy their time. *Kabuki* drama and woodblock prints became the rage, while stoneware and porcelain, silk brocade for kimono, and lacquerware improved in quality. In fact, it was probably the shogunate's rigid policies that actually fostered the arts. Because anything new was considered dangerous and quickly suppressed, Japanese were forced to retreat inward, focusing their energies on the arts and perfecting handicrafts down to the minutest detail, whether it was swords, textiles, or lacquered boxes. Only Japan's many festivals and pilgrimages to designated religious sites offered relief from harsh and restrictive social mores.

Yet even though the Tokugawa government took such extreme measures to ensure its supremacy, by the mid–19th century, it was clear that the feudal system was outdated and economic power had shifted into the hands of the merchants. Many samurai families were impoverished, and discontent with the shogunate became widespread. In 1853, American Commodore Matthew C. Perry sailed to Japan, seeking to gain trading

KEEPING THE daimyo IN CHECK

The Tokugawa government developed a clever system to ensure that no *daimyo* in the distant provinces would become too powerful and a threat to the shogun's power. Each *daimyo* was required to maintain a second mansion in Edo, leave his family there as permanent residents (effectively as hostages), and spend a prescribed number of months in Edo every year or two. Inns and townships sprang up along Japan's major highways to accommodate the elaborate processions of palanquins, samurai, and footmen traveling back and forth between Edo and the provinces. In expending so much time and money traveling back and forth and maintaining elaborate residences both in the provinces and in Edo, the *daimyo* had no resources left with which to wage a rebellion.

rights. He left unsuccessful, but returning a year later he forced the Shogun to sign an agreement despite the disapproval of the emperor, thus ending Japan's 2 centuries of isolation. In 1867, powerful families toppled the Tokugawa regime and restored the emperor as ruler, thus bringing the feudal era to a close.

MEIJI PERIOD THROUGH WORLD WAR II (1868–1945) In 1868, Emperor Meiji moved his imperial government from Kyoto to Edo, renamed it Tokyo (Eastern Capital), and designated it the official national capital. During the next few decades, known as the Meiji Restoration, Japan rapidly progressed from a feudal agricultural society of samurai and peasants to an industrial nation. The samurai were stripped of their power and no longer allowed to carry swords, thus ending a privileged way of life begun almost 700 years earlier in Kamakura. A prime minister and a cabinet were appointed, a constitution was drafted, and a parliament (called the Diet) was elected. With the enthusiastic support of Emperor Meiji, the latest in Western technological know-how was imported, including railway and postal systems, along with specialists and advisers: Between 1881 and 1898, about 10,000 Westerners were retained by the Japanese government to help modernize the country.

Meanwhile, Japan made incursions into neighboring lands. In 1894 to 1895, it fought and won a war against China; in 1904 to 1905, it attacked and defeated Russia; and in 1910, it annexed Korea. After militarists gained control of the government in the 1930s, these expansionist policies continued; Manchuria was annexed, and Japan went to war with China again in 1937. On December 7, 1941, Japan bombed Pearl Harbor, entering World War II against the United States. Although Japan went on to conquer Hong Kong, Singapore, Burma, Malaysia, the Philippines, the Dutch East Indies, and Guam, the tide eventually turned, and American bombers reduced every major Japanese city to rubble with the exception of historic Kyoto. On August 6, 1945, the United States dropped the world's first atomic bomb over Hiroshima, followed on August 9 by a second over Nagasaki. Japan submitted to unconditional surrender on August 14, with Emperor Hirohito's radio broadcast telling his people the time had come for "enduring the unendurable and suffering what is insufferable." American and other Allied occupation forces arrived and remained until 1952. For the first time in history, Japan had suffered defeat by a foreign power; the country had never before been invaded or occupied by a foreign nation.

POSTWAR JAPAN (1946–89) The experience of World War II had a profound effect on the Japanese, yet they emerged from their defeat and began to rebuild. In 1946, under the guidance of the Allied military authority headed by U.S. Gen. Douglas MacArthur, they adopted a democratic constitution renouncing war and the use of force to settle international disputes and divesting the emperor of divinity. A parliamentary system of government was set up, and 1947 witnessed the first general elections for the National Diet, the government's legislative body.

Avoiding involvement in foreign conflicts as outlined by its constitution, Japanese concentrated on economic recovery. Through a series of policies favoring domestic industries and shielding Japan from foreign competition, they achieved rapid economic growth. In 1964, Tokyo hosted the Summer Olympic Games, showing the world that not only had Japan recovered from the war's destruction but had also transformed into a formidable industrialized power. By the 1980s, Japan was by far the richest industrialized nation in Asia and the envy of its neighbors, who strove to emulate Japan's success. Sony had become a household word around the globe; books flooded the international market touting the economic secrets of Japan, Inc. Japan seemed to have it all: a good economy, political stability, safe streets, and great schools. As the yen soared, Japanese traveled abroad as never before, and Japanese companies gained international attention as they gobbled up real estate in foreign lands and purchased works of art at unheard-of prices.

In 1989, Emperor Hirohito died of cancer at age 87, bringing the 63-year Showa era to an end and ushering in the **Heisei period** under Akihito, the 125th emperor, who proclaimed the new "Era of Peace" (Heisei). When Akihito abdicated in April 2019, Crown Prince Naruhito ascended to the throne and Japan entered the era of "Beautiful Harmony" (Reiwa).

AFTER THE BUBBLE BURST (1990–PRESENT) In the early 1990s, shadows of financial doubt began to spread over the Land of the Rising Sun, with alarming reports of bad bank loans, inflated stock prices, and overextended corporate investment abroad. In 1992, recession hit Japan, bursting the economic bubble and plunging the country into its worst recession since World War II.

Part of Hiroshima's Peace Memorial Park (p. 433), the A-Bomb Dome is a shattered building left in ruins as a reminder of the atomic bomb's destructive power.

Japan, whose foremost trading partner had shifted from the United States to China, seemed to be on the economic mend by the mid-2000s. Then the 2008 global financial meltdown—referred to in Japan as the "Lehman Shock"—hijacked its recovery. Foreign trade spiraled downward, as demand for Japanese cars, electronics, and other exports dropped dramatically around the world. For Japan's young generation, economic stagnation was all they'd known. Instead of being envied as an Asian superpower,

Japan had become an example of an economy other nations wished to avoid. Furthermore, Japan continued to suffer a declining birthrate, coupled with one of the most rapidly aging populations in the world, a bleak demographic outlook indeed.

Japan is also in the unenviable position of having noisy geographic neighbors, like an expansionist China under Xi Jinping, the ever-unpredictable North Korea under the tyrannical Kim dynasty, and Russia under the bellicose stewardship of Vladimir Putin and his oligarchs. (For decades, Japan has waged a dispute with Russia about ownership of the Kuril Islands in the Sea of Okhotsk.)

But all of Japan's woes paled into insignificance on March 11, 2011, when one of the strongest quakes in recorded history struck off the Tohoku coast. With a magnitude of 9.0, the earthquake unleashed a massive tsunami that raced as far as 10km (6 miles) inland. More than 19,000 people died or vanished, entire towns and villages along the Tohoku coast (in eastern Honshu) were obliterated, and the Fukushima nuclear power plant was severely crippled. Although most of Tohoku has recovered, with gargantuan seawalls constructed near the shoreline and the opening of the 1,025km (637 miles) **Michinoku Coastal Trail** (p. 628), cleanup and decontamination in Fukushima continues. Experts say it could take 40 years to fully decommission the Fukushima power plant; 110,000 houses were contaminated in Fukushima Prefecture alone. Just as 9/11 remains seared in American minds, 3/11 is the day that for most Japanese changed their nation forever.

Despite being disaster-prone and having a currency that sends economists' heads spinning, Japan is in a good place in 2025. Much of this can be attributed to soft power. If I strike up a conversation with someone outside Japan and tell them I have lived more than half of my adult life there, they light up. They say they'd love to go someday, regale me with stories about their favorite anime or Japanese TV shows, mention that they keep hearing about some baseballer called Shohei Ohtani, and rave about how they just discovered okonomiyaki and Kewpie mayo. In 1983, then-Prime Minister Yasuhiro Nakasone told *Time* magazine, "In the past, we have been lacking in our efforts to publicize Japan culturally. We have done quite well in exporting products. But from now on, we must make greater efforts in exporting cultural information." Were the late Nakasone still with us now, I think he'd comfortably revise that statement.

TRADITIONAL ARTS

KABUKI Japan's best-known traditional theater art, *kabuki* is also one of the country's most popular forms of entertainment. Visit a performance and it's easy to see why—*kabuki* is eccentric and dramatic, the costumes are gorgeous, the stage settings are often fantastic, and the themes are universal—love, revenge, and the conflict between duty and personal feelings. Plots are easy to follow, though some theaters have English-language

A model of a Kabuki actor at the Edo-Tokyo Museum (p. 120).

programs and earphones that describe everything in minute detail.

Probably one of the reasons *kabuki* is so popular even today is that it developed centuries ago in feudal Japan as a form of entertainment for the common people, particularly the merchants. The founding of *kabuki* is generally credited to a shrine maiden from Izumo called Okuni, who travelled with a troupe of female prostitute-turned-actors, but since 1629 all roles—even those depicting women—have been played by men.

Altogether there are more than 300 *kabuki* plays, dating mostly from the 18th century. *Kabuki* stages almost always revolve and have an aisle that extends from the stage to the back of the spectator theater. For a Westerner, one of the more arresting things about a *kabuki* performance is the audience itself. Because this has always been entertainment for the masses, the audience can get quite lively with yells, guffaws, shouts of approval, and laughter. The best place to enjoy *kabuki* is at the **Kabukiza Theatre** (p. 199) in Ginza, Tokyo, where performances are held throughout the year.

NOH Whereas *kabuki* developed as a form of entertainment for the masses, *Noh* was a much more traditional and aristocratic form of theater. Most of Japan's shogun were patrons of *Noh;* during the Edo period, it became the exclusive entertainment of the samurai class. In contrast to *kabuki*'s extroverted liveliness, *Noh* is very calculated, slow, and restrained. One of the oldest forms of theater in Japan, it has changed very little in the past 600 years. The language is so archaic that Japanese cannot understand it at all, which also explains why *Noh* does not have the popularity of kabuki.

As in *kabuki,* all *Noh* performers are men. The principal characters are mostly ghosts or spirits, who illuminate foibles of human nature or tragic-heroic events. Performers often wear masks—probably a holdover from Japan's much more ancient theater styles, *gigaku* and *kagura,* both of which were mentioned in the *Nihon Shoki* (*The Chronicles of Japan*), published in 720 A.D. Spoken parts are chanted by a chorus of about eight; music is provided by a *Noh* orchestra that consists of several drums and a flute. In between *Noh* plays, short comic reliefs, called *kyogen,* usually make fun of life in the 1600s, depicting the lives of lazy husbands, conniving servants, and other characters with universal appeal. In addition to

Tokyo's **National Noh Theatre** (p. 200), Noh is staged throughout the country, including at shrines and private Noh venues.

BUNRAKU *Bunraku* is traditional Japanese puppet theater. Contrary to what you might expect, *bunraku* is for adults, and themes center on love and revenge, sacrifice and suicide. Many dramas now adapted for *kabuki* were first written for the *bunraku* stage, particularly by Chikamatsu Monzaemon, who often wears the lofty sobriquet "the Shakespeare of Japan." Popular in Japan since the 17th century, *bunraku* is fascinating to watch because the puppeteers are right onstage with their puppets, dressed in black and wonderfully skilled in making puppets seem like living beings. Usually, there are three puppeteers for each puppet, which is about three-fourths human size: One puppeteer is responsible for moving the puppet's head, right arm, and right hand, and controls the expression on its face; another puppeteer operates the puppet's left arm and hand; while the third moves the legs. Although at first the puppeteers are somewhat distracting, after a while you forget they're there as the puppets assume personalities of their own. The narrator, who tells the story and speaks the various parts, is accompanied by a *shamisen,* a three-stringed Japanese instrument. The

THE ART OF sumo

The Japanese form of wrestling known as **sumo** was first mentioned in written records in the 6th century, but it likely far predated that. Today it's still popular, with the best wrestlers revered as national heroes, much as baseball or basketball players are in North America. Often taller than 1.8m (6 ft.) and weighing well over 136kg (300 lb.)—a rarity for Japanese—sumo wrestlers follow a rigorous training period, which usually begins when they're in their teens and includes eating special foods to gain weight. Unmarried wrestlers even live together at their training schools, called sumo stables. Many sumo wrestlers nowadays are non-Japanese, with the majority from Mongolia.

A sumo match takes place on a sandy-floored ring less than 4.5m (15 ft.) in diameter. Wrestlers dress much as they did during the Edo Period—their hair in a samurai-style topknot, an ornamental belt/loincloth around their huge girths. Before each bout, the two contestants scatter salt in the ring to purify it from the last bout's loss; they also squat and then raise each leg, stamping it into the ground to crush, symbolically, any evil spirits. They then squat down and face each other, glaring to intimidate their opponent. Once they rush each other, each wrestler's object is to either eject his opponent from the ring or cause him to touch the ground with any part of his body other than his feet. This is accomplished by shoving, slapping, tripping, throwing, and even carrying the opponent, but punching with a closed fist and kicking are not allowed. Altogether there are 48 holds and throws, and sumo fans know all of them.

There are six 15-day sumo tournaments in Japan every year: Three are held in Tokyo (Jan, May, and Sept); the others are held in Osaka (Mar), Nagoya (July), and Fukuoka (Nov). Each wrestler in the tournament faces a new opponent every day; the winner of the tournament is the wrestler who maintains the best overall record. Tournament matches are also widely covered on television.

most famous *bunraku* presentations are at the **National Bunraku Theatre** (p. 477), but there are performances in Tokyo and other major cities, too.

THE TEA CEREMONY Tea was brought to Japan from China about 1,200 years ago. It first became popular among Buddhist priests as a means of staying awake during long hours of meditation; gradually, its use filtered down among the upper classes, and in the 16th century, the tea ceremony was perfected by a merchant named Sen-no-Rikyu. Using the principles of Zen and the spiritual discipline of the samurai, the tea ceremony became a highly stylized ritual, with detailed rules on how tea should be prepared, served, and drunk. The simplicity of movement and tranquility of setting are meant to free the mind from the banality of everyday life and to allow the spirit to enjoy peace. In a way, it is a form of spiritual therapy.

The tea ceremony, *cha-no-yu,* is still practiced in Japan today and is regarded as a form of training for mental composure, as well as for etiquette and manners. One can study the discipline for decades and still be confronted with an unequivocal truth: The more you come to know, the more you realize you don't know. *Oku ga fukai,* as the Buddhists say, "the way is deep." Confounding matters more, the study of the tea ceremony includes related subjects like the craftsmanship of tea vessels and implements, the design and construction of the teahouse, the landscaping of gardens, and literature related to the tea ceremony.

Several of Japan's more famous landscape gardens have teahouses on their grounds where you can sit on *tatami,* drink the frothy green tea (called *matcha*), eat sweets (meant to counteract the bitter taste of the tea), and contemplate the view. Tea pottery changes with the seasons, and the cups and pots are often valuable art objects.

IKEBANA Whereas a Westerner is likely to put a bunch of flowers into a vase and be done with it, the Japanese consider the arrangement of flowers an art in itself. Many young girls have at least some training in flower arranging, known as *ikebana.* First popularized among aristocrats during the Heian Period (A.D. 794–1192) and spread to the common people in the 14th to 16th centuries, traditional *ikebana,* in its simplest form, is supposed to represent heaven, man, and earth; it's often considered a truly Japanese art without outside influences. As important as the arrangement itself is the vase chosen to display it. Department store galleries sometimes have *ikebana* exhibitions, as do shrines; otherwise, check with the local tourist office.

GARDENS Nothing is left to chance in a Japanese landscape garden: The shapes of hills and trees, the placement of rocks and waterfalls—everything is skillfully arranged in a faithful reproduction of nature. To Westerners, it may seem a bit strange to arrange nature to look like nature; but to Japanese, even nature can be improved upon to make it more pleasing through the best possible use of limited space—the Japanese word for garden, *teien,* literally means "controlled nature." Japanese are masters at this, as a visit to any of their famous gardens will testify.

Japanese have been sculpting gardens for more than 1,000 years. At first, gardens were designed for walking and boating, with ponds, artificial islands, and pavilions. As with almost everything else in Japanese life, however, Zen Buddhism exerted an influence, making gardens simpler and attempting to create the illusion of boundless space within a small area. To the Buddhist, a garden was not for merriment but for contemplation—an uncluttered and simple landscape on which to rest the eyes. Japanese gardens often use the principle of "borrowed landscape"—that is, the incorporation of surrounding mountains and landscape into the overall design and impact of the garden.

ETIQUETTE

Much of Japan's system of etiquette and manners stems from its feudal days, when the social hierarchy dictated how a person spoke, sat, bowed, ate, walked, and lived. Failure to comply with the rules would bring severe punishment, even death. Many Japanese have literally lost their heads for committing social blunders. Today, Japanese still attach much importance to proper behavior—taking your shoes off when entering a house, addressing your elders with the correct honorifics, never passing anything with chopsticks (this is part of a Buddhist funeral process), washing yourself thoroughly before getting into a public onsen bath, and keeping noise to a bare minimum when using public transport—though as a foreigner, you can get away with a lot. Sometimes locals may scoff at your indiscretions, but you can't spend your entire holiday stressing over every minor social flub.

At any rate, if you're invited to a Japanese home, you should know that it's both a rarity and an honor. Most Japanese consider their homes too small and humble for entertaining guests, which is why there are so many restaurants, coffee shops, and bars. If you're invited to a home, don't show up empty-handed. Bring a small gift such as candy, fruit, flowers, alcohol, or perhaps a souvenir from your hometown.

BOWING The main form of greeting in Japan is the bow rather than the handshake. Although at first glance it may seem simple enough, the bow—together with its implications—is actually quite complicated. The depth of the bow and the number of seconds devoted to performing it, as well as the total number of bows, depend on who you are, to whom you're bowing, and how they're bowing back. In addition to bowing in greeting, Japanese also bow upon departing and to express gratitude. The proper form for a bow is to bend from the waist with a straight back, keeping your arms at your sides (if you're a man) or clasped in front of you (if you're a woman). If you're a foreigner, a simple nod of the head is enough. Knowing foreigners shake hands, a Japanese may extend his hand, although he probably won't be able to stop himself from giving a little bow as well. (I've even seen Japanese bow when talking on the telephone.) Although Japanese businessmen occasionally shake hands among themselves, the practice is still quite rare. Kimono-clad hostesses of a high-end traditional Japanese inn will often kneel on *tatami* and bow to the ground as they send you off on your journey.

SHOES Nothing is so distasteful to Japanese as the soles of shoes. Therefore, you should take off your shoes before entering a home, a Japanese-style inn, temple, or shrine, and even some museums and restaurants. Usually there are plastic slippers at the entryway for you to slip on, but whenever you encounter *tatami,* you should take off even these slippers—only bare feet or socks are allowed to tread upon *tatami.*

Restrooms present another set of slippers. If you're in a home, Japanese inn, or restaurant where you've removed your shoes, you'll notice another pair of slippers sitting right inside the restroom door. Slip out of the hallway plastic shoes and into the bathroom slippers and wear these the entire time you're in the restroom. When you're finished, change back into the hallway slippers. If you forget this last changeover, you'll regret it—it's both a breach of etiquette and sartorial elegance to waltz back into a room wearing toilet slippers.

BATHING In almost all circumstances, public bathing is gender segregated with no textiles allowed. There are some exceptions, primarily at outdoor hot-spring spas in the countryside, where you might be able to wrap yourself in a towel before entering the water. In cases where the bath is mixed and textiles are forbidden, it's mostly elderly bathers who have no time left for insecurities.

Whether large or small, the procedure at all Japanese baths is the same. After completely disrobing in the changing room, putting your clothes in either a locker or a basket, you walk into the bathing area. There you'll find plastic or wood basins and stools and faucets along the wall. Sit on the stool in front of a faucet and use the basin (or hand-held faucet if available) to splash water all over you. If there's no hot water from the faucet, it's acceptable to dip your basin into the hot bath, but your

PUBLIC BATHS: THE center OF JAPANESE SOCIAL LIFE

Japanese baths are delightful, perhaps the single greatest thing about winter (though warm sake and steamy bowls of ramen would run them close). You'll find baths at Japanese-style inns, at *onsen* (hot-spring spa resorts), and at *sento* (neighborhood baths). Sometimes they're elaborate affairs with indoor and outdoor tubs, and sometimes they're nothing more than a tiny tub. Public baths have long been regarded as social centers for Japanese—as a means of *hadaka no tsukiai,* naked companionship. Friends and coworkers will visit hot-spring resorts together, neighbors exchange gossip at the neighborhood bath, and even bathing with your boss on a business trip is by no means a faux pas. Sadly, neighborhood baths have been in great decline over the past decades, as most Japanese now have private baths in their homes. Hot-spring spas, however, remain hugely popular.

washcloth (if using one) should never touch the tub water. Rinsing yourself thoroughly is not only proper *onsen* manners; it also acclimatizes your body to the bath's hot temperature.

As in a Jacuzzi, everyone uses the same bath water. For that reason, you should never wash yourself in the tub, never put your washcloth into the bath (place it on your head or lay it beside the bath), and never pull the plug (if there is one) when you're done. After your bath is when you scrub your body and wash your hair. All *sento* provide shampoo and body soap, along with interesting products provided free by companies hoping to rope in new customers, but in small public baths you might have to provide your own.

The Japanese are so fond of baths that many take them nightly, especially in winter. At an *onsen,* where hot-spring waters are considered curative, Japanese will bathe both at night and again in the morning, often making several trips between the faucet and the tubs and being careful not to rinse off the curative waters when they're done. With time, you'll probably become addicted, too. ***Note:*** Because tattoos in Japan have long been associated with *yakuza* (Japanese mafia), most public baths do not admit people with tattoos—popular exceptions include Dogo Onsen and various public baths in Beppu, the largest concentration of hot springs in Japan. However, if your tattoo is discreet and you're at, say, a small Japanese inn, you probably won't have any problems.

THE JAPANESE LANGUAGE

No one knows the exact origins of the Japanese language, but we do know it existed only in spoken form until the 6th century. That's when the Japanese borrowed Chinese pictorial characters, called *kanji,* and used them to develop their own form of written language. Later, two phonetic alphabet systems, *hiragana* and *katakana,* were added to kanji to form the existing Japanese writing system. Thus, Chinese and Japanese use some of the same pictographs, but otherwise there's little similarity between the languages.

As for the spoken language, there are many levels of speech and forms of expression relating to a person's social status and sex. Even nonverbal communication is a vital part of understanding Japanese, because what isn't said is often more important than what is. It's little wonder that St. Francis Xavier, a Jesuit missionary who came to Japan in the 16th century, wrote that Japanese was an invention of the devil designed to thwart the spread of Christianity. And yet, astoundingly, adult literacy in Japan is estimated to be 99%.

It's worth noting that Japanese nouns do not have plural forms; thus, for example, *ryokan,* a Japanese-style inn, can be both singular and plural, as can kimono. Plural sense is indicated by context. In addition, the Japanese custom is to list the family name first followed by the given name, though nowadays Japanese working with international companies increasingly follow the Western custom of listing the family name last. In this

JAPANESE english

English-language words are often misspelled, sometimes with wonderful results. "Engrish" menus can be entertaining, listing dishes like "lice" (instead of rice) or "sandwitches." English is also fashionable in Japanese advertising, appearing on shop signs, posters, shopping bags, and T-shirts. Sometimes, however, you can only guess at the original intent. Who, for example, thought it was a good idea to print a T-shirt stating I LOVE BABY'S FANNY (which, by the way, is considerably more grotesque in British English)? I have treasured an ashtray that read DON'T NOT THROW CIGARETTES OR DRINKING INTO HERE, and I'll never forget ALL YOUR BASE ARE BELONG TO US from the opening cutscene of a classic SEGA video game. It might seem churlish to laugh at their linguistic discrepancies, but the Japanese often have a good sense of humor about it too. That said, if it's in an official business context, like signs in Narita Airport entreating you to have a good FRIGHT, then they'll quickly amend it once notified.

guide, I've favored listing names in the manner that people are most commonly known by: Yayoi Kusama (surname Kusama), Tokugawa Ieyasu (of the Tokugawa family).

Finally, you may find yourself confused because of suffixes attached to Japanese place names. For example, *dori* can mean street, avenue, or road; sometimes it's attached to a street name with a hyphen, while at other times it stands alone. Thus, you may see Chuo-dori, Chuo Dori, or even Chuo-dori Avenue on English-language maps and street signs, but they're all the same street. Likewise, *dera* and *ji* mean "temple" and are often included at the end of the name, as in Kiyomizudera, which may be translated into English as Kiyomizu Temple, or Nanzenji as Nanzen Temple. *Jo* inidicates a castle, while *jinja, jingu,* or *taisha* at the end of a word all mean "shrine."

DEALING WITH THE LANGUAGE BARRIER

Beyond using Google Translate or DeepL on your phone (both good tools that are only getting better), here's some advice for bridging the language gap. If you're heading out for a particular restaurant, shop, or sight, **have your destination written down in Japanese.** If you get lost along the way, look for one of the police boxes, called *koban,* found in virtually every neighborhood. They have maps of particular districts and can pinpoint exactly where you want to go if you have the address with you.

If you need to ask directions of strangers in Japan, your best bet is to ask younger people. They have all studied English in school and are more likely to be able to help you. Japanese businessmen also often know some English. And as strange as it sounds, if you're having problems communicating with someone, write it down so he or she can read it. The emphasis in schools is on written rather than oral English (many English teachers can't speak English themselves), so Japanese who can't understand a word you say may know the subtleties of syntax and English grammar.

EATING & DRINKING IN JAPAN

Whenever I leave Japan, apart from the toilets, it's the food I miss the most. Sure, there are sushi bars and other Japanese specialty restaurants in many major cities around the world, but they don't offer nearly the variety available in Japan, the quality would never pass muster for such discerning eaters as the Japanese, and they're usually way overpriced. Too few restaurants in the West realize that ramen and *yakitori* (chicken skewers) are cheap and cheerful dishes. Just as America has more to offer than hamburgers and steaks and the British Isles more than fish and chips, Japan has more than just sushi and *teppanyaki.* For both the gourmet and the uninitiated, Japan is a treasure trove of culinary surprises.

Japanese Cuisine

There are dozens of different and distinct types of Japanese cuisine, plus countless regional specialties. A good deal of what you eat may be completely new to you as well as completely unidentifiable. Don't worry; often even Japanese sometimes don't know what they're eating, so varied and so wide is the range of available produce—if you ask a Japanese person what an indistinguishable slice of raw fish is, they'll often say "yellowtail" as though it's a catchall term for things living under the sea. The rule is simply to enjoy, and enjoyment begins even before you raise your chopsticks to your mouth.

To the Japanese, **presentation** of food is as important as the food itself, and dishes are designed to appeal to the palate and to the eye. Japanese traditionally use lots of small plates, each arranged artfully with bite-size morsels of food, and often the colors are selected to reflect the season. After you've seen what can be done with maple leaves, flowers, bits of bamboo, and even pebbles to enhance the appearance of food, your relationship with what you eat may change forever. It's no surprise that traditional Japanese cuisine is on UNESCO's Intangible Cultural Heritage list.

Below are explanations of some of the most common types of Japanese cuisine. Generally, only one type of cuisine is served in a given restaurant—for example, seafood is the specialty in a sushi bar, whereas tempura is featured at a tempura counter. There are of course exceptions to this, especially in regards to raw fish, which is served as an appetizer in many restaurants, and set meals, which contain a variety of dishes. Hotel restaurants may also offer a great variety, and some Japanese drinking establishments (called *izakaya* or *nomiya*) offer a wide range of foods from soups to sushi to fried chicken.

KAISEKI The king of Japanese cuisine, *kaiseki* is the epitome of delicately and exquisitely arranged food, the ultimate in Japanese aesthetic appeal. It's also among the most expensive meals you can eat, though some restaurants do offer more affordable mini-*kaiseki* courses or reduce their prices at lunchtime. In addition, the better Japanese inns serve *kaiseki,* a reason for their high cost. *Kaiseki* is not a specific dish but rather a complete meal, and it's expensive because much time and skill are involved in preparing each of the many dishes. Even the plates are chosen with great care to enhance the color, texture, and shape of each piece of food.

Kaiseki cuisine is based on the four seasons—the selection of ingredients and their presentation depends upon the time of year. In fact, so strongly does a *kaiseki* preparation convey the mood of a particular season, the *kaiseki* gourmet can tell what season it is just by looking at a meal. A *kaiseki* meal is usually a lengthy affair with various dishes appearing in set order. Although meals vary greatly depending upon the region and what's fresh, common dishes include sashimi, tempura, cooked seasonal fish, miso soup, and bite-size pieces of various vegetables. Because *kaiseki* is always a set meal, there's no problem in ordering. Let your budget be your guide.

KUSHIAGE/KUSHIKATSU *Kushiage* foods (also called *kushikatsu*) are breaded and deep-fried on skewers and include chicken, beef, seafood, and lots of seasonal vegetables like snow peas, green pepper, gingko nuts, and lotus root. Their morsels are served with a slice of lemon and usually a specialty sauce. Ordering the set meal is easiest, and what you get is often determined by both the chef and the season.

Small, exquisitely presented dishes are part of a kaiseki meal at the Ryokan Kurashiki (p. 413), in the historic western Honshu town of Kurashiki.

OKONOMIYAKI *Okonomiyaki*, which originated in Osaka after World War II and literally means "what you like, cooked" is often referred to as Japanese pizza or pancake, to which meat or seafood, shredded cabbage, and vegetables are added, topped with a rich sauce similar to Worcestershire sauce. At some places the cook makes it for you, at others it's do-it-yourself at your table. *Yakisoba* (fried Chinese noodles with cabbage) is also usually offered at *okonomiyaki* restaurants, which are always very reasonably priced.

ROBATAYAKI *Robatayaki* refers to restaurants in which seafood, meat, and vegetables are cooked over an open charcoal grill. In days of yore, a *robata* (open fireplace) in the middle of an old Japanese house was the center of activity for cooking, eating, socializing, and keeping warm. Today's *robatayaki* restaurants, prevalent throughout Hokkaido, are therefore like nostalgia trips back into Japan's past and are often decorated in rustic farmhouse style with staff

rice: A MEAL IN A BOWL

As in other Asian countries, rice has been a Japanese staple for about 2,000 years. In fact, rice is so important to the Japanese diet that *gohan* means both "rice" and "meal." In Japan it's quite sticky, making it easier to pick up with chopsticks. Traditionally it was eaten plain, though nowadays trendy restaurants sprinkle rice with black sesame seeds, plum powder, or other seasoning. In the old days, not everyone could afford the expensive white kind, which was grown primarily to pay taxes or rent to the feudal lord; peasants had to make do with a mixture of brown rice, millet, and greens. Restaurants offering organic foods often serve *genmai* (unpolished brown rice).

dressed in traditional clothing. Robatayaki staples include *ginnan* (gingko nuts), asparagus wrapped in bacon, *piman* (a type of green pepper), mushrooms (various kinds), grilled skewers of beef and chicken, and just about any kind of fish.

SASHIMI & SUSHI Like rice, seafood is a staple of the Japanese diet. Although it may be served in any number of ways from grilled to boiled, a great deal of it is eaten raw. Sashimi is raw seafood that's not wrapped around rice, usually served as an appetizer and eaten with soy sauce. Sushi, which is raw fish with vinegared rice, comes in many varieties. The best known is *nigiri-zushi:* raw fish, seafood, or vegetables placed on top of vinegared rice with just a touch of wasabi. It's also dipped in soy sauce. Use chopsticks or your fingers to eat sushi; remember you're supposed to eat each piece in one bite—quite a mouthful, but about the only way to keep it from falling apart. Another trick is to turn it upside down when you dip it in the sauce, to keep the rice from crumbling.

Also popular is *maki-zushi,* which consists of seafood, vegetables, or pickles rolled with rice inside a sheet of *nori* seaweed. *Inari-zushi* is vinegared rice and chopped vegetables inside a pouch of fried tofu bean curd.

Typical sushi includes *maguro* (tuna), *hirame* (flounder), *tai* (sea bream), *ika* (squid), *tako* (octopus), *ebi* (shrimp), *anago* (sea eel), and *tamago* (omelet). If you don't want to order separately, there are always various *seto* (set meals or courses). Pickled ginger is part of any sushi meal.

One way to enjoy sushi without spending a fortune is at a *kaiten* sushi shop, in which plates of sushi circulate on a conveyor belt on the counter—customers reach for the dishes they want and pay for the number of dishes they take.

SHABU-SHABU & SUKIYAKI Until the Meiji Restoration beginning in 1868, which brought foreigners to Japan, meat was pretty much off the menu. It was considered unclean by Buddhists, and consuming it was banned by the emperor way back in the 7th century. It wasn't until Emperor Meiji himself announced his intention to eat meat that Japanese accepted the idea. Today, Japanese are quite skilled in preparing beef dishes.

Sukiyaki is among Japan's best-known dishes. Like fondue, it's cooked at the table and consists of thinly sliced beef cooked in a broth of soy sauce, stock, and sake along with scallions, spinach, mushrooms, tofu, bamboo shoots, and other vegetables. All diners serve themselves from the simmering pot and then dip their morsels into their own bowl of raw egg. You can skip the raw egg if you want (many Westerners do), but it adds to the taste and also cools the food down enough so that it doesn't burn.

Shabu-shabu is also prepared at your table and consists of thinly sliced beef cooked in a broth with vegetables in a kind of Japanese fondue. (It's named for the swishing sound the beef supposedly makes when cooking.) For dipping, there's typically sesame sauce or a more bitter fish stock sauce.

The main difference between the two dishes is the broth: Whereas in sukiyaki it consists of stock flavored with soy sauce and sake and is slightly sweet, in *shabu-shabu* it's relatively clear and has little taste of its own. The pots used are also different. Restaurants serving sukiyaki usually serve *shabu-shabu* as well, and they're often happy to show you the right way to prepare and eat it.

SHOJIN RYORI *Shojin Ryori* is the ultimate vegetarian meal, created centuries ago to serve the needs of Zen Buddhist priests and pilgrims. Dishes may include *yudofu* (simmered tofu) and an array of local vegetables. Kyoto is the best place to experience this type of cuisine.

SOBA, UDON & RAMEN Japanese love eating noodles, but I suspect at least part of the fascination stems from the way they eat them—they slurp, sucking in the noodles with gravity-defying speed. What's more, slurping noodles is considered proper etiquette; it signifies to the chef that you're enjoying the food and also helps cool the noodles when they're piping hot. In any case, noodles are among the least expensive dishes in Japan.

There are many different kinds of noodles, with seemingly every region proud of its own special style—some are eaten plain, some in combination with other foods such as shrimp tempura, some served hot, some served cold. *Soba,* made from unbleached buckwheat flour and enjoyed for its nutty flavor and high nutritional value, is eaten hot (*kake-soba*) or cold (*zaru-soba*). *Udon* is a thick white wheat noodle originally from Osaka, usually served hot. *Somen* is a fine white noodle eaten cold in the summer and dunked in a cold umami sauce. Establishments serving noodles range from stand-up eateries to more refined noodle restaurants with *tatami* seating.

Although technically considered Chinese fast food, **ramen** in recent years has been elevated from a cheap, late-night snack to celebrity status, with everyone weighing in on their own favorite restaurant. Many regions have their own style; chefs cultivate their own secret recipes. But what they have in common is noodles served in a broth that probably simmered for hours. In addition to ramen, you can also usually order rice or *gyoza* (fried pork dumplings).

TEMPURA Today a well-known Japanese food, tempura was actually introduced by the Portuguese in the 16th century. Tempura is fish and vegetables coated in a batter of egg, water, and wheat flour, delicately deep-fried, and served piping hot. To eat it, dip it in a sauce of soy, fish stock, *daikon* (radish), and grated ginger; in some restaurants, only some salt, powdered green tea, or a lemon wedge is provided as an accompaniment. Various tempura specialties may include *nasu* (eggplant), *shiitake* (mushroom), *satsumaimo* (sweet potato), *shishito* (small green pepper), *renkon* (sliced lotus root), *ebi* (shrimp), *ika* (squid), *shisho* (lemon-mint leaf), and various fish. Again, the easiest thing to do is to order the *teishoku* (set meal).

TEPPANYAKI A *teppanyaki* restaurant is a Japanese steakhouse. The chef slices, dices, and cooks your meal of tenderloin or sirloin steak and vegetables on a smooth, hot grill right in front of you—though with much less fanfare than most Japanese restaurants in the U.S. *Teppanyaki* restaurants tend to be expensive, simply because of the price of *wagyu* (Japanese beef), with Matsusaka Ushi, Ohmi Beef, and the globally acclaimed Kobe Beef the most prized brands.

TOFU Originally from China, tofu, or bean curd, is made from soy milk. It has little flavor of its own and is served cold in summer and *yudofu* (boiled) in winter. A by-product of tofu is *yuba,* thin sheets rich in protein often served with *soba* noodles.

TONKATSU *Tonkatsu* is Japanese comfort food, made by dredging pork in wheat flour, moistening it with egg and water, dipping it in bread crumbs, and deep-frying it in vegetable oil. Because *tonkatsu* restaurants are inexpensive, they're popular with office workers and families. It's easiest to order the *teishoku,* which usually features either the *hirekatsu* (pork fillet) or the *rosukatsu* (pork loin). In any case, *tonkatsu* is served on a bed of shredded cabbage, and one or two different sauces will be at your table, a Worcestershire sauce and perhaps a specialty sauce. If you order the *teishoku,* it will come with rice, miso soup, pickled vegetables, and often free refills. Pork cutlet served on a bowl of rice is *katsudon.*

UNAGI Popular as a health food because of its rich protein and high vitamin A content, *unagi* (freshwater eel) is supposed to help you fight fatigue during hot summer months but is eaten year-round. *Kabayaki* (broiled eel) is prepared by grilling fillet strips over a charcoal fire; the eel is repeatedly dipped in a sweetened barbecue soy sauce while cooking. A favorite way to eat broiled eel is on top of rice, in which case it's called *unaju* or *unagi donburi.*

YAKITORI *Yakitori* is chunks of chicken or chicken parts basted in a sweet soy sauce or rubbed with salt and grilled over a charcoal fire on thin skewers. The cheapest way to dine on yakitori is to order a set course, which will often include various parts of the chicken including the skin, heart, and liver. If this isn't to your taste, you may wish to order a la carte. Try *sasami* (chicken breast), *tsukune* (chicken meatballs), *piman* (green peppers), *negima* (chicken and leeks), *shiitake* (mushrooms), or *ginnan* (gingko nuts). Places that specialize in yakitori (*yakitori-ya*, often identifiable by a red paper lantern outside the front door) are technically not restaurants but drinking establishments; they usually don't open until 5 or 6pm.

OTHER CUISINES During your travels you might also run into these types of Japanese cuisine. *Kamameshi* is a rice casserole served in individual-size cast-iron pots with different toppings that might include seafood, meat, or vegetables. *Donburi* is also a rice dish, topped with tempura, eggs, and meat such as chicken or pork. *Nabe*, a stew cooked in an earthenware pot at your table, consists of chicken, sliced beef, pork, or seafood; noodles; and vegetables. *Oden* is a broth with fish cakes, tofu, eggs, and vegetables, served with hot mustard. If a restaurant advertises that it specializes in *Kyodo-Ryori*, it serves local specialties for which the region is famous and is often very rustic in decor. See individual city lists for more on regional cuisine.

KANPAI! WHAT'S ON THE drinks menu IN JAPAN

Most Japanese restaurants serve complimentary green tea with meals. You might also want to order **sake** (also known as *nihonshu*), an alcoholic beverage made from rice and served hot or cold. Produced since about the 3rd century, sake varies by region, production method, alcoholic content, color, aroma, and taste. There are around 1,000 sake breweries in Japan producing as many as 10,000 varieties. Miyabi is a prized classic sake; other brands are Gekkeikan, Koshinokanbai, Hakutsuru (meaning White Crane), and Ozeki. Hakkaisan, from Niigata, one of Japan's chief sake-brewing prefectures, tends to be palatable for the uninitiated and is found in many izakaya throughout the country.

Japanese **beer** is also very popular. The biggest sellers are Kirin, Sapporo, Asahi, and Suntory, with each brand offering a bewildering variety of brews. Microbreweries are also found everywhere in Japan and have become particularly popular in chic districts of Tokyo. Craft beer comes at a premium, though—it's not uncommon for a new IPA or saison to cost double the price of a *nama* (draft) Japanese lager.

Although cocktail lounges have become trendy in the big cities—so much so that in 2008 *Bon Appetit* magazine dubbed Tokyo the "cocktail capital of the world"—most Japanese stick with beer, sake, *shochu*, or whiskey. Businessmen gravitate to **whiskey,** which they usually drink with ice and water (Suntory and Nikka are the two biggest brands). Whiskey-soda highballs are one of the most popular drinks among the young. ***Shochu,*** a clear, distilled spirit usually made from rice but sometimes from wheat, sweet potatoes, barley, or sugar cane, can be consumed straight but is often combined with soda water in a drink called *chuhai*. *Ume-shu*, a plum-flavored *shochu*, is delicious, and quite potent to boot. **Wine,** usually available only at restaurants serving Western food, has become popular in recent years, with both domestic and imported brands available. Though **gin** isn't that widely drunk, Japanese brands like Roku, Ki No Bi, and Nozawa are garnering international attention.

Tips on Dining in Japan

UPON ARRIVAL As soon as you're seated in a Japanese restaurant (that is, a restaurant serving Japanese food), you'll be given a wet towel, which will be steaming hot in winter or pleasantly cool in summer. Called an *oshibori,* it's for wiping your hands. In all but the fancy restaurants, men can get away with wiping their faces as well, but women are not supposed to (although some ignore this if it's hot and humid outside). Sadly, many Japanese restaurants now resort to a paper towel wrapped in plastic, which isn't nearly the same.

ORDERING The biggest problem facing the hungry foreigner in Japan is ordering a meal in a restaurant without an English-language menu. This book alleviates the problem to some extent by recommending sample dishes and giving price ranges; I've also included restaurants offering English-language menus. It's also possible to get around the issue by using translation apps with scanning functionality.

Ordering is sometimes simplified with pictures of the food in the menu or the use of plastic food models in glass display cases either outside or just inside the front door of many restaurants, especially those in tourist areas and department stores. Simply decide what you want and point it out to staff.

Still, you'd be missing a lot of Japan's best cuisine if you restricted yourself to eating only at places with displays. If there's no display, English menu, or photographs in the Japanese menu, a simple solution is to order the *teishoku,* or daily special meal (also called "seto," "set course," or simply "course,"); these fixed-price meals consist of a main dish and several side dishes, including soup, rice, and Japanese pickles. Although most restaurants have set courses for dinner as well, lunch is the usual time for the *teishoku,* generally from 11 or 11:30am to 1:30 or 2pm.

Once you've decided what you want to eat, flag down a waiter or waitress; they will not hover around your table waiting for you to order but come only when summoned—the word for hailing them is *sumimasen,* akin to "excuse me." In most restaurants, servers are not assigned to specific tables but are multitaskers, so don't be shy about stopping any who pass by.

EATING & DRINKING ETIQUETTE The first thing you'll be confronted with in a Japanese restaurant is chopsticks (in restaurants serving Western food, knives and forks are provided instead). Chopstick etiquette says that if you're taking something from a communal bowl or tray, you're supposed to turn your chopsticks upside down and use the part that hasn't been in your mouth; after transferring the food to your plate, you turn the chopsticks back to their proper position. The exception is *shabu-shabu* and *sukiyaki.* To be honest, I don't often see people observe this etiquette.

You don't use a spoon with Japanese soup. Rather, you'll pick up the bowl and drink from it, using your chopsticks to fish out larger pieces of

Eating on the Move: A No-No

It's considered bad manners to walk down the street eating or drinking (except at a festival). You'll notice that if a Japanese buys a drink from a vending machine, he'll stand there, gulp it down, and throw away the container before going on. To the chagrin of their elders, young Japanese sometimes ignore this rule.

food. You should also pick up a bowl of rice to eat it. It's considered good taste to slurp with gusto, especially if you're eating hot noodles.

As for drinking etiquette, women should hold their glass or cup with both hands, but men do not. The main thing to remember if you're with a group is that you never pour your own glass (bottles of beer are so large that people often share one). The rule is that in turn, one person pours for everyone else in the group, so be sure to hold up your glass when someone is pouring for you. As the night progresses Japanese get sloppy about this rule. If someone wants to pour you a drink and your glass is full, the proper thing to do is to take a few gulps so that he or she can fill your glass. Because each person is continually filling everyone else's glass, you never know exactly how much you've had to drink, which (depending on how you look at it) is either very good or very bad. If you really don't want more to drink, leave your glass full and refuse refills.

PAYING THE BILL If you go out with a group of friends (not as a visiting guest of honor and not with business associates), it's customary to split the dinner bill equally, even if you all ordered different things. If you're with friends who do wish to pay for only what they ate, tell the cashier you want to pay *"betsu, betsu."*

EXTRA CHARGES & TAXES Japan's consumption tax imposed on goods and services, including restaurant meals, is 10%. Some restaurants include the tax in their menu prices, while others do not (it's usually stated on the menu whether taxes are included). In finer restaurants and nightlife establishments, a 10% to 15% service charge may also be levied (**there is no tipping in Japan**). You should also be aware of the "table charge" imposed on customers by some bars (especially *nomiya*), many cocktail lounges, and, only rarely, restaurants. Included in the table charge is usually a small appetizer—maybe nuts, chips, or a vegetable; for this reason, some locales call it an *otsumami* (also called *otoshi*), or snack charge. The charge is usually between ¥300 and ¥500 per person.

The Land of Karaoke

Literally meaning "empty orchestra," karaoke was introduced to the world by Japanese engineer Shigeichi Negishi in 1967. Today, every major city in the country is home to multi-floor karaoke parlors, where visitors rent private rooms, rather than the Western style of singing to a bar full of strangers (though these exist, too). It goes without saying that the more the liquor flows, the better everyone sounds.

HOURS In larger cities, most restaurants are open from about 11am to 9pm and later. Many close for a few hours in the afternoon, though inexpensive ones are open all day. In big cities like Tokyo or Osaka, try to avoid the lunchtime rush from noon to 1pm. In rural areas, restaurants tend to close early, often by 7:30 or 8pm. Traditional Japanese restaurants hang a *noren* (split curtain) over the front door to signify they're open. Keep in mind that the closing time posted for most restaurants is exactly that—everyone is expected to pay his or her bill and leave. A general rule of thumb is that the last order is taken at least a half-hour before closing time, sometimes an hour or more for *kaiseki* restaurants (staff members will usually alert you that they're taking last orders). To be on the safe side, try to arrive at least an hour before closing time so you have time to relax and enjoy your meal.

How to Eat Without Spending a Fortune

Japan feels cheaper than ever right now, but it's still worth noting some tips for getting the most for your yen.

BREAKFAST Buffet breakfasts are popular at Japanese hotels and can be an inexpensive way to eat your fill—though the eggs are usually piles of sloppy yellow goop. Otherwise, coffee shops offer what's called "morning service" until 10 or 11am; it generally consists of a cup of coffee, a small salad, a boiled egg, and thick toast. There are also many coffee-shop chains, including Doutour, Pronto, and the ever-expanding Starbucks. Except at most hotel breakfast buffets, there's no such thing as the bottomless cup in Japan.

SET LUNCHES Many restaurants serving Japanese food offer a daily set lunch, or *teishoku,* at a fraction of what the set dinners might be, from about 11am to around 2pm. A Japanese *teishoku* will include the main course (such as tempura, grilled fish, or the specialty of the house), soup, pickled vegetables, rice, and tea, while the set menu in a Western-style restaurant usually consists of a main dish, salad, bread, and coffee.

CHEAP EATS Inexpensive restaurants can be found in department stores (often one whole upper floor will be devoted to restaurants, most with plastic-food displays), underground shopping arcades, nightlife districts, and in and around train and subway stations. Hotel restaurants can also be good bargains for inexpensive set lunches or buffets (often called *viking* in Japanese), though often they're pretty meh.

Some of the cheapest establishments for a night out on the town are *yakitori-ya,* izakaya, noodle and ramen shops, coffee shops (which often offer inexpensive pastries and sandwiches), and conveyor-belt sushi restaurants. Restaurants serving Indian, Korean, Chinese, Thai, and Vietnamese cuisines are plentiful and usually inexpensive.

Street-side stalls, called *yatai,* are also good sources of inexpensive meals. These restaurants-on-wheels sell a variety of foods, including *oden* (fish cakes), *yakitori* (skewered barbecued chicken), and *yakisoba* (fried

A cheerful izakaya in Yokohama.

noodles), as well as sake and beer. They appear largely at night—and are a source of civic pride in the southern city of Fukuoka—lighted by a single lantern or a string of lights; most have a counter with stools as well, protected in winter by a wall of tarp. Sadly, traditional pushcarts are being replaced by motorized vans, which are not nearly as romantic and do not offer seating. You can still find yatai, however, at festivals.

PREPARED FOODS You'll save even more money by avoiding restaurants altogether and buying prepared foods. Some are even complete meals, perfect for picnics in a park or on a train journey. Perhaps the best known is the ***bento,*** or boxed lunch, commonly sold at train stations, in food sections of department stores, and at counter windows of tiny shops throughout Japan. Bento are also served by vendors on some Shinkansen trains (though they were recently discontinued on the most popular Tokaido route between Tokyo and Osaka). The basic bento contains animal protein (generally fish or chicken), various side dishes, rice, and pickled vegetables. Sushi boxed lunches are also readily available.

Department store **food sections** harken back to Japanese markets of yore, with vendors yelling out their wares and crowds of housewives deciding on the evening's dinner. Different counters specialize in different items—tempura, yakitori, Japanese pickles, cooked fish, sushi, salads, vegetables, and desserts. Practically the entire spectrum of Japanese cuisine is available, as are counters selling bento box meals. There's nothing like milling with Japanese housewives to make you feel like one of the locals.

Though not as colorful, 24-hour **convenience and grocery stores** also sell packaged foods like sandwiches, cup noodles, pastries, cooked foods, and bento. In recent years Japan's 7-Elevens and FamilyMarts have gained a lot of online attention, including best-of lists, YouTube reviews, and chat forums full of netizens arguing over which does the best *onigiri,* iced coffee, or fried chicken.

Japanese Fast Food in a Bowl

For a cheap, filling, and tasty meal, Japan has plenty of popular chain restaurants serving *gyudon* (beef bowls). **Yoshinoya** (yoshinoya.com) is the largest chain, though I personally prefer **Matsuya** (matsuyafoods.co.jp) and **Sukiya** (sukiya.jp), both of which have vending machine or tablet menus, with English translation, for ordering. **Curry House CoCo ICHIBANYA** (ichibanya.co.jp), better known as CoCo Curry, serves Japanese-style curry rice—a cheap and cheerful meal that's Japan's surprise national dish—including vegetarian, low-carb, and Halal options.

TIPS ON ACCOMMODATIONS

Accommodations in Japan range from Japanese-style inns (*ryokan*) to large Western-style hotels, in all price categories. Although you can theoretically travel throughout Japan without making reservations beforehand, it's essential to book in advance if you're visiting during peak travel seasons and is highly recommended at other times (see "When to Go," p. 55, for peak travel times). If you arrive in a town without reservations, most local tourist offices—generally located in or near the main train station—will find accommodations for you at no extra charge. ***Note:*** Most lodgings, especially in popular destinations, raise their rates in peak season and on weekends.

All accommodations levy a 10% consumption charge. Upper-end and some moderately priced hotels also add a 10% to 15% service charge, while expensive *ryokan* will add a 10% to 20% service charge. No service charge is levied at business hotels and inexpensive lodgings for the simple reason that no services are provided. In hot-spring resort areas, an *onsen* (spa) tax of ¥150 is added per night, though some regions are increasing this to ¥300 or more. Tokyo and Kyoto also levy their own local hotel tax (Kyoto's is set for a huge hike in 2026—see chapter 7 for more info). Unless otherwise stated, prices in this guide include all consumption taxes and service charges (but not *onsen* or local hotel tax) and range from the cheapest room in low season to the highest-priced deluxe room in peak season.

For bookings, check individual hotel websites first to see whether any special rates or packages are available, and then compare them to Japan's largest travel booking website **japanican.com** or other online sites like **booking.com** or **hotelscombined.com** (which Frommers.com found to have the lowest rates most consistently worldwide). Note that some smaller properties or independent guesthouses in rural Japan are either not listed on third-party sites or give much better rates to guests booking directly.

Japanese-Style Inns

Although an overnight stay in a *ryokan* can be astoundingly expensive, it's worth the splurge at least once during your stay. Nothing quite conveys the simplicity and beauty of old Japan more than these inns with their gleaming polished wood, *tatami* floors, rice-paper sliding doors, and meticulously pruned gardens. Personalized service by kimono-clad hostesses and exquisitely prepared *kaiseki* meals are the trademarks of such inns, some of which are of ancient vintage. Staying in one is like taking a trip back in time.

A night at a traditional ryokan inn can be one of the most memorable experiences of a trip to Japan.

If you want to experience a Japanese-style inn but can't afford the prices of a full-service *ryokan,* a few alternatives are described below. Although they don't offer the same personalized service, beautiful setting, or memorable cuisine, they do offer the chance to sleep on a futon in a simple *tatami* room and, in some cases, eat Japanese meals.

RYOKAN *Ryokan* developed during the Edo period, when *daimyo* (feudal lords) were required to travel to and from Edo (present-day Tokyo) every 1 or 2 years. The *daimyo* always traveled with a full entourage including family members, retainers, and servants. The best *ryokan* were reserved for the *daimyo* and members of the imperial family. Some of these still exist today, passed down from generation to generation.

Traditionally, *ryokan* are small, only one or two stories high, contain about 10 to 30 rooms, and are made of wood with a tile roof. Most guests arrive at their *ryokan* at around 3 or 4pm. The entrance is often through a gate and small courtyard garden; upon entering, you're met by the gate attendant or a bowing woman in a kimono. Take off your shoes, slide on the proffered plastic slippers, and follow your hostess down the long wooden corridors until you reach the sliding door of your room. After taking off your slippers, step into your *tatami* room, almost void of furniture except for a low table in the middle of the room, floor cushions, an antique scroll hanging in a *tokonoma* (alcove), and a simple flower arrangement. Best of all is the view past sliding screens of a Japanese landscaped garden with bonsai, stone lanterns, and a meandering pond filled with carp. Notice there's no bed in the room.

Almost immediately, your hostess serves you welcoming hot tea and a sweet at your low table so you can sit there for a while, recuperate from your travels, and appreciate the view. Next comes your hot bath, either in your own room or in a communal bath. Because *ryokan* are usually clustered around *onsen,* many offer the additional luxury of thermal baths,

Hotel Price Categories Used in This Guide

For most hotels, room rates are listed for doubles (which may have either twin or double beds), with prices for single rooms added in many cases. In the case of traditional inns, room rates are generally per person. Please assume that high-end suites, if the hotel has them, will be pricier. I use a slightly different price scale for Tokyo and Kyoto, where hotels tend to charge higher rates.

Tokyo & Kyoto
Inexpensive: ¥25,000 and under
Moderate: ¥25,000–¥50,000
Expensive: ¥50,000 and up
Elsewhere in Japan
Inexpensive: ¥15,000 and under
Moderate: ¥15,000–¥35,000
Expensive: ¥35,000 and up

including outdoor baths. (For bathing customs, see p. 35.) After soaking away all your travel fatigue, aches, and pains, change into your *yukata,* a cotton kimono provided by the *ryokan.* You can wear your *yukata* throughout the *ryokan,* even to its restaurant if there is one (in Western-style hotels, however, never wear a *yukata* outside your room unless you're going to its public bath or it's located in a resort *onsen* setting).

When you return to your room from your bath, you'll find the maid ready to serve your *kaiseki* dinner. Often the highlight of a *ryokan* stay, this is an elaborate spread of locally grown vegetables, sashimi (raw fish), grilled or baked fish, tempura, and various regional specialties, served on many tiny plates. (For more on kaiseki, see p. 38.) If you want, you can order sake or beer to accompany your meal (you'll pay extra for drinks).

After your meal, your maid will return to clear away the dishes and to lay out your futon, a two-layered mattress with quilts, on the *tatami* floor. The next morning, the maid will wake you, put away the futon, and serve a breakfast of fish, pickled vegetables, soup, dried seaweed, rice, and other dishes. Your hostess sees you off at the front gate, smiling and bowing as you set off for the rest of your travels.

Such is life at a good (read: expensive) *ryokan.* Sadly, the number of upper-class *ryokan* diminishes each year, and with staff shortages across the hotel industry, many others now have switched to serving diners in public dining halls. Unable to compete with high-rise hotels, many *ryokan* have closed down, especially in large cities; very few remain in Tokyo and Osaka. If you want to stay in a Japanese inn, it's best to do so in Kyoto, smaller towns like Takayama, or at a hot-spring spa like Hakone. In addition, many *ryokan* today, especially in hot-spring resort areas, are actually modern concrete affairs with as many as 100 or more rooms and communal dining rooms. What they lack in intimacy and personal service, however, is made up for

How to Wear Your *Yukata*

The proper way to wear a *yukata* is to first fold the right side over your body and then wrap over it with the left side on the outside; the opposite is done only when a person has died.

by cheaper prices, modern bathing facilities, and perhaps outdoor recreational facilities.

Although I heartily recommend you try spending at least 1 night in a *ryokan,* they do have some disadvantages. The most obvious problem is that you may be uncomfortable sitting on the floor. And because the futon is put away during the day, there's no easy place to lie down for an afternoon nap. *Ryokan* often supply horrible beaded pillows, and some older properties, though quaint, can be cold in the winter. As for breakfast, you might not be used to having raw egg, rice, and seaweed in the morning. (Some *ryokan* offer a Western-style breakfast if you order it the night before, though more often than not, the fried or scrambled eggs will arrive cold. Resort *ryokan* with dining halls, however, almost always offer breakfast buffets with both Western and Japanese dishes.) A traditional *ryokan* is also quite rigid in its schedule. You're expected to arrive between 3 and 5pm, take your bath, and then eat at around 6 or 7pm. Breakfast is served early, usually around 7am, and checkout is by 10am.

One potential workaround is to stay in a modern property that combines Western-style comforts—beds, sofas, proper pillows, no schedule—with *ryokan*-style aesthetics, like sliding screens, wood latticing, landscape gardens, and the sparing use of ornaments like pottery and hanging scrolls. Usually these hotels are expensive, like **Hoshinoya** in Tokyo (p. 144) or **Banyan Tree** in Kyoto (p. 324), but more affordable options exist, too, like the wonderful **Hotel Chupki** in Hokkaido (p. 667).

Roller-Bag Etiquette

Under no circumstances should you roll a piece of luggage onto *tatami* or on old wooden floors of Japanese inns.

RYOKAN RATES & RESERVATIONS Rates in a *ryokan* are always per person rather than per room and include breakfast, dinner, and often service and tax. Thus, while rates may seem high, they're actually competitively priced compared to what you'd pay for a hotel room and comparable meals in a restaurant. Although rates can vary from ¥10,000 to an astonishing ¥200,000 per person, the average cost is generally ¥15,000 to ¥35,000. Even within a single *ryokan* the rates can vary greatly, depending on the room you choose, the dinner courses you select, and the number of people in your room. Most rates for *ryokan* in this book are based on the cost per person per night; if there are more than two of you in one room, you can generally count on a slightly lower per-person rate (small children who sleep in the same bed as their parents often receive a discount as well). Most Japanese would never dream of checking into an exclusive *ryokan* solo, but lone travelers may be able to secure a room if it's not peak season.

For more information on *ryokan,* check the websites of the **Japan Ryokan & Hotel Association** (ryokan.or.jp), which lists some 1,200 inns and hotels, and **Japanese Guest Houses** (japaneseguesthouses.com), with more than 400 high-end and moderately priced Japanese inns. For some of the most luxurious *ryokan* in Japan, see **The Ryokan Collection** (ryokancollection.com).

MINSHUKU Technically, a *minshuku* is inexpensive Japanese-style lodging in a private home—the Japanese version of a bed-and-breakfast. Usually located in rural settings, small towns, or tourist areas like hot springs or ski resorts, *minshuku* can range from thatched farmhouses and rickety old wooden buildings to modern concrete structures. Because *minshuku* are family-run affairs, you may be expected to lay out your own futon at night, stow it away in the morning, and tidy up your room. Most do not supply a towel or *yukata,* nor do they generally have private bathrooms. There is, however, a public bathroom, and meals, usually included in the rates, are served in a communal dining room. Many *minshuku* owners have day jobs, so guests must be punctual for meals and checkout. Sadly, some *minshuku* owners are finding it easier to convert to a guesthouse, which is cheaper but provides less one-on-one interaction (see p. 54). The average per-person cost for 1 night in a *minshuku,* including two meals, is around ¥10,000 with two meals; most do not accept credit cards. At many, meals are now optional, so arrange in advance if you want them. Reservations for *minshuku* should be made directly with the establishment.

Western-Style Accommodations

HOTELS Both first-class and mid-priced hotels in Japan are known for excellent service and cleanliness. Japan's first-class hotels can compete with the best in the world (though many tourism industry insiders say there are fewer of these than there ought to be in a country of Japan's size and wealth). They offer exceptional service and wide-ranging facilities, including health clubs and spas, top-class restaurants, and shopping arcades. Sometimes health clubs and swimming pools cost extra—anywhere from ¥1,500 to an outrageous ¥5,000 per single use—though more hotels are mercifully doing away with this. In addition, outdoor pools are open only from about mid-July through August (the school holiday season).

Almost all hotels in Japan offer a spectrum of rooms at various prices. Room size is the biggest factor in pricing; other factors can include bed size, which floor you're on (higher floors are more expensive), and in-room amenities. Rooms with views—whether of the sea or a castle or even of cityscapes—are usually pricier.

Rooms come with such standard features as a minibar or fridge, TV, free Wi-Fi, *yukata* or pajamas, and a private bathroom with a tub/shower combination. (Because Japanese are used to soaping down and rinsing off before bathing, it is rare to find tubs without showers; showers without tubs are also rare in this nation of bathers.) Virtually all hotels also have "washlet" toilets, combination toilets and spray bidets with a range of speeds and temperatures.

Be sure to give your approximate time of arrival, especially if it's after 6pm, or they might give your room away. Check-in ranges from about 1 or

Western-style sleeping quarters at Hoshinoya Tokyo (p. 144), which blends the attentive service of a ryokan with modern amenities.

2pm in first-class hotels to 3 or 4pm for business hotels. Checkout is generally 10am for business hotels and 11am or noon for upper-range hotels.

BUSINESS HOTELS Catering traditionally to Japanese business travelers, a "business hotel" is a no-frills establishment with tiny, sparsely furnished rooms, most of them singles but usually with some twin and maybe double rooms also available (some also offer semi-double-size beds, wider than a single but narrower than a double, for one or two persons). Primarily just places to crash for the night, these rooms usually have everything you need, but in miniature form—minuscule bathroom, tiny bathtub/shower, small bed (or beds), TV, pajamas, free Wi-Fi, empty fridge, and barely enough space to unpack your bags. There are no bellhops, no room service, and sometimes not even a lobby or coffee shop, although usually there are vending machines selling beer, soda, cigarettes, and snacks. The advantages of staying in business hotels are price (starting as low as ¥6,000 for a single) and location—usually near major train and subway stations.

A Double or a Twin?

In Japan, a **twin room** refers to a room with twin beds, and a **double room** refers to one with a double bed or larger (many upper-range hotels also have king- or queen-size beds); most hotels charge more for a twin room, but some charge more for doubles. Because Japanese couples generally prefer twin beds, doubles are often in short supply, especially in business hotels.

As for business-hotel chains, **Toyoko Inn** (toyoko-inn.com) has locations around Japan and offers competitive prices. Other budget and medium-priced chains are **Tokyu REI Hotels** (tokyuhotels.co.jp), many with specially designed Ladies Rooms with female-oriented toiletries; **Hotel Gracery** brands (global.whg-hotels.jp/hotel-gracery); **Mitsui Garden Hotels** (gardenhotels.co.jp); and fast-growing **APA Hotels** (apahotel.com).

Other Accommodations Alternatives

SHUKUBO These are lodgings in a Buddhist temple, similar to inexpensive *ryokan,* except they're attached to temples and serve vegetarian food. There's usually an early morning service at 6am, which you're welcome to joi (in some *shukubo,* it's required). Probably the best place to experience life in a temple is at Mount Koya (see chapter 8) or in Kyoto. Prices at shukubo generally range from about ¥10,000 to ¥25,000 per person, including two meals.

GUESTHOUSES Virtually nonexistent more than a decade ago, low-cost guesthouses and private hostels have spread like wildfire in cities around the country, catering primarily to backpackers and travelers who don't mind close quarters. They often have a few tiny private rooms with *tatami* or beds for one or two people, sometimes with private bathrooms, but the majority are known primarily for their dorms, with shared bathrooms down the hall. Many have communal kitchens and lounge areas as well. Some independent properties that fall into this category are lovely, with friendly service and private rooms that are like small hotel guestrooms. Just be aware of the amenities offered before you book. Prices generally range from about ¥5,000 to ¥10,000.

BACKPACKER HOSTELS As Japan has become more affordable for young solo travelers, the number of hostels has increased. Rooms are usually dormitory-style with bunk beds or futons, though some have double rooms. A bunk bed in a dorm is usually between ¥3,000 and ¥7,000 per night, far cheaper than hotel rooms in similar locations. Hostels in Japan tend to be used by a broad demographic, including older couples and sometimes families, so they don't guarantee the lively youthful atmosphere found in hostels across Europe and Southeast Asia. But you may not view that as a bad thing.

CAPSULE HOTELS Capsule hotels became popular in the 1980s, used primarily by Japanese businessmen who'd spent an evening out drinking and missed the last train home. They've now become more mainstream, with many catering to both male and female guests. Costing around ¥5,000 per person, units are small—no larger than a coffin—and are usually stacked two deep in rows down a corridor; the only thing separating you from your probably inebriated neighbor is a curtain. A cotton kimono and a locker are provided, and bathrooms and toilets are communal.

AIRBNB Home-sharing became legal in Japan in 2017 (though Airbnb was widespread before then) and requires hosts to apply for a license and register with local authorities. Properties range from older traditional homes to apartments to a small room in a shared flat. On rare occasions, guesthouses or minshuku may be booked through Airbnb. You can find also beautiful home-sharing properties in the countryside, usually in places you can't really access by public transport. But generally Airbnb is not a popular form of accommodation in Japan.

CAMPSITES Some young Japanese and families head to campsites on summer weekends, usually located near beaches or on riverbanks where you can fish or swim. Often there's a fee, perhaps ¥1,000-¥2,000 per person, though sometimes even less. You'll probably only use them if you're on a long walk, like the Shikoku Pilgrimage (p. 496) or Michinoku Coastal Trail (p. 628).

LOVE HOTELS Finally, a word about Japan's so-called love hotels. Usually found close to entertainment districts and along major highways, such hotels do not offer sexual services; rather, they provide rooms for rent by the hour to couples (as well as overnight). You'll know that you've wandered into a love-hotel district when you notice hourly rates posted near the front door, though gaudy structures shaped like ocean liners or castles are also a dead giveaway. Because many have reasonable overnight rates, I am not averse to crashing in one solo when out late and too far from home to stomach the cost of a taxi.

WHEN TO GO

Weather-wise, the best times to visit Japan are spring (Apr to mid-June) and autumn (Sept–Nov). Most of the country lies in a temperate seasonal wind zone, similar to that of the East Coast of the United States, which means there are four distinct seasons—five if you count *tsuyu,* the rainy season. Japanese are very proud of their seasons and place much more emphasis on them than people do in the West. Kimono, dishes and bowls used for *kaiseki,* and even *Noh* plays change with the season. The cherry blossom signals the beginning of spring, and most festivals are tied to seasonal rites.

Summer, which begins in June, is heralded by the rainy season, which lasts from about mid-June to mid-July. Although it doesn't rain every day, it does rain a lot, sometimes quite heavily, making umbrellas imperative. After the rain stops, it turns unbearably hot and uncomfortably humid throughout the country, with the exception of mountaintop resorts such as those in the Japan Alps. You'll be more comfortable in light cottons, though you should bring a light jacket for unexpected cool evenings or air-conditioned rooms. You should also pack sunscreen and a hat (Japanese women are fond of parasols).

The period from the end of August to September is **typhoon season,** although the majority of storms stay out at sea and generally vent their fury on land only in thunderstorms. That said, typhoons with a rating of category 3 or higher (winds gusting at 178kmph/111mph and above) occasionally whip across the landmass, affecting transport networks and causing flooding in river basins. Though they can be deadly, Japan is well prepared for such events: You can stay up to date with disaster alerts in English through the NHK World apps, while the **Disaster Preparedness Tokyo App** is also worth downloading.

Autumn, lasting through November, is one of the best times to visit Japan, but it's also one of the most crowded seasons, with higher hotel prices to meet the demand. Days are pleasant and slightly cool, and the changing red and scarlet of leaves contrast brilliantly with deep blue skies. There are many chrysanthemum shows in Japan at this time, popular maple-viewing spots, and many autumn festivals. Bring a warm jacket.

Winter, lasting from December to March, is marked by snow in much of Japan, especially in the mountain ranges, attracting skiers and snowboarders chasing the fabled "Japow"—a somewhat cringy term for the powdery snow dumped on Japan's mountain slopes. It also draws Asian tourists who don't see snow in their own countries, while Japanese tourists enjoy a winter break at hot-spring resorts. The climate is generally dry, and on the Pacific coast the skies are often blue. Tokyo doesn't get much snow, though it can be cold, and wet.

Spring arrives in March and April with a magnificent fanfare of plum and cherry blossoms, an exquisite time when all of Japan is ablaze in whites and pinks. The blossoms themselves last only a few days, symbolizing to Japanese the fragile nature of beauty and of life itself. Other flowers blooming through May or June include azaleas and irises. Numerous festivals throughout Japan celebrate the rebirth of nature.

Tokyo's Average Daytime Temperatures & Rainfall

	JAN	FEB	MAR	APR	MAY	JUNE	JULY	AUG	SEPT	OCT	NOV	DEC
TEMP. (°F)	42	45	50	61	69	71	78	81	76	68	57	48
TEMP. (°C)	5	7	10	16	21	22	26	27	24	20	14	9
DAYS OF RAIN	4.3	6.1	8.9	10	9.6	12.1	10	8.2	10.9	8.9	6.4	3.8

BUSY SEASONS Japanese have a passion for travel, and they generally travel at the same time, leading to jam-packed trains and hotels. The worst times to travel are around **New Year's,** from the end of December to January 4; **Golden Week,** from April 29 to May 5; and during the **Obon Festival,** about a week in mid-August. Avoid traveling on these dates at all costs, since many long-distance trains and most accommodations are fully booked and prices are sky-high. The weekends before and after these holidays are also likely to be crowded. **Chinese New Year** is also considered high season, given the number of travelers from Japan's neighboring country.

Other busy times are during the **school summer vacation,** from around July 19 or 20 through August, **cherry blossom season,** and when leaves change in **autumn.** In addition, you can expect destinations to be packed during major festivals, so if one of these is high on your list, make plans well in advance. This, you may notice, covers most of the year; Japan is just that kind of destination now. Winter and the rainy season are quieter, but only to a degree.

HOLIDAYS National holidays are January 1 (New Year's Day), second Monday in January (Coming-of-Age Day), February 11 (National Foundation Day), February 23 (Emperor Naruhito's birthday), March 20 (Vernal Equinox Day), April 29 (Showa Day, after the late Emperor Showa),

May 3 (Constitution Memorial Day), May 4 (Greenery Day), May 5 (Children's Day), third Monday in July (Maritime Day), August 11 (Mountain Day); third Monday in September (Respect-for-the-Aged Day), September 23 (Autumn Equinox Day), second Monday in October (Health Sports Day), November 3 (Culture Day; many municipal museums are free), and November 23 (Labor Thanksgiving Day).

When a national holiday falls on a Sunday, the following Monday becomes a holiday. Although government offices and some businesses are closed on public holidays, most stores and restaurants remain open. The exception is during the New Year's celebration, January 1 through January 3 or 4, when virtually all restaurants, public and private offices, stores, and even some ATMs close; during that time, you may have to dine in hotels.

All museums close for New Year's for 1 to 4 days, but most major museums remain open for the other holidays. If a public holiday falls on a Monday (when most museums are closed), many museums will remain open but will close instead the following day, Tuesday. Note, however, that privately owned museums, such as art museums or special-interest museums, generally set more independent schedules. To avoid disappointment, be sure to phone ahead or check social media pages.

Calendar of Events

JANUARY

New Year's Day is the most important national holiday in Japan. Japanese are with their families and virtually all businesses, restaurants, museums, and shops close down. For visitors, your best bet is to head for shrines and temples, where Japanese come in their best kimono or dress to pray for health and happiness. It's said up to 1 million visit Ise Grand Shrine on this date every year. January 1.

Coming-of-Age Day. This national holiday honors young people who have reached the age of 20, when they can vote, drink alcohol, and assume other responsibilities. On this day, they visit shrines throughout the country to pray for their future, with many women dressed in kimono. In Tokyo, the most popular shrine is Meiji Jingu near Harajuku Station. Second Monday in January.

Toka Ebisu Festival, Imamiya Ebisu Shrine, Osaka. Ebisu is the patron saint of business and good fortune, so businesspeople come to pray for a successful year. The highlight of the festival is a parade of women dressed in colorful kimono and carried through the streets in palanquins (covered litters). Stalls sell good-luck charms. January 9 to January 11.

Toh-shiya, Kyoto. This traditional Japanese archery contest is held in the back corridor of Japan's longest wooden structure, Sanjusangendo Hall. Sunday closest to January 15.

Yamayaki (Grass Fire Ceremony), Nara. As evening approaches, Wakakusayama Hill is set ablaze and fireworks are displayed. The celebration marks a time more than 1,000 years ago when a dispute over the boundary of two major temples in Nara was settled peacefully. Fourth Saturday in January.

FEBRUARY

Sapporo Snow Festival, Sapporo. Held over a week in early February, this is one of Japan's grandest annual art showcases, featuring snow and ice sculptures depicting everything from feudal castles to grand cathedrals to the houses of heads of state. A week in early February.

Setsubun Mantoro (Lantern Festival), Kasuga Shrine, Nara. A beautiful sight in which more than 3,000 stone and bronze lanterns are lit from 6:30 to 9pm. February 3 and August 14 and 15.

MARCH

Omizutori (Water-Drawing Festival), Todaiji Temple, Nara. This festival includes a solemn evening rite in which young ascetics brandish large burning torches and draw circles of fire. The biggest event is on March 13, when water is drawn and offered to Buddhist deities, accompanied by ancient Japanese music. March 1 to March 14.

Hinamatsuri (Doll Festival), observed throughout Japan. It's held in honor of young girls to wish them a future of happiness. In homes where there are girls, dolls dressed in ancient costumes are displayed along with miniature household articles. Many hotels also display dolls in their lobbies. March 3.

AnimeJapan, Tokyo Big Sight, Odaiba (anime-japan.jp). One of the world's largest Japanese animation events draws production companies, film agencies, toy and game software companies, publishers, and other *anime*-related entities. Usually third weekend in March.

APRIL

Kanamara Matsuri, Kanayama Shrine, Kawasaki (just outside Tokyo). This festival extols the joys of sex and fertility (and, more recently, raises awareness about AIDS), featuring a parade of giant phalluses, some carried by members of the trans community. First Sunday in April.

Kamakura Matsuri, Tsurugaoka Hachimangu Shrine, Kamakura. This festival honors heroes from the past, including Minamoto Yoritomo, who made Kamakura his shogunate capital back in 1192. Highlights include horseback archery (truly spectacular to watch, although fewer and fewer men have the skill), a parade of portable shrines, and sacred dances. Second to third Sunday of April.

Takayama Spring Festival, Takayama. Supposedly dating from the 15th century, this festival is one of Japan's grandest, with a dozen huge, gorgeous floats wheeled through the village streets. April 14 and 15.

Yayoi Matsuri, Futarasan Shrine, Nikko. Yayoi Matsuri features parades of portable shrines and dance, with the biggest a parade of floats embellished with artificial cherry blossoms and paper lanterns on April 17. April 16 and April 17.

MAY

Takigi Noh Performances, Kofukuji Temple, Nara. *Noh* plays are presented outdoors after dark under the blaze of torches. Third Friday and Saturday in May.

Kanda Festival, Kanda Myojin Shrine, Tokyo. Commemorating Tokugawa Ieyasu's famous victory at Sekigahara in 1600, in feudal days this festival was the only time townspeople could enter the shogun's castle and parade before him. Today it features a parade of dozens of portable shrines carried through the district, plus geisha dances and a tea ceremony. Held in odd-numbered years (with a smaller festival in even years) on the Saturday and Sunday closest to May 15.

Aoi Matsuri (Hollyhock Festival), Shimogamo and Kamigamo Shrines, Kyoto. One of Kyoto's biggest events, this colorful parade features 500 participants wearing ancient costumes to commemorate the days when the imperial procession visited the city's shrines. May 15.

Shunki Reitaisai (Grand Spring Festival), Nikko. Commemorating the day in 1617 when Tokugawa Ieyasu's remains were brought to his mausoleum in Nikko, this festival re-creates that drama with more than 1,000 armor-clad people escorting three palanquins through the streets. May 17 and 18.

Sanja Matsuri, Asakusa Shrine, Tokyo. Tokyo's most celebrated festival features about 100 portable shrines carried through the district on the shoulders of men and women in traditional garb. Third Sunday and preceding Friday and Saturday of May.

JUNE

Takigi Noh Performances, Kyoto. Evening performances of *Noh* are presented on an open-air stage at Heian Shrine. June 1 and 2.

Hyakumangoku Matsuri (One Million Goku Festival), Kanazawa. Celebrating Kanazawa's production of 1 million *goku* of rice (1 *goku* is about 150kg/330 lb.), this extravaganza features folk songs and traditional dancing in the streets, illuminated paper lanterns floating downriver, public tea ceremonies, geisha performances, and—the highlight—a parade reenacting Lord Maeda Toshiie's triumphant arrival in Kanazawa on June 14, 1583, with lion dances, ladder-top acrobatics by firemen, and a torch-lit outdoor *Noh* performance. Three days centered on first Saturday in June.

Sanno Festival, Hie Shrine, Tokyo. This Edo Period festival, one of Tokyo's largest, features the usual portable shrines, transported through the busy streets of the Akasaka District. June 6 to June 17.

Otaue Rice-Planting Festival, Sumiyoshi Taisha Shrine, Osaka. In hopes of a successful harvest, young girls in traditional farmers' costumes transplant rice seedlings in the shrine's rice paddy to the sound of traditional music and songs. June 14.

JULY

Tanabata, nationwide. This festival of "star-crossed lovers" takes place on the 7th day of the 7th month each year, when, according to a Chinese legend, the two stars Altair and Vega, usually separated from each other by the Milky Way, were finally able to meet. Young singletons go out in search of love, usually in decorated shrine courtyards, where they write their desires on colorful strips of paper (*tanzaku*) and hang them on bamboo branches. Expect, music, dance, and festive food. July 7.

Gion Matsuri, Kyoto. One of the most famous festivals in Japan, this dates back to the 9th century, when the head priest at Yasaka Shrine organized a procession to ask the gods' help during a plague. Celebrations run throughout the month, but the highlight is on the 17th, when more than 30 spectacular wheeled floats wind through the city streets, accompanied by music and dances. July 17.

Tenjin Matsuri, Temmangu Shrine, Osaka. One of Japan's biggest festivals, this dates from the 10th century, when the people of Osaka visited the shrine to pray for protection against diseases prevalent during the long, hot summer. While the Shinto priest said prayers, they would use pieces of paper cut in human shapes to rub themselves in a ritual cleansing. Afterward, the paper pieces were taken by boat to the mouth of the river and disposed of. Today, events are reenacted with a procession of more than 100 sacred boats making their way downriver, followed by a fireworks display. There's also a parade of some 3,000 people in traditional costume. July 24 and 25.

Kangensai Music Festival, Itsukushima Shrine, Miyajima. There are classical court music and *Bugaku* dancing, and three barges carrying portable shrines, priests, and musicians across the bay along with a flotilla of other boats. Late July or early August, according to the lunar calendar.

Hanabi Taikai (Fireworks Display), Tokyo. Tokyo's largest summer celebration—first held in 1773 to commemorate lives lost in famine—draws the entire city (it seems) to sit along the banks of the Sumida River near Asakusa to watch the show. It's great fun, though frightfully busy. Last Saturday of July.

AUGUST

Peace Ceremony, Peace Memorial Park, Hiroshima. This ceremony is held annually at 8:15am to honor those who died in the atomic bomb blast of August 6, 1945. In the evening, thousands of lit lanterns are set adrift on the Ota River in a plea for world peace. August 6.

Obon Festival, nationwide. This festival commemorates the dead who, according to Buddhist belief, revisit the world during this period. Many Japanese return to their hometowns for religious rites, especially if a family member has recently died. Mid-July or mid-August, depending on the region.

Daimonji Bonfire, Mount Nyoigadake, Kyoto. A huge bonfire in the shape of the Chinese character *dai,* which means "large," and other motifs are lit near mountain peaks; it's the highlight of the Obon Festival (see above). August 16.

World Cosplay Summit, Nagoya. People from around the world dress up as their favorite manga, anime, and video game characters and descend on Nagoya over a weekend in August. The main event is a competition hosted in an arena, in which participants representing their countries—a la Eurovision—strut their stuff on the stage. A weekend in August.

SEPTEMBER

Reitaisai (Yabusame), Tsurugaoka Hachimangu Shrine, Kamakura. Archery performed on horseback recalls the days of the samurai, along with classical Japanese dance and a parade of portable shrines. September 16.

Tokyo Game Show (TGS), Chiba (just outside Tokyo). The largest gaming convention in Asia (more than 250,000 people attend each year), TGS is a showcase for Japanese video game developers like Bandai Namco, Atlus, Capcom, Square Enix, and Arc System Works. The third or fourth weekend in September.

OCTOBER

Takayama Matsuri (Autumn Festival), Takayama. As in the festival held here in April (see above), huge floats are paraded through the streets. October 9 and 10.

Doburoku Matsuri, Ogimachi, Shirakawago. This village festival honors unrefined sake, said to represent the spirit of God, with a parade, an evening lion dance, and plenty of eating and drinking. October 14 and 15.

Nikko Toshogu Shrine Festival, Nikko. A parade of warriors in early-17th-century dress are accompanied by spear-carriers, gun-carriers, flag-bearers, Shinto priests, pages, court musicians, and dancers as they escort a sacred portable shrine. October 17.

Jidai Matsuri (Festival of the Ages), Kyoto. Another of Kyoto's grand festivals, this one began in 1894 to commemorate the founding of the city in 794. It features a procession of more than 2,000 people in ancient costumes representing different epochs of Kyoto's 1,200-year history, who march from the Imperial Palace to Heian Shrine. October 22.

NOVEMBER

Daimyo Gyoretsu (Feudal Lord Procession), Yumoto Onsen, Hakone. The old Tokaido Highway, which once linked Kyoto and Tokyo, comes alive again with a faithful reproduction of a feudal lord's procession in the olden days. November 3.

Shichi-go-san (Children's Shrine-Visiting Day), held throughout Japan. Shichi-go-san literally means "seven-five-three" and refers to children of these ages who are dressed in their kimono best and taken to shrines by their elders to express thanks and pray for their future. November 15.

DECEMBER

Kasuga Wakamiya On-Matsuri, Kasuga Shrine, Nara. This festival features court music with traditional dance and a parade of people dressed as courtiers, retainers, and wrestlers of long ago. December 15 to December 18.

Hagoita-Ichi (Battledore Fair), Sensoji Temple, Tokyo. Popular since Japan's feudal days, this Asakusa festival features decorated paddles of all types and sizes. Most have designs of *kabuki* actors—images created by pasting together padded silk and brocade—and make great souvenirs and gifts. December 17 to December 19.

New Year's Eve. At midnight, temples ring huge bells 108 times to signal the end of the old year and the beginning of the new. Families visit temples and shrines throughout Japan to pray for the coming year. December 31.

SUGGESTED JAPAN ITINERARIES

3

With its rich culture, entertainment districts, and mountain scenery, Japan has much to offer the curious visitor, not only in and around the major cities like Tokyo, Kyoto, and Osaka but in outlying rural regions and villages as well. Many travelers to Japan never make it off Honshu, the largest of Japan's four major islands and home to most of the country's population—and there's no shame in that. Honshu is where the majority of Japan's important historical events have taken place; you'll find castles, imperial palaces, gardens, temples, shrines, and other attractions linked to the past here, many of them World Heritage Sites. Throw in museums displaying everything from avant-garde art to folk art, shops selling everything from lacquerware to designer fashion, and scenery ranging from the rugged Japan Alps to the picture-book Seto Inland Sea, and Honshu offers a great window into Japanese culture.

Most first-timers follow the Golden Route, which roughly follows the old Tokaido highway between Tokyo and Kyoto, including stops at Hakone and/or Mount Fuji, perhaps with a couple days in Osaka and Hiroshima. It's Japan's greatest hits, but it's also where you're most likely to encounter tourist hordes clogging major sites and historic districts. Consider traveling instead to the Western side of Honshu—to Nagano, Ishikawa, Gifu, and Shimane Prefectures—or perhaps including an excursion to Kyushu in the south or Tohoku in the north.

Repeat visitors may skip the most populated stretch of Japan altogether, instead doing a road trip in Hokkaido or spending more time in Kyushu and the islands in the south. If you're traveling for a specific activity, say hiking, or skiing, or wildlife viewing, scuba diving, this may take you to national parks and farther-flung locales.

This chapter is designed to help you decide on an itinerary, and figure out how you should travel—with rail passes or primarily by car or bus (see chapter 15 for details). If you're lucky enough to be in Japan for several weeks, you can combine several of these suggested itineraries and add a town or two from the chapters that follow.

THE REGIONS IN BRIEF

Separated from China and Korea by the Sea of Japan, Japan stretches in an arc about 2,900km (1,800 miles) long from northeast to southwest, yet it

PREVIOUS PAGE: 10,000 red torii line a long winding pathway behind Fushimi-Inari Shrine near Kyoto.

is only 403km (250 miles) wide at its broadest point. Japan consists primarily of four main islands—**Honshu, Hokkaido, Shikoku,** and **Kyushu,** sometimes collectively referred to as "the mainland"—surrounded by more than 14,000 smaller, mostly uninhabited islands and islets. These are divided into 47 administrative units (which includes **Okinawa**) called prefectures, not dissimilar to U.S. states or British counties.

If you were to superimpose Japan's four main islands onto a map of the United States, they would stretch all the way from Boston to Atlanta. Yet Japan's total landmass is slightly smaller than California in area. As much as 70% of it is mountainous and largely uninhabitable; another 20% is devoted to agriculture. That means that Japan's 123 million people are concentrated in only 10% of the country's landmass, mostly along Honshu's vast plains surrounding Tokyo, Nagoya, and Osaka. Imagine 39% of the U.S. population living in California—primarily in San Diego County—and you get an idea of how crowded Japan is.

For this island nation—isolated physically from the rest of the world, with only limited space for harmonious living—geography and topography have played major roles in shaping its culture, customs, and arts. One of Japan's most iconic artworks, Katushika Hokusai's *The Great Wave Off Kanagawa,* tellingly depicts the raw and destructive power of nature. One thing you'll notice, particularly on the populated eastern coast, is that Japan seems to be terrified of the sea. The coastline is covered in concrete embankments, ugly tetrapods designed to quell wave-power and erosion, and huge seawalls offering protection against tsunamis. Sadly, much of this is pork-barrel construction designed to line the pockets of ministry bureaucrats. But the desire to have solid wave defenses is well-founded—no one wants another 3/11.

Honshu

As Japan's largest island, Honshu might be considered the Japanese mainland (its name translates as "Main Province"). It holds 80% of Japan's population, Japan's tallest mountain (Mount Fuji), and 34 of Japan's 47 prefectures, each with its own capital. Honshu can be divided into five regions: **Kanto** (the Tokyo metropolitan area), **Chubu** (central Honshu,

SHADOWED BY earthquakes

Because Japan straddles four tectonic plates—the Philippine, Eurasian, Pacific, and North American—earthquakes have plagued the country throughout history. In the 20th century, the two most destructive earthquakes were the 1923 Great Kanto Earthquake, which killed more than 100,000 people in the Tokyo area, and the 1995 Great Hanshin Earthquake, which claimed more than 6,000 lives in Kobe. They were followed in March 2011 by Japan's largest earthquake in recorded history, the Great East Japan Earthquake, which struck off the northeast Honshu coast and triggered a massive tsunami that contributed to the loss of more than 20,000 lives.

Japan

0
100 mi
0
100 km
Changchun
Siping
Liaoyuan
Jilin
Songhua R.
Mudanjiang
Jixi
Lake Khanka
RUSSIA
CHINA
Yanji
Vladivostok
Nakhodka
Shenyang
Liaoyang
Tonghua
Baishan
Tumen R.
Yalu R.
Chongjin
NORTH KOREA
Hamhung
Pyongyang
SEA OF JAPAN
Incheon
SEOUL
Suwon
SOUTH KOREA
Daejeon
Daegu
Ulsan
Gwangju
Busan
Korea Strait
Tsushima
Tsushima Strait
Jeju
Dogojima
Matsue
Tottori
Tsuruga
L. Biwa
Chugoku
HO
Kyoto
Kansai
Okayama
Himeji
Hiroshima
Fukuyama
Kobe
Osaka
Inland Sea
Sakai
Kitakyushu
Shimonoseki
Takamatsu
Fukuoka
Matsuyama
SHIKOKU
Kurume
Kochi
Sasebo
Oita
Aso
Fukue
Nagasaki
Kumamoto
Simoshima
KYUSHU
Miyazaki
EAST CHINA SEA
Kagoshima
Osumi Pen.
Tanegashima

3

SUGGESTED JAPAN ITINERARIES | The Regions in Brief

Japan's tallest mountain, majestic Mount Fuji, towers over much of central Honshu and has long held a special place in the Japanese imagination.

including Nagoya), **Kansai** (home to Kyoto and Osaka), **Chugoku** (the westernmost end of Honshu), and **Tohoku** (a vast stretch of largely rural territory covering the north of the island).

TOKYO & THE KANTO REGION Located in east-central Honshu, this district is characterized by the vast Kanto Plain, the largest flatland in Japan. Development of the area didn't begin in earnest until 1603, with the establishment of the shogunate government in Edo (present-day Tokyo), but today Tokyo and surrounding mega-cities like Yokohama comprise the most densely populated region in Japan, if not the world, home to more than 40 million people. There are seven prefectures in Kanto, including Tokyo, the name of both the city and the larger prefecture (with 14 million inhabitants). Although Tokyo is the main tourist draw, worthwhile side trips include Nikko, Kamakura, Hakone, Yokohama, and hiking in the Okutama region.

CHUBU REGION The Chubu, or central, region straddles central Honshu from the Pacific Ocean to the Japan Sea, encompassing nine prefectures. The district features mountain ranges (including the **Japan Alps,** host of the 1998 Winter Olympics in Nagano), volcanoes (including **Mount Fuji**), large rivers, and coastal regions on both sides of the island. The quaint mountain villages of **Takayama** and **Shirakawa-go** have lovely historic districts and thatched-roof farmhouses. The Hokuriku Shinkansen makes **Kanazawa,** with its spectacular garden, wonderful museums, and Edo-era attractions, easily accessible from Tokyo.

KANSAI REGION Also called Kinki and encompassing seven prefectures, this is Japan's most historic region. **Nara** and **Kyoto**—two of Japan's ancient capitals—are here, as is Japan's third largest city, **Osaka.**

Since the 1994 opening of Kansai International Airport outside Osaka, some foreign visitors opt to bypass Tokyo altogether in favor of Kansai's many historic spots, including **Mount Koya** with its many temples, **Himeji** with what is widely considered to be Japan's most beautiful castle, and the spiritual walking trails of the **Kumano Kodo.**

CHUGOKU REGION Honshu's southwestern district has five prefectures divided by the Chugoku Mountain Range. Industrial giant **Hiroshima** is one of the region's biggest cities and draws many tourists to its Peace Memorial Park, dedicated to victims of the world's first atomic bomb. En route to Hiroshima is **Kurashiki,** renowned for its photogenic warehouse district. **Miyajima,** part of the Seto-Naikai (Inland Sea) National Park, is one of Japan's most beautiful islands. **Shimane,** a prefecture even many Japanese don't visit, hosts one of Japan's most significant Shinto shrines and is the heartland of *kagura,* arguably Japan's oldest performance art.

ISE-SHIMA Jutting into the Seto Inland Sea, Shima Peninsula is famous for **Ise-Shima National Park,** noted for its coastal scenery. The real reason to visit is to pay your respects at the **Ise Jingu Shrines,** also known as Ise Grand Shrines, where the sun goddess Amaterasu is enshrined. **Toba,** birthplace of the cultured pearl, is popular for its Mikimoto Pearl Island and the Toba Aquarium.

TOHOKU REGION Northeastern Honshu, with Sendai as its regional center, encompasses six prefectures. Known as Tohoku (literally "East North"), it isn't nearly as developed as the central and southern districts of Honshu, due in large part to its rugged, mountainous terrain and harsh climate. **Matsushima,** about halfway up the coast between Tokyo and the northern tip of Honshu, is the district's major tourist destination, with its scenic pine-clad islets dotting the bay. Inland **Kakunodate** is a former castle town offering preserved samurai houses; **Towada-Hachimantai National Park** has scenic lakes and rustic hot-spring spas. One of the best ways to see Tohoku is via the **Michinoku Coastal Trail,** a 1,025km (637-mile) walking path from Kabushima Shrine in Aomori Prefecture to Soma

TRAVEL WITH RESPECT: kyoto

Kyoto has long been considered a must-visit destination, and while that might still be the case, it's also now incumbent upon travelers to be more conscious of *how* they travel it. Kyoto has suffered more from overtourism than anywhere else in Japan. Some of the major sites are so busy that it's having adverse effects on the tourist experience, not to mention the day-to-day lives of locals and businesses. The streets leading to Kiyomizu Temple, for example, are so choked with visitors that the old-world atmosphere has been all but eroded, while nightlife areas like Pontocho are effectively devoid of Japanese customers. This doesn't mean you should avoid the major sites altogether, but rather plan more strategically when to visit and take note of our offbeat recommendations, which are just as impressive—and, in my view, often much more so—as their well-trodden counterparts.

City in Fukushima. The journey can take up to 2 months on foot; many travelers walk it in sections instead.

Hokkaido

Japan's second-largest island, Hokkaido lies to the north of Honshu and is regarded as the country's last frontier with its wide-open pastures, evergreen forests, mountains, gorges, crystal-clear lakes, and wildlife, much of it preserved in national parks. Originally occupied by the indigenous Ainu, it was colonized by Japanese settlers mostly after the Meiji Restoration in 1868. Today it's home to 5.3 million people, 1.9 million of whom live in **Sapporo,** the lively capital city known for its eclectic seafood, miso-based ramen, and nightlife. Though its landmass accounts for 22% of Japan's total area, Hokkaido has the nation's lowest population density: about 4.5% of the total population. That, together with the island's unspoiled natural beauty, make it a chief draw for nature lovers. Finish your journey at **Shiretoko National Park,** a place the Ainu called *siretok,* the "End of the Earth."

Shikoku

The smallest of the four main islands, Shikoku is off the beaten path for many foreign visitors, but culture buffs won't want to miss the **Art Islands,** installations of contemporary art scattered across a hazy, tree-swept archipelago in the Seto Inland Sea. For active travelers, the **Shimanami Kaido** route offers 70 scenic km (43 miles) of dedicated biking trails that connect Shikoku with Hiroshima Prefecture via six islands and a series of suspension bridges. A growing number of travelers also head to Shikoku to make the approximately 6-week **Shikoku Pilgrimage** to its 88 Buddhist temples, founded by the Buddhist priest Kukai (known posthumously as Kobo Daishi). Other major attractions are Ritsurin Park in **Takamatsu,** Matsuyama Castle in **Matsuyama,** and **Dogo Spa,** one of Japan's oldest hot-spring spas.

Kyushu

The southernmost of the four main islands, Kyushu has a mild subtropical climate, active volcanoes, and hot-spring spas. Because it's the closest major island to Korea and China, Kyushu served as a gateway to the continental mainland throughout much of Japan's history, later becoming the springboard for both traders and Christian missionaries from the West. **Fukuoka,** Kyushu's largest city, is diverse and vibrant, with a booming startup scene. From there, travelers continue on to hot springs in **Beppu** and **Unzen,** and to some of Japan's most livable cities in **Nagasaki** and **Kagoshima.** Off the south coast sits **Yakushima,** an island of towering mountains and rainy moss forests that's probably the most beautiful corner of Japan.

Okinawa

Okinawa is comprised of 160 islands stretching 400km (248 miles) north to south and 1,000km (620 miles) east to west. Part of the Ryukyu Island chain, Okinawa developed its own languages, culture, cuisine, and architecture under the Ryukyu Kingdom, which traded extensively with both Japan and China before being annexed to Japan after the 1868 Meiji Restoration. Okinawa Island, the largest Ryukyu island, is home to **Naha** (Okinawa Prefecture's capital), large U.S. military bases, war memorials, and natural attractions, including white sandy beaches and coral reefs popular with divers and snorkelers. Another popular destination is the mostly rural **Iriomote Island,** 80% of it protected in state and national parks, with dense forests, mangroves, and pristine beaches. Travel here is becoming harder, though, with a cap of 1,200 visitors per day to protect the island's sensitive ecosystem and its endangered species.

SUGGESTED ITINERARIES

FOR FIRST-TIMERS: JAPAN IN 1 WEEK

This trip, designed for first-timers, takes you to Japan's highlights, from fast-paced Tokyo to the quiet temples of Kyoto, along with a couple of other worthwhile destinations like Hiroshima. Plan on about a week, but if time permits, add destinations from the other two itineraries outlined below or one of the recommended side trips.

DAYS 1 & 2: Tokyo ♥♥♥

No one should miss this adrenaline rush of a metropolis; you'll need at least 2 full days to do it justice. Hit the highlights like the **Tsukiji** or **Toyosu Market,** the 45th-floor **observatory** in Shinjuku for its eye-popping views, and the **Tokyo National Museum** with the world's largest collection of Japanese art. Be sure to allow time for wandering Tokyo's diverse neighborhoods—**Asakusa** with its famous Sensoji Temple and old downtown atmosphere; electrifying **Akihabara** with stores selling everything from cameras to anime figurines; and **Harajuku** and **Omotesando** with their showstopping architecture and fashion boutiques. Top it off with a stroll through **Kabuki-cho,** Japan's most notorious nightlife district. See chapter 4.

DAY 3: Hakone ♥♥♥

Take an early train to Hakone Yumoto, gateway to the wonderful **Fuji-Hakone-Izu National Park,** where you can see some of Japan's most scenic countryside via a circuitous route that includes a three-car mountain train, a funicular, ropeway, and a boat. You'll take in sights like the wonderful **Hakone Open-Air Museum** and, if you're lucky, elusive **Mount Fuji.** Be sure to schedule some time for a dip in a hot-spring bath, and spend the night in the historic **Fujiya Hotel** or a Japanese inn. See chapter 5.

DAYS 4–6: Kyoto ♥♥♥

Capital for more than 1,000 years, Kyoto is atop many visitors' bucket lists. Top historic sites include **Nijo Castle,** former home of the

Japan Itineraries

JAPAN IN ONE WEEK

- **1–2** Tokyo
- **3** Hakone
- **4–6** Kyoto
- **7** Hiroshima

JAPAN IN TWO WEEKS

- **1–2** Tokyo
- **3** Nikko
- **4–5** Takayama
- **6** Shirakawa-go
- **7–8** Kanazawa
- **9** Mount Koya
- **10–12** Kyoto
- **13–14** Hiroshima

HONSHU WORLD HERITAGE TOUR

- **1** Nikko
- **2–4** Kyoto
- **5–6** Nara & Horyuji
- **7** Mount Koya
- **8** Himeji Castle
- **9** Hiroshima
- **10** Miyajima

JAPAN FOR FAMILIES

- **1–3** Tokyo
- **4–5** Kyoto
- **6** Nara
- **7–8** Osaka
- **9–10** Hiroshima
- **11–12** Beppu
- **13–14** Fukuoka

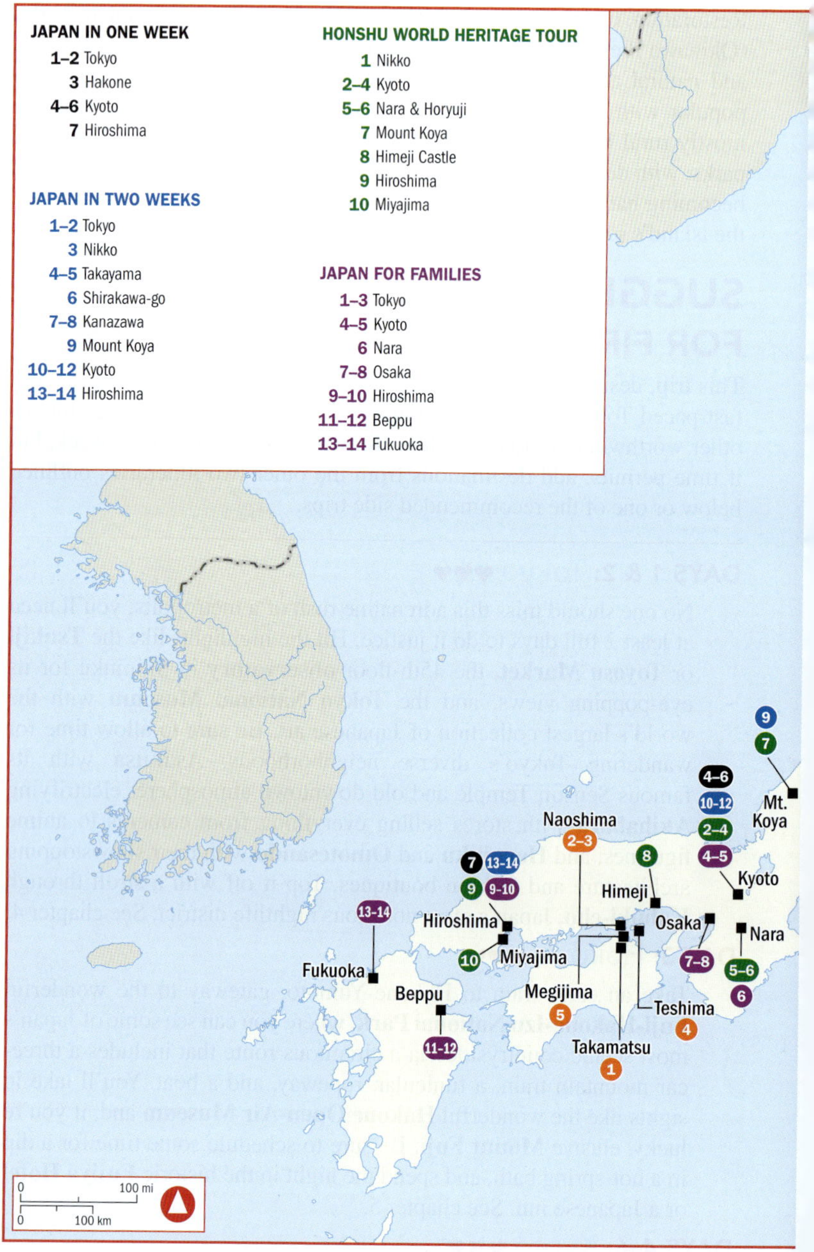

Mt. Koya
Naoshima
Kyoto
Himeji
Hiroshima
Osaka
Nara
Miyajima
Fukuoka
Beppu
Megijima
Teshima
Takamatsu

0 100 mi
0 100 km

7-8
Shiretoko N.P.
Akan-Mashu N.P.
9
5-6
Sapporo
Nibutani
Noboribetsu
4
3
2,10
Hakodate
Towada-Hachimantai N.P.
11-12
Matsushima
13
7-8
3
1
Kanazawa
Nikko
Shirakawa-go
Takayama
1-2
1-2
6
Tokyo
1-3
1,14
4-5
3
Hakone
NORTHERN JAPAN ROAD TRIP
1 Tokyo
2 Hakodate
3 Noboribetsu
4 Nibutani
5–6 Akan-Mashu National Park
7–8 Shiretoko National Park
9 Sapporo
10 Hakodate
11–12 Towada-Hachimantai National Park
13 Matshushima
14 Tokyo
FIVE-DAY SHIKOKU MODERN ART TOUR
1 Takamatsu
2–3 Naoshima
4 Teshima
5 Megijima & Ogijima

shogun; **Ryoanji Temple** with its famous Zen rock garden; the **Golden Pavilion,** and, with advance planning, the **Katsura Imperial Villa.** Take a self-guided walk through eastern Kyoto, seeing **Sanju-sangendo Hall** with its 1,001 wooden statues and **Kiyomizu Temple,** shopping for crafts along the way. Be sure to sample Kyoto's legendary Buddhist vegetarian cuisine and the food in **Nishiki Market.** Stroll through the famous geisha quarters, and spend at least 1 night in a Japanese-style inn. Pop culture fans should reserve entry to the **Nintendo Museum,** located just outside Kyoto in Uji. See chapter 7.

DAY 7: Hiroshima ♥♥

The top destination in Hiroshima is **Peace Memorial Park** with its memorials and museum detailing events surrounding the dropping of the atomic bomb in 1945. Within walking distance of the park is also a castle, garden, and art museum. If you have another day, include a trip to the nearby island of **Miyajima,** home of a famous shrine and considered one of Japan's most scenic places, or go for a short hike at **Mount Mitaki,** with its solemn temple grounds, bamboo groves, and quiet trails. See chapter 8.

JAPAN IN 2 WEEKS

This is something of a whirlwind trip, but it allows you to take in some of the best that Honshu has to offer. If you have 1 or 2 extra days, you might wish to bundle in Osaka or head over to Kyushu.

DAYS 1 & 2: Tokyo

Hit Tokyo's highlights as outlined above.

DAY 3: Nikko

An excellent choice for a day trip is **Nikko,** famous for its sumptuous mausoleum of Tokugawa Ieyasu, Japan's most famous shogun, set in a forest of majestic cedars. See chapter 5.

DAY 4: Takayama & the Japan Alps

Early in the morning, take the Shinkansen to **Nagoya** (about 2 hr.) and then a 3-hour train ride to **Takayama** in the Japan Alps (if you don't have a rail pass, there are also direct buses from Tokyo's Shinjuku Station). Explore the picturesque, narrow streets of this old castle town and its many interesting museums and merchants' homes.

DAY 5: Exploring Takayama

Start your day with a stroll through the **Miyagawa Morning Market** on the bank of a river. Of the many small museums and attractions in Takayama, must-sees include the **Hida Takayama Retro Museum** with its collection of postwar tech and merchandise, old **merchant homes** open to the public, and **Takayama Jinya** with its lovely garden and repository of art and artifacts used by the ruling elite during the Edo period. See chapter 6.

DAY 6: Overnight in Shirakawa-go

Take a 1-hour bus ride to Shirakawa-go, where you'll find the village of **Ogimachi,** a UNESCO World Cultural and Natural Heritage Site with thatch-roofed houses. Several farmhouses are open to the public as museums; you can also spend the night in one. See chapter 6.

DAYS 7 & 8: Kanazawa

Take the bus 1¼ hours to **Kanazawa,** famous for its artisans and crafts. It also has one of Japan's grandest gardens, **Kenrokuen,** several fine art museums, well-preserved former geisha and samurai districts, and the wonderful **Omicho Market,** full of seafood caught in the nearby Sea of Japan. See chapter 10.

DAY 9: Mount Koya

Take an early morning train to **Osaka,** transferring there for a train and cable car to **Mount Koya.** Japan's most sacred religious site, Mount Koya is achingly beautiful with more than 100 Buddhist temples spread through the forests. Be sure to take both a day and a nighttime stroll past towering cypress trees and countless tombs and memorial tablets to Okunoin, the burial ground of Kobo Daishi, one of Japan's most revered Buddhist priests. Spend the night in a temple, dining on vegetarian food. See chapter 8.

The pagoda at Kiyomizu Temple in eastern Kyoto.

DAYS 10–12: Kyoto

After a vegetarian breakfast and perhaps an early morning Buddhist service, return to Osaka and take the train to **Kyoto,** where you'll spend the next 3 days as outlined above in "Japan in 1 Week." If time permits, include an excursion to **Nara,** an ancient capital even older than Kyoto. Most of Nara's historic buildings and temples, including Todaiji Temple with its Great Buddha, are enclosed within an expansive park that is also home to free-roaming deer. For more sightseeing ideas, see chapter 7.

DAYS 13 & 14: Hiroshima

Take a bullet train bound for **Hiroshima.** En route, make a stopover in **Himeji** to see Himeji Castle, easily the most impressive castle in

Japan. In Hiroshima, you'll want to head to **Peace Memorial Park** with its sobering memorials and a museum that does an impressive job of detailing events surrounding the explosion of the atomic bomb. See chapter 8.

HONSHU WORLD HERITAGE TOUR

Japan has 21 cultural properties and 5 natural sites inscribed on the World Heritage List, most of them in central and western Honshu. It should be noted, however, that many listed sites actually consist of a collection of properties, such as the 17 temples, shrines, and castle that make up the "Historic Monuments of Ancient Kyoto." For that reason, you'd have to be pretty dedicated to visit all the World Heritage Sites contained in this book. This tour takes in the highlights, excluding Shirakawa-go, already mentioned above. If time is limited, I suggest skipping Nikko, flying directly into KIX airport and starting in Kyoto. But don't forget to schedule time for kicking back and enjoying the Japan of today, including that most satisfying of experiences, dining on Japanese cuisine. Even that could be considered part of this tour—*washoku,* traditional Japanese cuisine, was added to UNESCO's Intangible Cultural Heritage list in 2013.

DAY 1: Nikko ♥♥♥

About 2 hours north of Tokyo, **Nikko** is famous for its sumptuous mausoleum of Tokugawa Ieyasu, Japan's most famous shogun, set in a forest of majestic cedars. It's part of the World Heritage Site "Shrines and Temples of Nikko," which were constructed mostly in the 17th century. To get the most out of your stay, spend the night in a Japanese inn with hot-spring baths. See chapter 5.

DAYS 2–4: Kyoto ♥♥♥

En route to Kyoto on the Shinkansen, keep a lookout as you near Shizuoka Station for views of **Mount Fuji,** declared a World Heritage Site in 2013 as a sacred place and the source of artistic inspiration. Otherwise, **Kyoto,** Japan's capital and center of Japanese culture for more than 1,000 years, could be considered the epitome of World Heritage Sites in Japan. Its 16 religious structures and **Nijo Castle,** most built or designed from the 10th to the 17th centuries, include an astounding 189 buildings and 12 gardens. Among the most important are Nijo Castle (where the shogun stayed whenever he came to Kyoto), **Ryoanji** with its Zen rock garden, **Kiyomizu Temple, Ginkakuji** (Temple of the Silver Pavilion), and **Kinkakuji** (Temple of the Golden Pavilion). See chapter 7.

DAYS 5 & 6: Nara ♥♥♥ & Horyuji ♥♥♥

Less than an hour's train ride from Kyoto, **Nara** is even older than Kyoto and served as the nation's first official capital for 74 years in the

8th century. On the way, stop in Uji to visit **Byodoin Temple,** part of Kyoto's heritage sites and considered one of the best examples of temple architecture from the Heian Period (795–1192); its famed Phoenix Hall graces the back of ¥10 coins. Although Nara can be visited in a day's outing (rent a bicycle if pressed for time), I recommend you spend the night to explore the "Historic Monuments of Ancient Nara" and the "Buddhist Monuments in the Horyuji Area" at a more leisurely pace. Most of Nara's impressive sights are within expansive **Nara Park,** where deer (considered divine messengers) roam free; foremost here is the **Great Buddha,** housed inside the largest wooden structure in the world (p. 355). In **Horyuji** are Japan's earliest Buddhist monuments, some of them dating from the 7th century and considered the oldest surviving wooden buildings in the world (p. 357). Head on to **Osaka** to spend the night.

DAY 7: Mount Koya ♥♥♥

Accessible from Osaka via train and cable car, **Mount Koya** (p. 397) is Japan's most sacred religious site, achingly beautiful with more than 100 Buddhist temples spread through the dense forests of the Kii Mountain Range. Be sure to take both a day and a nighttime stroll past towering cypress trees and countless tombs and memorial tablets to **Okunoin,** the burial ground of Kobo Daishi, one of Japan's most revered Buddhist priests. Spend the night in a temple, dining on vegetarian food.

A pilgrim completes her journey by visiting the grave of Kobo Daishi on Mount Koya.

DAY 8: Himeji Castle ♥♥♥

Catch an early train to Osaka, where you'll transfer to another train to Himeji (travel time will be 3–3½ hr.). If you see only one castle in Japan, **Himeji Castle** (p. 407) is the one. Said to resemble a white heron poised in flight over the plains, it is quite simply Japan's finest example of early-17th-century Japanese castle architecture. In 1993, it became Japan's first World Heritage Site along with Horyuji. You'll want to spend at least 2 hours exploring the extensive grounds, where the ingenious defense mechanisms include a five-story keep, gates, moats, turrets, and maze of passageways that have survived virtually intact since feudal times. Then hop back on the Shinkansen for Hiroshima.

DAY 9: Hiroshima's Peace Memorial Park ♥♥♥

Hiroshima is most famous for its **Peace Memorial Park** (p. 433), which contains some 50 statues and memorials and the Peace Memorial Museum, dedicated to those who lost their lives in the atomic bomb explosion. While you'll certainly want to see it all, most eye-catching is **Genbaku Dome,** the only structure left standing from the World War II destruction; it was declared a World Heritage Site in 1996.

DAY 10: Miyajima ♥♥♥

Most visitors see **Miyajima** on a day trip from Hiroshima, but you'll get more out of this gem of an island, a holy Shinto site since early times, by spending the night. **Ikutsukushima Shrine,** built over the sea and with Mount Misen rising in the background, does an outstanding job of combining traditional Shinto architecture with nature. Although reconstructed twice, the shrine meticulously preserves its original styles from the late 12th and early 13th centuries. And if time permits, you should also hike or take the cable car up to **Mount Misen,** where you'll be rewarded with great views of the Inland Sea and hiking paths to religious sites. If it's summer, you might also want to hit Miyajima's beaches; in winter, try the region's famous oysters, shucked at street-side stalls. After this treasure-laden itinerary, you deserve it.

JAPAN FOR FAMILIES

There is no end to family entertainment in Japan. To keep your children's interest and preserve your sanity, this itinerary includes temples, shrines, museums, and castles for culture and a little education, along with a healthy dose of Japanese pop culture, from theme parks to sophisticated game arcades. Of course, you'll want to tailor your itinerary to fit your children's ages and interests; just be sure to schedule a lot of downtime so you don't suffer sensory overload. This tour has you arrive in Tokyo and depart from Fukuoka—there's an international airport with limited connectivity here, so you may prefer returning to Tokyo or Osaka for your flight home.

DAYS 1–3: Exploring Tokyo

Don't plan anything strenuous the first day, but do walk around to absorb your new environment (and adjust your body clocks). To help get your bearings, head for Shinjuku's **45th-floor observatory** in the Tokyo Metropolitan Government Office for eye-popping views. Then take the Yamanote Line directly to popular Ueno Park, where you can visit the **National Museum of Nature and Science** with its dinosaurs, Japanese mummy, and hands-on discovery room.

The next day head to one of teamLab's immersive digital art museums: **Borderless,** the flagship museum in the beautiful Azabudai Hills complex; or **Planets,** which in 2024 set the Guinness World Record for the world's most visited museum dedicated to a single group or artist. **Harajuku,** with its youthful fashions and lively street scene (keep hold of the little ones of Takeshita St.), is a must for kids and young adults. Walk along the main thoroughfare of **Omotesando** with its statement-making buildings designed by Japan's top architects; the Zelkova trees on either side are illuminated in December, creating a magical Christmasy atmosphere. If you want to bundle in some culture, visit nearby **Meiji Jingu,** Tokyo's most significant shrine, hidden in a forest of pine, oak, cypress, and camphor trees. See chapter 4.

A statue of three guardian lions on the grounds of Todaiji Temple in Nara Park.

DAYS 4 & 5: Exploring Kyoto

Take the bullet train to Kyoto, an awesome experience for both kids and adults, as you watch the countryside whizzing by. You may want to limit yourselves to Kyoto's highlights: **Kiyomizu Temple** is one of Kyoto's most famous temples, with plenty of food stalls and activities to keep little ones interested (though the crowds may feel overwhelming to younger kids). **Nijo Castle** is a painless introduction to the world of the shogun. Walk through **Nishiki Market** for an up-close look at the octopus, fish, crustaceans, seaweeds, and everything else Japanese eat. But probably the biggest hit with young children is the **Nintendo Museum** (advance reservations necessary), which celebrates modern games and consoles as well as the tech and software of yore—if your child has a Switch, they'll be in heaven here. Teenagers may also want to take in the **Kyoto International Manga Museum,** the largest manga museum in the world. See chapter 7.

DAY 6: Day Trip to Nara

Although your children may not care that Nara is even older than Kyoto and served as the nation's capital for 74 years, they'll be intrigued by **Nara Park,** where deer (considered divine messengers) roam free. They might also be impressed by the **Great Buddha,** Japan's largest bronze Buddha. See if they can crawl through a tiny passageway behind the Buddha—and supposedly attain enlightenment. Back in Kyoto, good evening diversions for older kids include a stroll through **Gion,** where they might catch a glimpse of a geisha, and **Gion Corner,** where they'll be exposed to traditional cultural pursuits, including Bunraku (Japanese puppetry). See chapter 7.

DAYS 7 & 8: Osaka

Take a short train ride to Osaka, with its colorful **Dotonbori** entertainment district surrounding a canal. **Osaka Castle** is the city's best-known sight, but follow the history lesson with a fun evening in **Shinsekai,** a carnivalesque area with an observatory, catch-your-own-fish restaurants, arcade centers, and archery ranges and shooting galleries. **Den Den Town,** with its electronics shops and pop culture merchandise stores is also a must. Spend the second day at **Universal Studios Japan,** a theme park with rides and attractions inspired by intellectual properties as diverse as Mario, Harry Potter, Jaws, and Hello Kitty. Consider forking out for express passes to avoid long queues. See chapter 9.

At Universal Studios Japan in Osaka, the popular Super Nintendo World features beloved characters like the Mario Brothers sidekick Yoshi.

DAYS 9 & 10: Hiroshima

Take a bullet train bound for Hiroshima, only 80 minutes away. If you have teenagers, they're old enough for **Peace Memorial Park,** where they'll learn about the horrors of war, particularly the devastation caused by an atomic bomb (pictures are too graphic for younger children). And don't skip **Okonomi-Mura,** a multistory building full of restaurants serving Hiroshima-style *okonomiyaki,* a savory and noodle-filled deconstructed pancake. Time permitting, the island of **Miyajima** is also a good destination, not only for the ferry ride and the free-roaming deer but also for the trails through the woods, its swimming beaches, and cable car. See chapter 8.

DAYS 11 & 12: Beppu

Take the Shinkansen to Beppu (with a change at Kokura; around 3 hr. total), the king of hot-spring resorts in Kyushu. There's probably no child who wouldn't be fascinated by the **Hells,** a series of thermal wonders ranging from red bubbling waters to hot springs with free-to-use footbaths. But the highlight will be **Suginoi Palace** with its hot-spring baths and heated outdoor pools on a wooded hill with a sweeping view of the city. See chapter 12.

DAYS 13 & 14: Fukuoka

It's a 2-hour train trip from Beppu to Fukuoka, a city with more than enough to keep families entertained, including **teamLab Forest Fukuoka,** a museum where visitors catch-and-release digital wildlife; a VR game center in the **BOSS E · ZO** building; the **Canal City**

Hakata mall, with its ramen shops, fountain shows, and regular live performances in the central plaza; and **Ohori Park** with its large central pond where you can feed the ducks. If it's baseball season, book tickets to see the **SoftBank Hawks,** Fukuoka's local team and one of the most successful franchises in the league. See chapter 13.

NORTHERN JAPAN ROAD TRIP

Tohoku and Hokkaido are still ignored by many travelers. Though it's true that the country's most significant historic treasures lie in the southern regions, vast northern Japan holds some of Japan's last truly unspoiled natural reserves. Traveling by car, either for the entirety or sections, will make it a more relaxed vacation, where the journey is as important as the destinations. I recommend renting a car in Hokkaido for the first leg of your trip, then using public transport when you get to Tohoku. See chapters 13 and 14.

DAY 1: Arrive in Tokyo or Osaka

Spend the night in Tokyo or Osaka, depending on which airport you fly into. If you wish to spend a couple days sightseeing, refer to the earlier itineraries.

DAY 2: Hakodate

Fly in the morning to Hakodate in Hokkaido, around 1½ hours from Tokyo; 1¾ hours from Osaka. Wander the waterfront **warehouse district** and historic **Motomachi,** a picturesque neighborhood of turn-of-the-20th-century clapboard homes and other buildings, relics of when Hakodate opened as one of Japan's first international ports after 2 centuries of isolation. Hakodate is also famous for its night views from **Mount Hakodate,** accessible by cable car, although you'll be up there with hordes of other sightseers. (I suggest a late-afternoon hike up the mountain instead—it only takes an hour or so and it's a much more pleasant experience.)

DAY 3: Noboribetsu

Visit the **Hakodate Morning Market** (open from 5am to lunchtime), famous for snow crabs, sea urchins, and other seafood delicacies. Then pick up a car at one of the rental shops near Hakodate Station and drive to **Noboribetsu**

Hell Valley in Noboribetsu Onsen.

Onsen (it takes 3 hr., or 4 hr. if you avoid toll roads), known for its curative hot springs. Hike through Hell Valley for a view of the bubbling hot water that has made Noboribetsu famous and then experience its magic at the Dai-ichi Takimotokan hot-spring baths.

DAY 4: Nibutani

The next day, a half-hour's drive from Noboribetsu Onsen will take you to **Upopoy** (**the National Ainu Museum and Park**) to learn about Hokkaido's indigenous population through museum exhibits, a recreated settlement, and craftwork demonstrations. Another 90 minutes' drive from there takes you to the **Nibutani Ainu Culture Museum,** which has even more artifacts and Ainu crafts to marvel over. Stay the night in a rural ryokan or inn, somewhere en route to Akan-Mashu National Park (it's a 4-hr. drive, so good to split it up.)

DAYS 5 & 6: Akan-Mashu National Park

Drive on to Akan-Mashu National Park, where you'll find hot springs, a crystal-clear caldera lake, an Ainu-style village, and a red crane observatory. Spend the first day in **Akanko Onsen,** a spa town, on the edge of the lake surrounded by forests and hiking trails. On the second day, take to the waters by boat or canoe, or head to the **Akan Kokusai Tsuru Center** to see rare red-crowned cranes in the wild, birds whose tremulous squawk was designated one of the 100 Soundscapes of Japan.

DAYS 7 & 8: Shiretoko National Park

The 2½-hour drive to Shiretoko is epic, including the 28km (17½-mile) "Road to Heaven," a pencil-straight highway disappearing into the horizon. One of the most beautiful stretches of Japan, the Shiretoko Peninsula juts into the sea of Okhotsk, its soaring mountain ranges full of alpine wildflowers. Engulfed by a national park, it's renowned for its biodiversity, with Ussuri brown bears, foxes, and deer on land, whales, porpoises, dolphins, and otters in the sea, and birds like Stellar's sea eagles and Blakiston's fish owl. Spend a couple days hiking to waterfalls and bird-watching in the forests, or in winter, walking on vast tracts of drift ice.

DAY 9: Sapporo

The drive back to Hakodate is long (around 10 hr. without stops). Better is to stay in **Sapporo,** just over halfway, and spend the evening in its bustling Susukino district, all neon-blazed streets, *robatayaki* restaurants, ramen shops, and cocktail and jazz bars. If you plan on getting up early, maybe skip the ¥500 bars (all drinks cost ¥500).

DAY 10: Return to Hakodate

The drive to Hakodate is around 4 or 5 hours; I'd recommend staying the night there, dropping off your rental car and leaving on a train for Tohoku the next morning. You'll be glad of the downtime.

DAYS 11 & 12: Towada-Hachimantai National Park

Take the 80-minute Shinkansen from Shin-Hakodate Station to Hachinohe in Aomori, then switch to a 2½-hour bus to **Yasumiya,** a small town on the shores of Lake Towada. It's a good base for exploring the many wonders of Towada-Hachimantai National Park, including boat trips across the lake or hiking through the old forests surrounding **Oirase Stream.** If you have time, consider a side trip to the **Towada Art Center,** one of Japan's best modern art museums, hosting indoor and outdoor works by Yayoi Kusama, Yoko Ono, Ron Mueck, Erwin Wurm, and Choi Jeong Hwa. If you want to take things at a slower pace, stay another night here, skip Matsushima (Day 13), and head straight back to Tokyo on the Shinkansen.

DAY 13: Matsushima

Return to Hachinohe and take the Shinkansen to Sendai (about 1½ hr.) and then board a sightseeing boat for a 50-minute trip to **Matsushima,** famous for its scenic coastline of pine-studded islets. Visit the venerable **Zuiganji Temple,** northern Japan's most famous Zen temple; **Entsuin Temple,** with its beautiful gardens; and a museum or two.

DAY 14: Back to Tokyo

Return to Sendai and take the Shinkansen south to Tokyo.

5-DAY SHIKOKU MODERN ART TOUR

Sure, Japan has exemplary old architecture and a seemingly endless repository of ancient arts and crafts. But true to the modern, cutting-edge image it likes to present to the world, it's also a global leader in contemporary art, with creatives like Takashi Murakami, Yayoi Kusama, teamLab, and Hiroshi Sugimoto well known outside Japan. Tokyo has an impressive selection of modern art museums, and Kanazawa, Kyoto, Fukuoka, and Hiroshima are no slouches in that department either. But nothing quite compares to the Art Islands off the coast of Shikoku, where immersive installations and museums and open-air centerpieces have given their host islands a new lease on life. Even better, try to coordinate this trip to coincide with the once-every-3-years **Setouchi Triennale** festival, when the Art Islands really come alive. See chapter 10.

DAY 1: Takamatsu

Fly to Takamatsu, around 90 minutes from Tokyo. Wander its miles of covered shopping arcades and 18th-century **Risturin Garden,** making a stop at the **Takamatsu Art Museum,** with 1,700 works covering postwar Japanese art, global art from the 20th and 21st centuries, and the crafts of Kagawa Prefecture. Before dinner, grab a can of beer or *chuhai* and watch the sunset from the port.

DAYS 2 & 3: Naoshima

Take a 50-minute ferry to Naoshima, the most famous of the Art Islands. Spend a couple of days exploring its museums and installations: the **Art House Projects,** where artists have used old homes and buildings as canvases for their work; the flagship **Benesse House Museum,** featuring art by Jasper Johns, Robert Rauschenberg, Frank Stella, Jackson Pollock, and Andy Warhol, and Hiroshi Sugimoto's ineffably profound *Time Corridors;* Yayoi Kusama's polka-dotted **pumpkin sculpture,** a symbol of the island; the **Lee Ufan Museum;** and a museum dedicated to one of the island's chief creatives, architect **Tadao Ando.** If you have the means, book a room at the **Benesse House Museum** hotel, which will elevate your stay to the realm of the exquisite.

DAY 4: Teshima

Naoshima's neighboring island (30 min. away by boat) is larger, but less frequented by tourists, making an ideal day trip. The **Teshima Art Museum** is the main reason to come; its smooth, globular shape is iconic—that of a raindrop as it strikes the ground—with a cavernous and contemplative interior. Shards of sunlight stream through an opening in the roof and water droplets meander across the floor's curvilinear surface; take your time to appreciate this interplay between the natural and the manmade. There are a couple of other interesting museums to visit, as well as the musical **La forêt des murmures** artwork on Mount Danyama.

DAY 5: Megijima & Ogijima

Take a ferry to **Megijima** via Takamatsu (50 min., not including transfer time), a charming little island with outdoor artworks along the coast and in the hills, and a cave network on its tallest mountain known as the "Ogre's Lair." Then jump over to **Ogijima** (15 min. by ferry), a speck of land with impact-driven art scattered around its coastline and along its narrow walking streets—like *Takotsuboru,* a giant octopus-trap-cum-playground serving as a symbol of hope that more youngsters will live on the rapidly depopulating island. (Note that both islands welcome many more artworks during the Setouchi Triennale.) It's 20 minutes back to Takamatsu from here; the final return ferry is at 4pm (later in Aug).

Bruce Naumann's "100 Live or Die" in the Benesse House Museum.

3

5-Day Shikoku Modern Art Tour

SUGGESTED JAPAN ITINERARIES

4

TOKYO

To the uninitiated, Tokyo may seem a whirlwind of traffic and people and LED screens and bleeding fluorescent lights, so dense and confusing it's a wonder that it functions at all. More than 13 million people reside in Greater Tokyo's 2,188 sq. km (845 sq. miles) and tens of millions visit each year; no matter where you go, you're never alone. Yet crowds and urban sprawl are what you'll see only if you don't bother to look beneath the surface.

Tokyo may be the posterchild for fast-paced urban efficiency, but it also has an often-overlooked side that feels less manufactured—atmospheric backstreets, generations-old businesses, neighborhood allotments with small produce stalls, and fresh food markets. Tokyo, more so than any other Japanese city, has woven these two distinct aspects into one cohesive tapestry.

Because it is so vast, the best way to visit as a traveler is to divide it in more digestible chunks. After all, Tokyo is nothing more than a sprawling series of small towns and neighborhoods clustered together, each with its own atmosphere and history and culinary treasures and nightlife haunts. What's more, beneath Tokyo's concrete shell, a thriving cultural life has been left very much intact. If you're interested in Japan's performing arts, like *kabuki,* or traditional activities such as sumo or seasonal flower-viewing, Tokyo is your best bet, offering the most at any one time. It is rich in museums, both historic and contemporary, and claims the largest repository of Japanese art in the world. It's also one of the world's pop-culture capitals, so if you're into video games, *manga* (Japanese comics), or anime, you'll be in high heaven. If style is your thing, you'll find Tokyo a mecca for cutting-edge fashion and innovative design. And if you're a foodie traveler, you'll be salivating from the outset: Tokyo has by far the highest number of Michelin-starred restaurants of any city in the world, many of which are excellent value for money, as well as more ramen shops, curry houses, and conveyor-belt sushi chains than your stomach will know what to do with. Many would argue this is the world's greatest metropolis, and I'd be hard pushed to disagree.

THE BEST TOKYO EXPERIENCES

- **Experiencing Digital Art at teamLab's Museums** Digital art collective teamLab has two Tokyo museums, Planets and Borderless, and they're among the most popular art spaces in the world. As you move through the space, dynamic artworks react to you and to each other, ensuring no two visitors share the same experience.

PREVIOUS PAGE: **The kaleidoscopic entrance to the chic Tokyu Plaza shopping mall in Omotesando.**

- **Seeing Sumo** Nothing beats watching huge sumo wrestlers (most weigh well over 135kg/300 lb.) throw each other around. Matches are held in Tokyo in January, May, and September; catch one on TV if you can't make it in person.
- **Browsing the Electronics and Anime Shops of Akihabara** Even if you don't buy anything, it's always entertaining—and very educational—to see the latest in electronic gadgetry in Japan's largest electronics district, which also has huge anime and manga emporiums catering to the growing number of local and foreign *otaku* (pop-culture fans).
- **Going to a Local Festival** Festivals in Tokyo attract huge crowds; they also give visitors a sense of how seriously the Japanese take their cultural celebrations. Ancient Shinto marches, Beerfests, food fairs, a festival that celebrates a mythological steel penis, and another where sumo wrestlers make babies cry—there's an event for people of every disposition.
- **Taking a Spin Through Kabuki-cho** Shinjuku's Kabuki-cho has the craziest nightlife in all of Tokyo, with countless strip joints, porn shops, restaurants, alleyways lined with bars, and the greatest concentration of neon you're likely to see anywhere.

For gamers, the arcades of Akihabara are endlessly enticing.

- **Sipping Whiskey in a Jazz Kissa** Tokyo is full of small, atmospheric jazz bars, also known as *kissa,* where locals go to drink whiskey, listen to old records on high-end sound systems, and forget about the world outside.
- **Singing the Night Away in a Karaoke Parlor** Few things feel more Tokyo than tumbling into a karaoke parlor in the wee hours and hogging the microphone till the sun comes up.

ESSENTIALS

Arriving

BY PLANE

Tokyo has two international airports. **Narita International Airport** (**NRT;** narita-airport.jp; ✆ **0476-34-8000**), located in Narita about 66km

A LOOK AT THE past

Though today the nation's capital, Tokyo is a relative newcomer to the pages of Japanese history. For centuries it was nothing more than a rather unimportant village called Edo, which means simply "mouth of the estuary." In 1603, Edo was catapulted into the limelight when the new shogun, Tokugawa Ieyasu, made the sleepy village the seat of his government. He expanded Edo Castle, making it the largest and most impressive in the land, and surrounded it with an ingenious system of moats that radiated from the castle in a great swirl, giving him easy access to the sea and an upper hand in thwarting enemy attacks.

The town developed quickly, due largely to the shogun's decree requiring all *daimyo* (feudal lords) to permanently leave their families in Edo, a shrewd move to thwart insurrection in the provinces. There were as many as 270 *daimyo* in Japan in the 17th century, all of whom maintained several mansions in Edo, complete with elaborate compounds and expansive gardens. The *daimyo*'s trusted samurai soon accounted for more than half of Edo's population, and the merchant class expanded as well. By 1787 the population had grown to 1.3 million, making Edo—even then—one of the largest cities in the world.

When the Tokugawas were overthrown in 1868, the Japanese emperor was restored to power and moved the capital from Kyoto to Edo, now renamed Tokyo (Eastern Capital). Japan's Feudal Era—and its isolation from the rest of the world—was over. As the capital city, Tokyo was the hardest hit in this new era of modernization, with fashion, architecture, food, and even people imported from the West. West was best, and things Japanese were forgotten or ignored.

It didn't help that Tokyo was almost totally destroyed twice in the first half of the 20th century: In 1923, a massive earthquake measuring 7.9 on the Richter scale destroyed more than a third of the city and claimed some 140,000 lives in Tokyo and Yokohama; disaster struck again in 1945, toward the end of World War II when Allied incendiary bombs laid more than half the city to waste and killed another 100,000 people.

But under Allied occupation, which lasted until 1952, Tokyo quickly rebuilt. By 1964 it showcased as one of Asia's most progressive cities when it hosted the Summer Olympics. Although the 6-minute 2011 Great East Japan Earthquake was the most terrifying most Tokyoites had ever experienced, there was virtually no damage to the city itself.

(41 miles) east of Tokyo, is by far the largest and serves the most flights. Closer at just 14km (8½ miles) is **Haneda Airport (HND;** tokyo-haneda.com/en/; ✆ **03/5757-8111**), which operates as Tokyo's domestic airport but also has an international terminal.

NARITA AIRPORT There are three terminals (3 is used mostly by regional low-cost airlines), all with ATMs and counters for money exchange. (See p. 103 for tips on currency exchange.) **Tourist Information Centers** in the arrival lobbies of terminals 1 and 2 are open daily 8am to 8pm and offer free maps and pamphlets. If you've purchased a Japan Rail Pass, you can turn in your voucher at the **Japan Railways (JR) Travel Service Center,** located in all terminals and open daily 6:30am to 9:45pm. Other facilities and services at terminals 1 and 2 include a Nintendo-themed visitor center, SIM card shops, post offices, medical clinics, shower rooms, day rooms for napping, beauty salons, children's playrooms, luggage storage and lockers, cellphone rentals, free Wi-Fi, and, in Terminal 2, a capsule hotel (useful if you have a very early flight). You can also have your suitcase delivered to your place of lodging no matter where you're staying in Japan; it costs about ¥2,190 to ¥2,850 per bag in the Tokyo area depending on the weight and size.

Getting from Narita into Tokyo The quickest way to reach Tokyo is by **train.** Trains depart directly from the airport's two underground stations, Narita Airport Terminal 1 and Airport Terminal 2-3. The JR **Narita Express** (**N'EX;** jreast.co.jp; ✆ **050/2016-1603**) is the fastest way to reach Tokyo Station, Shinagawa, Shibuya, Shinjuku, or Ikebukuro, with departures approximately twice an hour. The 56-minute trip to Tokyo Station costs ¥3,070 one-way. At Tokyo Station, the train splits, with some cars going to Shibuya, Shinjuku, and, less frequently, Ikebukuro, and other cars going to Shinagawa (cost to these stations: ¥3,250). Save money with the **N'EX Tokyo Round Trip Ticket,** which guarantees a round-trip journey to Tokyo, Shibuya, Shinjuku, Shinagawa, Yokohama, and Ofuna stations for only ¥5,000. Purchase online at jreast.co.jp or at JR ticket offices in Narita Airport. The ticket even allows you to transfer to another JR train line to reach your Tokyo destination. If you've validated your Japan Rail Pass as mentioned above, you can ride the N'EX free.

The privately owned **Keisei Skyliner** (keisei.co.jp; ✆ **0570-081-160**), which departs directly from terminals 1 and 2, travels to Ueno Station in Tokyo in as little as 41 minutes. Trains depart Narita approximately one to three times an hour from about 7:30am to 11pm. The Skyliner fare between Narita Airport and Ueno Station is ¥2,580 one-way; Keisei's slower limited express trains to Ueno Station take 80 minutes, with fares starting at ¥1,060. If your destination is Asakusa, Nihombashi, Higashi-Ginza, Shimbashi, or Shinagawa, you can also travel on the Narita Sky Access Line or Keisei Main Line. For details, check the Keisei website or drop by the Keisei ticket counters in the arrival lobbies of terminals 1 and 2.

The most popular and stress-free way to get from Narita to Tokyo is via the **Airport Limousine Bus** (limousinebus.co.jp; ✆ **03/3665-7220**), which picks up passengers and their luggage from just outside the arrival lobbies of Terminals 1 and 2 and delivers them to downtown hotels. It's a good option if you have heavy baggage or are staying at one of the 40 or so major hotels served by the bus. Buses depart for the various hotels generally once an hour, but note it can take almost 2 hours to reach a hotel in Shinjuku. Buses also travel to both Tokyo and Shinjuku stations, Haneda Airport, and the **Tokyo City Air Terminal** (**TCAT**) in downtown Tokyo, with more frequent departures (up to four times an hour in peak times). Even if your hotel is not served by limousine bus, you can still take it to the hotel or station nearest your destination. Check with the staff at the Airport Limousine Bus counter in the arrival lobbies to ask which bus stops

Saving on Transportation

If you plan to travel around Tokyo by public transportation (and who doesn't?), you can save money by purchasing a combination **Keisei Skyliner and Tokyo subway ticket,** available only at Narita Airport. One-, 2-, and 3-day tickets offering unlimited subway rides are ¥2,900, ¥3,300, and ¥3,600, respectively, for a one-way Skyliner ticket; and ¥4,900, ¥5,300, and ¥5,600 with a round-trip Skyliner ticket. Likewise, there are **Airport Limousine & Subway Pass** combination tickets that include a one-way or round-trip Airport Limousine Bus plus 24-, 48-, or 72-hour unlimited rides on all subways (it doesn't have to be the same day of arrival), with a one-way bus and 24-hour combination ticket costing ¥4,000. This ticket is available at Airport Limousine counters at the airport, TCAT, and Shinjuku Station West Exit in front of Keio Department Store. There are also combination tickets for visitors arriving at Haneda airport. Check websites for more information.

nearest your hotel and its departure time. The fare to most destinations is ¥3,100. Children 6 to 12 are charged half-fare; those 5 and under ride free.

Cheaper still is the **Airport Bus TYO-NRT,** departing from terminals 1, 2 and 3 to Tokyo Station (70–80 min.) and Ginza Station (80–90 min.). Run by different providers, the buses depart throughout the day from 7:30am to 11:30pm for only ¥1,500 one-way (later buses may be available for double fare). Purchase tickets and inquire about services from JR Travel Service Centers in the airport.

Jumping into a **taxi** is the easiest way to get to Tokyo, but it's also prohibitively expensive—and may not even be the quickest if you happen to hit rush-hour traffic. Taxis have both metered and—probably better—fixed-fare rates, but expect to spend around ¥25,000 to ¥32,000 for a 1½- to 2-hour taxi ride to areas in central Tokyo. Note that highway toll charges and a surcharge applied from 10pm to 5am will cost extra.

HANEDA AIRPORT **Haneda Airport** (officially Tokyo International Airport, though everyone calls it Haneda) has both domestic and international terminals. The international terminal has a **Tokyo Tourist Information Center** (on the second floor of the arrival lobby, open daily 24 hr.), currency exchange, free Wi-Fi, luggage storage and delivery, and cellphone rental. There are also short-term SIM card shops here. But the overriding benefit of Haneda is its central location compared to Narita. Taxi fares from Haneda are more reasonable than from Narita, though you can still expect to pay at least ¥7,000 to reach downtown Tokyo.

Like Narita, Haneda Airport is served by the **Airport Limousine Bus,** with service to Shinjuku Station, Tokyo Station, the Tokyo City Air Terminal (TCAT) in downtown Tokyo, and selected hotels in Ginza, Hibiya, Shinjuku, Ikebukuro, Shibuya, Roppongi, and Akasaka. Fares run ¥1,000 to ¥1,400 for most destinations. Locals, however, are more likely to take the **monorail** from Haneda 19 minutes to Hamamatsucho Station (fare: ¥520), or the **Keikyu Airport Line** 14 minutes to Shinagawa (fare:

¥330). Both Hamamatsucho and Shinagawa connect to the very useful Yamanote Line, which travels to major stations like Tokyo and Shinjuku.

BY TRAIN

If you're traveling to Tokyo from elsewhere in Japan, you'll most likely arrive via Shinkansen bullet train at Tokyo, Ueno, or Shinagawa stations. All are well served by trains (including the useful JR Yamanote Line), subways, and taxis.

BY BUS

Long-distance bus service from Hiroshima, Osaka, Kyoto, and other major cities delivers passengers mostly to Tokyo and Shinjuku stations, both of which are connected to the rest of the city via subway and commuter train, including the JR Yamanote Line, which loops around the city. For more info on long-distance bus service, check the websites bus.or.jp, jrbuskanto.co.jp, and travel.willer.co.jp/ (now the premier bus ticketing website in Japan) or go to the individual city descriptions in this guide.

Visitor Information

In addition to those located at both airports (see above), there's a **Tourist Information Center** (**TIC**) in the heart of Tokyo in the Shin-Tokyo Building, 3–3–1 Marunouchi (japantravelinfo.com; © **03/3201-3331;** station: Yurakucho), within walking distance of the Ginza. The TIC staff is courteous and efficient. In addition to city maps and sightseeing materials, this office (affiliated with the Japan National Tourism Organization) has more information on the rest of Japan than any other tourist office in town, including pamphlets and brochures on major cities and attractions such as Kyoto and Kamakura. Hours are daily 9am to 5pm.

A great source for local information is the **Tokyo Tourist Information Center,** operated by the Tokyo Metropolitan Government and located on the first floor of the Tokyo Metropolitan Government (TMG) Building no. 1, 2–8–1 Nishi-Shinjuku (gotokyo.org; © **03/5321-3077;** station: Tochomae or Shinjuku). You'll want to come here anyway for the great views from TMG's free observation floor. Other city-run information counters are at Keisei Ueno Station (© **03/3836-3471**), open daily 9:30am to 6:30pm, and at the Shinjuku Expressway Bus Terminal (© **03/6274-8198**), open daily 6:30am to 11pm.

Near Tokyo Station, the **TIC TOKYO,** facing the Nihombashi exit of Tokyo Station's north end at 1–8–1 Marunouchi (tictokyo.jp; © **03/5220-7055;** daily 10am–7pm), dispenses information on traveling in Tokyo and Japan and offers SIM cards and mobile Wi-Fi routers. Inside Tokyo Station at the Marunouchi north exit, the **JR EAST Travel Service Center** (jreast.co.jp; © **050/2016-1603;** daily 7:30am–8:30pm) provides tourist information as well as train tickets. **Tokyo City i,** in JP Tower next to the Central Post Office, 2–7–2 Marunouchi (tokyocity-i.jp; daily 8am–8pm), provides information to both international tourists and foreigners conducting business in Japan.

Among the increasing number of neighborhood tourist offices are the **Asakusa Culture Tourist Information Center,** 2–18–9 Kaminarimon (✆ **03/6280-6710;** daily 9:30am–8pm); the **Shibuya Tourist Information Center** in an old train car at the Hachiko exit of Shibuya Station (daily 10am–6pm); and the **Sumida City Tourist Information Office** outside Ryogoku Station (daily 10am–6pm).

Another good resource is the free **Foreign Residents' Advisory Center** (✆ **03-5320-7744**), which can answer questions on a wide range of topics concerning daily life in Japan, including legal matters, taxes, traffic accidents, emergency numbers, and even Japanese social customs; it's open Monday to Friday 9:30am to noon and 1 to 5pm. Finally, if you're staying in a first-class hotel, don't hesitate to make use of the concierge or guest-relations desk, where the staff can tell you how to reach your destination, answer general questions, and make taxi bookings or restaurant reservations.

City Layout

Tokyo, situated at one end of Tokyo Bay and spreading across the Kanto Plain, still retains some of its Edo Period features. If you look at a map, you'll find a large green oasis in the middle of the city, site of the Imperial Palace and its grounds. Surrounding it is the castle moat; a bit farther out are remnants of another circular moat built by the Tokugawa shogun. The JR Yamanote Line forms another loop around the inner city; most of Tokyo's major hotels, nightlife districts, and attractions are near or inside this oblong loop.

Greater Tokyo is Japan's most-populated prefecture (similar to a state or province), with more than 14 million inhabitants; it includes 26 cities, five towns, eight villages, and Pacific islands, in addition to Central Tokyo. For most purposes, however, references to Tokyo in this guide pertain mostly to central Tokyo. For administrative purposes, Central Tokyo is broken down into **23 wards,** known as ***ku.*** Its business districts of Marunouchi and Hibiya, for example, are in Chiyoda-ku, while Ginza is part of Chuo-ku (Central Ward). These two *ku* are the historic hearts of Tokyo, where the city had its humble beginnings.

MAIN STREETS & ARTERIES One difficulty in finding your way around Tokyo is that hardly any streets are named. Think about what that means: 14 million people living in a huge metropolis of nameless streets. Granted, major thoroughfares received names after World War II at the insistence of American occupation forces, and more have been labeled or given nicknames since then, but for the most part, Tokyo's address system is based on a complicated number scheme that before GPS must have made the postal worker's job a nightmare. To make matters worse, most streets in Tokyo zigzag—an arrangement apparently left over from olden days, to

Witnessing the urban energy of a big intersection like Shibuya Scramble is part of the whole Tokyo experience.

confuse potential attacking enemies. Now they confuse Tokyoites and visitors alike, though phones with mapping features do make getting around Tokyo less frustrating than in years past. Some tourists find the app **what3words** useful; it pinpoints precise locations by giving every single 3-sq.-m patch of land a unique three-word combination. In theory this leaves less up to chance than typing in an address that even Google struggles to identify. You can learn more about the app at what3words.com/products/what3words-app.

Among Tokyo's most important named streets are **Meiji Dori,** which follows the loop of the Yamanote Line and runs from Minato-ku in the south through Ebisu, Shibuya, Harajuku, Shinjuku, and Ikebukuro in the north; **Yasukuni Dori** and **Shinjuku Dori,** which cut across the heart of the city from Shinjuku to Chiyoda-ku; and **Sotobori Dori, Chuo Dori, Harumi Dori,** and **Showa Dori,** which pass through Ginza. Other major thoroughfares are named after the districts they're in, such as **Roppongi Dori** in Roppongi and **Aoyama Dori** in Aoyama (*dori* means "avenue" or "street," as does *michi*).

Intersections in Tokyo are called a crossing (and, more recently, a scramble); it seems every district has a famous crossing. **Ginza 4-chome Crossing** is the intersection of Chuo Dori and Harumi Dori. **Roppongi Crossing** is the intersection of Roppongi Dori and Gaien-Higashi Dori. The **Shibuya Scramble** became famous after being featured in the movie *Lost in Translation*—it's widely claimed to be the world's busiest intersection, and visiting it has become a tourist activity in its own right.

FINDING YOUR WAY AROUND Make use of your cellphone's mapping feature, as it will be a lifesaver. If your phone is dead and you're traveling

Tokyo at a Glance

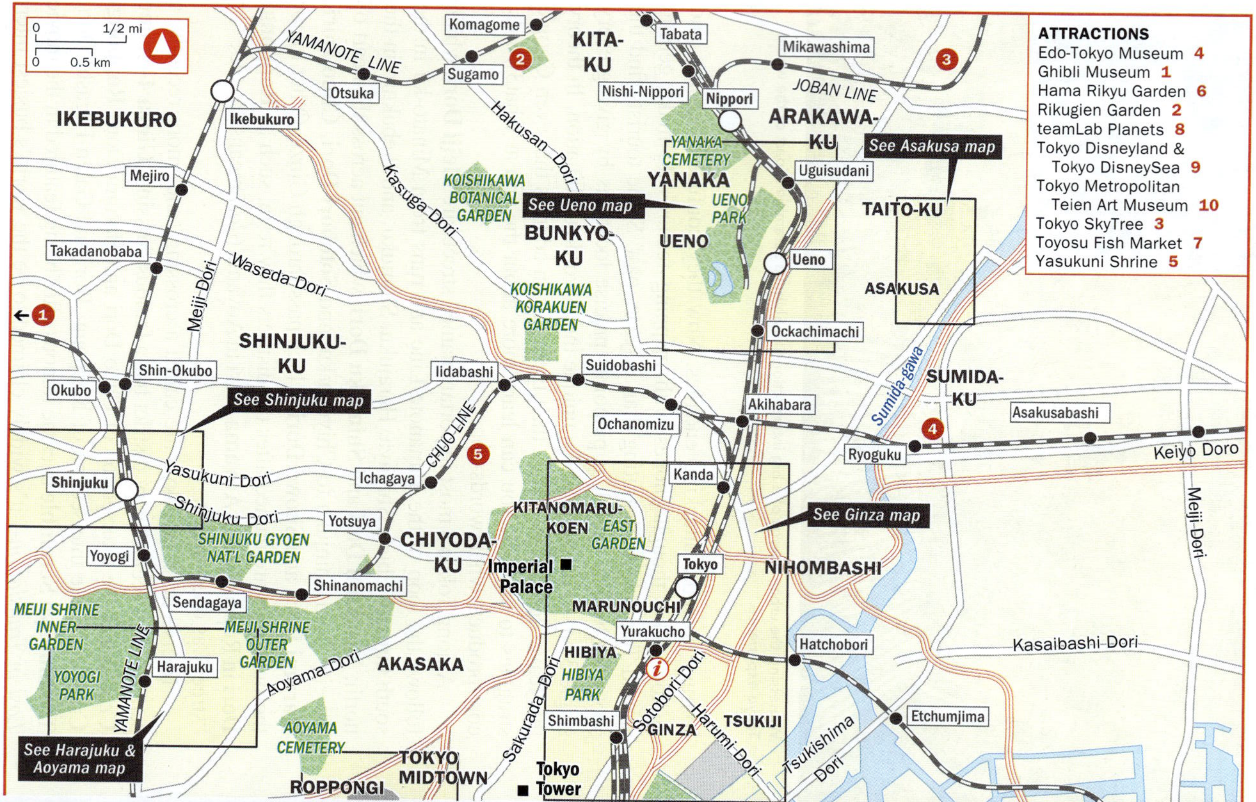

ATTRACTIONS
- Edo-Tokyo Museum 4
- Ghibli Museum 1
- Hama Rikyu Garden 6
- Rikugien Garden 2
- teamLab Planets 8
- Tokyo Disneyland & Tokyo DisneySea 9
- Tokyo Metropolitan Teien Art Museum 10
- Tokyo SkyTree 3
- Toyosu Fish Market 7
- Yasukuni Shrine 5

See Asakusa map
See Ueno map
See Ginza map
See Shinjuku map
See Harajuku & Aoyama map

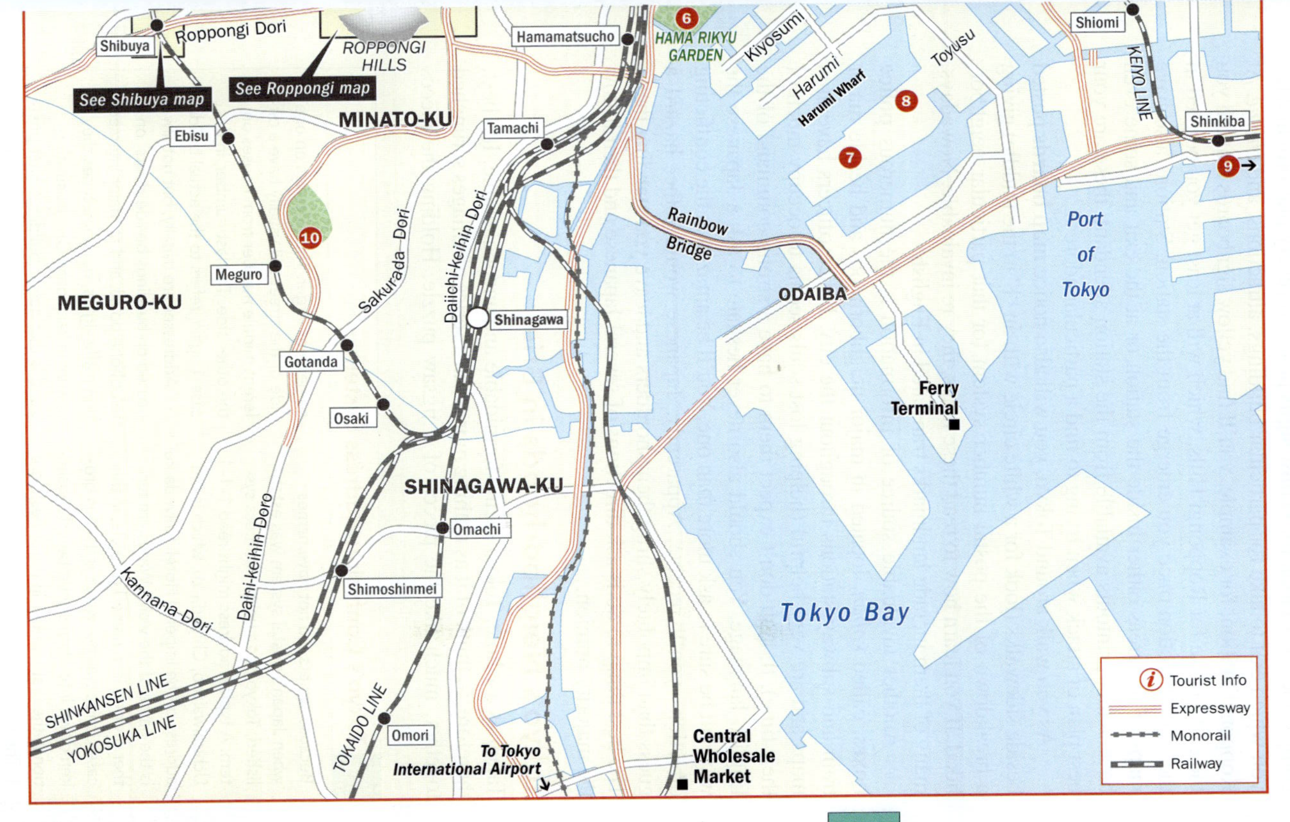
Shibuya
Roppongi Dori
ROPPONGI HILLS
See Shibuya map
See Roppongi map
MINATO-KU
Hamamatsucho
HAMA RIKYU GARDEN
Kiyosumi
Harumi
Harumi Wharf
Toyusu
Shiomi
KEIYO LINE
Shinkiba
Ebisu
Tamachi
Meguro
MEGURO-KU
Sakurada Dori
Daiichi-keihin Dori
Shinagawa
Rainbow Bridge
ODAIBA
Port of Tokyo
Gotanda
Osaki
Ferry Terminal
SHINAGAWA-KU
Omachi
Daini-keihin Doro
Kannana Dori
Shimoshinmei
Tokyo Bay
SHINKANSEN LINE
YOKOSUKA LINE
TOKAIDO LINE
Omori
To Tokyo International Airport
Central Wholesale Market
Tourist Info
Expressway
Monorail
Railway

by subway or JR train, the first thing you should do upon exiting your compartment is to look for **yellow signs** posted on every platform that tell you which exit to take for particular buildings, attractions, and *chome.* At Roppongi Station, for example, you'll find yellow signboards that tell you the exit to take for Roppongi Hills, which will at least get you pointed in the right direction once you emerge from the station. Stations also have maps of the areas either inside the station or at the exit and some even have actual printouts available from the station attendant; these are your best plan of attack when trying to find a particular address.

As you walk around Tokyo, you will also notice **map boards** posted beside sidewalks (look for a white circle with an "i" in the middle) giving a breakdown of the postal number system for that particular neighborhood. If you learn how to read these maps, they're invaluable. Nowadays, many of them include landmarks translated in English.

Another invaluable source of information is the numerous **police boxes,** called *koban,* located in major neighborhoods and beside major train and subway stations throughout the city. Police officers have area maps and are very helpful (helping lost souls seems to occupy much of their time), though don't expect them to have a strong command of the English language. You should also never hesitate to ask a Japanese the way, but be sure to ask more than one. You'll be amazed at the conflicting directions you'll receive. Apparently, Japanese would rather hazard a guess than impolitely shrug their shoulders and leave you standing there. The best thing to do is ask directions of several Japanese and then follow the majority opinion.

Tokyo's Neighborhoods in Brief

Taken as a whole, Tokyo seems formidable and unconquerable. It's best, therefore, to think of it as nothing more than a series of villages scrunched together, much like the pieces of a jigsaw puzzle. Holding the pieces

Tokyo's Confusing Address System

Because streets did not have names when Japan's postal system was established, Tokyo has a unique address system. A typical address might read 1–1–1 Uchisaiwaicho, Chiyoda-ku, which is the address of the Imperial Hotel. Chiyoda-ku is the name of the ward. Wards are further divided into named districts, in this case Uchisaiwaicho, which is itself is broken down into *chome* (numbered subsections), the first number in the series, here 1. The second number (also 1 in the example) refers to a smaller area within the *chome*—usually an entire block, sometimes larger. Thus, houses on one side of the street will usually have a different middle number from houses on the other side. The last number, in this case 1 again, refers to the actual building.

Addresses are usually, but not always, posted on buildings beside doors, on telephone poles, and at major intersection traffic lights, but sometimes they are written in kanji only. One frustrating trend is that newer buildings omit posting any address whatsoever on their facades, perhaps in the belief that no one understands the address system anyway.

together, so to speak, is the **Yamanote Line,** a commuter train loop around central Tokyo that passes through such important stations as Yurakucho, Tokyo, Akihabara, Ueno, Ikebukuro, Shinjuku, Harajuku, Shibuya, and Shinagawa. It surrounds the Imperial Palace grounds, which you can think of as a rough center point from which Tokyo unfurls.

MARUNOUCHI Bounded by the Imperial Palace to the west and Tokyo Station (used by about 1 million people daily) to the east, Marunouchi is one of Tokyo's oldest business districts. On the site of the **Imperial Palace** is where the Tokugawa shogun built his magnificent castle and the center of old Edo; many samurai had mansions here. Remnants of the castle can be seen in the wonderful **East Garden,** open free to the public. Marunouchi has undergone a massive revival since the turn of this century. It's home to swanky hotels and wide avenues, like tree-lined **Marunouchi Naka Dori** with its international boutiques from Armani to Tiffany (Marunouchi's winter illuminations are dazzling).

GINZA Across the train tracks and to the south of Marunouchi is Ginza, the most elegant and expensive shopping area in all Japan. When the country opened to foreign trade in the 1860s, after 2 centuries of self-imposed seclusion, it was here that Western imports and adopted Western architecture were first displayed. Today, you'll find the **Kabukiza Theatre,** department stores, international name-brand boutiques, exclusive restaurants, hotels, art galleries, and by some estimations, hundreds of craft cocktail bars.

TSUKIJI Located only two subway stops from Ginza, Tsukiji was born from reclaimed land during the Tokugawa shogunate. From 1935 to 2018, it was home to the famed **Tsukiji Fish Market,** one of the world's largest wholesale fish markets, which in 2018 moved to larger quarters in Toyosu. The old outer market is still home to stalls selling some of the finest seafood in the city; the inner market site is now a vacant lot that's being developed into a commercial and residential complex featuring a 50,000-seat stadium, a culinary center, and a transportation hub, set to open in the 2030s. Near Tsukiji is **Hama Rikyu Garden,** one of Tokyo's most famous gardens.

AKIHABARA Two stops north of Tokyo Station on the Yamanote Line, Akihabara has long been Japan's top shopping destination for electronics and electrical appliances, with hundreds of shops including **Yodobashi Camera,** Japan's (and possibly the world's) largest appliance store. It's also a mecca for *otaku* culture, home of anime and *manga* stores and maid cafes. See walking tour on p. 133.

ASAKUSA Northeast of central Tokyo, Asakusa and areas to its north served as the pleasure quarters for old Edo. Today it's known throughout Japan as the site of the venerable **Sensoji Temple,** one of Tokyo's top attractions. It also has a wealth of tiny shops selling traditional Japanese crafts. When Tokyoites talk about old *shitamachi* (downtown), they're referring to the traditional homes and tiny narrow streets of the Asakusa and Ueno areas. See walking tour on p. 128.

UENO Just west of Asakusa, on the northern edge of the JR Yamanote Line loop, Ueno is also part of the city's old downtown. It's home to **Ueno Park,** a huge green space comprising a zoo and several acclaimed museums, including the **Tokyo National Museum,** with its vast collection of Japanese art and antiquities. Under the train tracks of the JR Yamanote Line, the **Ameya Yokocho** is a thriving market for food, clothing, and accessories.

SHINJUKU Originating as a post town in 1698 to serve the needs of feudal lords and their retainers traveling between Edo and the provinces, Shinjuku was hardly touched by the 1923 Great Kanto Earthquake, making it a attractive place for businesses to relocate after the destruction. Today dozens of skyscrapers, including several hotels, dot the Shinjuku skyline; the **Tokyo Metropolitan Government Office** (**TMG;** with a great free observation floor) opened in 1991, sealing Shinjuku's transformation into the capital's business district. Separating eastern and western Shinjuku is **Shinjuku Station,** the nation's busiest and most confusing commuter station, on the western end of the Yamanote Line loop. Shinjuku is also known for its nightlife, especially in **Kabuki-cho,** one of Japan's most renowned—and naughtiest—amusement centers; and in **Shinjuku 2–chome,** Tokyo's premier gay nightlife district. An oasis in the middle of Shinjuku is **Shinjuku Gyoen Park,** with a tranquil Japanese garden at its center.

HARAJUKU A magnet for Tokyo's youth, Harajuku swarms throughout the week with teens in search of fashion and fun. **Takeshita Dori** is a narrow pedestrian lane packed with young people looking for the latest in inexpensive clothing. Harajuku is also home to one of Japan's major attractions, the **Meiji Jingu Shrine,** built in 1920 to deify Emperor and Empress Meiji; expansive **Yoyogi Park;** and the small but delightful **Ukiyo-e Ota Memorial Museum of Art,** with its woodblock prints. Linking Harajuku with Aoyama (below) is **Omotesando Dori,** a fashionable tree-lined avenue flanked by trendy shops, restaurants, and sidewalk cafes. The upscale **Omotesando Hills,** designed by Japan's king of concrete, Tadao Ando, is a shopping center on Omotesando Dori stretching from Harajuku to Aoyama.

AOYAMA While Harajuku is for Tokyo's teenyboppers, nearby chic Aoyama is its playground for trendsetting yuppies, with sophisticated restaurants, pricey boutiques, and cutting-edge designer-fashion outlets and sleek hair salons. It's on the eastern end of **Omotesando Dori,** centered on Aoyama Dori. Its cultural highlight is the **Tokyo SkyTree Museum,** devoted to items related to the tea ceremony, Chinese bronzes, and more. The **Japan Traditional Crafts Aoyama Square** sells beautifully crafted items made by artisans from around Japan.

SHIBUYA Located on the southwestern edge of the Yamanote Line loop, Shibuya is a vibrant nightlife and shopping area for the young. Tokyo is often described as a city that never sleeps and Shibuya is arguably its most insomniac district, with bars, speakeasys, clubs, and dens of the night still spilling weary patrons onto the streets come sunrise. In this dynamic neighborhood, construction never ceases and new businesses open (it seems) every week. More than a dozen department stores here specialize in everything from designer clothing to houseware, including **Rayard Miyashita Park,** a trendy shopping mall with a rooftop skatepark and garden, and **Shibuya Scramble Square,** a 47-story commercial and dining complex topped by a panoramic viewing platform. Shibuya also boasts Japan's first official Nintendo store, located in the **Parco** shopping mall. With its hordes of pedestrians, neon, and five video billboards, **Shibuya Scramble** (the crossing, not the skyscraper) has earned the nickname "Times Square of Tokyo." Please note, however, local drivers don't take too kindly to tourists who stand in the intersection to take photos after the traffic signal goes green, which they do all too often.

ROPPONGI One of Tokyo's best-known nightlife districts for young Japanese and foreigners, Roppongi has more bars and nightclubs than any other district outside Shinjuku, as well as a multitude of restaurants serving international cuisines. It's anchored by two sprawling developments: the eye-popping, 11-hectare (28-acre) **Roppongi Hills,** housing 230 shops and restaurants, a first-class hotel, a garden, a cinema complex, and Tokyo's highest art museum, on the 53rd floor of Mori Tower; and the smaller **Tokyo Midtown,** which has a luxury hotel, medical center, 130 restaurants and fashion boutiques, a garden, and the Suntory Museum of Art. Also in Roppongi is the **National Art Center, Tokyo,** focusing on changing exhibitions of modern and contemporary art. About a 15-miute walk from Roppongi Station, the new **Azabudai Hills** complex covers 8 hectares and was designed on the concept of a "forest city," peppered with foliage and centered on a broad green. The complex has the tallest skyscraper in Japan, along with high-end apparel shops, co-work spaces, a venture capital cluster, swanky apartments, the **Janu Tokyo** hotel, an international school, an indoor food market, art galleries, and the teamLab Borderless museum.

Getting Around Town

The first rule of getting around Tokyo: It will always take longer than you think. Taking a taxi is expensive and involves the probability of getting stuck interminably in traffic, with the meter ticking away. Taking the subway is usually more efficient, even though it's more complicated—choosing which route to take isn't always clear, and transfers between lines are sometimes quite a hike. If you're traveling across Tokyo, it's good to allow anywhere from 30 to 60 minutes, depending on the number of transfers; if you don't have to change trains, you can travel from one end of central Tokyo to the other (say, from Shibuya to Ueno) in about 30 minutes or less.

Your best bet for getting around Tokyo is to take the subway or a Japan Railways (JR) commuter train such as the Yamanote Line to the station nearest your destination. For all accommodations, restaurants, sights, shops, and nightlife venues listed in this chapter and the next, I've included both the nearest station and, in parentheses, the approximate time it takes to walk from the station to the destination. Unfortunately, Tokyo doesn't offer public transportation late at night (most services stop from around midnight to 4 or 5am).

This might sound silly given the sheer incomprehensible size of Tokyo, but it's actually a great city for walking, and if you're not traveling too far, the time difference between the train journey and journey on foot is often negligible (especially if you account for struggling to find the appropriate station exit). This also allows you to see parts of the city you'd otherwise skip over entirely—one of the great joys of Tokyo is its endless potential for discovery.

TIPS ON TAKING PUBLIC TRANSPORTATION Note that children 6 to 11 pay half-fare on public transportation in Japan; children 5 and under ride free. Note, too, that all cellphones should be switched to silent mode (called "manner mode" in Japanese) on public conveyances. Finally, avoid taking the subway or JR train during the weekday morning **rush hour,** from 8 to 9am—the stories you've heard about commuters packed like sardines into trains are all true. There are no dedicated "platform pushers" anymore, men who push people into compartments so that the doors can close, but sometimes station staff will fulfill this role when the carriage is full to bursting. If you want to witness Tokyo at its craziest, go to Shinjuku Station at 8:30am—but get there by taxi unless you want to experience the crowding firsthand. Most lines provide women-only compartments at the end of the train weekdays until 9:30am.

BY SUBWAY

To get around Tokyo on your own, it's imperative to learn how to ride its subways. Fortunately, the subway system is efficient, modern, clean, and easy to use; in fact, I think it's one of the most user-friendly systems on the planet. Comprehensive English-language signage and, particularly in the busiest stations, staff that can communicate in English are now commonplace. To remove the guessing game regarding which route to take, what it will cost, and the estimated ride time, download the invaluable free **Tokyo Subway Navigation app.** If Google Maps is your go to navigation app, it's usually spot on, too. Tokyo subway stations provide free Wi-Fi.

Altogether, some 13 underground subway lines crisscross the city, operated by two companies: **Tokyo Metro** (the bigger of the two, which uses a symbol "M" that is vaguely reminiscent of McDonald's arches) and **Toei,** which uses a gingko leaf symbol. Station names are written in English, and each subway line is color-coded and assigned a letter (usually the subway's initial). The Ginza Line, for example, is orange, which means that all its trains and signs are orange, and it's identified by the letter "G." Additionally, each station along each line is assigned a number in chronological order beginning with the first station (Shibuya Station, for example, is G1 because it's the first station on the Ginza Line, while Asakusa

STREAMLINE YOUR TRAVEL WITH fare passes

Each mode of transportation in Tokyo—**subway** (with two different companies), **JR train** (such as the Yamanote Line), **private rail companies,** and **bus**—has its own fare system and therefore requires a new ticket each time you transfer from one mode of transport to another. It's much more convenient to purchase a **Suica** (jreast.co.jp/e/pass/suica), issued by JR East and available at any JR station via ticket vending machine, or a **PASMO** (pasmo.co.jp), issued by Tokyo Metro subways and sold from ticket vending machines in subway stations. Both are contactless prepaid IC (integrated circuit) cards that automatically deduct fares and can be used on virtually all modes of transportation, including JR trains, private railways (such as the Rinkai Line to Odaiba), subways, and buses at a slight discount. They can even be used for purchases at designated vending machines, convenience stores, and fast-food outlets that display the Suica/PASMO sign. Best of all, the cards can be used on various modes of local transportation throughout Japan, whether you're in Kamakura or Kyoto.

Note that both cards come with a ¥500 deposit, plus any initial value between ¥1,000 to ¥10,000 that you choose to load. You can then reload them at ticket vending machines as needed. If you don't have enough balance on your card when you reach your destination, simply top off your card at the exit's fare adjustment machine. When you're ready to leave Tokyo, PASMO will refund the deposit and any remaining balance on the card, while Suica will refund the deposit but charge a handling fee of up to ¥220 for any remaining balance (so be sure the card is depleted).

Although other options are available, including 1-day cards and metro-only cards, the Suica and the Pasmo are by far the most convenient (and they can now be downloaded onto digital wallets on your phone or smartwatch). Because of a global IC chip shortage since the pandemic, these cards have been in short supply and only some major stations are currently stocking them. To streamline the transport experience for tourists, the government introduced a travel Suica, lasting 28 days, which you can purchase at Haneda and Narita Airports.

If you think you're going to be traveling a lot by public transportation on any given day, consider purchasing a **Tokyo Combination Ticket** (Tokyo Furii Kippu) for ¥1,590, which allows unlimited travel for 1 day on all subways, JR trains, and Toei buses within Tokyo's 23 wards. It's available at almost all JR and subway stations. There are also 1-day tickets that can be used only on Metro subway lines (¥600), on all subway lines of both companies (¥900), or only on JR trains (¥750). In addition, there are 24-hour, 48-hour, and 72-hour discount tickets just for visitors. See **tokyometro.jp/en/ticket** for details.

Station is G19). Before boarding, make sure the train is going in the right direction—signs at each station show both the previous and the next stop, so you can double-check that you're heading in the right direction. Tokyo's newest line, Toei's Oedo Line, makes a zigzag loop around the city and can be useful, but be aware that it's buried deep underground and platforms take a while to reach, despite escalators.

It used to be a matter of skill to know exactly which train compartment to board if making transfers down the line; nowadays, diagrams at each station (usually on a pillar at the platform entrance) show which end of the train and compartment is most useful for connections. Signs also show exactly how many minutes it takes to reach every destination on that line. Once you're on your way, digital signs in English above the doors display the next station, announce stops, and indicate which side to disembark from.

Comprehensive signs and ticket vending machines make Tokyo's subway system quite user-friendly.

Once you reach your destination, look for the yellow signs on station platforms designating which exit to take for major buildings, museums, and addresses. If you're confused about which exit to take, ask an attendant near the ticket gate. Taking the right exit can make a world of difference, especially in Shinjuku, where there are some 60 station exits.

Because buying individual tickets is a hassle, buy either a Suica or PASMO prepaid card (see box on p. 99). Otherwise, vending machines at all subway stations sell tickets; fares begin at ¥170 for the shortest distance and increase according to how far you're traveling. Vending machines give change, even for a ¥10,000 note. **To purchase your ticket,** insert money into the vending machine until the fare buttons light up, and then push the amount for the ticket you want.

Before purchasing your ticket, you first have to figure out your **fare.** Fares are posted on a large subway map above the vending machines, but they're sometimes in Japanese only. Some stations also have a signboard posting fares to other stations. If you can't figure out the fare, buy the cheapest ticket (¥170) and at your destination, look for the **fare adjustment machine;** insert your ticket to find out how much more you owe, or ask a subway employee at the ticket window to tell you how much you owe. In any case, be sure to hang onto your ticket, since you must give it up at the end of your journey. Once again, Suica or PASMO cards are much more convenient than buying individual tickets.

Most subways run from about 5am to midnight, although the times of the first and last trains depend on the line, the station, and whether it's a weekday or a weekend. Schedules are posted in the stations, and throughout most of the day, trains run every 3 to 5 minutes.

For more information on tickets, passes, and subway routes, as well as a detailed subway map, stop by **Metro Information desks** at Ueno, Ginza, Shinjuku, and Omotesando stations. Or check the websites **tokyometro.jp** or **kotsu.metro.tokyo.jp**.

BY TRAIN

In addition to subway lines, commuter trains operated by the **East Japan Railway Company** (**JR**) run aboveground throughout greater Tokyo. These are also color-coded, with fares beginning at ¥140. Buy your ticket from vending machines just as you would for the subway, or use the convenient Suica or PASMO cards (see p. 99). If you plan to travel a lot on JR lines on any given day, the **1-Day Metropolitan District Pass** (**Tokunai Pass**) allows unlimited travel within Tokyo's 23 wards for ¥750. If you have a validated Japan Rail Pass, you can travel on JR trains for free.

The best-known and most convenient JR line, the **Yamanote Line** (green-colored coaches) makes an oblong loop around the city in about an hour, stopping at 30 stations along the way, all of them announced in English and with digital signboards in each compartment. Another convenient JR line is the orange-colored **Chuo Line;** it's an express train that cuts across Tokyo between Shinjuku and Tokyo stations, with a stop at Ochanomizu. The yellow-colored **Sobu Line** runs between Shinjuku and Akihabara and beyond to Ryogoku and Chiba. Other JR lines serve outlying districts, including Yokohama and Kamakura. Because the Yamanote, Chuo, and Sobu lines are often not identified by their specific names at major stations, look for signs that say JR LINES.

For more information on JR trains, as well as train travel throughout Japan, stop by the **JR East Travel Service Center** at Tokyo Station's Marunouchi North Exit. Open daily 7:30am to 8:30pm, it also offers free Wi-Fi, hotel reservations, tourist information, currency exchange, and luggage delivery and storage. You can also exchange vouchers here for the Japan Rail Pass. There are also JR East Travel Service Centers at Ueno, Shinjuku, Shibuya, and Ikebukuro stations, which focus on Tokyo metro travel. You can also call the English-language **JR East Infoline** (✆ **050-2016-1603;** open daily 10am–6pm), or visit the website **www.jreast.co.jp**.

In addition to JR, private train companies provide service from Tokyo to outlying areas. **Tobu Railway,** for example, operates trains to Nikko, while **Odakyu Electric Railway** covers the Hakone area. Both offer discount travel passes. For more information, see individual destinations in chapter 5.

BY BUS

Toei buses are not as easy to use as trains or subways unless you know their routes, because only the end destination is written on the bus and many bus drivers don't speak English. However, I find they're more user-friendly than they used to be. Buses even offer free Wi-Fi onboard and are often convenient for short distances, such as traveling between Roppongi and Shibuya. Simply board the bus at the front and drop the exact fare (usually ¥210) into the box. If you don't have the exact amount, fare boxes accept coins or bills; your change minus the fare will come out below. Better yet, use a Suica or PASMO card (see p. 99). A signboard at the front of the bus displays the next stop, usually in English, and will be accompanied by a disembodied voice telling you the name of the stop that's next in line. When you wish to get off, press one of the purple buttons on the railing near the door or the seats. You can pick up an excellent Toei bus map showing all major routes at one of the Tokyo Tourist Information Centers operated by the Tokyo Metropolitan Government (see "Visitor Information," p. 89). The Toei website at **kotsu.metro.tokyo.jp** also provides information on routes, timetables, and fares.

In addition to Toei buses, the tourist-oriented **Sky Bus** (skybus.jp; ✆ **03-3215-0008**) offers 50-minute double-decker open-top bus tours around the Imperial Palace (¥1,600) and other tourist sites. It also offers hop-on, hop-off buses that travel three routes—Asakusa/Tokyo SkyTree, Odaiba, and Roppongi. These begin and end in Marunouchi near Tokyo Station and cost ¥3,500 for 24 hours. But frankly, taking public transportation is much cheaper.

Tokyo's High-Tech Transit Ambitions

Tokyo has made some big net-zero commitments and has put a lot of faith in the power of hydrogen energy. The city introduced a limited number of hydrogen fuel cell buses, partly to test their efficiency and partly to showcase Tokyo's high-tech ambitions as the world was set to arrive for the 2020 Olympics (which ended up being held in 2021 without spectators). Currently there's a free hydrogen-powered shuttle bus between Tokyo Station Marunouchi Exit and Tokyo Tower, stopping at WATERS Takeshiba and Hinode Pier. Tokyo hopes hydrogen will fuel up to 300 of its buses by 2030, but many members of the global commentariat are skeptical about Japan's hydrogen ambitions.

BY TAXI

Taxis are expensive in Tokyo, unless you're going a short distance. **Fares** start at ¥410 for the first 1.052km (.65 mile) but increase ¥80 for each additional 237m (924 ft.) or 90 seconds of waiting time. There are also smaller, more compact taxis that charge slightly less, but these are few in number. Fares are posted on the back of the front passenger seat. Note that from 10pm to 5am, an extra 20% is added to your fare. Perhaps as an admission of how expensive taxis are, fares can be paid by credit card.

With the exception of some major downtown thoroughfares, you can hail a taxi from any street or go to a taxi stand or a major hotel. A red light above the dashboard shows if a taxi is free to pick up a passenger; a greenish-yellow light indicates that the taxi is occupied. ***Note:*** Be sure to stand clear of the back left door—it swings open automatically. Likewise, it shuts automatically once you're in. Taxi drivers are quite perturbed if you try to maneuver the door yourself.

Because many taxi drivers don't speak English, it's best to have your destination written out in Japanese.

There are so many taxis cruising Tokyo (about 50,000) that you can hail one easily on most thoroughfares—except when you need it most: when it's raining, or just after 1am on weekends when subways and trains have stopped. To call a taxi for a pickup (which carries a ¥310 surcharge), try **Nihon Kotsu** (nihon-kotsu.co.jp; ✆ **03-5755-2336**) for an English-speaking operator.

Uber (uber.com/cities/tokyo) is tightly restricted in Tokyo, but even in the past few years it's become much more commonplace. It still works in conjunction with high-end private drivers and taxi companies, though, so don't expect fares to be much cheaper. **Go Taxi** is the most popular taxi booking app in Japan, servicing 45 of 47 prefectures. The fees are much the same as Uber, but worth downloading to increase your chances of hailing a cab when its busy.

[Fast FACTS] TOKYO

If you can't find answers to your questions here, check "Fast Facts: Japan," in chapter 15 or call one of the tourist offices listed on p. 89.

ATMs For ATMs that accept foreign credit cards, head to any post office, 7-Eleven or FamilyMart. I've even seen ATMs operated by 7-Eleven and JP Post in subway stations and other convenient locations. For details, see "Money & Costs," in chapter 15.

Currency Exchange **Narita Airport** and **Haneda Airport** have exchange counters for all incoming international flights; they offer better exchange rates than what you'd get abroad. Change enough money to last several days—the exchange rate is the same as you'd get at banks in town. Any bank displaying an AUTHORIZED FOREIGN EXCHANGE sign can exchange currency, with exchange rates usually displayed at the foreign-exchange counter.

Dentists The **Tokyo Clinic Dental Office,** 3–4–30 Shiba-koen, Minato-ku (tcdo.jp; ✆ **03-3431-4225**), is near Kamiyacho, Onari-mon, Akabanebashi, or Daimon stations and across from Tokyo Tower. Just a 3-minute walk away is the **United Dental Office,** 2–3–8 Azabudai, Minato-ku (uniteddentaloffice.com; ✆ **03-5570-4334**). Tokyo Midtown Medical Center (see "Doctors & Hospitals," below) also has a **Dental Clinic** (✆ **03-5413-7912**). All have English-speaking staff.

Doctors & Hospitals Many first-class hotels offer medical facilities or an in-house doctor. Tokyo Metropolitan Government's office for **Hospital Management** (byouin.metro.tokyo.jp/english/index.html) can refer you to medical professionals who speak English and has staff who can also explain the health insurance system in Japan; its emergency translation service (✆ **03-5285-8181;** daily 9am–8pm) is staffed with translators who can act as go-betweens during treatment if problems arise. Providing similar services is the **AMDA International Medical Information Center** (amda-imic.com; ✆ **03-5285-8088**), open Monday to Friday 9am–5pm. Embassies (see p. 696) also have lists of English-speaking health professionals.

Otherwise, clinics with English-speaking staff include **Tokyo Midtown Medical Center,** sixth floor of Midtown Tower, 9–7–1 Akasaka, Minato-ku, near Roppongi Station (tokyo-midtown-mc.jp; ✆ **03-5413-7911**), and **Tokyo Medical & Surgical Clinic** (tmsc.jp; ✆ **03-3436-3028**), in the same building as Tokyo Clinic Dental Office, above.

Large hospitals in Japan have limited public hours; designated hospitals remain open for emergencies (ambulances will automatically take you there). Hospitals with English-speaking staff include the **Seibo International Catholic Hospital,** 2–5–1

Naka-Ochiai, Shinjuku-ku, near Mejiro Station on the Yamanote Line (seibokai.or.jp; ✆ **03-3951-1111**); **St. Luke's International Hospital (Seiroka Byoin)**, 9–1 Akashi-cho, Chuo-ku, near Tsukiji Station on the Hibiya Line (luke.or.jp; ✆ **03-5550-7166**); and **Japanese Red Cross Medical Center (Nihon Sekijujisha Iryo Center)**, 4–1–22 Hiroo, Shibuya-ku (med.jrc.or.jp; ✆ **03-3400-1311**), whose closest subway stations are Roppongi, Hiroo, and Shibuya—from there, you should take a taxi.

Luggage Storage Major JR train stations have lockers for luggage, but with the increasing number of tourists, these can be full. **Sagawa** (sagawa-exp.co.jp) offers luggage storage and delivery, with offices in Tokyo Station, Tokyo SkyTree, Asakusa, and Shinjuku Expressway Bus Terminal. There's also a baggage storage room near the **JR East Travel Service Center** at the Marunouchi north exit of Tokyo Station (tokyostationcity.com/en/information/locker.html; ✆ **03-5221-8123**) open daily 7:30am to 8:30pm.

Newspapers & Magazines There are two daily English-language newspapers in Japan—the ***Japan Times*** (japantimes.co.jp), which comes distributed with the *International New York Times*, and the ***Japan News*** (the-japan-news.com). ***Metropolis*** (metropolisjapan.com) is a free quarterly with features on Tokyo, club listings, and restaurant and movie reviews. ***Tokyo Weekender*** (tokyoweekender.com), a free bi-monthly in-print magazine, offers more in-depth coverage of the city and its cultural figures. You can find these peppered around the city at various bars, train stations, and commercial buildings.

Pharmacies Tokyo has no 24-hour drugstores (*kusuri-ya*), but ubiquitous 24-hour convenience stores, such as 7-Eleven, Lawson, and FamilyMart, carry things like aspirin. If you're looking for specific pharmaceuticals, a good bet is the **American Pharmacy,** in the basement of the Marunouchi Building, 2–4–1 Marunouchi, Chiyoda-ku (✆ **03-5220-7716;** station: Tokyo or Marunouchi; Mon–Fri 9am–9pm, Sat 10am–9pm, Sun and holidays 10am–8pm), which has many of the same over-the-counter drugs you can find at home. It can also fill American prescriptions—but note that you *must first visit a doctor in Japan* before foreign prescriptions can be filled. It's best to bring an ample supply of any prescription medication with you. Japan has strict controls on bringing prescription drugs into the country, so check with the immigration authorities if a) you can bring said drugs with you, and b) what you need to declare at customs.

Post Offices Although all post offices (called a *yubinkyoku*) are open Monday to Friday 9am to 5pm, major post offices located in every ward remain open to 7pm (to mail a package, you'll need to go to one of these). Tokyo's **Central Post Office,** 2–7–2 Marunouchi, Chiyoda-ku (✆ **03-3217-5231;** station: Tokyo or Marunouchi), is open Monday to Friday 9am–9pm and Saturday and Sunday 9am–6pm; it also has a counter open 24 hours for mail and packages.

Safety Tokyo consistently ranks among the safest major urban destinations in the world. Petty crimes are exceedingly rare, though some Japanese caution women against walking through parks alone at night.

Wi-Fi All subway stations, JR Yamanote stations, and Toei buses provide free Wi-Fi. In addition, several neighborhoods offer their own free Wi-Fi at key spots, including Ginza, Marunouchi, Ueno, Asakusa, Shibuya, and Akihabara, as well as at most department stores. Many coffee shops, restaurants, and bars offer it to paying customers as well (you may need to ask for the password). Finally, many entities offer free Wi-Fi, most of which require you to sign up. The Tokyo Metropolitan Government, for example, offers **Free Wi-Fi & Tokyo** (wifi-tokyo.jp). Go to its website to register and see all the parks, museums, and other places where you can connect. For more on using the Internet and Wi-Fi in Japan, see "Fast Facts" in chapter 15.

EXPLORING TOKYO

Tokyo hasn't fared very well over the centuries. Fires and earthquakes have taken their toll, old buildings have been torn down in the zeal for modernization, and World War II left most of the city in ruins. Save your historical sightseeing, therefore, for places such as Kyoto, Kanazawa, or Takayama, and consider Tokyo an introduction to the newest of the new in Japan, showcasing the nation's accomplishments in the arts, technology, fashion, pop culture, and design. Tokyo also has more museums than any other city in Japan, as well as having a wide range of parks, temples, and shrines. In Tokyo you can explore mammoth department stores, sample unlimited cuisines, walk around atmospheric neighborhoods, drink in some of the world's best cocktail bars, sip draft beer in rustic *izakaya.* All the while it begins to become clear what is meant by *omotenashi,* Japan's gold-standard customer service. When planning your sightseeing itinerary, keep in mind that the city is huge, and it takes time to get from one end to the other. It's best, therefore, to cover Tokyo neighborhood by neighborhood, coordinating sightseeing with dinner and evening plans.

Most museums in Tokyo are closed 1 day of the week (usually Mon) and for New Year's (generally the last day or two in Dec and the first 1–3 days of Jan). If Monday happens to be a national holiday, most national and municipal museums will remain open but will close Tuesday instead. Some of the privately owned museums, however, are closed on national holidays, as well as for exhibition changes. Call beforehand or check websites to avoid disappointment. Remember, too, that you must enter museums at least 30 minutes before closing time.

For a listing of current exhibitions, including those being held at major department stores, consult museum websites or local culture news resources like ***Tokyo Weekender*** (tokyoweekender.com/), ***TimeOut Tokyo*** (timeout.com/tokyo), and ***Metropolis*** (metropolisjapan.com/).

Central Tokyo: Ginza & Around the Imperial Palace

See Ginza map on p. 143.

East Garden (Higashi Gyoen) ♥♥ GARDEN The 21 hectares (52 acres) of the formal Higashi Gyoen—once the main grounds of Edo Castle and located next to the Imperial Palace—are a wonderful respite in the middle of the city. Surprisingly, this garden is hardly ever crowded, except when cherry trees, azaleas, and other blossoms are in full bloom or at lunchtime when *bento*-eating office workers fill the benches. **Ninomaru** is laid out in Japanese style with a pond, steppingstones, and winding paths; it's particularly beautiful when the wisteria, azaleas, irises, and other flowers are at their peak. Near Ninomaru is the **Sannomaru Shozokan,** with free, changing exhibitions of art treasures belonging to the imperial family.

On the highest spot of East Garden is the **Honmaru** (inner citadel), where Tokugawa's main castle once stood, the mightiest in the land. Built in the first half of the 1600s, the massive castle was surrounded by a series of whirling moats and guarded by 29 watchtowers and 38 gates around its 15km (10-mile) perimeter. At its center was Japan's tallest building at the time, the five-story castle keep, soaring 50m (168 ft.) above its foundations and offering an expansive view over Edo. This is where Tokugawa Ieyasu would have taken refuge, had his empire ever been seriously threatened. Although most of the castle was a glimmering white, the keep was black with a gold roof, which must have been quite a sight in old Edo as it towered above the rest of the city. All that remains today of the shogun's castle are a few towers, gates, stone walls, moats, and the stone foundations of the keep.

1–1 Chiyoda, Chiyoda-ku. kunaicho.go.jp/e-event/higashigyoen02.html. ✆ **03-3213-1111.** Free admission. Tues–Thurs and Sat–Sun 9am–5pm (to 4:30pm Mar to mid-Apr and Sept–Oct; to 4pm Nov–Feb). Last entry 30 min. before closing. Closed Dec 23 and Dec 28–Jan 3; open other national holidays. Station: Otemachi, Takebashi, or Nijubashi-mae.

The Imperial Palace (Kyokyo) ♥ HISTORIC SITE The Imperial Palace, home of the imperial family, is the heart and soul of Tokyo. Built on the very spot where the massive Edo Castle compound used to stand during the Tokugawa shogunate, it became the imperial home upon its completion in 1888. It's now the residence of Emperor Naruhito, 126th emperor of Japan (who ascended to the throne in 2019, following the abdication of his father, Akihito). Destroyed during air raids in 1945, the palace was rebuilt in 1968 using the principles of traditional Japanese architecture. But don't expect to get a good look at it; most of the palace grounds' 114 hectares (282 acres) are off-limits to the public, with the exception of 2 days a year when the royal family makes an appearance before the throngs: January 2 and on the emperor's birthday (Feb 23).

You can visit the Imperial Palace grounds (not any buildings) on free **guided tours** conducted in Japanese and English Tuesday through Saturday at 10am and 1:30pm (1:30pm tour not available July 21–Aug 31). Reservations are accepted up to 1 month in advance, with a capacity of 200 persons per tour, but there are also walk-in options. Easiest is to book online, which you must do at least 4 days in advance at the website below. Alternatively, you can make a same-day or advance reservation by calling the number below. Tours last about 75 minutes and include official buildings, the inner moat, historic fortifications, and Nijubashi Bridge. This tour is only recommended if you have seen Tokyo's other top attractions (and it doesn't come close to the more impressive imperial palace tours in Kyoto).

Otherwise, you'll have to console yourself with a camera shot of the palace from the southeast side of **Nijubashi Bridge,** where an original palace turret rises above the trees. Most Japanese tourists make brief stops here to pay their respects. The wide moat, lined with cherry trees, is

While most of the Imperial Palace is off-limits to the public, you can get a good glimpse of it from the southeast side of Nijubashi Bridge.

especially beautiful in spring. You might even want to set aside an hour or two strolling or jogging the 5km (3 miles) around the palace and moat. But the most important thing to do in the palace's vicinity is visit its **East Garden (Higashi Gyoen;** see above).

Hibiya Dori Ave. sankan.kunaicho.go.jp/english/guide/koukyo.html. ✆ **03-5223-8071.** Station: Nijubashi-mae (1 min.) or Hibiya (5 min.).

National Museum of Modern Art (Tokyo Kokuritsu Kindai Bijutsukan) ♥♥ MUSEUM This is the place to go for Japan's largest collection of modern Japanese art. The inventory of 13,000 works includes paintings in both Japanese and Western styles, prints, watercolors, drawings, and sculpture, from the end of the Meiji Period to the present time. From that, about 200 are selected for exhibitions that change quarterly, but there are usually works by well-known Japanese artists like Ryusei Kishida, Shiko Munakata, Seiki Kuroda, and Yokoyama Taikan. Works by Western artists like Kokoschka, Van Gogh, Paul Klee, and others are included as examples of artistic styles from the same period. Expect to spend about 1 hour here. You might also want to head over to the nearby **Crafts Gallery** (it's included in the ticket price). Occupying a disappointingly small part of a Gothic-style 1910 brick building that once served as Imperial Guard headquarters, it holds changing exhibitions of contemporary crafts, from pottery and metalwork to glassware. It often includes works of living national treasures and great masters.

3 Kitanomaru Koen Park, Chiyoda-ku. momat.go.jp. ✆ **03-3214-2561.** ¥500 adults, ¥250 college students, free for children and seniors; special exhibits cost more. Free admission 1st Sun of every month. Tues–Sun 10am–5pm (Fri–Sat until 8pm). Station: Takebashi (exit 1B, 3 min.).

Works by both Japanese and Western artists are hung together in the National Museum of Modern Art (p. 107).

Yasukuni Shrine ♥ SHRINE/MUSEUM Built in 1869 to commemorate Japanese war dead, Yasukuni Shrine is constructed in classic Shinto style, with a huge steel *torii* gate at its entrance. During times of war, soldiers were told that if they died fighting for their country, their spirits would find glory here; even today, it's believed that the spirits of some 2.4 million Japanese war dead are at home here, where they are worshipped as deities. Every August 15, the shrine is thrust into the national spotlight when World War II memorials are held. Visits by prime ministers and other officials have caused national outrage among Japan's Asian neighbors, who think it improper to visit—and thereby condone—a shrine so closely tied to Japan's nationalistic and militaristic past.

The most important thing to see is the **Yushukan,** a war memorial museum outlining Japan's military history. It chronicles the rise and fall of the samurai, the colonization of Asia by Western powers by the late 1800s, the Sino-Japanese War, the Russo-Japanese War, and World Wars I and II, though explanations in English are rather vague and Japan's military aggression in Asia is barely touched. Still, you could spend a fascinating 90 minutes here gazing on samurai armor, swords, uniforms, tanks, artillery, and a Mitsubishi Zero fighter plane, as well as such thought-provoking displays as a human torpedo (a tiny submarine guided by one occupant and loaded with explosives) and a suicide attack plane. The most chilling displays are the seemingly endless photographs of war dead, some of them very young teenagers. In stark contrast to the museum's somberness, temporary exhibits of beautiful *ikebana* (Japanese flower arrangements) and bonsai are often held on the shrine grounds in rows of glass cases. Yasukuni Shrine is also famous for its cherry blossoms.

Yasukuni Shrine, 3–1–1 Kudan-kita, Chiyoda-ku. yasukuni.or.jp. ✆ **03-3261-8326.** Free admission to shrine; Yushukan ¥1,000 adults, ¥500 students, ¥300 seniors and junior-high to high-school students, free for younger children. Shrine daily 24 hr.; Yushukan daily 9am–4:30pm. Station: Kudanshita (5 min.) or Ichigaya or Iidabashi (10 min.).

Asakusa

For a map of Asakusa, see p. 149. On the corner of Kaminarimon Dori and Asakusa Dori (across from the entry gate to Sensoji Temple) is the **Asakusa Culture Tourist Information Center,** open daily 9am to 8pm, where you can get a map of the area and take in views of the temple from the 8th-floor observation terrace with a small coffee kiosk. On Saturdays and Sundays, volunteers give free 1-hour tours of Asakusa, departing here at 10:30am and 1:15pm.

Asakusa Sumo Club ♥♥♥ SUMO PERFORMANCE This is a fun—and after a few beers, quite riotous—introduction to one of Japan's most celebrated, not to mention mystifying, cultural touchstones: sumo wrestling. The event space is small, with tiered seating on either side of a sand-covered *dohyo* (wrestling ring), meaning you're close enough to fully appreciate the pre-bout rituals and mind-games, and to hear the slap of flesh on flesh as the wrestlers engage in a best-of-three-rounds battle. An English-speaking MC, whose job is also to rile up the crowd, explains the history of the sport, its connection to Shintoism, the process required to become a sumo wrestler (including the toll it takes on the body, often for little financial reward), the foodstuffs at the core of the sumo diet, and the techniques, foul plays, and rituals a sumo will encounter. All the while, you'll be treated to an all-you-can-eat feast: edamame, *karaage* (deep-fried chicken thigh), *inarizushi* (rice-filled sweetened tofu pouches that wrestlers believe to be auspicious), and *chanko nabe,* a calorie-filled hot-pot (wrestlers generally eat a whopping 30 portions of this at mealtimes). One drink is also included in the admission price, but you can order more using the QR codes at your table. As the event comes to a close, you'll have opportunities to ask the wrestlers questions, take photos with them, and if you're foolish enough, square off with a wrestler of your choice inside the ring (there's no guarantee they'll go easy on you). A short geisha dance also prefaces the sumo performance. Shows take place three to four times daily; you can book seats online using the website below. There are much more expensive V-VIP tickets, where you'll sit on sofas in front of the ring, but I'm not sure they justify the extra cost.

2-10-12-1F Asakusa, Taito-ku. asakusa-sumo.com. ✆ **03-5246-3344.** Standard tickets ¥16,000, VIP ¥20,000, V-VIP ¥60,000. Shows held 3 or 4 times daily, starting at noon. Irregular holidays. Station: Asakusa (Tsukuba Express A1 exit, 1 min.; Metro exits, 6–8 min.).

Hanayashiki ♥ AMUSEMENT PARK Opened in 1853 while the shogun still reigned, this small and rather corny amusement park is Japan's oldest. It has a small rollercoaster, a kiddie Ferris wheel, a carousel, a haunted house, a 3-D theater, and other diversions appealing to younger children. Grab a Telepathy Walker, a headset device that lets you "see" how Hanayashiki has changed over the years. Note, however, that after paying admission, you must still buy tickets for each ride (except for the

Telepathy Walker, which is free but available only to people 12 and older). Tickets are ¥100 each, and most rides require two to four tickets. 2–28–1 Asakusa (northwest of Sensoji Temple), Taito-ku. hanayashiki.net. ✆ **03-3842-8780.** ¥1,000 adults, ¥500 children 7–12 and seniors, free for children 6 and under. Daily 10am–6pm (to 5pm in winter). Station: Asakusa (5 min.).

Sensoji Temple ♥♥♥ TEMPLE Also popularly known as Asakusa Kannon, this is Tokyo's oldest and most celebrated temple. Its history dates to A.D. 628, when, according to popular lore, two brothers fishing in the nearby Sumida River netted the catch of their lives: a tiny golden statue of Kannon, the Buddhist goddess of mercy and happiness, who is empowered with the ability to release humans from all suffering. Sensoji Temple was erected in her honor. Although the statue is housed here, it's never shown to the public (you will find on your travels that Japan is fascinated with such secrets). Still, through the centuries, worshipers have flocked here seeking favors of Kannon, and when Sensoji Temple burned down during a 1945 bombing raid, it was rebuilt with donations from the Japanese people. After sunset, the temple and pagoda are illuminated until 11pm.

Entrance to the temple is via colorful Kaminarimon Gate onto lively **Nakamise Dori,** a pedestrian lane leading to the shrine and lined with more than 80 stalls selling souvenirs and traditional Japanese goods. Most tourists in Asakusa make a beeline for this linear path so it gets unbearably congested. Don't be afraid to take a detour onto the adjacent side streets,

Lined with souvenir stalls, Nakamise Dori leads to the popular Sensoji Temple.

where you'll find knife shops, kimono rental stores, artisanal crafts, and traditional cuisine restaurants.

The free weekend tours at the Asakusa Culture Tourist Information Center (see above) will take you to Sensoji, or you can book a tip-based tour with **Tokyo Localized** (tokyolocalized.com). Tours start at the Kaminarimon Gate and last about 2 hours; they should be booked 10–14 days in advance. Check the Tokyo Localized online schedule for availability.

2-3-1 Asakusa, Taito-ku. senso-ji.jp. ✆ **03-3842-0181.** Free admission. Daily 6:30am–5pm (from 6am in summer). Station: Asakusa (2 min.).

Ueno & Vicinity

For a map of Ueno, see p. 151. Ueno is a hugely popular family destination, making this a priority for those traveling with kids. Among family must-sees are Ueno Park and the National Museum of Nature and Science.

Asakura Choso Museum ♥♥ HISTORIC HOME This museum is actually a very unique home that once belonged to a famous artist. Of course, this isn't just any house. Designed by sculptor Fumio Asakura (1883–1964) to serve as his residence, studio, and Asakura Sculpture School, it's a delightful combination of both modern and traditional architecture, restored to reflect how it would have looked in 1955. Probably the most enviable feature is the inner courtyard pond, fed by a natural spring and visible from many rooms in the house. There's a library, his airy studio, and tatami rooms, including one for visitors where they could enjoy the rising sun. On the roof is a garden, where Asakura's students tended vegetables to sharpen their senses. And throughout the house are furniture, antiques, hundreds of orchids, and statues of statesmen, women, and cats (Asakura loved cats; he once had as many as 10). Visitors are asked to take off their shoes and wear socks through the museum.

7-18-10 Yanaka, Taito-ku. taitogeibun.net/asakura. ✆ **03-3821-4549.** Tues–Wed and Fri–Sun 9:30am–4:30pm. Station: Nippori (northwest exit, 5 min.).

National Museum of Nature and Science (Kokuritsu Kagaku Hakubutsukan) ♥♥ MUSEUM Of all of Tokyo's museums, this is probably the one that delights both kids and parents the most. As Japan's largest science museum, it has an informative section that concentrates just on Japan—making it a good learning tool—and lots of imaginative displays and exhibits geared toward youngsters. Of its two sections, a **Global Gallery** covers earth, space, the development of technology, the diversity of life, and the evolution of humans, dinosaurs, and other life forms; and the **Japan Gallery** focuses on the country's natural history. The **Animals of the Earth** hallway is filled with incredible taxidermic animals from around the world, including a polar bear, camel, gorilla, tiger, and bear; some of the animals are ones that died at nearby Ueno Zoo. Other highlights include dinosaur exhibits; a Japanese mummy from the Edo Period still curled up in a burial jar; the dog Hachiko (stuffed and

A cross-section of a sperm whale hangs overhead in an exhibit on biodiversity at the huge National Museum of Nature and Science.

so famous that there's a statue of him at Shibuya Station); and re-created woodland and marine habitats. **ComPaSS,** a playroom geared toward kids ages 4 to 6, costs ¥300 (free for babies) but requires a special ticket with a specified time stamp. On the roof are a **sky deck, herb garden,** and seasonal **coffee shop.** This museum is huge, so expect to spend a minimum of 2 hours here, though you'll likely stay longer if you rent the audio guide (¥320)—recommended since English-language descriptions are disappointingly limited.

Ueno Park, Taito-ku. kahaku.go.jp. ✆ **03-5777-8600.** ¥630 adults, free for seniors and children through high-school age. Sun and Tues–Thurs 9am–5pm; Fri–Sat 9am–8pm. Station: Ueno (5 min.).

The National Museum of Western Art (Kokuritsu Seiyo Bijutsukan) ♥♥ MUSEUM This is Japan's only national museum of Western art, and how it came to be is just as notable as its collection of sculpture and art from the late Middle Ages through the 20th century. Kojiro Matsukata was a wealthy shipbuilder who made frequent trips to Europe to buy art, eventually acquiring about 10,000 works that he intended to show in a Tokyo museum. The Great Depression interrupted those plans and forced him to sell off much of his collection, while those that had been left in a London warehouse perished in a 1939 fire. About 400 works remained, in Paris, but these were sequestrated by the French government during World War II and only returned to Japan in 1951, a year after Matsukata had died. Those works formed the basis of this museum, opened in 1959 in a building designed by Le Corbusier that is now a UNESCO World Heritage Site. The museum includes works by Old Masters like Lucas

Cranach the Elder, Rubens, El Greco, Murillo, Tintoretto, and Tiepolo, and by 19th- and 20th-century French painters like Delacroix, Monet (an entire room is devoted to his works alone), Manet, Renoir, Pissarro, Sisley, Courbet, Cézanne, Van Gogh, and Gauguin. Twentieth-century works by Picasso, Max Erst, Miró, Dubuffet, Pollock, and others round out the collection. Notably, the museum has one of the largest Rodin collections in the world, with 50-some sculptures that include "The Kiss," "The Thinker," and, outside the museum's front entrance, "The Gates of Hell." Plan on at least an hour here, unless you also take advantage of one of the special exhibitions—often from prestigious overseas collections—which almost always draw large crowds.

Ueno Park, Taito-ku. nmwa.go.jp. ✆ **03-3828-5131.** ¥500 adults, ¥250 college students, free for seniors and ages 17 and under; extra fee for special exhibits. Free admission to permanent collection 2nd Sun of month. Tues–Thurs 9:30am–5:30pm; Fri–Sat 9:30am–9pm. Station: Ueno (4 min.).

Tokyo National Museum (Tokyo Kokuritsu Hakubutsukan) ♥♥♥

MUSEUM Quite simply, this is the best fine art museum in Tokyo, if not in all of Japan. It has the largest collection of Japanese art in the world, making it the single best place to see a vast variety of Japanese antiques and art, including lacquerware, metalwork, pottery, old kimono, samurai armor, swords, scrolls, screens, *ukiyo-e* (woodblock prints), calligraphy, textiles, and ceramics. And that's just the main building (**Japanese Gallery**). Other galleries display Japanese archaeological finds, priceless treasures from Nara, art from other Asian countries, and frequent special exhibitions. As Japan's oldest museum, founded in 1872 and moved to

Like a visitor from ancient times, a 7th-century wooden mask from the traditional gigaku style of dance-drama is displayed at the Tokyo National Museum.

Ueno Park in 1882, it has amassed an inventory of more than 113,000 objects, with about 3,000 items on display at any one time, which means that there's something new to see every time you visit. Schedule a morning or afternoon to visit. Barring that, concentrate on the 24 exhibition rooms of the Japanese Gallery, which you can see in 1 or 2 hours, depending on your interest. The museum shop has reproductions of museum masterpieces and traditional crafts by contemporary artists, including jewelry and miniature fans.

If time allows, tour the **Gallery of Horyuji Treasures (Horyuji Homotsukan)**, which displays priceless Buddhist treasures from the Horyuji Temple in Nara, founded by Prince Shotoku in A.D. 607. Although it seems incongruous that antiquities should find a home in a building as starkly modern as this, low lighting and spacious displays allow the bronze Buddhist statues, ceremonial Gigaku masks (used in ritual dances), lacquerware, textiles, and paintings to shine.

The **Asian Gallery (Toyokan)** is the place to see art and archaeological artifacts from surrounding Asian regions, including China, Korea, Southeast and Central Asia, India, and Egypt. Chinese art, including jade, paintings, calligraphy, and ceramics, makes up the largest part of the collection, a reflection of China's tremendous influence on Japanese art, architecture, and religion. Although exhibitions change, items on display might include Buddhas from China and Gandhara, embroidered wall hangings and cloth from India, Iranian and Turkish carpets, Thai and Vietnamese ceramics, and Egyptian relics.

The **Heiseikan Gallery** houses archaeological finds of ancient Japan, including pottery and Haniwa clay burial figurines of the Jomon Period (10,000 B.C.–1000 B.C.) and ornamental, keyhole-shaped tombs from the Yayoi Period (400 B.C.–A.D. 200). The **Hyokeikan,** built in 1909 to honor the wedding of Emperor Taisho, has occasional special exhibitions.
Ueno Park, Taito-ku. tnm.jp. ✆ **03-3822-1111.** ¥1,000 adults, ¥500 college students, free for seniors and children. Special exhibits cost more. Tues–Thurs 9:30am–5pm; Fri–Sat 9:30–9pm. Station: Ueno (10 min.).

Toshogu Shrine ♥ SHRINE Come here to pay respects to the man who made Edo (present-day Tokyo) the seat of his government and thus elevated the small village to the most important city in the country. Erected in 1651, it's dedicated to Tokugawa Ieyasu, founder of the Tokugawa shogunate. Like Toshogu Shrine in Nikko, it was built by Ieyasu's grandson, Iemitsu, and boasts some of the same richly carved, ornate design favored by the Tokugawas, especially the Chinese-style main gate. Remarkably, it survived the civil war of 1868, the Great Kanto Earthquake of 1923, and even World War II. The pathway to the shrine is lined with massive stone lanterns, as well as 50 copper lanterns donated by *daimyo* from all over Japan, while the grounds themselves are shrouded by a 600-year-old camphor tree. Paying admission allows a closer look at the shrine's magnificent carvings. At the counter to the left you can buy good-luck charms that will supposedly bring you fortune, happiness, and other earthly desires. On a more somber note, a flame on shrine grounds, lit from flames burning in both Hiroshima and Nagasaki, appeals for world peace.

Ueno Park, Taito-ku. uenotoshogu.com. ✆ **03-3822-3455.** Free admission to shrine grounds; inner compound ¥500 adults, ¥200 children. Daily 9am–4:30pm Oct–Feb; 9am–5:30pm March–Sept. Station: Ueno (4 min.).

Shinjuku

For a map of Shinjuku, see p. 154.

Shinjuku Gyoen ♥♥ PARK/GARDEN Formerly the private estate of a feudal lord and then of the imperial family, this is considered one of the most important parks of the Meiji Era. It's wonderful for strolling because of the variety of its planted gardens; styles range from French and English to Japanese traditional. At 58 hectares (143 acres), it's one of the city's largest parks, and each bend in the pathway brings something completely different: Ponds and sculpted bushes give way to a promenade lined with sycamores that opens onto a rose garden. Cherry blossoms, azaleas, chrysanthemums, and other flowers provide splashes of color from spring through autumn. The Japanese garden, buried in the center, is exquisite; if you have time only for a quick look at traditional landscaping, you won't be disappointed here. Wide, grassy expanses are popular for picnics and playing, and a greenhouse is filled with tropical plants. You could easily spend a half-day of leisure here, but it's also good for a quick fix of rejuvenation.

11 Naitocho, Shinjuku-ku. env.go.jp/garden/shinjukugyoen. ✆ **03-3350-0151.** ¥500 adults, ¥250 students and seniors, free for children. Tues–Sun 9am–4:30pm Oct to mid-Mar; until 6pm mid-Mar to June and late Aug to Sept; until 7pm July to late Aug. Station: Shinjuku Gyoen-mae (5 min.) or Sendagaya (5 min.).

Yayoi Kusama Museum ♥♥♥ MUSEUM Dedicated to and founded by Yayoi Kusama, a pop art trailblazer and Japan's unofficial mother of the polka dot, this museum in Shinjuku is an absolute treat for fans of the still-active nonagenarian artist. Even if her name is unfamiliar, you may have seen photos of Kusama's polka-dotted pumpkin sculptures on the piers of Naoshima, which have become de facto symbols of Japan's Art Islands. Her work is also frequently displayed at special exhibitions in global art cities, like London, New York, L.A., Berlin, and Tel Aviv. An airy five-floor gallery in Shinjuku, this excellent museum displays canvases and artworks that serve as windows into the mind of their creator. Kusama was tortured by hallucinogenic visions from a young age, causing years of mental distress, ecstasy, and fear—and eventually prodigious artistic output. It's no surprise that her work is primal, psychedelic, unnerving, and difficult to take your eyes off, all in the same breath. The museum also features immersive 3-D exhibits, touching on themes of infinity, universal connection, and existential angst. But what you encounter depends on the time of your visit, as the artworks are always changing. The museum holds two exhibitions per year, each of which lasts around 5

Pop artist Yayoi Kusama founded this Shinjuku gallery devoted to her colorful, bold, arresting paintings and sculpture.

months, and it only opens Thursdays through Sundays (as well as on national holidays) during each exhibition period. Visitors must book tickets and 90-minute time slots in advance. Tickets go on sale at 10am (JST) on the 1st of each month for entry 2 months hence and are available through the museum's website until 30 minutes before the time slot starts. 107 Bentencho, Shinjuku-ku. yayoikusamamuseum.jp/. No telephone. ¥1,100 adults, ¥600 children. Thurs–Sun and holidays 11am–5:30pm during exhibition periods. Station: Waseda (7 min.), Ushigome Yanagicho (6 min.), or Kagurazaka (9 min.)

Tokyo Metropolitan Government Office (TMG) ♥♥♥ OBSERVATION DECK Tokyo's city hall—designed by one of Japan's best-known architects, Kenzo Tange—comprises three buildings—**TMG no. 1, TMG no. 2,** and the **Metropolitan Assembly Building.** Together they contain everything from Tokyo's Disaster Prevention Center to the governor's office. Most important for visitors is TMG no. 1, the tall building to the north, which offers the best free view of Tokyo. This 48-story, 240m (787-ft.) structure, among the tallest buildings in Shinjuku, has two observatories on the 45th floors of both its north and south towers. Both observatories offer the same spectacular views but have different opening hours and closed days (the North Tower was scheduled to

High above Tokyo's city hall, a free observation deck offers spectacular panoramic views of the metropolis.

reopen in spring 2025 after renovations). On clear winter days you get views of Mount Fuji, which, just after the sun has sunk behind the mountains in the west, looks like an old ink painting. Everyone will be snapping pictures here, but I suggest taking some time to burn the vision into your memory. It's spectacular. On the first floor is a **Tokyo Tourist Information Center,** open daily 9:30am to 6:30pm, where you can pick up maps and brochures; this is one of the city's best tourist offices, with detailed information on Tokyo's 23 wards and all 47 prefectures in Japan. It's also the meeting point for inexpensive city tours (see "Organized Tours," p. 140).
2–8–1 Nishi-Shinjuku. yokoso.metro.tokyo.lg.jp/tenbou/. ✆ **03-5321-1111.** Free admission. Daily 9:30am–10pm (last entry 9:30pm). Station: Tochomae (1 min.), Shinjuku (10 min.), or Nishi-Shinjuku (5 min.).

Harajuku & Aoyama

For a map of Harajuku & Aoyama, see p. 157.

Meiji Jingu Shrine ♥♥ SHRINE This is Tokyo's most venerable Shinto shrine, opened in 1920 in honor of Emperor and Empress Meiji, who were instrumental in opening Japan to the outside world in the late 1800s. Japan's two largest *torii* (the traditional entry gate of a shrine), built of cypress more than 1,700 years old, give dramatic entrance to the grounds, once the estate of a *daimyo.* The shaded pathway is lined with trees, shrubs, and dense woods, making it an incredible sanctuary in the middle of the city. In late May/June, the **Iris Garden** is in spectacular bloom, but its location in the Inner Garden makes it also a good respite from crowds all year round (admission ¥500). About a 10-minute walk from the first *torii,* the shrine is a fine example of dignified and refined

In full bloom in late spring, the Iris Garden on the grounds of the Meiji Jingu Shrine is a lovely place to relax year-round.

Shinto architecture, made of plain Japanese cypress and topped with green-copper roofs. It's not unusual to see a Shinto wedding procession here. Also note the twin camphor trees planted the year the shrine was established; bound by a *shimenawa* woven rope they represent the vitality and resilience of a healthy marriage. Meiji Jingu Shrine is also the place to be (or not, if you're crowd-averse) on New Year's Eve, when more than 2 million people squeeze onto the grounds to usher in the new year.
Meiji Shrine Inner Garden, 1–1 Kamizono-cho, Yoyogi, Shibuya-ku. meijijingu.or.jp. ✆ **03-3379-5511.** Free admission. Daily sunrise–sunset (about 6:40am–4pm in Dec, 5am–6:30pm in June). Station: Harajuku or Meiji-Jingumae (1 min.).

Ukiyo-e Ota Memorial Museum of Art (Ota Kinen Bijutsukan) ♥♥♥ MUSEUM Harajuku is teenybopper heaven, so it comes as something of a surprise to find this small but delightful museum tucked away on a side street. It specializes in *ukiyo-e* (woodblock prints), collected by businessman Seizo Ota over a period of more than 50 years to preserve this uniquely Japanese art form—Ota was becoming concerned that too many *ukiyo-e* works were flooding into overseas markets and foreign collectors' stashes during the Meiji era. Although the collection contains 12,000 prints, fewer than 100 are displayed at any one time, in thematic exhibitions that change monthly. You can tour it in about 30 minutes. Be sure to pop into the small basement shop with its *furoshiki* (traditional wrapping cloth), handkerchiefs, and other items (it has a separate basement entrance for those not visiting the museum).
1–10–10 Jingumae, Shibuya-ku. ukiyoe-ota-muse.jp. ✆ **03-3403-0880.** ¥700–¥1,000 adults, ¥500–¥700 high-school and college students, free–¥200 children; price depends on the exhibit. Tues–Sun 10:30am–5:30pm (last entry 5pm). Closed last few days of each month for exhibition changes. Station: Harajuku (2 min.) or Meiji-Jingumae (exit 5, 1 min.).

Roppongi

For a map of Roppongi, see p. 159.

Mori Art Museum (Mori Bijutsukan) ♥♥♥ MUSEUM/OBSERVATION DECK This is one of Tokyo's top museums, not only because its exhibits are always topnotch, but also because it's the highest museum in the city. Fifty-three stories high, in fact, providing unparalleled panoramas in virtually all directions. As for the art, exhibits change four times a year for innovative shows from both new and established artists, with past shows covering everything from

Changing exhibits at the Mori Art Museum include a wide range of art, like these colorful Keith Haring works from a recent show.

contemporary African art to art's role in shaping climate discourse to the largest Warhol exhibition ever presented in Japan. The art space is gorgeous, too, with 6m-tall (20-ft.) ceilings and controlled natural lighting. Most shows give access to a free audio guide. You'll want to spend at least 90 minutes here.

Roppongi Hills Mori Tower, 6–10–1 Roppongi, Minato-ku. mori.art.museum/jp/. ✆ **03/5777-8600.** Admission varies by exhibit; generally around ¥1,800 adults, ¥1,200 high-school and college students, ¥600 children. Daily 10am–10pm (closes 5pm Tues). Station: Roppongi (Roppongi Hills exit, 1 min.) or Azabu Juban (5 min.).

The National Art Center, Tokyo ♥♥ MUSEUM This museum has one of Japan's largest exhibition spaces—depending on how it's set up, it can become easy to lose your bearings—yet it doesn't have a permanent collection of its own. Rather, it serves as the canvas for Japanese artists' associations, shows organized by its own curators, and joint exhibitions in cooperation with other art institutions and even mass-media corporations. As such, its shows are both eclectic and impressive, with past exhibitions including a retrospective of Japanese government-sponsored art exhibitions from the last century; a powerful display of masks, religious idols, and other objects from around the world from Japan's National Museum of Ethnology; Impressionist works from Paris's Musée d'Orsay; and a Paintings Are Popstars exhibition that focused on performance art pieces and the queer experience in Japan. In other words, you never know what you might see. Many people drop by just to dine in the museum's **Brasserie Paul Bocuse Le Musée** or browse the expansive museum shop (you can enter both without paying admission). Of the three museums in the Art Triangle Roppongi (the others are the nearby Mori Art Museum and Suntory Museum of Art), this is by far the sexiest, with a seductive undulating facade that would entice visitors even without knowing what's inside.

7–22–2 Roppongi, Minato-ku. nact.jp. ✆ **03-5777-8600.** Admission varies by exhibit; top shows around ¥2,000 adults, ¥1,500 college students, ¥1,000 high-school students, free for children. Admission fee often reduced 1 hr before closing. Sun–Mon and Wed–Thurs 10am–6pm; Fri–Sat 10am–8pm. Station: Nogizakai (exit 6, 1 min.) or Roppongi (exit 4A or 7, 5 min.).

teamLab Borderless ♥♥♥ MUSEUM When international art collective teamLab opened its first flagship museum in Tokyo—called Borderless—in 2018, it became one of the world's most-visited museums dedicated to a single artist, group, or collective, welcoming 2.3 million people in its first year. Led by visionary creator Toshiyuki Inoko, the group of "ultratechnologists" creates immersive viewing spaces that engage the five senses. I had the honor of interviewing Inoko last year and he told me, with a glint in his eye, that Borderless is not even that high-tech; the digital artworks, soundscapes, and dynamic light projections are mere tools for exploring teamLab's ethos—that the world is not a static and independent thing we view from a fixed point, but rather a continuous and interdependent extension of ourselves. While this may sound like an arty-farty abstraction, you immediately understand what the collective is

Visitors interact with the dynamic digital effects at teamLab's wildly popular immersive art space Borderless.

trying to communicate when walking through cavernous spaces where spectral crows whizz past you, crashing wave patterns disappear in one room and reappear as swirling vortices in another, origami-like butterflies crush when you touch them, or flowers bloom as you give them room to breathe. This is a museum without a map—a "borderless" space—that challenges you to consider where the artwork ends and you begin. While the process behind Borderless is intellectual, the experience is catered to people of all ages, and kids are likely to get as much enjoyment out of the barrage of stimuli as are their parents. In 2024, the museum moved to a new location in the swanky Azabudai Hills complex, ushering in some new additions like the enthralling *Light Sculpture Series* and the perception-distorting *An Existence Without Center or Boundary.* Tickets should be booked in advance, and you must select an arrival time slot. Last entry is 1 hour before museum closing time—though you should give yourself at least 2 hours to play with.

1–2–4 Azabudai, Minato-ku. teamlab.art/e/tokyo/. ✆ **03-6894-3200.** ¥3,800 adults, ¥2,800 ages 13–17, ¥1,500 children 4–12, ¥1,900 persons with disability certificates + 1 companion (adult and disability tickets based on variable price system; these are base rates only). Daily 9am–9pm. Closed 1st and 3rd Tues every month. Station: Roppongi-itchome (4 min.) or Kamiyacho (5 min.).

Other Neighborhoods

Edo-Tokyo Museum (Edo-Tokyo Hakubutsukan) ♥♥♥ MUSEUM

Tokyo's history is riveting, making this museum's job easy as it vividly portrays the history, art, culture, architecture, and disasters of Tokyo from its founding in 1590—when the first shogun, Tokugawa Ieyasu, chose it as the seat of his government—to the 1964 Tokyo Olympics, the point at which Japan really announced itself as a global powerhouse. Displays begin on the sixth floor, where you'll begin your journey through the centuries with a walk over a replica Nihombashi Bridge, once the starting point for all roads leading out of Edo (old Tokyo). Displays of the Edo Period (1603–1868) center on the lives of the shogun, merchants, craftsmen, and townspeople, and though descriptions are mostly in Japanese, no explanations are necessary for the replica *kabuki* theater, models of Edo and a feudal lord's mansion, maps, photographs, portable festival floats, and a life-size replica row-house tenement, measuring only 10 sq. m (108 sq. ft.), where most of Edo's commoners lived. Other displays relay the events of the Meiji Restoration and Japan's opening to the rest of the world; the Great Kanto Earthquake of 1923 that killed more than 100,000 people; the bombing raids of World War II that destroyed much of the city (although Japan's role as aggressor is disappointingly glossed over); and Tokyo today. ***Note:*** The museum is expected to reopen in late 2025 after renovations, so there may be significant changes to the presentation of the material, as well as new admission fees and hours of operation.

A statue of a kabuki performer in an exhibit at the Edo-Tokyo Museum.

1-4-1 Yokoami, Sumida-ku. edo-tokyo-museum.or.jp. ✆ **03-3626-9974.** ¥600 adults, ¥480 college students, ¥300 seniors and junior-high/high-school students, free for younger children. Tues–Sun 9:30am–5:30pm (Sat to 7:30pm). Station: Ryogoku on the JR Sobu Line (west exit, 3 min.) and Oedo Line (exit A4, 1 min.).

Ghibli Museum ♥♥ MUSEUM A lot of '90s kids will have discovered Japanese anime through Saturday morning re-runs of *Yu-Gi-Oh!, Pokémon, Dragon Ball Z,* or *Sailor Moon.* But they were likely mere gateway drugs into the worlds of Studio Ghibli, a Japanese animation studio responsible for genre-defying films like the Oscar-winning *Spirited Away, My Neighbor Totoro* (adapted for the stage by the Royal Shakespeare Company in 2022), and *The Boy and the Heron,* which earned a record-breaking $12.8 million on its opening weekend in 2023, becoming the first original anime title to top the North American box office chart. True to the studio's surrealist and enigmatic style, visiting the museum is like falling through the looking glass. Inside a color-block building smothered in ivy, you'll find winding staircases, tiny doors, irregular hallways, a rooftop garden, and exhibits bringing fan-favorite characters like Kiki, Nausicaä, Catbus, and the Laputan Robot Troopers to life. The 80-seater

SPECTATOR sports

Baseball Japanese are so crazy about baseball, you'd think they invented the game. Actually, it was introduced to Japan by the United States way back in 1873. Today, it's as popular among Japanese as it is among Americans—even the annual high-school playoffs keep everyone glued to the TV set. As with other imports, the Japanese have added their own modifications, including cheerleaders and enthusiastic fan clubs, making the game a cultural experience. Several American players have proven very popular with local fans; there's also been a reverse exodus of top Japanese players defecting to American teams; most notably, the record-breaking force that is Shohei "Shotime" Ohtani of the L.A. Dodgers.

Japan has two professional leagues, the Central and the Pacific, which play from April to October and meet in the Japan Series. In Tokyo, the home teams are the **Yomiuri Giants,** who play at Tokyo Dome (tokyo-dome.co.jp; ✆ **03-5800-9999;** station: Korakuen or Suidobashi), and the **Yakult Swallows,** who play at Meiji Jingu Stadium (yakult-swallows.co.jp; ✆ **03-3404-8999;** station: Gaienmae). Just outside Tokyo, the **Yokohama DeNa BayStars** frequently sell out their home stadium, especially on weekends. Good English-language websites that follow Japanese baseball are japanesebaseball.com and japanball.com.

You can usually get tickets at the ballpark before the game, although Giants games often sell out. Otherwise, advance tickets can be purchased through each team's website, at convenience stores like Lawson, or at **Ticket Pia** locations around town (ask your hotel for the one nearest you). But probably the easiest method for obtaining tickets is through the website **japanballtickets.com;** tickets must be ordered at least 4 days in advance and can even be delivered to your hotel. Prices for Tokyo Dome, all for reserved seating, range from ¥2,800 in the outfield to ¥13,000 for seats directly behind the dugout; tickets for Jingu Stadium range from ¥1,300 to ¥7,200.

Sumo Sumo matches are held in Tokyo at the **Kokugikan,** 1–3–28 Yokoami, Sumida-ku (sumo.or.jp; ✆ **03-3622-1100;** station: Ryogoku, then a 1-min. walk). Matches are held in January, May, and September for 15 consecutive days, beginning at around 9:30am and lasting until 6pm; the top wrestlers compete after 3:30pm. The best seats are ringside box seats, but they're often snapped up by companies or the friends and families of sumo wrestlers. Usually available are balcony arena seats, which can be purchased at Ticket Pia locations around Tokyo or online tickets at sumo.pia.jp/en/ (these go on sale around 1 month in advance). Prices range from ¥2,200 for an unreserved seat (sold only on the day of the event at the stadium, with about 400 seats available); reserved seats start at ¥3,800.

Tournaments in Tokyo, as well as those that take place annually in Osaka, Nagoya, and Fukuoka, are broadcast on the NHK channel from 4 to 6pm daily while tournaments are taking place. For more information on sumo, see p. 32.

Saturn Theater in the museum basement plays Studio Ghibli animated shorts (usually lasting 10–15 min.), which are screened throughout the day; ask museum staff for the schedule.

The museum leans heavily on nostalgia, and rather than walloping visitors with the commercial thrust and bombast of a Disney park, it feels

The beloved anime character Totoro "sells tickets" at the entrance of the Ghibli Museum. In reality, getting tickets to visit the museum is a much more complicated process.

more like a love-letter, as though Hayao Miyazaki, one of the studio founders and Ghibli's best-known creative, drafted it as his last will and testament. This also means the museum is fiercely protective over what's inside: Taking pictures or videos is a no-go within the walls, and tickets are notoriously hard to get. Released on the 10th of each month for the following month, there are only 2,400 slots for each day (which sell immediately) and must be collected from a Lawson convenience store or purchased as part of a larger tour licensed by the Japan Tourism Bureau (which costs a pricey ¥26,000). The museum also does not field ticket-related enquires; instead use this contact form—faq.l-tike.com/contact/0145/—or see the tickets page on the Ghibli Museum website for more information. You can also use third-party sites like Klook or Viator, but going the official route is more reliable.

1-1-83 Shimorenjaku, Mitaka-shi. ghibli-museum.jp/en/. ✆ **0570-00-0403.** ¥1,000 adults, ¥700 ages 13–18, ¥400 children 7–12, ¥100 children 4–6. Wed–Mon 10am–6pm. Closed national holidays and selected days in May and Nov. Station: Telecom Center Station (2 min.).

Hama Rikyu Garden ♥♥♥ PARK/GARDEN Considered by some to be the best garden in Tokyo, this urban oasis has origins stretching back 300 years, when it served as a retreat for a former feudal lord and as duck-hunting and falconry grounds for the Tokugawa shogun. In 1871, possession of the garden passed to the imperial family, which used it to entertain such visiting dignitaries as Gen. Ulysses S. Grant. Come here to see how the upper classes enjoyed themselves during the Edo Period; to gain a better understanding, pick up the park's free audio guide. The garden contains an inner tidal pool, spanned by three bridges draped with wisteria (views from the south end of the garden are the most picturesque). The garden also has a refuge for ducks, herons, and migratory birds; a promenade along the bay lined with pine trees; a 300-year-old pine; moon-viewing pavilions; and teahouses (powdered green tea and steamed bun for ¥510, or tea with a sweet for ¥720). Plan on at least an hour's stroll to see everything, but the best reason for coming here is to board a ferry from the garden's pier bound for Asakusa, with departures every 30 minutes between 10:25am and 4:45pm; the fare is ¥940 one-way.

1–1 Hamarikyuteien, Chuo-ku. tokyo-park.or.jp. ✆ **03-3541-0200.** ¥300 adults, ¥150 seniors, free for ages 12 and under. Daily 9am–5pm. Station: Shiodome (exit 5, 5 min.) or Tsukiji-shjjo (7 min.).

Rikugien Garden ♥♥♥ GARDEN Though not as centrally located as Hama Rikyu, this one is a must for fans of traditional Japanese gardens; in fact, it might be the most sumptuous strolling garden in the city. It was created in 1702 by a trusted confidante of the shogun, who began as a page and rose to the highest rank as a feudal lord. During the Meiji Era, the founder of Mitsubishi took it over for his second residence and later donated it to the city. One of the garden's most distinguishing features is that it's dominated by a pond in its center, complete with islands and islets, viewing hills, and strolling paths around its perimeter, providing enchanting views. The landscape reflects themes of Chinese waka poetry and depicts characters from Shinto mythology, like Japan's mythical sibling creators Izanami and Izanagi (they appear as a pair of small hills, which is admittedly abstract). Rikugien is especially famous for its changing maple leaves in autumn and a huge weeping cherry that carries the melancholy of its years. Since it takes some effort to reach, you'll probably want to enjoy at least an hour here.

Autumn colors are especially lovely around the central pond of Rikugien Garden.

6–16–3 Hon-Komagome, Bunkyo-ku. tokyo-park.or.jp. ✆ **03-3941-2222.** ¥300 adults, ¥150 seniors, free for ages 12 and under. Daily 9am–5pm. Station: Komagome (8 min.) or Sengoku (10 min.).

teamLab Planets ♥♥ MUSEUM Borderless is, in my view, teamLab's greatest achievement and one of the finest contemporary art spaces in the world, but let's take nothing away from its sister museum, Planets, a similarly impressive feat of artistic conception (and implementation). Between April 2023 and March 2024, teamLab Planets welcomed 2,504,264 visitors, breaking the world record for museum attendance previously set by Borderless in 2019.

Planets is highly interactive: Visitors walk through water where light-projected koi fish swim and dart based on surface ripples, digital fire particles interact with a free-to-download smartphone app, crystal LEDs flash in rooms with mirrored walls creating a sense of infinity, and shapeless spaces filled with falling virtual petals or soft and glowing orbs encourage player agency. You can even eat vegan ramen noodles in the *Reversible Rotation-Non-Objective Space* installation, reinforcing teamLab's endeavor to engage all five senses. Tickets should be purchased in advance, and you must select an arrival time slot. See the museum website for apps that can be used to interact with the artworks.

Toyosu 6–1–16, Koto-ku. teamlab.art/e/planets/. ✆ **03-5500-1126.** ¥4,200 adults, ¥2,800 ages 13–17, ¥1,500 children 4–12; ¥2,100 persons with disability certificates + 1 companion. Wed–Mon 10am–6pm. Closed national holidays. Station: Shin-Toyosu (1 min.).

Tokyo Disneyland & Tokyo DisneySea ♥♥♥ THEME PARK A colorful, commercial ode to American pop culture, Tokyo Disneyland is still one of the most popular theme parks in the country. It includes popular rides like Pirates of the Caribbean, Snow White's Adventure, Peter Pan's Flight, and Pinocchio's Daring Journey. Other hot attractions include **Toontown,** a wacky theme park where Mickey and other Disney characters work and play, and **Star Tours,** a 3D thrill adventure created by Disney and George Lucas. This park is generally aimed at Disney superfans and young children. Adjacent to Disneyland, the **DisneySea** theme park is a better choice for older thrill-seekers. Based on ocean legends and myths, it offers 8 distinct "ports of call," including the futuristic Port Discovery marina with its Nemo & Friends SeaRider theater, which takes you on a pretend journey under the sea; the Lost River Delta with its Indiana Jones Adventure; Mermaid Lagoon, based on the film *The Little Mermaid;* the Arabian Coast, with its Sinbad's Seven Voyages boat ride; Mysterious Island with its 20,000 Leagues Under the Sea and Journey to the Center of the Earth attractions; and the American Waterfront with its Tower of Terror. Other areas include the Mediterranean Harbor and the newest addition, Fantasy Springs.

1–1 Maihama, Urayasu-shi, Chiba. tokyodisneyresort.jp. ✆ **0570-00-8632.** 1-day passports to either Disneyland or DisneySea (include park entry and use of all attractions) are offered on a variable price system, usually ¥8,000–¥11,000. Children pay around half price. Daily 9am–9pm (slightly shorter hours in winter). Station: Maihama, on the JR Keiyo Line from Tokyo Station (1 min.).

Tokyo Metropolitan Teien Art Museum ♥♥ MUSEUM Though nominally this is an art museum, people come here to marvel at the building itself, a masterclass in art deco design. During the post-Edo era, Japan's fascination with Western style and architecture was so prevalent that even members of the royal family—physical manifestations of Japan's national values—sought the great creative visionaries of Europe to design their home. Completed in 1933 as the residence of Prince Asaka, there is very little of traditional Japan in this geometric mansion bearing

Museumgoers come to the Tokyo Metropolitan Teien Art Museum as much to view its Art Deco design as for its excellent rotating exhibitions.

the artistic signatures of Henri Rapin and René Lalique. Instead, you'll find an echoey grand hallway, arched windows and intricate chandeliers, mosaics of natural stone, marbled fireplaces, walls paneled with walnut and fixed with magnificent glass reliefs, and a stately circular office. It's all so elaborate, so style-first-substance-later, you'll wonder how anyone could have lived in it. Turns out, the prince didn't last long—his wife, Princess Nobuko, died shortly after the mansion was complete, and following Japan's failed conquests in the Second World War, Asaka was stripped of his title and kicked out of his home.

Fronting the museum is a strolling *teien* (garden), populated by cherry, maple, and zelkova trees; a wooden teahouse overlooking a pond; a "European garden" with a seating area; a scattering of modern art sculptures; and a restaurant and box office from which you can purchase admission tickets (admission prices vary based on the special exhibition, usually held in the annex beside the gift shop). Exhibitions also take place in the teahouse each month—though most lectures, talks, and workshops are in Japanese.

5-21-9, Shirokanedai, Minato-ku. teien-art-museum.ne.jp/en/. ✆ **050-5541-8600.** Garden admission ¥200 adults, ¥160 students, ¥100 children. Average exhibition admission ¥1,400 adults, ¥1,120 students, ¥700 children, ¥700 65 and over; reduced prices for groups. Tues-Sun 10am–6pm (closed national holidays). Station: Meguro or Shirokanedai (9 min.).

Tokyo SkyTree ♥♥ OBSERVATION DECK When the world's tallest free-standing telecommunications tower (documented by Guinness World

Records) took over as Japan's tallest structure, it came with sky-high admissions to boot. Opened in 2012 to handle digital broadcasting and cellphone transmission, the 634m (2,080-ft.) tower contains two observatories, one at 350m (1,150 ft.) and the highest at 450m (1,476 ft.). Yet despite the steep price and potentially long queues, you can easily spend an hour in the 360-degree viewing spaces picking out Tokyo's iconic landmarks and highest-rising areas. For those less familiar with the capital's buildings, high-tech touch panels let you zoom in on the cityscape. Other diversions include a **cafe** in the first observatory and **Sky Restaurant 634** (restaurant. tokyo-skytree.jp/english; reservations required), offering Japanese/French fusion cuisine with what is certainly Tokyo's most expansive views. At the tower's base is **Solamachi,** a complex with 300 more shops and restaurants, including a Pokémon Center. To beat the long lines, go early on a weekday or head to the fourth-floor Fast SkyTree Ticket counter, open only to international visitors, though you'll pay extra for the privilege.

1–1–2 Oshiage, Sumida-ku. tokyo-skytree.jp. ✆ **0570-55-0634.** Lower observatory ¥2,100 adults, ¥1,550 ages 12–17, ¥950 children 6–11, ¥620 children 4–5; top observatory an extra ¥1,000, ¥800, ¥500, and ¥310, respectively. Combo ticket for both observatories ¥3,100 and ¥2,350, respectively. Daily 10am–9pm (last entry 8pm). Station: Oshiage (exit B3, 2 min.), Tokyo SkyTree (2 min.), or Asakusa (15 min.).

Toyosu Fish Market ♥♥ MARKET Iconic Tsukiji Market, which served as Japan's largest fish and produce market since 1935, closed on October 6, 2018, reopening as Toyosu Market just 4 days later. That's some feat, considering that this is one of the largest wholesale fish markets in the world, handling about 2,000 tons daily of seafood consumed in and around Tokyo. Whereas Tsukiji used to allow visitors to roam freely around its tuna auction site and wholesale stalls, over the years an increasing number of visitors forced ever more restrictions. To deal with its celebrity status, Toyosu Market prohibits visitors from its wholesale floor altogether, restricting them to observation platforms from which to view the action. This has diminished the quality of the experience, but there *is* still a lot going on, with men in black rubber boots rushing wheelbarrows and forklifts through the aisles, hawkers shouting, and knives chopping and slicing. As at Tsukiji, Toyosu has restaurants serving the freshest sushi you'll ever taste, but it also offers shops, displays relating to the market, and a rooftop garden with views of the waterfront. New is **Toyosu Senkyaku Banrai,** an Edo-style gourmet dining area. Introduced in 2024 to try to recreate the bustling market atmosphere of Tsukiji, it's full of street stalls and hole-in-the-walls selling sushi, sashimi, eel, crab, seafood barbecue, *donburi* (seafood rice bowls), fish-based ramen, and various seasonal delicacies. There's also a free-to-use garden with a public footbath looking toward the Tokyo Bay skyline. Restaurants are open 10am to 10pm, the footbath garden 10am to 8pm. Expect queues and waiting times during high season.

6–6–1 Toyosu, Koto-ku. toyosu-market.or.jp ✆ **03-3542-1111.** Free admission. Mon–Tues and Thurs–Sat 5am–3pm. Closed national holidays. Station: Shijo-mae (2 min.).

CITY STROLLS

WALKING TOUR 1: SEARCHING FOR OLD EDO, A WALKING TOUR OF ASAKUSA

START:	**Hama Rikyu Garden (Shiodome Station) or Asakusa Station (exit 1 or 3).**
FINISH:	**Kappabashi Dori (Station: Tawaramachi).**
TIME:	**Allow approximately 5 hours, including the boat ride.**
BEST TIMES:	**Tuesday through Friday, when the crowds aren't as big, or Sunday, when you can join a free tour of Asakusa, but:**
WORST TIMES:	**Sunday, when the shops on Kappabashi Dori are closed.**

If anything remains of old Tokyo, Asakusa is it. This is where you'll find narrow streets lined with small residential homes, women in kimono, Tokyo's oldest and most popular temple, and quaint shops selling boxwood combs, fans, kitchen knives, sweet pastries, and other products of yore. With its temple market, rickshaw drivers vying for the tourist trade, old-fashioned amusement park, traditional shops, and restaurants, Asakusa preserves the charm of old downtown Edo better than anyplace else in Tokyo. For many older Japanese, a visit to Asakusa is like stepping back to the days of their childhood; for tourists, it provides a glimpse of the way things were.

Pleasure-seekers have been flocking to Asakusa for centuries. Originating as a temple town back in the 7th century, it grew in popularity during the Tokugawa regime as merchants became wealthy and entirely new forms of popular entertainment arose to cater to them. Theaters for *kabuki* and *bunraku* flourished in Asakusa, as did restaurants and shops. By 1840, Asakusa had become Edo's main entertainment district. In stark contrast to the solemnity surrounding places of worship in the West, Asakusa's temple market had a carnival atmosphere reminiscent of medieval Europe, complete with street performers and exotic animals. It retains some of that festive atmosphere even today.

The most dramatic way to arrive in Asakusa is by boat, just as people did in the olden days. If you want to forgo the boat ride, take the subway to Asakusa Station and start from stop no. 2. Otherwise, begin at:

1 Hama Rikyu Garden

Located at the south end of Tokyo (Station: Shiodome, exit 5, then a 5-min. walk), this garden was laid out during the Edo Period in a style popular at the time, in which surrounding scenery was incorporated into its composition. Today, the only surrounding scenery you'll see is an overabundance of skyscrapers, but it does contain an inner tidal pool, bridges draped with wisteria, moon-viewing pavilions, and teahouses. (See p. 123 for more details.)

Walking Tour 1: Asakusa

In the shadow of skyscrapers, Hama Rikyu Garden is a riverside urban oasis where you can board a boat bound for Asakusa.

Boats depart the garden to make their way along the Sumida River every 30 to 60 minutes between 10:35am and 4:15pm, with the fare to Asakusa costing ¥940 (children ¥470). Although much of what you see along the working river today is only concrete embankments, the trip affords a different perspective of Tokyo—barges making their way down the river, high-rise apartment buildings with laundry fluttering from balconies, warehouses, and superhighways. The boat passes under approximately a dozen bridges during the 40-minute trip, each one completely different. During cherry-blossom season, thousands of cherry trees lining the bank make the ride particularly memorable.

After arriving in Asakusa, walk away from the boat pier a couple of blocks inland. You'll soon see the colorful Kaminarimon, or Thunder Gate, on your right. Across the street on your left is the:

2 Asakusa Information Center

Located at 2–18–9 Kaminarimon (✆ **03-6280-6710**), the center is staffed by English-speaking volunteers from 10am to 5pm. Stop here to pick up a map of the area, and perhaps use the restroom. Note the huge Seiko clock on the center's facade—every hour on the hour from 10am to 7pm, mechanical dolls reenact scenes from Asakusa's most famous festivals.

Head across the street to the:

3 Kaminarimon Gate

The gate is unmistakable with its bright red colors and 100-kilogram (220-lb.) lantern hanging in the middle. The statues inside the gate are the god of wind to the right and the god of thunder to the left, ready to protect the deity enshrined in the temple. The god of thunder is particularly fearsome: He supposedly has an insatiable appetite for navels.

To the left of the gate, on the corner, is:

4 Tokiwado Kaminari Okoshi

This open-fronted confectionery has been selling *okoshi* (rice-based sweets) for 250 years and is popular with visiting Japanese buying gifts for the folks back home. It's open daily from 9am to 9pm.

Past Kaminarimon Gate, you'll find yourself on a pedestrian lane called:

5 Nakamise Dori

The lane leads straight to the Sensoji Temple. *Nakamise* means "inside shops," and historical records show that vendors have sold wares here since the late 17th century. Today Nakamise Dori is lined on both sides with tiny stall after tiny stall, many owned by the same family for generations. If you're expecting austere religious artifacts, however, you're in for a surprise: Sweets, shoes, barking toy dogs, *sembei* (Japanese crackers), bags, umbrellas, Japanese dolls, T-shirts, fans, masks, and traditional Japanese accessories are all sold. How about a brightly colored straight hairpin—and a black hairpiece to go with it? Or a temporary tattoo in the shape of a dragon? This is a great place to shop for souvenirs, gifts, and items you have no earthly need for—a little bit of unabashed consumerism on the way to spiritual purification.

Take a Break

If you're hungry for lunch, there are many possibilities in the neighborhood. **Chinya,** 1–3–4 Asakusa, just west of Kaminarimon Gate on Kaminarimon Dori, has been serving sukiyaki and *shabu-shabu* since 1880. East of Kaminarimon Gate is **Ichiran Asakusa,** 1–1–16 Asakusa, a branch of the famous Kyushu-based ramen chain. Their specialty is noodles in *tonkotsu* (pork bone) broth, and it's a great shop for introverts—each customer is assigned a solo booth and orders via a slip of paper (English available), which is then slid under a divider. You'll see only the waiter's hands as they pass your bowl of noodles back through the same gap. Note this place gets very busy and queues are common.

Just 2 blocks north of Kaminarimon Gate are two:

6 Covered Shopping Arcades

Stretching to both the right and left of Nakamise Dori, these pedestrian-only covered lanes, called *shotengai,* are typical of what you'll see everywhere in Japan—regular streets that became instant shopping centers by covering them with roofs and banning vehicular traffic. This is where locals come to shop, with stores selling clothing, household goods, trinkets, and more.

Farther along Nakamise Dori, a second gate opens onto a square filled with pigeons and a large:

7 Incense Burner

This is where worshipers "wash" themselves to ward off or help cure illness. If, for example, you have a sore throat, be sure to rub some of the smoke over your throat for good measure.

The building dominating the square is:

8 Sensoji Temple

Worshippers stop by the incense burner to prepare themselves for visiting Sensoji Temple.

Sensoji is Tokyo's oldest temple. Founded in the 7th century and therefore already well established long before Tokugawa settled in Edo, Sensoji Temple is dedicated to Kannon, the Buddhist goddess of mercy, and is therefore popularly called the Asakusa Kannon Temple. According to legend, the temple was founded after two fishermen pulled a golden statue of Kannon from the sea. The sacred statue is still housed in the temple, carefully preserved inside three boxes; even though it's never on display, an estimated 30 million people flock to the temple annually to pay their respects.

Within the temple is a counter where you can buy your fortune by putting a 100-yen coin into a wooden box and shaking it until a long bamboo stick emerges from a small hole. The stick will have a Japanese number on it, which corresponds to one of the numbers on a set of drawers. Take the fortune, written in Japanese and half-comprehensible English, from the drawer that has your number. If you find that your fortune raises more questions than it answers or you simply don't like what it has to say, you can conveniently negate it by tying it to one of the wires provided for this purpose just outside the main hall.

Walk around the temple to the right. On the northeast corner of the grounds is the small orange:

9 Asakusa Jinja Shrine

Built in 1649 by Iemitsu Tokugawa, the third Tokugawa shogun, this shrine commemorates the two fishermen who found the statue of Kannon, as well as their village chief. Its architectural style, called *Gongen-zukuri,* is the same as the style of Toshogu Shrine in Nikko.

West of Sensoji Temple is a gardenlike area of lesser shrines and memorials, flowering bushes, and a stream filled with carp. The most picturesque photos of Sensoji Temple can be taken from here.

Farther west still is:

10 Hanayashiki

This is a small amusement park that first opened in 1853 and still draws in the little ones. (See p. 109 for more details.)

Most of the area west of Sensoji Temple (the area to the left if you stand facing the front of the temple) is a small but interesting part of Asakusa popular among Tokyo's older working class. This is where several of Asakusa's old-fashioned pleasure houses remain, including bars, restaurants, strip shows, traditional Japanese vaudeville, and so-called "love hotels," which rent rooms by the hour.

Keep walking west, past the Asakusa View Hotel. Within 10 minutes you'll reach:

11 Kappabashi-dougugai Dori

This district, generally referred to as Kappabashi Dori, is Tokyo's wholesale district for restaurant items. Shop after shop sells pottery, chairs, tableware, cookware, lacquerware, rice cookers, *noren* (short curtains hung outside shops and restaurants to signify they are open), and everything else needed to run a restaurant. Chefs, both local and foreign, love this area for high-quality kitchen knives. And yes, you can even buy those models of plastic food you've been drooling over in restaurant displays. Ice cream, pizza, sushi, mugs foaming with beer—they're all here, looking like the real thing, and boy, are they pricey. A full plastic meal can cost well upwards of ¥20,000. (Stores close about 5pm and are closed on Sun.)

WALKING TOUR 2: POP-CULTURE TOKYO, A STROLL THROUGH AKIHABARA & UENO

START:	**Kanda Station**
FINISH:	**Ameya Yokocho (Station: Ueno)**
TIME:	**Allow approximately 5 hours.**
BEST TIMES:	**Weekdays, when local *otaku* are at work or school**
WORST TIMES:	**Weekends, when half of Tokyo descends on Akihabara's Chuo Dori**

Akihabara, also known as Electric Town, or more pithily as "Akiba," should be at the top of the to-do list for Japanese pop-culture fans traveling to Tokyo. And that's a growing number of people: The global anime market was worth an estimated $31.23 billion in 2023. It's even been suggested that as many as 72% of Americans watch anime regularly (though

I doubt the veracity of that figure), and that's before we address the ongoing popularity of Japanese video game franchises and consoles, and the increasing number of manga titles found in English-language bookshops. The highest concentration of stores that honor Japan's historic pop-culture tradition is found in Akihabara. Whether you're old enough to remember the first Nintendo console, were reared on games like *Tekken* and *Street Fighter,* or first encountered Japanese entertainment through modern anime like *Attack on Titan* or *My Hero Academia,* there will be something for you in this carnival-esque neighborhood.

The end point of the tour, **Ueno,** is a bustling shopping and nightlife district, favored by many Japanese to the more youthful and cosmopolitan Shibuya. Here you'll make a beeline for Ameya Yokocho, typically shortened to Ameyoko, a lamplit warren of restaurants, izakaya, food stalls, sports shops, thrift stores, and market vendors.

Akihabara and Ueno are connected by the Yamanote (4 min.) and Keihin-Tohoku (3 min.) train lines, or you can walk from one to the other along Chuo Dori (20 min. approx.)

Start at Kanda Station, so you can approach Akihabara via a bridge over the Kanda River—giving you a great linear shot of the main thoroughfare (particularly impressive at night). Leave the station at exit 6 and head north toward Mansei Bridge, where you'll see:

1 Chuo Dori

Chuo Dori is one of Tokyo's main arterial routes, running through Ginza and Nihonbashi before bisecting Akihabara. The 1km (⅔-mile) stretch between Akihabara and Ueno-Hirokoji stations might be the world's largest concentration of pop-culture merchandise and retro arcade machines. There are shops selling '80s video game consoles in mint condition, old-school gaming mags and concept art books, and hundreds of Nintendo and SEGA titles never released outside Japan. You'll find manga stores specializing in *shonen, shojo, seinen,* shock horror, *doujinshi,* or boys love genres, and themed anime shops selling figurines of the most exquisite detail. Maid cafes, and appropriately attired female staff touting for business, are common sights on the side streets splitting off Chuo Dori, as are stores catering to more lascivious cartoon predilections. Chuo Dori is noisy and colorful and pullulating at the best of times, but this sense is heightened when the avenue is decorated in neon and fluorescent lighting come nightfall.

Cross Mansei Bridge and start making your way along the avenue. Many things will vie for your attention, so allow time for detours.

Not long after you cross the bridge, you'll find:

2 Radio Kaikan

Radio Kaikan is a great introduction to Akihabara, especially if you're new to the world of Japanese pop culture. This 10-floor

Walking Tour 2: Pop-Culture Tokyo

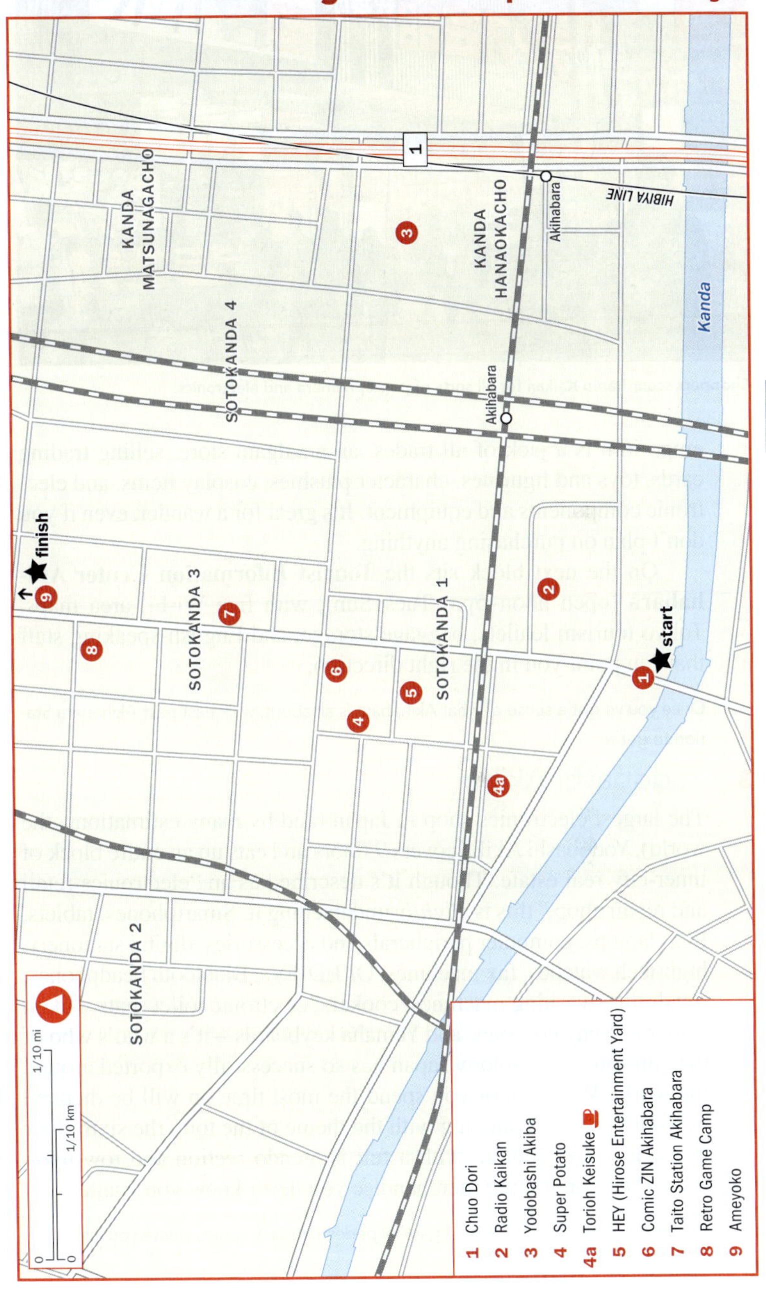

Shoppers scour Radio Kaikan for all sorts of pop ephemera and electronics.

emporium is a jack of all trades, an amalgam store, selling trading cards, toys and figurines, character plushies, cosplay items, and electronic components and equipment. It's great for a wander, even if you don't plan on purchasing anything.

On the next block sits the **Tourist Information Center Akihabara** (open noon–5pm Tues–Sun), with free Wi-Fi, area maps, Tokyo tourism leaflets, baggage storage, and English-speaking staff that can point you in the right direction.

Once you've got a sense of what Akihabara is all about, walk east past Akihabara Station to get to:

3 Yodobashi Akiba

The largest electronics shop in Japan (and by many estimations, the world), Yodobashi Akiba covers 9 floors and eats up an entire block of inner-city real estate. Though it's described as an "electronics retail and repair shop," this is *slightly* underselling it. Smartphones, tablets, PCs, laptops, computer peripherals and accessories, digital stationery, high-tech watches, fax machines, OLED TVs, Bluetooth headphones, treadmills, washing machines, cookers, electronic toilet seats, Nikon cameras, Sony consoles, and Yamaha keyboards—it's a who's who of the consumer technology Japan has so successfully exported around the world. Which floor you spend the most time on will be dictated by your tastes, but sticking with the theme of the tour, the sixth floor is *otaku* (geek) central, with a full Nintendo section and row upon row of the pop-culture merchandise you never knew you wanted.

Head back across Chuo Dori to a parallel pedestrian-only street, where you'll find:

4 Super Potato

The Akihabara branch of Super Potato (1–11–2 Sotokanda, floors 3–5) is famous in international *otaku* circles. You can buy the goods on display in here, but really it's a chronological archive of Japanese video game history. Floors 3 and 4 are a nostalgic romp for anyone who grew up playing Super Nintendo, Sega Genesis, the original PlayStation, or the heavy-as-a-brick Gameboy. Alongside old-school games, 16-bit consoles, and peripherals that never made it outside of Japan, there's a lot of cool merch—CD gaming soundtracks, game guidebooks with English and Japanese text, and themed T-shirts, pillows, teddies, hoodies, keyrings, and stickers. If this is your jam, prepare to dish out some yen in here. ***Note:*** For collector's items, like rare games and old consoles, the price will be commensurate with their availability and condition.

Floor 5 is a little less chaotic: There are several arcade machines, featuring games like *Metal Slug X, Bomber Man,* and *Double Dragon* (¥100 per go), a shop selling Japanese sweets, and a frequently photographed statue of Solid Snake (holding a suspiciously broken gun) from the *Metal Gear Solid* franchise.

Take a Break

Now might be a good time to grab a bite to eat. Akihabara is a secret big hitter in the ramen scene, with shops like Hakata Furyu, known for its sumptuous pork bone broth, and spicy-ramen specialist Kikanbo. My favorite, **Torioh Keisuke,** serves chicken ramen topped with crispy-skinned chicken thigh meat that will have you licking the bowl dry. It's a stone's throw from Super Potato at 1–3–4 Sotokanda.

On the block next to Super Potato is:

5 HEY (Hirose Entertainment Yard)

The HEY arcade is a noisy, flashing, all-encompassing throwback to the halcyon days of coin-op gaming; there is perhaps no better arcade in the country. You can play around 300 different games here—the likes of *Crazy Taxi* and *Street Fighter* will be familiar to most Western gamers, but there are more obscure titles from *Deathsmiles* and *Samurai Spirits* to *Fate/Grand Order, Cotton Rock 'n' Roll,* and *The Tower of Druaga.* Most games start at 100 yen per play, but some also require players to use collectible cards. There are machines that change notes to 100-yen coins on each floor.

Next, head north along Chuo Dori to 1–11–7 Sotokanda to find:

6 Comic ZIN Akihabara

As its name suggests, this is a manga store, known for its healthy stock of *doujinshi* titles—a meta-genre of manga fan fiction that doesn't fall foul of copyright laws and is generally seen as one of the most innovative spaces in Japan's pop-culture market. You won't find anything in translation here, though: Manga in English is still a fairly new phenomenon (barring the most popular franchises, like *Pokémon,*

Dragon Ball, and *Demon Slayer*), and even at that, English-language titles are often only available in international bookshops, like Kinokuniya Shinjuku South Store. That said, the colorful, jam-packed shelves of Comic ZIN Akihbara are fun to peruse. If you can't find the rare titles, special editions or art books you're looking for here, check out Comic Jiku-Chushinha down the street at 3–15–1 Sotokanda (it's on the fourth floor; closed Tues–Wed).

The buzzing Akihabara outpost of the Taito Station arcade station offers 5 floors of game machines of all stripes.

Two minutes to the north sits:

7 Taito Station Akihabara

Unmissable due to the giant Space Invaders—pixelated creatures from the classic game of the same name—pasted all over the front of the building, this five-story arcade is one of the best-known in Akihabara. You'll find local *otaku* and businessmen on their lunch breaks challenging each other to bouts of *Street Fighter* or showering zombies with bullets in *House of the Dead.* For the less pugilistic, have a crack at the claw machines, with *kawaii* plushies and anime figurines for prizes (¥100 per try), or head for the *purikura* photo booths on the basement floor, a popular pastime for Japanese teenage girls.

Continue north on Chuo Dori to:

8 Retro Game Camp

Smaller and less congested than Super Potato, Retro Game Camp stocks vintage Japanese games and consoles—handheld gaming enthusiasts will find much to swoon over here. The shop also has a free-to-play Super Nintendo, with one random game cartridge inserted, connected to a monitor at the entrance to the store. Basically next door, the Liberty figurine store at 3–14–6 Sotokanda stocks pieces from popular franchises like *Naruto, One Piece* and *Demon Slayer,* as well as toys that will be less recognizable to non-anime superfans. Around the side of the building, a staircase leads shoppers to the other floors—Full Comp on the fourth floor is for card collectors, with mint condition copies of *Pokémon, Yu-Gi-Oh!,* and *Dragon Ball* cards, the rarest of which cost hundreds of thousands of yen. If you have never witnessed a Japanese maid cafe in all its idiosyncratic glory, head to the concept shop in the basement of the same building. Though the theme may change in the future, at the time of writing the cafe is called **Lilian Plian** and it's styled as a snowy fantasy world populated by ice fairies. When you order a drink, it will come in a frosted glass and one of the maids will teach you how to "cast a spell" on the drink to make it taste "more delicious." You can also pay ¥2,200 for one of the maids to dance (to frankly dreadful music) on a hexagonal stage surrounded by the seating counter. Maid cafes are often thought of as highly sexualized places, but to be honest I find them more cheesy than salacious. In fact, children would likely enjoy this place more than their parents. Note you'll have to pay for entry (¥660; ¥880 after 4pm), you must order 1 drink per person and you'll have to keep paying by the hour if you choose to stay for longer.

From here, either walk 15–20 minutes north along Chuo Dori or take the train from Akihabara to Ueno Station. Leaving from exit 5a, another 5 minutes' walk will bring you to:

9 Ameyoko

Japan is often so prim and proper that it borders on sterile. Not so at Ameyoko, meaning "candy alley," the closest thing Tokyo has to a Southeast Asian bazaar. Staff tout outside shops for business, proprietors are open to haggling, bargains are aplenty, and everything appears patched together, charmingly unorganized. If you're looking for soccer shirts, baseball caps, jackets with garish Chinese motifs, leather shoes, fresh seafood, locally grown vegetables, suitcases, camping equipment, smartphone accessories, or various other trinkets, you might find them here. Many of the izakaya in Ameyoko have outdoor tables or terraced seating, generating a lively atmosphere in the evenings. **Coffee by Jalana** (6–10–1 Ueno) is always worth a stop, whether for an americano and a hot sandwich at lunch or for a craft beer from their hipster-y range of local and international brews after dinner. Opening hours are at the discretion of individual shops, but as a rule most operate from 10am to 8pm, while restaurants and bars stay open later.

The bazaarlike streets of Ameyoko.

Head to Ueno Station. This one of Tokyo's main transport hubs; you should be able to connect to your next destination from here.

ORGANIZED TOURS

With the help of this book and good online maps, you should be able to visit Tokyo's attractions easily on your own. Should you be pressed for time, however, consider taking a group tour of Tokyo and its environs offered by the **Japan Tourist Bureau** in partnership with **Viator.** These range from bar hopping in Shinjuku or private chauffeur trips around Tokyo to sumo experiences, sushi-making classes, bus tours to the city's most famous attractions, and Mt Fuji day trips. Be warned, however, that these itineraries do not allow much time for exploration and are more expensive than touring Tokyo on your own. Prices start at ¥10,000 and rise based on the nature of the experience, the size of your group, and the level of customization. Tours are easily booked online (japanican.com) or you can contact JTB through the JAPANiCAN Facebook page. Although its offerings are not nearly as extensive, **The Gray Line** (jgltraveljapan.jp/tokyo-tour; (✆ **03-5275-6525**) also offers a morning, afternoon, and full-day tour.

Walking Tours

The **Tokyo Metropolitan Government** offers 15 tours concentrating on specific areas or themes, such as Japanese gardens, Asakusa, or the tea ceremony. These tours are quite intimate, with a maximum tour-group size of only 5 persons. Lasting 2 to 6 hours, they are conducted mostly on foot or utilize public transportation and vary in price from free (a walking tour of Shinjuku and the food floor of Isetan department store) to ¥6,830 for a tour that combines Tokyo from the sky at Tokyo Tower and Tokyo from the sea at Odaiba—price includes transportation and admission costs of the volunteer guides. Tours depart from the Tokyo Tourist Information Center in the TMG Building No. 1 in Shinjuku (the same building as the free observatory; see p. 89) at 10am and/or 1pm Monday to Friday (excluding public holidays; some tours also adjust their times during summer). Preregistration 3 days in advance of the tour is required, and a minimum of one participant must be at least 20 years old. Prices may be cheaper for some tours if there's more than one participant. For info and bookings go to **gotokyo.org/en/guide-services**.

Tokyo Localized also offers a variety of free (tips welcome) Tokyo walking tours. Book online at tokyolocalized.com (✆ **090-7905-4185**). Volunteer guides are on hand at the **Ueno Green Salon** in Ueno Park every Wednesday, Friday, and Sunday for free 90-minute walking tours departing at 10:30am and 1:30pm; and at the **Asakusa Culture Tourist Information Center** every Saturday and Sunday for 1-hour tours departing at 10:30am and 1:15pm. No registration is required, but you should arrive 10 minutes beforehand. For more information, call ✆ **03-6280-6710.**

Boat Tours

For an alternative view of the Tokyo cityscape, from riverside promenades and a series of grand bridges to glittering apartment complexes and public artworks, take a cruise in the Tokyo ***Suijo Basu*** (Water Bus), with routes traveling between Asakusa and Odaiba, stopping at Hama Rikyu Garden or Toyosu. Covered in convex plate glass, the boat, designed by renowned Japanese cartoonist Leiji Matsumoto, was custom-built for sightseeing. Water Buses departing from Asakusa between 10am and 4:10pm are operated by the **Tokyo Cruise Ship Company** (suijobus.co.jp; ✆ **0120-97-7311**). The 50-minute journey to Odaiba is ¥2,000 for adults, ¥1,000 for children one-way. Similarly, an amphibious bus called **Tokyo no Kaba** (en.kaba-bus.com/tokyo; ✆ **03-3455-2211**) departs from Aqua City (station: Yurikamome Daiba) and tours Odaiba and Tokyo Bay. Departing multiple times a day from April to September on weekends and public holidays, it costs ¥3,800 adults and ¥1,900 children (¥500 for infants). This one tends to be a big hit with the kids.

Other Tour Options

One of the most recent introductions is the **Tokyo Premium Night Drive,** an open-top, double-decker bus that explores the city after dark. Operated by Hato Bus (hatobus.com/; ✆ **033-2012-725**), the tour begins at Tokyo Station Marunouchi South Exit and passes through Aoyama, Akasaka, Roppongi, Odaiba, Tsukiji, and Ginza before returning to Tokyo Station. It operates daily between 6:30pm and 8:50pm; tickets cost ¥3,200. The tour is in Japanese, but a GPS-based audio guide is available in English. It operates year-round but may be canceled due to inclement weather.

You can also see Tokyo on two wheels by joining one of 15 guided tours conducted by the **Tokyo Great Cycling Tour** company (tokyocycling.jp; ✆ **03-4590-2995**). Some tours are paired with a theme, such as the historic Edo-Tokyo Culture tour or the future-focused Tokyo Transformation tour. Full-day tours cost ¥5,000, half-day tours ¥3,000; kids' bikes and e-bikes available.

Lastly, food tours are all the rage in Japan these days, and one of the most highly rated services in Tokyo is **Arigato Travel** (arigatojapan.co.jp; ✆ **050-6860-7542**). Their tours can be pricey, averaging around ¥25,000 per person, but this includes the cost of meals (and drinks for bar tours), while Arigato's guides are founts of knowledge on local food and nightlife culture. Whether you want to sample ramen, traditional snacks, *karaage* and *kushikatsu, kawaii* foods and sweets, or cocktails and sake, there's a tour to accommodate you. The company's most bespoke offering is a wine country day trip to Yamanashi, Japan's top vintner region, costing ¥49,000. There's also an option to make tours private for an additional ¥19,500 plus tax (min. two people)—worth considering if you have specific dietary requirements.

WHERE TO STAY IN TOKYO

Tokyo has no old, grand hotels in the tradition of Hong Kong's Peninsula or Bangkok's Oriental; it has hardly any old hotels, period. But what the city's hotels lack in quaintness is more than made up for by excellent service—for which the Japanese are legendary—as well as cleanliness, efficiency, and, for higher-end hotels, gorgeous interior design. Be prepared, however, for small rooms. Space is at a premium in Tokyo, so with the exception of Tokyo's expensive hotels, rooms seem to come in only three sizes: small, minuscule, and barely adequate.

Unfortunately, Tokyo also doesn't have many first-class *ryokan,* or Japanese-style inns. You may, therefore, want to wait for your travels around the country to experience a first-rate *ryokan.* Otherwise, there are moderate and inexpensive Japanese-style inns in Tokyo, though don't expect much in the way of service or amenities. Most upper-bracket hotels offer at least a few Japanese-style rooms, with *tatami* mats, a Japanese bathtub (deeper and narrower than the Western version), and a futon. Although these rooms tend to be expensive, they're usually large enough for four people.

The hotel recommendations below are arranged by geographical location. However, there's no one location in Tokyo that's more convenient than another—Tokyo's attractions, restaurants, and nightlife are widely scattered, and the public transportation system is so fast and efficient that you can easily get anywhere, no matter where you're staying. The overriding factor in selecting accommodations will most likely be cost: Hotels here can be expensive, particularly in popular districts during peak season.

For details on the various types of accommodations, see "Tips on Accommodations" in chapter 2.

TAXES & SERVICE CHARGES All hotel rates below include a 10% government tax unless stated otherwise. An additional **local hotel tax** will be added to bills that cost more than ¥10,000 per person per night: ¥100 is levied per person per night for rates between ¥10,000 and ¥14,999; rates of ¥15,000 and up are taxed at ¥200. Furthermore, all upper-class hotels and most medium-range hotels add a **service charge** of 10% to 15% (cheaper establishments do not add a service charge, because no service is provided).

Central Tokyo & Ginza

EXPENSIVE

Conrad Tokyo ♥♥♥ Many attributes of this fine, contemporary hotel are exemplary, starting with the large *sumi-e* (Japanese brush painting) in the lobby by Toko Shinoda, just one of 23 leading Japanese craftsmen

price CATEGORIES FOR TOKYO

Expensive	¥45,000 and up	Inexpensive	Under ¥25,000
Moderate	¥25,000–¥45,000		

Central Tokyo & Ginza

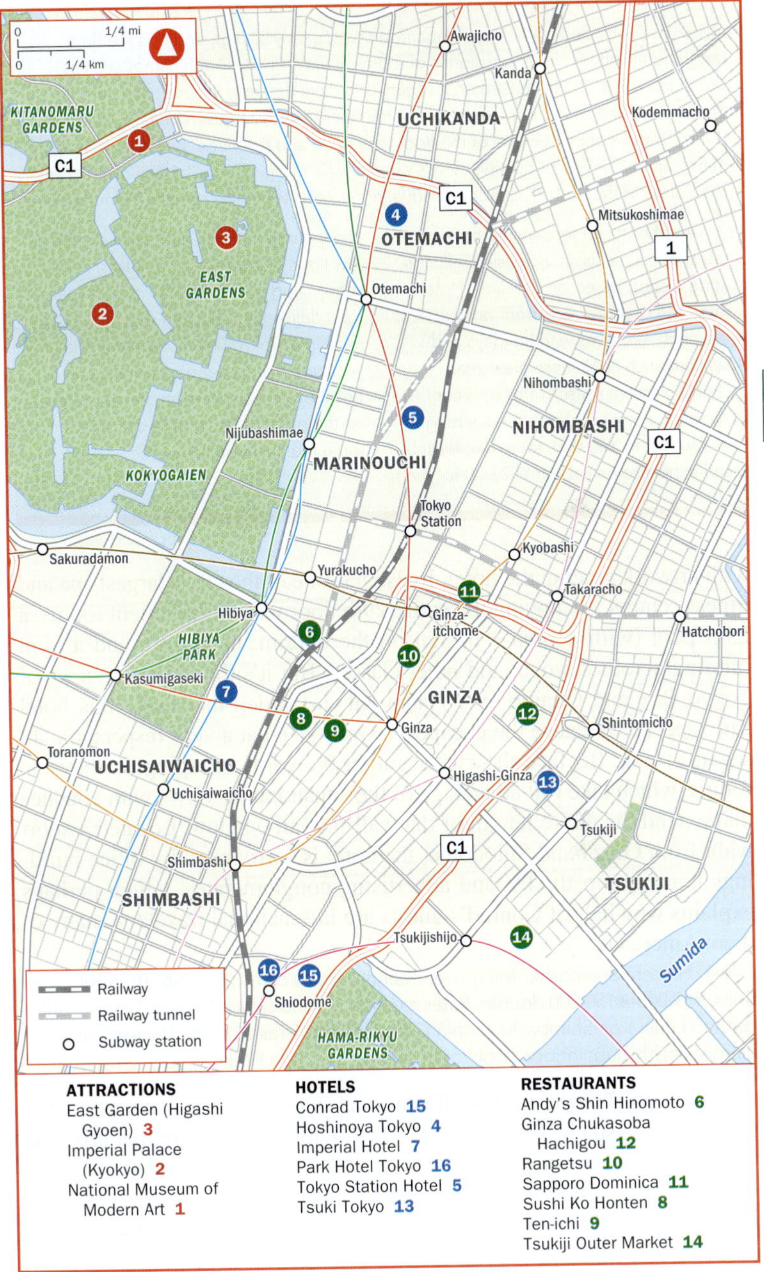

WHY THE big range IN HOTEL PRICES?

In Tokyo, Kyoto, and other major Japanese cities, nearly all high-end and medium-range hotels offer various categories of rooms at varying rates, with names such as premium, superior, etc., based on a variety of factors that may include room size, decor, view, and what floor they're on. Sometimes, rooms can even be fairly identical but still vary in price because of the floor they're on and the views. Because of those many different levels of quality, there's often a wide range of rates for any given hotel, regardless of the season. Check individual hotel websites to see specific room types.

Another factor influencing hotel rates, of course, is an increasingly fluctuating market based on demand. Hotel rates can change wildly from one week to the next, as well as with holidays and seasons such as Chinese New Year, cherry blossom season, and summer vacation. For a hotel with a price range of ¥30,000 to ¥60,000, for example, you can expect to pay about ¥30,000 for the cheapest room (such as a small one on a low floor facing another building) in low season and about ¥60,000 in high season for a deluxe bigger room with views of a garden or Tokyo Bay. For most of the year, you'll probably pay somewhere in between. Inexpensive accommodations, on the other hand, tend to charge the same rate year-round.

with artwork gracing the hotel. It also has one of the city's largest spa and fitness centers, occupying the entire 29th floor with 10 treatment rooms, a 25m pool (with a *sumi-e* design on the bottom, naturally), and a gym offering aerobics, yoga, and other classes. But it's the fantastic views of Tokyo Bay and Odaiba over Hama Rikyu Garden that make this hotel truly special. Because the cheapest rooms (sized at a very respectable 48 sq. m/516 sq. ft.) face the city, it might be worth splurging for bayside rooms, which take full advantage of those panoramic views with couches that extend the entire length of the wall-to-wall window. Located a short walk from Ginza and Shiodome, the hotel is surrounded by office buildings housing mostly TV and advertising conglomerates, which perhaps explains why half of Conrad's guests are international travelers, many of them American.

1–9–1 Higashi-Shinbashi, Minato-ku. conradhotels.com. ✆ **03-6388-8000.** 290 units. ¥69,000–¥150,000 double. Rates exclude tax and service charge. Station: Shiodome (1 min.) or Shimbashi (7 min.). **Amenities:** 4 restaurants, lounge/bar; concierge; health club; indoor pool; room service; spa; free Wi-Fi.

Hoshinoya Tokyo ♥♥♥ Traditional Japanese inns have gone the way of the geisha in Tokyo, and so it was with some fanfare that this gorgeous hotel recreating the atmosphere of a ryokan opened its discreet doors in 2016. Hidden among Otemachi's high-rises, it's an oasis of Japanese refinement. The moment you enter, you are greeted by a traditionally clad hostess, who will place your shoes in one of the decorative bamboo boxes that line the corridor like works of art. You won't wear shoes or

slippers at all during your stay (except for your own bathroom slippers), because tatami runs throughout the inn, inviting you to relax and feel at home. Rooms are decorated in a graceful minimalist style, resplendent with natural materials like wood, bamboo, slate-colored papered walls, and shoji covering floor-to-ceiling windows. There are no clocks in the rooms, and TVs are hidden behind full-body mirrors, encouraging guests to forget about worldly woes and slip into states of utter contentment. In keeping with the personalized service that's the trademark of a great ryokan, each of the inn's 14 floors has its own **Ochanoma Lounge,** where guests can relax and enjoy tea, sake, and snacks. Tea ceremony experiences are also available to guests on a tatami platform beside the reception area; the style of cup or the shape and flavor of the accompanying sweets changes with the seasons, entreating guests to tune into the natural ephemera hidden amongst the concrete cosmos of Tokyo. But the crowning glory is the top-floor hot-spring bath, a rarity in Tokyo, with water drawn from deep below ground and an open roof that lets you gaze up at passing clouds. It's hard to believe you're in one of the world's busiest cities.
1–9–2 Otemachi, Chiyoda-ku. hoshinoya.com/tokyo/en. ✆ **03-6214-5151.** ¥70,000–¥150,000 single or double. Rates include breakfast. Station: Otemachi (2 min.) or Tokyo (10 min.). **Amenities:** Restaurant; lounges; tea ceremony; spa; hot-spring bath; free Wi-Fi.

Imperial Hotel ♥♥♥ One of Tokyo's oldest and most respected hotels, the Imperial has a prime location near Ginza, Hibiya Park, and the Imperial Palace. First opened in 1890 at the request of the imperial family to house foreign visitors, it was rebuilt in 1922 by Frank Lloyd Wright—upon opening it was famously dubbed the "Jewel of the Orient"—and survived the horrific 1923 earthquake, only to succumb in 1970 to developers in a complete makeover. It's currently on its third-generation design, and more development projects in both the main and tower buildings, ongoing until 2036, are keeping true to Wright's original style. His legacy also lives on in the hotel's **Old Imperial Bar** and Wright-inspired designs and furniture in public spaces. Rooms in the main building are popular with Japanese guests because its showers are located outside of tubs (which allows them to bathe in traditional fashion). Access to the second

Hoshinoya Tokyo successfully blends the atmosphere of a traditional ryokan with elegant modern luxury.

Colorful wall murals brighten guest rooms at the Park Hotel Tokyo.

31-story tower, via a second-floor passageway, is a bit cumbersome, and tower rooms are smaller, yet foreign guests tend to prefer rooms here because views are better (with a choice of either the Ginza with its sparkling neon or Hibiya Park and the palace) and it's near the pool and gym. Though they're not as high up, rooms in the main building on the park side also have glorious views, and are emblematic of Wright's geometric design, with soft furnishings placed near windows so you can take it all in with your morning cup of coffee. The Executive Suite is by far the most impressive room—it might be the most impressive hotel room in Tokyo—but is prohibitively expensive to the average guest and is typically reserved for traveling dignitaries.

1-1-1 Uchisaiwaicho, Chiyoda-ku. imperialhotel.co.jp/e/tokyo. ✆ **03-3504-1111.** 1,019 units. ¥65,000–¥103,000 double. Rates exclude service charge. Station: Hibiya (1 min.). **Amenities:** 10 restaurants; 2 bars; lounge; concierge; gym, indoor pool and sauna; room service; tea-ceremony room; post office; free Wi-Fi.

A Double or a Twin?

For the sake of convenience, the price for two people in a room is typically listed as "double" in this book. Japanese hotels, however, differentiate between rooms with a double bed or two twin beds, usually with different prices. Although most hotels charge more for a twin room, sometimes the opposite is true; so be sure to inquire about prices for both. Note, too, that hotels usually have more twin rooms than doubles, for the simple reason that Japanese couples, used to their own futons, traditionally prefer twin beds.

Tokyo Station Hotel ♥♥

Tokyo Station was built in 1914 in the tradition of Europe's great train stations; the Tokyo Station Hotel opened a year later. Although the station itself has grown crazily over the years, the historic section containing the hotel, which faces Marunouchi with a handsome brick facade, retains its century-old glory. And luckily, the hotel has its own dedicated entrance (as well as direct access to subway and train stations, handy in inclement weather), so it's well away from the chaos that reigns in the station. As Japan Railway's flagship hotel, it retains many of its original features, including a high-ceilinged lobby lounge (once the first-class waiting lounge) and the original long corridor leading to rooms, which is about as long as the Tokyo Tower is tall. Bartender Hisashi Sugimoto, at the hotel since 1958, is at the historic **Bar Oak** concocting his signature cocktails. Six different styles of rooms, all with high-vaulted ceilings and expansive windows, are available, from Classic Queens (fairly standard and also dark, since they face another building) to Dome Side Rooms, which face a concourse with spectacularly restored reliefs from the train station's cupola ceiling. With both fine and casual dining and old-world ambience, this is a unique property in Tokyo. Train buffs won't want to stay anywhere else.

Tokyo Station, 1–9–1 Marunouchi, Chiyoda-ku. tokyostationhotel.jp. ✆ **03-5220-1111.** 150 units. ¥91,000–¥166,000 single or double. 10% discount for Japan Rail Pass holders. Station: Tokyo (1 min.). **Amenities:** 7 restaurants; 2 bars; lounge; concierge; gym and relaxation lounge; room service; spa; free Wi-Fi.

MODERATE

Park Hotel Tokyo ♥♥♥ Occupying the top 10 floors of a triangular-shaped building it shares with international media organizations (like Kyodo News), this hotel is within walking distance of Ginza and Hama Rikyu Garden. Its 25th-floor lobby, decorated with artworks that change each season, is bathed in the natural sunlight afforded by a 10-story atrium topped with an opaque ceiling—it's a great place to relax and take in the views either during the day or when the city is lit up at night. The front desk is one of the most dramatic I've seen, backed by superb views of Tokyo Tower and a cozy seating area in front of floor-to-ceiling windows. Books on Hokusai, Sotatsu, the concept of *wa,* and Studio Ghibli are placed on shelves beside the reception desk, serving as introductions to Japan's distinctive art styles. Rooms, decorated with original art and colorful wall murals, also provide views, the best of which can be found from the 30th floor and up. Art exhibits are also held on guest floor corridors (floors 26–34), while 42 rooms on the 31st floor are painted by Japanese artists, like the Bamboo Room with wall murals of greenery or the brightly colored Geisha Goldfish. The hotel is constantly iterating upon its art hotel concept, with new artists-in-residence redesigning rooms as this book goes to print.

Shiodome Media Tower, 1–7–1 Higashi Shimbashi, Minato-ku. parkhoteltokyo.com. ✆ **03-6252-1111.** 269 units. ¥32,000–¥70,000 single or double. Rates exclude service charge. Station: Shiodome (1 min.) or Shimbashi (8 min.). **Amenities:** 2 restaurants; bar; lounge; concierge; personal-size gym (free, on a reservation basis); room service; spa treatments; free Wi-Fi.

Tsuki Tokyo ♥♥♥ Tsuki is the archetypal slick, modern Japanese hotel. The entrance, fronted by a small landscape garden and soft ambient

Tsuki Tokyo's chic lobby sake bar.

lighting, gives way to an interior that marries concrete and bleached wood paneling. The lobby, staffed by receptionists with extensive knowledge of the Ginza and Tsukiji areas, doubles as a sake bar called Table Tsuki, open from 10am to 11pm. Here you can order sake tasting sets paired with small dishes like smoked quail eggs, squid marinated with hot pepper, or sake lees pickles. It also sells Japanese tea blends with sweet treats until 6pm, and from 7 to 10am, bread and coffee are available for hotel guests for free here. There's also a communal lounge and library with a free-to-use massage chair, and private cypress wood bathtubs (advanced reservation required) for ¥2,200 for 45 minutes. The guest rooms are equally chic, embodying a Japanese sense of style and comfort through aromatic wood, natural colors, plush bedding and towels, and handcrafted pottery and utensils. Across floors 3 to 10, five different types of room are available, ranging from 12 sq m (130 sq. ft.) to 28 sq m (301 sq. ft.), the larger of which come with private tubs.

1-9-4, Tsukiji, Chuo-ku. tsukihotel.com/en/. ✆ **03-6435-6288.** 31 units. ¥33,000–¥99,000 single or double. Station: Higashi Ginza (10 min.) or Shintomicho (4 min.). **Amenities:** Sake bar; private bathtubs, relaxation lounge; concierge; free Wi-Fi.

Asakusa

MODERATE

OMO3 Asakusa ♥♥♥ Part of the Hoshino Resorts hotel brand (which also owns Hoshinoya Tokyo, p. 144) this property is at the lower end of the luxury-budget spectrum, but it still has a sense of theater at almost every turn, from the rooms inspired by a *yose* (18th-c. vaudeville-style drama) playhouse, to the light-dappled OMO Base lounge area (with a view of Senso-ji Temple on one side and Tokyo SkyTree on the other), to *rakugo* (traditional spoken-word performances) delivered in the lounge every Friday and Saturday night. The location, of course, is premium, in the heart of one of Tokyo's most historic districts. Huge *go-kinjo* (neighborhood) maps in the lobby and lounge offer recommendations on local bars, restaurants, and craft shops, and free daily tours and events, available to all guests, focus on the food, culture, and history of Asakusa—a great way to meet local shop proprietors and artisans. Be sure to check out the 13th-floor rooftop terrace as evening looms; it's literally *the* Japan postcard image: The city's

Asakusa

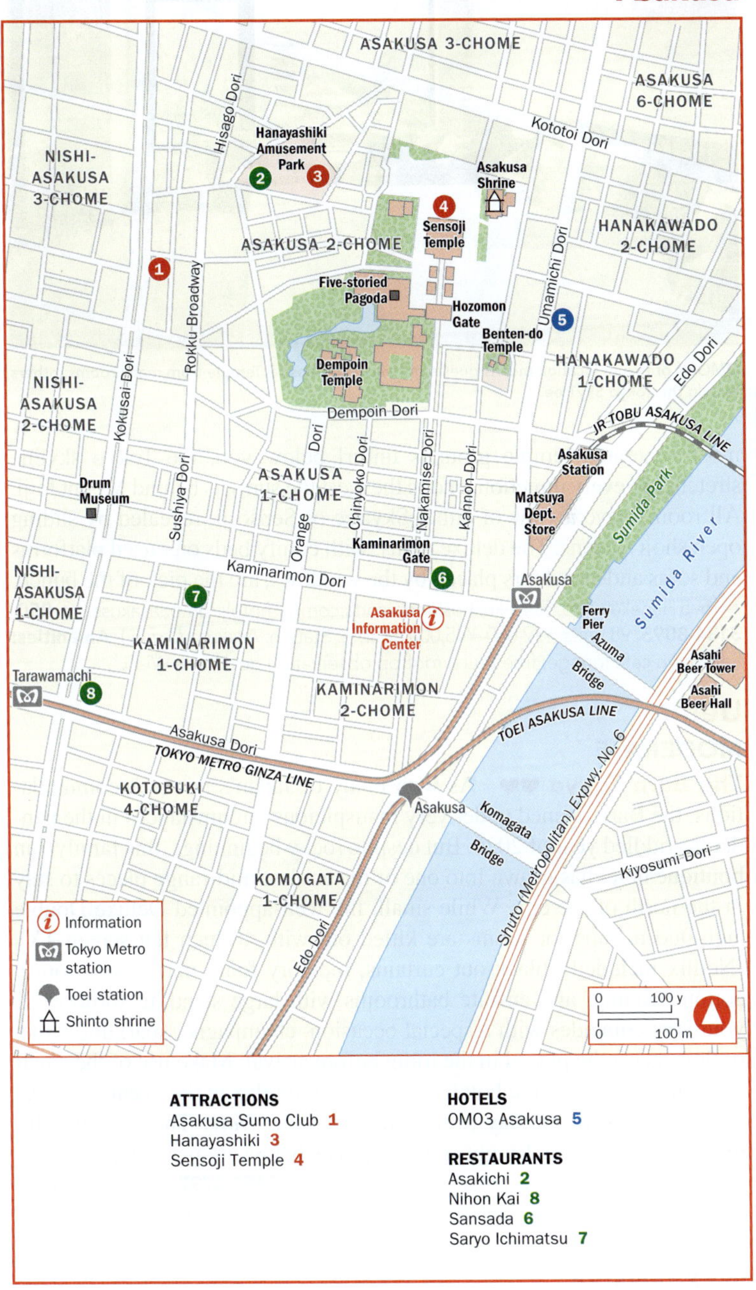

ATTRACTIONS
Asakusa Sumo Club 1
Hanayashiki 3
Sensoji Temple 4

HOTELS
OMO3 Asakusa 5

RESTAURANTS
Asakichi 2
Nihon Kai 8
Sansada 6
Saryo Ichimatsu 7

OMO3's premium location means guests get views of Senso-ji Temple from many rooms; others take in the Tokyo SkyTree.

most venerated temple grounds unfurl below you, the Tokyo skyline stretches in every direction, and in the west the sun sets behind Mount Fuji. All rooms have a view of either Skytree or Senso-ji, revealed by sliding open shoji screens. The deluxe twins, with comfy beds on raised platforms and sofas and armchairs placed by the windows, are the pick of the bunch. 1–15–5 Hanakawado, Taito-ku. hoshinoresorts.com/ja/hotels/omo3asakusa/. ✆ **050-3134-8095.** 98 units. ¥22,000–¥45,000 double. Station: Asakusa (7 min.). **Amenities:** Self-serve cafe lounge; free tours; rooftop observation deck; free Wi-Fi.

Ueno

MODERATE

The Barn Tokyo ♥♥ As with many of Japan's newer accommodations, the Barn opened under very inauspicious circumstances in the pandemic-riddled year of 2020. But despite rocky beginnings, this family-run boutique hotel has grown into one of the coolest mid-range places to stay in the north of the city. While small, the well-appointed Deluxe Double and Queen Superior rooms are kitted out with 40-inch flat screen TVs (Netflix included), black-out curtains, memory foam mattresses, comfy cotton bedding, and ensuite bathrooms with large standing showers. If your stay coincides with a special occasion, champagne, sparkling wine, or flowers can be placed in the room before arrival. Make use of the small Zen garden fronting the hotel, a great place to relax in the evening or formulate a plan for the day over a cup of coffee. ***Note:*** The Barn usually requires a minimum 2-night stay, but prices below are per night. 3–12–16 Negishi, Taito-ku. thebarntokyo.com. ✆ **050-5490-4797.** 16 units. ¥19,000–¥45,000 single or double. Station: Uguisudani (4 min.). **Amenities:** Concierge; free Wi-Fi.

INEXPENSIVE

Ryokan Sawanoya ♥♥♥ A family-run affair since 1949, this smoke-free inn is now in the capable hands of the original proprietress' grandson,

0 1/10 mi
0 100 m
Kanei-ji Temple
Uguisudani Station
TOKUGAWA SHOGUN CEMETERY
Tokyo National Museum
Tokyo Metropolitan Art Gallery
UENO PARK
Ueno Zoo
Five-story Pagoda
National Museum of Nature & Science
Toshogu Shrine
MONORAIL
Gojoten Shrine
National Museum of Western Art
Shinobazu Pond
CHIYODA LINE
Toho Cherry
Ueno Station
Tokyo Expressway No. 1
HIBIYA LINE
Kiyomizu-do Kannon Temple
Keisei Ueno Station
Shitamachi Museum
Shinobazu-dori
Chuo - dori
Uenohirokoji Station
Ameya Yokocho
Ueno Center Mall
Kasuga-dori
Matsuzakaya Dept. Store
Okachimachi Station
Kasuga-dori
ATTRACTIONS
Asakura Choso Museum 1
National Museum of Nature and Science 4
The National Museum of Western Art 5
Tokyo National Museum 3
Toshogu Shrine 7
HOTELS
The Barn Tokyo 2
Ryokan Sawanoya 9
RESTAURANTS
Innshoutei 6
Izu'ei Honten 8
Railway
Railway (tunnel)
Subway
Tourist Information

though the elder Sawa-san still pours his heart and soul into the business (he even wrote a book about the history of Sawanoya and his experiences as an innkeeper). Located about a 15-minute walk from Ueno Park and 5 minutes from Nezu Shrine, it's nestled in a residential area known for its *shitamachi* (old downtown) atmosphere and traditional architecture. Upon arrival, guests are given a short tour of the establishment, which includes two baths with views of a garden (which can be locked for privacy) and a nice laundry room with free detergent, before being led to their *tatami* room on the second or third floor (there's no elevator). Guests also receive a hand-drawn map outlining restaurants and other nearby facilities. The large lobby has free coffee and tea and a huge selection of brochures. A traditional Japanese lion dance is staged free of charge several times a month, and the inn is LGBT friendly. In short, Sawanoya has a long history of making travelers feel welcome in Tokyo and thus comes highly recommended.

2–3–11 Yanaka, Taito-ku. sawanoya.com. ✆ **03-3822-2251.** 12 units (2 w/ private bath). ¥7,400 single w/ shared bath; ¥13,420 double w/ shared bath, ¥15,070 double w/ bath. Closed Dec 29–Jan 3. Station: Nezu (exit 1, 7 min.). **Amenities:** Free Wi-Fi.

Shinjuku

EXPENSIVE

Park Hyatt Tokyo ♥♥♥ When the Park Hyatt opened in 1994 as Tokyo's first skyscraper hotel, it was bound for glory. No hotel yet offered views as surreal; and with its gorgeous layout, light-drenched rooms, and polished service (check-in is at one of three sit-down desks), it was light-years ahead of the competition. No wonder it starred in the 2003 hit film *Lost in Translation* and has inspired many competitors. Rooms are well above average in size and have walk-in closets, deep soaking tubs (and separate showers), original pieces of artwork, Japanese-style paper lamps, paneling made from 2,000-year-old wood from Hokkaido, and great views (east views of Shinjuku's nightlife and the greenery of several parks are the most popular, but the west side sometimes has glimpses of Mount Fuji). Other perks: the hotel's 2,000-book library; the **New York Bar** with outstanding views, live jazz, and creative in-house cocktails; free bike rentals for exploring nearby Yoyogi, Chuo, and Shinjuku parks; and the 47th-floor fitness facilities overlooking the city, with sky-lit lap pool, gym, and complimentary yoga, aerobics, Pilates, and a relaxing "Good Night Sleep Stretch." Note that the hotel is currently undergoing restoration, mostly in the public and event areas, scheduled for completion in October 2025. If history is anything to go by, the Park Hyatt will remain the cream of the Tokyo crop. Some amenities noted below are subject to change following the refurbishment.

3–7–1–2 Nishi-Shinjuku, Shinjuku-ku. tokyo.park.hyatt.com. ✆ **03-5322-1234.** 177 units. Room rates TBA upon reopening. Station: Shinjuku (a 13-min. walk or 5-min. free shuttle ride); Hatsudai, on the Keio Line (7 min.); or Tochomae (8 min.). **Amenities:** 3 restaurants; 2 bars; lounge; babysitting; concierge; gym; indoor pool; room service; free shuttle to Shinjuku Station up to 3 times per hour; spa; free Wi-Fi.

MODERATE

Hotel Century Southern Tower ♥♥♥ Conveniently located amid the skyscrapers of Shinjuku and connected to Takashimaya Shinjuku shopping complex via a footbridge, this superb choice offers smallish rooms with a view, at a fraction of the price of nearby competitors. Luggage carts instead of bellhops and vending machines in place of room service seem like no sacrifice at all when the rewards are mesmerizing panoramas from the 20th-floor lobby lounge and the rooms, which occupy the 22nd to 35th floors; rooms even come with skyline maps that help identify landmarks outside your window. The best—and most expensive—rooms (ask for one on a higher floor) face east or south, where views over central Tokyo take on a neon glow at night. Couples might note that doubles are much smaller than twins.

2–2–1 Yoyogi, Shibuya-ku. southerntower.co.jp. ✆ **03-5354-0111.** 375 units. ¥32,000–¥50,000 single or double. Station: Shinjuku (south exit, 3 min.). **Amenities:** 3 restaurants; lounge; free Wi-Fi.

Hotel Gracery Shinjuku ♥♥ Though there are several Hotel Gracery branches in Tokyo, the Shinjuku location, bang in the middle of Kabukicho, is far and away the most iconic, thanks to the towering Godzilla head (which roars every hour noon–8pm) rising from the eighth-floor terrace. (Appropriately, the hotel is right above Tokyo's flagship Toho Cinema, the parent company of the Godzilla movies.) One of the rooms, which I imagine appeals only to the most die-hard *kaiju* (Japanese monster film) fans, has a window that looks directly into Godzilla's blood-red eye. Another concept room is covered in black scaly wallpaper, movie posters chronicling the Godzilla franchise, and decor that depicts the Tokyo megalopolis under siege. Guests staying in this room also get goodie bags with Godzilla-themed merch. If this isn't your cup of tea, the other rooms, straddling 30 floors, offer standard business-hotel-style accommodation, and they're reasonably priced given the location and the potential views. Breakfast is served buffet-style in the Sakura cafe; the Gracery Lounge, located next to the lobby, serves coffee, tea, alcoholic drinks, (pricey) snacks, and items from the Godzilla specialty menu throughout the day.

1–19–1 Kabukicho, Shinjuku-ku. gracery.com/shinjuku/. ✆ **03-6833-2489.** 970 units. ¥26,200–¥70,000 single or double. Station: Seibu Sinjuku (3 min.), Shinjuku (east exit, 5 min.). **Amenities:** Restaurant; bar; terrace; concierge, self-check-in machines; laundry (fee); massages (fee); free Wi-Fi.

INEXPENSIVE

Book and Bed Tokyo ♥♥ A library room that doubles as a hostel? It's a bit gimmicky, and yet it works, mainly because it's well-done and the coffin-size sleeping cubbyholes are tucked away among a wall of bookshelves, making guests feel more insulated from their neighbors than the usual capsule hotel. But this is still a hostel, after all, with shared toilets and showers, and only a curtain separates you from the communal

Shinjuku

living space in the center of the room, where sofas invite guests to read some of the library's 4,000 books and comics, including many in English. There are three types of sleeping spaces available: single units, comfort singles/doubles, and a "superior room" with a king-size mattress and glass walls (with curtains) enveloping the space. All are fitted with reading lamps and electric outlets. At one end of the main room is a cafe offering coffee, tea, charcoal-bread sandwiches, and alcoholic drinks (happy hour 1–6pm), making sleep a challenge, perhaps, for those who like to turn in early or get up late. Note that payment can be made only with a credit card or the Suica or PASMO transportation card (no cash). Another Book and Bed hostel is in Shinsaibashi, Osaka. Alternatively, if manga is your literature of choice, the **Manga Art Hotel** in Kanda (1–14–13 Kanda Nishikocho, Chiyod-ku; mangaarthotel.com/maht/) takes a similar approach to Book and Bed, with 5,000 comics to read and cubby-hole beds hidden among the shelves.

Kabukicho APM Bldg. 8th floor, 1–27–5 Kabukicho, Shinjuku-ku. bookandbedtokyo.com. ✆ **03-6233-9511.** 46 units. ¥5,000–¥8,500 single; ¥11,000–¥15,000 double. Station: Seibu Shinjuku (1 min.). **Amenities:** Library; cafe; free Wi-Fi.

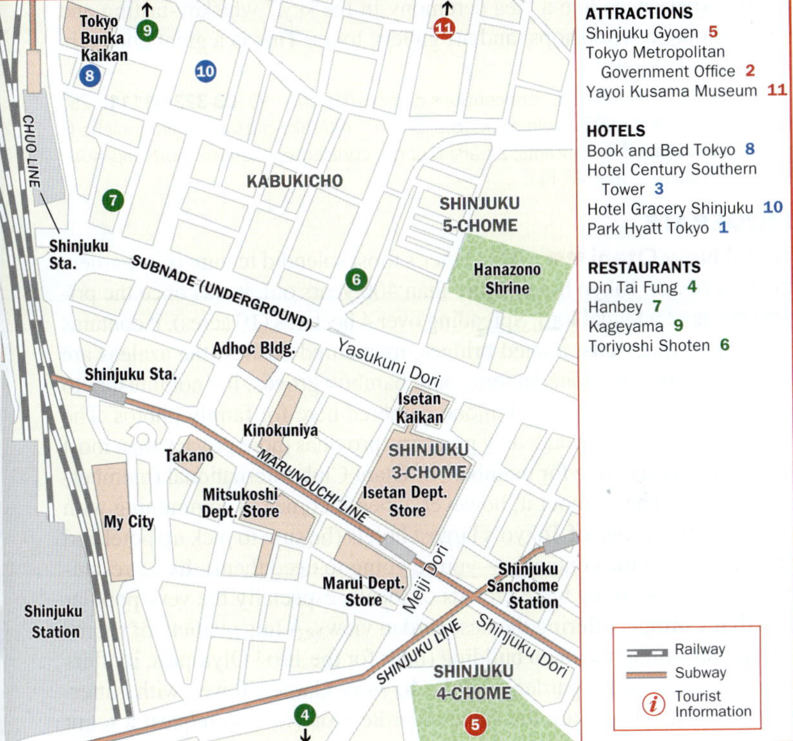

Aoyama & Akasaka

EXPENSIVE

The Prince Gallery Tokyo Kioicho ♥♥♥ It's all about the views at this striking hotel on the top seven floors of a 36-story high-rise in Akasaka. The moment you step out of the elevator, you behold an eye-catching cocktail bar framed by undulating glass walls, drawing attention to a huge picture window broadcasting Tokyo in all its glory. Rooms, too, capitalize on the views, with day beds spreading the length of wall-to-wall windows. Even bathrooms have views, either via glass walls that look out through the room to the window (thankfully, those glass walls turn opaque with the push of a button) or from window-side tubs in more deluxe rooms. The hotel is also high-tech: An iPad in each room controls everything from lighting and temperature to blackout drapes, and it's programmed with information on sightseeing, the weather, flight schedules, and more. The indoor lap pool and state-of-the-art gym (free for hotel guests) as well as restaurants also take advantage of Tokyo as a backdrop. Yet it's worth tearing your eyes away from the views to admire the 100 artworks by Japanese artists gracing the hotel's public spaces—they more than justify the word "gallery" in the hotel's name. Guests can also book (paid) experiences like a "tea ceremony in the sky," whiskey-tasting and sushi etiquette workshops, and art gallery tours. This is a great choice in the heart of the city.

1–2 Kioi-cho, Chiyoda-ku. princehotels.com/en/kioicho. ✆ **03-3234-1111.** 250 units. ¥70,000–¥103,000 single or double. Station: Akasaka-mitsuke or Nagatacho (1 min.). **Amenities:** 3 restaurants; 2 bars; lounge; concierge; exercise room; lap pool; spa; room service; free Wi-Fi.

MODERATE

Hotel New Otani ♥♥ This hotel's most splendid feature is its garden, the best of any Tokyo hotel: More than 400 years old, it was once the private estate of a feudal lord. Spreading over 4 hectares (10 acres), it contains koi ponds, waterfalls, arched bridges, manicured bushes (the azaleas are striking in spring), stone lanterns, and bamboo groves; it's not unusual to see Japanese in their finest kimono gathered here for family photos. The large outdoor pool, shrouded by greenery, provides more privacy than most hotel pools and is free for members of Otani Club International (membership is free). That's about it, however, when it comes to communing with nature, as this is one of Tokyo's largest hotels (be sure to pick up hotel and garden maps at the concierge—you're going to need them). Its 33 restaurants and 6 bars draw huge crowds of locals, especially the very popular **Garden Lounge,** offering the best garden views. A huge variety of rooms are spread among the main building (built for the 1964 Olympics, it offers up-close views of the garden) and the 40-story Garden Tower, with glittering city vistas. Rates are the same regardless of view, so request a room facing the garden. Hotel facilities are so exhaustive, this is like a city within a city; folks who shun crowds may be happier elsewhere.

4–1 Kioi-cho, Chiyoda-ku. newotani.co.jp. ✆ **03/3265-1111.** 1,479 units. ¥16,000–¥35,000 single or double; executive rooms ¥50,000 and up. Station: Akasaka-mitsuke or Nagatacho (3 min.). **Amenities:** 33 restaurants/cafes; 6 bars/lounges; children's day-care center (ages 2 months–5 years); concierge; exercise room; health club w/ indoor pool and spa; medical and dental clinics; art museum; outdoor pool; post office; room service; tea-ceremony room; lighted outdoor tennis courts; free Wi-Fi.

INEXPENSIVE

Hotel Asia Center of Japan (Asia Kaikan) ♥♥ A great location in central Tokyo, a Japanese restaurant popular with area office workers for its cheap rice balls and set meals (¥400–¥1,800), and reasonable rates for Western-style rooms have long made this a favorite for everyone from business travelers to youth groups. Established in 1957 and recently renovated, it has the atmosphere of a college dorm, with tiny, mostly single rooms equipped with the basics: a double-size bed (all beds are extra-long), wall-mounted TV, and desk. These are great for one person, but they're also sold for two people at the same price, making for inexpensive (if cramped) quarters. There are only 47 twin rooms (including twins with

Harajuku & Aoyama

CHAINS TO rely ON

Alongside the hotels mentioned above and below, you'll find clean and comfy, if admittedly cookie-cutter, business hotels throughout the city; those not in the busiest downtown neighborhoods tend to offer great deals throughout the year. The most popular chains include **APA** (apahotel.com), **MyStays** (mystays.com), **Dormy Inn** (dormy-hotels.com/en/dormyinn), and **Tokyu Stay** (tokyustay.co.jp). If you're the kind of traveler who views accommodation as simply somewhere to lay your head for the night, these chains are all reliable. Those hotels with "Premier" or "Premium" in the name tend to be in the mid-range, with more facilities and larger rooms, and therefore higher prices.

a sofa that can be turned into an extra bed). Best feature of the hotel is that it's in a quiet residential area only a 15-minute walk from Roppongi or Akasaka, or one station away by subway. Aoyama Dori, lined with shops and restaurants on its way to Omotesando, is a 5-minute walk away.

8–10–32 Akasaka, Minato-ku. asiacenter.or.jp. ✆ **03-3402-6111.** 175 units. ¥12,000–¥45,000 single or double. Station: Aoyama-Itchome (exit 4, 5 min.) or Nogizaka (exit 3, 5 min.). **Amenities:** Restaurant; free Wi-Fi.

Roppongi

EXPENSIVE

Janu Tokyo ♥♥♥ The flagship hotel of the new Azabudai Hills complex, this property is huge (you will almost certainly get lost during your initial reconnoiter) and has been designed in the most sumptuous modern style, with high-ceilinged atriums, wall-to-wall windows that flood public spaces and guest rooms with natural light, and furnishings and decor that blend urbane Japanese minimalism with Euro-chic accents. The name Janu comes from a Sanskrit word meaning "soul," and its designer, Belgian architect Jean-Michel Gathy, has created cool and sophisticated interiors, changing subtly from one area to the next, that do a good job of embodying the soul of this ever-dynamic city. That there are only 122 rooms here hints at their spaciousness: The smallest are 55 sq. m (592 sq. ft.), while the Janu Suite is a whopping 284 sq. m (3,037 sq. ft.) and can even be extended to include adjacent rooms, almost doubling its size. Whatever category you choose, south-facing rooms are probably the best, with views of Tokyo Tower, the greenery of Azabudai Hills below, and colorful sunsets from the private balconies. The restaurants and bar offerings are also top-drawer, including counter-style sushi at Igura; contemporary Cantonese cuisine at Hu Jing; steak and seafood at Janu Grill; a patisserie; the Janu Bar, whose cocktail menu is curated by one of the city's top mixologists, Shuzo Nagumo, and inspired by Tokyo's eclectic neighborhoods; and Mercato, yet another example of Japan's ability to deliver hearty Italian food with a deft touch. It also has one of the largest, best-equipped gyms and wellness centers of any hotel in the country—there's

Roppongi

Subway
Nogizaka Station (Chiyoda Line)
TOKYO MIDTOWN
TOEI-OEDO LINE
CHIYODA LINE
Aoyama Cemetery
National Art Center
Roppongi Station (Toei-Oedo Line)
Police Box
Roppongi Crossing
ROPPONGI
Roppongi Cemetery
Roppongi Dori
Almond Coffee Shop
Roppongi Station (Hibiya Line)
Gaien-Higashi Dori
Roppongi Dori
Roi Building
HIBIYA LINE
Expressway No. 3 (Elevated)
HIBIYA LINE
Mori Art Museum
ROPPONGI HILLS
TV Asahi
Imoarai-Zaka
TOEI-OEDO LINE
Tori-Zaka
Gaien Nishi Dori
0 1/10 mi
0 100 m
Roppongi 1-Chome Station (Nanboku Line)
NANBOKU LINE
Expressway No. 2 (Elevated)
RESTAURANTS
Florilège 6
Fukuzushi 3
Ganso Aburadou 6
Joumon Roppongi 4
Tokyo Shiba Toufuya Ukai 6
ATTRACTIONS
Mori Art Museum 2
The National Art Center, Tokyo 1
teamLab Borderless 8
HOTELS
Janu Tokyo 7
remm Roppongi 5
Shiba Park Hotel 7

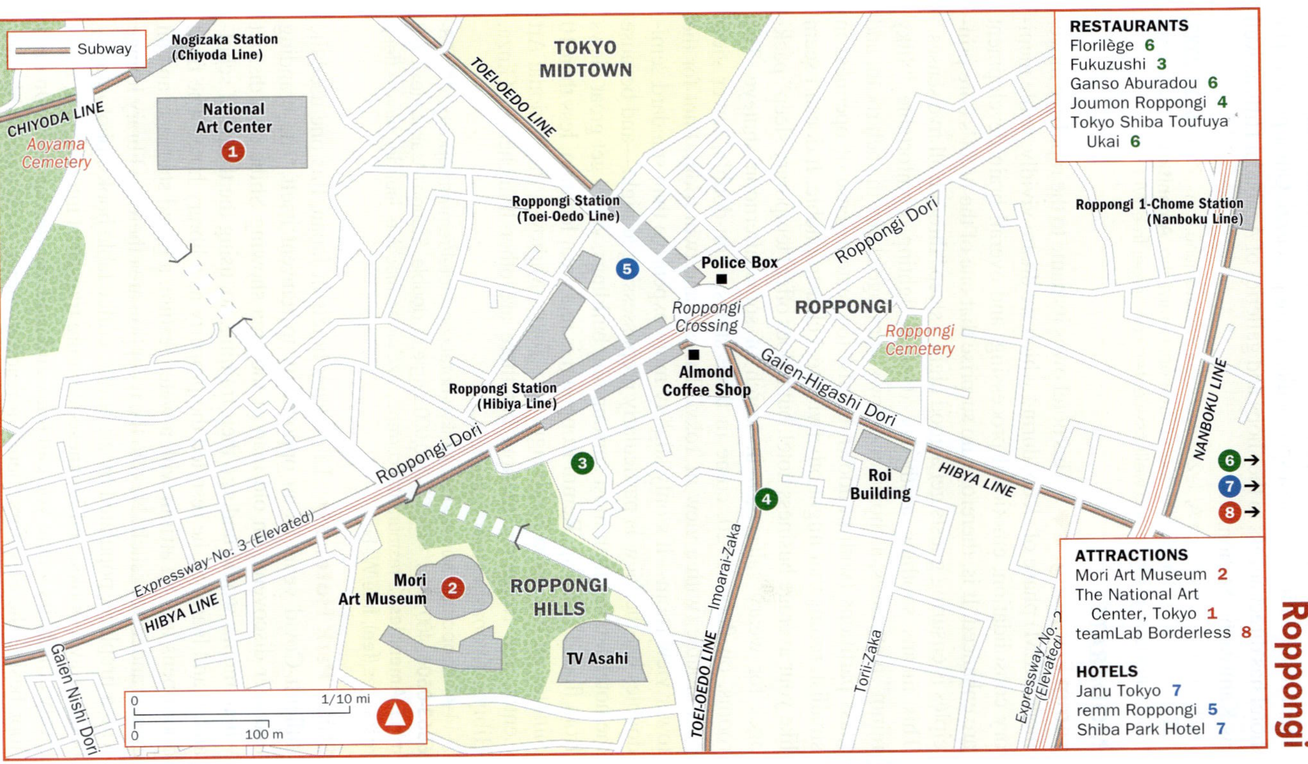

even a boxing ring and a spin room—including a private couples treatment room with access to a spectacular rooftop jacuzzi. Other pluses: The hotel has direct access to the shops and galleries of Azabudai Hills as well as Kamiyacho Station.

Azabudai Hills Residence A, 1–2–2 Azabudai, Minato. janu.com. ✆ **03-6731-2333.** 122 units. ¥150,000–¥350,000 double. Station: Kamiyacho. **Amenities:** 6 restaurants; 2 bars and lounges; gym and wellness center; concierge; free Wi-Fi.

MODERATE

remm Roppongi ♥♥ This hotel owes its name to the rapid eye movement (REM) phase of sleep, during which we dream vividly, wihle memory consolidation, emotional processing, and overall brain development are enhanced. It is, therefore, no surprise that one of the hotel's core principles is ensuring guests get a good night's sleep "through all five senses." This means soothing aesthetics, dreamy lighting, comfortable "Silky remm" mattresses, a choice of pillows, massage chairs in each room, and glass partitions (with pulldown blinds) to create a sense of openness in smallish rooms that might otherwise feel claustrophobic. It doesn't seem like your average business hotel, but it does offer "temporary sleep" packages for weary salarymen in search of some afternoon shuteye. The rooms, on floors 5–20, come in three styles: semi-double, tower view semi-double (with a view of Tokyo Tower), and twin room. Punt for the tower view room—it's only slightly more expensive than standard semi-doubles but the view is particularly prepossessing at night—and because the hotel is taller than most surrounding buildings, you'll get great views from floor 12 and up. Remm Roppongi is in a great location, less than 10 minutes on foot from Roppongi Hills, Tokyo Midtown, the National Art Center, and Roppongi Station, but there are other branches in Ginza, Hibiya, Kyobashi, and Akihabara.

7–14–4 Roppongi, Minato-ku. hankyu-hotel.com/hotel/remm/roppongi. ✆ **03-6863-0606.** 400 units. ¥12,000–¥40,000 single or double. Station: Asakusa (exit 2, 3 min.). **Amenities:** 2 restaurants; currency exchange machine; laundry service (fee); massages (fee); free Wi-Fi.

Shiba Park Hotel ♥♥ Like many hotels in Japan, this one used the difficult Covid years as an opportunity to reinvent itself. The branding manager discovered an old map of the area showing Shiba as a district where monks would undergo their training, so, using the theme of scholarship and learning, he restyled the property as a library hotel. The front door opens into an atrium with a water feature, a grand staircase, and an even grander bookshelf. Next to the reception area there's a library lounge with a fireplace, populated by art books, coffee table books, photography books, travel books, and Japanese literature translated into English; it has lovely armchairs where you can relax and read the various texts. On each floor beside the elevators there's a reading corner, with themes like art, photography, travel, architecture, craft, and fashion. Most rooms are kings or twins, though there are also smartly designed triples with deep bunks and raised seating areas, as well as junior suites on each floor that come with reading rooms and books on the shelves. Reception can also organize tea ceremony and *kintsugi* (gold-leaf crafting) experiences, but make sure you get in touch in advance to confirm availability for these.

1–5–10 Shibakoen, Minato-ku. shibaparkhotel.com. ✆ **03-3433-4141.** 400 units. ¥30,000–¥52,000 single or double. Station: Onarimon (3 min.), Daimon (5 min.), Hamamatsucho (10 min.). **Amenities:** Restaurant; breakfast buffet; self-serve coffee and alcohol bar; concierge; free Wi-Fi.

Shibuya

EXPENSIVE

Shibuya Excel Hotel Tokyu ♥♥ If you saw the movie *Lost in Translation,* you might remember a scene of an intersection that's crazy busy with pedestrians walking in all directions when the light turns red. That's Shibuya Scramble, and it's just a stone's throw from this hotel. The hotel's also across from bustling Shibuya Station, to which it's connected via underground passage and footbridge. (***Tip:*** The footbridge is a good place to photograph the scramble.) Set above the Mark City shopping mall, with reception on the fifth floor, it's mainly a business hotel but also appeals to women, with a women-only floor accessed by a special key (plus extras like face cream, jewelry boxes, and face steamers). Rooms are on the 7th to 24th floors; those higher up facing Shinjuku cost more but provide great night views. The 25th-floor French restaurant also has great views along with reasonable prices. There are many dining options near the hotel, including the Center Gai nightlife district, a pedestrian lane lined with restaurants and bars, and the Hikarie complex.

1–12–2 Dogenzaka, Shibuya-ku. tokyuhotelsjapan.com. ✆ **03-5457-0109.** 408 units. ¥31,000–¥90,000 single or double. Station: Shibuya (1 min. by footbridge). **Amenities:** 2 restaurants; lounge; room service; free Wi-Fi.

MODERATE

Shibuya Hotel En ♥♥ Also within striking distance of the Shibuya crossing, Hotel En is your best bet for staying in the area without burning a hole in your wallet. It may be nestled among the district's "love hotels" and late-night bars and clubs, but if you want to be close to the downtown action there are few more affordable options than this. That's not to say it's grubby or threadbare. The rooms, though small, are fitted with renowned Slumberland beds, as well as basic toiletries, slippers and pajamas, and 40-inch flatscreen TVs. The Executive Oriental suite is the fanciest pick for couples, with a veiled bed, wall-mounted woodcarvings, and a more spacious bathroom—typically it's only ¥5,000 to ¥10,000 per night more than a basic double. But if you sign up for En and The Court hotel membership (for free), you'll get 10% off the best rate and a complimentary 1-hour checkout extension. Note that, in most rooms, bathrooms have glass partitions, meaning you'll be in full view of your partner when attending to toilet-related business (blinds offer some semblance of privacy).

1–1 Maruyamacho, Shibuya-ku. shibuyahotel.jp. ✆ **03-5489-1010.** 58 units. ¥23,000–¥55,000 single or double. Station: Shibuya (7 min.). **Amenities:** Coffee shop; free Wi-Fi.

Other Neighborhoods

MODERATE

Hotel Balian Resort Kinshicho ♥♥ I'll come straight out with it: This is a love hotel, meaning a place where consenting adults go to enjoy each other's company, either overnight or for a few hours during the day—day-use rates start at ¥6,800. These accommodations are popular in Japanese cities, because many people live in small apartments with paper-thin walls separating them from family members, presenting a natural roadblock to physical intimacy with a partner. Some people are put off at the idea of staying in a hotel designed for people to have sex, but I hate to tell you, dear reader, rare is the hotel bed that can claim innocence. I like staying in love hotels because you get more space, comfier beds, and better in-room facilities than in your average mid-range business hotel. Hotel Balian, which also has branches in Shinjuku and Ikebukuro, recreates the atmosphere of the Indonesian tropics through floral decor, ornamentation, and the spirit of R&R. The Royal Balian suite is perfect for a honeymoon treat or special occasion, with its king-size canopy bed, a 75-inch wall-mounted TV, self-serve alcohol bar, massage chair, bubble bath, dry sauna, and open-air tub (hidden from prying eyes by a bamboo fence). Not bad at ¥25,800–¥29,800 per night. Note that, to increase the sense of privacy, love hotel rooms generally don't have windows, so you'll be glad of the balcony.

2-2-12 Kotobashi, Sumida-ku. balian.jp/shop/kinshicho/. ✆ **0120-759-170.** 49 units. Day use from ¥6,800; overnight stay from ¥11,800 (min. 2 guests). Station: Kinshichio (5 min.). **Amenities:** Room service; free drinks bar in lobby; free Wi-Fi.

OMO5 Otsuka ♥♥♥ One of the last neighborhoods in the city to still have a tram system, Otsuka conjures images of retro nostalgia in the Tokyoite mind. It's no surprise, then, that one of the themes of this hotel is to introduce guests to the little-known joys of wandering through Otsuka's Showa-style backstreets. Talk with a garrulous tea store owner, sip craft beer in the **Titans** or **Namachan** brewpubs, sample *dorayaki* (pancakes with fillings) at a generations-old sweetshop, or listen to bubble-era city pop records while eating sake affogato—these are the kinds of experiences hotel guests are treated to on daily tours and evening events. The rooms inspire a different kind of nostalgia by bringing out your inner child—like little treehouses overlooking the Tokyo skyline, they have cozy alcove windows perfect for curling up with a book, and twin beds tucked away in cubby-hole-sized mezzanines, letting the lounge areas take up most of the space. This place clearly caters to a younger crowd—think 20- to 40-year-olds—because older folks (not to mention those who are tall) may find it bothersome to maneuver in the low-ceilinged rooms.

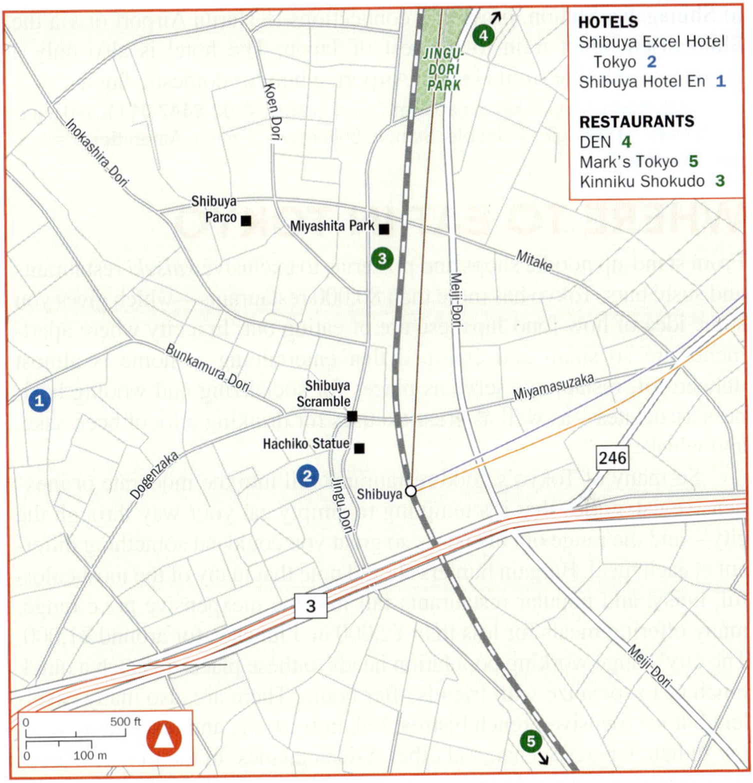

Shibuya

HOTELS
Shibuya Excel Hotel Tokyo 2
Shibuya Hotel En 1

RESTAURANTS
DEN 4
Mark's Tokyo 5
Kinniku Shokudo 3

As with all OMO hotels, there's a huge *go-kinjo* (neighborhood) map in the hallway, indicating cool bars, restaurants, and shops nearby, each of which has been chosen by the staff based on its openness to foreign clientele or how representative it is of Otsuka's urban culture. Staying here is a great way to see a relatively undiscovered Tokyo neighborhood, but you're also walking distance to Ikebukuro and a stone's throw from the Yamanote train line looping central Tokyo.

2–26–1 Kitaotsuka, Toshima-ku. hoshinoresorts.com/en/. ✆ **050-3143-8059.** 125 units. ¥20,000–¥40,000 double. Station: Otsuka (3 min.) **Amenities:** Cafe/lounge; tours; free Wi-Fi.

INEXPENSIVE

Shinagawa Tobu Hotel ♥♥ A step up from the usual business hotel, this property has red ceramic bowls on brown walls serving as artwork in the lobby and eye-catching red wingback chairs with black pillows, plus an Italian restaurant. Several different types of rooms are available, from the most common tiny economy double with a semi-double bed (okay for one person, but challenging for two) to six much larger standard doubles with a true double bed and twins that sleep from two to four people with the addition of extra beds. But the main reason to stay here is its proximity to Shinagawa Station, providing connections to Narita Airport or via the Shinkansen bullet train to the rest of Japan. The hotel is also only a 20-minute cab ride from Haneda Airport, a hub for domestic flights.

4–7–6 Takanawa, Minato-ku. shinagawatobuhotel.com. ✆ **03-3447-0111.** 190 units. ¥11,000–¥20,000 single or double. Station: Shinagawa (5 min.). **Amenities:** Restaurant; free Wi-Fi.

WHERE TO EAT IN TOKYO

From stand-up noodle shops and pizzerias to exclusive *kaiseki* restaurants and sushi bars, Tokyo has more than 80,000 restaurants—which gives you some idea of how fond Japanese are of eating out. In a city where apartments are so small and cramped that entertaining at home is almost unheard of, restaurants serve as places for socializing and wooing business associates—as well as great excuses for drinking a lot of beer, sake, and whiskey.

So many of Tokyo's good restaurants fall into the moderate or inexpensive categories that it's tempting to simply eat your way through the city—and the range of cuisines is so great you could eat something different at each meal. Bargain hunters should note that many of the most colorful, noisy, and popular restaurants fall into the inexpensive price range, many offering meals for less than ¥2,000 and lunches for around ¥1,000. The city's huge working population heads to these places to catch a quick lunch or to socialize with friends after hours. There are also many excellent but inexpensive French bistros, Italian *trattorie,* and restaurants serving Indian, Chinese, Thai, and other Asian cuisines. In the trendiest areas of downtown Tokyo, burger spots, taco shops, food trucks, and BBQ joints are becoming popular, too—noteworthy in case your palate gets homesick. I also suggest you look for gourmet maps in your hotel lobby or ask your concierge or hotel manager for recommendations; there's probably a great little place (or several) just around the corner.

deals ON MEALS

One of the best deals is the **fixed-price lunch,** usually available from 11am to 2pm. Called a *teishoku* in a Japanese restaurant and a *seto co-su* (or simply *seto* or *co-su*) in restaurants serving Western food, the set lunch lets you dine in style at reasonable prices. If possible, avoid the noon-to-1pm weekday crush when Tokyo's army of office workers floods area restaurants. Because Japanese tend to order fixed-price meals rather than a la carte, set dinners are also usually available (although they're not as cheap as set lunches). Many hotel restaurants offer all-you-can-eat buffets (called *baikingu,* meaning "viking," probably because Japan's first buffet was in a restaurant called Viking in Tokyo's Imperial Hotel), which are also bargains for hearty appetites. See p. 46 in chapter 2 for more recommendations on saving money.

Note that a 10% consumption tax is added to meals in restaurants. Most restaurants include the tax in their prices; some do not. In any case, menus usually state whether prices include taxes. The prices listed in this book are taken directly from menus, so be prepared for tax to be added to your check. In addition, first-class restaurants, as well as hotel restaurants, also add a 10% to 15% service charge. For information on Japanese food, see "Eating & Drinking in Japan," in chapter 2.

Finally, keep in mind that the **last order** is taken at least 30 minutes before the restaurant's actual closing time, sometimes even an hour before closing at the more exclusive restaurants. Some websites only in Japanese are included below, either because they have photos of dishes or maps that will help you find them.

In & Near Ginza

See Ginza map, p. 143.

EXPENSIVE

Sushi Ko Honten ♥♥ SUSHI Ginza is a hotspot for high-end sushi restaurants, most famously Sukiyabasho Jiro of Netflix documentary fame. But by all accounts, dining there is a rigid and pedantic affair that's finished in half an hour, and you'll pay a few hundred dollars for the courtesy. For sushi of similar quality, but in a more laidback and convivial atmosphere, try Sushi Ko (pay attention to the address below—there are several restaurants with this name in Tokyo). More than 130 years old and specializing in Edo-mae sushi (meaning "in front of Edo," referring to seafood caught in Tokyo Bay), Sushi Ko was a favorite Tokyo haunt for Anthony Bourdain—the number of international customers has increased markedly since he introduced it to the world in a 2016 episode of *Parts Unknown.* The sushi is served in a multicourse, seasonal showcase prepared by the chef in the *omakase* style, meaning what you eat is at his discretion (menus are superfluous). To reserve a space, download the app takeme.com.

6–3–8 Ginza, Chuo-ku. gawh001.gorp.jp. ✆ **050-5487-6726.** Dinner courses from ¥22,000 per person. Tues–Sun 11:30am–11pm. Closed Jan 1–6. Station: Ginza (3 min.), Hibiya (5 min.), Yurakucho (6 min.).

Ten-ichi ♥♥♥ TEMPURA Founded in 1930, this may well be the most famous tempura restaurant in the world, with many foreign dignitaries among its customers over the years. With branches all over Japan, its main shop is here on Namiki Dori, a street blazing with neon in Ginza's nightlife district. But indoors it's spartan, decorated with blond wood trim, sliding doors, and flower arrangements. Tempura counters on each floor seat no more than 10 customers, who get an intimate view of master chefs going about their work. Ten-ichi is famous for its delicately fried food, with a batter so refined and an oil so light, the flavor of fish, shrimp, scallop, eggplant, sweet potato, and other ingredients is enhanced rather than overwhelmed. The piping-hot morsels can be dipped into a variety of sauces, from the restaurant's own secret recipe to a simple lemon juice with a pinch of salt. Ten-ichi branches include those nearby in the basement of the Peninsula Hotel and three in the venerable Nihonbashi district, as well as locations in department stores, including Seibu in Ikebukuro, Takashimaya in Setagaya, and Isetan in Shinjuku.

6–6–5 Ginza. tenichi.co.jp. ✆ **03-3571-1949.** Set lunches ¥4,860–¥19,800; set dinners ¥16,550–¥27,500. Daily 11:30am–9pm (last order). Station: Ginza (3 min.).

MODERATE

Rangetsu (らん月) ♥♥ SUKIYAKI/SHABU-SHABU/KAISEKI/BENTO "Orchid moon" is the English translation of Rangetsu, a Ginza restaurant founded in 1947 and still under the same family ownership. It specializes in sukiyaki and shabu-shabu, made with A5-grade Japanese Wagyu beef and cooked at your table. The English-language menu with photos lists many other dishes, too, from yaki shabu-shabu cooked on a grill at your table and crab dishes (like the crab shabu-shabu set meal for ¥11,000) to bento, *kaiseki,* and more. Lunch sets, served until 4pm, are especially good deals, offering steaks, shabu-shabu, bento, and many other combinations. A sake bar in the basement stocks more than 80 varieties from all over Japan, all of which you can also order with your meal no matter which floor you dine on.

3–5–8 Ginza. ginza-rangetsu.com. ✆ **03-3567-1021.** Set dinners from ¥11,000 (premium wagyu cuts ¥21,000); set lunches ¥2,000–¥4,800. Daily 11:30am–10:30pm (last order 8pm). Station: Ginza (3 min.).

A Note on Establishments with Japanese Signs

Many establishments and attractions in Japan do not have signs in Roman (English-language) letters. For those that don't, we list the Japanese equivalent to help you locate them.

INEXPENSIVE

In addition to the following restaurants, check out the eighth floor of **Matsuya Ginza department store,** with restaurants serving everything from pastries and Chinese food to sushi, tempura, noodles, and more.

For atmospheric dining, head to an arch beneath the elevated Yamanote railway tracks located about halfway between Harumi Dori and the Imperial Hotel Tower; it has a handful of tiny ***yakitori* stands,** each with a few tables and chairs. These cater to a boisterous working-class clientele, mainly men. The atmosphere, unsophisticated and dingy, harks back to prewar Japan, somewhat of an anomaly in otherwise chic Ginza. Stalls are open from about 5pm to midnight Monday through Saturday.

Finally, in the basement of the behemoth that is Tokyo Station, the eight ramen shops along **Tokyo Ramen Street** offer specialties like Hirugao's delicious *shio* (salt-based) ramen broth and Oreshiki Jun's rich pork-stock ramen. There are instructions in English; you decide what you want and then buy a ticket from that shop's vending machine. Note, however, that Ramen Street is difficult to find—it's located off the **Ichibangai** (First Ave.) shopping arcade in the basement of the station, next to the

There's generally a queue waiting to eat at the shops in Tokyo Ramen Street in the basement of Tokyo Station.

Yaesu entrance ticket gates. Avoid the mealtime crunch or else get in the queue. The shops are open daily, some from as early as 7:30am; last orders at 10:30pm.

Andy's Shin Hinomoto ♥♥ VARIED JAPANESE This hole-in-the-wall underneath the Yamanote elevated train tracks looks like it's been here since the rubble of post–World War II…because it has. Founded in 1945 when there were cubbyholes like this throughout a bombed-out Tokyo, it is owned by the founder's son-in-law, a Brit named Andy. As tiny as it is, it has an upstairs with an arched ceiling, though that is only marginally better than the downstairs, which has the charm of a fallout shelter. Yet every night this place is packed elbow-to-elbow with office workers, and the only way you might get your foot in the door without a reservation is to come right when it opens. The food, made with seafood and vegetables bought fresh daily, includes tempura, a fish of the day, deep-fried chicken, chili prawns, salads (usually sold out by 8pm), and its signature stuffed *gyoza* chicken wings. Even with fluorescent lighting, soot-blackened walls, and a no-credit-card policy, this throwback is, in the words of Andy, always "insanely busy," and all from word of mouth.
2-4-4 Yurakucho (across from the Yurakucho Denki Bldg.). shin-hinomoto.com or andysfish.com/Shin-Hinomoto. ✆ **03-3214-8021.** Grilled dishes ¥850–¥1,500, set meals from ¥5,000, sashimi platters from ¥3,000. Mon–Sat 5pm–midnight. Station: Yurakucho or Ginza (1 min.).

Ginza Chukasoba Hachigou (銀座八五) ♥♥♥ RAMEN Ginza Chukasoba Hachigou, which earned a Michelin star in 2022, encapsulates how it's possible to eat gold-standard food on almost any budget while traveling in Japan. On the bottom floor of a multistory building on a nondescript side street, it's a location most would walk past without giving it a second glance. But that would be their loss. There are three ramen options available from the ticket vending machine, all made with the shop's signature broth, combining kombu (seaweed) and dried shiitake mushrooms with dried tomatoes, scallops, uncured ham, free-range chicken, and duck. If that sounds a little lavish, it's because chef Yasushi Matsumura had a glittering career in fine dining before returning to his humbler roots. Order the 特製中華そば, literally "special Chinese noodles," topped with a fatty slice of pork, a soft-boiled egg, and bamboo shoots. At ¥1,600 yen a bowl, it's an absolute steal. The restaurant is barely big enough to swing a chopstick in—*hachigou* means "eight-five"; the shop is 8 *tsubo* by 5 *tsubo,* about 35.58 square feet—so there are only six seats squeezed along the counter. When I last visited, I queued for an inordinate amount of time, but mercifully, the shop now takes online reservations, including a ¥500 booking fee. Use Table Check (tablecheck.com/ja/shops/ginza-hachigou/reserve) to reserve your spot; reservations accepted from 9am every Saturday for the following Tuesday to Sunday. From 11am, customers are served in the order of their arrival; from 12:30pm on, customers who have reservations will be seated. The shop closes when Matsumura-san runs out of ramen broth, usually around 3:30 or 4pm. (Ginza Chukasoba Hachigou now has a Michelin Bib Gourmand rather than a star, but that's down to Michelin restructuring its approval

A SEAFOOD feast AT TSUKIJI OUTER MARKET

Okay, Tsukiji has become utterly swarmed with tourists in recent years, but this 90-year-old fish market (tsukiji.or.jp; ✆ **03-3541-9444**), long referred to as "Japan's Kitchen," remains a vital destination on any Japan food pilgrimage. Walk the labyrinthine streets—the ramshackle stalls and market vendors give the place a Showa-era atmosphere—and note how they don't smell fishy; rather your nose detects the faintest notes of the sea. Then begin to feast, sampling food from various stalls: *otoro nigiri* (fatty tuna sushi), scallops seared with butter, oysters so big you won't know what to do with them, *uni donburi* (rice bowls topped with creamy sea urchin), and *omakase* sushi sets from tiny, counter-seating restaurants. The hole-in-the-walls selling raw beef sushi, *tamagoyaki* (sweet, rolled omelets), and *motsunabe* (offal and tofu hotpots) also do a healthy trade. Most of the restaurants here close around lunchtime, though some stay open until 2pm, so arrive around 9am and bring an empty stomach. Prices vary; expect to spend around **¥5,000 per person** (more for omakase sets).

Fresh king crab legs from a stall in Tsukiji Outer Market.

process rather than indicating a dip in the restaurant's quality.) Look for white half-curtains inscribed with the kanji 銀座八五.

3–14–2 Ginza, Chuo-ku. katsumoto-japan.com/ginza_hachigou.html. No phone. Ramen ¥1,200–¥1,600. Wed–Sun 11am till sold out (sometimes open Tues). Station: Shintomicho (4 min.), Tsukiji (6 min.), Ginza (10 min.).

Sapporo Dominica (札幌 Dominica) ♥♥ SOUP CURRY Soup curry, a wonderful winter warmer, is a salaryman staple in Sapporo, Japan's northernmost major city. This soup curry shop near Tokyo Station's Yaesu exit recreates this hearty repast for the diners who reliably fill its counter seats and three small tables during the lunch and post-work rushes. There are four base soup options to choose from—original, tomato, pork, soy (all delicious)—with toppings like chicken, pork, mixed vegetables, and hamburger steak. You can also increase the level of heat, and though the Japanese aren't known for their spicy food tolerance, level 10 is a real scorcher. I'd recommend a side of rice with melted cheese or crispy grilled cheese on top. Whatever you decide, it'll be unpretentious, bursting with flavor, and best enjoyed with a draft of Sapporo beer.

3–4–1 Kyobashi (TM Ginza Building, 2nd floor). No website. ✆ **03-3231-1347.** Soup curry with a side ¥1,200–¥1,600. Mon–Fri 11am–4pm and 5:30–9pm; Sat 11am–9pm; Sun 11am–3:30pm and 5:30–9pm. Station: Kyobashi (4 min.), Ginza-itchome (4 min.), Takaracho (5 min.), Tokyo (Yaesu exit, 9 min.).

Asakusa

See Asakusa map, p. 149.

EXPENSIVE

Saryo Ichimatsu (茶寮一松) ♥♥♥ KAISEKI Given Asakusa's reputation as the major entertainment district of old Edo, Saryo Ichimatsu is one of the most thematic places you can dine. Hidden away from the main drag, the building looks like it belongs in a temple precinct, ringed by coped-tile walls and fronted by a neatly manicured landscape garden and a wooden viewing platform overlooking a pond. The food served inside, a multicourse *kaiseki* feast, has an equally calming aesthetic, reflecting the season through produce, tone, texture, and color. On my last visit, autumn was segueing into winter, so we dined on persimmons, sesame tofu, seasonal steamed fish, and grilled grouper served with pickled yam, young ginger, and edible chrysanthemum. No overpowering flavors, no assaults on the palate, just Japan's philosophy of subtraction explored through the art of food.

While Saryo Ichimatsu is first and foremost a place to eat, geisha performances are often part of the dining experience (for an additional fee). Cleanse your palate mid-meal with a glass of sake, while geisha in full kimono regalia play the shamisen and perform traditional dances. They may engage you in party games, like rhythm-based *konpira fune fune* or *tora, tora, tora* (a local version of rock, paper, scissors). The kaiseki course menu is set at ¥17,600 per person, irrespective of the season; *fugu* (pufferfish) courses are also available upon request (at least 2 days in advance). A mini-kaiseki lunch option for ¥6,600 is served on weekdays, alongside the standard kaiseki lunch menu (from ¥11,000). Floor or table seating is available in the tatami dining rooms. The restaurant also offers a pick-up and drop-off service by rickshaw. As you arrive, look for a tile-roofed entrance gate with the kanji 茶寮一松 inscribed vertically on a wooden plaque. 1–15–1 Kaminarimon, Taito-ku. ichimatsu.co.jp. Reservations enquiries (2 or more people): yoyaku@ichimatsu.co.jp. ✆ **03-3841-0333.** Lunch from ¥6,600; dinners from ¥17,600 (plus 10% service charge). Wed–Mon 11am–2:30pm and 5–10:30pm (last admission 7pm). Closed Bon (mid-Aug) and New Year's holidays. Station: Tawaramachi (3 min.), Asakusa (5 min.).

MODERATE

Nihon Kai (日本海) ♥♥♥ SUSHI The name means "Japan Sea," so no prizes will be awarded for guessing Nihon Kai's style of cuisine. Falling somewhere between an omakase sushi restaurant and a pay-by-the-plate conveyor belt chain, Nihon Kai is a great place to eat high-quality sushi and sashimi without breaking the bank. The first floor is the more immersive of the two, with counter seats encircling a sushi kitchen where chefs slice, dice and prepare the food. The second floor has tables and private booths for larger groups. Walk-ins are usually fine unless you're part of a large party. Top sellers include the sashimi platters, crab *chawanmushi* (egg-drop custard), *tamagoyaki* (rolled omelet), and, surprisingly, the chicken wings, but the menu highlight is the Indian tuna set meals, featuring *akami* (lean tuna), *chutoro* (medium fatty tuna), and *otoro* (very fatty tuna) with pickled ginger to cleanse the palate. If you're willing to loosen your belt buckle and your purse strings, 6-course and 7-course seafood sets are available from ¥4,400 per person. Nihon Kai's food is best paired with Hakkaisan *nihonshu* from Niigata, one of Japan's chief sake-brewing prefectures. 1–6–5 Kaminarimon, Taito-ku. Reservations: r.gnavi.co.jp/a910500/drink. ✆ **050-5485-2696.** Tuna dinner from ¥1,520, 6-course dinner ¥4,400 (¥6,500 with unlimited drinks), 7-course dinner ¥5,500. Daily 11:30am–11pm (10:30pm last orders). Station: Tawaramachi (1 min.), Asakusa (5 min.).

INEXPENSIVE

Asakichi (浅吉) ♥ OKONOMIYAKI This atmospheric neighborhood restaurant specializes in *okonomiyaki,* a working-class meal that is basically an eggy Japanese pancake filled with your choice of beef, pork, and/or vegetables, and prepared by diners themselves as they sit at tables inset with griddles. Asakichi, which has been in business for the best part of 50 years, is also known for the okonomiyaki-adjacent dish *monjayaki* ("monja" for short). It's not the most aesthetically pleasing of foods—more water is added when the ingredients are mixed, resulting in a gelatinous gloop—but the flavors speak for themselves. Don't worry if you haven't cooked these dishes before, they're a breeze: Mix the bowl of raw egg, flour, and "toppings"; dump it onto the hotplate (preferably letting it form into something approximating a circle); and thermodynamics will do the rest. For *okonomiyaki,* you may also want to flip it when the underside is cooked. If you're feeling adventurous, order the cheese and octopus *okonomiyaki* or the tomato special *monja*.

2–28–6, Asakusa. No website. ✆ **03-6231-7478.** Lunch from ¥1,000, Dinner with drinks from ¥3,000. Mon–Fri noon–9pm (last order), Sat–Sun and holidays 11:30am–9pm (last order). Station: Tsukuba Express Asakusa (3 min.), Asakusa (5 min.).

Sansada (三定) ♥♥ TEMPURA Established in 1837 and located right beside Kaminarimon Gate, this simple tempura restaurant specializes in Edo-style tempura, fried in a light sesame oil. On the first floor, seating is either at tables or on *tatami,* while the upstairs is more traditional with *tatami* seating; one room overlooks the temple gate. Run by an army of very able grandmotherly types, the restaurant has an English-language menu with photos of various options, including *tendon* (tempura on rice), noodles with tempura, bento boxes, and full-course meals.

1–2–2 Asakusa. tempura-sansada.co.jp. ✆ **03-3841-3400.** *Tendon* ¥1,820–¥4,290; set meals ¥1,820–¥4,500. Daily 11am–8pm (last order). Station: Asakusa (1 min.).

Ueno

See Ueno map, p. 151.

MODERATE

You'll find a multitude of restaurants in all price categories between JR Ueno Station and Ueno Park in several new-ish buildings. **Mori Sakura Terrace** has more than a dozen eateries offering Italian and Chinese fare, as well as an oyster bar, noodles, sushi, yakitori, *udon,* and other Japanese foods.

Innshoutei (韻松亭) ♥♥♥ KAISEKI/BENTO A meal at this traditional restaurant makes an outing to Ueno even more special. A Tokyo

A top choice for a traditional kaiseki meal, Innshoutei has been a Tokyo landmark since 1875.

landmark since 1875, it has a simple tearoom with snacks on the ground floor and a restaurant upstairs, where meals are served in private *tatami* rooms or a small dining room overlooking greenery. There's an English-language menu, but let your budget be your guide in choosing a bento or *kaiseki* set lunch, all of which change with the seasons. Dinner offers more expensive *kaiseki* and chicken sukiyaki. This restaurant is extremely popular with older Japanese women, but reservations are accepted only for four or more, so be prepared to wait in line. During the cherry blossom season, when Ueno Park swarms with sightseers, Inshoutei limits its menu to only a few set meals complete with flowers to honor the season, but you'll be lucky to get your foot in the door then. Credit cards are not accepted.

In Ueno Park, beside the row of orange *torii* leading downhill. innsyoutei.jp. ✆ **03-3821-8126.** Lunch boxes from ¥1,690; kaiseki sets from ¥7,800. Daily 11am–3pm; Mon–Sat 5–9pm; Sun and holidays 5–8:30pm (last order). Station: JR Ueno (6 min.).

Izu'ei Honten (伊豆栄本店) ♥♥ EEL This restaurant's history goes back 270 years to the middle of the Edo Period, though you'd never know that from the modern multistoried building that stands here today. The dining rooms are pleasant and overlook Shinobazu Pond, but the star of the show here is grilled eel. The quality of charcoal used to grill the eel is considered paramount, and this restaurant is justly proud of its very own furnace in the mountains of Wakayama Prefecture, said to produce the best charcoal in Japan. An English-language menu with photos will help you select from about 15 different set meals featuring eel, but there's also tempura, bento, and, with advance reservations (made through Gurunavi: r.gnavi.co.jp/g063800), *kaiseki*.

2–12–22 Ueno. izuei.co.jp. ✆ **03-3831-0954.** Set meals from ¥3,630; *kaiseki* ¥8,800–¥22,000. Daily 11am–8:15pm (last order). Station: JR Ueno (3 min.).

Shinjuku

See Shinjuku map, p. 154.

MODERATE

Hanbey (半兵ヱ) ♥♥ IZAKAYA Hanbey takes diners back to the interwar years, when *motsu-yaki* (grilled guts) food stalls were crammed under railway bridges and positioned at the entrance to liquor stores. As soon as you walk through the sliding wooden door, you'll see Showa-period beer ads and movie posters covered in brooding protagonists and calligraphic kanji script. The pentatonic music is jaunty and quaint, yet somehow imperial, like a call to the "great adventure" of war. The menu also harkens back to the days when people ate things like fried swallows, simmered offal, and pig's uterus. Under different circumstances, Hanbey could come across as gimmicky, but the more familiar finger food and sharing plates—*yakitori* and fried vegetable skewers, sesame tofu salad, *tebasaki* (chicken wings), boiled dumplings—are as tasty as they are

Bustling Shinjuku is full of cozy izakaya restaurants, where locals spend their evenings drinking and eating.

cheap (some skewers are less than ¥100 a pop). Hanbey is a chain, but I particularly like the Shinjuku branch for its large dining room with low tables and floor seating, which fits the traditional Japanese vibe. It's also in the heart of Kabuki-cho, the high-rise epitome of modern Japan, offering a nice contrast to the retro aesthetic in the restaurant. There are English-language paper menus, and more recently, has introduced electronic menus from which you can place your orders. On the way out, there's a market stall selling old-world snacks, like pickled squid and cheese-fish paste, and toys, which make for unique (and cheap) souvenirs.
1–23–14 Kabuki-cho, 5th floor. hakuritabai-hanbey.com. ✆ **03-6861-3555.** Dinner and drinks ¥3,000 per person, special course menu (including all-you-can-drink) ¥5,500 per person. Daily 5pm–midnight. Station: Shinjuku (east exit, 7 min.).

INEXPENSIVE

Din Tai Fung ♥♥ CHINESE Tokyo's first branch of Taiwan's famous dumpling restaurant is so popular you'll probably have to join a long line of people waiting to get in. Luckily, the line moves fast and you'll soon find yourself dining inside the noisy restaurant or outside on the spacious terrace. The English-language menu lists various steamed and soup dumplings, including the signature pork dumplings served in piping-hot bamboo steamers, along with dishes like rice cakes and noodle soups. The *tantanmen* noodle soup and *xiaolongbao* combo sets are hard to beat. Din Tai Fung started out in 1958 as a retailer selling cooking oil in Taiwan and has been a smashing success across Asia (and now has branches in the U.K., the U.S., and Australia). The Japanese are among its most avid customers, with multiple locations in Tokyo alone, including in Ginza, Nihonbashi, and Tokyo Station.

Takashimaya Shinjuku, 12th floor, 5–24–2 Sendagaya. d.rt-c.co.jp/shinjuku. ✆ **03-5361-1381.** Dumplings from ¥680; set lunches ¥1,730–¥2,170. Daily 11am–10pm (last order). Station: Shinjuku (New South Exit, 1 min.).

Kageyama (蔭山) ♥♥♥ RAMEN This ramen joint in the wonderfully named neighborhood of Takadanobaba is easy to miss. What you're looking for is a coarse concrete building with a sliding door and a horizontal rectangular window. As at most ramen shops, the kitchen is surrounded by a counter and perhaps a dozen or so seats. Given this shop's proximity to Waseda University, you'll see the odd student or professor on their lunch break, but it's often surprisingly un-busy for what is pound-for-pound one of the best bowls of noodles in Tokyo. Kageyama's full name, 鶏白湯麺 蔭山, translates to "chicken white soup noodles Kageyama," which hints at their specialty. The signature chicken broth carries the heft of a *tonkotsu* with the lightness and zest of soy-based ramen and is served with a lemon wedge on the side. Next to the door there's a vending machine (which now has English translation) for placing orders—get the "chicken base soup salt noodle" topped with shredded chicken, boiled egg, and leafy greens for ¥880. Rice (¥100) and boiled gyoza (¥300) are available as sides, but I feel they're superfluous. Let the ramen take center stage.

1–4–18 Takadanobaba. No website. ✆ **03-6457-3160.** Ramen from ¥880. Daily 11am–11pm. Station: Takadanobaba (4 min.), Nishi-Waseda (6 min.).

Toriyoshi Shoten (鳥良商店) ♥♥ IZAKAYA Toriyoshi is a popular izakaya chain in Tokyo (and some other prefectures), specializing in chicken cooked various ways. The main branch, within earshot of the late-night bar streets of Golden Gai, is open 24/7 and is likely to be just as full at 4am as at 8pm. As with many major izakaya chains, Toriyoshi now has tablet menus with multilingual functionality, so ordering is straightforward (probably for the best if you've stumbled in after a night of bar hopping). The spicy sesame chicken wings are hard to beat, but I'd recommend the karaage and deep-fried *kawa* (chicken skin), or if you're feeling adventurous, the raw meat sets. The cocktails and highballs are pretty weak—not unusual for an izakaya—but the sake selection is surprisingly good.

1–2–2 Kabukicho, Shinjuku. toriyoshishoten.jp. ✆ **03-5291-8851.** Average ¥2,000–¥3,000 per person. Open 24/7. Station: Shinjuku (east exit, 5 min.).

Harajuku & Aoyama

See Harajuku & Aoyama map, p. 157.

EXPENSIVE

Two Rooms Grill/Bar ♥♥♥ CONTINENTAL Dress smartly to fit in with the fashion-conscious 40-somethings who gather here for high-powered business lunches and after-work cocktails. The sleek dining

Plastic displays of menu items outside Japanese restaurants not only make ordering easier, they are also works of art in themselves.

room looks like a setting in a black-and-white movie with its white walls and tablecloths, waiters decked out in black with crisp white aprons, and steel and glass architectural details. Bringing the scene to life are warm woods (including tables made of 50,000-year-old swamp kauri timber from New Zealand), jazz playing softly in the background, and an open kitchen briskly turning out orders. There's also a bar with an outdoor terrace over an infinity pool offering poster-perfect views of the city skyline from comfy sofas. As for the menu, wagyu beef reigns supreme, though other yum choices include the lamb chops or the slow-cooked pork sirloin. Weekday lunches and weekend brunches also are highly recommended (make reservations), but even if you don't dine here, a drink on the outdoor terrace will make Tokyo seem like the most relaxing place in the world. The bar is open until 2am (Sun until 10pm).
AO Building, 5th floor, 3–11–7 Kita-Aoyama. tworooms.jp. ✆ **03-3498-0002.** Main dishes ¥4,400–¥8,400 (premium steak cuts ¥14,000–¥15,000); set lunches ¥2,900–¥8,500; set dinners from ¥9,500. Daily 11:30am–2:30pm and 6–9:30pm (last order 8pm Sun). Station: Omotesando (exit B2, 1 min.).

MODERATE

Chao Bamboo ♥♥ THAI This semi-outdoor restaurant is popular throughout the year (wraparound plastic curtains shield diners during inclement weather) because of its relaxed street-food atmosphere and high-quality Thai fare. You can expect the classics: green curry, spicy papaya salad, *tom kha* soup, steamed chicken, and spring rolls. Other popular bites include fried soft-shell crab with curry egg sauce, tofu and coriander salad, and Indonesian *mi goreng*. In an area that's become excessively upscale, this homely backstreet joint is a perfect antidote. It's also a great place for a few Southeast Asian beers and light snacks during the lunch hour.
6–1–5 Jingumae. yasaiya-mei.com. ✆ **03-5785-0606.** ¥3,000–¥5,000 per person. Daily 11:30am–9pm (last order). Station: Meiji-Jingumae (3 min.), Harajuku (5 min.).

Yasaiya Mei (やさい家めい) ♥♥ VARIED JAPANESE If you like veggies, this restaurant is a must, specializing in fresh, seasonal, and mostly organic vegetables (note that because it uses fish stock for many of its dishes and meat dishes, it is not a strictly vegetarian restaurant). It's emblematic of Japan's traditional approach to cooking, in which vegetables are chosen when *shun,* at peak ripeness, to ensure the best taste and texture. Reservations are a must. Although it offers a few à la carte selections (carrot kimchi, say, or the Mei Special bagna cauda, served with a variety of veggies, such as eggplant, radish, and asparagus), set meals are the emphasis here. For lunch your meal might include vegetable pressed sushi with vegetable tempura and side dishes, while dinner offers sukiyaki and meals like the Vegetable Gozen, which comes with sweet potato soup, bagna cauda, and a slew of vegetables and other dishes. Seating is either at the U-shaped open kitchen or a table—try to snag one beside the large windows overlooking the zelkova trees of Omotesando Dori.

Omotesando Hills, 3rd floor, 4–12–10 Jingumae (on Omotesando Dori). yasaiya-mei.com. ✆ **03-5785-0606.** Set lunches ¥1,290–¥2,090; set dinners ¥3,650–¥4,900. Sun–Thurs 11am–9:30pm; Fri–Sat 11am–10:30pm (last order). Station: Meiji-Jingumae or Omotesando (4 min.).

INEXPENSIVE

Harajuku Gyozaro (原宿餃子樓) ♥♥ GYOZA The menu in this rub-elbows-with-locals *gyoza* joint is refreshingly sparse—only a few types of pork gyoza are offered, either steamed (*sui-gyoza*) or fried (*yaki-gyoza*), with or without garlic, or fried gyoza stuffed with *shiso* (Japanese basil)—but it's so tasty, it draws crowds daily. A few side dishes, such as boiled cabbage with vinegar, *moyashi* (bean sprouts) with a spicy minced-meat sauce, and rice, are also available, as are beer and sake. A U-shaped counter encloses the greasy open kitchen, which diners can watch as they chow down. There's usually a queue out the door, but this isn't the kind of place people linger, so waiting time is minimal. English language menu available.

6–2–4 Jingumae. ✆ **03-3406-4743.** Gyoza ¥380–¥420 for a plate of 6. Daily 11:30am–9:10pm (last order). No credit cards. Station: Meiji-Jingumae (3 min.), Harajuku (5 min.).

Maisen (まい泉) ♥♥ TONKATSU Plenty of Tokyoites consider this the best *tonkatsu* (deep-fried breaded pork cutlet) restaurant in the city. In business since 1965, it now has several locations around town, including the basement of Daimaru department store and the Hikarie Building in Shibuya. But this is the main store and the most atmospheric, with a dining hall ensconced in what was once the dressing room of a pre–World War II public bathhouse, where a tall ceiling and other original architectural details hint at its former life. The English-language menu lists various dishes and set meals, the most famous of which features *tonkatsu* made from black pig from Kagoshima, which has a sweet, more intense flavor than regular pork. *Tonkatsu* comes with finely shredded cabbage and Maisen's own sauce. Lunch specials, available until 4pm, are listed only in Japanese, but photos are provided. A takeout window offers various bento boxes, tonkatsu sandwiches, and Maisen products, including its own curry sauce.

4–8–5 Jingumae. mai-sen.com. ✆ **03-3470-0071.** Set lunches ¥1,150–¥1,680; set dinners ¥1,880–¥3,900. Daily 11am–9pm (last order). Station: Omotesando (A2 exit, 4 min.).

Roppongi

See Roppongi map, p. 159.

Because Roppongi is such a popular nighttime hangout for young Tokyoites and foreigners, it has a large number of both Japanese and Western restaurants. About a 12-minute walk west of Roppongi is **Nishi Azabu,** with more restaurants and bars. Between Roppongi Crossing and Nishi Azabu is **Roppongi Hills,** a sprawling urban development with many choices in dining. **Toranomon Yokocho,** an indoor marketplace on the third floor of **Tornamon Hills Business Tower** (located between Roppongi and Tokyo Stations), offers tasty and reasonably priced lunch deals, including Japanese soul food as well as Korean, Thai, Hong Kong, and Okinawan fare.

Meet Me in Roppongi

To find the location of any of the Roppongi addresses listed here, stop by the tiny police station on Roppongi Crossing (Roppongi's main intersection of Roppongi Dori and Gaien-Higashi Dori) to study a map of the area or ask for directions. Catty-corner from the police station, on the other side of the overhead expressway, is the number-one meeting spot in Roppongi, in front of Almond coffee shop. If you're meeting someone, this will likely be the spot.

EXPENSIVE

Florilège ♥♥♥ FRENCH-JAPANESE This high-end restaurant is dining as theater—not in the spatula-juggling fashion of American teppanyaki chefs, but in the meticulous approach that head chef Hiroyasu Kawate and his cadre of cooks use to prepare and present the multicourse tasting menu. Take a seat at the communal *table d'hôte* and sip your aperitif as the waiter introduces the restaurant and menu. The food is emblematic of classic French cooking techniques, but sustainability is core to Kawate's vision, so local ingredients are paramount. Most dishes celebrate Japanese vegetables and the accompanying season, while a buttery beef carpaccio (from breeding cows past their reproductive years) has long been a menu stalwart. Like a growing number of top-class Tokyo eateries, Florilège distances itself from traditional Japanese fine dining, in which cooking is a serious affair and a welcoming atmosphere irrelevant; its selling point is its warm vibe as much as the outstanding food. The restaurant, which moved to a new location in 2023, holds two Michelin stars and was voted the second-best in Asia in 2024, so don't expect it to be cheap. It's a special occasion dinner, a once-a-blue-moon kind of experience, and if you treat it as such, the bill at the end of the evening might not seem so egregious. (That said, you can slash the cost of the food by 50% if you go for lunch instead.) Reservations can be made online up to 1 month in advance (four guests maximum); dietary requirements may be accommodated upon request. 5–10–7 Toranomon, 2F Garden Plaza D Azabudai Hills. aoyama-florilege.jp/en/. ✆ **03-6435-8018.** Lunch menu ¥11,000 (wine and cocktail pairing ¥7,700), dinner menu ¥22,000 (wine and cocktail pairing ¥12,000). Station: Kamiyacho (5 min.), Roppongi-Itchome (10 min.).

Fukuzushi (福鮨) ♥♥♥ SUSHI Tokyo has thousands of sushi restaurants in all price ranges, but this classy spot has proven the test of time with its superb fresh fish and devoted following. Founded in 1917 and now in a new location under its fourth generation of owners—a wonderfully accommodating husband-and-wife team—it has a templelike entrance that beckons with lit lanterns, an overhanging maple tree, and beguiling dark wood slats. Yet inside it's all contemporary Tokyo, with pop-out reds contrasted against black furnishings, a now-iconic decor which enhances the theater of the dining experience. Because the solo chef goes to market daily, the menu is everchanging. Set dinners tell the story of the season through aquatic produce, and may feature tuna, bonito, *uni* (sea urchin), snapper, grouper, shrimp, *tai* (sea bream), and *anago* (saltwater eel), most served raw, some lightly seared. The *negitoro* (minced raw tuna roll) has been a specialty since the owner and host's great-grandfather ran the store in the mid-Taisho era and remains a menu highlight. Reservations should be made up to 35 days in advance—the easiest way to do this is through the reservation form on the website; you pick your course option before arriving. Lunch may be available upon request (English accommodated via email or telephone). Complex 665 1F, 6–5–24 Roppongi, Minato-ku. roppongifukuzushi.com. ✆ **03-3402-4116.** Tasting sets from ¥24,200. Mon–Sat 5–10pm. Station: Roppongi 1A exit (1 min.).

Tokyo Shiba Toufuya Ukai ♥♥♥ TOFU Practically in the shadows of Tokyo Tower, this restaurant has such a serene setting and lush gardens that it instantly transports customers to another time and place. Specializing in classic tofu cuisine, the restaurant is spread over several structures that are remakes of traditional architecture, from the *kura* (warehouse) with its thick, white walls and vaulted door to the main building with heavy beams and foot-thick lacquered pillars (once part of an old farmhouse in Takayama). Surrounding the buildings are exquisite gardens, tended by three full-time gardeners, with ponds, streams, gnarled pines, stone lanterns, arched bridges, and strolling paths (be sure to walk through the back garden after your meal). The main dining hall overlooks the back garden, but most guests opt for private *tatami* rooms, many also with garden views. It offers only set meals, which change with the seasons and are

Right by Tokyo Tower and Roppongi's nightlife scene, Tokyo Shiba Toufuya Ukai offers a contrast: a serene garden setting and traditional tofu cuisine.

explained on an English-language menu. The least expensive lunch (available only weekdays) may start with a lotus root cake with sea urchin and deep-fried tofu coated with miso sauce, followed by assorted sashimi, deep-fried simmered tofu with crab, a main dish, tofu boiled in a seasoned soy milk, rice with sweet potato, and dessert. Reservations are a must.

4-4-13 Shibakoen. ukai.co.jp. ✆ **03-3436-1028.** Set lunches ¥8,800; set dinners ¥14,000–¥22,000. Mon–Fri 11:45am–3pm and 5–9:30pm; Sat–Sun and holidays 11:30am–9:30pm (last order 7pm). Station: Akabanebashi (5 min.).

INEXPENSIVE

Ganso Aburadou (元祖油堂) ♥♥ NOODLES Diners queue for the *maze soba* (ramen without the broth) at this noodle shop in the swanky Kamiyacho area. What differentiates it from your standard soupless ramen, though, are the toppings: bacon slices, parmesan cheese, and raw egg yolk (it's like the offspring of ramen and spaghetti carbonara). Ramen is one of the most creative sectors of the Tokyo dining scene, and this seemingly bizarre combination (the brainchild of Taiwanese chefs) carries serious umami heft. Order at the vending machine, where you'll also find optional self-serve toppings like minced or pickled ginger, garlic, curry powder, nori seaweed, sesame seeds, and cajun spice. If you're visiting the Azabudai Hills complex, the location of teamLab Borderless and various other art galleries, this is an excellent and budget-friendly lunch option.

5-2-7 Toranomon, Minato-ku. shop.gift-group.co.jp/band/gansoaburadou. Maze soba ¥880–¥1,230. Daily 11am–10:30pm. Station: Kamiyacho (1 min.).

Joumon Roppongi ♥♥♥ KUSHIYAKI This hipster *kushiyaki* restaurant specializes in seasonal grilled delicacies, like scallops in butter soy sauce or yellowtail in teriyaki sauce, as well as serving other items like chicken breast with wasabi, seared Japanese beef, homemade sesame tofu, salads, and noodle dishes. Or, order eight skewers chosen by the chef for ¥1,780. Reservations are required, with seating either at the low counter (best for watching the action in the kitchen) or one of the tables in back.

5-9-17 Roppongi. teyandei.com. ✆ **03-3405-2585.** Skewers ¥200–¥500. Main dishes ¥580–¥1,680. Daily 5–10:30pm (last order). Station: Roppongi (4 min.).

Shibuya

See Shibuya map, p. 163.

In addition to the recommendations here, there's a food hall, called **Niku Yokocho** (meaning "Meat Alleyway") on the second/third floors of the Chitose Kaikan building (13–8 Udagawacho). Filled with 28 meat-themed restaurants serving everything from yakitori, yakiniku, and teppanyaki to meat sashimi, Mongolian mutton (a delicacy in the north), and Hamburg steaks, it's a great spot to try a few different cuisine styles in 1 night. See **nikuyokocho.jp/en/** to find out more.

EXPENSIVE

DEN ♥♥♥ JAPANESE It takes some gumption to run a two-Michelin-star restaurant and serve diners a single chicken wing in a cardboard box, or a garden salad that looks entirely unassuming except for a smiley face carved into a slice of carrot. But once you start chowing down on head chef Zaiyu Hasegawa's irreverent and playful dishes, you realize there's meticulous method to his (self-admitted) madness. DEN was anointed Asia's best restaurant in 2022, and such accolades don't come by accident. Sitting at the long cypress-wood chef's table, you'll gaze up into the open kitchen, where the chefs work in a state of collective calm. But that's not to suggest DEN is austere; conversation flows (as do the wine and sake), the atmosphere is vibrant and communal, and the tasting menu is one of endless creativity. In a way, the less you know about it the better—the restaurant likes to keep things mysterious—but let's just say it lives up to its billing. And the service? Exceptional, even by Japanese standards (I even got a hug from Hasegawa-san on the way out). If you only go to one fine-dining restaurant in Japan, make it this one. Reservations open 2 months in advance, accepted between noon and 5pm JST, but they are notoriously difficult to get. It's worth putting yourself on a waiting list, though, as cancellations can and do happen. 2–3–18 Jingumae, Shibuya-ku. jimbochoden.com/. ✆ **03-6455-5433.** Dinner ¥20,000 (price may fluctuate based on availability of ingredients). 10% service charge and 10% tax added. Mon–Sat dinner seating 6pm (starting at 7 or 8pm, may be available upon request). Closed irregular days. Station: Gaienmae (10 min.), Kokuritsu-Kyogijo (13 min.).

Mark's Tokyo ♥♥♥ ITALIAN-JAPANESE Eponymous head chef Mark Sekita has a pretty simple philosophy: Going out for a meal should feel like getting a warm hug. Fusing his Italian-American and Japanese heritages, his small chef's table restaurant has all the cool minimalism of modern Japan, while the menu brings the heart and simplified flavor of the land of la dolce vita. Sekita goes to market each week and grabs whatever local vegetables are in season—alongside scraps about to be discarded, to mitigate waste—and brings them to life in the kitchen. Dishes change every week, but follow a pattern of soup, seafood, pasta, meat dish, dessert, with Japanese flavors working as the undertones. Sekita also chats to diners (in Japanese and English) as though they were guests invited into his home—if you have questions about the wine list or the base flavor of a sauce, or simply want to know about his California childhood or his background working in finance, feel free to ask. Reservations recommended. Almost all dietary requirements can be accommodated. 1–23–14 Meguro. markstokyo.com/marks/. ✆ **03-6417-0664.** Omakase course ¥10,450, Hawaiian brunch ¥4,950. Wed–Fri and Sun 6–10pm; Sat 5–10pm; monthly Sat brunch 11am–2pm. Station: Kamiyacho (7 min.).

MODERATE

Kinniku Shokudo ♥♥ JAPANESE/HEALTHY Kinniku ("Muscle") Shokudo is all about eating heartily with none of the guilt. It markets itself as a "restaurant for your body," but by no means is this a substitute for taste. The menu features diced beef fillets, lean hamburger steaks, skinless chicken with salt *koji* (from a fungal mold containing up to 100 digestion-facilitating enzymes), raw horse meat, and eggs boiled, pickled, whipped into omelets, blitzed into sauces, shorn of their yokes, or sliced and stacked like pancakes. It's a worthwhile spot for proponents of paleo, keto, or primal diets who struggle to adhere to their eating regimes while traveling; if you're one for keeping score, every dish on the menu includes its calorific, protein, fat, and carbohydrate content. The chef's recommendations (unsurprisingly, the priciest items on the menu), are the wagyu and Australian fillet steaks (ordered by weight). You can also order the "Runner's Plate," featuring chicken, salmon, egg, tuna salad, almonds, rice or cabbage, soup, and a protein drink for ¥2,480. Or pick a main item off the menu and combine it with a rice (white or brown) and soup combo for an extra ¥400. English menu available. Between lunch and dinner, a coworking space and cafe serves only drinks.

Miyashita Park shopping complex, south wing, 3rd floor, 6–20–10 Jingumae. kin-nikushokudo.jp. ✆ **050-3188-5908.** Set lunches ¥1,000–¥1,800; steaks ¥4,500–**¥9,000;** main dishes ¥1,280–¥2,500. Mon–Fri lunch 11am–2:30pm (last order); dinner 5:30–10pm (last order). Station: Shibuya (Hachiko exit, 6 min.).

Other Neighborhoods

EXPENSIVE

Hachoji Ukai Tei ♥♥♥ TEPPANYAKI There are branches of Ukai Tei in Omotesando and Roppongi, but the Hachioji location, deep in the western suburbs on the tip of urban Tokyo, is the grandest of them all, in a building full of Taisho-era opulence, when Japanese and Euro-American aesthetics began to merge. Earthy colors, floral motifs, and East Asian spiritual iconography pair well with plush antique furnishings, art nouveau mosaics, and a courtyard with neoclassical flourishes. The set menus are an elegant reflection of the season, cooked by chefs who serve diners directly from the other side of a *teppan* (steel hot plate). The last time I visited, at the tail end of autumn, chestnut soup, buttery scallops, grass-fed wagyu beef, and a lighter-than-air chiffon cake with black sugar cream all featured in the meal—robust, no doubt, but unlike some hearty meals, it didn't leave me feeling as if I'd poured cement into my stomach. Private rooms are available, but the best atmosphere is around the crescent-shaped chef's table on the second floor.

2–14–6 Akatsukicho, Hachioji. ukai.co.jp/hachioji/. ✆ **042-626-1166.** Lunch ¥11,000–¥16,500, dinner ¥18,700–¥28,600. Daily 11:30am–4pm and 5–9:30pm. Station: Hachioji or Keio Hachoji (10 min. by taxi).

MODERATE

Hatos Bar ♥♥ BBQ Japanese meat is often sliced, diced, served as carpaccio, lightly battered, or presented in some kind of elegant, less-is-more fashion. But Hatos Bar in Nakameguro—part BBQ pit, part craft beer taproom—caters to carnivores who like their meat whole and generously portioned. Menu favorites include racks of smoky BBQ ribs, pork belly, pulled pork sandwiches, chili fries, and mac & cheese. The staff also place bottles of Frank's RedHot sauce on the tables, a surefire indicator of good taste. There's al fresco seating for balmy evenings; otherwise, try to snag the comfy seats in the corner of the restaurant (especially if you come in a group). For beers, check out the chalkboard menu and the fridge filled with bottles from various microbreweries. Ask staff for the natural wine selection.

1–3–5 Nakameguro, Meguro. hatosbar.org/top. ✆ **03-6452-4505.** Ribs ¥2,200–7,480; main dishes ¥1,100–1,980. Mon–Sat 3pm–midnight (10pm last food order). Station: Nakameguro (6 min.), Ebisu (Hibiya exit 4 or 5, 9 min.).

INEXPENSIVE

Dandan Sakaba (だんだん酒場) ♥♥ GYOZA Dandan Sakaba is a gyoza chain—many expats know it simply as "Juicy Dumpling"—but the menu also has salads and side items that appear prosaic until you chopstick them into your mouth and are hit with explosions of flavor. The *yaki*-gyoza (fried), *sui*-gyoza (boiled and served in soup), and *tebasaki*-gyoza (deboned chicken wings stuffed with minced meat) are musts, but I also recommend the *chashu* pork and the horse sashimi platter (a surprisingly common izakaya food), as well as the onion and ponzu salad, the coriander and sesame dressing salad, and the cabbage mountain salad doused in a creamy sauce and *katsuobushi* (dried and smoked bonito flakes). The Shimokitazawa branch is one of the liveliest, packed with students and young hipster types throughout the week (be sure to ask for the English menu), but you'll also find Dandan Sakaba shops in Gotanda, Asakusa, Aoyama, Kita-Senju, Ebisu, Shinjuku, Ikebukuro, and near Tokyo Station.

2–10–10 Kitazawa, Setagaya-ku. dandadan.jp. ✆ **03-6407-0804.** Dinner ¥2,500–¥3,500. Daily 11:45am–midnight. Station: Shimokitazawa (Inokashira exit, 1 min.).

Niigata Sanpoutei Tokyo Labo (新潟三宝亭 東京ラボ) ♥♥ RAMEN/FUSION Tokyo has the most innovative ramen scene in Japan, and it's becoming more and more common to find decidedly un-Japanese ingredients in shops' signature soups—parmesan and bacon, chicken mousse, pineapple, tomato, pizza toppings, even coffee. Niigata Sanpotei Tokyo Labo, which has another "noodle laboratory" in Bandai City, serves ramen inspired by *mapo tofu,* a Chinese dish of silken tofu, minced pork, Szechuan peppercorns, and *doubanjiang* chili paste. The combination of springy noodles, a gelatinous mapo soup, and numerous toppings makes an already dense meal even denser, but the unique and fiery flavor profile is undeniably addictive. There are three main menu options—hot-and-sour soup, Chinese chive and leek soba, and All-fatty Mapo Noodles (the signature dish)—all of which cost a mere ¥1,150. Beers and sake from some of the top breweries in Niigata Prefecture are also available. The menu is in Japanese only.

2–44–5 Kamimeguro, Meguro. sanpou-g.co.jp/tokyolab. ✆ **03-5725-3356.** Ramen ¥1,150. Mon–Fri 11:30am–3pm and 5:30–11pm (last orders), Sat–Sun and holidays 11:30am–11pm (last order). Station: Nakameguro (6 min.).

COOKING classes

With Japanese food firmly among the world's most popular cuisines, many travelers now view a journey through the archipelago as one extended culinary pilgrimage. This has led to a boom in English-language cooking classes, where guests learn how to prepare classic dishes like ramen, sukiyaki, sushi, okonomiyaki, and *teishoku* sets. You could easily spend a couple weeks in Tokyo attending a new class each day and honing your chopping, preparation, and cooking skills with kindly local chefs and cooks. While a love of food is expected, no real cooking expertise is required, and generally you'll get an instruction leaflet to take with you so you can recreate the meal at home.

Cooking Sun (cooking-sun.com; ✆ **03-6380-6028**) in Shinjuku is one of the most approachable cooking schools, offering two main classes. One teaches you how to cook a wagyu and a 7-dish set meal, including a sesame potato salad, *tamagoyaki* (a rolled omelet), miso soup, and a Japanese dessert; the other focuses on hand-pressed sushi techniques. Classes are ¥9,500 per person (with discounts if you're in a group); children pay ¥6,000. The cooking school also offers a more bespoke ramen and gyoza class—you'll cook both elements from scratch—starting at ¥40,000 per person. Cooking Sun classes last 3 hours; the school also has branches in Kyoto and Osaka.

Located in Asakusa's Kappabashi area (where chefs from Tokyo and beyond buy handmade knives and other high-quality kitchen utensils), **Chagohan** (chagohan.tokyo; ✆ **03-6802-8248**), run by husband-and-wife team Masa and Junko, offers a range of classes, from cooking traditional Japanese hotpots or Osaka-style okonomiyaki to handmaking soba and tempura; another option tours Adachi Market and uses local produce to craft *nigiri* sushi rolls. Some classes are private (and therefore much more expensive), but you will get discounts based on group size. Shared classes start at ¥13,200, private classes from ¥66,000. See website or enquire with the cooking school to find out more.

Rainbow Bird Rendezvous ♥♥ VEGAN Despite that fact that Zen monks have abstained from animal products for centuries, in Japanese food circles veganism is still treated as though it were an in-vogue health fad, rather than a dietary choice influenced by a wide variety of factors. But Tokyo has a growing cohort of vegan and vegetarian eateries, and this cafe in trendy Meguro-ku is one of the most popular, serving colorful salads, meat-substitute burgers, raw smoothies, and coffees with plant-based milks. The takeout bento boxes (¥750–¥1,300) are typical of traditional Japanese cuisine, featuring rice, veg, tofu, and pickles, but sans meat products or fish stock.

1-1-1 Yutneji, Meguro-ku. ls-adventure.com. ✆ **03-3791-5470.** Lunch ¥1,110, dinner ¥1,550–¥1,650. Mon and Thurs–Fri 11:30am–3pm and 5–8pm; Sat–Sun 11:30am–7pm (last orders). Station: Yutenji (7 min.), Naka-meguro (8 min.).

TOKYO SHOPPING

It won't take you long to become convinced that shopping is the number-one pastime in Tokyo. Women, men, couples, and even entire families go on buying expeditions in their free time, making Sunday the most crowded shopping day of the week. Even those on a budget can shop; 100-Yen discount stores are virtually everywhere.

The Shopping Scene

BEST BUYS Tokyo is the country's showcase for everything from the latest in camera, computer, or music equipment to original woodblock prints, anime products, and designer fashions. Traditional Japanese crafts and souvenirs that make good buys include traditional toys, kites, Japanese dolls, carp banners, swords, lacquerware, bamboo baskets, *ikebana* (flower-arranging) accessories, ceramics, pottery, iron teakettles, chopsticks, fans, masks, knives, scissors, sake, incense, and silk and cotton kimono. And you don't have to spend a fortune: You can pick up handmade Japanese paper (*washi*) products—lanterns, boxes, stationery, and other souvenirs—for a fraction of what they cost in import shops in the United States. In Harajuku, stores sell the latest fashion craze at cheap prices, and you can still find traditional shoe shops with cheap prices on everything from leather dress shoes to hiking boots. Reproductions of famous woodblock prints make great inexpensive gifts, and most items—from pearls to electronic video and audio equipment and even food—can be bought tax-free if you spend over a certain amount in one store (see "Taxes," below).

GREAT SHOPPING AREAS Another enjoyable aspect of shopping in Tokyo is that specific areas are often devoted to certain goods. **Asakusa** is the place to go for Japanese souvenirs from fans to T-shirts, while **Akihabara** is packed with shops selling new and retro electronics and pop-culture-related items. **Ginza** is the chic address for high-end international designer brands and art galleries. **Aoyama** (see box on p. 185) has the city's largest concentration of Japanese designer-clothing stores and an ever-increasing number of international names on **Omotesando Dori,** while nearby **Harajuku** and **Shibuya** are the places to go for youthful, fun, and streetwear fashions.

Kappabashi is the place to go for kitchen pottery and cookware.

Shimokitazawa is a great place for **vintage clothing**—the neighborhood draws comparisons to the likes of Williamsburg, NY, and Shoreditch in London—while Koenji, Kichijoji, and even Kita-Senju also have cool secondhand clothes at competitive prices.

HITTING THE designer boutiques IN AOYAMA

For top Japanese designers, the blocks between Omotesando Crossing and the Nezu Museum in Aoyama (station: Omotesando, 2 min.) are the Rodeo Drive of Japan. Even if you can't afford the steep prices, a stroll is de rigueur for clothes hounds and anyone interested in design. Most shops are open daily from 11am to 8pm. **Issey Miyake** (isseymiyake.com; ✆ **03-3423-1408**), on the left side as you walk from Aoyama Dori, offers two floors of cool, spacious displays of Miyake's interestingly structured and colorful designs for men and women. His very popular **Pleats Please** line is next door (✆ **03-5772-7750**). Across the street is **Comme des Garçons** (comme-des-garcons.com; (✆ **03-3406-3951**), Rei Kawakubo's showcase for her daring—and constantly evolving—men's and women's designs (even her shop is constantly evolving). The goddess of Japanese fashion and one of the few females in the business when she started, Kawakubo has remained on the cutting edge of design for 5 decades. Farther down the street on the right is **Yohji Yamamoto** (yohjiyamamoto.co.jp; ✆ **03-3409-6006**), where Yamamoto's unique, classically wearable clothes are sparingly hung, flaunting the avant-garde interior space.

Of the many non-Japanese designers to have invaded this trendy neighborhood, including **Alexander McQueen** and **Stella McCartney,** none stands out as much as **Prada** (✆ **03-6418-0400**), a bubble of convex/concave windows on the right side of the street.

The best place to shop for **cookware** is **Kappabashi-dougugai Dori** (kappabashi.or.jp; station: Tawaramachi), popularly known as Kappabashi; it's Japan's largest wholesale area for cookware, but most stores sell to individual shoppers as well. The approximately 150 specialty stores here sell everything a restaurant needs, including sukiyaki pots, woks, lunch boxes, pots and pans, aprons, knives, china, lacquerware, rice cookers, plastic food (the kind you see in restaurant display cases), *noren* (Japanese curtains), and disposable wooden chopsticks in bulk. Stores are closed on Sunday.

TAXES A 10% consumption tax is included in the price of marked goods, but all major department stores and tourist shops will refund the tax to foreign visitors if the total purchases in 1 day in any one store amount to more than ¥5,000 (excluding tax) for general items like household goods, clothing, and accessories, as well as for consumables like food and cosmetics, provided you don't consume them in Japan. Stores generally charge a service fee for the refund, equivalent to 1.1% of your total tax-free purchases, and you must present your passport. Note however that after an investigation concluded that most visitors were in fact consuming tax-free purchases in Japan, the government plans to revise the system, starting in November 2026. After that time, visitors will buy products at prices including the 10% consumption tax and have the tax refunded after their items are checked against their purchase records at customs.

omotenashi: SERVICE WITH AN EXTRA SOMETHING

One of the most wonderful aspects of the Japanese department store is the *omotenashi*, the **courteous service.** If you arrive at a store as its doors open at 10 or 10:30am, you'll witness a daily rite: Lined up at the entrance are staff members who bow in welcome. Some Japanese shoppers arrive just before opening time so as not to miss this favorite ritual. Salesclerks are everywhere, ready to help you. In some stores, you don't even have to go to the cash register once you've made your choice; just hand over the product, along with your money, to the salesclerk, who will return with your change, your purchase neatly wrapped, and an *"Arigatou gozaimashita"* ("Thank you very much"). Many department stores will also ship your purchases home for you, send them to your hotel, or hold them until you're ready to leave the store. A day spent in a Japanese department store could spoil you for the rest of your life.

Department Stores & Complexes

Japanese department stores are institutions in themselves. Enormous, well-designed, and chock-full of merchandise, they also sometimes include museums and art galleries, travel agencies, restaurants, grocery markets, and on the rooftop, playgrounds, greenhouses, and even shrines. You could easily spend an entire day in a department store—eating, attending cultural exhibitions, planning your next vacation, exchanging money, and of course, shopping.

Most department stores include **boutiques** by famous Japanese and international fashion designers, like Issey Miyake, Rei Kawakubo (creator of Comme des Garçons), Tsumori Chisato, Vivienne Westwood, Armani, and Paul Smith. Near the **kimono department** may also be a section of **traditional crafts,** including *ikebana* vases, pottery, and lacquerware. Many famous **restaurants** maintain branches in department stores, while in the basement (nicknamed *depachika,* a combination of *depa*—from department store—and *chika,* meaning "basement"), you'll find one or two levels devoted to **foodstuffs:** fresh fish, plant produce, green tea, sake, prepared snacks and dinners, and delectable pastries. There are often free samples of food, helpful if you just want a small snack.

To find out what's where, stop by the store's information booth on the ground floor near the front entrance and ask for the floor-by-floor English-language pamphlet (more and more department stores now have floor guides with English translation posted on walls near elevators and escalators). Be sure, too, to ask about **sales**—you never know what bargains you may chance upon. Department stores also have **tax-free counters** where you can get an immediate cash refund on taxes paid for items totaling more than a specific amount (see p. 700 in chapter 15), so make sure you bring your passport. They usually also have ATMs and Wi-Fi.

Commercial complexes (many owned by the Mori corporation and affixed with the name Hills—Roppongi Hills, Toranomon Hills, Omotesando Hills, Azabudai Hills) also draw in hordes of shoppers on weekends and weekday evenings. Usually, these will also have an art gallery and/or museum, open-air spaces with sculptures and artworks, dedicated floors of restaurants and cafes, perhaps an indoor market or a swanky new bar, as well as cinemas, event areas, hotels, offices, and private residences. They are like small cities in themselves and can take hours (or even days) to explore in any meaningful way.

Azabudai Hills ♥♥♥ Designed on the concept of a "forest city," including a huge central lawn and plaza and foliage sprouting from every nook of the seductively curving buildings, Azabudai Hills is a wonderful space to while away a few hours. Opened in fall 2023, it's an example of architecture as a social movement, where developments are designed to enhance the ways in which people interact with the city. Every part of the complex is interconnected, albeit in sometimes confusing ways, with sleek and airy interiors, all rounded edges and bathed in natural light. Foodies will delight at the huge indoor market with 31 specialist stores selling *meibutsu* (regional delicacies) from across Tokyo and Japan: *wagyu* beef, *yakitori, tonkatsu* (breaded pork cutlets), stocks and seasonings, French-style bread and pastries, and bento box sushi sets that would match the quality of Tsukiji or Toyosu's seafood fare. You can immerse yourself in the modern art scene at **teamLab Borderless** (p. 119) or genre-blending exhibitions at the Azabudai Hills Gallery. If you're in the mood to drop some yen on gladrags or extravagant jewelry, head to Hermes, Dior, or Cartier, each in a standalone building with a statement-making exterior design. And be sure to visit the Tower Plaza, with its fashion boutiques, the wonderful Ogaki Bookshop (with English-language coffee-table books on art, design, and architecture), and sleek bars and restaurants, like **Sawaan Bistro,** which serves innovative Thai cuisine. 1 Azabudai, Minato-ku. azabudai-hills.com/index.html. ✆ **03-6433-8100.** Station: Kamiyacho (1 min.). Opening hours vary by individual business.

The Azubudai Hills complex interconnects food, shopping, and modern art, with teamLab's Borderless.

Isetan ♥♥ With a history stretching some 130 years, Isetan is a favorite among foreigners visiting and living in Tokyo. Part of the Isetan-Mitsukoshi conglomerate, it has a good line of conservative work clothes, as well as contemporary and fashionable styles, including designer goods (Issey Miyake, Yohji Yamamoto, Junya Watanabe, and Tsumori Chisato), as well as a great kimono section along with all the traditional accessories (*obi,* shoes, purses). The tax-free counter is on the sixth floor. On the seventh floor are branches of well-known restaurants, including **Ten-ichi** (p. 165). The basement food hall is legendary, its dessert and massive chocolate sections an especially illuminating commentary on Japan's obsession with food. In its efforts to woo male shoppers, a 9-floor annex behind the main building caters entirely to men (it even has a golf school on the roof). 3–14–1 Shinjuku, Shinjuku-ku. isetan.mistore.jp/store/shinjuku. ✆ **03-3352-1111.** Daily 10am–8pm; restaurant floors open later. Station: Shinjuku Sanchome (1 min.) or Shinjuku (east exit, 6 min.).

Matsuya Ginza ♥♥ One of Tokyo's most famous department stores Matsuya—not to be confused with the cheap-and-cheerful beef bowl chain of the same name—has a good selection of Japanese folk crafts, kitchenware, and kimono, and beautifully designed contemporary housewares, in addition to the usual designer apparel ("queen" sizes are on the sixth floor). The seventh floor's Design Collection displays examples of fine design from around the world selected by the Japan Design Committee, from the Alessi teapot to Braun razors. Two basement floors are devoted to food. Also in the basement is the tax-free counter (Isetan does not charge a service fee). A branch is in Asakusa at 1–41–1 Hanakawado (✆ **03-3842-1111**). 3–6–1 Ginza, Chuo-ku. www.matsuya.com. ✆ **03-3567-1211.** Daily 11am–8pm; restaurant last order 9pm. Station: Ginza (2 min.).

Mitsukoshi ♥♥♥ This Nihombashi department store is one of Japan's oldest and grandest, founded in 1673 by the Mitsui family as a kimono store. In 1683, it became the first store in the world to deal only in cash sales; it was also one of the first stores in Japan to display goods on shelves rather than have merchants fetch bolts of cloth for each customer, as was the custom of the time. Today, housed in a building dating from 1935, it remains one of Tokyo's loveliest department stores, with a stately Renaissance-style facade and an entrance guarded by two bronze lions, replicas of the lions in

Mitsikoshi department store's elegant lobby.

Trafalgar Square. The store carries many name-brand boutiques, from Gucci to Prada. Its kimono, by the way, are still hot items. The tax-free counter is in the annex. Another branch is located at Ginza 4–chome Crossing (✆ **03/3562-1111**). 1–4–1 Nihombashi Muromachi, Chuo-ku. mitsukoshi.mistore.jp/store/nihombash. ✆ **03-3241-3311.** Daily 10:30am–7:30pm. Station: Mitsukoshimae (1 min.).

Omotesando Hills ♥♥ Architect Tadao Ando designed Omotesando Hills as an homage to the neighborhood; he wanted the 250m-long complex to befit its location on Omotesando Dori, the grand front approach to Meiji Shrine. Step inside to appreciate the depth of his vision: The seven-story mall plunges into the earth, with a triangular spiral walking platform that surrounds the main atrium, matching the look and angle of the main road outside. In classic Ando style, it's an exercise in marrying concrete with space, perspective, shadow, and light. Once you've taken in the epic interior, there are plenty of shops worth perusing, whether for apparel, jewelry, watches, cosmetics, or fashion accessories. The third-floor Galerie 412 usually has interesting exhibitions celebrating Japan's painters, sculptors, poets, writers, or musicians. And of course there's a restaurant floor with Italian, French, Japanese and Chinese cuisine, and the very reputable burger joint **Golden Brown.** 4–12–10 Jingumae. omotesandohills.com. ✆ **03-3497-0310.** Daily 11am–8pm; store opening hours vary. Station: Omotesando (2 min.).

Rayard Miyashita Park ♥♥♥ One of the many showcase architectural projects Tokyo hoped to reveal to the world for the 2020 Olympics, the Miyashita Park redevelopment spent its first 2 years hampered by Covid-19 conditions, but it's now one of Tokyo's finest shopping complex, a seamless extension of the Shibuya cityscape. The main shopping concourse hosts pop-up stores, mostly focusing on Japanese fashion and designer brands, as well as cafes, tea shops, and a souvenir store. Elsewhere you'll find international fashion brands, a dance studio, restaurants selling everything from burgers and tapas to dumplings and seafood rice bowls, and a store selling Studio Ghibli merchandise. The Miyashita Park rooftop, one of the mall's main draws, hosts a skatepark, a bouldering wall, a beach volleyball court, a manicured lawn, and the chic **Sequence Hotel,** with rooms offering some of the best views in the city. There's also a *yokocho* (dining alley) on the ground floor. Personally, I find it a little gimmicky—making something appear old and having an old-world atmosphere are not one and the same—but there are interesting hole-in-the-wall restaurants like **Rikishimeshi Man,** where sumo wrestlers cook steaming *chanko nabe* hotpots for diners. 6–20–10 Jingumae. miyashita-park.tokyo. ✆ **03-6712-5630.** Daily 11am–9pm. Station: Shibuya (3 min.).

Shibuya Parco ♥♥♥ This department store landed on many tourist's radars after a major 2019 redevelopment which included the opening of Japan's first official Nintendo store on the sixth floor—expect swooning tourists and long queues here. But there is much more to the 10-story behemoth. Walking through Parco is like wandering through the mind of Takashi Murakami: Everything is vibrant and arty and colorful and forever youthful. Each floor is themed, making it easier to find the right place to start browsing. The second floor ("Mode & Art") focuses on Japanese streetwear and creative fashion brands; the sixth floor ("Cyberspace Shibuya") is for pop-culture fans, with Capcom, Koei Tecmom and Pokémon shops alongside the Nintendo shop, an esports cafe, and Jump Shop for manga-related goods. You should also check out the galleries, pop-up apparel stores, collaboration events between manga artists and fashion designers, or the rooftop garden. And don't skip the basement floor, **Chaos Kitchen,** a social space designed by Sou Fujimoto, one of Tokyo's top young architects. It has a sake bar and a variety of delicious and innovative restaurants—**Masaka,** a fully vegan izakaya (the only one I've seen in Japan), is among the best. Udagawacho, 15–1. shibuya.parco.jp. ✆ **03-3464-5111.** Daily 11am–9pm (restaurants open later). Station: Shibuya (4 min.).

The Nintendo store at Shibuya Parco.

Shopping A to Z

ANIME & MANGA

In the past decade **Akihabara,** which has long had Japan's largest concentration of electronics shops, has also gained a reputation as *the* place to shop for manga (Japanese comic books and graphic novels) and items related to anime (Japanese animation) and cosplay (costume play), as well as for its maid cafes (see box on p. 192). For a guide on the best shops to visit, see the walking tour on p. 133. Serious shoppers will also want to make a pilgrimage to **Nakano Broadway Mall** at 5–52–15 Nakano (nbw.jp/#!/en; ✆ **03-3388-7004**), a 5-minute walk from the north exit of Nakano Station. It's known throughout the country as an *otaku* heaven for its slew of cubbyhole-size shops dedicated to both new and retro pop goods from Japan and overseas, including software, games, manga, figures, and anime and cosplay fare. Having gotten its start here, Mandarake is the biggest player, and the biggest in the world, with 30 different departments spread throughout the mall, each specializing in particular products, from manga and cosplay clothing to CDs of anime songs and figurines (✆ **03-3228-0007**). Nakano Broadway is open daily from 10am to 8pm.

Ikebukuro is as popular as Akihabara—if not more so—for female *otaku.* This energetic neighborhood on the northwestern side of Tokyo is a

Akihabara's maid cafes (see box on p. 192) are part of the district's otaku culture.

strange mix of highball-slugging salarymen and teenage girls hunting for popular *doujinshi* (fanzines) and Boys Love (BL) manga, a genre celebrating same-sex male relationships. The prime spot for manga and anime-related goods is Otome (Maiden) Road. Head to **K-books** for manga (1–13–13 Higashi-Ikebukuro); **Swallowtail** (3–12–12 Higashi-Ikebukuro) or **Suruga-ya** (1–32–1 Higashi-Ikebukuro) for wigs and cosplay items; or the **Animate Ikebukuro Main Store** to peruse 7 floors of pop-culture merchandise (1–20–7 Higashi-Ikebukuro)—the basement and floors 8 and 9 are dedicated event spaces. Cosplay is a thriving part of the Ikebukuro pop-culture trade. Every year, there's an **Ikebukuro Halloween Cosplay Festival** (ikebukurocosplay.jp), where you'll see some of the most accurate and creative depictions of cartoon heroes and heroines.

ANTIQUES, CURIOS & TRADITIONAL CRAFTS

In recent years, Japan's antiques trade has become a buyer-beware market, with fake antiques produced in China infiltrating the Japanese market. You shouldn't have any problems with the reputable dealers listed here, but if you're buying an expensive piece, be sure to ask whether it comes with papers of authenticity.

At **Nakamise Dori** (station: Asakusa), a pedestrian lane leading to Sensoji Temple in Asakusa, folk crafts are sold in a festival-like atmosphere. It's lined with stall after stall selling souvenirs galore, from hairpins worn by geisha to T-shirts, fans, umbrellas, toy swords, and dolls. Most are open daily from 10am to 6pm; some may close 1 day a week. The side streets surrounding Nakamise Dori, including Demboin Dori and a covered pedestrian lane stretching from both sides of Nakamise Dori, are also good bets.

Visiting Akihabara's Maid Cafes

While in Akihabara, you may want to experience the maid cafes, staffed by flirtatious young women in maid outfits. There are **@home Cafés** in the Mitsuwa Building, 1–11–4 Soto-Kanda (cafe-athome.com), on the fourth, fifth, sixth, and seventh floors, open daily 10am–10pm. It costs ¥780 to get in (discounts for students and children) and you must order at least one drink or set per person. These establishments are more cheesy than titillating, but you might still want to have your picture taken with a maid at an extra cost.

More good places to search for antiques and traditional crafts are **flea markets** (see p. 195), as well as **department stores** (p. 186), which usually have sections devoted to ceramics, pottery, bambooware, flower-arranging accessories, and kimono.

BEAMS ♥♥ Showcasing hip domestic Japanese brands, this six-story flagship store sells pottery, glassware, and other handicrafts as well as fashionable clothing and accessories, often with a pop-art emphasis. The inventory changes regularly and sometimes highlights a specific region in Japan. 3–32–6 Shinjuku. beams.co.jp/global/shop. ✆ **03-5368-7300.** Daily 11am–8pm. Station: Shinjuku Sanchome (2 min.) or Shinjuku (east exit, 5 min.).

Japan Traditional Crafts Aoyama Square (伝統工芸青山スクエア) ♥♥♥ Established to promote the country's artisans, this shop is a superb introduction to both traditional and contemporary Japanese design, with explanations in English about the products and where they're from. It sells top-quality crafts from all over Japan on a rotating basis, so there are always new items on hand. Crafts may include woodblock prints, lacquerware, ceramics, textiles, paper products, calligraphy brushes, fans, metalwork, knives, furniture, and sometimes even stone lanterns or Buddhist family altars (many items are also sold online). Be sure to look in the sliding drawers along the wall—these hold prints and other works of art. Prices are high, but rightfully so. Craftsmen are sometimes on hand, demonstrating their techniques—check the events calendar on the shop website. 8–1–22 Akasaka, Minato-ku. kougeihin.jp. ✆ **03-5787-1301.** Daily 11am–7pm (may change on first and last days of exhibitions). Station: Aoyama-Itchome (exit 4 north, 5 min.).

Yukari Antiques ♥ While not nearly as extensive as the old Antique Mall Ginza (now permanently closed), the half-dozen or so stalls here on the second floor of the Ginza 5 Building (located under an expressway) offer a variety of high-end antiques, including porcelain, furniture, dolls, swords, kimono, decorative items from the late-Edo, Meiji and Taisho periods, and other treasures from Japan and Europe, interspersed with stalls selling crafts, clothing, and jewelry. 5–1 Ginza, Chuo-ku. ✆ **03-5572-5559.** Daily 11am–7pm (some stalls closed Sun). Station: Ginza (exit C1, 1 min.) or JR Yurakucho (2 min.).

ELECTRONICS

Several areas around town are known for their electronics stores, especially just west of **Shinjuku Station,** where Yodobashi dominates with several shops devoted to electronics. The largest concentration of electronics and electrical-appliance shops in Japan, however, is in an area of Tokyo called **Akihabara,** also known simply as Akiba and centered on Chuo Dori (station: Akihabara). This is a must-see simply for its sheer size, with hundreds of multilevel stores, shops, and stalls. Even if you don't buy anything, it's great fun walking around. Most stores and stalls are open-fronted and painted in eye-catching colors. Salespeople yell out their wares, trying to get customers to look at cellphones, computers, digital cameras, TVs, watches, and rice cookers. This is the best place to see the latest models of everything electronic, as well as the retro goods that established Japan as an economic and cultural powerhouse in the latter half of the 20th century.

If you intend to buy, it pays to do some comparison shopping before you leave home so that you can spot a true deal—you can probably find these products just as cheaply, or even more cheaply, at home (laptops, for example, are expensive in Japan). On the other hand, you may be able to pick up something that's unavailable in your own country. Make sure that whatever you purchase is made for export—that is, with instructions in English, an international warranty, and the proper electrical connectors. Some of the old Japanese gaming consoles can only be used with power convertors, and games for these will also be region-linked—a Japanese PlayStation 1, for example, will only support discs made in Japan. All the larger stores have duty-free floors where products are made for export. Most shops are open daily from about 10am to 8pm or later.

A Haven for Booklovers

Jimbocho isn't on the wider tourism radar, but it's a personal favorite; a veritable haven for bibliophiles with as many as 200 bookshops. Some specialize in dusty old academic tomes—no surprise given Jimbocho is on the doorstep of Meiji University—some sell vintage magazines, others are full of arcane studies on Noh and kyogen theater. While many shops function like museum exhibits, there are some great English-language bookstores, too, like **@Wonder** for American comics and **Kitazawa Shoten,** a hub for antiquarian books since 1902.

Bic Camera ♥♥ This chain electronics store has about 40 shops in Japan, including its main shop in Ikebukuro and several locations in Shinjuku, Akihabara, and Shibuya. But this eight-floor store in Yurakucho is the largest, offering not only single-lens reflex, large and medium format, and digital cameras (plus all the accessories, including that all-important selfie extender), but also computers, cellphones, watches, eyeglasses, luggage, toys, home appliances, sporting goods, and much more. Note, however, that it caters primarily to Japanese; English-speaking salesclerks are scarce, and export models are limited. Ask for the English-language

The Yodobashi chain's huge Akihabara store is a mecca for electronics.

brochure, and, if you're buying sensitive equipment, make sure it will work outside Japan and comes with English-language instructions. 1–11–1 Yurakucho, Chiyoda-ku. biccamera.co.jp. ✆ **03-5221-1112.** Daily 10am–10pm. Station: Yurakucho (1 min.), Hibiya (exit D4, 3 min.), Ginza (6 min.).

Yodobashi Akiba ♥♥♥ Akihabara's largest store offers a staggering number of electronic-related goods such as phones, cameras, computers, printers, TVs, microwaves, vacuum cleaners, hair dryers, and more. It also offers a slew of other leisure-related items as well, including bicycles, games, luggage, and watches. Plus, it has 30 restaurants on the eighth floor. Yodobashi is found also in west Shinjuku, with a main shop and many branches specializing in various goods like watches or games. 1–1 Hanaoka-cho, Chiyoda-ku. yodobashi-akiba.com. ✆ **03-5209-1010.** Daily 9:30am–10pm. Station: Akihabara (1 min.).

FASHION

The **department stores** listed above (p. 186) are good places to check out the latest trends. For international designers, chic boutiques abound in **Ginza,** neighboring **Marunouchi,** and **Omotesando.** Otherwise, **Harajuku** and **Shibuya** are the places to go for hundreds of small shops selling inexpensive designer knockoffs, as well as fashion department stores—multistoried buildings filled with stores of various designers and labels, like **Shibuya 109,** which is always packed with teenagers.

Ginza Six ♥♥ The 13-story Ginza Six shopping complex houses 241 high-end international boutiques, restaurants, a basement food floor, and even a Noh theater and rooftop shrine and garden. Occupying what was once the full-block footprint of Matsuzakaya department store, this place is huge and especially popular with busloads of Chinese tourists with deep pockets. 6–10–1 Ginza. ginza6.tokyo. ✆ **03-6891-3390.** Daily 10:30am–8:30pm. Station: Ginza (2 min.).

La Forêt ♥♥♥ This is not only the largest store in Harajuku but also one of the most fashionable, appealing mostly to teenage and 20-something shoppers. Young and upcoming Japanese designers are here as well as established names, in boutiques spread on several floors. In addition to men's and women's fashions there are also shops selling jewelry, shoes, handbags, and other accessories. There's so much to see—from pink frilly dresses to Goth—you can easily kill a couple hours here. Note, however, that not all shops offer tax-free shopping, and since each shop is its own entity, you can't combine purchases to qualify for the tax refund. 1–11–6 Jingumae, Shibuya-ku. laforet.ne.jp. ✆ **03-3475-0411.** Daily 11am–9pm. Station: Meiji-Jingumae (1 min.) or Harajuku (4 min.).

Where to Buy Kimono

Chicago, on Omotesando Dori at 6–31–21 Jingumae in Harajuku (chicago.co.jp; ✆ **03-3409-5017;** station: Meiji-Jingumae or Harajuku), stocks hundreds of affordable used kimono, cotton *yukata* (casual kimono), and *obi* (sashes) back in the far left corner of the basement shop, past the used American clothes. It's so successful it has opened nearby branches, including a nicer and larger one practically next door. All are open daily from 11am to 8pm.

Department stores sell new kimono, notably **Takashimaya** and **Mitsukoshi** in Nihonbashi and **Isetan** in Shinjuku. They also hold sales for rental wedding kimono. Flea markets (see p. 195) are also good for used kimono and yukata.

Uniqlo ♥♥ Having taken the world by storm, Uniqlo specializes in inexpensive, basic clothing (think the Japanese version of Gap, but higher quality) and has 40-some outlets in Tokyo alone. This 12-story flagship store on Chuo Dori offers clothing for the whole family. Connected to Uniqlo in the back is the boutique **Dover Street Market,** with six small floors offering men's and women's fashions by Comme des Garçons, Miu Miu, Junya Watanabe, and other designers. 6–9–5 Ginza, Chuo-ku. uniqlo.com/jp. ✆ **03-6252-5161.** Daily 11am–9pm. Station: Ginza (2 min.). On Chuo Dori.

FLEA MARKETS

Flea markets are good places to shop for antiques and delightful junk. You can pick up secondhand kimono at very reasonable prices (usually around ¥1,000 or less), as well as kitchenware, vases, cast-iron teapots, woodblock prints, dolls, household items, and odds and ends. (Few good buys on furniture, though.) Bargaining is expected. Note that since most markets are outdoors, they tend to be canceled if it rains.

Ameya Yokocho ♥♥ (also referred to as Ameyoko, Ameyokocho, or Ameyacho; ameyoko.net) is the closest thing Tokyo has to a permanent flea market. It occupies a long but narrow area near Ueno Park that runs underneath the elevated tracks of the JR Yamanote Line, between Ueno and Okachimachi stations. Here you'll find stall after stall selling vegetables and discounted items ranging from cosmetics and handbags to tennis shoes, watches, and casual clothes. The scene retains something of the *shitamachi* spirit of old Tokyo. Housewives have been coming here for years, while more recently young Japanese have found it a good bargain spot for youthful fashions and accessories like baseball caps. Hours are usually daily from 10am to 7pm (some shops close on Wed); early evening is the most crowded time. Don't even think of coming here on a holiday—it's a standstill pedestrian traffic jam.

Hanazono Shrine ♥, 5–17–3 Shinjuku (✆ **03-3200-3093**), near the Yasukuni Dori/Meiji Dori intersection east of Shinjuku Station (Shinjuku Sanchome Station, 4 min.), has a small flea market every Sunday from about 8am to 2pm (except in May and Nov, due to festivals). Lots of wooden dolls, hair pins, obi sashes and kimono, woodblock prints and more. A 1-minute walk from Nogizaka Station, **Nogi Shrine ♥** (8–11–27 Akasaka; ✆ **03-3478-3001**) has an antiques flea market from 9am to dusk the fourth Sunday of each month except January and February. It has a lovely setting; the shrine commemorates General Nogi and his wife, both of whom committed suicide on September 13, 1912, to follow the Meiji

Weekends at the Farmer's Market

On the doorstep of Tokyo's United Nations University, the **Aoyama Farmer's Market ♥♥** (5–53–70 Jingumae; farmersmarkets.jp; info@farmersmarkets.jp) is a showcase of the best of Japanese produce—top Tokyo chefs will often source their ingredients from here. You'll find grapes and cherries with prices that surely include errant zeroes, corn cobs of the most magnificent size, fresh tangerine juice from oranges grown in Ehime, additive-free sweets made with seasonal fruits, ethically raised venison for dogs, apple jams and spreads from a farm in Azumino, and condiments of every color, derivation, and description. In amidst the colorful smorgasbords of fresh food, are traditional crafts and pop-up vintage clothing stalls, kitchenware and utensils for preparing and storing food, household antiques and curios, and craft beer and natural wine sellers. The market can feel a little boutique-y, and therefore expensive, but it's always worth a browse. Open 10am to 4pm every Saturday and Sunday.

Jars of artisanal pickles at the Aoyama Farmer's Market.

emperor into the afterlife. Their simple home and stable are on shrine grounds.

VARIETY STORES

Daiso ♥♥ The largest chain of 100-Yen shops in Japan (comparable to dollar stores in the U.S.), Daiso has more than 3,000 locations in the country and abroad. This four-story branch is one of the better discount stores, offering mostly its own brand goods, purchased directly from manufacturers (many of which are in China). Items, priced mostly at ¥100 or multiples thereof, include kitchenware, tableware, cosmetics, office supplies, candy, and other household goods and daily necessities, making it a good place to shop for cheap souvenirs such as chopsticks, plastic lunchboxes, and *ikebana* (flower-arranging) accessories. This place is so popular, there's usually a long queue at checkout. It adjoins **Bic Camera,** a discount electronics store. 1–19–24 Jingumae, Shibuya-ku. daisoglobal.com. ✆ **03-5775-9641.** Daily 9:30am–9pm. Station: Harajuku (north exit, 3 min.) or Meiji-Jingumae (4 min.).

Don Quijote (ドン・キホーテ) ♥ Teenagers and East Asian tourists don't seem to mind the jumble of everyday goods offered here, but the narrow aisles are claustrophobic and the incessant chatter of electronic voices advertising products is enough to send me into apoplexy. The shop offers household goods and gadgets, kitchen appliances, plastic lunchboxes, PEZ dispensers, sporting goods, electronics, clothing, cosmetics, toiletries, party items, Hello Kitty character goods, and much, much more, including cosplay fare such as maid costumes (a perennial favorite). Once you stumble into the adult goods section, usually behind a curtain with a sign warning off anyone under the age of 18, and see vibrators of every size and design imaginable, you'll realize there is probably nothing Don Quijote *doesn't* sell. Known for its discounted prices and late hours, Don Quijote has more than 50 branches in the Tokyo area. This Akihabara branch on Chuo Dori is open daily from 9am to 5am; branches on Yasukuni Dori (1–16–5 Kabuki-cho; ✆ **03-5291-9211;** station: Shinjuku) and in Roppongi (3–14–10 Roppongi; ✆ **03-5786-0811;** station: Roppongi) both open a mind-boggling 24 hours. 4–3–3 Soto-Kanda, Chiyoka-ku. donki.com. ✆ **03-5298-5411.** Station: Akihabara (3 min.).

Itoya ♥♥ If you're the sort of person who doesn't mind splurging on writing utensils, notebooks, journals, paper supplies, paintbrushes, coloring pencils, origami materials, book covers, canvases, photo frames, organizers, desk lights, or greeting cards, then Itoya in Ginza is the shop for you. "Stationery store" is an inadequate term to describe this narrow yet wonderfully stocked 12-floor shopping tower in the heart of Ginza. Items here can be pricey—I was given a diary cover that cost more than ¥13,000 yen—but the quality is undeniable. Behind the main store is a smaller Itoya (2–8–17 Ginza), where you can get neatly designed business cards or *hanko* (personal seals). There are also branches in department stores in

The Itoya store in Ginza stocks an inspiring wealth of beautiful stationery.

Tokyo—Keio Shinjuku and Tobu Ikebukuro; the smaller main shop, with less impressive stock, is on Yokohama's Motomachi shopping street. 2–7–15, Ginza, Chiyoda-ku. ito-ya.co.jp. ✆ **03-3567-1108.** Mon–Sat 10am–8pm; Sun 10am–7pm. Station: Ginza (2 min.) Ginza-itchome (1 min.).

Loft ♥ Seibu's store for the young homeowner sells tableware (chopsticks, *bento* boxes, sake cups, and so forth, on the third floor), cookware, glassware, bed linens, mobile phone accessories, cosmetics (the choice in face masks alone is bewildering), stationery and diaries, and more. Don't miss the fifth-floor variety goods department with character items, wind-up toys, and party goods, including some weird costumes and small plastic female figurines designed to hang from the side of a glass. 21–1 Udagawacho, Shibuya-ku. ✆ **03-3462-3807.** Daily 11am–9pm. Station: Shibuya (Hachiko exit, 4 min.).

Tokyu Hands ♥♥♥ Billing itself the "Creative Life Store," Tokyu Hands, part of the Tokyu chain, is a huge store for the serious homeowner and hobbyist, with everything from travel accessories (like padded eye masks), *noren* (doorway curtains), beauty products (including wigs), chopsticks, suitcases, miniature Shinkansen models, pet accessories, and kitchen knives. If there's a practical Japanese product you've decided you can't live without (lunchbox? bathroom slippers? hanging laundry rack?), this is a good place to look. You'll also find Tokyu Hands at 1–28–10 Higashi Ikebukuro beside the Sunshine City Building (✆ **03-3980-6111;** station: Higashi Ikebukuro or Ikebukuro) and in the Takashimaya Shinjuku complex (✆ **03-5361-3111;** station: Shinjuku). At the top of Inokashira Dori, 12–18 Udagawacho, Shibuya-ku. tokyu-hands.co.jp. ✆ **03-5489-5111.** Daily 10am–9pm. Station: Shibuya (Hachiko exit, 6 min.).

THE PERFORMING ARTS

For descriptions of Japanese traditional performance arts such as *kabuki* and *Noh,* see "Japanese Arts in a Nutshell," in chapter 2. In addition to the listings below, Tokyo also has occasional shows of more avant-garde or lesser-known performance art productions, including highly stylized Butoh dance performances and percussion demonstrations by Kodo drummers and other Japanese drum groups.

GETTING TICKETS If you're staying in a higher-end hotel, the concierge or guest-relations manager can usually get tickets for you. Otherwise, head to the theater or hall itself. An easier way is to go through one of many ticket services, such as **Ticket PIA;** ask your hotel concierge for the one nearest you. Lawson and FamilyMart convenience stores also sell tickets to many events from kiosks, but instructions are in Japanese only.

Kabukiza Theatre ♥♥♥ An easy walk from Ginza, Kabukiza Theatre Japan's largest and most famous *kabuki* theater. It has been rebuilt several times since it opened in 1889, but the most recent version thankfully preserves its eye-catching Momoyama-style facade (influenced by 16th-c. castle architecture). Like all *kabuki* theaters, its stage includes a revolving circle in its center, a platform that can be lowered below the floor level so that actors magically appear and disappear to dramatic effect, and a runway that extends into the audience. In the lobby, stalls sell *bento* lunch boxes and souvenirs (you're welcome to eat at your seat during intermission). There are *kabuki* productions most months of the year, with each production running for 25 days. Generally, each production consists of two shows—matinees staged from 11 or 11:30am to 4pm, and evening shows starting at around 4:30pm. Of course, unless you speak Japanese, you may not be able to understand what the actors are saying, but luckily English-language translation tablets (from ¥1,000) provide information about the plot, music, actors, and other aspects of *kabuki* so you can follow what's going on.

Tickets can be purchased at the box office in Basement Level 2 from 10am to 6pm and from automatic ticket dispensers. You can also make advance reservations by phone (✆ **03-6745-0888**) or online. Programs

The Popular Origins of *Kabuki*

Kabuki plays, all written before the 20th century, have plots that are easy to follow, with love, duty, and revenge popular themes. *Kabuki* developed as a form of entertainment for commoners in feudal Japan, so it doesn't have any of the highbrow seriousness attached to *Noh,* which was popular among the aristocracy. In fact, one of the best things about *kabuki* is the level of spectator engagement, with fans shouting out approval during particularly good performances. And of course, another interesting thing about *kabuki* is that all roles are played by men, even the female ones.

Opened in 1889, the grand Kabukiza Theatre is Japan's largest kabuki theater.

often run about 4 hours, but you can buy tickets for only part of a production. If you think one act (*makumi*) is enough and you don't mind being up in the balcony (on the fourth floor, a bit far from the stage), you can save money by buying single-act tickets (a single act may last 30 min.–2 hr.). These tickets, sold to the left of the main entrance, go on sale just before each act and are available on a first-come, first-served basis. Everyone in your party must be present and stand in line (that is, no substitutions and no one holding your place). Note that only 96 seats are available, with another 60 spaces for standing room only. You'll be assigned a number and allowed into the auditorium accordingly. There are no assigned seats, but by your place in line they'll be able to tell you whether you're standing or sitting. If you wish, you can buy tickets for consecutive acts as well.

On the fifth floor is a roof garden and the **Kabukiza Gallery,** where you can get a close look at *kabuki* costumes, stage props, old posters, and such daily from 10am to 6pm; admission is ¥600 for adults, ¥500 for children. It's a fun way to spend 20 minutes, especially if you aren't able to see a live performance (the museum shows kabuki videos). QR codes on the exhibit panels offer explanations in multiple languages.

4–12–15 Ginza, Chuo-ku. kabukiweb.net/theatres/kabukiza. ✆ **03-3545-6800;** ✆ 03-6745-0888 for reservations. Regular tickets ¥4,000–¥20,000, depending on program and seat location; single-act tickets ¥800–¥2,000, depending on time of day and length of show. Station: Higashi-Ginza (1 min.).

National Noh Theatre (Kokuritsu Nogakudo) ♥♥ *Noh* is performed at a number of locations in Tokyo, but this is the most famous stage. Opened in 1983, it's dedicated to presenting classical *Noh* and *kyogen,* with about three to five performances monthly, many of which have English subtitles. Tickets are often sold out in advance, but about 30 tickets are held back to be sold on the day of the performance. In addition, privately sponsored *Noh* performances are also held here, for which the admission varies. See **theatrenohgaku.org** for information on *Noh* performances staged throughout Japan.

4–18–1 Sendagaya, Shibuya-ku. ntj.jac.go.jp. ✆ **03-3432-1331** or 03-3230-3000 for reservations. Tickets ¥3,000–¥12,500. Station: Sendagaya or Kokuritsu Kyogijo (5 min.).

Tokyo Takarazuka Theater (Tokyo Takarazuka Kagekidan) ♥♥ The first Takarazuka troupe, formed in 1914 at a resort near Osaka, gained instant notoriety because all its performers were women, in contrast to the all-male *kabuki.* Today this world-famous, all-female troupe stages elaborate musical revues with dancing, singing, and gorgeous costumes. Performances range from Japanese versions of Broadway hits to original Japanese works based on local legends. Posters outside the box office show what's on and what's coming. Performances, with story synopses available in English, are scheduled throughout the year. Tickets are available at the box office, online or through **Ticket Pia.**

Tokyo Takarazuka Gekkjo, 1–1–3 Yurakucho, Chiyoda-ku. kageki.hankyu.co.jp/english. ✆ **03-5251-2001.** Cover ¥3,500–¥12,000. Same-day tickets (first-come, first-served) ¥2,500 for a seat, ¥1,500 for standing room. Station: Hibiya (1 min.).

Finding Out What's On

Keep an eye out for *Metropolis* (metropolisjapan.com) and *Tokyo Weekender* (tokyoweekender.com). Both publications have free print magazines, found in various locations around the city, like bars and restaurants, though these are published much less frequently than they used to be. Their respective websites have more regular listings for concerts, shows, festivals, and events. You should also check to see what's going on at www.timeout.jp. In addition, the *Japan Times* and *Daily Yomiuri* have entertainment sections. For an online rundown of what's happening at Tokyo's hundreds of venues, live houses, and clubs weekly, go to tokyogigguide.com.

Tokyu Theater Orb ♥♥ With a 2,000-seat auditorium, this is one of Tokyo's largest and most celebrated playhouses. The performance schedule includes Japanese-language adaptions of Western classics, such as *Les Miserables,* and English-language shows that have migrated to Tokyo from Broadway and London's West End, like the award-winning musical *Once* or Jonathan Larson's *Rent.* In typical Tokyo fashion, the theater engulfs the 11th floor of the Hikarie department store, and has all the bells and whistles necessary to allow big-budget productions to stay true to their original stagings. While seats are plentiful, tickets for the hottest shows can sell quickly, so it's best to buy in advance. Reservations should be made through the Bunkamura Ticket Center (✆ **03-3477-9999;** 10am–5pm), up to 15 days before the performance date. You can also buy tickets in person at the Tokyu Orb ticket desk (daily 11am–6pm) on the second floor of the Hikarie department store, next to the Shibuya station ticket gates, or on the same day in the theater's reception area. See theatre-orb.com/english/lineup/calendar/ for what's coming up.

Shibuya Hikarie 11th floor, 2–21–1 Shibuya. theatre-orb.com/english. ✆ **03-3477-9111.** Ticket average ¥12,000. Station: Shibuya (2 min.).

TOKYO NIGHTLIFE

By day, Tokyo's sprawl can make it seem monotonous and colorless. Come dusk, however, Tokyo comes into its own. The drabness fades, the city blossoms into a profusion of giant neon lights and billboards, and its streets fill with millions of overworked Japanese out to have a good time. Tokyo at night is one of the craziest cities in the world, a city that never gives up and never sleeps. Entertainment districts are as crowded at 3am as they are at 10pm, with many establishments open until the first subways start running after 5am. Whether it's jazz listening spaces, gay bars, secluded cocktail hideouts, or dance clubs that you're searching for, Tokyo has it all.

Tokyo's Top Nightlife Districts

Tokyo has several nightlife districts spread throughout the city, each with its own atmosphere, price range, and clientele. Before visiting any of the locales suggested below, be sure to just walk around one of these neighborhoods and absorb the atmosphere. The streets will be crowded, the neon lights will be overwhelming, and you never know what you might discover.

A chic and expensive shopping area by day, at night **Ginza** transforms itself into a dazzling entertainment district of restaurants, cocktail bars, and first-grade hostess bars at night. It's the most sophisticated of Tokyo's nightlife districts and can also be one of the most expensive. However, because Ginza has great restaurants and several hotels, I've included some reasonably priced recommendations for a drink if you happen to find yourself here after dinner. The cheapest way to absorb the atmosphere in Ginza is simply to wander about, particularly around **Namiki Dori** and its side streets. I also suggest looking up: A lot of the more interesting bars hide on the fifth or sixth floors of otherwise nondescript skyscrapers. Illuminated signage running vertically up the building will indicate the establishments you'll find on each floor.

Shibuya is as lively as it's ever been—and not just during the day when every tourist in Tokyo comes to take videos of the famous pedestrian crossing for their social media feeds. Imbibers here are naturally drawn towards ***Senta-gai*** (literally "Center District"), a neon-suffused street opposite Shibuya Station's Hachiko exit, the primary meeting spot in the area. There are some good bars here, like Whales of August (see p. 214), where all the cocktails are movie-themed, but the side streets off **Dogenzaka,** not far from the colloquially and accurately named "Love Hotel Hill," are much more charming. The cocktail bars, craft beer taprooms and izakaya here are by and large excellent, and some even

Mapping Out Tokyo's Nightlife

Once you've chosen a nightlife spot that appeals to you, you can locate it using the following neighborhood maps:

- To locate bars and clubs in **Ginza,** p. 143.
- To locate bars and clubs in **Shinjuku,** p. 154.
- To locate bars and clubs in **Roppongi,** p. 159.

Nightlife Spots for Every Taste

The most popular nightlife spots are drinking establishments, where the vast majority of Japan's office workers, college students, and expats go for an evening out. These places include **Western-style bars,** Japanese-style watering holes (***nomi-ya,*** literally "drinking place"), and ***izakaya,*** a Japanese-style pub serving food. ***Yakitori-ya,*** restaurant-bars that serve *yakitori* and other snacks, are included in this group. **Dancing** and **live-music venues** are also popular with young Tokyoites. At the low end of the spectrum are Tokyo's **topless bars, strip shows, massage parlors,** and **porn shops,** many of which are located in Kabuki-cho.

have outdoor seating (a rarity in Tokyo's busiest neighborhoods). You've also got the tiny but trendy bars on **Nonbei Yokocho,** an alleyway near Miyashita Park that keeps buzzing well into the wee hours. ***Note:*** At the end of 2024, in an attempt to curtail the nightly madness and its attendant litter, authorities enacted a street drinking ban on the streets surrounding Shibuya station, daily from 6pm to 5am.

In **Shinjuku,** northeast of Shinjuku Station, **Kabuki-cho** undoubtedly has the craziest nightlife in all of Tokyo: block after block of strip joints, massage parlors, porn shops, peep shows, love hotels, bars, restaurants, and, as the night wears on, drunken revelers. A world of its own, it's sleazy, chaotic, crowded, vibrant, yet surprisingly safe. (Despite its name, Shinjuku's primary night spot has nothing to do with *kabuki,* though at one time there was a plan to bring some culture to the area by introducing a *kabuki* theater—the plan never materialized, but the name stuck.) Kabuki-cho used to be the domain of businessmen out on the town, and was controlled by the *yakuza,* Japan's largest organized crime syndicate; nowadays, however, young Japanese, including college-age men and women, have claimed parts of it as their own, adding inexpensive eating and drinking venues to the mix. It has also become very popular with visiting tourists who enjoy simply walking about, passing everything from smoke-filled restaurants to street hawkers trying to tempt you onto the nth floor of a nondescript building. If you're looking for strip joints, topless or bottomless coffee shops, peep shows, or porn, I leave you to your own devices, but you certainly won't have any problems finding them. Just be sure you know what you're getting into; your bill may end up much higher than you bargained for, and drink spiking in such establishments is not unheard of.

About a 5-minute walk east of Kabuki-cho, just west of Hanazono Shrine, is a smaller district called **Golden Gai.** It's a warren of tiny alleyways leading past even tinier bars, each consisting of just a counter and a few chairs. Although many thought Golden Gai would succumb to land-hungry developers in the 1980s, the economic recession brought a stay of execution, and now Golden Gai has experienced a revival, with more than 200 miniature drinking dens lining the streets. Golden Gai first became popular with tourists for its uniquely Japanese vibe. That, however, has changed in recent years; most bars are now packed with drunk tourists, driving some establishments to post signs outside saying, "no tourists," or "regulars only." Table charges of ¥500 to ¥1,000 yen are common here, which may disincentivize you from bar hopping. When people visit Tokyo, I still like to show them Golden Gai, but there are similar areas elsewhere in the city (some mentioned below) that have retained their authenticity.

In the narrow alleys of Shinjuku's Golden Gai district, there are more than 200 tiny bars.

A 5-minute walk farther east is **Shinjuku Ni-chome** (pronounced "knee-chomay"). With 300-some bars, lounges, dance clubs, and shops, it's the largest LGBTQ-bar district in Japan, if not all of Asia. Its lively street scene makes this one of Tokyo's most vibrant nightlife districts.

To Tokyo's younger crowd, **Roppongi** is one of the city's most fashionable places to hang out. It's also a favorite with the foreign community, from models and business types to English-language teachers and tourists staying in Roppongi's posh hotels. Some Tokyoites complain that Roppongi is too crowded, too crass, and too commercialized (and has too many foreigners). However, for the casual visitor, Roppongi offers an excellent opportunity to see what's new and hot in the capital city. It's also easy to navigate because nightlife activity is so concentrated. There is one huge caveat, however: Roppongi's concentration of foreigners has also attracted the unscrupulous, with reports of spiked drinks and patrons passing out, only to awaken hours later to find credit cards missing or fraudulently charged for huge amounts. So never leave drinks unattended. Otherwise, consider signing up for a guided **Tokyo pub crawl** (see p. 212).

A little more off the beaten path, **Shimokitazawa,** "Shimo" for short, has long been viewed as a Tokyo renegade—a friend often calls it the "People's Republic of Shimokitazawa." A hub of artists, musicians, record collectors, and vintage fashion retailers, it has fought hard (not always successfully) against the corporate influence and major chain stores eating up the rest of the city. Shimo also has one of Tokyo's best nightlife scenes: The bars on **Chazawa Dori** often only close when the last customer decides to tumble out the door. **Good Heavens** (5–32–5 Daizawa), a pub run by affable Briton Paul Davies, has become the de facto home of international comedy in Tokyo. Despite its small size, headline acts have included Hannibal Buress, Aziz Ansari, and Ardal O'Hanlon.

Kichijoji is another neighborhood where nightlife pays no attention to the clock. The McDonalds by the station's Inokashira Park exit is packed on Saturday and Sunday mornings with revelers, hostesses, and door staff coming out of the pubs, clubs, and love hotels and heading straight for the Golden Arches. Most first-timers to Kichijoji will end up in **Harmonica Alley** (1–1–3 Kichijoji Honcho), an old flea market during the postwar

Harmonica Alley, in Kichijoji, stays busy well into the wee hours.

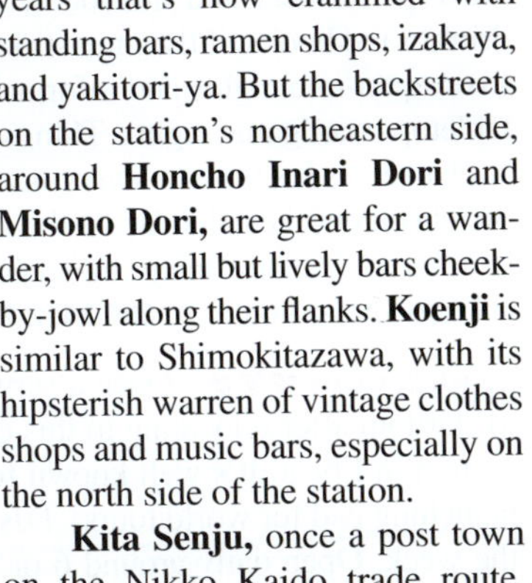

years that's now crammed with standing bars, ramen shops, izakaya, and yakitori-ya. But the backstreets on the station's northeastern side, around **Honcho Inari Dori** and **Misono Dori,** are great for a wander, with small but lively bars cheek-by-jowl along their flanks. **Koenji** is similar to Shimokitazawa, with its hipsterish warren of vintage clothes shops and music bars, especially on the north side of the station.

Kita Senju, once a post town on the Nikko Kaido trade route, deserves an honorable mention, too, and is worth visiting if you're staying in northern Tokyo, perhaps near Akihabara or Asakusa. Kita Senju's **Nomiya Yokocho,** "Drinking Place Alley," is one of the most authentically Japanese bar streets in the city, where you won't see large numbers of tourists. Standing beer bar **Beer-Ma** (2–62 Senju), is a great place to try local brews, while izakaya like **Agalico** (2–65 Senju) and **Pari-Pari** (2–39–18 Senju) mix their wide selections of alcoholic drinks with tasty finger food.

Live Music Clubs

The live-music scene exploded in the 1990s and is now available throughout the metropolis. In addition to the dedicated venues below, which represent only the tip of the iceberg, check out metropolis.co.jp, tokyoweekender.com, and tokyogigguide.com for more suggestions.

Crocodile ♥♥ Crocodile has spoken to generations of young Japanese with its casual rock-n-roll vibe and eclectic schedule of live bands, offering everything from rock and blues to jazz-fusion, reggae, soul, experimental, salsa, and country. It's a good place to mingle with a mostly Japanese crowd, except on the last Friday of every month, when the **Tokyo Comedy Store** (tokyocomedy.com) provides more than 2 hours of comedy and improv in English starting at 8pm for ¥2,200. Although it's a not a dance club per se, no one will mind if you just can't help yourself. Open daily 6pm to 1am; performances start around 7 or 8pm. 6–18–8 Jingumae, Shibuya-ku. crocodile-live.jp. ✆ **03-3499-5205.** Cover generally ¥2,500–¥3,500, more for big acts. Station: Meiji-Jingumae or Shibuya (10 min.).

Infinity Books ♥♥ Technically, this is a bookshop, with hand-built antique shelves and 15,000 secondhand English-language titles to choose from. But the proprietor, Yorkshireman Nick Ward, used to run pubs in Tokyo and has introduced elements from his old business into his new one. On Friday and Saturday evenings, local musicians and singers crowd around tables in the corner of the bookshop and jam or play sets to the other performers and attendees. Events are free of charge but buying drinks (and books, if the urge strikes) is encouraged. Event run the gamut from open-mic nights and informal live sessions to stand-up comedy and tabletop boardgame nights. Things usually start around 8pm and run until Nick decides it's time for everyone to leave (often very late). To see what's on, check out the calendar on the shop website. 1–2–4 Azumabashi, Sumida-ku. (past Azumabashi Bridge, turn right on main road after the Asahi Beer Tower). infinitybooksjapan.com. ✆ **080-3412-2564.** Station: Asakusa (10 min.).

Liquidroom ♥♥♥ Once a scruffy place in Shinjuku, this venue shot to stardom after relocating to this cavernous space with a fantastic sound system in Ebisu. It's well known for its concerts (bands often use it as a launching pad for world tours), DJs, and other stage events most nights of the week. Open daily around 6 or 7pm, with performances 1 hour later. 3–16–6 Higashi, Shibuya-ku. liquidroom.net. ✆ **03-5464-0800.** Cover around ¥5,000. Station: Ebisu (3 min.).

The Ruby Room ♥♥♥ It's hard to tell how big this second-floor venue is because it's always packed tight, with customers spilling out the door and down the stairway. Home to local acts, open-mic Tuesdays, house and techno DJs, and other events from poetry readings to comedy shows, it's one of the liveliest and most expat-heavy venues in the area. The crowd depends upon the act performing, and the band is close, close, close—any closer and you'd be in the drummer's lap. In any case, the energy in this place is great. Open daily from 7pm or later (some concerts start at midnight), until 2am (5am weekends). 2–25–17 Dogenzaka, Shibuya-ku. rubyroomtokyo.com. ✆ **03-3780-3022.** Cover ¥1,000–¥2,000 most nights, often including 1 drink. Station: Shibuya (Hachiko exit, 4 min.).

Sometime ♥♥♥ Founded in 1975, right around the time jazz was hitting an apex in Japan, Sometime quickly established itself as a major institution for the growing number of musicians looking to make it in the mysterious underworld of jazz. Fittingly, it looks exactly as you'd picture the great jazz clubs of yore: subterranean, cavernous, stocked with whiskey, surrounded by aging brickwork, and all about the music. The stage sits in the center of the bar with tables and seats so up-close-and-personal to the musicians you're likely to get sprayed by saliva from the bell of a trumpet. I also like the seats on the mezzanine for great views of the band without any deterioration in sound quality. Sometime is a great place to introduce newbies to the genre, because most arrangements tend towards lively cocktail jazz grooves rather than wild and chaotic free jazz. Performances here last quite long, but food is available throughout in case you get peckish. Daytime sessions run from 1pm to 3:30pm, evening sessions 7pm to 9:30pm (including 30-min. intervals). Talking loudly during performances is discouraged. 1–11–31 Kichijoji Honcho B1F (entrance on ground level, just off Kichijoji Sunroad). sometime.co.jp/sometime/live. ✆ **0422-21-6336.** Cover, ¥1,500–¥3,000. Station: Kichijoji (3 min.).

What the Dickens! ♥♥ This laid-back expat bar is kind of a dive, but it's been much loved for 30 years as a great place to kick back and hear free live music nightly. Bands play everything from rock to reggae, jazz, blues, folk, and even Dixieland jazz and ska, with live music from 8:30 to 11:30pm. It has British beer on tap, as well as a menu of steak pie, fish and chips, and other pub fare. Open Tuesday to Thursday 5pm to midnight, Friday and Saturday 5pm to 1am, and Sunday 3pm to midnight. 1–13–3 Ebisu Nishi, Shibuya-ku. 4th floor of Roob Bldg. whatthedickens.jp. ✆ **03-3780-2099.** Station: Ebisu (west exit, 3 min.).

Jazz Kissa & Listening Spaces

Jazz kissa, coming from the word *kissaten* (cafe), are enchanting, yet sadly disappearing, holdovers from Japan's 20th-century love affair with jazz. Small cafe-cum-bars, they sprung up in the postwar era as young people became interested in Western music. Records were expensive, so students would gather in jazz kissa to listen to the newest LPs, drink coffee or beer, smoke cigarettes, and plan the next riot or protest. In the 1960s and '70s, students' activist tendencies aligned spiritually with the tenets of jazz, an anti-establishment music for Black Americans at the same time. The greats of the Golden Age of Jazz—Art Blakey, Sonny Rollins, John Coltrane, Thelonious Monk, Billy Harper—performed to sold-out concert halls in Japan, a far cry from the dingy segregated clubs they were accustomed to back home. Many of these musicians met jazz kissa proprietors, also known as Masters, during their travels in the East, and the Masters still decorate their kissa with signed memorabilia, concert ticket stubs, and sepia-stained photographs to immortalize the memories.

In the 1970s, Tokyo had the highest concentration of these establishments—around 250 (even author Haruki Murakami owned one, called Peter Cat)—but the number has steadily declined since. The kissa that still exist, however, have changed little since the halcyon days. Their furniture and interior design are often shoddy, and the posters, artwork, record sleeves, old jazz mags, and memorabilia are like museum exhibits. The drinks menus will likely be functional at best, but the record collections are vast, rare, and religiously curated; the sound systems are of exceptional quality and huge sources of pride. The Master, usually a man, may engage customers sparingly, moving only to change the vinyl on the turntable. Phone numbers, websites, and opening hours are often irregular, all at the discretion of the Master. who opens the bar as and when he chooses. Nothing feels driven by commercial impulse—these places would exist, you feel, whether or not any customers came. Going to a jazz kissa is not only an experience for dedicated jazz fans; it's a window into Japan's musical past and the people who chose, through their love of music, to live on the margins of Japanese society.

Eigakan ♥♥♥ A favorite in the national jazz scene, Eigakan was once voted the best kissa in Japan. Its golden-brown sound system is legendary, filling an entire wall of the bar, while its low ceilings, faded vintage film posters (*Eigakan* means "movie theater"), and kitschy ornamentation give it a postwar speakeasy vibe. After decades of manning the bar and the turntables, owner Yoshida-san recently sought to pass the business on to new ownership. Though a Kickstarter-funded takeover fell through in 2024, there is hope that new owners will be in place to continue operations at some point in 2025. With a storied history that's apparent in every dusty lamp and retro electronic, one hopes Eigakan remains in good hands. 5–33–19 Hakusan, Bunkyo-ku (illuminated sign reads, "JAZZ & somethin' else 映画館.") No website (yet). ✆ **03-3811-8932.** Station: Hakusan (1 min.).

Jazz Bar Samurai ♥♥ When you walk into Jazz Bar Samurai, it's hard not to be struck by the sheer oddity of the space. The lighting is dim, the upholstery ragged, the walls yellowed by decades of tobacco smoke. The decor, however, is a monument to both Japan and jazz: A paper lantern illuminates a framed picture of John Coltrane, colorful *goshikimaku* Buddhist flags enwreathe a bar guarding a cabinet of vinyl LPs, innumerable *maneki neko* cat dolls bob to the transcendent saxophone melodies tumbling out of the speakers. It's like you've wandered into some strange parallel reality, a feeling enhanced by its location, cocooned on the fifth floor of a building in the heart of Shinjuku. Open daily 6pm to 1am. 3–35–5 Shinjuku. No website. ✆ **03-3341-0383.** ¥300 cover before 9pm, ¥500 after. Station: Shinjuku (south exit, 2 min.), Shinjuku-sanchome (exit E9, 2 min.).

Jazz Eagle Yotsuya ♥♥ Though it first opened in 1967, this bar is larger and more modern than most jazz kissa and attracts a lot of students from nearby Sofia University, who come to listen to the music and study without the distraction of background chatter (there's a "no talking" rule before 6pm). The sound system is super loud and clear, giving new verve to the vast collection of old records, and it does get livelier in the evenings. Open Monday to Friday 11:30am–11:20pm, Saturday noon–11:20pm; happy hour 5–7pm. Yotsuya 1–8, Shinjuku-ku. jazz-eagle.com. ✆ **03-3357-9857.** Station: Yotsuya (exit 2, 1 min.).

Little Soul Cafe ♥♥ Soul and funk are the musical preserve of this tiny, cinematic bar in Shimokitazawa that looks like a set from a Tarantino blaxploitation flick. With more than 14,000 records bunched up on the shelves, and an impressive selection of rum from across Central and South America and the Caribbean, this is a great kissa-adjacent bar for those less interested in jazz (though the Master sometimes plays jazz funk and jazz fusion). Open daily 7pm to 2am. 2F Taisei Bldg, 3–20–2, Kitazawa, Setagaya-ku (above Cuore Forte Italian restaurant). littlesoulcafe.com. ✆ **03-5454-9800.** Station: Shimokitazawa (Inokashira exit, 4 min.).

Pithecanthropus Erectus ♥♥♥ Named after a Charles Mingus album, this establishment on a side street in a lurid Tokyo suburb is the archetypal kissa: small, ancient, hidden, windowless, and endlessly atmospheric.

The Master, Ishizaki-san, is a man of few words, usually sitting in silence with an ember-ing cigarette in hand, listening to an album by Mingus or Hank Mobley or Lee Morgan. The only caveat is that Ishizaki-san tends to open up by chance rather than on schedule; your best bet is to head there between 6pm and midnight. A scribbled Thelonious Monk quote, now half-faded, at the top of the stairwell says it all: "Jazz and freedom go hand in hand." 3F, 7–61–8 Nishi-Kamata, Ota-Ku (green awning reads, "JAZZ 直立猿人"). kamata-enjin.com. ✆ **03-3737-1292.** Station: Kamata (west exit, 7 min.).

Bars, Cocktails & Dance Clubs

GINZA

Bar Orchard ♥♥♥ This quirky little enclave on the seventh floor of the Sunraku Building was my introduction to the breathtakingly innovative Japanese mixology scene, and an immediate love affair ensued. There is no menu—nothing unusual about that in a Tokyo cocktail bar—but rather a bowl of seasonal fruit on the counter: Pick a fruit, and the English-speaking husband-and-wife bar staff, Takuo and Sumire Miyanohara, will use that fruit as the base flavor for your drink, paired with a spirit of their choosing. (You select the strength of the drink—I usually punt for strong to get my money's worth.) Drinks are served in a variety of strange receptacles, like miniature bathtubs, trashcans, ceramic pots, and cast-iron teapots, which aren't just gimmicks but enhance the narrative of the experience. The owners also make classic cocktails upon request. 7f, 6–5–16 Ginza. instagram.com/barorchardginza. ✆ **03-3575-0333.** Mon–Sat 6pm–midnight. Station: Ginza (exit A1, 5 min.).

Old Imperial Bar ♥♥ A Tokyo institution, this clubby bar in the Imperial Hotel is where the legacy of the hotel's architect, Frank Lloyd Wright, really lives on. It has a subdued atmosphere, with dim lighting, comfy chairs, and reproduction Wright furniture, as well as Wright originals like the small desk at the entrance, standing lamp in the corner, the mural, and the Art Deco terra-cotta wall behind the bar. To pay tribute to Wright, order the bar's original Mount Fuji (which recently celebrated its 100th anniversary), a cocktail with dry gin, lemon juice, pineapple juice, egg white, and maraschino cherry. This is a quiet escape from busy Tokyo, but it's also good for an admittedly pricey lunchtime sandwich. Imperial Hotel, 1–1–1 Uchisaiwai-cho. wimperialhotel.co.jp. ✆ **03-3539-8088.** Daily 11:30am–midnight (last order 11:30pm). Station: Hibiya (1 min.).

SHINJUKU

Albatross ♥♥ Over the past 30 years Golden Gai has metamorphized from ramshackle alleyways frequented only by Japanese customers to a boarded-up place on the brink of extinction to the thriving hotspot it is today. Now you'll see fewer Japanese faces (unless they're in one of the "regulars only" bars or pouring your drinks), but it's still fun to walk around and see where the night takes you. Albatross has been a reliable option in Golden Gai for a while, with a mostly young clientele and an eclectic decor that ranges from chandeliers to a deer head. You'll have to squeeze in to find a seat, either at the counter or up the narrow stairs to one of two Lilliputian levels above. Once settled, you'll find it has a very welcoming vibe. There's a ¥500 snack charge per person. 1–1–7 Kabuki-cho. alba-s.com. ✆ **03-3203-3699.** Daily 7pm–5am. Station: Shinjuku Sanchome (7 min.).

Bar Aqua Cafe88 ♥ Perhaps there's nothing inherently special about Bar Aqua Cafe88, but it does have two principal selling points: proper-sized pints and outdoor seating, where you can watch the maelstrom of partygoers descending on the streets of Kabuki-cho. It also serves pub grub like sausages, fries, and *karaage* (deep-fried chicken thigh) to accompany the draft and bottled beers and a selection of international whiskies. If you're a sociable type, it's a good place to meet other tourists. 1–12–12 Kabuki-cho. No website. ✆ **03-6205-6678.** Open 24/7. Station: Shinjuku Station (exit B13, 6 min.).

New York Bar ♥♥♥ In *Lost in Translation,* one of the most iconic films ever made about Tokyo, doleful and lovesick actor Bob Harris (Bill Murray) spends most of his evenings drinking Suntory whiskey in a swanky bar overlooking the glittering city skyline. That location is the New York Bar on the 52nd floor of Shinjuku's Park Hyatt Hotel. Although there's an in-house restaurant, the cocktails, soaring views, live music, and jazzy atmosphere are the real reasons to come here. The bar is set to reopen in October 2025 after renovations; hours TBA. Park Hyatt Tokyo. restaurants.tokyo.park.hyatt.co.jp/nyb.html. ✆ **03-5323-3458.** Station: Shinjuku Station (west exit, 11 min.), Tochomae (8 min.).

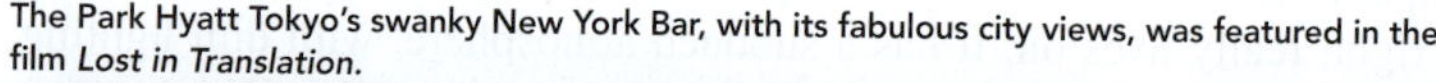

The Park Hyatt Tokyo's swanky New York Bar, with its fabulous city views, was featured in the film *Lost in Translation.*

Don't Be Surprised by Extra Charges

One thing you should be aware of is the **"table charge"** imposed on customers at some bars (especially *nomi-ya*) and many cocktail lounges—usually around ¥500 per person. Included in the table charge is usually a small snack—maybe nuts, chips, or a vegetable; for this reason, some locales call it an *otsumami*, or snack charge. Some establishments levy a table charge only after a certain time in the evening; others may add it only if you don't order food. If you're not sure, ask before you order anything. Remember, too, that there's a 10% consumption tax, though some menus already include it in their prices. Some higher-end establishments, especially nightclubs, hostess bars, and dance clubs, will also add a service charge ranging anywhere from 10% to 20%. In such establishments, men may be charged by the hour—sometimes in excess of ¥10,000—while women drink for free.

ROPPONGI

The center of Roppongi is **Roppongi Crossing** (the intersection of Roppongi Dori and Gaien-Higashi Dori), at the corner of which sits the Almond Coffee Shop with its pink decor. The shop has mediocre coffee and desserts at inflated prices, but the sidewalk in front is the number-one meeting spot in Roppongi. If you need directions, there's a conveniently located *koban* (police box) catty-corner from the Almond Coffee Shop and next to a bank. It has a big map of the Roppongi area showing the address system, and someone is always there to help.

Ant 'n Bee ♥♥ Not sure what ants and bees have to do with beer, but this cozy hideaway offers a laidback vibe and about 20 Japanese craft beers on tap, making it a great place to sample national brews, from wheat to stout. A friendly staff, limited but decent food (like buffalo wings and fish and chips), and free Wi-Fi make this a good place to hang out in Roppongi, away from all the hype. 5-1-5 Roppongi. antnbee.favy.jp. ✆ **03-3478-1250.** Daily 5pm–6am. Station: Roppongi (1 min.).

Geronimo Shot Bar ♥ In this tiny place, it is near impossible to elbow your way to the bar or avoid conversation with the people around you. It's a party scene most nights of the week, fueled no doubt by the 40 or so different shots available (the Russian Quaalude is quite a production). If you hear the drum, it means someone has bought a shot for everyone in the bar (it happens more than you'd think). Drink 15 shots in 1 night and you get a free T-shirt and your name listed on the Shot Hall of Fame. People seem to either love or hate the place, but there must be more of the former than the latter, because it's been in business 30 years and has many regulars, including expats. Happy hour is daily until 9pm. 7-14-10 Roppongi. geronimoshotbar.com. ✆ **03-3478-7449.** Mon–Fri 6pm–5am; Sat–Sun 7pm–5am. Station: Roppongi (1 min.).

A Drinking Tour of Roppongi

By yourself but still want to hit the town? Or maybe with friends but don't know where to go? Join the **Tokyo Pub Crawl** (tokyopub crawl.com; ✆ **070-1326-1423**), a roaming party every Friday and Saturday night when up to 120 people visit three bars and a club in Roppongi. The cost is ¥3,500 for men and ¥2,000 for women (which includes a shot at each venue). Interestingly, some 30% attendees are Japanese (many of whom come weekly), making for a diverse international crowd. Lots of fun. Book online for discounts.

R2 Supper Club ♥♥♥ The owners of this lounge decided that Roppongi needed a sophisticated hangout for expats with money, and it must be working—R2 can be crazy full from 10pm onward, with the targeted corporate types packing the dark interior. There's a huge bar center stage, offering mojitos (like yuzu mojito), martinis, cocktails, and margaritas. R2 gets kudos for promoting mostly local up-and-coming Japanese (and some international) DJs nightly, usually jazz paired with live instruments. 7–14–23 Roppongi. r2sc.jp. ✆ **03-6447-0002.** Mon–Sat 5pm–5am; Sun 5pm–3am. Station: Roppongi (2 min.).

SHIBUYA

Baia ♥♥ One of Tokyo's newest nightclubs, opened in 2022, Baia has quickly become a popular hangout for expats and yuppie types. It's hard not to be stopped in your tracks by its entrance: a neon-turquoise shard carved into a concrete facade. The crystal cave–like design—the work of New York–based artist Roy Nachum—continues across four sprawling floors and a rooftop garden. Events and the genre of music vary throughout the week; some of the biggest names in contemporary music, like DJ Skrillex and American rapper Fabulous, have headlined here. There's also a VIP karaoke room on the third floor. ***Note:*** Dress for a night on the town, or the venue may turn you away. 16–17 Udagawacho, Shibuya-ku (opposite Shibuya Parco department store). baiatokyo.com. ✆ **03-6455-3260.** Thurs–Sun 11pm–5am. Station: Shibuya (5 min.).

Baird Beer Harajuku Taproom ♥♥ This chain of brewpubs, started by American Brian Baird and his Japanese wife Sayuri, was at the cutting edge of Japan's craft beer boom. There are branches throughout Japan, but I'm often drawn to the Harajuku Taproom, partly for its welcome reprieve from chaotic Takeshita Dori nearby and partly because its signature brews stand the test of time. Year-round classics include the hoppy Rising Sun Pale Ale, the fruity Red Rose Amber Ale, and a chocolatey Kurofune Porter, but you'll also find seasonal specials. No matter what you choose, it'll pair well with the *yakitori* (chicken skewers) cooked in-house. Notice the excellent artwork on the bottles, too—like contemporary impressions of Edo-period landscape prints—reproduced on canvases throughout the bar. Other Tokyo taprooms are found in Kichijoji

(2–10–15 Kichijoji, Suginami-ku) and Takadanobaba (3–2–14 Takadanobaba, Shinjuku-ku). No-surrender Building 2F, 1–20–13 Jingumae, Shibuya-ku. bairdbeer.com/taprooms. ✆ **03-6438-0450.** Mon–Fri 5–11pm; Sat noon–11pm; Sun noon–10pm. Station: Harajuku (2 min.).

Liquid Factory ♥♥ With its metallic decor, exposed piping, and stacks of beakers, receptacles, and pipettes, Liquid Factory resembles the inside of a lab, so it should surprise no one that its mixologists are masters of experimentation. The menu features stiff drinks with flavor pairings you've likely never dreamed of—Warehouse Man (coffee, pu'er tea, pink pepper) or Beast Side (cranberry, artichoke, anise)—which helped the bar earn a place among Asia's 50 Best in 2021. If the flavor pairings sound a little rogue, consult the radar charts on the menu, which display the alcohol, sourness, sweetness, and bitterness levels of each drink. Coffees, milkshakes, and happy hour in the afternoon. 41–12–101 Udagawa, Shibuya-ku. liquidworks-jpn.com/liquid-factory. ✆ **03-6416-5252.** Tues–Fri 9am–1am; Sat 11am–1am; Sun 11am–midnight. Station: Shibuya (Hachiko exit, 11 min.).

ØL ♥♥ Since the craft beer scene exploded in Tokyo's trendier suburbs, it now seems as though almost every Shibuya side street has a taproom filled with young Japanese and expats slugging IPAs, witbiers, sours, and saisons. ØL, a Scandinavian craft beer bar on a quiet lane not far from the madness of Senta-gai, is prototypical: Expect a chalkboard menu, a minimalist interior, cosmopolitan clientele, and excellent beers from Japan and Norway at fairly steep prices (pints cost around ¥1,300, perhaps double what you'd normally pay for a draft beer). When the sun is out, grab a seat on the outdoor terrace and pair your beer with zesty tacos from the La Cabina food truck. Happy hour until 6pm. 37–10 Udagawacho, Shibuya-ku. oltokyo.jp. ✆ **03-3476-7238.** Sun–Tues noon–midnight; Wed–Thurs noon–1am; Fri–Sat noon–2am. Station: Shibuya (Hachiko exit, 10 min.).

Tight ♥♥ The name is certainly appropriate—this is one of the smallest bars I've ever drunk in, which is saying something in this city of Borrower-sized watering holes. A gleaming white box on the second floor of a building on Nonbei Yokocho, Tight is barely big enough for more than five or so patrons, but I've been there on nights when the number has exceeded double figures. The aesthetic is all cool minimalism and so is the menu: Two glass vats sit on the counter, one filled with a peppery gin-and-tonic and the other with an in-house cocktail. (Other drinks, like beer, wine, and sake, are available.) On the ground floor there's also a wine bar named **Loose,** which is somehow even smaller. 2F 1–25–10 Shibuya, Nonbei Yokocho. 2004-tight.com. ✆ **03-3499-7668.** Mon–Sat 7pm–2am. Station: Shibuya (Hachiko exit, 4 min.).

Tokyo Comedy Bar (TCB) ♥♥ Despite having a successful career in the video game industry, in 2022 longtime Tokyoite BJ Fox fulfilled his dream of opening Tokyo's first stand-up comedy club (alongside fellow expat JJ Wakrat). The small brick-walled room feels like a classic underground comedy joint, despite being on the third floor of a building beside Shibuya Station. You could fit 60 or 70 audience members in here, at a push—though apparently it was more like 80 on opening night—but it's best to get tickets in advance. Shows, mostly English-language, feature local journeyman comics and start from 7:30pm daily. Afternoon and early evening shows are on selected days; check the website for the schedule. Shows cost around ¥3,000; book at fienta.com/s/standup-comedy-tokyo. Renga Building 3F, 1–3–9 Dogenzaka, Shibuya-ku. tokyocomedybar.com. ✆ **03-6277-5610.** Station: Shibuya (Hachiko or Inokashira exit, 2 min.).

Whales of August ♥♥ Named after a 1987 film, this bar takes its love of cinema (and cocktail crafting) seriously. The decor commemorates movie classics from *A Clockwork Orange* to *Pulp Fiction* to *2001: A Space Odyssey,* and the menu (mostly in Japanese) features a series of film titles, each corresponding to a cocktail that reflects the movie. (The Titanic is a blue liqueur-based drink with a big chunk of ice in it; Se7en is blood-red and potent; Annie is an orange concoction topped by a tumbling frizz of orange-colored fruits.) You can request movies not on the menu and the owner will produce a drink on the spot—word has it he has seen more than 20,000 films, so he can probably accommodate your request; the other bartenders are also cinephiles. Most drinks are less than ¥1,000, so you can cycle through a few without breaking the bank, though there's also a ¥500 table charge. The bar covers three floors; the top floor is non-smoking. 28–13 Udagawacho, Shibuya-ku. No website. ✆ **03-3476-7238.** Daily 6pm–4am. Station: Shibuya (Hachiko exit, 5 min.).

OTHER NEIGHBORHOODS

Bar Ghetto ♥♥ One of the best spots to drink in Shimokitazawa, especially if you've missed your last train home (it stays open till 5am), cramped and cozy Bar Ghetto has the vermillion glow of a photographer's darkroom. Located among several bars on a boomerang-shaped bend of Chazawa Dori, it can get raucous when locals drift in from other neighborhood spots during the small hours. Take a seat at the counter if you're alone or in a pair, and the chat will flow as freely as the drinks and shots—linguistic barriers count for little here. It's a great spot for meeting fellow foreigners. 1–45–16 Kitazawa, Setagaya-ku. facebook.com/Ghetto.unko/. No phone. Daily 8:30pm–5am. Station: Shimo-Kitazawa (5 min.).

Meishu Center Ochanomizu ♥♥ If you're thirsting for a glass of *nihonshu,* more commonly referred to as "sake," but have no idea where to start, then you should schedule a visit here. A try-before-you-buy bottle shop, the Meishu Center has more than 150 types of sake on its refrigerated shelves, from breweries across Japan. Many staff members speak English, so don't worry about leaving more confused than when you entered—after an hour of sampling, you might even be able to pick a *daiginjo* or a *junmai* out of a lineup. There's also an all-you-can-drink plan for ¥5,500, including assorted sake nibbles like smoked cheese, fried monkfish, and pickled cucumber. 1F Lions Plaza Ochanomizu, 1–2–1 Yushima, Bunkyo-ku. nihonshu.com/ochanomizu/. ✆ **03-5207-2420.** Sun–Thurs noon–8pm; Fri–Sat noon–9:30pm (last orders). Station: Ochanomizu (5 min.), Shin-Ochanmoizu (5 min.), Akihabara (8 min.), Suehirocho (8 min.).

LGBTQ Bars

Shinjuku Ni-chome (pronounced "knee-chomay"), southeast of the Yasukuni-Gyoen Dori intersection (station: Shinjuku Sanchome), is Tokyo's LGBTQ quarter, with a lively street scene and countless establishments catering to a variety of age groups and preferences. The following are good starting points, but you'll find a lot more in the immediate area by exploring on your own.

AiiRO Café ♥♥ Where to start in Ni-chome? This is a good bet, right on the main drag, Naka-dori, with an open facade that overflows with partiers past the sidewalk to the street most nights. It's a good place to gain bearings, check out the people parading past, and connect with the friendly crowd. A few drinks here, and you'll probably have a list of several places you want to hit next. 2–18–1 Shinjuku. aliving.net/aiirocafe. ✆ **03-6273-0740.** Mon–Thurs 6pm–2am; Fri–Sat 6pm–5am; Sun 6pm–midnight. Station: Shinjuku Sanchome (4 min.).

Arty Farty ♥♥♥ One of Ni-chome's larger LGBTQ bars is also one of the best places to dance, thanks to a good sound system and music ranging from house to hip hop. On the first Saturday of the month, the nightly party turns into a major event, with a ¥1,500 cover (includes two drinks). Arty Farty used to be strictly males only, but it threw open its doors to all when it moved to this location across from the legendary **Pit Inn** jazz house. A fun climax to a pub crawl in Shinjuku. 2–11–7 Shinjuku. artyfarty.jp. ✆ **03-5362-9720.** Sun and Wed–Thurs 8pm–3am; Fri–Sat 8pm–5am. Station: Shinjuku Sanchome (3 min.).

Bar Goldfinger ♥ When Chiga Ogawa started Goldfinger as a women-only monthly event in 1991, she had no idea how successful it would become, bringing Tokyo's marginalized gay community together and being featured in media worldwide. Nor did she know that by 2007 she'd be running a bar in Ni-chome with the same name, its enduring popularity a testament to the space she has created. Bar Goldfinger welcomes a mixed LGBTQ crowd every night, except Saturdays, which is women only. On the third Saturday of every even-numbered month, the women-only Goldfinger Party takes place in the nearby Aisotope Lounge at 2–12–16 Shinjuku. Happy hour is from 5pm to 7pm; free popcorn and karaoke all night. 2–12–11 Shinjuku. goldfingerparty.com. ✆ **03-6383-4649.** Sun–Thurs 5–11pm; Fri–Sat 5pm–4am. Station: Shinjuku Sanchome (4 min.).

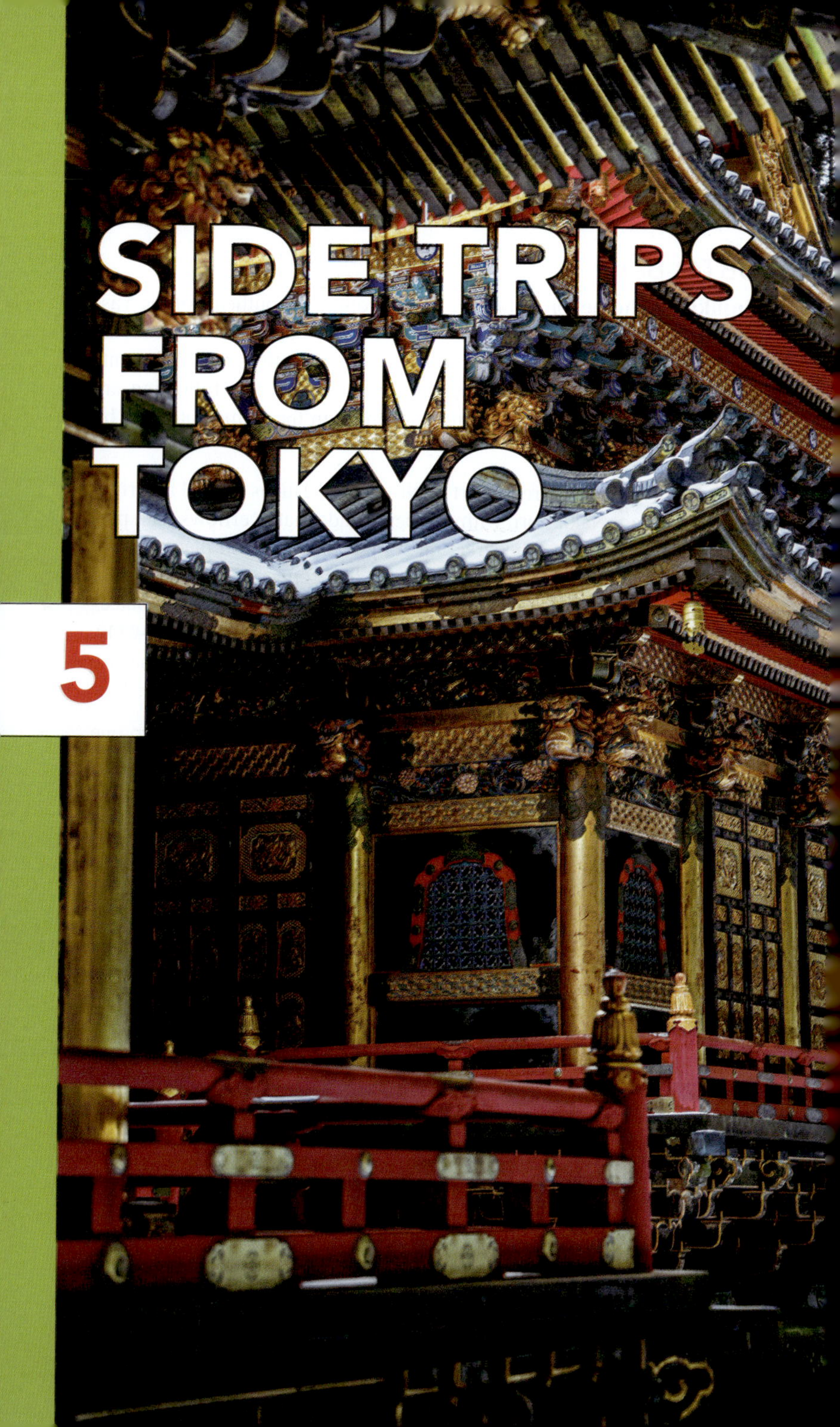

SIDE TRIPS FROM TOKYO

5

If your stay in Tokyo is long enough, consider taking an excursion or two. **Kamakura** and **Nikko** rank as two of the most important historical sites in Japan, renowned for temples and shrines that relate to former shogun (military dictators), while the **Fuji-Hakone-Izu National Park** serves as a huge recreational playground for the residents of Tokyo. **Yokohama,** with its thriving port and new waterfront developments, also makes an interesting day trip, as does **Mt. Fuji,** though the annual window for climbing it is quite small and overcrowding has caused restrictions to be placed on the most popular Yoshida trail. For an overnight stay, consider **Hakone,** famous for its hot-spring spas, beautiful ryokan inns, spectacular scenery, and unique modes of transportation that includes travel by ropeway and boat; you might even see Mt. Fuji on the way.

Your main problem will be deciding where to go. If you take only one day trip, Kamakura is a good option, especially if you're unable to include the ancient capitals of Kyoto and Nara in your travels, but it too has suffered from overcrowding in recent years. If you're going to Kyoto and Nara, and you enjoy communing with nature, Nikko is a great option, even though it's a much longer journey (especially if you're staying in south or west Tokyo). As for Hakone, it can be enjoyed as a side trip from Tokyo or seen en route to other destinations. Yokohama, only 30 minutes from Shibuya by express train, can be done easily in half a day if you're in a pinch for time.

FAVORITE TOKYO SIDE-TRIP EXPERIENCES

- **Coming Face to Face with the Great Buddha in Kamakura** There are larger bronze Buddhas in Japan, but this one with its serene expression and backdrop of wooded hills is the most memorable. See p. 222.
- **Exploring Nikko** With thousands of majestic cedars standing sentinel, the Nikko Sannai World Heritage Site will awe visitors, containing, as it does, the opulent **Toshogu Shrine,** the mausoleum of Japan's most famous shogun, an imperial villa, multiple craft stores, and more.
- **Being Charmed by Yokohama** Walk along the city's gorgeous harborside, making pit stops in the shops, bars, and restaurants of

FACING PAGE: **The ornate facade of the Toshugo Shrine at Nikko.**

Yokohama Hammerhead and the Red Brick Warehouses, or have a picnic in Yamashita Park.

- **Traveling in Hakone** With its mountain railway, cable car, ropeway, and sightseeing boat, the circuitous route through scenic Hakone is a delightful overnight adventure.

KAMAKURA, ANCIENT CAPITAL ♥♥♥

51km (32 miles) S of Tokyo

Kamakura is a delightful hamlet with no fewer than 65 Buddhist temples and 19 Shinto shrines spread throughout the town and surrounding wooded hills. Most of these were built centuries ago, when a warrior named Minamoto Yoritomo seized political power and established his shogunate government in Kamakura back in 1192. Wanting to set up his seat of government as far away as possible from what he considered to be the corrupt imperial court in Kyoto, Yoritomo selected Kamakura because it was easy to defend. The town is enclosed on three sides by wooded hills and on the fourth by the sea—a setting that lends a dramatic background to its many temples and shrines.

Although Kamakura remained the military and political center of the nation for a century and a half, the Minamoto clan was in power only a short time. After Yoritomo's death, both of his sons were assassinated, one after the other, after taking up military rule. Power then passed to the family of Yoritomo's widow, the Hojo clan, which ruled until 1333, when the emperor in Kyoto sent troops to crush the shogunate government. Unable to stop the invaders, 800 soldiers retired to the Hojo family temple at Toshoji, where they disemboweled themselves in ritualistic suicide known as *seppuku.*

The Great Buddha in Kamakura.

Today Kamakura is a thriving seaside resort (pop. 173,000), with old wooden homes, temples, shrines, and wooded hills—a pleasant 1-day trip from Tokyo. (There's also a beach in Kamakura called Yuigahama Beach—it can be crowded in summer, but it's one of the few decent places to surf or swim near the capital. Just beware, while Japan is renowned for cleanliness, its beaches often leave much to be desired.)

Side Trips from Tokyo

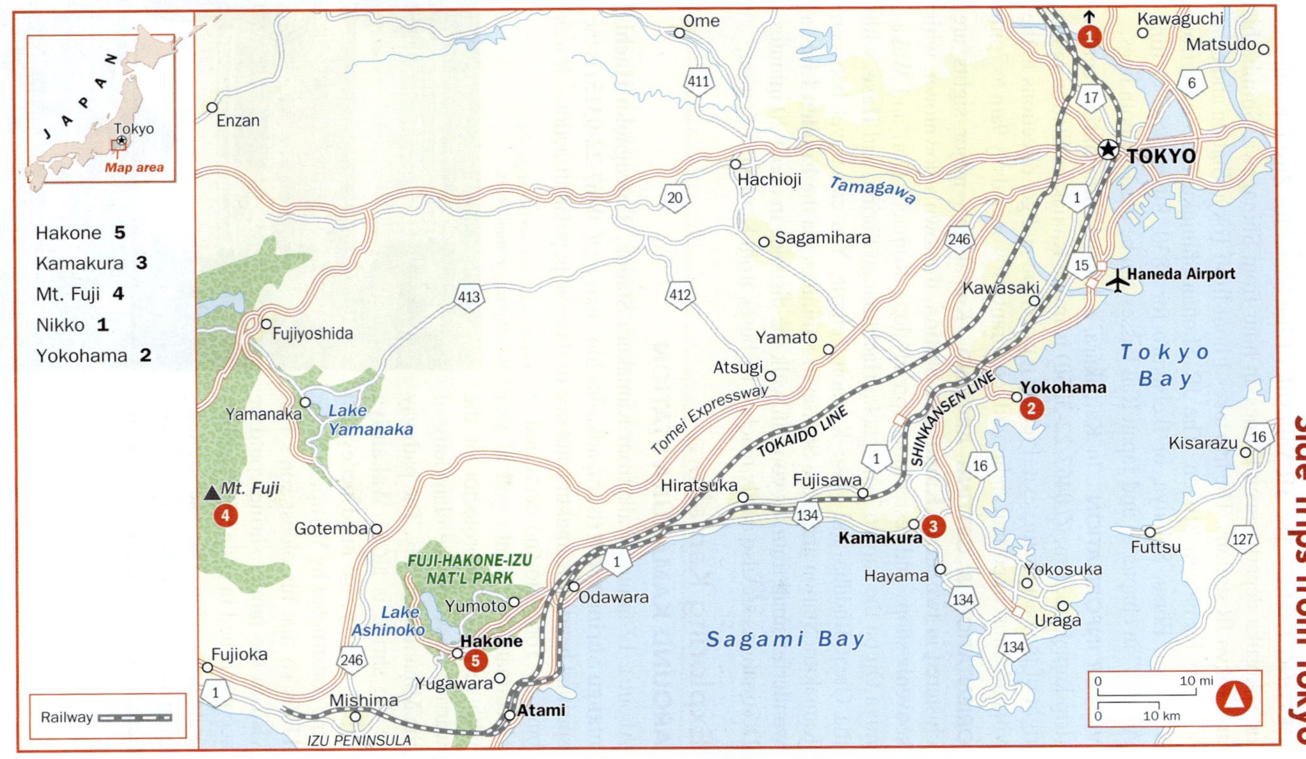

Essentials

GETTING THERE The **JR Yokosuka Line** bound for Zushi, Kurihama, or Yokosuka departs several times an hour from Shinagawa, Shimbashi, and Tokyo JR stations. The trip takes 1 hour from Tokyo Station and costs ¥740 to Kamakura Station. The JR Shonan-Shinjuku Line runs from Shinjuku, Ebisu, Shibuya, or Ikebukuro for ¥830. Suica (see "Getting Around" in chapter 4) and Japan Rail Passes can be used for both lines.

VISITOR INFORMATION In Kamakura, a **tourist information center** (trip-kamakura.com; ✆ **0467-22-3350**) is inside Kamakura Station to the right of the east (main) exit. Pick up a map here and get directions to the village's most important sights and restaurants. It's open daily 9am to 7pm.

ORIENTATION & GETTING AROUND Kamakura's major sights are clustered in two areas: **Kamakura Station,** the town's downtown, with souvenir shops and restaurants spread along Komachi Dori and Wakamiya Oji on the way to Tsurugaoka Hachimangu Shrine; and **Hase,** with the Great Buddha and Hase Kannon Temple. You can travel between Kamakura Station and Hase Station in 5 minutes via the **Enoden Line,** a wonderful small train, or you can walk the distance in about 20 minutes. Destinations are also easily reached by buses from Kamakura Station.

Exploring Kamakura

AROUND KAMAKURA STATION

About a 12-minute walk from Kamakura Station, **Tsurugaoka Hachimangu Shrine** ♥♥♥ (tsurugaoka-hachimangu.jp; ✆ **0467-22-0315**) is the spiritual heart of Kamakura and one of its most popular attractions. It was built by Yoritomo and dedicated to Hachiman, the Shinto god of war who served as a protector of the warrior class and the clan deity of the Minamoto family. The pathway to the shrine is along **Wakamiya Oji,** a cherry-tree-lined pedestrian lane constructed by Yoritomo in the 1190s so that his oldest son's first visit to the family shrine could be accomplished in style with an elaborate procession. The lane stretches from the shrine all the way to Yuigahama Beach, with three massive *torii* gates set at intervals along the route to signal the approach to the shrine. On both sides of the lane, souvenir and antiques shops sell lacquerware, pottery, and folk art.

The Tsurugaoka Hachimangu shrine, Kamakura's spiritual heart.

Kamakura

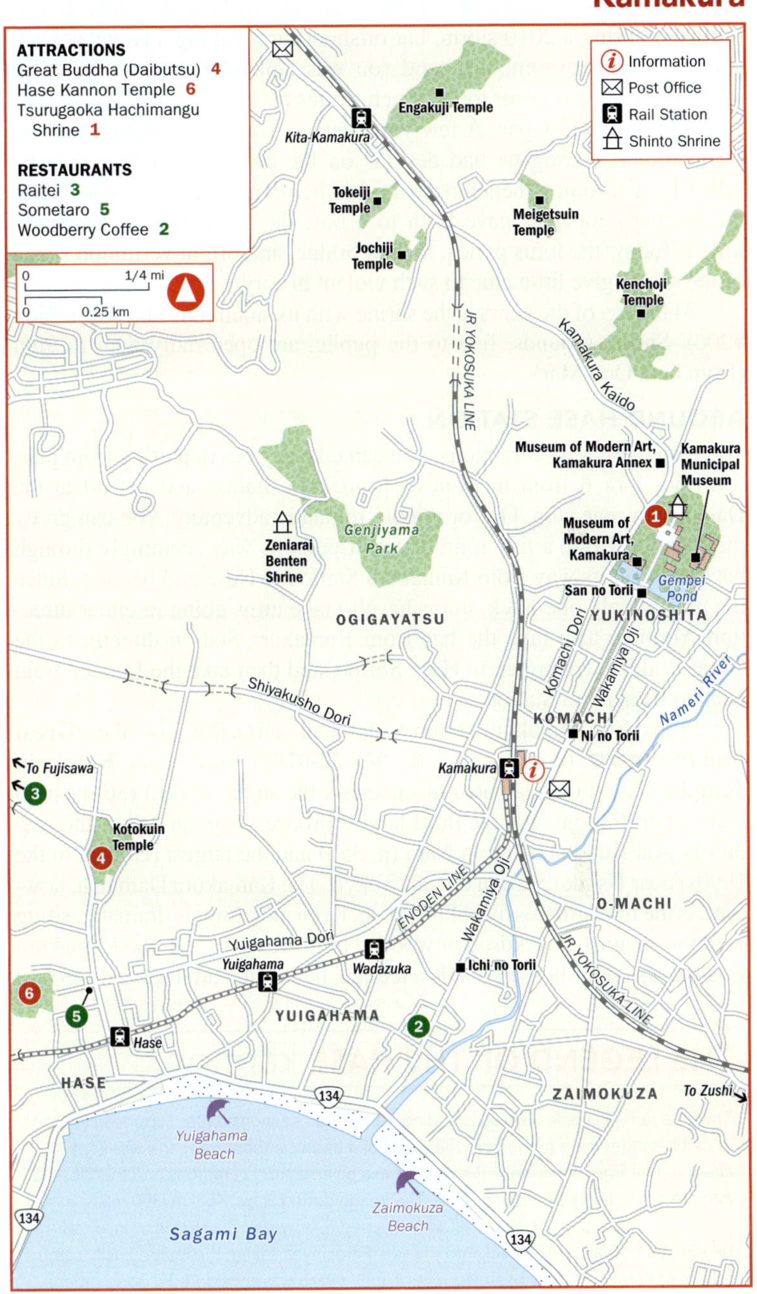

5

SIDE TRIPS FROM TOKYO | Kamakura, Ancient Capital

At the bottom of the 62 stairs leading to the vermilion-colored shrine, notice the massive trunk of a 1,000-year-old gingko tree (sadly, it was uprooted during a 2010 storm, but offshoots are making a comeback). It was here that Yoritomo's second son was ambushed and murdered in 1219; his head was never found. Such stories of murder and betrayal were common in feudal Japan. A few years earlier, Yoritomo had banished his own brother, fearing he had designs on the shogunate; rather than be killed by Yoritomo's henchmen, the brother committed *seppuku.* When the brother's mistress gave birth to a boy, the baby too was promptly killed. Today, the lotus ponds, arched bridge, and bright vermilion sheen of the shrine give little clue to such violent history.

At the top of the stairs is the shrine with its small museum (admission ¥200). Shrine grounds, free to the public, are open daily 5am to 9pm (from 6am Oct–Mar).

AROUND HASE STATION

To get to these next attractions, you can take any bus departing from platform no. 1 or 6 from in front of Kamakura Station and get off at the Daibutsuen-mae stop. Or, for a more romantic adventure, you can go by the **Enoden Line,** a tiny train that putt-putts its way seemingly through backyards on its way from Kamakura Station to Hase and beyond. Since it's mostly only one track, trains have to take turns going in either direction. You can also take the bus from Kamakura Station directly to the Great Buddha, backtrack to Hase Shrine, and then take the Enoden train back to Kamakura Station.

Probably Kamakura's most famous attraction is the **Great Buddha** ♥♥♥ (kotoku-in.jp; ✆ **046-22-0703**), located at **Kotokuin Temple.** Called the Daibutsu in Japanese, the statue is 11m (36 ft.) high and weighs 93 tons. It's the third-largest bronze image in Japan, the second-largest Buddha being in Nara (p. 355) and the largest (erected in the 1990s) near Ushiku Station outside Tokyo. The Kamakura Daibutsu, however, is the most impressive of the three. Even its setting is dramatic, siting outdoors against a backdrop of wooded hills. Cast in 1252, the Kamakura Buddha was once housed inside a temple, but a huge tidal wave destroyed

THE LEGEND OF THE HASE kannon

There's a remarkable legend surrounding Kamakura's Kannon statue. Supposedly, two wooden images were made from the wood of a huge camphor tree; one was kept in Hase, not far from Nara, while the second was given a short ceremony and then tossed into the sea to find a home of its own. The image drifted about 483km (300 miles) eastward, then washed up on shore; all who touched it, however, became ill or incurred bad luck, so it was thrown back into the sea. Fifteen years later, the image finally came ashore at Kamakura, now beaming rays of light, which was considered a good omen; the Hase Kannon Temple was promptly built here to give it its proper home.

The sea goddess Benzaiten with her lute in the Benten-kutsu Cave.

the wooden structure—and the statue has sat under sun, snow, and stars ever since. Even more arresting is the serene face of the Kamakura Buddha—it seems the embodiment of Nirvana, representing the plane above human suffering, the point at which birth and death, joy and sadness, merge and become one. The temple is open daily from 8am to 5:30pm (to 5pm Oct–Mar). Admission is ¥300 for adults and ¥150 for children. If you want, you can pay an extra ¥50 to go inside the statue—it's hollow—but there's usually a line.

About a 10-minute walk from the Daibutsu is **Hase Kannon Temple (Hasedera)** ♥♥♥ (hasedera.jp; ✆ **0467-22-6300**), located on a hill with sweeping views of the sea and a picturesque setting around a pond and flowering trees and bushes. This is the home of an 11-headed gilt **statue of Kannon,** the goddess of mercy, housed in the Kannon-do (Kannon Hall). More than 9m (30 ft.) high, it's the tallest wooden image in Japan, made in the 8th century from a single piece of camphor wood. Note how each face has a different expression, representing Kannon's compassion for various kinds of human suffering. Also in the Kannon-do is a museum with religious treasures from the Kamakura, Heian, Muromachi, and Edo periods. Beside the Kannon-do to the right, the Amida-do (Amida Hall) holds another golden statue, this one depicting **Amida,** a Buddha who promised rebirth in the Pure Land to the West to all who chanted his name. It was created by order of Yoritomo upon his 42nd birthday, considered an unlucky age for men. Also on the grounds, the **Benten-kutsu Cave** contains many stone images, including one of the sea goddess Benzaiten (seated, with a lute and a money box in front), the only female of Japan's Seven Lucky Gods. **Prospect Road** is a 10-minute hiking path featuring flowers in bloom and panoramic views. As you climb the steps to the Kannon-do, you'll encounter statues of a different sort: likenesses of **Jizo,** the guardian deity of children. Originally parents set up statues here to represent their children in hopes the deity would watch over them; over the years, however, the purpose of the Jizo statues changed. Now they represent miscarried, stillborn, or aborted infants. The hundred or so you see here will remain only a year before being burned or buried to make way for others. Some of the statues are fitted with hand-knitted caps, bibs, and sweaters; the effect is quite chilling. Hase Temple is open daily 8am to 5:30pm (to 5pm Oct–Feb); admission is ¥400 adults, ¥200 children.

The dining room at Hase Temple overlooks a beach

Where to Eat in Kamakura

Hase Temple's **Kaikoan,** with views of Yuigahama Beach, offers *udon,* spaghetti, curry, and Buddhist vegetarian dishes daily from 10am to 4pm.

Raitei (擂亭) ♥♥♥ NOODLES/BENTO Set in the hills on the edge of Kamakura, surrounded by verdant countryside, this restaurant occupies a house once owned by a wealthy landowner (it was moved to this site in 1929). In this magnificent setting, you'll be served inexpensive *soba* (Japanese noodles) and *bento* lunch boxes on pottery from the restaurant's own kiln. If you make a reservation in advance for kaiseki, you'll dine upstairs in your own private room in a refined traditional setting with awe-inspiring views. Note that guests to the estate pay an entry fee of ¥1,000, but that counts toward the price of your meal. Be sure to take the 20-minute looping path through the garden, past a bamboo grove, Buddhist stone images, and a miniature shrine; in fine weather, you can even see Mt. Fuji.

Takasago. raitei.com. ✆ **0467-32-5656.** Noodles ¥1,300–¥2,200; *bento* ¥4,235 (reservations required); *soba* set meal ¥3,025; *kaiseki* from ¥11,000. Daily 11am–sundown (about 7pm in summer). Closed New Year's and last week of July. Bus: 4 from Kamakura Station (platform 6) or Daibutsuen-mae. Get off at Takasago stop, then straight ahead on the left (or 15-min. taxi ride).

Sometaro (染太郎) ♥ OKONOMIYAKI Located on the left near the entrance to Hase Temple, this small second-floor restaurant offers do-it-yourself *okonomiyaki* (a kind of Japanese pancake; cooking instructions available in English) stuffed with cabbage, bean sprouts, and a choice of a main ingredient like beef, pork, or shrimp. It also serves *yakisoba* (fried noodles) and *teppanyaki* (grilled steak, seafood, or vegetables), all from an English-language menu.

3–12–11 Hase. ✆ **0467-22-8694.** Main dishes from ¥850. Fri–Mon 11:30am–9pm (last order); Tues 5–9pm; every other Thurs 11:30am–9pm. Station: Hase (2 min.).

Woodberry Coffee ♥♥ BRUNCH Despite its historical associations, a recent influx of young work-from-homers and surfers has made coastal Kamakura decidedly chic. This cafe near the beach end of Wakamiya Oji does proper Western-style brunches—something you don't find too often in Japan—and has a nice outdoor terrace for use in warm weather. Eggs benedict, vegan "Buddha Bowl" salads, avocado toast, pancake stacks, grilled cheese sandwiches, and acai and granola bowls—the menu is a real treat when you need a break from rice, noodles, and raw fish. The coffee, including cold brew, hand drip, and cortados, is excellent, too.

2–22–9 Yuigahama. instagram.com/woodberry_kamakura/. ✆ **0467-22-8694.** Brunch plates ¥1,680–¥2,200. Daily 8:30am–7pm. Station: Kamakura (13 min.).

NIKKO ♥♥♥

150km (93 miles) N of Tokyo

James Clavell's novel *Shogun* (recently adapted into a blockbuster TV series) was based on the life and times of Tokugawa Ieyasu, the powerful 1600s shogun who quashed all rebellions and unified Japan under his leadership. Tokugawa established such a military stronghold that his heirs ruled Japan for the next 250 years without serious challenge. Through the centuries, millions of Japanese have headed north of Tokyo to Nikko to pay homage to this great leader, one of the most important figures in Japanese history, at the **Toshogu Shrine ♥♥♥**, constructed in his honor in the 17th century. Nikko means "sunlight"—an apt description of the way the sun's rays play upon this sumptuous shrine of wood and gold leaf. Nothing else in Japan matches Toshogu Shrine for its opulence. Tokugawa's remains are entombed in a mausoleum here; nearby is another mausoleum, holding Tokugawa's grandson, as well as a temple, a shrine, and a garden. Surrounding the sacred grounds, known collectively as Nikko Sannai and designated a World Heritage Site by UNESCO in 1999, are thousands of majestic cedar trees in the 80,000-hectare (200,000-acre) **Nikko National Park ♥♥**. Another worthwhile sight is the **Nikko Tamozawa Imperial Villa ♥♥**, built in 1899.

I've included recommendations for an overnight stay, although you can visit Nikko on a very full day trip—4 to 5 hours for round-trip transportation, 2½ hours to see Toshogu Shrine and vicinity, and 1 hour for the imperial villa.

Essentials

GETTING THERE The fastest and most luxurious way to get to Nikko from Tokyo is on the Tobu Line's Limited Express **Spacia,** which departs

The famous "hear no evil, speak no evil, see no evil" monkeys above the stable door at Toshogu Shrine.

at least every hour from Tobu Asakusa Station. The cost is ¥3,050 one-way and the journey takes 1 hour and 50 minutes. There's free onboard Wi-Fi, and all seats are reserved, which means you're guaranteed a seat (on a holiday or a summer weekend, you may want to buy your ticket in advance). Otherwise, you can reach Nikko from Tokyo by local train. Take the Ryomo Line from Tobu Asakusa Station, then switch to Tobu's Nikko Line at Tobu Dobutsukoen Station. The journey to Nikko costs ¥1,950 and takes about 2½ hours.

To save yourself the hassle of buying individual tickets, consider purchasing Tobu's 2-Day Nikko Pass, which provides round-trip train travel between Asakusa and Nikko via rapid train, unlimited bus travel in Nikko, and other discounts listed on its website. Cost of the pass, valid for 2 days, is ¥2,120 for adults and ¥630 for children; you can upgrade to the Limited Express Spacia for an extra charge. Get info at **tobu.co.jp/en**, or visit the **Tobu Sightseeing Service Center** at Tobu Asakusa Station (✆ **03-3841-2871**), open daily 7:20am to 7pm.

To travel via Japan Rail trains, take the Tohoku Shinkansen bullet train from Tokyo Station to Utsunomiya (leaving every 20–40 min.; the trip takes about 50 min.), where you then change for the JR train to Nikko (45 min., with departures every hour or less).

VISITOR INFORMATION The **Tobu Sightseeing Service Center** in Tokyo (see above) stocks pamphlets on train schedules and sightseeing. In Nikko, you'll find the Tobu and JR stations located almost side by side in the village's downtown area. Inside Tobu Station, at the **Nikko Tobu Station tourist information counter** (daily 8:30am–5pm), staff can give you a map, answer basic questions, and point you in the right direction. If you arrive before noon, you can also leave your luggage here for delivery by 4pm to a limited list of area hotels and *ryokan* (¥500 per bag). Next to the

Nikko

0 1/10 mi
0 100 m
Bus stop
Information
Post Office
ATTRACTIONS
Futarasan Shrine 2
Ieyasu's Mausoleum 3
Nikko Tamozawa Imperial Villa 7
Rinnoji Temple 8
Sacred Bridge (Shinkyo) 9
Taiyuin Mausoleum 1
Toshogu Shrine 4
Yakushido 5
Yomeimon Gate 6
HOTELS
Annex Turtle Hotori-An 13
Nikko Kanaya Hotel 10
RESTAURANTS
Edokko 12
Hippari Tako 11
TOSHUGU SHRINE AREA
Ticket Office
Rinnoji Office
Ticket Office
Nishi-sando Bus Stop
Shinkyo Bus Stop
Ashikaga Bank
Shinkyo (Sacred) Bridge
Tamozawa Bus Stop
Stadium
Kirifuri Bridge
City Hall
Nikko Police Station
Tobu-Nikko Sta.
JR-Nikko Sta.
To Lake Chuzenji
To Mount Nakimushi

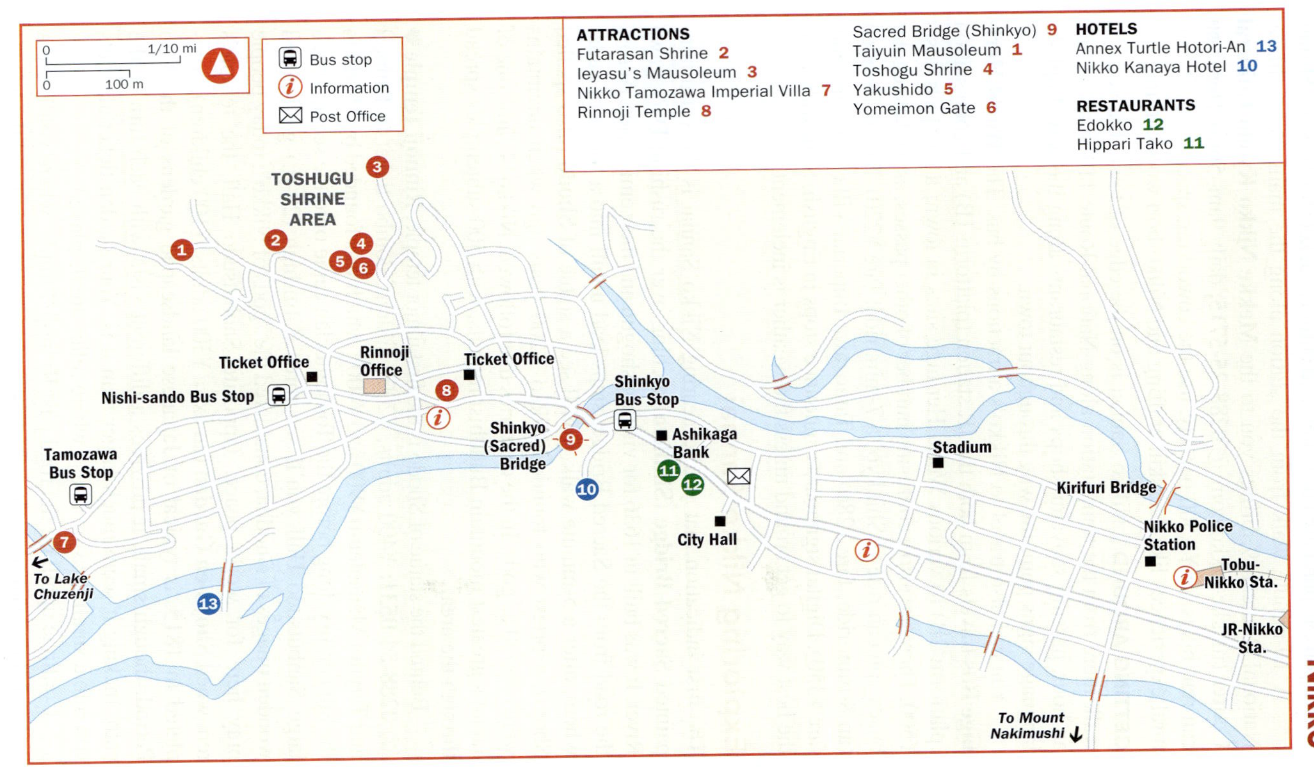

info counter in Tobu Station is the **Tourist Center** (daily 8:20am–5pm), where you can purchase bus tickets and entrance tickets for Toshogu Shrine.

A 10-minute walk from the station along the main thoroughfare, National Route 119, brings you to the **Mekke Nikko Kyodo Cultural Center** (mekke-nikko.com; ✆ **0288-25-5715;** daily 9am–5pm). Here you can rent bikes for ¥1,500 per day, use the coworking space, or book cultural experiences like deerskin crafting and Nikko-bori woodcarving.

GETTING AROUND Nikko Sannai is on the edge of town, but you can walk there from the train station along National Route 119 in about half an hour, passing souvenir shops and restaurants along the way. English-language signs point the way throughout town.

You can also travel to Nikko's attractions by bus. The **World Heritage Bus** travels from both the JR station (platform 1B) and Tobu station (platform 2B) to various World Heritage sites in town; a day pass costs ¥500. There are also a confusing number of other passes, as well as regular buses you can ride to Shinkyo (a 7-min. ride; fare ¥220), Nikko Toshogu (an 8-min. ride; fare ¥280) and Tamozawa Imperial Villa (a 9-min. ride; fare ¥350). Digital signboards announce stops in English. Still, walking is the best way to get around unless the weather is inclement.

Exploring Nikko Sannai

The first indication that you're nearing Nikko Sannai is the vermilion-painted **Sacred Bridge (Shinkyo)** arching over the rushing Daiyagawa River. It was built in 1636 for visiting shogun and their emissaries. Across the road from the Sacred Bridge, steps lead uphill into a forest of cedar where, after a 5-minute walk, you'll see a statue of **Shodo** (also spelled Shoto), a priest who founded Nikko 1,200 years ago when mountains were revered as gods. In the centuries that followed, Nikko became one of Japan's greatest mountain Buddhist retreats, with 500 subtemples spread through the area.

Behind the statue of Shodo is the first major temple, **Rinnoji Temple** ♥ (✆ **0288-54-0531;** ¥400 adults, ¥200 children; combo ticket to Rinnoji and Taiyuin Mausoleum ¥900 and ¥400), which was founded by Shodo in the 8th century, long before the Toshogu clan came onto the scene. In the large Sanbutsudo Hall you'll see three 8.4m-high (28-ft.) gold-plated wooden images of Buddha, considered the "gods of Nikko"; today people pray here for world peace. Opposite Sanbutsudo Hall, the temple's renowned **Shoyo-en Garden** (an extra ¥300 adults, ¥100 children), completed in 1815, is typical of Japanese landscaped gardens of the Edo Period; though small, it provides a different vista with each turn of the path, making it seem much larger than it is. Your garden ticket also lets you into a small treasure house where relics are displayed.

Continue uphill on the road past Rinnoji Temple, where you'll see a flight of stairs passing under a huge stone *torii* gateway, one of the largest in Japan. This is the entrance to the most important and famous structure

Dazzling Yomeimon Gate, the entrance to the main sanctuary at Toshogu Shrine.

in Nikko, **Toshogu Shrine ♥♥♥** (**✆ 0288-54-0560;** ¥1,300 adults, ¥450 children). On your left is a five-story **pagoda.** (Pagodas are normally found only at temples; this pagoda is just one example of how Buddhism and Shintoism are combined at Toshogu Shrine.) After climbing a second flight of stairs, turn left to see the **Sacred Stable,** which houses a sacred white horse. Horses are often kept at shrines, as they have long been dedicated to Shinto gods; shrines also kept monkeys as well, which were thought to protect horses from disease, and sure enough, you'll see three monkeys carved above the stable door, fixed in the poses of "see no evil, hear no evil, speak no evil." Across from the stable is **Kami-Jinko,** famous for its carving by Kano Tanyu, who painted the images of two elephants (under the eaves) after reading about them but without seeing what they actually looked like.

Continue on to the shrine's central showpiece, **Yomeimon Gate,** popularly known as the Twilight Gate because it could take you all day (until twilight) to see everything carved on it. Painted in red, blue, and green, and gilded and lacquered, this gate is carved with more than 500 flowers, dragons, birds, and other animals. Its opulence is very un-Japanese, more akin to Chinese architecture than to the usual austerity of most Japanese shrines. Past that you enter the shrine's main sanctuary, **Haiden,** comprised of three halls: one reserved for the imperial family, one for the shogun, and one (the central hall) for conducting ceremonies. You can buy good-luck charms here that guard against misfortunes, or others to ensure good health, success in business, easy childbirth, or other achievements in daily life. To the right of the main hall is the entrance to **Tokugawa Ieyasu's mausoleum**—look for the carving of a sleeping cat

BUILDING A SHRINE FOR A shogun

When Ieyasu Tokugawa died in 1616 at the age of 75, his wish was to be enshrined in Nikko so he could serve as a guardian against evil demons (who were thought to come from the north) and thereby ensure the Tokugawa regime a long reign. The modest shrine built in 1616 at Ieyasu's request wasn't enough, however, to satisfy his grandson, Tokugawa Iemitsu, the third Tokugawa shogun. No expense was too great for Iemitsu, who sought to create a grand monument as an act of devotion—and as a demonstration of the Tokugawa shogunate's wealth and power. It took some 4.5 million artisans and other workers 1½ years to erect this complex of buildings, designed to be more elaborate and gorgeous than any other Japanese temple or shrine. Rich in colors and carvings, Toshogu Shrine is gilded with no fewer than 2.4 million sheets of gold leaf (they could cover an area of almost 2.4 ha/6 acres). The mausoleum was completed in 1636, almost 20 years after Ieyasu's death. Its natural setting is magnificent as well, in a grove of ancient **Japanese cedars** planted over a 20-year period during the 1600s by a feudal lord named Matsudaira Masatsuna. Some 13,000 of the original trees still stand, adding a sense of dignity to the mausoleum and shrine.

above the door, famous today as a symbol of Nikko (you'll find many reproductions at souvenir shops). Beyond that, 200 stone steps lead past cedars to Tokugawa's tomb. After the riotous colors of the shrine, the tomb seems surprisingly simple.

On the way out you'll pass **Yakushido,** a Buddhist temple famous for the dragon painting on its ceiling. A monk gives a brief explanation (in Japanese) and demonstrates how two sticks struck together produce an echo that supposedly resonates like a bell. Twelve statues here represent the Chinese zodiac calendar.

Directly to the west of Toshogu Shrine is one of the oldest buildings in the district (ca. 1617), **Futarasan Shrine** ♥ (✆ **0288-54-0535;** ¥300 for adults, ¥100 for children). It has various miniature shrines dedicated to the gods of mountains surrounding Nikko—the god of fortune, the god of happiness, the god of trees, the god of water, and the god of good marriages. On the shrine's grounds, look for the so-called **ghost lantern,** enclosed in a small vermilion-colored wooden structure. According to legend, it used to come alive at night and sweep around Nikko in the form of a ghost. It apparently scared one guard so much that he struck it with his sword 70 times; the marks are still visible on the lamp's rim.

Past Futarasan Shrine, the ornately elegant **Taiyuin Mausoleum** ♥♥ (✆ **0288-53-1567;** ¥550 adults, ¥250 children, or combo ticket with Rinnoji Temple; see p. 228) is the final resting place of Iemitsu, the third Tokugawa shogun, who was responsible for building the Toshogu Shrine. (Look for his statue.) Completed in 1653, it's not nearly as large as Toshogu Shrine, but it's more serene, probably because most tourists bypass it. To show respect for the first shogun, Taiyuin's buildings face Toshogu Shrine.

Toshogu Shrine and the other sights in Nikko Sannai are open daily from 9am to 5pm April through October (to 4pm the rest of the year); you must enter at least 30 minutes before closing time.

Other Attractions in Nikko

Nikko Tamozawa Imperial Villa (Tamozawa Goyoutei Kinen Koen) ♥♥♥ HISTORIC HOME If you haven't seen the Imperial Villas of Kyoto (p. 308), this villa is a great alternative. Built in 1899 for Prince Yoshihito (who later became the Taisho emperor), it's been so painstakingly restored that it looks brand-new. It is the largest wooden Imperial villa of its era, with 106 rooms, 37 of which are open to the public. The central core of the villa is actually much older, constructed in 1632 by a feudal lord and brought to Nikko from Edo (present-day Tokyo). Altogether, three emperors and three princes used the villa between 1899 and 1947. A self-guided tour of the villa provides insight into traditional Japanese architectural methods—from its 11 layers of paper-plastered walls to its nail-less wood framing—as well as the lifestyle of Japan's aristocracy. It's about a 20-minute walk east from Nikko Sannai along National Road 120.

A peek into the garden at the exquisitely restored Tamozawa Imperial Villa.

8–27 Honcho. ✆ **0288-53-6767.** ¥600 adults, ¥300 children. Wed–Mon 9am–5pm (closes 4:30pm Nov–Mar), last entry 4pm. Bus: Tamozawa stop.

Where to Stay in Nikko

Annex Turtle Hotori-An ♥♥ Owned by a friendly family, this simple but spotless modern structure is one of the best places to stay in Nikko. One dip in the hot-spring bath overlooking the Daiyagawa River (which you can lock for privacy) will tell you why; at night, you're lulled to sleep by the sound of the rushing waters. It's in a nice rural setting on a quiet street with a few other houses; an adjoining park and playground make it an excellent choice for families. All rooms except one are Japanese style. The same family runs Turtle Inn at 2–16 Takumi-cho.

8–28 Takumi-cho. turtle-nikko.com. ✆ **0288-53-3663.** 11 units. ¥8,700–¥10,200 single; ¥13,500–¥19,800 double. Bus: Sogo Kaikan-mae stop, then a 10-min. walk. **Amenities:** Free Wi-Fi.

Hike Mount Nakimushi

Yes, Nikko is historic, but it's also blessed with forests, rivers, waterfalls, the sparkling Lake Chuzenji, and shaded walking trails. If you do plan on staying the night, it would be a shame to miss out on a long walk or hike. If you have a moderate level of fitness, the trek to Mt. Nakimushi should take 3 to 4 hours. The trail head is just a 5-minute walk from the Mekke Nikko Kyodo Cultural Center (see above); a sign reading "鳴虫山登山口" and an arrow will point you in the right direction. Once you're on track, it's hard to lose your way. The path, a mixture of tree roots, stone steps, and sections of rough (though trodden) terrain, culminates 7.2km (4½ miles) later at the Nakimushi summit, 596m (1,955 ft.) high. The name Nakimushi translates to "crying insect," and if you hike in summer, expect to be joined by a piercing orchestra of cicadas. You'll likely break a sweat, but it's worth it for gorgeous views of Nikko and its undulating landscape.

Nikko Kanaya Hotel ♥♥♥ Founded in 1873 as Nikko's first hotel (until then, visitors stayed in area temples), this distinguished-looking place on a hill above the Sacred Bridge combines the rustic heartiness of a European country lodge with elements of old Japan. The present complex, built in spurts over the past 150 years, has a rambling, delightfully old-fashioned atmosphere that fuses Western architecture with Japanese craftsmanship. Through the decades it has played host to a number of VIPs, from Charles Lindbergh to Indira Gandhi to Shirley MacLaine; Frank Lloyd Wright left a sketch for the bar fireplace, which was later built to his design. Even if you don't stay here, drop by for lunch and gaze at the old photos lining the hallways. Pathways lead to the Daiyagawa River and several short hiking trails. All rooms are Western-style twins, with price differences based on room size, view (river view is best), and facilities. Some 10 rooms have been updated, but the older rooms have more character; some have antiques and claw-foot tubs. The priciest room is the corner room in the 80-year-old wing where the emperor once stayed.
1300 Kami-Hatsuishi. kanayahotel.co.jp. ✆ **0288-54-0001.** 70 units. ¥15,000–¥83,000 double. Bus: Shinkyo stop. **Amenities:** 2 restaurants; cafe; bar; outdoor pool (mid-July through Aug); skating rink (Dec–Feb); shuttle bus from Tobu Nikko Station; free Wi-Fi.

Where to Eat in Nikko

In addition to rainbow trout, Nikko is famous for *yuba,* a high-protein soy by-product formed by boiling soy milk, which causes a thin film to rise to the liquid's surface. Thought to have originated in Kyoto, it was popular among monks training at Rinnoji Temple for its nutrition, meatlike protein, and light weight for carrying on mountain retreats. Until the Meiji Period, only priests and members of the imperial family were allowed to consume it. Now you can enjoy it, too, at many restaurants in Nikko. Another popular dish is *Mizu-yokan,* a traditional sweet made from the adzuki bean.

Edokko (江戸ッ子) YUBA/NOODLES The stretch of highway between Nikko Station and Toshogu Shrine is littered with restaurants specializing in yuba dishes. The best way to eat yuba, in my view, is on top of or alongside *soba* (buckwheat noodles). Edokko, a small mom-and-pop shop that only opens for about 4 hours each day, serves set meals that combine stewed or sliced yuba with soba or *udon* noodles, tempura vegetables, pickles, and miso soup. The English menu looks like it was created by a child on Microsoft Paint, but it does list the composite parts of each meal and pixelated photos to boot. There's nothing fancy in here—except the tables, perhaps, which are carved from fallen cedar trunks—but the food is superb and very reasonably priced. It's a 20-minutes walk from Tobu-Nikko Station, or 3 minutes from Shinkyo Bridge.
916 Nakahatsuishimachi. ✆ **0288-54-0293.** Set meals ¥1,300–¥1,800. Daily 11am–3pm (last order).

Hippari Dako (ひっぱり凧) ♥ VARIED JAPANESE This tiny three-table establishment offers a limited selection of noodle dishes, including ramen and stir-fried noodles with vegetables, as well as *yakitori* (skewered barbecued chicken), *gyoza* (dumplings), and vegetarian dishes that include *yuba*. The walls and ceiling are covered with business cards and messages left by travelers from around the world, and there's an English-language menu with photos. It's on the main street leading to Nikko Sannai, a 1-minute walk from Shinkyo Bridge.
1011 Kami-Hatsuishi. ✆ **0288-53-2933.** Main dishes average ¥1,000. Mon–Sat noon–5pm and 6:30–9pm.

MOUNT FUJI ♥♥

Affectionately called "Fuji-san" by Japanese, Mount Fuji has been revered since ancient times. Throughout the centuries, Japanese poets have written about it, painters have painted it, pilgrims have flocked to it, and more than a few people have died on it. Without a doubt, this mountain has been photographed more than anything else in Japan. At 3,766m (12,355 ft.), it's the country's tallest mountain, towering above everything around it, a cone of almost perfectly symmetrical proportions. To Japanese, it symbolizes the very spirit of their country.

Mount Fuji or Bust

The first documented case of someone scaling Mount Fuji is from the early 8th century. During the Edo Period, pilgrimages to the top were considered a purifying ritual, with strict rules governing dress and route. Women, however, were thought to defile sacred places and so were prohibited from climbing mountains until 1871.

Though it's visible on clear days (mostly in winter) from as far as 150km (100 miles) away, Fuji-san, unfortunately, is almost always cloaked in clouds. If you catch a glimpse of this elusive mountain (which you can sometimes do from the bullet train between Tokyo and Nagoya), consider yourself lucky. Some of the best spots for views of Mount Fuji are **Hakone** and **Izu,** though you can get great views from skyscrapers in Tokyo and Yokohama, and on the hiking trails webbing Kanagawa Prefecture, when the conditions are right.

Essentials

WHEN TO GO The "official" climbing season is very short, only from July 1 to August 31. Climbers are discouraged from climbing outside the season, due to low temperatures, superstrong winds, and no emergency services, but some guiding companies do climb in late June or early September. To beat the crowds—and it can still get busy despite the new restrictions—try to schedule your climb on a weekday during the first 2 weeks of July, before the start of Japan's school vacation (around July 20).

GETTING THERE There are four ascents to the summit of Mount Fuji (and four descents). The **Kawaguchiko-Yoshidaguchi Trail,** better known as the Yoshida Trail, is the most popular, easiest to access from Tokyo, and least steep. Most climbs start at the Go-go-me, or Fifth Station, about 1,400 to 2,400m (4,593–7,874 ft.) above sea level. In July and August, the peak climbing season, 13 **buses** daily travel directly from Tokyo's Shinjuku Station to the Yoshida Trail's Fifth Station; the trip takes almost 2½ hours and costs ¥3,800 one-way. Other buses go year-round to Kawaguchiko Station at the base of the mountain (trip time: 1 hr. 45 min.; ¥2,200 one-way); from Kawaguchiko Station you can catch a bus onward to the Fifth Station, which will take around 45 minutes and cost another ¥1,780 one-way (¥2,800 round-trip). From Tokyo, buses depart from the Yasuda Seimi no. 2 Building, a short walk from the west side of Shinjuku Station; they require reservations, which you can make at the **Keio Highway Bus Reservation Center** (**Keio Kosoku Bus Yoyaku Center; ✆ 03-5376-2222**) or online at highway-buses.jp.

If you want to use your Japan Rail Pass, you can take a **train** from Tokyo's Shinjuku Station via the **JR Chuo Line** to Otsuki, where you change to the **Fuji Kyuko Line** for Kawaguchiko Station. The entire trip takes about 3 hours. Note, however, that you must pay an extra ¥1,170 for the last leg of the journey, and from Kawaguchiko Station you must still take the 45-minute bus ride onward to the Fifth Station.

VISITOR INFORMATION A good online source is Fujiyoshida City's website, **fujiyoshida.net**, which carries info on the Kawaguchiko-Yoshidaguchi Trail, bus schedules from Tokyo, mountain huts, and other information. Finally, there's a tourist information office at Kawaguchiko Station (**✆ 0555-72-6700;** daily 9am–5pm during climbing season).

Climbing Mount Fuji

Mount Fuji is part of a larger national park called **Fuji-Hakone-Izu National Park.** Of the handful of trails leading to the top, the most popular is the Kawaguchiko-Yoshidaguchi Trail, which is divided into 10 different stages; the Fifth Station, located about 2,475m (8,120 ft.) up, is the usual

Climbing above the clouds that usually shroud Mount Fuji's peak.

starting point. From here it takes about 6 hours to reach the summit and 3 hours for the descent. Only 4,000 climbers are permitted to the trail each day (excluding those staying in mountain lodges), and they must pay a ¥4,000 access fee—arrive early if you want to guarantee entry. The gate to the trail is now closed 4pm to 3am to prevent overnight, or "bullet," climbers.

When your bus deposits you at the Fifth Station, you may feel bombarded with souvenir shops, restaurants, and busloads of tourists, but don't be discouraged—most of these tourists aren't climbing to the top. As soon as you get past them and the blaring loudspeakers, you'll find yourself on a steep rocky path, surrounded only by scrub brush and the hikers on the path below and above you. After a couple of hours, you'll probably be above the roily clouds, which stretch in all directions. It will seem as if you are on an island, barren and rocky, in the middle of an ocean.

PREPARING FOR YOUR CLIMB Because of snow and inclement weather from fall to late spring, the best time to make an ascent is during the "official" climbing season from July to August. Keep in mind that this is not a solitary pursuit. More than 300,000 people climb Fuji-san every year, mostly in July and August and mostly on weekends. (Restrictions on the trail, introduced in 2024, have reportedly reduced the number of climbers by about 10%.)

You don't need climbing experience to ascend Mount Fuji (you'll see everyone from grandmothers to children making the pilgrimage), but you do need stamina and a good pair of walking shoes. Climbing is possible in tennis shoes, but if the rocks are wet, they can get awfully slippery—if you're wearing sneakers, they should be ones designed for use on mountain trails. You should also bring a light plastic raincoat (don't buy the ones in souvenir shops at the Fifth Station; they're about as waterproof as filter paper) because it often rains on the mountain. You'll also want a sun hat, sunglasses, a bottle of water, a sweater for the evening, gloves, socks, tissues (for pay toilets, which may not have toilet paper), and a flashlight (or headlamp) in case you end up hiking at night. And it goes without saying, the bag in which you carry your supplies should also be waterproof. It gets very chilly on Mount Fuji at night. Even in August, the average temperature on the summit is 43°F (6°C). Finally, there are places to eat and rest on the way to the top, but prices are extortionate, so carry as many snacks and liquids with you as you can.

Souvenir walking sticks to commemorate climbing Mount Fuji, a bucket-list achievement for many Japanese.

STRATEGIES FOR CLIMBING TO THE TOP The usual procedure for climbing Mount Fuji is to take a morning bus, start climbing in early afternoon, spend the night near the summit, get up early in the morning to climb the rest of the way to the top, and then watch the sun rise (about 4:30am) from atop Mount Fuji. The summit is a 1-hour hiking trail that circles the crater. Hikers then begin the descent, reaching the Fifth Station before noon. In the past few decades, climbers had begun to arrive at the Fifth Station late in the evening and then climb to the top during the night with flashlights, which allowed them to watch the sunrise and make their descent without having to stay overnight in one of the mountain huts. Officials now shut off the trail between 4pm and 3am to prevent such climbers.

There are more than a dozen **mountain huts** along the Yoshida Trail above the Fifth Station, some with the capacity to house as many as 500 hikers. They're very primitive, providing only a futon and toilet facilities, yet many huts now charge over ¥10,000 per night with two meals. (Some huts also charge extra for Fri or Sat night.) Dinner will likely consist of dried fish, rice, miso soup, and pickled vegetables; breakfast will be exactly the same. Note that most huts are open only in July and August; book as early as you can to ensure a place. **Seikanso** at the sixth stage (✆ **0555-24-6090;** seikanso.jp) is a good option, with flush toilets and open from July to mid-October, but it leaves you with a lot of climbing to do in the morning. **Toyokan Hut** at the seventh stage (✆ **0555-22-1040**) and **Taishikan Hut** at the eighth stage (✆ **0555-22-1947**) are better if you want to stack more of your climbing on Day 1. See **japanmountainhuts.com** for more info.

Climbing Mount Fuji is a unique experience, but there's a saying in Japan: "Everyone should climb Mount Fuji once; only a fool would climb it twice."

HAKONE ♥♥♥

97km (60 miles) SW of Tokyo

Beautiful Hakone, which is part of **Fuji-Hakone-Izu National Park,** has about everything a vacationer could wish for: hot-spring resorts, mountains, lakes, breathtaking views of Mount Fuji when the weather is clear (mostly in cooler months), and interesting historical sites. Although you can conceivably tour Hakone on a day trip if you leave very early in the morning and limit your sightseeing to a few key attractions, it's much more rewarding to add an overnight stay or two—either round-trip from Tokyo or as a stopover between Tokyo and Kyoto. If you can, travel on a weekday, when modes of transportation are likely to be less crowded. Some hotels offer cheaper weekday rates in the off season.

Essentials

GETTING THERE & GETTING AROUND Getting to and around Hakone is half the fun. An easy loop tour through Hakone includes various forms of transportation: You start out by train from Tokyo, switch to a three-car mountain railway, change to a cable car and then a smaller ropeway, and finally end your trip with a boat ride across Lake Ashi. From Lake Ashi (that is, from the villages of Togendai, Hakone-machi, or Moto-Hakone), you then take a bus to Odawara Station (an hour's ride) to board the train back to Tokyo. Buses also connect all the recommendations listed below, which is useful if you wish to complete part of your sightseeing the first day before going to your hotel for the evening. A bus also runs directly between Togendai and Shinjuku in about 2¼ hours.

The most economical and by far easiest way to travel is Odakyu Railway's **Hakone Free Pass.** Despite its name, it isn't free, but it does give you a round-trip ticket on the express train from Shinjuku Station to Odawara or Hakone-Yumoto, then includes all modes of transportation in Hakone described above. The pass lets you avoid the hassle of buying individual tickets and gives nominal discounts on most Hakone attractions. A 2-day pass costs ¥6,100 and a 3-day pass is ¥6,500. Children pay ¥1,100 and ¥1,350, respectively.

The train from Shinjuku to Odawara via **Odakyu Express** takes 100 minutes, departing 2–4 times an hour. In Odawara, you then transfer to another train for a 15-minute trip to Hakone-Yumoto. If time is of the essence or if you want to ensure a seat during peak season, reserve a seat on the faster and more luxurious **Odakyu Romance Car,** which offers free onboard Wi-Fi; it travels from Shinjuku all the way to Hakone-Yumoto in 85 minutes, and costs an extra ¥1,150 one-way with a Hakone Pass.

Japan Rail Pass holders should take the Shinkansen bullet train to Odawara (not all bullet trains stop here, so make sure yours does), then do the rest of your traveling on a 2-day Hakone Free Pass for ¥5,000 or a 3-day Pass for ¥5,400 (children pay ¥1,000 and ¥1,250). This is also a good option if you are traveling onward to, say, Kyoto.

All passes described above can be purchased at any station of the Odakyu Railway, including Shinjuku, Odawara, and Hakone-Yumoto. In Tokyo, the **Odakyu Sightseeing Service Center,** located on the ground floor near the west exit of Odakyu Shinjuku Station (odakyu.jp/english/support/center/; (✆ **03-5909-0211;** daily 8am–4pm), sells the Hakone Free Pass and provides sightseeing information and maps in English.

Hakone also has an efficient bus network (included in the Free Pass), with lines conveniently identified by a letter that is also on the front of the bus. The Togendai (T) Line is the most useful, traveling between Togendai and Odawara and making stops near the three accommodations recommended below. Pick up the excellent route map for **Hakone Tozan Bus** (✆ **0465-35-1271**) at the Odawara or Yumoto tourist office, or online at hakonenavi.jp.

VISITOR INFORMATION In addition to the Odakyu Sightseeing Service Center in Tokyo (see above), there's the **Odawara Tourist Office** (✆ **0465-22-2339;** daily 9am–5pm) inside Odawara Station and the **Hakone Tourist Information Center** (✆ **0460-85-5700;** daily 9am–5:45pm) across the road from the east exit of Hakone-Yumoto Station. English-language information on Hakone is also available at **hakone-japan.com**.

LUGGAGE If you plan to return to Tokyo, I suggest you leave your luggage in storage at your Tokyo hotel or in Shinjuku Station and travel to Hakone with only an overnight bag. If you're heading onward to another destination, you can leave your bags at Odawara Station's **Yamato Luggage** (✆ **080-7776-3514;** daily 9am–8pm) for ¥500 per piece per day or ¥1,000 for larger items; or you can have it sent to your Hakone hotel if you deliver it by 12:30pm (around ¥1,350). Coin lockers are available for baggage storage at Hakone Yumoto Station, but you can't guarantee a locker, especially during peak season. Or, if you deliver your bags to the **Hakone Baggage Service** (✆ **0460-86-4140**) at Hakone-Yumoto Station between 8:30am and 12:30pm, it will transport your bags to your Hakone accommodations by 3pm. The next day, it can also pick up your bags at your hotel by 10am and deliver them to Hakone-Yumoto Station by 1pm, where they will keep them until 7pm. This service costs ¥900 to ¥1,600 per bag, depending on size and weight; a ¥100 discount is provided for holders of the Hakone Free Pass.

Exploring Hakone

If you plan on spending only a day in Hakone, you should leave Tokyo very early in the morning and plan on seeing only the top attractions, the **Hakone Open-Air Museum** (p. 241) and **Owakudani** (p. 242). Keep in

Hakone

HOTELS
Hanaori 5
The Fujiya Hotel 1
RESTAURANTS
Bella Foresta 3
ATTRACTIONS
Hakone Kowakien Yunessun 2
Hakone Check Point 9
Hakone Detached Palace Garden 7
Hakone Open-Air Museum 3
Narukawa Art Museum 6
Owakudani 4
Sengokuhara
138
Miyagino
Cable Car
Gora
Sounzan
Chokoku-no-Mori
Miyanoshita
Owakudani
Ropeway
Togendai
Kowakudani
1
Hakone-Tozan Railway
Tonosawa
Hakone-Yumoto
Odawara
Komagatake Cable Car
Komagatake Ropeway
BOAT TRIP
Sukomo River
Hakone Shindo Drive
TOKAIDO SHINKANSEN LINE
Hakone Shrine
Lake Ashi
Moto-Hakone
Hakone-machi
Hakone Turnpike
Sagami Sea
Tourist Info
Cable Car
Mountain Tram
Railway
Ropeway
Sightseeing boat
0
2 mi
2 km

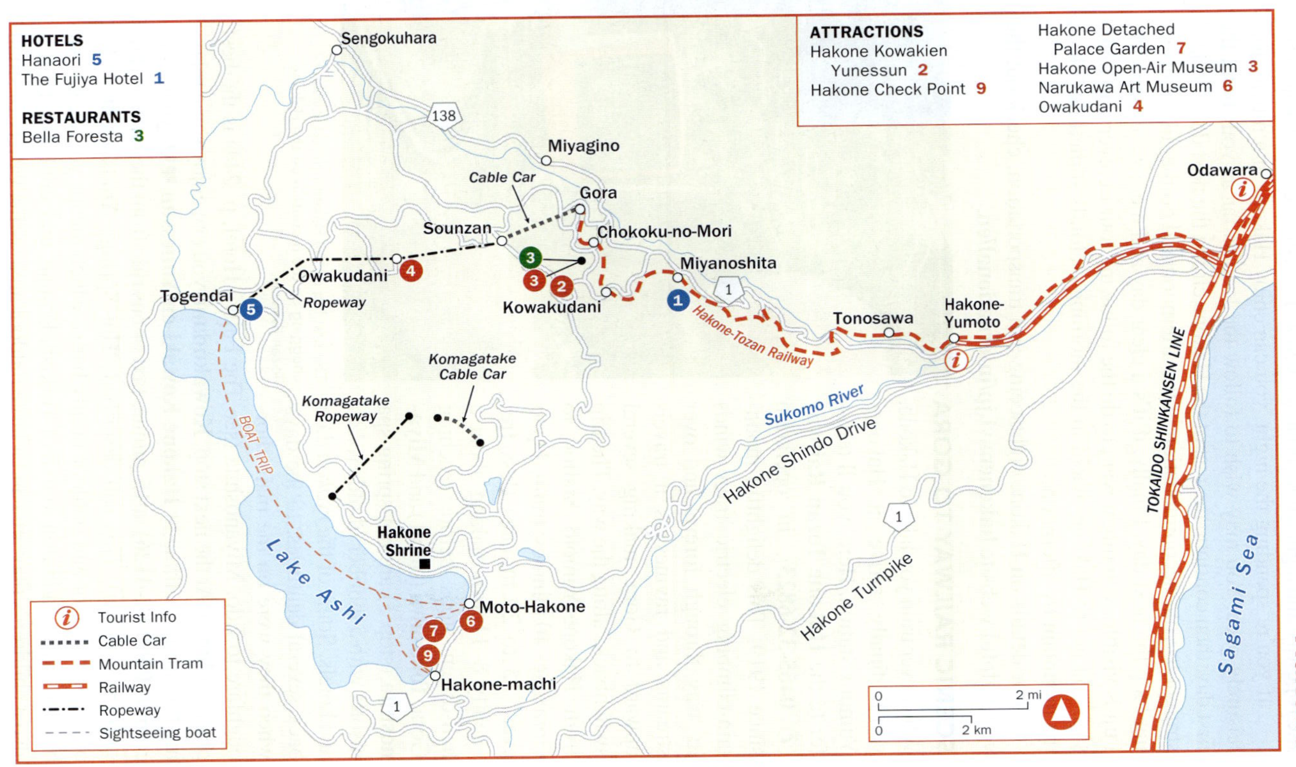

mind that it takes about 5 hours to travel the loop from Odawara and that the ropeway and sightseeing boat, as well as museums, close around 5pm.

If you're spending the night, you can enjoy Hakone at a much more leisurely pace. You may wish to follow the loop as far as your hotel the first day, then continue the rest of the Hakone circuit the next day. Or head straight to your accommodation in the afternoon and do the full sightseeing loop the next day. Finally, if it's a clear day and there's a chance Mt. Fuji is visible, you might want to do the following tour in reverse to make sure you get to Hakone-machi in the morning—clouds sometimes cloak the mountain by afternoon.

For details on Hakone sightseeing and transportation, check out the very helpful website **hakonenavi.jp/international/en**.

SCENIC RAILWAY TO GORA

Whichever train you take to Hakone, you'll finally arrive at Hakone-Yumoto Station. Here, you'll transfer to the **Hakone Tozan Railway** (✆ **0465-32-6823**), in operation since 1919. This delightful mountain-climbing electric train winds its way through forests and over streams and ravines as it travels upward to Gora, making several switchbacks along the way. The trip from Hakone-Yumoto Station to Gora takes 40 minutes; trains depart every 15 to 20 minutes (less frequently 8–11pm), making about a half-dozen stops before reaching Gora. **Tonosawa** (stop 1) and **Miyanoshita** (stop 3) are hot-spring spa resorts with a number of old *ryokan* and hotels. Some of the *ryokan* date back several centuries, to the days when they were on the main thoroughfare to Edo. Miyanoshita (see The Fujiya Hotel, p. 244) is the best place for lunch. At the next stop, **Kowakudani,** you can enjoy some relaxing hot-spring bathing at **Hakone Kowaki-en Yunessun** ♥♥ (yunessun.com; ✆ **0460-82-4126**), a 15-minute taxi or bus ride from the railway (bus stop: Kowaki-en). This self-described "Hot Springs Amusement Park" offers both indoor and outdoor family baths, which means you wear your bathing suit. In addition to indoor Turkish, Roman, and salt baths, there's also a children's play area and a large outdoor area with a variety of small baths, including those mixed with healthy minerals and—believe it or not—coffee, green tea, sake, or wine. For more traditional bathing, the

The first leg of the Hakone circuit involves chugging up the mountain on the Hakone Tozan Railway.

attached Mori No Yu has both indoor and outdoor baths separated for men and women (you don't wear your suit here). As with most public bathhouses, people with tattoos are not allowed. Most people stay 2 to 3 hours. Admission to Yunessun is ¥2,500 adults, ¥1,400 children; admission to Mori No Yu is ¥1,500 and ¥1,000; admission to both is ¥3,500 and ¥1,800. Upon admission, you'll be given a towel, robe, and wristband to pay for drinks and extras (rental suits are available; you'll leave your valuables in a locker). Yunessun is open daily 9am to 7pm; Mori No Yu is open daily 11am to 8pm.

The most important stop on the Hakone Tozan Railway is the next-to-the-last one, Chokoku-no-Mori, where you'll find the famous **Hakone Open-Air Museum (Chokoku-no-Mori Bijutsukan)** ♥♥♥ (hakone-oam.or.jp; ✆ **0460-82-1161;** daily 9am–5pm; ¥2,000 adults, ¥1,600 students, ¥800 children), a minute's walk from the station. With the possible exception of views of Mount Fuji, this is Hakone's number-one attraction, and it has inspired dozens of other open-air museums across the country. Using nature as a dramatic backdrop, it showcases (mostly) 20th-century sculpture in a spectacular setting of glens, formal gardens, ponds, streams, and meadows. Some 400 sculptures are on display, both outdoors and in several buildings, with works by Carl Milles, Manzu Giacomo, Jean Dubuffet, Willem de Kooning, Barbara Hepworth, Taro Okamoto, and Joan Miró, and more than 25 pieces by Henry Moore, shown on a rotating basis. Several installations geared toward children allow them to climb and play. The Picasso Pavilion contains works by Picasso from pastels to ceramics, one of the world's largest collections. Count on a visit of at least 2 hours. Be sure to stop off at the "foot *onsen,*" where you can immerse your tired feet in soothing, hot-spring water. The museum is open 9am–5pm year-round. Your Hakone Free Pass gives you a ¥100 discount. The museum's restaurant **Bella Foresta** (p. 244) serves an excellent buffet lunch.

Gabriel Loire's stunning Symphonic Sculpture at the Hakone Open-Air Museum.

CABLE CAR TO SOUNZAN & ROPEWAY TO TOGENDAI

Hakone Tozan cable cars leave Gora every 20 minutes or so and arrive 10 minutes later at Sounzan, making several stops along the way as they travel steeply uphill. At Sounzan, you board a gondola on the **Hakone Ropeway** for an 8-minute ride to **Owakudani ♥♥**, the ropeway's highest point. Before changing gondolas here for the rest of the ride, take some time to enjoy the views, including those of Mt. Fuji in winter. Owakudani means "Great Boiling Valley," and you'll soon understand how it got its name when you see (and smell) the sulfurous steam escaping from fissures in the rock, testament to the volcanic activity still present here (if you want to learn more, spend ¥100 to visit the small **Hakone Geomuseum;** hakone-geomuseum.jp; ✆ **0460-83-8140;** daily 9am–4pm). Most Japanese commemorate the trip by buying boiled eggs cooked here in the boiling waters. The ropeway continues another 16 minutes to Togendai, which lies beside Lake Ashi. Note that the ropeway stops running at around 5pm in summer and 4:15pm in winter.

ACROSS LAKE ASHI BY BOAT

From Togendai you can take a **Hakone Sightseeing Cruise** (hakone-kankosen.co.jp; ✆ **0460-83-7722**) across Lake Ashi, sailing on a replica of a man-of-war pirate ship. Lake Ashi, known as Ashinoko in Japanese, was formed by a volcanic eruption some 3,000 years ago. It takes about a half-hour to cross the lake to Hakone-machi (also called Hakonemachi-ko; *machi* means "city," and *ko* means "lake") and Moto-Hakone, two resort towns right next to each other on the southern edge of the lake. This end of the lake affords the best view of Mount Fuji, one you'll often see in tourist publications (you're more likely to catch this elusive sight in the morning in cooler months). Boats operate year-round, though they run less frequently in winter and not at all in stormy weather; the last boat

Hakone Sightseeing Cruises cross Lake Ashi on replica pirate ships.

departs around 5pm from April through November. If you miss it, you can get back from Togendai to Odawara by bus.

After the boat ride, you can get a bus back to Hakone-Yumoto and Odawara stations from the boat piers in Hakone-machi and Moto-Hakone. If you have time for more sightseeing, however, get off the boat in Hakone-machi, turn left, and walk about 5 minutes along the town's main road, following the signs to **Hakone Check Point** (**Hakone Sekisho**) ♥♥ (hakonesekisyo.jp; ✆ **0460-83-6635;** daily 9am–5pm, to 4:30pm Dec–Feb; ¥500 adults, ¥250 children). This reconstructed checkpoint, originally built in 1619, was used until 1869 as one of many along the famous Tokaido Highway, which connected Edo (present-day Tokyo) with Kyoto. In feudal days, local lords, called *daimyo,* were required to spend alternate years in Edo; their wives were kept in Edo as virtual hostages to discourage the lords from planning rebellions while in their homelands. This was one of 53 checkpoints in Japan set up to prevent the transport of guns, spies, and female travelers trying to flee Edo. Passes were necessary for travel, and anyone who was caught trying to sneak past were strictly punished—men were executed, while women had their heads shaved and then were given away to anyone who wanted them. This guardhouse was rebuilt using traditional carpenter tools and architectural techniques of the Edo Period; inside, life-size models reenact scenes from the era, and you can pore over displays of Edo Period artifacts—woodblock prints, photos of the old checkpoint, and items used for travel, including a tiny abacus and an even smaller case holding grooming supplies. Your Hakone Free Pass gives a ¥100 discount.

Just beyond the Hakone Check Point's exhibition hall, at a big parking lot with the traditional gate, the **Hakone Detached Palace Garden** (**Onshi-Hakone-Koen**) ♥, which lies on a small promontory on Lake Ashi, has spectacular views of the lake and, in clear weather, Mount Fuji. Originally part of an Imperial summer villa built in 1886 but destroyed by earthquake, the well-kept garden is free and open to the public and is a great place for wandering. Another fun option is to cross the highway and follow a shaded footpath lined with ancient and mighty cedars, once part of the old **Tokaido Highway.** During the Edo Period, more than 400 cedars were planted along this important road, which today stretches 2.5km (1½ miles) along the curve of Lake Ashi. It'll take about 5 minutes to reach the town of Moto-Hakone. Head up the hill to the right past the orange *torii* gate to the **Narukawa Art Museum** ♥♥ (narukawamuseum.co.jp; ✆ **0460-83-6828;** daily 9am–5pm; ¥1,500 adults, ¥1,000 students, ¥500 children), which offers both art and sweeping scenic views. It specializes in modern works of the *Nihonga* style of painting, a sparse style developed during the Heian Period (794–1185). Large paintings and screens by contemporary *Nihonga* artists are on display, from well-known artists to younger up-and-comers. Views of Lake Ashi and Mount Fuji, especially from its tea lounge, are a bonus. The Hakone Free Pass gives a ¥100 discount.

Buses depart 2 to 4 times an hour from both Hakone-machi and Moto-Hakone for Hakone-Yumoto and Odawara stations. (Be sure to check the time of the last bus; generally it's around 8pm, but this can change with the season and the day of the week.) The bus ride takes about 30 minutes to Hakone-Yumoto, 50 minutes to Odawara.

Where to Stay & Eat in Hakone

Most accommodations cost more during peak travel times like Golden Week, school holidays, New Year's, weekends, national holidays, cherry blossom season in spring, and the changing of the leaves in autumn.

For casual dining, the Hakone Open-Air Museum has a pleasant restaurant, **Bella Foresta** ♥, overlooking the park's fantastic scenery and offering a buffet lunch of mostly Western fare daily from 11am to 3pm for ¥2,200. There are also informal restaurants at the **Owakudani** Ropeway Station and **Togendai** boat cruise building, both with scenic views and serving meals for around ¥1,500.

The **Fujiya** ♥♥♥ is one of Hakone's prime spots for a meal, located in its grandest, oldest hotel (see below).

The Fujiya Hotel ♥♥♥ The Fujiya, established in 1878, is quite simply the grandest, most majestic old hotel in Hakone; indeed, it might be the loveliest historic hotel in Japan. Its comfortably old-fashioned atmosphere includes such Asian touches as a Japanese-style roof and long wooden corridors with photographs of famous guests, from Einstein to Eisenhower. A landscaped garden out back, with a waterfall, pond, greenhouse, outdoor pool, and stunning views over the valley, is great for strolls and meditation. There's also an indoor thermal pool and public hot-spring baths (hot-spring water is piped into each guest's bathroom). There are five separate buildings, all different and added on at various times in the hotel's long history, but management has been meticulous in retaining its historic traditions. Rooms are spacious with high ceilings and antique furnishings. The most expensive rooms are the largest, but the most evocative are in the Flower Palace, built in 1936 in an architectural style reminiscent of a Japanese temple. Even if you don't stay here, come for a meal or tea in the bright, cheerful main dining hall, dating from 1930, with its intricately detailed high ceiling, large windows with Japanese screens, wooden floor, and white tablecloths. It's famous for its curry, but other options include rainbow trout, sirloin steak, and set lunches (set lunches start at ¥8,000, set dinners at ¥19,000; a la carte options are also available).

359 Miyanoshita, Hakone. fujiyahotel.jp. ✆ **0460-82-2211.** 146 units. Twins ¥51,000–¥83,000; suites ¥130,000–¥200,000. Station: Miyanoshita (Hakone Tozan Railway; 5 min.). Bus: Miyanoshita Onsen stop (1 min.). **Amenities:** 3 restaurants; lounge; bar; hot-spring baths; Jacuzzi; indoor/outdoor pools; room service; sauna; free Wi-Fi.

Hanaori (はなおり) ♥♥ Only an 11-minute walk from Togendai Port, this beautiful property fuses traditional ryokan aesthetics with modern hotel comforts. It's a great option if you want to start your second day with

A Phallic Festival in Kawasaki

Every April in Kawasaki, a city squeezed between Tokyo and Yokohama, one of Japan's most unusual, and arguably misunderstood, festivals takes place. The **Kanamara Matsuri,** otherwise known as the "Festival of the Steel Phallus," places the penis as the primary object of veneration. Participants carry floats topped with huge phallic iconography, covered in sacred *shide* streamers, through the old market streets en route to **Kanayama Shrine.** The festival's origins are rooted in a folktale in which a blacksmith creates a steel penis to exorcise a demon that's taken refuge inside a newlywed woman's vagina. Nowadays, tens of thousands of festivalgoers show up the first Sunday of April each year to pray for fertility, healthy sex lives, and prevention of STDS (a regular act, since Kawasaki was a town full of brothels on the old Tokaido trade route). The festival is also a significant celebration for Japan's gay, drag, and trans communities, who use it normalize different sexual orientations and sex positivity, going against the grain of this socially conservative nation. The festival is free to attend, and though the main parade, starting around midday, is obscenely busy, the crowds soon disperse across the shrine grounds and nearby Daishi Park, and throughout the **Kawasaki Daishi Temple** complex, where you'll find lots of street food and souvenir stalls. The parade begins at **Kawasaki-Daishi Station,** 35 minutes from Shinagawa Station by train; the journey, requiring a change at Keikyu-Kawasaki Station, costs ¥560.

a boat trip across Lake Ashi (see p. 242)—or you can walk around the lake on an undulating footpath from here (1½–2 hr. to Hakone Check Point). When you enter the hotel's handsome wooden lobby, you'll notice the Hana ("Flower") Stage on the other side of a plate-glass wall. A sunken seating area surrounded by water, it's primed for enjoying the sunset with a local craft beer or glass of sake from the cafe counter. (Guests can't resist posing for photos on the Hana Stage, which keeps the staff busy offering to take their pictures.) This region is a hotbed of geothermal activity, and Hanaori's *onsen* baths are another reason to book yourself in for the night. One of the public baths looks toward Lake Ashi, another views a nicely curated Japanese garden. The baths (open 5–10am and 3pm–midnight) alternate between men-only and women-only, so each sex has access to one bath in the evening, the other the following morning. There's also a private bath, which guests can reserve for 40 minutes for ¥3,000; alternatively, book a lakeside room with a tub on the balcony. Buffet-style dinner and breakfast (included in the price) use seasonal ingredients.

160 Motohakone Togendai, Hakone-machi. ashinoko-hanaori.orixhotelsandresorts.com. ✆ **0460-83-8739.** 154 units. Twins ¥35,000–¥63,000; twins with open-air bath ¥68,000–¥80,000; includes dinner and breakfast. Free shuttle from Odawara Station (1-hr; call hotel to reserve), 45-min. bus ride. from Hakone-Yumoto Station (Izu Hakone Bus J Line). **Amenities:** Hot-spring bath; cafe; souvenir shop; free Wi-Fi.

YOKOHAMA ♥♥

Many tourists skip Yokohama, assuming it's just an extension of the Tokyo urban sprawl. But to see it as such is to do it a great disservice.

Yokohama is one of Japan's most multicultural cities, with a redeveloped bay area providing the kind of picturesque waterfront strolls you can't find elsewhere in the country. It's also home to two ramen museums, some of Japan's most storied jazz cafes, a resplendent strolling garden, an amusement park hosting one of the world's largest Ferris wheels, the lively bars and *izakaya* of the old Noge pleasure district, the best Chinatown in Japan, the uber-popular DeNa Baystars baseball team (fresh off their first Japan Series title in 26 years), and the Yokohama International Stadium, host of Rugby World Cup and FIFA World Cup finals this century. Many Yokohamaites commute to Tokyo for work, but they also know on which side their bread was buttered, retaining a strong, and I would argue well-placed, sense of hometown pride. It's so much more than simply Tokyo by the sea.

Although Yokohama was ravaged by both the Great Kanto Earthquake of 1923 and firebombing raids during World War II, some of the administrative buildings and grand hotels built to serve the growing number of Western diplomats, emissaries, businessmen, scholars, and writers remain in the Naka-ku area, including the **Red Brick Warehouses** retail and dining complex (p. 253); the **Hotel New Grand** (10 Yamashitacho), widely viewed as the birthplace of cocktails in Japan; the **Yokohama**

WHAT MADE YOKOHAMA yokohama?

Though it's now Japan's second most populous city, Yokohama was a place of little historical note until the final days of the Edo period (1603–1868)—a fishing village of 600 people, enclosed by the hills and bluffs of eastern Kanagawa Prefecture on one side and Tokyo Bay on the other. When Commodore Matthew Galbraith Perry of the U.S. Navy sailed past Yokohama in 1853, he dropped anchor in Tokyo Bay and, by way of presidential decree, demanded that Japan end its policy of national isolation and open the borders to trade. Fearing the power of the U.S. fleet's modern weapons and accepting Japan had fallen well behind the West's pace of technological progress, Lord Abe Masahiro, acting on behalf of the shogun, acceded to Perry's demands.

Masahiro identified ports in Shimoda and Hakodate for foreign trade; Yokohama, only 32km (20 miles) south of the capital, was added to the list in 1859. It was close enough to Edo (now Tokyo) that trade could be streamlined and immigration monitored, but it was not *too* close to Tokyo, nor was it part of the Tokaido Highway—meaning it was easier there to keep foreign residents segregated from the greater public.

As the colonial powers of Europe and North America set sail for Japan, Yokohama was their primary point of entry. Many would go on to settle in a district still known as Kannai, literally "inside the barrier." The settlement and population ballooned. By 1890, when Lafcadio Hearn (see p. 418), one of the most famous 19th-century travelers to Japan, stepped off a wooden sampan and onto the port of Yokohama, he found a blue-grey city of large houses, temples, coped walls, tile roofs, rickshaws, and markets, where lattice-fronted shops housed curios of the most bewitching designs and labyrinthine streets contained the hubbub of a growing metropolitan area. The population of this village so recently lost in time had by then surpassed 100,000.

Yokohama

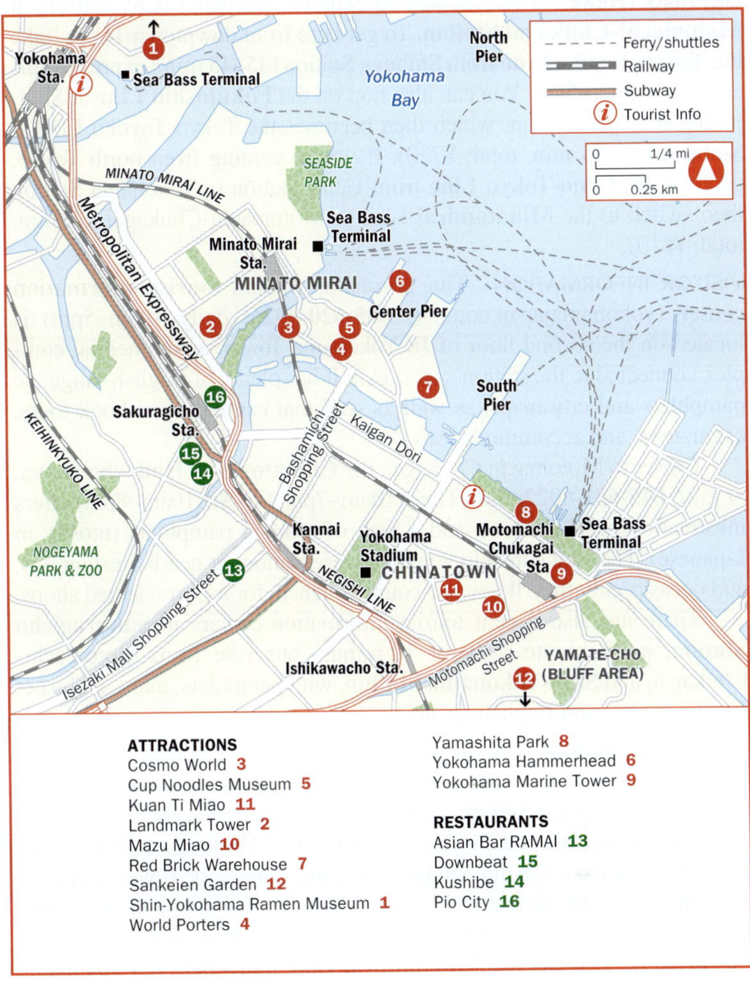

Archives of History Museum (3 Nihonodori), used as the British Consulate from 1931 to 1972; and the beautiful **Yokohama Port Opening Memorial Hall** (1–6–6 Honcho).

Yokohama retains this cosmopolitan air. Many major companies have established their Japanese HQs here, and multiple international schools cluster near the bay area. Walking down the charming, pedestrian-only shopping street Motomachi, you'll be struck by how many non-Japanese faces you see and how often you hear English-language accents (primarily American) filling the air. Japan is still a homogenous country; but Yokohama gives a view of what might have been and, perhaps in the future, what the country may yet become.

Essentials

GETTING THERE The best way to explore Yokohama is by starting at **Motomachi-Chukagai Station.** To get here from downtown Tokyo, take the **Tokyo-Toyoko Line** from Shibuya Station (35–45 min.; express trains every 15 min.; ¥540). You can also hop on the **Fukutoshin Line** at Shinjuku-sanchome Station, which then becomes the Tokyo-Toyoko Line at Shibuya (45–55 min. total; ¥720). If you're coming from north Tokyo, take the **JR Ueno-Tokyo Line** from Ueno Station to Yokohama Station then switch to the **Minatomirai Line** to Motomachi-Chukagai (50 min. total; ¥810).

VISITOR INFORMATION The Yokohama Station **tourist information center** (yokohamajapan.com; ✆ **045-620-9926;** daily 10am–5pm) is located on the second floor of JR Yokohama Tower, a commercial complex connected to the station's west exit. It has plenty of English-language pamphlets and city maps, as well as staff that can help you book tours, excursions, and accommodations.

Closer to Motomachi Chukagai, the **Chinatown 80 Hall** (chinatown.or.jp; ✆ **045-681-6022;** Sun–Thurs 10am–7pm, Fri–Sat 10am–8pm) offers information on Chinatown and a rack of tourism pamphlets (mostly in Japanese). The staff can help you make reservations at nearby restaurants, and occasionally they'll have discount vouchers for use in selected shops.

There are also decent tourist information centers in **Sakuragicho Station,** a 30-minute walk or 10-minute bus ride from Motomachi-Chukagai, and **Shin-Yokohama Station,** with pamphlets, maps, sightseeing itineraries, and English-speaking staff.

GETTING AROUND For the areas covered in this guidebook, I suggest walking as much as weather and your physical condition allow. From Motomachi-Chukgai Station, right next to Chinatown, you can walk to Yamashita Park, Marine Tower, the Red Brick Warehouses, World Porters, Hammerhead, Cosmo Amusement Park, Landmark Tower, and various other points of interest without having to worry about public transport. Yokohama is, however, connected by various train lines and an extensive bus network. You can use **Minatomirai Line** trains between Yokohama and Motomachi-Chukagai stations, with useful stops at Nihon-Odori, Bashamichi, and Minatomirai. The 008, 058 and 026 bus routes connect the Chukagai-iriguchi (Chinatown Entrance) and Sakuragicho Station (¥220). Another, and perhaps the most interesting option, is the **Sea Bass** water bus, connecting Yokohama Station with Hammerhead, Akarenga Pier, and (currently closed for renovation) Yamashita Park. It runs daily 10am to 7pm. Depending on where you get on and off, fares start at ¥500 and can take anywhere from 10 to 45 minutes. Children pay half-price.

Exploring Yokohama

Yokohama is sprawling, but unless you're here for something that specifically brings you away from the coast—like a baseball game, soccer game,

The vibrant Yokohama waterfront dazzles at night.

concert, or the **Shin-Yokohama Ramen Museum** (p. 255)—you'll want to spend most of your time in the bay area.

AROUND MOTOMACHI-CHUKAGAI STATION

There are two sides to Motomachi-Chukagai: **Motomachi,** a pretty walking street lined with pottery shops, craft boutiques, clothing stores, yoga studios, beauty salons, restaurants, coffee bars, and pubs; and **Chukagai,** or "Chinatown," one of the largest districts of its kind in the world.

The stores on **Motomachi** are mostly geared toward deep-pocketed shoppers, but with the yen at historically low levels, the number of visitors who could accurately be described as "deep-pocketed" has grown. I'd recommend browsing in **Iwano Toki-ten** (3–129 Motomachi) for porcelain goods and curios; **Itoya** (3–123 Motomachi) for handicrafts, notebooks, and beautiful stationery; and for pre-loved or quirky apparel, **Branksta** (1–28–1 Motomachi), **Junky Classics** (1–50 Motomachi), and **Base-1** (3–131 Motomachi). For a nice bar with local expats watching baseball and indulging in hearty pub food, check out **Laser Rush** (1–33 Motomachi; instagram.com/barlaserrush; ✆ **045-662-5210**). It's open till midnight weekdays, 2am weekends (closed Mon). Or see **motomachi.or.jp/en/shop/** for a comprehensive list of the shops and establishments in the area.

On the other side of the station is **Chinatown,** which has been around in some capacity since the 1860s. After Yokohama opened its port to the outside world, Chinese settlers and middlemen who helped facilitate trade with local businesses began flooding into the country, establishing their bases of operations in this still-thriving neighborhood. Perhaps unsurprisingly, it's so brash and gaudy that it hits you like a cudgel to the head—all blood-red wood and gilded roofs with mythical iconography, lanterns strung from end to end like festival bunting, vertical calligraphic script on every wall and signboard, hole-in-the-wall dumpling shops pumping out saliva-inducing smells, and store clerks yelling offers at passersby. You're probably here for the food—and with an estimated 500 restaurants, you'll be spoilt for choice. (See "A Food Tour of Chinatown," p. 257.) Still, it's worth also setting aside a little time to visit the area's temples, **Mazu Miao** and **Kuan Ti Miao.** Though they may not have the historical significance of the country's great centers of worship, they have a sheer stop-you-in-your-tracks, kaleidoscopic grandeur that few other religious monuments in Japan can match. Both temples are free to enter and hold events with extended opening hours on New Year's Eve and the Lunar New Year's Eve.

The older of the two, **Kuan Ti Miao** (140 Yamashita-cho; ✆ **045-226-2636;** daily 9am–7pm), was first established in 1862 to honor the warrior Guan Yu, who played a pivotal role in the Three Kingdoms era of Chinese history (A.D. 220–80). Destroyed during the Great Kanto Earthquake, then again in the Second World War, and for a third time during a fire in 1986, the opulent modern structure was opened to the public in 1990; Chinese immigrants in Yokohama, Tokyo, Osaka, and Kobe raised ¥600 million for the reconstruction. The newer temple, inaugurated in 2006, is **Mazu Miao** (136 Yamashitacho, Naka-ku; ✆ **045-681-0909;** daily 9am–7pm), constructed on what was originally the Qing Dynasty Consulate during the Meiji Era (1868–1912). It is dedicated to Mazu, goddess of the sea and a Heavenly Mother figure in Chinese mythology.

As a multicultural port city, it's no surprise that Yokohama has a thriving Chinatown district, perhaps Japan's best.

A GARDEN FOR ALL seasons

On the southern side of the peninsula, closer to Negishi Bay, **Sankeien ♥♥** (sankeien.or.jp; ✆ **045-621-0634**) is one of Yokohama's loveliest refuges, a strolling garden of lotus ponds, chuckling streams, thatched-roof dwellings, teahouses, and a three-storied pagoda. Constructed in 1910 at the behest of a wealthy silk merchant, Tomitaro "Sankei" Hara, the 175,000-sq-m garden changes face with the seasons, whether it's the cherry trees blooming in spring, the vibrant lotus blossoms erupting across the ponds in summer, or the fiery colors of maple trees in fall. When entering the garden, your attention will naturally be drawn to the **pagoda,** an iconic structure built in Kyoto in the mid-1400s before being moved to Sankeien. But I recommend seeking out the **Former Yanohara Family Residence,** a 19th-century thatched-roof farmhouse emblematic of the *gassho zukuri,* or "praying hands," architectural style, which was relocated from Gifu in 1960. Inside has all the trappings of pre-industrial farm life, from the sunken hearth used to cook food and warm the cavernous interior to the sooty black pillars and smoky smells that envelop the space. Tickets to the garden cost ¥900; ¥200 for children. Technically, you can walk to Sankeien from Motomachi-Chukagai, though it takes about 50 minutes and is not all that interesting a walk. Otherwise, take bus number 8 or 148 from the east exit of Yokohama Station (30–35 min.; ¥220), or from Sakuragicho Station (20–25 min.; ¥220); the garden's stop is Sankeien-Iriguchi.

THE BAY AREA

A 5-minute walk from Chinatown's Eastern Gate, you'll arrive at Yokohama's charming waterfront. Head straight for **Yokohama Marine Tower** (p. 255), a converted lighthouse offering epic views of the harbor and beyond. Across from Yokohama Marine Tower is the seaside **Yamashita Park** (p. 254), popular with joggers and elderly folk practicing tai chi and other martial art forms in the mornings, and with picnickers and students choreographing dances or playing sports on weekend afternoons. The broad lawn in the middle of the park is a great place to relax, eat bento lunch boxes, drink a few cans of beer or *chuhai* (an alcoholic drink combing shochu and a fruity mixer), and people-watch.

Head along the Yamashita Rinko Line Promenade, past Osanbashi Pier, Yokohama's "gateway to the sea" for more than 130 years, to **Shinko,** a manmade island and pier on which you'll find many focal points of social and commercial life in Yokohama. Three popular commercial complexes draw visitors here for shopping and eating: Akarenga, commonly referred to by its English title, the **Red Brick Warehouses** (p. 253); **World Porters** (p. 253); and **Yokohama Hammerhead** (p. 254), which takes its name from a now-defunct crane that's been watching over Shinko Pier since 1914. Two other fun stops on Shinko are the **Cup Noodles Museum** (p. 252) and the family-friendly **Cosmo World Amusement Park** (p. 252). The pier beside Yokohama Hammerhead is served by the Sea Bass waterbus, which takes 15 minutes from Yokohama Station and costs ¥700 (children ¥350). You can also ride a gondola, or "Air

Cabin," from World Porter's Unga Park Station to Sakuragicho Station, carving a line across the bay. Running from 10am to 10pm, the 5-minute ride (¥1,000 or ¥1,800 for a return-trip; children pay half price) is pretty special around dusk when the city begins to light up.

Leaving Shinko island, head northwest toward the stylish Minatomirai district, where you can end your stroll as you began it, with an even-higher view from atop the famous **Landmark Tower** (p. 253).

Cosmo World Amusement Park ♥♥ ATTRACTION Cosmo World is best known for its huge Ferris wheel—called Cosmo Clock 21, for the immense digital clock at its center—which is visible from most corners of the bay area. (Until 1992, it was the world's tallest Ferris wheel.) The park is split into three zones. In the Kids Carnival Zone you'll find bumper cars, a mini-Shinkansen ride, and a merry-go-round; the Burano Street Zone has higher-octane, more disorienting rides with cosmic names like Super Planet and Galaxy; and the Wonder Amuse Zone has a trio of classics—a roller coaster, a log flume, and the Ferris wheel.

A roller coaster splashes down at Cosmo World Amusement Park.

Shinko. cosmoworld.jp. ✆ **045-641-6591.** Admission free; buy tickets in park for rides. Mon–Wed and Fri 11am–9pm; Sat–Sun 11am–10pm.

Cup Noodles Museum ♥♥ MUSEUM Though less comprehensive than the Shin-Yokohama Ramen Museum (p. 255). This huge orangey-red block of a building contains so much more than your run-of-the-mill museum exhibits. Rather, it's an engaging and educational character study, portraying the creator of the dish, Momufuku Ando, as an ambitious DIY inventor and one of Asia's great 20th-century visionaries. A broke businessman, Ando created the world's first instant noodles when he was 48, inspired by seeing people queueing at soup kitchens in postwar Osaka; he then shared his main piece of intellectual property (the flash-frying method to preserve the noodles) with competitors to prevent sub-standard products flooding the market. Years later, he came up with the idea of presenting the noodles in a cup after an inauspicious meeting with American investors who couldn't figure out how to eat the thing. At the age of 95, he embarked upon his final act: developing noodles that could be eaten in space. The second-floor Instant Noodles History Cube, a gallery with more than 3,000 instant noodle packets, details how this simple labor-and-cost-saving meal—invented to help a society crawl out of the wreckage of World War II—morphed into a global culinary subculture. You can also make your own instant ramen (with up to 5,460 possible flavor combinations) in the My Cup Noodles Factory (¥500 fee), see the instant noodle manufacturing process at the Cup Noodles Park, watch a subtitled 15-minute animated short about Ando in the Momofuku Theater, or sample noodle dishes from around the world in the Noodles Bazaar.

Shinko (5 min. walk from Hammerhead). cupnoodles-museum.jp/en/Yokohama. ✆ **045-345-0918.** ¥500 adults, children free. Daily (except Tues) 10am–6pm.

Landmark Tower ♥ OBSERVATION DECK This skyscraper is one of Japan's tallest at almost 300m, and while its slightly angled institutional-grey exterior is not that pretty, there is something incredibly imposing (perhaps even dystopian) about the structure, as though it's the center of a panopticon, casting its all-seeing eye across the city. Landmark Tower has the usual helping of shopping floors, restaurants, offices, and event spaces, but the main reason to come here is to check out the 69th-floor **Sky Garden.** It's a splendid place to watch the sun set behind Mt Fuji in the west.

2 Chome–2–1, Minatomirai. yokohama-landmark.jp. ✆ **045-222-5015.** Sky Garden entry ¥1,000 adults, ¥800 seniors and high school students, ¥500 children. Daily 10–9pm (Sat until 10pm), last entry 30 min. before closing.

Red Brick Warehouses ♥♥ SHOPPING COMPLEX Built in the early 20th century to store unprocessed imported goods, the warehouses of **Akarenga** (to use its Japanese name) have been converted into shops, restaurants, markets, and an adjacent events plaza. The shopping concourses, on the first floor of Warehouse 1 and on floors 1 and 2 of Warehouse 2, feature souvenirs, toys, crafts, apparel, and jewelry, while the culinary fare runs the gamut from Hawaiian burgers and grilled seafood to pastries and Disney-themed desserts. **Shogun Burger** (shogun-burger.com; ✆ **045-306-7567;** daily 11am–11pm) on the third floor of Warehouse 2 might be the pick of the bunch, with a less-is-more menu that lets its award-winning signature wagyu patties shine, rather than dousing them in toppings and sauces. The Akarenga event plaza draws crowds with seasonal showcases like food expos, live music, urban sports events, Oktoberfest for a couple weeks each autumn, and an annual Christmas Market (one of Japan's best) beginning in late November. A temporary ice-skating rink (admission and skate rental ¥1,500 adults, ¥1,000 children) is set up every winter from early December to late February. For the full events calendar, see **yokohama-akarenga.jp/event/**.

Shinko. yokohama-akarenga.jp. ✆ **045-227-2002.** Warehouse 1 10am–7pm; Warehouse 2 11am–8pm; restaurants open until 10pm.

World Porters ♥ SHOPPING COMPLEX This massive modern indoor mall, opened in 1999, offers fashion and apparel shops, pop-culture souvenir stores, a global gourmet hall, an "Entertainment Sweets Zone" (including a shop selling an array of Japan's famously eccentric

Seaside Yamashita Park offers many pleasant corners where locals as well as visitors can enjoy the flowers, fountains, and greenery.

flavored KitKats), a branch of the Village Vanguard variety store, a karaoke parlor, and a movie theater.

Shinko. yim.co.jp. ✆ **045-222-2000.** Shops open 10:30am–9pm, restaurants 11am–11pm.

Yamashita Park ♥♥ GARDEN Once a commercial district destroyed in the Great Kanto Earthquake of 1923, this seaside area makes a great place to take a break. Features include the Guardian of Water, a fountain and statue donated by the people of San Diego in 1960 to commemorate their sister-city relationship with Yokohama; The Little Girl with the Red Shoes statue, honoring *Akai Kutsu,* a popular nursery rhyme from the 1920s; the Indian Water Tower, donated by Yokohama's Indian community to commemorate lives lost in the 1923 earthquake and tsunami; the Future Rose Garden, home to 160 species of rose, which bloom in May-June and October-November; and the *Hikawa Maru,* a luxury passenger liner that traveled between Japan and the USA, crossing the Pacific 254 times between 1929 and 1960. If you're partial to a pint of craft beer, visit **The Wharf House** (wharfhouse-yokohama.zetton.co.jp; ✆ **045-228-7737**) on the park's western fringe, where you can sit in the beer garden and enjoy a selection of ales, pilsners, lagers, and weizens from a local brewery (350mL ¥900, 500mL ¥1,200). From mid-March through November, it also offers BBQ meals from ¥6,000 per person, including 2 hours of all-you-can-drink beer (craft beer not included, but ¥350mL drafts are discounted to ¥600). It's open 9am to 9pm.

Yokohama Hammerhead ♥♥ SHOPPING COMPLEX While World Porters feels like a '90s boardroom vision of the future, Hammerhead is smart, sleek, modern and very much in keeping with Yokohama's

continued reinvention. There are some delightful sweets shops in here, like **Masaki, Caramellabo,** and **Kuromicco Factory,** all on the second floor—the concourses here are suffused with the scent of burnt sugar and melted butter. The first-floor ramen food hall hosts four ramen shops, each with its own umami-filled signature broth. Even the ground floor **7-Eleven** convenience store is famous for its beer selection, with more than 500 (and ever-increasing) canned and bottled craft beers from breweries throughout Japan and across the world. You can also purchase bespoke glassware and other brewery merch to accompany your tipple of choice.
Shinko. hammerhead.co.jp. ✆ **045-211-8080.** Stores open 10 or 11am to 8pm; restaurants open later.

Yokohama Marine Tower ♥ OBSERVATION DECK A functioning lighthouse from its inception in 1961 until 2008, the needle-shaped Marine Tower now serves as a tourist attraction, with observation decks on its 29th and 30th floors. You'll get epic views of the Yokohama skyline from here, as well as the harbor, the 890m-long Yokohama Bay Bridge, and when visibility is clear, Mount Fuji in the distance. Digital art pieces are projected onto the windows of the 30th-floor observation deck at night, and there's also a tourist information desk and a free-to-enter art gallery on the second floor with new exhibitions every month. It costs ¥1,500 to access the observation areas before 5:30pm, while the cost of night tickets varies depending on the artworks on display.
14–1 Yamashitacho. marinetower.yokohama. ✆ **045-664-1100.** Daily 10am–9:30pm.

SHIN-YOKOHAMA

Though it's a little out of the way, and not all that interesting in itself, Shin-Yokohama draws a lot of visitors to two attractions: **Yokohama International Stadium,** which hosts soccer and rugby matches and occasional concerts, and the **Shin-Yokohama Ramen Museum** (below). It has its own stop on the bullet train route—18 minutes from Tokyo Station, 10 minutes from Shinagawa—so you can travel here for free using the Japan Rail Pass. Alternatively, from Yokohama Station take the Blue Line (8 min.; ¥250) or the Yokohama Line (11 min.; ¥180) to Shin-Yokohama Station.

Shin-Yokohama Ramen Museum ♥ MUSEUM The history of (arguably) Japan's most famous culinary export is told in great detail on the ground floor exhibition space and gallery of this museum. You'll learn that the first proto-ramen dishes were eaten by nobles and priests in the feudal era; you'll also learn about the founding of Rairaiken, the restaurant credited as the progenitor of modern ramen after chef Kanichi Ozaki embellished a Chinese dish called *shina-soba* with Japanese ingredients. Among the exhibits are the recreated Raraiken shop exterior (ca. 1910), plastic models of regional ramen dishes, 1,000-plus books on ramen and its history, almost 400 wall-mounted bowls from famous ramen shops in

The food hall at Shin-Yokohama Ramen Museum, designed to look like a Showa-era streetscape.

Japan, and a display of instant ramen packets from times past. What most visitors come for, however, is the food hall. In a vaultlike, two-storied basement, designed to resemble lamplit Showa-era *yokocho* (alleyways), you'll find 8 hole-in-the-wall ramen shops, each specializing in a different style of regional broth. It's a whistlestop cuisine tour of the country, from Yamagata to Tokyo, Okinawa to Kumamoto, Fukuoka to Hokkaido. One shop, **Asakusa Rairaiken,** has recreated the first ever ramen recipe, based on period testimonies and historical research. Bowls of ramen cost around ¥1,000, or you can buy mini bowls for around ¥680 and try to sample as many as your stomach will allow. Note, however, that there are often long waiting times during busy periods. Be sure to order tickets from the vending machines on the B2F floor before joining the queue.

2–14–21 Shinyokohama, Kohoku-ku. raumen.co.jp. ✆ **045-471-0503.** ¥450 adults; ¥100 children. Mon–Fri 11am–9pm; Sat–Sun 10:30am–9pm. Shin-Yokohama Station (5 min.).

Where to Eat & Drink in Yokohama

Besides the wealth of eating spots in Chinatown (see “A Food Tour of Chinatown,” p. 257) and the host of restaurants and cafes at the big shopping complexes on Shinko island (p. 251), a great place to finish your day in Yokohama is strolling around Noge, or Nogecho, an area of backstreets populated by small bars and restaurants that somehow escaped the waves of major redevelopment in the 1980s. If you're looking for an *izakaya* or yakitori joint, I recommend walking around the area and letting your instincts guide you. The fare is mostly finger food and *akachochin* (red lantern) late-night eateries serving chicken skewers, deep-fried vegetables, or seafood. Also worth visiting is **Pio City,** a low-ceilinged underground corridor connecting Noge and Sakuragicho Station. Lined with counter-seating izakaya and bars that fill up on weekday evenings with twentysomethings and red-faced salarymen, it's one of those places that feels like it could only exist in Japan.

Noge is a 12-minute walk south from Landmark Tower and a stone's throw from Sakuragicho Station, from where you can return to Tokyo on the JR Negishi Line to Shinagawa (33 min.; ¥410), Tokyo (44 min.; ¥580) or Akihabara (50 min.; ¥580) stations.

Asian Bar RAMAI ♥♥♥ SOUP CURRY This is the best soup curry restaurant I've eaten in—the main branch is in Sapporo, where soup curry was invented in 1970—so it's worth making the short journey to Kannai (a 10-min. walk from Noge) to indulge in this hearty northern repast. The menu is in Japanese, but the ordering process is quite simple: Pick the main filling in your curry—beef, chicken, pork, vegetables, fried fish—and then select toppings, like mushrooms, cheese, or extra meat, and choose whether you want rice on the side. You can also make your soup curry large for free (or extra-large for an additional ¥100) or increase the

A FOOD TOUR OF chinatown

There *are* cultural pursuits, museums and trinket shops in Chinatown, but when walking around you could be convinced the entire district was built to showcase the great culinary culture of Japan's neighbor across the East China Sea. Part of the fun is letting your senses guide you: following the rich umami smells, looking for cooked ducks hanging in restaurant windows, and searching for hidden alleyways where queues form outside lantern-lit shops. I like starting with a couple of takeout Peking duck rolls at **Ocho,** 北京ダック専門店 王朝 (ocho.gorp.jp/; ✆ **050-5486-2751**), 30 seconds on foot from the Chinatown Higashimon (Eastern Gate). The rolls are basically on-the-go duck pancakes with the traditional toppings of hoisin sauce, shredded cucumber and spring onion, and cost ¥420 apiece. Order from the shop window.

Around the corner on Shanghai Road, at **Houtenkaku Shinkan** (houtenkaku.com/shinkan/; ✆ **045-681-9016**), the top seller is *yaki-shoronpo*, a pan-fried variety of the soup dumpling known in Mandarin as *xiaolongbao*. Watch the chefs prepare dumplings through large street-facing windows, then order from the shop counter on the ground floor. Yaki-shoronpo are stuffed with pork or seafood and cost ¥750 for 4 pieces or ¥1,100 for 6 pieces. Top tip: Take a small bite of the dumpling and then suck out the hot soup from inside, or risk scalding your mouth.

Chinese food is, to put it mildly, not well-known for its vegan-friendliness. But **Koukien** (好記園; ✆ **050-5868-5801**), a Taiwanese restaurant across the street from Kuan Ti Miao Temple, makes vegan-friendly versions of popular dishes like mapo tofu, *tantanmen* noodle soup, fried or steamed dumplings, and spring rolls. The animal products may be lacking, but the flavors are there in abundance. Lunch ¥1,500 per person approx., dinner ¥3,000 per person.

level of spiciness from 1 up to 10 for no additional cost—spice levels 3 to 5 are plenty if you have a decent tolerance for hot food. Counter seats are available, but your view of the kitchen is obscured, so I prefer the booths—ask for *teberu seki,* "table seats."

7F Kameraku Building, 1–6–5 Isezakicho, Naka-ku. ramai.co.jp/shop_yokohama.html ✆ **045-308-8338.** Soup curry with toppings and sides ¥1,500–¥2,500. Daily 11:30am–9:30pm (last order). Station: Kannai (5 min.) or Noge (10 min.).

Downbeat ♥ JAZZ KISSA Noge also hosts some of Japan's most storied jazz *kissa* (p. 207), cozy music listening spaces where the owners, known affectionately as "Masters," play old-school vinyl records on turntables through immaculate speaker systems. In the heart of Noge, Downbeat is a legendary spot in the jazz kissa scene, dating back to 1956. It's now on its third owner, Yoshihisa-san, who is adding to the collection of nearly 4,000 records representing myriad jazz genres and subgenres. The (very loud) speakers are at the far end of the bar on the left, so take a seat at the counter if you want to make conversation (these seats are also nonsmoking).

2F Miyamoto Bldg., 1–43 Hanasakicho. yokohama-downbeat.com. ✆ **045-241-6167.** Coffee ¥750 (refill ¥500), beers ¥850 and up, whiskeys ¥750 and up. Tues–Sun 4–11:30pm.

Kushibe (野毛 串兵衛) ♥ IZAKAYA For a catch-all izakaya with a lively atmosphere, grab a counter seat at this welcoming spot in Noge. The selection of 30-plus meat and veg skewers are cooked over hardwood *binchotan* charcoal, imbuing them with juicy textures and charred, smoky flavors. If you're feeling adventurous, try the pork heart steak (¥490) served with onion and sesame oil—it's a Kushibe specialty. Skewers like pork belly, shiitake mushrooms, or asparagus wrapped in pork cost between ¥180 and ¥350 apiece, and they combine well with the vast selection of sake from across Japan. If you're overwhelmed by the sake menu, order the Kubota Chitose (¥650); it's light on the palate and agrees with most food pairings.

231–0064 Kanagawa. kushibe-noge.com. ✆ **050-5385-3655.** Dinner ¥2,000–¥3,000 per person. Mon–Fri 3–11pm; Sat–Sun noon–11pm.

6

THE JAPAN ALPS

Aside from Mount Fuji (p. 233), all of Japan's loftiest mountains are found in several volcanic mountain ranges that stretch across central Honshu. This craggy landscape, designated the **Japan Alps National Park (Chubu Sangaku Kokuritsu Koen)** ♥♥♥, is a popular destination for hikers in summer and skiers in winter (Nagano, near Matsumoto, hosted the XVIII Winter Olympics in 1998). For many, the gateway to the Japan Alps is **Matsumoto,** with its fine feudal castle; others gravitate to picturesque **Shirakawa-go** and **Ogimachi,** with their thatched-roof farmhouses; while yet others seek out the old Edo-style town of **Hida Takayama,** often described as the "Little Kyoto of the Alps."

Because towns and villages in this region are spread out—with lots of mountains in between—traveling isn't all that fast in this part of the country. If you're unable to rent a car, your best strategy for visiting all the destinations covered in this chapter is to take the **Limited Express Azusa** from Tokyo's Shinjuku Station to Matsumoto (around 2 hr., 40 min.; ¥6,850; JR Pass accepted). From Matsumoto, you'll travel by bus onward to Takayama and then on to Ogimachi (in Shirakawa-go). From there you can return to Takayama to catch the train to Nagoya, or take a bus onward to Kanazawa (see chapter 8 for information on Nagoya and Kanazawa). You may also consider renting a car between certain destinations, perhaps to visit Shirakawa-go as a day trip from Matsumoto or Kanazawa.

THE BEST EXPERIENCES IN THE JAPAN ALPS

- **Traipsing Around Matsumoto Castle** Popularly known as the Crow Castle due to its black color, it has the oldest donjon in Japan (more than 400 years old) and contains a superb collection of Japanese matchlocks and samurai armor from the mid–16th century through the Edo Period. See p. 262.
- **Seeing How Mountain Folk Lived in Ogimachi** Shirakawa-go is famous for its thatched-roof farmhouses. Learn how they're constructed and about the extended families who once lived in them at Ogimachi's open-air museum, and the many homes now open to the public. See p. 269.

 PREVIOUS PAGE: Hiking in the Japan Alps National Park.

- **Greeting the Morning at Takayama's Market** Set on a picturesque riverbank, it's a photographer's dream with its stalls of flowers, vegetables, and locally made crafts. See p. 277.
- **Takayama's Higashiyama Walking Course** Sure, you should visit the city's many museums and sights, but this leafy hiking path winding past temples and shrines gives a more relaxing view of Takayama. See p. 278.

MATSUMOTO ♥♥

235km (146 miles) NW of Tokyo

Located in the middle of a wide plateau about 200m (660 ft.) above sea level and surrounded on all sides by mountain ranges, **Matsumoto ♥♥** hosts a fine feudal castle with the oldest existing *tenshu* (keep) in Japan, as well as an outstanding modern art museum. Although the city itself (pop. 230,000) is modern with little remaining from its castle days, it has approximately 100 *kura* (storehouses) scattered throughout town, built more than a century ago after a devastating fire destroyed much of the town. Made of earth and straw, these kura were painted many times to protect against future flames. Several have been renovated into shops, restaurants, and other establishments, especially on Nakamachi Street.

Overall Matsumoto is quite pleasant, the air fresh, and its people among the nicest in Japan. Encircled by towering peaks, sparkling mountain lakes, and colorful wildflowers, Matsumoto also is the starting point for the hiking trails of Japan Alps National Park; most travelers heading to the more remote regions of the Japan Alps pass through here on their way.

On Nakamachi Street in Matsumoto, historic storehouses have been converted to shops and restaurants.

Essentials

GETTING THERE The JR Chuo Honsen Line runs **trains** directly to Matsumoto from Tokyo's Shinjuku Station. Its Limited Express Azusa, departing every hour or so, reaches Matsumoto in about 2½ to 3 hours and costs ¥6,850 one-way for an unreserved seat. There's also a direct JR train from Nagoya, the Limited Express Shinano, which departs about every hour, takes about 2 hours, and costs ¥5,940 for an unreserved seat. Keio Highway **buses** (✆ **03-5376-2222**) also depart hourly from Shinjuku Station (west exit) for Matsumoto; they take about 3¼ hours and cost ¥4,500. From Nagoya, the ride is 3½ hours and ¥3,400; from Osaka, there is an overnight bus that takes about 8½ hours and cost ¥6,400; from Takayama, the ride is 2½ hours and ¥4,400.

VISITOR INFORMATION The **Matsumoto Tourist Information** (✆ **0263-32-2814;** daily 9am–5:45pm) is just across from the main wicket of Matsumoto Station. It has a good English-language map of the city, and English-speaking staff. Another tourist information center is located 1 block south of Matsumoto Castle (visitmatsumoto.com; ✆ **0263-39-7176;** daily 9am–5:45pm). Speak to staff in here about recommended tours of the city and surrounding areas.

GETTING AROUND You can **walk** to Matsumoto Castle, about 1.5km (1 mile) northeast of the station, in about 20 minutes; signs in English point the way. Alternatively, take the dedicated tourist bus, **Town Sneaker Bus,** which has three sightseeing routes departing from Matsumoto Station every 30 minutes (most useful for the sights below is the Kita, or Northern, Course). It costs ¥200 each time you get off or ¥500 for an all-day pass (half-price for children). Free **bicycles** are available daily 8:30am to 5pm at various locations throughout town, including the Matsumoto City Museum (next to Matsumoto Castle) and the Kaichi Gakko Primary School. They're convenient for visiting sights not accessible by Sneaker Bus; ask the Matsumoto Tourist Information staff for details. To visit the Japan Ukiyo-e Museum, you'll have to go by local **train** or **taxi;** see the listing on p. 265 for details.

Exploring Matsumoto

In addition to the sights below, good places for strolling and shopping include the **Nakamachi** district in the heart of the city with its *kura,* restaurants, and shops selling Matsumoto furniture, crafts, and antiques; and **Nawate Dori,** a narrow pedestrian lane flanking the Metoba River where vendors sell fruit, vegetables, flowers, and souvenirs.

MATSUMOTO CASTLE & ENVIRONS

Matsumoto Castle ♥♥ CASTLE Originally built in 1504 when Japan was in the throes of bloody civil wars, Matsumoto Castle is a fine, if rather small, specimen of a feudal castle—its 400-year-old *tenshu* is the oldest existing keep in the country. Surrounded by a moat with ducks and white swans and lined with willow and cherry trees, the outside walls of

The Japan Alps

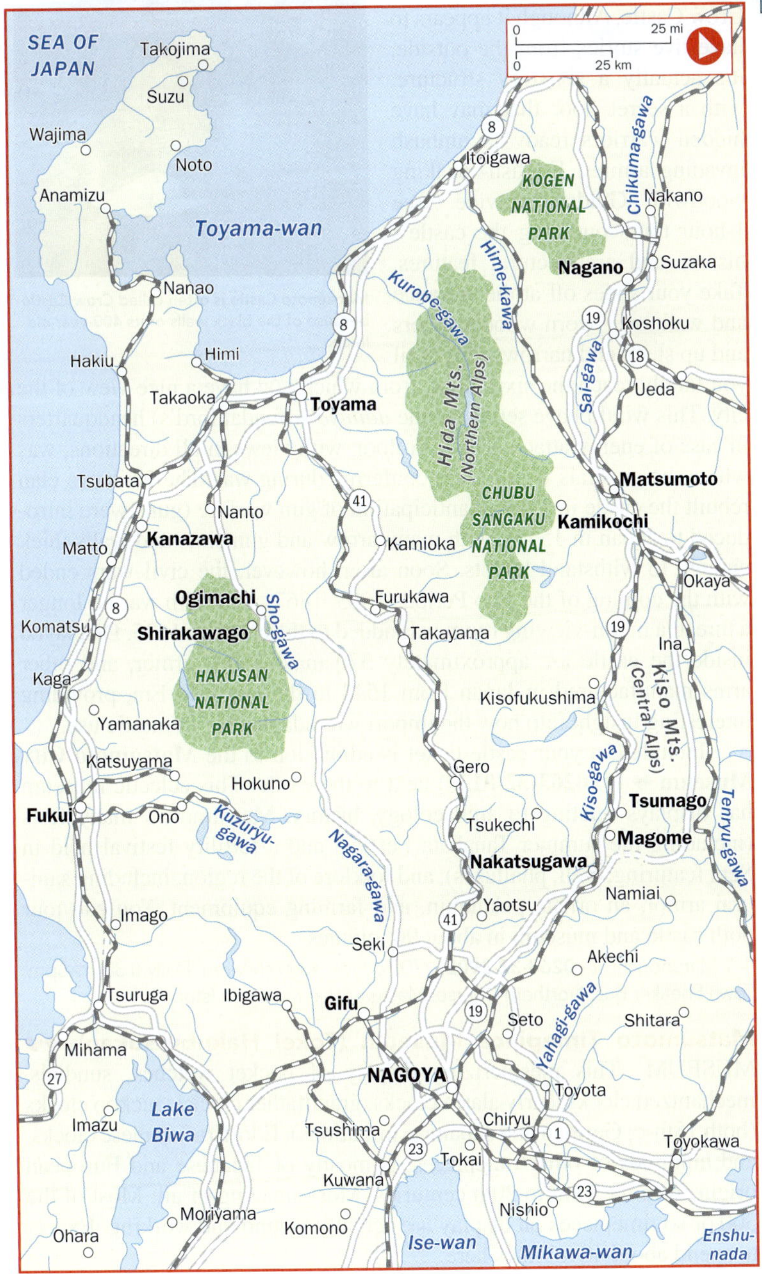

the keep are black, earning the place the nickname of Karasu-jo, or Crow Castle. Although it appears to have five stories from the outside, it's actually a six-story structure, with a secret floor that may have hidden warriors ready to ambush invading armies. English-speaking Goodwill Guides provide free 1-hour tours outlining the castle's history and architectural features. Take your shoes off at the entrance and walk over worn wooden floors and up steep and narrow steps until you finally reach the sixth floor, from which you have a nice view of the city. This would have served as the *daimyo*'s (feudal lord's) headquarters in case of enemy attack. The fifth floor, with views in all directions, was where the generals would have conferred during war. The Ishikawa clan rebuilt the castle in 1593 in anticipation of gun warfare (guns were introduced to Japan in 1543), with many arrow and gun slots and walls thick enough to withstand bullets. Soon after, however, the civil wars ended with the coming of the Edo Period (1603–1867), and with war no longer a threat, a moon-viewing room was added to the castle in 1635. Displayed inside the castle are approximately 370 matchlocks, armor, and other arms manufactured in Japan from 1543 to the late Edo Era, providing interesting insight into how the import was adapted for domestic use.

Matsumoto Castle is often called Crow Castle because of the black walls of its 400-year-old keep.

Included in your castle ticket is admission to the **Matsumoto City Museum** ♥ (✆ **0263-32-0133**) next to the castle. This eclectic museum has displays relating to archaeology, history, Matsumoto's many fests (including the summer Tanabata Festival and a fertility festival held in Sept featuring, well, phalluses), and folklore of the region, including samurai armor, an ornate palanquin, and farming equipment. You can tour both castle and museum in about 90 minutes.

4–1 Marunouchi. ✆ **0263-32-2902.** ¥700 adults, ¥300 children. Daily 8:30am–5pm. Town Sneaker Bus, Northern Course: Matsumotojo Kuromon (stop 6).

Matsumoto Timepiece Museum (Tokei Hakubutsukan) ♥♥

MUSEUM This mesmerizing display of pocket watches, sundials, mechanized clocks, early alarm clocks, grandfather clocks, cuckoo clocks (both 18th-c. German and Japanese imitations), Edo-Era Japanese clocks, and hundreds of other timepieces, is mostly of Japanese and European origin from the 18th to 20th centuries. Most amazing of all: Most of the 300 or so timepieces on display are actually wound and working. Expect to spend about 40 minutes here.

1–21–15 Chuo. matsu-haku.com/tokei. ✆ **0263-36-0969.** ¥310 adults, ¥150 children. Tues–Sun 9am–5pm. Town Sneaker Bus, Eastern Course: Tokei Hakubutsukan (stop 15).

OTHER ATTRACTIONS

Japan Ukiyo-e Museum (Nihon Ukiyo-e Hakubutsukan) ♥♥♥

MUSEUM The ultramodern building housing the private collection of the Sakai family, is, quite simply, one of the best museums of woodblock prints in Japan. With more than 100,000 prints, it's believed to be the largest collection of its kind in the world and includes representative masterpieces of all known Ukiyo-e artists. The exhibition changes every 3 months, with approximately 100 prints on display at any one time. A 15-minute slide show with English-language explanations introduces the current exhibition, and an English-language pamphlet describes the history of the collection and how woodblock prints are made.

2206–1 Koshiba, Shimadachi. ✆ **0263-47-4440.** japan-ukiyoe-museum.com. ¥1,000 adults, ¥500 children. Tues–Sun 10am–5pm. From Matsumoto Train Station (platform 7) take Kamikochi Line 10 min. to Oniwa Station (¥170; JR Rail Pass not accepted); 15-min. walk or 10-min. taxi ride from there. By bike, about 20 min. from Matsumoto Station.

Matsumoto City Museum of Art (Matsumoto-shi Bijutsukan) ♥

MUSEUM This inviting museum showcases the talents of artists with connections to Matsumoto, including Kamijyo Shinzan, who elevated calligraphy to an art; landscape artist Tamura Kazuo; and Yayoi Kusama, a female artist known for her exuberant colors and polka-dot modern art. The Kusama exhibits are particularly fascinating, beginning with a hallucinogenic, writhing flower sculpture in the museum's front plaza. The Yayoi Kusama Museum in Tokyo (p. 115) showcases some of the still-active nonagenarian artist's greatest work, but this museum in her

Colorful sculptures by Yayoi Kusama brighten the front plaza of the Matsumoto City Museum of art.

hometown is the definitive entry point into her work. You could easily spend an hour here.

4-2-22 Chuo. matsumoto-artmuse.jp. ✆ **0263-39-7400.** ¥400 adults, ¥200 college and high-school students, children and seniors free. Tues–Sun 9am–5pm. Town Sneaker Bus, Southern Course: Matsumoto-shi Bijutsukan (stop 30).

Matsumoto Folkcraft Museum (Matsumoto Mingei-kan) ♥ MUSEUM Housed in a *kura* originally built to store fish, this small museum contains folk art made primarily of wood, glass, bamboo, and porcelain from Japan and other countries. Exhibits change three times a year; on display may be items as diverse as combs from around the world to Japanese store signs designed during the Edo Period for people who couldn't read. Particularly beautiful are the wooden chests. It's about a 17-minute walk from Matsumoto Station, or you can take a bus from the bus terminal (platform 1) to the Shimoganai Mingeikan Guchi stop.

1313-1 Satoyamabe. ✆ **0263-33-1569.** ¥410 adults, students ¥200, free for children 15 and younger. Tues–Sun 9am–5pm.

Where to Stay in Matsumoto

Because Matsumoto is popular primarily with hikers used to roughing it along nature trails, accommodations are geared mainly toward convenience.

MODERATE

Matsumoto Hotel Kagetsu ♥ This *ryokan,* in a newer building constructed in the style of a *kura* (storehouse) but with a history going back more than 100 years, imparts a pleasant, old-fashioned atmosphere with its antique wooden furnishings in public spaces. Both Western- and Japanese-style rooms are available, comfortably large for the price. For the best views, book a room on one of the upper-floor rooms facing the castle and mountains. For a splurge, deluxe corner rooms have more windows, larger sitting areas, and toilets separate from the bathrooms.

4-8-9 Ote, Matsumoto. matsumotohotel-kagetsu.com. ✆ **0263-32-0114.** 80 units. ¥6,750–¥15,000 per person. Town Sneaker Bus, Northern Course: Agetsuchimachi (stop 10). **Amenities:** 2 restaurants; room service, free Wi-Fi.

Ryokan Sugimoto ♥♥♥ Overlooking the city from the hills to the east, this *ryokan* is in many ways traditionally Japanese, but the designers have borrowed tastefully (and quite liberally) from the styles of 20th-century Western decorators. The rooms are modular units with futons and cedar wood bathtubs, and there's a gorgeous bamboo-lined hallway burrowing underneath the property to connect the courtyard and hot springs with the kaiseki dining rooms. Dinners (included in room price) feature *nabe* (hotpots), wild local herbs, sashimi, cooked seafood, and stewed boar (specifics will vary from season to season). There are two bars in the property, both of which look like scenes from an Agatha Christie novel, with antique tables, a selection of international whiskies and liqueurs, plush seating, reading lamps, and a sense that Detective Poirot might be sitting in the corner twiddling his moustache. It's the kind of hotel that invites investigation and discovery, so give yourself time after dinner to explore its nooks and crannies.

451–7 Satoyamabe, Matsumoto. ryokan-sugimoto.com. ✆ **0263-32-3379.** 17 units. ¥15,500–¥40,000 per person, includes kaiseki dinner. Bus stop: Utsukushigahara Onsen Station (20 min. from Matsumoto Station). **Amenities:** 2 bars; outdoor hot springs; free Wi-Fi.

INEXPENSIVE

In addition to the more atmospheric choice below, the **Toyoko Inn Matsumoto Ekimae Honmachi,** at 2–1–23 Chuo (✆ **0263-36-1045**), a 6-minute walk west of Matsumoto Station, offers the budget chain's usual freebies, including loungewear, complimentary breakfast, and free Internet access in the rooms. Rates are around ¥6,500 for a single and ¥8,000 to ¥9,000 for a double.

Marumo ♥♥ This accommodation offers a taste of old-fashioned Matsumoto during the Meiji Era. Located in the traditional district of Nakamachi, a 15-minute walk from Matsumoto Station, it occupies a *kura* and a traditional Japanese inn constructed after the great 1888 fire that destroyed much of Matsumoto. It has a diminutive but eye-catching entryway of polished woods and antiques, very narrow stairs and corridors leading to Japanese-style rooms, and a wonderful coffee shop that has changed little over the decades. Rooms are simple and without the usual creature comforts, but the location is tiptop and the atmosphere is truly "traditional Japan."

3–3–10 Chuo. marumoryokan.jp/eng. ✆ **0263-32-0115.** 8 units, all w/ shared bath. Rooms from ¥5,280 per person, Japanese breakfast included. Town Sneaker Bus, Eastern Course: Kurashikkukan (stop 17). **Amenities:** Coffee shop; free Wi-Fi.

Where to Eat in Matsumoto

Ishii Miso Brewery ♥♥♥ MISO Now on its sixth-generation owner, the Ishii Miso Brewery offers interesting free tours of its facilities, but for most visitors the restaurant is the highlight. Reserve at least 2 days in advance if you want to try the pork set meals—one marinated in two kinds of aged miso, the other marinated in salt *koji,* a delicious enzyme-packed fermented marinade that facilitates digestion. Otherwise, the order-on-the-day menu includes rice ball and miso soup sets, miso dumplings, and a margherita and rice terrace miso pizza. If you would like a tour, ask the staff (they may not be

Matsumoto, Soba Capital

Matsumoto is famous for its buckwheat noodles, which are fairly thick with a hearty flavor and can be served hot or cold, with several kinds of dips and sauces. **Kobayashi Soba** (3–3–20 Ote; ✆ **0263-32-1298;** Fri–Wed 11am–4pm) serves classic soba tempura for around ¥2,000 (and it has an English-language menu). The tourism association lists 20 more downtown locations where you can slurp these noodles (see **visitmatsumoto.com/en/genre/soba-and-ramen**). Matsumoto is also known for its *basashi* (raw horse meat), a delicacy served in many of its izakaya and local cuisine restaurants.

able to accommodate you during busy periods); on your own, you can also poke around some of the miso storehouses that are open to the public. Reservations recommended.

1–8–1 Uzuhashi. ishiimiso.com. ✆ **0263-32-0534.** Set meals ¥1,760, rice balls ¥550, pork soup ¥770. Daily 9am–5pm (lunch 11am–2pm). Town Sneaker Bus, Eastern Course: Shimingeijutsukanmae stop.

Nomugi ♥♥ NOODLES There are only three tables in this well-known eatery popular with the locals (you may have to wait for a seat and can't dawdle over a meal). Its handmade buckwheat noodles are served until they run out, which is why the restaurant has a flexible closing time. You'll be given a *tsuyu* sauce to pour into a cup; add green onion, wasabi, and *daikon* radish, and then dip your *soba* into the mix. At the end of your meal, make a soup from the soba water stock (served in a teapot), called *soba yu,* and the soba sauce. In winter, the soba is served with boiled toppings.

2–9–11 Chuo. ✆ **0263-36-3753.** Soba ¥1,200–¥1,450; half portion ¥800. Thurs–Mon 11:30am–2pm. Town Sneaker Bus, Northern Course: Kuranomachi Nakamachi (stop 16).

SHIRAKAWA-GO & OGIMACHI ♥♥

555km (347 miles) NW of Tokyo; 77km (48 miles) S of Kanazawa; 47km (29 miles) NE of Takayama

With its thatched-roof farmhouses, paddies trimmed with flowerbeds, roaring river, and pine-covered mountains rising on all sides, **Shirakawa-go** is one of the most picturesque regions in Japan. Unfortunately, it also has more than its fair share of tour buses (especially in May, Aug–Oct,

The traditional thatched-roof farmhouse of Ogimachi were built to accommodate large extended families.

THE thatched roofs OF SHIRAGAWA-GO

Although Shirakawa-go stretches about 39km (24 miles) beside the Shokawa River and covers 229 sq. km (88 sq. miles), mountains and forest account for 95% of the region—the region's cultivated land is squeezed into a valley averaging less than 3km (2 miles) in width. Land for growing rice and other crops has always been scarce and valuable here. Because there wasn't much land for young couples to start their own farms, only the eldest son in a family was allowed to marry; other children were required to stay on with their parents and help with the farming. Farmhouses were built large enough to hold extended families, with as many as several dozen people under one roof. Even though younger children weren't allowed to marry, a man was allowed to choose a young woman, visit her in her parents' home, and father her children; those children then grew up with the mother's family, adding to the labor force.

Before the roads came to Shirakawa-go, winter always meant complete isolation as snow 2m (6 ft.) deep blanketed the entire region. Summer vegetables were pickled and preserved for winter sustenance, and *irori* (open-hearth fireplaces) in the middle of a communal room were used for cooking, as well as warmth and light during the long, harsh winters. The family lived on the ground floor; upper floors were used for silk cultivation and storing utensils. Because of the heavy snowfall, thatched roofs were constructed at steep angles (known as *gassho-zukuri*, "hands in prayer," because the rooftops look like clasped hands). The steep angle also allowed rain to run off quickly, and the thatch (Japanese pampas grass) dried quickly in the sun, preventing decay. There were no chimneys; smoke from the *irori* simply rose into the levels above, helping to ward off insects in the thatch and to dry it out.

Remarkably, these massive homes were built without nails; sturdy ropes held the framework together and helped withstand earthquakes. Most were constructed on a north-south orientation, so that the ends of the buildings would bear the brunt of winds and precipitation whipping through the valley, and to allow sunlight to melt snow more quickly, therefore adding extra years to the life of the thatched roofs.

Today, Shirakawa-go has about 114 thatched farmhouses, barns, and sheds, most of them built around 200 to 300 years ago. The thatched roofs are about .6m (2 ft.) thick and last some 40 years. Every April, one to four roofs in a village are replaced on successive weekends. The entire process involves about 200 or more people—a communal event known as *yui*—who can replace one roof in a couple of days.

and during the snowy months, which attract many Asian travelers), with an astounding 2 million-plus visitors annually. Shirakawa-go may no longer be off the beaten path, but I think there's still a magic to this rural region in Gifu Prefecture. The adjective "fairytale" is thrown around wantonly these days, but in winter, Shirakawa-go really does look like a town from which the Grinch would try to steal Christmas. If you can, spend the night—since most tourists are day-trippers, you'll have the village pretty much to yourself by late afternoon.

Shirakawa-go's inhabitants live in several small villages. Of these, **Ogimachi ♥♥♥**, declared a UNESCO World Cultural and Natural Heritage site in 1995 and often referred to as Shirakawa, boasts the greatest concentration of thatched-roof buildings. With just 600 residents, it's a delightful hamlet of narrow lanes winding past thatched-roof farmhouses, which stand like island sentinels surrounded by paddies. Many of the farmhouses have been turned into *minshuku,* souvenir shops, restaurants, and museums, including an open-air museum that depicts life in the region before roads opened it to the rest of the world.

Essentials

GETTING THERE Two bus companies serve Shirakawa-go: **Hokutetsu Bus** (hokutetsu.co.jp/en; ✆ **076-234-0123**) based in Kanazawa, and **Nohi Bus** (nouhibus.co.jp; ✆ **0577-32-1688**) in Takayama. Hokutetsu requires reservations, which you can do on the spot if there's room, but in high season it's best to reserve as early as possible. Nohi is first-come, first-served to Ogimachi but requires reservations if the bus is continuing to Kanazawa. From Takayama Station, Nohi buses take 50 minutes and cost ¥2,800, with about 15 departures daily; from Kanazawa Station, Hokutetsu runs 10 daily buses, costing ¥2,800 for a 1½-hour trip. Note that weather can cancel bus services. Buses deliver you to the center of Ogimachi, with a nearby luggage storage room (¥600 and up per bag) and coin lockers (¥500 for smaller bags, ¥1,000 for larger ones) if you need to store bags. The Nagoya Railroad's **Shoryudo Bus** (meitetsu.co.jp/eng) is another option, offering open-ended travel between Matsumoto, Shirawaka-go, Takayama, Kanazawa, Nagoya, and elsewhere in central western Japan. There are 3- and 5-day passes available from ¥14,000.

VISITOR INFORMATION Next to the bus parking lot in Ogimachi is a **tourist office** (vill.shirakawa.lg.jp/en; ✆ **05769-6-1013;** daily 8:30am–5pm) where you can pick up an English-language map.

Seeing the Sights in & Around Ogimachi

In addition to an open-air museum, several old farmhouses in Ogimachi are open to the public. ***Note:*** Because Ogimachi is so small, few addresses are given below. The village has basically one main street and some side

A View of Ogimachi

For an overview (and the best vantage point for photos) of the entire village, walk 20 minutes along the gently sloping road that leads from the north side of Ogimachi to the **Shiroyama Viewing Point ♥♥** (in winter, you have to take a shuttle bus, ¥200 each way). There's a souvenir shop/restaurant here, but the best thing to do is to turn left at the crest of the hill and walk to the hill's westernmost point (toward the river), where there are some secluded benches. From here, you'll have a marvelous view of the entire valley, made even more picturesque because all the thatched houses face north and south. If you're thirsty or hungry, head to the restaurant (also with an outdoor viewing point) to buy a drink or a snack and then take it with you to the lookout.

Traditional cooking and farming equipment is displayed in the upper loft of an old house in the Gassho Zukuri Minka-En open-air museum.

streets; it takes about 15 minutes to walk from one end to the other. English-language signs direct you to the various attractions.

Gassho Zukuri Minka-en ♥♥♥ MUSEUM To see how rural people lived in centuries past, visit Shirakawa-go's top attraction, an open-air museum with 25 *gassho-zukuri* houses and sheds, relocated mostly from Kazura village, which was abandoned in 1967. Filled with the tools of everyday life and displays ranging from silk production to straw clothing, the buildings are picturesquely situated around ponds, paddies, flowerbeds, and streams. Artisans are occasionally on hand making traditional crafts. A couple of the structures show videos, including one that depicts rural life more than 50 years ago in Kazura; another shows *gassho-zukuri* construction and re-thatching.

✆ **05769-6-1231.** ¥600 adults, ¥400 children 7–15. Mar–Nov daily 8:40am–5pm; Dec–Feb 9am–4pm (closed Thurs Dec–Mar; if Thurs is a holiday, it closes Wed instead).

Kanda House (神田家) ♥♥ HISTORIC FARMHOUSE The Kanda family that once lived here raised silkworms, much like the rest of the village, and made extra cash by fuming nitric acid for gunpowder in a subterranean chamber. Located just north of the main street, the house is perfumed by woodsmoke from crackling wooden logs in the sunken hearth, a contrast to the crisp mountain air. This heats the entire property, dries out the thatch after heavy rainfall, and allows soot to accumulate on the wooden beams, imbuing everything with a dark, smoky aesthetic. QR codes are dotted around giving context to some of the exhibits.

✆ **05769-6-1047.** ¥300 adults, ¥150 children. Daily 9am–5pm. Occasionally closed.

Nagase Ke (長瀬家) ♥♥ HISTORIC FARMHOUSE Across the road from the Kanda house (see above), the Nagase house is the village's largest home. Built in 1890 using centuries-old cypress and chestnut, it once housed 44 people (three generations of the Nagase family still live here). The enormous cross beam is 18m (59 ft.) long, and the height of the five-story house is more than 17m (55 ft.) high. A 15-minute video shows the 2001 re-thatching in which 500 people took part, including 40 women involved just in cooking meals for the workers. Nagase ancestors were personal doctors of the powerful Maeda lords from the Kanazawa region, and the house displays gifts from the Maedas as well as medical tools. Like other homes, it contains a family altar, this one 500 years old and adjoined to the house so it could be quickly removed in case of fire. Upstairs is a mezzanine where 17 laborers lived, while the next level displays tools used for everything from threshing rice and making rope to weaving cloth. The fourth floor, where silk production once took place, contains tools related to the business, including flat trays where the silkworms were bred.

✆ **05769-6-1047.** ¥400 adults, ¥200 children. Daily 9am–5pm. Occasionally closed.

Where to Stay in Ogimachi

Because huge extended families living under one roof are a thing of the past, some residents of Ogimachi have turned their *gassho-zukuri* homes into *minshuku* (bed-and-breakfasts). Staying in one gives you the unique chance to lodge in a thatched farmhouse with a family that might consist of grandparents, parents, and children. English is often limited to the basics of "bath," "breakfast," and "dinner," but smiles go a long way. Most likely, the family will drag out their photo album with pictures of winter snowfall and the momentous occasion when the thatched roof was repaired.

Most *minshuku* are small, with about four to nine *tatami* rooms open to guests. Rooms are basic without bathroom or toilet, and you may be expected to roll out your own futon. Privacy may be limited, with only a flimsy sliding partition separating you from the guest next door. Typically, check-in is at 3pm; checkout is 9am. The tourist office can make a reservation for you at these or any others around town.

Although *minshuku* have baths, the best place to soak is in the town's only hot-spring indoor and outdoor baths, at **Shirakawa-go no Yu** (**白川郷の温泉; ✆ 05769-6-0026**), across the street from the bus stop. Open Saturday-Wednesday from 7am to 9pm (open 3pm Fri), it charges ¥800 for adults and ¥400 for children, but ask your *minshuku* for a ¥200 discount coupon.

Koemon (幸エ門) ♥♥♥ Now run and managed by fifth- and sixth-generation family members, this 200-year-old farmhouse became a *minshuku* almost 50 years ago. It has been modernized with a cafe in the lobby, a heated floor, automatic sensor lights, and even dimmer switches to enhance the mood around the *irori* fireplace, where you'll have your meals and watch a video during dinner showing the re-thatching of the farmhouse. Rooms are spotless, with the best one facing a pond. If you have heavy luggage, you'll be happy to know that this one is closest to the bus stop, only a 10-minute walk away via Nishi Dori.

456 Ogimachi. shirakawago-kataribe.com/koemon.html. ✆ **05769-6-1446.** 4 units, all w/ shared bath. ¥9,000 per person.

Shimizu (志みづ) On the edge of town, mercifully far from the tourist crowds and souvenir shops, this small *minshuku* in a 200-year-old thatched house surrounded by a pastoral setting is a good choice for travelers who desire more privacy—guests aren't living with a family, since the owner, who speaks some English, lives in the house next door. There's a communal room with an *irori,* where you can serve yourself coffee and tea and where meals are served. Although you can stay here without opting for meals, note that dinner options in the village are minimal.

2613 Ogimachi, south edge of the village. shimizu-inn.com. ✆ **05769-6-1914.** 3 units w/ shared bath. ¥16,500–¥22,000 per person. Rates include 2 meals. Reservations accepted through Airbnb only.

Where to Eat in Ogimachi

Keyaki (けやき) ♥♥♥ GRILLED MEAT When the doors to this restaurant on the highway bisecting the town are left ajar, the smell of rendering meat fat will probably lure you inside. Using portable burners at their tables, diners cook Hida beef, a specialty in Gifu prefecture, or Yui-uma, a local brand of pork known for being lean yet tender. Non-DIY options like boneless short rib rice bowls, fried shrimp curry, and tempura udon are also available to order on the electronic tablet menus. The tea is

GOING green IN THE MOUNTAINS

The whole sustainability craze took a while to land in Japan, but once it did, numerous hotels made spurious claims as to their green, waste-free, zero-carbon, or environmentally friendly credentials. In contrast, a few km west of Ogimachi village, the **Shirakawa-go Eco Institute** (**志みづ;** toyota.eco-inst.jp; ✆ **05769-6-1187**) shows how sustainability is done right. Opened in 2005 under the stewardship of Toyota Motors, this hotel actually puts its money where its mouth is, combining nature preservation, eco-education, and the implementation of green technologies. For example, to cut back on its carbon footprint, the hotel stores cold winter air in a gigantic chamber and uses it to ventilate the lodging in summer. Guests are encouraged to enjoy the serene surroundings of the Japan Alps and staff can organize hiking trips, nature walks, snowshoe tours, sled rental, and river rafting excursions. Japanese and Western rooms are both available, but the tatami rooms are much more charming. Indoor and open-air hot spring baths and a French restaurant using local produce are also on site. Room rates run about ¥20,000 to ¥40,000. One caveat: While it's only a 10-minute drive from the village, the hotel is more than an hour's walk (and includes possibly slushy uphill terrain) from Ogimachi. If you don't have access to a car, contact the hotel to enquire about pickup.

self-serve. Keyaki might not have the rustic interior for which Shirakawa-go's buildings known, but it serves arguably the best pound-for-pound lunch in the village.

305–1 Ogimachi. keyaki-shirakawago.com. ✆ **05769-6-1072.** Set meal ¥1,600. Wed–Mon 10:30am–2:30pm.

Ochudo (落人) CAFE Because *minshuku* provide dinner and breakfast, all you'll probably need is lunch. With its small front porch and rocking chairs overlooking a paddy, and a welcoming old-fashioned interior in a thatched house, this tea and coffee shop with soothing music makes for a relaxing place for a snack or light meal. It's owned by charming Miyako-san (whose husband is from the Nagase family; see p. 272), who lets you choose your own cup for tea or coffee and offers a yummy daily beef curry that strays from the usual (with, for example, asparagus). Order it with the sweet red bean soup, which you can refill at your leisure from pots on the central hearth. Miyako-san will probably hand you a bound booklet with information on Shirakawa-go to skim through with lunch, and before you leave, a postcard to take home.

In middle of Shirakawa Mura, near the Kanda House. ✆ **090-5458-0418.** Set meal ¥1,600. Daily 11am–5pm (to 6pm in summer if there are customers).

Satou Café (喫茶さとう) VARIED JAPANESE The concept at Satou Cafe is to imbue the flavors of Shirakawa-go with a mother's magic touch. Run by kindly couple Noboru and Nao-chan, Satou serves homemade food with ingredients cultivated and harvested without the use of pesticides or inorganic farming techniques. Expect *shiso* dumplings, *kinako dango* (mochi rice balls with soybean powder), wild pickled vegetables, soba noodles, and horse chestnuts. You can also book *onigiri*-making workshops with Nao-chan (enquire with the tourism office for availability), though these will be in Japanese only. Language is no barrier to her admonishing you, however, especially if you lack a deft touch at pressing the rice ball together. That said, combinations like black rice, wild mushrooms, and sweet *kabocha* (pumpkin), served on a bed of magnolia leaves with freshly brewed tea, are worthy compensation. It's a 15-minute walk from the Ogimachi bus stop, next to the Shirakawa-go no Yu baths.

1163–1 Ogimachi. satou-shirakawa.wixsite.com/satou-shirakawa. ✆ **05769-6-1432.** Set meal ¥900–¥1,200. Daily 9am–5pm (irregular holidays).

HIDA TAKAYAMA ♥♥♥

533km (331 miles) NW of Tokyo; 165km (103 miles) NE of Nagoya

Located in the Hida Mountains (part of the Japan Alps National Park) in Gifu Prefecture, **Hida Takayama** is surrounded by a series of craggy, 3,000m (10,000-ft.) peaks, providing a lovely backdrop to the old Edo-style town. Situated along a river on a wide plateau with a population of about 82,000, it was founded in the 16th century by Lord Kanamori, who selected the site for the impregnable position afforded by the surrounding

A lookout point over Hida Takayama from the Higashiyama Walking Route in the forested hills east of town (see box on p. 278).

mountains. Modeled after Kyoto but also with strong ties to Edo (Tokyo), Takayama borrowed from both cultural centers in developing its own architecture, food, and crafts, all well-preserved today thanks to centuries of isolation. With a rich supply of timber from surrounding forests, its carpenters were legendary, creating not only beautifully crafted traditional merchants' homes in Takayama but also the Imperial Palace and temples in Kyoto.

Though Takayama hasn't completely evaded the ravages of Japan's construction magnates, it does have a delightful and well-preserved historic district, **Sanmachi,** with homes of classical design typical of 18th-century Hida. The streets are narrow and clean, flanked on both sides by tiny canals that in centuries past were useful for fire prevention, washing clothes, and dumping winter snow. Rising from the canals are one- and two-story homes and shops of gleaming dark wood with overhanging roofs; latticed windows and slats of wood play games of light and shadow in the white of the sunshine. In the doorways of many shops, curtains flutter in the breeze.

With its quaint old character, great shopping (including a lively city market), and museums, Takayama invites exploration. It's well on the tourism radar now—those old walking streets can get jam-packed in the late-morning and afternoon—but deviate from the trodden trail and you'll find lively bars and restaurants, and walking paths that feel relatively undiscovered. Look for huge cedar balls hanging from the eaves in front of several shops, indicating one of Takayama's six sake breweries, most of them small affairs. Go inside, sample the sake, and watch the men stirring rice in large vats.

Essentials

GETTING THERE The easiest way to reach Takayama is by direct **train** from Nagoya (which is on the Shinkansen line), with departures approximately every hour. The 2½-hour trip costs ¥6,340 for an unreserved seat. There's also one early-morning train that departs Osaka and Kyoto directly for Takayama. From Tokyo, **Nohi buses** (nouhibus.co.jp; ✆ **03-5376-2222**) depart Shinjuku Station four times daily, arriving in Takayama 5½ hours later and costing ¥7,000; they depart Osaka (with a stop in Kyoto) three times daily and cost ¥5,500 to ¥8,500 for a 5½-hour trip. Nohi buses also serve Takayama from Kanazawa (with a stop in Shirakawa-go) several times a day; reservations are usually required and the fare is ¥4,000 for the 2¼-hour trip.

VISITOR INFORMATION The **Takayama Tourist Information Office** (hida.jp/english; ✆ **0577-32-5328;** daily 8:30am–5pm) is just outside the main (east) exit of Takayama Station. You can pick up an English-language map of the town showing the location of all museums and attractions. Or stop by the **Hidatakayama Tourist Information Center** (daily 9am–6pm), on the corner of Honmachi Dori opposite Takayama Jinya (p. 279), to pick up English language pamphlets and route maps, including a Hida Takayama Audio Guide Map with a scannable QR code. You can also store luggage here for ¥500 per item per day.

GETTING AROUND Takayama is one of Japan's easiest towns to navigate. Most of its attractions lie east of the train station in the historic Sanmachi district and are easily reached from the station in about 10 to 15 minutes on foot. Throughout the town, English-language signs give directions to many attractions; they're even embedded in sidewalks and streets. Tourist shuttles, the **Takumi, Sarubobo,** and **Machinami** buses (day passes **¥500**), travel north-south and east-west through the old town, and also stop at the Hida Folk Village and Takayama Museum of Art in the western outskirts; pick up the schedule and route map at the tourist office.

Lots of shops and hotels rent **bicycles,** charging ¥1,000 and up for the day (less for a few hours). The **Hara Cycle Shop** at 61 Suehirocho (✆ **0577-32-1657;** Wed–Mon 9am–8pm) rents bikes for ¥300 per hour, ¥200 per hour for the second hour, and ¥1,300 for 6 hours or more. Note however that Takayama's old town has narrow streets—you won't get far on two wheels when it's busy—and Hida Folk Village and Hida Takayama Museum of Art are both up a very long hill.

Exploring Takayama

Takayama's main attraction is **Sanmachi,** its historic center of traditional homes and businesses. Be sure to allow time to wander around; you'll likely want to sample the Hida beef skewers, seared beef *nigiri, dango* (grilled mochi), and *taiyaki* (wafflelike pastries filled with custard cream or sweet bean paste), or investigate shops selling folk crafts, cypress

The well-preserved streets of Sanmachi still look much as they did in the 18th century.

antiques, yew woodcarvings, retro trinkets, a unique type of lacquerware called *shunkei-nuri,* and Japanese rice wine.

Be sure, too, to visit the **Miyagawa Morning Market ♥♥**, which stretches on the east bank of the Miyagawa River between Kajibashi and Yayoibashi bridges. Held every morning from 7am (8am in winter) to noon, it's very picturesque, with cloth-covered stalls selling fresh produce, flowers, pickled vegetables, street food, and locally made crafts. Note that it gets very busy here, so you might prefer the smaller morning market held in front of Takayama Jinya.

Hida Folk Village (Hida no Sato) ♥♥ MUSEUM An open-air museum of more than 30 old thatched and shingled farmhouses, sheds, and buildings, the entire village is picturesque, with swans swimming in the central pond, green moss growing on the thatched roofs, and flowers blooming in season. Many structures were brought here from other parts of the region to illustrate how farmers and artisans used to live in the Hida Mountains. Some houses have *gassho-zukuri*-style roofs, built steeply to withstand the region's heavy snowfalls. All the buildings, which range from 100 to 500 years old, are open to the public and filled with furniture, old spindles and looms, utensils for cooking and dining, instruments used in the silk industry, farm tools, sleds, and straw boots and snow capes for winter. Some even have smoldering fires in the *irori* fire pits. Workshops set up in one corner of the village grounds demonstrate Takayama's well-known woodcarving, weaving, and other cottage industries. You can also enquire through the website about craft workshops, like making *sarubobo* (baby monkey stuffed toys that have long been a symbol of the region), weaving braids, painting small bells, or making puzzles from hardwood scraps. You could spend about 1½ hours at the village, but you many want to skip it if you're heading to Shirakawa-go, where there's a similar, more accessible folk village (p. 269).

1–590 Kamiokamoto-choi. hidanosato.com. ✆ **0577-34-4711.** ¥700 adults, ¥200 children. Daily 8:30am–5pm. Bus: Sarubobo Bus to Hida-no-Sato.

Hida Takayama Museum of Art (Hida Takayama Bijutsukan) ♥♥ MUSEUM Serious glass lovers will not want to miss this museum with its collection of mostly European Art Nouveau and Art Deco glassware, including works by Tiffany, Lalique, and Gallé, as well as some contemporary works by glassmakers like Fujita Kyohei and Dale Chihuly. Several rooms are furnished in decorative and applied arts by masters such as Louis Majorelle, Mackintosh, and Vienna's Secessionist artists.

1–124–1 Kamiokamoto-cho. htma.rtg.jp. ✆ **0577-35-3535.** ¥1,000 adults, children free. Daily 10am–5pm (closed irregular days). Bus: Sarubobo Bus to Hida Takayama Museum of Art.

Merchants' Houses ♥♥♥ HISTORIC HOMES In contrast to other castle towns during the Edo Period, Takayama was under the direct control of the Tokugawa government rather than a feudal lord, which meant its homes were built and owned by merchants and commoners rather than the samurai class that dominated other Japanese cities. Located side by side in the historic center and both toured easily in less than 30 minutes, **Yoshijima-ke** and **Kusakabe Heritage House** are merchants' mansions that once belonged to two of Takayama's richest families.

A WALK IN THE woods

Carving through wooded hills on the eastern edge of town, the well-marked **Higashiyama Walking Course ♥♥♥** leads past a string of 12 temples, a couple of shrines, and a moss-covered mausoleum (where you might hear the rhythmic chanting of local monks), offering a glimpse into the nature and topography of Takayama before civilization arrived. It's particularly resplendent in autumn when the hillsides are bedecked in vermillion, ochre, lime yellow, and golden leaves. In a country that's hacked down a dispiriting portion of its native deciduous forest and replaced it with industrial cedar—even from the town you'll notice blocks of identical conifers wedged in between the rest of the foliage—it's heartwarming to see such a diverse array of old trees. While tourists clog the walking streets of the old town, you'll get to explore this lovely stretch of forest in comparative solitude. The course also leads to **Shiroyama Park,** site of the Kanamori clan castle until it was torn down in 1695 by order of the Tokugawa shogunate; parts of its stone foundations still remain. It's worth marching up here for the views of the Hida Mountains—a sign (in English) tells you which ones you're looking at and how tall they are. The hiking course stretches 5.5km (3 miles) end to end; there are English-language signs, but be sure to get the map provided by the tourist office. If you get lost, consider it part of the fun; there are seductive-looking paths splitting off from the main trail that will doubtless grab your attention. From the tourist office on the corner of Honmachi dori, cross the red footbridge and keep walking straight, heading up a set of steps. You'll see signs indicating the trail.

With its exposed attic, heavy crossbeams, sunken open-hearth fireplace, and sliding doors, **Yoshijima-ke ♥♥♥** (also called Yoshijima Heritage House; ✆ **0577-32-0038**) is a masterpiece of geometric design. It feels like it was constructed from modular blocks—accentuated by interlocking tatami floorboards—as though any part of the house could be unplugged, rotated 90 degrees, and refitted elsewhere. There's also an expert use of space and framing; with sliding doors left open to reveal views of a pine tree in the front garden from several rooms away or shafts of light spilling through the shoji screens to create a seamless balance between nature and the interior. The manor was built in 1907 as both the home and factory of the Yoshijima family, well-to-do sake brewers. Notice how the beams and wooden accents gleam from decades of polishing, as each generation of women did their share in bringing the wood to a luster. Yoshijima-ke is also famous for its lattices, typical of Takayama yet showing an elegance influenced by Kyoto. Its walls serve as an art gallery for the lithographs of female artist Shinoda Toko, a distant relative of present owner Yoshijima Tadao, who also uses the house for his other passion, jazz, heard softly in the back gallery. If you only choose one of these houses to visit, this should be it.

Built in 1879 for a merchant dealing in silk, lamp oil, and finance, **Kusakabe Heritage House ♥♥** (kusakabe-mingeikan.com; ✆ **0577-32-0072**) is more imposing, if not quite as intricate. Its architectural style is considered unique to Hida—the woodworking techniques have a lineage that goes back to the Asuka period (A.D. 538–710) when the region's carpenters first garnered acclaim—but it has many characteristics common during the Edo Period, including a two-story warehouse at the back with open beams and an earthen floor, now filled with folk art and other items, plus artwork by Shoji Hamada and Kanjiro Kawai. On display, too, are personal items such as a lacquered pillow box that could be filled with incense to perfume the hair and imports from other countries, handed down through the generations. Scan the QR code at the entrance (free Wi-Fi available) to get detailed English explanations on the various rooms and exhibits.

North end of Nino-machi St., Oshinmachi. **Yoshijima-ke:** ¥500 adults, ¥300 children; Wed-Sun 9:30am-3:30pm. **Kusakabe Heritage House:** ¥1,000 adults, high-school students ¥500, children ¥300; Wed–Mon 10am–4pm. Both may extend opening hours in spring and summer.

Takayama Jinya ♥♥ HISTORIC BUILDING This building served as the Tokugawa government's administrative building for 177 years (1692–1868). Of some 60 local Tokugawa government offices once spread throughout Japan, it is the only one still in existence. Resembling a miniature palace with its outer wall and imposing entrance gate, the sprawling complex consists of both original buildings and reconstructions. In addition to offices, chambers, and courts, the complex contained living quarters, a huge kitchen, an interrogation room for criminals with torture

A demonstration of traditional musical instruments at the Takayama Jinya, once the Takayama headquarters of the Tokugawa government.

devices, a tearoom, and a 400-year-old rice granary, the oldest and biggest in Japan, where rice collected from farmers as a form of taxation was stored. If it's quiet, take a few minutes on the veranda to appreciate the lovely landscape garden in the inner courtyard; when scattered with fallen maple leaves in autumn, it's a reminder that even Japan's dictatorial rulers understood the natural world was a source of poetry and enlightenment. Some exhibits have QR codes supplying information in multiple languages, but the explanations aren't particularly detailed.

1–5 Hachi-ken-machi. ✆ **0577-32-0643.** ¥440 adults, free high-school age and younger. Mar–Oct daily 8:45am–5pm; Nov–Feb daily 8:45am–4:30pm.

For history of a more recent era, check out the delightful clutter of 20th-century artifacts at the Takayama Showa Museum.

Takayama Showa Museum (昭和館) ♥♥♥ MUSEUM We may think of minimalism—an appreciation of the *spare*—as Japan's aesthetic ideal. But at this eclectic museum, packed to the rafters with items used in daily life during the Showa era (the reign of Emperor Hirohito, 1926–89), we are reminded that the Japanese also have an almost artistic sense of clutter. This collection includes tiny family cars from the 1960s, movie posters of blood-spattered mobsters or sword-wielding samurai, tinplate shop signs, old Minolta cameras, and posters for wrestling events featuring Hulk Hogan and his Japanese counterparts, as well as rusty bikes, typewriters, washing machines, rice cookers, and much more, most of it arranged in themed rooms. You can step inside a toy shop, photo studio, doctor's office, barbershop, appliance store (it's fun to see what was considered high-tech back then), schoolroom, beauty salon, a typical living room (playing cartoon reruns like *Tom and Jerry* in Japanese), and even a movie theater showing black-and-white action flicks, all providing a unique perspective on how much Japan—and the world—has changed in just a few short decades. If, like me, you're a sucker for this kind of stuff, buy a combination ticket (¥1,600) for this museum and the **Takayama Retro Museum ♥♥**, a 10-minute walk south at 4–7 Shinmeimachi (daily 10am–5pm). Though what you get here is more of the same, including a prized display of soft vinyl dolls, the focus is more on retro video games. Arcade games like *Street Fighter, Space Invaders, Galaga,* and *Pac Man* (mostly free), slot and pachinko machines, and puzzles and board games are there for visitors to play. The upstairs room is a treat, designed like a child's gaming room with Nintendo consoles and early home gaming systems like the Color TV-Game and Racing 112 (unknown even to many diehard gamers). Even if games aren't your thing, walking around to the sound of clanging pachinko balls, *bip-bop* arcade sounds, whirring slot machines, and some out-of-synch *jidaigeki* (period drama) dialog does harken back to a simpler, somehow more carefree, age. You could easily spend 30 or 40 minutes in each location, swooning over what was clearly a labor of love for the collector.

6 Shimoichino-machi. showakan.jp/takayama. ✆ **057-33-7836.** ¥1,000 adults, ¥800 high-school students, ¥600 junior highl students, ¥400 grade-school students, free children under 4. Daily 9am–5pm.

Zazen at Zennoji Temple ♥♥ MEDITATION EXPERIENCE The frequent use of the word "Zen" in temple and restaurant names around Takayama is a giveaway that this region has a deep-seated connection to Buddhism—some temples were founded well over 1,000 years ago. It makes sense that Zen practitioners would have chosen life in the mountains, where they could contemplate the nature of the universe and our bizarre place of suffering within it, far from the squabbles of land-grabbing warlords. If you want to take the first baby steps in your own Zen tutelage, try a zazen meditation experience at Zennoji Temple, one of the 12 temples along the Higashimyama Walking Course (see "A Walk in the Woods," p. 278). After being greeted with tea and *wagashi* (a Japanese sweet), you'll make your way to the meditation room (freezing in winter), assume the lotus position on a small round pillow, form an "O" shape with your fingers (known as the "cosmic mudra") to allow the free flow of energy, begin to breathe deeply, and finally let all internal thoughts wash over you until, hopefully, they dissipate altogether. ***Note:*** This experience last around 1.5 hours and is mostly conducted in Japanese, so you may prefer to bring a translator to get the most value for your money. Enquire with the temple or the tourism office about translation services in the area. 177 Soyujimachi. ✆ **0577-32-4516.** Zazen ¥1,000 per person. Daily 9am–3pm (unavailable irregular days). Reservations made by phone only.

Where to Stay in Takayama

Antique Inn Sumiyoshi (寿美よし) ♥♥♥ This place calls itself a *ryokan,* but its size, homey atmosphere, and the family that runs it make it seem more like a *minshuku.* Built more than 100 years ago by a well-known local carpenter to house a silkworm industry (and then operating as a pawnshop), it opened in 1950 as a *ryokan* and hasn't changed much since then. An open-hearth fireplace, samurai armor, and antiques and folk toys fill the reception area, where you are invited to have tea or coffee. On the second floor a lovely outdoor deck faces the river, across which is the morning market. *Tatami* rooms are comfortable and old-fashioned, many with painted screens and antiques; request one facing the river. Minami-san, the man running the *ryokan,* is a fifth-generation innkeeper and speaks English. In addition to Japanese and vegetarian dinners (order when making reservations), both Japanese and Western breakfasts are available. Meals are served in your room. No credit cards accepted. 4–21 Honmachi. sumiyoshi-ryokan.com/en. ✆ **0577-32-0228.** 8 units (1 w/ private bath, 2 with sink/toilet). From ¥12,100–¥16,500 per person, meals included. **Amenities:** Private hot spring baths; free Wi-Fi.

Takayama Green Hotel ♥♥ This large resort hotel on the west side of the station might not have the character of some of Takayama's smaller properties, but the rooms are smartly designed and traditionally Japanese, if somewhat old-fashioned, and room sizes are decent. The deluxe Japanese-Western rooms have large double beds, a *washitsu*-style living area with low tables and chairs on the tatami, and views across the town and surrounding mountains. The main reasons to stay here, however, are the large public bathing areas with atmospheric open-air rock pools, and the Hida beef banquet dinners at the Ryokutei restaurant, served overlooking a Japanese garden.
2–180 Nishinoichiirocho. takayama-gh.com. ✆ **0577-33-5500.** 238 units (4 w/ private bath). ¥13,500–¥45,000 double. **Amenities:** 7 restaurants; large hot-spring baths; free shuttle from the station; free Wi-Fi.

Takayama Ouan ♥♥ This cool, modern property run by the ever-reliable Dormy Inn chain is a no-shoes hotel, with tatami flooring throughout, that makes it feel like you're staying in somebody's home. The rooms are designed in a simple, modular style, with sliding fusuma door frames, compact seating areas, and either mattresses set on the tatami or Western-style beds. Tea-making facilities, funky crockery, and *samue* (pajama-like clothes for wearing around the hotel) are also provided in all rooms. The best aspect of the hotel, though, is the hot spring baths on the 13th floor—one for men, one for women, and three private baths operating on a

first-come-first-served basis (maximum 30 min. bathing time)—offering lovely views of the Hida Mountains. A freezer in the spa lobby offers free ice pops and frozen chocolates to help you cool down after a steamy dip, or if you'd prefer something savory, a half-bowl of ramen is served free to guests each night between 9:30 and 10:30pm. Breakfast can be included, but I'm not sure it's necessary with a couple of morning markets nearby.
4–313 Hanasatomachi. dormy-hotels.com. ✆ **0577-37-2230.** 155 units. ¥9,000–¥30,000 double. **Amenities:** Restaurant (breakfast and late-night ramen); hot-spring baths; free Wi-Fi.

Where to Eat in Takayama

The best-known of Takayama's local specialties is *hoba miso,* soybean paste mixed with dried scallions, ginger, and mushrooms and cooked on a dry magnolia leaf at your table above a small clay burner. Other dishes include Takayama's own style of *soba* (buckwheat noodles), soy sauce-based ramen, *mitarashi-dango* (grilled rice balls with soy sauce), and Hida brand beef. *Sansai* are mountain vegetables, including edible ferns and other wild plants; and *ayu* is a small river fish, grilled with soy sauce or salt.

Takayama's local specialty, *hoba miso* is a savory mixture piled onto a dry magnolia leaf and cooked at your table.

EXPENSIVE

Kakusho (角正) ♥♥♥ VEGETARIAN For a big splurge, dine at Kakusho, established 250 years ago and now under the helm of the 12th-generation head chef. It offers local vegetarian fare called *shojin ryori,* typically served at Buddhist temples. Situated on the slope of a hill in the eastern part of the city, a 5-minute walk from Sanmachi, this delightful restaurant serves meals either in small private *tatami* rooms dating from the Edo Period or in a larger room from the Meiji Period that can be opened to the elements on three sides, all of which overlook a dreamy, mossy garden enclosed by a clay wall. The least expensive meals consist of various mountain vegetables, mushrooms, nuts, tofu, and other dishes, with more dishes added for more expensive meals (tax and service charge will be added to prices below). Reservations are required.
2–98 Babacho. ✆ **0577-32-0174.** Kaiseki dinners from ¥19,360; lunches from ¥15,730. Daily 11:30am–2pm and 5:30–7pm (last order). Irregular closing days.

MODERATE

Suzuya (寿々や) ♥♥ TAKAYAMA CUISINE Darkly lit with traditional Takayama country decor, this restaurant specializing in Takayama cuisine has been a mainstay for decades. It's not uncommon for queues to form outside, but even when long they move quite quickly. There's an English-language menu complete with photographs and explanations of each dish, including such local specialties as mountain vegetables, *hoba miso* (including a vegetarian option), and Hida beef, as well as *shabu-shabu, sukiyaki,* and deep-fried breaded shrimp and pork. But Hida beef is what the restaurant is known for.

24 Hanakawa-machi. ✆ **0577-32-2484.** Set meals ¥1,500–¥5,000. Daily 11am–2pm and 5–8pm (last order). Closed irregularly.

Yakiniku Kaede ♥♥ HIDA BEEF Hida beef is *everywhere* in town, be it at chic new restaurants, venerable family-run joints, or hole-in-the-walls dishing out beef sushi for the tourist trade. This restaurant on Honmachi Dori is one of the most approachable places to eat Hida beef in all its forms. The menu is in English, the lunch sets are seriously good value, and if you opt for the pricier (and super delicious) dinner courses, you'll get simple instructions on how to use the grill at your table. Beef *donburi* rice bowls and beef curry plates are ¥1,650 during lunch (served until 2pm); at dinner you can order beef cuts a la carte or set menus with chateaubriand, fillet, sirloin, and rump, as well as vegetables, salad, and bread or rice. Takayama sake flights are popular, too, costing ¥1,980 for a set of three—one cloudy, one *junami* (pure rice with no additives), and one *daiginjo* (the highest-quality sake, showcasing the brewer's prowess).

2-63-63 Honmachi. kaede-hidatakayama.com/yakiniku. ✆ **0577-62-9270.** Lunch from ¥1,650; dinner courses ¥3,685–¥13,475. Wed–Mon 11:30am–2pm and 5–9pm (last order).

INEXPENSIVE

Hanbee (半兵衛) ♥♥ RAMEN *Shoyu* (soy sauce) ramen is one of Takayama's regional specialties—after Hida beef, it's probably the style of cuisine you'll see most around town—and is much lighter than the dense, oily soups favored in Kyushu or Hokkaido. This shop, hiding in a little alcove down a side street near Takayama Jinya, has several seats along the shop counter (you'll sit on the ground with your legs dangling in the footwells) and three low tables overlooking a small garden. The top-seller is the classic Takayama ramen (order the deluxe to get an egg and some extra toppings), but there's also spicy ramen, ramen with a beef bowl on the side, and a la carte beef skewers. The menu has pictures and English translation.

54 Kawaharamachi. ✆ **0577-34-8451.** Ramen ¥850–¥1,100; beef skewers ¥1,200. Wed–Mon 11am–2pm and 5–10pm.

Hashizen (はし善) ♥♥♥ TAKAYAMA CUISINE A few streets away from the hubbub of the town center, while queues form outside the restaurants trending on social media, this family-run shop serves classic Takayama dishes, like *hoba miso* sets with vegetable tempura and Hida beef courses, in relative anonymity. The restaurant is on the ground floor of the owner's home, and it feels that way; you can hear the commotion of family life tumbling down the staircase and the TV chattering in the background, probably playing baseball reruns or one of the many food programs populating the Japanese airwaves. It all feels low-key until the food arrives, a baroque serving of vegetables, pickles, condiments, rice, soup, and egg custard in ceramic or lacquered receptacles. The tempura set, using *sansai* vegetables grown locally in the mountains, served with a *hoba miso* grilled at the table (or counter) is superb. A dining experience that will stay long in the memory.
1–93 Hachikenmachi. ✆ **0577-32-3821.** Tempura or beef sets ¥1,000–¥2,500; dinner courses ¥2,500–¥3,500. Tues–Sun 11:30am–2pm and 5–8pm.

7 KYOTO & NARA

For any first-time traveler to Japan, **Kyoto ♥♥♥** richly deserves a spot on your itinerary. Not only is it the most historically significant city in the nation, this former capital was also the only major Japanese city spared the bombs of World War II. Unfortunately, much of Kyoto has succumbed to Japan's near-ceaseless urban development projects, eroding the old-world atmosphere that characterized the city as recently as the 1950s. That said, thanks to special designations handed to historic sites and buildings, it's still filled with temples, shrines, imperial palaces, gardens, and *machiya* (traditional wooden houses) amid the unsightly modernity. Spend a few days exploring the city's back streets and off-beat neighborhoods, and you'll probably agree that Kyoto is one of Japan's most romantic cities.

Home to the Imperial court for 1,000 years, Kyoto has the nation's greatest concentration of craft artisans, whose works are displayed in museums and shops dealing in textiles, dyed fabrics, pottery, bambooware, cutlery, fans, metalwork, umbrellas, and other goods. Kyoto is also famous for its own style of *kaiseki,* which blends ceremonial court cuisine with Zen vegetarian food. No fewer than 17 heritage sites in Kyoto Prefecture comprise UNESCO's Historic Monuments of Ancient Kyoto, including Kiyomizu Temple, Kinkakuji, Ginkakuji, Ryoanji Temple, and Nijo Castle, but there are also cool modern attractions like the Kyoto International Manga Museum and Japan's first ever Nintendo Museum. The city's small but vibrant nightlife still features geisha performers, known locally as *geiko,* decked out in all their finery.

FAVORITE KYOTO EXPERIENCES

- **Admiring a Japanese Garden** Kyoto has a wide range of traditional gardens, from austerely beautiful Zen rock gardens to miniature bonsai-like landscapes.
- **Strolling Through Eastern Kyoto** Temples, shrines, gardens, craft shops, traditional neighborhoods—these are highlights of a day spent walking through this historic part of Kyoto, a rare slice of old Japan.
- **Taking an Evening Stroll Through Pontocho** A small, narrow pedestrian lane, Pontocho is lined with a dazzling collection of brightly lit hostess bars, restaurants, and drinking establishments. On

FACING PAGE: A demonstration of the traditional art of the tea-ceremony.

In eastern Kyoto, the atmosphere of old Kyoto lives on in Higashiyama-ku, along stone-cobbled Sannenzaka street.

a warm night, sit for a while along the banks of the nearby Kamo River, a popular spot for Kyoto's young couples.

- **Cycling Through the City** Kyoto's flat topography lends itself to cycling; rent a bike and visit Kyoto's top attractions without clogging the commuter buses.
- **Visiting the Nintendo Museum** On the site of a former Nintendo factory, this museum is a nostalgia-fueled love-letter to the most famous brand name in gaming. See and play the consoles of yore in what's quickly become one of Kyoto's premier attractions.

ESSENTIALS

Getting There

BY PLANE

Kyoto is served by two airports, **Kansai International Airport (KIX;** kansai-airport.or.jp) outside Osaka for international and domestic flights and **Itami Airport** (osaka-airport.co.jp) for domestic flights.

KANSAI INTERNATIONAL AIRPORT The **JR Kansai-Airport Express Haruka** has direct service every 30 to 60 minutes to Kyoto Station, an 80-minute trip that costs ¥3,110 for a non-reserved seat (free for JR Rail Pass holders). Foreign tourists can also use the **Haruka One-Way Ticket**

(¥2,200) from the airport to Kyoto Station, though it must be purchased from the JR website or selected travel agents before arrival in Japan—see westjr.co.jp/global/en/ticket/pass for more information. A cheaper, though slower and less convenient, alternative is the **JR Kanku Kaisoku,** which departs every 30 minutes or so from Kansai Airport and arrives in Kyoto 1 hour and 50 minutes later, with a change at Osaka Station. It costs ¥1,910. Also consider taking the **Kansai Airport Limousine Bus** (kate.co.jp; ✆ **072-461-1374**) from Kansai Airport; buses depart every hour or less for the 1¾-hour trip to Kyoto Station and cost ¥2,800 (¥1,400 children).

BY TRAIN

Kyoto is a major stop on the Shinkansen bullet train; trip time from **Tokyo** is about 2¼ hours, with the fare for a nonreserved seat ¥13,320 one-way. If you're coming from **Osaka,** Kyoto is only 15 minutes from outlying Shin-Osaka (Osaka's bullet train station), but you may find it more convenient to take the JR Tokaido Line, which connects Kyoto directly with centrally located Osaka Station in 30 minutes. From **Kobe,** you can reach Kyoto from Sannomiya and Motomachi stations on the Tokaido Line in 50 minutes.

Strikingly modern **Kyoto Station**—which is an affront to its more historic environs—is like a city in itself with tourist offices, restaurants, a hotel, a department store, a shopping arcade, a theater, and stage events; it is connected to the rest of the city by subway and bus.

BY BUS

Lots of long-distance buses travel between Tokyo and Kyoto; reservations are necessary and prices depend on the bus, the type of seat selected, time of day, and season. **Willer Express** buses (willerexpress.com; ✆ **050-5805-0383**) depart Tokyo, Shinjuku, and Ikebukuro stations nightly, arriving at Kyoto Station the next morning. Fares are ¥4,400 to ¥8,900. Booking platform **Kosoku Bus** (kosokubus.com/en) also offers tickets from various bus providers for as low as ¥2,300 one-way, or you can purchase tickets at station counters or in some convenience stores.

Visitor Information

The **Kyoto Tourist Information Center** (kyoto.travel; ✆ **075-343-0548;** daily 8:30am–7pm), in the central passageway on the second floor of Kyoto Station near Isetan department store, has city and bus maps, as well as many brochures. For information on the wider Kansai area, the Kansai Tourist Information Center Kyoto (tourist-information-center.jp/kansai; ✆ **075-341-0280;** daily 10am–5:30pm) is located across from Kyoto Station in Kyoto Tower.

A monthly tabloid distributed free at hotels and restaurants, the ***Kyoto Visitor's Guide*** (kyotoguide.com) has maps, a calendar of events, and information on sightseeing and shopping (it's available at the Kyoto Tourist Information Center, too, but you have to ask for it). ***Kansai Scene*** (kansaiscene.

com) is a monthly giveaway with information on nightlife, festivals, and other events in Osaka, Kobe, Kyoto, and Nara. The booklet ***Explorer Kyoto*** has excellent maps.

City Layout

Most of Kyoto's attractions and hotels are north of Kyoto Station (take the Central exit), spreading like a fan toward the northeast and northwest. The **northern and eastern edges** of the city contain the most famous temples. The heart of the city is **central Kyoto (Nakagyo Ward**), which has the largest concentration of restaurants, shops, and bars; it radiates outward from the intersection of Kawaramachi Dori and Shijo Dori. It includes a narrow street called Pontocho, a nightlife mecca that runs along the western bank of the Kamo River. Across the Kamo River to the east is the ancient geisha district of Gion.

At twilight, couples gather along the Kamo River near the nightlife district of Pontocho.

Kyoto's Neighborhoods in Brief

The following are Kyoto's main tourist areas; to locate them, see the Kyoto map on p. 296.

AROUND KYOTO STATION The southern ward of **Shimogyo-ku,** which stretches from Kyoto Station north to Shijo Dori Avenue, caters to tourists with its cluster of hotels and to commuters with shops and restaurants. One of Japan's largest station buildings, Kyoto Station caused quite a controversy when it opened in 1997 because of its size, height, and futuristic appearance, but it is now this area's top attraction. It's very contemporary (*too* contemporary, in my opinion), with soaring glass atriums, dramatic public spaces, and a rooftop plaza.

CENTRAL KYOTO **Nakagyo-ku,** the central part of Kyoto west of the Kamo River and north of Shimogyo-ku, embraces Kyoto's main shopping and nightlife districts, with most of the action on **Kawaramachi Dori** and **Shijo Dori** and the **Teramachi** and **Shin-kyogoku** covered shopping arcades. It's home to city hall, **Nijo Castle,** and numerous restaurants and hotels, including a number of exclusive *ryokan* tucked away in delightful neighborhoods typical of old Kyoto. Nakagyo-ku is one of the most desirable places to stay in terms of convenience and atmosphere, but downtown is changing fast, with new shopping and entertainment complexes such as the **Kyoto International Manga Museum,** housed in a former elementary school.

How to Find an Address in Kyoto

Kyoto's streets are laid out in a grid pattern with named streets (a rarity in Japan). Locals tend to use an unofficial address system based on directional terms. The major streets north of Kyoto Station that run east-west are numbered; for example, *shi* means "four," and *dori* means "avenue," so Shijo Dori means "Fourth Avenue." *Agaru* equates to "to the north," *sagaru* to "to the south," *nishi-iru* means "to the west," and *higashi-iru* means "to the east." Thus, an address that reads Shijo-agaru, Teramachi Higashi-iru means "north of Fourth Avenue, east of Teramachi." On non-numbered streets, addresses generally indicate cross streets. Take the restaurant Kushi Kura, for example: Its address is Takakura Dori, Oike-agaru, which tells you it's just north of Oike Dori on Takakura Dori. Addresses for attractions, hotels, and restaurants below will be the establishment's preferred address.

Just a stone's throw from the Kawaramachi-Shijo Dori intersection, Kyoto's most famous street for nightlife is **Pontocho,** a narrow lane paralleling the Kamo River's western bank; many of its bars and restaurants feature outdoor verandas over the river. Paralleling Pontocho to the east is **Kiyamachi,** a narrow lane beside a canal lined with bars and restaurants that bustle with nighttime revelers.

EASTERN KYOTO East of the Kamo River, the wards of **Higashiyama-ku** and **Sakyo-ku** host some of the city's most famous temples and shrines, as well as restaurants specializing in Kyoto cuisine and Buddhist vegetarian dishes, and shops selling local pottery and other crafts. **Gion,** Kyoto's most famous geisha entertainment district, is part of Higashiyama-ku. The traditional wooden geisha houses are not open to the public—you can only gain entry through introductions from someone who's already a customer—but the area makes for a fascinating stroll. Note, however, that Gion is not as welcoming to tourists as it used to be, with visitors barred from certain areas following a spate of "bad behavior," like people chasing geisha down the streets trying to take photos of them. Be mindful of this when strolling through here.

NORTHERN KYOTO Embracing the **Kita-ku, Kamigyo-ku,** and **Ukyo-ku** wards, northern Kyoto is primarily residential but contains a number of Kyoto's top sights, including the **Kyoto Imperial Palace, Kinkakuji** (Temple of the Golden Pavilion), and **Ryoanji Temple,** site of Kyoto's most famous Zen rock garden.

GETTING AROUND

Though a larger city than most people give it credit for, Kyoto has lots of English-language signs and an easy-to-navigate transportation system. making it a breeze to travel in. Its subway and bus networks are especially efficient and quite easy to use, though it's worth noting that the clogging of commuter buses has caused a flurry of anti-tourist sentiment in recent years. You'd be doing Kyoto residents a big favor if you avoided using these, particularly during rush hour. Using bicycles and your own two feet are also good ways to see parts of the city you might otherwise miss, without disrupting local lives.

BY SUBWAY & COMMUTER TRAIN Kyoto has two subway lines, with stops announced in English. The older **Karasuma Line** runs north and south, from Takeda in the south to Kokusai Kaikan in the north, with stops at Kyoto Station, central Kyoto, and Imadegawa Station (convenient for visiting the Imperial Palace). The **Tozai Line** runs in a curve from east to west and is convenient for visiting Nijo Castle and Higashiyama-ku. The two lines intersect in central Kyoto at Karasuma Oike Station (if you find station names cumbersome, go by their numbers; Karasuma Oike, for example, is K08 on the Karasuma Line and T13 on the Tozai Line). Fares start at ¥220 (children pay half-fare) and service runs from about 5:30am to 11:30pm. In addition to subways, the private **Keihan Railway** runs north-south along the Kamo River on the east side of town and is convenient to Gion and some hotels.

BY BUS The most direct way to get to most of Kyoto's attractions in eastern or northern Kyoto is by bus. Buses depart from Kyoto Station's Central (north/Karasuma) Exit, with platforms clearly marked in English listing destinations. Both the Kyoto Tourist Information Center (p. 289) and the Bus and Subway Information counter give out excellent maps showing major bus routes. Some of the buses loop around the city, while others go back and forth between two destinations. Most convenient for sightseeing is **EX100 bus,** which makes a run every 10 minutes from Kyoto Station to major attractions in east Kyoto, including the Kyoto National Museum, Gojo-zaka (the approach to Kiyomizu Temple), Gion, Heian Shrine, Nanzenji, and Ginkakuji. Tickets cost ¥500 adults, ¥250 children, or ¥1,100 for a day pass that can also be used on other bus routes and train lines. The **EX101** departs Kyoto Station for Nijo Castle and Kinkakuji. Unfortunately, at Kyoto Station there are often long queues of foreigners waiting to board these two buses.

The fare for traveling in central Kyoto is ¥230 for a single ride (¥120 for children). If you don't have the exact fare, a fare box can make change for coins and ¥1,000 notes. If the bus is traveling a **long distance** out to the suburbs, you might find a ticket machine right beside the door—take the ticket and hold onto it. It has a number on it and will tell the bus driver when you got on and how much you owe. You can see

Bus Riders: Enter or Exit at the Back?

For more than 40 years, Kyoto bus riders have boarded buses at the rear entrance and paid upon exiting the front door. Recently, however, a dramatic increase in foreign visitors (some with very large suitcases) has prompted the city to gradually switch to a front entry, where you pay upon boarding, and a rear exit. As you navigate around town, expect to encounter both systems.

for yourself how much you owe by looking for your number on a lighted panel at the front of the bus; the longer you ride, the higher the fare. Digital signboards on buses announce each stop in English.

Instead of purchasing individual tickets, you can save time with a prepaid **ICOCA** card (Tokyo's IC cards Suica and PASMO also work in Kyoto; see p. 99 in chapter 4 for a description of IC cards).

For journeys farther afield, there are regional passes available only to foreign tourists that provide travel throughout the Kansai area (including Osaka, Kyoto, Kobe, Nara, and Himeji) and some even as far away as Hiroshima or Kanazawa. For more information, see p. 689 in chapter 15.

BY BICYCLE Kyoto has few hills, and a popular way to get around is by bike—in peak season, you might even be faster on a bike than a bus. The ride along the Kamo River is especially wonderful. You do have to be on guard for vehicular and pedestrian traffic, and in central Kyoto it's illegal to leave your bike parked on the street (ask the rental company for a map of bike parking lots; bikes left outside a designated bicycle parking area will be removed, and you'll be fined). **Kyoto Cycling Tour Project,** a 3-minute walk from the Central (north) Exit of Kyoto Station (kctp.net; ✆ **075-354-3636;** daily 9am–6pm), rents bikes starting at ¥1,200/day. It has several rental terminals throughout the city, including at Nijo Castle and Kinkakuji Temple, and offers guided cycling tours as well.

[Fast FACTS] KYOTO

In addition to the information here, see "Fast Facts: Japan" in chapter 15.

ATMS The most convenient ATMs accepting foreign bank cards are at post offices (like the Kyoto Central Post Office next to Kyoto Station; see "Mail," below) or at one of the many convenience stores in Kyoto.

Climate Kyoto is generally hotter and more humid than Tokyo in summer and colder than Tokyo in winter.

Currency Exchange In addition to banks all over town, you can also exchange money at large department stores like Isetan (which also has a currency-exchange machine on the second floor), Takashimaya, and Daimaru. When changing money, be sure to bring your passport, and note that you'll usually get better exchange rates at banks.

Dentists, Doctors & Hospitals Most hospitals are not equipped to handle emergencies 24 hours a day, but a system has been set up in which hospitals handle emergencies on a rotating basis. **Kyoto University Hospital** (**Kyoto Daigaku Byoin**), Shogoin Kawahara-cho, Sakyo-ku (kuhp.kyoto-u.ac.jp; ✆ **075-751-3111**), has English-speaking doctors. For less urgent care, **Sakabe International Clinic,** Gokomachi, Nijo-sagaru, Nakagyo-ku (sakabeclinic.com; ✆ **075-231-1624**), also has English-speaking staff, as does **Nakai Dental Office,** 724–1 Yohoji-mae-cho, Teramachi Nijo-agaru, Nakagyo-ku (ndo-kyoto.jp; ✆ **075-252-1020**).

Luggage Storage & Delivery **Kyoto Station** has lockers for storing luggage beginning at ¥300 for 24 hours, including lockers large enough for big suitcases (¥700) on its south (Shinkansen) side. However, these can fill up during peak season, in which case head to the basement's **Crosta** check-in baggage room

(✆ **075-352-5437;** daily 8am–8pm), where you can store luggage for ¥700 per bag, or ¥1,000 per large bag, for up to 15 days (price is per day). You can also drop off bags here by 2pm for delivery to most hotels in town; this service costs ¥1,500 per bag and is great if you want to sightsee before check-in.

Mail The **Kyoto Central Post Office** (✆ **075-365-2471**), located just west of Kyoto Station's Central Exit, is open Monday–Friday 9am–7pm, weekends and holidays till 6pm. To the south of the Central Post Office's main entrance is a counter offering 24-hour postal service. There are also ATMs here.

Wi-Fi Access Kyoto City offers 24 hours of free Wi-Fi, with hotspots all over town, including Kyoto Station, bus stops, and subway stations; for more information, go to kanko.city.kyoto.lg.jp/wifi/en. Many restaurants, stores and hotels also offer free Wi-Fi.

EXPLORING KYOTO

As Japan's seventh-largest city, with a population of almost 1.5 million people, Kyoto hasn't escaped the afflictions of the modern age. In fact, if you arrive in Kyoto by train, your first reaction is likely to be great disappointment. There's Kyoto Tower looming in the foreground like a giant middle finger to the architectural tradition of this great city, and Kyoto Station itself is strikingly modern and unabashedly high-tech, looking as though it was airlifted straight from Tokyo. Modern buildings and hotels surround the station on all sides, making Kyoto look like any other Japanese town.

Once you escape to Kyoto's old neighborhoods, however, you'll find yourself in an entirely different place. Kyoto has an astonishing 2,000 temples and shrines and 20% of Japan's National Treasures, hidden among the crush of modernity. Discovering these—and you will happen upon plenty by accident—is the city's chief virtue. Because there are so many worthwhile sights, you must plan your itinerary carefully. Even the most avid sightseer can become jaded after days of visiting temples and shrines, no matter how beautiful or peaceful, so be sure to temper your visits to cultural sites with time spent simply walking around. Kyoto is a city best seen on foot; take time to explore small alleyways and artisan shops, pausing from time to time to soak in the beauty and atmosphere. If you spend your days in Kyoto racing around in a taxi or a bus from one temple to another, the essence of this ancient capital and its charm may literally pass you by.

"Light Up": Kyoto Illuminated

When the cherry blossoms spring forth or leaves change color, many Kyoto temples (like Kiyomizu) are open at night, their buildings and gardens dramatically lit. It's a great way to see these wondrous spaces, literally in a different light. Ask the tourist office or concierge at your hotel for a list of temples offering "light up."

Keep in mind that you must enter Kyoto's museums, shrines, and temples at least a half-hour before closing time.

A LOOK AT THE past

Kyoto served as Japan's capital for more than 1,000 years, from 794 to the Meiji Restoration in 1868. Originally known as Heian-kyo, it was laid out in a grid pattern borrowed from the Chinese with streets running north, south, east, and west. Its first few hundred years—from about A.D. 800 to the 12th century—were perhaps its grandest, a time when culture blossomed and court nobility led luxurious lives of poetry-composing parties and moon-gazing events. Buddhism flourished and temples were built. A number of learning institutions were set up for the sons and daughters of aristocratic families, run by scholars versed in both Japanese and Chinese.

Toward the end of the Heian Period, military clans began clashing as the samurai class grew more powerful. A series of civil wars eventually pushed Japan into the Feudal Era of military government, which lasted nearly 680 years—until 1868. The first shogun to rise to power was Minamoto Yoritomo, who set up his shogunate government in Kamakura (p. 218). With the downfall of the Kamakura government in 1336, however, Kyoto once again became the seat of power, home to both the imperial family and the shogun.

The beginning of this era, known as the Muromachi and Azuchi-Momoyama periods, was marked by extravagant luxury, expressed in such splendid shogun villas as Kyoto's Gold Pavilion and Silver Pavilion. Lacquerware, landscape paintings, and the art of metal engraving came into their own. Zen Buddhism was the rage, giving rise to such temples as the Ryoanji rock garden. And, despite civil wars that rocked the nation in the 15th and 16th centuries and destroyed much of Kyoto, culture flourished. During these turbulent times, *Noh* drama, the tea ceremony, flower arranging, and landscape gardening took form.

Emerging as the victor in the civil wars, Tokugawa Ieyasu established himself as shogun in 1603 and set up his military rule in Edo (presently Tokyo) far to the east. For the next 250 years, Kyoto remained the capital in name only. In 1868, with the downfall of the shogunate and the restoration of the emperor to power, the capital was officially moved from Kyoto to Tokyo.

Central Kyoto

Although much of downtown Kyoto has been taken over by the 21st century, it still has wonderful old neighborhoods with *machiya* (traditional townhouses) and historic treasures. And it is a joy to explore the backstreets, especially those contained within the square of Shijo, Kawaramachi, Oike, and Karasuma streets.

Kyoto Imperial Palace (Kyoto Gosho) ♥♥ PALACE This is where Japan's imperial family lived from 1331 until 1868, when they moved to Tokyo. The palace was destroyed several times by fire but was always rebuilt in its original style; the present buildings date from 1855. Modestly furnished with delicate decorations, the palace shows the restful designs of the peaceful Heian Period, and the emperor's private garden is a study in grace. Visitors used to be able to enter the palace grounds only on 1-hour guided tours; now you can stroll the grounds on your own, but to better understand court life and palace architecture it's still a good idea

Kyoto

ATTRACTIONS
Boydo-in (Temple of the Phoenix) 50
Fushimi-Inari Shrine 50
Ginkakuji (Temple of the Silver Pavilion) 6
Heian Shrine 8
Kinkakuji (Temple of the Golden Pavilion) 1
Kiyomizu Temple 37
Kodai-ji Temple 35
Kyoto Imperial Palace 5
Kyoto International Manga Museum 16
Kyoto Museum of Crafts and Design 30
Kyoto National Museum 40
Nanzenji Temple 34
Nijo Castle 10
Nintendo Museum 50
Nishijin Textile Center 4
Ryoanji Temple 2
Sanjusangendo Hall 41
Ginkakuji Temple
Shirakawa Dori
Okazakimichi
Heian Shrine
Kyoto Handicraft Center
Yoshidahon Dori
Mototanaka
SAKYO WARD
Higashioji Dori
EIZAN MAIN LINE
Demachiyanagi
Ichijo Dori
Kyu Shirakawa Dori
Konoe Dori
Kasugakita Dori
Keihan Marutamachi
KEIHAN OTO LINE
Takano River
Kamo River
Shimogamohon Dori
Shimogamohon Shrine
Kawaramachi Dori
Imperial Household Agency Office
Kyoto Imperial Palace
Marutamachi Dori
Takeyamachi Dori
Kitayama
KYOTO PREFECTUAL BOTANICAL GARDEN
Kitaoji Dori
Kuramaguchi Dori
Kiuramaguchi
Shokokuji Temple
Imadegawa
Imadegawa Dori
Karasuma Dori
KYOTO MUNICIPAL SUBWAY KARASUMA LINE
Kitaoji
Shimei Dori
KAMIGYO WARD
Ichijo Dori
Aburanokoji Dori
Horikawa Dori
Shimodachiuri Dori
Muratamachi
Kitayama Dori
KITA WARD
Kitaoji Dori
Kuramaguchi Dori
Senbon Dori
Kinkakuji Temple
Kitano-Hakubaicho
Nishioji Dori
0 1/2 mi
0 0.5 km

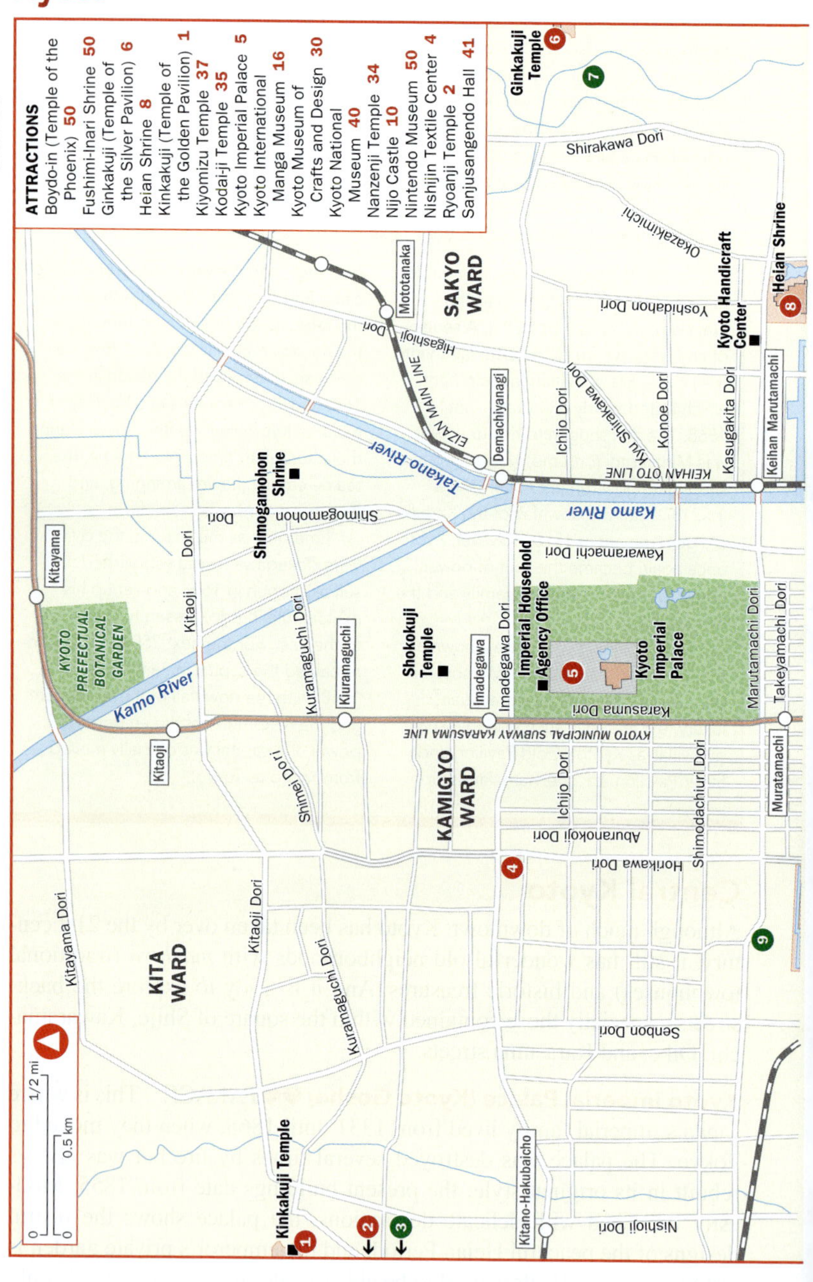

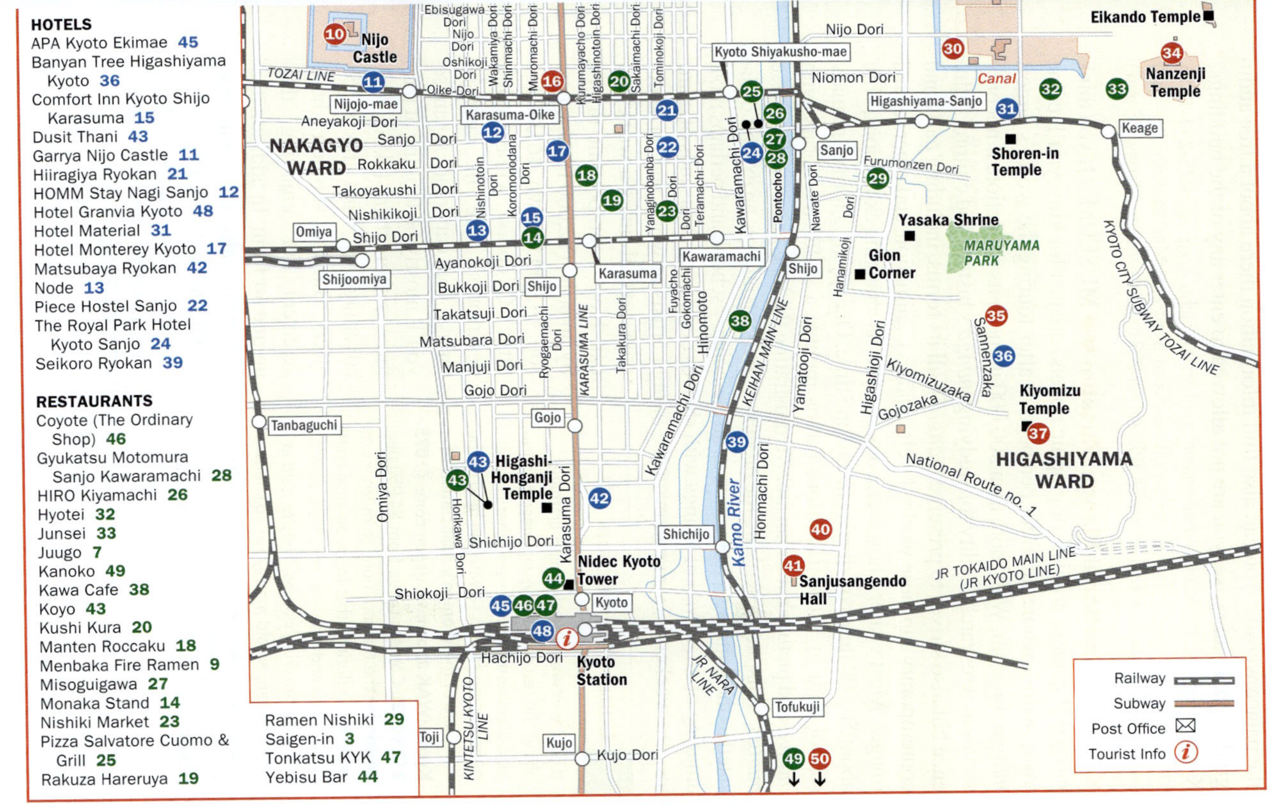
HOTELS
APA Kyoto Ekimae 45
Banyan Tree Higashiyama Kyoto 36
Comfort Inn Kyoto Shijo Karasuma 15
Dusit Thani 43
Garrya Nijo Castle 11
Hiiragiya Ryokan 21
HOMM Stay Nagi Sanjo 12
Hotel Granvia Kyoto 48
Hotel Material 31
Hotel Monterey Kyoto 17
Matsubaya Ryokan 42
Node 13
Piece Hostel Sanjo 22
The Royal Park Hotel Kyoto Sanjo 24
Seikoro Ryokan 39
RESTAURANTS
Coyote (The Ordinary Shop) 46
Gyukatsu Motomura Sanjo Kawaramachi 28
HIRO Kiyamachi 26
Hyotei 32
Junsei 33
Juugo 7
Kanoko 49
Kawa Cafe 38
Koyo 43
Kushi Kura 20
Manten Roccaku 18
Menbaka Fire Ramen 9
Misoguigawa 27
Monaka Stand 14
Nishiki Market 23
Pizza Salvatore Cuomo & Grill 25
Rakuza Hareruya 19
Ramen Nishiki 29
Saigen-in 3
Tonkatsu KYK 47
Yebisu Bar 44
Nijo Castle
NAKAGYO WARD
HIGASHIYAMA WARD
Eikando Temple
Nanzenji Temple
Shoren-in Temple
Yasaka Shrine
MARUYAMA PARK
Gion Corner
Kiyomizu Temple
Higashi-Honganji Temple
Nidec Kyoto Tower
Kyoto Station
Sanjusangendo Hall
Kamo River
Canal
TOZAI LINE
KYOTO CITY SUBWAY TOZAI LINE
KARASUMA LINE
KEIHAN MAIN LINE
JR TOKAIDO MAIN LINE (JR KYOTO LINE)
JR NARA LINE
KINTETSU KYOTO LINE
National Route no. 1
Nijo Dori
Niomon Dori
Oike-Dori
Aneyakoji Dori
Sanjo Dori
Rokkaku Dori
Takoyakushi Dori
Nishikikoji Dori
Shijo Dori
Ayanokoji Dori
Bukkoji Dori
Takatsuji Dori
Matsubara Dori
Manjuji Dori
Gojo Dori
Shichijo Dori
Shiokoji Dori
Hachijo Dori
Kujo Dori
Omiya Dori
Horikawa Dori
Karasuma Dori
Ebisugawa Dori
Nijo Dori
Oshikoji Dori
Wakamiya Dori
Shinmachi Dori
Muromachi Dori
Kurumayacho Dori
Higashinotoin Dori
Sakaimachi Dori
Tominokoji Dori
Nishinotoin Dori
Koromonodana Dori
Yanaginobanba Dori
Teramachi Dori
Kawaramachi Dori
Pontocho
Nawate Dori
Hanamikoji Dori
Furumonzen Dori
Fuyacho
Gokomachi
Hinomoto
Takakura Dori
Ryogaemachi Dori
Yamatooji Dori
Higashioji Dori
Kiyomizuzaka
Gojozaka
Sannenzaka
Honmachi Dori
Kyoto Shiyakusho-mae
Higashiyama-Sanjo
Keage
Sanjo
Shijo
Kawaramachi
Karasuma
Karasuma-Oike
Nijojo-mae
Omiya
Shijoomiya
Tanbaguchi
Gojo
Shichijo
Kyoto
Tofukuji
Kujo
Toji
Railway
Subway
Post Office
Tourist Info

to join the free, 50-minute guided tour in English, conducted at 10am or 1:30pm. Tours tend to fill up quickly, but you can register in advance on the palace website. You can also find information there about a free audio guide app. In any case, you are not allowed to enter any of the buildings. Kyotogyoen-nai, Karasuma-Imadegawa. sankan.kunaicho.go.jp. ✆ **075-211-1215.** Free admission. Tues–Sun 9am–5pm (to 4:30pm Sept and Mar, to 4pm Oct–Feb). Subway: Imadegawa (5 min.). Bus: 59, 102, 201, or 203 to Karasuma Imadegawa (5 min.).

Kyoto International Manga Museum ♥♥ MUSEUM If you think *manga* (Japanese comics, or graphic novels) are just for kids, you'll come away with a whole different perspective after touring the world's largest *manga* museum. With more than 300,000 items in its collection, it not only serves as a research facility for studying *manga*'s history and cultural influence but also strives to preserve *manga* in all its forms, including early and contemporary Japanese works, foreign *manga,* animation, and other related images. Most visitors, however, come to view its changing exhibitions, with about 50,000 items on display at any one time. Occupying a former primary school built in 1869, its various rooms include a children's library with *manga* and picture books, an archive illustrating the long history of Japanese *manga,* a display describing the process of making *manga,* an exhibit dedicated to the building's former life as an elementary school, and perhaps most amazing of all, a Wall of Manga with shelves containing thousands of comics. On weekends, you can even see *manga* artists at work, and on select days several times a week you can have your portrait drawn by an artist (¥2,000 for one person, ¥4,000 for two, ¥6,000 for three). Of course, while display descriptions are in English, unless you can read Japanese you'll mostly be looking at pictures rather than taking full advantage of what this place offers. But that shouldn't be a deterrent for enjoying this unique art form. In addition to a cafe, there's also a museum shop selling *manga* (including *manga* translated into English), figurines, notepads, and other items. 452 Kinbuki-cho, Karasuma Oike. kyotomm.jp. ✆ **075-254-7414.** ¥1,200 adults, ¥400 junior-high and high-school students, ¥200 children. Thurs–Tues 10am–6pm. Subway: Karasuma-Oike (1 min.). Bus: 15, 51, 61, 62, 63 or 65 to Karasuma Oike (1 min.).

Cultural Immersion

If you're interested in learning firsthand about the tea ceremony, Japanese calligraphy, Japanese cooking, and other cultural pursuits, you can do so with the help of the members of the **Women's Association of Kyoto** (**WAK Japan;** wakjapan.com; ✆ **075-212-9993**). Courses range from ¥4,950 per person for the tea ceremony to much more expensive offerings that focus on local crafts, like origami and ikebana, or private cooking and sweet-making classes. They're held at Wakwak-kan, an old *machiya* at 761 Tenshucho (subway Karasuma Oike, exit 7, 5 min.). You can also opt for lessons in a private home, though those are the most expensive courses.

Nijo Castle (Nijojo) ♥♥♥ CASTLE The Tokugawa shogun's Kyoto home stands in stark contrast to most of Japan's other remaining castles, which were constructed purely for defense. Built by the first Tokugawa

Look up as you pass through Nijo Castle's Karamon Gate to admire its intricate colored woodwork.

shogun, Ieyasu, in 1603, Nijo Castle, a UNESCO World Heritage Site, is considered the quintessence of Momoyama architecture, built almost entirely of Japanese cypress and housing delicate transom woodcarvings and paintings by the Kano School on sliding doors. (***Note:*** No interior photos are allowed.) The main building, **Ninomaru Palace,** has 33 rooms, some 800 *tatami* mats, and an understated elegance, especially compared with castles being built in Europe at the same time. All the sliding doors on the outside walls can be removed in summer, permitting breezes into the building. Typical for Japan at the time, rooms were unfurnished, with futon stored in closets during the day. Astoundingly, considering the expense of its construction, no shogun visited the castle between 1634, when the third Tokugawa shogun Iemitsu stayed here, and 1867, when the 15th and last Tokugawa shogun Yoshinobu came to announce the restoration of imperial rule.

Outside the castle is the **Ninomaru Garden,** designed by the renowned gardener Kobori Enshu and famous in its own right, with two other gardens added in 1895 and 1965. For ¥100 extra, you can also visit the castle's **Anniversary Gallery,** with original screens, murals, and paintings from the castle.

Plan on spending at least an hour here; or, for ¥2,500, join a 60-minute English guided tour offered daily at 10am and noon—enquire at the ticket counter or book online at the castle's website.

541 Nijojo-cho. nijo-jocastle.city.kyoto.lg.jp. ✆ **075-841-0096.** ¥800 adults, ¥400 junior-high and high-school students, ¥300 children. Daily 8:45am–5pm (last entry 4pm). Closed Tues Dec–Jan and July–Aug. Subway: Nijojo-mae Station (1 min.). Bus: 9, 12, 50, or 101 to Nijojo-mae (1 min.).

Guarded by Nightingales

One of Nijo Castle's most intriguing features is its so-called **nightingale floors.** To guard the shogun from real or imagined enemies, the castle was protected by a moat, stone walls, and these special floorboards in the castle corridors, which creaked when trod upon. The distinct birdsong sound was originally an accident, caused by the rubbing of nails against clamps when the floorboard moves, but it became useful as an alarm. The nightingale floors were supplemented by hidden alcoves for bodyguards. As a further precaution, only female attendants were allowed in the shogun's private living quarters.

Nishijin Textile Center (Nishijin-Ori Kaikan) ♥♥ MUSEUM Kyoto's Nishijin weavers, whose history can be traced back to Kyoto's earliest years, are famous for richly decorative textiles, made into clothing worn by the imperial family, Buddhist monks, and Shinto priests. During the Edo Period (1603–1867), an estimated 7,000 looms were crammed into 160 city blocks comprising the Nishijin District. Unsurprisingly, the district suffered a terrible blow when the capital was moved to Tokyo, but the industry bounced back by adopting Western weaving technology and equipment, which allowed them to produce inexpensive machine-woven clothing alongside luxurious hand-woven fabrics. Today, Nishijin remains one of the country's largest districts for hand weaving. This commemorative museum is located on the very spot where merchants once gathered to bid for textiles sold at auction.

On display are silkworms and descriptions of how they produce silk, old and modern Nishijin fabrics, and looms, with frequent demonstrations of handlooms using the Jacquard system of perforated cards for weaving. A shop sells Nishijin products and fabrics, including kimono, sashes, purses, and more. If you have 40 minutes to spare, you can also weave your own table cloth for ¥2,530. Reservations are required if you'd like to dress up as a *maiko* (geisha apprentice), *geiko* (professional entertainer), or lady of the Imperial court in a 12-layer kimono. (There's also an option for men to wear ancient ceremonial court dress.) These experiences cost ¥19,800, including hair styling, makeup, and photo. You can also try on a simpler everyday kimono for ¥3,895 and wander around Kyoto in it until 5pm for an extra ¥1,100, a popular activity (other stores rent kimono, too). 414 Tatemonzen-cho, Kamikyho-ku. nishijin.or.jp. ✆ **075-451-9231.** Free admission. Tues–Sun 9am–4pm. Subway: Imadegawa (8 min.). Bus: 9, 12, 59, 101, 102, 201, or 203 to Horikawa Imadegawa (2 min.).

Eastern Kyoto

The eastern part of Kyoto, encompassing the area of Higashiyama-ku with its Kiyomizu Temple and stretching up all the way to the Temple of the Silver Pavilion (Ginkakuji Temple), is probably the richest in terms of culture and charm. Although temples and gardens are the primary attractions, Higashiyama-ku also has several fine museums, forested hills and running streams, great shopping opportunities, and some of Kyoto's oldest and finest restaurants. See also our walking tour on p. 313, which visits the district's top attractions as well as some intriguing lesser-known sights.

Ginkakuji (Temple of the Silver Pavilion) ♥♥♥ TEMPLE Ginkakuji, considered one of Kyoto's more beautiful structures, was built in 1482 as a retirement villa for Shogun Ashikaga Yoshimasa, who intended to coat the structure with silver in imitation of the Golden Pavilion built by his grandfather. He died before this could be accomplished, however, so the Silver Pavilion is not silver at all but remains a simple two-story wood structure enshrining the goddess of mercy and Jizo, the guardian god of children. The entire complex is designed for enjoyment of the tea ceremony, moon viewing, and other aesthetic pursuits. Note the sand mound in the garden, shaped to resemble Mount Fuji, and the sand raked in the shape of waves, created to enhance the views during a full moon. It's easy to imagine the splendor, formality, and grandeur of the life of Japan's upper class as you wander the grounds and climb the hillside path to its lookout point. While the temple is worth seeing, for me this place is all about its garden, a masterclass in composition, framing, and perspective. 2 Ginkakuji-cho. ✆ **075-771-5725.** ¥500 adults, ¥300 junior-high and grade-school students, younger children free. Mar–Nov daily 8:30am–5:30pm; Dec–Feb daily 9am–4:30pm. Bus: 5, 17, 102, 203, or 204 to Ginkakuji-michi (10 min.); or 32 or 100 to Ginkakuji-mae (5 min.).

Heian Shrine ♥♥♥ SHRINE Although it dates only from 1895, Kyoto's most famous Shinto shrine, built in commemoration of the 1,100th anniversary of the founding of Kyoto, is a replica of the first Imperial

The gardens surrounding the Temple of the Silver Pavilion are its loveliest feature.

Performers dressed as demons help celebrate the Setsubun festival at Heian Shrine.

Palace, though on a less grand scale. As the story goes, when the capital was moved to Tokyo during the Meiji Restoration, Kyotoites become so depressed that authorities commissioned Heian Shrine to remind them their city was still one of the world's cultural powerhouses. To that end, the surrounding area has long been dedicated to artistic pursuits. The shrine deifies two of Japan's emperors: Emperor Kammu, 50th emperor of Japan, who founded Heian-kyo in 794; and Emperor Komei, the 121st ruler of Japan, who ruled from 1831 to 1866. Although the orange, green, and white structure is interesting for its Heian-Era architectural style, the most important thing to see here is the 33,000-sq.-m (8-acre) **Shinen Garden** (its entrance is on your left as you face the main hall). Typical of Meiji Era gardens, it's famous for its weeping cherry trees in spring, its irises and water lilies in summer, and the changing maple leaves in the fall, all beautifully arranged around a central pond. (It even appears in a scene in the movie *Lost in Translation.*) Generally Japanese gardens are about curation and control—the word for garden, *teien,* literally means "controlled nature"—but much like the age it's commemorating, the Shinen Garden is wild and free. Don't miss it.

Nishi Tennocho, Okazaki. heianjingu.or.jp. ✆ **075-761-0221.** Free admission to grounds; Shinen Garden ¥600 adults, ¥300 children. Garden mid-Mar to Sept daily 8:30am–5:30pm (to 4:30pm Nov–Feb, to 5pm Mar 1–14 and Oct). Subway: Higashiyama (10 min.). Bus: 5, 32, 46, or 100 to Okazaki Koen Bijitsukan Heian Jingu-mae (5 min.).

Kiyomizu Temple (Kiyomizudera) ♥♥♥ TEMPLE Higashiyama-ku's most famous temple is well known throughout Japan for the grand views from its main hall—in fact, there's even a Japanese idiom, "jumping from the veranda of Kiyomizu Temple," meaning to undertake some particularly bold or daring adventure. Occupying an exalted spot on Mount Otowa, the main hall is constructed over a cliff and features a large wooden veranda supported by 139 massive pillars, each 15m (49 ft.) high. Founded in 778 and rebuilt in 1633 by the third Tokugawa shogun, Iemitsu, the temple is dedicated to the goddess of mercy and compassion, but most visitors come for the magnificent view. Kiyomizu's grounds are spectacular (and crowded) in spring during cherry-blossom season and in fall when the maple leaves turn. Thanks to the proliferation of online Kyoto travel content in our digital age, this has become arguably Kyoto's most congested tourist attraction (which is no mean feat). If you're an early bird, I suggest making your way to Kiyomizu at the crack of dawn—the temple opens at 6am daily.

Also worth checking out are the three-story pagoda and Otowa Falls (known for the purity of its water; *kiyomizu* translates as "pure water"), but don't spite the gods by neglecting to visit **Jishu Shrine** (✆ **075-541-2097**), a vermilion-hued Shinto shrine behind Kiyomizu's main hall that has long been considered the dwelling place of the god of love and matchmaking. Be sure to take the ultimate test: On the shrine's grounds are two "love fortune-telling" stones placed 9m (30 ft.) apart; if you're able to walk from one to the other with your eyes closed, your desires for love will be granted.

1–294 Kiyomizu. kiyomizudera.or.jp. ✆ **075-551-1234.** ¥500 adults, ¥200 children 7–15, children 6 and under free. Daily 6am–6pm (until 6:30pm in summer; special evening hours several times a year). Jishu Shrine daily 9am–5pm. Bus: 86, 100, 106, 110, 202, 206, or 207 to Gojo-zaka (10 min.).

Visitors flock to Kiyomizu Temple's Jishu Shrine, associated with the god of love and matchmaking.

The teahouse at Kodaiji Temple.

Kodaiji Temple ♥♥ TEMPLE Located between Kiyomizu Temple and Yasaka Shrine, this temple was founded in 1605 by Toyotomi Hideyoshi's widow (popularly known as Nene) to commemorate her husband and pacify his spirit. Shogun Tokugawa Ieyasu, who served under Toyotomi before becoming shogun, financed its construction. Its lovely gardens were laid out by Kobori Enshu. You'll can visit Nene's grave (the Otama-ya) and a shaded bamboo grove leading to a tearoom where visitors drink matcha and eat *wagashi* sweets. A memorial hall, connected to the Founder's Hall by a stepped walkway known as Garyoro (the "Reclining Dragon Corridor"), enshrines wooden images of Hideyoshi and Nene. Nene, by the way, became a Buddhist nun after her husband's death, as was the custom of noblewomen at the time, and remained a highly respected figure in Japan until her own death in 1624. The one-room **Kodaiji Sho Museum,** across the street from the temple and included in the admission price, contains artifacts relating to Nene and the temple, but skip it if your time is limited.

526 Shimogawara-cho. kodaiji.com. ✆ **075-561-9966.** ¥600 adults, ¥250 children 17 and under. Daily 9am–5:30pm (last entry 5pm). Bus: 86, 202, 206, or 207 to Higashiyama Yasui (5 min.).

Kyoto Museum of Crafts and Design (Fureaikan) ♥♥ MUSEUM Near Heian Shrine this excellent museum focuses on the many crafts that flourished during Kyoto's long reign as the imperial capital, 17 of which are considered *kogei,* or nationally dedicated traditional crafts. Displays and videos demonstrate the step-by-step production of items from stone lanterns and fishing rods to textiles, paper fans, umbrellas, boxwood combs, lacquerware, Buddhist altars, *Noh* masks, musical instruments, and more. The displays are fascinating, the crafts beautiful, and explanations are in English—a digital information board has a slide description page for each of the 74 crafts on show—making even a 30-minute stop here well worth the effort. Artisans demonstrate their skills most days

except Mondays and Thursdays, while occasional special events may include sake tasting or *geiko* (what geisha are called in Kyoto) and *maiko* (geisha apprentices) performing traditional dance on selected Sundays (check website for times and further information).
B1F, 9–1 Seishoji-cho, Okazaki, in basement of Miyako Messe. kmtc.jp/en. ✆ **075-762-2670.** ¥500 adults, ¥400 children. Daily 9am–6pm (last entry 5:30pm). Subway: Higashiyama (7 min.). Bus: 5, 32, 46, or 100 to Okazaki Koen Bijitsukan Heian Jingu-mae (5 min.), or 201, 202, 203, or 206 to Higashiyama-Nijo/Okazakikoenguchi.

Kyoto National Museum (Kokuritsu Hakubutsukan) ♥♥ MUSEUM Housed in an imposing French baroque–style building constructed in 1897 expressly for the collection, as well as in a new wing completed in 2014, this museum displays stone and bronze Buddhist and Shinto sculpture, paintings, ceramics from the Nara through Edo periods, textiles, lacquerware, swords and other metalworks, archaeological relics (like 6th-c. *Haniwa* clay figures excavated from burial mounds), and much more, displayed on a rotating basis from the vast collection. The museum is especially famous for its artifacts from the Heian Period (794–1192) and ancient sutras. Many of the treasures were once in Kyoto's temples, shrines, and imperial palaces, while others—like Chinese sculpture or paintings—were imported to Japan at different times during its history. If you've seen the larger Tokyo National Museum (p. 113), you may want to skip this one if your time in Kyoto is short, though special exhibitions concentrating on a specific period or genre draw huge crowds.
527 Chaya-machi (across from Sanjusangendo Hall). kyohaku.go.jp. ✆ **075-525-2473.** ¥700 adults, ¥350 college students, free for children (higher for some special exhibitions). Tues–Sun 9:30am–5pm (till 8pm for special exhibits). Bus: 86, 88, 100, 106, 110, 206, or 208 to Hakubutsukan Sanjusangendo-mae (1 min.).

Nanzenji Temple ♥♥ TEMPLE Part of a broad campus that once hosted up to 70 temples, this Rinzai Zen temple with its massive front gate is set amid a grove of spruce and maple. One of Kyoto's best-known, it was founded in 1291, though the present buildings date from the later 16th century during the Momoyama Period. Attached to the main hall is a Zen rock garden attributed to Kobori Enshu; it's sometimes called "Young Tigers Crossing the Water" because of the shape of one of the rocks, but looking at it is more like taking a Rorschach's test, with each viewer's experience colored by their perception and imagination. Whatever you think it resembles, it's a place of startling tranquility. If peace and calm are what you're searching for in Kyoto, this is one place you can still find it. In the building behind the main hall, look for a sliding door with a famous painting by Kano Tanyu of a tiger drinking water in a bamboo grove. Spread throughout the temple precincts are a dozen other lesser temples and buildings worth exploring if you have the time, including Nanzen-in with its moss, ponds, natural waterfall, and rock garden—built before Nanzenji Temple, it served as the emperor's vacation house whenever he visited the grounds. The gardens at Konchi-in temple are among the most

Sanjusangendo Hall is the longest wooden structure in Japan, built to hold 1,001 statues of the goddess Kannon.

transcendentally beautiful I've ever laid eyes on. There's so much to see, in fact, including an old aqueduct from the Meiji Period, you'll probably wish you had more time (allow a couple of hours).

Nanzenji-Fukuchi-cho. nanzenji.or.jp. ✆ **075-771-0365.** ¥600 adults, ¥500 high-school students, ¥400 children; Nanzen-in ¥300, ¥250, and ¥150 extra, respectively. Daily 8:40am–5pm (till 4:30pm Dec–Feb). Bus: 5 to Nanzenji, Eikando-michi (3 min.).

Sanjusangendo Hall ♥♥♥ TEMPLE Originally founded as Rengeoin Temple in 1164 and rebuilt in 1266, Sanjusangendo Hall has one of the most visually stunning sights of any Japanese temple: 1,001 wooden statues of the thousand-handed goddess Kannon. Marvel at the row upon row of life-size figures, carved from Japanese cypress in the 12th and 13th centuries, and in the middle, a large seated Kannon carved in 1254 by Tankei, a famous sculptor from the Kamakura Period, when he was 82 years old. You won't actually see a thousand arms on each statue; there are only 40, the idea being that each hand has the power to save 25 worlds. In front of the 1,001 Kannon are a row of 28 guardian deities; not only are they all National Treasures, but it's rare to find a whole set like this one still intact. To accommodate all the statues, the hall stretches nearly 120m (400 ft.), making it the longest wooden building in Japan (no cameras or video allowed inside, which helps move the crowds along quickly). Its length was too hard to ignore—archery competitions have been held for centuries in the corridor behind the statues (you can see how difficult it might be to hit a piece of sacred cloth attached to the wall at the opposite end!). The greatest record was set in 1686, when a competitor fired off 13,053 arrows for 24 hours nonstop, hitting the target 8,133 times.

Shichijo Dori. ✆ **075-525-0033.** ¥600 adults, ¥400 junior-high and high-school students, ¥300 children. Apr to mid-Nov daily 8am–5pm; mid-Nov to Mar daily 9am–4pm. Bus: 86, 88, 100, 106, 110, 206, or 208 to Hakubutsukan Sanjusangendo-mae (1 min.).

Near Mount Inari

Fushimi–Inari Shrine ♥♥♥ SHRINE One of Japan's most celebrated Shinto shrines, Fushimi-Inari is consistently voted Japan's top attraction for foreign visitors, so its procession of torii gates is typically clogged with people wielding selfie sticks. To see it at its best, come early in the day. Founded in 711, it's dedicated to the goddess of rice (rice was collected as tax during the shogun era) and has therefore long been popular with merchants, who come here to pray for prosperity. The 4km (2½-mile) pathway behind the shrine is lined with more than 10,000 red *torii,* presented by worshipers through the ages; the tunnel of vermilion-colored gates gradually climbs a hill, for a view of Kyoto. There are also stone foxes, which are considered messengers of the gods, usually with a key to the rice granary hanging from their mouths. At several places along the path are small shops (open from 9am) where you can dine on a bowl of noodles or other refreshments. The most popular visiting days are the first of each month and New Year's; avoid these at all costs. ***Note:*** The same JR line continues to Nara (p. 352), making this a good stop if you plan to spend the night in Nara. Just be sure you take a local train—the Nara express train does not stop at JR Inari Station.

68 Fukakusa Yabunouchicho, Fushimi-ku. inari.jp. ✆ **075-641-7331.** Free admission. Open 24 hr. Train: JR Inari Station (2 stops from Kyoto Station), then a 2-min. walk.

Western Kyoto

Two of Kyoto's most famous sights are northwest of downtown Kyoto.

A bronze phoenix tops the dazzling gold-covered pavilion at Kinkakuji.

Kinkakuji (Temple of the Golden Pavilion) ♥♥ TEMPLE One of Kyoto's best-known (and most crowded) attractions—and the inspiration for the Temple of the Silver Pavilion (p. 301)—Kinkakuji was constructed in the 1390s as a retirement villa for Shogun Ashikaga Yoshimitsu. It features a three-story pavilion covered in gold leaf with a roof topped by a bronze phoenix. The first floor is built in the style of a Heian court noble, the second in the martial style of samurai, and the third in Zen Buddhist style. Apparently, the retired shogun lived in shameless luxury while the rest of the nation suffered from famine, earthquakes, and plague. If you come on a clear day (best is late afternoon), the Golden Pavilion

JUST OUTSIDE KYOTO: imperial VILLAS

If this is your first visit to Kyoto, you should concentrate on seeing sights in Kyoto itself. If, however, this is your second trip to Kyoto, or you're here for an extended period, or you have a passion for traditional Japanese architecture, either of these former royal residences makes a worthwhile short excursion from Kyoto. You'll need advance permission, however. The easiest way to apply is online in English at **sankan.kunaicho.go.jp** at least 4 days before your visit (earlier if possible—applications are accepted up to 3 months in advance). Alternatively, you can go in person to the **Imperial Household Agency Office** (✆ **075-211-1215;** they don't speak English, but you can have a Japanese speaker call on your behalf), on the northwest grounds of the **Kyoto Imperial Palace** near Inui Gomon Gate, a 5-minute walk from Imadegawa subway station. It's open Monday through Friday 8:45am–5pm. Here you'll be able to apply for a tour the next day if there's room. If all else fails, you can head directly to Katsura or Shugakuin villas for a same-day application; a limited number of tickets for afternoon tours are distributed on a first-come, first-served basis starting at 11am (you'll want to get there much earlier). Regardless of how you apply, everyone must present their passports, and **participants must be at least 18 years old.** Tours take place Wednesday through Sunday (and selected Mon and Tues). Tour times at Katsura Imperial Villa are 9:20am, 11:20am, 1:20pm, 3:20pm, and 4:20pm; and at Shugakuin Imperial Villa at 9am, 10am, 11am, 1:30pm, and 3pm. Katsura Imperial Village Tours are in English, Shugakuin tours are conducted in Japanese only, but there are videos and a free handheld audio guide in English.

Katsura Imperial Villa ♥♥♥ Considered the jewel of traditional Japanese architecture and landscape gardening, this villa was built between 1620 and 1624 by Prince Toshihito, brother of the emperor, with construction continued by Toshihito's son. The garden, markedly influenced by Kobori Enshu, Japan's most

shimmers against a blue sky, its reflection captured in the waters of a calm pond. This pavilion is not the original, however; in 1950, a disturbed student monk burned Kinkakuji to the ground (the story is told by Yukio Mishima in his famous novel *The Temple of the Golden Pavilion*). The temple was rebuilt in 1955; in 1987 it was recovered in gold leaf that was five times thicker than the original coating (you almost need sunglasses). Be sure to explore the surrounding **park** with its moss-covered grounds and teahouses.

1 Kinkakuji-cho. ✆ **075-461-0013.** ¥500 adults, ¥300 children. Daily 9am–5pm. Bus: 12 or 59 to Kinkakuji-mae (1 min.) or 101, 102, 204, or 205 to Kinkakuji-michi (3 min.).

Ryoanji Temple ♥♥♥ TEMPLE About a 20-minute walk southwest of the Golden Pavilion is Ryoanji—home to what is probably the most famous **Zen rock garden** in all of Japan, laid out at the end of the 15th century during the Muromachi Period. Fifteen rocks set in waves of raked white pebbles are surrounded on three sides by a clay wall and on the fourth by a wooden veranda, in an area that measures about 25m (80 ft.) long and 10m (30 ft.) wide. Sit down and contemplate what the artist was famous garden designer, is a "stroll garden" in which each turn of the path brings an entirely new view. The first thing you notice upon entering Katsura is its simplicity—the buildings were all made of natural materials, with close attention paid to the grain, texture, and color of the various woods. Every garden detail was carefully planned, down to the stones used in the path, the way the trees twist, and how scenes are reflected in the water. A pavilion for moon viewing, a hall for imperial visits, a teahouse, and other buildings are situated around a pond; islets, stone lanterns, and manicured trees are strategically placed, and bridges of stone, earth, or wood arch gracefully over the water. It's about a half-hour ride from Kyoto Station on the bus (bus no. 33 to the Katsura Rikyu-mae stop, then an 8-min. walk) or train (the Hankyu railway line to Katsura Station, then a 20-min. walk).

Shugakuin Imperial Villa ♥♥

Built in the mid-1600s, this was a retirement retreat for Emperor Go-Mizunoo, who came to the throne at age 15 and suddenly abdicated 18 years later to become a monk, passing the throne to his daughter in 1629. Amazingly, though the villa was just 2 hours from the Imperial Palace, the emperor came here only on day trips; he never once spent the night. Set at the foot of Mount Hiei, the 53-hectare (133-acre) grounds are among Kyoto's largest; they're famous for the principle known as *shakkei*, or "borrowed landscape," in which the surrounding landscape is naturalistically incorporated into the design. Grounds are divided into three levels: The **upper garden,** with its lake, islands, and waterfalls, is the most extensive, offering grand countryside views from a hillside pavilion; the **middle garden,** built as a residence for the emperor's daughter, contains a villa with the famous "Shelves of Mist," a 5-paneled shelf designed to look like drifting wisps of mist. It's about a 40-minute bus ride from Kyoto Station; take bus no. 5 to the Shugakuin Rikyu-michi bus stop and then a 15-minute walk.

trying to communicate; the interpretation of the rocks is up to the individual. This kind of garden is called a *karesansui,* which means "dry, mountain, water," so you may well see something like summits piercing through cloud cover, pebbles skimming across a lake, or even the humps of a dragon cavorting in the sea. Unfortunately, this "peaceful" garden is not always peaceful, with perpetual crowds destroying any chance for meditation. A cap on the number of entrants would be a good idea, and personally, I'd ban smartphones, too; constant camera clicks and people posing for Instagram snaps hardly fosters a space of quiet repose. If you get here early enough, you may be able to escape both the crowds and the noise. After visiting the rock garden, be sure to take a walk around the temple grounds. There's a 1,000-year-old **pond,** on the rim of which sits a beautiful little restaurant, **Seigein-in** (p. 336), with *tatami* rooms and screens, where you can eat *yudofu* and enjoy the view.

13 Ryoanji-Goryo-shita-machi. ryoanji.jp. ✆ **075-463-2216.** ¥600 adults, ¥500 high school students, ¥300 children. Mar–Nov daily 8am–5pm; Dec–Feb daily 8:30am–4:30pm. Bus: 59 to Ryoanji-mae (2 min.); or 12 or 50 to Ritsumeikan Daigaku-mae (6 min.).

Uji

Uji, lying to the south of Kyoto (22 min. from Kyoto Station on the Nara Line; fare ¥240), has one of Japan's oldest Shinto shrines, Ujigami Jinja, as well two attractions representing opposite sides of Japanese culture—the ancient **Temple of the Phoenix** and the up-to-the-minute **Nintendo Museum.** It's even better known as a tea-producing region, where you can sample high-quality matcha, *sencha* (whole-leaf tea), and *gyokuro* (tea grown in the shade). Stroll down **Byodo-in Omotesando,** a traditional street marking the front approach to the Temple of the Phoenix, and you'll pass several tea shops and souvenir stores, where you can sip green tea, eat tea-flavored ice cream and tea-infused gyoza dumplings or ramen with matcha noodles, and buy all manner of tea-related souvenirs and brewing paraphernalia. For a green feast of matcha ramen, matcha beer, and matcha ice cream, head to **Tanaka Kyu Shoten** (Renge–99–2 Uji; ✆ **0774-22-5797**) or **Mitsuboshien Kanbayashi** (Renge–27–2 Uji; ✆ **0774-21-2636**) to try the various blends of tea popular in Uji.

Boydo-in (Temple of the Phoenix) ♥♥♥ TEMPLE Byodo-in is an exercise in abstract impressionism. A regal structure of vermillion-pained cypress wood, it was built in 1053 at the behest of Yorimichi Fujiwara, a powerful lord and then-regent to the emperor, who held staunch views about the world coming to an end and wanted therefore to create a physical manifestation of his vision of the Pure Land. It later became known as the Temple of the Phoenix because of its unique shape—the wings expand outwards with another hallway trailing behind like a great red bird in flight—and for the two golden phoenix statues surmounting the roof. Fujiwara came close to achieving perfection: on a summer's day, when sunshine irradiates the exterior and the temple's distorted reflection is mirrored on the green lake in the foreground, there are few comparable sights in Japan. The temple's design is so famous and revered, it was immortalized on the tail side of the 10-yen coin.

If you want to step inside the Phoenix Hall to see the **statue of Amida Buddha** enshrined there, you'll have to pay an extra ¥300. The basic admission price does, however, cover the **Hosho-kan Museum,** located within the temple precinct. The English-language explanations in here aren't great, but the collection of statuary, artworks, and national treasures are worth examining. Thursdays to Sundays you can also try Uji's feted green tea at the temple's **Toka Teahouse.** Popular offerings include Uji matcha or *sencha* served with *wagashi* treats for ¥600, and the *gyokuro* cold-brew for ¥900. Though Byodo-in is hardly Kyoto's best-kept secret, compared with some of the busier temples and shrines in Kyoto proper its atmosphere is much more contemplative and restful.

Renge–116 Uji. byodoin.or.jp/en. ✆ **0774-21-2861.** ¥700 adults, ¥400 high-school students, ¥300 children. Daily 8:30am–5:30pm (Phoenix Hall last entry 4:10pm; Hoshokan Museum last entry 4:45pm). Toka Tea Room: Thurs–Sun 10am–4:30pm (last order 4pm). Train station: Uji (8 min.).

Nintendo Museum ♥♥♥ MUSEUM Built in a renovated Nintendo factory on the Kyoto outskirts, the recently opened Nintendo Museum is a temple to the origins of Japanese video games, with exhibits celebrating the titles, machines, characters, and ingenious innovation that helped Nintendo go from selling *hanafuda* playing cards for the domestic market to one of the best-known brands in global entertainment. The main section of the museum, located on the second floor, features dedicated displays for each of the major consoles and handhelds Nintendo has developed since it transitioned from arcade to home gaming in the late 1970s. Whichever console generation you remember most fondly, there'll be something to send you frolicking down memory lane: The bricklike NES; iconic box art from series like Mega Man and Metroid; the Pokémon games from *Red* and *Green* through *Scarlet* and *Violet;* the Virtual Boy and NES Robot and SNES Superscope peripherals; the controversial Wii U console; and charming homages to key Nintendo franchises including Super Mario Bros, Donkey Kong, Star Fox, Kirby, Luigi's Mansion, and Animal Crossing. Interesting exhibits around the perimeter of the room focus on game instruction manuals, in-game music, Nintendo advertising campaigns, and perhaps most interesting of all, little-known prototypes, one of which shows that the original Nintendo 64 controller design was even worse than the one they finally greenlighted. Avid fans could easily spend an hour or two in this section. The one thing lacking is a more detailed history of the company, perhaps focusing on pioneering creatives like Shigeru Miyamoto (father of both *Mario* and *The Legend of Zelda* games) or Gunpei Yokoi (designer of the original Gameboy). But then again, Nintendo is a traditionally Japanese company and often it is the Japanese way to celebrate the achievements of the whole rather than the individual. Please note that **no photos** are allowed in this section, which shows

Getting Tickets to the Nintendo Museum

Demand to visit this museum is so high that Nintendo has created an obnoxious lottery system, the only way you can get into the museum. Be aware that you'll have to start the process **several weeks before you visit Kyoto.**

Join the lottery through the website **museum.nintendo.com/en** (you'll need a Nintendo account) and select three preferred date-and-time slots. After a random selection process, successful applicants are announced on the first day of the month after your application. If you're one of them, you will have to call a Japanese number from the phone number you applied with. **This is important:** even though the call will not be answered, you must be able to call a Japanese number from your phone or your ticket will be void. There is no other way to confirm your identity. From the date on which you get selected in the draw, you have 48 hours to confirm your identity via phone call, after which you pay ¥3,300 for the ticket, which is sent as a QR code a couple days before your entry date. While I applaud Nintendo's decision to cap visitor numbers (some other Japanese museums could learn from this), the booking system just isn't user-friendly.

commendable restraint on behalf of the museum organizers; constantly battling past live streamers and people posing for photos would seriously hinder the experience.

On the ground floor you can play games from classic Nintendo consoles: A card preloaded with virtual coins lets you use one of the machines for 7 minutes (you can extend this by using another coin, though the number you can use is limited). It's in this area that the museum transitions from surprisingly earnest to a colorful, noisy, lighthearted, and joyous experience, capturing the essence of what made Nintendo so beloved in the first place. People queue up for the giant controllers that allow you to team up with a partner to play games from the Nintendo archives, such as 1990's *Super Mario World.* There's also a gift shop down here, but most of the merch is tatty and quite expensive.

Kaguraden–56 Oguracho, Uji. museum.nintendo.com/en. ✆ **0570-011-120.** ¥3,300 adults, ¥2,200 ages 12–17, ¥1,100 kids 6–11, free children 5 and under. Daily 10am–6pm. Train station: Ogura (6 min.).

A STROLL THROUGH HIGASHIYAMA-KU

START:	**Kyoto National Museum on Shichijo Dori a couple of blocks east of the Kamo River; to get there, walk 20 min. from Kyoto Station or take bus no. 86, 88, 100, 106, 110, 206, or 208 to Hakubutsukan Sanjusangendo-mae.**
FINISH:	**Maruyama Park.**
TIME:	**Allow approximately 4½ hr., including stops for shopping and museums.**
BEST TIMES:	**Weekdays, when temples and shops aren't as crowded.**
WORST TIMES:	**Monday, when museums are closed.**

A stroll through Higashiyama-ku will take you to Kiyomizu Temple, one of Kyoto's most famous sights, and other worthwhile attractions like Sanjusangendo Hall. It will also take you through some of Kyoto's most charming neighborhoods, with plenty of shopping opportunities en route.

Start your stroll at:

1 Kyoto National Museum (Kokuritsu Hakubutsukan)

In 1889, the Meiji government, fearful that Japan's cultural objects were going the way of the samurai with the increasing import of Western ways and products, established three national museums—one in Tokyo, one in Nara, and this one in Kyoto (p. 305), which serves as a repository for art objects and treasures that once belonged to Kyoto's temples and royal court. In addition, special exhibitions are mounted several times a year.

Walking Tour: Higashiyama-ku

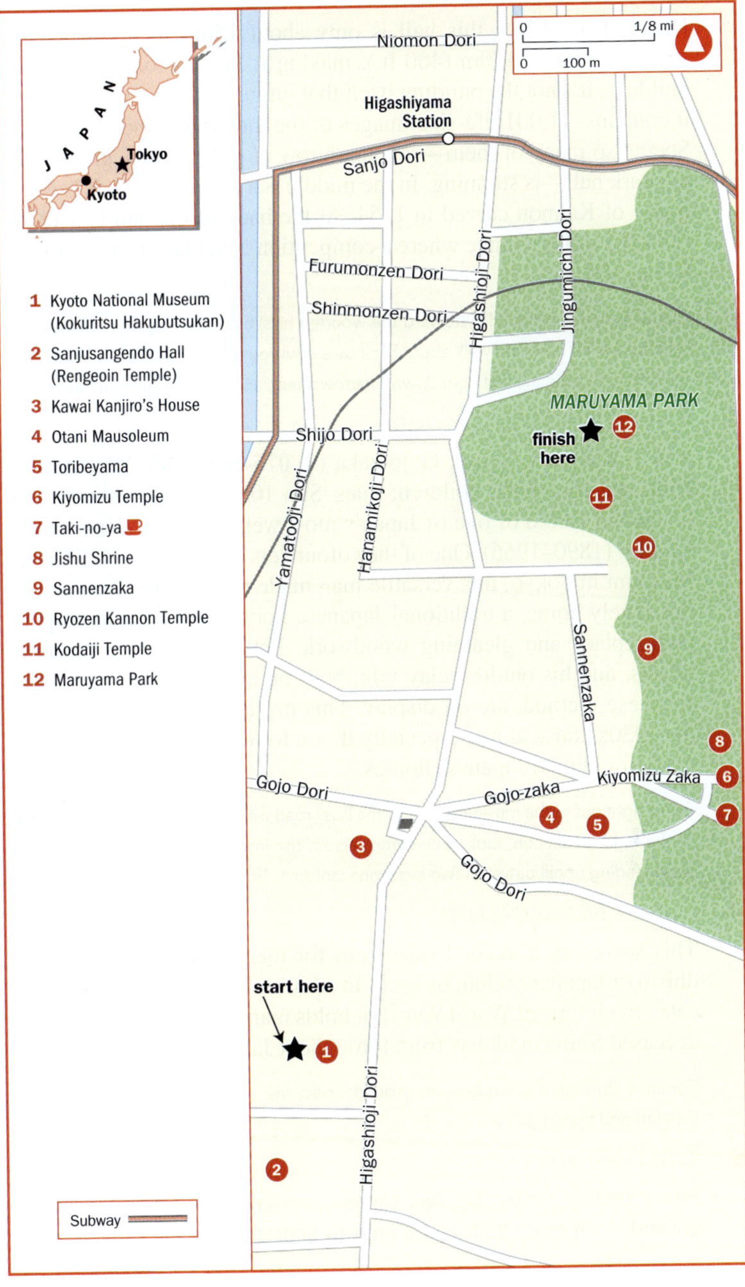

Across the street is:

2 Sanjusangendo Hall

Dating from 1266, this hall is only about 15m (50 ft.) wide, but stretches almost 120m (400 ft.), making it Japan's longest wooden building. It's not the building itself that impresses, however, but what it contains—1,001 life-size images of the thousand-handed Kannon. Seeing so many of them—row upon row of gold figures, glowing in the dark hall—is stunning. In the middle is a 3.3m-tall (11-ft.) seated figure of Kannon carved in 1254. At the back of the hall is a 117m (384-ft.) archery range where a competition is held every January 15. See p. 306.

East of Sanjusangendo Hall (toward the wooded hills) are Higashioji Dori and a stoplight; take a left here and walk about 5 minutes until you come to the second stoplight. Turn left here, take the first right down a narrow street, and to your right you'll soon see:

3 Kawai Kanjiro's House

Kawai Kanjiro's House, Gojo-zaka (✆ **075-561-3585;** ¥900 adults, ¥500 students, ¥300 children; Tues–Sun 10am–5pm), is the former home and studio of one of Japan's most well-known potters, Kawai Kanjiro (1890–1966). One of the cofounders of the Japan Folk Crafts Museum in Tokyo, this versatile man made much of the furniture in this lovely home, a traditional Japanese house with an indoor open-pit fireplace and gleaming woodwork. Pottery, folkcraft, personal effects, and his outdoor clay kiln, built on a slope in the traditional Japanese method, are on display. This museum is worth seeing for the 1930s house alone, especially if you haven't seen the interiors of many traditional Japanese homes.

Take a right out of the museum, walk to the busy road with the overpass, and turn right. At the big intersection, look catty-corner across the intersection to the left to find a slope leading uphill between two big stone lanterns. This marks the entrance to the:

4 Otani Mausoleum

This serves as a major mausoleum for members of Shinshu Buddhism (a Japanese religious sect). In addition to a memorial hall dedicated to victims of World War II, it holds many memorial services for deceased Shin Buddhists from throughout Japan.

Continue through the mausoleum grounds, past the second 2-story wooden gate. Turn left and then right for:

5 Toribeyama

Since ancient times this has served as a cremation site and burial ground, with more than 15,000 tombs spread along the slopes.

Follow the pathway uphill for about 10 minutes to the top. Turn left and follow the street to the vermilion-colored tower gate, which marks the entrance to:

6 Kiyomizu Temple

Visitors drink the healing waters at Kiyomizu Temple.

This temple (p. 302) is the star attraction of this stroll. First founded in 798 and rebuilt in 1633 by the third Tokugawa shogun, Iemitsu, the temple occupies an exalted spot. The recently renovated main hall is built over a cliff with a large wooden veranda, supported by 139 pillars, offering a panoramic view of Kyoto. For a better view of the grandeur of the main hall itself, head to the nearby three-story **pagoda,** cunningly built without the use of a single nail. From the pagoda, descend the stone steps to **Otowa Falls,** where you'll see Japanese lined up to drink the refreshing spring water; Kiyomizu's name translates as "pure water" and it's supposedly good for health. From here you'll also have the best view of the temple's impressive pillars. (***Note:*** To avoid the midday crowds, you may want to start your walking tour here, since Kiyomizu Temple is open from 6am. After exploring the temple precincts [stops #6–8], double back to the Kyoto National Museum [a 20-min. walk] and follow the itinerary from there. After Toribeyama [stop #5], skip ahead to Ryozen Kannon Temple [stop #10], a 15-min. walk.)

7 Temple Dining

On the grounds of Kiyomizu Temple, just beside Otowa Falls, is **Taki-no-ya** (✆ **075-561-5117;** Fri–Wed 10am–5pm), an open-air pavilion where you can sit on *tatami* and enjoy *yudofu*, noodles, a beer, or flavored shaved ice from the English-language menu. This is a great place to stop; if you're lucky to be here in autumn, the fiery reds of the maple trees will set the countryside around you aflame.

Before departing Kiyomizu Temple, make a stop at the vermilion-colored Shinto shrine behind the temple's main hall:

8 Jishu Shrine

This shrine is regarded as a dwelling place of the deity of love and matchmaking. Throughout the grounds, English-language signs describe the shrine's good-luck stations (for once, nonnatives can be enlightened as to the purpose of the various statues and memorials). You can buy good-luck charms for anything from a happy marriage to easy childbirth to success in passing an exam. Look for two stones placed about 9m (30 ft.) apart—if you're able to walk from one stone to the other with your eyes closed, you're allegedly guaranteed success in your love life. It sure doesn't hurt to try. There's also a place where you can write down your troubles on a piece of paper and then submerge it in a bucket of water, which supposedly will cause both the paper and your troubles to dissolve. If you failed the rock test, you might make a point of stopping here.

Retrace your route to the vermilion-colored entry tower gate to Kiyomizu Temple. Follow a downhill slope called Kiyomizu-zaka past shop after shop selling tea, coffee, flavored ice cream, ***zenzai*** (a hot and sweet soup made with stewed adzuki beans and mochi), and Kyoto-famous ***wagashi*** sweets. (Lots of stores will have samples out front.) Other stores sell crafts and souvenirs. After a couple of small shrines nestled in among the shops, you'll come to a split in the road and a small tree-shaded shrine on the right. Just beside this shrine, steps lead downhill (north) to a stone-cobbled street called:

9 Sannenzaka

The slope leads past lovely antiques stores, upscale craft shops, and restaurants and winds through neighborhoods of wooden buildings reminiscent of old Kyoto.

When the street curves left, keep your eyes peeled for downhill stairs to the right leading onto a similar stone path, **Ninen-zaka.** Follow this downhill to a T intersection. Take the stairs opposite the road and look to the right for:

10 Ryozen Kannon Temple

This temple (✆ **075-561-2205;** daily 8:40am–4:20pm) has a 24m-high (80-ft.) white statue dedicated to unknown soldiers who died in World War II. Memorial services are conducted four times daily at a shrine that contains tablets memorializing the 2 million Japanese who perished during the war. A Memorial Hall also commemorates the more than 48,000 foreign soldiers who died on Japanese territory.

The giant goddess figure at Ryozen Kannon Temple, a memorial to the dead of World War II.

Just past Ryozen Kannon Temple, across the parking lot, is:

11 Kodaiji Temple

This temple (p. 304) was founded by the widow Nene to commemorate her husband, Toyotomi Hideyoshi, who succeeded in unifying Japan at the end of the 16th century. In addition to teahouses and a memorial hall containing wooden images of the couple, there's a beautiful garden designed by master gardener Kobori Enshu. Don't miss it (a one-room museum is included in admission, but skip it if time is of the essence).

Exit Kodaiji Temple via the main steps leading downhill and turn right, continuing north. Turn right at the pagoda with the crane and then take an immediate left, which marks the beginning of:

12 Maruyama Park

Once an unkempt field of shrubs and weeds, this was designated a public park in 1886, and now it's one of Kyoto's most popular outdoor refuges, filled with ponds, pigeons, and gardens. In spring, it's a popular spot for viewing cherry blossoms; to the left after you enter the park is one of the oldest, most famous cherry trees in Kyoto.

WHERE TO STAY IN KYOTO

Accommodations are expensive in Kyoto, about on par with Tokyo and sometimes even higher. Because Kyoto is a big tourist destination, be sure to make reservations in advance, particularly in spring when flowers bloom, in autumn (Oct–Nov) for the changing of the leaves, during summer vacation from mid-July through August, and during major festivals (see "Calendar of Events," in chapter 2). With the exception of inexpensive lodgings, most accommodations raise their rates during these times, sometimes shockingly so: A hotel that may charge ¥30,000 to ¥40,000 for a double most of the year, for example, may charge ¥60,000 or more in high season, with some lodgings requiring a minimum two-night stay. In the off-season (mid-Dec, after New Year's to the beginning of Mar, and June), that same double might go for as little as ¥18,000. "Expensive" accommodations below cost more than ¥45,000 per room or per person per night; "Moderate" range from ¥25,000 to ¥45,000; and "Inexpensive" are priced at less than ¥25,000. Keep in mind, however, that a modestly priced hotel could very well be in the expensive category in peak season and in the inexpensive category in February. Furthermore, the wide range of prices for each accommodation runs the spectrum from the cheapest room in off-season to its most expensive room in peak season. Inexpensive accommodations, on the other hand, tend to have the similar rates year round.

Because Kyoto is relatively small and has such good bus and subway systems, whereever you stay you won't be too far away from the heart of the city. Most lodgings are concentrated around Kyoto Station (Shimogyo

ONLY IN JAPAN: THE ryokan EXPERIENCE

If you've never stayed in a *ryokan,* Kyoto is one of the best places to do so. With the exception of hot-spring resorts, Kyoto has more choices of *ryokan* in all price categories than any other city in Japan. Small, traditionally made of wood, and often situated in delightfully quaint neighborhoods, these *ryokan* can enrich your stay in Kyoto by putting you in direct touch with the city's traditional past.

The prices at upper- and mid-priced *ryokan* may seem prohibitive at first glance, until you consider that the per-person charge includes two meals and usually tax and service charge. These meals are feasts, not unlike *kaiseki* meals you'd receive at a top restaurant (where they could easily cost in excess of ¥10,000). Ryokan in the budget category, on the other hand, usually don't serve meals unless stated otherwise and often charge per room rather than per person, but they do provide the futon experience. For more, see p. 49.

Ward), in central Kyoto not far from the Kawaramachi-Shijo Dori intersection (Nakagyo-ku Ward), and east of the Kamo River (in the Higashiyama-ku and Sakyo-ku Wards). Some properties also have shuttle buses to Kyoto Station.

TAXES & SERVICE CHARGES All accommodations levy a federal 10% consumption tax on room rates, while mid- and upper-range ones also add a 10% to 15% service fee; in *ryokan,* the service charge can be as high as 20%. Unless noted otherwise, all rates below include consumption tax and service charge. Kyoto also has its own accommodations tax. Per person, per night, it is ¥200 for rooms costing less than ¥20,000 a night, ¥500 for rooms costing ¥20,000 to ¥50,000, and ¥1,000 for rates ¥50,000 and more. The prices below are *without* this local tax. If your room is pre-paid, you may have to pay it in cash on arrival.

Note: Proposed tax hikes are expected to come into effect in Kyoto in March 2026, and it's fair to say many hoteliers aren't thrilled about it (nor will prospective guests be when they hear about it). The new taxes fall into five categories: ¥200 a night for rooms costing ¥6,000 or less; ¥400 a night for rooms costing ¥6,000 to ¥20,000; ¥1,000 a night for rooms costing ¥20,000 to ¥50,000; ¥4,000 a night for rooms costing ¥50,000 to ¥100,000; and ¥10,000 a night for rooms costing ¥100,000 or more.

Around Kyoto Station

EXPENSIVE

Dusit Thani ♥♥♥ This chain of luxury hotels rose to prominence in Thailand, but you wouldn't know if from Dusit Thani Kyoto. The wood latticing that surrounds the hotel exterior, the clever interplay of light and shadow in the hallways, subtle art pieces reflecting the craft culture of Japan's ancient capital, a tatami tea lounge, and a rock garden in the basement courtyard (where you'll find an exceptional teppanyaki restaurant;

see Koyo in the "Where to Eat" section for a full review) make this property feel like it could only exist in Japan. The customer service is of distinctly Japanese quality: from the moment you walk in your luggage will be on a trolley (before rematerializing in your room) and you'll be reclining on a comfy sofa in the lobby drinking a cup of Japanese tea and wiping your brow with a towel. Guest rooms are on floors 2 to 4, and though they vary in size from 40 sq m to the outrageously extravagant 173 sq m Imperial Suite, sliding shoji frames on the windows of all rooms lend both a sense of theater and privacy. Don't skip on sampling the rare and craft spirits sold in the hotel's Den Kyoto bar (a fine place for a night cap), or shaking off the cobwebs in the gym and spa each morning.

466 Nishinotoincho, Shimogyo-ku. dusit.com/dusitthani-kyoto/. ✆ **075-343-7150.** 147 units. ¥40,000–¥110,000 double. Train station: Kyoto (Central Exit, 12 min.). **Amenities:** 3 restaurants; tea lounge; bar; breakfast hall; concierge; room service; gym and pool; spa; free Wi-Fi.

MODERATE

Hotel Granvia Kyoto ♥♥ You can't beat this hotel for convenience, since it's located in Kyoto Station and is only a minute's walk to buses and subways serving the rest of the city. Luckily, the lobby is on the second floor, away from the station's foot traffic, though it can still hum with the hotel's many guests. It's LGBTQ-friendly and also offers amenities geared toward Muslims, including Halal menus and, on request, a prayer mat and Qibla direction sign in all guest rooms. The hotel also has a list of privately guided tour options, from antiques shopping to walking and cycling tours; it even offers a gay wedding package, with a ceremony at a temple. The cheapest standard rooms are small, have unexciting views of the station's glass roof, and are rather dark, so you might want to spend a bit more for a standard facing outside. The best rooms are large deluxe rooms facing north with great views of Kyoto. Because Granvia is owned by the West Japan Railway Company, if you have a valid Japan Rail pass you can get a discount off certain rooms. In any case, if you're in Kyoto only a night or two, this is a convenient choice, but it can't compete with the ambience of hotels in central Kyoto.

JR Kyoto Station, Central Exit, Karasuma Dori Shiokoji-sagaru. granviakyoto.com. ✆ **075-344-8888.** 537 units. ¥20,000–¥60,000 double. **Amenities:** 11 restaurants and cafes; bar; lounge; concierge; health club w/ indoor pool, gym; sauna; room service; free Wi-Fi.

A Double or a Twin?

For the sake of convenience, the price for two people in a room is typically listed as a "double" in this book. Japanese hotels, however, differentiate between rooms with a double bed or two twin beds, usually with different prices. Most hotels charge more for a twin room, but sometimes the opposite is true; if you're looking for a bargain, therefore, be sure to inquire about prices for both. Note, too, that hotels usually have more twin rooms than doubles, for the simple reason that Japanese couples, used to their own futon, traditionally prefer twin beds.

INEXPENSIVE

APA Kyoto Ekimae ♥♥ Apart from the ornate lobby, there's nothing too fancy about this business hotel on the western side of Kyoto Station. That said, if you're on a budget, need to book a room last minute, or just want somewhere to lay your head before jumping on the Shinkansen the next day, this is a great option (and one I use frequently). APA is Japan's most popular business hotel chain for a reason: they do the simple things right. Bedding is comfy, toiletries and pajamas are provided, express check-in/check-out is speedy, and in-room aromatherapy treatments are often available. Plus, all rooms are kitted out with large flatscreen TVs and desks with lights in case you need to catch up on some emails or pen a couple of postcards. There's also a basement bierkeller which doubles as a breakfast banquet hall each morning at 7am (breakfast costs extra).

806 Minamifudodocho. apahotel.com. ✆ **075-365-4111.** 193 units. ¥6,000–¥20,000 double. Train station: Kyoto (Central exit, 5 min.). **Amenities:** Spa treatments (additional cost); free Wi-Fi.

Matsubaya Ryokan ♥♥ The Hayashi family has managed this inn, just east of Higashi Honganji Temple, since the late Edo Period; it's now under ownership of the fifth Hayashi generation. Long an old wooden *ryokan* with character, in 2008 it was torn down and enlarged, though some architectural details were salvaged. Still, the ground-floor courtyard garden and lounge remains a good place to connect with other travelers. Rooms are mostly Japanese style, with the best overlooking the garden. Also good bets are five Western-style rooms on the fifth floor with kitchenettes and tiny balconies. For families, a combination suite is big enough for six people, with beds and futon along with two bathrooms. Nearby is a company that rents bicycles.

Higashinotoin Nishi, Kamijuzuyamachi Dori. matsubayainn.com. ✆ **075-351-3727.** 32 units (2 w/ shared bath). ¥5,000–¥15,000 single; ¥10,000–¥20,000 double. Train station: Kyoto (Central Exit, 10 min.). **Amenities:** Free Wi-Fi.

Central Kyoto

EXPENSIVE

Garrya Nijo Castle ♥♥♥ Garrya makes a strong first impression—its entrance hidden at the end of a bamboo-lined passageway, its lobby pointed towards a pretty garden of maple and moss. You'll be checked in while sitting upon a sofa, being served a welcome drink on a polished volcanic-rock table reflecting the slowly shifting scenes from the garden. Whereas the communal spaces are all about the poetry of the natural world and the aesthetic of the spare, the guestrooms are bolder, their cabinets covered in red *urushi* lacquer. Rooms on the upper floors offer views of nearby Nijo Castle, the former seat of the Tokugawa Shogunate, and room decor evokes the power of the samurai—red, among its many other connotations in Japanese lore, symbolizes strength, authority, and sacrifice. All guestrooms are large and have separate shower rooms with deep

A guest meditates in the mossy garden off the lobby of the Garrya Nijo Castle hotel.

tubs; Rikyu Terrace and Bamboo Garden rooms also offer outdoor seating areas, a rarity in Kyoto hotels. The hotel can organize experiences like flower arranging, tea ceremony, and forest meditation sessions. Guests should consider reserving a table at Singular, the hotel's farm-to-table restaurant, where the chef de cuisine applies classic French cooking techniques to seasonal, Kyoto-sourced ingredients. For the best seats in the house, request a table next the garden.

180–1 Ichinocho. garrya.com/en/destinations/kyoto. ✆ **075-366-5806.** 25 units. ¥70,000–¥185,000 double. Subway: Nijojo-mae Station (2 min.). Bus: 9, 12, 50, or 101 to Nijojo-mae (2 min.). **Amenities:** Restaurant; bar; free Wi-Fi.

Hiiragiya Ryokan ♥♥♥ This exquisite *ryokan* is as fine an example of a traditional inn as you'll find in Japan. Built in 1818 and nestled in the heart of old Kyoto, it has all the quintessential design characteristics of an old inn, making artful use of wood, bamboo, screens, and stones in its simple yet elegant *tatami* rooms. Art and antiques decorate the rooms, many of which have garden views and cypress baths. Even modern conveniences are cleverly hidden, like the gourd-shaped lacquered remote controls for the lights and curtains. Dinners, served in your room in true *ryokan* fashion, are multi-course *kaiseki* feasts (Western-style breakfasts are available on request). No wonder Hiiragiya has played host to writers, artists, politicians, and even members of the imperial family over the decades. Its level of service and hospitality is intuitive and about as perfect as it gets, honed over the years and now under the watchful and caring eye of Ms. Nishimura, the inn's seventh-generation innkeeper.

277 Nakahakusancho, Fuyacho Anekoji-agaru (corner of Fuyacho and Oike sts.). hiiragiya.co.jp. ✆ **075-221-1136.** 24 units. ¥35,000–¥90,000 per person, excluding tax. Rates include 2 meals. Subway: Kyoto Shiyakusho-mae (4 min.) or Karasuma-Oike (7 min.). Bus: 4, 17, or 205 to Kyoto Shiyakusho-mae (5 min.). **Amenities:** Free Wi-Fi.

MODERATE

Comfort Inn Kyoto Shijo Karasuma ♥♥ As business hotels go, this property has a lot going for it: super-friendly reception staff, comfortable and quite sizable rooms, and a location that couldn't get much better. Gion and Nijo Castle are equidistant (each under 2km away) and charming old-world streets like Pontocho and Miyagawacho can be reached in 20 minutes on foot. Karasuma and Shijo stations, connecting you to all corners of the city, are practically on your doorstep, as is the always-crammed Nishiki Market and a host of great restaurants. Guests also get free access to the hotel's public bathhouse—it's small and steamy, but quiet in the evenings when your walk-weary muscles are most likely to appreciate a soak. There's a good selection of tourist pamphlets and gourmet maps in the lobby.

284–1 Tenjinyama-cho, Muromachi-nishiiru, Nishikikoji-dori. choicehotels.com. ✆ **075-2113-611.** 63 units. ¥10,000–¥30,000 double. Subway: Karasuma Oike (3 min.), Shijo (4 min.). **Amenities:** Breakfast buffet; public bathhouse; free Wi-Fi.

HOMM Stay Nagi Sanjo ♥♥ This hotel quite clearly reflects Kyoto's cultural heritage: guestroom walls are painted with spiritual motifs like screen doors in a feudal lord's palace, and varied art pieces sit in alcoves in the earth-toned welcome room (note the Oriental white stork sculpture, an ode to this long-endangered species). There's something refreshing about the quirky style, a reflection of the owner's personal tastes, even if the artworks occasionally clash. Guestrooms are all generously sized, with large comfy beds, seating areas, work desks, reading lights, and espresso machines. As with many Kyoto hotels, there's little in the way of natural light, but this does lend itself to coziness. Shower rooms are separate from the toilets and feature black enamel baths, a material chosen for its ability to retain heat. It's worth the extra charge for breakfast, cooked in a nearby restaurant and served in your room, much in the fashion of Japan's traditional inns.

524 Anenishinotoin-cho. hommhotels.com. ✆ **075-212-7707.** 28 units. ¥20,000–¥55,000 r double. Subway: Karasuma-Oike (8 min.). Bus: 9 or 50 to Horikawa Sanjo (6 min.). **Amenities:** Breakfast in room; free Wi-Fi.

Hotel Monterey Kyoto ♥♥ The Monterey hotel chain is known for its old-world designs, but always with some connection to the city it's located in. Monterey Kyoto, occupying a former bank, centers on the Arts & Crafts style of Edinburgh (Kyoto and the Scottish capital are sister cities). The lobby is dark and subdued, with marbled flooring, bookcases, and period European artwork. Rooms, on the other hand, are remarkably bold, most with striped wallpaper in navy blue or crimson red. There are great views across the city from the top-floor spa, an extra incentive to stay; it utilizes thermal waters obtained by drilling more than 1,000m (3,300 ft.) below ground.

604 Manjuya-cho, Karasuma Dori, Sanjo-sagaru. hotelmonterey.co.jp/kyoto. ✆ **075-251-7111.** 327 units. ¥8,000–¥45,000 double. Subway: Karasuma Oike (exit 6, 3 min.). **Amenities:** 2 restaurants; concierge; spa; free Wi-Fi.

Node ♥♥♥ Minimalist, urbane, and designed with real intention, this artsy hotel in central Kyoto is exactly the kind of place that's shaking up the local hotel market. Grey walls and exposed concrete serve as a canvas for a thoughtfully curated selection of contemporary artworks dotted throughout the lobby-restaurant, hallways, and guestrooms. Abstract photography hangs over beds, *wabi sabi* pottery and metalworks sit in illuminated alcoves, and paintings fusing principles of Zen and impression add texture and color to otherwise neutral spaces. Guestrooms include singles, twins, and doubles, along with three beautiful junior suites that can accommodate 4 people. All have nice features, like natural wood bedframes, white-oak flooring, handwoven rugs, large walk-in showers, vintage-style Tivoli speakers with Bluetooth, marble paperweights in desk drawers, and booklets with information on the art found in your room. Because of its location and relatively low height (there are only five floors), you won't get much of a view, but the rooms so soothing you probably won't mind. And the breakfast served to guests in the ground-floor restaurant is far better than your standard buffet fare.
461 Toroyamacho. nodehotel.com. ✆ **075-221-8800.** 25 units. ¥30,000–¥55,000 single or double. Subway: Karasuma Oike (5 min.). Bus: 26 or 50 Shijo Nishinotoin (3 min.). **Amenities:** Restaurant; concierge; free Wi-Fi.

The Royal Park Hotel Kyoto Sanjo ♥♥ Close to sightseeing, shopping, nightlife, and transportation, this hotel is stylish, comfy, and up to date. A hidden (some might say *too* hidden) entryway down a dramatic, darkened corridor leads to a subdued lobby, with spotlights trained on artworks behind the desk and statues arranged on shelves. Rooms are fairly standard and small, though deluxe rooms provide more space and have bathrooms with separate showers and soaking tubs. All have custom-designed mattresses and playful artwork of rabbits jumping over the moon or other motifs that add a dash of color and whimsy.
74 Nakajimacho. royalparkhotels.co.jp/the/kyotosanjo. ✆ **075-241-1111.** 172 units. ¥15,000–¥50,000 double. Subway: Kyoto Shiyakusho-mae (3 min.). **Amenities:** Restaurant; bar; concierge; free Wi-Fi.

INEXPENSIVE

Piece Hostel Sanjo ♥♥ A good example of how far budget accommodations have come in Japan, this spotless hostel was converted from a former ryokan. It has a contemporary yet traditional facade, with big chunks of rock lining a long entryway. The communal kitchen is huge, allowing several people to cook at once, and overlooks a dining area that includes a small outdoor terrace. In addition to four dormitory rooms sleeping four to 10 people (including two just for women), it has single, twin, and double rooms without private bathrooms, plus a family room for up to six people and double rooms with private bathrooms. This local brand has big aspirations, with various other Piece properties located in central Kyoto; this one is undoubtedly one of the best spots for backpackers visiting the city.

531 Asakura-cho. piecehostel.com/sanjo/en. ✆ **075-746-3688.** 50 units, 28 dormitory beds. ¥3,000–¥10,000 dorm bed; ¥7,000–¥18,000 private twin/double. Subway: Karasuma Oike (10 min.). **Amenities:** Cafe; rental bikes (fee); free Wi-Fi.

Eastern Kyoto

EXPENSIVE

Banyan Tree Higashiyama Kyoto ♥♥♥ Opened in summer 2024 and designed by Kengo Kuma, Japan's inimitable Master of Wood and one of the nation's best-known architects, this property might just be the cream of the Kyoto crop, surveying the city from atop a hill in the old-world Higashiyama district. The lobby is all natural woods, soft furnishings, beautifully bound artbooks, and local craftworks including Nishijin textiles. Floor-to-ceiling windows look upon a sculpted Japanese garden, which you can walk through to visit the hotel's private bamboo forest, its stalks rustling in the breeze like a wooden orchestra. The restaurant, serving Western and Japanese breakfasts in the morning and a modern take on *kaiseki* in the evening, faces a grand Noh stage on the garden patio, where performances are held on special occasions. Guestrooms—aptly given names like Serenity, Wellbeing Sanctuary, and Onsen Retreat—are bathed in natural light (control panels allow you to close the blinds if you're averse to waking up at sunrise) and decorated with a combination of stone and tatami flooring, Kyo-yaki pottery sculptures, and wall features accented with goldleaf. There are deep tubs carved from *hiba* cypress (some rooms use hot spring water tapped from deep below the surface), and raised seating areas let you drink tea or coffee in the morning while admiring views of Kyoto's surrounding hillscape and the city below. Guests also get Banyan's own brand of kimono to wear around the property, to the public bathhouse (including a *rotenburo,* or "outdoor bath"), or when strolling the narrow, lantern-fringed streets between the hotel and nearby Kiyomizu Temple. Rooms even include huge safes, to encourage guests to place their laptops inside and embrace a digital detox. Undoubtedly, Banyan Tree requires a splurge, but if you're in Japan for a honeymoon or special occasion, I can think of few better places to stay.

7 Seikanji Ryozan-cho. banyantree.com/japan/kyoto. ✆ **075-531-0500.** 52 units. ¥115,000–¥550,000 double. Bus: 80, 86, 206, or 207 to Higashiyama Yasui (12 min.). Taxi ¥2,000–¥3,500 from most areas in the city. **Amenities:** Restaurant; bar; concierge; gym; room service; spa with yoga classes; hot-spring baths; free Wi-Fi.

MODERATE

Hotel Material ♥♥ Kyoto may have some of Japan's finest traditional accommodations, but the boutique craze that's disrupted the national hotel market has found a footing here, too. And there's no two ways about it, this is a cool, modern, art-house property. Rooms blend smooth concrete furnishings with brick walls, delicate lighting, color-popping upholstery, and wooden stages with sunken beds, giving each room a sense of contrast and playfulness. With only 6 rooms total, the property feels exclusive without being snobby, thanks to its communal atmosphere—the rooftop BBQ area is a great place to meet fellow guests, cook produce from Nishiki Market over open flame, and sit back with a bottle of sake and admire the hills to the east (the hotel provides the BBQ materials, but guests are required to purchase the food and drink). There's also a ramen restaurant on the ground floor—with outdoor terrace seating—serving noodles in meaty broths made with hydroponic vegetables grown in-house.

210–4 Nakanocho. hotelmaterial.kyoto. ✆ **075-762-1777.** 6 units. ¥15,000–¥35,000 double. Subway: Higashiyama (8 min.). **Amenities:** BBQ area; ramen shop; concierge; free Wi-Fi.

Seikoro Ryokan ♥♥♥ This *ryokan* just east of the Kamo River was established in 1831, with the present building dating from about 115 years ago. After passing through a traditional front gate and small courtyard, you'll find yourself in one of the most charming entryways in Kyoto, which adjoins a cozy parlor decorated with an eclectic mix of Japanese and Western antiques. Guest rooms are comfortable, decorated with antiques, and have wooden bathtubs. Rooms in the older main building consist of old and renovated *tatami* rooms, most with sliding doors and *shoji* screens that open onto the garden; those in the annex, which was built just before the 1964 Olympics, include three combination rooms with beds and tatami areas, and only provide views over the surrounding rooftops. The nice public bath has a tub made of 400-year-old hinoki cypress, making it one of the inn's most treasured possessions. Though meals are typically included in the rates, the English-speaking, seventh-generation innkeeper doesn't mind if you dine elsewhere in the off-season, especially if you're here for a while.

Tonyamachi Dori, Gojo-sagaru. seikoro.com. ✆ **075-561-0771.** 20 units. ¥30,000–¥50,00 per person, incl. meals (from ¥20,000 per person w/o meals if staying 3 or more nights). Bus: 4, 17, or 205 to Kawaramachi (5 min.). Keihan Railway: Gojo Station (2 min.). **Amenities:** Public bath; free Wi-Fi.

A zen retreat IN WEST KYOTO

For a different kind of Kyoto experience, consider staying at the **Shunko-In Temple and Guesthouse ♥♥♥** (42 Myoshinji-cho, Hanazono; shunkoin.com; ✆ **075-462-5488**) in west Kyoto. Established in 1590, this Buddhist temple serves as a sub-temple of Myoshinji, with its expansive grounds. Although the Japanese-style rooms are rather basic and located in a nondescript building (with the great name "Cave of Enlightened Dragon"), a stay here includes Zen meditation sessions led by head priest Rev. Taka Kawakami, who speaks flawless English and is the fifth generation of his family to have presided over the temple the past 150 years. The temple no longer takes individual bookings, but it welcomes overnight guests for occasional retreats, a great way to begin your Zen tutelage in one of the most spiritual corners of Japan. Retreat dates, contents, and price are listed on the temple's Peatix page: zenwithtakakawakami.peatix.com. It's a 6-minute walk from Hanazono train station, or you can take bus 26 to the Myoshim-ji Kitamon stop.

WHERE TO EAT IN KYOTO

Kyoto cuisine, known as ***Kyo-ryori,*** is linked to Kyoto's long history and to seasonal foods produced in the surrounding region. Among the various types of Kyo-ryori available, most famous are the vegetarian dishes, or ***shojin ryori,*** created to serve the needs of Zen Buddhist priests and pilgrims making the rounds of Kyoto's many temples, These vegetarian set meals may include *yudofu* (blocks of tofu simmered in a pot at your table and served with dipping sauce), filmy sheets of *yuba* (soy milk curd), and an array of local vegetables. Kyoto is also renowned for its own style of *kaiseki* called ***Kyo-kaiseki,*** originally conceived as a meal to be taken before the tea ceremony but eventually becoming an elaborate feast enjoyed by the capital's nobility with a blend of ceremonial court cuisine, Zen vegetarian food, and simple tea-ceremony dishes. You'll typically need a reservation for *kaiseki* (Kyoto's better *ryokan* also serve *kaiseki* as the evening meal). Simpler restaurants specialize in ***obanzai,*** home-style Kyoto cooking using traditional seasonal ingredients. ***Remember:*** Last orders are taken 30 to 60 minutes before the restaurant's actual closing time, even earlier for *kaiseki* restaurants.

Around Kyoto Station

In addition to the restaurants listed here, Kyoto Station houses dozens of restaurants in underground arcades, at major exits, and in Isetan department store, which has more than 20 outlets alone, mostly on the 10th and 11th floors. A cheap standout is **Ramen Koji** (拉麺小路) ♥♥♥ (✆ **075-361-4401**)where nine of the best ramen shops from around the country are assembled on the 10th floor of Isetan. Dishes, most priced around ¥1,000, run from Sapporo-style miso ramen (ramen in miso broth) to so-thick-it's-almost-creamy *tonkotsu* (pork broth) from Hakata (Fukuoka). After choosing what you want, buy a ticket from vending machines outside each shop (English-speaking staff is usually on hand to help) and then line up in that restaurant's queue. Ramen Koji is open daily from 11am to 10pm.

EXPENSIVE

Koyo ♥♥♥ TEPPANYAKI This cinematic teppanyaki restaurant in the basement courtyard of the Dusit Thani hotel stays true to the seasonal cuisine heritage of old Kyoto, yet clearly the executive chef has been given room to innovate—don't be surprised if your degustation contains a shellfish bisque or a meaty jus. The tasting menu features the likes of crab and sea urchin sushi, grilled shellfish and mushrooms, Hajime or Kobe beef, a buttery medley of Kyoto-grown vegetables, a teppan-fried rice dish, and a delicate, palate-cleansing dessert, and it's all definitely cooking as art—food is steamed under luminous copper cloches or is sliced and diced on the grill as though the chefs are carrying out surgery. (And there's no question the ingredients are fresh: My abalone was literally trying to crawl off the plate.) I'd recommend trying the sake pairing as well—rather than just several versions of clear, highly polished rice wine, you'll get to try sake that's been brewed with malt, wine yeast, or an unfiltered foamy concoction called *doburoku.* This being a hotel, the maître'd-cum-waiter speaks English, as do some of the chefs (as a foreign customer, you'll likely be assigned one of these), and the menu is also presented in English. Reservations recommended.

Dusit Thani Hotel. dusit.com/dusitthani-kyoto/dining. ✆ **075-585-4746.** Daily noon–2pm and 5:30–8pm (last order). Lunch ¥6,000–¥18,000, dinner ¥25,000–¥40,000; omakase wine pairing ¥25,000. Train station: Kyoto (Central exit, 12 min.).

MODERATE

Yebisu Bar ♥♥ PUB It's hard to walk past the Yebisu Bar on a sunny day and not feel like joining the crowd. With al fresco seating and drafts from the Yebisu Brewery populating the sun-drenched tables, it offers diners and imbibers the kind of piazza-esque people-watching experience that doesn't come around too often in Japan. Beer drinkers will have a field day swiping through the tablet menus, from which you can order (in English) Yebisu lagers, meisters, black beer, and ales, as well as not-too-appealing beer cocktails mixed with green tea or strawberry iced tea. The food menu is a combo of pub grub classics and izakaya finger food. An interesting option is the ¥1,600 *karaage* (deep-fried chicken thigh) set, with five different options each designed to pair with a specific beer. Or try an all-you-can-drink course—90- and 120-minute options available—which come with five or six sharing dishes, including pizza, fish and chips, carpaccio, sausages, and hors d'oeuvres. These start at ¥4,500 per person.

Yodobashi Camera bldg., 590–2 Higashishiokojicho. ginzalion.jp. ✆ **075-353-2201.** Set menu ¥4,500–¥6,000, a la carte ¥2,000–¥3,000 per person. Daily 11am–11pm. Train station: Kyoto (Central exit, 2 min.).

INEXPENSIVE

Coyote (The Ordinary Shop) ♥♥ COFFEE SHOP It's perhaps not that well known, but Japan has one of the world's great coffee cultures, with artisans applying the nation's trademark attention to detail to the sourcing, roasting and brewing of beans. At Coyote, which also has branches in Shimogyo-ku and Sakyo-ku, the baristas make hand-drip and cold-brew coffee from beans bought directly from producers in the Chalatenango region of northwestern El Salvador. Clean, mellow, mildly fruity, and gently acidic, the coffee pairs well with the menu's Western breakfast staples of fluffy eggs on toast, banana bread, and vegan cookies—a good choice if rice, fish, and miso don't appeal to you first thing in the morning. Coyote also opens at 8:30am, earlier than many coffee shops in Japan, meaning you don't have to start your day deprived of caffeine. If the coffee hits the mark, beans are available at the cafe counter, from ¥1,800 per 150g.

939 Higashishiokojicho. coyote-coffee.stores.jp. ✆ **075-3539-154.** Coffee and breakfast ¥1,000–¥1,500. Tues–Sun 8:30am–5pm. Train station: Kyoto (Central exit, 4 min.).

Tonkatsu KYK ♥♥ TONKATSU *Tonkatsu* (breaded pork cutlet) is inexpensive comfort food in Japan. This restaurant, in the underground **Porta Dining** concourse at Kyoto Station, has both a display case of popular dishes and an English-language tablet menu to help you choose your meal. Set meals are the way to go, with combinations like tonkatsu and oyster croquettes, plus rice, miso soup, shredded cabbage, and pickled vegetables (as at most tonkatsu restaurants, you get free refills of rice, cabbage, and soup). Glass jars with tonkatsu sauce are placed on the table along with KYK's own-brand sesame and creamy dressings, the latter of which is basically Big Mac sauce. The Japanese pork loin cutlet and KYK special pork tenderloin sets are both delicious, but either way I'd recommend ordering some breaded oysters on the side at ¥250 a pop. Porta, JR Kyoto Station. tonkatu-kyk.co.jp. ✆ **075-343-3265.** Set meals ¥1,600–¥2,730. Daily 11am–9:30pm (last order).

A Note on Japanese Characters

Many hotels, restaurants, attractions, and other establishments in Japan do not have signs giving their names in Roman (English-language) letters. Where they don't, I've given the Japanese script here, next to the restaurant name.

Central Kyoto

The heart of Kyoto's shopping, dining, and nightlife district is in Nakagyo-ku, especially on Kawaramachi and Shijo Dori and along the many side streets. In summer, restaurants on the west bank of the Kamo River erect large wooden outdoor platforms that extend over the water and offer open-air dining.

The food court at bustling Nishiki Market is a great place to grab lunch in Central Kyoto.

EXPENSIVE

Misoguigawa (禊川) ♥♥♥ FRENCH KAISEKI An idyllic location on the Kamo River, historic ambience, and innovative cuisine all make Misoguigawa Kyoto's finest dining experience. Master-chef/owner Teruo Inoue created his own take on fusion cuisine long before it became fashionable. Trained by a three-star Michelin chef, Inoue is a genius at blending classic French cuisine with Japanese ingredients. Served on Kyoto tableware, his dishes are works of art, arranged to please both the eye and the palate. Open since 1981, Misoguigawa occupies a century-old former teahouse on Pontocho that once belonged to a geisha. It has several dining options: private *tatami* rooms; a casual counter (dinner only, a la carte) where you can watch the chef at work; and an outdoor summer veranda extending over the Kamo River. Three set dinners and a lunch set are available, but chef Inoue always asks about allergies and preferences and makes changes accordingly. One of the conveniences of dining here is the English-speaking staff, with explanations of each dish as it's presented.

Sanjo-sagaru, Pontocho. misogui.jp. ✆ **075-221-2270.** Lunch ¥15,730; dinners ¥21,700–¥47,190 (prices exclude tax and 10% service charge). Thurs–Mon 11:30am–1pm and 5:30–8:30pm (last order). Bus: 4, 5, 17, or 205 to Kawaramachi Sanjo (5 min.).

MODERATE

Gyukatsu Motomura Sanjo Kawaramachi ♥♥ GYUKATSU *Gyukatsu* (breaded steak cutlet) is a popular dish in Kyoto and this restaurant on the western side of the Kamo River is one of the best places to try it. The gyukastu sets, starting at ¥1,930 and rising based on the weight of the cutlets, feature breaded raw sirloin beef, which diners cook at their tables on stone hotplates. Sides include shredded cabbage, barley rice, pickles, and dipping sauces. Many of the staff speak English, so if you're unsure about how to cook the beef, just ask. But given the cutlets have a good amount of marbling, if you cook them medium or, God forbid, well done, they should retain their buttery umami flavor. Counter seating here is atmospheric, but I like watching the city go by from the tables by the wall-length window.

110 Nakajimacho, Forum Sanjo Building 2F. gyukatsu-motomura.com. ✆ **050-1721-9130.** Gyukatsu sets ¥1,930–¥3,660. Bus: 4, 5, 7, 205 to Kawaramachi Sanjo (4 min.). Subway: Sanjo (2 min.).

HIRO Kiyamachi ♥♥ YAKINIKU The bamboo-lined entry to this superb *yakiniku* (grilled meat) restaurant suggests you're about to check into an old Kyoto inn. But the second floor, where HIRO Kiyamachi is located, has been revamped, with an urbane design and sunken grills in the center of each table that marry well with rustic wooden beams and pretty views of the Kamo River lit up at night. There are some interesting a la carte items, like thick-sliced *gyutan* (beef tongue), wagyu sushi, and pot-marinated dragon ribs (named for their appearance rather than source), which are worth trying, especially if this is your first yakiniku experience. Better, though, are the set menus, featuring a range of high-quality meat cuts (mostly beef) with some sides and veggies, as well as 2 hours of all-you-can-drink on selected drink items. Another good sharing option is the Daily Special Meat Plate, a curation of cuts from the day's meat stock. Note that some set menus require a minimum of 6 diners. The indoor dining hall at HIRO Kiyamachi is convivial, but in the warmer months (May–Sept), ask for a table on the outdoor terrace.

527 Kamiosakacho (off Kiyamachi-dori). kakiniku-hiro.com. ✆ **075-213-5000.** Set meals ¥5,000–¥10,000; a la carte items ¥480–¥1,380. Daily 5–11pm (food last order 10pm; drinks 10:30pm). Bus: 4 or 205 to Kawaramachi Sanjo (3 min.). Subway: Kyoto Shiyakusho-mae (3 min.).

Kushi Kura (串くら) ♥♥ YAKITORI Built in a century-old warehouse where heavy beams and dark polished wood contrast with whitewashed walls, this restaurant maintains the atmosphere of old Kyoto. Seating is at tables, on *tatami,* or at a counter where you can watch the chefs. The restaurant's specialty is grilled chicken, using top-grade charcoal, served *yakitori*-style on skewers, although the English-language menu, with photos, lists other possibilities as well, along with set meals and a variety of individual meat and vegetable skewers you can order à la carte. The least expensive set dinner includes an appetizer, raw veggies with dipping sauce, and six skewers that may include chicken breast, Kyoto-style wheat gluten, chicken and leeks, ground chicken, and small sweet green peppers; most diners prefer to select their own meals to get exactly what they want. Try the locally made Fushimi sake.

584 Hiiragi-cho. kushikura.jp. ✆ **075-213-2211.** Lunches ¥1,200–¥3,800; dinners ¥2,500–¥6,000. Daily 11:30am–2pm and 5–9pm (last order). Subway: Karasuma-Oike (2 min.).

Manten Roccaku (串焼 満天 六角編) ♥♥♥ GRILLED MEAT If you like barbecued meat, you'll want to ink this spot atop your Kyoto food itinerary. A creative take on a *yakitori-ya* (grilled chicken shop), the menu features a wide variety of skewered meats, such as pork-wrapped asparagus and lettuce, eggs wrapped in bacon, eggplant meat rolls, spinach meat rolls with carbonara and parmesan cheese, grilled ray fin, and *unagi* (freshwater eel) with butter, alongside classic dishes like the five-piece yakitori set (usually chicken thigh, breast heart, minced, and a skin-and-cartilage combo). More robust plates are available, too, like beef sushi sets and *wagyu* steak and green peppers, which diners grill on portable grills at their table. You certainly won't lack for protein here. There's a dining area with tables at the back for groups, but it's much more atmospheric to sit at the counter, surrounded by the hubbub of beer-swilling customers, where you can watch the chefs on a raised platform sizzling the skewers over wild flames. The menu has pictures, but the staff will likely hand you a QR code from which you place orders in English.

231 Donomaecho. manten-kusatsu.owst.jp. ✆ **075-606-5035.** Dinner and drinks ¥3,000–¥6,000 per person. Daily 5pm–midnight (last order). Bus: 3, 5, 11, 12, 31, 32, 46, or 58. to Shijo Takakura (6 min.). Subway: Karasamu-Oike (5 min.).

A STANDING feast: NISHIKI MARKET FOOD COURT

Every foodie in Kyoto should make a pilgrimage to **Nishiki Market ♥♥** (485 Nakauoyacho, on Nishikikoji-dori, near the intersection with Sakaimachi-dori). Yes, it's one of the most congested corners of the city, a series of shopping arcades lined by produce stalls and restaurants that's far too narrow for the many thousands that visit it daily. But they call it "Kyoto's Kitchen" for a reason: you can find everything from *age-dashi* tofu and bags of pickled vegetables to butter *taiyaki* (a fish-shaped pastry) and deep-fried *fugu* (pufferfish). The Nishiki Food Court was set up to thin the crowds and prevent tourists from walking while eating (a social faux pas in Japan) by cramming some of the best-selling food stalls into a lively hallway illuminated by colorful lanterns and saturated by the smells of grilled meat and seafood. The wagyu sushi (one piece for ¥800, three pieces for ¥2,000), the Kyoto gyoza and karaage combo (¥1,000), and the seasonal seafood skewers are all good options, but there's plenty else to choose from—let your gut guide you. You'll also notice an eye-catching display of sake bottles running along the wall. Sample a few different styles here, starting at only ¥100 for a small glass—a good way to see if you like the drink before diving in at the deep end. It's open daily noon to 8pm; take bus 5 to Shijo Takakura (4 min.) or take a 9-minute walk from Shijo subway station.

Menbaka Fire Ramen ♥♥ RAMEN This ramen shop has a very Instagram-able gimmick—setting a bowl of noodles ablaze at the counter—but there's more to it than shock factor. The recipe for the soy sauce-based ramen, blended with chicken broth and charred spring onions, is more than 200 years old, while the technique of pouring flaming oil onto the bowl before serving was introduced in the 1980s to enhance the flavor of the onions on top. It's more expensive than your average bowl of noodles—the standard Fire Ramen now cost ¥3,000—but you're paying for both the experience and a rich, charry taste that differentiates it from its peers. After you order, the chef will show you instructions in English, asking you not to touch the noodles, stand up, scream, or run away (from which we can assume all the above have happened), and to put your arms behind your back for safety. Photos and videos are prohibited until after the flames peter out, but the chefs will happily take one of you once the dish is served. Note that this shop doesn't take reservations, so it's best to come outside peak lunch and dinner hours.

757–2, Minamiiseyacho. fireramen.com. ✆ **075-812-5818.** Ramen ¥3,000; ramen sets from ¥3,550. Bus: 6 or 206 to Senbon Marutamachi (7 min.).

Monaka Stand (もなかスタンド) ♥♥ VARIED JAPANESE Typical of a style of restaurant that's becoming common in Japan's major cities, this fusion of an izakaya and a gastropub has chefs whipping up Japanese classics with a European twist in an open kitchen. The staff are all young, attentive, and speak decent English. Take a seat at the counter, or one of the larger tables if you're in a group, and ask for the English menu—basically just the chef's recommendations in scrawled handwriting—where you'll find seasonal dishes like conger eel frites, eggplant steak, vegetable teppanyaki, tomato and sesame salad, green beans with butter and soy, and *omakase* sashimi. If you've never tried a Japanese sour—a shochu-based drink popular among the young—here's a good place to do so, with tasty concoctions such as watermelon, *sudachi* (a limelike citrus fruit), and "mojito style" sours. The plates are pretty small, but don't worry if you under-judge it—you can keep ordering as you go.

468 Kannondocho. instagram.com/monaka_stand. ✆ **075-366-4144.** Dinner ¥2,500–¥4,500. Daily 5pm–midnight (food last order 11pm; drinks 11:30pm). Bus: 50 to Nishinotoin (5 min.). Subway: Shijo-Karasuma (2 min.)

Pizza Salvatore Cuomo & Grill ♥♥ ITALIAN Instead of the usual Japanese greeting of *irashaimase!* when you walk into this restaurant, here you'll get a *buona sera!* And if it is indeed a fine evening and you're dying for pizza, there's no better place to be than here, with its very cool setting alongside the Kiyamachi canal. Seating is either outdoors or indoors, where a wall of glass faces the canal. The emphasis here is clearly on pizza, with more than a half-dozen varieties available in two different sizes (hearty appetites will find even the small one ample; daintier diners might want to share). Salads, pasta, and a few meat entrees like chicken or spareribs round out the menu.

90 Nakajima-cho. salvatore.jp. ✆ **075-212-4965.** Small pizzas ¥1,800–¥2,500; large pizzas ¥2,300–¥3,200. Daily 11:30am–3pm (last order 2:30pm) and 5–11pm (food last order 10pm; drinks 10:30pm). Subway: Kyoto Shiyakusho-mae (3 min.). Bus: 4, 5, 17, or 205 to Kawaramachi Sanjo (2 min.).

Rakuza Hareruya (楽坐青天家　四条烏丸, ハレルヤ) ♥♥ OBANZAI This shop serves classic *obanzai* (finger-food dishes native to Kyoto), not surprising given it's on the doorstep of Nishiki Market, colloquially known as "Kyoto's Kitchen" (see box on p. 331). The sharing plates are small but good value, so be liberal with your orders. Raw oysters, Kamo eggplant in umami stock, corn tempura, *oden* (fish, tofu, and veg stewed in a dashi broth) served with mushrooms, grilled Manganji chili peppers, simmered burdock with boiled spinach, steamed pork belly, and salt-grilled mackerel—this is dining in Kyoto as the locals do. There is an English menu, but it's a watered-down version of the Japanese one, so ask for both and use a translation app if you can. The restaurant has a cozy, traditional feel with sliding doors, polished wooden floors, and Japanese artworks; the large second-floor tatami room has the best seats in the house.

568 Kaiyacho. rakuza-0066.owst.jp. ✆ **075-251-1155.** Dinner ¥3,500–¥5,500. Mon–Sat 5–10:30pm (last order). Subway: Shijo (8 min.).

INEXPENSIVE

Kawa Cafe ♥♥♥ SWEETS This place is perfect for a coffee and dessert to break up a midday stroll. Take a seat on the shaded veranda overlooking the Kamo River and order a Mont Blanc or slice of cheesecake—two of the many European sweets Japan has made its own—and pair it with an espresso, a glass of wine, sake, ice green tea, or a locally brewed beer. If you need something more robust, the ¥1,600 set menu includes a main course (pizza, pasta, quiche, croque monsieur, or ramen), a soft drink, and a dessert. Provided the weather is decent, grab a table closest to the railing and keep an eye out for grey herons, majestic wading birds that glide along the Kamo River, which often carry creepy connotations in Japanese folklore. 176–1, Minoya-cho. kawa-cafe.com. ✆ **075-341-0115.** Lunch ¥1,600; sweets ¥900. Bus: 4, 7, 205 to Kawaramachi Gojo (8 min.).

Eastern Kyoto

EXPENSIVE

Hyotei (瓢亭) ♥♥♥ KAISEKI/BENTO Opened around 400 years ago as a teahouse to serve pilgrims on their way to Nanzenji Temple, this is one of Kyoto's oldest and most famous restaurants. It specializes in *kyo-kaiseki,* a multi-course meal that originated with the tea ceremony but has evolved into Kyoto's special cuisine. The setting is rustic and lovely, with individual teahouses spread around a beautiful garden with a pond. Kimono-clad women deliver your *kaiseki* meal to your private *tatami* room, much as they have been doing for centuries. The cuisine, the dishes they're served on, the outdoor scenery, and the gracious service all conspire to create the ultimate traditional Japanese experience. For travelers who find *kaiseki* prices prohibitive, adjoining the main restaurant is a modern annex (*bekkan*) with its own separate entrance, specializing in *shokado bento* (lunch boxes), served in a communal dining room with views of a garden, though the experience doesn't match that in the main restaurant.

In addition to set meals, there are also seasonal options. In July and August, a special breakfast called *asagayu* is available in the main restaurant (8–10am, ¥7,590); in the annex, it's available mid-March to November (8–11am, ¥5,445). From December to mid-March, the main restaurant offers the seasonal *uzuragayu* (quail porridge) meal (noon–1:30pm, ¥18,975). No matter where or when you dine, a boiled egg, traditionally served to Hyotei's guests since its founding, will be part of your meal. Note that reservations are required, secured with a credit card, and must be made either by your hotel or via secure reservation platforms Pocket Concierge and Table Check. Note, too, that you should dress respectfully (no T-shirts, shorts, or sandals). Only children older than 10 are allowed. If you want a time machine to old Kyoto, you can't get any closer than this. 35 Kusakawa-cho, Nanzenji. hyotei.co.jp/en. ✆ **075-771-4116.** Kaiseki lunches from ¥31,625, dinners from ¥37,950; shokado bento ¥7,260. Kaiseki Thurs–Tues noon–7:30pm; shokado bento Fri–Wed noon–2:30pm (last order). Subway: Keage (5 min.). Bus: 5 or 100 to Dobutsuen-mae (7 min.).

MODERATE

Junsei (順正) ♥♥ TOFU/KAISEKI/BENTO This well-known tofu restaurant near Nanzenji has been open since 1961, but its extensive garden and thatched-roof main building are even older, remnants of a medical school established in 1839 during the shogun era. It attracts tour groups, but it's still an authentic experience, and everything runs with smooth Japanese efficiency. As soon as you arrive you'll be given an English-language menu and asked what you'd like to eat, because that determines where you'll be seated in the restaurant's various buildings. If you order the house specialty—one of the *yudofu* set meals that includes tofu simmered in an earthen pot, vegetable tempura, grilled skewers of tofu, and an assortment of other dishes—you'll probably be led to an older building near the front of the property filled with antiques and overlooking the garden. Other set meals offer *yuba* and shabu-shabu.

Nanzenjimon-mae. to-fu.co.jp. ✆ **075-761-2311.** Yudofu meals ¥3,630–¥5,500; shabu-shabu from ¥11,000; kaiseki ¥11,000–¥16,500. Daily 11am–8pm (last order). Subway: Keage (5 min.). Bus: 5 to Nanzenji-Eikando-michi (7 min.).

Juugo (十五) ♥♥♥ SOBA Since appearing in an episode of the Netflix travel and cooking show, *Somebody Feed Phil,* this little white building has become one of Kyoto's most popular noodle shops. Its amiable head chef Akiya Ishibashi, who formerly worked in the women's fashion industry in Shanghai, now farms buckwheat in Otsu, just over the eastern hills that mark the edge of Kyoto City, and handmakes it into soba noodles. Why the drastic career change? He says he simply wanted to make soba for a living. The restaurant is sparsely designed, with only six seats and some cooking utensils on the wooden counter, with large windows looking onto the cherry tree–lined Tetsugaku-no-michi ("Philosopher's Path"). A glass partition divides the kitchen and the dining area; through this opening, you can watch Ishibashi, towel around his head like a samurai's *hachimaki,* as he sprinkles and sieves the brown flour, whacks and rolls the dough, and then hacks at it with large cleavers. The menu is refreshingly simple, with two options: cold soba with *tsuyu* dipping broth and soy sauce, or a buckwheat dumplinglike dish called *sobagaki.* The cold soba is the most popular. The noodles are thicker and chewier than those you'll find elsewhere in Japan, but they're perfect vehicles for the umami broth and pair wonderfully with the mildly sweet soy sauce. You'll have to reserve a seat at Juugo in advance—use the Table Check booking link on the restaurant's Instagram page, where you'll also order and pay for your food. Reservations open on the 15th of each month for the following month. The restaurant closes occasional days here and there, and shuts down completely July through August and December through mid-March. Ishibashi is considering opening another branch, tentatively called Juugo Farm, near where he cultivates his buckwheat.

71–6 Jodoji Kamiminamidacho. instagram.com/15_soba. Daily 10am–4pm. Closed July–Aug and Dec to mid-Mar. Soba or sobagaki ¥3,500. Bus: 5 or 7 to Jodoji (6 min.).

Ramen Nishiki (らーめん錦) ♥♥ RAMEN When people say that ramen is one of the most innovative spaces in Japan's culinary world, it's places like Ramen Nishiki they're referring too. Sure, the deep-green matcha and citrus soup is gimmicky, but there's no denying the jolt of umami in the salt-based broth flavored with slow-cooked sea bream or the zingy

A cup of the deeply flavorful green soup at Nishiki Ramen.

dipping sauce for the *tsukemen* sets. The sides aren't your standard gyoza-and-rice fare, but include deep-fried eggplant, grilled duck meat, smorgasbords of grade A4 wagyu, and assorted vegetables like *shishito* peppers and king trumpet mushrooms cooked over flame. Other boons for foreign visitors: menus are in English and vegan ramen options are available.
416 Hashimotocho. ramen-nishiki.com. ✆ **075-606-5210.** Ramen ¥1,200–¥1,650, set meals ¥2,080–¥6,600. Tues–Sat 11am–2:30pm and 6–10:30pm; Sun 11am–3:30pm (last order). Bus: 46, 201, 203, or 206 to Gion (3 min.). Subway: Sanjo Keihan (9 min.).

INEXPENSIVE

Kanoko (可乃古) ♥♥ SOBA This noodle shop combines two of Japan's best traditional ingredients, *soba* (buckwheat noodles) and green tea, to make an umami-filled, knock-out lunch. To create the handmade *cha-soba* (tea noodles), the chefs add green tea powder sourced from nearby Uji, one of Japan's chief tea-producing regions, and add it to the buckwheat flour mixture. With an earthy flavor and chewy texture, the resulting noodles are a perfect match for the restaurant's sweet and mild dashi broth, a secret in-house recipe. Lots of appealing options are on the menu: the Uji set; cha-soba with shrimp and veg tempura; or the Tempura Zen set, featuring two kinds of soba, three side dishes, a selection of tempura, and *inari-zushi* (rice in sweet, deep-fried tofu pouches). Ask for an *ozashiki* (banquet room) table, where you'll sit on the floor with your feet nestled in a well under the table and get great views of the property's miniature landscape garden. There are only 24 seats in the banquet room, and it closes at 3pm, so reservations are recommended. This shop is also on the doorstep of Fushimi Inari (p. 307), so consider lunching here after paying your respects at the hilltop shrine.
59 Fukakusa Inari Nakanocho. inari-kanoco.com. ✆ **075-641-4507.** Soba sets ¥1,150–¥2,750. Thurs–Mon 11am–3pm (last order). Train station: Inari (3 min.).

Western Kyoto

Seigein-in ♥♥ TOFU/VEGETARIAN If you're visiting Ryoanji Temple (p. 308) in northeastern Kyoto, there's no lovelier setting for a meal than this traditional restaurant, which calls itself the Ryoanji Seven Herb Tofu Restaurant in honor of its signature dish, *yudofu,* boiled tofu and vegetables topped with seven herbs. You can order it by itself, or as a set meal of *shojin ryori* (Buddhist vegetarian) with side dishes (no credit cards accepted; there's an English menu). Entrance to the restaurant, situated beside the Kyoyoike Pond on temple grounds, is along a small path that takes you past a stream, a small pond, a grove of maple and pine, and moss-covered grounds, which are also what you see as you dine seated on *tatami.* You'll know you're getting close to the place when you hear the *thonk* of a bamboo trough fed by a stream, which fills and hits against stone as it empties.

Ryoanji Temple. ✆ **075-462-4742.** Yudofu ¥1,800; yudofu vegetarian meal ¥3,800. Daily 10am–3pm (last order). Bus: 59 from Shijo Kawaramachi to Ryoanji-mae (2 min.), or 50 to Ritsumeikan Daigaku-mae (4 min.).

KYOTO SHOPPING

As the nation's capital for more than 1,000 years, Kyoto spawned numerous crafts and exquisite art forms that catered to the elaborate tastes of the imperial court and the upper classes. Kyoto today is still renowned for its **crafts,** including Nishijin textiles, Yuzen-dyed fabrics, Kyo-yaki (pottery fired in Kyoto), fans, dolls, cutlery, gold-leaf work, umbrellas, paper lanterns, bamboo crafts, combs, *Noh* masks, cloisonné, and lacquerware.

GREAT SHOPPING AREAS The majority of Kyoto's tiny specialty shops are in central Kyoto's downtown. The rectangular grid formed by **Kawaramachi Dori, Shijo Dori, Nijo Dori,** and **Teramachi Dori** includes two covered shopping arcades and specialized shops selling lacquerware, combs and hairpins, knives and swords, tea and tea-ceremony implements, and more—including, of course, clothing and accessories for customers of all ages. Here, too, is the **Nishiki Food Market** (p. 331).

For antiques, woodblock prints, and art galleries, head toward the high-end **Shinmonzen Dori** and **Furumonzen Dori** in Gion, which parallel Shijo Dori to the north on the east side of the Kamo River, as well as **Teramachi Dori** north of Oike, home also of the **Kyoto Antiques Center** (p. 338). You'll find pottery and souvenir shops in abundance on the roads leading to Kiyomizu Temple, particularly the hill known as **Chawanzaka** (Teacup Slope).

For clothing, accessories, and modern goods, **department stores** (see p. 339) are conveniently located in central Kyoto near the Shijo-Kawaramachi intersection and Kyoto Station. Near Kyoto Station are also two large **shopping malls** selling everything from clothing and shoes to stationery and local souvenirs: an underground mall beneath the station, and Aeon, southwest of the station across Hachijo Dori. The **Kyoto-Yodobashi** mall, on Karasuma Dori a block north of Kyoto Tower, contains the Yodobashi Camera electronics store, fashion boutiques, and restaurants.

Crafts & Specialty Shops

Aritsugu (有次) ♥♥ The fact that this family-owned business is located at the Nishiki Food Market is appropriate, as it sells hand-wrought knives and other handmade cooking implements—sushi knives, bamboo steamers, pots, pans, and cookware used in the preparation of traditional Kyoto cuisine—as well as *ikebana* scissors. In business for more than 450 years, the shop counts the city's top chefs among its customers; look for its display cases of knives. Nishiki-Koji Dori, Gokomachi Nishi-iru. aritsugu.co.jp. ✆ **075-221-1091.** Thurs–Tues 10am–4pm. Subway: Shijo (8 min.). Bus: 4, 5, 10, 11, 12, 17, 32, 46, 59, 62, 63, 64, 65, 66, 67, 104, 201, 203, 207, or 205 to Shijo Kawaramachi (5 min.).

Harada Chagu Shoten Tea Ceremony Shop (有原田茶具商店) ♥♥ This family-run shop near Nishiki Market has everything you'd need for a DIY Japanese tea ceremony: bowls painted with seasonal imagery, cast-iron *chagama* (water pots), bamboo whisks, matcha powder, tea scoops, lacquered caddies, dessert plates, and serving trays. Of the husband-and-wife duo who own the place, the wife speaks better English and can point you in the right direction if you're not sure what you're looking for. A set including a tea bowl, whisk, scoop, and powdered tea may go for as little as ¥6,000, rising commensurately with the quality of the craftsmanship. These sets also come with English-language instructions on how to make matcha the traditional way. ***Note:*** This is not a duty-free shop, because all

Anchoring the mall of the same name, the Kyoto Yodobashi store is bursting with the latest electronic gadgets.

SHOPPING FOR SECONDHAND kimono

Flea markets, especially the one at Toji Temple (see "Markets," p. 339), are good hunting grounds for inexpensive used kimono. **Kikuya,** tucked away in a residential neighborhood on Manjuji Dori, east of Sakaimachi (✆ **075-351-0033;** Mon–Sat 9am–7:30pm), on the second floor of a nondescript building, has three rooms packed with used kimono (both antique and modern), *haori* (short kimono-like jackets, traditionally worn by men), *obi* (kimono sashes, often worn as scarves), and kimono accessories for both adults and kids. Another good place is **Chicago,** a thrift shop about halfway down the Teramachi covered shopping arcade (✆ **075-212-5391;** daily 11am–8pm); its entire second floor is devoted to used kimono (including wedding kimono), *obi, jinbei* (men's pajamas), and *yukata* (cotton sleeping kimono). **Vintage Kimono AN Gion** (37–4 Bishamoncho; ✆ **075-201-9949;** Mon–Sat 11am–7pm) is in amongst the action in Higashiyama, although it's hidden down an entryway and easy to miss. The kimono inside run the gamut from cheap (and kind of ugly) to elaborately expensive and everything in between. Men shopping for kimono might appreciate the neutral-toned robes with old samurai crests emblazoned on the fabric; you can purchase a set with a sash for around ¥6,000.

items are made by independent Kyoto artisans and are already sold at fair rates. Tachiuri Higashi-machi, Fuyacho Nishiiru, Shijo-Dori. ✆ **075-351-2608.** Mon–Tues and Thurs–Sat 10am–5pm. Bus: 5, 17, or 19 to Shijo Takakura (4 min.). Subway: Shijo (9 min.).

Ippodo (一保堂) ♥♥ In business since 1717, this famous shop is a good place not only to buy high-quality Japanese green teas but to learn more about them. Pick up the shop's English-language brochure, which explains the different varieties, from *matcha* to *sencha* to *genmaicha,* or sample them at the shop's hands-on tearoom, **Kaboku,** where you can experience brewing techniques for the tea of your choice. In a nod to modern times, Ippodo also sells teabags. Teramachi Dori, north of Nijo. global.ippodo-tea.co.jp. ✆ **075-211-3421.** Daily 10am–5pm (Kaboku 10am–4:30pm), closed 2nd Wed of month. Subway: Kyoto Shiyakusho-mae (5 min.). Bus: 4, 10, 17, 32, 59, 104, or 205 (5 min.).

Kyoto Antiques Center ♥ On Teramachi, known for its antiques and specialty shops, this store is the largest, with about 20 vendors offering both Western and Japanese antiques and curios. It's a fun place to browse for jewelry, lacquerware, pottery, and dolls. East side of Teramachi, north of Nijo Dori. ✆ **075-222-0793.** Wed–Mon 10:30am–6pm; closed 3rd Mon of month. Bus: 4, 10, 17, 32, 59, 104, and 205 to Kyoto Shiyakushomae (7 min.).

Kyoto Handicraft Center ♥♥♥ For one-stop shopping for Japanese souvenirs and crafts, your best bet is the city's largest craft, gift, and souvenir center, in business more than 80 years and founded by the present owner's grandfather. Its two buildings offer pearls, woodblock prints, lacquerware, pottery, dolls, kimono, ornamental swords, samurai armor, iron teapots, wind chimes, chopsticks, cloisonné, lunch boxes, incense, Nishijin textile goods, sake and sake cup sets, food items, *furoshiki* (cloth used for wrapping gifts), T-shirts, and refrigerator magnets—and that's just for starters. In addition to a tourist office (where you can also exchange money) and a kimono rental service, it provides workspace for artisans producing their various crafts, including woodblock printing and the production of damascene. You can also try your own hand at craft activities, including cloisonne, clay bell doll painting, and woodblock printing. Classes are ¥2,200 each and last between 45 minutes and an hour; they usually require a minimum of 10 persons and reservation 2 weeks in advance. 17 Shogoin Entomi-cho, on Marutamachi Dori, north of Heian Shrine. kyotohandicraftcenter.com. ✆ **075-761-8001.** Daily 10am–7pm. Bus: 93, 201, 202, 203, 204, or 206 to Kumano-jinja-mae (1 min.).

Department Stores

Department stores are good places to shop for Japanese items and souvenirs, including pottery, lacquerware, and kimono as well as clothing, foodstuffs, and everyday items. **JR Kyoto Isetan,** located in Kyoto Station (kyoto.wjr-isetan.co.jp; ✆ **075-352-1111;** daily 10am–8pm), is Kyoto's most fashionable department store, specializing in women's imported and domestic clothing. In central Kyoto, **Daimaru,** on Shijo Dori west of Takakura (daimaru.co.jp/kyoto; ✆ **075-211-8111;** daily 10am–8pm), is Kyoto's largest department store, with everything from clothing to electronic goods spread over nine floors (and branches of well-known restaurants on the eighth floor). Nearby are **Marui,** on the southeast corner of the Shijo-Kawaramachi intersection (✆ **075-257-0101;** daily 10:30am–8:30pm), aimed at young shoppers with nine floors of fashion, housewares, and restaurants; and **Takashimaya,** across the street at the southwest corner of the Shijo-Kawaramachi intersection (takashimaya.co.jp/kyoto; ✆ **075-221-8811;** daily 10am–8pm), one of Japan's oldest and most respected department stores with a good selection of traditional crafts. **Tokyu Hands** (kyoto.tokyu-hands.co.jp; ✆ **075-254-3109;** daily 10am–8:30pm), on Shijo Dori east of Karasuma Dori, sells tools and gadgets for hobbyists, as well as kitchenware, beauty goods, and other items.

Markets

Many shrines and temples in Kyoto hold outdoor markets one day a month. The largest flea market in Japan is held at **Toji Temple** (15-min. walk southwest of Kyoto Station; toji.or.jp/en/index.html; ✆ **075-691-3325;** 8am–4pm), on the 21st of each month. Its history stretches back more than 700 years, when pilgrims began flocking to Toji Temple to pay their respects to Kobo Daishi, who founded the Shingon sect of Buddhism. Today, Toji Temple, a World Heritage Site, is still a center for the Shingon sect, and its market (popularly known as Kobo-san) is a colorful affair with booths selling Japanese antiques, old kimono, ethnic goods, flowers, bonsai, dried foods, foodstuffs, crafts, odds and ends, and many other items. Worshipers come to pray before a statue of Kobo Daishi and to have their wishes written on wooden slats by temple calligraphers. Even if you don't buy anything, the festive atmosphere makes it worth checking out. The largest Kobo-san markets are in December and January. A smaller market, devoted entirely to Japanese antiques, is held at Toji Temple on the first Sunday of each month.

Toji Temple's monthly flea market is Japan's largest.

Commemorating the scholar/poet Sugawara Michizane, the **Tenjin-san market** held at **Kitano Tenmangu Shrine** (✆ **075-461-0005;** 8am–dusk) the 25th of every month is a large market with a bit of everything—antiques, used clothing, ceramics, food—in a beautiful setting, especially in spring when plum trees are in bloom. Kitano Shrine is on Imadegawa Dori between Nishi-oji and Senbon; take bus no. 10, 50, 101, 102, and 203 to the Kitano Tenmangu-mae stop. Next to Chion-Ji Temple in northeast Kyoto, the **Chion-ji market** (✆ **075-691-3325;** 9am–4pm), held the 15th of each month, is devoted to handmade goods and crafts, including pottery and clothing. To reach it, take bus no. 17, 102, 201, 203, or 206 to Hyakumanben at the Higashioji and Imadegawa intersection.

If you're keen on bringing Japanese foodstuffs home with you—like *katsuobushi, konbu* seaweed, *tsukemono* pickles, or dried shiitake—or you want to sample a variety of meat skewers and sweets, pencil in a trip to **Nishiki Food Market** (see box on p. 331). With a 400-plus-year history, this covered shopping arcade in the heart of downtown Kyoto on Nishiki-Koji Dori (1 block north of Shijo Dori) has approximately 135 open-fronted shops and stalls selling fish, seasonal produce (like chestnuts in the fall), flowers, eggs, dried, fresh and pickled vegetables, teas, confectionary, fruit, kitchenware, and—to cash in on an increasing number of foreign visitors—crafts, souvenirs, and street food. This is where locals, as well as the city's finest restaurants and inns, buy their food. It's open from the early hours to about 6pm; some shops close on either Wednesday or Sunday.

ENTERTAINMENT & NIGHTLIFE

From the geisha district of Gion to the bars and restaurants lining Pontocho, Kyoto is utterly charming and romantic at night. Begin with a walk along the banks of the Kamo River—it's a favorite place for young couples in love. In summer, restaurants stretching north and south of Shijo Dori along the river erect outdoor wooden platforms on stilts over the water.

There are many annual events and dances, including **Miyako Odori** dances in April and **Gion Odori** dances in November, featuring *geiko* and *maiko* (geisha and apprentice geisha) dressed in elaborate costume. In December, ***kabuki*** is presented at the Minamiza Theater. Every spring, coinciding with cherry blossom season, the **Kyotographie** festival (kyotographie.jp/en) celebrates photography, using atmospheric exhibition spaces like temple courtyards and traditional streets.

To find out what's happening during your stay, check online at **kyoto.travel** and **kansaiscene.com**.

The Major Nightlife Districts

PONTOCHO & KIYAMACHI

Pontocho is a narrow alley that parallels the Kamo River's western bank, stretching from Shijo Dori north to Sanjo Dori. Once riddled with geisha houses and other members-only establishments, it's now lined with bars, clubs, restaurants, and hostess bars. Pontocho makes for a fun walk as you watch Japanese and visitors from around the world engaging in revelry.

Kyoto's liveliest nightlife district, with bar after bar, is along **Kiyamachi,** another small street that parallels Pontocho just to the west and runs beside a small canal.

GION

A small neighborhood of plain wooden buildings in Higashiyama-ku on the eastern side of the Kamo River, Gion doesn't look anything like what you'd expect of a nightlife district—there's little neon in sight, and the atmosphere is almost austere and solemn. Gion instead is a shrine to Kyoto's past, an era when geisha numbered in the thousands. The geisha district is centered primarily on Hanamikoji Dori, which translates as "Narrow Street for Flower Viewing." Gion's narrow streets are great for strolling; a popular time to take a walk through the neighborhood is around dusk, when geisha are on their way to their evening appointments. Perhaps you'll see one clattering in her high *geta* (wooden shoes). She'll be dressed in a brilliant kimono, her face a chalky white, and her hair adorned with hairpins and ornaments. From geisha houses, music and laughter lilt from behind paper screens, sounding all the more inviting because you can't enter. Don't take it personally; not even Japanese venture inside without the proper introductions. A number of bars and restaurants in Gion are open to outsiders, however. ***Note:*** Suppress any urge to take photos; Kyoto's geisha have been treated like zoo exhibits by some tourists in the past couple years, which has caused locals to ban non-residents from certain areas of the neighborhood. Please exercise restraint, don't get in their way, and don't try to coerce them into taking photographs with you.

As part of your stroll around Gion, you may want to visit **Gion Corner ♥♥** (Yasaka Hall, 570–2 Minamigawa; kyoto-gioncorner.com;

THE ART OF THE geisha

Contrary to popular Western misconceptions, geisha are not prostitutes; the word "courtesan" is often used as an inelegant, and frankly misguided, translation (though it would be a stretch to claim sex was never part of the geisha-customer dynamic). Rather, they're trained experts in conversation and the traditional arts of music and dance (*geiko*, as they're usually referred to in Kyoto, translates as "art professional"). Their primary role is to make men feel like kings when they're in the soothing enclave of the geisha house. Estimates put the number of working geisha in Kyoto at somewhere between 100 and 200, with perhaps fewer than 70 in Gion, the largest of the five geisha districts. (For purposes of comparison, prior to World War II, there were around 80,000.) In today's high-tech world, few women are willing to undergo the years of rigorous training necessary to learn how to conduct the tea ceremony, play the *shamisen* (a three-stringed instrument), and perform ancient court dances. *Maiko* (geisha in training) are not even allowed to have cellphones.

Though you will probably not be able to enter a geisha house, the recently opened **Gion Museum** (gion-museum.com; ¥1,500 adults, ¥700 students, free for children under 5; daily 11am–7pm, closed first and third Wed of the month) is a good introduction to the world of geiko and maiko culture. **Gion Corner** on Hanamikoji Dori (p. 341) also offers a taste of geisha culture, with nightly performances of dance, puppetry, and other traditional arts. You may also want to consider joining a guided **Gion Night Tour ♥♥** (waraido.com/gion-walk-en; ¥3,000; Mon, Wed, and Fri 5:30–7:30pm). Lasting about 1 hour and 40 minutes, these informative tours stroll past entertainment and boardinghouses while describing what life is like for a *maiko* as she prepares to become a *geiko*.

✆ **075-561-1119**), which presents a quick and convenient introduction to Japan's ancient cultural arts: Short demonstrations of the tea ceremony, Japanese flower arranging, *koto* (Japanese harp) music, *gagaku* (ancient court music and dance), *kyogen* (*Noh* comic plays), *kyomai* (Kyoto-style dance) performed by *maiko,* and *bunraku* (puppetry), all described in detail in an English-language program. The shows are definitely tourist-oriented, but not a bad way to spend an hour. Before or after the show, visit the Maiko Gallery with its small display of *maiko* hairstyles and accessories. Performances are held nightly at 6pm and 7pm (Dec to mid-Mar Tues–Fri only; no performances July 16 or August 16); tickets cost ¥5,000 adults (¥6,500 premium seats), ¥3,850 high-school and university students, ¥3,300 children.

The Live Music Scene

Hello Dolly ♥♥ Open since 1939 but with a retro look more reminiscent of the 1950s—velvet-upholstered chairs and old album covers in the front window—Hello Dolly offers regular live jazz nights, with three sets at 8, 9:30, and 11pm. When no event is on, it plays classic jazz recordings. It's a very civilized and old-school place in fast-changing Pontocho. Pontocho. hello-dolly.webnode.jp. ✆ **075-241-1728.** Daily 5:30pm–12:30am. Cover

¥900, live charge ¥950–¥1,100 (more if staying for 2-plus performances). Bus: 4, 5, 10, 11, 12, 17, 32, 46, 59, 62, 63, 64, 65, 66, 67, 104, 201, 203, 207, or 205 to Shijo Kawaramachi (4 min.).

Le Club Jazz ♥♥ For serious jazz fans, this has been the real deal for more than 25 years, with musicians from around Japan performing on a simple stage six nights a week. It's in a contemporary concrete building on Sanjo Dori, but its upstairs entrance can be hard to find. The website is in Japanese only, and looks like it's riddled with malware, but there is a contents section with some English so you can at least get an idea of the schedule and cover fee. Arimoto Building, 2nd floor, Sanjo Dori Gokomachi. web.kyoto-inet.or.jp/people/ktsin. ✆ **075-211-5800.** Cover ¥1,500–¥3,000, including 1 or 2 drinks (may be higher for special shows). Tues–Sat 7pm–midnight, Sun 6–11pm. Subway: Kyoto Shiyakusho-mae (3 min.). Bus: 4, 5, 10, 11, 17, 32, 59, 62, 63, 64, 65, 66, 67, 104 or 205 to Kawaramachi Sanjo (4 min.).

Live Spot RAG ♥♥♥ This is one of Kyoto's oldest live clubs, established in 1981 and still pulling in the college-age crowd with mostly Japanese bands that play jazz but also rock, acoustic, and fusion. It's popular and can fill up fast, so try to buy tickets in advance (you also get a slight discount with advance purchases); students also often get discounts. Live music usually starts around 7 or 7:30pm. After the events end, it winds down to become a mellow bar, so you might just want to drop in for a drink. Empire Building, 5th floor, Kiyamachi Dori, Sanjo Agaru. ragnet.co.jp. ✆ **075-241-0446.** Nightly 6pm–midnight (weekends may open earlier). Cover ¥2,000–¥10,000, plus 2-drink/dish min. Subway: Kyoto Shiyakusho-mae (3 min.). Bus: 4, 5, 10, 11, 17, 32, 59, 62, 63, 64, 65, 66, 67, 104, or 205 to Kawaramachi Sanjo (2 min.).

The Bar Scene

Atlantis ♥ Located on Pontocho's east (river) side not far from Shijo Dori, this cocktail lounge is recommended mostly for its outside deck overlooking the Kamo River. Otherwise, it's a small, pleasant bar, where you might try one of its signature drinks, such as its orange liqueur and tonic with a green-tea flavor; it also stocks scotch, bourbon, rum, and brandy. There's a ¥1,000 cover charge, but only when it's busy. 161 Matsumoto-cho. atlantis.net.co.jp. ✆ **075-241-1621.** Daily 6pm–1am. Bus: 4, 5, 10, 11, 12, 17, 32, 46, 59, 59, 62, 63, 64, 65, 66, 67, 104, 201, 203, 207, or 205 to Shijo Kawaramachi (4 min.).

Bar Cask ♥♥ Right in the thick of Pontocho, this second-floor bar is usually crammed full after dark, mostly with foreigners (probably because there's a sign in English outside). While that could be a plus or negative, depending on your disposition, it makes it a good place to meet other travelers. The drinks menu is extensive and features a wide range of whiskeys, including Japanese brands like Hibiki and Taketsuru, as well as smoky Islay scotches like Laphroaig. Everything's reasonably priced, even with the 10% charge levied on foreign visitors for all drinks. Tables are available but the bar seats are more communal. If this place is full, there's a similar establishment on the floor above that might be able to host you. 2F 203 Shimokorikicho. barcaskponto.wixsite.com/barcask. ✆ **075-256-8337.** Daily 6pm–2am. Bus: 4, 5, 7, 205, 17, or 19 to Shijo Kawaramachi (6 min.). Subway: Gion-Shijo (7 min.).

Bars and restaurants line narrow Pontocho, drawing crowds of revelers.

Gear ♥♥ Hidden down a gloomy alleyway, the weather-beaten wooden door is barely noticeable but for the illuminated "G" above it. It might look creepy, but when you push it open, pass the red drapery in the anteroom, and survey the scene, you'll be pleasantly surprised. Comfy leather seats, guitars on floor stands and hanging from the walls, liqueurs and spirts glinting on the shelves behind the bar, bluesy rock *kerranging* out of the sound system—perhaps the owner is there, too, wearing his Stetson like a Japanese Billy Rae Cyrus and smoking a cigar. Gear *feels* exclusive but is actually super welcoming, and the cover charge is only ¥300. You can also purchase a range of cigars, like Cohiba, Hoyo de Monterrey and Montecristo, from ¥800 apiece. Basically, if you jibe with Gear's mantra—"Alcohol, movies, rock and roll, and sometimes cigars"—you'll probably be right at home here. 242 Kugigakushikakucho, Nishi-iru Fukouji, Karasuma-dori. bar-gear.biz. ✆ **075-201-3622.** Daily 7pm–3am. Subway: Shijo (4 min.).

Spring Valley Brewery ♥♥ The lure here is Spring Valley's own craft beer, as well as brews from other small Japanese breweries. Ensconced in a renovated *machiya,* it's big also on farm-to-table dishes, like smoked lamb, grilled fish with miso, craft pizzas, and rice and noodles. Beer flights, 3 for ¥1,200 or 6 for ¥2,000, are good value. Takamiya-cho 287–2. springvalleybrewery.jp2. ✆ **075-231-4960.** Daily 11:30am–11pm. Subway: Shijo (7 min.) or Kawaramachi (5 min.). Bus: 5, 11, 12, 17, 32, 46, 201, 203, or 207 to Shijo Takakura (5 min.).

Umineko (スタンドうみねこ コト) ♥♥ Named after a species of seagull, this taproom is housed in a building reminiscent of old Kyoto, but the stripped-back interior of smooth concrete, stainless steel, wall gauges, and seats made from scrap wood is very much that of a modern craft beer bar. Fridges host hundreds of artsy beer cans and bottles from around the world, but it's the drafts from Japanese microbreweries that make this place worth the visit, with a rotating menu of 20 on offer on any given day. Rather than drawing in tourist crowds, this is the kind of place locals go for a beer after work. That said, the menu is in English, so you should have no problem ordering. 160–3 Takoyacho. cyclo-inc.jp/services/umineko-koto.php. ✆ **050-3134-4635.** Mon–Fri 4–11pm (from 1pm weekends). Bus: 4, 5, 7, 205, 17, or 19 to Shijo Kawaramachi (4 min.). Subway: Gion-Shijo (10 min.).

EXCURSIONS FROM KYOTO

The Tango Peninsula ♥♥♥

100km (26 miles) NW of Kyoto

Kyoto City is so famous and romanticized throughout the world that it's easy to forget there's more to Kyoto Prefecture than Japan's former capital city. On the **Tango Peninsula,** an area known also as Kyotango and Kyoto by the Sea, you can venture deep into Japan's ancient past, because everything in Tango harks back to something ancestral. Some even argue that this peninsula on the Sea of Japan coast, with its humid climate and frequent rainfall, is where rice was first planted, and sake first brewed as a potent tonic and spiritual offering to the *kami,* or Shinto spirits. Artifacts uncovered near the coast suggest humans have been here for more than 30,000 years.

The peninsula also has a 1,300-year tradition of silk production—it was the starting point of a de facto silk road to Kyoto during the Edo period, when *chirimen* silk, known for its puckered texture and durability, was invented here. An even older technique called *fuji-ori* (wisteria weaving) had its roots in the Jomon period (14,000–300 B.C.). *Fuji-ori* was thought to have died out, until in 1962 it was discovered that women in Kamiseya Village were still making clothes and materials, as well as bags for female pearl divers, from woven wisteria fibers. The nearly extinct craft has seen a minor revival since, with the Tango Wisteria Preservation Society established in 1989. Tango is also home to lacquerware and washi paper artisans, swordsmiths and lantern makers, and a small but legendary kimono producer, **Tamiya Raden,** that uses a secret technique to weave kimono fabric inlaid with mother-of-pearl shell. The rural landscape is dotted with sake and craft beer breweries, home cooks extolling the virtues of local cuisine culture, innovative chefs retracing their culinary roots, and fisheries aiming for more sustainable farming methods.

THE TANGO PENINSULA'S blue zone SECRETS

The Tango Peninsula has been identified as a Blue Zone: a region abundant in centenarians, people who live to be 100 years old. The Japanese, and Okinawans in particular, are famed for their longevity, but according to a 2019 study the Tango Peninsula might be the longest-lived region in the country, with 2.8 times more centenarians than the national average. The oldest man in history, Jiroemon Kimura, spent his life here, dying in 2013 at the age of 116. Residents credit their diet: red meat is eaten sparingly, fish and seaweed are consumed in abundance, and the volcanic soil grows a wide range of produce, from edamame to Manganji peppers to sweet potatoes to an array of fruits, from melons and grapes to berries and peaches. But arguably the most important ingredient of all is a humble one: the fungal mold *koji,* containing up to 100 enzymes that facilitate digestion and a vital ingredient in miso, soy sauce, vinegar, and sake, all of which are produced prolifically in the region.

If you want to get a holistic view of life in Tango, an overnight stay is a good idea (so I've recommended some accommodation options), but a day trip is feasible if you're willing to leave Kyoto early in the morning; so much the better if you can rent a car.

ESSENTIALS

GETTING THERE Amanohashidate is the main entry point to the peninsula. Take the **JR Hashidate Line** from Kyoto Station to Amanohashidate Station (some trains require you to switch to the **Tango Relay Line** at Fukuchiyama), which takes 2 hours and costs ¥5,000. You can use your JR Pass or IC card, but if you have to switch to the Tango Relay Line, you'll need to buy a separate ticket for that leg of the journey; look for the kanji "天橋立"on the ticket vending machine at Fukuchiyama (cash only) or tell a staff member where you're going to and they should be able to help. The transit time can be quite quick, so the safest option is to purchase a ticket at Kyoto Station. Passes enabling travel on local, rapid, and limited express Kyoto Tango Railway trains, local buses from Amanohashidate, and some other forms of transport, are available at Kyoto Station or online at **willer-travel.com/en/train/tantetsu**. One-day passes cost ¥3,550; 2-day passes ¥4,550. Alternatively, you can get a bus from the north side of Kyoto Station on Shiokoji-dori to Amanohashidate Station. The journey takes around 2 hours and costs ¥3,200.

Having a car will make your journey through Kyotango much easier. **Times Car Rental** (timescar-rental.com), **Nippon-Rent-a-Car** (nippon-rentacar.co.jp), and **Toyota** (rent.toyota.co.jp) all have branches at Kyoto Station. I prefer Times, whose fees start at ¥7,700 for a compact car for 24 hours, but that's a matter of brand loyalty more than anything else; Toyota and Nippon-Rent-a-Car are equally reliable and have similar prices. The drive from Kyoto Station to Amanohashidate takes around 1¾ hours.

VISITOR INFORMATION You'll find the **Amanohashidate Tourist Information Center** in the train station; look for the counter with a rack

Where to Start in Tango?

As more tourists cotton on to the beauty and heritage of the Tango Peninsula, suppliers in the region are dealing with unprecedented demand. To help locals mitigate overtourism, consider using Kyoto by the Sea (**kyotobythesea.com**), an English-language destination management organization (DMO) that helps guests book travel experiences and liaises with local service providers. This will come at a cost but saves a lot of hassle. The DMO has a platform on its website where guests can reserve experiences directly, such as sake tasting, a tea ceremony, cooking workshops, fruit picking, or fishing experiences. Prices for these range from ¥4,000 to ¥30,000, but some may not offer English support. **Tabel Table** (p. 350), which offers cooking classes, can also help with bookings and transport, or you can book a tour with **Get Your Guide** (getyourguide.com/) for ¥9,800 that includes transport to and from Kyoto, as well as visits to Amanohashidate, Chionji Temple, a hot spring, and Ine.

of pamphlets and maps beside it. You can enquire about excursions, bike rentals, hotels, and seasonal discount coupons here. For more info, call ✆ **0772-22-8030** or go to amanohashidate.jp. There's also a tourist information center in **Ine** (491 Hitara, Yosa-gun Ine-cho; ine-kankou.jp; ✆ **0772-32-0277**), a seaside town that makes it onto most Tango Peninsula travel itineraries. The staff here can help you book lodging in one of the village boathouses or arrange ferry cruises and cycling tours.

GETTING AROUND The Tango Peninsula is not the best-connected corner of Japan; trains are infrequent and buses seem to stop at every homestead between the mountains and the sea. If you've purchased one of the Tango Relay Line travel passes (see p. 346), you can use most buses and trains in the region for no additional cost. Two trains you may find useful are the **Tantetsu Miyamai-Miyatoyo Line** and the **Tango Relay Line,** both of which travel east-west across the peninsula. Otherwise, you can use local buses between Amanohashidate and Ine. But given that not all areas are accessible by public transport, it's wise to organize excursions through local providers with transport included, or even better, rent your own car.

EXPLORING THE TANGO PENINSULA

Arrive early; the 7:32am train from Kyoto Station will get you to **Amanohashidate** by 9:33am. Exit the station and walk 5 minutes to Kaisen Bridge, connecting the mainland to the famous sandbar from which the station takes its name. *Amanohashidate* means "**Bridge of Heaven,**" and it's little wonder those who first viewed the sandbar from above remarked on it with divine exultation. Swerving dragonlike across Miyazu Bay (dragons tend to be sea-dwelling creatures in Japanese lore), covered in dense thickets of pine, it was once considered a connective thread between heaven and earth. It's only 20m (66 ft.) across at its widest, and at its narrowest points you may feel like you're walking across the sea. On the eastern side, sedimentary deposits have formed white sand beaches, from which you can wade into the water if the weather's nice and watch the small cruise ferries drift by. There's also a tea shop and cafe here, **Hashidate Chaya** (amanohashidate.jp; ✆ **077-2223-363;** daily 9am–5pm except Thurs). Stop for clams and rice, sweetened *zenzai* soup, or tea and coffee.

Cloaked in pine forest, Amanohashidate is a beautiful long sandbar snaking across Miyazu Bay.

It'll take about 45 minutes to walk the length of the sandbar (15 min. by bicycle). At the far end, you'll reach the **Fuchu** cable car and chairlift station. From here you can take a 4-minute cable car or 6-minute chair lift (return tickets ¥800, ¥400 children, free with Kyoto Tango Railway pass) to the **Kasamatsu Park Sky Deck Observatory.** The name makes it sound grandiose and soaring, but in reality it's a small wooden platform, 130m (425 ft.) above sea level, offering great views of Amanohashidate. If you're so inclined you can look at the sandbar *matanozoki*-style, by turning your back and bending down to look at it through your legs. The logic goes that this flips sea and sky, making the sandbar *really* look like a bridge across heaven. (It's also possible to hike up to Kasamatsu Park, but the route is a circuitous 6.5km/4 miles from the end of the sandbar and could take a couple of hours.) After this, return to Amanohashidate Station—if you've rented a bike, take the longer route back around the Miyazu Bay coastline (around 45 min.).

A half hour's drive north up the coast from Amanohashidate, **Ine** ♥♥ (pronounced "ee-nay") was the first town on the Tango Peninsula to land on the wider tourism radar, after it was designated one of The Most Beautiful Villages in Japan in 2008. The main attraction here is the 200 or so *funaya,* literally "boathouses," built on wooden stilts along the bay with domiciles on their upper floors and boat garages on their bottom floors—when reflected upon the water's looking-glass surface, they create a charming picture-book setting. Some of these properties now accommodate overnight guests, though they tend to fill up quickly; most can be booked three months in advance (see the Ine tourism accommodation page, **ine-kankou.jp/inns**, for available options). Because this is just a

Ine is known for its picturesque bayfront, lined with boathouses on stilts.

normal workaday fishing town with few shops and restaurants, the best way to appreciate Ine's charm is to view it from the water. Sightseeing boats depart the ferry port every 30 minutes between 9am and 4pm (¥1,200 per person, ¥600 children, free with Kyoto Tango Railway pass) for a 25-minute cruise. You can also book a 30-minute "sea taxi" across Ine bay—the boat holds between 11 and 20 passengers—for ¥1,000 per person (free for children). Staff in the tourism information center can help arrange this for you. You can also explore the area by bicycle, from ¥2,000 per hour, or take a guided e-bike tour of the Ine boat houses for ¥8,000 with **Kyoto Ocean** (kyoto-ocean.com/; ✆ **050-1743-3085**). And for lunch with a view, consider **Restaurant Funaya** (ine-aburaya.com/michi-no-eki; ✆ **0772-32-0680;** Wed–Mon 10am–7pm), where you can eat *kaisen-don* (seafood rice bowls) on tatami mats overlooking the bay. To get to Ine by bus from Amanohashidate Station, take the Ine Line (伊根線) bus (51 min.; fare ¥400).

For the rest of your time on the Tango Peninsula, choose from among the attractions below, based on your interests and available timeframe. Advance booking is essential.

Iio Jozo Vinegar Brewery ♥♥ A trip to a vinegar brewery might not sound like the most enlivening of travel experiences, but this isn't your average vinegar brewery. Now on its fifth-generation owner, this is the brewery from which many top sushi chefs and French haute cuisine restaurants source their rice wine vinegar, grown pesticide-free since 1964 on rainy rice terraces in the nearby mountains. Iio Jozo's vinegar is prized for its therapeutic properties—the *koji* is credited for that—with the most sought-after blend a secret recipe, aged for 14 years, that few are lucky enough to get their hands on. Thankfully, the brewery is less restrictive when it comes to touring the property, and organized tours (book through Kyoto by the Sea, p. 346, or Tabel Table, p. 350) include a tasting experience at the end. You can also buy Iio Jozo products in the brewery shop; the purple sweet potato and rice wine vinegar is an interesting option. The (now-retired) previous owner, Tsuyoshi Iio, drinks a cup every morning diluted with water, and claims it has done wonders for his gut health and brain functions. In fairness, he does look younger than his 70-some years. 373 Odasyukuno, Miyazu-shi. iio-jozo.co.jp. ✆ **0772-25-0015.** Brewery tour ¥5,500. Mon–Fri 9am–5pm. No public transport; arrange private transport when booking. Bicycle: 45 min. from Amanohashidate. Car: 15 min. from Amanohashidate.

Nippon Genshosha ♥♥ The three thirtysomething swordsmiths at Nippon Genshosha are young pups in an old dogs' field. Only around 200 people have a license to make samurai swords in Japan, and perhaps only half that number are doing so, most of them men in their 60s, 70s and 80s. But Nippon Genshosha, working out of a small sooty workshop amid the Tango farmlands, is striving to reinvent this dying craft, creating beautiful steel blades that can function as both statement-making art pieces and instruments of death. The trio of artisans has been raising the profile of their business and industry through a seriously polished website and high-production-quality YouTube videos, and they are open to showing visitors around their workshop and display hall. While this is one of the best ways to see the blade-forging process in action, you will need a translator if you don't speak Japanese. Best booked through Kyoto by the Sea (p. 346).

314 Tangochomiyake. gensho.jpn.com. ✆ **0772-66-3606.** Bus: From Amanohashidate Station take Tantetsu Miyamai-Miyatoyo Line to Mineyama Station, then Taiza Circular Line bus (間人循環線) to Miyake (三宅). Car: 40-min. drive west from Amanohashidate.

Tabel Table ♥♥♥ In a renovated traditional home, all smoky wooden beams and sliding doors, Junko Hamilton, a Kyoto native who spent 10 years living in Ireland, teaches Japanese cooking techniques to visitors—preparing local dishes with *koji*-based seasonings, or perhaps making miso from fermented soy beans. The classes are wonderful introductions to Tango produce as much as chances to hone your kitchen skills. Hamilton's approachable teaching style and *genki* (energetic) personality more than justifies the ¥30,000 price point for two guests (plus ¥10,000 for each additional guest). Classes last around 2½ hours, but you can customize them if you have more time. Hamilton also runs a cafe and restaurant service upon request, including a hearty Irish brunch or an *omakase* (chef's choice dinner course), using Tango ingredients. Multiday cooking courses are also available and feature transport and visits to the breweries mentioned below—enquire via email for details.

510 Okuono, Omiya-cho. tabeltable.net. ✆ **090-8448-6966.** Classes ¥30,000 for 2 guests. Bus: Take Tantetsu Miyamai-Miyatoyo Line from Amanohashidate to Kyo-Tango-Omiya Station, then 20 min. walk or request pickup in advance. Car: 20 min. from Amanohashidate.

Yosamusume Sake Brewery ♥♥ Sixth-generation sake brewer Shiro Nishihara now helms this brewery in the Yosa district of Tango, balancing his creativity with tried-and-tested methods of sake production. *Yosamusume* means daughter of Yosa, so celebrating the district's terroir is close to Nishihara's heart. But he also likes throwing paint over the canvas, developing unique sake blends that enhance the tartness and punch by using white wine yeast or local fruits. His farm-to-table rice wine owes its high quality to the mineral properties and cleanliness of Yosa spring water. Of course, similar claims are made in every sake brewing region of the country, but there's no denying the brewery's *daiginjo* (sake brewed from 50% polished rice) is super crisp and clean, while the sour and fizzy blends offer up some interesting variation. Tours and tastings can be organized though Tabel Table (above), and though he doesn't speak much English, Nishihara-san is a friendly and engaging host. You'll also want to peruse the small shop and set aside a few thousand yen for bringing some bottles home.

2–2 Yoza, Yosano, Yosa. yosamusume.com. ✆ **0772-42-2834.** Daily 8am–6pm. Bus: From Amanohashidate Station take Tantetsu Miyamai-Miyatoyo Line or Tango Relay Line to Yosano Station, then Yosa Line (与謝線) bus to Futatsu Iwa (二ツ岩). Car: A 25-min. drive south of Amanohashidate.

WHERE TO STAY & EAT ON THE TANGO PENINSULA

Kissuien ♥♥ If you're not staying in a *funaya* in Ine (see p. 348), this property is a good alternative, located in the heart of the peninsula and within walking distance of Mineyama Station. The business hotel-style rooms are good for an in-and-out stay, but there are also six spacious concept rooms, mixing Japanese and Western aesthetics, that offer cozier, more bespoke accommodation—these start at ¥15,000 per night. The facilities are generous and include a breakfast buffet and restaurant, a souvenir shop, a communal work and reading space, and an indoor public bath.

943 Mineyamacho Sugitani. kissuien.jp. ✆ **0772-62-5111.** 68 units. **Amenities:** Breakfast buffet; restaurant; souvenir shop; public bath; free Wi-Fi.

Suginoya ♥♥ UDON Adjoining a souvenir shop, this *udon* restaurant doesn't look like much. But after eating a bowl of thick, chewy noodles in the restaurant's signature umami soup, I told my dining companion that I'd happily bathe in a tub of it. Maybe that's why people come from all over the peninsula to eat at Suginoya. The food is cheap too, from ¥650 for *kake* udon (noodles in soup) to ¥1,350 for udon served with a basket of tempura. Most popular is udon with a tempura set of mochi and black *chikuwa* (a tubular fishcake made from sardines and horse mackerel; famous in Tango) for ¥1,000.

71 Ejiri, Miyazu (5-min. walk from north end of Amanohashidate sandbar). suginoyaudon.com. ✆ **0772-27-0040.** Udon (hot or cold) ¥650–¥1350. Daily 11:30am–3:30pm (last order).

Nara ♥♥

42km (26 miles) S of Kyoto; 48km (30 miles) E of Osaka

In early Japanese history, the nation's capital was moved to a new site each time a new emperor came to the throne. In 710, however, the first permanent Japanese capital was set up at **Nara.** Not that it turned out to be so permanent: After only 74 years, the capital was moved first to Nagaoka and shortly thereafter to Kyoto, where it remained for more than 1,000 years. What's important about those 74 years, however, is that they witnessed the birth of Japan's arts, crafts, and literature, as Nara imported everything from religion to art and architecture from China. Even the city was laid out in a rectangular grid pattern, modeled after the Tang Dynasty capital of Chang'an. It was during the Nara Period that Japan's first historical account, first mythological chronicle, and first poetry anthology (with 4,173 poems) were written. Buddhism flourished, and Nara grew as the political and cultural center of the land with temples, shrines, pagodas, and palaces.

Japanese still flock to Nara because it gives them the feeling that they're communing with ancestors. Foreigners come here to get a glimpse of Japan's past. Remarkably, many of Nara's historic buildings and temples remain intact, and long ago someone had the foresight to enclose many of these historical structures in the peaceful confines of a spacious park, which has the added attraction of free-roaming deer. I would add the

Your Own Personal Guide

Nara has many volunteer guides (from students and housewives to retirees), who will happily show you the town's sights in exchange for the chance to practice their English. There's no charge, but you pay your own admission and are requested to cover the guide's transportation expenses to meet you (guides do not have to pay admission to attractions); it's also a good idea to pay for the guide's lunch. Although guides are sometimes waiting at tourist offices, it's better make reservations at least 3 days in advance with one of the following organizations: **YMCA Goodwill Guides** (application form at egg-nara.org/booking.html; ✆ **0742-45-5920**), **Nara Guide Club** (nara-guide-club.com/en/; ✆ **0742-43-2938**), or **Nara SGG Club** (narasgg.com/en/; ✆ **0742-22-5595**).

caveat, however, that Nara has been terribly mismanaged in recent years. Bus parking lots sit on the doorstep of every major attraction (or in the case of Kofukuji Temple, literally between the main building and the hall of treasures), disrupting the serenity of the old-world atmosphere. And though the tacky signage has finally been removed from the columns upholding Todaiji Temple, one of Asia's most imposing religious structures, placing a handful of souvenir stalls behind the great statue of the Buddha feels sacrilegious. So much for Buddhism foregoing materialism.

Those issues aside, Nara can be a worthwhile day trip, particularly when autumn descends on the public park (usually in mid-Nov). Note, however, that fall is mating season for the deer, so stags tend to become frisky and their behavior patterns more erratic.

ESSENTIALS

GETTING THERE From Kyoto Station, Nara is easily reached on two lines: the JR Nara Line and the private Kintetsu Limited Express. Japan Rail Pass holders generally opt for the commuter **JR Nara Rapid (Kaisoku) Line,** which departs about four times an hour and takes 43 to 57 minutes depending on the train; if you don't have a pass, the trip costs ¥720 one-way. The deluxe **Kintetsu Special Limited Express** whisks you to Nara in 35 minutes, guarantees you a seat (all seats are reserved), costs ¥1,280, and departs every 30 minutes (advance purchase suggested in peak season).

From Osaka, there are two train lines running to Nara. The **Kintetsu Nara Line,** from Namba Station, takes 36 minutes and costs ¥680. The **JR Yamatoji Rapid Line** from Osaka Station takes 50 minutes and costs ¥820 (or 33 min. and ¥510 from Tennoji Station).

VISITOR INFORMATION Tourist info offices at **JR Nara Station** and **Kintetsu Nara Station** are both open daily 9am to 7pm. At JR Station, the **Tourist Information Center** is just outside the JR Station, to the left in the attractive former JR station. In between both JR and Kintetsu stations, on Sanjo Dori about a 5-minute walk from either, is the main **Nara City Information Center,** called **Naranicle.** There's also a tourist information center just beyond the southern gate to Todaiji Temple, next to the museum. For more info, call ✆ **0742-22-3900** or go to **visitnara.jp**.

GETTING AROUND Both Kintetsu Nara Station and JR Nara Station are in Nara's small downtown. Sanjo Dori, the main shopping street, runs from JR Nara Station to Nara Park, a 15-minute walk. Kintetsu Station is closer, about a 5-minute walk to the entrance of the park. Keep in mind, however, that Nara Park is quite large and its attractions far-flung; it takes about 20 minutes to walk from Kintetsu Nara Station to Todaiji Temple and another 20 minutes to Kasuga Taisha Shrine. Buses travel from both stations all the way to Kasuga Shrine. The **Loop Line bus** runs every 10 minutes, circling past both JR and Kintetsu train stations, Kofukiji and Todaiji temples, and the Naramachi historic district (no. 2 follows the loop clockwise, no. 1 goes counter-clockwise). You can also rent **bicycles** near the east exit of JR Nara Station, opposite the AB Hotel (the rental shop looks like a parking garage). Standard bikes are ¥700 for a day, or you can rent e-bikes for ¥1,000 (¥1,500 if using for more than 4 hr.). Pedestrian thoroughfares can get quite congested and having two wheels lets you explore more of the park and surrounding areas. There are designated bicycle parking sites near Nara's main attractions.

EXPLORING NARA

The best way to enjoy Nara is to arrive early in the morning before the first tour buses start pulling in. If your time is limited, the most important attractions to see are **Todaiji Temple, Kasuga Taisha Shrine,** and **Kofukuji Temple,** all part of the World Heritage Site; you can tour all three in about 3 or 4 hours. If you have more time, make a side trip to **Horyuji Temple** (p. 357), or take a stroll south of downtown and Nara Park through

Among Nara's many charms are the friendly deer that roam free in historic Nara Park.

Naramachi, the historic part of town, with its narrow streets, well-preserved *machiya* (traditional wooden residences), and plenty of restaurants.

AROUND NARA PARK With ponds, grassy lawns, tree groves, and temples, Nara Park covers about 520 hectares (1,300 acres). It's also home to more than 1,300 deer, which are considered divine messengers and are therefore allowed to roam freely. The deer are generally quite friendly; throughout the park you can buy "deer crackers," which all but the shyest fawns will usually snatch right out of your hand. If you're unsure of what to expect, you'll see rule boards dotted around the place instructing visitors on how to "protect" the animals, though it's mostly common-sense stuff, like "do not hit or chase deer."

All the below listings are within Nara Park, in the order you'll reach them walking east from the stations.

Kasuga Taisha Shrine ♥♥ Originally the tutelary shrine of the powerful Fujiwara family, this shrine was founded in 768, and according to Shinto concepts of purity it was torn down and rebuilt every 20 years in its original form (the last time it was torn down and rebuilt was in 2015–16). As virtually all empresses hailed from the Fujiwara family, the shrine enjoyed a privileged status with the imperial family. Nestled amid verdant woods (the Kasugayama Primeval Forest rising behind it has been protected since the 9th c.), it's a shrine of vermilion-colored pillars and an astounding 3,000 stone and bronze lanterns. The most spectacular time to visit is mid-August or the beginning of February, when all 3,000 lanterns are lit. Also cool is the **Fujinami-no-ya Hall,** a near-pitch-black room in which lanterns dangle and flicker, creating a mystical night-world effect; walk through and try not to clatter into anything. Although admission to the shrine's outer grounds is free, admission is charged for the inner cloister, the **Man'yo Botanical Garden,** preserving about 300 varieties of native Japanese plants and famous for its wisteria (it's on the left on the approach to the shrine), and to the **Kasuga Taisha Museum,** displaying costumes, swords, and armor in exhibitions that change four times a year. Fork out the extra yen only if you have time and the interest.

Nara Park. kasugataisha.or.jp. ✆ **0742-22-7788.** Inner cloister ¥700; Man'yo garden ¥500 adults, ¥200 children; museum ¥500 adults, ¥300 junior- and senior-high students, ¥200 children. Grounds daily 6am–6pm Apr–Sept, 6:30am–5pm Oct–Mar; inner cloister daily 8:30am–4pm (periodically closed); botanical garden daily 9am–5pm (till 4:30pm Dec–Feb); museum daily 10am–5pm.

Kofukuji Temple ♥♥ Established in 710, this was the family temple of the Fujiwaras, the second-most powerful clan after the imperial family from the 8th to 12th centuries. There were once as many as 175 buildings on the Kofukuji Temple grounds, giving it significant religious and political power up until the 16th century; through centuries of civil wars and fires, however, most of the structures were destroyed. Only a handful of buildings remain, and even these were rebuilt after the 13th century.

Survivor: Todaji's Great Buddha

At a height of more than 15m (50 ft.), the Daibutsu is made of 437 tons of bronze, 286 pounds of pure gold, 165 pounds of mercury, and 7 tons of vegetable wax. Thanks to Japan's frequent natural calamities, however, the Buddha of today isn't quite what it used to be. In 855, in what must have been a whopper of an earthquake, the statue lost its head. It was repaired in 861, but alas, the huge wooden building housing the Buddha, the **Daibutsuden,** was burned twice during wars, melting the Buddha's head. The present head dates from 1692. As for the Daibutsuden, it was also destroyed several times through the centuries; the present structure dates from 1709. Measuring 48m (160 ft.) tall, 57m (187 ft.) long, and 50m (165 ft.) wide, it's one of the largest wooden structures in the world, but only two-thirds its original size.

The **five-story pagoda,** first erected in 730, burned down five times. The present pagoda dates from 1426 and is an exact replica of the original; at 50m (164 ft.) tall, it's the second-tallest pagoda in Japan (the tallest is at Toji Temple in Kyoto). It's currently undergoing major renovation work, so for the foreseeable future you'll see a towering mess of steel, rather than the upturned tile roofs that have surveyed the surrounding area for centuries. The renovation is projected to be complete by 2031. The **Eastern Golden Hall** (**Tokondo**) was originally constructed in 726 by Emperor Shomu to speed the recovery of the ailing Empress Gensho. Rebuilt in 1415, it houses several priceless images, including a bronze statue of Yakushi Nyorai (the healing Buddha) installed by Emperor Shomu on behalf of his sick aunt; a 12th-century wooden bodhisattva of wisdom, long worshiped by scholar monks and today by pupils hoping to pass university entrance exams; and the 12 Heavenly Guards, wooden reliefs carved in the 12th century. The **Central Golden Hall,** reopened in 2018 after 18 years of renovation, is historically the most important building in the complex, though it's been rebuilt many times since the 8th century; its current incarnation enshrines several Buddhas, bodhisattvas, and Heavenly Kings. But the best thing to see is the **Treasure House** (**Kokuhokan**), which displays works of art originally contained in the temple buildings, many of them National Treasures. Most famous are the standing 8th-century Ashura statue and a bronze head of Yakushi Nyorai, but the six 12th-century carved wooden statues representing priests of the Kamakura Period are equally striking.

Nara Park. kofukuji.com. ✆ **0742-22-7755.** Treasure House ¥700 adults, ¥600 junior- and high-school students, ¥300 children; Central Golden Hall ¥500 adults, ¥300 junior- and high-school students, ¥100 children; Eastern Golden Hall ¥300 adults, ¥200 junior- and high-school students, ¥100 children. Combination tickets available. Daily 9am–5pm.

Todaiji Temple ♥♥♥ Nara's premier attraction is Todaiji Temple and its **Great Buddha** (**Daibutsu**), Japan's second-largest bronze Buddha. When Emperor Shomu ordered construction of the Todaiji temple in the mid-700s, he intended to make it the headquarters of all Buddhist temples in the land. As part of his plans for a Buddhist utopia, he commissioned work for the Daibutsu, a remarkable work of art that took eight castings. Be sure to circle around the Great Buddha to take it in from all angles. Behind the statue is a model of how the Daibutsuden used to look, flanked by two massive pagodas. Even at a scale of 1/50, you get a sense of how colossal the original Todaiji must have appeared. Behind the Great Buddha to the right is a huge wooden column with a small hole in it near the ground. According to popular belief, if you can manage to crawl through this opening, you'll be sure to reach enlightenment (a snap for children, though people of all ages seem eager to give it a go). The **Todaiji Museum** displays the temple's priceless Buddhist statues and other artworks (entry ¥800; combo tickets available for ¥1,200), but most visitors skip this one. Nara Park. todaiji.or.jp. ✆ **0742-22-5511.** ¥800 adults, ¥400 children. Nov–Mar daily 8am–5pm; Apr–Oct daily 7:30am–5:30pm (museum opens at 9:30am).

The Great Buddha of Todaiji Temple.

WHERE TO EAT IN NARA

Besides the recommendations below, **Rokumei Coffee** (rokumei.coffee; ✆ **0742-23-4075**), just off Sanjo Dori, is worth stopping at for a boost of caffeine en route to the park. Coffee and croissant sets are ¥820 or ¥920 (depending on which croissant you choose) until 11am, and it has the added bonus of opening at 8am (early for a Japanese coffee shop).

Restaurants in the park can get quite crowded, with queues forming outside during peak season. **Wakakusa Mountain Plate,** sitting atop a stairway near Mount Wakakusa in Nara Park, is a good takeout option, serving sandwiches for ¥950 using vegetables and eggs farmed on a nearby plateau and seasonal juices made with local fruits. There's plenty of green space here to sit and tuck into your lunch.

I also recommend swinging by **Alcohol Library** (お酒の美術館; ✆ **0742-22-0787;** daily 11am–11pm) before returning to Kyoto or Osaka, especially if you're traveling from JR Nara Station. Sitting in a glass-walled building by the station's east exit, you'll see a long bar counter and signs advertising a range of Japanese whiskey and sake brands. Glasses of whiskey start at ¥500 and climb steeply the more aged and rarer it is—Hibiki 21 goes for ¥15,000—while sake samplers start at ¥700. Side dishes and snacks also available from ¥300 to ¥700.

Mizuya Chaya (お酒の美術館) ♥♥ UDON & SWEETS This charming thatched-roof teahouse outside the northern entrance to Kasuga Shrine is reliably filled with diners, either at the indoor tables surrounding small hearths for boiling water, or on the outdoor seats shaded by old trees. The specialty here is twofold: *udon* noodle bowls and traditional Japanese

THE HISTORIC BUILDINGS OF horyuji temple

Founded in 607 by Prince Shotoku as the center for Buddhism in Japan, **Horyuji Temple** ♥♥♥ (horyuji.or.jp; ✆ **0745-75-2555**) is one of Japan's most significant spaces for historic architecture, art, and religion. It was from here that Buddhism blossomed and spread throughout the land. Today about 45 buildings remain in the complex, some dating from the end of the 7th century and comprising what are thought to be the oldest wooden structures in the world. But this is more than just another ancient temple—Yaskon quieter days, the serene atmosphere of the compound elevates the experience to a higher plane. It's a fitting tribute to Prince Shotoku, founder of Buddhism in Japan and still revered today. Little wonder Horyuji was selected as one of Japan's first UNESCO World Heritage Sites, in 1993.

At the western end of the grounds, the two-story, 17m-high (58-ft.) ***kondo,*** or main hall, is considered to be the temple's oldest building, erected sometime between the 6th and 8th centuries. It holds Buddhas commemorating Prince Shotoku's parents, protected by Japan's oldest set of four heavenly guardians (from the late 7th or early 8th c.). Next to the main hall is Japan's oldest **five-story pagoda,** dating from the foundation of the temple and cleverly built to withstand earthquakes; it has four scenes from the life of Buddha around its base. The **Gallery of Temple Treasures** contains statues, tabernacles, and other works of art from the 7th and 8th centuries, many of them national treasures. On the eastern temple precincts, the octagonal **Yumedono Hall,** or Hall of Visions, was built in 739 as a sanctuary to pray for the repose of Prince Shotoku. Admission to these Horyuji treasures costs ¥1,500 adults, ¥750 children; the grounds are open daily 8am to 5pm (till 4:30pm Nov 4–Feb 21).

Just behind Yumedono is **Chuguji Temple** (中宮寺; chuguji.jp; ✆ **0745-75-2106**), once part of a large nunnery built for members of the imperial family. It contains two outstanding national treasures: the graceful wooden statue of **Nyoirin Kannon Bosatsu,** dating from the 7th century and noted for its compassionate expression (inviting comparisons to da Vinci's *Mona Lisa*), and the **Tenjukoku Mandala,** the oldest piece of embroidery in Japan. Originally about 5m (16 ft.) long, it was created by Shotoku's consort and her female companions after Shotoku's death at the age of 48. It depicts scenes from the Land of Heavenly Longevity, where only those with good karma are invited by the Buddha in the afterlife, and where Shotoku surely resides. Only a replica of the fragile embroidery is now on display. Chuguji is open daily 9am–4:30pm (till 4pm Oct–Mar 20); admission is ¥600 adults, ¥450 ages 13 to 15, ¥300 children.

To get to Horyuji Temple from Nara, take the JR Yamatoji Rapid Line, which departs every 10 to 15 minutes; it's only an 11-minute trip (fare ¥230). From Horyuji Station, you can walk to the temple area in about 20 minutes, or take bus no. 72 (maps available at the small tourist office in Horyuji Station).

sweets. The udon comes in a soy and dashi broth and can be paired with wild vegetables, prawn tempura, fried chicken, or seasoned tofu (vegetarian options are available). Treats include a hot sweet bean soup called *zenzai,* jellylike *warabi* mochi and tea sets, and matcha dumplings with sweet bean paste and *kinako* (roasted soybean flour).

Nara Park. ✆ **0742-22-0627.** Udon ¥600–¥1,050; sweets ¥500–¥850. Thurs–Tues 11am–3:30pm.

Nara Sagakura Nabe (なら酒蔵なべ) ♥♥ VARIED JAPANESE Many tourists never see Naramachi, a lovely area with narrow lanes and traditional wooden homes and shops. This restaurant, with its sliding doors, low seating, and tatami floorboards, is one of many rejuvenating the town's old buildings. Seating is at cozy *kotatsu*-esque tables. While it's technically a *nabemono* (hotpot) shop, it also does seasonal specialties like a set of three oysters (one steamed, one grilled, one vinegared) and a glass of sake for ¥1,000 in autumn and winter. The hotpot meals feature marbly cuts of beef or high-quality pork with seasonal vegetables all swimming in a savory soup. You can add toppings like more meat, rice, noodles, fettucine, eggs, or fondue cheese. Note that the hotpot menu is in Japanese but the staff speak English and will explain it to you as necessary.

34–1 Imamikadocho. narasakeguranabe.foodre.jp. ✆ **050-5462-0948.** Hotpots ¥1,900–¥2,200 per person. Wed–Mon 11:30am–10pm.

Unagiku (うな菊奈良本店) ♥♥♥ EEL Hidden in the century-old Kikusuiro building at the eastern end of Sanjo Dori, this wedding and kaiseki venue is the picture of timeworn Japanese elegance, seductively located at the end of a cobbled path around the side of the building and marked by billowing white curtains. Luckily, the culinary fare matches the restaurant's elegant looks. Unagiku's set meals, presented in lacquered boxes and delicate porcelain, include eel fillets, *chawanmushi* (steamed egg custard), pickles, tofu, rice, miso soup, and a sweet. The eels, sourced from high-quality fishmongers, are steamed, grilled over charcoal, and basted with famed Amano soy sauce and Kankyo Shuzo mirin. For those in a rush, takeaway sets from ¥2,300 are also available.

15 Nakashinya-cho (right before the red *torii* gate). ✆ **0742-22-2669.** Set meals ¥3,700–¥9,400. Wed–Mon 11am–2:45pm and 5–7pm (last order).

WESTERN HONSHU

8

When we think of Honshu, it's usually in terms of Tokyo in the east or Kyoto and Osaka in the west. But elsewhere in the western half of the island you'll find regions and cities that feature heavily in the history books and have helped Japan forge an understanding of itself.

The **Kumano Kodo** walking trail holds the key to Japan's origin story. Mountainous **Koyasan** is the home of Shingon Buddhism and resting place of the famous monk Kobo Daishi, while **Izumo** and **Ise,** and their eponymous shrines, are among the most important locations in Shinto lore. **Kanazawa,** where both Buddhism and samurai culture flourished, has been a center of handicrafts and refined arts for centuries. And then there's **Hiroshima,** a city that used the darkest day in modern global warfare to reinvent itself and strive for a world of peace and prosperity. Whether it's history, art, philosophy, or religion, Western Honshu has much to offer the culture-hungry traveler.

FAVORITE EXPERIENCES IN WESTERN HONSHU

- **Making a Pilgrimage to Ise Grand Shrines** Follow the age-old route to see the most venerated shrines in all of Japan. Amazingly, the Inner Shrine is razed and reconstructed on a new site every 20 years, according to the strict rules of the Shinto religion. See p. 374.
- **Walking the Kumano Kodo** This pilgrimage trail in Wakayama holds the key to Japan's mythical origin story and connects three major Shinto shrines, the Kumano Sanzan, with Koyasan, the home of Shingon Buddhism. See p. 403.
- **Watching a Kagura Performance in Yunotsu Onsen** Kagura, an ancient fusion of theater and dance performed for the Shinto deities, might be Japan's most-approachable performance art; book a seat for the weekly performance at Yunotsu's Tatsu no Gozen shrine. See p. 427.
- **Learning & Mourning at Hiroshima's Peace Memorial Museum** The devastating story of the bombing of Hiroshima is told here in a detailed, multifaceted manner, that leaves viewers sadder but far wiser about this world-changing event. See p. 435.
- **Sleeping with the Monks in Koyasan** In Koyasan, a mountaintop town and the most sacred site in Shingon Buddhism, you can

PREVIOUS PAGE: Moss-covered stone lanterns light the path for worshippers on Mount Koya.

meditate with monks, learn to copy sutras, eat *shojin ryori* cuisine, and walk through one of the world's most magnificent ancient cemeteries. See p. 397.

Along the Kumano Kodo pilgrimage route, shops rent traditional outfits for pilgrims to wear.

NAGOYA ♥

366km (227 miles) W of Tokyo; 147km (92 miles) E of Kyoto; 186km (116 miles) E of Osaka

It's telling, perhaps, that Nagoya's expat community has adopted the mantra "Nagoya is not boring"—which gives you an idea of how it's viewed by the residents of Japan's marquee urban areas. Nagoya may be Japan's largest seaport and fourth-largest city, with a population of 2.2 million, yet most foreign visitors pass it by. A frank assessment would be that Nagoya *is* a little boring when compared to its peers. It doesn't have the bombastic nightlife or world-class culinary scene of Tokyo, Osaka, or even Sapporo. Culturally it's not as rich as Kyoto or Kanazawa, and it doesn't have as handsome a harborside as Yokohama or Nagasaki. Yes, it was leveled during World War II, but so was Hiroshima, which today draws plenty of tourist traffic.

Yet this historic crossroads, strategically planted right in the middle of the country almost 400 years ago on orders of Tokugawa Ieyasu, still has a few cards up its sleeve: a castle built by the first Tokugawa shogun, a museum housing ornate Tokugawa-owned art pieces, and one of Japan's most important Shinto shrines. You can spend hours at an open-air museum north of the city, which houses the most magnificent work of Frank Lloyd Wright architecture still standing in Japan. It makes an excellent 1-night stopover if you're on your way to visitng Ise Shima National Park and its surrounding towns.

Essentials

ARRIVING Known officially as the Central Japan International Airport (NGO) but dubbed **Centrair** (✆ **0569-38-1195;** centrair.jp/en), this airport occupies a man-made island in Ise Bay about 35km (22 miles) outside Nagoya. Tourist information desks in the airport include the **Meitetsu Tourist Information Center** (✆ **0569-38-7091;** daily 9am–7pm), located on the second-floor Access Plaza. **Meitetsu** trains (meitetsu.co.jp) connect Centrair with Nagoya Station in 28 minutes by express (¥1,430). A taxi from Centrair to downtown Nagoya will run about ¥20,000 and take 50 minutes.

The fastest way to get to Nagoya from Tokyo is by **Shinkansen bullet train,** which takes 1½ to 2 hours from Tokyo Station to **JR Nagoya Station** (depending on the train) and costs ¥10,560 for an unreserved seat. Kyoto and Shin-Osaka stations are less than an hour away and are the next stops on the fastest Nozomi trains.

From Shinjuku Station and Tokyo Station, regular **highway buses** (willer-travel.com/en/; ✆ **050-5805-0383**) travel 6 hours to Nagoya Station, costing between ¥3,000 and ¥6,000. From Kyoto, the highway bus costs ¥2,800 and takes 2½ hours; from Osaka, the trip takes around 3 hours and costs ¥3,100.

The modern towers above Nagoya Station comprise the world's largest building containing a train station.

VISITOR INFORMATION In Nagoya Station's central concourse, the **Nagoya Tourist Information Center** (✆ **052-541-4301;** daily 8:30am–7pm) has maps and brochures. There's another one downtown, in the basement of Oasis 21 (which looks like a spaceship) on Hisaya Dori near Sakae Station (✆ **052-963-5252;** daily 10am–8pm).

ORIENTATION Almost completely destroyed during World War II, Nagoya was rebuilt with wide, straight streets, many of which are named. This makes the city a pain to walk around, as vehicular traffic has been given pride of place, and its major attractions are quite spread out.

Soaring more than 50 stories above the skyline, the ultramodern twin-towered **JR Nagoya Station,** with its many train lines (including the Shinkansen), contains the Takashimaya department store, many restaurants, and an observatory. Built in 1999, it has been recognized by Guinness World Records as the world's largest building containing a railway station. Clustered nearby are the Meitetsu Bus Terminal, Meitetsu Nagoya Station, the city bus terminal (on the second floor of the Matsuzakaya department store), Kintetsu Station, and a subway station for the Sakuradori and Higashiyama lines, as well as many hotels and a huge underground shopping arcade that stretches 6km (3¾ miles) and includes about 600 shops.

East of Nagoya Station is **Sakae,** the city's downtown area, located two subway stops from Nagoya Station. The wide boulevard **Hisaya Odori** runs north-south through Sakae, with a park and a TV tower in its green meridian. North of Hisaya Odori is **Nagoya Castle,** south is **Atsuta Jingu Shrine.**

Western Honshu

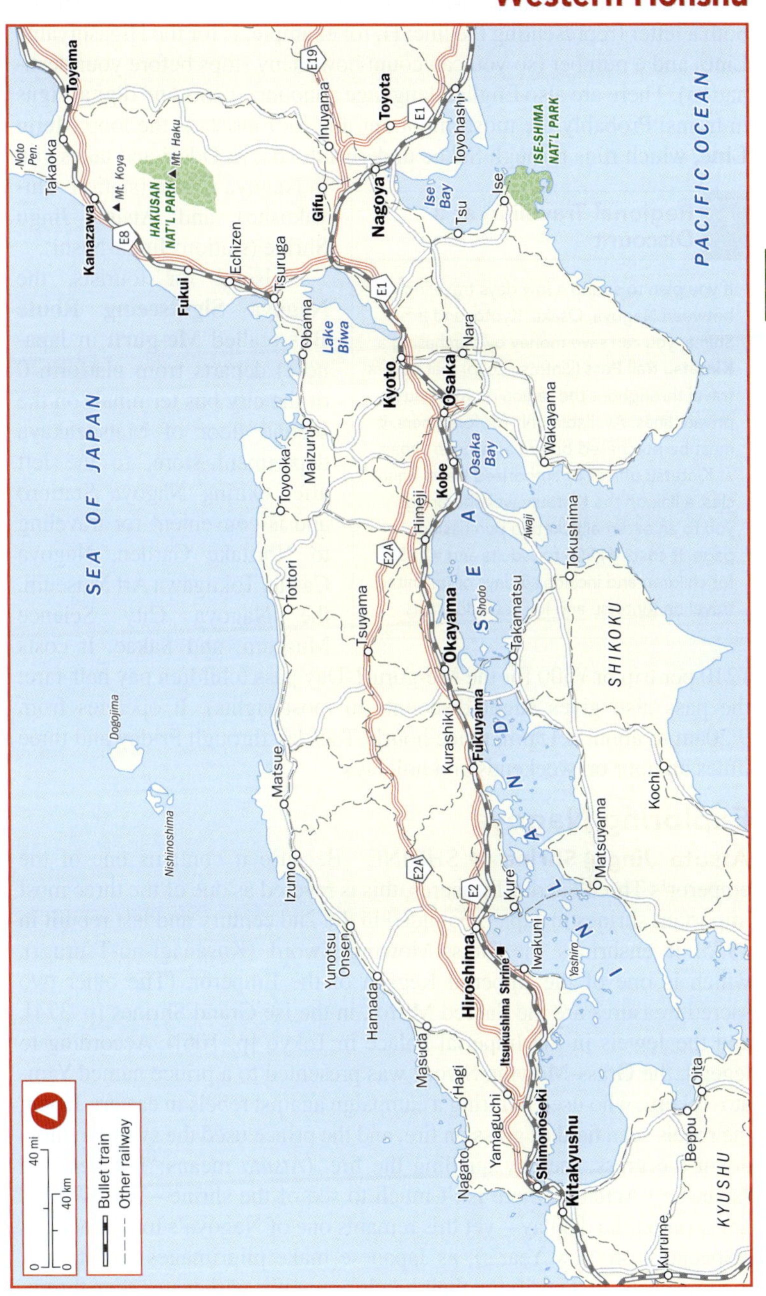

GETTING AROUND Nagoya's eight-line **subway** system is simple to use because station names, written in English and Japanese, are assigned both a letter (representing the line; H, for example, is for the Higashiyama Line) and a number (so you can count how many stops before your destination). There are also English-language announcements and digital signs in trains. Probably the most important line for tourists is the loop **Meijo Line,** which runs through Sakae underneath Hisaya Odori and takes you to Nagoya Castle (station: Shiyakusho) and Atsuta Jingu Shrine (station: Jingu-Nishi).

Useful for tourists, the **Nagoya Sightseeing Route Bus** (called **Me-guru** in Japanese) departs from platform 0 of the city bus terminal (on the second floor of Matsuzakaya department store, to the left after exiting Nagoya Station) and is convenient for traveling to Noritake Garden, Nagoya Castle, Tokugawa Art Museum, the Nagoya City Science Museum, and Sakae. It costs ¥210 per trip or ¥500 for the Me-guru 1-Day pass (children pay half-fare; the pass also gives slight discounts to most sights). It operates from 9:20am to about 6:15pm, twice hourly Tuesday through Friday and three times an hour on weekends and holidays.

Regional Traveling at a Discount

If you plan to spend a few days traveling between Nagoya, Osaka, Kyoto, and Ise-Shima, you can save money by purchasing a **Kintetsu Rail Pass** (kintetsu.co.jp) that covers travel throughout the region on Kintetsu's private lines. Available only for foreigners, it must be purchased *before arriving in Japan* at Kintetsu offices or authorized travel agencies; a link on the Kintetsu website brings you to an external ticketing purchasing page. It costs ¥4,900 for adults and ¥2,450 for children and includes 5 days of unlimited travel on Kintetsu and Iga Tetsudo trains.

Exploring Nagoya

Atsuta Jingu Shrine ♥ SHRINE Because it contains one of the emperor's Three Sacred Treasures, this is revered as one of the three most important shrines in Japan. Founded in the 2nd century and last rebuilt in 1955, it enshrines the Grass-Mowing Sword (Kusanagi-no-Tsurugi), which is one of the Imperial Regalia of the Emperor. (The other two sacred treasures are the Sacred Mirror, in the Ise Grand Shrines [p. 374], and the Jewels in the Imperial Palace in Tokyo [p. 106]). According to legend, the Grass-Mowing Sword was presented to a prince named Yamato-Takeru, who used it during a campaign against rebels in eastern Japan; the rebels set a field of grass on fire, and the prince used the sword to mow down the grass, thereby quelling the fire. (*Atsuta* means "hot field" in Japanese.) Actually, there isn't much to see of the shrine—the sword is never on public display—yet this remains one of Nagoya's top attractions (especially on New Year's), as Japanese make pilgrimages here to pay their respects, first purifying their hands or mouths with water, then throwing coins into the money box, clapping to gain the attention of the gods, and bowing as they pray. A Treasure Hall displays an ever-changing

Nagoya

0 1/4 mi
0 0.25 km
Kikunoo Dori
Sengen-cho Sta.
Nagoya Castle
Shiyakusho Sta.
Airport Bus Stop
Ote Sta.
Dekimachi Dori
To Inuyama City
MEITETSU SETO LINE
Railway
Subway
Tourist Info
Kamejima Sta.
Solobori Dori
Misono Dori
Kuwanamachi Dori
Nagashimacho Dori
Chojamachi Dori
Hommachi Dori
Shichikencho Dori
Gofukucho Dori
Isemachi Dori
Hisaya Odori
Toyota Motor Corporation
Takaoka Sta.
SAKURA-DORI LINE
City Bus Terminal
Sakura Dori
Hisaya-odori Sta.
Nagoya TV Tower
Kokusai Center Sta.
Marunouchi Sta.
Fushimi Sta.
Sakaemachi Sta.
Sakae Sta.
Shinsakae-machi Sta.
HIGASHIYAMA LINE
Nakamura Police Station
Nagoya Sta.
TSURUMAI LINE (SUBWAY)
Taiko Dori
Hirokoji Dori
Iriecho Dori
Mitsukura Dori
Shirakawa Dori
Otsu Dori
MEIJO LINE
Hisaya Odori Park
Kurokawa-hondori
Nagoya Expressway
Horikawa River
Fushimi Dori
SHIRAKAWA PARK
Yabacho Sta.
KINTETSU LINE
JR KANSAI LINE
JR TOKAIDO SHINKANSEN
Wakamiya Odori
KEY BUS ROUTE
Sapporo Beer
Osu Kannon Sta.
Komeno Sta.
Osu Dori
JR CHUO LINE
ATTRACTIONS
Atsuta Jinja Shrine 12
Nagoya Castle 7
Ninomaru Garden 8
Tokugawa Art Museum 13
HOTELS
the b nagoya 10
Lamp Light Books Hotel 5
Nagoya Marriott Associa Hotel 1
Toyoko Inn Nagoya-eki Sakuradori-guchi Honkan 3
RESTAURANTS
Hacchi 4
Hitsumabushi Bincho 9
Mikuni 1
Torisoba Susuru 6
Yabaton 11
Yamamoto-ya Honten 2

variety of items donated through the ages by members of the Imperial family, shoguns, feudal lords, and common people, including furniture, household goods, and, thanks to the legend of the Kusanagi-no-Tsurugi, an impressive number of swords and daggers.

1–1–1 Jingu, Atsuta-ku. atsutajingu.or.jp. ✆ **052-671-4151.** Free admission to grounds; Treasure Hall ¥300 adults, ¥150 children. Grounds daily dawn–dusk; treasure house daily 9am–4:30pm (closed last Wed and the following day of every month). Station: Jingu-mae (3 min.) or Jingu-Nishi (7 min.).

Nagoya Castle ♥♥ CASTLE Built for his ninth son by Tokugawa Ieyasu, the first Tokugawa shogun, Nagoya Castle was completed in 1612 and served as both a strategic stronghold on the Tokaido Highway and a residence for members of the Owari branch of the Tokugawa family for almost 250 years, until the Meiji Restoration ended their rule in 1868. A shrewd and calculating shogun, Tokugawa forced feudal lords throughout Japan to contribute to the castle's construction, thereby depleting their resources and making it harder for them to rebel. Although Nagoya Castle was largely destroyed in World War II (only three turrets and three gates escaped destruction), the main keep and other structures were rebuilt in 1959 exactly like the originals, only in ferroconcrete, as were most reconstructed castles in Japan. The current keep, however, is not considered suitably earthquake resistant and was closed off to visitors; at the time of writing it is scheduled to be torn down and reconstructed with wood, which is slated for completion in 2032. Once it's rebuilt, the two iconic

Stunning painted sliding doors and screens decorated the shogun's living quarters in Nagoya Castle.

golden dolphins—replicas of ones destroyed in World War II—will be returned to the castle roof. Long thought to protect the castle from fires, the dolphins each weigh about 1,190 kilograms (2,650 lb.) and are made of cast bronze covered with 18-karat-gold scales (the gold scales have been repeatedly stolen through the centuries).

Meanwhile, the reconstructed **Honmaru Goten** (castle palace) houses treasures that escaped the bombing during World War II, including beautiful paintings on sliding doors and screens. Glimmering gold-leaf artworks and decorative transom panels pair with spacious *tatami* rooms and soft lighting to express old Japan's wonderful sense of aesthetics. These artworks, depicting courtly life and seasonal ephemera, take on different shapes, shadows and meaning when viewed from various angles in the wooden corridors.

East of the castle is **Ninomaru Garden,** laid out at the time of the castle's construction, converted to a dry Japanese landscape garden in 1716 and today one of the few remaining castle gardens in Japan. Besides providing a lovely setting, it served as an emergency shelter for the lord in case of enemy attack. Stop by the **Ninomaru Tea House**—it's said that if you drink tea here when it's made with a golden kettle (available only on Fri), 5 years will be added to your life. You can tour the castle and grounds in less than 1½ hours.

1–1 Honmaru, Naka-ku. nagoyajo.city.nagoya.jp. ✆ **052-231-1700.** ¥500 adults, free for junior-high students and younger. Daily 9am–4:30pm. Station: Shiyakusho (5 min.). Me-guru sightseeing bus: Osakajo (1 min.).

Tokugawa Art Museum ♥♥ MUSEUM Located on the grounds of a former mansion owned by the Owari branch of the Tokugawa clan—with the original entry gate and a guardhouse still intact—this worthwhile museum houses a changing display of documents, samurai armor, swords, matchlocks, helmets, pottery, lacquerware, *noh* costumes, and paintings that once belonged to the Tokugawa family, including objects inherited from the first Tokugawa shogun, Ieyasu. There are also replicas of structures and items that once adorned Nagoya Castle, including decorative alcoves, a teahouse, and a *noh* stage. Of the museum's nine National Treasures, most famous is the 12th-century picture scrolls of *The Tale of Genji,* but they're displayed only 1 week a year at the end of November; otherwise, replicas are on display. English-language explanations throughout the museum put the exhibits in historical context. You can easily spend 90 minutes here and in the museum's garden, the Tokugawaen, with a pond, waterfalls, and strolling paths. In the late afternoon, lanterns made from bamboo, wood, and porcelain flicker to life, filling the darkening walkways with a mystical air.

1017 Tokugawa-cho, Higashi-ku. ✆ **052-935-6262.** tokugawa-art-museum.jp. Art museum ¥1,400 adults, ¥800 college and high-school students, ¥500 children; combination ticket to museum and garden ¥1,550, ¥950, and ¥500 respectively. Tues–Sun 10am–5pm (garden 9:30am–5:30pm). Me-guru sightseeing bus: Tokugawaen (1 min.). Station: Ozone (exit 3, 10 min.), Morishita (12 min.).

TAKE A TRIP IN TIME TO THE meiji era

In Inuyama City, a 25-minute train ride north of Nagoya, you can spend a glorious afternoon roaming the landscaped grounds of **Museum Meiji Mura ♥♥♥** (meiji mura.com; ✆ **0568-67-0314**), an open-air architectural museum devoted to buildings dating from the Meiji Period (1868–1912). Before Japan opened its doors in the mid-1800s, unpainted wooden structures dominated Japanese architecture; after Western influences began infiltrating Japan, however, stone, brick, painted wood, towers, turrets, and Victorian features came into play. Earthquakes, war, fire, and developer greed have destroyed most of Japan's Meiji-Era buildings, making this a priceless collection. On the grounds are official government buildings, schools, two churches and a cathedral, a post office, a bathhouse, a *kabuki* theater, Western homes that once belonged to foreigners living in Nagasaki and Kobe, Japanese-style homes (including one that belonged to Japanese novelists Mori Ogai and Natsume Soseki), a martial-arts hall, an assembly hall used by Japanese immigrants in Hawaii, and a prison. There's even a steam locomotive, a streetcar, and an old village bus for shuttling visitors around the park. The northern section is the most impressive—you'll find the Renaissance-style entrance to Kanazawa Bank, a corridor of jail cells identical to one used in the opening scene of the classic 1973 film *Lady Snowblood,* and the unmissable front facade and lobby of the original Imperial Hotel in Tokyo, designed by Frank Lloyd Wright. Containing original Wright-designed furniture, it's an exceptional feat of architectural design, with intricate *hiraki-no-kagobashira* ("box columns of light") that hold up the entire structure as if by some magical force. You can mail a postcard from the post office, buy candy and toys at a shop in what was once the writer Lafcadio Hearn's summer house, or stop for coffee and cake in the Imperial Hotel lobby cafe. Plan on spending at least 3 hours here. Admission is ¥2,500 adults, ¥1,500 high-school students, ¥700 junior-high and elementary students. It's open daily 9:30am–5pm (to 4pm Nov–Feb; it's also closed Mon Dec–Feb).

To reach Inuyama, take the Meitetsu rapid limited express from Meitetsu Nagoya Station (beside Nagoya Station) to Inuyama Station (a 25-min. trip; fare ¥630). Then catch a bus from platform no. 2 and ride 20 minutes to Meiji Mura (¥500 one-way). While you're in Inuyama, you can also make a quick visit to Japan's oldest standing castle, **Inuyama Castle ♥** (Kitakoken–65–2; inuyama-castle.jp; ✆ **0568-61-1711**), constructed in 1537 atop a bluff overlooking the Kiso River. This four-story donjon—much smaller than most of Japan's castles—was owned by the same family from 1618 to 2004 (it's now under management of a foundation). Step inside to see a few samurai outfits on display and take in the expansive views over the river. Admission costs ¥550 adults, ¥110 children; it's open daily 9am to 5pm.

Where to Stay in Nagoya

In addition to the choices here, Toyoko Inn has several properties in Nagoya. Most convenient to Nagoya Station is **Toyoko Inn Nagoya-eki Sakuradori-guchi Honkan,** 3–16–1 Meieki (toyoko-inn.com; ✆ **052-571-1045**), with an annex catty-corner across the street. Expect to pay less than ¥10,000 per night for a room and breakfast (perhaps a little more in peak season).

the b nagoya ♥ Japanese business hotels used to be dingy, depressing affairs, but this stylish chain illustrates how far they've come. Known for its upbeat contemporary decor, reasonable rates, and good downtown locations, the b offers smallish, spotless rooms with focused bed lights and deep tubs, free coffee in the lobby, and a convenience store on-site. Sakae, with its shops, restaurants, and nightlife, is a few minutes' walk away. On Hisaya Odori, 4–15–23 Sakae, Naka-ku. ✆ **052-241-1500.** en.theb-hotels.com. 219 units. ¥10,000–¥20,000 double. Station: Sakae (exit 13, 3 min.). **Amenities:** Restaurant; smoke-free rooms; free Wi-Fi.

Lamp Light Books Hotel ♥♥ This is one of the best affordable hotel chains in Japan, with a focus on simple pleasures: a reading corner in each room, bookshelves for guests to browse, and communal library-cum-work spaces with jazz drifting out of the speaker systems. You'll even get a few coffee-table or picture books placed around your room, in case you forget to bring reading material. As Cicero once said, "A room without books is like a body without a soul." This branch is well located between Nagoya Station and Sakae, with good access to bars and restaurants and Nagoya Castle. A cafe in the lobby makes decent coffee and sells fruit juices, morning snacks, and mini burgers. 1 Chome–13–18 Nishiki, Naka-ku. ✆ **052-914-2867.** lamplightbookshotel.com. 70 units. ¥11,000–¥25,000 double. Station: Fushimi (5 min.), Marunouchi (9 min.). **Amenities:** Cafe; free Wi-Fi.

Nagoya Marriott Associa Hotel ♥♥ A location right over Nagoya Station makes this Nagoya's most convenient hotel. Occupying the 15th to 52nd floors of the JR Central Towers building, it offers the city's best views (ask for a room facing the castle and downtown; higher floors cost more), not to mention quick access to the many restaurants and shops on the lower floors of this "vertical city." It doesn't skimp on facilities, either, offering a health club; good-sized up-to-date guest rooms; and a wide range of in-house dining possibilities (to eat at French restaurant Mikuni, considered Nagoya's top restaurant, make reservations months in advance). Don't miss having a drink at the 52nd-floor Sky Lounge Zenith (open 11:30am–midnight on weekends; from 1pm weekdays). 1–1–4 Meieki, Nakamura-ku. associa.com/nma ✆ **052-584-1113.** 774 units. ¥29,000–¥60,000 double. Station: Nagoya. **Amenities:** 6 restaurants, 2 bars; concierge; pool, Jacuzzi, and spa; gym; room service; Wi-Fi.

Where to Eat in Nagoya

One of Nagoya's specialties is ***kishimen,*** fettuccine-like broad and flat white noodles usually served in a soup stock with soy sauce, tofu, dried bonito shavings, and chopped green onions. Nagoya is also famous for ***miso nikomi udon***—udon noodles served in a bean-paste soup and flavored with such ingredients as chicken and green onions. ***Cochin*** (free-range) chicken and ***tonkatsu*** (breaded pork cutlets) with red miso sauce are also Nagoya favorites.

Kishimen noodles, a Nagoya specialty.

The best place for one-stop dining is Nagoya Station itself, on the 12th and 13th floors of one of the twin towers atop the station. Called **Towers Plaza,** it offers about 40 food-and-beverage outlets, most with plastic-food displays.

If you reserve early enough (at least 2 months in advance; Table Check reservations possible), you might also get one of the coveted tables at French restaurant **Mikuni** on the 52nd floor of the Nagoya Marriott Associa Hotel (✆ **052-584-1111**). Decorated in Art Nouveau style and considered by some to be the city's finest restaurant due to its celebrated chef Kiyomi Mikuni (who has restaurants also in Tokyo and Sapporo), it offers set lunches for ¥8,500 (11:30am–1:30pm) and set dinners from ¥15,000 (5:30–9pm), with a menu that changes monthly. Prices increase with choice of course menu and additions like champagne pairing or guaranteed window seats.

Hacchi ♥♥ YAKINIKU This *yakiniku* (grilled meat) restaurant is a no-frills place, with a dining counter along one side and a few tables on the other, where locals char meat and occasionally look at up at the TV in the corner (probably showing baseball). Each table is inset with a gas grill on which you'll cook items ordered from the English-language menu, like boneless short rib, pork skirt, or cheek. There's also a Japanese menu with a la carte items, including chicken thigh and breast, as well as shiitake, *shishito* peppers, eringi mushrooms, and green onions. The staff don't speak much English, but they're friendly so don't hesitate to ask them for a recommendation.

1–14–3 Nishiki, Naka-ku. ✆ **052-222-2986.** Dinner ¥4,000–¥5,000 per person. Daily 5–11pm. Station: Fushimi (5 min.), Kokusai Center (5 min.). Look for a sign (white lettering on black background) that says "ホルモン ハッチ".

Hitsumabushi Bincho (ひつまぶし備長) ♥♥♥ EEL Though the main branch of this highly regarded eel restaurant is way up in the north of the city, there are four other branches clustered close together in the downtown area. This branch, on the seventh floor of the Lachic Shopping mall (note there's another branch in the basement food court), gets busy quickly, so I'd recommend arriving a few minutes before the 5pm opening time or be prepared to wait. It's become a popular stop for foodie tourists, and now has an English-language menu and several English-speaking staff. The *hitsumabushi* set meals are you're best option. Alongside grilled eel presented on top of rice in a lacquered box, you'll get the usual set-meal helping of pickles, rice, and soup, as well as dashi broth, sliced *nori* seaweed, green onions, and wasabi. Don't worry if it's overwhelming; the staff will supply an instruction sheet on how to eat it. This is a ritual in itself: Start by eating it "plain," then add green onion and wasabi, then finish with the dashi and nori, creating a new dish called *una-chazuke.* Hitsumabushi sets start at ¥3,980, but eel donburi bowls and other a la carte options are cheaper.

7th floor, Lachic Shopping Mall, 3–6–1 Sakae, Naka-ku. ✆ **050-3164-0145.** Set meal from ¥3,980. Daily 11am–3pm and 5–9pm. Station: Sakae (exit 16, 2 min.).

Torisoba Susuru ♥♥ RAMEN This ramen, served in a rich and foamy chicken broth, feels like an amalgamation of Nagoya and Fukuoka cuisines, blending the local love of chicken with the kind of thick umami soup found in noodle shops in the south. The shop claims it's a big hit with women, but judging by the queues of salarymen forming outside during the lunch hour it doesn't do too badly amongst the unfairer sex either. Taste-wise, it certainly packs a wallop, with a richness that lingers on the palate—but never unpleasantly—long after you've left the shop. There's no English on the vending machine from which you order, but a sign points to the top left button letting you know this is the recommendation: noodles in the signature broth with chashu slices and bean sprouts. It's a filling dish for ¥900, but you can make it large for an extra ¥100.

2–15–28 Marunouchi, Naka-ku. torisoba-susuru.com. ✆ **052-218-3308.** Ramen from ¥900. Mon–Fri 11am–2pm and 6–9pm; Sat 11am–2pm. Station: Marunocuhi (exit 3, 2 min.).

Yabaton ♥♥♥ TONKATSU You'll recognize this everyman's eatery on Kinshachi Yokocho, a small restaurant street on the grounds of Nagoya Castle, by its branding: a comical pig dressed like a sumo wrestler, pasted onto the door, the menu, your order number ticket, and the merch for sale in the restaurant lobby. Even the "stand here" sign for the queues that form outside shows trotters instead of feet. Established in 1947, the Yabaton chain has grown into a source of civic pride for Nagoya because of its reliably delicious *tonkatsu* (pork cutlet) meals. Depending on what you order, you may be asked whether you want yours with homemade sauce or red *miso;* the former is thicker and sweeter, but the latter is the specialty here (if you don't specify, you'll be served the miso; if you can't decide, ask

A local favorite, the Yabaton chain is known for its sumo pig mascot and its delicious pork cutlets.

for a little of both). *Donburi,* a breaded and fried pork cutlet on rice, is the cheapest (pay a little more to get the fattier Taiwan fillet cutlets), but recommended are the prime rib teppan or Kagoshima black pork set meals. Main dishes all come with cabbage; rice or miso soup costs extra but rice refills are free. The main branch (located at 3–6–18 Osu) opens daily 11am to 9pm.

1–2–5 Sannomaru, Naka-ku. ✆ **052-231-8810.** Tonkatsu-don ¥1,470–¥1,780; set meals ¥1,690–¥3,050. Daily 10:30am–5pm.

Yamamoto-ya Honten ♥♥ UDON NOODLES This chain noodle shop, a 2-minute walk from Nagoya Station, specializes in *miso nikomi udon.* Its noodles, all handmade, are thick, hard, and chewy and are served in a type of bean paste that's special to Nagoya. You can order it plain or with additions like tofu, cochin chicken, or pork (an English-language menu with explanations makes ordering easy), and if you like your noodles spicy, add spices to your food from the large bamboo container on your table. A small dish of vegetables (cabbage, shaved onion, cucumber) is brought to your table as soon as you're seated and is replenished free of charge.

3–25–9 Meieki, basement of Horiuchi Bld., Sakura Dori, Nakamura-ku. ✆ **052-565-0278.** Udon dishes ¥1,090–¥2,000. Daily 11am–3pm and 5–9pm (last orders). Station: Nagoya (exit 6, 2 min.).

ISE-SHIMA NATIONAL PARK ♥♥

465km (289 miles) W of Tokyo; 100km (60 miles) S of Nagoya

Blessed with subtropical vegetation, small islands dotting its shoreline, and the most revered Shinto shrine in Japan, **Ise-Shima National Park** could be visited on a day's outing from Nagoya, but it really merits a 1- or 2-night stopover. Covering 518 sq. km (200 sq. miles) on and around Shima Peninsula, its ragged coastline is full of bays and inlets that make up the home of the Mikimoto pearl divers and thousands of pearl-cultivating rafts. The Inner and Outer Shrines and sub-shrines of Ise Jingu are concentrated in the town of **Ise,** also called Ise-Shi, which translates as Ise City. Nearby **Toba** contains Mikimoto Pearl Island, which offers a pearl museum and demonstrations by its famous women divers, as well as the Toba Aquarium and sightseeing boat trips around the bay. There are lots of good seaside accommodation options in Toba, with free shuttle buses ferrying guests between them and Toba Station, so if you're planning on staying a couple of nights here, it's a good base.

Essentials

ARRIVING The easiest way to get to Ise-Shima is from Nagoya on the private Kintetsu Railway's **Ise Shima Liner,** which departs every 30 minutes or so from Kintetsu Station, next to the JR Nagoya Station. It takes about 90 minutes via limited express to reach Ise, 15 minutes more to reach Toba. The train costs ¥3,410 to Toba; see p. 364 for information on buying a Kintetsu Rail Pass. Less frequent is the **JR Rapid Mie Line** from Nagoya to Ise-Shi (¥2,370) or Toba (¥2,830); this train is free for holders of the Japan Rail Pass.

Overnight **buses** depart nightly from Tokyo's Ikebukuro Station's east exit at 9pm, arriving at Ise-Shi Station at 7:15am and Toba 40 minutes later. Buses leaving Shinjuku Station at midnight arrive in Ise around 9am. The fare to Ise-Shi Station ranges from ¥7,000 to ¥12,000, depending on the date and the bus company. See **Willer Express** (willer-travel.com/en; ✆ **050-5805-0383**) for bookings.

VISITOR INFORMATION There's a **tourist information center** in Ise-Shi Station (✆ **0596-65-6091;** daily 9am–5:30pm). The **Toba Tourist Office** on the main concourse of Toba Station (✆ **0599-25-2844**) is open daily 9am to 5:30pm. More information on the area is available at **en.ise-kanko.jp**, **iseshima-kanko.jp/en**, and **toba.gr.jp**.

GETTING AROUND Transportation within Ise-Shima National Park is either by train or by bus. **Trains** are convenient if your destinations are Ise City and Toba, but some major sites, including the Ise Grand Shrines, are best reached by bus or bicycle. For sightseers, there's the **CAN Bus,** which you can board in front of the JR stations in Ise City and Toba. Buses, departing about once an hour on weekdays and twice an hour on weekends, travel from Ujiyamada and Ise-Shi stations to both Outer and Inner Shrines of Ise Jingu before continuing onward to Toba. One-day passes for ¥1,200 and 2-day passes for ¥1,800 can be bought aboard the buses and at train stations. In Ise, you can rent a **bicycle** at Ise-Shi Station's baggage storage center (go left after you exit the station) for ¥800 for 4 hours or ¥1,000 for a full day up to 5pm; cost is ¥1,500 and ¥2,000 for e-assist bikes. You can keep the bike overnight for an extra ¥100, but be sure to drop it back by 10am. There are also luggage storage facilities at Ujiyamada and Toba stations, as well as at the entrance to the Inner Shrine in Ise.

Exploring Ise-Shima National Park

ISE CITY (ISE-SHI)

Tied historically to the imperial family and considered the spiritual home of the Japanese people, Japan's most venerable Shinto shrines, the Ise Grand Shrines, consist of an Outer Shrine and an Inner Shrine, plus more than 100 minor shrines spread through a dense forest of Japanese cypress. As the Outer and Inner shrines are about 6.5km (4 miles) apart, your best bet is to first visit the Outer Shrine, which is a 5-minute walk from Ise-Shi Station along a flagstone street lined with shops and cafes, and then either cycle or take a bus to the Inner Shrine. Because of the distance between the shrines, their large grounds, and the numerous handicraft shops and charming restaurants sandwiched into the old-world streets, plan on spending at least 4 hours exploring Ise.

The Inner Sanctuary of the Ise Grand Shrine reflects the simplicity of traditional Shinto architecture.

The Ise Grand Shrines (Ise Jingu) ♥♥♥ SHRINES The Grand Shrines are among the few Shinto shrines in Japan without any Chinese Buddhist influences and are therefore thought to be the purest style of Shinto architecture. Constructed of plain cypress wood with thick thatched roofs in the oldest style of architecture in Japan, they're starkly simple and have no ornamentation except for gold and copper facing on beams and doors. In fact, if you've come all the way to Shima Peninsula just to see the shrines, you may be disappointed—there's nothing much to see (and no photos are allowed). But in this country fascinated by both secrets and its own mythos, there is a powerful allure to the mystery surrounding it all. The shrines are so sacred, in fact, that no one is allowed near them except members of the imperial family and high-ranking Shinto priests, yet an estimated 10 million Japanese come here annually because they regard the shrines as the embodiment of Japanese Shinto itself.

The **Outer Shrine (Geku)** was founded in 478 and is dedicated to the Shinto goddess of industry, agriculture, clothing, and housing. The **Inner Shrine (Naiku)** was founded a few centuries earlier and is dedicated to Amaterasu, the sun goddess. Both shrines are surrounded by four wooden fences; lesser mortals are allowed only as far as the third gate. The Inner Shrine is by far the more important because it's dedicated to the sun goddess, considered to be the legendary ancestress of the imperial family. It contains the *Yata-no-Kagami* (Sacred Mirror), one of the Three Sacred Treasures of the emperor (see "The Legend of the Sacred Mirror of Ise," p. 375).

Perhaps the most amazing thing about the Outer and Inner shrines is that, even though they were founded centuries ago, the buildings themselves have never been more than 20 years old; for more than 1,300 years, they have been completely torn down and rebuilt exactly as they were on neighboring sites every 20 years. Not only does the practice ensure that the shrines don't deteriorate but also that ancient building techniques are preserved. The 62nd rebuilding will take place in the fall of 2033. **Sengakukan,** a museum on the fringe of the Outer Shrine, takes visitors through this process and explains the traditional building techniques employed. Almost all the information is in Japanese, but you will receive an information sheet in English on arrival, and there's a model of the entire Geku sanctuary grounds and a to-scale recreation of the eastern edge of the main hall. Museum admission is ¥300 (¥100 children, free for preschoolers and babies). You don't have to pay, however, to sit on the terrace here; with seats looking across a small lake, it's a nice spot to enjoy a packed lunch.

The Legend of the Sacred Mirror of Ise

According to legend, the sun goddess sent her grandson to Japan so that he and his descendants could rule over the country. Before he left, she gave him three insignia—a mirror, a sword, and a set of jewels. As she handed him the mirror, she is said to have remarked, "When you look upon this mirror, let it be as if you look upon me." The mirror, therefore, is a manifestation of the sun goddess and is regarded as the most sacred object in the Shinto religion. It's kept in the deep recesses of the Inner Shrine in a special casket and is never shown to the public. (The sword is in the Atsuta Shrine in Nagoya, and the jewels are in the Imperial Palace in Tokyo.)

After taking a bus or bicycle ride from the Outer Shrine, you'll approach the Inner Shrine by crossing the Isuzu River via the elegant Uji Bridge (also rebuilt every 20 years), passing through a manicured garden, and then entering a dark forest of 800-year-old cypress trees. Watch how Japanese stop after crossing the second small bridge on the approach to the shrine to wash and purify their hands and mouths with water from the Isuzu River. Its source lies on the Inner Shrine, and it's considered sacred. Also note that it's not only the buildings that are venerated—Shinto, in its oldest form, was a celebration of nature immemorial, with all its beauty, grandeur, unpredictability, and wildness, and you'll probably notice people, particularly elderly Japanese, communing with trees, praying to stones, and paying obeisance to other natural ephemera within the shrine grounds. Even the thatched roofs of the shrines are beautifully unkempt, smothered in moss and grasses. The belief is that the *kami,* Shinto spirits, are not just responsible for nature; they are nature itself.

Ise's Historic Districts ♥♥♥ HISTORIC QUARTER After visiting the Inner Shrine (a 45-min. walk round-trip), turn right after recrossing Uji Bridge for the nearby historic district of **Oharai-machi,** whose 800m-long

(½-mile) main street is lined with beautiful wooden buildings and *kura* (storehouses). Some date from the Edo and Meiji periods, others are newly constructed but faithful to traditional architecture. It's hard to tell what is new and what is old: Everything is made of dark wood, coped tiles, and sliding doors; the buildings all low-rise and clustered together, allowing the tree-covered mountains to form an imposing backdrop. This area once served as the main pilgrimage road leading to Ise Jingu, and during the Edo Period when travel was strictly controlled, joining a mass pilgrimage to Ise was for many Japanese a once-in-a-lifetime opportunity. It's estimated a fifth of the population joined pilgrimages to Ise during that time.

Okage Yokocho is a retail district built to look like a Meiji-era village.

About halfway down is **Okage Yokocho,** a re-created Meiji Era village with teahouses, restaurants, and shops selling Japanese candies, traditional toys, and folk crafts. If you have time, stop by **Okageza** ♥ (✆ **0596-23-8844;** daily 10am–5:30pm, till 4:30pm in winter; ¥400 adults, ¥200 children), a museum housed in an authentic Edo-style building that captures the spirit of Oharai-machi during the Edo Period; dioramas of half-scale models and lively street scenes vividly convey what life was like for both the residents and the pilgrims passing through. On a bridge overlooking a model of the city, take note of the small man: He's not half-scale; the average Edo man measured 4 feet, 11 inches. You'll spend about 20 minutes here. For a traditional sweet, head to **Akafuku** (赤福**;** akafuku.co.jp; ✆ **0596-22-7000;** daily 9am–5pm), which serves *zenzai,* a hot sweet bean soup with grilled mochi cakes. A bowl costs ¥800 and comes with tea and savory snacks.

A 15-minute walk north from Ujiyamada Station or northeast from Ise-shi Station, you'll find **Kawasaki,** which was Ise City's business district during the Edo Period, when boats traversing the Setagawa River delivered goods to storehouses along the river. A grass-roots movement has restored four of these storehouses along with an Edo-Era house, grouped together in the **Merchant's House Museum (Ise-Kawasaki Shonin-Kan)**, 2–25–32 Kawasaki (✆ **0596-22-4810;** Wed–Mon 9:30am–5pm; ¥300). In addition to a high-class teahouse, displays include Ise's own paper money, the first paper money in Japan (developed to lessen the load of pilgrims who might otherwise be forced to carry heavy gold or silver). Surrounding buildings now house restaurants and shops selling crafts, food, and antiques (ask for a map of the area at the museum).

TOBA

Toba's best-known attraction, located on a small island connected to the mainland by a pedestrian bridge and consisting of several buildings, is touristy but still quite enjoyable, especially if you have a weakness for pearls or have ever wondered how they're cultivated.

Mikimoto Pearl Island ♥♥ MUSEUM Once you're on Pearl Island, head for the **Pearl Museum,** which tells all you'd probably ever want to know about the creation of pearls. English-language videos show the insertion of the round nucleus into the shell and the harvesting of the pearls 2 years later, while other exhibits explain the process of making a pearl necklace by hand and the criteria used for pricing pearls. The museum also contains some of Mikimoto's earliest jewelry and some intriguing models made with pearls—the five-story Pearl Pagoda, for example, which has 12,760 Mikimoto pearls and took 750 artisans 6 months to complete (it was exhibited at the Philadelphia World Exhibition in 1926), or the Liberty Bell, with 12,250 pearls and 366 diamonds, which caused such a frenzy when it was exhibited at the 1939 New York Exhibition, the American viewing public dubbed it the "Million Dollar Bell."

Once every hour ***ama* (women divers)** in traditional white outfits demonstrate how women of the Shima Peninsula through the ages have dived in search of abalone, seaweed, and other edibles. They were also essential to the pearl industry, diving to collect the oysters and then returning them to the seabed following insertion of the nuclei. At one time, there

THE FATHER OF pearl island

Born in Toba in 1858 as the eldest son of a noodle-shop owner, Kokichi Mikimoto went to Yokohama as a young man and was surprised to see stalls selling pearls with great success. He reasoned that if oysters produced pearls as the result of an irritant inside the shell, why couldn't humans introduce the irritant themselves and induce oysters to make pearls? It turned out to be harder than it sounded. It wasn't until 5 years after he started his research that Mikimoto finally succeeded in cultivating his first pearl, here on what is today called Mikimoto Pearl Island. In 1905, Mikimoto cultivated his first perfectly round pearl, after which he built what is probably the most successful pearl empire in the world.

Visiting Pearl Island, you can learn all about Mikimoto in **Kokichi Mikimoto Memorial Hall,** built in 1993 to commemorate the 100th anniversary of his success. The exhibitions here do something many other Japanese museums fail at: creating a sense of character. Through excellent English-language explanations paired with playful cartoon sketches, as well as an anime short film (in Japanese only), the kind-hearted, eccentric, and ambitious father of pearl culturing comes vividly to life.

In the Pearl Museum on Mikimoto Pearl Island, displays show pearl-studded luxury items like these model crowns.

were thousands of *ama,* known for their skill in diving to great depths for extended periods. It is said that there are still more than 1,000 of these women divers left in Mie Prefecture, but you're only likely to see them during demonstrations for tourists. Of course, there's also a shop selling Mikimoto pearl jewelry and a restaurant. You can easily spend 1½ hours here.

1–7–1 Toba. ✆ **0599-25-2028.** mikimoto-pearl-museum.co.jp. ¥1,650 adults, ¥820 children. Daily 8:30am–5pm (Dec 9am–4:30pm), closed 2nd Tues–Thurs of Dec. Station: Toba (3 min.).

Toba Aquarium ♥ ATTRACTION First, a note on aquariums in Japan. In recent years, Japan has come under scrutiny for its lack of animal rights and welfare practices, and a lot of the negativity has focused on its treatment of aquatic creatures, particularly dolphins and whales (this was even the subject of a Netflix documentary). JAZA, the Japanese Association of Zoos and Aquariums, is now working with NGOs and other animal welfare bodies to ensure that any animals remaining in captivity are being protected and not subjected to poor living conditions. When I visited this aquarium recently, most of the animals appeared to meet these standards, and some of the aquatic mammals, like the sea lions and otters, looked happy enough. That said, seeing a lolling walrus in a small(ish) tank, wading birds like pelicans and ibises in cages that prevent meaningful flight, and penguins with their flippers banded stirs conflicting emotions. Nevertheless, aquariums are still incredibly popular in Japan and they're undoubtedly a great way for kids and enquiring adults to learn more about the natural world—where else would you get to see poisonous tree frogs, deep-sea jellyfish, and feeding dugongs up close? This aquarium next to Pearl Island is one of Japan's largest, containing more than 850 species of animals and some 20,000 creatures. Various zones and themes make it easy to navigate. The display of marine animals from around Ise-Shima and Japan includes giant spider crabs and the finless porpoise, the world's smallest whale. The exhibit of "living fossils"—creatures relatively unchanged since ancient times—includes sharks, horseshoe crabs, and the nautilus (which are bred here; babies are often on display), while the marine mammals include Commerson's dolphins, Russian walruses, Baikal seals, and sea lions, with sea-lion shows several times a day. The aquarium also has exotic creatures such as African manatees, Amazonian turtles, and even some wildcats. If you take in some of the feeding shows or demonstrations, you'll likely spend at least 90 minutes here.

3–3–6 Toba. ✆ **0599-25-2555.** aquarium.co.jp. ¥2,800 adults, ¥1,600 junior-high and grade-school students, ¥800 children. Daly 9am–5pm (mid-July to Aug 8:30am–5:30pm). Station: Toba (10 min.).

Where to Stay Near Ise-Shima

ISE

Asakichi ♥ During the Edo Period, a pilgrimage to Ise Jingu was often the only trip a commoner might make in his lifetime, so visiting pilgrims often indulged themselves in Furuichi, Ise's former red-light district. Located between the Inner and Outer shrines, it was filled with many *ryokan,* brothels, and restaurants. Now only Asakichi remains, a ramshackle ryokan founded more than 200 years ago by the present owner's family. It seems little changed since then, built on a slope on an impossibly narrow street with steep stairs inside; there's even a museum of sorts filled with dusty Edo-Era family memorabilia, which you can request to see. The *tatami* rooms are simple. Japanese course meals are served at dinner (be sure to ask for a sake recommendation to accompany the food); breakfast is also available on request. Doors are locked and lights turned off at 10pm, so let staff know if you're arriving or staying out late.

109 Nakanocho, Ise-Shi. ✆ **0596-22-4101.** 6 units (2 w/ private bath). ¥10,000–¥15,000 per person. No credit cards. Station: Ise-Shi, then bus no. 01 or 02 from platform 7 another 9 min. to the Nakanocho stop (1 min.). **Amenities:** Free Wi-Fi.

TOBA

TAOYA Shima ♥♥ Everything about this sophisticated hotel is focused on its stunningly beautiful setting on the sea, with nary another building in sight and sweeping views through floor-to-ceiling windows (see if you can spot one of Yayoi Kusama's famous pumpkin sculptures on the hotel grounds). It exudes a soothing, subdued atmosphere, fitting for a resort dedicated to healing. Aromatherapy, reflexology, and other treatments are offered, as well as free-to-use high-performance massage chairs (perfect for post-bath reclining). Rooms, decorated in cool, crisp whites, have small balconies. Due to the hotel's isolation, you'll want to take your meals here. The gourmet buffets, including many dishes served directly from the kitchen, are a seasonal reflection of local produce: spring vegetables, bamboo shoots, and firefly squid from March to June; duck, roast chicken, and root vegetables in autumn; and beef, bonito, and Ise udon year-round.

1826–1 Shirahama, Uramura-cho, Toba. ooedoonsen.jp/taoya-shima. ✆ **050-3615-3456.** 123 units. ¥25,000–¥90,000 double. Rates include 2 meals. Free 25-min. shuttle bus hourly from JR or Kintetsu Toba Station (reservations recommended). **Amenities:** Restaurant; bar; exercise room; spa; hot-spring baths; room service; free Wi-Fi.

Toba Seaside Hotel ♥♥ This hotel has all the trappings of those grand resorts that sprang up during the economic bubble years, combining traditional aspects of a *ryokan* (*tatami* rooms, hot-spring baths, guests walking around in *yukata* robes) with the size and scope of a large Western hotel. In fact, it's like a mini town center with three separate buildings connected by a confusing array of escalators, elevators, and stairways. You'll find the "You Road" corridor, with restaurants, karaoke rooms, and a small arcade; a large souvenir store selling everything from sake and pearls to dried seaweed and beef; an outdoor swimming pool and private beach; a golf simulator; and a public bath in each building (two of which have outdoor sections). It's got a nice location, overlooking the islands of Ise Bay, and with most rooms on the sea-facing side you're pretty much guaranteed a decent view (concrete embankments on the coast notwithstanding). You can opt for meals included, which might make sense given there's no real nightlife or restaurant scene nearby, but with a cafe that opens from 9 to 5 and the You Road restaurants open between 8pm and midnight, a meal plan may feel superfluous. There are also 6 Western-style rooms if you really can't hack another futon. Free shuttle buses run hourly to and from Toba Station (15 min.).

1084 Arashimacho, Toba. ✆ **0599-25-5151.** tobaseasidehotel.co.jp. 204 units. ¥9,000–¥25,000 per person. **Amenities:** Buffet hall; 2 restaurants; souvenir store; games room; karaoke rooms; golf simulator; indoor/outdoor hot-spring baths; free Wi-Fi.

Where to Eat Near Ise-Shima

ISE

Mishokan Morishita Liquor Store (味匠館 森下酒店) ♥♥ This popular restaurant and bar in Okage Yokocho (p. 376) serves raw tuna rice bowls, shellfish skewers, beef sushi, and sake from across the country. It gets quite lively after customary respects have been paid at the nearby shrine. You can sit in or (better when the weather's nice) order from the shop window and eat al fresco—there's a little Shinto-style pavilion, the **Daiko-Yagura Drum Tower,** directly opposite. The *temari* sushi (circular sushi balls) with Matsusaka black beef or tuna are superb; you can order a mix with two of each for ¥2,400. Use pictures on the Japanese-only menu to guide you. ***Note:*** There's nothing in English to help you identify this place—Ise is generally lacking in translation—so look for three stone monkeys on the corner of a tiled roof (one is looking through a spyglass). 52 Ujinakanokiricho, Ise. ✆ **0596-23-8850.** 2 pieces of sushi ¥1,200, 4 pieces ¥2,400; tuna rice bowls from ¥2,500. Daily 9:30am–5:30pm.

Tofuya ♥♥♥ TOFU Hidden off the main road towards the inner shrine, this lovely old building with its dark wooden floors, raised seating areas, sunken *irori* hearth, and half-shoji-half-glass windows looking over the river is a delight. Tofu is the specialty here, and though some meals come with deep-fried or grilled *anago* (saltwater eel), I'd recommend letting the tofu take center stage. The menu outside has pictures, though it's hard to tell from them whether the smooth white blobs are tofu or *shirako* (fish sperm sacs that many Japanese love but have a distinctly acquired taste). There's also not a lick of English on it—even the prices use kanji symbols instead of numbers—but inside the shop uses a QR code menu with multilingual functionality, so you'll know exactly what you're getting. The standard tofu set meal (¥1,450, an extra ¥100 if you want seasoned rice) is huge—I counted 8 individual plates on the tray, featuring things like pickles, savory egg custard, a rich miso soup, and a slightly sweet tofu milk—and is served with a complimentary pot of roasted tea. The tofu, made fresh each morning, has a rich satiny texture and is perfectly delicious eaten plain, with a pinch of salt, and then finished off with a light *tare* broth, green onions, and minced ginger. To get here, take the third left off Ise Highway; Tofuya is at the end of the street on the left. 1 Chome-4-1 Ujiurata, Ise. ✆ **0596-28-1028.** Tofu meals ¥1,450–¥1,800; eel meals ¥1,880–¥4,000. Daily 11am–5pm.

TOBA

Connected to Toba Station via a raised walkway (toward exit 2), you'll find **Toba Ichibangai,** a commercial complex of souvenir shops, snack shops, pearl jewelers, and on the third floor, restaurants. It's a good place to try out some of the local seafood, including seasonal sashimi, fried prawn *teishoku,* oysters, or Toba *meibutsu* (delicacies), like spiny lobster and Toba burgers (known locally as *Tob-ba-ga,* these typically include some combination of lobster, octopus, oysters, turban shells, and other marine creatures). Sashimi platters go for as little as ¥900; seafood set meals start from around ¥1,500. Restaurants have pictures on their menus and plastic food in glass cabinets out front.

Furusato-kan (ふる里館) ♥♥ Meaning "hometown hall," this seafood restaurant looks like it's been around forever, with a raised *tatami* seating area, low dining tables, and all manner of traditional Japanese ornamentation, from Noh masks hanging on the wall and *manekineko* cat dolls to ceramic depictions of the Shinto god Ebisu and old photos of the shop's proprietors. The menu features four lunch sets, featuring sashimi, raw oysters, fried oysters, or fried fish, served with seafood miso soup, rice, pickles, and green tea. There's no English on the menu but pictures should make ordering easy. There are also a la carte options like udon noodles and *onigiri* (rice balls).

1–6–9 Toba. ✆ **0599-26-6818.** Lunch sets ¥1,650; a la carte items from ¥300. Station: Toba (6 min.).

KANAZAWA ♥♥

622km (386 miles) W of Tokyo; 224km (140 miles) NE of Kyoto

Near the northwest coast of Honshu on the Sea of Japan, Kanazawa is the gateway to the rugged, sea-swept Noto Peninsula. It was the second-largest city (after Kyoto) to escape bombing during World War II, and some of the old city has been left intact, including a district of former samurai mansions, old geisha quarters, temple towns, Edo-era canals, and tiny narrow streets that run crookedly without rhyme or reason (apparently to confuse any enemies foolish enough to attack). Kanazawa is most famous for its **Kenrokuen Garden,** one of the most celebrated gardens in all of Japan. It's the main reason people come here, though several fine museums and excellent restaurants add to the experience. Kanazawa is also renowned for its crafts dating from the shogun era, particularly Kutani ware, Yuzen silk dyeing, lacquerware, and *Noh* theater. In 2009, it was named Japan's first UNESCO Creative City of Crafts and Folk Art. Kanazawa also gets 160 rainy days a year, inspiring a local proverb you'd be wise to heed: "Even if you forget your packed lunch, don't forget your umbrella."

Essentials

ARRIVING From **Tokyo,** the Hokuriku Shinkansen takes about 2½ hours and costs ¥13,850 for an unreserved seat. From **Osaka** (via Kyoto), direct JR trains depart once or twice an hour; the ride takes 2 hours and 45 minutes and costs ¥7,590 for an unreserved seat. **Highway buses** (willerxpress.com; ✆ **050-5805-0383**) offer multiple departures from

THE feudal lords OF KANAZAWA

About 500 years ago, Kanazawa first gained notoriety with an act of rebellion. A militant Buddhist sect joined with peasant rebels to overthrow the feudal lord, establishing its own autonomous government—an event unprecedented in Japanese history. Kanazawa survived as an independent republic almost 100 years, until it was attacked by an army commanded by Oda Nobunaga, who was trying to unite Japan at a time when civil wars wracked the nation. Kanazawa was subsequently granted to one of Nobunaga's retainers, Maeda Toshiie, who built a castle and transformed the small community into a thriving castle town. The Maeda clan continued to rule over Kanazawa for the next 300 years, amassing wealth in land and rice and encouraging development of the arts. Throughout the Tokugawa shogunate, the Maedas remained the second-most powerful family in Japan and controlled the largest domain in the country. At the end of the Feudal Era, Kanazawa was Japan's fourth-largest city, and much of its historic atmosphere can still be felt even today.

Shinjuku and Ikebukuro stations, with prices dependent on the month, day of the week, and even the type of seat chosen; expect to pay between ¥5,000 and ¥10,000 for the 5-hour-plus journey.

VISITOR INFORMATION In Kanazawa Station, the **Tourist Information Center** (✆ **076-232-6200;** daily 8:30am–8pm) distributes maps, bus schedules, and brochures. The **Central Tourist Information Center** (✆ **076-254-5020;** daily 10am–9pm), next to Oyama Shrine (p. 385), has lots of excellent English-language information and is especially useful if you plan on heading to Shirakawa-go or to the Noto Peninsula. For more information, see **visitkanazawa.jp**.

GETTING AROUND Kanazawa's attractions spread south and southeast from the station's Kenrokuen Gate exit. **Katamachi** and adjacent **Korinbo,** 3km (2 miles) southeast of the station, are Kanazawa's downtown. Kanazawa is a great city for walking, but if it's raining you may find the sights too far-flung to see everything on foot. Dedicated tourist buses go to major attractions, departing every 15 minutes from about 8:30am to 7pm. The **Kanazawa Loop Bus,** makes a circular route in both directions from the station to all the tourist sights (stops are announced in English) and costs ¥210 per journey or ¥800 for a day pass; children pay half-fare. Sunday night **Light-up Buses** allow visitors to experience Kanazawa's sights after dark; they leave Kanazawa Station every 20 minutes between 7 and 9:40pm and cost ¥500 for an unlimited pass. You can purchase bus passes at ticket counters in the station, tourist information centers, and many hotels. If you have a Japan Rail Pass, you can ride for free on **JR buses,** which depart up to three times hourly from platform 4 and also go to major sights. Pick up maps and schedules at the tourist office.

Exploring Kanazawa

Much of Kanazawa's charm lies in its atmospheric old neighborhoods. The best way to explore various parts of the city is via your own two feet, so be sure to wear good walking shoes. One suggested itinerary for tackling the city's sights is to take the Loop Bus to the Higashi Chaya district, then another Loop bus onward to Kanazawa Castle Park and Kenrokuen, then walk 15 minutes to the Naga-machi Samurai district, stopping at Seisonkaku Villa, the 21st Century Museum of Contemporary Art, and other sights along the way. Directional English-language signs to major sights are posted throughout the city.

AROUND KENROKUEN GARDEN

The sights here are listed in the order you reach them on foot from Kenrokuen. See Kanazawa Castle Park *before* entering Kenrokuen.

Kanazawa Castle Park ♥ PARK/GARDEN At one time, Kanazawa had an impressive castle belonging to the powerful Maeda clan for 14 generations, but it was destroyed by fire several times, most recently in 1881. The only remnant of it, **Ishikawamon Gate**—visible from the northwest corner of Kenrokuen and reached via a bridge over a busy thoroughfare—is big and grand, giving you some sense of the magnitude of the original Maeda castle. Note that the roof tiles are made of lead (so that in an emergency they could be melted down for musket balls). The area just beyond the gate is **Kanazawa Castle Park,** where several castle fortifications have been reconstructed using traditional Japanese construction techniques, including Kahokumon Gate and two watchtowers linked by an incredibly long arsenal that doubled as a protective wall. (Note the various stone masonry techniques used for the castle's many walls.) You can skip these empty buildings, if time is of the essence, but do check out **Gyokusen'inmaru Garden,** originally constructed in 1634 and re-created in 2015 based on excavations, drawings, and literature. Goodwill Guides can be found at the garden's rest house and near Ishikawamon Gate daily from 9:30am to 3:30pm (Sat only Jan–Feb) for free tours of the park.

Kenroku-machi. pref.ishikawa.jp/siro-niwa/kanazawajou. ✆ **076-234-3800.** Free admission to Castle Park, garden, and Kahokumon; watchtowers/storehouse ¥320 adults, ¥100 children. Park daily 7am–6pm (mid-Oct to Feb 8am–5pm); watchtowers/storehouse daily 9am–4:30pm. Loop Bus: Kenrokuen.

Kenrokuen Garden ♥♥♥ PARK/GARDEN Kanazawa's main attraction, the 10-hectare (25-acre) **Kenrokuen Garden,** is the largest of what are considered Japan's three best landscape gardens (the other two are Kairakuen Garden in Mito and Korakuen Garden in Okayama), and many consider it to be the grandest. Its name can be translated as "a refined garden incorporating six attributes": spaciousness, careful arrangement, seclusion, antiquity, elaborate use of water, and scenic charm. Ponds, trees, winding streams, rocks, mounds, and footpaths are combined to create a spellbinding effect. Best of all, unlike most other gardens in Japan, there are no surrounding skyscrapers to detract from splendid views.

One of Kenrokuen Garden's loveliest spots is the Yugaotei Teahouse, set overlooking a tranquil pond.

Originally laid out as Kanazawa Castle's outer garden, Kenrokuen took about 150 years to complete. The fifth Maeda lord started construction in the 1670s, and successive lords added to it according to their individual tastes. The garden as you now see it was finished by the 13th Maeda lord in 1837; only after the Meiji Restoration was it opened to the public, in 1874. Several historic structures are worth seeking out, including the **Yugaotei tea-ceremony house,** dating from 1774, and, most important, **Seisonkaku Villa** (p. 386). Plan on 1½ hours of blissful wanderings. ***Tip:*** You may want to arrive early in the morning or near the end of the day, as Kenrokuen Garden is a favorite destination of camera-toting tour groups. 1–4 Kenroku-machi. pref.ishikawa.jp/siro-niwa/kenrokuen. ✆ **076-234-3800.** ¥320 adults, free for seniors, ¥100 children. Daily 7am–6pm (mid-Oct to Feb 8am–5pm). Loop Bus: Kenrokuen.

Oyama Shrine ♥♥♥ SHRINE You'll probably end up visiting this shrine even if it's not on your initial itinerary, because its main entrance gate stops visitors in their tracks. A three-storied structure, constructed in 1875, it's famous for its fusion of Japanese, Chinese, and Western architectural styles. The arched first story, built using Kanazawa granite, is surmounted by a pagoda-like tower with polychromatic stained-glass windows. Designed by a Dutch architect—evidence of the unique relationship the Netherlands and Japan developed from the 17th to the 19th centuries—it actually served as a lighthouse, until land reclamation efforts and urban development meant it was no longer visible from the sea. The shrine itself is dedicated to Maeda Toshiie, a general who was given Kanazawa after it was overtaken by Japan's first unifier, Oda Nobunaga. When Maeda died in 1599, a shrine was dedicated to him at the foot of Utatsuyama, a small mountain on the city outskirts; in 1873 it was moved to its current location, on the former site of Kanaya Palace (used as a retirement home for Maeda lords during the Edo period)—and not just moved, but reconstructed on a grander scale. The most impressive feature of the complex is the **Shin-en,** or "Divine Garden." Inspired by the courtly revelry once common here, the garden's main pond features a lute-shaped

Designed by a Dutch architect, the front gate of the Oyama Shrine blends Japanese, Chinese, and Western styles.

island, a bridge representing a *koto* (stringed zither instrument), and stones arranged in the shape of *sho* (panpipe). It provides a lovely, if short, stroll any time of year, but the best time to visit is in May when the wisteria is in bloom.

11–1 Oyamamachi. oyama-jinja.or.jp. ✆ **076-231-7210.** Free admission. Open 24/7. Loop Bus: Minami-cho Oyama Jinja Shrine (1 min.).

Ishikawa Prefectural Museum of Traditional Arts and Crafts ♥♥ MUSEUM Located next to Seisonkaku Villa (see below), this the best place in town to view the range of handcrafts for which Ishikawa Prefecture has long been famous (the Maeda lords promoted crafts over warfare). You'll learn about the famous Kutani pottery, first produced under the patronage of the Maeda clan in the 1600s and known for its hues of green, red, purple, navy blue, and yellow, as well as Kaga Yuzen dyeing and hand-painting on silk, Kanazawa lacquerware (which uses raised lacquer painting), paulownia woodcrafts, metalwork, family Buddhist altars, Kanazawa gold leaf, *taiko* drums, *koto* and *shamisen* stringed instruments, lion masks, fishing lures (using feathers of wild birds), folk toys, *washi* (Japanese paper), umbrellas, and even fireworks. Plan on 1 hour.

1–1 Kenroku-machi. ishikawa-densankan.jp. ✆ **076-262-2020.** ¥260 adults, ¥210 seniors, ¥100 children. Daily 9am–5pm (closed 3rd Thurs of every month Apr–Nov and every Thurs Dec–Mar). Loop Bus: Hirosaka (6 min.).

Seisonkaku Villa (成巽閣) ♥♥ HISTORIC HOME Just outside the Kodatsuno (southeast) exit of Kenrokuen Garden, this villa was built in 1863 by the 13th Maeda lord as a retirement home for his widowed mother. Elegant and graceful, it has a distinctly feminine atmosphere with delicately carved, brightly painted wood transoms and *shoji* wainscoting painted with seashells, butterflies, flowers, and other motifs. In the ground-floor bedroom, notice the tortoises painted on its *shoji* wainscoting; tortoises were associated with long life. Upstairs, rooms are painted in brilliant blue, red, and purple. A visit here will take 20 minutes or so.

1–2 Kenroku-machi. seisonkaku.com. ✆ **076-221-0580.** Admission ¥700 adults, ¥300 junior-high and high-school students, ¥250 children. Thurs–Tues 9am–5pm. Loop Bus: Hirosaka-21st Century Museum (5 min.).

21st Century Museum of Contemporary Art, Kanazawa ♥♥ MUSEUM In a word, this museum is fun. Centrally located between Kenrokuen and the Katamachi shopping district, it's ensconced in a striking circular building that has no front or back, allowing visitors to explore it from all directions (and, from time to time, get lost). Galleries, which range from bright spaces with sunlight pouring through glass ceilings to darkened rooms with no natural light, display a collection that concentrates on works of the past 50 years, particularly from Japanese artists born after 1965, along with contemporary works from around the world shown in changing exhibitions. Top sights: Leandro Erlich's outdoor "swimming pool" topped with a roof of glass and shallow water; look in, and you might see people who, having entered through a subterranean tunnel, look like they're walking underwater. (To enter said tunnel yourself, reserve ahead through a link on the museum website.) James Turrell's *Blue Planet Sky Room* is also compelling, a white courtyard open to the sky, making the heavens appear as a work of art. Visitors rush inside, only to be told by the artist to stop for a moment, and remember, the sky is always there, if only we'd look up. Note that galleries may be temporarily closed for exhibition changes.

1–2–1 Hirosaka. kanazawa21.jp/en. ✆ **076-220-2800.** ¥450 adults, ¥360 seniors, ¥310 university students, free for ages 17 and under (special exhibits may cost more). Sun and Tues–Thurs 10am–6pm; Fri–Sat 10am–8pm. Loop Bus: Hirosaka-21st Century Museum (2 min.).

D.T. Suzuki Museum ♥♥♥ MUSEUM This wonderful museum—in my view the best Kanazawa has to offer—is dedicated to the life and work of the city's favorite son, a Buddhist philosopher, Zen scholar, and essayist called Daisetz Teitaro "D.T." Suzuki, who penned over 100 books in English and Japanese and was influential in introducing some of the most arcane forms of Eastern spirituality to the West. Inside, everything is spare, pared back to its basic, most essential elements; it is the essence of "Zen." Pictures of Suzuki in the first exhibition room depict a man who looked exactly as you'd imagine he would: a kind if somewhat studious face; a monkish bald pate; and eyebrows bushier than a fox's tail. There's a "Learning Space" where you can read Suzuki's writings—like *Essays on Zen Buddhism, Shin Buddhism,* or *The Zen Monk's Life*—while looking out at a dry rock garden, where one flowering tree rises from a mound of moss. The Mirror Water Garden is perhaps the most contemplative space of all, a shallow pool surrounded by blank walls and overhanging trees, including willows, maples, and gingkoes. Some falling leaves drift across the surface like tiny toy boats, and ripples are occasionally sent across the pool—a simple act that occurs everywhere in nature but somehow exudes a cosmic significance in this carefully orchestrated space. Because there's not a lot to "see" here, per se, the museum remains mercifully quiet.

3–4–20 Hondamachi. kanazawa-museum.jp/daisetz. ✆ **076-221-8011.** ¥310 adults, ¥210 seniors, free for children. Tues–Sun 9:30am–5pm. Loop Bus: Honda-machi (3 min.). In Honda Koen Park (there are 5 museums and a garden here, look for maps dotted around the park).

NAGA-MACHI SAMURAI DISTRICT

About a 15-minute walk west of Kenrokuen Garden and just a couple minutes' walk west of Kanazawa's downtown, the Naga-machi Samurai District is basically a few streets lined with beautiful wooden homes hidden behind gold-colored mud walls (higher-ranked samurai had higher walls; the lowest rank had only hedges) and bordered by canals left over from the Edo Period. An unhurried stroll in the neighborhood will give you an idea of what a feudal castle town might have looked like, though on a much reduced scale. Lord Maeda had as many as 8,000 samurai retainers, who in turn had their own retainers, making the samurai population here very large indeed. Go to the free-to-enter **Takada Family House** (旧加賀藩士高田家跡) to find a large map that'll give you an idea of how far the city's samurai districts used to sprawl. To see how those in the lowest military class lived, stop by the **Kanazawa Ashigaru Museum,** consisting of two modest homes: the Shimizu house and the Takanishi house, both occupied until the 1990s and open free to the public daily 9:30am to 5pm. In addition, the **Kanazawa Shinise Kinenkan (✆ 076-220-2524;** Tues–Sun 9:30am–5pm), a former Chinese pharmacy established in 1579, displays the old store and family residence and, upstairs, Kanazawa crafts and products from some 60 local stores; admission here is well worth the ¥100.

A warrior's suit of armor, displayed in the Nobura Samurai House.

Nomura Samurai House (Buke Yashiki Ato Nomura Ke; 武家屋敷跡野村家) ♥ HISTORIC HOME Stop 20 minutes here to see how higher-ranking samurai lived back in the Edo Period. Occupied by 11 generations of the Nomura family for 400 years, this traditional Japanese home has a drawing room made of Japanese cypress, with elaborate designs in rosewood and *shoji* screens painted with landscapes, and a tea-ceremony room upstairs (*matcha* tea and a sweet cost ¥300 extra). Rooms overlook a small, charming garden with a miniature waterfall, a winding stream, huge carp, a 400-year-old bayberry tree, and stone lanterns (many come just for the garden). Personal effects of the Nomura family and objects from the Edo Period are on display, including a samurai outfit, swords, lacquerware, the family altar, and a box for bush warblers (deliberately dark so the birds would sing).

1–3–32 Naga-machi. ✆ **076-221-3553.** ¥550 adults, ¥400 high-school students, ¥250 children. Apr–Sept daily 8:30am–5:30pm; Oct–Mar daily 8:30am–4:30pm. Loop Bus: Korinbo (5 min.).

HIGASHI CHAYA DISTRICT

Approximately 40 geisha, or *geigi* as they're known in Kanazawa, practice their trade in three old entertainment quarters in the city, including this one. A walk here reveals rather solemn-looking, wood-slatted facades of geisha houses dating from the 1820s, where men of means have long come to be entertained with music, dancing, songs, the tea ceremony, poem recitals, and other pleasure pursuits. Geisha still perform at a handful of houses in the Higashi Chaya district, but most of the other former geisha homes have been turned into shops, inns, and restaurants. For an inside peek at the geisha world, visit the 200-year-old **Shima Geisha House** (志摩) ♥♥, 1–13–21 Higashiyama (✆ **076-252-5675;** daily 9:30am–5:30pm), a former tearoom where geisha performed. Inside, you'll find rooms that were allotted to personal use and/or performing, along with displays of ordinary artifacts, from hair ornaments, pipes, and game boards to cooking utensils. Architectural details worth noting include several stairways (so that customers could come and go discreetly); a small Shinto shrine at the entrance; a more elaborate family Buddhist altar in a place of honor in a front room; the gleaming wood-lacquered surfaces of furniture; cloisonné door pulls on sliding doors; and a calming *tsubo-niwa* (courtyard garden). Admission is ¥500 for adults, ¥300 for children; you can also enjoy tea in a room facing another garden, which, depending on the accompanying sweet, costs ¥600 to ¥800. Plan on 15 minutes to tour the house; add another 15 if you visit the tearoom.

If you have the time, it's also worth following the walking course east towards Utatsuyama Park's **Overlook Hill.** It's outlined on a map near the western entrance to Higashi Chaya, though it may be just as easy to rely on Google and occasional signposts. A 10-minute walk from Shima Geisha House will bring you to Hosenji Temple, where you can see the cluster of tile roofs in Higashi Chaya slowly giving way to functional modern architecture in the heart of Kanazawa, with a chain of mountains dominating the skyline to the southeast. Another 10 to 15 minutes brings you to Overlook Hill, where you can see the Japan Sea bordering the Kanazawa coastline, though the scenery is somewhat obscured by foliage and the high-rise skyline of modern Kanazawa.

The traditional streets of Kanazawa's Higashi Chaya quarter.

Where to Stay in Kanazawa

Keep in mind that most accommodations charge higher rates on Saturday and nights before public holidays. You'll also pay more during peak season—New Year's, Golden Week (Apr 29–May 5), and mid-July through mid-November. Low season is generally January through March.

EXPENSIVE

Hotel Nikko Kanazawa ♥♥♥ Rising 30 stories high, Kanazawa's tallest building was designed by a Japanese-French team, who succeeded in giving it a boutique-hotel ambience despite its size. The lobby exudes a French Colonial drawing-room atmosphere, with intimate groups of sofas and armchairs spread throughout and Asian decorative art ranging from ginger jars to Japanese lacquered boxes. The English-speaking concierge staff receives high marks, and the location, in front of Kanazawa Station and connected by underground passageway, can't be beat for convenience. The spacious rooms, from the 17th to 28th floors, reflect Kanazawa's craft heritage, with accents of Yuzen cloth, ceramics, and artwork trimmed with gold leaf created by local artisans. Twin rooms, which are larger, cost more than rooms with a double bed. On the highest floors, Luxe Rooms offer great views of either mountains or the Japan Sea in the distance.
2–15–1 Hon-machi. hnkanazawa.jp. ✆ **076-234-1111.** 254 units. ¥15,000–¥65,000 double. Station: Kanazawa (east exit, 1 min.). **Amenities:** 5 restaurants; 2 bars; lounge; concierge; access to next-door health club and spa w/ indoor pool; room service; free Wi-Fi.

Korinkyo ♥♥♥ It's hard not to feel completely at ease in this new boutique hotel, opened in 2021. Designed by creatives from Kanazawa, Nara, and the U.S., it has an monochrome grey color palette, with a feeling of warmth instilled by soft tones and round shapes, from curving corners to arched doorways. Suite rooms on floors 7 to 9 look plucked straight

Minimalist contemporary decor sets a serene tone at the Korinkyo hotel.

from the pages of an interior design magazine, with space used to bind the minimalist decor together, drawing your focus to a potted plant, natural light flooding through the windows, or king-sized beds on woven platforms that create an impression of *tatami* flooring. City view suites have deep bathtubs overlooking Kanazawa Castle Park (particularly beautiful in the fall or when submerged in snow in winter), while suites on the backside of the hotel have saunas to make up for the lack of a view. Handmade crockery and utensils are placed in all rooms—as art pieces as much as for any utilitarian purpose—and Italian-designed loungewear is provided for guests to use. Guests also have access to the private sauna and open-air tubs (90 min. for ¥7,480), an hour spent floating in an isolation tank (¥9,900), and various aromatherapy treatments. Another interesting aspect is the tasty, if somewhat unusual breakfast; based on the concept of Oriental medicine, it features chicken, seafood, or vegetable congee, dumplings, pickles, tea-infused eggs, steamed vegetables and wontons, and tofu pudding with ginger syrup.

1–1–31 Katamachi. korinkyo.com. ✆ **076-209-7766.** 18 units. ¥45,000–¥100,000 double. Rates include breakfast Loop Bus: Korinbo (5 min.). **Amenities:** Concierge; room service; sauna; open-air bath; isolation tanks; aromatherapy treatments; free Wi-Fi.

MODERATE/INEXPENSIVE

In addition to the recommendations here, Kanazawa has two **Toyoko Inns** (toyoko-inn.com): **Toyoko Inn Kanazawa-eki Higashi-guchi,** just a 4-minute walk from the east exit of Kanazawa Station, and **Toyoko Inn Kanazawa Kenrokuen Korinbo,** in the heart of downtown. Rooms often go for less than ¥10,000 per night.

APA Hotel Kanazawa-Ekimae ♥ Although a business hotel, this place does have a special feature that sets it apart: large public baths complete with sauna and open-air bath, free to hotel guests. Other pluses include a convenient location just steps from Kanazawa Station (but on the opposite side from where buses depart) and bold use of bright colors—a welcome relief from the usual blandness of business hotels. On the downside, rooms here are so minuscule that if you open your luggage you may have to leap to reach your bed (there are no closets). Double rooms are about right for one person, and twins provide barely enough room for two people to move about. APA also has three downtown hotels, including **APA Hotel Kanazawa-Chuo,** 1–5–24 Katamachi (✆ **076-235-2111**), which offers similar-size rooms at similar rates, but the water tapped for its indoor and rooftop outdoor baths comes from hot springs.

1–9–28 Hirooka. apahotel.com. ✆ **076-231-8111.** 456 units. ¥7,000–¥25,000 double. Station: Kanazawa (west exit, 1 min.). **Amenities:** 2 restaurants; bar; sauna; breakfast buffet; Wi-Fi.

Hotel Pacific Kanazawa ♥♥ This hotel on the doorstep of Omicho Market has the feel and vibe of a hostel, with a cafe-reception that serves granola bowls and coffee in the morning and craft beer and snacks in the evening. The staff, mostly young, speak English and will recommend restaurants and bars nearby. You'll also find Kanazawa Machi-Navi pamphlets on the cafe counter with information on everything from bike rentals and food to bus routes and tax-free shopping. There are seven different types of room, all small but functionally designed, with desks, TVs, reading lights, and armchairs. Bathrooms are private but minuscule with a toilet and shower squeezed into a space that's equal to about one *tatami*. In any case, this is still a great option for travelers who want quick access to the morning market or Kanazawa Castle Park.

46 Jikkenmachi. hotel-pacific.jp. ✆ **076-264-3201.** 32 units. ¥8,000–¥12,000 single; ¥10,000–¥25,000 double. Loop Bus: Musashigatsuji-Omicho Market (3 min.). **Amenities:** Cafe-bar; free Wi-Fi.

Kanazawa Manten ♥ A small fountain outside the entrance, a front desk backed by trees, jazz playing in the hotel restaurant, indoor/outdoor hot-spring baths, and attentive service all conspire to make this business hotel seem more expensive than it is. Window panels in the guest rooms can be closed for complete darkness, and designated ladies' rooms provide face steamers and women's toiletries. Alas, the mostly single rooms (there are 141 twin rooms and 42 doubles) are otherwise no different, and certainly no larger, than those of any other business hotel. Couples might want to opt for twin rooms, which are roomier than doubles but also more expensive. Book a room on a higher floor; those facing the station give views of trains coming and going. Note that the hotel is located on the opposite side of the station from where the buses depart.

1–6–1 Kita-yasue. manten-hotel.com/kanazawa. ✆ **076-265-0100.** 509 units. ¥6,000–¥10,000 single; ¥9,000–¥15,000 double. Station: Kanazawa (west exit, 4 min.). **Amenities:** Restaurant; hot-spring baths w/ Jacuzzi; sauna; free Wi-Fi.

Where to Eat in Kanazawa

Kanazawa's local specialties, known collectively as ***Kaga Ryori,*** consist of seafood such as tiny shrimp and winter crabs, as well as freshwater fish, duck, and mountain vegetables. Popular in winter is *jibuni,* a duck-and-vegetable stew.

AROUND KANAZAWA STATION

Forus, a shopping center located next to Kanazawa Station, has a slew of restaurants on its sixth floor, including two branches of the super-popular Mori Mori Zushi (see below), as well as others serving *shabu shabu, okonomiyaki, tonkatsu,* and Indian, Korean and Chinese fare. Most are open daily from 11am to 10pm.

Mori Mori Zushi (もりもり寿し) ♥♥ SUSHI This hugely popular sushi restaurant—you'll almost certainly have to wait in line after grabbing a ticket from the touch panel outside—has colored plates, each signifying a specific price, and another touch panel at each seat with photos (as well as daily specials) for ordering. Sushi set meals including *nodoguro* (blackthroat seaperch) are popular. There are spigots for hot water at the counter; serve yourself and add powdered tea. A more colorful branch at Omicho Market (✆ **076-262-7477**) is open daily 8am to 4pm.

Forus, 6th floor, 3–1 Horikawashinmachi. ✆ **076-265-3510.** Sushi plates ¥140–¥500, tasting sets ¥900–¥2,500. Daily 11am–9pm (last order). Station: Kanazawa (east exit, 1 min.).

KENROKUEN GARDEN

Miyoshian (三芳庵) ♥♥ KAGA KAISEKI A great place to try the local *Kaga* cuisine right in Kenrokuen Garden, this century-old restaurant by the park's Renchimon Gate consists of two separate wooden buildings, the best of which is a traditional room extending over a large pond. This is where you'll probably dine, seated on *tatami* with a view of a waterfall and an ancient pond with giant carp swimming in the murky waters. Only set meals of *Kaga* cuisine are served, all featuring *jibuni* stew. The more expensive the meal, the more dishes it adds. The ¥1,800 *yugao* bento includes soup, *jibuni,* sashimi, and rice and pickles; the ¥2,400 *hisago* bento adds such dishes as seasonal fish, crab, tofu, and various small delicacies. Matcha, hot or iced, with a *wagashi* sweet is also available for ¥750.

Kenrokuen Garden, 1–11 Kenrokumachi. ✆ **076-221-0127.** *Kaga teishoku* ¥1,800–¥2,400. Thurs–Tues 11am–2:30pm. Loop Bus: Kenrokuen Garden (5 min.).

OMICHO MARKET AREA

Coil ♥♥ SUSHI & TEA With its artsy, minimalist interior, Coll offers a fresh take on a pillar of the Japanese culinary pantheon: sushi. On one

OMICHO MARKET: FEASTS FROM THE sea of japan

Every morning and afternoon, 300-year-old **Omicho Market** ♥♥♥ (50 Kamiomicho; ohmicho-ichiba.com; ✆ **076-231-1462**), on the northwestern side of Kanazawa Castle Park, is the pulsing heart of the town, as fishmongers, butchers, flower shops, food stalls, restaurants, and craft shops sell their wares to streams of passersby. Specializing in *Nihon Kai* ("Sea of Japan") seafood, prized throughout the country, the market is *the* place to eat sashimi rice bowls, steamed crabs, turban shells, sushi tasting sets (often including *nodoguro,* or blackthroat seaperch, a local favorite), or a la carte sushi delicacies like *uni* (sea urchin), *fugu* (pufferfish), and vinegared sea cucumber. There are dozens of restaurants here—many with counter seats and tables out front—including a branch of Mori Mori Zushi (p. 392) and the popular **Kaisendon Ichiba.** You're spoilt for choice, but a good indicator of a shop's quality is to look for those with queues of Japanese people forming outside. There's also a food court, with shop windows offering the likes of oysters, scallops, clams, and squid, as well as a sake tasting counter (¥500 per glass). You can also wet your whistle at the **Hyakuman Johana Craft Beer** shop, with four-beer tasting flights for ¥1,500. Cooking experiences, including a tour of the market and lunch made with market produce, can be booked online at **in-kanazawa.com/cooking** (costly unless you're in a group, at ¥90,000 for two people, plus ¥8,500 for each adult up to 14 people). Foodies intent on eating their way around could easily spend 2 or 3 hours here at the market; it's open daily from 9am to 5pm (some shops close earlier). Loop Bus: Musashigatsuji-Omicho Market.

side of the restaurant is the dining area, with six tables arranged in a hexagon around a central art piece—a potted bonsai or a flowering plant in a mostly empty space—and diners making their *hosomaki* ("thin roll") sushi themselves, using bamboo rollers. The most popular menu item is the hosomaki sushi and tempura set meal, for which you'll choose either 5, 6, or 8 types of sushi filling—from crab, octopus, and yellowtail to avocado, mustard leaf, and plum jellyfish—to put in your rolls (sushi-making instructions included). Unlike most sushi places, Coil also caters to dietary requirements with veggie options and low-carb alternatives like cauliflower rice. Order the self-serve tea ceremony for ¥880 (¥670 if part of a hosomaki sushi set) and pick your brews from a carefully curated section at the restaurant's tea bar.

1–1 Fukuromachi. coil-japan.jp. ✆ **076-256-5076.** Hosomaki sushi meals ¥1,980–¥2,580. Daily 11am–8:30pm (last order). Loop Bus: Katamachi (2 min.).

Kadocho ♥♥ NOODLES & TEMPURA Serving udon, soba, tempura, *jibuni* set meals, and Kanazawa-style desserts like *kinako* mochi and matcha *daifuku* ice cream, this cheap and cheerful restaurant is a great spot to sample the local cuisine at little expense—one of the reasons it's popular with families. The "recommended" section of the English-language menu, replete with pictures, suggests ordering a warm bowl of udon with duck meat, shrimp tempura, or *mentaiko* (cured pollack roe), but the cold soba and set meals are also good options. Sake, hot or cold, is available for ¥900 yen for a flask.

42 Shimoomicho. ✆ **076-221-0435.** Udon ¥950–¥1,400, set meals ¥1,200–¥1,500, desserts ¥500–¥1,000. Thur–Tues 11am–9pm. Loop Bus: Musashigatsuji-Omicho Market (3 min.).

Toritake ♥♥♥ CHICKEN *Yakitori* is usually viewed as soul food, the kind of fare salarymen wolf down with their colleagues in smoky izakaya after the workday finishes. At this modern counter-seat restaurant near Omicho Market, however, the Master chef elevates this simple repast to a higher culinary plane, selecting the best cuts of meat—the chicken is from a free-range producer in Aomori Prefecture—and seasonal vegetables which he then grills over charcoal in the open kitchen. The ¥5,500 set menu (additions can be made) may include chicken thigh, neck, skin, heart, liver, meatballs, and different parts of the wing, either salted, with a dash of wasabi, or basted with *tare* sauce, as well as quail eggs, gingko nuts, eggplant, Japanese yam, lotus root, mushrooms, and a final rice-based dish like soup *chazuke* (a light chicken soup on rice). The vibe is cool in an understated Japanese way, with smooth jazz playing softly in the background and the Master engaging diners in conversation as the meal begins to wind down. The sake menu is also extensive and comes with English translation. Reservations recommended.

2–15 Fukuromachi. ✆ **076-255-0353.** Set menu ¥5,500. Wed–Mon 6–11pm. Loop Bus: Musashigatsuji-Omicho Market (5 min.).

NAGA-MACHI SAMURAI DISTRICT

The canal fringing Naga-machi is a joy to walk along at night, illuminated by old street lamps and lined with diverse restaurants, including a burger joint, a chic French-Italian bistro, a pizza parlor, a handful of izakaya, and the popular Indian restaurant **Aashirwad** (see below).

Aashirwad ♥♥ INDIAN/NEPALESE/VEGETARIAN You'll be met by a welcoming Nepalese woman in this small but warm two-story building, decorated in the vibrant colors of the Himalayas and with calming Indian music adding to the ambience. There's a lot to choose from, including tandoori chicken, *aloo sadeko* (a Nepalese potato dish made with spicy oil, black sesame, and coriander), paneer butter masala, Kerala fish curry, and the restaurant's signature deep-fried eggplants stuffed with coconut and potatoes. If you can't make up your mind, order a *thali* meal (meat or vegetarian), which will include your choice of curry/curries and sides like *papad,* samosa, salad, raita, rice, and naan, served in bowls on a metallic tray. A selection of Indian bottled beers is also available.
1–4–59 Naga-machi. ✆ **076-231-262-2170.** Main dishes ¥1,100–¥1,500; thali ¥2,550–¥2,800. Tues–Sun 11:30am–2pm and 6–9pm (last order). Loop Bus: Korinbo (3 min.).

Kanazawa Shopping

Kanazawa's most famous products are **Kutani pottery,** with its bright five-color overglaze patterns, and hand-painted **Yuzen silk.** Kanazawa also produces *maki-e* lacquerware, sweets, toys, wooden products, and almost all of Japan's gold leaf. For convenient shopping for these and other souvenirs, including food products, there's the **100 bangai shopping arcade** right in Kanazawa Station, open daily 8:30am to 8pm.

Kanazawa artisans are known for their brightly colored Kutani pottery.

For department stores, boutiques, and contemporary shops, visit downtown **Katamachi** and the pedestrian **Tatemachi shopping street** with its many youth-oriented shops, hair salons, and cafes.

Ishikawa Prefectural Products Center (Kanko Bussankan) ♥♥ Located just north of Kenrokuen Garden, this place on Hyakumangoku Dori is good for one-stop shopping of all the products Ishikawa Prefecture is famous for. The ground floor sells crafts ranging from lacquerware and pottery to glassware, as well as foodstuffs like confectionary and sake, while the second floor has drop-in craft classes (no reservations necessary; small fee charged) and a sushi restaurant. The third floor offers more in-depth workshops on sandblasting glass, gold-leaf painting, or making confectionary (reservations required), while the basement floor has a permanent art gallery, including an exhibition on the history of *wagashi* (sweets) in Kanazawa and their significance to the ruling Maeda family. 2–20 Kenroku-machi. ✆ **076-222-7788.** Loop Bus: Kenrokuen Garden.

Juen (寿苑) ♥♥ Selling colorful Kutani ware, like soy sauce dishes, *chawanmuchi* cups, teapots, tea caddies, chopstick rests, spoons, incense holders, vases, sake receptacles, daruma dolls, and folkloric ornamentation, this shop in the Higashi Chaya district does a good trade among pottery-loving tourists. With a dizzying array of patterns and generously priced items—teapots cost between ¥2,000 and ¥5,000—it's worth perusing if you're in the area. 1–5–6 Higashiyama. No phone.

Sakuda (さくだ) ♥♥ Thinking about wallpapering a room in gold leaf? Then you'll want to pay a visit to Sakuda, located in a modern building in the Higashi Chaya District. (As much as 98% of Japan's entire national output of gold leaf is produced in Kanazawa.) You can watch artisans pounding the gold leaf and spreading it until it's paper-thin and translucent (reservations required); it's the equivalent of pounding a ¥10 coin into the size of a *tatami* mat. But most people come here to shop for gold-leafed vases, boxes, chopsticks, bowls, trays, screens, furniture, and—this being Japan—golf balls and iPhone covers. You can even buy gold flakes to add to your coffee or sake or gold-laden skincare products. Don't miss the second-floor bathrooms; the women's room is done entirely in gold leaf, the men's in platinum. 1–3–27 Higashiyama. goldleaf-sakuda.jp. ✆ **076-251-6777.** Apr–Oct daily 9am–6pm; Nov–Mar Wed–Mon 10am–5pm (upstairs closes 4pm). Loop Bus: Hashiba-cho (4 min.).

Soil ♥♥ One of many new shops in the Nagamachi district—if they open any more, the area will begin to lose its authenticity—this concept store focuses on handcrafted items made of diatomaceous earth (made from the powdered remains of fossils) using traditional plastering techniques. The idea is that every product is born of the earth, the *soil,* of the land of Japan. The products, mostly in neutral colors, are placed carefully around the uncluttered shop, while bilingual staff attend to individual customers. You can buy drying boards, knife trays, coasters, ikebana vases, toothbrush holders, ornaments, aroma pots, salt and pepper shakers, cutlery rests, and champagne coolers, all of which showcase traditional techniques, yet evince a style that is emblematic of present-day Japan. 1–3–18 Nagamachi. soil-isurugi.jp. ✆ **076-201-8603.** Daily 10am–5:30pm. Loop Bus: Korinbo (4 min.).

TEMPLES OF KOYASAN ♥♥♥

748km (465 miles) W of Tokyo; 199km (124 miles) S of Osaka

If you've harbored visions of wooden temples nestled among trees whenever you've thought of Japan, then sacred **Mount Koya** is the place to go. It's all here: head-shaven monks, religious chanting at the crack of dawn, the wafting of incense, towering cypress trees, tombs, and early-morning mist rising above the treetops. Mount Koya—called Koyasan by Japanese—is one of Japan's most sacred places and the mecca of the Shingon esoteric sect of Buddhism. Standing almost 900m (3,000 ft.) above the world, the top of Mount Koya is home to 117 Shingon Buddhist temples as well as Japan's most magnificent graveyard. Fifty-plus temples offer accommodations, making this one of the top places in Japan to observe temple life firsthand.

Koyasan also serves as a terminal point on the **Kumano Kodo,** a pilgrimage route connecting the home of Shingon Buddhism with the Kumano Sanzan, three of the most significant Shinto shrines in Japan. We recommend at least a 2-day hike along its most popular route, Nakahechi (see p. 403).

Essentials

ARRIVING Osaka is the gateway to Koyasan. **Nankai Railway**'s rapid express **Koya Line** departs from Osaka's Namba Station (with a stop at Shin-Imamiya, on the Osaka Loop Line) every half-hour or hour, bound for Gokurakubashi (trip time about 1½ hr.). From Gokurakubashi, you

KOBO DAISHI, beloved BUDDHIST PRIEST

Koyasan, located in the Kii Mountain Range, first became a place of meditation and religious learning 1,200 years ago when Kukai, known posthumously as Kobo Daishi, was granted the mountaintop by the imperial court in 816 as a place to establish his Shingon sect of Buddhism. Kobo Daishi was a charismatic priest who had spent 2 years in China studying esoteric Buddhism before returning to his native land to spread his teachings among Japanese. Admired for his excellent calligraphy, his humanitarianism, and his teachings, Kobo Daishi remains one of the most beloved figures in Japanese history. When he died in the 9th century, he was laid to rest in a mausoleum on Mount Koya. His followers believe Kobo Daishi is not dead but simply in a deep state of meditation, awaiting the arrival of the last bodhisattva, or Buddha messiah. According to popular belief, priests opening his mausoleum decades after his death found his body still warm. Through the centuries, many of Kobo Daishi's followers, wishing to be close at hand when the great priest awakens, have had huge tombs or tablets constructed close to Kobo Daishi's mausoleum, and many have had their ashes interred here. Pilgrims over the last thousand years have included emperors, feudal lords, samurai, and common people, all climbing to the top of the mountain to pay their respects. Originally women were barred from entering the sacred grounds of Koyasan, but in 1872 they too were finally permitted to pay their respects here.

can take a 5-minute cable car ride to the top of Mount Koya. A more luxurious option is the Nankai limited-express (also called super-express) train with reserved seating; these depart less frequently (three times in the morning) and arrive in Gokurakubashi about 1 hour, 10 minutes later (the last stretch through the mountains is beautiful). The entire journey from Namba Station to Mount Koya costs ¥1,430 one-way, including the cable car; if you take the faster express, it'll cost ¥510 extra. You'll save money, however, with Nankai's **Koyasan World Heritage Digital Ticket** (purchase through howto-osaka.com/en/ticket/koyasan), which includes round-trip travel from Namba Station and the cable car, plus unlimited rides on Koya's buses for 2 days and a 20% discount to the attractions listed below. You can also purchase a round-trip digital pass between Koyasan and other stations, like Sakai (¥3,190), Wakayama (¥3,690), and Kansai Airport (¥3,820). Children pay half-fare. For info on travel to and around Koyasan, including booking temple accommodation, go to **eng-shukubo.net** or **koyasan.net**.

VISITOR INFORMATION The **Koyasan Tourism Association** (koya.org; ✆ **0736-56-2468**) is located in the center of Koyasan village, on Odawara street near Kongobuji Temple. It offers a few lockers for luggage, bicycle rental for ¥1,000, and compact EV rental for ¥3,000 (a useful mode of transport if you have an international driver permit). Also available are 90-minute rental audio guides for ¥500, explaining what you're seeing throughout Koyasan, including the location of famous mausoleums and tombstones in Okunoin cemetery. There's also a phone app for a self-guided tour, though it's pricy, at $100.) You can book *shukubo* (temple lodgings) here, though it's better if you reserve those ahead, a minimum of 7 business days in advance (check eng.shukubo.net or call ✆ **0736-56-2616** for details). The tourist office is open weekdays 9am to 5pm.

GETTING AROUND Upon reaching Koyasan via cable car, you must board a **bus** that travels 2km (1¼ miles) on a narrow, winding road (no pedestrians allowed) before going through the village of Koyasan along the main street all the way to the Okunoin-guchi and Okunoin-mae bus stops, the location of Kobo Daishi's mausoleum. The bus passes most sights along the way. Buses depart about 5 minutes after every cable car arrival; the trip to Okunoin-mae takes 20 minutes and costs ¥610. Once you've dropped off your luggage or settled into your temple lodging, you can walk to Okunoin and other locations mentioned below. You can rent bikes or compact EVs at the tourist office (see above); the number of bikes is limited, so reserve in advance if possible.

Exploring Mount Koya

The most awe-inspiring and magnificent of Koyasan's sights, **Okunoin** ♥♥♥ is the cemetery containing the mausoleum of Kobo Daishi. The most dramatic approach to Okunoin is from the Okunoin-guchi bus stop along the Sando pathway, which leads 2km (1¼ miles) to the

A statue of Buddha in Koayasan's Okunoin cemetery, Kobo Daishi's final resting place.

mausoleum. Huge cypress trees form a canopy overhead as you pass monument after monument, tomb after tomb—some 200,000 of them, all belonging to faithful followers from past centuries. It is a marriage between the natural and the manmade: the sheer density of tombstones, the iridescent green moss, the shafts of light streaking through the treetops, the stone lanterns, and the gnarled bark of the old cypress trees. The audio guide from the tourist office (see above) will guide you to the most famous tombstones, including those of the Toyotomi, Shimadzu, Maeda, Asano, and Matsudaira clans. You'll also notice many small *Jizo* statues, believed to protect children in the afterlife, wearing red bibs donated by parents who have lost a child. Altogether, the dramatic scene represents more than a thousand years of Japanese Buddhist history; each step into the depths of the cemetery feels like another step back in time. ***Tip:*** Tour buses park at a newer entrance to the mausoleum at the bus stop called Okunoin-mae. The route from there to mausoleum is shorter, but its crowds lessen the impact of this place considerably. Also be sure to return to the mausoleum at night; the stone lanterns (now lit electrically) create a numinous and powerful effect.

At the end of the pathway, about a 30-minute walk away, is the **Lantern Temple,** or Torodo, which houses about 10,000 lanterns, donated by prime ministers, emperors, and commoners. Two sacred fires, which reportedly have been burning since the 11th century, are kept safely inside. The mausoleum itself, the **Okunoin Gyobo,** is behind the Lantern Hall to the left. Buy a white candle, light it, and make a wish. Then sit back and watch respectfully as Buddhists come to chant and pay respects to one of Japan's greatest Buddhist leaders. Many who have successfully completed the pilgrimage to Shikoku Island's 88 Buddhist temples, often dressed in white and carrying a staff, conclude their journey here. Twice a day, at 6am and 10:30am, monks ritually offer meals to Kobo Daishi.

MORE TO SEE & DO ON MOUNT KOYA

Kongobuji Temple (金剛峯寺) ♥♥, located near the Koyasan Tourist Association in the center of town (✆ **0736-56-2011**), is the central monastery headquarters of the Shingon sect in Japan. It was originally built in the 16th century by Toyotomi Hideyoshi to commemorate his mother's death, although the present building dates from 1869. Pictures by famous artists from long ago decorate sliding screens and depict Kobo Daishi's trip to China. The huge kitchen, big enough to feed multitudes of monks, is also on view. The most important thing to see, however, is the temple's magnificent **rock garden,** the largest in Japan. It's said to represent a pair of dragons in a sea of clouds. If it's raining, consider yourself lucky—the wetness adds sheen and color to the rocks. Admission is ¥1,000 for adults, ¥300 for children.

The daito, or pagoda, is the most striking building at the Garan on Mount Koya.

A short walk farther west is the **Garan** ♥ (✆ **0736-56-3215**), the first buildings constructed on Koyasan and still considered the center of religious life in the community. Its huge *kondo* (main hall) was first built in 819 by Kobo Daishi; you'll also see the oldest remaining building on Mount Koya, the Fudodo, which was built in 1198. The Garan's large vermilion-colored *daito* (pagoda), which many consider to be Koyasan's most magnificent structure, is very much worth entering for its brightly colored murals and statues (¥500 each for the *kondo* and *daito*). All of the sites above are open daily 8:30am to 5pm (enter by 4:30pm).

Where to Stay & Eat Near Mount Koya

Although this community of 4,000 residents has the usual stores, schools, and offices of any small town, *shukubo* (temple lodgings) are where most visitors stay. I strongly urge you to do so, too, traveling only with an overnight bag if possible. To guarantee a spot, reserve a minimum of 7 days in advance, especially in peak season. See "Visitor Information" on p. 398 for details.

Prices for an overnight temple stay, including two vegetarian meals, range from about ¥10,000 to ¥50,000-plus per person, depending on the temple, room, and meal. Check-in is around 2 or 3pm (5pm at the latest) and checkout is at 9 or 10am (you can leave your luggage at the temple while sightseeing).

Your room will be *tatami* and may include a nice view of a garden. Both baths and toilets are communal in some temples (you may need to supply your own towel and toiletries), but more and more temples are adding private bathrooms (and charging much more). College students studying at Koyasan's Buddhist university and living at the temple might attend you, bringing your meals to your room (or serving in the dining hall), making up your futon, and cleaning your room. The *shojin ryori* (Buddhist vegetarian meals) are generally quite good, and because Buddhist monks are vegetarians but not teetotalers (beer and sake are made of rice and grain), alcoholic drinks are readily available at the temples for an extra charge. Dinner is at 5:30pm, and breakfast is usually served by 7:30am. The morning religious service is at 6 or 6:30am; you don't have to attend, but it's worth doing so if you don't mind waking up at the crack of dawn. There's something uplifting about meditative chanting when sleep-deprived, even for nonbelievers. Some temples include sacred fire ceremonies as well.

Unfortunately, since Koyasan became a World Heritage Site in 2004, the flood of tourists has taken its toll, with some temples seemingly more interested in cashing in than helping souls. Some guests show little respect for their surroundings; don't be one of them. On the flip side, some of the head priests now speak great English and can communicate the nuances of their sermons and morning ceremonies with international visitors.

Below are a few of the dozens of area temples open to overnight guests. Rates are based on two people to a room.

A Guest House for Budget Travelers

Koyasan Guest House Kokuu (koyasanguesthouse.com; ✆ **0736-26-7216**) is a compact A-frame inn that squeezes in eight capsule beds (¥4,500), three private rooms (¥11,000–¥14,000 for a double), plus a cozy bar offering food and drink. Owner Ryochi Takai, a Mt. Koya native, is happy to give tips on sightseeing.

Bon On Shya ♥ CAFE A Japanese and French couple, Takeshi and Veronique, run this small, casual cafe on Koyasan's main street. Simply outfitted with wooden tables and a play corner for children, it offers coffees, cakes (try the baked tofu cheesecake), and a daily set meal from 11:30am until they run out. The meal may include rice and beans, potato salad, cake, and a drink (vegan and vegetarian options available; gluten-free, too, with 24-hr. notice). Credit cards aren't accepted and business hours are sometimes irregular. It's that kind of place.

730 Koyasan. ✆ **0736-56-5535.** Set meal ¥1,300. Wed–Sun 7am–5pm. Bus: Odawaradori.

Chuoshokudo Sanbo (中央食堂 さんぼう) ♥♥ ZEN CUISINE This mom-and-pop *shojin ryori* restaurant may have a charmless interior, but the vegan-friendly set meals are exemplary. You can get a full spread for ¥2,500, including sesame tofu, vegetable tempura, local produce simmered in sweet soy sauce, *tsukemono* (pickles), and barley-soy rice—basically the menu's greatest hits. Smaller set meals, most around ¥1,500 and centered on tofu prepared in one or multiple ways, are plenty hefty, despite the lack of animal protein, thanks to the abundance of satiating umami. If you haven't tried *yuba* (tofu skin), this an ideal place to do so.

Overnight stays at Mount Koya's temples include two Buddhist vegetarian meals.

772 Koyasan. ✆ **0736-56-2345.** Set meal ¥1,300–¥2500. Daily 11am–4pm. Bus: Senjuin-bashi.

Ekoin (恵光院) ♥♥ TEMPLE LODGING This 100-year-old temple, with origins stretching back almost 1,100 years when Kukai was said to have erected a stupa on this site, has nice grounds, nestled in a wooded slope an easy walk from Okunoin. It's known for its excellent Buddhist cuisine (gluten-free available) and free meditation lessons at 4:30pm, usually in English. Every morning there's both a chanting service and a fire ceremony. All rooms have views of the garden (some even have a balcony) and info on how to wear a *yukata* (cotton kimono) and take a bath.

497 Koyasan. ekoin.jp. ✆ **0736-56-2514.** 37 units (34 w/ shared bath). Rooms from ¥19,000 per person. Rates include 2 meals. Bus: Karukayado-mae. **Amenities:** Hot-spring bath; Wi-Fi.

Miroku-ishi (みろく石本舗 かさ國) ♥♥ CONFECTIONERY STORE This delightful little confectionary is popular enough that you'll see people queuing outside in peak tourist season. It sells local treats arranged neatly in glass display cases, like *imo-yaki* (a sweet potato dessert), *kusa-yaki-mochi* (mugwort mochi and sweet bean paste), *kurumi-mochi* (flavored with crushed walnuts), *waka-ayu* (sweet mochi wrapped in a thin pancake), and *sake-manjyu* (made with leavened dough, rice, and *koji*). Most cost between ¥150 and ¥200.

764 Koyasan. ✆ **0736-56-2327.** Confections ¥150–¥200. Bus: Karukayado-mae. Odawaradori.

Rengejoin Temple (蓮華定院) ♥♥ TEMPLE LODGING This temple was established 900 years ago but rebuilt 150 years ago after a fire.

Lodging, up the hill in a newer annex, ranges from simple *tatami* rooms to those nicely decorated with painted screens and antiques, the best with views of a garden with a pond. The walkway between the boarding annex and the dining hall wraps around the main landscape garden, which is impossibly atmospheric when lit up at night (especially in the rain), while a simple yet elegant rock garden draws your gaze in the front courtyard; it fuses Zen principles of space, framing, and perspective with an *ajikan* meditation symbol raked into the gravel. Also pluses: The *shojin ryori* meals are tasty and inventive, and morning services are conducted in both Japanese and English. Rengejoin is on the opposite end of town from Okunoin, about a 40-minute walk away, but given you'll have lots of time on your hands in Koyasan—that's part of the reason people come—it's not much of an issue.

700 Koyasan. rengejoin.jp/en ✆ **0736-56-2233.** 46 units (all w/ shared bath). Rooms from ¥20,000 per person. Rates include 2 meals. Bus: Ishinguchi stop.

Shojoshinin (清浄心院) ♥♥♥ TEMPLE LODGING Of all Koyasan's temples, this one has the most curbside appeal. It has a great location at the beginning of the tomb-lined pathway to Okunoin, making it convenient for a late-night stroll to the mausoleum. Originating as a thatched hut built by Kobo Daishi almost 1,200 years ago, it was once the second-largest temple in Koyasan after Kongobuji; today it has attractive 150-plus-year-old buildings set against a wooded backdrop, including a large wooden structure with rooms overlooking a small garden and pond. There are free temple tours at 11am, noon, and 4pm daily (¥1,000 for non-guests); QR code audio guides are available. It's usually full in August and peak seasons, so make reservations early.

566 Koyasan. ✆ **0736-56-2006.** 30 units (29 w/ shared bath). Rooms from ¥13,000 per person. Rates include 2 meals. Bus: Okunoin-guchi. **Amenities:** Free Wi-Fi.

HIKING THE KUMANO KODO ♥♥♥

Kumano Honga Taisha: 45km (28 miles) SE of Koyasan.

The Kumano Kodo trail network links the Buddhist mecca of Koyasan with three of Japan's most revered Shinto sites, standing as a physical manifestation of *shinbutsu-shugo* (the syncretic relationship between Shinto and Buddhism). It cover hundreds of kilometers, with six main routes for modern pilgrims to choose from: Kiiji, Kohechi, Nakahechi, Ohechi, Iseji, and Omine Okugake-michi. Some of these paths, particularly those hugging the coastline, have succumbed to development and roadworks; the **Kohechi** trail, leading up through the peninsula en route to Koyasan (p. 397), is challenging, with three separate passes that have elevations of more than 1,000m (even seasoned hikers need around 4 days to walk it). The **Nakahechi** trail is therefore the most popular; it misses Koyasan, but it connects the three major Kumano shrines, Kumano Hongu Taisha, Kumano Nachi Taisha, and Kumano Hayatama Taisha, with inns, guesthouses, and small towns along the way. Nakahechi can be divided into

EMPEROR JIMMU & THE kumano kodo

In many ways, the Kumano Kodo holds the key to Japan's origin story. Legend has it that around 660 BC, Emperor Jimmu, the fabled first emperor of Japan, was marching with his legion of warriors through the Kii Peninsula, hoping to launch an assault on Nagasunehiko, the most powerful ruler in the land. Jimmu failed to realize how dense and mazelike the Kii forests were, and before he knew it, he and his troops were walking in circles. One evening, when Jimmu had all but given up, he received a visitor—a three-legged crow the Japanese call *Yatagarasu*, a messenger of the gods from which Jimmu was descended. Yatagarasu charted a path for Jimmu and his army to reach the other side of the peninsula. Jimmu quickly regrouped and attacked his enemies from the East, the sun rising at his back. Upon victory, he founded the Empire of Japan. Japanese believe that to walk Kumano Kodo roads today is to mirror Jimmu's ancient journey.

manageable sections; the following 2-day hike journeys through one of Honshu's finest mountain landscapes, linking Kumano Hongu Taisha and Kumano Nachi Taisha. The second day poses a stiff challenge, so you may choose to do the first day only; there are wonderful views across the peninsula on day 1, but you'll miss some of the Kodo's greatest hits on day 2.

You'll begin your walk at **Kumano Hongu Taisha,** which is a 4½-hour bus ride from Koyasan, with a stop at Gomadanzan (bus fare ¥6,050). If you leave Koyasan at 9:45am, you'll reach Kumano Hongu Taisha around 2:30pm, which leaves you tight on time for walking the trail. I recommend you spend the afternoon exploring the Kumano Hongu Shrine and stay overnight, starting on your hike in the morning. The **Kumano Hongu Heritage Center** (city.tanabe.lg.jp/hongukan; ✆ **0735-42-0751;** daily 9am–5pm) next to the shrine has some excellent trail maps and English-language brochures. **Kumano Backpackers** (✆ **0735-42-0220**) offers bunks in mixed dorms from around ¥4,500 and private twins with beds or futons for ¥9,000 to ¥13,000. For the trek, a hiking pack, waterproof clothing, and a decent pair of walking shoes are musts.

DAY 1: UKEGAWA TO KOGUCHI

From the Kumano Hongu Heritage Center it's a mostly flat 3km (1.85-mile) walk to the **Ukegawa Trail Head.** From here, you'll walk for 2½ to 5 hours on unpaved roads to the quaint, scenic town of Koguchi. The total elevation gain is around 670m (2,200 ft.), with excellent views across the mountain range at the **Hyakken-gura** viewpoint. You'll also pass by the **Ishido-chaya Teahouse,** a nice spot to enjoy a packed lunch. You'll want to rest well overnight in **Koguchi,** where a few river tributaries converge (you can swim here when the weather is nice). I recommend staying at **Koguchi Shizen-no-ie** (/小口自然の家/; kgch-go.jimdofree.com; ✆ **0735-45-2434**), an inn in a renovated junior high school, with 11 Japanese-style twin guest rooms and 2 detached Japanese-style rooms behind the dining hall. Out front is a multi-purpose lawn with benches, outdoor cooking facilities, and a free-to-use camping area. Dinner and breakfast are served in the dining hall and there are male and female communal *sento* (indoor bathhouses). One night with dinner and breakfast costs ¥9,000; pay an extra ¥550 for a packed lunch to bring on your hike the following day.

DAY 2: KOGUCHI TO NACHISAN

Koguchi is a 10-minute walk from the **Ogumotori-noe Trail Head;** it's a good idea to start early, as the trek to Kumano Nachi Taisha can take anywhere from 4 to 8 hours. Apart from a winding logging road near the midway point, the path is almost exclusively unpaved roads and stone stopes, with a total elevation gain of 1,260m (4,134ft.). You'll pass the remains of ancient teahouses, chuckling streams and waterfalls, groves of fern and flowering bamboo, an abandoned adventure park home to roaming deer, and a mountain ridge known as **Moja-no-Deai,** "The Abode of the Dead," where hikers supposedly meet deceased loved ones. At the highest point of the trail, the **Echizen-toge Pass,** a plaque quotes the Kamakura-period poet Fujiwara no Teika: "This route is very rough and difficult; it is impossible to describe precisely how tough it is." That makes it all the more rewarding when you finally arrive at your destination, **Kumano Nachi Taisha,** a structure of glinting vermillion-painted cypress overlooking the valley below. Tens of thousands of pilgrims annually come to pay their respects to the 12 gods enshrined there, including Izanami-no-Mikoto, one of the sibling creators of the land of Japan. While it's a significant site for Shinto adherents, the real object of veneration here is **Nachi-no-Otaki,** Japan's tallest single-tiered waterfall, believed to be the physical manifestation of a Shinto water deity. The best views of the waterfall are from the three-story **Seiganto-ji** pagoda (admission ¥300; daily 9:30am–3:30pm).

The waterfall at Kumano Nachi Taisha is believed to be the incarnation of a Shinto water deity.

After this demanding hike, take the no. 31 bus from Nachisan (30 min.; ¥630) to the seaside town of **Katsuura.** (Note that the last bus is at 6:01pm.) Most accommodations in Katsura are within walking distance of the station; I recommend **Kosakaya** (kosakaya.jp; ✆ **0735-52-0335**), a 120-year-old guesthouse with small but perfectly pleasant *tatami* rooms. Rates start at ¥8,800 per night, and there's an indoor hot spring bath. Dinner and breakfast, usually featuring local seafood, are served in the dining hall, or you can head to **Kumano-no-mezame** (instagram.com/kumano_no_mezame_restaurant; ✆ **070-8912-1367;** Wed–Sun 11am–2pm and 5–9pm) for high-quality sashimi, tempura, and wagyu set meals (**¥1,200–¥3,000**). The next morning, a direct train from Kii-Katsuura Station takes 4 hours to Osaka (fare **¥7,660**), with departures at 6:46am, 8:49am, and 11:49am; other trains require at least one change.

HIMEJI ♥♥

640km (400 miles) W of Tokyo; 130km (81 miles) W of Kyoto; 250km (155 miles) E of Hiroshima

Himeji, in Hyogo Prefecture, is home to a magnificent 400-year-old castle, which embodies the best in Japan's military architecture. If you were to see only one castle in Japan, this World Heritage Site should be it—though Matsumoto Castle (p. 262) would run it a close second. If time permits, it's also worth strolling the delightful garden next to the castle, Koko-en.

Essentials

ARRIVING A stop on the **Tokaido/Sanyo Shinkansen** bullet train, which runs between Tokyo and Kyushu, Himeji is about 3½ hours from Tokyo, 1 hour from Kyoto, and 2 hours from Hiroshima. The fare from Tokyo is ¥15,400 for a non-reserved seat. From Osaka Station, the JR commuter Tokaido line arrives in Himeji 1 hour later; the Shinkansen from Kyoto also takes an hour.

VISITOR INFORMATION The **Himeji Tourist Information Center** (officially called the Himeji Kanko Navi Port; ✆ **079-287-0003;** daily 8:30am–6:30pm) is located at the Central (north) exit of Himeji Station. It offers maps and free Wi-Fi. For online information, see **visit-himeji.com/en**. Most people come just for the day; the station has coin lockers.

GETTING AROUND You can walk to Himeji's attractions. The main road in town is **Otemae Dori,** a wide boulevard stretching from Himeji Station north to Himeji Castle (you can walk it in about 15 min.). To the east (right) of Otemae Dori are two parallel covered shopping arcades, Miyukidori and Omizosuji. The retro-looking **Himeji Castle Loop Bus** makes runs weekdays every half-hour from 9am to 4:30pm and every 15 minutes on weekends (no weekday service Dec–Feb) from the station to the castle, Koko-en, and beyond. It costs ¥210 per ride; an all-day ticket (¥600) includes discounts to Himeji Castle and Koko-en, but frankly, you can easily walk and save money by buying a combination ticket to the castle and garden.

Exploring Himeji

Himeji Castle ♥♥♥ CASTLE Probably the most beautiful castle in all of Japan, Himeji Castle is nicknamed "White Heron Castle" in reference to its white walls, which stretch out on either side of the *tenshu* (castle keep) like a white heron poised in flight over the plain. Whether or not you see the resemblance, the view of the white five-story donjon under a blue sky is striking, especially when the area's 1,000-some cherry trees are in bloom. This is one of the few castles in Japan that has remained virtually as it was since its completion, surviving even World War II bombings that left Himeji in ruins. In 1993, the castle, along with Horyuji Temple in Nara, became Japan's first UNESCO World Heritage Site.

A tour inside Himeji Castle reveals its sophisticated defense systems.

Originating as a fort in the 14th century, Himeji Castle took a more majestic form in 1581 when a three-story donjon was built by Toyotomi Hideyoshi during one of his military campaigns in the district. In the early 1600s, the castle became the residence of Ikeda Terumasa, one of Hideyoshi's generals and a son-in-law of Tokugawa Ieyasu. In 1609 he remodeled the castle into its present five-story structure, though it actually has a hidden sixth floor and a basement.

On weekends (and some weekdays), volunteers hanging around the castle ticket office offer guided tours of the castle for free. It gives them an opportunity to practice their English while you learn about the history of the castle and even old castle gossip. One oft-told story is that of Okiku, a servant working in the castle who was thrown down a well by a samurai after she rejected his advances. Okiku tormented the offending samurai from beyond the grave and still supposedly haunts the well in the castle's central grounds. The story has since been developed into a famous *bunraku* (puppet theater) play, *Bancho Sarayashiki,* and served as inspiration for the Japanese book and film *Ringu,* adapted for Hollywood in 2002 as *The Ring*. Even if you explore the castle on your own, you won't have any problems understanding what you're seeing: There are good English-language explanations throughout. With or without a guide, you'll spend at least 2 hours here. But beware, the grounds are huge, with lots of stairs. ***Tip:*** A combination ticket, allowing discounted admission to both the castle and Koko-en (see below), is available at either entrance. Also note that the castle now receives 1.5 million annual visitors, and the mayor of Himeji, concerned about overtourism, has touted quadrupling prices for non-residents. How much the price hike will actually be is still under debate, but it is expected to come into effect by spring 2026.

68 Honmachi. himejicastle.jp/en. ✆ **079-285-1146.** ¥1,000 adults, ¥300 children. Combination ticket Himeji Castle/Koko-en ¥1,050 adults, ¥360 children. May–Aug daily 9am–6pm; Sept–Apr daily 9am–5pm (last entry 1 hr. before closing).

Koko-en (好古園) ♥♥♥ PARK/GARDEN Although only laid out in 1992, this garden is a splendid tip of the hat to the Edo period, occupying land where samurai mansions once stood at the base of Himeji Castle, a 5-minute walk away. It's actually composed of nine separate small gardens, each one different and enclosed by traditional walls. The gardens, typical of those in the Edo Period, include an area of deciduous trees, a garden of pine trees, a bamboo grove, a garden of flowers popular during the Edo era, tea-ceremony gardens, and traditional Japanese gardens with ponds, waterfalls, and running streams. Stop off at the Souju-an teahouse in the Cha-no-niwa (tea ceremony garden), where kimono-clad women serve powdered green tea and a sweet (¥700; daily noon–4pm). Or, dine at a restaurant overlooking a carp pond (see below). If you don't stop, you can stroll all the gardens in about 45 minutes.

68 Honmachi. himeji-machishin.jp/ryokka/kokoen. ✆ **079-289-4120.** ¥310 adults, ¥150 children. Combination ticket Himeji Castle/Koko-en ¥1,050 adults, ¥360 children. Daily 9am–5pm (to 6pm May–Aug).

The carp pond at Koko-En Garden (notice Himeji Castle peeking over the treetops).

THE CUNNING ENGINEERING OF himeji castle

With its 21 gates, three moats, turrets, and a secret entrance, Himeji Castle had one of the most sophisticated defense systems in Japan. The maze of passageways leading to the donjon is so complicated that intruders would find themselves trapped in dead ends. The castle walls, made of fireproof white plaster, were constructed with square, triangular, or circular holes through which gun muzzles could poke; the rectangular holes were for archers. There are also drop chutes where stones or boiling water could be dumped on enemies trying to scale the walls. Roof eaves were designed to collect rainwater, a bonus if the castle were ever under siege.

Where to Eat in Himeji

In addition to the choices below, **Kassui-ken** (✆ **079-289-4131**) in Koko-en garden, is the most picturesque place in town to try Himeji's specialty, conger eel. It also serves a few noodle dishes and beef curry, as well as set meals (¥1,480–¥2,680). Last order is an hour before Koko-en closes.

Banshu Sakaba (播州酒場) ♥♥ IZAKAYA A few minutes' walk north of Himeji Station, this festive-looking izakaya, framed by a display of white paper lanterns (the script on each one indicates a different menu item), is ostensibly a gyoza bar, but it also serves deep-fried skewers, sashimi, grilled conger eel, yakitori, rice bowls, and other popular sharing plates like edamame and Japanese salads. Pair your food with a glass of local sake—Hyogo is one of Japan's chief rice wine-brewing regions—which can be enjoyed hot or cold.
308 Ekimaecho, just off Myukidori. ✆ **079-224-5661.** Most sharing plates ¥300–¥900. Daily 11am–11pm.

Le Chat Botté ♥♥♥ FRENCH Chef/owner Dimitri somehow has the time to greet customers, take orders, cook, and send guests happily on their way, all with a friendly demeanor (his Japanese wife also helps out). The place is small, with a counter and some tables that seat only 20 or so diners. The menu, written in Japanese on a blackboard (Dimitri can translate), ranges from a simple set lunch of appetizer, soup, and quiche to dinner entrees that may include French-style hamburger, salmon, roast duck with orange sauce, or lamb. Delicious food and welcoming service.
71 Shiroganemachi. lechatbotte.owst.jp. ✆ **079-280-3107.** Llunches ¥1,500–¥2,900; dinners ¥4,000–¥6,600; small items ¥600. Tues–Sat 11:30am–2pm and 5:30–10pm; Sun 11:30am–2pm.

Menme (めんめ) ♥♥ UDON NOODLES The friendly husband-and-wife team here has been dishing out delicous *udon* noodles at this same spot for 40 years, with tempura *udon,* curry *udon,* and other *udon* listed on the English menu. Tanimoto-san makes all of his *udon* on the spot, so though you might have to wait, it's interesting to watch the process, which he accomplishes practically at the speed of light. The restaurant's handy location—on Otemae Dori, a couple blocks from Himeji Castle—draws in many passing tourists, but it's also popular with locals.

68 Honmachi. ✆ **079-225-0118.** *Udon* ¥750–¥1,000. Thurs–Mon noon–4pm. No credit cards.

KURASHIKI ♥♥

750km (465 miles) W of Tokyo, 235km (380 miles) W of Kyoto, 177km (110 miles) E of Hiroshima

Kurashiki is a top contender for the title of Japan's most picturesque town, with a small but delightful historic district set around a willow-fringed canal. As an administrative center of the shogunate in the 17th century, Kurashiki blossomed into a prosperous market town where rice, sake, and cotton were collected from the surrounding region and shipped off to Osaka and beyond. Back in those days, wealth was measured in rice; large granaries were built to store the mountains of granules passing through the town, and canals were dug so that barges laden with grain could work their way to ships anchored in the Seto Inland Sea. (Kurashiki, in fact, means "Warehouse Village.") It's these warehouses, still standing and now converted into restaurants, shops, and *ryokan,* that give Kurashiki its distinctive charm. Kurashiki is also known for its museums, especially the prestigious **Ohara Museum of Art,** with a collection of European and Japanese art. Kurashiki is hardly undiscovered—visitors flock here in droves, especially in summer, and bus lots beside the old town mar the atmosphere—but Kurashiki is still worth visiting if you're in this corner of Japan.

Essentials

ARRIVING Although Kurashiki has a Shinkansen station (**Shin-Kurashiki**), most Shinkansen trains do not stop there, and the station is inconveniently located about 9.5km (6 miles) west of the city center (a frequent local train connects Shin-Kurashiki and Kurashiki stations, a 9-min. ride). From most destinations, you're better off getting off the Shinkansen in Okayama and transferring to the **JR Sanyo Line** to **Kurashiki Station,** in the heart of the city (trip time: 17 min.; fare ¥330). From Tokyo, an unreserved seat on the Shinkansen to Okayama followed by the JR Sanyo Line to Kurashiki Station takes about 4½ hours and costs ¥17,330. An overnight **highway bus** (willer-travel.com/en; ✆ **050-5805-0383**) departs Tokyo's Shinjuku Station nightly at 9:30pm, arriving in Kurashiki at 8:10am, and can cost anywhere from ¥5,000 to ¥13,000 one-way.

VISITOR INFORMATION A **tourist information office** located outside Kurashiki Station to the right (✆ **086-424-1220**) is open daily 9am to 6pm. Another tourist information office, called the **Kurashiki-Kan** (kurashiki-tabi.jp; ✆ **086-422-0542**), is right on the canal in the historic district. It was built in 1916 and is the only Western-looking wooden building in the area.

GETTING AROUND You can walk to virtually everywhere of interest in Kurashiki; the historic district is zoned mostly for pedestrians. The historic warehouse district is only a 10-minute walk south from Kurashiki Station.

Exploring Kurashiki's Bikan Historical Quarter

Kurashiki's **historic old town** is centered on a canal lined with graceful willows and 200-year-old granaries made of black-tile walls topped with white mortar. Many of the granaries have been turned into museums, *ryokan,* restaurants, and boutiques selling hand-blown glass, Bizen pottery, papier-mâché toys, women's clothing imported from Bali and India, and the two local specialties—mats and handbags made of *igusa* (rush grass), or clothing and decorative items made from denim. Street vendors sell jewelry, their wares laid out beside the canal, and healthy young men stand ready to give visitors rides in rickshaws.

It's best to awaken early, before shops and museums open, to explore this tiny area while it's still under the magical spell of the early morning glow, when there's little moving except for the odd heron perched on a rowboat preening its feathers. Pray for rain—it keeps others indoors and enhances the poetry of the setting. Early evenings are pretty, too, when lights along the narrow walkways flicker to life. And don't overlook the side streets between the canal and Achi Shrine in Tsurugatayama Park, especially the neighborhoods of Honmachi and Higashimachi, with cafes, antique stores, and boutiques.

Ohara Museum of Art (Ohara Bijutsukan) ♥♥♥ ART MUSEUM
Believing that people even in remote Kurashiki should have the opportunity to view great works of art, industrialist Ohara Magosaburo (that's his

Kurishiki's picturesque historic district centers on a willow-lined canal.

stately mansion across the canal from the museum) founded this impressive institution in 1930, Japan's first museum of Western art. The main building, a two-story stone structure resembling a Greek temple, is small but manages to contain the works of Picasso, Matisse, Vlaminck, Monet, Pissarro, Sisley, Chagall, Toulouse-Lautrec, Gauguin, Cézanne, El Greco, Modigliani, Renoir, Miró, Kandinsky, Pollack, Rothko, Jasper Johns, De Kooning, Warhol, and many more. The museum has expanded so much over the years that several annexes have been added. A *mingei* (Japan's 20th-c. folkcrafts) gallery housed in a series of renovated Edo-era granaries contains exquisite ceramics by Hamada Shoji, Bernard Leach, and Kawai Kanjiro, and woodblock prints by Shiko Munakata, who lived in Kurashiki for 3 years. It connects to the Asian Art Gallery, which displays ancient Chinese art, primarily from prehistoric times to the Tang Dynasty (A.D. 618–907). A walk through a garden brings you to an annex devoted to Japanese artists painting in the Western style and to contemporary Japanese artists like Shigeru Aoki, Ryusei Kishida, and Ryuzaburo Umehara. Allow up to 2 hours to see everything—your ticket is good all day, so you don't have to see it all at once.

1–1–15 Chuo. ohara.or.jp. ✆ **086-422-0005.** ¥2,000 adults, ¥500 children. Tues–Sun 9am–5pm (Dec–Feb closes at 3pm).

The Ohashi House (Ohashi-ke; 大橋家住宅) ♥ HISTORIC HOME

Built in 1796 by a wealthy salt and rice merchant, this traditional mansion is typical of the era, with front rooms used for entertaining guests and conducting business (the doorsill leading to the warehouse can be removed for easy transport), and the rear used as family living quarters. An imposing front gate, usually allowed only in homes belonging to the samurai class, is proof of how important the Ohashi family was (remarkably, the Ohashi family still owns the house). Once much larger (sadly, a hotel occupies the former garden), the home's 20 remaining rooms contain some family heirlooms. Listen to a short audio introduction in English and take a 15-minute spin through if you've never seen the inside of a traditional Japanese home. There's no sign in English, but you'll find it across Chuo Dori from Bikan Historical Quarter, on the left side behind the Royal Art Hotel.

3–21–31 Achi. ohashi-ke.com. ✆ **086-422-0007.** ¥550 adults, ¥350 seniors and children. Daily 9am–5pm (Apr–Sept Sat to 6pm; Dec–Feb closed Fri).

Where to Stay in Kurashiki

Cuore Kurashiki ♥♥♥ Hidden in the Bikan Historical Quarter, this super cool hostel feels like it could be on a beach in Thailand's Phi Phi islands. Check-in is downstairs in a comfy cafe/bar, at a reception desk cleverly constructed out of stacked old suitcases. It's the kind of place you won't mind hanging out in—quite literally, as it even has a small separate room strung with hammocks—with free Wi-Fi, sofas, an alcove library, bar food like pizza and fish and chips, and a full-service bar. A central glass ceiling hints at the rooms above, lined along an atrium corridor on the second and third floors (there's no elevator). In addition to three six-person dormitory rooms with bunkbeds (one is for women only, the other two for both genders), there are single, twin, and double rooms, small but with funky decor that's different in each. The two most expensive rooms, for one or two persons, have private showers and toilets. The hostel also offers two one-room apartments with kitchenettes a minute's walk away. Breakfast, served at the bar 7 to 8:30am daily, costs ¥500.

1–9–4 Chuo. bs-cuore.com. ✆ **086-486-3443.** 19 units. ¥3,000–¥5,000 dorm bed; ¥4,000–¥12,000 private room. **Amenities:** Cafe/bar; free Wi-Fi.

Kurashiki Ivy Square Hotel ♥♥ When this 1882 brick cotton mill was converted to a hotel in 1974, much of the old architectural style was left intact, making for an interesting setting. The rooms, renovated during the pandemic, are simple, cozy, and spotlessly clean, with some facing a tiny expanse of green grass and an ivy-covered wall or a koi-filled canal. They range from small, inexpensive economy rooms with very narrow beds to deluxe two-room suites with sofas and living areas. The historic quarter is a minute's walk away.

7–2 Honmachi. ivysquare.co.jp. ✆ **086-422-0011.** 145 units. ¥15,000–¥45,000 double. **Amenities:** Restaurant; bar; summer beer garden; free Wi-Fi.

Ryokan Kurashiki (旅館くらしき) ♥♥♥ This venerable *ryokan* in the Bikan Historical Quarter consists of an old mansion and three converted rice-and-sugar warehouses more than 260 years old, all in its own little compound connected by a corridor of black marble polished to a sheen. It's set right on the willow-lined canal. Filled with antiques and curios, it has long narrow corridors, nooks and crannies, and the peaceful sanctuary of an inner garden. There's no other *ryokan* in Japan quite like this one. Its eight rooms are actually two- and three-room suites consisting of a *tatami* living room and sleeping quarters with Western-style beds, and they are simply elegant, with antiques placed here and there, and Jacuzzi tubs. Two are big enough for up to six people (although no children younger than 13 are allowed), and three overlook the canal.

4–1 Honmachi. ryokan-kurashiki.jp/en. ✆ **086-422-0730.** 8 units, 2 villas. ¥25,000–¥60,000 per person; villas ¥20,000–¥50,000 per person. Rates include 2 meals. **Amenities:** Restaurant; free Wi-Fi.

Set in the historic district, Ryokan Kurashiki offers a twist on the traditional inn set-up: *Tatami* living rooms with Western-style beds.

Tsurugata (鶴形) ♥♥ Rustic furniture, aged wood, and memorable meals of seasonal specialties are trademarks of this *ryokan,* on the canal in the Bikan Historical Quarter's oldest building, constructed in 1744. It was once a merchant's house and shop selling rice, cotton, seafood, and cooking oil. The most expensive rooms have a view of the garden (even from their cypress tubs) with its 400-year-old pine trees and stone lanterns, while the least expensive, rather ordinary six-mat *tatami* rooms, are on the second floor with views over the historic district. All rooms have private toilets, but all but the more expensive rooms share a common bath.
1–3–15 Chuo. turugata.jp ✆ **086-424-1635.** 11 units (3 w/ private bath). ¥30,000–¥45,000 per person. Rates include 2 meals. **Amenities:** Restaurant; free Wi-Fi.

Where to Eat in Kurashiki

In addition to the options below, **Ryokan Kurashiki** (Tues–Sun 11am–2pm) serves elegant, seasonal set lunches (the mini *kaiseki* meals cost ¥4,500) in a tea lounge with views of its garden. Evening summer beer gardens are located in the courtyard of **Ivy Square** (p. 413). Next to the Ohara Museum, the one-room **El Greco Coffeehouse** (✆ **086-422-0297;** Tues–Sun 10am–5pm) is Kurashiki's most famous coffee shop, open since 1959. With an ivy-covered stone facade and simply decorated with a wooden floor, wooden tables, vases of fresh flowers, and El Greco photos, it serves coffee, green tea, fruit juice, milkshakes, ice cream, and cake.

Hachikengura ♥♥ FRENCH Occupying a converted rice granary that once belonged to the Ohashi family (see p. 412), Hachikengura offers an atmospheric meal in a room with a soaring wood-beamed ceiling, tiled walls, worn wooden floor, and tables widely spaced for privacy. The food is French, with a number of Japanese touches. You can eat here more economically at lunch; even the least expensive set meal is delicious. Reservations recommended.
Kurashiki Royal Art Hotel, 3–21–19 Achi, across Chuo Dori from Bikan Historical Quarter. royal-art-hotel.co.jp. ✆ **086-423-2122.** Main dishes 2,400–¥7,000; set lunches ¥2,750–¥6,050; set dinners ¥5,500–¥16,500. Daily 11:30am–1:30pm and 5:30–8:30pm (last order).

Kamoi (カモ井) ♥♥ VARIED JAPANESE Set in a 200-year-old rice granary on Kurashiki's willow-fringed canal, across from the Ohara Museum, Kamoi is sparingly decorated with stark white walls, dark wooden beams, and hanging white paper lamps. But that's just fine, because the view of the canal through the windows is mesmerizing. Best item on the (English language) menu is the *Kurashiki bento* with tempura, vegetables, and seasonable goodies. Noodle dishes, and the *Kamoi teishoku* (featuring sashimi and *chirashi-zushi*—seafood rice bowl) are also available. The restaurant stocks bottles of local beer, including the Okayama Pale Ale and Kurashiki Hazy IPA.
1–3–17 Chuo. ✆ **086-422-0606.** Set meals ¥1,600–¥3,300. Thurs–Tues 11am–5pm (Sat–Sun from 10:30am; closed 2nd Mon of month).

Kurashiki Takataya (亀遊亭) ♥♥ YAKITORI With seats running along the counter, the customers here are almost on top of the hibachi grills, where the chefs cook a myriad of tasty chicken and veg skewers. This creates a lively atmosphere, not to mention that you'll be bathed in beautiful umami smells all evening (be prepared to do some laundry on returning home). Whether it's bacon-wrapped asparagus, chicken breast with *shiso* leaf, crispy chicken skin, *negima* (chicken thigh and spring onion), *shishito* peppers, or shitake mushrooms—or more delicate offerings like steamed tofu with soy sauce and shredded seaweed—expect the fare to be high-quality. The menu is in Japanese, but pictures of the skewers make ordering easy.
11–36 Honmachi, east of the historic quarter. instagram.com/yakitori_takataya/. ✆ **086-425-9262.** Around ¥4,000 per person for dinner and drinks. Tues–Sun 5–10pm (last order).

MATSUE ♥♥

724km (450 miles) SW of Tokyo; 186km (116 miles) NW of Okayama; 402km (251 miles) NE of Hakata (Fukuoka)

Lying near the northern coast of western Honshu, Matsue is off the beaten track for most foreign tourists, who tend to keep to a southerly route in their travels toward Hiroshima and Kyushu. Japanese, however, are quite fond of Matsue, the capital of Shimane Prefecture, with a population of about 195,000. A fair number of them choose to spend their summer vacation in and around this pleasant town, visiting its castle and other sights, including a nearby museum highlighting contemporary Japanese art in a fantastic garden setting and a museum dedicated to Lafcadio Hearn (also known as Koizumi Yakumo), one of the foremost cultural interpreters of Japan in the late 19th century. Hugging the shores of Lake Shinji and Nakaumi Lagoon, cut in half by the Ohashi River, and crisscrossed by a network of canals, Matsue is a pretty castle town—in fact, I'd argue it might be Japan's most attractive city—blessed with Edo-Era architecture, particularly along the castle moat where many samurai settled. All these things conspire to make a trip to Matsue—despite its out-of-the-way location—very worthwhile.

Essentials

ARRIVING The easiest way to reach Matsue is from Okayama via the 2¾-hour **JR limited express Yakumo train** ride (¥6,140 for an unreserved seat). You can also fly to Izumo Airport from Tokyo with **Japan Airline** (**JAL**) for ¥15,000, then take the airport limousine bus to Matsue, which takes 35 minutes and costs ¥1,050. A **highway bus** (willer-travel.com/en; ✆ **050-5805-0383**) departs from Tokyo's Shinjuku Station at 7:40pm and arrives at Matsue Station at 7:30am (fare ¥9,000–¥15,000 one-way). From Hiroshima, 14 buses depart daily, taking 3½ hours and costing ¥4,200 one-way.

VISITOR INFORMATION Upon arrival at Matsue Station, stop at the **Matsue International Tourist Information Office** (✆ **0852-21-4034;** daily 8:30am–6pm), located in a contemporary-looking kiosk in front of the station's north exit, where you can pick up English-language brochures and a good map of the city. Be sure to ask for a brochure listing discounts (up to 50%) available to international visitors for nine tourist sights in and around Matsue, including Matsue Castle and the Adachi Museum of Art (you'll have to show your passport at each site for the discount). Go to **visit-matsue.com** and **www.kankou-shimane.com/en** for more information on Matsue.

GETTING AROUND Matsue's attractions lie to the northwest of the station and across the Ohashi River. Buses run virtually everywhere, but you can easily cover most distances on foot. **Matsue Castle** is about a 30-minute walk from Matsue Station, with most attractions located just north of the castle along a picturesque moat on a street called Shiomi Nawate. To the west of Matsue Station, about a 10-minute walk away, is **Lake Shinji,** famous for its sunsets.

If you prefer to ride, ¥520 (children pay half-price) buys you an all-day pass for the **Lake Line,** which features red old-fashioned buses running every 20 minutes in a 50-minute loop through the city. They begin at Matsue Station and stop at most tourist sights daily between 8:40am and 6:56pm (8:20am–6:11pm Dec–Feb). Single trips cost ¥210.

Goodwill Guides in Matsue

Although Matsue's sights are concentrated in one area of town and are easy to find on your own, you may want a "goodwill guide" to show you around, especially if you're going to Izumo Taisha Shrine. Established by the Japan National Tourist Organization, the goodwill guide network is composed of volunteers with foreign-language abilities who act as guides in their city. All you have to do is pay their transportation costs and entrance fees into museums and sights—and it's nice if you buy them lunch, too. If you wish to have a guide, apply at the tourist information office 2 or 3 days in advance (kankou-shimane.com/en; ✆ **0852-21-4035**).

Exploring Matsue

International visitors are entitled to 50% discounts at Matsue Castle, Buke Yashiki, Lafcadio Hearn Memorial Museum, Adachi Museum of Art, and a few other attractions by showing their passport at attraction entrances. The prices below are the regular fare, without the discount.

Matsue Castle ♥♥ CASTLE First built in 1611 and partly reconstructed in 1642 and again in the 1950s, Matsue Castle is the only castle along this northern stretch of coast built for warfare (as opposed to serving merely as a residence). It's also one of Japan's few remaining original castles—that is, its main keep is not a ferroconcrete reconstruction. Rising

Afloat on the Moat

On the **Horikawa Pleasure Boat Tour ♥♥** (matsue-horikawameguri.jp/language/en/; ✆ **0852-27-0417**), you can cruise along Matsue Castle's moat aboard flat-bottom boats (take off your shoes and sit on *tatami*) with a rooftop canopy that lowers for tight squeezes under bridges. It's a picturesque, relaxing way to see the city, with trips around the castle lasting about an hour. In winter, you can keep warm huddled under a *kotatsu* (a kind of heated blanket). Note, however, that commentary is in Japanese only. Boarding spots are at Karakoro Hiroba near the Kyobashi Bridge (Lake Line Bus stop no. 6) and Otemae near Matsue Castle (Lake Line Bus stop no. 8). Boats run every 20 minutes daily from 9am to 5pm (Nov–Feb to 4pm). An all-day ticket allowing you to disembark and embark as much as you like costs ¥1,600 for adults and half-price for children; foreigners get a 33% discount by showing their passport.

from a hill about 1.5km (1 mile) northwest of Matsue Station, with a good view of the city, the five-story donjon (which actually conceals six floors to give its warriors a fighting advantage) houses the usual *daimyo* and samurai gear, including armor, swords, helmets, and lacquerware that belonged to the Matsudaira clan, who ruled for 10 generations.

Lafcadio Hearn, an American writer who moved to Matsue in the 1890s (see box on p. 418), said of Matsue Castle: "Crested at its summit, like a feudal helmet . . . the creation is a veritable architectural dragon, made up of magnificent monstrosities." He also described it as "moldering," but it is well-maintained today. As you walk through the castle up to the top floor, notice the staircase: Although it looks sturdy, it's light enough to be pulled up to halt enemy intrusions. Concealed holes on the second floor could serve as drop chutes for raining stones down on invaders. The top floor, with windows on all four sides from which the feudal lord could command his army, is one of the few watchtowers remaining in Japan. And to think the castle almost met its demise during the Meiji Restoration, when the ministry of armed forces auctioned it off, hoping to rid the city of its feudal-era landmark. Luckily, former vassals of the clan pooled their resources and bought the castle. In 1927, the grounds were donated to the city.

Also on castle grounds is the Matsue Kyodo Kan, a Western-style Meiji-Era building built in 1903 to accommodate Emperor Meiji should he ever turn up (he never did). Today it houses the **Matsue Historical Museum,** with free admission to its changing exhibits. Jozan Park surrounds the castle, providing some lovely strolling paths, where you walk in the company of herons, turtles, frogs, cicadae, and various other animals prevalent in Japanese folktales. Give yourself an hour to tour the grounds in full.

1–5 Tonomachi. matsue-castle.jp. ✆ **0852-21-4030.** ¥680 adults, ¥290 children. Daily 8:30am–5pm (Apr–Sept 7am–7:30pm). Last entry to castle tower 30–60 min. before closing. Lake Line bus: stop no. 7, Matsue-jo Otemae (1 min.).

ATTRACTIONS NEAR THE CASTLE

Most of these attractions are located on Shiomi Nawate, a small, picturesque street beside the castle's north moat. They are listed in geographic order, walking east to west.

Teahouse Meimei-an ♥ TEAHOUSE This is one of Japan's most renowned and well-preserved thatch-roofed teahouses, built in 1779 upon orders of a 29-year-old lord of the Matsudaira clan. It's located at the top of a flight of stairs, from which you have a good view of Matsue Castle. Note the waiting room (and its ancient toilet) for guests awaiting a summons to the teahouse. A separate building offers bitter Japanese green tea and sweets for an additional ¥410, which you might find refreshing before you move on to your next destination.

278 Kitahori-cho. meimeian.jp/meimeian. ✆ **0852-21-9863.** ¥410 adults, ¥300 students, free for children. Daily 8:30am–5pm (Apr–Sept until 6:30pm). Tea served 9:50am–4pm (Apr–Sept until 4:30pm). Lake Line bus: stop no. 9, Shiomi Nawate (4 min.).

Buke Yashiki ♥ HISTORIC HOME This ancient samurai house, facing the castle moat, was built in 1730 and belonged to the Shiomi family, one of the chief retainers of the Matsudaira feudal clan residing in the castle. High-ranking samurai, the Shiomi family lived pretty much like kings themselves, having separate servants' quarters, a tearoom, and even a shed for their palanquin, though it's a bit austere compared with samurai

WHO WAS lafcadio hearn?

Japanese are fascinated with Lafcadio Hearn, a Greek-Irish writer who married the daughter of a Matsue samurai and adopted the name Koizumi Yakumo. Born in 1850 in Lefkada, Greece, and raised in Dublin, Ireland, he moved to the U.S. at age 19, where he cut his literary teeth at the *Cincinnati Enquirer,* followed by years in New Orleans and the French West Indies. In 1890 a newspaper assignment sent the 40-year-old Hearn to Japan. He immediately fell in love with the country and never left, becoming a Japanese citizen and converting to Buddhism. Curiously, Hearn never properly learned the Japanese language—in fact, he thought it an impossible task for any "occidental" to achieve (even though friends and mentors, like Japanologist Basil Hall Chamberlain, proved otherwise).

Hearn was one of the first writers to give Japanese the chance to see themselves through the eyes of a foreigner and to describe Japan to the outside world. But the real reason Japanese, and particularly the people of Matsue, fell in love with Hearn was his body of work on Japanese ghost stories. Hearn traveled widely in Izumo Province, collecting old tales from vagabonds, countryfolk, fishermen, and drifters, then reimagined them in his lucid prose style. (He's regarded by many as the father of the Japanese ghost story.) He wasn't just researching the macabre and the grotesque for pleasure; he believed "the ghostly represents always some shadow of the truth." *Kwaidan* (meaning "Strange Stories") is widely regarded as his magnum opus and remains on local literature curricula today.

Next to the Lafcadio Hearn Memorial Museum, you can visit his former home and gaze out at the garden he wrote about in a famous essay.

residences in wealthier regions of Japan. As you walk around it, peering into rooms with their wooden walls slid open to the outside breeze, you'll see furniture and objects used in daily life by samurai during the Edo Period. You can see it all in 10 minutes.

305 Kitahori-cho. matsue-bukeyashiki.jp. ✆ **0852-22-2243.** ¥310 adults, ¥150 children. Daily 8:30am–5pm (Apr–Sept to 6:30pm). Lake Line bus: stop no. 10, Koizumi Yakumo Kinenkan-mae (3 min.).

Lafcadio Hearn Memorial Museum (Koizumi Yakumo Kinenkan) ♥♥♥ MUSEUM Here you'll find memorabilia of writer Lafcadio Hearn (1850–1904) including his desk, manuscripts, photographs, and smoking pipes, as well as extensive information on his tormented childhood and the remarkable journey that led him from abandoned pauper to one of the most respected travel writers and cultural ethnographers of his age. (Bon Koizumi, Hearn's great-grandson and a folklorist at Shimane University, is the museum director, ensuring the attention to detail is exquisite.) Original editions of his many books can be found in the upstairs library (and some are available for purchase in the museum store), provide insight into Japanese life at the turn of the 20th century.

For die-hard Hearn fans, next to the museum is **Lafcadio Hearn's Old Residence** (✆ **0852-23-0714**), a Japanese-style house (and former samurai mansion) where Hearn lived in 1891. It has a pleasant, small garden immortalized in Hearn's essay "In a Japanese Garden"—if you grab a copy of *Lafcadio Hearn's Japan* (probably the best introduction to his work) in the museum shop next door, I recommend flicking through this essay while overlooking the garden from the veranda. It gives context to the sights, sounds, and natural phenomena that so enchanted his words. Depending on how invested you are in the subject, you can tour the museum and the residence in 30 minutes to an hour (though some stay much longer).

322 Okudani-cho. hearn-museum-matsue.jp. ✆ **0852-21-2147.** ¥410 adults, ¥200 children. Combination ticket w/ Lafcadio Hearn's Old Residence ¥560 Daily 8:30am–5pm (Apr–Sept till 6:30pm). Lake Line bus: stop no. 10, Koizumi Yakumo Kinenkan-mae (1 min.).

Gesshoji Temple ♥ TEMPLE/CEMETERY This family temple and burial ground of the Matsudaira clan, feudal lords of Matsue and the surrounding region, was established in 1664 by Matsudaira Naomasa (his grandfather was the powerful Tokugawa Ieyasu). Nine generations of the Matsudaira clan are buried here, each in his own small compound spread throughout the solemn grounds. Naomasa's grave, the grandest and largest, is at the far left. At the grave of the sixth lord, look for a stone turtle (described by Lafcadio Hearn as "the monster tortoise") famous for midnight strolls that terrorized residents; if you rub its head, you'll have good luck. In June, the temple grounds are famous for stunning hydrangeas. This cemetery feels ancient and forgotten; you might find yourself the only living soul here.

Sotonakabara-cho. gesshoji-matsue.com. ✆ **0852-21-6056.** ¥500 adults, ¥300 high-school students, ¥150 younger children. Daily 8:30am–5:30pm (Nov–Mar till 5pm). Lake Line bus: stop no. 15, Gesshoji-mae (4 min.).

ON THE SHORES OF LAKE SHINJI

Shimane Art Museum (Kenritsu Bijitsukan) ♥♥ MUSEUM With huge glass windows overlooking Lake Shinji, this modern museum showcases works by artists of Shimane Prefecture, as well as art that employs water as a theme. Most of the permanent collection consists of works by Japanese artists, though there are also a few pieces by Monet, Courbet, and Rodin. In addition to its many paintings, woodblock prints, photography, crafts, and ceramics, there's a rooftop terrace and an outdoor sculpture garden (free of charge) along Lake Shinji, perfect for a sunset stroll. In fact, the museum is so attuned to sunsets that in summer it remains open 30 minutes past sunset.

1–5 Sodeshi-cho, a 15-min. walk W of Matsue Station. shimane-art-museum.jp. ✆ **0852-55-4700.** ¥300 adults, ¥200 students, free for children. Special exhibitions typically around ¥1,000. Wed–Mon 10am–6:30pm (Mar–Sept closes 30 min. after sunset). Lake Line bus: stop no. 27, Kenritsu Bijitsukan.

Half-Day Excursions from Matsue

Adachi Museum ♥♥♥ MUSEUM/GARDEN This is one of Japan's premier collections of Japanese modern art (from the Meiji, Taisho, and Showa periods) set amid a meticulously sculpted garden that has been voted the most beautiful in Japan for 20 years in a row by *Sukiya Living* magazine, also known as the Journal of Japanese Gardening. Exhibitions in the main building, which are changed four times a year to reflect the seasons, are drawn from some 200 early modern Japanese works, including the largest collection of distinguished painter Yokoyama Taikan, with at least 20 of his works always on display. Also on display are Japanese *douga* (illustrations from children's books and magazines), as well as pottery by Kawai Kanjiro and Kitaoji Rosanjin. An annex displays another 120 paintings of late-modern Japanese artists. Some of the English translations are pretty erratic; don't expect to glean too much from the info boards beside the artworks.

Surrounding the museum, the **Adachi Museum Garden** ♥♥♥ was perfectly crafted to complement Taikan's masterpieces; it's continually visible through cleverly designed windows to incorporate it into the museum's artwork. The effect is surreal, as though the garden is a "living picture," in the words of the museum's founder, like a scroll that changes with the seasons. There are several outdoor viewing spots, as well as a coffee shop overlooking a koi pond and two teahouses serving traditional cakes and powdered green tea (one with a nice view of a moss garden).

Getting There: Take the JR train from Matsue Station 20 minutes to Yasugi, and then board one of the free shuttle buses that depart nine times a day for the 20-minute ride to the museum. There are also city buses directly from Matsue, but they're infrequent; check online for a schedule. The Yakumo limited express train traveling between Okayama and Matsue also stops at Yasugi Station.

320 Furukawa-cho, Yasugi. adachi-museum.or.jp. ✆ **0854-28-7111.** ¥2,300 adults, ¥1,800 college students, ¥1,000 high-school students, ¥500 children. Daily 9am–5:30pm (Oct–Mar till 5pm). Foreigners can get a 50% discount by showing their passport.

Enormous shinemawa ropes hang over the entrance to Izumo Shrine's Kagura Hall.

Izumo Grand Shrine (Izumo Taisha) ♥♥♥ SHRINE Many shrines claim to be Japan's oldest or most significant, but there *is* something special to this ancient Shinto complex in Izumo City. It's been an important site for Shinto adherents since at least the 8th century, when it was discussed at length in the *Kojiki* (A.D. 710) and *Nihon Shoki* (A.D. 720), Japan's founding historical texts, and it is believed to be much older than that. The main deity enshrined here, Okuninushi no Okami, was considered the first godly ruler of the known earth, then called *Ashihara no Nakatsukuni*, the "Central Land of Reed Plains." He also introduced to the people of proto-Japan things like agriculture, medicine, control of national disasters, the desire to build nations, and the importance of interpersonal relations (the last of these is why visitors to the shrine clap four times, as opposed to the usual two times, during prayer rituals: twice for themselves and twice for their partners).

The shrine complex is north of the city, near the coast, and sprawls across 27,000 sq. m (42 sq. miles), full of statuary, cedar and pine trees, and broad lawns. A flagstone walkway leads to the prayer hall and ceremonial buildings. The most famous building in the compound is **Kagura Hall,** used for performances and rituals since the 1770s. Notice the enormous *shimenawa*—ropes woven from rice straw or hemp that demarcate the natural and supernatural worlds—hanging over the entrance to the hall; they're the largest of their kind in Japan, weighing nearly 5 tons. You may want to visit the **Shimane Prefecture Ancient Izumo History Museum** (✆ **0853-53-8600;** ¥300 adults, ¥100 children; daily 9am–6pm), due east of the Iron Torii Gate, though most of the information is in Japanese.

A statue in the shrine grounds depicts Okuninushi no Okami handing Japan over to the Heavens; the god kneels with his arms in the air, facing a planetary object riding the crest of a wave. This epochal event supposedly took place at **Inasa Beach,** which you can walk to in about 15 minutes. It's considered one of Japan's finest beaches, a fabled power spot where visitors can acquire otherworldly energy; it's also a scenic viewpoint, especially if you take in the sunset from the rocky outcrop here, called *Benten-jima,* with a small shrine and *torii* gate on top.

The traditional street leading to the temple grounds, **Shinmon-dori,** is lined with soba shops, tea and coffee houses, souvenir stores, and a small market.

Getting There: Take the Yakumo Line from Matsue Station to Izumoshi, then switch to the Ishibata Line to Izumotaisha-Mae Station, with a change at Kawato. The train journey should take between 90 minutes and 2 hours. The shrine is a 5- minute walk north from the station.

195 Taishacho Kizukihigashi, Izumo. izumooyashiro.or.jp. ✆ **0853-53-3100.** Free admission. Daily 6am–7pm.

Where to Stay in Matsue

Hotel Ichibata ♥♥ Matsue's best-known hotel opened its doors more than 40 years ago in a part of town called Matsue Shinjiko Onsen, a hot-spring spa. Pluses include the hotel's indoor and outdoor hot-spring public baths with views over Lake Shinji and a nearby jogging path that hugs the shores of the lake. Just behind the hotel is the private Ichibata Line train to Izumo Taisha (p. 421). None of the singles or doubles have a view of the lake, but the more expensive twins and all the Japanese-style rooms do, including some combination-style rooms with both beds and *tatami* area.

30 Chidori-cho. hotel.ichibata.co.jp. ✆ **0852-22-0188.** 142 units. ¥20,000–¥80,000 double. Lake Line bus: stop no. 18, Chidori Minami Koen (1 min.). **Amenities:** 4 restaurants; bar; lounge; indoor/outdoor hot-spring baths; room service; free Wi-Fi.

Minami-Kan ♥♥ You'll be treated like royalty at this *ryokan,* located right beside Lake Shinji. Although parts of the ryokan, including its lobby and rooms with private bathroom, are modern, the original building stems from 1888 and has several handsome *tatami* rooms with nice wood detailing (these have private toilets, but no tubs). Most rooms have views of the lake, but if you really want to feel special, stay in the two-room garden cottage right beside the lake with views of the lake and a garden. Three new "spa suites," equipped with saunas—a couple also have open-air baths (rooms 208 and 209)—opened in summer 2024. Minami-Kan is also renowned for its restaurant, open to the public daily for lunch and dinner. It's a good place to try *taimeshi,* a local specialty of steamed rice and freshwater fish. 14 Suetsugu Honmachi. minami-g.co.jp/minamikan. ✆ **0852-21-5131.** 19 units. ¥30,000–¥70,000 per person, including 2 meals. Lake Line bus: stop no. 6, Kyobashi (2 min.). **Amenities:** Restaurant; hot-spring baths; free Wi-Fi.

Ryokan Terazuya ♥♥♥ Terazuya offers good value for your money, but it also offers something money can't buy: true hospitality. This Japanese inn has been in business since 1893, owned by the Terazu family, who has shown so much kindness to foreigners that many consider their stay here a highlight of their trip. The Terazus treat guests like family, teaching them the tea ceremony in the tearoom, showing them how to make sushi in the communal dining hall, giving calligraphy lessons, and singing traditional *noh* songs in the *tatami* party room. They've even been known to escort guests to the *onsen.* The postwar building, while nothing special on the outside, is spotless and colorfully decorated inside. Located near the Shimane Art Museum and Lake Shinji, it's convenient for watching those famous sunsets. And although it's only a 10-minute walk from Matsue Station, you can call ahead to request a pickup. 60–3 Tenjin-machi. mable.ne.jp/~terazuya. ✆ **0852-21-3480.** 9 units w/ shared bath. From ¥9,300 per person, 2 meals included (from ¥5,100 w/o meals; free morning coffee and bread). Lake Line bus: stop no. 27, Kenritsu Bijutsukan (3 min.). **Amenities:** Restaurant; free Wi-Fi.

Where to Eat in Matsue

Much of Matsue's regional cuisine comes from Lake Shinji, including sea bass, smelt, carp, freshwater eel, and a small black clam called *shijimi,* popular in soups. *Warigo soba,* which comes with stacked layers of noodles, to which you add grated *daikon* radish, yam, fish flakes, and seaweed, is also popular.

Bankichi ♥ YAKITORI A branch of an Osaka yakitori-ya, Bankichi is a lively, friendly place, presided over by the grinning English-speaking owner/cook. The English-language menu offers various yakitori, including chicken, minced chicken meatballs, and chicken with leek or green pepper (which come with two sticks per dish), as well as its own brand of sake and wine. 491–1 Asahimachi. yakitori-bankichi.com. ✆ **0852-31-8308.** Yakitori ¥200–¥500. Daily 5–10pm (last order). A 2-min. walk from Matsue Station.

Ji Beer Kan ♥♥ GRILLED MEAT In a large, airy setting beside the castle moat west of the Hearn Memorial Museum, this is Matsue's microbrewery/restaurant (every town seems to have one now). You'll find it on the second floor above a souvenir shop. Four different kinds of beer are brewed: a pilsner, a hoppy pale ale, a wheat beer, and a milk stout; a beer flight with three styles costs ¥1,250. Set lunches, including those with grilled meats, are popular. Or, for gluttonous abandon, try the *yakiniku* courses; the most expensive features high-grade Shimane wagyu. These include vegetables, appetizers, and strips of beef and/or pork you cook yourself at a grill at your table.

509–1 Kuroda-cho. jibeer.ichibata.co.jp. ✆ **0852-55-8877.** Yakiniku courses ¥1,870–¥3,630, beer flights ¥1,250. Daily 9:30am–5pm. Lake Line bus: stop no. 11, Horikawa Yuransen Noribo (1 min.).

Kaneyasu ♥ FISH/VARIED JAPANESE Around for more than 60 years, this modest one-counter place with *tatami* rooms upstairs has good food and is run by bustling grandmotherly women. Most of its customers are local working people, so avoid the noontime rush. It has a great lunch *teishoku,* which includes a piece of *yakizakana* (grilled fish), vegetable, soup, tofu, rice, and tea. In the evening, both set meals feature locally caught seafood.

569–3 Otesemba-cho. ✆ **0852-21-0550.** Lunch teishoku ¥780, set dinners ¥3,000. Mon–Fri 11am–2pm; Sat and Sun 5–9pm. Closed holidays. A 5-min. walk north of Matsue Station.

Kyoragi ♥♥ LOCAL SPECIALTIES Located across from Ji Beer Kan (above), this woodsy modern eatery with lots of windows and both *tatami* and table seating specializes in dishes based on original Izumo recipes, using organic meats and vegetables whenever possible. The lunch menu, which comes with English translation, features sashimi bowls, soba sets, and beef steak plates. Alternatively, you can reserve (at least 3 days in advance) a private room with kaiseki for dinner from ¥4,000 per person, excluding tax.

512–5 Kuroda-cho. kyoragi55.com. ✆ **0852-25-2233.** Set lunches ¥1,500–¥2,500; dinner sets from ¥3,000. Wed–Sun 11am–2pm and 5–8pm. Lake Line bus: stop no. 11, Horikawa Yuransen Noribo (1 min.).

Menya Hibari ♥♥ RAMEN The owner of this ramen shop near Matsue Castle trained in a traditional Japanese restaurant, which has allowed him to elevate the flavors of his signature broth, a combination of slow-cooked pork bones and locally caught *tobiuo* (flying fish) stock. This is what I recommend you order, but there are other options, like chicken broth and truffle ramen, spicy miso ramen, and shrimp and shellfish broth salt ramen. Usually, an abundance of different ramen styles indicates that the kitchen is spreading itself too thin, putting out a handful of good ramen, rather than one *great* ramen. Not so here; all of the soups are complex and super tasty in their own ways. There are also pictures on the menu to help you order.

189 Kitahoricho. menya-hibari.jp. ✆ **0852-21-5062.** Ramen ¥880–¥1,580. Tues–Sun 11:30am–2:30pm and 5–8:30pm (last orders). Lake Line bus: stop no. 5, Shiomi Niwate (2 min.).

Yakumoan ♥♥ SOBA NOODLES A great place to stop off for lunch if you're sightseeing along Shiomi Nawate north of Matsue Castle, this lovely *soba* shop has a teahouselike atmosphere, surrounded by a stone wall with a large wooden entryway, a grove of bamboo, bonsai, a Japanese garden, and a pond full of prize carp. Part of the restaurant, a former samurai residence, dates from 200 years ago. Its specialty is noodles, all handmade, including the local specialty Warigo *soba* and *udon*. Seating is at either tables or *tatami*.

308 Kitabori-cho. yakumoan.jp. ✆ **0852-22-2400.** Noodle sets ¥900–¥2,300. Daily 11am–1:30pm (last order) or when noodles run out. Lake Line bus: stop no. 10, Koizumi Yakumo Kinenkan-mae (1 min.).

YUNOTSU ONSEN ♥♥

675km (419 miles) SW of Tokyo; 76km (47 miles) SW of Matsue; 65km (40 miles) NE of Masuda; 78km (48 miles) N of Hiroshima

Mythology runs deep in this relatively sleepy corner of west Japan, and in the hot-springs town of Yunotsu Onsen, an ancient ritual called ***kagura*** ♥♥♥ is performed weekly to a small audience of locals and travelers. A theatrical style of dance, with little dialogue, kagura has one primary objective: To entertain the gods. Kagura is mentioned in Japan's ancient 8th-century texts, but it's believed to be much older, with a primitive version likely appearing not long after Shintoism itself. It's also performed in other parts of Japan, including Hiroshima and Miyazaki, but Yunotsu Onsen is a true heartland of the craft, with 130 troupes in the surrounding Iwami region; 8 artisans still make papier-mâché masks, the most important of kagura props. Yunotsu Onsen itself is charming, with hot-spring bathhouses, old-world buildings, and spiritual iconography lining the narrow streets, and the World Heritage Iwami Ginzan Silver Mine nearby. But the kagura performances every Saturday night at **Tatsugozen Shrine** are the real reason to visit. I'd argue kagura is Japan's most approachable performance art: At its best, it simply presents timeworn stories of good vs evil or a god's journey of self-discovery, and it's an absolutely joy to watch.

You can visit Yunotsu as a day trip from Matsue or Izumo, but I recommend staying the night, which will be necessary if you're here to see the evening kagura performance.

Essentials

ARRIVING The **San'in Line Limited Express** from Matsue Station runs every couple of hours from around 8:30am. Some of these trains

Plan well in advance to attend an authentic kagura performance in Yunotsu Onsen.

involve a transfer in Izumo, increasing both travel time and cost, but the direct train takes 70 minutes and is ¥3,250. From Tokyo, you can fly on All Nippon Airways to Hagi-Iwami Airport in Masuda (fare from ¥9,000; flight time around 95 min.), take a bus to Masuda Station, then switch to the San'in Line to Yunotsu Onsen, a total trip time of less than 2 hours.

VISITOR INFORMATION The **Yu Yu Kan Tourist Information Center** (ginzan-wm.jp; ✆ **0855-65-2065;** daily 8:45am–5:30pm), overlooking the river port at 794–1 Yunotsucho, has information leaflets; some exhibits upstairs focus on the Iwami region, which includes Yunotsu. Most of the material is in Japanese, but there is a handy gourmet map, and the staff are super friendly. They can help you book a kagura performance, but it's simpler to do it through your accommodation.

Exploring Yunostu Onsen

Iwami Ginzan Silver Mine ♥♥ Northeast of Yunotsu Onsen in the town of Omori (about 20 min. by car, though it can take an hour by public transport), this historic silver mine was awarded World Heritage status in 2007. Active for almost 400 years, from the 16th through the 20th century, in its heyday this mine produced a third of the world's silver—silver was one of the premier commodities Japan traded with the Dutch East India Company during the Edo period (1603–1868). What's most impressive is how the mine is spread throughout mountains and river valleys, with 1,000 individual shafts, thus maintaining a balance between silver yield and preserving the region's nature. Visitors can go down into the **Ryugenji Mabu Mine Shaft,** opened in 1715, where you can learn about the different ways in which silver was mined throughout the centuries. The old mining town of **Omori,** 2km on foot from the Ryugenji shaft, is worth exploring, with its old samurai residences, traditional souvenir and confectionary shops, hidden temples and shrines, and the wonderfully named **Imo Daikan Museum** ("Potato Magistrate" Museum)—a nice old building containing mining tools, ore, scrolls, documents, and other period artifacts. Because the mining site is so large, around 440 hectares (1,087 acres), you can easily spend half a day trudging about. For a more streamlined experience, enlist the services of an English-speaking goodwill guide, who will guide you to the major attractions in the area in about 2½ hours. For more information on guides, go to **kankou-shimane.com** or call the **Iwami Ginzan Omori Tourist Information Center** (✆ **0854-88-9950;** daily 8:30am–5pm). E-bikes are available to rent next to the Omori Daikansho Ruins bus stop (¥700 for 2 hr.), or regular bikes (¥500 for 3 hr.), if you want to cover more ground more quickly.

HOW TO SEE A *kagura* PERFORMANCE

Backed by taiko drums, symbols, and wooden flute music, kagura performances take place on Saturday nights from 8pm to 9:30pm to a crowd of 55 people at **Tatsugozen** shrine, an unassuming wooden building at 736 Yunotsucho, only a few minutes' walk from the river port. It's intimate, like a tribal ritual, with guests encircling the foot of the stage and occasionally getting showered by bits of colored paper tumbling from the roof display or the actor's makeshift props. This is guaranteed to be one of the most memorable experiences you have in Japan.

Kagura performances are part theater, part dance, usually presenting three stories plucked from the grand bible of kagura scripts, which has been passed down the generations since the 8th century (sometimes it may include a piece written by a member of the local troupe). Each story involves some dialogue at the beginning—usually a god or some mythical warrior from the Shinto canon explaining the epic battle that's about to ensue—but there's little left to interpretation. The showstopper to close out the performance is typically the tale of Orochi, the eight-headed serpent who was defeated by the god Susano-o in one of the great, violent encounters in Shinto lore.

The actors are amateurs, but they deliver their performances with aplomb, cavorting around the stage in magnificent multicolored livery and intricate papier-mâché masks depicting demons, warriors, gods, dragons, and anguished commoners. Taizo Kobayashi, a local mask maker, heads the troupe, building props, writing scripts, playing music, and sometimes acting in the stories. Having been involved in kagura since he was a boy, he approaches what is essentially a community theater effort with professional levels of detail—and it shows.

The simplest way to book a kagura performance is through your hotel. Make sure you call or email beforehand—a few months in advance, if possible—and ask them to reserve a space for you. Request a front row seat, if possible. Admission is ¥2,000.

At **kankou-shimane.com**, you can find out more about kagura performances throughout the Iwami region.

Getting There: Take the San'in Line train from Yunotsu Onsen to Odashi, then take the Omorisen Bus to Omori. Total cost ¥1,100.

Omoricho, Oda. hajimeteno.iwamiginzan.jp. Mine shaft admission: ¥200 for tourists (you'll need to present your passport). Daily 9am–5pm (mine shaft closes 4pm in winter).

Moto-yu Bathhouse ♥ As this an onsen town, you should probably set aside some time to soak in Yunotsu's hot spring water. The milky-brown, mineral-rich waters of this bathhouse, usually clocking in at around 45 degrees, have been used by travelers and locals for 1,300 years, renowned for their beautifying properties as well as for alleviating chronic pain, stress, hypertension, and fatigue. There's nothing overly decorative about the bathhouse—if anything, there's charm in its rusticity—but it's a great place to warm your bones in winter and literally soak up the town's history. It's just a few minute's walk up the street from the Tatsugozen shrine.

208–1 Yunotsucho. matsue-bukeyashiki.jp. ✆ **0855-65-2052.** ¥500 adults, ¥250 children. Daily 6am–8pm (shortened hours on selected days).

Where to Stay & Eat in Yunotsu Onsen

The main walking street of Yunotsu is lined by old inns and guesthouses, like the 115-year-old **Masuya Ryokan** (ryokan-masuya.com; ✆ **0855-65-2515**) with its stylish and beautifully named rooms—Evening Tide and The Sound of Waves are a couple of examples—and an imposing wall relief in the lobby made by the local craftsman Taizo Kobayashi (see "How to See a Kagura Performance," p. 427). Rooms go for around ¥10,000 to ¥30,000 per person (cheapest rates exclude meals). Next door to Masuya, **Nogawaya** (nogawaya.com; ✆ **0855-65-2811**) is not quite as dramatic, but it does have cozy rooms that look out at a Japanese garden and a private hot-spring bath for guests to reserve. Rooms usually cost ¥10,000 to ¥20,000 per person including two meals (those at the more expensive end of the scale have private baths and toilets).

Boonies Diner ♥♥ BURGERS This eatery would feel out of place in most onsen towns, but it's a sign that Yunotsu has modernized, in its own understated way. The traditional exterior and sliding wooden entrance door remain, but the inside is decidedly urbane, all polished wood and metal illuminated by naked bulbs. Expect burger joint classics like a double cheeseburger, chili cheeseburger, wagyu smash patty burger, and a Mexican salsa burger, all of which are served in pretzel dough buns. Non-burger options such as chili cheese fries and fish and chips, as well craft beer served on a rotating basis, are also available.

176–1 Yunotsucho. instagram.com/boonies_and_moonlit. ✆ **090-4436-7044.** Burgers ¥1,200–¥2,800; non-burger items ¥600–¥1,500; craft beer ¥900–¥1,300. Thurs–Mon 11am–2pm and 6pm–10pm.

Genshosha ♥♥ CURRY Genshosha is an artsy little restaurant and cafe in a traditional building on Yunotsu's main street; dark wooden beams and ambient lighting pair well with the *wabi sabi* pottery, modern art pieces, minimalist floral bouquets, and a communal dining table carved from a giant tree trunk. The owner, who used to work in Tokyo's corporate world, somehow convinced her husband to move to this forgotten corner of Japan and open a curry house, despite neither of them having experience in the dining scene. You wouldn't know it: The food is a delightful fusion of Asian flavors. The English-language menu features a three-curry dish for ¥1,600 and a two-curry dish for ¥1,400, both served with rice and Japanese pickles. You can choose which curries you want to combine from the likes of pork vindaloo, a mild dal, soybean keema, and lamb keema with Sichuan pepper. Sides, like falafel and stewed Iwami pork, are available, as is an extensive selection of wild grass teas, including cherry blossom and horsetail, Manchurian wild rice and mint, and Japanese Mallotus and bamboo grass. The owner is fluent in English and passionate about her adopted hometown, so if you want any advice for exploring the area, be sure to ask her.

160 Yunotsucho. shop.genshosha.jp. ✆ **0852-31-8308.** Mon–Wed and Fri 11am–2pm and 5–10:30pm (last orders), Sat–Sun 2–5pm most weekends.

Kazeto (カゼト) ♥♥ Right on the waterfront on the road into town, this guesthouse in a pair of refurbished buildings has the feel of a youth hostel without any of the partying, chaos or general disturbances. Rooms are private (twins available), while the bathrooms, shower area (toiletries provided), and kitchens are shared. The main building has three floors, with a lobby and seafood restaurant (see below) on the ground floor, and rooms spread across the other two; the two-story annex holds another five rooms. Ask for a port-facing room—202 in the annex is the best option, as it has a balcony—from which you can watch seafowl skimming across the water's surface, fishermen bringing in the day's haul, or the glorious sunsets of western Japan. Kazeto can arrange tickets for the weekly kagura performance, but note that if you're communicating by email or via a third-party channel like booking.com, you may have to translate your messages into Japanese to ensure prompt communication.

1109–17 Kohama, Yunotsucho. kazeto.snack.chillnn.com/snack/kazeto. ✆ **050-1807-9277.** 12 units w/ shared bath. ¥7,000–¥20,000 single or twin. An 8-min. walk from Yunotsu Station. **Amenities:** Restaurant; free Wi-Fi.

Port Restaurant Kan ♥♥ SEAFOODI Downstairs in the Kazeto guesthouse (see above), this seafood restaurant is open for breakfast, lunch, and dinner. Given its proximity to the Sea of Japan, you won't be surprised to hear that the fish is super fresh. There are various food options like ginger soy sauce ramen, stewed oden, and whitebait rice bowl set meals, but the fishermen's meal, featuring 4 kinds of seafood and/or shellfish caught by local fishermen, is the most popular option. Premium versions of this meal add such delicacies as cod roe, sea urchin, and *nodoguro* (blackthroat seaperch). The morning breakfasts (7:30–9am), are superb, too, provided you don't mind starting your day with sashimi bowls, tofu, pickles, stewed mushrooms, and miso soup.

1109–17 Kohama, Yunotsucho. kazeto.snack.chillnn.com/snack/kazeto-kan or instagram.com/kan_yunotsu. ✆ **0855-65-3344.** Fishermen's meal ¥1,980–¥3,960; breakfast ¥1,400. Tues–Sun 7:30–9am, 11:30am–2pm, and 5:30–9pm (sometimes closed weekday mornings).

HIROSHIMA ♥♥♥

894km (554 miles) W of Tokyo; 376km (235 miles) W of Kyoto

With a population of 1.19 million, Hiroshima, capital of Hiroshima Prefecture and the largest metropolis in the Chugoku region, looks just like any other city in Japan. With modern buildings and an industry that includes the manufacture of cars and ships, it's a town full of vitality and purpose, with a steady flow of both Japanese and foreign business executives. But Hiroshima's past is forever clouded, for it has the unfortunate distinction of being the first city ever destroyed by an atomic bomb. (The second city—and, it is hoped, the last—was Nagasaki, on Kyushu island.)

It happened one clear summer morning, August 6, 1945, at 8:15am, when a B-29 approached Hiroshima from the northeast, passed over the central part of the city, dropped the bomb, and then took off at full speed. The bomb exploded 43 seconds later at an altitude of 600m (1,980 ft.) in a huge fireball, followed by a mushroom cloud of smoke that rose 8,910m (29,700 ft.) in the air.

Approximately 350,000 people were living in Hiroshima at the time of the bombing, and almost a third lost their lives that day. The heat from the blast was so intense that it seared people's skin, while the pressure caused by the explosion tore clothes off bodies and caused the rupture and explosion of internal organs. Flying glass tore through flesh like bullets, and fires broke out all over the city. But that wasn't the end of it: Victims who survived the blast were subsequently exposed to huge doses of radioactive particles. Even people who showed no outward signs of sickness suddenly died, creating panic and helplessness among survivors. In the years that followed, blast survivors continued to suffer from the effects of the bomb, with a high incidence of cancer, disfigurement, scars, and keloid skin tissue. There are still a number of *hibakusha,* A-bomb survivors, living in the city (those in utero at the time of the blast are included), who are striving, along with younger residents, to reframe the city's narrative through the lens of peace. To that end, many of the city's landmarks have "peace" in their name, from Peace Boulevard and the Peace Line to the city's main attractions, Peace Memorial Park and the Peace Memorial Museum.

Ironically, Hiroshima's tragedy is now the city's largest tourist draw, and visitors from around the world come to see its haunting museum and memorials. But Hiroshima, laced with rivers and wide, tree-lined boulevards, has other worthwhile attractions, and it is the most popular gateway

for trips to nearby **Miyajima,** a small island renowned for its shrine and nature (p. 443).

Essentials

ARRIVING Hiroshima is about 5 hours from Tokyo by **Shinkansen** bullet train (with a change of trains in Shin-Osaka or Shin-Kobe) or 4 hours on the **Nozomi** bullet train (Japan Rail Pass users must pay a supplemental fee to use the Nozomi). It's a little less than 2 hours from Kyoto via bullet train; the fastest trains from Osaka take only 85 minutes. The fare for an unreserved seat is ¥18,380 from Tokyo on the Nozomi train, ¥10,770 from Kyoto, and ¥9,890 from Osaka.

A **highway bus** (willerexpress.com; ✆ **050-5805-0383**) departs nightly from Tokyo Yeasu Station at 7:30pm, stops at Shinjuku Station at 8:10pm, and arrives at Koikikoen-Mae Station in Hiroshima at 5:50am; it costs ¥6,400 to ¥11,500, depending on the seat and day. From Kyoto (with a stop in Osaka), buses depart three times a day, taking more than 7 hours to reach Hiroshima and costing ¥3,600 to ¥9,000 (there are also night buses).

VISITOR INFORMATION There's a **Hiroshima Tourist Information Center** (✆ **082-263-5120**) at Hiroshima Station at the north exit where Shinkansen bullet trains arrive; it's open daily 6am to midnight. A small tourist and transportation information kiosk at the station's south exit, where streetcars depart, is open daily 9am to 6pm. A third tourist office is in **Peace Memorial Park** in the Rest House (✆ **082-247-6738**)—check out the basement here, with the harrowing testimony of an A-bomb survivor, collected from diary entries, printed on the walls. It's open daily 8:30am to 6pm March to November (Aug to 7pm), 8:30am to 5pm the rest of the year. All three facilities carry pamphlets with information on Hiorshima and Miyajima, including transportation, maps, and sightseeing. They can also give you access to the city's free WiFi system. Online info is available at **dive-hiroshima.com** and **gethiroshima.com**.

City Layout

One legacy of Hiroshima's total destruction was its rebirth into one of Japan's most navigable cities, with wide, open boulevards. Hiroshima's main attractions, including Peace Memorial Park, Hiroshima Castle, Shukkei-en Garden, and Hiroshima Museum of Art, lie to the west and southwest of Hiroshima Station. From Hiroshima Station, you can walk west to **Shukkei-en Garden** in about 15 minutes, from which it's another 10-minute walk west to **Hiroshima Castle.** You can walk on south to **Peace Memorial Park** in about 15 minutes, passing the Hiroshima Museum of Art and the A-Bomb Dome on the way. To the north of the Peace Park lies **Gate Park,** a new development of shops and restaurants encircling a central plaza, that continues the city's **Peace Line,** a series of spacious postwar projects aimed at maintaining a clear view behind the Atomic Bomb Dome. Just east of Peace Park is the **Hondori** covered shopping arcade and its neighboring streets, considered the heart of the city with its many department stores, shops, and restaurants.

GETTING AROUND Most of the main attractions are easy enough to walk to. Othrwise, the most convenient mode of transportation is **streetcar,** which costs ¥220 per ride (children pay half-fare). A 1-day pass, which you can buy from the conductor, costs ¥700. You can pick up a streetcar map from the tourist office, which also describes how to use the streetcar and how to ask for a streetcar transfer ticket (*norikae*) if transferring to another line. There is also a **sightseeing loop bus,** the "Hiroshima Meipuru-pu," with three color-coded routes departing from the backside

Save on Hiroshima Public Transport

If you plan on using public transport while in Hiroshima, consider getting the Hiroshima Tourist Pass, purchased online at **mobiry.jp**. It provides free access to all streetcar routes and the Meipuru-pu, as well as ferries to Miyajima (see p. 443). It's a great value at ¥1,000 for 24 hours, ¥1,500 for 48 hours, or ¥2,000 for 72 hours. If you purchase a digital pass, you'll also get coupons to use at various tourist facilities and restaurants throughout the city.

of Hiroshima Station from around 9am to 5:30pm daily and traveling to Peace Memorial Park, among other attractions. The fare is ¥220 for one ride or ¥600 all day; holders of the Japan Rail Pass ride for free. Ask the tourist office for a bus map. Finally, bikes are available from 7am to 11pm at cycle ports around town through the city's **bike-sharing system,** called **Peacecle.** A 1-day pass costs ¥1,100; you can purchase these online by registering at mobiry.jp. Pick up a flyer at the tourist office or go to city.hiroshima.lg.jp for details.

Exploring Hiroshima

Hiroshima draws a steady flow of travelers, including Japanese school groups, who come to see Peace Memorial Park, the city's best-known landmark. Dedicated to peace, the city also seems committed to art: In addition to art museums, you'll find statues, stone lanterns, memorials, and sculptures lining the streets, many drawing on the theme of peace.

A good place to start is with a bird's-eye view of Peace Memorial Park and the mountains ringing the city from **Hiroshima Orizuru Tower** (*orizuru* means "paper crane"; orizurutower.jp; ✆ **082-569-6200**), just steps from the A-Bomb Dome at 1–2–1 Otemachi. Inside is the rooftop Hiroshima Hills wooden deck and the 12th-floor Orizuru Square, where you can make paper cranes and experience interactive displays; one lets you drop your paper crane into a glass chamber facing the street. From the outside you can see this chamber filling up with thousands of paper cranes, connecting people from across the world in one collaborative artwork. Check website for admission fees and opening hours as they vary throughout the complex. On the ground floor is a shop selling Hiroshima products, a cafe, and a tourist office open daily 10am to 6pm.

EXPLORING PEACE MEMORIAL PARK ♥♥♥

Needless to say, visiting Peace Memorial Park is a sobering experience but a necessary one, and for most visitors, their main reason for coming to Hiroshima.

It's best to start on the northern side of the park; the Meipuru-pu bus and streetcar stop here (Genbaku Domu mae stop), or you can approach from Gate Park.

The first structure you'll see as you approach the park is the **A-Bomb Dome** (**Genbaku Domu**), the shattered ruins of the former Industrial Promotion Hall, left as a visual reminder of the death and destruction caused by the atomic bomb. Inscribed on the ground to the southeast of the dome is a poem by the activist and writer Tamiki Hara, summing up the futility of nuclear war and the resilience of the human spirit: "Engraved in stone long ago / Lost in the shifting sand / In the midst of a crumbling world / The vision of one flower."

A figure of Sadako Sasaki tops the Children's Peace Monument.

Across Motoyasubashi Bridge is the park. Its main attraction, the Peace Memorial Museum, is a 10-minute walk away, at the park's southern end, but you'll likely take longer to get there, as there are 50-some statues and memorials to visit along the way. Most touching is the **Children's Peace Monument,** dedicated to the war's most innocent victims, not only those who died instantly in the blast but also those who died afterward from the effects of radiation. It's a statue of a girl with outstretched arms; rising above her is a crane, a Japanese symbol of happiness and longevity. The statue is based on the true story of a young girl, Sadako, who suffered from the effects of radiation. She believed that if she could fold 1,000 paper cranes she would become well again. Tragically, even though she folded 1,000 cranes (and many more), she still died of leukemia. Today, all Japanese children are familiar with her story, and around the memorial are streamers of paper cranes donated by schoolchildren from all over Japan. Across the road from the statue, the **Rest House** holds a branch of the Hiroshima Tourist Office, as well as an exhibit in the basement presenting the testimony of Nomura Eizo. Nomura was a staff member of the Hiroshima Prefectural Fuel Rationing Control Union who happened to go looking for his papers in the basement of this very building—a kimono shop, at the time—around 8:15am on August 6, 1945. Knocked out by the blast, he awoke to the blood-curdling screams of his colleagues and other soon-to-be-victims of the bomb. Despite the extreme levels of radiation he was subjected to, suffering from fever, diarrhea, and bleeding gums, he still managed to live till he was 84. Excerpts from his diary printed on the wall are among the most haunting pieces of survivor testimony.

To the west of the children's monument, you'll see a huge stone turtle, adorned with colorful paper streamers, with a stone stele rising from its back topped by dragon iconography. This is the **Cenotaph for Korean Victims** (the turtle is a revered Korean symbol of guardianship, longevity, and the connection between celestial and terrestrial realms). It's a little-publicized fact that some 20,000 Koreans were killed that fateful summer day, most of them brought to Japan as forced laborers. For 29 years, the cenotaph was outside the park, until 1999, when Hiroshima's mayor gave the memorial a new home here, calling for an end to prejudice against Korean residents in Japan. Nowadays the local Korean community leaves bottles of water at the base of the monument, in tribute to bomb victims who cried out for water to cool their scorched and rapidly blistering skin.

Cross the road again and head south to the **Cenotaph for the A-bomb Victims,** designed by Japan's famous architect Kenzo Tange (considered the godfather of modern Japanese architecture, he also designed the Tokyo Metropolitan Government offices in Shinjuku, p. 116). Set at the end of a long reflecting pool, it is shaped like a figurine clay saddle found in ancient tombs, arching over a stone chest that holds the names of all of those killed by the bomb and its aftereffects (more than 314,118 names have been registered so far; the number still increases each year). An epitaph, written in Japanese, carries the hopeful phrase, "Let all the souls here rest in peace, for we shall not repeat the evil." If you stand in front of the cenotaph, you'll have a view north through the hollow arch of the **Flame of Peace** and the A-Bomb Dome. It is said that the Flame of Peace will continue to burn until all atomic weapons vanish from the face of the earth and nuclear war is no longer a threat to humanity—one fears it'll keep burning for some time yet. East of the Peace Flame is the **Hiroshima National Peace Memorial Hall for the Atomic Bomb Victims** (hiro-tsuitokinenkan.go.jp; ✆ **082-543-6271**). Its circular Hall of Remembrance, a 360-degree panorama re-creating the bombed city as seen from the hypocenter, is made of 140,000 tiles, the number of people estimated to have died by the end of 1945. The rest of the memorial serves as a computerized audiovisual library with information on victims, and photos. Admission is free, and it's open the same hours as the Peace Memorial Museum.

The Cenotaph for the A-bomb Victims, with the Flame of Peace and the A-Bomb Dome beyond.

South of here, you finally come to the park's highlight, the **Peace Memorial Museum (Heiwa Kinen Shiryokan)** ♥♥♥ (1–2 Nakajima-cho; hpmmuseum.jp; ✆ **082-241-4004**), which illuminates the inhumanity of atomic bombs, the A-bomb's enormous destruction (92% of Hiroshima's buildings were destroyed or burned), and the indescribable suffering on that awful day. Exhibits show in graphic detail how Hiroshima looked before and after its destruction and the effects of the blast on bodies, buildings, and materials. There are photographs of scorched earth, charred remains of bodies, and people with open wounds, while displays explain the devastating effects of radiation. Many personal items have been donated by families of victims and survivors—tattered clothing, diaries, a wristwatch stopped at exactly 8:15—accompanied by short biographies of their owners, many of them children and teenagers. Survivor accounts describe their sufferings, not only on the day of the blast but in the many years afterward. Other displays describe the development of the atomic bomb, why Hiroshima was chosen as a target (an exhibition that explores some of the worst traits of human behavior), and the danger of nuclear proliferation. Museum admission costs ¥200 adults, ¥100 high-school students and seniors, free for children; it's open daily 7:30am to 7pm (Aug until 8pm, Dec–Feb until 6pm). Audio guides are available for ¥400, but you won't need one, as there is plenty to see and read; plan on spending 1½ hours here to do the museum justice.

EXPLORING HIROSHIMA'S OTHER ATTRACTIONS

Hiroshima Castle ♥♥♥ CASTLE Completed in 1591 but destroyed in the atomic blast, Hiroshima Castle was reconstructed in 1958, its five-story wooden donjon a faithful reproduction of the original. The main reason to come here, however, is the museum housed in the castle's modern interior. Devoted to Hiroshima's history as a flourishing castle town, it has excellent English-language presentations, including a look at castles across Japan, explaining differences in architecture between those built on hills (for defense) and those built on plains (mainly administrative, as Hiroshima's was). Videos, with English translations via earphones, describe Hiroshima's founding and the construction of Hiroshima Castle as a hub for transportation. Displays illuminate the differences in lifestyle between samurai and townspeople, the hierarchy of the feudal administration system, and other aspects of Edo life; you'll see samurai gear, swords, and models of old Hiroshima and the castle, as well as a kimono and helmet and breast plate you can try on for free. The top of the donjon provides a panoramic view of the city. Elsewhere in the castle compound, you can find trees that somehow survived the A-bomb, including a camphor on the northeastern banks of the moat and a eucalyptus to the south. Notice how the eucalyptus,

Rebuilt after WWII, Hiroshima Castle is a faithful reproduction of its 16th-century original, with an excellent museum inside.

THE FIRST CALL FOR help

Just to the east of Hiroshima Castle's shrine, look for the ruins of the **Chugoku Regional Military Headquarters Air Defense Room.** In this military bunker, a group of teenage girls known as "mobilized students" were finishing their night shifts the morning the bomb went off. One girl, Yoshie Oka, sent the first distress call to the military headquarters in Fukuyama. Unsurprisingly, they assumed there'd been a mistake when she said the *entire* city was destroyed. Not until Oka repeated the words of a burnt soldier—"the city was hit by a new type of bomb"—did they believe her. Oka died in 2017 from malignant lymphoma, a probably resulting from her radiation exposure 70 years earlier. Though she played a pivotal role in the final days of the war, there's little to commemorate her and her fellow student-workers, bar the bunker itself, now mostly overgrown, and a small commemorative plaque.

hanging over the moat, has two different types of foliage—a rare phenomenon, supposedly caused by radiation scrambling the tree's DNA.

21–1 Moto-machi. rijo-castle.jp. ✆ **082-221-7512.** Castle grounds: free admission. Main keep: ¥370 adults, ¥180 high-school students and seniors, free for children. Daily 9am–5:30pm (Dec–Feb to 4:30pm). Streetcar: Kamiya-cho-higashi (10 min.). Meipuru-pu: Hiroshima Castle.

Hiroshima Museum of Art (Hiroshima Bijutsukan) ♥♥ MUSEUM Surrounded by trees in a park just south of Hiroshima Castle, this is a gem of a private museum, housed in a modern one-story building. Its permanent collection of some 300 paintings, half by French painters from Romanticism to Ecole de Paris, is presented in chronological order, with about 100 on display at any one time. It's small, with only four rooms, but virtually every piece is by a well-known artist, including Delacroix, Courbet, Manet, Monet, Renoir, Sisley, Degas, Rousseau, Cézanne, Gauguin, van Gogh, Matisse, Picasso, Braque, Utrillo, Chagall, and Modigliani. An annex is devoted to special exhibits by both Western and Japanese artists. Plan on an hour here.

3–2 Motomachi. hiroshima-museum.jp. ✆ **082-223-2530.** ¥2,000 adults, ¥1,000 college and high-school students, ¥500 junior-high and grade school students. Higher prices during special exhibits. Tues–Sun 9am–5pm (last entry 4:30pm). Streetcar: Kamiya-cho-higashi (3 min.). Meipuru-pu: Hiroshima Museum of Art.

Mitaki-dera ♥♥ TEMPLE/HIKE It's hard to believe this temple complex and hiking trail sits on the fringe of a Japanese city. Once you enter, you're in a world of tumbling waterfalls and streams, singing cicadae and squawking birds, moss-covered statuary and gravestones, and pretty wooden structures. The main temple, moved here from Wakayama in 1951 to guide the souls of A-bomb victims into the next life, is dedicated to Kannon, the bodhisattva of compassion. But the real reason to come is to drink in how the beautiful natural surroundings enhance the religious monuments—which you'll truly appreciate by hiking to the summit of Mitakiyama, or "Three Waterfall Mountain." A signboard at the entrance to the temple grounds shows a few different hiking trails; I recommend the A course. This takes you up through an atmospheric bamboo forest to a viewpoint overlooking Hiroshima, where you'll see the city unfurling towards a cluster of islands in the Inland Sea. A photo board indicates (in Japanese only) the different landmarks you're able to see. There's also a bench here where you can rest before the descent. If you don't want to return the same way, you can take the B course back to the temple grounds. Just note that it's not particularly well signposted, and where you have to skirt around a massive concrete wall—perhaps some form of dam or rockfall prevention structure—the path is not that clear. You will see "beware of bears" signs on the trail, but these creatures are quite docile and exceedingly rare this close to civilization. In any case, it's a lovely hike and quite isolated, unlike many trails near Japanese cities. It should only take between 1 and 3 hours, depending on your hiking ability.

411 Mitakiyama, Nishi-ku. ✆ **082-237-0811.** Free admission (donation box near the entrance). Daily 8am–5pm. Take Kabe Line from Hiroshima Station to Mitaki Station, then walk 10 min. west to the temple grounds.

Shukkei-en Garden ♥ PARK/GARDEN Shukkei-en Garden, which means "landscape garden in miniature," was first laid out in 1620 by a master of the tea ceremony, with a pond constructed in imitation of famous Lake Xi Hu in Hangzhou, China. Using streams, ponds, islets, and bridges, the feudal lord's garden was designed to appear much larger than it actually is. It's best viewed on a 30-minute circular stroll. Like everything else in Hiroshima, it was destroyed in 1945, but amazingly it looks like it's been here forever. Unfortunately, as with most gardens in Japan, tall neighboring buildings detract from the garden's beauty, but there are vantage points where you can't see any buildings and lots of places to sit and relax.

2–11 Kaminobori-cho. shukkeien.jp. ✆ **082-221-3620.** ¥260 adults, ¥150 college and high-school students, ¥100 children. Daily 9am–6pm (Sept 15–Mar 15 until 5pm). Streetcar: Shukkeien-mae (1 min.). Meipuru-pu: Hiroshima Prefectural Art Museum.

Where to Stay in Hiroshima

Hotel Flex ♥♥♥ This is Hiroshima's most unconventional hotel, apparent the moment you walk in and find yourself in a cafe that doubles as the front desk and opens out onto a terrace overlooking the tree-lined Kyobashi river and promenade. A modern concrete structure, it offers tiny but fashionable rooms, some with relaxing river views and/or floor-to-ceiling windows. All are crisply decorated with blue-and-green pillows and bed runners, stark white walls, and wooden floors. The best and most expensive are three top-floor rooms that are almost like mini-apartments, without kitchens; one even has an outdoor terrace.

7–1 Kaminobori-cho. hotel-flex.co.jp. ✆ **082-223-1000.** 64 units. ¥7,500–¥27,500 double. Hiroshima Station (7 min.). **Amenities:** Cafe/restaurant; free Wi-Fi.

Hotel Park Side ♥♥ This business hotel is fairly cookie-cutter, but given the Peace Memorial Park is on its doorstep, it's a great place to stay for in-and-out travelers. The single rooms are barely large enough to stretch in, though the twins are a little more generous in size; if you book one on the higher floors (8–10), you'll also get a decent view of the park and the mountains to the west of the city. Despite their spatial shortcomings, all rooms are equipped with ultra-high density pocket mattresses, conducive to a good night's sleep.

2–6–8 Otemachi. park-side.co.jp. ✆ **082-244-7131.** 91 units. ¥6,800–¥7,300 double. Streetcar: 1 to Fukuromachi (2 min.). **Amenities:** Free Wi-Fi.

The Knot ♥♥♥ Hotels as stylish and centrally located as this one, overlooking the southern end of the Peace Park, have every right to be much more expensive, but The Knot is excellent value and by any metric one of the best places to stay in Hiroshima. On the ground floor is a cafe and restaurant called MORETHAN, one of the most popular non-Japanese restaurants in town, serving freshly baked focaccia, omelets, and acai bowls at breakfast, and pizza, pasta, and other Italian-inspired fare for lunch and dinner. To check in, you'll have to shoot up the elevator to the 14th-floor lobby, with its artsy decor of greenery and interlocking wooden floorboards, plus tremendous city views through floor-to-ceiling windows. On check-in you'll receive 2 Knot coins, which can be exchanged for drink and food items at the Kei bar, located next to the reception desk. With an outdoor terrace that also offers sublime views, this bar is a great place to start your evening with a cocktail or glass of sake before heading into town. The rooms are also smart, with soothing color palettes, funky lighting fixtures, comfortable furnishings, and nice views that get better with each floor. Deluxe twins with panoramic city views on the Peace Boulevard side of the hotel are the pick of the bunch.

3–1–1, Otemachi. hotel-the-knot.jp. ✆ **0570-009-015.** 201 units. ¥7,000–¥29,160 double. Streetcar: 1 to Chuden-mae (3 min.). Meipuru-pu: The Peace Memorial Park. **Amenities:** 2 restaurants; bar; free Wi-Fi.

Rihga Royal Hotel Hiroshima ♥♥♥ The 33-story Rihga Royal stands out as Hiroshima's tallest hotel, with a convenient location in the heart of the city between Hiroshima Castle and Peace Park; it's also connected to a large complex that includes the Pacela shopping mall and Sogo department store. Large rooms with luxurious furnishings come with plenty of features, including magnifying mirrors and lots of counter space in the bathrooms. Rates are based on floor height and room size, but even some of the cheapest twins have views of a park across the street and the distant castle. The best views, however, are from top floors with panoramas of the Seto Inland Sea (you can even see Miyajima). A nice touch are the pictorial maps in each room describing the view. The best view of all is from the 33rd-floor **Rihga Top** lounge (no cover charge if you sit at the bar).

6–78 Motomachi. rihga.co.jp. ✆ **082-502-1121.** 488 units. ¥14,300–¥47,500 single or double. Streetcar: 1 or 6 to Kamiya-cho-nishi. Meipuru-pu: Kamiyacho. **Amenities:** 5 restaurants; 2 bars; concierge; health/dental clinic; gym; pool, Jacuzzi, and sauna (¥3,250 for pool and sauna; ¥6,480 for all); room service; free Wi-Fi.

Where to Eat in Hiroshima

Although the people of Osaka claim to have made *okonomiyaki* popular among the masses, the people of Hiroshima claim to have made it an art. *Okonomiyaki* is a kind of savory Japanese pancake (or perhaps an omelet) filled with cabbage, meat, and other ingredients. Whereas in Osaka the ingredients are mixed together, in Hiroshima each layer is prepared separately, which means the chefs must be quite skilled at keeping the whole thing together. Hiroshima is also famous for its oysters (among the largest I've ever seen), with thousands of rafts cultivating oysters in Hiroshima Bay and producing 20,000 tons of shelled oysters yearly.

The recommendations below focus on restaurants, but a few cafes are also worth mentioning. **Caffé Ponte** (caffeponte.com; ✆ **082-247-7471**) offers outdoor seating under white umbrellas, even in winter thanks to heaters, and nice views of the Peace Memorial Park across the Motoyasu River. Vegans have a tough time of it in Japan, but at **Croissant Marche** (croissant-marche.blogspot.com; ✆ **082-234-8133**) on the other side of the park, you can get tasty vegan curry lunches or vegan plates, including five dishes and brown rice, for ¥1,000.

Bus Town Food Hall (バスマチフードホール) ♥♥ VARIED ASIAN Granted, there's little about the name of this place that screams "gourmet." But it's located in Hiroshima Station, your probable point of arrival and departure, and has a handful of great lunch options. Korean ramen, Thai curry, and Japanese yakisoba meals for less than ¥1,000, *teishoku* (sets featuring a main with rice, pickles, and miso soup) for ¥1,000, and an indulgent beef stew *omurice* for ¥1,100. The number of diners filling up the tables in between the hole-in-the-wall restaurant counters is a good indication that this is more than your average food hall.

6 Motomachi, next to the Bus Center. h-buscenter.com/basumachi. ✆ **082-225-3332.** Lunches ¥720–¥1,300.

Kokoroya Otemachi (心屋 大手町店) ♥♥ IZAKAYA This lively izakaya is unapologetically authentic, filling up with locals during the post-work dinner rush; you won't find many tourists in here. It serves an array of sashimi, maki rolls, fried chicken and fish, beef cutlets, Japanese potato salads, unusual bar snacks like deep-fried eel bones (these are delicious, almost like pork scratchings), and a Hiroshima favorite: oysters. Bottles of sake line shelves throughout the shop, with 140 types of sake available at ¥140 per glass. There's a good selection of shochu and fruit wine, too, if you've acquired a taste for either. The best seats are on the main floor by the counter, with wells for your feet (you'll have to take your shoes off). The menu, scribbled on sheets of paper, is in Japanese only and not very legible, so you might have to throw caution to the wind when ordering. But isn't that the joy of dining out of your comfort zone?

2-6-21 Otemachi. syokudouhyogen.com. ✆ **082-241-2210.** Dinner and drinks ¥3,000–¥5,000 per person. Tues–Sun 6pm–12:30am (last order). Streetcar: 1 to Fukuromachi (2 min.).

A CAFE DEDICATED TO peace

Hiroshima's most unconventional cafe, and one that could only exist here (or perhaps in Nagasaki), is **Hachidorisha** (hachidorisha.com/home/; ✆ **082-576-4368**), meaning "Hummingbird Cafe." Run by local peace activist Erika Abiko, it's full of bookshelves and colorful wall displays, and has a cozy raised seating area with low tables and floor cushions. People come here to discuss social issues, give presentations on peace, or brush up on peace literature—some of the books are in English, like the serialized manga, *Barefoot Gen*, following a boy who survives the atomic bombing. On occasion, they can even speak with *hibakusha* (A-bomb survivors). Abiko speaks some English but also employs the services of English guides and translators for the hibakusha events on the 6th of each month (others on the 16th and 26th are in Japanese only), so that international visitors can communicate with those who still remember the city's darkest day in 1945. The purpose isn't dark tourist voyeurism, but to gain a better understanding of the long-term effects of manmade disasters and how we as a species can make sure such a catastrophe never happens again. Given the age profile of the *hibakusha*, events may not happen as regularly as planned.

Kushinobo (串の坊) ♥♥♥ KUSHIYAKI Decorated with Japanese knickknacks, this is a friendly, rub-elbows-with-the-locals kind of place. Although kushiyaki connoisseurs prefer ordering skewers a la carte, you're probably better off ordering one of two set meals from the English-language menu. The *Kushinobo-gozen* with 10 skewers of vegetables, meat, and seafood plus pickled vegetables and soup is a good option. For dipping, there's soy sauce, mustard, and coarse salt, while a ceramic fish with an open mouth serves as the receptacle for empty skewers. Kushinobo is located off the east end of the Hondori covered arcade, behind Parco department store.

Parco-mae, 7–4 Horikawa-cho. ✆ **082-245-9300.** Dinner and drinks ¥3,500–¥5,000 per person. Daily 11:30am–1pm and 5–9pm (last order). Streetcar or Meipuru-pu: Hatchobori (3 min.).

Maruken (マルケン) ♥♥ GYOZA Sitting northwest of the Peace Memorial Park, this shop specializes in dumplings served myriad ways: classic fried gyoza, deep-fried gyoza with chili and coriander, *hanetsuki* gyoza (fried with crispy "wings"), *sui* gyoza (boiled and served in broth or soup), and *tebasaki* gyoza (deboned chicken wings stuffed with pork mince). You can also order other sharing bites, like *karaage* (deep-fried chicken thigh), crispy gyoza skin crackers, edamame, kimchi, bean sprouts with ponzu sauce, *torishimi* (raw chicken, seared on the outside), and *basashi* (raw horse meat)—don't be put off by the last two, they're tasty and perfectly safe to eat. The food is good value here, so don't be surprised if you end up working your way through the menu.

2–10–7 Yokogawacho. gyoza-maruken.jp. ✆ **082-297-7055.** Gyoza plates ¥240–¥660. Daily 5am–midnight. From Peace Memorial Park, take streetcar no. 7 to Yokogawa 1-Chome Station (2 min.).

Okonomi-Mura (お好み村) ♥♥ OKONOMIYAKI Open since 1963 as one of Hiroshima's most beloved establishments, this is the best place in town to witness okonomiyaki short-order cooks plying their trade. Although the shabby building doesn't look like it contains restaurants, its name means "okonomiyaki village," and that's what it is—three floors of some 20 individual stalls dishing out okonomiyaki. All offer basically the same menu—sit down at one of the counters and watch as the chef first spreads pancake mix on a hot griddle, then adds a layer of cabbage, bean sprouts, and bacon, and finally tops it off with an egg. If you want, you can have yours with Chinese noodles. Portions are huge. I suggest wandering through and choosing one that catches your fancy.

5–13 Shintenchi. okonomimura.jp. ✆ **082-241-2210.** Set meals ¥860–¥1,600. Most open daily 11am–10pm or 11pm. Streetcar or Meipuru-pu: Hatchobori (2 min.).

Onigiri Nitaya (お好み村) ♥♥ RICE BALLS *Onigiri* (Japanese rice balls) have become all the rage abroad, with Asian-inspired delis and restaurants serving this convenience store snack as though it were a revolutionary concept. Typically, it's the kind of thing you grab when in a rush, costing somewhere between ¥100 and ¥200, to wolf down when you get a spare minute on your commute. But some places elevate the humble rice ball to a higher culinary plane; one such shop is Onigiri Nitaya on Peace Boulevard, just east of the Peace Memorial Museum. You can buy onigiri fresh, including classic flavors like tuna mayo and *umeboshi* (pickled plum), as well as maki roll bento boxes and in-house onigiri meals that come with sides like fried fish, pickles, and soup. The last of these is the best option if you want a sit-down lunch. Note, though, there are only a few tables, so you may have opt for a meal to go.

2–11–15 Otemachi. nitaya.jp/peaceblvd. ✆ **082-546-0144.** Onigiri ¥200–¥400, onigiri meals ¥1,500–¥1,800, bento boxes ¥630–¥850. Mon–Fri 11am–1:30pm; Sat–Sun 10am–4:30pm (last order).

Yakitori Ya Yo-chan Rukawa (焼鳥酒場 ようちゃん) ♥♥ YAKITORI With sliding doors open to the streets on summer evenings, this *yakitori-ya* has the atmosphere of a steamy street market, especially if you sit at the counter and watch the chefs manning the grills. The fare is typical of a Japanese chicken joint: chicken skewers with salt or sweet *tare* dressing, raw meat sets, and grilled vegetables, including tomatoes, peppers, onions, and mushrooms like shiitake and king oyster. Located east of the Peace Memorial Park, where you'll find most of Hiroshima's real nightlife spots, this shop stays open till 3am, attracting lots of bleary-eyed revelers in search of a late-night feast.

6–21 Nagarekawacho. ✆ **082-229-7766.** Skewers from ¥220. Mon–Sat 6pm–3am. Streetcar nos. 1, 2 and 6 to Ebisucho (5 min.).

Side Trip to Miyajima Island ♥♥♥

13km (8 miles) SW of Hiroshima

Easily reached in about 40 minutes from Hiroshima, **Miyajima** is a treasure of an island only 2km (1¼ miles) off the mainland in the Seto Inland Sea. No doubt you've seen pictures of its most famous landmark: a huge red *torii,* or shrine gate, rising out of the water. Erected in 1875 and made of camphor wood, it's one of the largest *torii* in Japan, measuring more than 16m (53 ft.) tall. It guards Miyajima's main attraction, **Itsukushima Shrine,** designated a World Heritage Site in 1996. With the Japanese penchant for categorizing the "three best" of virtually everything in their country—the three best gardens, the three best waterfalls, and so on—it's no surprise that Miyajima's shrine is ranked as one of the three most scenic sights in Japan (the other two are Matsushima in Tohoku, [p. 608], and Amanohashidate, a remote sand spit, on the Japan Sea coast [p. 347]). Of course, this distinction means the shrine can be **extremely crowded** with visitors, particularly in summer and autumn. If you can, avoid coming on a weekend.

Miyajima Island itself is only 31 sq. km (12 sq. miles) in area, most of it steep wooded hills, but it's exceptionally beautiful, part of the Seto-Naikai (Inland Sea) National Park, which is mostly water, islands, and islets. Covered with cherry trees that illuminate the island with snowy petals in spring, and with maple trees that emblazon it in reds and golds in autumn, Miyajima is home to tame deer that roam freely.

Although you can see Miyajima in a day's trip from Hiroshima, you'll enjoy the island much more if you stay behind after the droves of day-trippers leave. An added benefit of a longer stay: Itsukushima Shrine is illuminated at night, a gorgeous sight (despite the ghastly night cruises

Ranked as one of Japan's most scenic sights, Itsukushima Shrine was built to appear as if it is floating above the Seto Inland Sea.

Miyajima: A Sacred Island

Miyajima has been held sacred since ancient times. In the olden days, no one was allowed to do anything so human as to give birth or die on the island; the pregnant and the ill were quickly ferried across to the mainland. Even today there's no cemetery on Miyajima.

offered around the *torii*). Below you'll find a couple recommendations on where to stay. Avoid Golden Week and weekends in spring, July, August, October, and November, when accommodations are usually full. even if you don't spend the night.

ESSENTIALS

ARRIVING The easiest way to reach Miyajima is from Hiroshima, via JR train, streetcar, or boat. **Trains** depart from Hiroshima Station approximately every 15 minutes; from downtown or near Peace Memorial Park, you can catch the train at Nishi-Hiroshima Station. The ride to Miyajimaguchi takes 28 minutes and costs ¥420 (free for JR Rail Pass holders). **Streetcar no. 2** takes about an hour from Hiroshima Station through town to Hiroden Miyajimaguchi, the last stop, and costs ¥270. Both the train and streetcar deposit you at Miyajimaguchi, from which it's just a 3-minute walk to the **ferry** bound for Miyajima. Two ferry companies (JR and Matsudai) offer the 10-minute ride to Miyajima for ¥200; if you have a Japan Rail Pass you can ride the JR ferry for free. **Boats** from downtown Hiroshima travel directly to Miyajima in about 45 minutes, operated by **Aqua Net Hiroshima** (aqua-net-h.co.jp; ✆ **082-240-5955**). They leave from Motoyasu-bashi bridge, south of the A-Bomb Dome, 10 to 15 times daily depending on the season. Fare is ¥2,200 one-way (¥4,000 roundtrip); children pay half fare. Note that service is suspended during inclement weather and when the tide is low.

VISITOR INFORMATION The **Tourist Information Office** (miyajima.or.jp; ✆ **0829-44-2011;** daily 9am–6pm) is in the Miyajima ferry terminal. For more info, go to **visit-miyajima-japan.com**.

EXPLORING MIYAJIMA ISLAND

You can walk from the ferry to all the sights, accommodations, and restaurants listed below. **Omotesando Dori,** the long, narrow main street leading to the shrine, is lined with shops and restaurants. Miyajima is also known for its beaches—west of the town and shrine, look for **Suginoura** and **Tsutsumigaura Natural Park** (you can also camp here; rental tents and cabins are available; tsutsumigaura.com/en/index.html).

Daisho-in Temple ♥♥ TEMPLE Set on the slope of Mount Misen, Daisho-in is one of the most famous Shingon Buddhist temples in western Japan. Numerous sights are spread around on its leafy grounds, including a mandala made of colored sand that was created by Tibetan priests; a main hall where worshipers pray for health and contentment; and a hall dedicated to Kobo Daishi, founder of the Shingon sect (his remains are interred on Mount Koya; see p. 397). In Henshokutsu Cave are Buddhist icons and sand gathered from all 88 pilgrimage temples on Shikoku; making a round here is considered as auspicious as visiting the temples themselves. Other halls contain deities thought to bring good health and to save humans from earthly sexual desires. Every April 15 and November 15 worshipers walk over hot coals in fire-walking festivals here; in March there's a ceremony to give thanks to retired old kitchen knives. An excellent brochure at the entrance describes the various sights, free to the public. From Daisho-in, a path leads to Mount Misen (see below), which you can hike in about 90 minutes.

Miyajima Island. daisho-in.com. ✆ **0829-44-0111.** Free admission. Daily 8am–5pm.

Itsukushima Shrine ♥♥♥ SHRINE Founded in 593 to honor three female deities, Miyajima's major attraction is famous for its arresting setting: The wooden shrine is built over the water so that, when the tide is in, it appears as though the shrine is floating. A brilliant vermilion, it contrasts starkly with the wooded hills in the background and the blue sky above, casting its reflection on the waters below. If you do happen to see Itsukushima Shrine when the tide is in, consider yourself lucky—most of the time it floats above mucky shallows, so you'll need a little imagination to summon up the intended effect. The majority of the shrine buildings are thought to date from the 16th century, preserving the original Shinden style of 12th-century architecture; they have been repaired repeatedly through the centuries. Most are closed, but you can still enter the main shrine, or walk along the 230m (770-ft.) covered dock, which threads its way past the outer part of the main shrine and one of the oldest *Noh* stages in Japan. From the shrine, you'll have a good view of the red *torii* standing even farther out in the water. The shrine is a 10-minute walk from the ferry pier (turn right from the terminal), reached by walking along the seawall or via Omotesando Dori.

Miyajima Island, itsukushimajinja.jp. ✆ **0829-44-2020.** ¥300 adults, ¥200 high-school students, ¥100 children. Daily 6:30am–sunset (usually 6pm in summer, 5 or 5:30pm in winter).

Mount Misen ♥♥ NATURAL ATTRACTION Miyajima's highest peak, 535m (1,755-ft.) seems light years away from the crowds down below. Signs direct you to Momijidani Park, a pleasant hillside park covered with maple trees (spectacular in the fall) and cherry trees (heavenly in the spring) and marked by a picturesque stream. A 10-minute walk or free shuttle bus through the park brings you to the **Miyajima Ropeway** (miyajima-ropeway.info; ✆ **0829-44-0316**) to Mount Misen; round-trip tickets cost ¥2,100 for adults (half-fare for children), or you can buy a one-way ticket (¥1,100) and enjoy more scenery by walking back down; it takes about 60 to 90 minutes, down one of three different pathways. From the cable-car terminus, it's about a 30-minute walk over a strenuous

> **The Eternal Flame of Mount Mizen**
>
> Mount Misen is best known for Kobo Daishi's visit in 806, when he spent a 100-day retreat here. On that visit, he is said to have lit the Eternal Fire (located in the Kiezu-no Reikado Hall, one of several temples on the mountain), which has reputedly been burning for more than 1,200 years. The same flame was used to light the Peace Flame in Hiroshima's Peace Memorial Park (p. 433). In recent years, the Eternal Fire has come to symbolize the eternal fire of love, making it popular also with couples.

up-and-down pathway to the actual summit of Mount Misen, which has several temples (see "The Eternal Flame of Mount Mizen," above) as well as splendid 360-degree views of the Seto-Naikai (Inland Sea) National Park. Plan on at least 2 hours round-trip for visiting the summit; note that the last ropeway departure from Mount Misen is at 5 or 5:30pm most of the year. If you're hiking up and down, plan on a minimum of 3 to 4 hours.

WHERE TO STAY ON MIYAJIMA

Kurayado Iroha (厳島いろは) ♥♥♥ Located on the main Omotesando Dori pedestrian shopping street, this is modern Japanese elegance at its finest, with remarkably gracious and personalized service. Dinners (served in a dining room) are a feast of organic vegetables, seafood from the Seto Inland, and other local dishes; the meal typically lasts 2 hours and is a highlight of staying here. Several types of rooms are available, with the cheapest on the second floor offering only inner courtyard or Omotesando Dori views. Other rooms have beds and face inland or toward the sea (seaside is more expensive); the best is a combination room with both beds and *tatami* with sweeping views of the sea, including Ikutushima Shrine's torii. In any case, don't miss the top-floor indoor/outdoor baths.

589–4 Miyajima-cho. i-iroha.jp ✆ **0829-44-0168.** 18 units. ¥40,000–¥100,000 double. Rates include 2 meals. **Amenities:** Restaurant (hotel guests only); free Wi-Fi.

Nakaya Bed & Breakfast ♥♥♥ Hiroshima transplant Rie Nakaya, who speaks fluent English, lives in the front house and offers three rooms in another house out back: a Japanese-style two-room suite for three people or more, with a carved transom, a view of the pagoda over rooftops, and a toilet; a room with twin beds for one or two people; and two connecting rooms with four single beds (this room can accommodate six guests upon request).

511 Miyajima-cho. nakaya-bandb.com. ✆ **0829-44-0725.** 3 units w/ shared bath. ¥8,000–¥11,000 per person. **Amenities:** Free Wi-Fi.

WHERE TO EAT ON MIYAJIMA

Most Miyajima inns will offer at least one meal, but you should also explore the island's culinary heritage. Grilled conger eel and fresh oysters (in season Nov–Mar) are two of Miyajima's specialties; it even celebrates an oyster festival in early February. Stalls along Omotesando Dori, the main street, sell oysters on the half shell. If you're a foodie, you'll be a regular at these.

Kakiya (牡蠣屋) ♥♥ OYSTERS Located on Miyajima's main street, this open-fronted and very narrow shop, with the motto "We're so shuckin' good," is one of several selling humongous oysters cooked over a grill, along with products you might want to take home, like oyster pesto or truffle and oyster shavings. An English-language menu offers oysters prepared a half-dozen ways, including raw when in season, barbecued in the shell, and breaded and fried. It offers wine, beer, shochu, and sake to wash it all down.
539 Miyajima-cho, on Omotesando Dori. kaki-ya.jp. ✆ **0829-44-2747.** Oyster dishes ¥1330–¥1,800; set meals ¥1,450–¥2,600. Mon–Fri 10am–5pm; Sat–Sun 10am–6pm. Stays open later in autumn.

Shibaisaryo Mizuha (芝居茶寮 水羽) ♥ JAPANESE CUISINE Occupying an old rice granary, this bustling restaurant offers set meals of local specialties like conger eel and oysters, as well as more ordinary choices like tempura and *kamameshi* (rice casserole with toppings) from an English-language menu, with a choice of table and *tatami* seating.
Omachi 1–2 Miyajima-cho. mizuhaso.com. ✆ **0829-44-1570.** Set meals ¥1,480–¥2,400. Daily 10am–5pm.

9

OSAKA & KOBE

Though Osaka is firmly on the tourist trail, it all too often plays second fiddle to Tokyo and Kyoto. But more visitors are catching on to the city's virtues: its world-class food scene and youthful energy, its hipster subcultures and trend-setting fashion districts, and its laidback people with their fierce independence and hometown pride. If you want to spend your trip eating and drinking and hobnobbing with locals, there's nowhere better to do it.

Although its history stretches back almost 1,500 years, Osaka first gained prominence when Hideyoshi Toyotomi, the most powerful lord in the land, built Japan's most magnificent castle here in the 16th century. To develop resources for his castle town, he persuaded merchants from other parts of the nation to resettle in Osaka. During the Edo period (1603–1868), the city became an important distribution center as feudal lords from the surrounding region sent their rice to merchants in Osaka, who in turn sent the rice onward to Edo (present-day Tokyo) and other cities. As the merchants prospered, the town grew, and such arts as *kabuki* and *bunraku* flourished, pioneered by playwright Chikamatsu Monzaemon, known as "Japan's Shakespeare." With money and leisure to spare, the merchants also developed a refined taste for food.

Today, with a population of about 2.6 million, it's Japan's third largest city, after Tokyo and Yokohama. The legacy of the city's commercial beginnings is still felt: Osaka is the mover and shaker of the Kansai region, known for its international and progressive business and high-tech industries. Osakans are usually characterized as being outgoing and clever at money affairs. (One Osakan greeting is *mokari makka,* which means "Are you making any money?") Yet the city is also known for its soul food, vibrant nightlife, castle, port, and shopping arcades. It's home to the first Universal Studios outside the United States, and in 2025 is hosting the World Expo, which is expected to welcome close to 30 million visitors, including 3 million from overseas. Because of its international airport, it also serves as a gateway to the rest of Japan, with many travelers basing themselves in Osaka and taking side trips to Kyoto, Nara, Himeji, and Mount Koya. Kobe, one of Japan's most cosmopolitan cities, is only 30 minutes away from Osaka by train and makes another interesting side trip.

PREVIOUS PAGE: **Rooftop landscaping atop Osaka's Namba Parks, one of many retail complexes in a city long known for its merchants.**

Osaka

ATTRACTIONS
Floating Garden Observatory 2
Harukas 300 33
Museum of Oriental Ceramics 9
Osaka Castle 10
Osaka Museum of History 11
Shitennoji Temple 27
Spa World 30
teamLab: Field of Wind, Rain and Sun 13
teamLab Osaka Botanical Garden 31
Tsutenkaku 29
Universal Studios Japan 14
0 1/4 mi
0 0.25 km
Railway
Subway
Tourist Info
KITA-KU (NORTH WARD)
HIGASHI (EAST)
NISHI (WEST)
Osaka Visitors' Information Center Umeda
JR Osaka Station
Osaka
Umeda
Nishi-Umeda
Higashiumeda
Nakazakicho
Ogimachi
Temma
Sakuranomiya
Minamimorimachi
Naniwabashi
Kitahama
Yodoya-bashi
Oebashi
Higobashi
Watanabebashi
Nakanoshima
Fukushima
Temmabashi
Tanimachi-4-Chome
Morinomiya
Osakajo-Koen
Katamachi
Sakaisuji Hommachi
Hommachi
Awaza
OGIMACHI PARK
NAKANOSHIMA PARK
MINAMI-TEMMA PARK
UTSUBO PARK
OSAKA CASTLE PARK
NISHINOMARU GARDEN
Remains of Naniwa Palace
Aqua Bus Port
O-Kawa River
Neya River
Dojima River
Tosabori River
Oimatsucho Dori
Macchamachisuji Dori
Hanshin Expressway Loop Route
Sakai Suji
SAKAISUJI LINE
Kusuri-Tokyagai (wholesale street)
Hommachi Dori
Chuo Odori
CHUO LINE
TANIMACHI LINE
Midosuji Dori
MIDOSUJI LINE
Yotsubashisuji Dori
YOTSUBASHI LINE
Naniwa Suji
Tosabori Dori
KEIHAN NAKANOSHIMA LINE
HANSHIN RWY. MAIN LINE
JR LOOP LINE

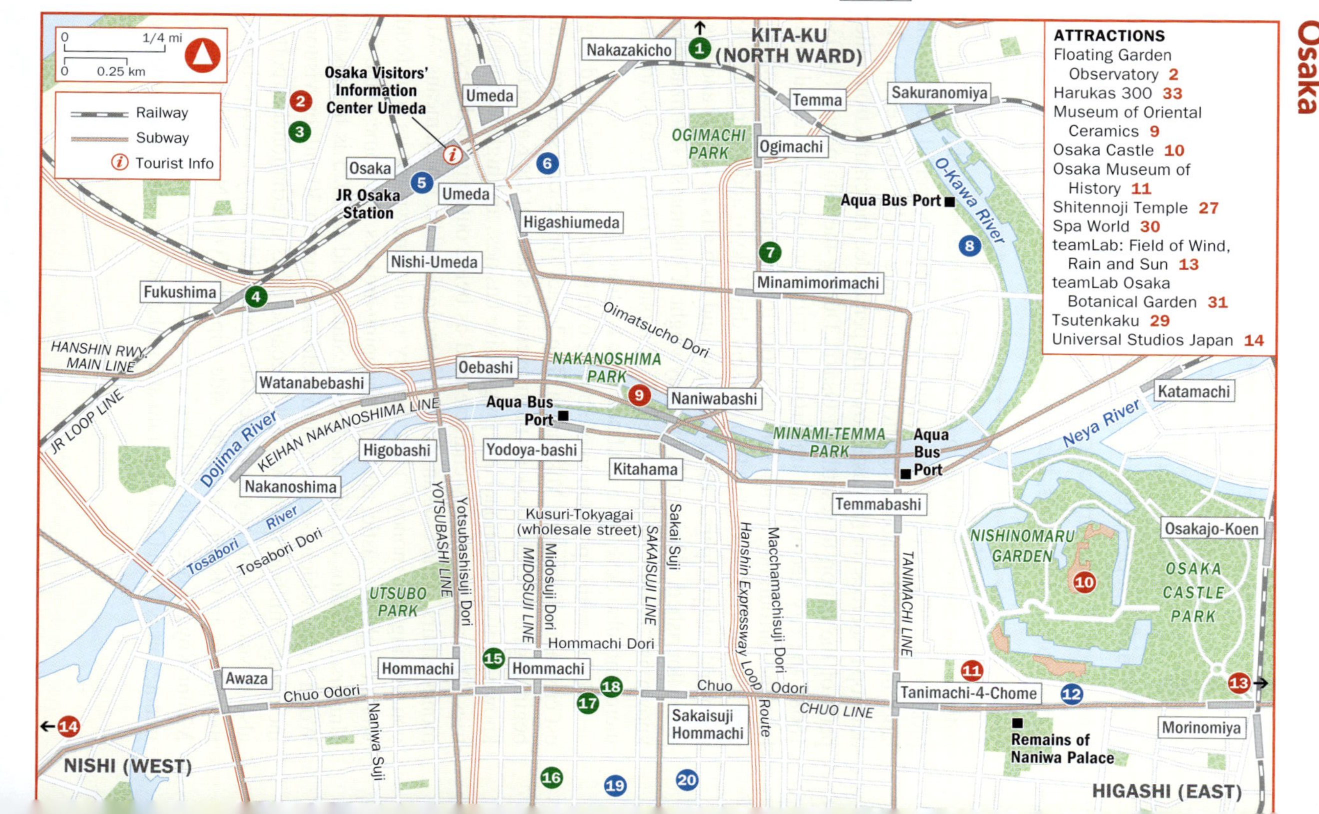

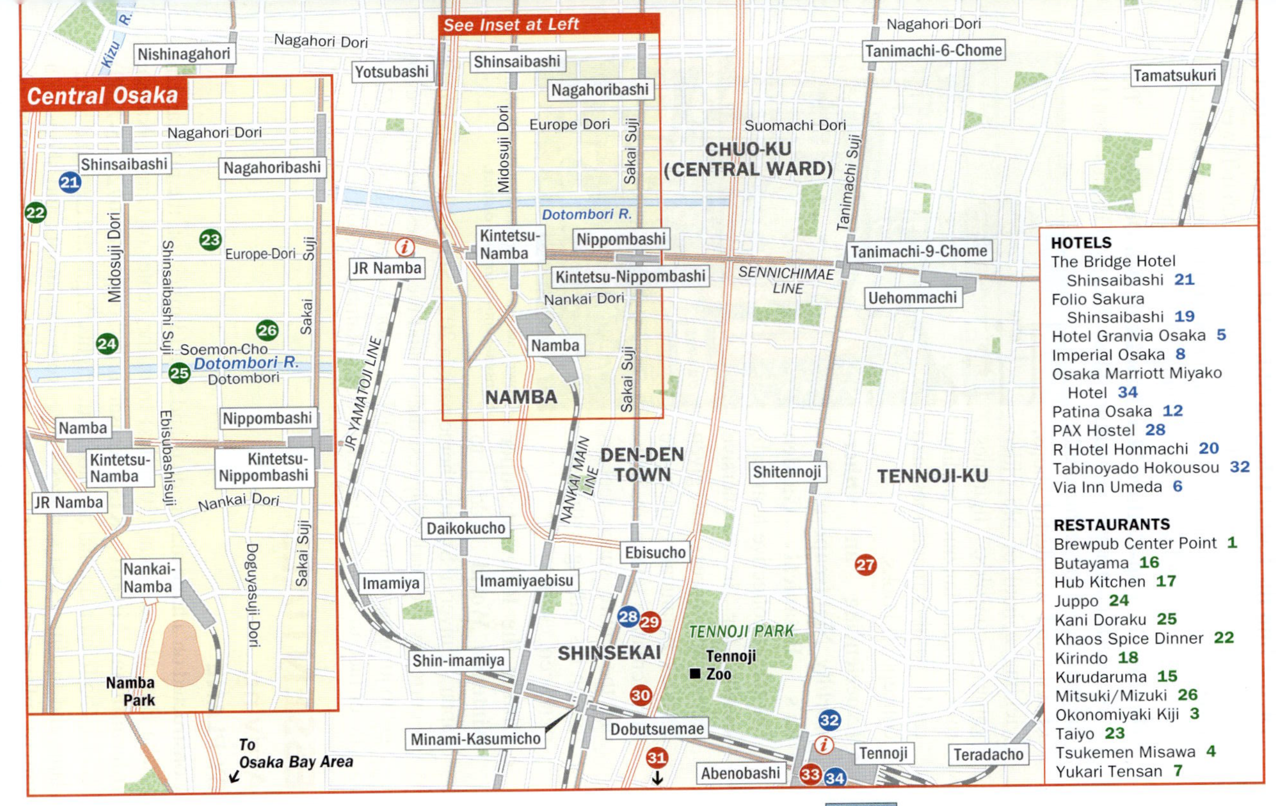

Central Osaka
See Inset at Left
HOTELS
The Bridge Hotel Shinsaibashi 21
Folio Sakura Shinsaibashi 19
Hotel Granvia Osaka 5
Imperial Osaka 8
Osaka Marriott Miyako Hotel 34
Patina Osaka 12
PAX Hostel 28
R Hotel Honmachi 20
Tabinoyado Hokousou 32
Via Inn Umeda 6
RESTAURANTS
Brewpub Center Point 1
Butayama 16
Hub Kitchen 17
Juppo 24
Kani Doraku 25
Khaos Spice Dinner 22
Kirindo 18
Kurudaruma 15
Mitsuki/Mizuki 26
Okonomiyaki Kiji 3
Taiyo 23
Tsukemen Misawa 4
Yukari Tensan 7
Nishinagahori
Nagahori Dori
Yotsubashi
Shinsaibashi
Nagahoribashi
Europe Dori
Midosuji Dori
Sakai Suji
Suomachi Dori
CHUO-KU (CENTRAL WARD)
Tanimachi Suji
Tanimachi-6-Chome
Tamatsukuri
Dotombori R.
Kintetsu-Namba
Nippombashi
Kintetsu-Nippombashi
Nankai Dori
Namba
NAMBA
Tanimachi-9-Chome
SENNICHIMAE LINE
Uehommachi
JR Namba
JR YAMATOJI LINE
NANKAI MAIN LINE
DEN-DEN TOWN
Shitennoji
TENNOJI-KU
Daikokucho
Ebisucho
Imamiya
Imamiyaebisu
TENNOJI PARK
Tennoji Zoo
SHINSEKAI
Shin-imamiya
Minami-Kasumicho
Dobutsuemae
Abenobashi
Tennoji
Teradacho
To Osaka Bay Area
Kizu R.
Shinsaibashi Suji
Europe-Dori
Soemon-Cho
Dotombori
Ebisubashisuji
Doguyasuji Dori
Nankai-Namba
Namba Park

FAVORITE OSAKA EXPERIENCES

- **Diving Into the Faded Glory of Shinsekai** In the retro district of Shinsekai, you can ascend the Sputnik-like Tsutenkaku Tower, play 8-bit games in an old arcade, dine in a restaurant where you can catch your own fish, and soak in the country's largest bathhouse.
- **Hunting for Pop-Culture Merchandise in Den Den Town** Traveling *otaku* (Japanese pop-culture fans) flock to Osaka's Den Den neighborhood for its hundreds of wild and wonderful shops, yielding a haul of old video games, consoles, figurines, toys, *manga,* fanzines, trading cards, gaming magazines, and concept-art books.
- **Experiencing an Otherworldly Nightscape at Osaka's Botanical Garden** Digital art collective teamLab, known for its immersive indoor art spaces, has given Osaka's botanical garden the same creative treatment, making the entire space feel as though it's pulsing with bioluminescent energy.
- **Hitting the Rides at Super Nintendo World** Added to Japan's Universal Studios theme park in 2021, Super Nintendo World is currently the park's biggest draw—and the closest you may ever get to jumping through an old CRT monitor to explore Bowser's Castle or race in a four-wheeled kart down Rainbow Road.

Crowds swarm the carnival-like streets of the Shinsekai entertainment district.

ESSENTIALS

Arriving

BY PLANE

Constructed on a huge manmade island 5km (3 miles) off the mainland in Osaka Bay, almost 50km (30 miles) from the center of Osaka, **Kansai International Airport** (**KIX;** kansai-airport.or.jp; ✆ **072-455-2500**) receives both international and domestic flights. Signs are clear and abundant, and facilities and services range from restaurants and shops to a **tourist information center** (p. 454), **post office, ATMs** that accept foreign credit cards, a **children's play area,** doctor and dental clinics, **SIM card** rental counters, and free **Wi-Fi.**

GETTING FROM KIX TO OSAKA **Taxis** are prohibitively expensive: Expect to spend ¥20,000-plus for an hour's cab ride to the city center. Easiest if you have luggage is the **Kansai Airport Transportation Enterprise** (kate.co.jp; ✆ **072-461-1374**), which provides bus services to major stations and some hotels in Osaka, as well as to Kyoto, Kobe, Nara, and Himeji. Fares to Osaka average ¥1,800; purchase tickets at counters in the arrival lobby. The same company also offers more frequent service from KIX to the Osaka City Air Terminal (OCAT), located in the heart of Osaka next to JR Namba Station; it serves as a major bus terminal for express buses to cities throughout Japan (buses depart every 30 min.; trip time: 50 min.; ¥1,300 one-way, ¥2,300 round-trip with return within 14 days).

There are also several trains into Osaka. The **JR Airport Express Haruka** (westjr.co.jp; ✆ **0570-00-2486**), which travels to Tennoji and Shin-Osaka stations (but not Osaka Station) before continuing to Kyoto, departs about twice an hour; the fare to Shin-Osaka is ¥3,320 for the 50-minute trip. The **Kansaikuko Line** travels to Osaka station, a 70-minute trip costing ¥1,210. Both are free for Japan Rail Pass holders (exchange your voucher at the Kansai Airport rail station on the third floor, open daily 5:30am–11pm). Across from the JR trains in the same airport station, the private **Nankai Line** (howto-osaka.com; ✆ **06-6643-1005**) runs a sleek **rapi:t** (pronounced "rapito") train that reaches Namba Nankai Station in 38 minutes. There are usually two trains an hour, and ordinary reserved seats cost ¥1,490, though discounts are often available if purchased in advance online, including tickets that bundle airport transfer with local transportation. If you're on a budget, take an ordinary **Nankai Express Line** for ¥970 and reach Namba in 47 minutes.

BY TRAIN

Osaka is 2½ to 3 hours from Tokyo and about 80 minutes to almost 3 hours from Hiroshima, via the **Shinkansen bullet train.** The fare from Tokyo costs ¥13,870 for an unreserved seat. All Shinkansen bullet trains arrive at **Shin-Osaka Station** at the city's northern edge. Take the Midosuji subway line from Shin-Osaka Station to Osaka Station (the subway station here is called Umeda Station), Namba, Tennoji, and other points south. JR trains also run between Shin-Osaka and Osaka stations. If you haven't turned in your voucher for your Japan Rail Pass yet, you can do so at either Osaka Station or Shin-Osaka Station daily from 5:30am to 11pm.

From Kobe or Kyoto, the **commuter lines** will deliver you directly to Osaka Station in the heart of the city. Take note that Osaka Station is huge; in fact, the entire complex is called **Osaka Station City** (osakastationcity.com), with department stores, restaurants, and more.

BY BUS

Willer Express (willerexpress.com; ✆ **050-5805-0383**) operates a bus departing Tokyo's Shinjuku Station each morning at 8:40am, arriving at Osaka Station around 9 hours later. Night buses leave Tokyo Station

Kajibashi at 8:55pm and arrive in Osaka at 6:30am (with a stop in Kyoto an hour earlier). Prices range from ¥3,800 to ¥9,500.

Visitor Information

At KIX Airport, the **Kansai Tourist Information Center** (✆ **072-456-6160;** daily 9am–7pm) is in the international arrivals lobby of Terminal 1. The multilingual staff dispenses general travel information about Japan and maps and brochures of the Kansai area, including Kyoto and Kobe, and can make hotel reservations. There's also a Tourist Information Center in Terminal 2 (✆ **072-456-8630;** daily 11:30am–7:30pm).

In Osaka, the **Tourist Information Osaka** (✆ **06-6345-2189;** daily 7am–10pm) is in front of Osaka Station's central ticket gates. The downtown **Tourist Information Namba** (✆ **06-6631-9100;** daily 9am–8pm) is located in Nankai Namba Station across from Takashimaya Department Store.

To find out what's going on in Osaka, look for ***Kansai Scene*** (kansai scene.com), a free bilingual quarterly magazine. Information on Osaka city is also available at **osaka-info.jp**. The publication *Tokyo Weekender* (tokyoweekender.com) releases an annual ***Kansai Weekender*** edition, which gives information and travel recommendations on the Kansai region.

City Layout

Osaka is divided into various wards, or *ku,* the most important of which for visitors are **Kita-ku** (North Ward), which encompasses the area around Osaka and Umeda stations; and **Chuo-ku** (Central Ward), where you'll find Osaka Castle and **Namba,** the heart of the city, also often referred to as **Minami** (**South**). Dividing Kita-ku and Chuo-ku, a tributary of the Yodo River runs east-west, which confusingly goes by different names (the O, Tosahori, Dojima, or Ajii River) at different stretches. Three subway stops north of Osaka Station, **Shin-Osaka Station** is a tourist wasteland with a scattering of hotels, but it does field bullet trains from around the country.

AROUND OSAKA STATION Kita, the area around Osaka and Umeda stations, includes many of the city's top hotels, office and entertainment complexes, shopping malls, lots of restaurants, and Nakanoshima Island. Its maze of buildings and streets make it frustrating to navigate, even for Japanese. Flanking the station, **Umekita Park** is the centerpiece of Grand Green Osaka, an ambitious redevelopment project aimed at making the Kita area more visitor-friendly, with greenspaces, new restaurants, and shopping and entertainment venues. Farther east, the narrow alleyways of **Tenma** (see "Where to Eat in Osaka," p. 467) are worth seeking out for their many tiny bars and restaurants.

AROUND OSAKA CASTLE Osaka Castle, which lies to the east, is the historic center of the city and is surrounded by a huge park.

MINAMI/NAMBA Four subway stops south of Umeda Station, Namba has a cluster of stations serving subways, JR trains, and Kintetsu and

Nankai lines, all connected to one another via underground passageways. This is the heart of the city, bustling with the spirit of old Osaka, where you'll find hotels; Osaka's liveliest shopping and entertainment district, **Shinsaibashi;** the National Bunraku Theatre, and major shopping areas. Connecting Kita-ku with Namba is Osaka's main street, **Midosuji Dori,** a wide boulevard lined with gingko trees and international name-brand shops.

World Expo at the Technoport

The 2025 World Expo, Japan's first since 1970, took place from April through October on Yumeshima, one of three artificial islands in Osaka Bay. These islands were an element of the 1988 Technoport Osaka plan, part of the government's bid to create a second Osaka city center. Though impressive feats of construction, these manmade islands haven't diverted much activity away from central Osaka. The Technoport is worth visiting for specific attractions, but not particularly atmospheric to walk around—and still is years away from achieving its aim of becoming city center 2.0. It remains to be seen what will be done with the left-over infrastructure once the Expo has finished.

TENNOJI/ABENO At the south end of the JR Loop Line, **Tennoji-ku** was once a thriving temple town with Shitennoji Temple at its center. In addition to a park with a zoo, it hosts the retro Shinsekai amusement area and Spa World, one of Japan's biggest and most luxurious public bathhouses. In neighboring **Abeno-ku** is the Abeno Harukas skyscraper, once Japan's tallest building, with an observatory, Japan's largest department store, a luxury hotel, shops, and restaurants.

OSAKA BAY & PORT West of the city, Osaka's well-developed waterfront has domestic and international ferry terminals. Osaka Bay also has a popular aquarium and **Universal Studios Japan,** one of Japan's major attractions.

Getting Around

Despite its size, Osaka is easy to navigate, thanks to lots of English-language signs and information. The exception is Osaka Station (used for JR trains) and adjoining Umeda Station (subway lines and private railway lines Hankyu and Hanshin). Underground passages and shopping arcades make it even more confusing; there's no escaping—you will get lost.

When exploring by foot, it helps to know that most roads running east and west end in *dori* (street), while roads running north and south end in *suji* (avenue).

The **Osaka Municipal Transportation Bureau** (osakametro.co.jp; ✆ **06-6582-1400**) operates Osaka's user-friendly subway network. All lines are color-coded and identified with a letter ("M" for the Midosuji Line, etc.), while stations are assigned a number (M20 for Namba Station on the Midosuji Line); there's English signage in stations and in-car announcements are in English. Lines run from about 5am to midnight. Of the eight lines, the red **Midosuji Line** is the most important one for

Transportation Passes

If you think you'll be traveling a lot by subway on a given day, consider purchasing a **1-Day Enjoy Eco Card** for ¥820 (¥620 weekends and holidays), which allows unlimited rides on subways and buses and offers slight discounts (usually ¥100 or less) to 30 attractions, including Osaka Castle, Shitennoji Temple, and Spa World. The **Osaka Amazing Pass** (¥3,300 for 1 day) allows unlimited rides on subways, city buses, and private railways in Osaka plus free entrance to 30-some attractions (none of these passes include Osaka Aquarium or Universal Studios). A 2-day Osaka Amazing Pass costs ¥5,500 but doesn't include private railways. Note that JR trains are not included in any of these passes, and it would take a lot of travel and sightseeing to get your money's worth. Passes are available at subway stations and tourist information offices. For information on the Amazing Pass, go to osaka-amazing-pass.com.

For trips outside Osaka, the **Kansai Thru Pass** (**Surutto Kansai;** surutto.com) allows foreigners (you must show your passport) to ride subways, private railways (no JR trains), and buses throughout Kansai, including Osaka, Kyoto, Kobe, Nara, Himeji, and Mount Koya, for 2 or 3 days (¥5,600 and ¥7,000, respectively), and they don't have to be consecutive days. The pass also offers slight discounts to tourist sights. JR West Passes allow travel on JR trains that cover a wider area. For more information on regional passes, see p. 689 in chapter 15.

visitors; it passes through Shin-Osaka Station and on to Umeda (the subway station next to Osaka Station), Shinsaibashi, Namba, and Tennoji. Fares begin at ¥190 and increase according to the distance traveled. More convenient, however, are prepaid **ICOCA cards.** Various cards are available, all of which include a ¥500 deposit that can be refunded when you turn in the card, minus an annoying ¥220 handling fee. Note that if you already have an IC card, such as a Suica from Tokyo, you can use it in Osaka, too. Although there are also city buses, it's more convenient to travel by subway.

A Japan Railways train called the **JR Loop Line** passes through Osaka Station and makes a loop around the central part of the city (similar to the Yamanote Line in Tokyo); take it to visit Osaka Castle. Fares begin at ¥140, but you can ride free with a valid Japan Rail Pass. For trips outside Osaka, JR-West (westjr.co.jp) has several passes, with a **1-day Kansai Area Pass** offering unlimited rides to and around Osaka, Kyoto, Nara, Himeji, and Kobe for ¥2,800 (children pay half-price). Two-, 3- and 4-day Kansai Area Passes are also available.

EXPLORING OSAKA

Near Osaka Station

Floating Garden Observatory (Kuchu Teien Tenbodai) ♥♥

OBSERVATION DECK This futuristic observatory 167m (557 ft.) high looks like a space ship floating between the two towers of the Umeda Sky Building. Take the superfast glass elevator from the East Tower building's third floor; you'll then take a glass-enclosed escalator that also bridges the two towers before depositing you on the 39th floor. From here, you have an unparalleled view of Osaka, making it a popular nightspot for couples on dates.

Umeda Sky Building, 1–1–88 Oyodo-naka. ✆ **06-6440-3901.** skybldg.co.jp/observatory. ¥2,000 adults, ¥500 children. Daily 9:30am–10:30pm (until 1am on New Year's). Station: JR Osaka or Umeda (Central North exit of JR Osaka Station, 9 min.).

Museum of Oriental Ceramics (Toyotoji Bijutsukan) ♥♥♥ MUSEUM With its 6,000-piece collection of Chinese, Korean, and Japanese ceramics—of which 400 are on display at any one time on a rotating basis—this ranks as one of the world's finest ceramics museums. Korean celadon, Chinese ceramics from the Eastern Han, Song and Ming dynasties, Chinese snuff bottles, Aritaware from the Edo period, Imari ware that once graced European palaces, and works by Hamada Shoji are just some of the items that might be on display. Built specifically for this collection (it even has shock-absorbent platforms to protect its fragile wares), the museum does a superb job showcasing the exquisite pieces, in darkened rooms that utilize natural light and computerized natural-light simulation. Even if you've never given ceramics more than a passing glance, you're likely to come away with a heightened sense of appreciation. You'll want to spend up to an hour here. The museum is a 15-minute walk south of Osaka Station, on Nakanoshima Island between the Dojima and Tosabori rivers.

1–1–26 Nakanoshima. moco.or.jp. ✆ **06-6223-0055.** ¥1,800 adults, ¥800 high-school and college students, free for children. Tues–Sun 9:30am–5pm (occasionally closed for exhibition changes). Station: Naniwabashi on the Keihan Nakanoshima Line (exit 1, 1 min.) or Yodoyabashi (exit 1, 5 min.).

Around Osaka Castle

Osaka Castle (Osaka-jo) ♥♥ CASTLE First built in the 1580s on the order of the great shogun Toyotomi Hideyoshi, Osaka Castle was the largest castle in Japan, a magnificent structure used by Toyotomi as a military stronghold from which to wage war against rebellious feudal lords in far-flung provinces. Destroyed a few times over the ages (see "The Battle for Osaka Castle," p. 459), the present Osaka Castle is a ferroconcrete replica from 1931 and was extensively renovated in 1997. Though not as massive as the original, it's still one of Japan's most famous and impressive castles, with its huge stone walls, black and gold-leaf trim, and copper roof, surrounded by moats and an expansive park famous for its cherry trees. Its eight-story *tenshu* (keep) rises 39m (130 ft.), with a top-floor observatory offering bird's-eye views of the city. The rest of the keep is a little modern-looking for my taste, but it does house a high-tech museum that uses videos, holograms, models, replicas, and artifacts to describe the life and times of Toyotomi Hideyoshi and the history of the castle—be sure to pick up the free audio guide, as some explanations are in Japanese only. Among the prized artifacts here are samurai armor and gear; a magnificent folding screen with meticulously painted scenes of the battle

Originally built by the great shogun Toyotomi Hideyoshi, copper-roofed Osaka Castle has a towering eight-story keep.

between the Toyotomi and Tokugawa forces; a full-scale reproduction of Toyotomi's Gold Tea Room; and a model of Osaka Castle during the Toyotomi Era. For ¥500 you can dress up in period clothing, including some awe-inspiring samurai helmets.

1–1 Osakajo. osakacastle.net. ✆ **06-6941-3044.** ¥600 adults, free for ages 15 and under. Daily 9am–5pm. Station: Osakajo Koen on JR Loop Line or Morinomiya (15 min.); or Temmabashi or Osaka Business Park (10 min.).

Osaka Museum of History ♥♥ MUSEUM Set in a modern building on the site of former Naniwa Palace (built in 645 by Emperor Kotoku), this museum brings to life Osaka's long history and growth into a metropolis, with smart interactive exhibits, videos, archaeological displays, and a life-size re-creation of Naniwa's Daikokuden Hall. A highlight is the realistic reproduction of Dotonbori from a century ago. And because the museum begins on the 10th floor, it offers multiple stunning views of Osaka Castle and its park. In the basement are archaeological remains of Naniwa Palace, while a reconstruction of a 5th-century warehouse is on the museum grounds. Plan on at least an hour here.

4–1–32 Otemae. osakamushis.jp. ✆ **06-6946-5728.** ¥600 adults, ¥400 high-school and college students, free for younger children. Wed–Mon 9:30am–5pm. Station: Tanimachi 4-chome (3 min.).

Around Tennoji/Abeno

Harukas 300 ♥ OBSERVATION DECK Sunlight bathes this 300m-high (990 ft.) glass-walled observatory in Japan's tallest building (if it's raining or foggy, spend your time elsewhere). Not as memorable as Tokyo SkyTree (p. 126), but also not as expensive, the observatory on floors 58, 59, and 60 is a good place to get some perspective on sprawling Osaka. If you squint you may be able to pick out Osaka Castle or the bay, and on clear days you can see even farther. You can up the ante with the ¥3,000 **Edge the Harukas** experience: Strapped into a harness and holding onto a safety rail, you can edge your way along a 60cm-wide (8-in.), 20m-long (66-ft.) platform skirting the building, 300m (984 ft.) above the city. The experience lasts approximately 1 hour and is scheduled every 90 minutes from 10am to 7pm. Book tickets online or at the application center on the 60th floor. There's also a free public outdoor terrace down on the building's 16th floor, with views north toward the city, but it doesn't compare to those from the observatory. Other diversions in Abeno Harukas include restaurants, shops, and Japan's largest department store with over 100,000 sq m of retail space.

Abeno Harukas (ticket counter 2nd floor), 1-1-43 Abeno-suji. abenoharukas-300.jp. ✆ **06-6621-0300.** ¥2,000 adults, ¥1,200 ages 12–17, ¥700 kids 6–11, ¥500 children 4–5. Daily 9am–10pm. Station: Tennoji or Osaka Abenobashi (1 min.).

Shitennoji Temple ♥♥ TEMPLE Founded some 1,400 years ago as the first—and therefore oldest—officially established temple in Japan, Shitennoji Temple is the spiritual heart of Osaka. It was constructed in 593 by Prince Shotoku, who is credited with introducing Buddhism to Japan and remains a revered and popular figure even today. However, like most wooden structures in Japan, the temple's buildings have been destroyed repeatedly through the centuries by fire and war, including the 1615 Tokugawa raid on Osaka Castle and World War II. And through the centuries, the buildings have been faithfully reconstructed exactly as they were in the 6th century, with the Central Precinct (*Garan*) consisting of

THE battle FOR OSAKA CASTLE

By the time he died in 1598, Toyotomi Hideyoshi had accomplished what no man had done before: crushed his enemies and unified all of Japan under his command. After Toyotomi's death, Tokugawa Ieyasu seized power and established his shogunate government in Edo. But Toyotomi's heirs had ideas of their own: Considering Osaka Castle impregnable, they plotted to overthrow Tokugawa.

Sensing an uprising, in 1615 Tokugawa sent 155,000 soldiers to Osaka. After a long siege, they not only annihilated the 55,000 Toyotomi insurrectionists, but in the process also destroyed Osaka Castle. The victorious Tokugawas rebuilt the castle a few years later, in 1629, though the main tower was destroyed by lightning 36 years later.

Centuries later, in 1868, much of the remaining Osaka Castle burned down as the shogunate made its last stand against imperial forces in what later became known as the Meiji Restoration. It was then partly replaced and used as an arsenal. The 1931 version you see today was extensively damaged in World War II bombings—but Osaka Castle rose again from the ashes and has been rebuilt to its present glory.

A STROLL AROUND shinsekai ♥♥

If you ever needed evidence of Japan's often misguided soul-searching in the Meiji era, consider this now-abandoned amusement park and commercial district just east of Tennoji Park. In the wake of 1903's successful National Industrial Exposition in Osaka, work began on Shinsekai—a name meaning "New World," reflecting the era's passion for modernization. Paris was the model for the northern half, New York's Coney Island for the south. The only nod to Paris remaining in Shinsekai today is the ugly metallic tower rising from the center, **Tsutenkaku,** and even that looks more like a Cold-War Soviet satellite than it does the Eiffel Tower. Built in 1912, scrapped during the war, then reconstructed in the 1950s, Tsutenkaku is 103m (338 ft.) tall, with a relatively inexpensive observation deck (adults ¥900, ages 5–17 ¥400, free for children 4 and under; daily 10am–7:30pm). The Coney Island influence is a little easier to spot, given that the area hosted the Osaka Luna amusement park from 1912 to 1923, and a carnival-esque atmosphere still reigns here at night. Along the streets you'll find shooting galleries, retro game centers, hand-drawn rickshaws, seafood restaurants where you can fish for your own dinner, and **Spa World** (see below). The closed market streets are worth ambling around, offering a variety of fresh produce and street food, as well as a handful of 24/7 *kushikatsu* (deep-fried skewers) shops. There may be an air of melancholy to Shinsekai—ultimately the entire thing is a symbol of failed ambition—but if you're into retro aesthetics, you'll find much to swoon over here. To get here, take the subway to Ebisucho (5 min.) or Dobutsuen-Mae (8 min.).

the Inner Gate, the five-story Buddhist Pagoda, the Main Hall with its statue of Prince Shotoku as the Buddha of Infinite Mercy, and the Lecture Hall all on a north-south axis. Be sure, too, to wander the temple's Gokuraku-Jodo Teien, a restored Japanese landscape garden first laid out during the Tokugawa regime. Buddhists believe that if you follow the path between the two streams representing greed and anger, you will symbolically reach Paradise, a place of sublime beauty, tranquility, and peace. A **flea market** is held on the temple grounds on the 21st and 22nd of each month.

1–11–18 Shitennoji. ✆ **06-6771-0066.** Admission to either Garan or garden, ¥300 adults, ¥200 students and children. Apr–Sept daily 8:30am–4:30pm; Oct–Mar daily 8:30–4pm. Station: Shitennoji-mae Yuhigaoka (exit 4, 5 min.); or JR Tennoji (north exit, 10 min.).

Spa World ♥♥ SPA One of the most ambitious bathhouses in Japan, Spa World accommodates up to 5,000 people and draws upon hot springs 890m (2,970 ft.) below the earth's surface. On its roof, in a large hangar-like room, a covered swimming complex for families includes a kiddies' pool, two large water slides, a kids' amusement pool with aquatic activities, and an outdoor sunning terrace with a small pool and a Jacuzzi overlooking retro Tsutenkaku Tower. You wear your swimsuits here (rental suits available). For a more grown-up experience, two *onsen* are divided into themed geographical bathing zones, alternated between the sexes (no suits are allowed here). The Asian Zone, for example, has Persian- and Bali-themed baths, as well as a Japanese cypress bath and an outdoor

Japanese bath; while the European Zone features baths that evoke the cultures of ancient Rome and Greece—it's a little gimmicky, but that's par for the course in Shinsekai. By paying extra (¥800 weekdays, ¥1,000 weekends and holidays), you can also use six themed saunas. Spa World also has a gym (included in admission price), a kids' playroom, and restaurants, plus treatment rooms that cost extra—and even a hotel. If you're timid about visiting a public bath, this one will convert you. But sorry, people with tattoos aren't allowed—they're associated with the Japanese mafia. 3-4-24 Ebisu-higashi. spaworld.co.jp. ✆ **06-6631-0001.** Weekdays ¥2,400 adults, ¥1,300 children for 3 hr.; day pass ¥2,700 adults, ¥1,500 children. Weekends ¥2,700 adults, ¥1,500 children for 3 hr.; day pass ¥3,000 adults, ¥1,700 children. Baths daily 10am–8:45am the next morning; top floor Mon–Fri 10am–7pm; Sat–Sun 10am–10pm. Station: Shin-Imamiya or Dobutsuenmae (2 min.).

teamLab Osaka Botanical Garden ♥♥♥ ART GARDEN Deep in Osaka's southern suburbs sits Nagai Botanical Garden, a lovely expanse of strolling paths, groves of native trees, and symbolic flowers often celebrated in old Japanese poems and artworks, from wisteria and hydrangeas to roses and peonies. It may seem strange to turn something so naturally lovely into a digitized artwork, but teamLab has treated the garden as a collaborator rather than simply a canvas, infusing the whole space with a quasi-magical energy that pulses across its 24 hectares (60 acres) after dark. Cosmic illuminations projected over the lake, glowing "ovoids" that shine brightly when hit by rain or roaming hands, autumnal trees burnished by nightlights, and huge rubbery eggs congregated in a woodland thicket—the impression each artwork makes is entirely attuned to its setting. The most extreme examples are the *Sculptures of Dissipative Birds in the Wind,* covered in fluid digitized swirls depicting energy sent out into the world by the wind and the birds. If birds don't fly around the artwork and the wind comes to a halt, the "sculptures" will dissolve into the darkness. Though the whole space is undeniably photogenic, I'd implore you not to use your phone or camera too much—as always with teamLab, there is player agency, and you'll want to pay close attention to how your movements influence the fantastical

teamLab has transformed Osaka's botanical garden into an enchanting immersive experience.

world around you. Bear in mind this is a popular excursion for visitors to Osaka, so make sure you get tickets well in advance.

1–23 Nagaikoen. teamlab.art/e/botanicalgarden. Variable pricing, but usually ¥1,800–¥2,400 per adult (children pay around ⅓ of the price). Hours change across the season, usually open daily from sunset until around 9:30 or 10pm. Irregular holidays. Station: Nagai (11 min.).

Osaka Bay Area

Universal Studios Japan ♥♥♥ THEME PARK Following the tradition of Universal's Hollywood and Orlando theme parks, this park takes guests on a fantasy trip through the world of American blockbuster movies, with thrill rides, live entertainment, shows, back-lot streets, restaurants, shops, and other attractions based on movie franchises like *Jaws, Jurassic Park,* and *Spider-Man.* Universal **Wonderland** features rides and attractions (think Snoopy, Sesame Street, and Hello Kitty) for the wee ones; **WaterWorld™** is an action-packed stunt show in a dramatic setting. For years the most popular attraction was the **Wizarding World of Harry Potter™,** which re-creates Hogsmeade village; inside Hogwarts Castle is the motion-simulation ride Harry Potter and the Forbidden Journey, which many argue is the best theme-park ride on the planet. But **Super Nintendo World,** one of the park's most recent additions, may have now eclipsed the wizards' popularity. While there are rides here, the zone's main appeal is capitalizing on visitor nostalgia. Designed in

Opened in 2021, Super Nintendo World has become a blockbuster hit for Universal Studios Japan.

concert with Nintendo game designers, it's endlessly interactive. Power-Up Bands allow you to forage for digital collectibles, you can wander through the famous green Warp Pipes from the Super Mario games, and park employees walk around in hyper-realistic Mario and Luigi costumes, Also popular is the park's **virtual-reality jet coaster,** which operates intermittently throughout the year, transporting visitors into one of Japan's most-popular anime universes—recent editions have included *Lupin III* and *Demon Slayer.* Plan for an entire day here, but note that the park is immensely popular: Avoid weekends, arrive early, and consider buying a Universal Express Pass (various packages run ¥10,000–¥30,000), which allows priority entry into designated rides.

2-1-33 Sakurajima, Konohana. usj.co.jp/e. ✆ **06-6465-4005.** Studio Pass to all attractions ¥7,900 adults, ¥7,100 seniors, ¥5,400 children 4–11. Hours vary by season; generally daily 10am–6pm winter, 9am–9pm summer. Station: JR Universal City (5 min.).

In Higashiosaka

teamLab: Field of Wind, Rain and Sun ♥♥ ARTWORK & CAFE On the face of it, this is a cafe with a garden view, cocooned (ever so strangely) on the overgrown grounds of a former factory in eastern Osaka. But teamLab's ethos essentially states that an artwork is not something one views at a comfortable remove, but rather something that's influenced by environmental factors, with you, the viewer, being one of those factors. As this dawns on you, the *Field of Wind, Rain and Sun* begins to make more sense. teamLab orchestrated the space by tearing down the old building, but then simply allowed the return of wind, rain, and sun to influence the artwork's design. You'll start in the cafe, drinking tea or coffee with a sweet treat while looking at the rustling grasses and stalks of bamboo clinking outside; jets of water shooting across an old warehouse ladder generate shards of rainbow-light every time the sun splits through the clouds. Perhaps another visitor decides to enter the garden and the scene changes focus, a subject moving through the slowly shifting landscape. You decide to follow, looking for colorful kaleidoscopes of noontime light or raindrops glittering like liquid crystals. How the artwork presents itself is highly dependent on weather conditions; sunny afternoons and drizzly evenings are when it's at its best. Either way, a visit here is an engaging way to spend an hour, but I suspect only diehard contemporary art fans will consider it worth the detour (an hour round-trip from central Osaka). ***Note:*** Reservations required; tickets include a drink (alcohol available at night) and a snack.

1-1-15 Wakae Higashimachi, Higashiosaka. teamlab.art/e/field/. ¥1,500 daytime, ¥3,000 nighttime. Thurs–Mon 10:30am–4:30pm and 6:30–9:30pm. Station: Wakaeiwata (10 min.).

WHERE TO STAY IN OSAKA

Many hotels are clustered around Osaka Station, but Namba in the city's downtown offers more interesting surroundings. The Tennoji/Abeno area is also emerging as a vibrant place to stay. The prices below reflect demand and can vary markedly; note too, that many hotels charge more on Saturday and nights before a holiday.

For more budget-priced lodgings, there are 20-plus **Toyoko Inn** hotels in Osaka (see toyoko-inn.com), including those near Osaka and Shin-Osaka stations and in Namba and Tennoji. There are lots of capsule hotels in Kita-ke, like the old-school **Capsule Inn Osaka** (capsulehotel-inn-osaka.com) and the smart-looking **Frist Cabin Nishi Umeda** (first-cabin.jp/hotels/nishiumeda). They're not the most private of accommodations, but they're cheap, and offer a lens into Japan's enduring approach to maximizing space.

Around Osaka Station

Hotel Granvia Osaka ♥♥ You can't get any closer to Osaka Station than this hotel, with discounts for Japan Rail Pass holders making it even more attractive for train travelers. But there are prices to pay: The ground-floor lobby is hard to find in the maze that is Osaka Station, and elevators are crowded with hungry masses on their way to the hotel's many 19th-floor restaurants (overnight guests get discounts up to 20% at hotel restaurants). Rooms, on floors 21 to 27, offer many choices, with top-floor Granvia Floor club rooms providing the best views, through large windows. Note, however, that standard rooms are tiny, some of which face an inner courtyard and are dark (on the plus side, they tend to be quieter).
3–1–1 Umeda. granvia-osaka.jp. ✆ **06-6344-1235.** 726 units. ¥25,000–¥70,000 double. Station: Osaka or Umeda (1 min.; above the station). **Amenities:** 5 restaurants; 2 bars; 2 lounges; room service; free Wi-Fi.

Imperial Osaka ♥♥ Much like its namesake in Tokyo, the Imperial Osaka is a sprawling hotel complex inspired by the work of Frank Lloyd Wright, utilizing his organic design philosophy and love of geometry and space, and featuring iconic box columns of light—pillars and wall features that Wright hoped would evoke images of sliding shoji screens. Across its 24 floors, you'll find grand banquet halls, a basement shopping concourse, high-end restaurants, cocktail lounges, a light-drenched atrium with a water feature and buffet, and hundreds of art deco-y rooms, many with views of the Osaka cityscape and the mountains to the east and south. The best rooms are the corner suites, which make use of the curving exterior wall with wrapround windows providing fine views. Guests staying in the Imperial Rooms (floors 19–21) will have to fork out extra cash, but in return get access to the private 23rd-floor Imperial Lounge, with a self-serve bar stocked with champagne, fine wines, and a selection of spirits (a staff member is also on hand, should you need any assistance). The views from here are immense—seats by the window become hot commodities in spring for viewing the cherry blossom-lined river below or when the summer *hanabi* (firework) festival takes place. The hotel is a little far from Osaka-Umeda Station, but there are free shuttle buses every 20 minutes between

10am and 10pm, and to make up for it you're within walking distance of the lively Tenma nightlife district (see "Where to Eat in Osaka," p. 467).

1–8–50 Tenmabashi. imperialhotel.co.jp/en/osaka. ✆ **06-6881-1111.** 378 units. ¥35,000–¥70,000 double; Imperial Floor ¥50,000–¥150,000. Station: Sakuranomiya or Osaka-tenmangu (13 min.); or free shuttle from Osaka-Umeda Station. **Amenities:** 7 restaurants; 2 bars and lounges; access to health club and pool (fee); room service; concierge; free Wi-Fi.

Via Inn Umeda ♥♥ With a convenient location near Osaka Station, Via Inn offers a sleek lobby with slate-gray walls and overstuffed chairs and sofas, and most importantly, very comfortable rooms done up in beige with purple pillows and bedrunners. Rooms are mostly singles and twins, but the doubles are all corner rooms with two windows and a loveseat. In addition to the usual in-room amenities like shampoo and tea, a basket next to the elevator offers additional packets of coffee and other items, allowing you to take as much as you want. Another plus is the door off the lobby providing direct access to a 7-Eleven.

1–20 Komatsubaracho. viainn.com/en/umeda. ✆ **06-6314-5489.** 217 units. ¥10,000–¥20,000 single; ¥15,000–¥35,000 double. Station: Osaka (5 min.) or Higashi-Umeda (3 min.). **Amenities:** Free Wi-Fi.

Minami

The Bridge Hotel Shinsaibashi ♥♥♥ The location of this hotel couldn't be any better, with coffee bars, restaurants, and the bustling Triangle Park and Amemura on your doorstep, and Shinsaibashi Station right around the corner. A recreated vermillion footbridge, the type you see in castle parks and strolling gardens, marks the entrance to the hotel, with a row of massage chairs in the lobby adding to the welcoming atmosphere. The rooms are small and simply designed, albeit with a soothing Japanese aesthetic, but it's the communal lounge space, decorated in traditional umbrellas and its adjoining bamboo-lined terrace, that really makes The Bridge stand out. From 3pm to 9:30pm daily, there's a free self-serve bar here, including beer, highballs, and spirits. (Depending on your appetite for alcohol, you can quickly reclaim a portion of the already-reasonable room rate.) Also noteworthy is a kimono-wearing experience, Mondays and Thursdays at 5pm, during which you can take photos in front of a stylish glass-and-tatami art piece on the hotel's roof terrace.

1–10–24 Nishi-Shinsaibashi bridge-h.co.jp ✆ **06-4963-6501.** 207 units. ¥20,000–¥40,000 double. Station: Shinsaibashi (3 min.) or Yotsubashi (3 min.). **Amenities:** Bar and lounge; free Wi-Fi.

Folio Sakura Shinsaibashi ♥♥♥ Having recently been drafted into the Banyan Group, this simple "micro-hotel" in Shinsaibashi has been given an official seal of approval, yet it remains unpretentious and affordable to most travelers. The rooms are small and, given the hotel is surrounded by similarly sized buildings, you won't get much of a view, but the beds are super comfy and shower rooms and toilets are kept separate in the Japanese style. The rooms are also fitted out with desks and chairs, and you'll get English-language instructions on how to use the aircon/heating unit remote (something that's conspicuously lacking in many hotels). The breakfast, free to all guests, is basic, but the hotel's best quality is its location; you're really in the heart of Osaka here.

2–7–8 Minamisenba. foliohotels.com. ✆ **06-4963-2111.** 48 units. ¥14,000–¥32,000 double. Rates include breakfast. Station: Nagahoribashi (5 min.), Shinsaibashi (8 min.). **Amenities:** Breakfast lounge; free Wi-Fi.

Patina Osaka ♥♥♥ Opened on the south side of Osaka Castle in 2025, this is one of the city's newest luxury properties, as you'll know from the moment the elevator doors open onto its statement-making 20th-floor Sky Lobby. The public spaces and guestrooms are decidedly modern, but draw inspiration from ancient palace architecture, with features like wood latticing, simple floral arrangements, wabi-sabi pottery, and the use of space to bind the design elements together. Rooms come in six styles, from Deluxe Suites, with double beds and tea-platforms placed by the floor-to-ceiling windows, to the epic Patina Suite, with its stone walls, spacious lounge, and state-of-the-art audio system. The hotel's signature restaurant, P72—named after the 72 *ko,* or "micro-seasons," dictated by which flowers are in bloom and which produce is at peak ripeness—serves innovative plant-forward cuisine using ingredients from the hotel's pesticide-free garden or sourced from local farmers. The Listening Room, with its ambient atmosphere and large record collection, designed in concert with Brooklyn-based "speaker sculptor" Devon Turnbull (OJAS), is the ideal space for a post-dinner tipple. No matter which room you choose you'll be paying a pretty penny, but for the best views, request a room on the north side facing Osaka Castle and its surrounding gardens.

3–91 Banbacho. patinahotels.com/osaka. ✆ **06-6941-8888.** 221 units. ¥100,000–¥200,000 double. Station: Morinomiya (10 min.), Tanimachi 4-chome (8 min.). **Amenities:** 4 restaurants; bar and lounge; spa and pool; room service; concierge; free Wi-Fi.

R Hotel Honmachi ♥♥♥ This is about as sleek as budget hotels come, with a charmingly Japanese lobby and communal workspace staffed by English-speaking receptionists. The Honmachi area is one of my favorite places to stay in the city: In between Kita and Tennoji wards, it's a 20-minute walk from Shinsaibashi, so you're not too reliant on public transport and you've got some great authentic restaurants nearby. This makes the miniscule bedrooms worth it (and they really are small). If you want to increase the sense of space, ask for a room with a street view; others have frosted windows facing the adjacent buildings.

1–7–15 Bakuromachi. r-hotel.jp. ✆ **06-6266-1515.** 55 units. ¥8,000–¥14,000 single or double. Station: Sakaisuji Honmachi (6 min.). **Amenities:** Communal workspace; free Wi-Fi.

Around Tennoji/Abeno

Osaka Marriott Miyako Hotel ♥♥♥ Located in one of Japan's tallest buildings, this hotel is strikingly different from any other in Japan.

Its 19th-floor lobby features a soaring 7m-high (23-ft.) ceiling and huge windows on three sides revealing sweeping views of Osaka, making it seem more like a continuation of the 58th-floor Harukas 300 observatory (p. 458) than a hotel. For even more eye-popping panoramas, there's **Restaurant ZK** on the 57th floor, serving *teppanyaki*—the chefs are literally framed by sprawling views of the cityscape as they prepare your food. Rooms, on the 38th to 55th floors, all have a wall of glass providing outstanding views of the city, and deluxe rooms have views even from the bathroom. Probably best are corner kings, offering views in two directions and from windowside tubs. Many rooms also have a round table and comfortable desk chair right beside the window, great for making those working vacations hardly seem like work at all. Clearly, vast views are the emphasis here, though the hotel's exuberantly contemporary decor ensures guests enjoy all aspects of staying here.

1–1–32 Abeno-suji. miyakohotels.ne.jp. ✆ **06-6628-6111.** 360 units. ¥40,000–¥90,000 double. Station: Tennoji or Osaka Abenobashi (1 min.). **Amenities:** 2 restaurants; bar; lounge; concierge; gym; room service; free Wi-Fi.

PAX Hostel ♥♥ Right in the middle of Shinsekai, this backpacker hostel is a favorite among young travelers to the city, with its handsome cafe-lobby-workspace (there's also a record store here) and an entertainment district on its doorstep—you don't have to stray far for fun or food. If you're looking for a bite to eat before heading out for the day, the cafe serves coffee and banh mi. Dorm rooms are located upstairs (no elevator access) and retain the unpolished wood finishing from the old building before it was refurbished. They're not super spacious, but they are cozy, and the beds have private reading lights and charging ports and curtains you can draw for privacy. ***Note:*** The minimum length of stay is 2 nights.

1–20–5 Ebisu-higashi. thepax.jp. ✆ **070-3899-3605.** 3 units. ¥8,000–¥18,000 dorm bed for 2 nights (minimum stay). Station: Doubutsuen-mae (7 min.), Ebisucho (5 min.). **Amenities:** Cafe-bar; free Wi-Fi.

Tabinoyado Hokousou (旅ｷの宿葆晃荘) ♥♥ This family-owned, 130-year-old traditional Japanese guesthouse has many charming features, including a breakfast room with a soaring ceiling and heavy wooden beams; even the big bouquet of fake flowers by the front door has class. Rooms vary in style and size; the best is a 10-tatami-mat room sleeping up to five people and overlooking a small garden. It has a top location, within walking distance of Shitennoji Temple and Spa World and with direct access to Kansai airport, Osaka and Shin-Osaka Stations, Osaka Castle, and Nara.

14–16 Horikoshi-cho. hokousou.com. ✆ **06-6771-7242.** 13 units w/ shared bath. ¥5,000–¥7,500 per person, an extra ¥650 for breakfast. Station: Tennoji (north exit, 1 min.).

WHERE TO EAT IN OSAKA

There's a saying among Japanese: A Kyotoite will spend his last yen on a fine kimono, but an Osakan will spend it on food. Osaka is known as the "nation's kitchen," and that's not just because of its historic role as a distribution center for rice and produce. You don't have to spend a lot of money to eat well here. Local specialties include ***Oshi-zushi*** (pressed square-shaped sushi), ***udon*** noodles with white soy sauce, ***omurice*** (a rice omelet topped with ketchup), ***takoyaki*** (wheat-flour dumplings with octopus), and Naniwa black beef. *Kushikatsu* (deep-fried vegetable skewers), *butaman* (steamed pork buns), meat and noodle hotpots, and fish prepared myriad ways are other bites you'll encounter on your culinary excursions in Osaka.

Hot off the griddle, a savory okonomiyaki pancake is one of Osaka's signature dishes.

Kyoto may have Japan's most refined cuisine, and Tokyo may be the standard-bearer for quantity and quality of delicious food on offer. But if we're judging Japan's food scene in terms of sheer gustatory pleasure, I think Osaka takes the biscuit. You could easily spend half your trip sitting at restaurant counters and flipping indulgent pancakes in okonomiyaki shops—and frankly, you'd be better off for it. This is the city of *kuidaore,* "eating oneself bankrupt," so while you might not have the constitution to hit every restaurant recommended below, it would be the Osaka way to try.

Around Osaka Station

There are a multitude of possibilities in and around Osaka Station, including the eighth floor of **Yodobashi-Umeda** on the station's north side, where more than 30 restaurants offer pizza, pasta, sushi, dim sum, *udon,* ramen, *shabu-shabu, omurice, tonkatsu,* and morel many of them offer excellent lunch deals. Also worth checking out is **Hanadako** (**✆ 06-6372-0313**), a hole-in-the-wall selling *takoyaki* on Shin-Umeda Shokudogai Street under Osaka Station. Expect queues here, but also whip-fast service.

Brewpub Center Point ♥♥♥ MEAT & BEER This trendy taproom and restaurant in one of Osaka's most understated neighborhoods is a great place to try craft beer and feast on barbecued meat. Alongside award-winning ales, you can order beef brisket and pulled pork by the pound, paired with sides like pickles, chili, French fries, jambalaya, and mac-n-cheese. Meat platters, with all-you-can-drink craft beer, are also available from ¥5,000. There's none of the pretension of a Western gastropub here; the vibe is super-chilled, and the staff are happy to let customers sample beer from the chalkboard menu before committing to a full glass. Great for casual group dining.

2–5–8 Ukida. brewpub.co.jp ✆ **06-6450-8296.** Meat combos from ¥3,500; platters with all-you-can-drink from ¥5,000. Mon and Wed–Fri 3–11pm; Sat–Sun noon–11pm. Station: Nakazakicho (4 min.), Tenma (12 min.).

Okonomiyaki Kiji (お好み焼きじ) ♥ OKONOMIYAKI Takimikoji Village is a fun place for a meal, a re-created 1920s and 1930s Japanese village filled with period relics, from a post office to a police box and a miniature shrine, with a soundtrack of music of the era. There are about a dozen small restaurants here, including ones serving ramen, *soba, shabu-shabu,* sushi, tempura, etc.—and this spot, which offers what some Osakans swear is the best *okonomiyaki* in town. Customer photos and *meishi* (business cards) paper the walls and ceiling, testifying to customer appreciation.

Umeda Sky Building basement, 1–1–90 Oyodo-naka. takimikoji.jp/shop/kiji. ✆ **06-6440-5970.** Okonomiyaki ¥780–¥1060. Daily 11:30am–9:30pm (last order). Station: JR Osaka or Umeda (Central North exit of JR Osaka Station, 8 min.).

Tsukemen Misawa ♥♥ TSUKEMEN Ramen is so globally renowned that its culinary cousin, *tsukemen* (dipping ramen), often gets neglected by non-Japanese diners. But in many ways, I find it a more accomplished dish. The noodles come in a bowl or on a tray with a concentrated helping of the broth served in a separate receptacle. This means the noodles retain their original chewy texture, and with each mouthful you can taste every ounce of umami in the soup. Misawa's owners have been honing its

EAT YOURSELF BANKRUPT IN tenma

Splitting off from the Tenjinbashisuji shopping arcade near Tenma Station, you'll find this network of alleyways with dozens of tiny old restaurants packed tightly together like dusty records on a shelf, many with counter seats or standing-only, serving all kinds of classic Japanese fare. Okonomiyaki, sushi, yakitori, yakiniku, *kushikastu*, tempura, udon, gyoza, and izakaya bites are just the beginning. This is still mainly an area for locals—don't expect too many English menus or staff that can communicate with you fluently. Still, some spots have open kitchens and glass counters showcasing the food, which makes ordering easier. Prices and opening times vary, but you can dine in many restaurants for around ¥1,000–¥2,000 per person.

For okonomiyaki, **Chigusa** (✆ **06-6351-4072**) is one of the most popular shops in town, while **Tensho** (✆ **090-8445-8004**) does great oden and tempura. **Tayutayu** (temma-tayutayu.com; ✆ **06-6354-8108**) has a wide selection of meat skewers and around 100 types of shochu on the menu. Many restaurants open late here, so if you need to kill a couple hours before the morning train service resumes, head to the nearby karaoke parlor, **Big Echo Temma Ekimae** at 4–11–6 Tenjimbashi, which closes at 5am daily.

To get here, look for the McDonald's on the north side of Tenma station, then head down one of the alleyways on either side. It's easy to miss, but definitely worth seeking out—great packages sometimes come in the least expected of places.

Osaka, the Capital of Okonomiyaki

Osaka is probably best known for ***okonomiyaki,*** which literally means "what you like, cooked." Its origins date from about 1700, when a type of thin flour pancake cooked on a hot plate and filled with miso paste was served during Buddhist ceremonies. It wasn't until the 20th century, however, that it became popular, primarily during food shortages. Gradually other ingredients such as pork, egg, and cabbage were added. Today, Osaka is riddled with inexpensive *okonomiyaki* restaurants—more than 4,000 of them—many of which have made it onto the Michelin food guide.

recipes for four generations; their complex meat-and-fish-based broth, topped with *naruto* (cured fish cakes) and *menma* (bamboo shoots), is a culinary treasure. Order your noodles from the vending machine—pictures and English-language instructions should make this a breeze—then hand your ticket stub to the staff once you've taken a seat. The tsukemen costs around ¥1,000 yen, but you can also add extras, such as eggs, *sudachi* (a limelike citrus), slices of *chashu* (pork belly), or a beer. You'll also be given a light dashi-based soup, called "soup *wari,*" in case you want to dilute or add some extra volume to your dipping broth.

3–6–1 Minami-Honmachi. smile-c.co.jp/tsukemen-misawa. ✆ **06-6281-3380.** *Tsukemen ¥900–¥1,200.* Mon–Sat 11am–11:45pm (closed 4–5pm Mon–Fri), Sun 11am–7:45pm (last order). Station: Osaka (14 min.).

Yukari Tensan ♥♥ OKONOMIYAKI The interior of this small okonomiyaki shop is rustic-looking, with wooden beams, decorative lanterns, and sunken tables at which you cook your food. If you're not sure how to make okonomiyaki—though really, there's little technique involved—the staff will lend a helping hand. Classic flavor profiles such as seafood medleys or pork and squid (a kind of okonomiyaki surf 'n turf) are popular menu items. There's also a recommended 5-cheese okonomiyaki that's been featured on TV segments—it's more like a pizza than a pancake, but worth a try at ¥1,680.

3–1–12 Tenjinbashi, yukarichan.co.jp. ✆ **06-6353-1414.** *Okonomiyaki* ¥980–¥1,680. Daily 11:30am–9pm (last order). Closed 1st and 3rd Mon. of month, plus other irregular holidays Station: JR Osaka Tenmangu (5 min.), Minamimorimachi Station (5 min.).

Minami

The stretch of city from Shinsaibashi through Namba and southward to Shinsekai must have one of the greatest concentrations of star-quality restaurants in the world—that might be based on observation alone, but I say it without a hint of hyperbole. If you make this journey on foot after dark, you will pass atmospheric restaurants on nearly every street corner; diners hunched over counters, chefs at work on crackling *hibachi* grills, small plates on delicate crockery being fizzed out of restaurant kitchens, and open doorways funneling stomach-rumbling smells onto the street. And that's just what you can see at ground level; never mind the hundreds of innovative restaurants on buildings' upper floors, most of which you will never discover.

If you're heading to the popular nightlife street Dotombori (see p. 478), a good spot for a quick meal is **Acchichi Honpo Dotonbori** (kd4h000.gorp.jp; ✆ **050-5487-0593**), a popular hole-in-the-wall joint where a portion of *takoyaki* costs ¥800; throw in a beer for an extra ¥300.

Butayama (豚山 南船場店) ♥♥ RAMEN Osaka might be the home of okonomiyaki and takoyaki, but the city's ramen restaurants are no chumps. The meaty bowls of noodles and *tonkotsu* broth served in this shop—whose names translates to "Pork Mountain"—are a glutton's dream. Place your order at the vending machine as you enter the shop (it's mostly in Japanese, but there are pictures that offer some help), then hand your ticket stub to the chefs behind the counter. They may ask you how you like your noodles, but if you just say "futsu" (normal), that should clear up any miscommunication. A standard bowl of pork ramen costs ¥950 or you can order a large bowl (大ぶた) with 375g of noodles, extra slices of *chashu* (pork belly), and a heap of bean sprouts for ¥1,300. Even the "small" bowls are indulgent, though, so best to come here on an empty stomach.

3–9–6 Minamisenba. butayama.com. ✆ **06-6440-5970.** Ramen ¥900–¥1,600. Daily 11am–10:30pm. Station: Shinsaibashi (4 min.), Honamchi (7 min.).

Hub Kitchen ♥♥ FOOD COURT This indoor street market is a great place to sample various cuisines under one roof; it epitomizes Osaka's more-is-more approach to food. The line-up of stalls changes often (it's a breeding ground for food start-ups), offering the likes of shawarma, on-the-go curry cups, bowls of ramen, pizza slices, tempura, cookies, smoothies, and more, in a funky and communal setting. Lunch times are popular with workers in the Honmachi area; in the evenings, there's a great atmosphere as commuters and young professionals begin populating the tables in the central concourse.

3–1–27 Kyutaromachi. hub-kitchen.jp. ✆ **06-4708-4222.** Prices vary, most meals ¥1,000–**¥2,000.** Daily 11am–3pm and 5–11pm (individual stall hours may vary). Station: Honmachi (2 min.).

Developing a Taste for Cheese Tarts

A popular hole-in-the-wall food in Osaka is the cheese tart, a fluffy cheesecake wrapped in pastry. **Bonbomy Honmachi** (2–3–4 Minamihonmachi, in Chuo-ku; bombomy.com; ✆ **06-6261-6222**) gets creative in the kitchen, serving delicious chestnut, pistachio, matcha, and berry cheese tarts for ¥380, or ¥2,000 for a set of six. **Cheese Tart Pablo Shinsaibashi** (2–8–1 Shinsaibashisuji, Chuo-ku; pablo3.com; ✆ **06-6211-8260**) also has a good selection, with plain cheese tarts for ¥290 and mouthwatering Uji matcha tarts for ¥320.

Juppo (十方) ♥♥♥ KAISEKI This traditional restaurant near Dotonbori takes the essence of kaiseki cuisine—with its seasonal raw fish, steamed dishes, stewed tofu, wagyu, and miso soup, all plated on pretty ceramics and delicate lacquerware—and delivers it without posturing. It's

one of the more approachable kaiseki restaurants, with an English drinks menu and a simple online booking system where you select your dinner course in advance. Dinners start at ¥6,600 (a very fair price for kaiseki) and go all the way up to ¥15,200 for the 10-dish Arima course, including 2 hours of all-you-can-drink. If you're unsure what to order, the Japanese black beef sukiyaki course, including sashimi, an appetizer, a hotpot, and dessert, is a sumptuous deal. For the best atmosphere, request a table in a tatami room (you'll have to take your shoes off and sit on the floor), though on busier nights these are reserved for groups only.
2–4–14 Nishishinsaibashi. restaurant.ikyu.com/106349/dinner. ✆ **06-6212-0086.** Lunch from ¥3,300; dinner ¥6,600–¥15,200. Mon–Sat 11:30am–2pm and 5–9:30pm (last orders). Station: Namba (6 min.), Shinsaibashi (7 min.).

Kani Doraku (かに道楽) ♥♥ CRAB Specializing in *kani* (crab), this very popular restaurant on Dotonbori beside the Ebisu-bashi Bridge.is difficult to miss: It has a huge model crab on its facade, waving its legs and claws. It's the signature eatery of a chain originating in Osaka 60-plus years ago, now with dozens of branches in Japan, including two others just down the street (there are 16 in Osaka altogether). The English-language menu lists crab sukiyaki and other dishes, but it's easiest to simply order a set meal or bento box. Crab sushi boxes average around ¥2,000, while set meals can go up to ¥22,000, depending on how fancy you want to be. There are several floors for dining, all with kimono-clad waitresses; some have tables offering a view of the canal. Avoid peak times if you can (lunch is served until 4pm); otherwise, to avoid making customers wait in line, the restaurant assigns them a specific dining time to come back.
1–6–18 Dotonbori. douraku.co.jp. ✆ **06-6211-8975.** Bento lunches ¥1,728–¥2,646; dinners ¥3,200–¥22,000. Daily 11am–9pm (last order). Station: Namba (exit 14, 2 min.).

Khaos Spice Diner ♥♥ CURRY This fusion curry house merits repeat visits because the menu is constantly changing. The Khaos keema curry, a dish originating in the Indian subcontinent that's become a staple in Japan, is a menu stalwart, while the other two options change weekly: One is chicken-based (such as spicy Mexican chicken or butter chicken), the other is the "weekly whimsical curry," which really is at the discretion of the chef (veggie options are becoming more popular). You can order one curry, or a mix of two or three, alongside plain or turmeric rice (rice refills are only ¥100). Extra toppings include spiced eggs, cilantro, potato salad, Thai *gaiyan* chicken, and *achar* (Indian pickle). The beer menu is interesting, too, featuring Lion lager from Sri Lanka, Singha from Thailand, Jamaican Red Stripe, and Heartland, a malt-and-hops pale lager produced in Ibaraki Prefecture.
1–2–17 Kitahorie. khaos-spicediner.com. ✆ **06-6534-2600.** Set meals ¥800—1,280, toppings ¥150–¥*200.* Mon–Sat 11:30am–10pm (weekdays closed 3:30–5pm); Sun 11:30am–9pm. Station: Yotsubashi (2 min.), Shinsaibashi (6 min.).

Kirindo (麒麟堂) ♥♥♥ IZAKYA There's something quintessentially Osakan about this (mostly) standing-only izakaya, located in an underground concourse connected to Honmachi Station. A little cube that looks like it's been hacked out of the station's concrete wall, it caters to customers in need of a few quick bar snacks before heading home and those who want to lean on the counter, drink highballs for a couple hours, and chew the rag with the staff. The Japanese-only menu might cause some ordering headaches, but the items are all quite familiar (provided this isn't your first izakaya)—sashimi, chicken salad, meat skewers, edamame, fried oysters, quail eggs, steamed eggplant, tofu dishes, and small hotpots. But the food is a little more elevated than you'd find in most chain izakayas, so don't be surprised if you end up ordering a lot of small plates (most cost ¥200–¥500) and running up a decent tab. There's also a good selection of sake from ¥400 per glass—tell the staff either *karakushi* (dry) or *amai* (sweet), and they'll pick a bottle to suit your taste.

B1F Semba Center Building 9, 4–1–10 Senbachuo. instagram.com/kirindo_senba. ✆ **070-8390-6363.** Small plates ¥190–680. Mon–Fri 4–10pm; Sat–Sun 3–9:30pm (last order). Station: Honamchi.

Kurodaruma ♥♥♥ IZAKAYA Always lively, this bar-cum-izakaya has a standing-only counter surrounding the kitchen, and when the weather's good, long tables placed outside. The English-speaking owner spent time living and traveling abroad, which has translated into a menu of izakaya-style sharing plates imbued with foreign flavors. Just a few examples of the delectable dishes that fly out of the kitchen: seafood tartare with plum, miso, and truffle; red shrimp pickled in Shaoxing wine; Korean-style

GRAZE YOUR WAY THROUGH shinsekai

In the retro district of Shinsekai (see p. 460), head for **Jan-Jan Yokocho,** a narrow arcade street lined with busy eateries, running alongside Spa World (p. 460). **Tengu** ♥♥ (てんぐ; ✆ **06-6641-3577;** Tues–Sun 10:30am–8pm) is among the most popular *kushikatsu* spots here. The chefs somehow make the deep-fried meat and veg skewers not seem overindulgent, and with diners sitting at a counter surrounding the kitchen, there's always a jovial, communal vibe. Skewers cost between ¥100 and ¥500. **Sushi Kinga** ♥♥ (✆ **050-5461-1671;** daily 11am–11pm) serves hand-pressed sushi meals, as well as a la carte dishes like clam soup, grilled salmon belly, deep-fried pufferfish, and vegetable tempura. It's popular with foreigners because of its English-language menu; most meals cost between ¥1,000 and ¥4,000.

A few blocks farther north, on the street leading to Tsutenkaku Tower, **Janbo-tsuribune Tsurikichi** ♥ (ジャンボ釣船 つり吉; ✆ **06-6630-9026;** daily 10:30am–11pm) is a classic place to try the catch-your-own fish dining gimmick. It's a huge restaurant with maritime decor and open-top fish tanks along one side. The overwhelming menu has all manner of raw, grilled, steamed, stewed, and deep-fried seafoods to pair with whatever you choose to catch. The live produce is dictated by the season (a noticeboard outside announces the fish scheduled for arrival) and includes lobsters, shellfish, breams, flounders, mackerels, and even small sharks. Pricier catches can cost up to ¥10,000; you then request two methods of preparation from a list that includes sashimi, carpaccio, salt-grilled, served as bone crackers, or simmered in a vegetable hotpot.

octopus stir-fry with bamboo shoots; seaweed- and cheese-wrapped pork tempura with demi-glace sauce; oven-baked eggplant "black beauty" Bolognese; shiitake mushrooms in gorgonzola sauce; and Pacific saury with muscat-grapes. If you're staying in the Honmachi area, don't skip this place. 4–8–8 Honmachi. instagram.com/kuro_daruma.honmachi/. ✆ **050-1353-5792.** Sharing plates ¥500–¥1250; around ¥4,000–¥5,000 per person for dinner and drinks. Daily 4pm–midnight. Station: Honmachi (2 min.).

Mitsuki/Mizuki (美月のお好み焼き) ♥♥ OKONOMIYAKI Not only is this one of the tastiest okonomiyaki spots in town, but the chefs also cook the food at the counter before delivering it to the hotplates at the center of your table—handy if you're not comfortable with the DIY okonomiyaki style. There's an English menu with classic combos like pork and seafood, or pork, udon, green onion, and egg. Or you can concoct your own, picking a base protein and adding toppings (egg, green onion, cheese, kimchi, rice cakes, or oysters). I recommend mixing pork, cheese, and kimchi—three ingredients that work in perfect harmony—or if you're feeling frivolous, order the special Japanese black beef and seafood okonomiyaki for ¥4,290. ***Note:*** The pronunciation of this restaurant is *Mizuki,* but in English-language listings online, it's often rendered as *Mitsuki.* 2–26 Souemoncho. ✆ **06-6214-6001.** Okonomiyaki ¥990–¥4,290. Mon–Sat noon–3pm and 5–11pm. Station: Kintetsu-Nippombashi (7 min.), Shinsaibashi (11 min.).

Taiyo (心斎橋本店) ♥♥♥ UDON Hiding at the end of a corridor in the middle of the pulsating Shinsaibashi district (look for a white lantern reading "肉しょうがう)ん"), this easy-to-miss noodle shop specializes in *udon* served in a light yet deceptively complex broth. The most popular item is the *niku-shouga* (beef and ginger) udon for ¥1,000 (another ¥100 to make it a large), which is a gift from umami heaven. If you're hungry enough, consider adding toppings like tempura chicken or eggplant, raw or soft-boiled egg, or extra meat and spring onions. Given its late-night hours, you may happen upon this place after an evening of drunken revelry, when it makes for an excellent noodle nightcap. 1–16–7 Higashishinsaibashi. ✆ **06-6210-4774.** Udon ¥1,000–¥1,500. Daily 7pm–4am. Station: Shinsaibashi (7 min.).

OSAKA SHOPPING

Osaka is famous for shopping, in no small part because Osaka developed as a commercial town of merchants—and who knows merchandise better than the merchants themselves? It's one of the world's leading cities in underground shopping arcades—check out the vast underground arcades in Umeda (where the JR, Hanshin, subway, and Hankyu train lines intersect) and downtown's **Crysta Nagahori,** one of the most attractive underground malls in Japan, with a glass atrium ceiling and 100 shops.

There are plenty of aboveground options as well. **Tenjinbashisuji,** in Kita-ku, is said to be Japan's longest shopping street, stretching 2.6km/1.6 miles and lined with some 800 shops and restaurants—but because retail space is expensive here, the shops are often chains and big-name brands. **Midosuji Dori,** a wide boulevard with gingko trees running north and south in the heart of the city, is Osaka's calling card for name-brand international boutiques, as well as the lovely old **Daimaru** department store, with newer annexes on both sides. Just to the east is **Shinsaibashi-suji,** a covered promenade with many long-established shops, some dating back to the Edo Period. Teens flock to **Marui 0101,** a seven-story department store on the corner of Shinsaibashi-suji and Nankai Dori, and to **HEP FIVE,** a huge shopping complex near Umeda Station with a Joypolis amusement arcade and a Ferris wheel on top. At JR Osaka Station are two LUCUA, Daimaru, and flagship **Hankyu** department stores, plus **Yodobashi,** with computers, cameras, toys, bikes, luggage, and more. The granddaddy department store of them all is **Kintetsu Abeno Harukas** near Tennoji Station, boasting more floor space than any other department store in Japan.

And of course, this being Osaka, there are shopping areas dedicated to food and cooking. In the heart of the city, just east of Sakaisuji Avenue near Nipponbashi Station, is **Kuromon Ichiba,** a covered street where professional chefs shop for seafood, fruit, vegetables, pickles, and other edibles, and tourists munch on grilled scallops, tempura, sushi, and street food. To the south, a few blocks east of Nankai Namba Station, is **Sennichimae Doguya-suji,** a covered shopping lane with about 45 open-fronted shops selling pots, pans, dishes, chopsticks, kitchen knives, aprons, plastic food, and any other implement you need to prepare and serve Japanese food, at very inexpensive prices.

Amemura: Street Fashion Central

In the heart of Shinsaibashi, **Amemura,** meaning "American Village," has been a popular spot for young Japanese shopping for American secondhand clothing since the 1960s. Today, it still hosts thrift stores selling Americana, particularly around **Triangle Park,** but a new wave of young Japanese apparel shop owners is reinventing the area. Fusing Japanese and Korean streetwear—both major influences on the global fashion scene—with elements of North American fashion, these shops have cemented Amemura's status in shaping millennial sartorial trends, comparable to the likes of Harajuku in Tokyo. Many floor staff speak decent English—at least enough to drive a hard sell and tell you how cool their products are—streamlining the shopping experience for the twenty-something Western tourists who now scout the area. Clothes hanging in windows and on racks outside will indicate whether the shop is worth perusing, but there are a few I'd recommend to give you a sense of Amemura's stock (all are within a block or two from Triangle Park). **E.S.P Osaka** (espwebstore.com; ✆ **06-6244-2005**) sells high-quality T-shirts and jumpers with artistic prints and vintage-style sports jackets. **Cherish** stocks one-size-fits-all, baggy T-shirts by Japanese and Korean designers—plus, the shop owner is super friendly and is happy to cut a bargain—while sister shops **Jolly Clan** and **Jolly Clan 2** (be-in.online) are showcase reels for

21st-century Japanese street fashion. **Pigsty** (pigsty1999.com; ✆ **06-6251-0289**) sells secondhand American clothing and patterned button-down shirts. Most apparel shops here open daily from late morning till around 8pm. Another trendy spot is **ADD CBD** at 1–8–23 Nishishinsaibashi, a shop selling coffee, chocolates, oils, and vapes infused with CBD, a cannabis-derived cure-all that's surprisingly booming in Japan, a country with a zero-tolerance policy towards illicit drugs.

Den Den Town: Pop-Culture Heaven

Just south of Namba Station is **Nipponbashi Den Den Town,** stretching along Sakaisuji Avenue and its side streets. This is Osaka's electronics and pop-culture shopping mecca (*Den* is short for "electric"), similar to Tokyo's Akihabara, and is becoming very popular with international tourists, who flock to the shops specializing in *manga,* anime, retro video games, and cosplay items, as well as its arcades and maid cafes. Stop by the **Nipponbashi Information Center,** just north of Ebisucho Station on Sakaisuji (✆ **06-6655-1717;** daily 11am–7pm), for an English map of the area listing approximately 500 stores. Some are multifloored emporiums crammed with decades' worth of pop-culture merchandise, while others are obscure trading card centers that would appeal only to the most die-hard otaku. You're best identifying a few shops that cater to your interests.

The shops of Den Den Town offer a bewildering array of pop-culture finds.

Animate ♥♥ Animate is one of Japan's best-known pop-culture megastore chains. Focusing on manga, this branch is spread across several floors and stocks a dizzying number of serialized comics and related merch, including soundtracks, figurines, dolls, and soft toys. Most of the material is in Japanese, but on the ground floor, just to the right of the main entrance, are a few shelves of manga in English, featuring titles like *Dragon Ball, Case Closed, One Piece, Demon Slayer,* and *Hunter x Hunter.* Granted, manga in translation is increasingly available in the West now, but you may still find something that's hard to get your hands on at home. 1–1–3 Nipponbashinishi. animate.co.jp. ✆ **06-6636-0628.** Daily 11am–8pm.

Gee Store ♥♥ Known as a "hobby shop," meaning it's stocked with miscellaneous pop-culture goods, this store sells comics, T-shirts, accessories, souvenirs, trinkets, and most importantly for cosplayers, props and costumes to transform shoppers into their favorite animated heroes and heroines. 2–18–18 Nishi-Shinsaibashi. geestore.com ✆ **06-6630-7655.** Daily 11am–8pm.

Guf ♥♥ Most shoppers in Guf won't stray beyond the ground floor, with its impressive selection of tees, jumpers, jackets, socks, boxers, bags, and badges depicting fan-favorite animated characters, from Charizard and Godzilla to the Kamen Riders and Snorlax. IF you plan on wandering upstairs, know that the upper floors (over-18s only) cater to raunchier predilections, selling themed sex toys, animated-porn fanzines, life-sized love dolls, and other items I'd thought were the stuff of urban legend. Not for prudish eyes. 4–10–5 Nipponbashi. ✆ **06-6630-7521.** Daily 10am–11pm.

Super Potato ♥♥♥ Super Potato in Akihabara, Tokyo, is probably Japan's most famous retro video game store, but the Den Den Town branch on Ota Road (which also hosts the trademark Solid Snake statue) might be even better. It's easier to navigate, with wide aisles and the merchandise all on one floor, and the haul of memorabilia is museum-worthy, including old tech in mint condition, only-in-Japan video game releases, obscure peripherals—the Nintendo Family Trainer or the 1987 Famicom 3D System, anyone?—commemorative console catalogues, and ancient handhelds like Bandai Namco's SwanCrystal. A must-visit for collectors. 3–18–18 Nipponbashi. superpotato.com. ✆ **06-6647-3505.** Daily 10am–8pm.

Torejaras (とれじゃらす) ♥♥ This shop on Ota Road is a good hunting ground for toys and figurines, especially characters from gaming, anime, and manga franchises that achieved popularity outside Japan, like Resident Evil, Kingdom Hearts, Digimon, NieR, Gundam, Splatoon, and Final Fantasy. Use the floor map (with English translation) to find what you're looking for. 3–6–16 Nipponbashi. torejaras.com. ✆ **06-4396-8328.** Daily 11am–8pm.

ENTERTAINMENT & NIGHTLIFE

Performing Arts

The **National Bunraku Theater,** 1–12–10 Nipponbashi (ntj.jac.go.jp; ✆ **06-6212-2531**), was completed in 1984 as the only theater in Japan dedicated to Japanese traditional puppet theater. Five different productions are staged a year, each generally running for about 3 weeks. Prices range from about ¥2,500 to ¥6,000 (more for reserved seating). English-language programs are available. The theater is located just east of Namba and Dotombori, a 1-minute walk from exit 7 of Nipponbashi Station.

Northwest of Osaka, the town of Takarazuka (in Hyogo Prefecture) is synonymous with the all-female **Takarazuka Revue.** Founded in 1914 to attract vacationers to Takarazuka, the troupe proved instantly popular with the general public of that era, whose tastes had turned from traditional Japanese drama to lively Western musicals and entertainment. Performances are held at the **Takarazuka Grand Theatre** (kageki.hankyu.co.jp/english; ✆ **0570-00-5100**) most days throughout the year (closed Mon), usually at 1pm on weekdays and at 11am and 3:30pm on weekends and holidays. Tickets range from about ¥3,500 to ¥11,000.

The Bar Scene

Dotombori (or Dotonbori), a narrow pedestrian lane just off Midosuji Dori that flanks the south bank of the Dotombori River Walk, is the center of Osaka's most famous nightlife district, with lots of restaurants and bars, and huge mechanical signage and 3D billboards depicting crabs, dragons, chefs, pufferfish, squid, and pieces of sushi. This is one of the busiest parts of town, with the Glico Man (a huge billboard erected in 1935 that advertises the Glico confectionary company) serving as a popular meeting and Instagramming spot. The tourist crowds swell to such numbers here that the reinforced footbridge seems to creak and buckle under their weight, so don't be afraid to explore the adjacent streets and narrow alleys splitting off the main shopping arcade—this is where you'll find lots of the most interesting foodstuffs.

North of Dotonbori and Shinsaibashi, in **Honmachi** you'll find lots of cool late-night establishments that cater more to locals than tourists.

Bar Lit ♥♥ "Bar Dimly Lit," would be a more fitting name for this cocktail lounge in Honmachi; enter late at night after a few warm-up drinks and you may feel your vision has left you. The chief mixologist here used to work at Osaka's Conrad Hotel, so he speaks good English and is accustomed to dealing with foreign customers. Take a seat at the counter and tell him what you like or ask for a recommendation. His concoctions are pricier than elsewhere—many cost ¥2,000 to ¥3,000—but they're layered and complex and pack an alcoholic punch. 4-3-14 Kawaramachi. instagram.com/bar_lit_honmachi. ✆ **06-6202-6682.** Station: Honmachi (5 min.). Daily 5pm–2am.

Bird/56 ♥♥♥ This classy *kissa* shows why Japan's underground jazz culture is so enchanting: cozy, atmospheric, nostalgia-fueled, and crammed with whiskey bottles and old jazz records. An English menu and a friendly proprietor make this establishment approachable (some *kissa* can be a little intimidating). The previous owner, or "Master," as they are known in the jazz *kissa* world, died a couple years back, and the current Master, a former customer, places a glass of whiskey on the shelf every evening in commemoration—a sign of how hallowed these places are for the people that frequent them. The impressive selection of Japanese whiskeys, from ¥1,500 a glass, and a recommended drinks list featuring plum wine, yuzu sake with soda, and an Old Fashioned with your choice of whiskey, are the alcohol highlights. 3F 1-6-18 Namba. ✆ **090-1590-4126.** Station: Namba (4 min.). Usually 6pm–midnight or later.

RAID THE VAULT AT THE whisky bank

One of Japan's finest whiskey stores, **Whisky Bank** ♥♥ (1–3–5 Shinsaibashisuji; whiskybank.jp; ✆ **06-6210-3310**) stocks blends from the Suntory and Yamazaki distilleries rare enough to fetch north of ¥1 million per bottle. Others are noteworthy for their design, sold in bottles shaped like samurai warriors, Templar knights, saxophones, trumpets, accordions, or violins—and from their six-figure price tags, you can guess that the quality of the liquid inside ain't half-bad either. While some blends are clearly aimed at deep-pocketed collectors, there's also a list of more common (yet still high-quality) whiskeys for customers to try. McCallan, Yamazaki, Ichiro's Malt, Hakushu, Karuizawa, and Taketsuru all feature, with 30ml samples costing anywhere from ¥900 to ¥10,000. The staff in here speak excellent English, and as you can imagine, they know their way around a whiskey, so feel free to pepper them with questions.

Dublin Bay ♥♥ Japan doesn't have too many authentic Irish pubs, but this one gets top marks for its seventh-floor beer garden—a great place to sample the bar's selection of ales and lagers on pleasant evenings. If you're in a group you can reserve a 3-hour all-you-can-drink BBQ plan for ¥5,000 per person (food and equipment provided, but cooking is DIY). The main basement bar is cavernous, with decent pints of Guiness and a good atmosphere; it's *the* place to go to watch live international sporting events. 2–1–5 Dotombori. irishpubdublinbay.com. ✆ **06-6213-1122.** Station: Namba (5 min.). Daily 3pm–2am.

Escapé ♥♥ This standalone building looks like it belongs on a Wes Anderson film set, with its textured green walls and a sense of balance and symmetry, all focused on the diffused glow of the espresso lounge within. It's popular with young women and couples on coffee dates, who come here for cups of fresh roast and sweet snacks. Beer, wine, whiskey, rum, and simple cocktails are also served. If you're standing at the counter, don't be surprised if the regulars start chatting to you; it's that kind of place. Most drinks are between ¥500 and ¥1,000. 1–1–6 Kawaramachi. ✆ **06-4963-2718.** Station: Honmachi (7 min.). Sun–Wed 3pm–midnight, Fri–Sat 3pm–2am.

Fanny Mae ♥♥ Located on the ground floor of the same building that hosts Bird/56 (see above), this rock n' roll bar is so narrow and clouded in cigarette smoke you can barely make your way past the customers squeezed along the counter. But with its Rolling Stones-loving proprietor and a fitting soundtrack (very loud), it attracts old school rock fans and lots of young tourists who scream over the music to converse with one another. It's not for everybody, but if you like the rock music of yesteryear and don't mind having your eardrums blown out, you'll enjoy yourself. 1–6–18 Namba. ✆ **090-3429-9886.** Station: Namba (4 min.). Daily 7pm–5am.

Kopimal ♥♥♥ In a maze of narrow, flagstone-paved walking streets near Den Den Town (p. 476), this small craft beer and coffee bar feels like someone's living room, with soft chairs, coffee tables, card games, and shelves of pop-culture merch probably bought in the nearby electronics and comic book stores. The friendly English-speaking proprietor seems to enjoy practicing his English with foreign customers and readily dishes out recommendations for other bars in Osaka—if you order a craft beer, he may offer you a map listing trendy taprooms throughout the city. The hand-written menu features Osaka-brewed craft beers and other weekly specials, as well as rice wine and foods like spicy quail eggs, chicken liver pate, prosciutto-and-cheese boards, and sumptuous stewed beef tendon. ***Note:*** There are two shops side-by-side here, both under the same ownership, but they are listed under two different names: Kopimal and 月のアムリタ (*Getsu no Amurita*). 4–17–3 and 4–17–4 Nipponbashi. ✆ **090-5617-1415.** Station: Ebisucho (5 min.). Daily 10am–midnight.

Otachi (お立ち) ♥♥ This bar's name means "standing," and that's probably what you'll do here (though there some makeshift seats). It's little more than a hole-in-the-wall with wrapround translucent curtains, space for a few imbibers, and a huge picture over the bar of Ken Takakura (known as "Ken-san" by Japanese), an actor famous for playing gangsters in the '60s and '70s. The proprietor, having lived in New York, speaks good English and will engage you in conversation, as will any other customers who wander in. Definitely worth swinging by for a drink (most are ¥500–¥1,000) if you're in the Honmachi area. 1–10–2 Awaza. No phone. Station: Honmachi (3 min.). Mon–Sat 7pm–2am.

7UP Bar ♥♥ This expat-friendly bar and karaoke joint spills out onto the street—as do the dulcet tones of those singing inside—which works as both an advertisement or a deterrent, depending on how you look at it. Cocktails and beers from ¥700, a wide range of shots, English-speaking staff, and a youthful clientele make this a great spot for young travelers looking to meet like-minded souls. 2–9–36 Nishishinsaibashi. No phone. Contact info N/A. Station: Yotsubashi (6 min.) or Shinsaibashi (5 min.). Mon–Thurs 2pm–2am; Fri 2pm–3am; Sat–Sun 1pm–3am.

Tsuzuru ♥♥♥ This bar has a cocktail-lounge atmosphere and an excellent selection of domestic and international whiskies, without usual pretension or high prices those usually imply. The staff speak little English, but smiling and pointing at which whiskey you want works just fine. There's no menu, either, but you can tell the staff what you like with words like "single-malt," "smoky," "smooth," etc. and they'll get the drift. Glasses of top-end whiskey sometimes go for ¥1,000 or less, far cheaper than what you'll pay in most other whiskey bars. ***Note:*** It's on the second floor, atop an unassuming staircase, and therefore easy to miss. 2F 4–7–5 Hiranomachi. ✆ **06-4400-3796.** Station: Honmachi or Higobashi (10 min.). Mon–Sat 6pm–4am; Sun 8pm–4am.

SIDE TRIP TO KOBE ♥♥

589km (366 miles) W of Tokyo; 75km (47 miles) W of Kyoto; 31km (19 miles) W of Osaka

Blessed with the calm waters of the Seto Inland Sea, Kobe (the capital of Hyogo Prefecture) has been an important port town for centuries. Even today its port is the heart of the city, its raison d'être. It was one of the first ports to begin accepting foreign traders in 1868; many of them lived in **Kitano,** an attractive neighborhood of Western-style residences built around the turn of the 20th century. This vibrant city of 1.5 million inhabitants is still quite multicultural, with foreigners from more than 120 different nations residing here.

Despite the devastation of the Great Hanshin Earthquake in 1995, Kobe has risen from the ashes with more attractions, hotels, and urban redevelopment than ever before. Indeed, if it weren't for several earthquake memorials and a museum dedicated to the event, visitors would never guess at the widespread destruction of 30 years ago. Nowadays, the name "Kobe" probably is most associated with the local brand of beef. The city also offers excellent international cuisine, most notably in the restaurant-filled Chinatown, and is one of Japan's major sake-producing regions.

Essentials

ARRIVING Take the **Tokaido-Sanyo Line** from Osaka Station to Sannomiya in the heart of Kobe City. The half-hour ride costs ¥420.

VISITOR INFORMATION There's a **tourist information center** in Sannomiya Station (✆ **078-241-1050;** daily 9am–6pm), where English-speaking staff provide maps and sightseeing information. Another tourist office is in the hilly **Kitano** district (✆ **078-251-8360;** daily 9am–6pm), with its old Western-style clapboard residences. Enquire here for a

An important port town for centuries, Kobe has been vibrantly rebuilt since the 1995 Great Hanshin Earthquake leveled much of the city.

walking map with points of interest. More tourist information is available at **feel-kobe.jp/en**.

CITY LAYOUT Squeezed between Mount Rokko rising in the north and the shores of the Seto Inland Sea to the south, Kobe stretches some 29km (18 miles) along the coastline but in many places is less than 3km (2 miles) wide. The heart of the city lies around Sannomiya, Motomachi, and Kobe stations in the **Chuo-ku (Central Ward)**; here, you'll find the city's nightlife, its port, many restaurants and shopping centers, and most of its hotels. South of Sannomiya Station is the **Sannomiya Center Gai** covered-arcade shopping street. To the north you'll find bars and restaurants clustered around narrow streets such as **Higashimon Street.** Kitano-zaka leads uphill to **Kitano-cho** (usually shortened to Kitano) with its colonial houses. Manmade **Rocco Island,** lying east of the city, has apartments and a port zone, separated by a green belt.

GETTING AROUND Old-fashioned-looking **City Loop** buses follow a 13km (8-mile) route passing all major attractions, including Kitano, Chinatown, Meriken Park, and Harborland. Buses run three to four times an hour from about 8:30am to 7:30pm (to midnight on weekends). It costs ¥300 for adults and ¥150 for children per ride; a 1-day pass, allowing you to get on and off as often as you like and offering slight discounts to some attractions (mainly in Kitano) costs ¥700 for adults and ¥350 for children.

You can also use the **JR Local Commuter train,** which stops at Sannomiya, Motomachi, and Kobe stations, if you don't mind walking a bit to reach attractions. The **subway** is useful only for traveling between Shin-Kobe and Sannomiya stations. There are also two monorails, the **Portliner** connecting Sannomiya with Port Island, and the **Rokkoliner** between JR Sumiyoshi Station and Rokko Island.

Exploring Kobe

In addition to the sights below, you might wish to drop by **City Hall,** on Flower Road, to visit its 24th-floor **observatory** (✆ **078-331-8181**), open free to the public Monday to Friday 9am to 10pm, Saturday and Sunday 10am to 10pm.

Evidence of the damage wrought by Kobe's horrific earthquake can be found at **Meriken Park,** a 10-minute walk south of Motomachi Station. On its eastern edge is the **Port of Kobe Earthquake Memorial,** dedicated to the thousands of people who lost their lives in the tragic 1995 earthquake. As a haunting reminder of the quake's horrific force (240,000 buildings and homes were destroyed), it shows unrepaired damage, including tilted lampposts and a submerged and broken pier.

Disaster Reduction Museum ♥♥♥ In January 1995, the world was riveted by news of one of the worst natural disasters of that decade: the Great Hanshin Earthquake that struck Kobe. Measuring 7.3 on the Richter scale, it killed more than 6,400 people and destroyed much of the city. Despite its rather official-sounding name, this facility gives a human

The picturesque Kitano district reflects Kobe's 19th-century role as one of the first Japanese cities to welcome Westerners.

dimension to the Great Hanshin Earthquake. Sheathed in glass and built to withstand both vertical and horizontal earthquakes, it vividly conveys what happened during the first moments of the 1995 earthquake and the weeks, months, and years that followed. A visit begins with a powerful 7-minute film that re-creates the exact moment the earthquake struck, with computer-generated scenes showing buildings imploding or bursting into flames and highways collapsing (the graphics might be too much for young children). From the movie theater, visitors emerge into a life-size diorama depicting a typical Kobe neighborhood destroyed by the quake. They then enter another movie theater where a 15-minute documentary shows actual footage shot shortly after the quake and during the weeks that followed, presented through the eyes of a teenage survivor. Other displays in the museum concentrate on the individual experiences of survivors, emergency relief, and reconstruction. A hands-on section helps visitors learn how construction techniques can minimize and even prevent earthquake damage and dispenses information on disaster management. There is no other facility in Japan quite like this one; you can easily spend an hour here.

1–5–2 Wakinohama Kaigan-Dori. dri.ne.jp. ✆ **078-262-5050.** ¥600 adults, ¥450 college students, children free. Tues–Sun 9:30am–5:30pm (last entry 4:30). Station: JR Nada (12 min.).

Hakutsuru Sake Brewery Museum ♥ Everything you ever wanted to know about sake production is available at this former brewery, with English-language videos and pamphlets describing the various painstaking steps of brewing sake, and comparing the old techniques to those used today. Hakutsuru, established in 1743, is one of many sake breweries in this part of Kobe; its actual brewery is now across the street (closed to the public). Thirty-minute self-guided tours end with hints on how to enjoy sake and—what would a brewery tour be without this?—free tastings.

4–5–5 Sumiyoshi-minami-machi. hakutsuru.co.jp. ✆ **078-822-8907.** Free admission. Daily 9:30am–4:30pm; closed most of summer. Station: Hanshin Sumiyoshi (5 min.); JR Sumiyoshi (15 min.).

kitano: A LITTLE BIT OF HOME

When Kobe was chosen as one of five international ports following the Meiji Restoration, foreign traders and diplomats who settled here built homes in much the same style as those they left behind in their native lands. Approximately 30 of these Western-style homes, called ***ijinkan,*** remain on a hill north of Sannomiya Station called Kitano-cho, along with a surprising number of churches, synagogues, and other religious centers to serve Kobe's international community. Because the area seems so exotic to young Japanese, this is the number-one draw for domestic visitors, who come also to shop the area's boutiques, including its many bridal stores (there are also many wedding venues in Kitano).

Approximately 20 Victorian- and Gothic-style homes are open to the public, many with lovely views of the sea from verandas and bay windows. Although you may not be interested in visiting most of them, Kitano is very pleasant for an hour's stroll. It's located about a 15-minute walk north of Sannomiya Station (via Kitano-zaka) or a 10-minute walk west of Shin-Kobe Station. Or take the City Loop bus to Kitano Ijinkan.

Two of the more interesting homes open to the public are the **Moegi no Yakata,** 3–10–11 Kitano-cho (✆ **078-222-3310**), a pale-green 107-year-old home built for a former American consul general, Hunter Sharp, and filled with antiques; and **Kasamidori-no-Yakata,** 3–13–3 Kitano-cho (✆ **078-242-3223**), popularly referred to as the Weathercock House because of its rooster weather vane. This 1909 brick residence was built by a German merchant and is probably Kobe's most famous home if not its most elaborate. The two houses are across the street from each other. Admission to each is ¥500; a combination ticket to both costs ¥650. Children enter free, and City Loop pass-holders pay ¥450. They're open daily from 9am to 6pm (Dec–Mar until 5pm). The Weathercock House is also closed the first Tuesday in June and February.

Another home of note (because it contains porcelain, glass, and art, not because of its historical value) is **Uroko no Ie,** 2–20–4 Kitano-cho (✆ **078-242-6530;** ¥1,100 adults, ¥220 children; daily 9am–6pm in summer, to 5pm in winter). It has a castlelike exterior and slate walls that have earned it the nickname the Fish-Scale House. Inside are lovely antiques, including Meissen porcelain and Tiffany glass, as well as a small private museum of Western 18th- to 20th-century art, with a few works by Andrew Wyeth, Utrillo, and others. It also offers lovely views of the city below.

A lovely, meandering, fragrant collection of gardens planted with various flowering shrubs and herbs, the **Nunobiki Herb Garden** ♥ (1–4–3 Kitano-cho; ✆ **078-271-1160;** ¥2,000 adults, half-price for children; daily 10am–5pm, until 8:30pm weekends and in summer) offers postcard-perfect views over Kobe. You get here via a ropeway and must take it to the end (don't get off at the first stop), then walk downhill past gardens planted with sage, mint, lavender, roses, seasonal herbs, Japanese plants, and a greenhouse.

Hyogo Prefectural Museum of Art ♥ MUSEUM If you're on your way to the Disaster Reduction Museum (p. 482), check out what's being shown at this art museum, which is practically next door. Designed by renowned Japanese architect Tadao Ando, it displays contemporary art, prints, sculpture, and other works produced by artists with connections to Hyogo Prefecture, as well as temporary exhibits from around the world. 1–1–1 Wakinohama Kaigan-dori. artm.pref.hyogo.jp. ✆ **078-262-0901.** ¥500 adults, ¥400 high-school and college students, ¥250 children. Tues–Sun 10am–6pm.

Kobe Fashion Museum ♥♥ Japan's first museum devoted to fashion is housed on Rokko Island in a contemporary, sophisticated structure that does justice to the highbrow costumes it contains. Temporary displays devoted to individual designers allow closer inspection than you could ever get at a fashion show. Other displays, which are imaginative tableaux complete with visual images, music, and lighting, may feature anything from 20th-century gowns by Christian Dior to extravagant *kabuki* costumes or ethnic clothing worn by indigenous peoples from around the world. Displays change four or five times a year, rotating the many costumes owned by the museum. To get here, take the local JR train to Sumiyoshi Station and transfer for the Rokkoliner monorail to Island Center. 2–9 Koyocho-naka, Rokko Island. fashionmuseum.jp. ✆ **078-858-0050.** Exhibition admission varies, usually around ¥1,000 adults, ¥500 children. Tues–Sun 10am–6pm (occasionally closed for exhibit changes). Station: Island Center (1 min.).

Where to Eat in Kobe

With its sizable foreign population, Kobe is a good place to dine on international cuisine, including French, Indian, Korean, and Chinese food.

A sidewalk stall in Kobe's lively Chinatown.

The greatest concentration of Chinese restaurants is along a pedestrian lane in **Chinatown ♥♥**, called **Nankin-machi** by the locals, just a 2-minute walk south of Motomachi Station. It's worth wandering through for its lively street scene, with sidewalk vendors selling snacks and open-fronted souvenir shops and produce stands. If the vendors tempt you with their Kobe beef sushi, steamed dumplings, and fluffy bao buns, grab a bite and eat it in the central square called **Nankin Park,** adorned with statues representing the animals of the 12-year Chinese astrological calendar. Chinatown's public restroom, called **Garyoden,** which means "palace of a secluded wise man," is certainly one of Japan's most colorful—its outer wall is decorated with five-clawed dragons and is based on a famous Chinese epic about a dragonlike hero; it's located a block off the main street. While here, I'd recommend stopping for a quick drink at **Kamome ♥♥**, meaning "seagull," a tiny bar and cafe above Gyoza Daigaku (see below). The owner was a former ship captain—his uniform still hangs on the wall—and though his current job keeps him on dry land, he hasn't lost his sense of adventure, regaling guests in Japanese and broken English with tales of his travels. The drinks are simple—beer, coffee, spirits, and mixers—but there's a lovely nostalgic feel to the place and you'll be welcomed with warmth from the moment you open the door.

Chonju (全州) ♥♥♥ The local Korean community makes a point of eating in this no-frills Korean barbecue joint north of Sannomiya Station, and though the interior design—pallid lighting, scuffed tables and chairs, kitschy gold pulldown blinds, an old TV droning in the corner—is in dire need of refurbishment, it's in no way a reflection of the food. The portions are large (better for sharing than dining solo), so you should come here with an appetite. From *buchimgae* (Korean pacakes) and *tteok-bokki* (rice cakes) to *sundubu-jjigae* (spicy stewed tofu) and marinated pork cuts (cooked on portable grills at your table), the food is both hearty and delicious. The menu is in Japanese only, but the staff are accommodating, so ask for *osusme* (recommendations).

4–6–5 Ninomiya-cho. ✆ **078-242-6244.** Main courses ¥300–¥1,500. Tues–Thurs 4:30–10:30pm; Fri–Sun 4–11pm. Station: Sannomiya (5 min.).

Gyoza Daigaku ♥♥ Queues are guaranteed at this dumpling shop on a narrow Chinatown side street, but given those waiting are mostly locals, you can view this as quality assurance. There's nothing flashy about the menu, it's just simple gyoza dumplings done well: light skin, crispy on top, with a juicy and un-oily pork filling, served with zingy dipping sauces. Once it's your turn to enter, you'll be squeezed into a small, featureless room with a handful of other diners and a yellow menu (in Japanese only) on the wall. But if anything, the lack of decor sharpens your taste buds and olfactory senses, allowing you to enjoy the dumplings to the fullest.

2–3–5 Motomachidori. ✆ **078-332-2233.** Gyoza ¥350–¥1,000. Wed–Sat 11:30am–2pm and 5–8pm; Sun 11:30am–7:30pm. Station: Motomachi (2 min.).

SHIKOKU

10

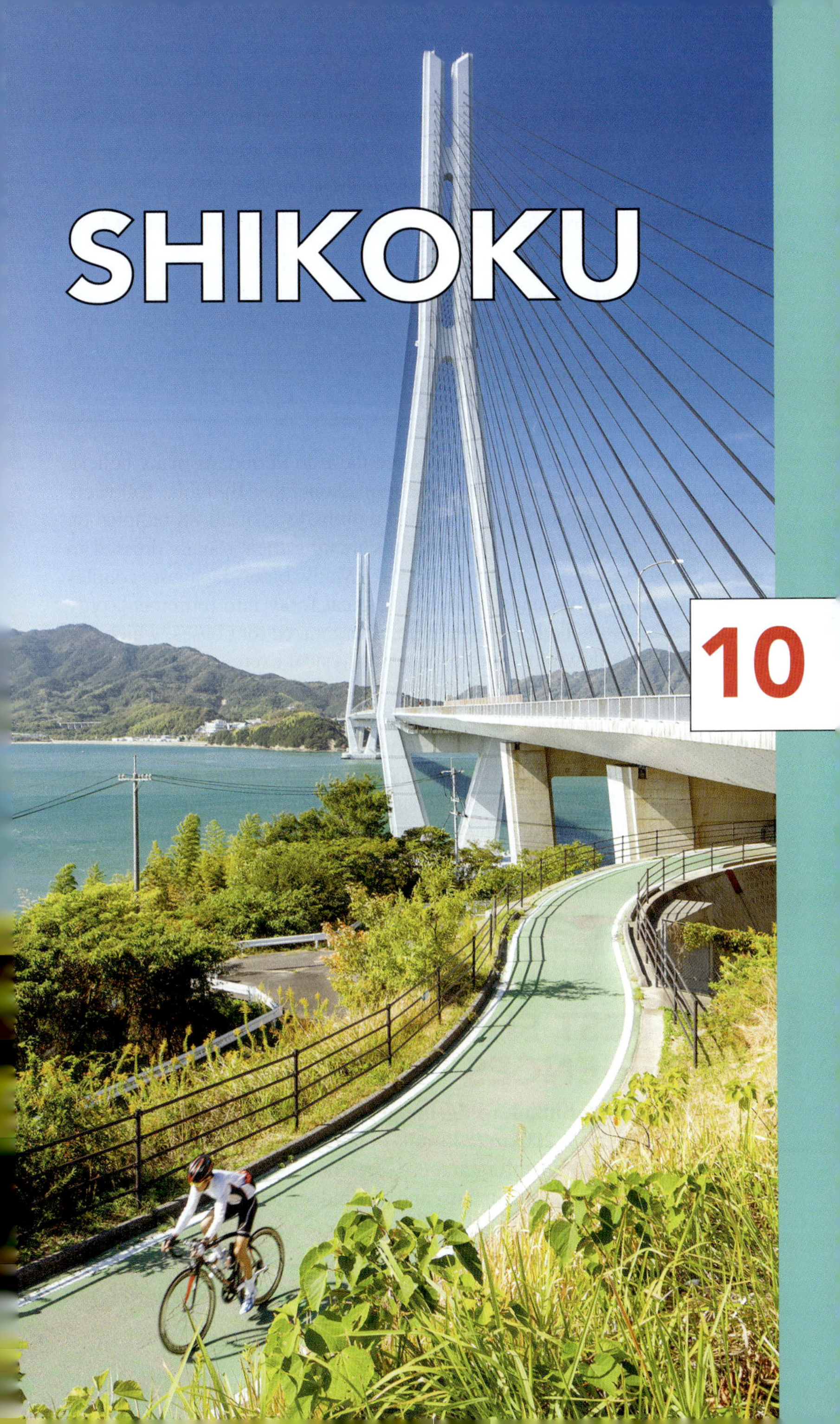

The smallest of Japan's four main islands, Shikoku is also the one least visited by foreigners. That's surprising considering the natural beauty of its rugged mountains, its mild climate, and its most famous monuments—88 sacred Buddhist temples. Many Japanese wish to make a pilgrimage to all 88 temples at least once in their lifetime as a tribute to the great Buddhist priest Kobo Daishi, who was born on Shikoku in 774 and who founded the Shingon sect of Buddhism.

This pilgrimage has been popular since the Edo Period, as many believe that a successful completion of the tour exonerates Buddhist followers from rebirth. It used to take almost 2 months to visit all 88 temples on foot. Even today, you can see pilgrims making their rounds dressed in white and wearing conical straw hats. Many older Japanese couples embark on the pilgrimage as their first great foray into retirement, only now they're more likely to drive or go by organized tour buses, which can cut travel time down to 2 weeks or less. Physical exercise is reserved for the temples, whose stone steps must be scaled before sutras can be read at the main prayer hall.

For centuries, the only way to reach Shikoku was by boat. However, in 1988 the Seto Ohashi Bridge was completed, linking Shikoku with Okayama Prefecture by car and train. In 1998 another bridge, for cars only, was opened, linking Shikoku with Kobe. In 1999 it was followed by a series of bridges spanning six scenic islands in the Seto Inland Sea, which connected Shikoku with Hiroshima Prefecture (complete with cycling paths offering scenic views—it's now one of Shikoku's hottest attractions). Shikoku is no longer as far off the beaten track as it used to be, because access is now so easy.

THE BEST SHIKOKU EXPERIENCES

- **Walking the Shikoku Pilgrimage:** You'll need at least 6 weeks to complete this 1,200km (746-mile) pilgrimage, and a decent level of fitness. But it's an unforgettable experience, as you navigate clifftops, meet locals in mountain huts, and find hidden temples in near-impenetrable forests. See p. 496.
- **Admiring Modern Art on the Art Islands:** An ambitious series of open-air and indoor museums scattered across the Seto Inland Sea

PREVIOUS PAGE: The Shimanami Kaido cycling route crosses a series of suspension bridges over the Seto Inland Sea.

has proven a creative shot in the arm for regional tourism. Best time to visit is during the once-every-3-years Setouchi Triennale festival. See p. 497.

- **Bathing in Dogo Onsen Honkan (Matsuyama):** The wooden 1894 bathhouse has baths, yes, but it's the upstairs tatami relaxation rooms where people lounge in yukata and drink tea that make a visit here special. See p. 513.
- **Learning About Japan's First Zero-Waste Village:** Kamikatsu became Internet famous because of a zero-waste declaration it made back in 2003. Now, with an English-language homestay program, you can learn about the village's unique approach to waste mitigation, upcycling, and environmental sustainability. See p. 508.

Wearing a traditional pilgrim straw hat, a walker follows the Shikoku Pilgrimage route.

TAKAMATSU ♥♥

805km (500 miles) W of Tokyo; 71km (44 miles) S of Okayama

The second-largest town on Shikoku, with a population of 427,000, Takamatsu, the capital of Kagawa Prefecture, is on the northeastern coast of the island, overlooking the Seto Inland Sea. Takamatsu means "high pine," and the city served as the feudal capital of the powerful Matsudaira clan from 1642 until the Meiji Restoration in 1868. The Matsudairas are responsible for Takamatsu's most famous site, **Ritsurin Garden,** one of the most outstanding gardens in Japan. Takamatsu also has more bonsai nurseries than anywhere else in the country.

Essentials

ARRIVING ANA flies from Tokyo's Haneda Airport to Takamatsu Airport in 1 hour and 20 minutes; flights start around ¥8,000. Jetstar flies from Haneda for as low as ¥5,000 (though it's not the most reliable of airlines in my experience). There is also air service from Kagoshima and Okinawa. An airport limousine bus and the Shino Line train deliver passengers downtown in about 45 minutes (an hour on the train) both for ¥1,000. Seto Ohashi Line trains depart from Okayama Station approximately twice an hour, reaching Takamatsu in an hour; the fare is ¥2,500. From Matsuyama, trains take about 2½ hours and cost ¥6,690. A highway bus (willer-travel.com/en/bus; ✆ **050-5805-0383**) departs Tokyo Station's Yaesu south exit nightly at 8:40pm (picking up passengers at Shinjuku

Station at 9:15pm and Yokohama Station at 10:15pm) and reaches Takamatsu at 7:45am the next day. The one-way fare is around ¥11,000. From Matsuyama Station, buses take 2¾ hours and cost ¥4,400.

VISITOR INFORMATION The **Takamatsu Information Center** (art-takamatsu.com; ✆ **087-826-0170;** daily 9am–8pm) is located in the Orne shopping mall on the northeast side of the station.

CITY LAYOUT Takamatsu Station, Takamatsu Port, and the local streetcar terminus are clustered at the north edge of the city on the coast of the Seto Inland Sea, in an urban development called **Sunport Takamatsu,** which also includes the 30-story Takamatsu Symbol Tower, exhibition and concert facilities, restaurants, shops, and offices. Office workers take respite along the Waterfront Harbor Walk and Tamamo Park, site of Takamatsu Castle's remains. Most of the hotels and restaurants listed below, as well as Ritsurin Garden, are located south and southeast of Sunport Takamatsu. **Chuo Dori** is the town's main avenue, running south from Sunport to Ritsurin Garden and beyond. Bisecting Chuo Dori and paralleling it to the east are shopping arcades—in fact, Takamatsu has a total of 4km (2½ miles) of covered shopping arcades, more than any other Japanese city.

GETTING AROUND Although the main attractions of Takamatsu are spread out, they're easily reached from Takamatsu Station by **JR train** or by a commuter streetcar called the **Kotoden,** which operates three lines: the Kotohira Line, heading south and southwest; the Nagao Line, heading southeast; and the Shido Line, heading east. The Kotoden streetcar terminus, **Takamatsu Chikko Station,** is a 2-minute walk from Takamatsu Station's main exit, past the JR hotel and to the right. Fares start at ¥200. Two stops south on the Kotoden streetcar (or a 25-min. walk from Takamatsu Station), Kawaramachi Station lies in the heart of the city, where you'll find many department stores, restaurants, and nightspots.

Exploring Takamatsu

Ritsurin Garden ♥♥♥ GARDEN Once the summer retreat of the Matsudaira family, Ritsurin Garden was first laid out in the 1600s and took about 100 years to complete. Using the backdrop of adjacent Mount Shiun in a principle known as *shakkei,* or "borrowed landscaping," the 75-hectare (185-acre) park, Japan's largest Cultural Heritage Garden, incorporates the pine-clad mountain into its overall visual design. The garden, arranged around six spring-fed ponds and 13 scenic mounds, can be divided into two parts: a traditional, classical southern garden; and a modern northern garden, once a lord's private hunting grounds, with wide grassy lawns and huge lotus ponds. No matter the season, something is always in bloom, from plum and cherry trees in spring to camellias in winter (a bulletin board at the entrance identifies what's in bloom). English-speaking volunteers are on hand most days to provide free tours if you wish. It takes about an hour to see the southern garden; add another half-hour if you also take in the northern garden.

The **southern garden** is the more interesting one, representing what's called a strolling garden, in which each bend of the footpath brings another perspective into view, another combination of rock, tree, and mountain. The garden is absolutely exquisite, and what sets it apart are its twisted, contorted pines. If you're lucky, a mist will be rolling off Mount Shiun, lending mystery to the landscape; what better fits the image of traditional Japan than mist and pine trees? Altogether, there are some 1,400 pine trees and 350 cherry trees in Ritsurin Garden, which you should tour in a counterclockwise route to fully appreciate the changing views. Alas, tall buildings on its eastern periphery detract from the garden's overall effect.

Besides beautiful landscapes, the park contains a couple of attractions worth visiting; entry is included in the park's admission fee. In the northern garden, the **Sanuki Folk Art Museum** (**Sanuki Mingei Kan**) displays local folk art and handicrafts such as ceramics, lacquerware, furniture, and items used in daily Edo life (regrettably, there are no English-language descriptions). Next to it, the **Commerce and Industry Hall** (**Shoko-shoreikan**) sells local products, including kites, masks, woodcarvings,

Every element of the landscaping in Ritsurin Gardens has been carefully planned.

umbrellas, fans, and food items; it also sponsors craft-making demonstrations on weekends and holidays. In the southern garden, **Scooping the Moon House (Kikugetsu-tei)** ♥♥ has a teahouse dating from feudal days overlooking a pond. Matcha, used in the ceremonies, is ¥700, *sencha* (infused leaf tea) is ¥500.

1–20–16 Ritsurin-cho. ✆ **087-833-7411.** my-kagawa.jp/static/en/ritsurin. ¥410 adults, ¥170 children. Daily sunrise–sunset. Streetcar: Ritsurin-koen Station (10 min.). JR train: Ritsurin-koen Kita Guchi (4 min.).

Shikoku Mura Village ♥♥ OPEN-AIR MUSEUM On the northeastern edge of town, this open-air museum has more than 30 traditional houses, sheds, and storehouses dating from the Edo Period and collected from all over Shikoku. The structures, picturesquely situated on the wooded slope of Yashima Hill, include thatch-roofed homes of farmers and fishermen, century-old cottages used by lighthouse keepers, a rustic tea-ceremony house, a 250-year-old rural *kabuki* stage, rice and soy-sauce storehouses, and sheds for pressing sugar and for producing paper out of mulberry bark. There's also a suspended bridge made of vines, once a familiar sight in Shikoku as a means for crossing the island's many gorges and ravines; if you look closely, however, you'll see that this one is reinforced by cables. **Waraya** (wara-ya.co.jp; ✆ **087-843-3115**), a noodle shop in a thatched-roof building, opened in 1975 and still specializes in the same recipe half a century later;, stop in to try the region's famed Sanuki udon noodles—bowls cost between ¥540 and ¥1,250. Touring the village takes at least 1½ hours (and there are lots of stairs). If you haven't had the opportunity to see similar villages in Takayama or Shirakawago, take the time to include this one—there's no better way to get a sense of rural Japanese life in centuries past.

91 Yashima-naka-machi. shikokumura.or.jp. ✆ **087-843-3111.** ¥1,600 adults, ¥1,000 students, ¥600 high-school students, children free. Daily 9:30am–5pm (last entry 4:30pm). Streetcar: Kotoden Yashima Station (5 min.). JR train (Tokushima-bound): Yashima Station (15 min.).

Takamatsu Art Museum ♥♥ MUSEUM If you've come to Takamatsu to visit the Art Islands (p. 497), this museum is a little taste of what you're about to experience. Opened in 1988, it was one of many art projects in Kagawa Prefecture designed to rejuvenate an area that had suffered from population decline, low tourism numbers, and brain drain to the major cities. The drafty steel-and-glass entrance hall feels a bit like an airplane hangar—and frankly a massive waste of space (though occasional works are displayed in here)—but the surrounding exhibition rooms are compact and enriching. Among its collection of 1,600-plus artworks, you'll find postwar Japanese art, local crafts of Kagawa Prefecture, and innovative contemporary art, including prints, oil paintings, photography, sculpture and others that defy classification. The Gutai Association, a group of avant-garde iconoclasts that rose to prominence in the 1950s, are among the Japanese artists celebrated here—don't miss the *Electric Dress,* a wearable artwork made of electrical wires and hundreds of colored neon light bulbs. Local craft exhibits include beautiful Sanuki lacquerware (this region was once called Sanuki province). There are regular special exhibitions, too, the most impressive of which are showcased during the Setouchi Triennale.

10–4 Konyacho. city.takamatsu.kagawa.jp. ✆ **087-823-1711.** ¥200 adults, ¥150 students, high school students and younger children free. Tues–Sun 9:30am–5pm (until 7pm on weekends during special exhibitions). Streetcar: Takamatsu Chiko Station (10 min.).

BONSAI IS BIG IN kinashi

The art of **bonsai**—the crafting of miniature pines and other trees through skillful manipulation—is on magnificent display in **Kinashi ♥♥♥**, a western suburb of Takamatsu. With more than 80 nurseries, half of them cultivating bonsai, Kinashi has been a center of bonsai since the Edo Period and remains the largest bonsai-growing region in Japan. To reach it, take a local JR train from Takamatsu Station two stations to Kinashi, walk north a few minutes, and then turn right into Bonsai Street. One of the largest nurseries, **Nakanishi Chinshouen** (chinshoen.jp; ✆ **087-882-0526**), across the street from the station, is owned by a fifth-generation bonsai cultivator; some of the larger pines here were started by his ancestors. You're welcome to walk through this and other nearby nurseries. The **Kinashi Green Fair 21** (takamatsu-bonsai.com/en/), a 3-day exhibition and sale of bonsai trees, is held in the area each April. It's worth a visit, even if you don't plan on buying. A similar event is held each October. Enquire at the tourist information center for more info.

Bonsai cultivator at Nakanishi Chinshouen.

Where to Stay in Takamatsu

In addition to the choices below, there's the **Toyoko Inn Takamatsu Hyogomachi,** 3–1 Hyogomachi (toyoko-inn.com; ✆ **087-821-1045**), an 8-minute walk southeast of Takamatsu Station on Chuo Dori beside the Hyogomachi arcade. Singles go for as little as ¥8,000, including breakfast. The **Takamatsu Tokyu Rei Hotel,** 9–9 Hyogamachi (tokyuhotels.co.jp; ✆ **087-821-0109**), is a similar option; the rooms are cookie-cutter hotel suites, but you can walk to most of Takamatsu's top attractions and the ferry port from here. You can expect to pay around ¥7,000 to ¥12,000 per person, depending on season.

Business Hotel Parkside Takamatsu ♥ Although a business hotel, this small, boutiquelike hotel has a great location across from Ritsurin Garden. Rooms are small, but who cares when you can open the window and look out over the fabled garden? Some rooms have only a partial view or none at all, so be sure to request a ringside seat on an upper floor. A bonus: The hotel provides discount tickets to Ritsurin Garden.

1–3–1 Ritsurin-cho. ✆ **087-837-5555.** 116 units. ¥8,000–¥13,000 double. Streetcar: Ritsurin Koen (10 min.). **Amenities:** Restaurant; rental bikes; free Wi-Fi.

Century Hotel Takamatsu ♥ Five minutes on foot from Takamatsu Station, this hotel has a selection of decent-sized rooms across 6 floors, and family rooms with a raised tatami area on which you can request futons to be placed (maximum capacity five people). Food plans are available too, from a breakfast buffet (¥1,200) and bento box dinner (¥1,000) to beer plans that provide guests with local Sanuki beer and snacks on check-in. A small *sento,* indoor bathhouse, makes this a great winter option.

1–chome–4–19 Nishikimachi. takamatsu-century.com. ✆ **087-851-0558.** 126 units. ¥6,000–¥15,000 single or double. Station: Takamatsu (5 min.). **Amenities:** Breakfast buffet; bento box dinner; public bathhouse; free Wi-Fi.

JR Hotel Clement Takamatsu ♥♥ In Sunport across from Takamatsu Station (and offering a discount to Japan Rail Pass holders), the city's most expensive hotel is also its most conspicuous: sleek, 21 stories high, cutting across the landscape like a white sail. It's by far the best place in town. It's designed with an aquatic theme, with a cascading fountain in the sunlit lobby lounge, carpets and chandeliers with wavy patterns, bubbled or crackled glass in public places, and curving, seductive lines everywhere, even in corridors. It's the kind of place sightseers happily return to after a busy day out and about. Room rates are based on size, floor, view, and amenities, with the best twin and double rooms offering views of the sea or nearby Tamamo Park, even from bathroom windows. But the least expensive rooms are also recommendable—spacious and chic with contemporary furnishings and good bedside reading lamps. Ask for a room on the highest available floor. Note that the cheapest double has only a semi-double bed.

1–1 Hamano-cho. ✆ **087-811-1111.** jrclement.co.jp. 300 units. ¥20,000–¥50,000 double. 10% discount with Japan Rail Pass, or Shikoku Passport. Station: Takamatsu (1 min.). **Amenities:** 4 restaurants; bar; lounge; beer garden (summer only); concierge; room service; free Wi-Fi.

Rihga Hotel Zest ♥ This beige-brick hotel, consisting of a main building and newer annex, appeals to both business and leisure travelers with its convenient location on Chuo Dori next to Hyogomachi shopping arcade. It has accommodating staff and offers a variety of rooms at different price ranges. The cheapest rooms, including all singles, are in the main building and are narrow with tiny bathrooms. More expensive and spacious annex rooms sport shoji screens and window panels that close for complete darkness. There are also four combination rooms with both tatami areas and beds.

9–1 Furujinmachi. rihga.com. ✆ **08-822-3555.** 122 units. ¥15,00–¥40,000 double. Station: Takamatsu (10 min.). **Amenities:** 4 restaurants; lounge; rooftop beer garden (summer only); free Wi-Fi.

Where to Eat in Takamatsu

Takamatsu is known throughout Japan for its ***Sanuki udon***—thick white noodles made from wheat flour—and a fresh supply of fish from the Seto Inland Sea. If you want a tipple after dinner, consider **Music Inn Granfather's** at 1–6–4 Tokiwacho (✆ **087-837-5177**), a basement record bar where the owner serves classic cocktails, whiskey, and jazz. **Melobar** at 10–3 Furujinmachi plays classic rock and disco and is good place to mingle with locals late into the night.

Tenkatsu ♥ TEMPURA/SUSHI This well-known tempura and sushi restaurant is in a modern-looking building with a plastic-food display case and a window where passersby can watch a chef prepare sushi. Inside the restaurant are tatami mats and tables, but better is sitting at the counter, which encircles a large pool filled with fish. As customers order, fish are swept out of the tanks with nets—they certainly couldn't be fresher. A photo menu (along with prices for fish in the tanks) and a display case help you choose.

7–8 Hyogomachi. ✆ **087-821-5380.** Lunches ¥1,200–¥2,400; sushi courses ¥6,600–¥11,000. Mon–Fri 11am–2pm and 4–10pm; Sat–Sun 11am–9pm. Station: Takamatsu (5 min.).

Sanuki udon, a local specialty to try in Takamatsu.

WALKING THE shikoku pilgrimage

The Shikoku Pilgrimage is not something one does on a whim, but it has the potential to be one the most rewarding trips you can undertake in Japan. The route, 1,200km in total, is a physical journey mapped onto a spiritual one. The 88 temples, beginning in Tokushima and culminating in Kagawa, form a circuit around the island, with the inland mountain temples serving as rough central points, as though the island were a giant Buddhist mandala, a diagram of eternal truths. You don't need to be an expert in esoteric Shingon Buddhism—the sect founded by Kobo Daishi (whom the pilgrimage is dedicated to)—to understand the life-altering power of disconnecting yourself from the digital world and embarking on a one-foot-after-the-other journey for 6 to 8 weeks. After all, around 150,000 people attempt it each year (though many now do it in cars or on bus tours).

Few have the luxury of being able to take a 2-month vacation, but there are shorter, more digestible chunks you can tackle. The four prefectures of Shikoku each represent different parts of the spiritual journey, which maps out one way to break up the pilgrimage. **Tokushima** is the spiritual "Awakening," with 23 temples in the east and southeast of the island; **Kochi,** the "Ascetic Training" section, has 16 temples running along the south coast (it's the largest prefecture, however, and could take the most time to traverse); **Ehime,** "Enlightenment," has 26 temples, mostly crammed into the island's northwestern tip; and **Kagawa,** the journey's end, offers one final shot at "Nirvana," with 22 temples. Walking a single prefecture could still take anywhere from 1 to 3 weeks, depending on your fitness level and the location you choose.

When to Go Spring is pleasant, when the cherry blossoms come into bloom and the temperature typically stays between 12°C (54°F) and 18°C (64°F). Late autumn is the most popular with pilgrims, when the temperature hovers around 20°C (68°F) and the leaves begin to fall. The stifling humidity of summer and the snowfall at higher elevations in winter make these more challenging seasons for walkers.

Where to Stay Pilgrimage lodgings come in various forms, from *shukubo*

Ueharaya ♥♥ SANUKI UDON One of the most popular udon shops in town, Ueharaya serves thick, chewy, elastic noodles that are expert vehicles for soaking up the in-house dashi-based broth. The canteenlike vibe isn't the most convivial, but you're here for the flavor. In winter, order the *kake* or *bukkake* udon in hot soup (toppings include shredded ginger and spring onions). In summer, the cold *zaru udon,* served on a bamboo tray with a light dipping sauce, is the best option. If you're hungry enough, there's a selection of fish tempura and vegetable croquettes displayed on the counter which you can add to your noodles.

1–18–8 Ritsurin-cho. ueharayahonten.com. ✆ **087-831-6779.** Udon and tempura meals ¥500–¥1,500. Mon–Sat 9:30am–2:30pm. Streetcar: Ritsurin-Koen Station (10 min.).

Wakadaisho ♥♥ YAKITORI This jaunty-looking izakaya near the port is easy to spot, enwreathed by *akachochin* (red lanterns) and fronted (temple stays) and *minshuku* (family-run guesthouses) to campgrounds and hotels. Many of these are good value—you can find a map with accommodation options on the official *henro* (pilgrims) website: **henro.org/shikoku-pilgrimage**. Other more bare-bones forms of lodging, *tsuyado* (temples with spare futons for pilgrims) and *zenkonyado* (inns catering exclusively to pilgrims), are free of charge, but are good for those with limited funds or as a last resort when you can't find accommodation elsewhere. Other websites, like **shikokuhenrotrail.com**, provide databases of free lodgings for pilgrims, but these are not always up to date; your best bet is to check each temple's website or call ahead.

What to Expect Your journey may involve some grueling ascents, and with so much time spent outdoors, you'll be at the whims of Mother Nature. But you'll get wonderful coastal scenery, contemplative time in Shikoku's forests, and a chance to experience the culture of *osettai*—locals giving gifts, well-wishes, and tokens to pilgrims. This might be a spare bottle of water handed through a car window, a box of local snacks, fruit from nearby farms, plastic ponchos when it's raining, or a few hundred yen to use at the next convenience store or roadside vending machine. Alongside meals provided at temples and lodgings, this means a lot of your food will come in the form of donations. After all, the way of the pilgrim is frugal.

What You'll Need It's easy to spot pilgrims when traveling the coastal roads of Shikoku: They'll be wearing white cotton vests called *hakui* (with sleeves) or *oizuru* (sleeveless), conical straw hats, sometimes a silk *wagesa* scarf, and carrying a wooden walking stick. Using these will help people identify you as a pilgrim, which is useful for donations, meeting fellow walkers, and when checking in to free lodgings. Stores near temples often sell pilgrim clothing, like Mozen Ichibangai (monzen-ichibangai.com; ✆ **088-689-4388;** daily 8am–5pm) across the street from Ryozenji, the first of the 88 temples and official starting point of the Shikoku pilgrimage. Having an ergonomic backpack, proper waterproof clothes, and camping equipment will also be useful.

by a large menu with pictures indicating the fare inside. It's mostly tasty chicken skewers, like *negima* (chicken thigh with spring onions) and *tsukune* (chicken meatballs), with various seasonings and condiments. Other bites include pork belly and vegetable skewers, grilled rice balls, seared tuna with salad, and deep-fried fish. The restaurant is small, generating a lively vibe, whether you sit at the counter or the tables. The fug of cigarette smoke might add some atmosphere, too, but it's worth noting in case that's a dealbreaker for you.

5–1 Nishinomarucho. ✆ **087-821-2824.** Dinner ¥2,000–¥4,000. Daily 4pm–1am. Station: Takamatsu (2 min.).

THE ART ISLANDS ♥♥♥

The Art Islands once served as a cautionary tale for rural Japan. Now they're a shining example of what's possible when artistic vision, regional

HOW THE art islands CAME TO BE

In the 1980s, the islands in the Seto Inland Sea—a lakelike body of water between Honshu, Shikoku, and Kyushu—were a sorry sight. Villages had been abandoned and reclaimed by nature, or were stewing in illegally dumped toxic waste. Fisherman and farmers had traded their tools for hard hats and trucks, commuting to the refineries and industrial sites that blotted the no-longer bucolic coastline. Young people were fleeing to Osaka, Kobe, Hiroshima, Fukuoka, and as far as Tokyo in search of better employment and education opportunities.

When Soichiro Fukutake, a billionaire publishing magnate and patron of the arts, saw the state of disrepair, he was aghast that this region of hazy, pine-cloaked islands, home to some of Japan's most poetic sunrises, had become another victim of postwar rapid urbanization. But rather turn a blind eye, he sought to fight back—using art as his weapon. He enlisted the services of Japan's King of Concrete and Pritzker Prize-winning architect Tadao Ando to design numerous buildings. He identified three islands—Naoshima, Teshima, and Inujima—for revitalization. (Others later came on board, bringing the total to 12.) Hundreds of millions of dollars, thousands of commissioned artworks, and more than 3 decades later, the Art Islands are now among the most attractive destinations in the country.

redevelopment, and financial wherewithal work in concert. Thanks to Soichiro Fukutake and his Benesse Foundation (see "How the Art Islands Came to Be," above), there are permanent works scattered throughout the region; during the **Setouchi Triennale,** which takes place every third year (the most recent is in 2025), the smaller islands not under Benesse's stewardship kick into gear as well. The window for attending the festival is quite long, with three sessions in every Triennale year—spring, summer, autumn—each of which lasts for several weeks.

What makes the islands special is how art, people, and the environment are married to each other. Instead of white-box gallery spaces, installations are mounted in parks and on coastlines, artworks are placed in abandoned homes as an evocation of the region's history, and new museums were built that play with light, shadow, space, and meaning. There's little room for navel-gazing blowhards or esoteric pieces that are heavy on style, light on substance. Art functions best not when it stratifies its audiences, but when it works as a great equalizer. And on the Art Islands, that's exactly what you get.

Essentials

ARRIVING Scattered across the sea as they are, you can only access the islands by boat from Takamatsu or Uno Port in Okayama Prefecture. Most ferries run regularly from morning till early evening (the Uno Port to Naoshima route also runs until after midnight) and can cost anywhere from ¥240 to ¥1,350 one-way, depending on the route and type of boat (high-speeds are more expensive). Routes, travel times, and cost are detailed in each island entry below. If you don't want your sojourn to be dictated by ferry schedules—and you aren't afraid to splurge—the **Setouchi Islands Concierge Service** (setouchi-sics.com; ✆ **087-811-7923**) can arrange private transfers for you. Some of these options are decent value if you're in a small group, like a chartered speed boat from Ogijima to Takamatsu for ¥13,000. At the current exchange rate, the service's Setouchi Sunset Cruise for ¥66,000 (maximum capacity 40 people) is also a good deal.

VISITOR INFORMATION The **Takamatsu Information Center** (p. 490) contains info on the Art Islands; you'll find it particularly useful during the Triennale. The information desk at **Marine Station Naoshima** (naoshima.net; ✆ **087-892-2299;** daily 9am–6pm), the **Onigashima Oni Hall** (oninoyakata.mystrikingly.com/#5; ✆ **087-873-0728;** daily 8:20am–5:15pm) at the port of Megijima, and the Jaume Plensa–designed **Ogi Island Exchange Center** (✆ **087-873-0006;** daily 6:30am–5pm), also called Ogijima's Soul, are equally valuable sources of information. Enquire at these about maps, English-language pamphlets, bike rentals, and where appropriate, bus schedules.

WHERE TO STAY & EAT Visitors to the Art Islands often stay in Takamatsu (p. 494). Alternatively, there are some nice hotels and inns on Naoshima (p. 503), which works well as a base for visiting other islands. Dining options on the islands are limited, so it's best to eat at museum cafes and hotel restaurants wherever possible. You can also buy simple foodstuffs in tourist information centers or bring a packed lunch from Takamatsu.

Naoshima

This is the most popular of the Art Islands, the epitome of Fukutake's vision realized. Naoshima is small—less than 8 sq. km (3 sq. miles)—but this only enhances the impact of the works exhibited here; a thought-provoking sculpture, modern art centerpiece, or Zen-like viewing space lurks around every corner. There are striking museums, interactive installations housed in traditional buildings, and outdoor sculptures spread throughout. The entire island is effectively a canvas, splashed in proverbial paint by world-renowned artists. But more than that, Naoshima is a place of discovery, with a symbiotic relationship between natural scenic beauty and manmade creations. ***Note:*** For art venues closed on Monday, if Monday is a national holiday, they stay open but will close the next day, on Tuesday, instead.

ARRIVING From Tamono's Uno Port, the ferry takes 15–20 minutes and costs ¥300. From Takamatsu, the ferry takes 50 minutes and costs ¥520, the high-speed takes 30 to 40 minutes and costs ¥1,220. For full schedule and suspensions visit the **Naoshima Tourism Association** website (naoshima.net; ✆ **087-892-2299**). Ferries to Naoshima arrive at either

Miyanoura or Honmura Port, which are connected by bus (5 min.; ¥100 adults, ¥50 children).

EXPLORING NAOSHIMA

From March through September, free shuttle buses run between the island's main museums (Benesse House Museum, Chichu Art Museum, and the Lee Ufan Museum), which are only a 5-minute walk from each other. In addition to the art sites mentioned below, another Tadao Ando-designed museum, the **Naoshima New Museum of Art** (located on a hilltop near Honmura, at 3299–73 Naoshima), will open its doors in 2025, after this book goes to press. Celebrating contemporary Asian art placed in dramatic light-filled gallery spaces, it looks to be another fine addition to the island's already stellar roster.

A Yayoi Kusama pumpkin by the water on Naoshima island.

Ando Museum ♥♥ A good introduction to the work of Tadao Ando, this renovated 100-year-old house shows that wood and concrete needn't always be foes. From the outside, not much looks amiss; only the swirling reliefs on the exterior garden wall and a *noren* curtain covered in vivid green leaves suggest there might be more to this place than meets the eye. Inside is a different story, where irregular concrete walls allow past and present, light and darkness, the natural and the manmade, to work as one. Photographs and sketches are placed throughout, detailing Ando's oeuvre and the history of art on the island.

736–2 Naoshima. benesse-artsite.jp. ✆ **087-892-3754.** ¥700 adults (¥600 online), ages 15 and under free. Tues–Sun 10am–1pm and 2–4:30pm. Honmura Port (5 min.).

Art House Projects ♥♥♥ INSTALLATIONS In the port town of Honmura, you'll find a handful of old buildings that have been remodeled by artists into interactive art installations. At **Kadoya** (by Tatsuo Miyajima), a 200-year-old farmhouse contains a darkened room with a shallow pool of water and submerged colored numbers that blink on and off at varying frequencies; the speed of each number is controlled by an islander, and each number represents a human life. **Go'o Jinja** is an Edo-Era shrine that has been transformed by Hiroshi Sugimoto, with glass stairs, white rocks, and a narrow underground passageway that leads to a tomblike space. You'll need to reserve in advance to see **Kinza,** an installation by Rei Naito in a tiny 200-year-old cottage that can only be viewed by one person at a time. **Ishibashi** is a restored family home of a salt-producing family now housing paintings by Hiroshi Senji, while **Gokaisho,** where residents once gathered to play the Japanese game *go,* contains Yoshiro

Suda's *Camelia* artwork. **Haisha** is a transformed dental clinic now housing sculptures and graphic art, and **Minamidera** is a stark wooden building designed by Tadao Ando, with an installation by James Turrell called *Backside of the Moon.* After being led into a pitch-black room by staff, you wait about 10 minutes until your eyes adjust, when you see a faint glow ahead. You're told you can walk to the light to touch it, only to find . . . well, you'll have to "see" for yourself.

Honmura. benesse-artsite.jp. ¥600 adults for Minamidera or Kinza; combination ticket to other 5 other projects ¥1,400 adults (¥1,200 online), ages 15 and under free. Tues–Sun 10am–4:30pm. Bus stop: Nokyo-Mae (in front of JA Bank).

Benesse House Museum ♥♥♥ MUSEUM Designed by Tadao Ando, this museum contains site-specific works by Jasper Johns, Robert Rauschenberg, Frank Stella, Jackson Pollock, Andy Warhol, and others, all conceived with Ando's architecture and Naoshima's natural beauty in mind. It's easy to spend hours here, examining every piece from all possible angles, seeing how the scenery has been "borrowed" and incorporated into the art. The **Valley Gallery,** an Ando-designed structure resembling a shrine, sits in a bowl of mountains and has a semi-open exterior allowing the sounds and pulses of nature to flow freely through the space. In the museum proper are artworks exploring topical themes, like Richard Long's *Circle of Driftwood in the Seto Inland Sea,* where trees gaze through apertures in the museum wall at a formation of driftwood, as though seeing their own future in a world of deforestation and rising sea levels. Outdoor galleries bring the Seto Inland Sea into view and work it into the compositions, be it Cai Guo-Qiang's *Cultural Mixing Bath,* a collection of gnarled rock features placed around a hot tub on a sloping lawn that invokes the principles of Feng Shui, or Walter de Maria's

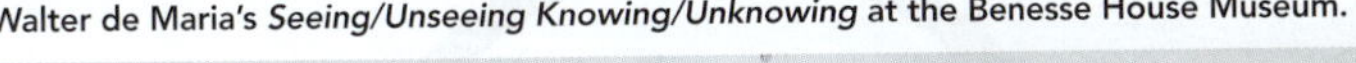

Walter de Maria's *Seeing/Unseeing Knowing/Unknowing* at the Benesse House Museum.

Seeing/Unseeing Knowing/Unknowing, two smooth granite spheres, mystical and imposing, like eyes looking searchingly across the waves. One of the most famous pieces is a yellow polka-dotted pumpkin—a symbol of the island and also of its visionary creator, Yayoi Kusama—sitting alone on the coast, framed by the stunning Seto backdrop.

Godanji. benesse-artsite.jp. ✆ **087-892-3223.** ¥1,500 adults (¥1,300 online), ages 15 and under free. Daily 8am–9pm (last entry 8pm). Bus stop: Tsutsuji-So.

Chichu Art Museum ♥♥ Unsurprisingly, this space was also designed by Ando, a striking concrete structure with sharp angles, contemplative viewing spaces, and only a few works of art. These include light installations by James Turrell, a room of Monet paintings—a nod to the late-20th-century fad for *japonisme* in France that inspired some of his work—and a room by Walter De Maria containing a huge granite ball and gold-leaf-covered bars. The trickery of this museum is that despite looking like a subterranean *kofun* (megalithic burial mound) from the early centuries A.D., it's incredibly airy and so bathed in light that the interplay of light, darkness, and shadow is incorporated into every piece.

3449–1 Naoshima. benesse-artsite.jp. ✆ **087-892-3755.** ¥2,800 adults (¥2,500 online), weekends and holidays ¥3,000 (¥2,700 online), ages 15 and under free. Tues–Sun 10am–6pm (to 5pm Oct–Feb). Bus stop: Chichu Art Museum or Tsutsuji-So.

Lee Ufan Museum ♥♥ Though born in Korea in the 1930s, the octogenarian Lee Ufan has spent most of his career in Japan and was a pioneer of the *Mono-ha* (School of Things) movement that emerged in Tokyo in the 1960s. An exploration of materials and their properties, Mono-ha was

Tadao Ando's *Infinity Gate* outside the Lee Ufan Museum.

a reaction to the rapid industrialization of postwar Japan. Using compositions of stone and steel—the materials of construction—Lee's namesake museum, created in collaboration with (you guessed it) Tadao Ando, is one of minimalism and simplicity. Angular corridors and the natural environment create a sense of rhythm and theater, enhancing the artworks within.

1390 Naoshima. benesse-artsite.jp. ✆ **087-892-3754.** ¥1,400 adults (¥1,200 online), ages 15 and under free. Tues–Sun 10am–6pm (until 5pm Oct–Feb). Bus stop: Chichu Art Museum or Tsutsuji-So.

WHERE TO STAY ON NAOSHIMA

Traditionally most visitors to the Art Islands stayed in Takamatsu, or perhaps Okayama, but with beautiful hotels and restaurants, plenty of art spaces, and pleasant beaches for swimming in the summer, there's now enough justification to consider staying overnight on Naoshima. **Batonworks** (beds24.com/book-batonworks; no phone) offers good value apartment rentals in the heart of the island, either with a garden or mountain view. You can rent free e-bikes here, which you'll be glad of given the island's hilly topography. Apartments cost around ¥20,000 per night for 2 guests; a minimum 2-night stay is required. **Shimacoya** (shimacoya.com; ✆ **090-4107-8821**) is an interesting budget option, where guests sleep in tents in the garden or rent a tent placed inside the building (sliding glass doors are open to the elements in summer). There's also a bookshop/cafe here that serves nice coffee. Nightly fee and equipment rental ¥3,500 or ¥6,000 for 2 people.

Benesse House Hotel ♥♥♥ The best hotel on the island—and in terms of sheer wow factor, maybe the best I've ever stayed in—is this boutique hotel set in the Benesse House Museum. There are four different guestroom sections. Museum is part of the main building, with drawings, paintings, and artworks in the minimalist, yet smartly styled rooms. Oval, reached by "monorail" (a 5-min. funicular railway ride) from the museum, has rooms with floor-to-ceiling windows offering epic views of the Seto Inland Sea. Beach suite rooms overlook the coast and sit within earshot of gently lapping waves. In Park, the rooms have verandas built on top of a gentle slope that's dotted with art pieces—you'll get views of Hiroshi Sugimoto's deeply profound *Time Corridors* artwork, which begins in a concrete bunker before making its way outside and unfurling across the lawn. Because high-quality food options on the island are limited, I'd recommend dining in the hotel's Terrace restaurant around twilight, where you'll be treated to a French fine-dining course menu with local produce, alongside seasonal cocktails and a well-curated selection of wines, as the shadows shift and change beyond the building-length glass wall. ***Note:*** Rooms often sell out immediately after the reservation window opens 6 months in advance, so don't delay in making your reservations.

Godanji. benesse-artsite.jp. ✆ **087-892-3223.** ¥50,000–¥80,000 double, but it can vary during peak season. **Amenities:** Restaurant; free Wi-Fi.

Teshima

Though it's larger than Naoshima, Teshima is often ignored in favor of its more popular neighbor. It probably didn't help that Teshima was hit by an environmental scandal in the 1970s, when a company masquerading under the name Teshima Comprehensive Tourism Development dumped as much as 900,000 tons of industrial waste—heavy metals, PCB, oil, and shredded materials—on the island, toxifying the land and its surrounding waters. Thanks to grass-roots campaigning and sponsorship from the Benesse Corporation, the toxins have been removed, and with the opening of the Teshima Art Museum in 2010, the restored island is once again a jewel in the Seto Inland Sea. It might not generate the same online fervor as Naoshima, but Teshima is worthy of a half-day of exploration.

Spring waters from Danyama, a mountain rising from the island's center, ensured Teshima was a land of plenty, encouraging seafaring people to settle here as far back as the early Jomon period (around 12,000 B.C.), and those waters still feed the island's rice terraces, which is where you'll find its most impressive museum. Danyama is also an object of veneration in the art: Halfway up the mountain, an installation of wind chimes dangling from trees, called **La forêt des murmures,** creates a whispery, orchestral soundtrack to an otherwise quiet woodland stroll.

ARRIVING From Tamano's Uno Port, the ferry to Teshima's Ieura Port takes 20–30 minutes and costs ¥780; to Teshima's Karato Port is another 15 minutes and costs ¥1,050. From Takamatsu, the ferry to Ieura takes 35 minutes (or 50 min. with a stop at Naoshima) and costs ¥1,350. Ferries from Naoshima (Miyanoura Port) to Ieura take 22 minutes and cost ¥630. For full schedule visit the **Teshima Tourism Association** website (teshima-navi.jp; ✆ **0879-68-3135**). Ieura and Karato ports are connected by boat and bus (both around 15 min.).

EXPLORING TESHIMA

Les Archives du Cœur ♥♥ In a small wooden building on the coast, a 10-minute walk from Karato Port, this work by Christian Boltanski is a hymn to existence, to human connectivity, and perhaps, the fragility of life. Botlanski, a French multimedia artist who often explored themes of life and death in his work, began recording people's heartbeats in 2008. Here, you can listen to this archive of human heartbeats, along with recorded audio messages, in a strangely profound artistic experience. There are three rooms: one for recording your own heartbeat and an accompanying message (additional cost required), one for listening to heartbeats already stored in the archive, and a third with a thematic installation. If you choose to record your own heartbeat, you'll get a CD of it with an information booklet to take home.

2801–1 Teshimakarato. benesse-artsite.jp. ✆ **0879-68-3555.** ¥700 adults (¥600 online), ages 15 and under free. Recording fee (incl. CD and booklet) ¥1,570. Wed–Mon 10am–5pm (until 4pm Oct–Feb; also closed Tues–Thurs in winter).

The sinuous concrete shapes of the Teshima Art Museum enclose a wondrous work of art composed of sunlight and water.

Teshima Art Museum ♥♥ The most famous artwork on the island, this concrete museum is out of the Tadao Ando playbook, but was designed by artist Rei Naito and architect Ryue Nishizawa. Its smooth, globular shape is iconic—that of a raindrop as it strikes the ground—though I'd liken it to a frictionless spaceship that has crash landed amid the island's terraced rice fields. The museum structure is what you're here to see: pillarless, cavernous, and echoey, with apertures that allow shards of sunlight to stream in, as water droplets, pushed through 168 two-millimeter holes in the ground, meander around following wind movements and the floor's curvilinear shape. You can "see" this place in 20 minutes if you wish, but it's worth spending more time, perhaps sitting in a state of quiet repose and contemplating the artists' intent. There's a cafe, also designed by Nishizawa, next to the museum, with small treats like lemon roll cake and strawberry soda made from Teshima produce.
607 Teshimakarato. benesse-artsite.jp. ✆ **0879-68-3555.** ¥2,000 adults (¥1,800 online), ages 15 and under free. Wed–Mon 10am–5pm (until 4pm Oct–Feb; closed Tues–Thurs in winter). 9-min. bus ride (¥200) or 20-min. walk from Karato Port.

Teshima Yokoo House ♥♥ It's initially hard to figure out if this small museum-cum-artwork makes sense, until you decide it doesn't matter because it's strangely beautiful anyway. An old Japanese home, with its white gravel garden, wooden framing, tatami floors, and generally subdued color palette has been injected with vibrant primary colors and ostentatious paintings that adhere to no real style nor format. The guilty parties are architect Yuko Nagayama and artist Tadanori Yokoo (who's known for dealing in psychedelia and pastiche), and after those initial impressions fade away, you might just wish they'd give similar treatment to more disused Japanese homes.
2359 Teshimaieura. benesse-artsite.jp. ✆ **0879-68-35554.** ¥700 adults (¥600 online), ages 15 and under free. Wed–Mon 10am–5pm (closed Tues–Thurs in winter; also closes 11:30am–12:30pm in Mar). 6-min. walk from Ieura Port.

THE haunting HISTORY OF OSHIMA ISLAND

There are dozens of islands in Japan called or known as Oshima—the typical translation is "Big Island," though this one isn't very big at all, just a fertile little mound adrift in the sea. Once you learn its story, however, you won't confuse it with any of its namesakes. Oshima has skeletons buried in its closet.

Japan enacted a Leprosy Prevention Law in 1907, which saw sufferers of leprosy, or Hansen's disease, sequestered in remote regions and uninhabited islands where they could supposedly cause no harm to the public. Though barely a kilometer across the sea from the Takamatsu outskirts, Oshima was deemed obscure enough to host one of these island leprosaria. Passage to the island was often involuntary and almost always a one-way ticket. "Patients" were checked in, stripped of their belongings, often subjected to brutal treatments, and forced to live out the rest of their lives with only their fellow victims for company (most were cut from family registers due to the stigma of the disease).

Unbelievably, the law was only repealed in 1996, even though the disease has been treatable since the '40s. A few dozen former patients still live on the island, and reparations have been sought in court for much of the 21st century. Yet they also believed in the power of art to tell their story. Oshima is now one of the most evocative stops on the Triennale map, with a heart-wrenching and detailed museum inside the former leprosarium, visceral artworks that capture the extent of the human suffering, and forward-looking installations that leave you with a sense of hope.

A 20-minute ferry ride from Takamatsu (¥690) operates twice daily, with the last return ferry leaving at 4pm (extended hours in Aug).

Other Art Islands

Some of the Art Islands, while enchanting in their own rights, are best visited during the **Setouchi Triennale** (setouchi-artfest.jp; ✆ **087-813-0853**), one of Asia's greatest modern art showcases. There are permanent installations on the non-Benesse-sponsored islands, but they really spring to life during the festival, becoming vital destinations on an Inland Sea itinerary. Tickets to the festival are sold as passports (but don't include regular Benesse Art Sites): A three-season passport (¥5,000) allows access to all artworks and installations across spring, summer, and autumn; a seasonal limited passport (¥4,200) is valid for only one of the three seasons; a 1-day pass is ¥1,800, and a 2-day pass is ¥3,200 (must be used on consecutive days). Entry to individual installations is around ¥300 to ¥500 per site. During the festival, you can also purchase a **3-Day Ferry Pass** at Takamatsu Port Terminal (1–1 Sunport, Takamatsu; ✆ **087-831-1111**) for ¥2,600, which allows unlimited use on many ferries operating in the region for 3 consecutive days. ***Note:*** All prices are subject to change with each edition of the festival.

MEGIJIMA

ARRIVING The ferry from Takamatsu (¥370) takes about 20 minutes; the last return ferry is at 5:20pm (extended hours in Aug). See full schedule at **meon.co.jp/access#timetable**.

This tiny island off the coast of Takamatsu has a permanent population of fewer than 150 inhabitants, but its legend is known throughout Japan. The story of Momotaro, the "Peach Boy," one of Japan's most popular children's fables, follows the titular hero and his unruly animal accomplices—a pheasant, a dog, and a monkey—in their bid to defeat a gang of ogres. The island where the final showdown takes place is thought to be Megijima, because of a cave network, or **Ogre's Lair,** on its tallest mountain. Many visitors make the pilgrimage to these caves (a 10-min. bus ride from the ferry port; ¥800 round-trip), which are covered in ogre-face tiles created in 2013 by 3,000 local middle school students for the second edition of the Triennale. A 10-minute walk from the cave brings you to the summit of **Mount Washigamine,** where you'll get 360-degree views of the Inland Sea. Enquire at the Onigashima Oni Hall (p. 499) for the bus schedule, which is irregular during the off-season.

New artworks are exhibited during each edition of the Triennale, but popular recurring installations include Shinro Ohtake's ***MECON*** and Rintaro Hara+Yu Hara's ***Ping Pong Sea,*** both of which reanimate abandoned school buildings; ***Island Theater Megi,*** a disused warehouse converted into a mid-20th-century Manhattan picture house; and Yasuyoshi Sugiura's ***Terrace Winds,*** an installation of 400 ceramic blocks overlooking the village from a former rice field (this is also open to the public in the off-season). Pop up restaurants and cooking classes sometimes grace the island during the Triennale—see the website for what's featured in the current/next edition.

A recent installation of hanging glass bottles, each containing an islander's memories, on Ogijima.

OGIJIMA

ARRIVING The ferry from Takamatsu (¥510) takes 40 minutes, including a stop at Megijima. From Megijima to Ogijima is 15 minutes (¥240). A round trip from Takamatsu to Megijima/Ogijima costs ¥1,020. The last return ferry leaves at 5pm (extended hours in Aug). See full schedule at **meon.co.jp/access#timetable**.

Ogijima is a mere speck of land, basically a few forested peaks protruding from the sea—you can walk it from top to tail in about half an hour—but the place and its people exude warmth, resilience, and heart. It helps that the artworks have a strong sense of narrative here, celebrating not only the island's environment but also the 100-plus people who call it home. ***Takotusboru,*** for example, is a giant octopus trap, a nod to the fishermen's favorite catch, serving as a children's playground in the hope that more youngsters will one day live on the rapidly depopulating island. Previous exhibitions have included artistic *onba* (wheeled walking aids) for the elderly inhabitants, and a room of memories, each one donated by an Ogijima resident, captured in glass bottles. From ***Ogijima's Soul,*** the island's curved and shadow-warping welcome center, to Keisuke Yamaguchi's ***Walking Ark,*** four large mushroomlike protrusions walking in the direction of a city halfway across the country, there's plenty squeezed into this lovely little package. You'll probably break a sweat walking from installation to installation along the undulating paths and slopes, but doubtless you'll find your exertions well rewarded.

SIDE TRIP TO KAMIKATSU ♥♥

Kamikatsu's zero-waste declaration in 2003 was bold for a town of fewer than 2,000 people, with a mostly elderly population, located high in the forests of Tokushima Prefecture on the eastern end of Shikoku. It had no real record of adept waste management up to then, in a country that had become one of the world's great producers of single-use plastics (those vending machines on every street corner from Hokkaido to Okinawa have their downsides).

But by 2018, Kamikatsu was recycling 80% of its waste, four times the national average. Residents compost organic waste and separate the rest into 45 distinct categories for recycling at the **Zero Waste Center,** a now famous facility shaped like a question mark that asks two prominent questions: Why do we generate so much waste? and What can we do to mitigate it? For anyone interested in environmental issues, Kamikatsu makes a fascinating case study.

ARRIVING You can **fly** directly to Tokushima Airport from Tokyo Narita or Haneda with JAL and ANA, for around ¥8,000 to ¥20,000 one-way. Tokushoma is also 1 hour by **train** from Takamatsu, via the JR Uzushio Express (¥3,570 one-way). From Tokushima Station in the city center take the 82 Katsuura Line **bus** to Yokose-nishi then switch to Kamikatsu Choei bus to the town's Zero Waste Center (1½ hr. total; ¥1,450). If you can **rent a car** in either Takamatsu or Tokushima (there are many rental offices around the train stations in both cities), it makes travel to and around Kamikatsu much easier.

Visiting Kamikatsu

There was no real way for visitors to get a better understanding of how Kamikatsu had worked its wonders until 2021, when local chef Terumi Azuma and her Canadian co-founders Kana Watando and Linda Ding founded **INOW** (inowkamikatsu.com; ✆ **0885-46-0338**). INOW, meaning "let's go home" in the local dialect, is an English-language educational program that brings guests into the Kamikastu fold, where they can learn about waste mitigation, circular economies, sustainable farming techniques, farm-to-table produce, and lessons from rural life that can be applied to urban areas. Alongside enquiring tourists, the program has welcomed tourism professionals, chefs, architects, and startup founders.

INOW programs are curated based on guests' specific requests and goals—you'll have plenty of chances to discuss these with the program managers before committing to a trip. It's a great opportunity for travelers who want to leave a positive impact on the places they visit, whether you're helping local farmers during harvest season, upcyling materials to be used by local artisans, or attending cooking classes or craft workshops that inject money into the local economy. The length and specifics of the program vary greatly, and therefore so does the cost, but if you're interested get in touch with the managers via the email address on the website or phone number above. INOW can arrange transport for specific experiences, like cultivating and drinking tea with a local farmer or attending waste-mitigation workshops.

You can consult INOW about accommodation options, but the best hotel in the area, and the best for understanding the sustainable principles at play in Kamikatsu, is **Hotel WHY** at Shimohiura–7–2 Fukuhara (chillnn.com/177bcc0b991336; ✆ **070-2616-9012**), located right next to the Zero Waste Center. Ask for a room with a mountain view, where you'll be able to watch mist rolling through the valley from your private terrace each morning. Rates for the four rooms, which are cozy two-story lodges, vary based on length of stay and season; enquire with the hotel or INOW. Note that guests will have to arrange their own waste into specific categories, so try not to bring too many disposable items with you,

At a nearby Italian restaurant, called **PERTONARE,** served *omakase* style dinners cooked with local ingredients, as well as breakfasts and bento box packed lunches. Or you can reserve a *kaiseki* dinner at **Tsugikatani Onsen** (e-kamikatsu.jp; ✆ **0885-46-0203**), a hot-spring hotel on the banks of the Katsuura River. The set dinners cost between ¥4,400 and ¥7,700 and feature sashimi, pickles, tempura, konjac, soup, rice, and dessert. There's also a shop here where you can purchase local souvenirs, snacks, and beer from the Kamikatz microbrewery. The inn is 12 minutes from Hotel WHY on the Kamikatsu Choei bus, or a hilly 44-minute walk.

MATSUYAMA & DOGO SPA ♥♥

947km (588 miles) W of Tokyo; 192km (120 miles) E of Takamatsu; 211km (132 miles) SW of Okayama

Although Matsuyama is Shikoku's largest city and the capital of Ehime Prefecture, with a population of more than 515,000, it has the relaxed atmosphere of a small town. Located on the island's northwest coast, Matsuyama features one of Japan's best-preserved feudal castles and what is arguably the most delightful historic public bathhouse in the country, located in Dogo Onsen. The nearby Shimanami Kaido, a series of bridges skipping from island to island from Ehime over to Hiroshima prefecture, has a dedicated cycling lane, with fantastic views of the Seto Inland Sea.

Essentials

ARRIVING There are flights into Matsuyama airport from Tokyo, Osaka, Nagoya, Fukuoka, Sapporo, Kumamoto, Kagoshima, and Okinawa. The flight from Tokyo takes 1 hour and 25 minutes and is as low as ¥5,000 with **Jetstar,** ¥8,000 with **ANA.** Buses connect the airport to downtown in 20 minutes for ¥490. Frequent **JR trains** from Okayama (on Honshu Island) take 2 hours and 40 minutes to reach Matsuyama; the fare is ¥7,350. Trains from Takamatsu leave hourly and take about 2½ hours to reach Matsuyama (fare ¥6,690). An **overnight bus** (willer-travel.com/en/bus; ✆ **050-5805-0383**) leaves Shinjuku Station in Tokyo at 7:50pm and arrives in Matsuyama at 8:20am the next day; tickets cost ¥9,900 to ¥13,800.

Matsuyama is also linked by ferry to several ports on Honshu and Kyushu islands, including Osaka (overnight: 8 hr.; fare ¥6,300) and Hiroshima (2 hr., 40 min. by ferry for ¥3,600, or 70 min. by high-speed boat for ¥7,100). Osaka ferries dock at Toyo Port; from nearby Nyugawa Station the train to Matsuyama takes 46 minutes and costs ¥3,160. Boats from Hiroshima dock at **Matsuyama Port** (**Matsuyama Kanko Ko**), where trains (¥430) and buses (¥920) transport passengers to Matsuyama Station in about 20 minutes.

An old-fashioned-looking streetcar trundles passengers from downtown Matsuyama out to the hot springs of Dogo Onsen.

VISITOR INFORMATION The **Matsuyama City Tourist Information Office** (✆ **089-931-3914;** daily 8:30am–8:30pm) is inside JR Matsuyama Station to the left as you exit the wicket. Be sure to pick up the detailed Matsuyama Offical Guide and Maps and enquire with staff about possible discounts on attractions, hotels, and restaurants. The **Dogo Tourist Information Center** (✆ **089-943-8342;** daily 8am–8pm) is across the street from the Dogo Onsen streetcar stop. The **Ehime Prefectural International Center** (**EPIC**), located between Matsuyama Castle and Dogo Onsen (epic.or.jp; ✆ **089-917-5678;** Mon–Sat 8:30am–5pm), provides information on Ehime Prefecture, including Uchiko, Tobe, and the Shimanami Kaido cycling path.

CITY LAYOUT **JR Matsuyama Station,** which serves long-distance trains, is on the west edge of town, with most attractions, hotels, shopping, and restaurants spreading to the east. **Matsuyama Castle** lies less than 2.5km (1½ miles) due east of the station. Just southwest of the castle is the **Okaido** shopping arcade, a covered pedestrian passageway lined with restaurants and shops and considered to be the heart of the city. **Dogo Onsen,** Japan's oldest hot-spring spa, is on the eastern edge of the city.

GETTING AROUND The easiest and most convenient form of transportation in Matsuyama is **streetcar.** The no. 5 line runs from Matsuyama Station to the Okaido arcade, Matsuyama Castle, and Dogo Onsen. The fare is ¥200 per trip or ¥800 for a **1-day pass** (**Ichinichi Joshaken**). An old-fashioned locomotive-style streetcar nicknamed "Botchan" (after a novel by Natsume Soseki set in Matsuyama) runs between Matsuyama Station and Dogo Onsen. This costs ¥1,300 per ride (children half-price).

Exploring Matsuyama

Ehime Museum of Art ♥♥ MUSEUM Originally opened on the grounds of Matsuyama Castle in 1970, the Ehime Museum of Art has a collection of more than 10,000 works including paintings by European masters, such as Cezanne, Boudin and Monet, and works by contemporary and Meiji-era Japanese artists; its special exhibitions have covered everything from Banksy to the Silk Road to the history of nearby Dogo Onsen. The permanent collection is showcased in rotating exhibitions that change five or six times a year. The New Wing buildings, which opened in 1998, are also noteworthy: curved concrete and plate-glass structures built on the site of the castle's *sannomaru* (outer circle). Divided in two to preserve the old Edo-Period road and a stand of ancient camphor trees, the building is deliberately monotone, in deference to Matsuyama Castle. It's also only 3 stories high so as not to mar the old-world cityscape. You'll get excellent views of the castle from the second-floor lobby.

Horinouchi. ehime-art.jp. ✆ **089-932-0010.** ¥330 adults, ¥220 children. Tues–Sun 9:40am–6pm (last entry 5:30pm). Hours may differ during special exhibitions. Streetcar: Minamihorihata stop (3 min.).

Matsuyama Castle ♥♥ CASTLE Right in the heart of the city, Matsuyama Castle crowns the top of a 131m (435-ft.) hill, commanding an impressive view. It was built by feudal lord Kato Yoshiakira more than 400 years ago, later falling into the hands of the powerful Matsudaira family that ruled the surrounding region from here during the Edo Period. Like most structures in Japan, Matsuyama Castle has suffered fire and destruction through the ages, but unlike many other castles (such as those in Osaka and Nagoya), this one was renovated with original materials in the 1850s. There's only one entrance, a pathway leading through a series of gates that could be swung shut to trap attacking enemies. A secret gate allowed a surprise rear attack, while drop chutes could be used to rain stones onto the enemy. Drums were used to communicate, whether it was to warn of invaders or simply give the time. The granary could store enough rice to feed 2,000 people for a year. The three-story donjon houses some samurai gear, swords, screens, and scrolls from the Matsudaira family, as well as photos of Japan's other castles. Allow yourself 30 minutes to tour.

A set of samurai armor on display in Matsuyama Castle.

Surrounding the castle is a park; if you're feeling energetic, you can walk uphill through the park to the castle in about 15 minutes. Otherwise, the easiest way to reach the castle is to take the streetcar to the Okaido stop, then take a cable car or chairlift (more fun) from the modern cable station (the walking path to the castle also begins here). A round-trip ticket for either the cable car or the chairlift, and including admission to the castle, costs ¥1,040 for adults and ¥420 for children.

1 Marinouchi. matsuyamajo.jp. ✆ **089-921-4873.** ¥520 adults, ¥160 children. Daily 9am–5pm (closes 4:30pm Dec–Jan and 5:30pm Aug). Streetcar: Okaido stop, then chairlift.

Exploring Dogo Onsen ♥♥♥

Dogo Onsen boasts a 3,000-year history and claims to be the oldest hot-spring spa in Japan. According to legend, the hot springs were discovered after a white heron healed an injured leg by soaking it in the thermal mineral waters. Nowadays, Dogo Spa can accommodate about 7,000 people in 34 hotels and *ryokan,* which means the narrow streets resound at night with the slap of thonged slippers and the occasional clatter of *geta* (wooden platform sandals) as vacationers go to the various bathhouses dressed in *yukata* (cotton robes). Friendly conversations start as tourists gather on the hour to see the Botchan clock (across from the historic Dogo Onsen streetcar station, built in 1895), an animated clock featuring characters from Natsume Soseki's novel, and soak their feet in the nearby foot bath, one of 10 foot baths scattered through Dogo Onsen.

The spa is in the city's northeast, about a 20-minute streetcar ride from Matsuyama Station (take streetcar no. 5 to Dogo Onsen, the last stop). Most of the hotels and ryokan in Dogo have their own *onsen,* but I suggest that no matter where you stay, you make at least one trip to **Dogo Onsen Honkan ♥♥♥**, 5–6 Yunomachi (✆ **089-921-5141**), a wonderful three-story public bathhouse built in 1894. A wooden structure with shoji screens, tatami rooms, creaking wooden stairways, and the legendary white heron topping the crest of its castlelike roof, this Momoyama-style building is as much a social institution as it is a place to soak and scrub. On busy days, as many as 4,000 people pass through its front doors. The water here is transparent, colorless, tasteless, and alkaline, helpful for rheumatism and neuralgia. At the very least, it makes your skin feel soft and smooth. The hottest spring water coming into the spa is 120°F (49°C); the coolest, 70°F (21°C). But don't worry—the waters are mixed to achieve a comfortable 108°F (42°C). Bathing in the ground-floor granite bath is just a small part of the experience; most people come to relax and socialize. Although you can bathe for as little as ¥700 for adults (¥350 for children 2–11), it's worth it to pay extra (¥1,300 for 1 hr.) for the privilege of relaxing on tatami mats in a communal room on the second floor,

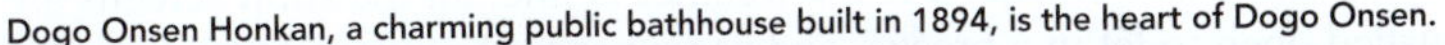

Dogo Onsen Honkan, a charming public bathhouse built in 1894, is the heart of Dogo Onsen.

cycling THE SHIMANAMI KAIDO

Matsuyama is a convenient base for cycling the **Shimanami Kaido ♥♥**, generally viewed as one of Japan's most rewarding cycling routes. Opened in 1999, this dedicated biking and pedestrian lane connects Ehime Prefecture on Shikoku with Onomichi in Hiroshima Prefecture on Honshu (Japan's main island). Also called the Setouchi Shimanami Sea Route, it follows a series of seven suspension bridges that hopscotch across the Seto Inland Sea via six islands.

The cycling path runs beside vehicular traffic on the bridges but often diverges from the highway on the islands. Views of the sea and surrounding countryside are occasionally splendid, with a faded, watercolor-esque quality that is typical of the Inland Sea, though some of the old towns have become depressed industrial sites covered in tons of concrete. It's a popular ride, however, for good reasons: The pathway, clearly marked in blue, is well-paved and easy to follow (though steep in some areas, which can pose a challenge when the wind is swirling).

If you're up for it, you can cycle the entire 70km (43-mile) distance between Shikoku and Honshu in less than 7 hours, whereupon you could either return to Shikoku by bus or continue your travels onward (send your luggage beforehand to your next hotel by TA-Q-BIN; see p. 697). If you prefer to break your ride into 2 days, you can stay in a hostel around the halfway point, like **I-Link** on the east coast of Omishima Island (shimanami.bike; ✆ **0897-72-8308**), which is set up for cyclists, with a garage for bike storage, mounts for hanging bikes in your room, lockers and towels, a cafe and bar, a laundry service across the street, and single rooms, bunks, and dorm capsules. Capsules start at ¥7,120. Other riders may choose to cycle for a

dressed in a rented *yukata,* drinking tea from a lacquered tea set, and eating Japanese rice crackers. If the weather is fine, all the shoji screens are pushed open to let in a breeze, and as you sprawl on the tatami, listening to the voices of people coming and going, you can imagine that you've landed in ancient Japan. The entire scene looks like an old woodblock print come to life. Be sure to take a peek inside the Botchan Room, said to be the favorite room of novelist Natsume Soseki. Want even more of a splurge? Rent a private tatami room on the third floor, which also come with tea, sweets, and yukata, for ¥3,000 or ¥6,000 per group for 90 minutes. (These different levels of luxury probably date from the early days when there were separate baths for the upper class, priests, commoners, and even animals.) While at the bathhouse, you can also tour the **Yushinden,** special rooms built for the imperial family in 1899 for their visits to the spa and last used in 1952 (¥270 adults, ¥130 children). Dogo Onsen Honkan is open daily 6am until 11pm (last entry 10:30pm), though the second and third floors close at 10pm (last entry 9 and 8:40pm respectively), and last entry to the Yushinden is 9pm.

After your bath visit **Ishiteji Temple ♥**, 2–9–21 Ishite (✆ **089-977-0870**), about a 15-minute walk east of Dogo Onsen Station. Established in 728, it's the 51st of Shikoku's 88 sacred temples (see "Walking the Shikoku few hours and then double back, or to ride a little further, dropping off their rental bikes (there are 13 bike drop-off sites along the route) and catching a bus back (check bus schedules beforehand, as buses do not go to all drop-off sites). If this is your choice, it may help to know that the stretch from Shikoku is more scenic and easier to follow than the stretch closer to Hiroshima.

To get to the Shimanami Kaido's starting point on Shokoku, **Sunrise Itoyama** (sunrise-itoyama.jp; ✆ **0898-41-3196**), take an express train from Matsuyama Station to Imabari (30 min.). From there, three to five buses a day go all the way to Sunrise Itoyama; alternatively, take a local train 5 minutes from Imabari to Hashihama Station, which is a 20-minute walk from the cycling center. If you notify Sunrise Itoyama in advance, they also offer pickup and drop-off service at Hashihama Station. Sunrise Itoyama, which lies at the foot of the first bridge (the Kurushima Kaikyo Bridge), offers a restaurant, showers, and rooms without private bathrooms beginning at ¥4,400 for a single and ¥6,600 for a twin; perhaps more importantly, it also offers bike rentals daily 8am to 8pm (to 5pm Oct–Mar). Bikes rent for ¥1,000 a day, plus a ¥1,000 deposit which you forfeit if you decide to ditch your bike at one of the drop-off sites; be sure to ask the folks at Sunrise Itoyama for a bus schedule back. (There are also power-assisted bikes for ¥1,500; however, these bikes must be returned to Sunrise Itoyama, and they have only enough juice to run about 4 hr. or so.) At Sunrise Itoyama, it's also a good idea to buy a coupon for ¥500 covering all the bridge tolls along the route; otherwise you'll have to pay them individually, dropping the money into boxes on the honor system.

Pilgrimage," p. 496). Its main Nio-mon Gate, built in 1318 with a blend of Chinese and Japanese styles, is a good example of architecture of the Kamakura Period. You'll see statues of Kobo Daishi, as well as an old-fashioned arcade of stalls that seems little changed over the decades. Notice the huge straw sandals at the main gate; those with feet or leg ailments are thought to regain their health by touching them. You'll also see regular-size sandals at the temple, donated by older Japanese in hopes of regaining new strength in their legs. Behind the main temple is a tunnel containing stone statues representing the 88 temples of Shikoku; pausing in front of each statue is considered a short circuit to the actual pilgrimage, convenient for those who don't have time for the real thing but still hope for the pilgrimage's blessings. And, by the way, all those paper cranes you see in front of the main hall were folded in prayer for world peace, a practice that started with the American invasion of Iraq. The temple is open 24 hours.

Where to Stay in Matsuyama

EXPENSIVE

Yamatoya Besso ♥♥♥ The ultimate ryokan experience awaits you at this famous lodging in Dogo Onsen. It's the little things that make it special: the rustle of kimono as you're met by bowing, smiling women in the front courtyard; pillars of salt at the front door in good Shinto fashion; lit shoji lanterns guiding the way through hushed hallways; scrolls of haiku poems, in beautiful calligraphy, decorating all the rooms (changed seven times a year to fit the season). With a history dating back 140 years, it offers rooms that preserve the integrity of the past with TVs hidden behind shoji screens and old-fashioned cypress tubs that use water from the hot springs. For a real splurge, there are even four rooms with their own open-air tubs. Lavish kaiseki meals feature seafood of the Seto Inland Sea. The only thing lacking at this superb ryokan is the requisite garden.

2–27 Dogo Sagidani-cho. ✆ **089-931-7771.** 19 units. ¥25,000–¥100,000 per person. Rates include 2 meals. Weekday and off-season discount available. Streetcar: Dogo Onsen (5 min.). **Amenities:** Indoor/outdoor hot-spring baths; free Wi-Fi.

MODERATE

ANA Crowne Plaza ♥♥ Matsuyama's premier hotel (called Zenniku Hotel in Japanese) is located in the heart of the city, just a few minutes' walk from the Matsuyama Castle ropeway and the Okaido covered shopping arcade; streetcars heading for Dogo Onsen pass right in front of the hotel. Built in 1979 but constantly updated, it offers business hotel-like inexpensive singles, as well as larger and well-appointed singles, twins, and doubles; ask for a double or twin with a castle view.

3–2–1 Ichiban-cho. ichotelsgroup.com. ✆ **089-933-5511.** 327 units. ¥11,000–¥20,000 single or double. Streetcar: Okaido (1 min.). **Amenities:** 3 restaurants; bar; tea lounge; rooftop beer garden (summer only); room service; free Wi-Fi.

Old England Dogo Yamanote Hotel ♥♥ An outdoor terrace cafe; a lobby decorated in old-world style with wainscoting, chandeliers, and antique-filled cabinets; and classical music playing in the background bring a sense of English grandeur to the heart of Dogo Onsen. A slightly deceptive sign outside declaring SINCE 1886 refers to a *ryokan* that once stood here; the owner tore it down and opened this hotel in 2003. Still, this is a classy choice if you prefer a bed to a futon—rooms sport brocade bedspreads and curtains, wood floors, and roomy bathrooms (but note that the cheapest doubles have only semi-double-size beds). The rates below are for rooms only, but many guests pay rates that include meals in the hotel's good French restaurant. The hotel doesn't offer much in the way of services, but it does have both indoor and outdoor public baths.

1–13 Dogosagidani-cho. ✆ **089-998-2111.** 70 units. ¥30,000–¥40,000 double. Streetcar: Dogo Onsen (10 min.). **Amenities:** Restaurant; coffee shop; indoor/outdoor hot-spring baths; free Wi-Fi.

Tsubakikan ♥♥ This may look like a large, cookie-cutter business hotel from the outside, but there's a touch of Meiji-era romance within. From the antique lobby and secluded *kaiseki* dining rooms to the outdoor baths cocooned by Japanese gardens and the 3-minute stroll to Dogo Onsen Honkan, there are plenty of good reasons to stay at this property. During special events, which all guests can attend free of charge, the hotel rearranges the furniture in the lobby to point towards a stage, where a taiko drum troupe makes full use of the room's acoustics—a great way to punctuate dinner. Tatami rooms, Japanese-Western fusion rooms, retro Western rooms, and (rare for a 100-plus-year-old Japanese hotel) a spacious barrier-free room accessible by elevator are all available.

5–32 Dogosagidani-cho. tsubakikan.co.jp ✆ **089-945-1000.** 92 units. ¥30,000–¥60,000 double. Streetcar: Dogo Onsen (8 min.). **Amenities:** Kaiseki dinner; indoor/outdoor hot-spring baths; free Wi-Fi.

INEXPENSIVE

Toyoko Inn Matsuyama Ichibancho ♥ Yes, it's a chain business hotel, but its handy location in front of Katsuyama-cho streetcar stop (near the castle and nightlife area) and its long list of freebies, including free rental bikes and breakfast, make it highly recommendable. That said, rooms are cookie-cutter identical and tiny, though otherwise well-maintained and comfortable.

1–10–8 Ichiban-cho. toyoko-inn.com. ✆ **089-941-1045.** 216 units. ¥7,000–¥11,500 single or double. Rates include Japanese breakfast. Streetcar: Katsuyama-cho (1 min.). **Amenities:** Free rental bikes; free Wi-Fi.

Where to Eat in Matsuyama

Bocchan ♥♥ SEAFOOD The system is Bocchan is simple: Each item can be purchased using a single coin (¥500), whether it's Japanese curry rice, pork and rice set meals, yakisoba, deep-fried fish and salad, beer, or sake. A small kitchen with counter seating, it looks like some entrepreneurial resident has converted an unused space in the family residence to make homecooked food for tourists. There are no frills, but the food is tasty given its ridiculously low price tag.

6–23 Dogoyunomachi. All items ¥500. Daily 10:30am–8pm. Streetcar: Dogo Onsen (3 min.).

Dogo Beer Hall ♥♥ BEER/PUB GRUB If you agree that "One gulp of beer taken just after a bath is the time when you feel most refreshed," as proclaimed in this microbrewery's pamphlet, then after bathing at Dogo Onsen Honkan head straight across the street for some sake or beer. (The parent company, which has been a sake producer for more than a century, opened a brewery in 1996 following deregulation, which had long assured a beer monopoly by the major players.) An upbeat establishment with an eclectic decor mixing the traditional (bamboo ceilings) and the modern (artworks), it offers German beers (Cologne-style Kolsch, alt, and stout), along with typical Japanese pub grub, including boiled *edamame* (soybeans), *yakitori,* sashimi, and fried chicken; it's most famous for its deep-fried *jyakoten* (fish paste).

20–13 Yuno-machi. minakuchi-shuzo.jp. ✆ **089-945-6866.** Main courses ¥500–¥2,300. Mon–Fri noon–2pm and 5–8:30pm; Sat–Sun 11am–9pm. Streetcar: Dogo Onsen (4 min.).

Goshiki ♥♥ SEAFOOD Stringy *somen* (wheat noodles) with grilled sea bream is the specialty in this traditional Matsuyama restaurant, and it's an absolute treat—the fish falls right off the bone, and the somen is so texturally satisfying, you'll probably ask for second helpings. You can also order assorted sashimi meals, or a la carte items including grilled octopus, tempura, seasonal grilled fish, even pork belly and wagyu. The best place to dine is in a private room with a low table at the back of the restaurant, though these usually require reservation. The front of the shop doubles as a souvenir store, where you can buy local snacks, juices and condiments. 3-5-4 Sambancho. s422500.gorp.jp. ✆ **050-5486-6517.** Set meals ¥1,580–¥6,000. Daily 11am–1:30pm; weekends also 5–8:20pm (last order). Closed on irregular days. Streetcar: Okaido (6 min.).

Kadota ♥♥ FRENCH Chef Kadota, a gold medalist in the Culinary Olympics, worked at both the Okura Hotel and ANA Hotel Matsuyama before opening his own restaurant here in 1993. Small and cozy, with classical music playing in the background, flowers on every table, and French cuisine served on elegant tableware, it offers homemade appetizers, organic vegetables whenever possible, and—the house specialty—steaks and seafood. Your dinner may start with yellowtail sashimi in mandarin orange sauce or fish bouillabaisse, followed by Seto Inland Sea bream served in a white-wine sauce. Reservations recommended. 3-4-25 Sanban-cho. kadota.co.jp. ✆ **089-931-3511.** Lunches ¥2,900–¥7,700; dinners ¥7,700–¥16,500. Thurs–Tues 11am–2pm and 5–9pm (last order). Streetcar: Kencho-mae (5 min.).

KOCHI ♥♥

617 km (383 miles) W of Tokyo, 127km (79 miles) S of Okayama, 80km (50 miles) SE of Matsuyama, 96km (60 miles) SW of Takamatsu.

It's often the case as you travel further south and west from Tokyo that cities feel less buttoned up, more laidback, at ease with themselves—and that's inarguably the case in Kochi. As dusk approaches, this compact, walkable city starts to hum, the izakaya fill up, the large market in the

An imposing statue of Ryoma Sakamoto looks out to sea in Kochi's Katsurahama Park.

LOCAL HERO: ryoma sakamoto

Kochi, or Tosa as it was once known, rarely features in the history books until the end of the Edo period (1603–1868), when a young samurai called Ryoma Sakamoto began to make a name for himself. Despite being part of the samurai class, Ryoma was in favor of democracy, Westernization, and modernization, as well as (somewhat paradoxically) the return of power to the imperial throne. In 1866 he took part in clandestine negotiations to unite two domains in the west of the country, Satsuma and Choshu. As their forces proved capable of standing up to the shogun's armies, Ryoma and his allies increasingly were seen as enemies of the state. In 1866, the shogun's assassins tried to kill Ryoma. Luckily he escaped, thanks to a young woman who soon became his wife.

Undaunted, Ryoma returned to his hometown of Tosa and persuaded its leaders to join the cause as well. With so many forces now united against him, in 1867 the embattled shogun agreed to a plan, largely crafted by Ryoma, to restore supreme power back to the emperor. Not surprisingly, however, Ryoma had made too many enemies by then, and his luck eventually ran out. Visiting a friend in Kyoto, he was assassinated the following year at the age of 31.

Over the years, this pioneer of modern Japan has also become romanticized as a figure of legend, and no more so than in his home territory: Museums have been dedicated to him, statues have been carved in his likeness, numerous TV shows and manga have him as their protagonist, and Kochi airport carries his name.

center of town is packed with hungry revelers, and even the seedy side streets with their snack bars and men's clubs carry a certain cinematic allure. Add to that one of Japan's best-preserved castles, a huge modern art museum, possibly the country's most important botanical garden, and the nearby gorges of Niyodo, and you have a complete package that punches well above its diminutive weight.

Essentials

GETTING THERE Jetstar **planes** fly from Tokyo's Narita Airport (¥5,000–¥10,000) in 1 hour and 25 minutes. Flights also go from Fukuoka and Chubu. An airport limousine costs ¥900 and takes 30 minutes to get to the city center. The Dosan Line **train** departs from Okayama Station every hour reaching Kochi in 2½ hours; the fare is ¥6,470. From Matsuyama, trains take about 2½ hours and cost ¥6,690. An **overnight bus** (willer-travel.com/en/bus; ✆ **050-5805-0383**) departs Tokyo Station's Yaesu south exit at 8:45pm, with intermediate stops at Shinjuku Station and Yokohama City Air Terminal, reaching Kochi at 8:30am the next day. The one-way fare is usually between ¥9,900 and ¥11,900. From Matsuyama Station, buses take 2¾ hours and cost ¥4,400; from Takamatsu, it's a 2¼-hour ride and costs ¥3,900.

VISITOR INFORMATION The **Kochi Tourist Information Center** (navi.kochi.jp; ✆ **088-856-8670;** daily 10am–6:30pm) is located in the Obiyamachi shopping arcade in the city center; it has English-language brochures and pamphlets, and helpful staff. You can store luggage here for

¥500 per piece. Another information desk is on the south side of Kochi Station at 2–10–17 Kitahonmach (✆ **088-879-0515**); look for a big red banner with an "i." You'll also find the website **visitkochijapan.com** a valuable source of information.

GETTING AROUND Kochi is a city made for walking, with many of its attractions, and the best restaurants and nightlife, squeezed into a tract of land between the Kuma and Kagami rivers. There's also good bus service, and the **Tosanden streetcar,** running north-south and east-west, covers more than 25km (16 miles), the longest of any tram system in Japan. Streetcar tickets are ¥200 per journey, ¥500 for a day ticket in the central city (the "flat-rate" zone), or ¥1,000 for a day ticket covering all routes. There's also a 1-day pass for all streetcar and bus routes for ¥1,800. Children pay half price.

Exploring Kochi

Kochi Castle ♥♥ Built in the early 17th century, this is one of Japan's 12 "original" castles—those with a main keep that has remained intact since the Edo period—and the only one of those 12 with mostly original structures in the *honmaru* (innermost circle of defense). But if this suggests Kochi Castle is a brooding, impregnable fortress, that only tells half the tale. One of its most distinguishing features is that the Yamauchi lords—who ruled over what was then Tosa domain for more than 250 years—saw this as their permanent home, rather than as just a place to retreat when their lands were under siege. So, while there are sturdy cyclopean foundations, archer's perches, and a dry moat, you'll also find well-kept gardens, handsome strolling paths, cherry blossom groves, and the lord's residence decorated with ornate transom panels, shoji doors, and calligraphic wall scrolls. A path guides you through the palace living quarters, exhibition rooms (with period artifacts and models of the castle's construction), and the various levels of the main keep. The keep surmounts a hill, with rivers meandering on either side, which gave a strategic vantage point during its years a fortress and a lovely view of low-rising Kochi today. As one of the city's easiest-to-spot landmarks, it cuts a regal figure anytime of the day, but even more so after dark when its illuminated against the night sky.

Well-preserved Kochi Castle is more gracious than most Edo-period fortresses.

There are two volunteer tours of the castle grounds daily (lasting approx. 1½ hr.), departing from Kochi Castle tourist kiosk at 9:10am and 1:30pm; no reservation required. You can enquire here about shorter tours of the *honmaru* conducted on request throughout the day. If you have time, also nip across to the **Kochi Castle Museum of History** on the east side of the castle grounds, which has 67,000 materials and artworks, formerly owned by the Yamauchi family, that tell the story of Tosa Domain under their rule. An English audio guide app can be downloaded for free.
1–2–1 Marunouchi. kochipark.jp. ✆ **088-872-4344.** ¥420 adults; children free; combination ticket w/ museum ¥740 (¥900 during special exhibitions). Daily 7:30am–6:30pm. Museum 9am–6pm (from 8am Sun). Streetcar: Kenchomae (4 min.).

Makino Botanical Garden ♥♥ GARDEN Born in a rural village in Kochi Prefecture in 1862, Tomitaro Makino soon developed a deep fascination with plants, ecology, and the fundamental components of the natural world. He would go on to become the country's greatest ever botanist, the aptly titled Father of Japanese Botany, collecting 400,000 specimens, discovering 1,500 new species and subspecies, and eventually publishing his legendary *Illustrated Flora of Japan.* This garden, which opened the year after his death in 1958 and was significantly expanded at the turn of the 21st century, is a love letter to Makino's life and work. Across 8 hectares, shaded pathways and winding trails showcase 3,000 different botanical species, including cherry trees, azaleas, yellow Patrinia, clover flowers, canna lilies, roses, and hundreds of other plants with tongue-twisting Latin names. Changes in topography bring different scenery into view, allowing the mountains and plains of Kochi prefecture to enhance the bucolic setting. The conservatory is worth visiting, with rare varieties of tropical flora that thrive in jungles, as is the exhibition hall, exploring the life of Dr. Makino through photos, illustrations, and text. You'll want to spend at least an hour here.
4200–6 Godaisan. makino.or.jp. ✆ **088-882-2601.** ¥730 adults, children free. Daily 9am–5pm (last entry 4:30pm). Bus: My-Yu bus from Kochi Station.

The Museum of Art, Kochi ♥♥ MUSEUM Built with slats of timber and a tiled roof, this museum has none of the neomodern design tropes that are so often the preserve of Japan's contemporary architects. Add that to the location—lying just outside the main thrust of the town, a featureless expressway on one side, a river hugging the other—and it's almost as if this place been forgotten about, or more likely, earmarked for demolition. But when you step inside you quickly realize this is one of the finest modern art museums in the country. More than 41,000 works and 440 artists are included in the permanent collection: the photography of Yasuhiro Ishimoto, who explored modernist themes and depicted the works of Japan's greatest 20th-century architects; the cubist and surrealist paintings of Marc Chagall; calligraphers and painters who rose to prominence in Kochi during the Edo period; and virtuosic European artists including Max Pechstein, Paul Klee, George Grosz, and Wassily Kandinsky. The special exhibitions are excellent, too—whether celebrating the architecture of Kengo Kuma, the films of Studio Ghibli, the prints of Katsushika Hokusai, the kinetic sculptures of Theo Jansen, or European art in the post-Renaissance era, the museum has no problem luring in heavyweights of the arts scene from both Japan and overseas. There's also a theater hall, staging dance, music, screenings, and traditional performance arts like Noh and *kagura.*

353–2 Takasu. moak.jp. ✆ **088-866-8000.** ¥360 adults, ¥250 students, children free; price varies for special exhibitions. Daily 9am–5pm (last entry 4:30pm). Streetcar: Kenritsu Bijutsukan-Dori (8 min.).

Excursion to Niyodo ♥♥

When the poets of yore spoke about Japan as the Land of the Gods, it was places like Niyodo that inspired such assertions. Ancient forests and heavy mists enshroud the mountains; huge gorges, as though hacked out of the landscape by a giant pickaxe, funnel rivers towards the distant coastline. Hamlets sit on vertigo-inducing precipices, their centuries-old structures only one landslide away from becoming driftwood. There's a freshness in the air, a cleanliness in the water, a peacefulness in the solitude, and a kindness in the heart of the people that is impossible not to love. While it's a 2-hour drive each way to get there from Kochi City, as you wind up through the mountains in the heart of the prefecture you slowly find yourself in a kind of Japan that only exists in snapshots today.

A hike along the famously blue waters of Niyodo Gorge makes for a rewarding day trip from Kochi.

If you get off the bus at Nanokawa, you'll be 10 minutes on foot from **Nakatsu Gorge,** where the water is so clean it acquired the epithet "Niyodo Blue." The walking path winds gently upstream, occasionally over bridges crossing the ravine, passing waterfalls plunging over cliffs, mossy slabs of granite and limestone, rock pools that beg to be swum in, Buddhist iconography hiding amongst overgrown foliage, and a handful of echoey caves, nooks, and crannies. Take your time here; there is no need to rush. This is Japanese nature at its finest.

To experience the gorge more actively, of course, you can go packrafting or canyoning with **Niyodo Adventure** (niyodoadventure.

com; ✆ **080-5026-3288**). Outings cost ¥8,500, last around 3 to 4 hours, and take place twice a day (early in the morning and again in the afternoon). Or to take things at a slower pace, go for a soak in the hot spring baths at **Yunomori** (yunomori.jp; ✆ **0889-36-0680;** Thurs–Mon 11am–7:30pm, also same hours every other Wed) for ¥800; children pay half price. Both Niyodo Adventure and Yunomori are located near the entrance of the walking trail.

Next head to **Blue Brew Taproom** (mukaicraftbrewing.com; ✆ **050-3701-9091;** Sun–Mon noon–6pm, occasional Wed–Thurs noon–6pm, Fri–Sat noon–8pm), a small brewpub 15 minutes' drive upriver from Nakatsu Gorge. It was founded by Ken Mukai, a California native, who fell in love with the place while visiting Japan every year since the 1990s; in 2020 he quit his job as a high school science teacher in the U.S., moved to the mountains of Kochi Prefecture, and decided to turn his homebrewing hobby into the Mukai Craft Brewing company. Mukai spends a lot of time tinkering with his concoctions—a *satsumaimo* stout made with Japanese sweet potato, a Belgian white flavored with ginger and homegrown *sansho* peppers, an IPA combined with green tea leaves—or developing new brews with local produce, like a Mountain Fruits sour ale that harnesses the flavors of *goumi* (a cherry native to East Asia), *kuwa* (mulberry), and *yamamomo* (red bayberry). Mukai says the water source from the artesian springspure, the famed Niyodo Blue, is so pure that he basically has a blank canvas to produce whatever beer he fancies. And his taproom is a lovely place to while away a few hours, with its wood-paneled seating area and front porch overlooking the gorge. Pints cost around ¥1,250, halfs ¥720, and bottles of the seven regular Mukai beers are ¥880. If you bring your own meat and veg, you can rent BBQ equipment for ¥3,000 per person and cook in the front yard of the brewpub.

You may not want to take a 2-hour bus journey back into Kochi City after this (especially since the last bus leaves at 5:15pm), but the **Shimonanosato inn** ♥♥ (shimona23.com; ✆ **0889-36-0005**) on the opposite riverbank is a great option if you'd prefer to leave the next morning. It's built in a repurposed elementary school that some former students turned it into a *minshuku* (guesthouse) about 20 years ago. The rooms, in former classrooms, are equipped with tatami flooring and have balconies with views along the gorge. The inn runs on a self-catering system, where guests can use the kitchen or rent BBQ equipment (the cafeteria-esque dining room stocks Mukai craft beers, in case you didn't get to try everything at Blue Brew Taproom). You can make reservations through the website or by getting in touch with Blue Brew Taproom. Rooms cost ¥5,500 to ¥6,600 per night (¥8,700–¥9,700 with BBQ rental), all with shared bathroom.

To get to Nakatsu Gorge, you can take the train from Kochi to Sakawa Station, then change to the Kawado Line bus to Nanokawa (¥1,610), but renting a car is much more convenient, especially once you get to

Nanokawa (the local **Nanokawa Bus,** which can ferry you between the locations mentioned above, only runs three times a day). **Times Car Rental** (timescar-rental.com) has branches at Kochi Ryoma Airport and Kochi Station starting at ¥7,700 for 24 hours for a compact vehicle. **Nippon Rent-a-Car** (nipponrentacar.co.jp) also has branches at the airport and train station and offers compact cars from ¥9,020 per day.

Where to Stay in Kochi

Kochi has lots of affordable and mid-range business hotels from popular hotel groups like **APA** (apahotel.com), **MyStays** (mystays.com/en-us/ and) and **Dormy Inn** (dormy-hotels.com), each of which has built a reputation on nailing simple comforts. Singles usually go for less than ¥10,000.

Jyoseikan ♥♥ Running for more than 150 years, this fine inn has hosted members of the Imperial family on several occasions and has won lots of awards for its accommodation and services. You'll be in no rush to leave, with traditional Japanese rooms that have beautiful views of the nearby hills, Western style suites if you prefer more comfortable bedding, and an eighth-floor VIP room that looks towards the illuminated Kochi Castle by night. Add to that kaiseki dinners, a tea lounge (daily 10am–6pm), an outdoor bath, and concierge service and it's easy to see why this has become the prime spot in Kochi City for those willing to splurge. You can also enquire with the front desk about a tuna tataki cooking demonstration carried out by the hotel chefs—though you'll get as much by walking the halls of Hirome Market (below).

2-5-34 Kamimachi. jyoseikan.co.jp. ✆ **088-875-0111.** 61 units. ¥25,000–¥45,000 per person. Streetcar: Kamimachi 1-Chome (1 min.). **Amenities:** Restaurant; tearoom; public bath; concierge; free Wi-Fi.

Kochi Hotel ♥♥ This businesslike property gets extra marks for location—near Kochi Station and walking distance from good bars, restaurants, and Hirome Market (below)—and for the morning buffet (valuable in Japan, where breakfast that suits the Western palate is hard to come by). The largest rooms are a respectable size and those on floors 5 and above offer nice views of the cityscape and surrounding countryside. It's recommended for travelers who want somewhere clean and comfortable in the city center to lay their heads for the night.

4-10 Ekimae-cho. kochihotel.co.jp. ✆ **088-822-8008.** 79 units. ¥9,000–¥19,000 single or double. Station: Kochi (2 min.). **Amenities:** Breakfast buffet; free Wi-Fi.

Where to Eat & Drink in Kochi

Many travelers to Kochi make **Hirome Market ♥♥** (2-3-1 Obiyamachi; hirome.co.jp; ✆ **088-822-5287**) their first port of call. A huge indoor seafood market in the heart of the city, open daily from 10am until 11pm (open at 9am Sun), it's a constant hive of activity, with diners crammed around the long wooden tables, workmen in overalls drinking sake after their shifts, around 70 stalls peddling all kinds of Kochi delicacies, and numerous chefs charring huge fillets of tuna over open flame. The last of these is what many diners come to eat, because tuna *tataki*—fillets seared on the outside but left raw and tender within—is Kochi's number-one *meibutsu,* or regional specialty.

Technically, there are different sections of the market—Ryoma Street (fisheries and butchers), Castle Square (mostly seafood restaurants), Igosso Yokocho (bars and snacks), and several others—but it's such a chaotic mishmash and a joy to amble around that I'd recommend just letting your instincts (and your stomach) guide you. There's a lot to choose from, so pick a stall that looks appealing, place your order, then bring the food to a table anywhere in the market once you've been served (some stalls will have their own stools or chairs, too). You can find a full selection of shops on the market website (see below), but **Yairo-tei** (© **088-871-3434;** Mon–Sat 10am–9:20pm, Sun 9am–9pm) near the market's north entrance serves delicious tuna tataki with garlic, grated wasabi, *shiso* leaves, and *daikon* radish. Price here is dictated by the number of slices: ¥1,300 for 5 pieces, ¥1,560 for 6 pieces, ¥2,600 for 10 pieces—a steal for fish of that quality. If you plan on doing a culinary tour of the market—and I suggest that you do—budget around ¥5,000 per head. It's a 10-minute walk from the Hasuikemachidori streetcar stop.

Gyozaya Yokojii (餃子家 よこじぃ) ♥♥ DUMPLINGS This small, counter-seat izakaya specializes in dumplings, alcohol, and conviviality. The menu is concise, consisting mostly of *shumai* (ground pork dumpling parcels) served with different Asian spices and condiments, like spring onions, chilies, wasabi, ponzu, *umeboshi* plum, yuzu mayonnaise, kimchi, and soy sauce. The owner, Hiro, who recently acquired the bar, spent a year living in Australia so he's got a pretty good command of the English language and is likely to engage you in conversation. Depending on the inertia of the evening, Hiro might finish the night by putting on the karaoke machine or plugging his Nintendo Switch into the TV and challenging customers to bouts of *Super Smash Bros.*

1–3–9 Obiyamachi. gyozaya-yokojii.com. No phone. Shumai and drinks ¥2,000–¥3,000. Fri–Wed 11am–2pm and 7pm–3am. Streetcar: Hasuikemachidori (2 min.).

Mokuba ♥♥ JAZZ KISSA This bar, whose name means "Wooden Horse," is legendary in the Japanese *kissa* (jazz cafe) scene. Hiding down a noodle-thin alleyway near Hirome Market, it was founded in 1963 by local musician Uga Tosao, who passed away prematurely in his 50s, Mokuba is now on its third owner, a former customer who has maintained the longstanding tradition of the establishment. It's small, dim, smoky, and redolent of the jazz clubs of old, as though immune to the passage of time beyond its walls. Live gigs are staged every Saturday, usually around 7:30pm, and the price of entry comes with a free drink. On other nights, customers just sit back, sip whiskey, and listen to vinyl. It's a little hard to find; look for the red semi-circular awning, with a sign saying "WHISKEY & COFFEE" above it.

1–12–8 Obiyamachi. eiji-dr.wixsite.com/mokuba-jazz-kochi. ✆ **088-822-3955.** Live events ¥2,500–¥3,500. Drinks ¥500–¥800. Tues–Sat 2–9pm. Irregular holidays. Streetcar: Harimayabashi (5 min.).

Suninareru Basho (素になれる場所す) ♥♥♥ IZAKAYA This lively izakaya is one of Kochi's hottest food spots, filling up with diners of all ages as the workday comes to a close. The menu is in Japanese only and is written in a barely legible scrawl, so you might have to get creative when ordering, but it's worth taking some risks in here—all the food is tasty, and there's some genuine inventiveness going on in the kitchen. Izakaya favorites like pork-wrapped asparagus, *tsukune* (chicken meatballs), and *tamago kake gohan* (rice with raw egg and seasoning, usually eaten at the end of a meal), are delivered with an extra bit of polish and punched full of flavor. You can also order bowls of sashimi, *karaage* with a zingy garnish, grilled shiitake mushrooms, and various skewers cooked over open flame. For a drink, order a *tokkuri* (flask) of sake, which is served in an iced bamboo trunk alongside a small cup carved out of bamboo. Ask for a counter seat if you're alone or in a pair so you can watch the industrious chefs at work. This also means you can point at plates of food as they come out (a decent plan B for ordering when the menu is indecipherable).

4–12 Nijudaimachi. ✆ **088-8741-261.** Dinner and drinks: ¥3,000–¥5,000 per person. Daily 5pm–midnight (until 11pm Sun). Streetcar: Kochibashi (5 min.).

Yasube ♥♥ GYOZA This collection of *yatai* stalls on the banks of the Enokuchi tributary is the go-to gyoza spot for Kochi locals; expect long queues on most days. The hanging red lanterns, outdoor seating, and the sizzle of grills and hot plates give Yasube a bustling market atmosphere; prices are commensurate with what you'd expect in a market, too. Plates of 7 gyoza go for ¥600, stewed oden is ¥500, and bowls of ramen are ¥600 (or ¥1,000 with chashu pork). This is the perfect spot to kick off an evening of restaurant hopping in Kochi.

4–19 Nijudaimachi. mfc-group.jp/yasube. ✆ **088-873-2773.** Gyoza: ¥600, ramen ¥600–¥1,000. Mon–Sat 7pm–2:30am. Streetcar: Kochibashi (6 min.).

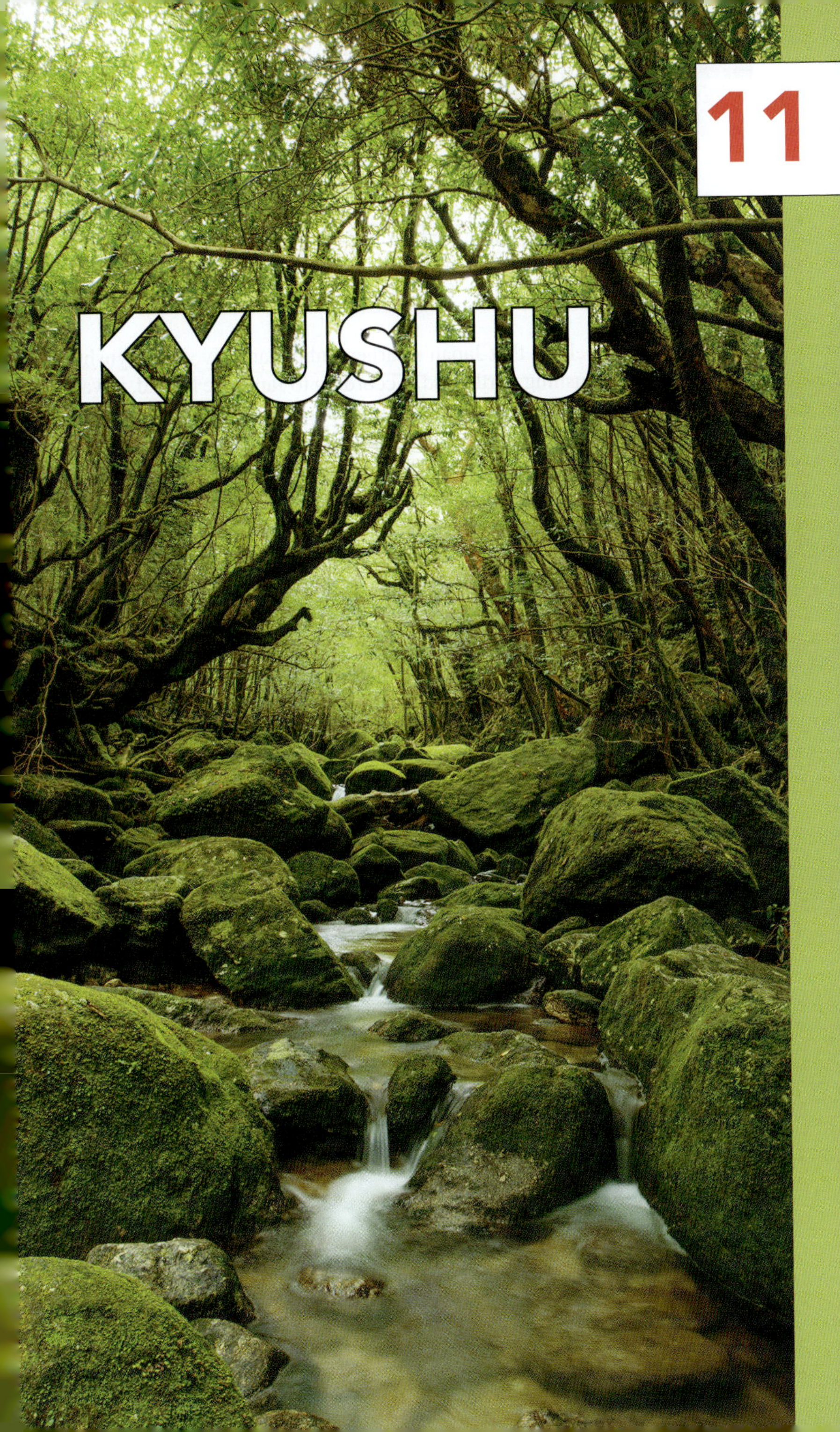
11
KYUSHU

The southernmost of Japan's four main islands, Kyushu offers a mild climate, famous hot-spring spas, handsome bays and coastlines, national parks, and warm, friendly people. It also surrounded by smaller islands on its west and south sides, where visitors can explore some of Japan's last true stretches of wilderness.

Many historians believe that Japan's earliest inhabitants lived on Kyushu before gradually pushing northward. According to Japanese legend, it was from Kyushu that the first emperor, Jimmu, began his campaign to unify Japan. Kyushu is therefore considered the cradle of Japanese civilization. And because Kyushu is the island closest to Korea and China, it has served through the centuries as a point of influx for people and ideas from abroad, including those from the West.

THE BEST KYUSHU EXPERIENCES

- **Exploring Nagasaki, Japan's First Cultural Melting Pot:** Having hosted Chinese merchants, Korean potters, Dutch traders, and European and South American Christian missionaries over the centuries, Nagasaki is one of Japan's most cosmopolitan settlements, as reflected in its culture, cuisine and architecture. See p. 544.
- **Cheering the Local Baseball Team:** Baseball in Japan is a completely different spectator experience; join avid fans at a Fukuoka Softbank Hawks game. If they win, there's fireworks. See p. 535.
- **See One of Japan's Most Active Volcanoes: Sakurajima,** a stratovolcano off the coast of Kagoshima, is the city's most famous landmark, experiencing minor eruptions daily and constantly puffing volcanic smoke into the air. See p. 565.
- **Walking the Forests of Yakushima:** If there is a true land of the Shinto gods left in Japan, the UNESCO-protected moss forest of Yakushima island is it. There's nothing else in the country like it. See p. 572.
- **Getting Buried in Hot Steaming Sand:** In the onsen town of Beppu, this relaxing and curative activity takes place in an old wooden bathhouse. See p. 583.

FUKUOKA ♥♥

1,174km (730 miles) W of Tokyo; 450km (281 miles) W of Hiroshima

Kyushu's largest city (population 1.6 million), Fukuoka is a major international and domestic gateway to the island, with its location on the

PREVIOUS PAGE: **Mysterious, moss-covered Yakushima Island is one of the world's most biodiverse landscapes.**

northern coast of Kyushu lying closer to Seoul and Shanghai than to Tokyo. In recent years, the city's maverick mayor, Soichiro Takashima, has looked to capitalize on Fukuoka's geostrategic position, turning into a startup hub for early-stage Asian and Western companies looking to break into the Japanese market. Thanks to more relaxed visa regulations and various financial and logistical incentives, Fukuoka has become arguably Japan's easiest city to get a new business up and running in. As a result, it's one of the country's most internationalized and youthful urban areas, and has become a favorite city break destination for young Japanese.

During Japan's feudal days, Fukuoka was divided into two distinct towns separated by the Nakagawa River: Fukuoka, the castle town of the local feudal lord, where the samurai lived; and Hakata, the commercial center of the area, where merchants lived. Both cities were joined in 1889 under the common name of Fukuoka. Fukuoka's main train station, however, is in Hakata and is therefore called Hakata Station.

In the 13th century, Fukuoka was selected by Mongol forces under Kublai Khan as the best place to invade Japan. The first attack came in 1274, but Japanese were able to repel the invasion, with a little help from difficult conditions for the Mongols at sea. Convinced they would attack again, the Japanese built a 3m-high (10-ft.) stone wall along the coast. The second invasion came in 1281. Not only did the Mongols find the wall impossible to scale, but a typhoon blew in and destroyed the entire Mongol fleet. Japanese called this gift from heaven "divine wind," or *kamikaze,* a word that took on a different meaning during World War II when young Japanese pilots crashed their planes into American ships in a last-ditch attempt to win the war.

Essentials

ARRIVING Direct flights connect **Fukuoka Airport** (FUK; fuk-ab.co.jp; ✆ **092-621-6059**) to a variety of international cities, as well as numerous domestic cities. Flying time from Tokyo's airport is around 2 hours, with Jetstar, Peach, and ANA all operating flights. Expect to pay between ¥7,000 and ¥15,000 for a one-way ticket. To get into town, there's a subway station located directly under the domestic terminal (if you've arrived at the international terminal, take the free shuttle bus to the domestic terminal). The trip to Hakata Station takes only 5 minutes and to Tenjin, 11 minutes; the fare is ¥260, or you can purchase a 1-day subway pass for ¥640. There's also the **Nishitetsu** bus service, which leaves directly from the domestic terminal every 20 to 30 minutes to Hakata Station's bus terminal; the cost is ¥310.

Fukuoka's Hakata Station is the last stop on the **Nozomi Shinkansen bullet train** from Tokyo, which takes approximately 5 hours and costs ¥22,220 for an unreserved seat. If you have a Japan Rail Pass, which doesn't cover Nozomi trains (unless you pay a supplemental fee), you can take the **Hikari Shinkansen,** changing trains in Osaka or Okayama; the trip takes almost 6 hours, not including transfers. Hiroshima is 1 hour away by train; Kyoto is 2 hours and 45 minutes.

A **bus** departs Tokyo's Shinjuku Station nightly at 9pm, arriving at Hakata Station at 11:20am the next morning. The fare is usually between ¥10,000 and ¥20,000 one-way. Book through **Willer Express** (willer-travel.com; ✆ **0570-200-770**).

VISITOR INFORMATION **Fukuoka Tourist Information Office** (✆ **092-431-3003;** daily 8am–7pm) is in Hakata Station near the East Gate. You'll find pamphlets, brochures, and electronic information tablets here. Sightseeing information is available at **yokanavi.com** and **city.fukuoka.lg.jp**. Other useful sites include **fukuoka-now.com** (good for restaurants,

Only a few walls and turrets remain of Fukuoka's feudal-era castle, but they are beautifully lit up at night in Maizuru Park.

exhibitions, events, and nightlife) and **crossroadfukuoka.jp/en**, with information on and sightseeing recommendations in Fukuoka Prefecture.

CITY LAYOUT Hakata Station is the terminus for the Shinkansen bullet train and trains departing for the rest of Kyushu, with most of Fukuoka's hotels clustered nearby, but the heart and business center of Fukuoka is an area to the west called **Tenjin.** It's home to several department stores, its own train station and bus center, a large underground shopping arcade, and many restaurants, bars, and nightlife haunts. Tenjin even has its own train station, **Nishitetsu Fukuoka Station,** located inside the Mitsukoshi department store building Just a few minutes' walk east from Tenjin, **Nakasu** is one of Kyushu's most famous nightlife districts, with more than 2,000 bars, restaurants, and small clubs clustered on what's actually an islet bounded by the Nakagawa River. Just upriver from Nakasu, **Canal City Hakata** is an intriguingly designed (by American architect Jon Jerde) entertainment, hotel, and shopping complex with 125 shops and restaurants.

GETTING AROUND You can **walk** from Hakata Station or Tenjin to most of the attractions recommended below. There are also three main **subway** lines—the **Airport, Hakozaki,** and **Nanakuma** lines—which are super easy to use and may come in handy during inclement weather. Fares start at ¥210. Or you can get a 1-day subway pass for ¥640. City **buses** running inside the central Hakata-Tenjin District charge a flat fare of ¥150.

Exploring Fukuoka

AROUND HAKATA

An easy stroll around the Hakata area takes in most of Fukuoka's historic sites. Head northwest from Hakata Station for about 8 minutes to find, on the right side of Taihaku-Dori, **Tochoji Temple,** 2–4 Gokushomachi (✆ **092-291-4459;** daily 9am–5pm). This modern reconstruction of a long-established temple may not look like much when compared to venerable religious structures elsewhere around the country, but up on the second floor is Japan's largest seated wooden Buddha, measuring 10m (33 ft.) tall and carved in 1988. Sitting in the lotus position, fingers forming the circular "cosmic mudra" shape associated with meditation, and framed by an intricate mandala, the Buddha is well worth the paltry ¥50 admission fee (put coins in an honesty box). Then enter the small room to the left of the Buddha for a trip through the Hells of Buddhism—you'll view colored reliefs of unfortunate souls suffering all sorts of tortures, then walk through a darkened (read "pitch black") twisting passageway guided only by a rail, until you reach the end, or as the Buddhists would have it: *enlightenment.*

About a 5-minute walk southwest from the temple, in an area referred to as Hakata Old Town, is the **Hakata Machiya Folk Museum (Hakata Machiya Furusato-Kan)** ♥, 6–10 Reisen-machi (hakatamachiya.com; ✆ **092-281-7761;** daily 10am–6pm; ¥200 adults, free for children). This museum celebrates the history and cultural heritage of Hakata, the old merchants' town, concentrating primarily on the Meiji and Taisho eras. It occupies three buildings, two of which are Meiji-Era replicas; the third is an authentic 150-year-old house of a weaver. On display are items used in everyday life, a film about the city's Yamakasa Festival (featuring races of men carrying enormous floats), dioramas depicting everyday street scenes, and a home typical of a Hakata merchant family. You can also watch artisans at work on Hakata's most famous wares, including the highly refined Hakata dolls, tops, wooden containers, and *Hakata-ori* cloth, used for *obi* sashes and loincloths worn by sumo wrestlers.

A mask-maker demonstrates his art at the Hakata Machiya Folk Museum.

Beyond the Hakata Machiya Folk Museum is **Kushida Shrine,** 1 Kamikawabata-machi (✆ **092-291-2951;** shrine grounds open 24 hr.), Fukuoka's oldest shrine, traditionally a shrine for merchants praying for good health and prosperity. Most interesting is a towering, intricately detailed float decorated with dolls made by Hakata doll makers. These floats are used in the annual Yamakasa Festival, which has been held here for nearly 800 years; the festival is in mid-July (if you come

A festival float festooned with dolls by Hakata doll makers is displayed at the Kushida Shrine.

in June, the float won't be on view because it's off being rebuilt for the festival). It's particularly lively around here during one of the many annual cultural celebrations, reminders of the days when shrine courtyards were the heart of a town's social life.

Walk through Kushida Shrine and turn right into the **Kawabata-dori** covered shopping arcade. Halfway down is another Yamakasa Festival float on view year-round in **Kawabata Zenzai Square,** where you can also order sets of hot sweet bean soup with mochi and tea for ¥700. At the end of the arcade, across the street, is Riverain, where up on the seventh and eighth floors is the **Fukuoka Asian Art Museum ♥♥♥**, 3–1 Shimo-Kawabatamachi (faam.city.fukuoka.lg.jp; ✆ **092-263-1100;** Thurs–Tues 9:30am–8pm; ¥200 adults, ¥150 college and high-school students, ¥100 children), which claims to be "the only museum in the world that systematically collects and exhibits Asian modern and contemporary art." Though I'm not convinced this is entirely true, the museum's exhibitions are excellent, shining a light on edgy and iconoclastic Asian artists whose work has yet to feature prominently in the West. From folk art to political art, the permanent exhibition presents changing displays pulled from the museum's own collection. It's very much worth the hour you'll spend here—though that time may be extended if you visit one of the regular special exhibitions, which cost extra.

Head back through the Kawabata-dori arcade to end your walk in **Canal City Hakata ♥♥**, 1–2 Sumiyoshi (canalcity.co.jp; ✆ **092-282-2525;** daily 10am–11pm), a colorful modern open-air shopping mall. Along the canal that bisects the complex, a set of fountains spray in synch with epic orchestral pieces, like *Time to Say Goodbye* or *Ride of the Valkyries,* a la the Fountains of Bellagio in Vegas (albeit on a smaller scale). Fountain shows take place throughout the day (at night they may also feature 3D projection mapping) and the plaza by the fountains also sometimes stages high-quality taiko drum and other traditional musical performances. The curving mall functions like an amphitheater, with viewing balconies on each floor. Between shows, there's plenty to see and do here, with brand-name shops (Doc Martens, The North Face, Calvin Klein, Guess), cafes, restaurants, an arcade, an IMAX cinema, and pop culture shops, including Gundam Base, Jump Shop, and the huge Bandai Namco Cross Store, which has merchandise from many of Japan's most famous anime, manga, and gaming franchises. It even has a couple of smart hotels (see p. 538).

AROUND OHORI PARK

East of Tenjin lies another arts and culture hub, in the area around **Ohori Park ♥♥**. If you're coming from the Ohori Park/Fukuoka Art Museum subway station, you can first walk into **Maizuru Park,** site of the former Fukuoka Castle, Kyushu's largest during the Edo period (1603–1868); rugged stone walls and a few turrets still remain. Unless the park's cherry trees are in full bloom (late Mar to early Apr), the main thing to do here is walk up to the base of the castle keep to get sweeping views across the city, providing a sense of Fukuoka's geography, with the sea to the north and mountains forming a horseshoe shape around the city from west to south to east.

Then head into Ohori Park proper. Constructed in the 1920s in the mold of the West Lake in Hangzhou, China, it's a popular spot for morning joggers and dog walkers—if you're partial to people watching, grab a coffee and a window seat at one of the three cafes on the park perimeter. The park's main feature is a huge **central pond,** bisecting by a string of pine-clad islets and stone bridges; a 2km (1¼-mile) path circles around it. As you walk around the pond, keep an eye out for the many avian species that either live in the park or stop over here during migration. You'll see children feeding ducks, mallards, wigeons, and pochards; spot gulls, cormorants, and grey herons perched on sunken posts or gliding across the

Grey herons make their home around the beautifully landscaped central pond in Ohori Park.

TAKE ME OUT TO THE ballgame

If you're in town March through September, seeing **Fukuoka Softbank Hawks** baseball team play a home game is an unmissable cultural experience. They play in Mizuho PayPay Dome Fukuoka (softbankhawks.co.jp; ✆ **092-847-1006**), the first retractable-roof stadium in Japan. Tickets start at ¥1,600 for an unreserved seat in the outfield and are available at major convenience stores or at the box office. Frankly, watching the spectators is as much fun as watching the game, with their coordinated cheering, flag waving, trumpet blowing, and more. Oddly enough, the roof is generally kept closed (in case it rains and so that players aren't distracted by their shadows), but when the Hawks win, they open the roof and celebrate with specialty fireworks. To reach the stadium, take the subway to the Tojinmachi stop, from which it's about a 15-minute walk. On game days, there are also special shuttle buses departing from the bus centers in Tenjin and Kotsu Center near Hakata Station.

water's surface; and hear dusky thrushes, tree sparrows, bush warblers, woodpeckers, starlings, and greenfinches twittering in the treetops. Winter is the best time to see the 30 or so species that visit the park annually. To get an even better view, rent a Swan-shaped pedalo or rowboat from the **boathouse** on the north bank. For a half-hour on the water, 2-person swan boats cost ¥1,200, 4-person boats ¥1,600, and rowboats ¥800. Boats are available from 11am weekdays, 10am weekends and holidays, until 1 hour before sunset. Other sites of interest include a **wooden pavilion** that juts into the pond from one of the central islets (you may have to queue to get a photo here), a **Noh theater,** a **playpark,** and a lovely **Japanese garden,** enclosed by a forest and whitewashed earthen walls befitting an old samurai manor. The admission price (¥250 adults, ¥120 children) is meager for a tranquil space that conveys the tenets of eastern philosophy, from the carefully raked dry Zen garden to the three Taoist immortal islands adrift in the pond. The garden is open Tuesday to Sunday 9am to 5pm (later in summer).

On the southeast fringe of the park, the **Fukuoka Art Museum** (fukuoka-art-museum.jp; ✆ **092-714-6051;** Tues–Sun 9:30am–5:30pm, until 8pm Fri–Sat July–Oct) is also worth an hour's visit. Its permanent exhibition features works from its own eclectic collection; special exhibitions range from traditional craft showcases to a retrospective on the works of Marc Chagall, a traveling show of Salvador Dali portraits. or a celebration of 85 years of *Tom and Jerry*—see the website for what's currently on. General admission is ¥200 (¥150 high-school and college students, free for children); special exhibitions cost extra.

A 20-minute walk north of Ohori Park, another destination I'd heartily recommend, especially if you're traveling with kids, is **Boss E · ZO ♥♥♥**, 2–2–6 Jigyohama (e-zofukuoka.com; ✆ **092-400-0515;** Mon–Fri 11am–10pm, Sat–Sun 10am–10pm). This multifaceted entertainment complex sits next to Mizuho PayPay Dome, home of the SoftBank Hawks (see

"Take Me Out to the Ball Game," p. 535). Inside the seven-story building, you'll find an MLB-themed **cafe** with the obligatory stock of Shohei Ohtani merch and a museum dedicated to Sadaharu Oh, a Japanese baseball legend who played for the Yomiuri Giants from 1959–80; there's also a **VR zone** where you can chase down dinosaurs and ride bikes and racecars in 3D virtual space or play games like the popular *Beat Saber.* The premier attraction, however, is **teamLab Forest Fukuoka ♥♥♥** (teamlab.art/jp/e/forest; Mon–Fri 11am–7pm, Sat–Sun 10am–7pm), an immersive art space inspired by woodland wildernesses. teamLab takes interactive digitized artworks and adds a catch, study, and release system—visitors use their smartphones to capture bioluminescent creatures living in various 3D computerized biomes (large cats prowling the forests, amphibians and lizards in the swampy underbrush, fish and crustaceans on the seabed); a profile of the captured creature appears on your smartphone screen with relevant details of its classification, physical characteristics, behavior patterns, and habitat; and then you release the creatures back into the wild and continue Pokémon-like in the quest to catch all 59 animals. There's also a sketch factory where your animal drawings can be printed onto t-shirts and totes, plus various other spaces where digital woodland life forms dissipate away and sprout anew, as if repeating the cycle of life, in reaction to the movements of visitors. This sense of discovery and player agency are among teamLab's most impressive achievements, ensuring that no two visitors have the same experience. Tickets cost ¥2,400 adults, ¥2,000 students, ¥1,000 ages 4 to 15, free for kids under 4. Either purchase from the website above or from the third-floor ticketing machines—there's also an information desk here if you have questions about any of the attractions in Boss E · ZO.

teamLab's immersive art installation Forest Fukuoka was inspired by the thriving woodlands of Kyushu.

Side Trip to Dazaifu

An easy half-day excursion inland from Fukuoka, the town of Dazaifu has a festive atmosphere, thanks to its immensely popular shrine and an important contemporary museum. The main attraction, **Dazaifu Tenmangu Shrine ♥♥♥**, 4–7–1 Saifu Dazaifu (dazaifutenmangu.or.jp; ✆ **092-922-8225**), is a 5-minute walk from the train station (see "Getting to Dazaifu," p. 537); you'll take a right onto a pedestrian lane lined with shops selling

Getting to Dazaifu

The best way to reach Dazaifu is from Nishitetsu Fukuoka Station in Tenjin (in the Mitsukoshi department store). Take a *tokkyu* (limited express) of the Nishitetsu Tenjin Omuta Line (departures every 30 min.) 12 minutes to Futsukaichi (the second stop) and transfer across the platform for an 8-minute train ride on the Nishitetsu Dazaifu Line (two stops) to Dazaifu Station, the last stop. If you're lucky, you may catch one of the few trains that go directly from Fukuoka Station to Dazaifu. In any case, the fare is ¥420 one-way. The **Dazaifu City Tourist Information Desk** (**© 092-925-1880;** daily 9am–5:30pm) in Dazaifu Station has English-language pamphlets.

souvenirs, followed by three bridges (representing the past, present, and future) spanning a turtle-filled pond shaped in the kanji for "heart." The shrine itself was established in 903, soon after the death of the scholar-poet Michizane Sugawara, who'd been demoted from his position as Minister of the Right in Kyoto and exiled to Dazaifu. Today, there are some 12,000 Tenmangu shrines throughout Japan, all dedicated to Michizane, who is deified as the Shinto god of literature and calligraphy. This is one of the oldest and most important ones, drawing six million visitors a year, many of them high-school students praying to pass tough university entrance exams. Behind the main hall, which dates from 1591, hang wooden tablets, written with the wishes of visitors—mostly for successful examination scores. Also behind the main hall is an extensive plum grove with 6,000 trees; the plum blossom, in bloom from late January to March, is considered the symbol of scholarship.

A 2-minute walk south from the shrine, the Zen temple **Komyozenji Temple ♥♥** (**© 092-922-4053;** daily 8am–5pm), built in 1275, has Kyushu's only significant Zen rock garden, arranged to form the Chinese character for "light." In the back is a combination moss-rock garden, representing the sea and land. It's a glorious sight and almost never crowded, except in autumn when the changing colors of the overhanging maple leaves make it even more spectacular. To see it, take your shoes off, throw ¥500 into the donation box, and walk to the wooden veranda in back where you can sit and meditate.

Students submit prayers for high exam scores to the Shinto god of scholarship at Dazaifu Tenmangu shrine.

Return to the grounds of Dazaifu Tenmangu Shrine and bear right, where an escalator will take you up to the **Kyushu National Museum ♥♥**, 4–7–2 Ishizaka (kyuhaku.jp; **© 092-918-2807;** Tues–Sun 9:30am–5pm; ¥700 adults, ¥350 college students, free for children under 18). Perched on a hillside, it's a strikingly modern structure (opened in 2005) that undulates down the slope in imitation of the hills around it; surrounding woods are reflected on its glass facade. Through permanent and special exhibits, it focuses on how Japan's cultural heritage has been influenced by other Asian cultures through the ages, and the vital role Kyushu has played in cultural exchange. Religious objects, musical instruments, ceramics, lacquerware, art, and other items from ancient to modern times are on display, including goods that reached Japan via the Silk Road and European trading ships.

Where to Stay in Fukuoka

In addition to the choices here, Toyoko Inn (toyoko-inn.com) has four locations within walking distance of Hakata Station, all with free internet access and complimentary breakfast. You'll also find several APA Hotel (apahotel.com) branches in Hakata, and another in Tenjin at 1–9–39 Daimyo. Unless you're booking during a busy period, you should be able to nab rooms for around ¥10,000 or less per night.

Canal City Fukuoka Washington Hotel ♥♥ Though part of a nationwide business-hotel chain, this Washington has more style: It's located in Canal City Hakata, Fukuoka's number-one shopping and entertainment complex, offering convenience right outside the front door. Higher-priced, large singles and all twins and triples have views outward toward the city. The downside: Its good location makes it popular; you'll likely find the lobby and common areas crowded.

1–2–20 Sumiyoshi. washington-hotels.jp. ✆ **092-282-8800.** 423 units. ¥15,000–¥20,000 single; ¥20,000–¥40,000 double. Station: Gion (10 min.). **Amenities:** Coffee shop; breakfast buffet; free Wi-Fi.

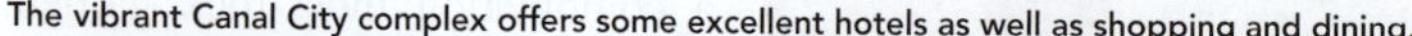

The vibrant Canal City complex offers some excellent hotels as well as shopping and dining.

Grand Hyatt Fukuoka ♥♥♥ Fukuoka's top hotel commands a grand setting in the innovative Canal City Hakata, with easy pedestrian access to some of the city's main sights. Its black-marbled lobby has a curved facade that overlooks the shopping complex and its fountain shows, but for guests who desire solitude, the hotel also has a private roof garden. Service throughout the hotel is superb—along the order of "Your wish is our command." Small but stylish rooms provide views of the private garden or the river and its night scenes. Besides all the luxury, a stay at the Grand Hyatt is fun, with Canal City's many shops and restaurants right outside the door.

1–2–82 Sumiyoshi. ✆ **092-282-1234.** fukuoka.grand.hyatt.com. 370 units. ¥30,000–¥80,000 single or double. Station: Gion (10 min.). **Amenities:** 2 restaurants; bar; lounge; concierge; fitness center and spa w/ indoor pool; room service; free Wi-Fi.

Hotel Etwas Tenjin ♥ Located in the lively Tenjin area, where late-night bars and karaoke parlors are aplenty, this property is also within walking distance of Hakata's historic attractions to the east and Ohori park to the west. The rooms are spotless, if a little pokey, and you'll get the usual free amenities, like toiletries and pajamas, that are the preserve of Japanese budget hotels. The two main reasons to stay here are the large communal lounge and the ground-floor food market. In the former, jazz standards are piped in through the speaker system and you can help yourself to free tea or coffee, read on one of the sofas (magazines are available from the shelves), or check your emails at the desks (replete with charging ports). In the latter, you can eat seafood bowls for lunch, izakaya food at dinner, and stop in for the 5 to 6pm happy hour, when drinks cost ¥300 and food items go for as little as ¥190. All-you-can-eat breakfast is also available here for ¥1,500.

3–5–18 Tenjin. hoteletwas.co.jp. ✆ **092-737-3233.** 59 units. ¥10,000–¥15,000 double. Subway: Tenjin (6 min.). **Amenities:** Free Wi-Fi.

Mistui Garden Hotel Fukuoka Gion ♥♥ A branch of the reliable Mitsui Garden chain of chic (if slightly cookie-cutter) hotels, this property gets top marks for location, set between Tenjin and Hakata, as well as for its cozy, neutral-toned decor and a rooftop communal bath. The simply designed rooms are accented with patterned motifs using the five colors (purple, red, yellow, blue, navy) of Hakata-*ori* textiles. They range from comfort doubles to junior suites; even those towards the lower end of the spectrum have ample space. A good base for business or leisure purposes.

2–8–5 Hakataeki-mae. gardenhotels.co.jp. ✆ **092-414-3131.** 300 units. ¥20,000–¥40,000 double. Streetcar: Kushida Shrine (1 min.). **Amenities:** Breakfast buffet; sauna and communal bath; free Wi-Fi.

Where to Eat in Fukuoka

For one-stop dining, head to **Canal City Hakata** (**✆ 092-282-2525**), a 10-minute walk west of Hakata Station or a 1-minute walk from the Canal City Hakata-mae bus stop. You'll find dozens of restaurants in this shopping complex, offering everything from Chinese, Italian, and Japanese cuisine to fast food and bar snacks. **Hakata Station** has an even greater selection of culinary fare, with a sprawling hall of food counters on the ground floor—take your pick from hot bento boxes, rice balls, fresh pastries, fried chicken, cakes, muffins, and Japanese sweets—and an underground corridor, called **Hakata Ichibangai,** lined with popular restaurants; it's not unusual for queues to form before a shop's 10 or 11am opening time. Udon, soba, beef tongue, ramen, *okonomiyaki* (Osaka-style savory pancakes), teppanyaki, Korean and Chinese food, and craft beer are all available. If you're planning on dining here before hopping on a Shinkansen or an inter-prefectural express train, be sure to leave some buffer time.

For a bit more local flavor, head to one of Fukuoka's famous 200 ***yatai*** ♥♥ (street-side food stalls), mostly located in Tenjin and along the

EAT A BOWL OF hakata ramen

Eating Hakata ramen—more commonly known as *tonkotsu*, a style of broth made from boiling pork bones for 12 to 24 hours—is as important a cultural activity when in Fukuoka as visiting any of the city's attractions. And you won't have to go far; estimates have put the number of ramen shops in Fukuoka Prefecture at around 1,700.

On the fifth floor of the Canal City mall is **Ramen Stadium,** with eight ramen shops offering noodles, *gyoza* (dumplings), and other dishes from different regions of Japan Pick your meal from the ticket vending machine outside each shop; there are photos of most selections, priced from ¥700 to ¥1,300. Like most restaurants in Canal City, they're open daily from 11am to 11pm.

Two major national Hakata ramen chains, **Ichiran** (ichiran.com) and **Ippudo** (ippudo.com), were founded in Fukuoka in 1960 and 1985, respectively. There are multiple branches of each, but if you want to dine in the main shops, head to **Ippudo Daimyo** at 1–13–14 Daimyo in Tenjin, or **Ichiran Souhonten** at 5–3–2 Nakasu in Hakata; in both you can expect to pay around ¥1,000 for a bowl (or a little more, if you add extra toppings). Note that neither accepts reservations. Ichiran is probably Japan's best-known ramen chain, partly because of its unique, introvert-friendly style of service—placing diners in separate cubicles where they receive bowls under a divider so that neither kitchen staff nor customer ever interact—which has become internet famous as an example of "only in Japan" customs. The ramen is excellent, mind, but I struggle to see the sense in queuing for 30-plus minutes (as is common here) to eat it when so many other gold-standard restaurants are within a stone's throw.

There are a couple other options worth noting. On the top-floor food court of the **Mark IS** shopping mall at 2–2–1 Jigyohama, next to Boss E · ZO (p. 535), is a branch of the award-winning **Najimatei** ramen chain. Open 10am to 9pm daily, it serves bowls of Hakata ramen for ¥850 to ¥1,200; cost depends on how liberal you want to be with your toppings. Or for a super-cheap, but still high-quality, bowlful of local tonkotsu, dine in **Hakataya Kawabata** (9–151 Kamikawabatamachi; ✆ **092-291-3080;** open 24/7), adjacent to the Kawabata-dori shopping arcade in Hakata (p. 533). Believe it or not, you can get a bowl of ramen in here for only ¥290—add ¥180 to make it a large.

Nakagawa River on Nakasu Island south of Kokutai-Doro Avenue. Most stalls sell ramen, though some also serve *oden, yakitori,* tempura, and other simple fare. They're open daily from about 6pm to 2am. Many nighttime revelers stop here before or after a spin through the Nakasu entertainment district. Choose a stall, sit down, and you'll be served a steaming bowl of ramen for about ¥800.

Brooklyn Parlor ♥♥ BURGERS/CRAFT BEER Occasionally when one is on the road it's nice to find something that resembles a home comfort, and Brooklyn Parlor provides exactly that, with its brickwork decor, American rock and Britpop soundtrack, hefty burgers and French fries, a range of craft beer, and even slices of warm apple pie. The food is good, but I'd argue the main reason to come is to cycle through the beer menu, featuring a lager and pale ale from the eponymous Brooklyn brewery, as well as local drops like a Heartland pilsner, a Sorachi Ace saison, and a fruit beer and stout by Spring Valley Brewery. Half pints cost ¥600, pints ¥1,000.
3–1 Shimokawabatamachi (Riverain mall, ground floor). brooklynparlor.co.jp. ✆ **092-283-5622.** Burger and fries ¥1,350–¥1,650. Daily 11:30am–9pm. Station: Nakasu-Kawabata (1 min.).

Kazaguruma ♥♥ IZAKAYA In a relocated 200-year-old farmhouse accented with heavy wooden beams, this lively izakaya near Hakata station specializes in locally brewed *shochu,* a clear rice-based spirit often called Japanese vodka. It also offers a fish of the day, *yakitori,* sashimi, and other local favorite foods. The ¥5,000 set menu features 10 dishes selected by the chef and 2 hours of all-you-can-drink.
Dangam Building 1F, 1–13–1 Hakata-eki Higashi. ✆ **092-481-3456.** Dinner and drinks ¥4,000–¥5,000 per person. Mon–Sat 5pm–1am. Station: Hakata (1-min. walk from east exit).

Nichinan Pho ♥♥ VIETNAMESE Hakata ramen may be the soupy noodle dish of choice in Fukuoka, but if you're looking for a change of pace this Vietnamese restaurant serves a mean bowl of pho. You'll have to walk down a dingy, odd-smelling corridor and take an elevator to the second floor to get here, but that's little sacrifice to taste the shop's umami-filled clear soup topped with tender meat and fresh, zingy herbs and vegetables. A regular-sized pho costs around ¥850; all orders are made via multilingual tablets at your table.
2F 3–4–15, Chuo-ku. nichinanpho.com/ja/home-japan ✆ **090-1362-6789.** Pho ¥850–¥1,000; lunch ¥1,050–¥1,450. Daily 11am–midnight. Station: Tenjin (6 min.).

NAGASAKI ♥♥

1,329km (826 miles) SW of Tokyo; 152km (95 miles) SW of Fukuoka

Many people in Japan—including foreign residents—consider this city one of the country's most beautiful. It's a place of hills rising from the deep, U-shaped harbor with boats and ferries chugging back and forth, of houses perched on terraced slopes, of small streets and distinctive neighborhoods, of jutting church spires and classical Chinese architecture, and of people extremely proud of their hometown. Without a doubt, Nagasaki is one of Japan's most livable cities. It's also perhaps Japan's most cosmopolitan city, with a unique blend of outside cultures interwoven into its history, architecture, food, and festivals. Nagasaki doesn't have a castle, a famous landscaped garden, or hot-spring spas, and it's perhaps best known as the second city to be destroyed by a nuclear bomb (its memorials about that tragic event are moving and important to visit). But it's still well worth fitting into your Japan itinerary.

Located on the northwest coast of Kyushu, Nagasaki opened its harbor to European vessels in 1571 and became a port of call for Portuguese and Dutch ships; Chinese merchants soon followed and set up their own community. Along with traders came St. Francis Xavier and other Christian missionaries, primarily from Portugal and Spain, who found many converts among the local Japanese. During Japan's more than 200 years of isolation, only Nagasaki was allowed to conduct trade with outsiders, based on a fan-shaped manmade islet called Dejima, and thus served as the nation's window to the rest of the world.

Essentials

ARRIVING JAL, ANA, and budget airline Solaseed serve **Nagasaki Airport** from Tokyo's Haneda Airport. Flight time is around 2 hours; the one-way fare costs between ¥7,000 and ¥20,000. Jetstar also offers cheap flights from Narita Airport. Airport buses travel to Nagasaki Station in about 45 minutes for ¥920. If you're traveling by train, take the **Nozomi Shinkansen bullet train** from Tokyo to Hakata Station in Fukuoka, and transfer there for a train to Nagasaki; travel time is about 7½ hours, depending on connections, and the total fare is ¥28,000 for an unreserved seat. There are roughly 2 trains an hour from Fukuoka; you'll have to transfer at Takeo Onsen Station. If you're just traveling from Fukuoka to Nagasaki, the train trip takes about 2 hours and costs ¥5,520 for an unreserved seat.

VISITOR INFORMATION The **Nagasaki City Tourist Information Office** (✆ **095-823-3631;** daily 8am–7pm) is located just outside the main ticket gates of Nagasaki Station; you'll get maps, pamphlets, and information on tours here. More information is available at **discover-nagasaki.com**.

CITY LAYOUT Nagasaki is one of Japan's most navigable cities, with lots of English-language signs pointing the way to attractions. The city layout follows natural boundaries set by the Urakami River, long narrow Nagasaki Bay, and many steep-sloped hills. **Nagasaki Station** isn't in the downtown part of the city; most nightspots, shops, and restaurants are southeast of the station, clustered around an area that contains **Shianbashi Dori** and **Kanko Dori streets,** the **Hamano-machi** covered shopping arcade, and a waterfront area called **Dejima Wharf** that includes restaurants and Seaside Park. Just west of Dejima is **Chinatown,** with Chinese restaurants and shops selling Chinese-made souvenirs and

Post Office
Shrine
Railway
Tourist Info
0 1/10 mi
0 100 m
Twenty-Six
Martyrs Museum
Ken-ei
Bus Station
Nagasaki
Station
Honrenji
Temple
NAGASAKI
PARK
Suwa
Shrine
Central
Post Office
Nishi
Nakamachi
Umamachi Dori
City Hall
Chamber
of Commerce
Imauomachi
Dori
Nagasaki River
GOTO
MACHI
Fukuromachi Dori
Kofukuji
Temple
KOZEN
MACHI
City Hall Street
Manzaimachi Dori
Megane-bashi
Ohato Dori
Gowa
Kanko Dori
Teramachi Dori
Nakajima
Nagaski Port
Terminal
Hamanomachi Arcade
Sofukuji
Temple
Dejima
Wharf
DEJIMA
WHARF
CHINATOWN
Nagasaki Bus
Station
Nagasaki
Prefectural
Art Museum
Nagasaki
Harbor
MOTOKAGO
MACHI
Oura Gawa
ATTRACTIONS
Confucius Shrine 25
Dejima 20
Glover Garden 27
Hollander Slope 23
Nagasaki Atomic Bomb Museum 1
Nagasaki Museum of History & Culture 9
Nagasaki Ropeway to Mt. Inasa 2
Nishizaka Hill 3
Oura Cathedral 27
Peace Park (Hirano-machi) 2
Sofukuji Temple 15
Spectacles Bridge 13
Suwa Shrine 10
HOTELS
Candeo Hotel Nagasaki Shinchi Chinatown 19
Coruscant Hotel Nagasaki Station 8
Hotel New Nagasaki 7
Hotel Wing Port Nagasaki 5
JR Kyushu Hotel Nagasaki 4
Nagasaki Hotel Monterey 24
Sakamoto-ya 12
RESTAURANTS
Kadoya 17
Kagetsu 28
Katsushika 14
Khao Ken 11
Lao Lee Main Branch 22
Miraizaka 6
Sazio 18
Seafood Market Dejima Wharf 21
Shikanoko 26
Shippoku Hamakatsu 16

clothing. Farther south is **Glover Garden,** where many foreigners settled in the 19th century. **Peace Park** and its atomic-bomb museum are located north of Nagasaki Station on the other end of town.

GETTING AROUND Streetcars have been hauling passengers in Nagasaki since 1915 and have changed little in the ensuing years; they're still the easiest—and most charming—way to get around. Four lines run through the heart of the city, with stops written in English. Because streetcars have their own lanes of traffic here, during rush hour they're usually the fastest on the road. It costs a mere ¥140 (half-price for children) to ride one, or ¥100 if going two stops or fewer; pay at the front when you get off or use your IC card. You are allowed to transfer to another line only at **Tsukimachi Station** (ask the driver for a transfer ticket, a *norisugi,* when you disembark from the first streetcar); otherwise, you must pay each time you disembark. If you think you'll be riding more than five times in 1 day, save a few yen with a ¥600 **pass,** sold at the tourist office and at many hotels, which allows unlimited rides for 1 day. Streetcars run from about 6am to 11pm. With the exception of Peace Park, you can get around Nagasaki easily **on foot,** which is certainly the most intimate way to experience the city and its atmosphere. You can walk from the Hamano-machi downtown shopping district to Glover Garden, for example, in 20 minutes, passing Chinatown, Dejima, and the Dutch Slope on the way.

Exploring Nagasaki

Nagasaki's long history of contact with foreign cultures have left it with several historic sites that are refreshingly different from what you'll see in other Japanese cities. Most visitors come to visit the **Peace Park** and, within it, the **Nagasaki Atomic Bomb Museum** (p. 549), but the museums, temples, churches, and gardens clustered around the harbor and center city are just as worthy of your attention.

Confucius Shrine (Koushi-byo) and Historical Museum of China ♥♥ SHRINE Chinese residents living in Nagasaki built this colorful red-and-yellow shrine in 1893, aided by the Ch'ing Dynasty in China. This is the only Confucian mausoleum outside China built by the Chinese—in fact, the land upon which it stands belongs to China and is administered by the Chinese embassy in Tokyo. The main hall contains a statue of Confucius, attended by courtyard statues representing his 72 disciples. More fascinating, however, is the small **Historical Museum of China** located behind the main hall, with bronze jars, ceramics, jade carvings, painted enamel vases, and other treasures on loan from Beijing's National Museum of Chinese History and Beijing Palace's Museum of Historical Treasures.

10–36 Oura-machi. ✆ **095-824-4022.** ¥660 adults, ¥440 high-school students, ¥330 children. Daily 9:30am–6pm. Streetcar: Oura Cathedral (3 min.).

Dejima ♥♥♥ OPEN-AIR MUSEUM When the Tokugawa shogunate adopted a national policy of isolation in the 1630s, only Nagasaki was

Among the restored buildings on Dejima Island, the Chief Factor's Residence shows how Dutch trade officials lived during their Nagasaki postings.

allowed to remain open as a port of trade with foreigners. The Portuguese and Spaniards were expelled in 1639 because of their Christian faith; only the Dutch and Chinese were allowed to remain, and 2 years later, in 1641, the Dutch were confined to a tiny fan-shaped artificial island called Dejima—meaning "Exit Island"—where they remained for 218 years. (See "Life on Dejima Island," p. 546.) Today, after land reclamation re-connected it to the mainland, Dejima has been reborn as a semi-open-air museum, recreating the island as it was in the early 19th century. More than a dozen period structures have been resurrected based on old maps and artists' renderings. Pick up an English-language map at the entrance, and get an overview of the restoration process in No. 1 Warehouse; exhibits in the No. 2 Warehouse describe Dejima's role in introducing Western science and culture to Japan. Another warehouse, under the head honcho's living quarters, has a hands-on experience, where you can stare down the barrel of a cannon or inspect an old badminton racket, a billiards table, and a cooking pan used by Dejima's former residents. You'll also find various audiovisual panels dotted throughout these buildings, detailing the building of Dejima's lone bridge, the role of the Dutch East India Company in facilitating trade in the Orient, and how Dejima functioned as a conduit for imported goods to be spread across Japan.

While Dejima's function as a trading hub is interesting enough, the museum is at its best when giving visitors a glimpse into the life of its inhabitants. For this you'll want to visit the **Chief Factor's Residence.** In stark contrast to the spare decor of the Japanese administrative office at the back of the compound, the residence may have tatami flooring and modular spaces, but its walls and ceilings are covered in colorful *karakami* wallpaper (a product of China's Tang Dynasty); chandeliers and elaborate light fixtures dangle from the roof; door and window frames are painted in a bluish-green color popular in the Netherlands at the time; geometric rugs, possibly picked up in the Middle East on trading expeditions, cover the floors; and rooms for conducting official business are furnished with sofas, armchairs, timepieces, and cabinets stocked with demijohns, tumblers, and decanters. One room depicts a Chief Factor, or *Opperhooft,* overseeing the transition of power to his predecessor. Another shows a grand feast on a banquet table; all candles, roasted meat joints,

LIFE ON dejima island

Tiny Dejima Island in Nagasaki harbor was for centuries (1641–1854) Japan's only official contact with the outside world; the director of Dejima was required to travel to Edo every 1 to 4 years to report to the shogun. Otherwise, the only people allowed to cross the bridge into the Dutch community were Japanese prostitutes, translators, traders, and Buddhist priests. The Dutch often maligned life on Dejima, quickly tiring of the stultifying summers and lack of home comforts, and were baffled by the arcane etiquette and communication style of their hosts. Having to hide their Christian faith (Christmas, for example, was celebrated under the guise of "Dutch Winter Solstice") was another point of ongoing tension. The Japanese, for what it's worth, looked on the Dutch with equal amounts of distrust and disgust, believing that their vulgar ways and oafish appearances justified their being essentially imprisoned on this thin strip of land. This fascinating period of Japanese history is wonderfully fictionalized in David Mitchell's historical novel *The Thousand Autumns of Jacob de Zoet,* following the travails of a Dutch clerk stationed on Dejima at the turn of the 18th century: It's nigh-on required reading for modern visitors to Dejima.

red wine, rich colors, and merriment—the annual Dutch Winter Solstice dinner. Next walk over to the **Siebold Repatriated Plant Garden,** where botanist Philipp Franz Von Siebold, who wrote the revolutionary *Flora Japonica* and helped introduce Western science to the Japanese, would have conducted much of his work. Next to this is a 1:15 scale model of Dejima as it looked c. 1820, based on a painting by Nagasaki artist Kawahara Keiga. Also of note is a blue colonial-style wooden building constructed in 1877 as Japan's first **Protestant seminary,** and a green and white clapboard structure next door, built in 1903, which was once the **Nagasaki International Club** (it now houses a decent restaurant). Opposite, a replica of an old stone warehouse has artifacts unearthed during Dejima excavations.

6–3 Dejima-machi. nagasakidejima.jp. ✆ **095-821-7200.** ¥520 adults, ¥200 high-school students, ¥100 children. Daily 8am–9pm. Streetcar: Dejima (1 min.).

Glover Garden ♥♥ OPEN-AIR MUSEUM After Japan opened its doors to the rest of the world and established Nagasaki as one of its international ports, Nagasaki emerged as one of Japan's most progressive cities, with many foreign residents. A number of Western-style houses were built during the Meiji Period (1868–1912), many of them on a hill overlooking Nagasaki and the harbor. Today, that hill has been developed into Glover Garden, which showcases nine Meiji-Era buildings on lushly landscaped grounds. (Some stand on their original site; others were moved here.) The stone-and-clapboard houses have sweeping verandas, Western parlors, the most modern conveniences of the time, and Japanese-style roofs. Most famous is **Glover Mansion,** Japan's oldest Western-style house, built in 1863. It's often romanticized as the home of Madame Butterfly, the fictitious heroine of Puccini's opera. Its owner, Thomas Glover, was a Scotsman who was indeed married to a Japanese woman, but he was much more faithful than his Puccini counterpart; he also, among other things, financially backed and managed ship-repair yards in Nagasaki, brought the first steam locomotive to Japan, sold guns and ships, and exported tea. The **Ringer House,** dating from the early Meiji Period, contains a display of photos, clothes, and artifacts of Kiba Teiko, a Japanese opera singer who played Madame Butterfly. A former **boys' academy** houses photographs of old Nagasaki, including portraits of foreigners who used to live here. The **Mitsubishi Dock House,** built in 1896 as a rest house for ship crews, offers great views of the harbor. One of Nagasaki's first Western restaurants is now a quaint **cafe.** And don't miss the **Nagasaki Traditional Performing Arts Center,** which displays floats and dragons used in Nagasaki's most famous festival, the Kunchi Festival, held in October. The museum's highlight is an excellent film of the colorful parade, featuring massive ships on wheels and Chinese dragon dances. Views from Glover Garden of the harbor are among the best in the city. Plan on spending about 1 hour here.

8–1 Minami Yamate-machi. glover-garden.jp. ✆ **095-822-8223.** ¥620 adults, ¥310 high-school students, ¥180 children. Daily 8am–6pm; open at night selected periods, see website for info. Streetcar: Oura Cathedral (7 min.).

A Little Slice of Europe

About a 10-minute walk northeast from Glover Garden (follow Glover St. north, then go 2 blocks on Holland St.), you'll find another remnant of Nagasaki's Western influences, on **Hollander Slope** (**Oranda-zaka,** also referred to as Dutch Slope). It's undoubtedly Nagasaki's prettiest street, a cobbled lane lined with wooden houses built by former European residents. A century ago, the people of Nagasaki referred to all Europeans as Hollanders.

Nagasaki Museum of History and Culture ♥♥ MUSEUM To understand Nagasaki's pivotal role in Japan's exchange of culture, trade, and ideas with the outside world, visit this museum. With the help of English-language explanations, you'll learn about how Western languages, medicine, astronomy, and other sciences were introduced via Nagasaki's contact with the Dutch; Japan's cultural exchanges with China and Korea; Christianity in Japan; and Nagasaki's role as a trading port. There are also displays of Nagasaki arts and crafts, including local artwork influenced by Western and Chinese styles, from porcelain and lacquerware to glass and tortoiseshell objects. The adjoining *Bugyosho* (Magistrate's Office) is a faithfully reconstructed example of mid-1600s Japanese architecture (note the *shoji* panels that slide around corners to be stored away, completely opening the interior to the exterior). A short 3D movie (with an English-language written explanation) recounts a year in the life of the magistrate, and you'll see rooms where smugglers were interrogated and brought to trial. Plan on spending an hour here.

1–1–1 Tateyama. nmhc.jp. ✆ **095-818-8366.** ¥630 adults, ¥310 children. Daily 8:30am–6pm. Closed 3rd Tues of month. Streetcar: Sakuramachi (5 min.).

On Nishizaka Hill, a sculptural panel commemorates the 26 Christians—20 of them Japanese converts—crucified here in 1597.

Nishizaka Hill ♥ MONUMENT/MUSEUM After Nagasaki opened its port to European vessels, missionaries came to the city to convert Japanese to Christianity. Gradually, however, the Japanese rulers began to fear that these Christian missionaries would try to exert political and financial influence through their converts. Who was to say that conversion to Christianity wasn't the first step toward colonization? So in 1587, Toyotomi Hideyoshi, ruler of Japan, officially banned Christianity. In 1597, 26 male Christians (20 Japanese and 6 foreigners) were arrested in Kyoto and Osaka, marched 30 days through the snow to Nagasaki, and crucified on Nishizaka Hill as warning examples. Through the ensuing decades, there were more than 600 documented cases of Japanese, Portuguese, and Spanish Christians being put to death in the Nishizaka area. Today, a short but steep walk from nearby Nagasaki Station brings you to the hilltop site, where the **Monument to the 26 Saints** bears statues of the victims carved in stone relief. (In 1862, the 26 martyrs were canonized by the pope.) You'll immediately notice that three of them look very young—indeed, the youngest was only 12. Behind the relief, the small **Twenty-Six Martyrs Museum** displays artifacts relating to the history of Christianity in Japan, including paintings and drawings of the 26 saints, reward notices for those turning in Christians to authorities, and religious objects. Perhaps most amazing about the history of Christianity in Japan is that the religion continued to be practiced secretly by the faithful throughout Japan's isolation policy, surviving more than 200 years underground. 7–8 Nishizakamachi. japan26martyrs.studio.site; ✆ **095-822-6000.** Museum: ¥500 adults, ¥300 high-school students, ¥150 children. Daily 9am–5pm. Station: Nagasaki (7 min.).

Oura Cathedral ♥ CHURCH Also known as the Basilica of the Twenty-Six Holy Martyrs of Japan, this cathedral atop a hill overlooking Nagasaki Port is Japan's oldest standing church. It is also, in my view, the prettiest Christian building in the country. Built by French missionaries—Fathers Furet and Petitjean—in 1864 to accommodate the growing number of foreigners living in Nagasaki, the church was dedicated to the 26 martyrs killed on nearby Nishizaka Hill (p. 548) and those "hidden Christians" who kept their faith despite centuries of persecution. Inside you'll find high-vaulted Gothic-style ceilings, an ornate dais, and colorful light refracted through stained-glass windows. If you don't want to pay the ¥1,000 admission fee (expensive, given that you'll only spend 10 or 15 min. inside), it's still worth walking up the hill to have a look at the exterior, with its white-washed walls, arched apertures, and an octagonal mint-green spire, all fronted by palm trees.

5–3 Minamiyamatemachi. ✆ **095-823-2628.** ¥1,000 adults, ¥400 seniors and high-school students, ¥300 children. Daily 8:30am–5:30pm. Streetcar: Oura Cathedral (5 min.).

Peace Park/Nagasaki Atomic Bomb Museum ♥♥♥ MEMORIAL On August 9, 1945, at 11:02am, American forces dropped an atomic bomb over Nagasaki, 3 days after they had dropped one on Hiroshima. The bomb, which exploded 480m (1,600 ft.) above ground, destroyed about a third of the city, killed an estimated 74,000 people, and injured 75,000 more. Today, Peace Park, located north of Nagasaki Station, serves as a reminder of that day of destruction. Nagasaki's citizens are among the most vigorous peace activists in the world; a peace demonstration is held in Peace Park every year on the anniversary of the bombing.

At the south end of the park, a black pillar marks the exact epicenter of the atomic blast; a black casket contains names of the bomb's victims. Ironically, the bomb exploded almost directly over the Urakami Catholic Church, built after centuries of persecution in Japan; only a fragmented wall remains, to the right of the pillar. A few minutes' walk farther north, across Urakami Cathedral Street, the largest part of Peace Park covers the

Exhibits in the Nagasaki Atomic Bomb Museum give context to the tragic events of August 9, 1945.

site of a former prison (all 134 of its inmates died in the blast). A fountain is dedicated to the wounded who begged for water; many of them died thirsty. Statues donated by countries from around the world line a pathway leading to **Peace Statue,** a 9m-high (30-ft.) statue of a male deity. One hand points to the sky from where the bomb came (meant as a warning?), and the other hand points to the horizon (representing hope?).

Return to the south end of the park for the main attraction, the **Nagasaki Atomic Bomb Museum.** Upon entering, guests circle an empty glass-domed foyer via a spiraling ramp—bringing to mind, perhaps, the atomic mushroom cloud. This is followed by photographs of the city as it looked before the bomb, accompanied by the ominous, loud ticking of a clock. Displays, all with English-language explanations, illustrate events leading up to the bombing, the devastation afterward, Nagasaki's postwar restoration, the history of nuclear weapons, and the subsequent peace movement. Objects, photos, and artifacts graphically depict the bomb's destruction, including a clock stopped precisely at 11:02am, personal belongings ranging from mangled spectacles to a student's singed trousers, hand bones encased in a clump of melted glass, and photographs of victims, including a dead mother and her baby and a 14-year-old whose face has been hideously burned. On video, survivors describe their personal experiences on that fateful day. The adjoining **Peace Memorial Hall for Atomic Bomb Victims** contains a Remembrance Hall, with portraits of those who lost their lives. The museum noticeably omits Japan's role in the war (the same is also true of Hiroshima's Peace Memorial Museum), but a visit here can be both disturbing and illuminating in equal measure. 7–8 Hirano-machi. ✆ **095-844-1231.** nabmuseum.jp. ¥200 adults, ¥100 children. Daily 8:30am–5:30pm (until 6:30pm May–Aug). Streetcar: Atomic Bomb Museum (1 min.).

Sofukuji Temple ♥♥ TEMPLE Distinctly Chinese-looking with its Ming architecture, Nagasaki's most famous temple dates back to 1629, when it was founded by Chinese residents. Its Buddha Hall, erected in 1646, is the oldest building in Nagasaki and a designated National Treasure; painted a brilliant red and decorated with Chinese lanterns, it was

A View from the Top

The best panoramic view of Nagasaki is from atop 330m (1,090-ft.) **Mount Inasa,** which you can reach in 7 minutes from Nagasaki Station by taking bus no. 3 or 4 to the Ropeway-mae stop (fare ¥160). A 2-minute walk from the bus stop is **Fuchi Shrine,** where believers come to pray for a good marriage, safe childbirth, and academic success. Beside the shrine is the **Nagasaki Ropeway** (✆ **095-861-3640;** daily 9am–10pm), which delivers you to the top of Mount Inasa in 5 minutes (round-trip ¥1,200 adults, ¥940 junior-high and high-school students, ¥620 children). A hilltop observation deck provides 360-degree panoramic views; it's most beautiful (and also busiest) if you arrive before sunset and stay for the zillion twinkling lights.

designed and cut in China before transportation to Nagasaki. Another National Treasure is the temple's beautiful gate, which employs a complex jointing system and features brightly painted detailing. But arguably most fascinating is the temple's gigantic cauldron, built by a priest during a terrible famine in the 1680s to cook enough porridge to feed more than 3,000 people a day.

7–8 Kayjiya-machi. ✆ **095-823-2645.** ¥300 (place in a box in the main hall). Daily 8am–5pm. Streetcar: Sofukuji Temple (2 min.).

Spectacles Bridge (Megane-bashi) ♥ LANDMARK The Chinese also left their mark on Nagasaki with several bridges, the most famous being the so-called Spectacles Bridge, built in 1634 by a Chinese Zen priest. One of Nagasaki's most photographed objects, it's the oldest stone-arched bridge in Japan and is named after the reflection its two arches cast in the water. It's a 5-minute walk from the Hamano-machi shopping arcade.

Streetcar: Megane-bashi Bridge.

Suwa Shrine ♥♥ SHRINE Although Nagasaki's famous Kunchi Festival has Chinese roots, it's celebrated at this Shinto shrine, built to promote Shintoism at a time when the feudal government was trying to stamp out Christianity. Today, with a location on top of a hill with views over the city, the shrine symbolizes the spiritual heart of the Japanese community. When Japanese women turn 33 and men turn 40, they come here to pray for good health and a long life. Newborns are brought 30 days after their birth to receive special blessings and then again for their 3rd, 5th, and 7th birthdays. On New Year's, the grounds are packed with those seeking good fortune in the coming year. People also visit to ask the shrine's many deities for favors—good marriage, safe childbirth, good health, and more. You can even have your automobile blessed here. The shrine sells English-language fortunes and has an info board with a touch screen expanding the *omikuji* (fortune-telling) process and other info on Shinto traditions. If you're satisfied with your fortune, keep it; if not, tie it to the branch of a tree and the fortune is conveniently negated.

18–15 Kami-Nishiyama-machi. ✆ **095-824-0445.** Free admission. Daily 24 hr. Streetcar: Suwa Jinja-mae (4 min.); take underground passage and follow signs up stone stairs.

Where to Stay in Nagasaki

Nagasaki has reasonably priced hotels, but keep in mind that some accommodations raise their rates during peak times—cherry blossom season (late Mar through early Apr), Golden Week (Apr 29–May 5), Obon (mid-Aug), and most of the fall.

EXPENSIVE

Hotel New Nagasaki ♥♥ One of Nagasaki's deluxe hotels, with a grand marbled lobby, the Hotel New Nagasaki is right next to the train station, offering convenient access to locations throughout the city (and beyond). Its rooms are among the city's largest; some even offer a view of Nagasaki's busy port. Add the hotel's wide range of facilities—a beauty salon and spa, a chic bar, three restaurants—and you have what amounts to one of Nagasaki's best top-tier choices.

14–5 Daikoku-machi. newnaga.com. ✆ **095-826-8000.** 153 units. ¥15,000–¥50,000 double. Station: Nagasaki (1 min.). **Amenities:** 3 restaurants; bar; lounge; concierge; room service; free Wi-Fi.

MODERATE

Candeo Hotel Nagasaki Shinchi Chinatown ♥♥ The wraparound, floor-to-ceiling windows of the 11th-floor reception area in this smart hotel make a great first impression, offering panoramic views of Nagasaki's mountainous cityscape. The rooms are modern and nicely designed, with L-shaped seating areas by the windows that make for cozy reading corners. To get the most out of the view, book a room on the eighth floor or higher. The 12th floor has a sauna and sky spa, in which you soak in hot water amongst the skyscrapers, as well as guestrooms with private open-air baths. The hotel's location between Dejima and Chinatown is another great reason to stay.

3–12 Dozamachi. candeohotels.com. ✆ **095-829-3300.** 207 units. ¥10,000–¥25,000 double. Streetcar: Shinchi Chinatown (2 min.). **Amenities:** Spa; sauna; free Wi-Fi.

JR Kyushu Hotel Nagasaki ♥ You can't get closer to Nagasaki Station than this business hotel on the station's second floor; those traveling with a Japan Rail Pass get a 10% discount. Otherwise, rooms are your basic boxes, with small bathrooms, alcoves serving as closets, and no views. The adjoining Amu Plaza has many shops and restaurants where guests can while away their free time.

1–1 Onoue-machi. jrhotelgroup.com. ✆ **095-832-8000.** 144 units. ¥10,000–¥30,000 double. **Amenities:** Coffee shop; free Wi-Fi.

Nagasaki Hotel Monterey ♥♥ Step into old Portugal in this whimsical hotel decorated with whitewashed walls, shuttered windows, imported tiles, and hand-painted furnishings. A small chapel on site has relics and decor from Portugal, too, and there's a kerosene lamp museum on hotel premises, free to hotel guests. The hotel is conveniently located at the bottom of Hollander Slope (p. 547).

1–22 Oura-machi. hotelmonterey.co.jp. ✆ **095-827-7111.** 123 units. ¥10,000–¥25,000 double. Streetcar: O-Urakaigandori (2 min.). **Amenities:** Restaurant; free Wi-Fi.

Sakamoto-ya ♥♥♥ This beautiful 130-year-old *ryokan* (Nagasaki's oldest) right in the heart of the city is a wonderful place to stay, especially when you consider how rare traditional ryokan are nowadays. All rooms, which are named after plants, flowers, and trees, have a Japanese-style bathtub made of cypress wood, as well as traditional artwork on the walls. The best room is *Matsu No Ma* (Pine Room), which even has its own miniature garden with a tiny shrine. Rates vary according to the room and the meals served; you may opt for the *shippoku* dinner, a Nagasaki specialty consisting of a variety of dishes showing European and Chinese influences. Note that at the time of writing the accommodation section is closed (it's still taking reservations for the restaurant); check the website to see if it has reopened.

2–13 Kanayamachi. ✆ **095-826-8211.** 16 units. ¥23,100–¥25,300 per person. Rates include 2 meals. Streetcar: Gotomachi (5 min.). **Amenities:** Breakfast and dinner; free Wi-Fi.

INEXPENSIVE

As well as the hotels listed below, reliable budget chains like **Toyoko Inn** (toyoko-inn.com) and **APA Hotels** (apahotel.com) have branches in Nagasaki, where you'll get basic amenities and clean, cookie-cutter rooms for around ¥10,000 or less; perhaps a little more during busier seasons.

Coruscant Hotel Nagasaki Station ♥ There are absolutely no frills in this hotel opposite Nagasaki Station, but the rooms do function like small apartments, each with a galley kitchen stocked with a refrigerator, kettle, microwave, sink, and washing machine. Some also have a stove top and dining table. Early bird discounts, if booked more than 45 days in advance, offer rooms for as little as ¥9,576.

7–5 Daikokumachi. go-coruscant-hotel.com. ✆ **095-818-2919.** 14 units. ¥9,576–¥12,000 double. Station: Nagasaki (2 min.). **Amenities:** Free Wi-Fi.

Hotel Wing Port Nagasaki This business hotel offers mostly singles that couldn't get much smaller. However, the fact that they're spotless, with white walls and cheerful bedspreads, helps alleviate claustrophobia, as do good bed lights and windows that can be opened. Panels close for complete darkness; note that some rooms face another building. The deluxe twins are actually quite roomy for a business hotel, with a sofa, a semi-double-size bed, and a single bed. A cheap place to stay, even during busy holiday seasons.

9–2 Daikoku-machi. wingport.com. ✆free **095-833-2800.** 200 units. ¥8,500–¥13,000 double. Station: Nagasaki (3 min.). **Amenities:** Free Wi-Fi.

Where to Eat in Nagasaki

Nagasaki's most famous food, called *shippoku,* is actually an entire meal of various courses with Chinese, European, and Japanese influences. It's a feast generally shared by a group of four or more and includes such dishes as fish soup, sashimi, and fried, boiled, and seasonal delicacies from land and sea.

Another Nagasaki specialty is *champon,* a Chinese noodle usually served in soup with pork, seafood, and vegetables. A popular place to eat *champon* is **Shikanoko** (4–5 Matsugaemachi; shikairou.com; ✆ **095-822-1296**), formerly called Shikairo, which supposedly created the dish at the turn of the 20th century. There's a free museum here, too, with displays relating to the history of *champon.*

Nagasaki's nightlife district centers on a small area south of Hamanomachi known as **Shianbashi,** which begins just off the streetcar stop of the

A street vendor offers fresh steamed pork buns in Nagasaki's bustling Chinatown.

same name and is easily recognizable by the neon arch that stretches over the entrance of a street called Shianbashi Dori. Shianbashi shimmers with the lights of various drinking establishments and *yakitori-ya,* which are often the cheapest places to go for a light dinner. Another good hunting ground for restaurants is **Nagasaki Shinchi Chinatown** (see Lao Lee, p. 556); you'll also find street vendors selling *xialongbao* (soup dumplings), *nikuman* (steamed pork buns), and *dongpo* pork (braised and served in a bao bun), as well as shops serving *champon* and Chinese regional cuisine.

EXPENSIVE

Kagetsu ♥♥♥ SHIPPOKU/KAISEKI This traditional restaurant is the ultimate Japanese dining experience, an oasis of dignified old Japan, where kimono-clad waitresses shuffle down wooden corridors and serve guests constantly changing exquisite dishes in *tatami* rooms. First established in 1642 and formerly a geisha house, Kagetsu is one of Japan's longest-running restaurants; the oldest part of the present wooden building is about 360 years old. Display cases exhibit treasures related to Kagetsu's history. Behind the restaurant, which is set back from the road, is a beautiful 300-year-old garden with gnarled, stunted pines. There must be at least two of you if you want to feast on *shippoku* or *kaiseki.*

2–1 Maruyama-machi. ryoutei-kagetsu.co.jp. ✆ **095-822-0191.** Reservations required. Lunch obento sets ¥10,560–¥17,160; shippoku or kaiseki dinner ¥23,760–¥33,000. Wed–Mon noon–3pm and 6–10pm (last order). Streetcar: Shianbashi (3 min.).

MODERATE

Katsushika ♥♥ TONKATSU The breaded meat cutlets in this restaurant at the northern end of the Bellenade arcade street are sublime. Order a large beef or pork set meal and you'll basically get a full steak, cooked

in panko crumbs, served with rice, shredded cabbage, miso soup, pickles, and "special" tonkatsu sauce. If you chow through the salad and/or rice with haste, ask for a refill (they're free). The smaller set meals, as well as the chicken and seafood cutlet options, might work better for less voracious diners. Japanese menus are set out on the tables but ask for an English one and they'll bring it over. There's also a pretty good alcohol selection, including wine, beer, sake, shochu, whiskey, and fruit sours.
3–13 Yorozuyamachi. katsu-shika.com. ✆ **095-801-0828.** Tonkatsu meals ¥1,000–¥2,800. Daily 11:30am–3pm and 5–9pm. Streetcar: Kankodori (4 min.).

Sazio (サジオ) ♥♥ ITALIAN There's a seductively cinematic atmosphere at this small Italian trattoria, with a counter running along the kitchen-bar, the husband-and-wife owners chatting to wine-slurping customers, and wraparound windows looking down on the lamplit streets below. The menu (in Japanese) features classic antipasto dishes—beef and seafood carpaccio, bruschetta, chicken liver pâté—and pastas include carbonara, arrabbiata, salmon and cream, gorgonzola, and amatriciana. Specials, perhaps steak or ragu, are written on the chalkboard (also in Japanese) behind the bar, but the owners can explain the contents in basic English. On busy evenings, all diners are required to order an in-house appetizer (¥1,400), usually an insalata of fresh greens and capers with a mix of cured meats and raw fish. The restaurant also levies a ¥300 per person table charge.
2F 5–13 Dozamachi. ✆ **095-820-2369.** Pasta/risotto meal ¥2,700; average ¥4,000–¥5,000 with drinks. Tues–Sat 6–11pm; Sun 6–9pm. Streetcar: Shinchi Chinatown (2 min.).

Seafood Market Dejima Wharf ♥♥ SEAFOOD Diners are spoiled for choice in this aptly located seafood restaurant overlooking Nagasaki port. Take a seat by the pool, where various crustaceans and fish mill about in ignorant bliss, or under the silvery wall relief depicting Dejima and old Nagasaki, and order from a menu—with English translation and pictures—that includes *kaisen don* (seafood rice bowls), sashimi platters, sushi sets, prawn tempura, grilled yellowtail, oysters, Nagasaki-style seafood salad, and much more. Though some people are, understandably, uncomfortable with this, you can even order whale bacon, tongue, or lean meat (whale is famous in Nagasaki). The rice bowls are good if you're dining solo, but I'd suggest mixing some platters if you're here in a group. If the weather conditions are right, you can also dine on the front terrace beside the sea.
Dejima Wharf. nagasakikou.com. ✆ **095-811-1677.** Rice bowls ¥1,485–¥3,168; sushi and sashimi platters ¥1,155–¥7,480. Daily 11am–2pm and 5–9pm (last orders). Streetcar: Dejima (1 min.).

Shippoku Hamakatsu ♥♥ SHIPPOKU Just a minute's walk from the Hamano-machi covered shopping arcade, this modern spot is one of Nagasaki's best-known *shippoku* restaurants. The ground floor, with Western-style table seating, is made private with alcoves and pull-down screens; upstairs is a large *tatami* room with individual low tables and seat cushions. It offers shippoku set meals for lone diners or groups, as well as more manageable lunch sets (these still feature around seven or eight dishes) served by women in elegant kimono between 11am and 2:30pm, making it a good place to try this unique cuisine.

6–50 Kajiya-machi. ✆ **095-826-8321.** Lunches ¥1,650–¥3,600; shippoku meals ¥4,800–¥18,500. Daily 11am–8:30pm (last order). Streetcar: Shianbashi (4 min.).

INEXPENSIVE

Kadoya (濃厚豚骨 かどや) ♥♥ RAMEN & CHAMPON This ramen shop next to the Shianbashi nightlife district serves a seriously good bowl of *champon,* the *tonkotsu*-style broth imbued with a charred flavor from the stir-fried pork. It's a generous portion of food and wonderfully joyous looking, with green cabbage leaves and pink *narutomaki* (cured fish cake) adding pops of color. If you want to add some spice to the dish, order the red *champon* ("赤ちゃんぽん" on the vending machine; there are pictures to help you out), served with a chili-garlic dressing. Gyoza, rice, extra slices of pork, and bottles of Asahi beer are available, too.

6–23 Hamamachi. ✆ **095-895-7310.** *Champon* ¥860–¥930; ramen ¥690–¥990. Daily 11:30am–2:30am. Streetcar: Kankodori (1 min.).

Khao Ken (かうけん) ♥♥ THAI Hidden in an alcove that looks like it was once an automobile garage, this tiny Thai restaurant is a delight. The lone room, a full third of which is taken up by the kitchen, has some bunting hanging from the roof, a few 3D prints of Thai dishes on the wall, a narrow table running around the perimeter, and the spicy, herbaceous smells of Thai cuisine pervading the air. The menu (mostly in Japanese, but with pictures) features some classic noodle and rice dishes like tom yum, pad Thai, green curry, gapao, khao tom goong, and khao man gai, all for less than ¥1,000. Whatever you order, you can't really go wrong.

AYU Bldg, 10–1 Furumachi (under the Total Care salon). ✆ **095-808-1557.** Dishes ¥600–¥950. Mon–Fri 11:30am–2:30pm. Streetcar: Sakuramachi (6 min.).

Lao Lee Main Branch (老李総本店) ♥♥ TAIWANESE With its blood-red decor, mythical iconography, and plaintive string music playing in the background, this Taiwanese restaurant is one of Chinatown's most popular haunts. Several styles of boiled dumpling are available—with pork or prawn, or flavored with perilla or coriander—and you know they're confident about these because the staff advise to you to eat it *sono mama* ("as it is"—that is, without dipping sauce). Other dishes include *champon,* stir-fried meat and veg, *xiaolongbao* (soup dumplings), bao buns with braised pork belly, and fried rice. Set meals are also available, mixing small versions of select menu items. Note the kanji name above, as there are two Lao Lee's in Chinatown.

12–7 Shinchimachi. ✆ **095-820-3717.** Main dishes ¥390–¥1,250; set meals ¥1,200–¥1,600. Daily 11:30am–3pm and 5–9:30pm. Streetcar: Shinchi Chinatown (3 min.).

Miraizaka (ミライザカ 長崎駅前) ♥♥ IZAKAYA A good place to get your evening going near Nagasaki Station, this lively izakaya serves fried chicken, grilled meat skewers, noodle bowls, fish grilled or raw, gyoza, and sides like tofu, *tsukemono* (Japanese pickles), quail eggs, and edamame. All dishes are cheap, and beer is ¥299 a glass, highballs ¥199. There's another branch in **Shianbashi** at 14–21 Dozamachi (✆ **050-2019-7266**). 9–30 Daikokumachi. ✆ **050-2019-7205.** Dishes ¥299–¥999. Mon–Thurs 5pm–1am; Fri 4pm–2am; Sat 2pm–2am; Sun 2pm–1am. Station: Nagasaki (3 min.).

UNZEN SPA ♥♥

66km (41 miles) SE of Nagasaki

Thanks to its high altitude, cool mountain air, great scenery, and hot sulfur springs, this small resort town in the pine-covered hills of the Shimabara Peninsula became popular in the 1890s as a summer resort for American and European visitors, who came from as far away as Shanghai, Hong Kong, Harbin, and Singapore to escape the oppressively humid summers. They arrived in Unzen by bamboo palanquin from Obama, 11km (6¾ miles) away. In 1911, Unzen became the first prefectural park in Japan; in 1934, the area became **Unzen-Amakusa National Park ♥♥**, one of the nation's first national parks; it covers 282 sq. km (113 sq. miles).

Unzen Spa is small and navigable, consisting basically of just a few streets with hotels and *ryokan* spread along them, a welcome relief if you've been spending hectic weeks rushing through big cities and catching buses and trains. Hiking paths wind into the tree-covered hills, and dense clouds of steam arise from solfataras (vents) and fumaroles, evidence of volcanic activity. For visitors, the best result of all that thermal activity is the abundance of hot springs: Unzen's name derives from "*Onsen*," meaning "hot spring."

Essentials

ARRIVING The only way to get to Unzen via public transportation is by bus. From Nagasaki, buses depart three times a day from the **Ken-ei Bus Terminal** (✆ **095-826-6221**) across the street from Nagasaki Station. The ride takes about 1 hour and 40 minutes and costs ¥1,850 one-way. You could also take the train from Nagasaki to Isahaya Station, then walk over to the **Shimatetsu Bus Center** (en.shimatetsu.co.jp/bus; ✆ **0957-22-4091**), where you can catch one of 10 buses a day to Unzen at a cost of ¥1,400 for the 75-minute trip. And by the way, both these buses pass through Obama, which sports flags with "I heart Obama" and a cartoon drawing of the former U.S. president.

Most convenient is to rent a car, which will also make it easier to visit Mount Fugen, the most popular excursion from Unzen. The drive from Nagasaki to Unzen takes between 1 hour and 90 minutes. **Times Car Rental** has a branch near Nagasaki Station (timescar-rental.com; ✆ **095-843-5656**), with compact cars from ¥7,700 per day.

VISITOR INFORMATION The **Tourist Information Center** (unzen.org; ✆ **0957-73-3434;** daily 9am–5pm), is in the heart of Unzen Spa across from the police station. Not much English is spoken, but it has a good English-language map of Unzen and the surrounding area and a hiking map. Nearby is the park's **Mount Unzen Visitor Center** (✆ **0957-73-3636;** Fri–Wed 9am–6pm, to 5pm Nov–Mar), with displays and info on the national park and a knowledgeable park ranger who can provide hiking information. You'll also find info on buses and road closures pinned to noticeboards.

GETTING AROUND Buses stop at the Mount Unzen Visitor Center in the center of town and the Shimatetsu Bus Center (which is a little farther out). Unzen is so small you can walk from one end to the other in less than 20 minutes. If you don't have a car and want to visit Mount Fugen, make a reservation for a taxi with **Heisei Kanko Taxi** (✆ **0975-73-2010**), which departs from the Visitor's Center to Nita Pass, about a 20-minute ride.

Exploring Unzen Spa

When the area around Unzen Spa was designated a national park in 1934, it was named after what was thought to be an extinct volcanic chain, collectively called Mount Unzen. In 1990, however, a peak in Mount Unzen—Mount Fugen—erupted for the first time in almost 200 years, killing several dozen people on its eastern slope and leaving behind a huge lava dome. Luckily, Unzen Spa, on the opposite side, was untouched.

On the main street of Unzen are a finger spa and two foot spas, where you can soak the appropriate appendages in outdoor baths for free. If you'd like to get more than your feet wet (though all accommodations below offer hot-spring baths), the **Yunosato Public Spa** (303–1 Obamacho; ✆ **080-5286-2576;** Wed–Mon 9am–10pm) and **Chocotto Yokayu**

Sulphurous steam rises amidst craggy boulders from the hot springs of Unzen Spa's Jigoku area, otherwise known as The Hells.

HIKING THE panoramic peak OF MOUNT FUGEN

About a 20-minute drive northeast of Unzen Spa, up the twists and turns of National Road 389, **Nita Pass** is the gateway to Mount Fugen. A 3-minute ride on the ropeway here (¥1,500 round-trip, ¥700 children) takes you up to **Mount Myoken,** which at 1,333m (4,399 ft.) offers spectacular views of the volcanic peninsula on which Unzen sits. From there you can walk another hour or so along a marked path leading starkly uphill to the summit of **Mount Fugen ♥♥**, once Unzen's highest peak at 1,359m (4,485 ft.) above sea level—this is the peak that erupted in 1990. On a clear day, you'll be rewarded with splendid views of other volcanic peaks as far away as Mount Aso in the middle of Kyushu, as well as the lava dome Mount Heisei Shinzan, born during Mount Fugen's last eruption; it's now Unzen's loftiest peak at 1,483m (4,894 ft.). Allow at least 2 hours for the hike to Mount Fugen and back.

Of course, if you want to do some real hiking, start at Ikenohara Park, about 5 minutes from town on Route 389. From here, a trail of stony steps leads through the forest to Nita Pass. Instead of riding the ropeway at Nita Pass, take the path on your left before the ropeway station to reach the top of Mount Myoken (where the ropeway terminates), then follow it on to Mount Fugen. A round-trip from Ikenohara to the summit of Fugen could take between 3 and 5 hours, depending on your hiking ability and accounting for lunch or rest stops. ***Note:*** There's nowhere to buy food or water on the trail, so make sure you bring provisions. The **Yamazaki Daily Store** on Unzen Spa's main street sells fruit, drinks, dry snacks, and a limited number of rice balls and sandwiches.

Public Spa (299–37 Obamacho; ✆ **0957-73-2004;** Thurs–Tues 10am–8pm) both have small indoor bath facilities.

Konohanasakuya-Hime Jinja ♥, a hillside shrine established 300 years ago above the Gensei-Numa Marsh on the edge of Unzen Spa, is the perfect endpoint for a gentle hike. The shrine is dedicated to the deity of flowers, where people come to pray for fertility, safe childbirth, and family harmony. What that means is you'll see two unmistakable statues of—well, you'll just have to see for yourself. Benches provide views over Unzen to Mount Myoken and the ropeway.

The Hells (Jigoku) ♥♥ NATURAL ATTRACTION Unzen Spa literally bubbles with activity, as sulfurous hot springs erupt into surface cauldrons of scalding water in an area known as the Hells (Jigoku). Indeed, in the 1600s, these cauldrons were used for hellish punishment, as some 30 Christians were boiled alive here after Christianity was outlawed in Japan. (A simple cross erected on stones serves as a memorial to these martyrs.) Today, Unzen Spa has more than 30 solfataras and fumaroles, with the Hells providing the most geothermal activity, making this spot Unzen's number-one attraction. It's a favorite hangout of huge black ravens. Through the centuries the barren land has been baked a chalky white, and sulfur vapors rise thickly to veil pine trees on surrounding hills.

Where to Stay in Unzen Spa

As with most resort areas in Japan, Unzen tends to be crowded and sometimes even fully booked during Golden Week and New Year's, and from mid-July to August. The best times of year are late April to June, when Unzen's famous azalea bushes are in glorious bloom, and late October and early November, when the maple leaves turn brilliant reds. All the *ryokan* and hotels listed here are on the main street running through town.

Kyushu Hotel ♥♥♥ Originally built in 1917, this is a lovely old-style *ryokan* with modern touches added during a 2018 refurbishment. Pluses include gracious and accommodating staff and fusion cuisine served in the dining hall that successfully blends Western and Japanese styles. Best of all, the Kyushu Hotel offers some of the most scenic views in town; many of its rooms look towards the hills as well as the Hells. All rooms are Japanese-Western style with tatami areas and alcoves with chairs next to large windows, affording relaxing places to take in the view. The communal baths are spacious and inviting with both indoor and outdoor bathing, but if you don't care to bathe with everyone, all rooms are equipped with their own hot-spring baths.

320 Obamacho. kyushuhtl.co.jp. ✆ **0957-73-3234.** 38 units. ¥30,000–¥70,000 double. Rates include 2 meals. **Amenities:** 2 restaurants; bar; rooftop lounge; indoor/outdoor hot-spring baths; free Wi-Fi.

Miyazaki Ryokan ♥♥ One of the largest Japanese inns in Unzen, this modern *ryokan* first opened more than 90 years ago and overlooks a beautiful, gracefully manicured garden with hills and sulfur vapors rising in the background—absolutely exquisite when the azaleas are in bloom. Upon arrival, you'll be served green tea and sweets by women in kimono. Afterward, you'll want to ease into the large marble hot-spring bath overlooking a rock-lined outdoor bath, separated for men and women. Or, if you're shy about bathing with others or want to make it a family affair, make a reservation (¥3,300 for 50 min.) for the private family bath. Japanese-style breakfast and *kaiseki*-fusion dinner are served in the Miyama Dining hall overlooking the garden. Rooms are combination Japanese-Western-style, some also equipped with semi-open-air baths. Rates are the same regardless of which direction the rooms face, so try to get one that looks out over the garden.

320–1 Obamacho. miyazaki-ryokan.co.jp. ✆ **0957-73-3331.** 96 units. ¥60,000–¥70,000 double. Rates include 2 meals. **Amenities:** Lounge; restaurant; indoor/outdoor hot-spring baths; sauna; free Wi-Fi.

Unzen Kanko Hotel ♥♥♥ If you're the least bit romantic, you won't be able to resist staying at this old-fashioned mountain lodge, built in 1935 of stone and wood, covered in ivy, and resembling a Swiss chalet. No wonder it's been designated an Important Tangible Cultural Heritage Site. The lobby, main dining hall, and public spaces have changed little over the decades, with whitewashed walls, dark-beamed ceilings, and

The Swiss chalet look of the Unzen Kanko Hotel reflects how popular this spa town has long been with American and European visitors.

inviting sofas and chairs. The rooms are rustic and old-fashioned, too, with heavy ceiling-to-floor curtains tied back to reveal a balcony (ask for a room facing the front), brass doorsills, a high ceiling, and wooden beams, along with modern additions such as duvet-covered beds.

320 Obamacho. unzenkankohotel.com. ✆ **0957-73-3263.** 48 units. ¥30,000–¥60,000 single or double. Rates include meals. **Amenities:** Restaurant; bar; lounge; billiard room; hot-spring baths; library; free Wi-Fi.

Yukai Resort Unzen Toyokan ♥♥ I have a soft spot for these kinds of properties; large postwar *ryokan* hotels with grand lobbies, *meibutsu* (local specialty) stores, bathhouses, games areas, karaoke rooms, and a selection of *yukata* for guests to slip into until their check-out time a couple days hence. Like many of its ilk, this place grew to accommodate the growing thirst for travel during Japan's economic revival years, so if its decor feels dated, try to think of it as retro charm. The rooms, most facing the mountains to the west and Oshidorino "Pond" (really, it's a lake), mix traditional Japanese elements like sliding doors, tatami, and futons with Western additions, such as vanity mirrors, armchairs, and balconies. For those averse to sleeping on the floor, rooms with Western beds are also available. The bathrooms, with their deep tiled tubs, are really in need of some upkeep, and you will have to contend with occasional creaking and rattling noises which have no obvious source. The property has two bathhouses, one on the rooftop with views of the lake and surrounding countryside, the other a large steamy indoor facility that alternates between men (3pm–midnight) and women (2am–10am).

128 Obamacho. ooedoonsen.jp/unzen-toyokan/. ✆ **050-3615-3456.** 149 units. ¥15,000–¥25,000 per person. Some rates include 2 meals. **Amenities:** Hot-spring baths; karaoke and games rooms; manga library; free Wi-Fi.

Where to Eat in Unzen Spa

Food options in Unzen are limited, so consider booking meals as part of your hotel plan (all those listed above offer this option). Even if you don't stay at the **Unzen Kanko Hotel** (p. 560), you may want to have lunch in its old-fashioned dining hall, with a high ceiling, wainscoting, wooden floors, white tablecloths, and flowers on each table. It serves both Japanese and Western selections daily from noon to 2pm and for dinner starting at 6pm, with last orders taken at 7pm.

Izakaya Yuuchan (居酒屋 祐ちゃん) ♥♥ IZAKAYA Just off the main street, this is one of the liveliest restaurants in town, by Unzen's typically sleepy standards, where you'll find locals at the counter on most nights engaging the staff in boisterous conversation. Take a seat among them or head to one of the booths, one of which is inset with a hotplate for making *okonomiyaki* (savory pancakes). The Japanese-only menu offers fare you'd find in izakaya across the country: grilled meat skewers, boiled and fried gyoza, deep-fried tofu and fish, fried potatoes, and noodle and rice dishes, like ramen and *ochazuke* (rice with seaweed and fish with green tea poured on top). A few different tipples are available, too; a flask of sake, hot or cold, cost only ¥600.

327 Obamacho. ✆ **0957-73-3575.** Dinner and drinks ¥3,000–¥5,000. Daily 7pm–midnight.

Wachaku Kiku (喜久) ♥ JAPANESE VARIED The old women who run this threadbare restaurant don't speak a lick of English, but they're perfectly sweet, dishing out Japanese classics like *omurice* (an omelet wrapped around a mound of flavored rice), pork cutlet sets, rice bowls, udon, gyoza, and *champon* (noodles, broth, and stir-fried veg and pork) with customary smiles and politeness. You'll be served tea hot or cold on arrival; if you want a stiffer drink to accompany your meal, pick one from the fridge near the doorway, stocked with beer and other beverages. There is no English menu, but there is a glass cabinet with plastic recreations of the food built into the exterior wall. Take a photo and show them what you want if communication is proving difficult.

323 Obamacho. ✆ **0957-73-3555.** Main dishes ¥400–¥850, set meals ¥850–¥1,000. Daily 9:30am–8:30pm.

KAGOSHIMA ♥♥

1,483km (927 miles) SW of Tokyo; 315km (197 miles) S of Fukuoka

With a population of 580,000 residents, the capital of Kagoshima Prefecture is a city of palm trees, flowering trees and bushes, wide avenues, and people who are like the weather—warm, mild-tempered, and easygoing. The city spreads along Kinko Bay with one of the world's most unusual coastal vistas: Sakurajima, an active volcano, rising from the waters and puffing volcanic smoke into the atmosphere all day long. During summer vacation (July 21–Aug), there are nightly fireworks displays over the bay.

THE INDEPENDENT SPIRIT OF kagoshima

Relatively isolated at the southern tip of Japan, far from the capitals of Kyoto and Tokyo, through the centuries Kagoshima developed an independent spirit that fostered a number of great men and accomplishments. Foremost is the **Shimadzu clan** (also spelled Shimazu), a remarkable family that for 29 generations—almost 700 years—ruled over Kagoshima and its vicinity (Satsuma and Osami provinces, as they were then known) before the Meiji Restoration in 1868. Much of Japan's early contact with the outside world was via Kagoshima, first with China and then with the Western world. Japan's first contact with Christianity occurred in Kagoshima when **St. Francis Xavier** landed here in 1549; although he stayed only 10 months, he converted more than 600 Japanese to Christianity. Kagoshima is also where firearms were introduced to Japan.

By the mid–19th century, as the Tokugawa shogunate began losing strength and the confidence of the people, the Shimadzu family was already looking toward the future. In the mid-1850s, they built the **first Western-style factory** in the country (see p. 568), employing 200 men to make cannons, glass, ceramics, land mines, ships, and farming tools. In 1865, while Japan's doors were still officially closed to the outside world, the Shimadzu family smuggled 19 young men to Britain to learn foreign languages and technology. After returning to Japan, they became a driving force in the Meiji Restoration and Japan's modernization.

Kagoshima is also home to Sengan-en Garden, one of the grandest old gardens in south Japan.

Kagoshima is a fun city to explore, whether drinking *shochu* (most locals' favorite spirit) and eating black pork in a lively izakaya or visiting monuments to the city's rebellious history (see "The Independent Spirit of Kagoshima," above). It's also the entryway to Yakushima (p. 572), a subtropical island off Kyushu's southern tip that offers a peek into the mysteries of pre-civilization Japan.

Essentials

ARRIVING You can reach **Kagoshima Airport** from Tokyo in around 2 hours. Flights from budget airlines Solaseed and Jetstar cost ¥6,000 to ¥12,000; flights with JAL and ANA are ¥15,000 to ¥25,000. The airport is linked to Kagoshima Chuo Station in 45 minutes by limousine bus, which departs every 10–15 minutes and costs ¥1,400. While Kyushu isn't that well connected by train, you can get to Kagoshima by **Shinkansen train** from Tokyo, changing at Hakata Station in Fukuoka (6½–7½ hr.), or taking a Shinkansen directly to Kagoshima from Okayama or Shin-Osaka stations (4–4½ hr.). Tickets cost around ¥30,000, varying a little depending on the route you choose. If coming directly from Fukuoka (Hakata Station), the train trip takes 1½ hours and costs ¥10,110 for an unreserved seat. All trains travel to Kagoshima Chuo (Central) Station. **Buses** connect Kyushu's cities more cheaply than the train. From Fukuoka's Tenjin

Station, the 4- to 5-hour trip costs around ¥5,000. See **willer-travel.com** (✆ **050-5805-0383**) for timetables and reservations.

VISITOR INFORMATION In Kagoshima, there's a Tourist Information Center at **Kagoshima Chuo Station** (✆ **099-253-2500;** daily 8am–7pm) near the East Exit, as well as at the airport (✆ **0995-58-4686;** daily 7:30am–arrival of last flight). More information is available at **kagoshima-kankou.com/for** and **kagoshima-yokanavi.jp/en**.

CITY LAYOUT Downtown Kagoshima lies between Kagoshima Chuo Station, with its adjacent Amu Plaza (a shopping, restaurant, and recreation complex—you'll see the Ferris wheel on top), and Kinko Bay, northeast of the station. **Tenmonkan-Dori** (a covered shopping street) serves as the heart of the city.

GETTING AROUND You can walk from the station to downtown in about 20 minutes, but the city is easy to get around by **streetcar** and **bus.** There are two streetcar lines (fare ¥170), as well as two types of buses—City View buses and Kagoshima City buses. **Kagoshima City buses** are regular buses used for commuter travel by local residents, while **City View buses** are geared toward tourists. Running every 30 minutes from 8:30am to 6:50pm daily, City View buses look like old-time streetcars, have English-language announcements, and travel a 14km (9-mile) circuit through the city, beginning at Kagoshima Chuo Station. They stop at all tourist sights, including Sengan-en, Sakurajima Ferry Terminal, and Kagoshima Aquarium. The fare is ¥230, ¥120 for children; you pay when you get off. Day passes cost ¥600 for adults, ¥300 children. If you plan on being very mobile, you may want to purchase a **CUTE Pass,** which allows unlimited travel on City View buses, commuter buses, and streetcars, the Sakurajima Ferry, and the Sakurajima Island View buses. A 1-day CUTE Pass is ¥1,300 adults, ¥650 children; 2-day passes cost ¥1,900 yen and ¥950 yen, respectively. Passes can be purchased at the Tourist Information Center in Kagoshima Chuo Station and aboard buses and streetcars.

Exploring Kagoshima

Kagoshima City Museum of Art (Kagoshima Shiritsu Bijutsukan) ♥ MUSEUM Only a few minutes' walk away from the Prefectural Museum (see below), this city museum holds a collection of Western-style works by artists from Kagoshima Prefecture. Look for the portrait of Saigo Takamori ("Local Hero: Saigo Takamori," p. 565), painted by Masayoshi Tokonomi, to the left upon entering the permanent gallery. A small selection of paintings by Western artists is also displayed (Pissarro, Monet, Renoir, Matisse, Kandinsky, Picasso, Warhol), as well as decorative art including the famous Satsuma pottery and cut glass. You can see everything in about 20 minutes.

4–36 Shiroyma-cho. ✆ **099-224-3400.** ¥300 adults, ¥200 college and high-school students, ¥150 children. Tues–Sun 9:30am–6pm. City View stop: Statue of Saigo Takamori (5 min.). Streetcar: Asahidori (5 min.).

LOCAL HERO: saigo takamori

Born in Kagoshima Prefecture, Saigo Takamori was a philosopher, scholar, educator, and poet who played a major role in helping restore Emperor Meiji to power in 1868. But because he was also a samurai, he became disillusioned when the ancient rights of the samurai class were rescinded and the wearing of swords was forbidden. In 1877 he led a force of samurai against the government in what is called the Seinan Rebellion. After they were defeated, he withdrew to Shiroyama in Kagoshima, where he committed suicide. Today, Saigo has many fans who still visit the cave on Shiroyama Hill where he committed suicide.

Kagoshima Prefectural Museum of Culture (Reimeikan) ♥ MUSEUM Tracing the history of the people of Kagoshima over the last 30,000 years, the museum occupies the former site of Tsurumaru Castle, of which only the stone ramparts and moat remain. Among the stories it covers are the rise of the Shimadzu clan in the 11th century and Kagoshima's preeminence as a pottery center after Korean potters were brought here in the late 1500s. There are models of an 18th-century samurai settlement, Tsurumaru Castle, and, best of all, Tenmonkan-Dori as it might have looked 80 years ago. The second floor is devoted to folklore and everyday life. The third floor shows Satsuma swords, pottery, scrolls, and paintings and has a hands-on learning room for children with old-fashioned toys and samurai outfits that can be tried on.

7–2 Shiroyama-cho. ✆ **099-222-5100.** ¥420 adults, ¥260 college and high-school students, ¥160 children. Tues–Sun 9am–6pm; closed 25th of month unless it's Sat or Sun. City View stop: Statue of Saigo Takamori (3 min.). Streetcar: Asahidori (8 min.).

Mount Sakurajima ♥♥ NATURAL ATTRACTION/HIKE With ties to Naples, Italy, as its sister city, Kagoshima bills itself the "Naples of the Orient." That's perhaps stretching things a bit, but Kagoshima is balmy most of the year and even has its own Mount Vesuvius: Mount Sakurajima, an active volcano across Kinko Bay that has erupted 30 times through recorded history and continues to puff smoke into the sky and occasionally cover the city with fine soot and ash. In 1914, Sakurajima had a whopper of an eruption and belched up 3 billion tons of lava. When the eruption was over, the townspeople were surprised to discover that the flow was so great it now blocked the channel separating the volcano from a neighboring peninsula; Sakurajima, which had once been an island, was now part of the mainland.

Magnificent from far away and even more impressive from observation areas near the crater, Sakurajima can be visited by a 15-minute **ferry** ride, which departs from the Sakurajima Ferry Terminal. (See ferry information below.) Upon reaching Sakurajima, stop off at the small tourist counter by the ferry pier for a map of the area. The **Nagisa Lava Trail** is a 3km (1¾-mile) trail that begins near the ferry pier and travels through

Rising dramatically over Kinko Bay, Mount Sakurajima still puffs smoke into the skies over Kagoshima.

the lava fields, past huge lava boulders and pine trees (many, unfortunately, dying of disease). At the **Sakurajima Visitor Center** (✆ **099-293-2443**), a 5-minute walk from the ferry pier, you can find displays relating the history and natural history of Sakurajima; from here, longer trails lead past stone monuments to Kagoshima's past and pine trees sprouted from the volcanic soil, ending at the **Karasujima Observation Point.** Sakurajima has only limited public transportation, so joining a tour can be a smart move. On weekends, E-bike tours, conducted by **Volcano Life Journey** and led by experienced guides, take visitors on an 8km (5-mile) journey that covers 360m (1,181 ft.) of elevation and enters a usually off-limits zone, 2km (1¼ miles) from the Sakurajima crater. Tours cost ¥22,000 per person; participants must be at least 12 years old. Book at least 2 days in advance through the Sakurajima Museum Office (✆ **099-245-2550**) or email r.oshikawa@sakurajima.gr.jp.

Mount Sakurajima's Produce

Mount Sakurajima's rich soil grows the world's largest radishes, averaging about 17 kilograms (37 lb.) but sometimes weighing in at as much as 36 kilograms (80 lb.), and the world's smallest oranges, only 3 centimeters (1¼ in.) in diameter.

Sakurajima Ferry: ¥250 adults, ¥130 children. Ferries run 24/7, every 10–15 min. daytimes, hourly through the night. Terminal is 2-min. walk from Kagoshima Suizokukan-mae/Sakurajima-sanbashi City View bus stop, or 8-min. walk from downtown Kagoshima or Shiyakusho-mae streetcar stop.

Nagashima Museum ♥♥ MUSEUM Sitting on a hill high atop the city, with excellent views of Sakurajima and Kagoshima, this splendid private museum focuses mostly on works by such Kagoshima artists as Kuroda Seiki, but it also contains works by well-known Western artists such as Picasso, Braque, Kandinsky, Renoir, and Chagall, as well as pottery from South America. Most impressive is an outstanding collection of mainly 19th-century white Satsuma pottery, including many pieces that were originally imported to London, Paris, and New York, and the more utilitarian 17th- to 20th-century black Satsuma pottery.

3–42–18 Take. ngp.jp/nagashima-museum. ✆ **099-250-5400.** ¥1,000 adults, ¥800 college and high-school students, ¥400 children. Wed–Mon 9am–5pm. Taxi: 7-min. ride from Kagoshima Chuo Station.

Sengan-en Garden ♥♥♥ GARDEN Whereas Sakurajima, rising dramatically out of the bay, is Kagoshima's best-known landmark, Sengan-en is its most widely visited attraction. The grounds of a countryside villa, it's a garden laid out more than 300 years ago by the Shimadzu clan, incorporating Sakurajima and Kinko Bay into its design scheme in a principle known as *shakkei,* or "borrowed scenery." There's a lovely grove of bamboo, a waterfall located a 30-minute walk up a nature trail with good views over the bay, and the requisite pond. It's Japan's only garden with its original *kyokusui* (poem-composing garden) still intact, an idyllic spot where the 21st lord of the Shimadzu family held famous poem-composing garden parties. Guests seated themselves on stones beside a gently meandering rivulet and were requested to have completed a poem by the time a cup filled with sake came drifting by on the tiny brook. Ah, those were the days!

The good life is also present in the **Iso Residence,** which was built as a villa by the Shimadzu clan about 350 years ago and became the family's

Intricate floral displays in Sengan-en Garden, laid out more than 3 centuries ago for what was then home of Kagoshima's ruling family.

main residence when the Meiji Restoration made feudal lords obsolete. You'll see 11 of the villa's 25 rooms, including a bedroom, a bathroom, a dressing room, living quarters, and reception rooms; throughout are furnishings and artifacts that once belonged to the Shimadzu clan.

After visiting the garden, head to the **Shoko Shuseikan Museum,** located next to the garden and included in the admission. Built in the mid-1850s as Japan's first industrial factory, it houses items relating to the 800-year history of the Shimadzu clan, including family heirlooms ranging from lacquerware to tea-ceremony objects, palanquins used to carry Shimadzu lords back and forth to Edo (present-day Tokyo; the trip from Kagoshima took 40–60 days), everyday items used by the family, and photographs. An exhibit explores southern Kyushu's role in maritime trade and the Shuseikan factory's manufacture of cannons, textiles, and other products. In all, you'll probably spend at least 2 hours seeing everything, especially if you stop off at souvenir shops selling Satsuma glassware, pongee silk, and other Kagoshima products.

9700–1 Yoshino-cho. senganen.jp. ✆ **099-247-1551.** ¥1,600 adults, ¥800 children. Daily 9am–5pm; closed for Kagoshima Marathon 1st Sun in Mar. City View bus: Sen-gan-en-mae stop (40 min. from Kagoshima Chuo Station).

Where to Stay in Kagoshima

In addition to the choices here, there are several **Toyoko Inns** (toyoko-inn.com) and **APA Hotels** (apahotel.com) in town that are well maintained and reasonably priced (that is, rooms for ¥10,000 or less).

Art Hotel Kagoshima ♥♥ This medium-priced hotel is in a newer area of Kagoshima, smack-dab on the waterfront with a good view of the volcano, even from its lobby lounge. Its twins and doubles face the water with balconies—great for watching the sunrise over Sakurajima. Outdoor pools, including a children's pool, and connecting rooms make this a good bet for families. The outdoor hot-spring pool and Jacuzzi (you wear your bathing suit here) are open year-round free to hotel guests. The main disadvantage is that it's a 15-minute bus ride from the station and downtown.

22–1 Kamoike Shinmachi. art-kagoshima.com. ✆ **099-257-2411.** 208 units. ¥5,000–¥40,000 double. Bus: 146 from Kagoshima Chuo Station to Sea Fishing Park (5 min.). **Amenities:** 3 restaurants; bar; outdoor pools; hot-spring bath; Jacuzzi; room service; free Wi-Fi.

Gasthof Hotel ♥ After traveling to Europe, the owner of the founder of this hotel decided to re-create the coziness of a German bed-and-breakfast with a cafe in the lobby, antiques in the hallway, and rooms that vary in decor, furniture, and bedspreads, including four-poster beds in some. Although it falls short, the Gasthof has a lot more character than a regular business hotel and has a convenient location near Kagoshima Chuo Station. Another plus is the Japanese restaurant and an *izakaya* (Japanese pub-diner) in the same building.

7–1 Chuo-cho. ✆ **099-252-1401.** 38 units. ¥5,000–¥15,000 single or double. Station: Kagoshima Chuo (3 min.). **Amenities:** 2 restaurants/bars; free Wi-Fi.

Nakazono Ryokan ♥ A member of the Japanese Inn Group, this simple laid-back *ryokan* has tatami-style rooms and the atmosphere of an old Japanese home, with sliding doors and simple artworks hanging in alcoves. It is located near Kagoshima Station (not to be confused with Kagoshima Chuo Station), about a 10-minute walk from the Tenmonkan-Dori covered shopping street and a 3-minute walk from the Sakurajima ferry pier. Its English-speaking owner is knowledgeable about area sightseeing and has prepared handouts on how to get to nearby towns such as Ibusuki and Chiran. No meals are served, but there's a communal refrigerator, and the staff will direct you to nearby restaurants. ***Note:*** Bookings are now made through Airbnb.

1–18 Yasui-cho. ✆ **099-226-5125.** 10 units w/ shared bath. ¥5,000–¥10,000 per person. Streetcar: Shiyakusho-mae (3 min.). **Amenities:** Free Wi-Fi.

Richmond Hotel Kagoshima Kinseicho ♥ Located in the heart of downtown, this business hotel has easy access from Kagoshima Chuo Station via streetcar passing right outside the front door. Check-in and check-out is accomplished via automatic machines, though humans (sometimes wearing flowery shirts in summer, a nod to the city's laidback atmosphere) are on hand to help guide you through the process. Otherwise, this is your run-of-the-mill business hotel with small clean rooms furnished with the standard toiletries and loungewear. In any case, you're paying for location. Note that the cheapest singles and doubles are actually the same room, fine for one person but cramped for two.

5–3 Kinseicho. richmondhotel.jp/kagoshima. ✆ **099-219-6655.** 220 units. ¥5,000–¥12,000 single; ¥10,000–¥25,000 double. Streetcar: Asahidori (1 min.). **Amenities:** Restaurant; free Wi-Fi.

Shiroyama Hotel ♥♥ Kagoshima's foremost hotel sits high atop tree-covered Shiroyama Hill, commanding a sweeping view of the city below and Sakurajima across the bay. Opened more than 60 years ago, it offers updated, comfortable rooms; the most recommended (and more expensive) ones face the volcano and city with the best views in town. Other pluses include hot-spring (including open-air) baths with views of Kinko Bay, an ion sauna using steam pumped from deep below the surface, and good restaurants that take advantage of the hotel's views and gardenlike setting. There's also a microbrewery, the Shiroyama Brewery, that infuses its beers with local flavors, like Sakurajima oranges and loquat leaves, and a Satsuma *kiriko* (cut-glass) boutique, displaying colorful and intricately detailed glassware. In short, this is a great respite from city life, and to offset its main drawback—a location far from the city center—it offers free regular shuttle buses to Kagoshima Chuo Station and Tenmonkan-Dori in the heart of the city.

41–1 Shinshoin-cho. shiroyama-g.co.jp. ✆ **099-224-2211.** 355 units. ¥20,000–¥60,000 double. Taxi or free shuttle bus 12 min. from Kagoshima Chuo Station. City View Bus: Shiroyama (1 min.). **Amenities:** 11 restaurants; lounge; 2 bars; outdoor/indoor hot-spring baths; room service; sauna; free Wi-Fi.

Where to Eat in Kagoshima

While in Kagoshima, be sure to try its local dishes, known as ***Satsuma ryori*** (Satsuma was the original name of the Kagoshima area). This style of cooking supposedly has its origins in food cooked on battlefields centuries ago; if that's the case, it certainly has improved greatly since then. Popular Satsuma specialties include ***Satsuma-age*** (ground fish mixed with tofu and sake and then deep-fried), ***tonkotsu*** (black pork boiled for several hours in miso, *shochu,* and brown sugar—absolutely delicious), ***sakezushi*** (a rice dish flavored with sake and mixed with vegetables and seafood), and ***Satsuma-jiru*** (miso soup with chicken and locally grown vegetables, including Sakurajima radishes). ***Kibinago*** is a small fish belonging to the herring family that can be caught in the waters around Kagoshima; a silver color with brown stripes, it's often eaten raw and arranged on a dish to resemble a chrysanthemum.

Know Your Shochu

Don't forget to wash your food down with *shochu,* a spirit that's inseparable from Kagoshima's cuisine culture. To be considered *honkaku* (genuine), it must be distilled from one of 53 specified crops; Kagoshima prefecture produces more than 2,000 varieties. Taste varies greatly; the most popular forms in Kagoshima City include *imo shochu,* made from sweet potatoes, and *kokuto,* made from brown sugar grown in the nearby Amami Islands. While it may take some time to grow on you, the flavor is somewhere between vodka and whiskey.

Ajimori ♥♥♥ BLACK PORK This near-50-year-old establishment specializes in pork from small black pigs, which the locals claim is more tender and succulent than regular pork. The restaurant is divided into two parts: The upper floors, with both table seating and private *tatami* rooms, serve *Satsuma Kuroshabu,* a Kagoshima specialty of black-pork *shabu-shabu;* the first floor is a casual dining room specializing in *tonkatsu,* breaded black-pork cutlet. If you order the Kuroshabu, you'll eat it just like the more common beef shabu-shabu, cooking it yourself at your table by dipping it into a boiling broth and then in raw egg or sauce. Portions are generous, but if you wish, you can also order tonkatsu as a side dish. Otherwise, go to the first floor for perhaps the lightest, best-tasting tonkatsu you'll ever have.

13–21 Sennichi-cho. ✆ **099-224-7634.** Shabu-shabu dinners ¥4,400–¥8,800, lunches ¥1,600–¥4,400. Thurs–Tues 11:30am–2:15pm (1:30pm last order for shabu-shabu) and 5:30–8:45pm (8pm last order for shabu-shabu). Streetcar: Tenmonkan-Dori (3 min.).

Kumasotei ♥♥ SATSUMA RYORI Located in the city center, this restaurant specializes in local Satsuma dishes but carries them one step further by featuring them as part of *kaiseki* set meals. If there isn't a crowd, you'll probably have your own private tatami room; otherwise, you'll

share. Alongside an information sheet explaining the elements of Satsuma ryori, there's an English-language menu with photos of the various set meals, which may include such local dishes as *Satsuma-age, tonkotsu, Satsuma-jiru, kibinago,* or *sakezushi,* as well as *shabu-shabu.* Reservations recommended; you can make one through the website below.
6–10 Higashi Sengoku-cho. kumasotei.com. ✆ **099-222-6356.** Lunches ¥2,200–¥4,400; dinners ¥5,500–¥22,000. Daily 11am–1:30pm and 5:30–9pm (last order). Streetcar: Tenmonkan-Dori (4 min.).

Meli Melo ♥♥♥ ITALIAN This trattoria on a handsome side street will certainly catch your eye, with its cream-colored walls, aging brickwork, and iron-fenced balconies, as though plucked straight from the corner of an Italian piazza. Inside is all wood paneling, colorful paint, ragtag furniture, and stained glass, with character oozing from every inch. The pizzas, most costing around ¥1,500, are superb, too; marinara, margarita, *melanzane,* spicy meat, and Bolognese are some of the flavor profiles you can expect. Salads, pastas, *ajillo,* meat dishes, and desserts, as well as a small selection of Italian wines, are also available.
7–1 Higashisengokucho. instagram.com/trattoria_melimelo/?hl=en. ✆ **099-239-7373.** Pizza ¥1,200–¥2,000. Daily 5pm–1am. Streetcar: Tenmokan-Dori (4 min.). City View Bus: Tenmokan (4 min.).

Onlygne ♥ CAFE & RESTAURANT Pronounced "Onlee Gan," this small, chic cafe and restaurant serves plates of food that are colorful, fresh (mostly), healthy, and full of flavor. The menu is a bit of mixed bag, featuring jambalaya, taco rice, tom yum ramen, paella, and couscous, using local ingredients. It also has a great selection of tea, hot or cold, and spirits. The bar, decorated with illuminated bottles, is where to sit if you're mainly here for drinks; the sofas and tables will be preferable for diners. In any case, the vibe's usually good here in the evenings and it seems to attract a cosmopolitan clientele.
7–19 Higashisengokucho. instagram.com/cafe_onlygne. ✆ **090-8801-4651.** Main dishes around ¥1,000. Daily noon–1am. Streetcar: Tenmokan-Dori (4 min.). City View Bus: Tenmokan (4 min.).

Yokaban ♥♥♥ YAKITORI & SHOCHU The name means "a wonderful night," and this small izakaya on a curving pedestrian street (also jauntily named, "Flamingo-dori") really comes alive after dark. Alongside *yakitori* (chicken skewers) grilled on hot magma rock, the bar is stacked with shochu from local distilleries. The owner, Reina-san, is a lively character and doesn't let a lack of English get in the way of chitchat or making foreign guests feel at home. Don't be surprised if you spend an extra hour or two in here drinking and raconteuring.
17–17 Higashisengokucho. ✆ **099-227-1010.** Dinner and drinks ¥3,000–¥5,000 per person. Tues–Sun 2–11pm. Streetcar: Shiyakusho-mae (8 min.). City View Bus: Kagoshima Suizokukan-mae/Sakurajima-sanbashi (3 min.).

11

YAKUSHIMA ♥♥♥

140km (87 miles) S of Kagoshima

Nothing in Japan has quite stopped me in my tracks like the first time I stepped onto the tarmac at Yakushima Airport. Huge tree-swarmed mountains thrust upwards in the middle of the island, fog spilling over them like liquid nitrogen; I felt an electricity in the air like a storm was looming beyond the hazy horizon, and the dampness that clung to my skin was totally different from the stifling humidity of the mainland cities in summer. Modern Japan and its neon nightscapes and pachinko parlors and all-night karaoke joints and steamy alleyways seemed not just a different place, but a different reality altogether.

Lying 60km (37 miles) adrift off Kyushu's southern tip, Yakushima is part of the volcanic Osumi archipelago. One of the world's most biodiverse islands, it was formed by a combination of sediment accumulation, magma activity, and granite protrusion beginning in the Paleogene Period (66 to 22 million years ago)—but one senses divine intervention may also have played a role.

Most travelers who venture to Yakushima come for nature—to see the forest that inspired Studio Ghibli's fantastical 1997 anime, *Princess Mononoke,* or to hike to Jomon Sugi, a gnarled old tree that is estimated to be close to 7,000 years old. But while Yakushima's landscape is admittedly sublime, coming *only* to commune with nature overlooks the rich cultural heritage and spiritual folklore that is woven into the very fabric of island life. A fabled white deer carrying messages from the gods, blood-sucking sprites and trees with humanlike characteristics, a scheming Confucian scholar who exploited the *yakusugi* timber for commercial benefit, a cave that howls like a conch shell to warn of typhoons—Yakushima is a place of endless stories.

One final note is that Yakushima has experienced a **surge in tourism** over the last decade, to the point that local guides and accommodations now struggle to meet the demand. More importantly, increased tourism may be a threat to the forest biome. One of the major matters of contention is a government-approved plan to build a new runway at the airport to handle larger jet planes, which would increase pollution and noise levels, affecting wildlife habitats. Tourism is vital to the local economy, but visitors must consider how their presence will impact the environment. For this reason, I'd recommend **traveling with a guide,** which can limit environmental damage and turn your travel experience into a education in ecology, myth, philosophy, and history. Yakushima English Services, more commonly known as **YES! Yakushima** (yesyakushima.com), is the premier guide and information service for English-speaking travelers to the island. The staff can also help with accommodation and car rental, or booking other activities like rafting, canyoning, and river walking.

Traveling with a guide is highly recommended when visiting Yakushima Island, as local outfitters know best how to explore its walking trails, carved through the island's extraordinary forest biome.

Essentials

ARRIVING Yakushima's small **airport** receives five JAL flights a day from Kagoshima (40 min.), as well as one flight each from Fukuoka (70 min.) and Osaka (95 min.). These are small planes, so the ride can get bumpy. If you're coming from Kagoshima or Fukuoka, you'll pay ¥15,000 to ¥25,000 one-way; from Osaka, the cost will be closer to ¥30,000. **Hydrofoil ferries** make several runs daily from Kagoshima Port to Yakushima, often with a stop at either Ibusuki on the Kyushu mainland or Tanegashima, another of the Osumi Islands. The 2- to 3-hour trip costs ¥12,200 (¥22,300 round-trip); book through **Tane Yaku Jetfoil** (tykousoku.jp; ✆ **0570-004015**) or at the Kagoshima Ferry Terminal. Yakushima has two main ports: Anbo on the east coast and Miyanoura on the north coast. Miyanoura is the larger of the two towns, but Anbo is closer to most of the accommodation and restaurants recommended below, so know in advance which port your ferry arrives in. There's also an overnight **Hibiscus Ferry** (yakushimaferry.com; ✆ **0997-42-0140**), which leaves Kagoshima's Taniyama Port at 6pm and arrives in Miyanoura the next morning at 7am. This option takes longer but costs less (round-trip ¥7,800), and you can bring a car with you on the ferry for another ¥30,000-plus.

VISITOR INFORMATION You'll find tourist offices in both Miyanoura (**Yakushima Travel Center;** 799 Miyanoura; ✆ **0997-42-0091;** daily 9am–6pm) and Anbo (**Yakushima Anbo Tourist Information;** 187–1 Anbo; ✆ **0997-46-2333;** daily 8:30am–5:15pm). But **yesyakushima.com**

is a better source of information and guidance; **town.yakushima.kagoshima.jp** and **kagoshima-kankou.com** may also come in handy.

GETTING AROUND There are buses on Yakushima, but public transport is limited, so I don't recommend coming here unless you can rent a car or hire a guide service. Car rentals are found at both main ports, all offering similar prices; I tend to use **Navi Rent-a-Car** (yakushima-navi.com; ✆ **0120-894071**) near the airport, because the cars are cheap (starting at ¥6,600 for 24 hr.), they supply good maps and information, and the woman who runs the place is super friendly.

Yakushima has one road circumnavigating the island, with smaller roads and dirt tracks shooting inland, though you'll rarely use these, unless heading to a specific cafe, restaurant, or accommodation. It takes about an hour to get from one side of the island to the other; the whole island can be circled in less than 2 hours. Use a your sat nav or map app to find addresses listed below.

Exploring Yakushima

YAKUSHIMA NATIONAL PARK

With 45 mountains taller than 1,000m (3,280 ft.), **Yakushima National Park**—which covers the entire interior of the island—ranges from low-lying laurel forests, mixed broadleaf and needle trees at medium elevations, and at the highest, windswept zones, broad moors, and dwarf bamboo grasslands where winter temperatures can plunge towards freezing. The park charges an entry fee of ¥500, paid in cash. The three routes which most visitors follow to explore the forest are the **Yakusugi Land Trail,** the **Shiratani Unsuikyo Gorge,** and the **Jomon Sugi** hike. You can attempt these yourself by following trail markers and signs (in Japanese and English), but if you want to gain a deeper understanding of what makes Yakushima tick, there's no substitute for a local guide. More importantly, guides are well attuned to the whims of the forest and can help you avoid getting caught in a landslide or stuck in the mountains during heavy showers. (Unfortunately, it's not unheard of for solo hikers to enter the forest trails in a downpour and never return.) Besides YES! Yakushima (p. 572), other reputable English-language companies offering forest-trekking tours include **Yakushima Experience** (yakushimaexperience.com; ✆ **090-3239-3592**) and **Yakushima Geographic Tour** (yaku-geo.com; ✆ **090-2718-2753**). Also note that it rains *a lot* on Yakushima, so you'll want waterproof clothing and walking shoes with decent grip on the soles. If you don't have these or can't bring them with you, tour companies also rent hiking gear.).

The **Yakusugi Land Trail** ♥♥ is a great introduction to the forest and culture of Yakushima, and is recommended for less confident hikers. A 30-minute drive from Anbo, the tour takes around 2½ hours, though this can be extended to 4 hours if you've got time. Alongside views of Mount Tachudake—topped by a 40m (131-ft.) tall granite monolith called Tenchu

YAKUSHIMA: LAND OF biodiversity

Though it's only 130km (75 miles) in circumference, Yakushima island supports an incredible 600 species of moss and almost 2,000 species of flora, including ancient *yakusugi* trees (also known as *cryptomeria japonica*, or Japanese cedar), many of them well over 1,000 years old. It's often nicknamed the "Alps of the Sea" because its highest peaks rise almost 2,000m (6,562 ft.) in height, yet it's covered in subtropical rainforest. Endemic subspecies of mammals like Yakushima macaques, Yakushima Dsinezumi shrews, and Yakushima deer roam the forest, while more than 150 bird species, 15 reptiles, 8 amphibians, and 1,900 insects also call the island home. In 1993, such biodiversity helped Yakushima gain UNESCO World Heritage status for Natural Beauty.

Yakusugi trees may be the island's most iconic plants, but most travelers end up most impressed by the moss. Thanks to Yakushima's approximately 8,000mm (315 in.) of annual rainfall, moss coats every surface it can cling to: slabs of granite, wooden steps, trail markers, the gnarled bark of *yakusugi* trees, and fallen trunks and branches scattered across the underbrush, making every stretch of forest look like a scene from a Brothers Grimm fable. The moss, however, serves an important function: Because the island's interior is soil-deficient, moss replaces soil as a nutrient-rich platform in which trees can plant their roots. And because moss absorbs water directly from its environment, it can live on a host plant without damaging it. This locks the forest in a virtuous cycle of growth, with moss and trees growing on top of one another, essentially ad infinitum.

Rock, an otherworldly structure that has been a site of pilgrimage for centuries—you'll visit several venerable *yakusugi* trees with names like Old Longbeard, the Buddha, and the Mother and Child, as well as impressive hemlock and fir trees. Some of the most memorable parts of the hike are river crossings by way of suspension bridges, where the water emits a thunderous roar after heavy rainfall.

The **Shiratani Unsuikyo Gorge** ♥♥♥ is the most popular forest trail, a mildly challenging hike of 6km (3.7 miles) with around 450m (1,476 ft.) of elevation. You'll climb through fog and folklore to a bulbous granite boulder called the *Taiko Iwa* ("Drum Rock") looking down on the river valley below. On the way you'll pass the stretch of moss forest said to have inspired *Princess Mononoke* and a windy path flanked by hanging vines and fruiting camellia trees, where macaques tend to cavort in the warmer months. An alternative course, called the *genseirin* ("primeval forest") route, goes through a quiet expanse of moss forest carved up by small rivers and home to famous trees like *Sanbonashi-sugi* (the "Three-Legged Cedar"). Which route you walk depends on weather conditions and your own preferences.

The **Jomon Sugi** ♥♥♥ trail is a long 22km (13.7-mile) round-trip hike, taking approximately 10 hours with a lot of altitude gain; it's recommended for hikers who are in good physical condition. Its endpoint, deep in the interior of the island, is the Jomon Sugi, believed to be Japan's oldest tree. Some argue it's as much as 7,000 years old, while more conservative

Moss seems to drape every available surface in the forest of the Shiratani Unsuikyo Gorge.

estimates suggest it's closer to 2,200 years old. Either way, it has seen a lot—the rise and fall of the Roman Empire, the Golden Age of Japan, Genghis Khan and his Mongol hordes, the invention of electricity, the first atomic bombs—all the while growing in solemn isolation. The tree was "rediscovered" in 1966 by an amateur hiker and civil servant. Other sites of interest on the trail include an old lumber-ferrying railway line built 100 years ago; the abandoned village of Kosugidani; a 2,000-year-old fallen *yakusugi* tree, now home to a new generation of moss and plant life; and the huge Wilson Stump, cut down around the late 16th century and famed for its heart-shaped opening facing the sky. The trail culminates at viewing platforms around 15m (50 ft.) from the Jomon Sugi, which can get busy during the main tourism season from March to mid-December.

A COASTAL ROAD TRIP

Tracing the island's perimeter, Yakushima's costal drive takes in a range of scenery: the misty mountains in the heart of the island, the Anbo and Miyanoura Rivers carving through steep-sided valleys, rockpools on the south and west coasts, or islands like Mishima, Kuchinoerabu, and Tanegashima, lying somewhere beyond the fog. If you're moving leisurely—and really, why wouldn't you be?—a drive around the island with stops for swimming, trekking, bathing, or eating could easily eat up most of the day.

Starting in the east, somewhere around Anbo, and traveling clockwise, one of the first points of interest is the **Sarukawa Banyan Tree,** a 10-minute drive from Anbo Port. A tangled mess of roots, branches, vines, and foliage, it looks more like an entire ecosystem than a single organism, covering an area of around 100 sq. m (1,076 sq. ft.). A little further along the coast road you'll pass over the Taino River, after which you can take a winding road on your right leading to the **Mocchomudake Trailhead.**

From here, walk down a short steep path to the **Senpiro Falls Observation Deck** to see ta lovely waterfall cascading down a 60m (197-ft.) cliff. The waterfall was named after an old unit of measurement—one *hiro* is equal to the length of a reaching arm; *senpiro* means "one thousand reaching arms."

Your next stop along the coastal road is **Hirauchi Kaichu Onsen,** about 25 minutes away on the tip of the south coast. This hot spring, steaming in naturally formed rock pools overlooking the craggy shoreline, is a boon for weary hikers. Throw ¥300 into the honesty box, then sink into one of the mixed-sex hot baths. Women are permitted to wear some form of clothing or cover up using a towel, though older Japanese men may grumble at males who try to enter the water with trunks or underwear on—using a small modesty towel, however, is deemed okay. In any case, it rarely gets busy here; you might have the baths all to yourself.

On the west coast, you'll find more waterfalls, V-shaped valleys, tracts of protected forest, and the World Heritage Coastal Road (note that it's often closed in inclement weather). This is a good place to spot Yakushima macaques and deer, as well as avian species like kites, kestrels, and falcons. At the northern end of the road is the **Yakushima Todai Lighthouse,** where there's a small shrine to Ebisu, the god of fishermen and fortune, and epic views across the sea towards Kuchinoerabu Island. If the weather is decent (never a guarantee on this drizzly little island), go for a swim at **Inakahama Beach.** (Though all sorts of flotsam and jetsam wash up here during winter, authorities try to keep it clean during the main tourism season.) While here, you might consider eating some satiny white tofu at **Shiba Tofu Shop** (a 4-min. drive or 20-min. walk from the beach; see p. 580) or catching the last rays of twilight at **Sunset Hill Observation Deck.** It takes about 45 minutes to get back to Anbo from here. If it's not yet dark, you'll get some wonderful scenery on the drive back, particularly of mist settling amid the creases of the mountains, but less so on the road between Miyanoura and Anbo, the most developed corner of the island.

Yakusugi Trees: Protected by the Gods

During the Edo-period (1603–1867), Yakushima's *yakusugi* trees were sought after for their wood, which yielded the country's best and most durable *hiragi* (roof tiles). (Note that the three kanji characters making up Yakushima, 屋久島, can be read as "roof," "longtime," and "island.") To address the moral uncertainty of cutting down such spiritually significant trees, loggers would place their axes against the trunks overnight. If, in the morning, the axe was in the same place, it meant that the gods had granted them permission to hack the tree down; if the axe had fallen over, they were required to take their business elsewhere.

Where to Stay in Yakushima

Accommodations in Yakushima often offer better rates if you book with them directly. Some may close between mid-December and the beginning of March, so be sure to get in touch early if traveling here in winter. Also note that it's best to book well in advance if staying during the high season—the island is often at max capacity in spring, August (especially around the Obon holidays), and most of the autumn.

Guesthouse Manmaru ♥♥ This guesthouse on Yakushima's east coast was inspired an old island maxim—"Ten days in the mountains, ten days at sea, ten days in the fields"—offering simple instruction on how to live a happy life. It's a small u-shaped complex with rooms on either side and a communal lounge and dining area at the far end, all surrounded by verdant foliage and pointing towards the coast. The simple rooms open straight into the outdoors and there's a communal hot spring bath, carved from stone, with a large sea-facing window. Breakfast is served in the dining area at 7:30am, and "mountaineering" packed lunches are available on request. The husband-and-wife owners, both Yakushima natives, speak only a smattering of English but are extremely accommodating. They also offer "workation" plans, with highspeed internet connection in the lounge, outdoor power outlets, free bicycle rental, and 5% to 30% discounts for guests staying 4 or more nights; stay longer for a larger discount.

540–19 Anbo. manmaru-yakushima.com. ✆ **0997-49-7107.** 10 units. ¥6,600 per person. Rates include breakfast. **Amenities:** Lounge and dining area; indoor hot-spring bath; free Wi-Fi.

Mori no Fairy ♥♥♥ These cottages are just perfect: Spend your mornings drinking coffee on the terrace and watching butterflies float among the hibiscus; by night dip into your hot tub, sunken into the floor of the deck, while listening to singing cicadas and the sound of waves crashing softly on the shore. While you won't have hotel-like amenities, the privacy and extra space are a decent trade-off. Cottages have beautiful, cedar-paneled interiors and kitchens for rustling up dinner or lunch; each has a loft with bedding to accommodate families and groups. The owners can help organize excursions like sea or river kayaking. There are small discounts (¥800 per person per night) if you reserve through the Mori no Fairy homepage or directly with the property via telephone or email (morinofairy@air.ocn.ne.jp).

165–5 Mugio. morinofairy-y.p2.weblife.me. ✆ **080-8382-4847.** 4 units. ¥4,600–¥5,800 per person (minimum 2 guests). **Amenities:** Outdoor bath; garden; kitchen; free Wi-Fi.

TIDA Resort Yakushima ♥♥ Don't be fooled by the name; this is *not* a sprawling complex catering to tour groups and holidaymakers. A collection of four maisonette-style units, each facing the East China Sea, these wood-paneled lodges have kitchen-dining-lounge areas, bedrooms that can sleep five guests, semi-open-air baths, and terraces overlooking the coast. Dinner and breakfast, served in a separate building, fuse Japanese and Western cuisines, including sashimi plates, soups, grilled fish, and other entrees, all prepared and executed with aplomb.

211–52 Yudomari. yakushima-tida.com. ✆ **0997-49-8750.** 4 units. ¥15,000–¥25,000 per person (some rates include 2 meals). **Amenities:** Restaurant; semi-open-air bath; free Wi-Fi.

Where to Eat in Yakushima

Yakushima's produce differs from on the mainland. Venison is the most common meat, though beef from Jomon cows is also popular, while protein from the sea includes flying fish (often served minced), blue and spotted chub mackerel, silver-stripe herring, cuttlefish, freshwater prawns, and a type of sea snail known as silver-mouth turban. The fruits and vegetables also have a more exotic flair, with papaya, bananas, sweet potatoes, passion fruit, and orangelike citruses called *ponkan* and *tankan*.

Also worth noting is that Yakushima residents often operate on "island time"—shops and restaurants don't always hold to their stated hours of operation, particularly in the winter months (in fact, some close altogether or open only for limited weekend hours)—so it's a good idea to call ahead, ask accommodation staff for food recommendations, and make use of dinners and packed lunches at your lodging whenever available.

Kirankuya ♥♥ SOBA If you come here at night, it might at first feel like a wild goose chase, the restaurant hidden between forest and sea near the eastern coast, with barely a flicker of light from the doorway. But inside is a lovely family-run *soba* (buckwheat noodle) restaurant, serving the dish, hot or cold, with tempura, as well as other sides like pickles, raw egg, seafood, and beef. There's no English on the menu; use the pictures or translation apps to guide you.

891–4311 Anbo. kirankuya.travel.coocan.jp. ✆ **0997-46-4610.** Soba ¥600–¥1,300. Wed–Mon 11am–1:30pm and 6–7:30pm (last order), or until soba runs out.

Nakarase (食彩なからせ) ♥♥ YAKUSHIMA CUISINE *Teishoku* (set meals) made with local ingredients is the fare in this homey little restaurant in Yakushima's Hara township. Meals usually include seasonal tempura, a stewed dish with radishes and root vegetables, an array of pickles using the likes of spinach and zedoary (similar to ginger), perhaps a fishcake or some mushrooms, rice, white miso soup, and a papaya and chili salad. Good, wholesome, fresh food with lots of flavor. The menu is in Japanese but there's usually only one thing on it.

896–4 Hara. ✆ **0997-49-3011.** Meals around ¥1,500 per person. Fri–Tues 11:30am–2pm.

Renga (焼肉れんが屋) ♥♥♥ YAKINIKU Take a seat on the floor of the communal tatami dining room and get ready to grill cuts of sumptuous meat—mostly marbled beef and venison—at portable grills on your table. The vibe here is always joyous, like you've all descended on someone's living room and been welcomed by an obliging host; this is only enhanced by the smells of cooked meat and sounds of merriment wafting around the room. Even the low tables are cool, carved from fallen *yakusugi* trees and retaining the trunks' exterior shape. Tablet menus were recently introduced here, so ordering should be a breeze.

410–74 Anbo. instagram.com/yakushimarengaya. ✆ **0997-46-3439.** Average ¥5,000 per person. Thurs–Tues 5:30–10pm.

Shiba Tofu Shop ♥♥♥ TOFU A good place to stop on a road trip around the island, this tiny tofu shop sells soybean curd steamed or fried, and as *yuba* (bean curd skin) or tofu milk, all of them delicious. There's nowhere to sit (you'll have to grab a seat outside) but if you've been driving all day, the lack of seating will be of little consequence.
1377–2 Nagata. ✆ **0997-45-2048.** Tofu items ¥150–¥450; meals ¥700. Tues–Sat 8am–5pm.

BEPPU ♥♥

1,228km (763 miles) SW of Tokyo; 186km (116 miles) SE of Fukuoka

Beppu gushes forth more hot-spring water than anywhere else in Japan. With approximately 3,000 hot springs spewing forth 130,000 kiloliters (34 million gal.) of water daily, it has long been one of the country's best-known spa resorts. Some 8 million people come to Beppu every year to relax and rejuvenate themselves in one of the city's 100-plus bathhouses, and they do so in a number of unique ways: They sit in mud baths up to their necks, they bury themselves in hot black sand, they soak in hot springs, and on New Year's they bathe in water filled with floating orange peels. They even drink hot-spring water and eat food cooked by its steam. Bathing reigns supreme here—and I suggest you join in the fun. After all, visiting Beppu without enjoying the baths would be like going to a world-class restaurant with your own TV dinner.

Not a very large town, with a population of 113,000, Beppu is situated on Kyushu's eastern coast in a curve of Beppu Bay, bounded on one side by the sea and on the other by steep hills and mountains. On cold days, steam rises everywhere throughout the city, escaping from springs and pipes and giving the town an otherworldly appearance. Indeed, seven of the hot springs look so much like hell that that's what they're called—Jigoku, the Hells. But rather than a place most people try to avoid, the Hells are a major tourist attraction. In fact, everything in Beppu is geared toward tourism, and if you're interested in rubbing elbows with Japanese on vacation—particularly the older generation—this is one of the best places to do so.

Essentials

ARRIVING Direct JR **trains** run daily from Hakata Station in Fukuoka (trip time: 2 hr.) and cost ¥5,940 for an unreserved seat. You can also get here directly from Shikoku via the **Uwajima Unyu Ferry** (uwajimaunyu.co.jp; ✆ **0894-22-2100**) from Yawatahama in Ehime Prefecture (it's 1½–2 hr. from Matsuyama City by train). There are six ferries a day; the trip takes around 3 hours. Fares start at ¥4,200 for a second-class seat; children pay half-price.

VISITOR INFORMATION The **Beppu Tourist Information Office** (beppu-tourism.com; ✆ **0977-21-6220;** daily 8:45am–6pm) is in Beppu Station at the east (main) exit. The **Beppu International Plaza Kannawa**

Office (✆ **0977-66-3855;** daily 9am–5pm) is located near the Hells. Both locations offer friendly staff and lots of useful information in English.

GETTING AROUND Most destinations are not within walking distance, so you'll probably need to travel around Beppu by bus and by taxi. The largest bus company, **Kamenoi Bus Company** (kamenoibus.com; ✆ **0977-23-0141**), serves most of the city. Bus fares begin at ¥170 and increase according to the distance; a 1-day pass called **My Beppu Free** (buy at the tourist office in the train station) costs ¥1,100 for adults (¥1,700 for 2 days); children 11 and under pay half-fare. It allows unlimited travel on Kamenoi Company buses (which are blue).

Exploring Beppu

Beppu City Traditional Bamboo Crafts Center ♥ MUSEUM

Beppu is famous for its bamboo crafts, and the best place to learn more about this amazingly durable material is this museum. Exhibits explain how bamboo grows, the different varieties of bamboo (620 kinds are found in Japan; 1,250 grow worldwide), and the role bamboo has played in daily Japanese life, with displays that include palanquins, fish traps, lunch boxes, toys, fans, hats, bows, and arrows, and a beautiful 1920s stationery box. Even Edison's electric light bulb used a bamboo filament. You can see everything in 15 minutes, but with your new appreciation for bamboo, you'll easily spend an additional 15 minutes in the museum shop.

8–3 Higashisoen. ✆ **0977-23-1072.** ¥300 adults, ¥100 children. Tues–Sun 8:30am–5pm. Bus: no. 1 or 41 to Soen Jutaku Mae stop (5 min.).

Tourists snap selfies and try to boil eggs in the steaming Kamado pond, one of many hot springs in Beppu's Hells.

The Hells (Jigoku) ♥ NATURAL ATTRACTION Boiling ponds of various colors created by volcanic activity, their Japanese name, *Jigoku,* refers to the burning hell of Buddhist sutras. Seven Hells are clustered together in the Kannawa hot-spring area, within walking distance of each other, and they can be toured in about 90 minutes or so. Each hell has its own attraction, but because a few are kind of hokey, you might want to pick and choose which to visit. **Umi Jigoku,** or Sea Hell, has a nice garden setting (spectacular in spring when azaleas are in bloom), a cobalt-blue pond, a gallery displaying pieces from recent Beppu art projects, and a foot bath where you can soak your feet in hot springs. **Oniishibozu Jigoku** features bubbling mud said to look like monks' heads and a foot bath; **Kamado Jigoku,** the Oven Hell, was used for cooking and has a statue of a red devil (a good place to try eggs boiled in onsen water); and **Shiraike Jigoku** features a large bluish-white pond and a small aquarium. A little farther out (take the no. 16 bus; 10 min.) **Chinoike Jigoku,** the Blood-Pond Hell, is blood-red in color because of the red clay dissolved in the hot water; and **Tatsumaki Jigoku,** or Waterspout Hell, has one of the largest geysers in Japan. I recommend skipping **Oniyama Jigoku,** featuring crocodiles living in cramped enclosures.

Kannawa hot-spring area. ¥450 adults for each Hell; combination ticket for all 7 Hells ¥2,200 adults, ¥1,000 children. Daily 8am–5pm. Bus: no. 2 to Umijigoku-mae stop (25 min. from Beppu Station's west exit).

Jigoku Onsen Museum ♥♥♥ MUSEUM Set in the center of the Hells, this museum is a wonderfully engaging introduction to this natural phenomenon, taking visitors on the journey of an individual water droplet, from striking the Beppu ground as rainfall to reappearing on the surface as hot spring water 50 years later. The first of four "scenes" is like an acid trip, as you sit on soft seats in a dark room staring at a raised polyhedral screen on the floor that sucks you in with dynamic audiovisual displays—when at last you're asked to imagine that you're now a water droplet, it doesn't feel too much of a stretch. The next room is a maze of curtains, explaining how these droplets meander through subterranean chambers until they encounter red-hot magma deep in the earth's crust—turning them into steam that dissolves chemicals from the rock, like salts, sulfates, silica, carbonates, and metals that humans will later seek out for their curative properties. A hall of mirrors leads to another area where you'll answer a quiz on the information you've gleaned so far—get all the answers right and you'll get some rock salts to take home—and where you'll learn about the different mineral springs and their attendant benefits. The final section features a short movie (in a theater styled after an old wooden bathhouse) about the water droplet's journey back to the surface, and some artworks that symbolize the importance of hot springs to life in Beppu. There's clearly been a lot of money spent on this place, and it shows. Well worth the 1 hour visiting time.

321–1 Kannawa. jigoku-museum.com ✆ **0977-84-7858.** ¥1,500 adults, ¥1,000 children (¥1,050 and ¥700 with Hells combination ticket). Daily 9am–6pm.

Taking the Waters

Beppu is divided into eight hot-spring areas, each with its own mineral content and natural characteristics. Although any hot-spring bath can help stimulate metabolism and blood circulation and create a general feeling of well-being, specific springs have various mineral contents that the Japanese believe help relieve ailments ranging from rheumatism and diabetes to skin disease. The tourist office has a pamphlet so you can select the baths that will benefit you the most. And whatever you do, don't rinse off with plain water after taking your bath—that will only wash away all those helpful minerals. You should bring your own towel and, for some places, a *yukata* (cotton kimono), though these are often available for sale or for rent.

Suginoi Palace ♥♥♥ HOT-SPRING BATH While your accommodation is likely to have a hot-spring bath, while you're here it would a shame not to experience the deluxe package. This hotel and amusement center has one of the best-known baths in all of Japan, called **Tanayu.** Built of natural woods, stone, and glass, it's refined and spacious, with different kinds of baths both inside and out, taking advantage of its hillside perch with great views over the town toward the sea. In addition to an indoor bath and a sauna with a view, there are outdoor stone tubs, a cavelike onsen room where soothing music fills the steamy air, shallow pools with headrests so you can recline and take in the scenery, and an onsen infinity pool that descends in steps towards the cliff face. If you're shy about disrobing in front of strangers or have kids in tow, you might want to visit the Suginoi Palace's **Aqua Garden** instead, a collection of heated pools and seating areas with sun loungers overlooking the town below. Given it's mostly families and young kids here, it won't be a serene as the main onsen, but this is still a good option, and it's included in the Tanayu admission price. Also in the complex is **Spa the Caeda,** where you can get aromatherapy and massage treatments, starting at ¥9,900 for a 40-minute "refresh course." Guests staying at the Suginoi Hotel (p. 585) can use the bath and Aqua Garden for free but will be charged for spa treatments.

Kankajii. suginoi.orixhotelsandresorts.com. ✆ **0977-24-1141.** ¥2,900 adults, ¥2,000 children. Daily 9am–11pm. Free shuttle (15 min.) from Beppu Station (Mon–Thurs 8am–6:40pm; Fri–Sun 8am–10pm).

Takegawara Bathhouse ♥♥♥ HOT-SAND BATH One of the unique things you can do in Beppu is take a bath in hot sand, considered useful for treating muscle pain, arthritis, and indigestion. Several public baths offer hot-sand baths, but this beautiful wooden structure is one of the most atmospheric places to try the treatment. Built in 1879 in traditional Meiji-Era style, it's one of the oldest public baths in the city. Its interior resembles an ancient gymnasium, dominated by a pit filled with black sand. The attendants are used to foreigners here; they'll instruct you to change into the provided *yukata* and lie down in a hollow they've dug

One of Beppu's signature spa experiences: Lying in a pit submerged in hot black sand.

in the sand. An attendant will then shovel sand on top of you and pack you in until only your head and feet are sticking out. The sand isn't all that hot, but it is relaxing as the heat soaks into your body. You stay buried for 15 minutes—at which point you'll be on the verge of a nap—contemplating the wooden ceiling high above and hoping you don't get an itch somewhere. When the time is up, the attendant will tell you to stand up, shower off the sand, and then jump into a bath of hot water. Note that you will be naked under the yukata and should be prepared to shower, rinse off, and bathe naked in a semi-open space (albeit one that's separated by sexes). 16–23 Motomachi. ✆ **0977-23-1585.** ¥1,500. Daily 8am–10:30pm; closed 3rd Wed of month. Beppu Station: 10-min. walk.

Where to Stay in Beppu

As with most hot-spring spas, Beppu levies a hot-springs tax: ¥150 per person, per night. In addition, some places raise their rates for New Year's, Golden Week (Apr 29–May 5), Obon (mid-Aug), Saturdays, and evenings before holidays.

Hotel Beppu Pastoral ♥♥ Situated on the banks of the Sakai River, this large property has a retro—some might argue *dated*—vibe, with its yellowy-brown color scheme and beds that have old radios and alarm clocks built into the frames. Nevertheless, its outdoor baths have a timeless beauty, surrounded by small Japanese gardens and rocks shaped by the hand of nature. These are free for hotel guests to use, as is a selection

of colorful *yukata* robes for wearing around the building. Rooms on the mountain-facing side are spacious enough, if a little bland; those looking towards the sea are fancier, many equipped with outdoor terraces and open-air baths enclosed by fences and foliage to give a sense of privacy.
1–4 Higashisoen. pastoral.jp. ✆ **0977-23-4201.** 67 units. ¥8,000–¥10,000 single; ¥15,000–¥30,000 double. Kamenoi Bus no. 6 to Sakaigawa Shogakko Mae (2 min.). **Amenities:** Restaurant; hot-spring bath; free Wi-Fi.

Kokage ♥ This *minshuku* offers simply furnished Japanese-style rooms. Those with bathrooms have hot-spring water, while the rooms for three people have only a sink and toilet. There's also a rock-lined public hot-spring bath. Meals are served in a homey dining room with a cluttered but interesting collection of antique lamps, clocks, and other items. Note that there's a midnight curfew.
8–9 Ekimaecho. ✆ **0977-23-1753.** 13 units (10 w/ private bath, 3 w/ toilet only). ¥4,350 single w/ bath; ¥7,650 double w/ bath. Station: Beppu (2 min.). **Amenities:** Free Wi-Fi.

Suginoi Hotel ♥♥ One of the best-known hotels in Beppu, Suginoi is famous for its adjoining Suginoi Palace with its hot-spring baths (p. 583). Situated on a wooded hill with a sweeping view of the city and sea below, it's a lively and noisy hotel, filled with good-natured holidaymakers; if you

One of many bathing areas at the Suginoi Hotel's Suginoi Palace complex, the Aqua Garden overlooks the town of Beppu and Beppu Bay beyond.

like being in the middle of the action, this is the place for you. Occupying several buildings, it offers many accommodation options, from Western-style rooms (with beds), to combination rooms (with both beds and *tatami* area), to rooms with epic sea views and those complete with open-air baths. With its baths, spa facilities, arcade machines, games room, lounges, restaurants, and water park (currently closed for renovation; check website to see if it's reopened), you could easily vacation here without leaving the complex. On the other hand, the place is so vast you have to hike to its various facilities, and it's inconvenient to the rest of Beppu.

Kankaiji. suginoi.orixhotelsandresorts.com. ✆ **0977-24-1141.** 587 units. ¥20,000–¥40,000 per person, including 2 meals. Free hotel shuttle bus from Beppu Station. Taxi: 8 min. **Amenities:** Multiple restaurants, cafes, and lounges; hot-spring baths (p. 583); free Wi-Fi.

Yanagiya ♥♥ The oldest family-run inn in the city, this is one of the best places to stay near the Hells. Several interesting features here utilize the hot springs, including old radiators heated naturally from hot springs and a *jigokugama* (stone oven) in the courtyard that uses steam from hot springs for cooking (many older homes in Beppu still use such ovens). Use of the oven is free in case you want to cook your own meals, but there's also a modern kitchen you can use. If you opt for rates that include meals, most of your dinner will be steamed using the hot springs and then served in a Japanese dining room with whitewashed walls and a heavy timbered ceiling. In winter, the *kotatsu* in the dining room (a table with a heating element and covered with a blanket to keep legs warm) is steam-heated. All rooms are Japanese style, the oldest of which don't have bathrooms but are very nice, dating from the Meiji Period (1868–1912); those with private bathroom are in a newer addition that nonetheless maintains a traditional atmosphere.

Ida, Kannawa. ✆ **0977-66-6234.** 12 units, 7 w/ private bath. From ¥4,860 per person w/o meals; from ¥13,770 with 2 meals. Bus: Kannawa (5 min.). **Amenities:** Indoor hot-spring baths; free Wi-Fi.

Where to Eat in Beppu

Bungo Chaya Beppu ♥♥ LOCAL SPECIALTIES From the outside, this restaurant in Beppu train station looks like a run-of-mill eatery you'd find in any mall across the country. But it's a surprisingly good place to sample Oita cuisine, like chicken tempura, wheat dumpling soup, and mochi with *kinako* (roasted soybean flour). Some set meals include all of the above, or you can order a la carte from the English-language menu. The five-piece chicken tempura set, served with rice, pickles, and miso soup, for ¥1,050 is hard to beat.

In Beppu Station. ✆ **0977-25-1800.** Set meals ¥1,050–¥1,900. Daily 10am–8pm.

Genki ♥♥ VARIED JAPANESE When you name your shop *Genki,* meaning "energetic" or "full of spirit," it's imperative you follow it up with the kind of lively atmosphere that's customary here. In true izakaya fashion, the menu includes everything from fried horse mackerel and assorted sashimi to dumplings, pork belly slices, and grilled tomato and cheese. Despite the quantity, the quality is still there. The shochu menu is also extensive, if that's your thing. Located on Yayoi Tengu-Dori, one of the town's busy-after-dark arcade streets, it's a good place to start a night of restaurant hopping.
1–1–18 Kitahama. ✆ **090-1450-1282.** Wed–Mon 5–11pm. Beppu Station (5-min. walk).

Kawahachi (焼肉川八(かわはち) ♥♥ YAKINIKU Grab a private room with sliding doors or a table in the small communal dining area in this cook-it-yourself *yakiniku* (grilled meat) meat joint. The English-language menu with pictures features yakiniku staples: beef skirt, beef loin, pork rib, chicken thigh, offal, and sides including rice, kimchi, corn, and egg drop soup. You'll receive a pair of tongs for flipping the meat, a slab of fat for basting the griddle in the center of your table, and a couple of sauces for dipping. All seating is shoes off, on the floor, at low tables.
16–38 Tenmancho. instagram.com/yakinikukawahachi/. ✆ **0977-21-0191.** Dinner and drinks around ¥5,000 per person. Wed–Mon 11:30am–2pm and 5–10pm (last order 20 min. before closing). Bus: Kamenoi Bus no. 6 to Noguchibaru (1 min.).

Menkichi (うどん・そば めん吉) ♥♥ NOODLES In one of the covered arcade streets to the east of Beppu Station, this small udon shop fits the Showa-era vibe of the area, with cramped confines, vintage beer posters, and low-hanging paper lanterns. The elderly owner-chef comes across as testy, but the fact that there's an English-language menu shows his openness to new clientele, and personally, I don't mind a cold shoulder when the food is this good. Curry udon, beef udon, udon with tempura, udon with deep-fried tofu, and udon with chicken and burdock all feature.
1–4–19 Kitahama. ✆ **080-6455-3042.** Udon ¥600–¥1,100. Daily noon–3am (hours may vary). Beppu Station (5 min.), in Sol Paseo Ginza shopping arcade.

12 OKINAWA

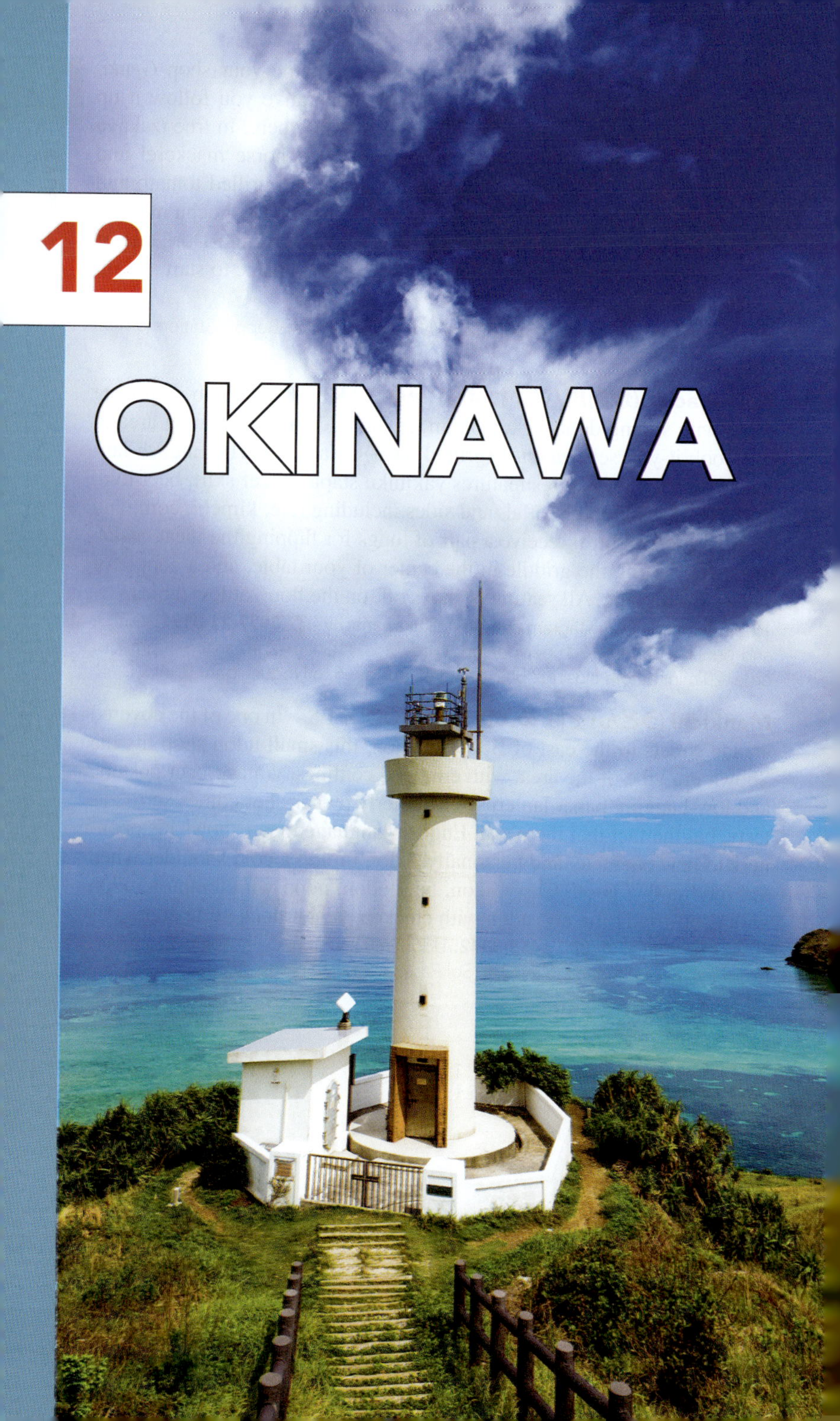

Okinawa Prefecture, an archipelago of 160 islands between Kyushu and Taiwan, seems like its own country. Maybe that's because once upon a time it was its own kingdom—the Ryukyu Kingdom—with dynasties and castles (constructed mostly between the 14th and 18th c.), as well as its own languages, culture, and cuisine. Although it was invaded in the early 1600s by Satsuma (what is now Kagoshima in southern Kyushu), the Ryukyu Kingdom retained domestic autonomy, trading freely with China and elsewhere, until it was annexed to Japan after the 1868 Meiji Restoration. In 1879 it was renamed Okinawa Prefecture.

Today Okinawa is perhaps better known as a site of brutal combat during World War II (several sites and memorials recount the horrific battle and massive casualties). Yet Okinawa is also one of the best diving spots in the world, with some of Japan's prettiest coral reefs, and what may be most appealing about the island is its laid-back, rural atmosphere. In fact, parts of Okinawa are so off the beaten path that they're caught in a time warp of decades past.

Of Okinawa's 160 islands, only 40-some are inhabited. The largest, Okinawa Island (Okinawa-honto), is home to Naha, capital of Okinawa Prefecture and gateway to the rest of the islands by sea and by air. After visiting Okinawa Island's many attractions, you might wish to fly or take a ferry onward to one or more of my other favorites, like Ishigaki, known for its crystal-clear waters and rare blue coral, or Iriomote, famous for its pristine wilderness and for scuba diving.

THE BEST OKINAWA EXPERIENCES

- **Being Dazzled by Shuri Castle** Unlike Japanese castles on the mainland, Okinawa's vermillion-painted Shuri Castle has a unique look—constructed in the traditional Ryukyu Kingdom style, influenced by both Chinese and Japanese designs.
- **Plunging into the Reefs** Scuba diving is one of the main reasons travelers flock to Okinawa, which is famous for coral reefs, illuminated underwater caves, and a diverse array of tropical fish. Dive spots are dotted around the coast of the main island, as well as near Ishigaki and Iriomote.

FACING PAGE: **Hirakubozaki Lighthouse, on the northern tip of Ishigaki Island, part of the Yaeyama Islands.**

- **Trying New Fish in Naha's Seafood Markets** At the Makishi Public Market in the center of Naha, discover the originality of Okinawa's cuisine culture, with delicacies like parrot fish, shellfish tempura, and locally famous *umi budo* (a seaweed whose name translates to "sea grapes").
- **Paying Respect to Lives Lost in WWII** Through impactful museums and monuments, you can learn about the Battle of Okinawa, the bloodiest, most devastating conflict in World War II's Pacific Theater.

The delicate seaweed umi budo, or "sea grapes," is just one of Okinawa's many seafood specialties.

OKINAWA ISLAND ♥

1,539km (956 miles) SW of Tokyo

Okinawa Island, the largest in the Ryukyu island chain, has plenty of attractions that make a 2- or 3-day stay particularly worthwhile. There are no less than nine castle sites here dating from the Ryukyu Kingdom era, all on the UNESCO World Heritage list. The **Okinawa World** theme park contain Japan's second-longest limestone cave and exhibits related to Okinawa history and culture, and there are several memorials for victims of the Battle of Okinawa (see "Okinawa & the U.S., a Troubled History," p. 592). More lighthearted pursuits include shopping and dining in downtown Naha, sunning and swimming on the island's many white sandy beaches, and snorkeling and scuba diving among the island's surrounding coral reefs.

U.S. military bases are mostly in central Okinawa Island, where you'll also find **Okinawa City,** the island's second-largest town, and **Chatan,** both with many establishments, shops, and services geared toward military personnel and their families. Chatan, is an especially trendy corner of the island, with a mall, dive and surf shops, parks, and beaches. North Okinawa Island, the least populated, is a hilly region with resorts, golf courses, beaches, snorkeling and diving spots, and the **Okinawa Churaumi Aquarium.**

Essentials

ARRIVING Multiple **airlines** fly from both Narita and Haneda airports in Tokyo, taking around 3 hours to reach Okinawa. Budget airlines fly for as little as or as little as ¥7,000; JAL and ANA flights usually cost ¥10,000 to ¥20,000. Flights from Osaka's Kansai Airport take 2 hours; costs are similar, depending on the airline. After stopping by the **tourist information**

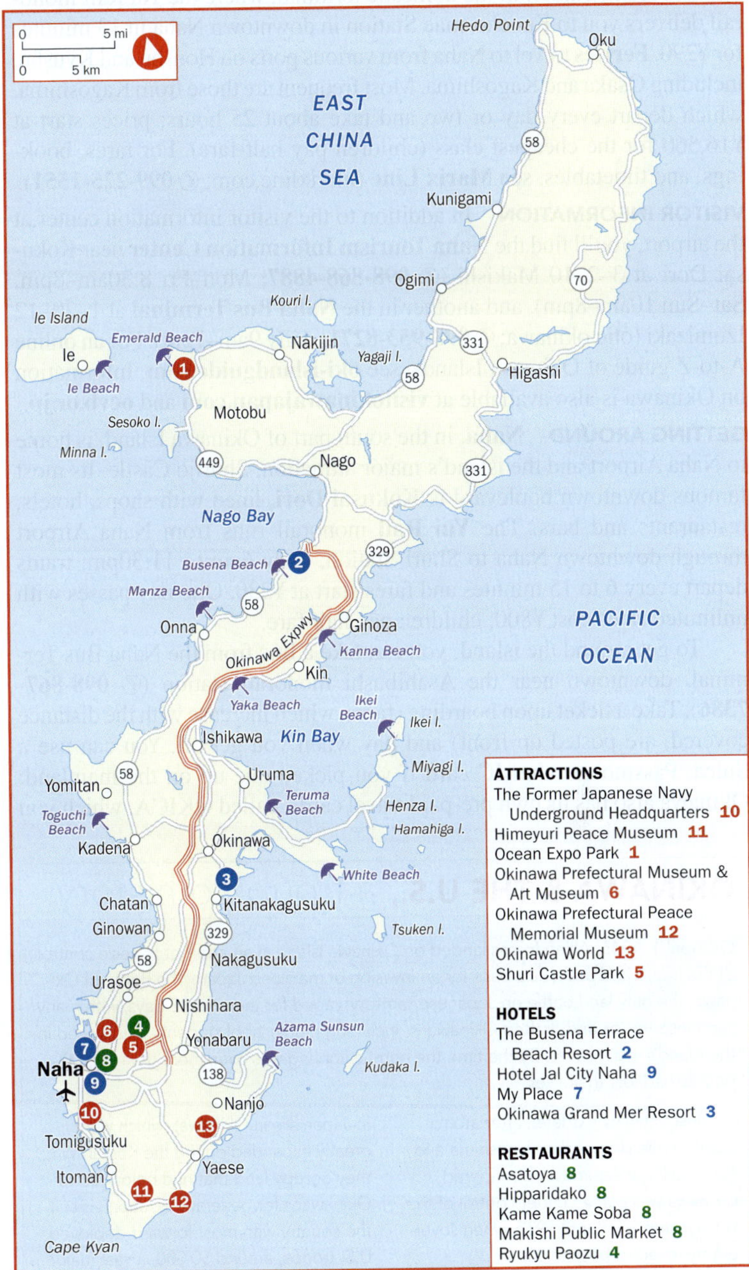

ATTRACTIONS
The Former Japanese Navy Underground Headquarters **10**
Himeyuri Peace Museum **11**
Ocean Expo Park **1**
Okinawa Prefectural Museum & Art Museum **6**
Okinawa Prefectural Peace Memorial Museum **12**
Okinawa World **13**
Shuri Castle Park **5**

HOTELS
The Busena Terrace Beach Resort **2**
Hotel Jal City Naha **9**
My Place **7**
Okinawa Grand Mer Resort **3**

RESTAURANTS
Asatoya **8**
Hipparidako **8**
Kame Kame Soba **8**
Makishi Public Market **8**
Ryukyu Paozu **4**

center in the domestic terminal (✆ **098-857-6884;** daily 9am–9pm), head to Naha Kuko Station in the domestic terminal, where the Yui Rail monorail delivers you to Kencho-mae Station in downtown Naha in 13 minutes for ¥290. **Ferries** travel to Naha from various ports on Honshu and Kyushu, including Osaka and Kagoshima. Most frequent are those from Kagoshima, which depart every day or two and take about 25 hours; prices start at ¥16,560 for the cheapest class (children pay half-fare). For fares, bookings, and timetables, see **Marix Line** (marixline.com; ✆ **099-225-1551**).

VISITOR INFORMATION In addition to the visitor information center at the airport, you'll find the **Naha Tourism Information Center** near Kokusai Dori at 3–2–10 Makishi (✆ **098-868-4887;** Mon–Fri 8:30am–8pm, Sat–Sun 10am–8pm), and another in the **Naha Bus Terminal** at 1–20–12 Izumizaki (otic.okinawa; ✆ **098-953-8271;** daily 9am–7pm). For an online A-to-Z guide of Okinawa Islands, see **oki-islandguide.com**. Information on Okinawa is also available at **visitokinawajapan.com** and **ocvb.or.jp**.

GETTING AROUND **Naha,** in the south part of Okinawa Island, is home to Naha Airport and the island's major attraction, Shurijo Castle. Its most famous downtown boulevard is **Kokusai Dori,** lined with shops, hotels, restaurants and bars. The **Yui Rail** monorail runs from Naha Airport through downtown Naha to Shuri Station, daily 6am to 11:30pm; trains depart every 6 to 15 minutes and fares start at ¥230. One-day passes with unlimited rides cost ¥800; children pay half fare.

To get around the island, you can take a **bus** from the Naha Bus Terminal, downtown near the Asahibashi monorail station (✆ **098-867-7386**). Take a ticket upon boarding (fares, which increase with the distance covered, are posted up front) and pay when you get off. You can use a Suica, Passmo or other IC card if you picked one up on the mainland; Okinawa also has its own pre-paid travel cards, called OKICA, which you

OKINAWA & THE U.S., a troubled history

On April 1, 1945, Allied forces landed on Okinawa Island in an attempt to seize control of the island and use it as a base for an invasion of mainland Japan. The Battle of Okinawa, the only land battle on Japanese territory, raged for the next 82 days, with many Japanese troops and drafted Okinawans, including high-school students, ensconced in the island's many caves. By the time the horrific fighting was over, more than 200,000 people had lost their lives.

Just a few weeks later, after atomic bombs were dropped on Hiroshima and Nagasaki, the Japanese surrendered. Okinawa was placed under control of the U.S. government until 1972, when sovereignty reverted back to Japan.

Some American military bases remain, however (75% of American bases in Japan are in Okinawa), which were greatly expanded during the Korean War; they occupy land that had belonged to Okinawans for generations. Japan is still the country with most forward-deployed U.S. troops, around 50,000, a vast majority of which are stationed in Okinawa. This is not uncontroversial in Japan.

can purchase at monorail stations, bus depots, and some Family Mart convenience stores.

If you have an international driver's license, you might wish to **rent a car.** There are many rental agencies, with locations at the airport, in Naha, at hotels and other locations. Prices start around ¥7,000 or ¥8,000 per day for a compact vehicle for 24 hours. For more information contact **Times Car Rental** (timescar-rental.com; ✆ **098-858-1536**) or **Toyota Rent-A-Car** (rent.toyota.co.jp; ✆ **098-857-0100**), both of which have branches at Naha Airport.

Exploring Naha

The Former Japanese Navy Underground Headquarters (Kyukaigun Shireigo) ♥ HISTORIC SITE Just outside of Naha, this haunting site is where the Japanese Navy, under Rear Admiral Ota, took its last stand in the Battle of Okinawa. A system of underground tunnels stretching 450m (1,475 ft.), built by civilians using shovels and pickaxes, it remains almost exactly as it was, including the operations room and where Ota killed himself with a grenade. Rather than surrender, many of his staff also committed suicide; 2,400 bodies were eventually recovered after the war. Before touring the tunnels, which are rather bare but convey what it must have been like to live here (audio explanations throughout the tunnels are also in English), first tour the one-room museum. Most poignant are farewell letters written to family members.

236 Aza Tomishiro. kaigungou.ocvb.or.jp. ✆ **098-850-4055.** ¥450 adults, ¥230 children, or ¥360 and ¥160 with 1-day monorail pass. Daily 8:30am–5pm (until 5:30pm July–Sept). Bus: 55, 88, or 98 to Uebaru Danchi-mae (3 min.).

Okinawa Prefectural Museum & Art Museum (Okinawa Kenritsu Hakubutsukan & Bijutsukan) ♥♥ MUSEUM Make these two museums under one roof your first stop. While the art museum is interesting for its changing exhibitions of contemporary art, including works by artists with a connection to Okinawa, the Prefectural Museum is a superb way to get some background on Okinawa's history, culture, and natural history. You'll learn about the formation of the Ryukyu archipelago; the rise and fall of the mighty Ryukyu Kingdom with its extensive trade routes to China, Japan, and Southeast Asia; the Battle of Okinawa and subsequent U.S. occupation; and Okinawan folklore, crafts, and culture. A discovery room for children is equipped with traditional toys, clothing, musical instruments, and more.

Omoromachi 3–1–1. okimu.jp. ✆ **098-941-8200.** Prefectural Museum ¥530 adults, ¥270 college and high-school students, ¥150 children; Art Museum ¥400, ¥220, and ¥100 respectively (special exhibits cost more). Tues–Thurs and Sun 9am–6pm; Fri–Sat 9am–8pm. Yui Rail: Omoromachi Station (10 min.).

Shuri Castle Park (Shurijo Koen) ♥♥♥ CASTLE Naha's top attraction was first constructed between the 13th and 14th centuries and served as the epicenter of the Ryukyu Kingdom for about 500 years, until

Colorful Shuri Castle, with its unique Ryukyuan architectural style, is unlike most other Japanese castles.

the establishment of Okinawa Prefecture in 1897. Serving as both a residence for the king and an administrative and religious center, it shows architectural influences from both China and Japan but is uniquely Ryukyuan in style. If you've visited other castles in the country and they're starting to blur together in your mind, then Shurijo will be a pleasant surprise, its vermillion walls glinting like lacquer in the afternoon sun and its spacious courtyard more like Beijing's Forbidden City than the cloistered halls of Japan's feudal-era structures. Even the approach to the entrance gate, under swaying palm fronds and banyan trees, contrasts with the cherry blossom groves and manicured lawns of castles on the mainland. Though the original buildings were destroyed in the Battle of Okinawa, as a reflection of the site's importance, this partial re-creation went up in its place. (Along with eight other historic properties in Okinawa Prefecture, it has been designated as a World Heritage Site, formally titled "Gusuku Sites and Related Properties of the Ryukyu Kingdom.") Unfortunately, in 2019 a fire in the middle of the night, likely caused by an electrical malfunction, set the main hall ablaze, spreading to six other buildings and destroying all of them before the conflagration was contained. Restoration work has been ongoing since, and the castle is expected to be reopened to the public in 2026 alongside a subterranean complex which housed the command of the Japanese imperial forces' 32nd army headquarters in the 1940s.

1–2 Kinjocho, Shuri. oki-park.jp/shurijo. ✆ **098-886-2020.** Castle park ¥400 adults, ¥300 high-school students, ¥160 younger students, free for ages 6 and under. Castle interior admission TBA upon reopening. Daily 8:30am–7:30pm (closes 8:30pm July–Sept; closes 6:30pm Dec–Mar); castle hours may change upon reopening. Yui Rail: Shurijo Station, then a 15-min. walk. Bus 8 to Shurijo-mae stop.

Elsewhere on Okinawa Island

Ocean Expo Park (Kaiyohaku Kinen Koen) ♥♥ ATTRACTION

Site of the 1975 International Ocean Expo, this expansive park on the northwestern coast contains several attractions. The most popular is the **Okinawa Churaumi Aquarium** (kaiyouhaku.com; ✆ **098-48-3740**), which concentrates on the oceans and currents surrounding the Ryukyu Islands, from coral reef habitats to the deep sea. Like all Japanese aquariums, this place has had its critics, many of whom question the ethics of keeping dolphins, manatees, sea turtles, and whale sharks in captivity. Also popular is the free-to-enter **Native Okinawan Village (Okinawa Kyoudo Mura)**, featuring more than a dozen sites modeled after a village from the Ryukyu Kingdom period, including thatch-roofed houses and storehouses, grand homes where the manor lord and priestess lived, and an *utaki* (sacred forest). Nearby, the **Oceanic Culture Museum and Planetarium (Kaiyo Bunka-kan;** ✆ **098-48-2741**) displays items relating to oceanic people from Asia through the South Pacific, including replica boats and canoes, fishing gear, money (like the Yap's stone currency), clothing, and more. It also has a planetarium with up to 140 million stars displayed on the domed screen. At the north end of the park is **Emerald Beach,** where you can swim free (open only Mar–Oct).

Motobu. oki-park.jp. Aquarium: ¥2,180 adults, ¥1,440 high-school students, younger students ¥710, children under 6 free; open daily 8:30am–8pm (closes 6:30pm Oct–Feb). Oceanic Culture Museum: ¥190 adults, children free; daily 8:30am–5:30pm (open until 7pm May–Aug). Express bus no. 111 from Naha Bus Terminal to Nago Bus Terminal (105 min.), then bus no. 65, 66 to Expo Park (55 min.), or YKB888 bus from Okinawa Prefectural Office in Naha (Kencho Kitaguchi) to Hotel Mahaina Wellness Resort (2 hr.), then 5 min. on foot to Expo Park.

Viewing a tank of whale sharks at Okinawa Churaumi Aquarium.

Okinawa World ♥♥ ATTRACTION About 40 to 60 minutes southeast of Naha, Okinawa's largest theme park promotes the region's history, culture, and natural sciences with a variety of attractions. Top among them is **Gyokusendo Cave,** which you can walk through in about 30 minutes along an 890m (2,900-ft.) walkway suspended above water and filled with impressive stalagmite and stalactite formations. There's also a museum devoted to the *habu,* Okinawa's indigenous poisonous snake; an orchard of 450 tropical fruit trees; an outdoor plaza for performances of the local Eisa dance; and workshops for potters, glass blowers, weavers, and other artisans housed in restored century-old Okinawan homes. While not a theme park in the Disneyland sense, it's certainly entertaining, as well as enlightening. Plan on 3 hours to see everything.

1336 Maekawa, Tamagusuku gyokusendo.co.jp/okinawaworld. ✆ **098-949-7421.** ¥2,000 adults, ¥1,000 children. Daily 9am–5:30pm (last entry 4pm). Bus: 54 or 83 to Gyokusendo-mae.

Gyokusendo Cave, a central attraction at Okinawa World.

Outdoor Activities

BEACHES With a swimming season that runs from about March through October, Okinawa has a huge variety of white sandy beaches, most with gentle slopes. Most accessible is **Naminoue Beach,** located right in Naha (bus no. 5 or 15 to Seibumon stop), but there are prettier beaches outside the city, especially to the north. Some are public beaches and some are resort beaches open to the public; many also have coral reefs popular with snorkelers (see below). Some charge small fees. Top options for bathing include **Emerald Beach** (in Ocean Expo Park, p. 594), **Manza Beach** (on a peninsula halfway up the west coast), and **Ikei Beach** and **White Beach** (both to the east of Okinawa City). **Busena Beach** (p. 598) is popular for watersports like windsurfing, and beaches on outlying islands like **Ie** and **Iheya** are ideal for travelers who prefer more secluded places to swim. Beach buffs will definitely benefit from having a car, and therefore, access to most secluded swimming and sunbathing spots.

DIVING & SNORKELING Due to its crystal-clear waters and coral reefs full of marine life, Okinawa is a diving mecca year-round. **Maeda Point,**

THE WAR MEMORIALS OF itoman

Some 40 minutes' drive southeast of Naha in the town of Itoman, the story of the Battle of Okinawa is told affectingly in a pair of memorial museums.

Of all the war memorials, the **Himeyuri Peace Museum (Himeyuri Heiwa Kinen Shiryokan)** ♥♥♥ (671–1 Aza-Ihara; himeyuri.or.jp; ✆ **098-997-2100**) is the most affecting, perhaps because it gives a personal dimension to the tragedy of war. It tells the story of 240 girls and teachers who in March 1945 were assigned to serve as nurse assistants in an army hospital buried inside a series of caves, where they were faced with indescribably filthy conditions and duties, including disposal of amputated limbs and burying the dead. As U.S. forces approached, the girls were thrown out of the caves to fend for themselves, where they were killed in battle or, fearing rape, took their lives. In all, 226 perished; this museum, filled with portraits and personal accounts, was founded by the survivors. Admission is ¥450 adults, ¥250 high-school students, ¥150 children; it's open daily 9am–5pm.

Head east to the waterfront Peace Memorial Park, where the **Okinawa Prefectural Peace Memorial Museum (Heiwa Kinen Shiryokan)** ♥♥♥ (614–1 Aza-Mabuni; peace-museum.pref.okinawa.jp; ✆ **098-997-3844**) will give you a broader picture of the impact of the Battle of Okinawa on the Okinawan people, through dioramas, videos, photographs, testimonials, and a free audio guide in English. You'll learn about the last days of battle, when many conscripted civilians died in caves from artillery fire, flamethrowers, or starvation, at the hands of Japanese soldiers or from forced suicide. But it doesn't stop there: The museum also describes Okinawan life before and after the war, from forced assimilation under the Japanese to postwar protests over the vast seizure of land for U.S. occupation. An exploration of this place will make you reflect not only on the human cost of war, but also on what Okinawans have endured for more than a century. Admission is ¥300 adults, ¥150 children; it's also open daily 9am–5pm.

It's a 40-minute bus ride (bus 34 or 89) from Naha to the Itoman Bus Terminal, then another half-hour on local bus 82; the two museums are 15 minutes apart by bus. It's much more convenient to visit them by car.

on the west coast, is the most popular dive spot on Okinawa Island. There are numerous dive shops offering instruction in English for everything from certification courses to *taiken* diving (experience dives for uncertified divers) to guided dives for those already certified. **Aloha Divers,** based mid-island in Yomitan (41–9 Toguchi; alohadiversokinawa.com; ✆ **090-6676-8807**), uses dive sites across the archipelago. Diving trips, starting at ¥11,000 per person (¥15,000 for two dives), include the teeming-with-life waters of the Kerama Islands, exploring an American warship sunk by a kamikaze pilot, and journeys to Yonaguni, where underwater ruins have leant themselves to theories of an as-yet-undiscovered ancient civilization. Snorkeling trips start at ¥5,500. In Naha, the local dive shop **Honu Honu Divers** (hhdivers.com; ✆ **098-988-8877**) also offers a broad range of tours, from beach dives and reef dives to exploring underwater

Diving with a hawksbill turtle in the teeming waters off the Kerama Islands.

caves or nearby islands. Trial dives for beginners start from ¥16,000, while certified divers will pay around ¥25,000 to ¥35,000 depending on the area chosen and the equipment needed.

Where to Stay on Okinawa Island

Most hotels charge extra during peak season (New Year's, Golden Week, and summer school vacation), with discounts in the off season. Directions are from Naha Airport.

NAGO CITY

The Busena Terrace Beach Resort ♥♥ Located on the northern end of Okinawa Island, on a peninsula surrounded on three sides by water, this resort with an elegant yet tropical atmosphere is the ultimate getaway. In addition to many on-site facilities, including a spa and indoor and outdoor pools, you're just a short walk or free shuttle ride away from Busena Beach and Busena Marine Park (with an underwater observatory and glass-bottom boats), and Ocean Expo Park (p. 594) is a 45-minute drive away. The resort also offers a wide range of activities, from whale watching and scuba diving to a star-gazing night walk on the beach, along with rentals for beach umbrellas, sea kayaks, and windsurfing. Rooms range from standard ones facing inland to more expensive ocean-facing rooms with balconies; for true luxury there are "gazebo" suites with huge balconies and views from both bedroom and living room. Restaurants also take advantage of the beautiful views, making this a good choice for a romantic retreat.

1808 Kise, Nago City. terrace.co.jp. ✆ **098-51-1333.** 410 units. ¥45,000–¥105,000 double. 120 min. via Airport Limousine from Naha Airport. **Amenities:** 8 restaurants; 4 lounges and bars; rental bikes; gym; indoor/outdoor pools; spa; free Wi-Fi.

NAHA

Of four Toyoko Inns (toyoko-inn.com) in Naha, most centrally located are **Toyoko Inn Naha Asahibashi Ekimae,** 2–1–20 Kume (✆ **098-951-1045;** Yui Rail to Asahibashi Station), and **Toyoko Inn Naha Miebashi-eki,** 1–20–1 Makishi (✆ **098-867-1045;** Yui Rail to Miebashi), both with doubles usually available for less than ¥10,000 (perhaps a little more in high season). Rates include breakfast.

Hotel Jal City Naha ♥ This is a good choice if you're basing yourself in Naha, in transit to another island, or prefer this hotel's location right on Kokusai Dori. Rooms are small but stylish, with good views out over the city from its higher floors.

1–3–70 Makishi. naha.jalcity.co.jp. ✆ **098-866-2580.** 304 units. ¥15,015–¥35,000 single or double. Yui Rail: Makishi Station (8 min.). **Amenities:** Restaurant; free Wi-Fi.

My Place ♥ Backpackers stay in this guesthouse because of the cheap dorm beds; couples often prefer private rooms so they can stay in a shared space without bunking with strangers. Rooms are clean if unremarkable, but the lounge area is nice, with exposed timber, raised tatami areas, the embalmed tail fin of a whale, and a hammock. The location is decent, too, on the doorstep of Tomari Iyumachi Fish Market and the ferry terminal, though the closest monorail station is about a 15-min. walk.

3–1–18 Tomari. myplace-guesthouse.com. ✆ **080-8569-2887.** 35 units, all w/ shared bath. Dorms from ¥2,000; private rooms from ¥4,000. Yui Rail: Miebashi (5 min.). **Amenities:** Free Wi-Fi.

OKINAWA CITY

Okinawa Grand Mer Resort ♥♥ It isn't on the coast, but this family hotel on top of a hill outside Okinawa City has lots of pluses, including free shuttle service from the airport (you can also take it to the airport and then board the monorail for Naha), a multilingual staff, and activities like marine walks, deserted island tours, parasailing, fishing, sunset kayaking, and coral dyeing experiences. All rooms have balconies; best are studio rooms for two people, complete with kitchenette.

2–8–1 Yogi. okinawa-grandmer.com. ✆ **098-931-1500.** 297 units. ¥15,000–¥30,000 double. 50 min. via free shuttle from Naha Airport (reservations required). **Amenities:** 2 restaurants; lounge; fitness center; indoor pool; sauna; spa; free Wi-Fi.

Where to Eat in Naha

Okinawan cuisine is big on pork, including *tebichi* (pigs' feet), simmered for hours in soy sauce and sake to make it soft and glutinous, and *rafute,* pork belly simmered in fish broth and *awamori* liquor. Other favorites include Okinawa *soba,* made with white flour instead of the mainland's usual buckwheat; and dishes made with *goya* (bitter gourd), like stir-fried *goya champuru* containing tofu, pork, egg, and other ingredients. *Champuru* means to "mix together" in Okinawan dialect; perhaps the ultimate example of this concept is taco rice, an adaptation of Mexican tacos (introduced by Americans stationed here) served with rice instead of tortillas. *Kyutei* cuisine, blending Chinese and Okinawan flavors and ingredients, originated with the Ryukyuan royal court; you can still occasionally find *irabu jiru,* a soup served to distinguished guests that mixes smoked sea snake, pork rib, and kelp. Pair local foods with the local Orion Beer or awamori, Japan's oldest distilled liquor, introduced to the Ryukyu Kingdom from Siam (present-day Thailand) in the early 15th century and made with Thai rice.

For seafood, in addition to the Makishi Public Market (see below), check out the **Tomari Iyumachi Fish Market** overlooking Tomari Port. Open daily 9am to 5pm, it's frequented in the mornings by fishmongers and restaurants scouting for the prize catch, but is also lined with stalls selling seafood delicacies at fair prices.

Asatoya ♥♥ PORK HOTPOTS This *shabu shabu* (hotpot dish) restaurant serves textured cuts of pork, including brisket, thigh, and shoulder, that diners swish in the simmering broth. This cooks the meat in about the length of time it takes to say *shabu shabu,* while the meat fat in turn adds flavor to the slowly reducing soup. You can order a la carte, or all you-can-eat sets for around ¥5,000 per person (a little more for the highest quality cuts), and it's worth adding sides like Okinawa tofu, *mozuku* seaweed, *goya champuru,* and pork *rafute.* The setting, in an old-style building with rustic wooden beams, shoji screens, and on-the-floor seating also adds to the ambience of the experience.

2F 1–3–3 Asato. ✆ **098-911-3537.** Dinner and drinks ¥4,000–¥7,000 per person. Daily 5–11pm. Yui Rail: Makishi (4 min.).

Hipparidako ♥♥ OKINAWAN DISHES This izakaya shows how varied and colorful the local diet can be, serving assorted sashimi sets in bamboo trays (often with *umi budo* hanging from the edges), raw horse meat

OKINAWA'S blue zone DIET

The traditional Okinawan diet was centered on seafood, fresh island fruits and vegetables, and nutrient-rich and anti-inflammatory seaweeds like kelp, reddish-brown *mozuku, hijki* (often found in salads and soups), and *umi budo* ("sea grapes"). The last of these, named so because its tendrils look like little green grapes hanging from vines, is loved for its *puchi-puchi* ("popping") texture and salty bursts of flavor, and is still a staple in every Okinawan kitchen. There's evidence to suggest this was one of the healthiest diets going; after all, Okinawa is a Blue Zone, its people among the longest-lived in the world. The island's centenarians also credit portion control, or *haru hachi bu* (eating until one is 80% full), as vital to their endurance. Unfortunately, the introduction of American fast foods, convenience stores, ready meals, and cheap ultra-processed foods to feed the struggling postwar populous (like spam, still far too common an item on restaurant menus) has vastly changed the Okinawan diet over the last 50 years.

Add a Little Snake to That?

An unusual drink to try while you're in Okinawa—provided you've no major aversion to reptiles—is *habushu,* made with the local distilled spirit *awamori* and a venomous pit viper. The snake is either drowned in the liquor or killed and gutted before being submerged in the bottle for months, resulting in a sweet and mildly spicy concoction not unlike a rum or maple-barrel whiskey. Look for vats of it on shelves in bars and restaurants throughout Okinawa—you can recognize it by the preserved snake still coiled up inside.

with perilla and *daikon* radish, seafood pokes, spicy chicken salads, and even seaweed tempura. You can start eyeing up what you want before entering—the fish tanks facing the road host all matter of aquatic life that has no idea it's about to be dinner. Once inside, grab a seat at the counter if it's available. ***Note:*** The price for some seafood changes depending on availability and season.

1–9–3 Makishi. hipparidako4832.owst.jp. ✆ **098-943-4832.** Sashimi meals ¥1,320–¥2,970; salads and sides ¥400–¥1,000. Daily 2pm–2am (last food order 12:30am). Irregular holidays. Yui Rail: Miebashi (6 min.).

Kame Kame Soba ♥♥ SOBA In business for more than 25 years, this small, down-to-earth soba shop makes a great lunch spot if you're spending the day on Naha's Naminoue Beach. The décor is sparse and the pallid ceiling lights suggest this was once an office or conference room, but don't let that deceive you. The white-flour soba is delicious, its springy texture pairing well with toppings like braised pork belly, spring onions, mugwort leaves, and *kamaboko* (fishcakes). Despite the quality, the dishes are still super cheap (all soba is less than ¥1,000); order from the vending machine when you enter.

1–3–6 Wakasa. kamekamesoba.wixsite.com/website. ✆ **098-869-5253.** Soba ¥500–¥900. Mon–Sat 10:30am–4pm. Yui Rail: Prefectural Office Station (12 min.) or a 4-min. walk from Namimoue Beach.

Makishi Public Market ♥♥♥ SEAFOOD Of the many fish markets you'll find in Okinawa, this is most accessible, located in the heart of Naha City and humming with the energy of shoppers and eaters day and night. It's not only fish on offer, mind. Pigs (every last bit of them: face, feet, and all) also line the stalls, as do fruits delivered that morning from nearby farms, wild vegetables and herbs, fresh and dried seaweeds, and sauces and marinades made from local produce. The seafood fare is, however, the most extensive and the real reason to come. Order shellfish tempura or a slow-boiled seafood soup; buy lobster, turban snails, or parrotfish on the ground floor and ask for it to be cooked at the hole-in-the-walls upstairs; try the many different versions of *umi budo* (you'll begin to realize it's an excellent beer snack); or hop from shop to shop, slowly loosening your belt buckle along the way. If you're a foodie, you won't be leaving this place in a hurry.

2–10–1 Matsuo. makishi-public-market.jp ✆ **098-867-6560.** Prices vary widely; you could easily spend ¥5,000–¥10,000. Daily 8am–10pm. Yui Rail: Makishi (9 min.), Miebashi (10 min.).

Makishi Public Market in Naha (p. 601).

Ryukyu Paozu ♥♥ DUMPLINGS Set high on a hilltop, Shuri Castle feels like it has little going on around it. So it was a delight to discover this superb dumpling shop between the castle park and the monorail station, serving various kinds of pork and prawn dumpling, and *xiaolongbao* (soup dumplings) as good as those from the stalls in Yokohama's Chinatown. Order dumpling plates a la carte, or if you're here at lunch, go for a set meal that may include rice, salad, soup, pickles, small veg plates, and a dessert.

1–46–2 Shuritorihoricho ryupao.com. ✆ **098-943-7950.** Dumplings ¥450–¥600, lunches ¥1,080–¥1,200. Tues–Sat 11am–2:30pm and 5–8pm (last order); Sun 11am–2:30pm. Yui Rail: Shuri (3 min.). The sign to the right of the door says, "Ryukyu Baozi."

Excursion to the Yaeyama Islands

Closer to Taiwan than to Okinawa Island, the **Yaeyama archipelago** is a chain of 19 islands, most of them small. Lying at about the same latitude as the Bahamas, the Yaeyama Islands are blessed with beautiful beaches and coral reefs. Eighty percent of the chain's population lives on **Ishigaki Island,** the area's gateway and administrative center.

Most famous of the Yaeyama Islands is **Iriomote ♥♥♥**, a rather mysterious island covered mostly with subtropical primeval forests preserved in a national park that you can explore by kayak and on foot. In recent years, tourists have begun flooding into Iriomote; though its population is around 2,400, more than 300,000 visit annually. Iriomote has thus capped the maximum number of daily visitors at 1,200, hoping to combat the water shortages, increased traffic accidents, damage to endangered wildcat habitats, and general disruption to local lives caused by tourism. While the cap is not yet official law, it's being enforced at the community level through tourism providers and lodgings. Check before booking to make sure the island can accommodate you.

ARRIVING & GETTING AROUND Peach, JAL, and ANA fly from Tokyo directly to **Ishigaki Airport,** a 3½-hour flight costing from ¥10,000 to ¥30,000 one-way. Planes from Naha on Okinawa Island depart for Ishigaki every hour; prices start at ¥6,000 for the cheapest flights. To continue on to Iriomote, catch a ferry from the **Outer Islands Ferry Terminal** in Ishigaki City; boats depart two to four times an hour for the 40-minute trip. There are three different ferry companies; most boats go to Ohara Port on the east coast (¥1,830 one-way) but some go to Uehara Port on the west coast (¥2,390). Each of the ferry companies operates its own buses on Iriomote, which you can ride free only if you purchased their ferry ticket (some drivers, however, don't seem to care).

EXPLORING THE YAEYAMA ISLANDS

Ishigaki City has a nice **public market** and is surrounded by lovely beaches, like **Sukuji Beach** with its long, sandy shoreline; **Kabira Bay,**

It's best to visit mystical Irimote Island with a guide, to explore its primeval forests without damaging their rare ecosystems.

famous for its black pearl cultivation, and the **Yonehara Coast,** with its beach, campground, and grove of Yaeyama Palm Trees, found only on these islands. It's also famous among divers for its coral reefs, manta rays, and steep drop-offs. **Prime Scuba,** 345–9 Maesato, Ishigaki City (primescuba-ishigaki.com/en/; ✆ **0980-87-5980**), offers diving excursions for the novice and expert alike. Programs start at ¥13,000 (additional dives only ¥5,500).

Your main reason for coming this far, however, is **Iriomote Island (Iriomotejima)**. At 289 sq. km (115 sq. miles), it's actually the second-largest Okinawan island, but it is almost entirely covered by a dense subtropical forest laced by rivers that drain into Japan's largest mangrove swamp. Its most famous resident is the Iriomote cat, a shy nocturnal wildcat found only here. There are only 100 or so remaining in the wild. There are also, however, many crabs, birds, butterflies, and other creatures to see in what is sometimes called "Asia's Amazon."

It's highly recommended that you visit Iriomote with a guide or tour. **Hirata Tourism Company,** 1 Misaki-cho in Ishigaki City (hirata-group.co.jp; ✆ **0980-82-6711**), offers several guided tours in English into Iriomote's remote wilderness that involve hiking, kayaking, and boat trips. Tours start at ¥14,770 adults, ¥10,900 children. The Sangara Falls itinerary, which involves a full day of kayaking through jungle rivers and trekking through the island's verdant walking trails, costs ¥18,200 adults, ¥14,100 children. Check the website for seasonal discounts.

WHERE TO STAY ON THE YAEYAMA ISLANDS

In Ishigaki, **Hotel East China Sea** (eastchinasea.jp; ✆ **0980-88-1155**), near bus and ferry terminals, is a convenient choice, offering rooms with rattan furniture that impart a sense of island style, as well as Japanese-style rooms. Balconies from all rooms face the busy port with its fleet of ferries, fishing boats, and pleasure boats. Rooms go for around ¥20,000 to ¥35,000 per night. This place often requires a minimum 2-night stay.

On Iriomote, **Pension Hoshinosuna** (✆ **0980-85-6448**) sits on a hill above the famous Hoshizuma no Hama beach with its pretty islet-studded bay and sand shaped like stars. It's popular with overnighters because of its dive shop, rental snorkeling equipment, and restaurant with an outdoor terrace facing the sea offering Okinawan specialties. Expect to pay around ¥5,000 to ¥10,000 per person, including two meals. Pickup is available from Uehara Port.

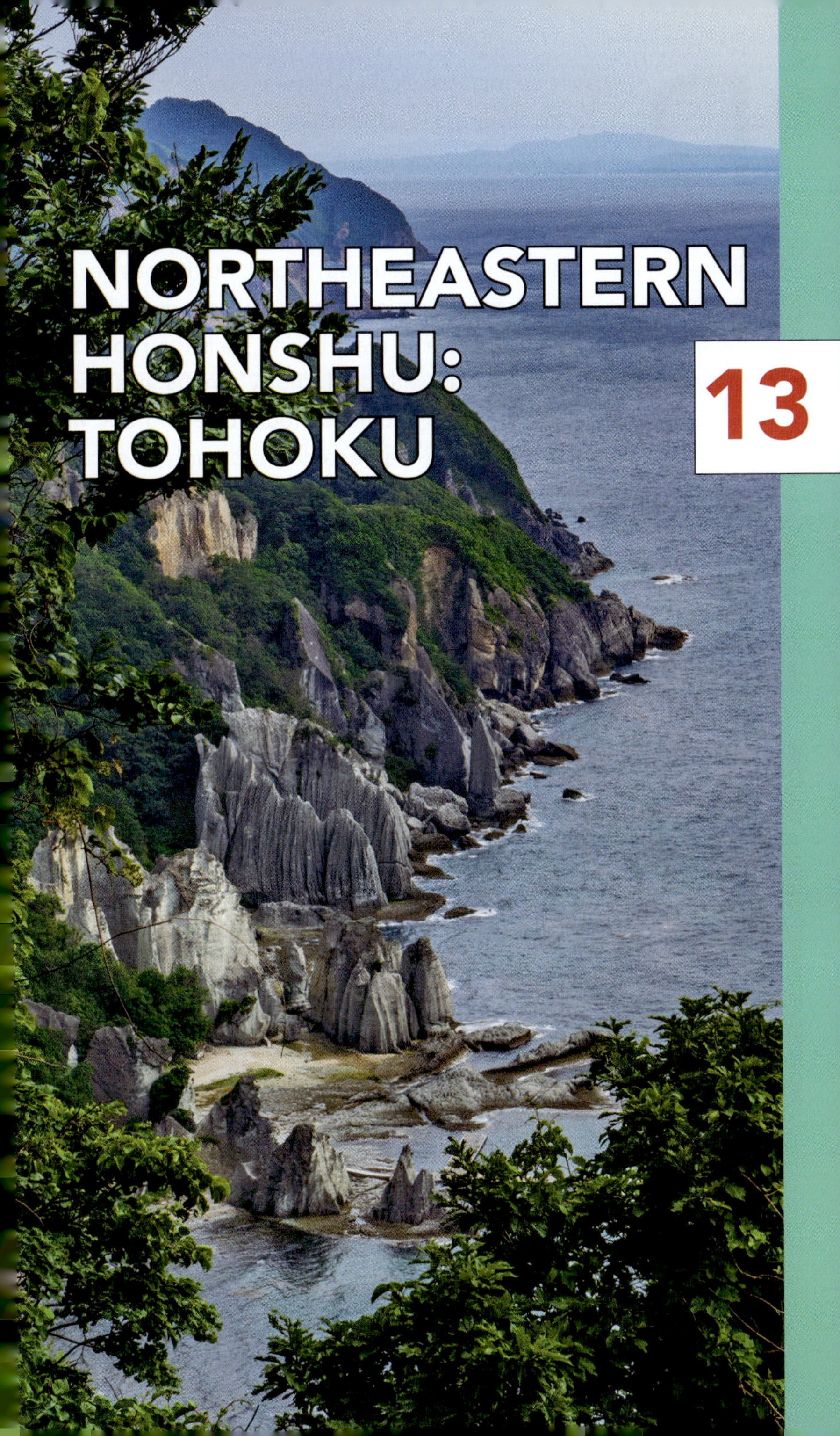

NORTHEASTERN HONSHU: TOHOKU

13

Because so many of Japan's historic events took place in Kyoto, Tokyo, and other cities in southern Honshu, most visitors to Japan never venture farther north than Tokyo. True, northeastern Honshu (Tohoku; literally "East North") does not have the famous temples, shrines, gardens, and castles of southern Japan, but it does have spectacular mountain scenery, national parks, hot springs in abundance, excellent ski resorts, and many hiking trails. Its rugged, mountainous terrain, coupled with cold, snowy winters, has also helped preserve the region's traditions. You won't find any of Tokyo's edgy flashiness here, but rather a down-to-earth practicality, warm hospitality, and a way of life that harks back generations.

Matsushima, about 3 hours north of Tokyo, is considered one of Japan's most scenic spots, with pine-covered islets dotting its bay. Farther north, the pleasant village of **Kakunodate,** once a thriving castle town, is renowned for its samurai houses and cherry trees. Sprawling over 862 sq. km (333 sq. miles) of northern Tohoku, the resplendent **Towada-Hachimantai National Park** draws visitors with scenic lakes, rustic hot-spring spas, skiing, and hiking, including a trail that flanks the picture-perfect Oirase Stream.

THE BEST TOHOKU EXPERIENCES

- **Exploring the Pine-Clad Islets of Matsushima** The sea around Matsushima, sprinkled with pine-covered islets, has been regarded for centuries as one of the finest natural scenes in all Japan. See p. 608.
- **Learning the Ways of the Mountain Monks** In Bandai-Asahi National Park you can walk through ancient forests with *yamabushi,* mountain monks, a sect of ascetic practitioners in search of quasi-magical powers. See p. 627.
- **Spending the night at Nyuto Onsen** There is no other hot spring quite like this one, consisting of a string of new and ancient inns. See p. 620.
- **Hiking Along the Oirase Stream** Set beside a rushing stream beneath a dense canopy of trees, this is one of Japan's loveliest hiking paths. See p. 624.
- **Walking the Michinoku Coastal Trail** This 1,025km walking trail winds along the Tohoku coast, past some of Japan's most magnificent geological features and through towns and villages still recovering from the 2011 earthquake and tsunami. See p. 628.

 PREVIOUS PAGE: **Northern Honshu's rugged coast.**

Northeastern Honshu: Tohoku

13

NORTHEASTERN HONSHU: TOHOKU | The Best Tohoku Experiences

MATSUSHIMA ♥♥

375km (234 miles) NE of Tokyo

The scenic Sea of Matsushima, dotted with tiny wooded islands.

Matsushima means "Pine Tree Islands"—and that's exactly what this region is known for. Around 260 pine-covered islets and islands dot Matsushima Bay, giving it the appearance of a giant pond in a Japanese landscape garden where twisted and gnarled pines sweep upward from volcanic tuff and white sandstone, creating bizarre and beautiful shapes. Matsushima is so dear to Japanese hearts that it's considered one of the three most scenic spots in Japan (the other two are Miyajima in Hiroshima Bay and Amanohashidate on the north coast of Honshu), so designated about 380 years ago in a book written by a Confucian philosopher of the Edo government. Matsuo Basho (1644–94), the famous Japanese haiku poet, was so struck by Matsushima's beauty that, almost as if a loss for words, he wrote: "Matsushima, Ah! Matsushima! Matsushima!"

Unfortunately, motorboats have been invented since Basho's time, detracting from the immemorial beauty that evoked such ecstasy in him long ago, but this is still a fetching corner of Japan's vast north.

Essentials

ARRIVING From Tokyo, take the **Tohoku Shinkansen** train from Ueno or Tokyo Station to Sendai, a 1½-hour trip that costs ¥10,560 for an unreserved seat. In Sendai change to the **JR Senseki Line**—it's well marked in English and trains depart every half-hour or so. From Sendai, the trip to **Matsushima Kaigan Station** takes about 25 minutes by express train and costs ¥420.

VISITOR INFORMATION There's a **Matsushima Tourist Association office** (✆ **022-354-2233;** daily 9am–5pm, to 4pm in winter) located inside the Sightseeing Boat building at **Matsushima Kaigan Pier,** with informative leaflets and an English-speaking staff. Information is available also at **matsushima-kanko.com** and **discoversendai.travel**.

CITY LAYOUT **Matsushima Kaigan Station** lies to the west of the boat pier and Matsushima's main attractions; the train station and pier are about a 6-minute walk apart. All of Matsushima's major attractions are within walking distance of both the station and the pier (though the pier is more centrally located); you can cover the entire area on foot in a half-day of sightseeing. To really explore the beauties of Matsushima, however, be sure to get out onto the bay with a scenic boat cruise (see p. 613).

Exploring Matsushima

Date Masamune Historical Museum (Date Masamune Rekishikan) ♥ MUSEUM This museum details the life and times of the feudal lord Date Masamune (see box on p. 610) through 25 life-size, audiovisual diorama displays involving more than 200 wax figures. Showing everything from how he lost sight in one of his eyes at age 5 to his marriage at age 13 to his victories in battle (he fought his first battle at age 15), the dioramas may be a little cheesy, but they bring to life what might otherwise be dull history. If you download a special discount coupon from the website below, you can get a 20% discount on the admission fee for up to five people.

13–13 Fugendo. date-masamune.jp. ✆ **022-354-4131.** ¥1,000 adults, ¥500 children. Daily 8:30am–5pm (9am–4:30pm in winter). A 3-min. walk east of the pier.

Entsuin ♥♥ TEMPLE Built in the early Edo Period, more than 360 years ago, by the Date clan, this lesser-known temple next to Zuiganji (p. 611) is admired for its gardens—a small rock garden (with seven rocks representing the Seven Deities of Good Fortune) inspired by the islets of Matsushima Bay, a moss garden with six different types of moss, a lovely rose garden, and an Edo-period garden with a pond and "borrowed landscaping." The small temple houses an elaborate equestrian statue of Lord Date Mitsumune, Date Masamune's grandson, who was reportedly poisoned by the Tokugawa shogunate and died at the tender age of 19 in Edo Castle. Seven statues surround him, representing retainers who committed

The rock garden at Entsuin Temple was inspired by the Sea of Matsushima, with boulders set around the gravel like the sea's famous islands.

LOCAL HERO: date masumune

A name you'll hear often in your travels around this area is **Date Matsumune** (1567–1636), the most powerful and important lord of northern Honshu in the early Edo period. Somewhat romantically nicknamed the One-Eyed Dragon (in fact, he lost his eye in a childhood illness, not in battle), he was a fearless warrior, leading a powerful army dressed in black armor and golden headgear. Unifying the region known as Tohoku, Date built his castle in nearby Sendai, and today almost all sites in and around Sendai and Matsushima are tied to the Date family. He was also a wily political survivor—though he eventually submitted to the Tokugawa shogunate, as a powerful regional lord he maintained some independence, building many castles, expanding trade with other countries, and even embracing, or at least tolerating, Christianity. His legend lives on in video games, anime, manga, and television historical dramas.

ritual suicide to follow their master into death. The interior walls are all covered with an overlay of gold. The painting of an occidental rose on the right-hand door is thought to be the first in Japan (hence, the rose garden); other Western flowers include narcissus and corona. Be on the lookout for "hidden" joined crosses above the door that are slanted; Christianity was banned in Edo Japan, but the Date clan used crosses as a symbol for silent revolt. Expect to spend about 45 minutes here, enjoying the serenity (this temple rarely gets as many crowds as nearby Zuiganji does).

67 Aza-chonai. ✆ **022-354-3206.** ¥500 adults, ¥300 children. Daily 9am–4pm (to 3:30pm Dec–Mar).

Fukuurajima ♥ ISLAND/GARDEN About a 10-minute walk east from the boat pier, a long red concrete bridge with orange-colored railings connects Fukuurajima to the mainland. It's a botanical garden of sorts, with several hundred labeled plants and trees, but mostly it's unkempt and overgrown—which comes as a surprise in cultivated Japan. It will take you less than an hour to circle the island, and there are many resting spots along the way, including a snack shop. The island gate is open daily 8am to 5pm (4:30pm in winter); admission is ¥200 for adults, half-price for children.

Kanrantei ♥ HISTORIC TEAHOUSE The name means the "Water-Viewing Pavilion," and this simple wooden teahouse, just a 1-minute walk west from the pier, was indoor used by generations of the Date family for such aesthetic pursuits as watching the moon cast its silver beam across the water's surface, or contemplating the ripples of the tide. Originally it belonged to warlord Toyotomi Hideyoshi as part of his estate at Fushimi Castle near Kyoto, but he presented it to the Date family at the end of the 16th century; it was moved here in 1645, where it remains one of the largest teahouses in Japan. For an additional ¥400 or more, depending on the accompanying sweet, you can drink ceremonial green tea while sitting on *tatami* and contemplating the bay, its islands, and the boats carving ribbons through the water—this is the main reason to come. After tea, wander through the small museum containing samurai armor, ceramics, lacquerware, and tea-ceremony utensils belonging to the Date family.

56–1 Aza-chonai. ✆ **022-353-3355.** ¥200 adults, ¥150 college and high-school students, ¥100 children. Daily 8:30am–5pm (to 4:30pm Nov–Mar); tea and sweets served till 1 hour before closing time.

Matsushima Retro Museum ♥♥ MUSEUM It's not uncommon to find museums dedicated to Showa-period (1926–89) toys, games, pop culture, and trinkets in small-town Japan, perhaps because people actually had the space and time to amass collections. Among the colorful cluttered displays in this delightful little archive are old manga series, sumo programs, and pulpy sports rags; mechanical pachinko machines and spring-loaded tabletop games; baseball cards and an ancient catcher's mitt; vintage movie posters and record sleeves promoting the hottest names in Japanese city pop; soft vinyl dolls depicting Ultraman and various pop culture *kaiju* (monsters); and a wooden stereoscope with cardboard slides showing scenes from around the world (a lotus pond in Yokohama, a horsedrawn cart in Singapore, a Sioux chieftain astride his steed). Even the ugly carpet-tile floor evokes the questionable styles of the '80s. Though you might only spend 20 minutes here, it's a hands-on experience, where you can touch, inspect, and play with any of the items (you can even request records to be played on the old hi-fi system) that's well worth the admission fee.

48–1 Funendo. ✆ **022-355-0280.** ¥400, ¥300 junior high and high-school students, ¥200 children. Daily 9am–5pm. A 5-min. walk east of the pier.

Oshima ♥♥ ISLAND On the southern edge of Matsushima, about an 8-minute walk from Matsushima Kaigan Station, this small island was once used as a retreat by priests (women were forbidden on the island). Long ago there were more than 100 hand-dug caves carved with scriptures, Buddhist images, and sutras, but today the island and its remaining 50 caves and stone images are rather neglected. There's no fee, there's no gate, and the island never closes. Connected to the mainland by bridge, it's a nice quiet spot in which to sit and view the harbor; you can walk around the entire island in about 15 minutes. If you want an even better view of the bay, walk to the end of **Matsushima Seaside Park,** then join the footpath ascending alongside the main road. After about 15 minutes, you'll come to **Sokanzan,** a small headland with a wooden veranda and a stone-viewing platform overlooking the bay.

Zuiganji Temple ♥♥♥ TEMPLE The most famous Zen temple in northern Japan, Zuiganji Temple is a designated National Treasure. It's just a couple minutes' walk from Matsushima Kaigan Pier, 10 minutes from the train station. On the right side of the pathway leading to the temple are impressive caves and grottoes dug out by priests long ago; adorned with Buddhist statues and memorial tablets, they were used for practicing *zazen* (sitting meditation). The rock wall appears to be an object of veneration itself, a concept more associated with the Shinto faith—but this is a

A small sub-temple of Zuiganji, Godaido is connected to the Matsushima mainland by picturesque red bridges.

reminder that Buddhism and Shinto, though they have diverged somewhat since the heyday of *shinbutsu-shugo* (the syncretization of two belief systems), are still, by religious standards, close siblings.

Originally founded in the Heian Period (828) as a Tendai temple, Zuignji became a Zen temple in the 13th century. After a period of decline, it was remodeled in 1604 by order of Date Masamune to serve as the Date family temple. It took hundreds of workers 5 years to build the grand hall, a large wooden structure constructed in the *shoin-zukuri* style typical of the Momoyama Period. The temple's interior is what really impresses, especially the wood-carved transoms and brilliantly painted, gold-plated *fusuma* (sliding doors). A room at the back is dedicated to the samurai who were laid to rest here, having followed their Date lord into death by committing ritualistic suicide.

Also on the temple grounds and included in the admission price, the **Zuiganji Art Museum (Seiryuden)** houses temple and Date family treasures, including painted sliding doors, portraits and statues of the Date clan, teacups, scrolls, calligraphy, and woodblock prints, many of Matsushima as it looked in former times.

91 Aza-chonai. ✆ **022-354-2023.** ¥700 adults, ¥400 children. Daily 8am–5pm (to 3:30pm Dec–Jan, to 4pm Nov and Feb, to 4:30pm Oct and Mar).

Crossing the Bridge to Godaido

On a tiny island just east of the pier, **Godaido** is a small wooden worship hall under the supervision of Zuiganji Temple (p. 611). It's connected to the mainland by three short bridges, built with spaced wooden slats. If you trip while crossing, so the legend goes, you're not yet ready to attain the temple's wisdom. Godaido's grounds are open night and day and are free to enter, though there's not much to see other than the bay. Nevertheless, Godaido is often featured in brochures of Matsushima, making this delicate wooden temple one of the town's best-known landmarks.

BOAT CRUISES

Regular sightseeing boats depart from the Matsushima pier once an hour between 9am and 4pm (3pm in winter), making 50-minute trips around the bay; they charge between ¥1,000 and ¥1,500 for adults, half-price for children. More expensive tickets are for larger, more state-of-the-art boats, but whichever you choose you're getting the same experience. Boat excursions are the best way to get a sense of the bay's topography, and the symbolism attached to the more eye-catching pine-topped islets. A disembodied voice—a little annoying, in my opinion, but providing context all the same—will draw your attention to Kujiira-jima ("Whale Island") and Kame-jima ("Turtle Island"), so named for their distinctive shapes; you'll see an island where Lord Date Masamune once conducted moon-viewing parties, and another which inspired a monk to write a tanka poem after seeing two herons take flight from it. A stony outcrop is said to have weathered into the likeness of a Nio guardian—usually found warding off evil spirits at temple gates—which protects the bay from the destructive power of the open ocean. (Incidentally, during the 2011 tsunami, Matsushima didn't fare as badly as other parts of the Tohoku coastline because the islets acted as barriers between the mainland and the waves.) In the winter, snow-topped mountains to the south form a lovely backdrop, which is just reward for braving the fierce winds whipping across the deck (though indoor seating is available on all boats). The only blot on the journey is the ghastly Tohoku Electric Power station, which for some reason the disembodied voice takes time to point out—not that you could miss it.

Where to Stay in Matsushima

Because this is a popular tourist destination, accommodations in Matsushima are not cheap, especially during the peak months of May through November. For the Tanabata Festival (Aug 6–8 in Sendai) and the Toronagashi Festival (Aug 15–16 in Matsushima), rooms may be fully booked 6 months in advance and rates are at their highest. Rates are generally lower during the off-season (Dec–Apr).

Hotel Ichinobo ♥♥ Despite its large size, modern facilities, and the word "hotel" in its name, this property has the atmosphere of a traditional *ryokan* (albeit a rather large, modern one) and offers mostly Japanese-style rooms. It's surrounded by pine trees and has charming landscaped grounds and ponds, with views of the sea and islands from all its rooms and the wonderful public baths, including outdoor baths. Smartly furnished View Bath twin rooms include use of a private lounge and have glassed-in, private whirlpool baths off private balconies. Dinner is served in a dining hall that blends the buffet model with an order-as-you-go Japanese counter restaurant (notably, it has a well-stocked wine cellar). Ichinobo's location

on the northern edge of Matsushima—about a 20-minute walk from the pier—is inconvenient, but staff will fetch you upon arrival.
1–4 Takagi Azahama. ichinobo.com/matsushima. ✆ **022-353-3333.** 126 units. ¥50,000–¥100,000 double. Rates include 2 meals. Free shuttle bus from pier or train station. **Amenities:** Restaurant; bar; tea lounge; outdoor pool; sauna; free Wi-Fi.

Matsushima Koumura (まつしま香村) ♥♥ Fronted by a small landscape garden, this family-run ryokan continues the old-world aesthetic inside; its hallways are like Edo-period streets, with pebbles and irregular flagstones, bamboo stalks lining the walls, wood-latticed sliding doors, and soft ambient lighting. The husband-and-wife owners are exemplary hosts—they even give gifts to guests staying on special occasions—and despite having only a smattering of English, enthusiastically help with restaurant bookings or marking points of interest on the map. The rooms are in a basic Japanese style, with tatami, futons, shoji window frames, and an alcove displaying a hanging scroll. Traditional *koto* music is piped into the rooms throughout the day, starting around 7:30am. (I find it quite meditative, but I can see how some guests might tire of it.) There's a public bath facility on the top floor, albeit a small one with no open-air section. Upon request, the staff can also organize a breakfast of rice balls with fillings like salmon, pickled plum, and kelp. It's a 15-minute walk east of the pier, or 10 minutes walk from Takagimachi Station.
37–7 Takagi Hama. ✆ **022-354-4361.** 8 units. ¥6,000–¥15,000 per person. **Amenities:** Indoor bath; free Wi-Fi (though connection is sketchy).

Taikanso ♥♥ Able to accommodate more than 1,000 guests, Matsushima's largest hotel sprawls atop a plateau surrounded by pine-covered hills and offers the best views in town, including views of the island-studded bay from its indoor and outdoor public baths. Both Western- and Japanese-style rooms are available. The cheapest rooms (singles and twins) face inland, but all the Japanese-style rooms face the sea, though views are marred for some by a parking lot. Wonderful combination rooms (the most expensive) offer the best of both worlds with *tatami* areas and beds. A plus here is that you can choose from several restaurants to dine in. Though the hotel is a bit of a hike from town, it offers regular shuttle buses to the train station and the pier.
10–76 Aza Inuta. taikanso.co.jp. ✆ **022-354-2161.** 256 units. ¥15,000–¥25,000 per person. Rates include 2 meals. **Amenities:** 4 restaurants; bar; outdoor pool; room service; free Wi-Fi.

Where to Eat in Matsushima

In summer, stalls up and down the main street of Matsushima sell grilled octopus, corn on the cob, and crab; in winter oysters are all the rage. Most of the permanent eateries are clustered around the pier, but many operate during the day only. Matsushima turns into a bit of a ghost town at night, so consider adding dinner to your accommodation plan, unless you plan on going to one of the izakaya mentioned below (even these take last orders by 9pm at the latest).

Fresh Off the Boat

It wouldn't be a Japanese coastal city without a good fish market, and the **Matsushima Fish Market** ♥♥ (4–10 Fugendo; sakana-ichiba.co.jp; ✆ **0120-502-3180**) still very much caters to the locals, with its aisles of frozen fish, dried seafood hanging on racks, and shelves of seaweeds, snacks, and dashi-based sauces. That said, its restaurant stalls now attract the tourist crowds, too, thanks to multilingual vending machines for placing orders. There's a sushi stall selling omakase boards and tuna sets (¥1,500–¥3,000); a hole-in-the-wall offering deep-fried oysters, seafood skewers, and Miyagi-famous beef tongue; and an upstairs soup shop specializing in seafood ramen (¥1,050–¥2,000). Collect your order then bring it to one of the tables on the second floor. There's also an outdoor seating area connected to the **Yakigaki Grilled Oyster House** at the market's entrance, though technically it's reserved for customers ordering food from this shop, like the ¥1,800 Matsushima grilled oyster set. The market is open Monday to Friday 9am to 4pm, weekends 8am to 4pm, and is (handily) just a 3-minute walk from the pier.

Café Knit ♥♥ VARIED JAPANESE Café by day, izakaya by night, this cheerful little restaurant with its friendly husband-and-wife owners makes a good rest stop for families—with ice cream, cakes, coffee, and tea on the menu, and a small kids play area—or dinner and a nightcap after dark. From the English-language menu, order minced meat curry, *omurice* (an omelet draped over a portion of rice served with demi-glace or ketchup), Japanese curry rice, and hamburger steak, or appetizers like tofu and *wakame* seaweed salad, French fries, shrimp and scallops cooked in oil and garlic, and *karaage* (deep-fried chicken thigh). It's classic izakaya fare, but it's done well. If you're primarily here for a drink, consider the evening set meal, featuring two alcoholic drinks and three *otsumami* (small appetizers, probably some pickles and tofu) for ¥1,500.
13–1 Kakinouchi. instagram.com/cafeknit_matsushima. ✆ **080-3145-2100.** Lunches ¥1,300–¥1,800, dinner ¥3,000–¥4,000 per person. Wed–Mon 11am–9pm. A 5-min. walk east of the pier; opposite the Matsushima Retro Museum (p. 611).

Kitchen Table Matsushima ♥ VARIED JAPANESE There's nothing too fancy about this restaurant squeezed between Entsuin and Zuiganji temples, dishing out seafood rice bowls and *soba* (buckwheat noodle) and tempura sets for sightseers seeking lunch amidst the town's main attractions. The front room is for customers having tea and sweets, the large dining area out back (tables and floor seating available) is for those having hot food. The most popular item is the *anago* (saltwater eel) rice bowl, and I suggest opting for that or the tempura, which nicely batters up whatever's in season; I find the soba here to be too al dente.
67 Azamachi. ✆ **022-393-9275.** Lunches ¥1,000–¥2,000. Daily 9:30am–6:30pm.

Umechaya ♥♥ IZAKAYA In this one-room izakaya, run by a kindly husband-and-wife duo, the restaurant experience becomes something akin to a homestay. Seated at one of tables in the tatami-floored dining room, a

VISITING THE samurai town OF KAKUNODATE

Just 3 hours by Shinkansen train from Tokyo, this historic town in the heart of Tohoku offers a wonderfully well-preserved window into the feudal samurai culture; it makes a nice day trip for those traveling on to Towada-Hachimantai National Park (see below).

Founded in 1620 by Lord Ashina Yoshikatsu, Kakunodate was a samurai settlement of modest thatched-roof homes behind dark wooden fences along wide streets lined with weeping cherry trees imported from Kyoto. To help support themselves, the samurai engaged in cottage industry, crafting beautiful products made from cherry bark. Merchants, who were despised by other social classes during the Edo period, settled in their own district nearby in narrow, cramped quarters. Today, many of Kakunadate's 13,000 residents are direct descendants of the original samurai and merchant residents. The town is at its most glorious (and crowded) in late April, when its hundreds of cherry trees are in full bloom.

The main thing to see is **The Samurai District** (**Bukeyashiki**), 15 to 20 minutes from the station on foot. Even though only seven of the original 80

Cherry-blossom season in Kakunodate, known for its well-preserved samurai houses.

TV at one end playing some crappy food or fishing show, you'll dine on the likes of sashimi, tofu, miso-flavored rice balls, yakitori skewers, and breaded pork cutlets, all prepared in the adjacent open kitchen. The owners are keen on foreign clientele, engaging them in conversation (language barriers notwithstanding); you may be asked to mark your home country on the map on the wall. You'll feel at ease dining here; don't be surprised if you stay for a couple extra draft beers upon finishing your meal.
35–2 Fugendo. ✆ **090-317-72471.** ¥3,000–¥5,000 per person. Tues–Sun 5–9pm (last order). On a backstreet behind the Matsushima Fish Market.

TOWADA-HACHIMANTAI NATIONAL PARK ♥♥♥

Blessed with mountain ranges, lakes, streams, and hot-spring spas, the vast unblemished wilderness of Towada-Hachimantai National Park spreads through north-central Tohoku across three prefectures (Akita, homes remain, the old-world atmosphere is still intact, with traditional entry gates and beautifully kept gardens. Walking from the station, you'll pass several samurai houses on Bukeyashiki Dori that are open free to the public (though in some, only limited areas can be viewed), including the **Odano Samurai House,** the **Kawarada Samurai House** next door, the **Matsumoto Samurai House** across the street, and the city-owned **Iwahashi Samurai House,** which has appeared in movies. The first major place of interest, however, is the **Aoyagi Samurai Manor** (**Kakunodate Rekishi-mura Aoyagi**) ♥♥, 26 Higashi Katuraku-cho (✆ **0187-54-3257;** daily 9am–5pm; ¥500 adults, ¥300 junior-high and high-school students, ¥200 children), with its impressive entry gate and several buildings full of treasures—samurai armor, rifles, swords, dolls, kimono, sake cups, *ukiyo-e* (woodblock prints), scrolls and screens, Meiji-Era uniforms and medals, farm tools, antique phonographs, and even cameras. Next door, the thatched-roof **Ishiguro Samurai House** ♥♥, Omotemachi (✆ **0187-55-1496;** daily 9am–5pm; ¥500 adults, ¥300 children), remains almost exactly as it might have looked when it was constructed 200 years ago. English-speaking 12th-generation descendant Ishiguro Naotsugi continues to live here; he has opened five simple but elegant rooms to the public in the main house; a former warehouse displays family heirlooms including samurai gear, winter *geta* (fur-lined and with spikes), scales for weighing rice, and old maps of Kakunodate. The medical illustrations, by the way, are from Japan's first book on anatomy, copied from a Dutch book in 1774 by Kakunodate samurai Odano Naotake.

From Tokyo, the **Akita Shinkansen** to Kakunodate takes 3 hours and costs ¥16.820 for a non-reserved seat; you could also take the **Tohoku Shinkansen** to Morioka then change to the **JR Tazawako Line,** but this will take 4-plus hours with changes.

Iwate, Aomori). It's perfect for the outdoor enthusiast, offering hiking in summer and skiing in winter, as well as wonderful woodland walks and nighttime skies primed for stargazing. Most easily accessible from Tokyo is **Lake Tazawa** at the southern end of the park, with its ski lifts, hot-springs, and biking, kayaking, and hiking opportunities. Far to the north, and a good choice if you're heading onward to Hokkaido, are the pristine **Lake Towada** and delightful **Oirase Stream** with its riverbank hiking trail. Bus service through the national park is either infrequent or nonexistent, so the easiest way to get around is by rental car. That said, if you travel only in and around the Lake Tazawa area, it's possible to do this using public transport.

Lake Tazawa ♥♥♥

At 423m (1,387 ft.) deep, crystal-clear Lake Tazawa (Tazawako) has the distinction of being the deepest lake in Japan. Set in a mountain caldera, it offers swimming and kayaking as well as cycling along its rim. Nearby are several ski resorts, as well as the **Nyuto Onsen** rustic hot-spring spa hotels at the base of Mount Nyuto, which make good bases for exploring the area. **Mount Komagatake** is a popular destination for trekkers.

A highlight of the drive around Lake Tazawa: the famous statue of Princess Tatsuko.

ESSENTIALS

ARRIVING From Tokyo, take the **Akita Shinkansen** to Tazawako Station. The trip takes 2¾ hours and costs ¥19,050 for a reserved seat on the fastest train.

VISITOR INFORMATION Inside Tazawako Station, the **Tazawako Tourist Information Center** (**© 0187-43-2111;** daily 8:30am–5:15pm) provides luggage storage until 4:30pm daily for ¥500 per piece; luggage delivery costs ¥650 per piece, though registration closes at noon. You'll find more information at **tazawako-kakunodate.com** and **akita-tourism.com**. For information on Nyuto Onsen, see **nyuto-onsenkyo.com**.

GETTING AROUND The town of **Tazawako** is the best base for visiting the southern region of Towada-Hachimantai National Park. **Buses** depart from the Tazawako Bus Terminal (across from Tazawako Station) for Lake Tazawa, ski resorts, Mount Komagatake, and Nyuto Onsen. Lake Tazawa is a 15-minute bus ride from Tazawako Station on the **Lake Circular Line** bus or the **Nyuto Line;** the Nyuto Line goes on to Tazawa Ski Resort (27 min.), Kogen Onsen (37 min.), Nyuto Onsen (45 min.), and Akita-Komagatake 8th Station (approximately 1 hr.).

In **Nyuto Onsen,** a bus runs between the seven hot-spring spas; after purchasing the Yumeguri-cho ticket book for ¥2,500 (¥1,000 children) at your inn, you can make reservations for the bus and enter all seven hot-spring baths at no extra charge.

If you plan to drive through Towado-Hachimantai National Park, **Toyota Rent-A-Car** (rent.toyota.co.jp; **© 0187-43-2100**) has a branch near Tazawako Station. Rates average around ¥8,000 per day for a compact car.

LOCAL BEAUTY: PRINCESS tatsuko

According to folk tales, a princess named Tatsuko once drank from Lake Tazawa hoping for eternal beauty. Instead, as punishment for her vanity she was turned into a dragonlike serpent. Despite her misfortune, her statue on the lake shore stands as a symbol of *Akita bijin*, usually translated as "Akita beauty." Thet term was popularized during the Heian Period (794–1185), referring to the striking looks of Akita women, often said to be Japan's most beautiful. While that's ultimately in the eye of the beholder—though I can't say I've heard anyone from Akita disagree—the term is still synonymous with the prefecture.

EXPLORING THE LAKE TAZAWA AREA

Deep as it is, Lake Tazawa is only 20km (13 miles) in circumference, an easy and scenic circuit to make by bike. A 15-minute bus ride from Tazawako Station will get you to the Tazawakohan bus stop (fare ¥370) at the lake shore. A couple minutes' walk from there, there's a small beach (generally quiet outside the July–Aug swimming season) where you can rent bicycles of all types—tandem bikes, road bikes, cross bikes, mountain bikes, and e-bikes—for around ¥2,000 to ¥3,000 for 3 hours, which should be plenty of time to circumnavigate the lake at a leisurely pace. You'll have to share the road with vehicular traffic, but it's a popular cycling route so motorists know to keep a lookout. Except for one small stretch, the road is mostly flat and is pleasantly wooded and relatively unspoiled. Circle the lake counterclockwise in the left lane, which puts you on the inside track closer to the water. Along the way you'll pass a couple of water-facing shrines, a trout museum, a microbrewery and taproom (see p. 622), and just off the shoreline a famous local landmark—a golden statue of Princess Tatsuko, a legendary nymphlike beauty.

Sightseeing boats, some of which make stops to explore the surrounding woods, operate on Lake Tazawa from late April to early November; a 40-minute trip costs ¥1,400. A better option is at **Tazawako Outdoor Tours** (tazawako.net; ✆ **0187-43-2990**), located next to a campsite by the beach, which offers 3-hour kayak tours of the lake for ¥5,500. Note, however, the guide's English-language ability may be limited. Kayak tours are available from late April until early November.

From the lake, you should be able to spot **Mount Komagatake,** Akita Prefecture's tallest mountain, at 1,637m (5,402 ft.). It's actually an active

The Gozanoishi Jinga shrine sits serenely on the north shore of Lake Tazawa.

Strap On Your Skis

Of several ski resorts in the Lake Tazawa area, the largest is **Tazawako Ski Resort** (tazawako-ski.com; ✆ **0187-46-2011**), with 14 runs, including beginner, intermediate, and advanced slopes, and the steep, 1,000m-long Mizusawa Championship Course. A 1-day lift ticket costs ¥4,800 and ski-equipment rental costs ¥4,700 for everything (another ¥3,700 if you need to rent clothing, too); snowboarding is also available. Discounts, including equipment rental, ski pass, and half-board, are available if you book your accommodation through the ski resort. Buses from Tazawako Station (traveling in the direction of Nyuto Onsen) reach Tazawako Ski Resort in 27 minutes and cost ¥560.

volcano (it last erupted in the early 1970s) and is a popular destination for hikers. Most start their hikes at the 8th Station, which you can reach by bus in 1 hour from Tazawako Station (fare ¥1,050). From there, you can reach the top in about 1½ hours, where you're rewarded with grand views of the surrounding mountains, as well as more hiking trails, many of them awash in alpine wildflowers in summer. Note that buses to the 8th Station run daily in July and August but only on weekends June, September, and October; as buses take up most of the limited parking space, private car access is restricted at those times. The roads are closed due to snow November through late May.

WHERE TO STAY AROUND LAKE TAZAWA

Most visitors to this area stay in the rustic hot-springs area of **Nyuto Onsen,** about 14km (8¾ miles) northeast of Tazawako.

Kamenoi ♥♥ There are some cookie-cutter features to this large property—a local souvenir and sweets store, grand banquet halls, a mix of nice if unexciting Japanese- and Western-style rooms—but it isn't completely devoid of style. A secret bar that requires reservations, a hallway lined with 26 artworks depicting natural scenes of Akita prefecture, and a traditional *izakaya* mean there's more to this place than first meets the eye. It also has a wonderful outdoor hot spring bath, lit up seductively amid the rocks and foliage (or snowfall) at night. Most rooms offer views of the surrounding forests. Those in the main building are most convenient (in annex buildings, you may have to cross a breezeway or lug your bags up stairs in lieu of an elevator). Families will appreciate the extra space in the larger suites, with many rooms able to fit at least 4 guests. Breakfast and dinner buffets are served in the hotel's Mountain Resort restaurant; in the evenings, there's sometimes as many as 60 different dishes offered, though the quality remains quite high across the board.

2–32 Komagatake. kamenoi-hotels.com/en/tazawako. ✆ **0187-46-2131.** 121 units. ¥10,000–¥25,000 per person. Rates include 2 meals. Bus stop: Sugiyachi (35 min. from Tazawako Station). **Amenities:** 2 restaurants; bar; indoor/outdoor hot-spring baths; free Wi-Fi.

Kyukamura Nyuto Onsenkyo ♥ This lodging offers the convenience of being on Nyuto Onsen's main road, with buses from Tazawako Station stopping right outside. While it may lack the charm of a traditional inn, it offers both indoor and outdoor hot-spring baths (daily 24 hr.) and nearby hiking paths through the forests of beech (gorgeous in autumn) enveloping the property. It's a good place to stay if you're an active traveler and/or prefer Western-style rooms, though Japanese *tatami* rooms are also available. Rooms are simple but clean and pleasant, with sinks and toilets (three Western-style rooms have bathrooms), and buffet-style meals are served in the dining room. If you stay here, you can still sample the other ryokans' hot-spring baths for a modest fee.

2–1 Komagatake. hotel.qkamura.or.jp/en/nyuto-onsenkyo. ✆ **0187-46-2244.** 38 units (3 w/ private bath). ¥15,000–¥22,000 per person. Rates include 2 meals. Bus stop: Kyukamura (45 min. from Tazawako Station). **Amenities:** Indoor/outdoor hot-spring baths; free Wi-Fi.

Tsuru-no-yu Onsen ♥♥♥ Though this is the best place to stay in Nyuto Onsen, it's not because it's refined or elegant; it's not even expensive. Rather, nestled in a wooded valley more than 2.5km (1½ miles) off the main Nyuto Onsen road, it's restfully remote and charmingly old-fashioned, with a thatched-roof row house of tiny *tatami* rooms lit by oil lamps, complemented by the sound of rushing water and steam rising from the outdoor baths. Tsuru-no-yu opened as an *onsen* (hot-spring spa) in the 17th century; its oldest building—the thatched row house of connected rooms—is more than 100 years old. Your dinner will be cooked on your own *irori* (open-hearth fireplace); breakfast is served in a tatami

Steam rises from the milky hot springs at old-fashioned Tsuru-no-yu Onsen.

dining hall, with all the guests dressed in *yukata* (cotton kimono). Additional buildings constructed over the years ramble across the hillside, along a rushing stream that serenades you to sleep. Outdoor sulfurous baths are separated for men and women, but there is one mixed bath where you can wrap a towel around you. Unfortunately, day-trippers spoil some of the fun of staying here (baths are open to the public daily 10am–3pm for ¥700). Evenings, however, are magical.

50 Kokuyurin. tsurunoyu.com. ✆ **0187-46-2139.** 35 units w/ shared bath. ¥9,930–¥19,950 per person. Rates include 2 meals. Bus stop: Alpa Komakusa (35 min. from Tazawako Station), hotel will pick guests up from stop. **Amenities:** Indoor/outdoor hot-spring baths; free Wi-Fi (connection is poor).

WHERE TO EAT AROUND LAKE TAZAWA

You're likely to do most of your eating around Lake Tazawa in your hotel (all the abovementioned offer breakfast and dinner). But it's worth stopping at the following cafe and taproom for lunch, especially if you're partial to craft beer:

Orae (Tazawa Lakeside Forest Beer; 田沢湖 湖畔の杜ビール) ♥♥
WESTERN FOOD & BEER Located beside Lake Tazawa, this casual restaurant merits a visit for its on-site Tazawako microbrewery (the beer brand is called Kohan no Mori) and views of the lake from its airy, glass-enclosed dining room and outdoor terrace. The menu, in Japanese only but with pictures, offers a limited selection of Western dishes like pizza and mezze-style sharing plates, often featuring produce fished out of the nearby lake.

37–5 Haruyama. orae.net/beer. ✆ **0187-58-0608.** Pizza and beer ¥2,000–¥4,000 per person. Mon–Fri 11:30am–3pm (last order); Sat–Sun 11:30am–3:30pm and 5–7pm (reserve ahead for dinner). Lake Circular Line Bus: Hourai-no-matsu (1 min.).

Lake Towada ♥♥

At the northern end of Towada-Hachimantai National Park, on the border between Aomori and Akita prefectures, **Lake Towada** (Towadako in Japanese) is considered one of the park's most scenic areas. It's certainly one of Japan's least spoiled lakes, with only two small villages on its perimeter and encircled by wooded cliffs and mountains. People also visit to see **Oirase Stream ♥♥♥**, the only river flowing out of Lake Towada and one of the few in Japan not to have been subjected to ugly concrete embankments and significant course diversions. In this sense, it is a real treasure; a shaded mountain stream coursing over boulders and down waterfalls, it's flanked by a hiking trail offering one of the prettiest walks in Tohoku. In autumn, leaves of gold and red render the scenery truly spectacular.

ESSENTIALS

ARRIVING Lake Towada isn't close to any train station, but you can travel by bus to Yasumiya, a small village on Lake Towada with a tourist office and a few accommodations. From Tokyo, take the 3-hour **Tohoku Shinkansen** to Hachinohe (¥19,320 for a reserved seat on the fastest

Hiking along the Oirase Stream is particularly gorgeous in autumn.

train), and then board a **JR bus** to Yasumiya (bus stop: Towadako), which takes about 2½ hours and costs ¥3,050. From Hokkaido, take the train to Aomori, then a **JR bus** to Yasumiya, which takes 3 hours and costs ¥3,480. JR Rail Pass holders can ride both these buses for free. You must make a reservation for the JR bus at a major JR train station or travel agency; each makes five or six runs daily (less frequently in winter). For more information, visit **jrbustohoku.co.jp**.

If you have a car, it's about a 3-hour drive from Lake Tazawa to Lake Towada, with some spectacular scenery at times. It's a 2-hour drive from Aomori, and 1¾ hours from Hachinohe. **Times Car Rental** (rental.timescar.jp) has offices at Shin-Aomori Station (✆ **017-761-5356**) and Morioka Station (✆ **019-625-0666**), both of which are served by bullet trains from Tokyo. **Toyota Rent-A-Car** (rent.toyota.co.jp) has offices near Aomori (✆ **017-734-0100**) and Shin-Aomori (✆ **017-782-0100**) stations. Rates usually start around ¥7,000 to ¥9,000 per day.

VISITOR INFORMATION There are two tourist office near the Yasumiya bus station: the **Lake Towada Tourist Information Center** (✆ **0176-75-1531;** daily 9am–5pm) and the **Towada Visitor Center** (env.go.jp/park/towada; ✆ **0176-75-1015;** daily 9am–4:30pm). More information can be found at **towada.travel**.

GETTING AROUND The **JR buses** that run between Yasumiya and Aomori or Hachinohe also stop at Nenokuchi and several locations along the Oirase hiking trail (including Oirase Keiryu Grand Hotel), from April to early November. Otherwise, your best bet for travel between Yasumiya and Nenokuchi is via **sightseeing boat** (see below).

EXPLORING LAKE TOWADA

There are two villages on the shores of Lake Towada—**Yasumiya** on the southwestern shore and **Nenokuchi** on the eastern side of the lake, which is the trail head for hikes along Oirase Stream.

Pristine, crystal-clear **Lake Towada (Towadako)** ♥♥ is one of Towada-Hachimantai National Park's major draws, with about 44km (27 miles) of undulating coastline marked by capes, inlets, cliffs, and trees that put on a spectacular autumn show. It's actually a double caldera, formed some 20,000 years ago by a volcanic eruption. The best way to enjoy the lake's beauty is aboard excursion boats, which depart year-round from Yasumiya; from April through early November, there are also cruises that travel between Yasumiya and Nenokuchi, which is handy if you want to get off at Nenokuchi for a hike along Oirase Stream (see below). Cruises are 50 minutes long and cost ¥1,650 (pay ¥550 extra to sit in the top lounge); children pay half-fare. For more information go to **toutetsu.co.jp** (you can get up-to-date timetables and downloadable Oriase walking maps from here) or call **0176-75-2909.**

Running 67km (42 miles) on its way from Lake Towada to the Pacific Ocean, **Oirase Stream** ♥♥ is at its picture-perfect best in **Oirase Gorge,** where hikers are treated to waterfalls, rapids coursing over moss-covered boulders, and a dense wood of ferns, Japanese beech, oaks, and other broadleaf trees, particularly stunning in autumn (these forests are actually more representative of indigenous Japanese nature than the pine- and cedar-choked hillsides of central and southern Honshu). A trail runs beside the stream from Nenokuchi to Yakeyama, a distance of 14km (8¾ miles); most hikers only do the 9km (5½-mile) stretch between Nenokuchi and Ishigedo, which takes about 2 hours. Disappointingly, a road runs through the gorge beside the stream, but the pathway often diverges from the road, and the roar of the swift-running river and the 13 waterfalls masks the sound of vehicles. The hike upstream (toward Nenokuchi) is the most picturesque, as it affords a full view of the cascading rapids. There are nine bus stops on the road beside Oirase Stream, including Nenokuchi, Ishigedo, and Yakeyama. Because buses run only once an hour or so, you might consider taking a bus first and then hiking back.

In Yasumiya, the major point of interest is **Towada Jinja Shrine,** surrounded by giant cedars and hosting marvelous woodcarvings of animals. A curious custom here is to buy a fortune, put money or rice inside, twist it into the shape of a missile, and then hike up the steep flight of wooden steps beside the shrine 20 minutes to a scenic spot (the last part of the hike is down metal ladders—only for the adventurous on a rainy day) where you then throw your missile into the

A modern statue of two young women, near the Towada Jinja shrine.

TAKE AN art break AT THE TOWADA ART CENTER

While it's not as spectacular as the Art Islands of the Seto Inland Sea (p. 497), the **Towada Art Center** ♥♥ (towadaartcenter.com; ✆ **0176-20-1127**) has been just as successful in injecting some culture into a formerly tired and aging urban area. It's about a 70-minute drive from Lake Towada and well worth an excursion if you have a car. Opened in 2008, it's a colorful, irreverent, and strikingly contemporary museum. Green spaces and plazas host huge sculptures by some of the art world's marquee names, like Yayoi Kusama, Erwin Wurm, Choi Jeong Hwa, and Igness Idee. White-box gallery spaces focus your gaze on the lone pieces exhibited there: Ana Laura Alaez's *Bridge of Light;* Seo Do-ho's *Cause and Effect* (one of the strangest chandeliers you'll ever see); or the frighteningly realistic, Trunchbull-like *Standing Woman,* crafted by Ron Mueck. It's all connected by glass-walled hallways and small courtyards, allowing light to flood into the building and making the entire structure feel like it's part of the fabric of the city. Even street furniture has been given the modern-art treatment, with benches that look like giant pillows, amorphous flowerpots, shards of glass, blocks from an old 8-bit SEGA game, and tree stumps surmounted by balancing apples.

Located in Towada City, at 10–9 Nishinibancho, museum is open 9am to 5pm, Tuesday through Sunday (closed Mon). Admission is ¥1,800 adults (¥1,000 during special exhibitions), free for ages 18 and under. Many outdoor artworks are not within the confines of the main museum and therefore free for visitors to see. A bus from Hachinohe (around 1¾ hr. with a change at Chuo) is also available.

lake. If it sinks, your wish will come true. Near Towada Jinja Shrine, look for the **sculpture of two young women.** Unlike the golden nymph at Lake Tazawa (p. 619), these broad-shouldered, wide-hipped young ladies were sculpted just after the war, when such proportions were promoted as a way to rebuild the nation.

WHERE TO STAY AROUND LAKE TOWADA

Peak season is August through autumn; book far in advance for these months.

Oirase Keiryu Hotel ♥♥ The main reason for staying in this large hotel is its location on Oirase Stream, making it an easy base for hiking the trail. It's also part of the Hoshino Resorts brand, a reliable indicator of style and quality. The hotel offers both Japanese *tatami* and twin rooms, many with views of Oirase Stream. Public hot-spring baths also take advantage of river views and the changing scenery of the deciduous forest. The hotel is divided into east and west wings, both with giant fireplace sculptures by eccentric artist Taro Okamoto, who was enchanted by Oirase when he first visited the region. The west wing fireplace is known as *Kashin* (River God); the east wing's is called *Mori no Shinwa* (Myth of the Forest). The latter, overlooking the river and maples trees, becomes a cocktail lounge at night—try the Apple Salty Dog, an in-house specialty.

Alongside standard half-board plans, you can opt for a tasting-menu dinner in a chic French bistro, an apple-themed buffet, or have breakfast on a breezy outdoor terrace each morning. The hotel also offers tours and craft workshops, chief of which is the Frozen Waterfall Night Tour for ¥1,500 per person (available in winter only). Buses that traverse Oirase Stream stop here, but the hotel also offers its own shuttle buses from Aomori station (¥3,500 per person, reservations required) and Hachinohe station (free). Enquire about departure times when making reservations. By car, it's a 45-minute drive northeast from Lake Towada.

231 Aza Tochikubo, Oaza Okuse, Towada-shi. ✆ **0176-74-2121.** 187 units. ¥25,000–¥60,000 Japanese-style room or twin. Bus: Yakeyama (1 min.). **Amenities:** 3 restaurants; cocktail lounge; indoor and outdoor hot-spring baths; aromatherapy treatments; EV charging; tours and workshops (mostly for a fee); free Wi-Fi.

Towada Hotel ♥♥♥ Secluded on a wooded hill overlooking the lake, this imposing and elegant hotel was built in 1938 using huge cedar logs in a Western-lodge-meets-Japanese-temple style, with a modern addition built years later. Former U.S. ambassador Edwin Reischauer and Emperor Showa have stayed here; nowadays most American guests are high-ranking officers from a nearby U.S. military base. Although all rooms face the lake, best are the Japanese rooms, all in the older part of the hotel with fantastic views. Western-style rooms, though spacious and beautifully designed, do not have as good a view; be sure to ask for a room on the top floor and be sure, too, to wander over to the older wing for a look at its beautiful wood details in the old lobby (crafted by shrine and temple carpenters). Unfortunately, the public baths do not have hot-spring waters (instead, it's heated water from a mountain stream), but they do have lakeside views and outdoor tubs. Meals, served in a communal dining room with a mix of Japanese and Western dishes, are substantial. It's a 15-minute drive up the lake's west shore from Yasumiya.

Nishi-kohan Towada, Kosaka-machi, Kazuno-gun. ✆ **0176-75-1122.** 50 units (8 w/ shared bath). ¥40,000–¥66,000 Japanese room or twin. Pickup service available from Yasumiya bus stop. **Amenities:** Restaurant and lounge; indoor/outdoor public baths; sauna; free Wi-Fi.

Tsuta Onsen ♥♥ One of Tohoku's most famous traditional *ryokan,* this classic inn dates from 1909. *Tsuta* means "ivy" in Japanese, a theme carried out not only in pillars, transoms, and other architectural details but also in the dense, surrounding beech forest. Rooms in the oldest wooden structure (built in 1918) and an annex (built in 1960), both up a long flight of stairs, have striking wood-carved details and good views; the west wing 1989 addition, with gleaming wood floors salvaged from an old ryokan, has an elevator, but its rooms lack the character of the older rooms. For those who don't like sleeping on futons, combination units offer *tatami* areas, beds, and bathrooms. The hot-spring baths are new but preserve traditional bathhouse architecture, with high ceilings and cypress walls. Breakfast and dinner are served in a charming, wood-paneled dining hall and often feature

Aomori favorites like apple-infused desserts and a root-vegetable soup called *kenoshiru.* Although it's a 30-minute drive north of Lake Towada, Tsuta Onsen has its own 1-hour hiking trail to a nearby lake; at night here in autumn and winter you'll see the star-studded firmament in all its glory. 1 Tsutanoyu, Okuse, Towada-shi. tsutaonsen.com. ✆ **0176-74-2311.** 35 units. ¥30,000–¥60,000 per person. Rates include 2 meals. Bus: Tsuta Onsen stop (1 min.). **Amenities:** Hot-spring indoor bath; free Wi-Fi.

WHERE TO EAT AROUND LAKE TOWADA

Most accommodations serve breakfast and dinner. It's wise to bring a packed lunch if you're walking the Oirase trail, although there is a small snack bar at Ishigedo that sells inexpensive ramen noodles, tempura soba, ice cream (dubbed Ishigato), and drinks.

Shinshuya ♥ LOCAL SPECIALTIES There's nothing unique about this restaurant in Yasumiya, but it does have views of Lake Towada and is conveniently near the bus stop and ferry pier, near the path to Towada Jinja Shrine. Among the local specialties offered are Towada beefsteaks, fish, *Inaniwa udon* (noodles with mountain vegetables), and *kiritampo nabe* (a one-pot stew consisting of newly harvested rice pounded into a paste and

THE mountain monks OF BANDAI-ASAHI

In the northern end of sprawling, mountainous Bandai-Asahi National Park, the **Dewa Sanzan**—the "Three Spiritual Mountains of Dewa"—have for centuries been the domain of *yamabushi* (mountain monks), practitioners of the ancient Shugendo religion, an arcane belief system fusing Shintoism, Buddhism, Taoism, and shamanism. Viewed as hermits for centuries, yamabushi wear white robes inspired by Buddhist cosmology and carry large conch shells, which they believe are instruments for communing with the gods. They are in search of a quasi-magical force achieved through a lifestyle of toil; they believe in both the power of Shinto spirts and Buddhist ideas of enlightenment.

Ascetism is one of Shugendo's defining features. Monks bathe in ice-cold water, march daily up vertiginous mountain trails, and practice dietary austerity, some eating only food foraged in the mountains: pine needles, bark, chestnuts, seeds, grasses, and roots. In rare cases, yamabushi have even practiced mummification as a physical and spiritual attempt at attaining Buddhahood.

To those of us that enjoy modern life's conveniences, this all sounds rather extreme. But at the 414m-tall (1,358-ft.) **Mount Haguro,** the shortest of the three Dewa Sanzan peaks, you can walk in the footsteps of (or alongside) the yamabushi. For centuries, this mountain has been a place of spiritual pilgrimage; with the famous five-story **Goju-To Pagoda** (a designated National Treasure) and a path of 2,446 stone steps leading to the summit. To experience it as the monks would, your "training" will likely involve walking, meditation, chanting, becoming one with your environment, and perhaps strange rituals like jumping over a bonfire or standing under a plunging waterfall. Contact the Haguro Tourism Association (hagurokanko.jp; ✆ **0235-62-4727**) to find out more about yamabushi experiences and rates (some involve overnight stays). ***Note:*** You may need to organize your own translator. Mount Haguro is a half-hour east of the town of Tsuruoka, in Yamagata Prefecture.

then charcoal-grilled before simmering in chicken broth with vegetables). Use pictures to help you order or ask for the English-language menu. 16–11 Towadakohan-Yasumiya. ✆ **0176-75-3131.** Main dishes ¥1,000–¥3,300. Daily 8am–6pm (10am–4pm in winter). A 7-min. walk from the Towadako Bus Station.

THE MICHINOKU COASTAL TRAIL ♥♥♥

Running 1,025km along the Tohoku coastline, the Michinoku Coastal Trail is one of Japan's longest unbroken walking routes—and it's arguably its wildest, marching northward into the depths of a region once known as *Michinoku,* the "End of the Road." In a sense the trail has existed for centuries, parts well-trodden by pilgrims, fishermen, villagers, brigands, *ronin* (masterless samurai), and the occasional lord and his retainers. But it was officially opened in 2019, with all loose ends connected and markers and signposts in Japanese and English erected throughout. Local municipalities, national parks, and private landowners worked together to establish the trail in order to bring more tourism to the region and to help revive the coastal cities, towns, and villages ravaged by the 2011 earthquake and tsunami.

The trail starts in **Soma,** a city in Fukushima Prefecture, and travels north through Miyagi and Iwate Prefectures en route to **Hachinohe** in Aomori. To walk it from tip to tip takes around 6 or 7 weeks, even for experienced hikers, so many tackle it in increments instead, ranging from half-day strolls to dedicated multi-week treks. As you'd expect in this final frontier of the Honshu mainland, much of the scenery is the nature of times past: striated sea stacks buffeted by foamy waves, bays and inlets with picture-perfect views of the morning sun, grassy bluffs and headlands accentuating the vastness of the Tohoku landscape, and thick forests cloaked in fog, home to Shinto spirits and the region's wildlife: deer, serows, foxes,

THE bear FACTS ON THE MICHINOKU TRAIL

Asiatic black bears are beautiful creatures, with pillowy bodies, smiling-childlike faces, and yellowish crescents of fur on their breasts, earning them the epithet, "moon bears." They are usually happy to forage for fruits, grasses, nuts, seeds, berries, and tubers, perhaps eating the odd invertebrate if push comes to shove. However, as their habitats have expanded in recent years due to rural villages dying out, the black bear population is growing and food sourcing has become more competitive. This has coincided with a rise in bear attacks. Sometimes they walk into a small-town supermarket and make a beeline for the fresh produce aisles, other times they get spooked by hikers when already hungry and irascible. Hikers should take necessary precautions, like brushing up on what to do if you encounter a bear on the trail and packing bear spray in your bag. You may also want to use trail-walking community pages on social media to find hiking partners or look for a local walking guide. (See "Visitor Information" and "What to Bring" sections below.)

songbirds, owls, cicadae, rat snakes and pit vipers, salamanders and newts, frogs and toads, and Asiatic black bears. And yes, you may also pass through some charmless towns and cities, new buildings of concrete, prefab, and tin, and a reinforced bastion of sea walls, built as defense against the next once-in-a-thousand-years tsunami. They speak to Tohoku's history, in a way, which has long been defined ironclad resilience. And if you're going to walk the Michinoku Coastal Trail, you'll need plenty of that, too.

Essentials

ARRIVING The eastern side of Tohoku isn't as well connected by train as central and southern Honshu, so you may need to plan a combination of Shinkansen or flight followed by car rental or local trains and buses. In the "Recommended 2-Day Hikes" section below, I've included information on how to get to each starting point from Tokyo. If you're hiking the entire trail—firstly, good on ya—you can get to the **Soma trailhead** in Matsukawa-ura Kankyo Park by taking the Shinkansen to Sendai Station, followed by a JR train to Soma Station and then a local bus. The entire journey from Tokyo takes 3½ to 4 hours and costs around ¥15,000. Once you've arrived, look for the trailhead sign among the park's flower beds and strange wooden totems. To reach the **Hachinohe trailhead** at the north end of the trail at Kabushima Shrine, take a Shinkansen to Hachinohe, then switch to a local JR train to Same Station, a 15-minute walk from the traihead. From Tokyo, this will take 3½ to 4 hours (ironically, the same trip time as the journey to Soma, so much farther south) and costs around ¥20,000 for a reserved seat on the fastest train.

VISITOR INFORMATION You'll find some information on the trail in tourist offices at major stops along the way, including at the northern trailhead, the **Kabushima Kyuukeijo Rest Space** (✆ **0178-51-6464;** daily 9am–5pm, to 4pm in winter), and the **Natori Trail Center** (mct-natori-tc.jp; ✆ **022-398-6181;** daily 9am–5pm, until 4pm in winter) in Miyagi Prefecture, which serves as the trail's HQ. Outside of that, the best places for information, advice, accommodation options, and route maps are **michinokutrail.com** and the Michinoku Coastal Trail Community Facebook page (facebook.com/groups/michinokucoastaltrail/), a great place for getting up-to-date information on weather, trail conditions, where bears have been spotted, and general advice on choosing a course that fits your hiking ability. Also consider downloading the Michinoku Trail Club online map at **m-tc.org**.

Preparing for Your Hike

CHOOSING A ROUTE While most through-hikers travel southbound, starting in Hachinohe, traveling north from the Soma trailhead has logistical benefits: You can hit the main visitor center early in the journey, you'll travel mostly with the sun at your back, and you can get into a good rhythm on flat terrain before the trail starts to really undulate.

Accommodation options vary from simple guesthouses and traditional ryokan to cheap business hotels and campsites. Online maps through the

The Luck of the Seagulls?

The northern trailhead of the Michinoku Trail, Kabushima Shrine, sits perched on a rocky outcrop and covered in seagull droppings. So many birds call the shrine home, in fact, that you can grab a free umbrella to protect yourself from their poo as you walk up the stone steps to pay your respects. This is the more common place to begin a hike of the entire trail—after all, the old wisdom maintains that getting defecated on by a bird will bring luck in the days ahead.

above resources have pinpointed locations where you can stay. Or consult Tokyo-based **Michinoku Hikers** (michinoku-hikers.com; ✆ **090-4393-4469**), a tour company that offers multi-day excursions and can also help with accommodation bookings.

WHEN TO GO Given you'll be walking, and perhaps walking *a lot,* you'll want to go when the climate is at its most agreeable. In **winter,** Tohoku can be freezing (nighttime temperatures plunge regularly below zero) and receives heavy snowfall, making hiking tough, falls more likely, and camping next-to impossible. (On the other hand, the black bears will be hibernating!) In **late June and July,** parts of Tohoku get hit by the rainy season, making the trails slushy and washing out the scenery; hikers in **August** face stifling, sticky, arduous treks with potentially limited access to water. From **late March through June** and **late September to mid-November,** however, the weather is at its most pleasant, and you'll get the added bonus of seeing either flowers coming into spring bloom or deciduous forests in all their autumn glory. The caveat is that the black bear population is active and unpredictable in spring (when mothers are protecting newborn cubs) and autumn (when they're stocking up on nutrients for the winter hibernation).

WHAT TO BRING Obviously you'll want good walking shoes, and your clothes and pack should be waterproof, or at least highly water-repellent. A refillable water bottle, sugar tablets or energy drink packets, a towel (especially if using campsites and cheap lodgings), a tent and sleeping bag, a flashlight, retractable walking sticks, mosquito spray, a portable power boiler, and a plastic bag or similar for collecting your rubbish are also recommended. Bear spray—which can cost around ¥10,000 in an outdoor goods shop—is also a good idea, if only for peace of mind. Some people like to walk with a bell, too, to warn bears of their presence, but I find these infuriating. Occasional loud clapping and shouting is a less-persistent way of letting wildlife know you're approaching; many forest guides prefer this method. ***Note:*** If you're only hiking a short section of the trail, consider using luggage storage or delivery services to avoid carrying unnecessary belongings. For more info on sending luggage, see p. 697 in chapter 15.

Recommended 2-Day Hikes

Below are three options for 2-day hikes on sections of the Michinoku trail. In theory, you could shorten any of them to 1 day, but why travel all this way for just 1 day of hiking? Plus, the more time you spend on the trail, the more you'll come to appreciate Tohoku's wilderness, the recovery efforts following one of Japan's worst natural disasters, and the warm-hearted, genuine kindness of the country folk who call this place home.

TANESASHI COAST ROUND-TRIP

Consider this an easy starter set. Beginning at Kabushima Shrine at the northern trailhead and culminating 11km (6.8 miles) later at Okuki Station (where you can catch a train back to your starting point), it's a relatively gentle trail, with a total elevation rise of 200m (656 ft.). Its scenery varies from the aggressive beauty of the northern Aomori coastline to a Viking-like scene of impetuous seas with curtains of grey hanging over the horizon, to crags and weather-beaten headlands in which only the foolhardiest of seamen would moor their boats, to tracts of grassland where wildflowers try their darndest to grow. Though views are quite special for most of the way, the best vantage point is the Takaiwa Lookout not far from Okuki Station. Overnighters should consider booking a space at **Tanesashi Campground** (**✆ 0178-51-8500;** rates are ¥500–¥2,500 per night, depending on tent size).

Though the entire Michinoku Coastal Trail is 1,025km (637 miles), there are plenty of shorter sections that can make great 2- or 3-day scenic hikes.

To get to the starting point from Tokyo, take a Shinkansen to Hachinohe then switch to a local JR train to Same Station and walk for about 15 minutes, a total journey of between 3 and 4 hours, costing around ¥20,000.

TANOHATA TO FUDAI

This 2-day hike features 1 challenging day and 1 easier day; I suggest doing the difficult stretch first—from Tanohata north to Kurosaki—because it allows you to travel onward to another destination on the second evening if necessary. Starting at Tanohata, you'll soon notice an old sea wall, left destroyed on the beach like an art piece, a result of Mother Nature at her most wicked and inevitable. For the next 20km or so (12½ miles), with an ascent of around 1,000m (3,280 ft.), you'll slog through forests choked with deciduous trees and species of fir and pine (try not to let the "Warning! Bear habitat" signs freak you out), along the rambling cliffs of Kitayamazaki Cape, through hand-dug tunnels burrowing into the promontories, and over wooded ridges that offer some of the finest coastal views in Japan. Only then will you reach your accommodation for the

A swim among the rocks at Jodogahama Beach is a refreshing way to end the 2-day hike from Taro.

evening, the **Kurosakiso Lodge and Campsite** (kurosakisou.jp; ✆ **0194-35-2611**), located right next to the Rikuchu-Kurosaki Lighthouse, one of Tohoku's highest at 130m (427 ft.) above sea level. The campsite is cheap (¥300 per person), but if you're willing to pay ¥10,000-plus for room and board, your legs will be glad to soak in the hotel's hot spring baths and your stomach will appreciate the generous kaiseki dinner. The next day, you'll walk around 7km north and west to Fudai Station, mostly through woodland and along paths carved into the headlands; it will be a cinch compared to the previous day's undertaking.

To get from Tokyo to the starting point in Tanohata, take the Shinkansen to Morioka, then switch to a local train and ride to Tanohata with a change at Miyako. This will take 6 hours and cost around ¥17,000.

TARO TO JODOGAHAMA

This hike is a little less taxing than the Tanohata-to-Fudai route, and you have the incentive of finishing at Jodogahama, a white pebble beach with crystal clear waters that many a hiker has used for a celebratory cool off. With more than 900m (2,953 ft.) of elevation and covering 22km (13¾ miles) from north to south, you'll need a decent level of fitness. Around the midway point there's a campsite (**Anegasaki Campground; ✆ 0193-62-9911;** ¥1,340 per person) next to hotel (**Kyukamura Rikuchu-Miyako; ✆ 0119-362-9911;** ¥13,000–¥17,000 per person). The scenery is a mix of forests, beaches, and headlands, some better preserved than others, with highlights including the Sakiyama Blowhole, a cave opening that shoots water 30m into the sky like a geyser; the Tsunami Memorial Park Nakanohama, which has some English-language info boards; and of course Jodogahama, whose rock outcroppings look like fossilized mega-creatures—it's named after *Jodo,* the Buddhist "Way to the Pure Land."

To get from Tokyo to the starting point in Taro, take the Shinkansen to Morioka, then switch to a JR Line and ride to Taro with a change at Miyako. This will take 5½ hours and cost around ¥17,000.

HOKKAIDO
14

Hokkaido, the northernmost of Japan's four main islands, has a landscape strikingly different from that of any other place in Japan. Covering more than 83,000 sq. km (32,000 sq. miles), it accounts for 22% of Japan's total landmass, yet it has only 4.5% of its population. In other words, Hokkaido has what the rest of Japan doesn't: space. The iconic symbols of Japan—cherry blossoms and ginkgo trees, shrines and temples, feudal-era castles and old samurai manors, and (dare I say it) ceaseless construction and a rapacious logging industry—are also less in evidence here. Even the convenience stores, called Seico Marts, have their own branding. This is all to say: Hokkaido is the Japan you don't know. But the epic scale, harsh climate, and lack of development mean it's also your best bet for avoiding the crowds that plague Japan's more well-known playgrounds.

Hokkaido didn't open up to development until after the Meiji Restoration in 1868, when the government began encouraging Japanese to migrate to the island (at the expense of Hokkaido's indigenous people, the Ainu). Even today, Hokkaido has a frontier feel. Many young Japanese come here to backpack, ski, camp, and tour the countryside on motorcycles and bicycles, or behind the wheel of a car. There are dairy farms, silos, and broad fields of wheat, corn, and potatoes. Where the fields end, the land becomes craggy with bare volcanoes, deep gorges, and hills densely covered with virgin forests and dotted with clear spring lakes, rugged wilderness, and bubbling hot springs. The people of Hokkaido are as open and hearty as the wide expanses of land around them.

Much of Hokkaido's wilderness has been set aside as national and prefectural parkland, offering a wide range of activities from hiking and skiing to bathing at *onsen,* or hot-spring spas. Located on a frosty peninsula on Hokkaido's northern coast, **Shiretoko National Park** is probably the most entrancing of them all, a thrust of volcanic rock rising so steeply from the coast that the rivers plunge straight into the Sea of Okhotsk without ever forming "downstream" meanders. Road networks are sparse, brown bears are aplenty, and Stellar's sea eagles dive bomb for prey amid huge sheets of drift ice, while whales, dolphins, sea lions, and sea otters use the shallow coastal waters as refuge for their young.

PREVIOUS PAGE: Three hours west of Sapporo, Niseko is the top ski area in Hokkaido, known for its fabulous powdered snow, aka "japow."

Hokkaido's main tourist season is in July, when days are cool and pleasant with an average temperature of 70°F (21°C). While the rest of the nation is afflicted by the rainy season, Hokkaido's summers are usually bright and clear. Winters are long and severe, but ski enthusiasts flock to slopes near **Sapporo**—Japan's largest city north of Tokyo—and to resorts such as Niseko and Rusutsu. February marks the annual Sapporo Snow Festival, featuring huge ice and snow sculptures.

The best way to explore Hokkaido is on a road trip. Driving through Hokkaido is a reminder that Japan has a sense of scale that the denizens of Honshu's urban belt rarely recognize. One day you're driving over a flatland plain, craggy peaks looming in the distance, the next you're weaving through sleepy woodlands thick with fog or bypassing places with names of strange origin: Maruseppu, Nibutani, Urahoro, or Shakotan. You might see bears, foxes, or deer darting across the asphalt, raptorial birds swooping over the sea or forest canopy, and even in the depths of winter, one of the rarest creatures of all: the hitchhiker. Driving itself is a huge part of the Hokkaido experience; traveling by public transport simply doesn't compare. No matter where you are, there's always another road that begs to be driven down, another corner demanding to be turned.

THE BEST HOKKAIDO EXPERIENCES

- **Eating at Hakodate's Morning Market** There are dozens of excellent morning seafood markets in Japan, but this on the southern tip of Hokkaido is one of the finest. Be sure to sample sea urchins and hairy crabs, both local delicacies.
- **Spending a Night in Susukino** The neon-splashed Susukino district in Sapporo is one of the country's top spots for a night on the town, packed with jazz clubs, cocktail bars, dive bars, robatayaki restaurants, and miso-style ramen shops.
- **Getting to Know the Ainu** Forcibly assimilated into Japanese society in the 19th century, Northern Japan's indigenous Ainu population has reasserted its culture and ways of life in recent years, as proudly demonstrated at recreated village settlements and eye-opening museums.

In the gateway city of Hakodate, the Morning Market offers a profusion of local seafood.

- **Visiting Shiretoko National Park** The closest thing you'll get to a final frontier in Japan, this wild peninsula is home to bears, foxes, deer, whales, dolphins, sea otters, and a menagerie of birds, all of which you see in their natural habitat.

ESSENTIALS

ARRIVING The fastest way to reach Hokkaido is to fly. Flights from Tokyo to Sapporo's **New Chitose Airport** take about 1¾ hours and can cost anywhere from ¥6,000 to ¥20,000, depending on the air carrier. Flights to **Hakodate** on the western side of the island and to **Kushiro** on the eastern side are typically more expensive (¥15,000–¥25,000).

For centuries, the only way to travel between Honshu and Hokkaido was via a ferry ride, but the opening of the Seikan Tunnel in 1988 allowed the entire trip between the islands to be made by train in little more than 2 hours—more than a fourth of which is in the 55km (34-mile) tunnel. Today, travel to Hokkaido by land is generally via the **Hayabusa Shinkansen** bullet train from Ueno or Tokyo Station in Tokyo to Shin-Hakodate. The entire takes about 4 hours and costs ¥26,160 for a reserved seat one-way. You can then take the **Limited Express Hokuto** to Sapporo Station for ¥9,440. Your **JR Rail Pass** is good for all trains.

VISITOR INFORMATION Additional information on Hokkaido is available online at **visit-hokkaido.jp**.

GETTING AROUND Public transportation around Hokkaido is by train and bus. In addition to regular bus lines, sightseeing buses link the national parks and major attractions. Although they're more expensive than trains and regular buses, and although commentaries are usually in Japanese only, they offer unparalleled views of the countryside and usually stop at scenic places, albeit sometimes only long enough for the obligatory photo. Keep in mind that bus schedules fluctuate with the seasons and can be infrequent; some lines don't run during snowy winter months. Try to get

JR Hokkaido Passes

If you plan to travel a lot in Hokkaido and don't have a Japan Rail Pass (see chapter 15 for information), consider purchasing one of several special passes issued by Japan Railways that allow unlimited travel on JR trains and buses in Hokkaido. The **Hokkaido Rail Pass** works just like the Japan Rail Pass—it's valid for travel throughout Hokkaido, but available only to foreign tourists visiting Japan. It can be purchased abroad (through JTB or other authorized travel agencies; see **jrhokkaido.co.jp**) or at train stations in Hakodate, Sapporo, Kushiro, and a few other cities in Hokkaido. It costs ¥20,000 for 5 consecutive days, ¥27,000 for 7 days, or ¥32,000 for 10 days (add an extra ¥1,000 to the price if purchasing in Hokkaido). Other passes, like the **Sapporo-Noboribetsu Area Pass** (¥9,000) and **Sapporo-Furano Pass** (¥10,000), allow for unlimited transfers between a handful of areas over a 4-day period. See **jrhokkaido.co.jp** for more info on travel passes and discounts.

Hokkaido

bus and train schedules before setting out on each leg of your journey. Otherwise, you might find yourself waiting to make a transfer.

CAR RENTALS Because distances are long and traffic is rather light, Hokkaido is one of the few places in Japan where driving your own car is recommended. Rates for a 1-day rental of a compact car are around ¥7,000 to ¥9,000 per day, with each additional day costing less than the base rate. In autumn and winter, it's worth paying extra for snow tires or 4WD. Car-rental agencies are found throughout Hokkaido, often near train stations and airports. In Sapporo, **Toyota Rent-A-Car** (toyotorentacar.net; ✆ **011-281-0100**) is located east of Sapporo Station. You'll also find **Times Car Rental** (timescar-rental.com) and **Nippon-Rent-a-Car** (nipponrentacar.co.jp) branches here, both of which offer competitive prices and can supply English-language insurance and breakdown information booklets. You'll also find a **Times** branch at 22–7 Wakamatsu-cho in Hakodate, near the main entrance of Hakodate Station. Or for something a little different, enquire at **Arigato Campervan Rental Hokkaido** (arigatocampervan.com; ✆ **080-1623-5099**) about renting a campervan or RV; depending on the model you'll pay somewhere between ¥10,000 and ¥40,000 per night. For routes and road conditions, go to **northern-road.ceri.go.jp**, and for a recommended road trip route through Hokkaido, see p. 79 in chapter 3.

HAKODATE ♥♥

888km (549 miles) NE of Tokyo; 283km (177 miles) SW of Sapporo

If you arrive in Hokkaido from Tokyo by train, **Hakodate**—Hokkaido's third-largest city, with a population of 250,000—makes a good first-night stopover. Even if you have only a few hours here, you can see a lot. After checking into your hotel, head to **Mount Hakodate** for its famous nighttime views; the next morning before you set out for your next destination, check out the colorful **morning market.** For those with time to linger longer, it also has quaint historic districts of renovated warehouses (now housing restaurants and shops) and century-old Western-style homes, churches, and administrative buildings. Founded during the Feudal Era, Hakodate was one of Japan's first ports opened to international trade following the Meiji Restoration. With its clanking streetcars, sloping streets lined with historic buildings, and port, it retains the atmosphere of a provincial outpost even today.

Essentials

ARRIVING JAL, ANA, and Air Do fly from Tokyo's Haneda Airport to **Hakodate Airport** (**HKD**) in 1¼ hours for around ¥20,000. Limousine buses travel to JR Hakodate Station in 20 minutes for ¥500. You can also take the **Shinkansen bullet train** from Tokyo to Shin-Hakodate (4 hr.), and then transfer to a direct train for Hakodate (20 min.). The total fare is ¥26,160.

VISITOR INFORMATION The **Hakodate Tourist Office** (hakodatekankou.com; ✆ **0138-23-5440;** daily 9am–7pm) is inside the train station to your left as you exit the wicket. Pick up timetables, pamphlets, and maps here.

GETTING AROUND The most pleasant way to see Hakodate is on foot. The city is easy to navigate, and there are many English-language signs. Otherwise, streetcars are the major form of transportation (stops are announced in English), with fares starting at ¥210; take a ticket upon entering the back door and pay when you get off, or use your Suica or PASMO Card. There's also a 1-day streetcar pass for ¥600.

Exploring Hakodate

Only about a 12-minute walk south from the train station, past the morning market (p. 642) and along the seaside promenade, Hakodate's renovated **waterfront warehouse district** is fun to prowl around, full of shops and restaurants. A block inland, look for the **Meijikan** (12 Toyokawacho; ✆ **0138-27-7070**), a former 1911 brick post office now housing glassware boutiques. A few minutes' walk inland is historic **Motomachi,**

Stroll around Hakodate's Warehouse District to find the city's hippest shops and restaurants.

a picturesque hilltop neighborhood of turn-of-the-20th-century Western-style clapboard homes, consulates, churches, and other buildings. Most impressive is the pillared **Old Branch Office of the Hokkaido Government** in Motomachi Park (✆ **0138-27-3333**), which now has a casual snack bar inside as well as some historic photos on display. The nearest streetcar stop is Suehiro-cho.

Motomachi is actually on the lower slopes of **Mount Hakodate ♥**, which rises 330m (1,100 ft.) about 3km (1¾ miles) southwest of Hakodate Station. Few vacationing Japanese spend the night in Hakodate without taking the cable car to the top of this lava cone, formed by the eruption of an undersea volcano. From the peak at night, the lights of Hakodate shimmer and glitter like jewels on black velvet. There's an informal restaurant here (where you can indulge in a drink or a snack while admiring the view) as well as the usual souvenir shops. However, I have long contended that cable cars cause more problems than they solve, and Mount Hakodate is a perfect case in point. Goodness, what a mess. Because the view has become so popular, out-of-town tour buses start pulling up to a huge parking lot at the ropeway station as dusk nears. Queues quickly form and the cable car begins depositing a fresh load of people onto the top of the mountain *every 5 minutes.* By the time the sun dips behind the horizon, the observation decks have turned into heaving masses of flesh, which spoils the enjoyment of everyone involved. People block one another's view and the scenery becomes obscured by selfie sticks in rows three or four deep. So my advice is **to hike up the mountain.** There's a trailhead right next to the **Mount Hakodate Fureai Center** at 6–12 Aoyagicho, about 5 minutes on foot from the ropeway station. The walk is lovely, well-signposted, only takes an hour (less if you're quick), and you'll see few other hikers on the trail. Rather you'll be accompanied by the sound of rustling grasses, trees creaking in the wind, and birds filling

On the slopes of Mount Hakodate, Motomachi's Western-style buildings include this old government building, which now holds some historic exhibits.

the air with their strange songs. If you walk up in late afternoon, you'll get to see the city bathed in a warm, pre-sunset glow. Then, as the light begins to fade, you can either walk back down or get on the cable car—and ask the driver to step on it.

If you still want to travel by ropeway, the round-trip costs ¥1,800 for adults and ¥900 for children (or ¥1,200 and ¥600 one-way). Ropeway hours are daily 10am to 10pm early May through October (from 9am during Golden Week and July 25–Aug 20), and 10am to 9pm November through April. From April 20 to November you can also reach the top of Mount Hakodate directly by bus from Hakodate Station; the 30-minute trip costs ¥500 for adults and half-price for children.

Where to Stay in Hakodate

Hakodate's peak tourist season is in July and August, and some hotels raise their rates then. May also sees a spike in prices at some hotels. In addition to the options below, there's a 260-room **Toyoko Inn Hakodate Ekimae Asa-ichi** just a couple minutes' walk from Hakodate Station at 22–7 Otemachi (toyoko-inn.com; ✆ **0138-23-1045**), and the slightly newer **Toyoko Inn Hakodate Daimon** (✆ **0138-24-1045**), a 4-minute walk from the station, both with the usual freebies for which this chain is famous. Double rooms at both start at ¥8,000, including breakfast.

APA Hakodate Ekimae ♥ Even though the rooms in APA hotels are small, and this one is no different, there is a comfortable familiarity to Japan's number-one budget chain. Close to the station and walking distance from the main attractions in the area (even the ropeway can be reached in about 20 min.), this hotel is a good option if location is a priority. English-speaking staff, free maps and brochures (mostly in Japanese) in the lobby, and aromatherapy treatments and a breakfast buffet (extra fees for both) are other bonuses. Note that floors 3 and 5 of B building and floor 5 of A building are smoking rooms.

19–13 Otemachi. apahotel.com. ✆ **0138-23-2200.** 143 units. ¥5,000–¥20,000 single or double. Station: Hakodate (6 min.).

Hakodate Danshaku Club Hotel & Resorts ♥♥ With a convenient location near Hakodate Station and the morning market, this locally owned hotel is named after the *danshaku,* a Hokkaido potato; in the modern lobby you'll see a 1902 horseless carriage that once belonged to the farmer/shipbuilder who developed said potato. Standard rooms would qualify as suites elsewhere, with one or two bedrooms (sleeping up to four persons) that can be closed off from the living area by shoji-like doors, as well as a fully stocked kitchen. Balconies face Mount Hakodate, and spacious bathrooms complete with generous tubs also have windows providing views.

22–10 Otemachi. danshaku-club.com. ✆ **0138-21-1111.** 52 units. ¥18,000–¥40,000 double. Station: Hakodate (3 min.). **Amenities:** Restaurant; cafe; free Wi-Fi.

La Jolie Motomachi ♥ The antique vibe of this hotel matches its location in the Motomachi area of town, though the cozy lounge (free juice and coffee here) with its sofas, armchairs, bookshelves, and grand piano make it feel more like an old B&B. The rooms are spacious, clean, and equipped with TVs (Netflix included) and CD players (you can borrow CDs from a shelf in the lobby), making them nice places to chill when the weather gets harsh in winter. If you don't fancy breakfast at the morning market, you can ask for a meal plan, which includes a breakfast of rice balls or scrambled eggs and toast served with salad and/or soup, all made with homegrown ingredients and served at **NK2 FARM Shop&Café** (nk2farm.co.jp; ✆ **0138-83-1233**), just around the corner from the hotel.

6–6 Suehiro-cho. lajolie-hakodate.com. ✆ **0138-23-3322.** 29 units. ¥10,000–¥30,000 double. Streetcar: Jujigai (2 min.).

Take a Soak with the Locals

In addition to the sights here, you might wish to soak away the aches of travel in one of Hakodate's hot-spring spas. Yunokawa Spa is Hokkaido's oldest, but it's 25 minutes away by streetcar. More accessible is **Yachigashira Public Hot-Springs Bath** (✆ **0138-22-8371**), handily located right at the foot of Mount Hakodate. It's famous for its rust-colored waters, but what's most striking about it is its size, capable of accommodating—it claims—more than 500 bathers. Refreshingly, it feels like it was built for locals, rather than to accommodate Japanese day-trippers and foreign tourists. Sitting in the huge indoor tubs, or smaller outdoor baths, you'll be joined by grizzled fishermen straight off the morning market shift and local retirees who consider a trip to this bathhouse a daily ritual. (Bath areas are designated as men-only or women-only—I can only assume the female baths appeal to a similar demographic.) Entrance is ¥460, and you can purchase a towel at the front desk for ¥150. Use the vending machine at the entrance to buy tickets. It's open daily 6am–9:30pm (closed 2nd and 4th Tues of the month); the closest streetcar stop is Yachigashira.

start your day AT THE MORNING MARKET

A must-visit for foodies, Hakodate's **morning market** ♥♥ is spread out just south of the train station daily from about 5am to noon. In many ways it's the heart and soul of this small port city. Walk around and look at the variety of foods for sale from about 300 vendors, especially the hairy crabs for which Hokkaido is famous. You can make an unusual breakfast of fruit, raw sea urchin, or grilled crab from the stalls here. Don't miss **Donburi Yokocho,** literally "Rice Bowl Alley," a hallway of sushi and *donburi* restaurants, serving eclectic seafood fare, from sea urchin, cod roe, and crab to tuna, squid, and scallops seared in butter. A lot of the hubbub is centered on **Hakodate Morning Market Square** and **Ekini Market,** two side-by-side indoor spaces full of stalls offering seafood rice bowls, squid tempura, crab croquettes, fresh seaweed, shaved kelp, and sashimi, and others handing out samples of delicacies like chili-spiced dried squid. A lot of the crab is sold by weight, and giving the hulking size of the creatures, one can cost a pretty penny. A cheaper option is to have crab sushi or similar options at one of the small vendors—around the midway point of the Ekini Market, you'll find a small sushi counter tucked into the wall, run by an elderly lady that does just that. Two pieces of crab sushi here costs ¥864; you can also order *otoro* (fatty tuna), sea urchin, flounder, salmon roe, and surf clam. You could try several different kinds of sushi for about ¥4,000 to ¥5,000. The nearest streetcar stop is Hakodate Ekimae.

Where to Eat in Hakodate

Several of Hakodate's harborfront warehouses have been renovated into smart-looking shopping and dining complexes. They're about a 12-minute walk from Hakodate Station; you can reach the complexes by walking past the morning market and continuing along the seaside promenade.

Daimon Hitsuji-tei (大門ひつじ亭) ♥♥ BBQ MEAT This place looks like a gutted old office space—as a matter of fact, it probably is—replaced with a BBQ restaurant. But don't judge this book by its cover: The meat is super tender, and when put on the convex grill, liquid fat dribbles toward the base and flavors the vegetables lying in wait. Every diner must order the course menu (featuring three cuts of lamb, assorted vegetables, and either kimchi or crispy salt-and-sesame seaweed), and cook it at their table. The friendly, engaging ladies who run the restaurant will explain how to cook the meat before letting you have at it. If you're still hungry, you can order more items for the grill, though the a la carte menu is in Japanese only. 8–4 Suehirocho. ✆ **0138-83-5973.** BBQ course ¥3,190. Daily 6–9:30pm (last order). Irregular holidays. Streetcar: Jujigai (1 min.).

Hakodate Beer ♥ BAR FOOD/SEAFOOD In a brick building about halfway between the waterfront warehouse district and the station, this beer hall has four kinds of beer brewed in large copper vats. You'll dine on such fare as boiled shrimp, squid (Hakodate is famous for squid), fish and chips, sausages by Carl Raymon (a famous Hakodate sausage maker), Japanese-style fried chicken, or Italian dishes like ravioli, Bolognese, and unusual pizzas (whoever dreamed up mayonnaise and chicken curry?) all ordered from an English-language tablet menu with photos. Beer flights are also available; a set of three costs ¥1,320 or four for ¥1,760. There's live music in the evenings, usually a stringed-instrument performance followed by a pianist, and in summer there are tables outside. It's a local institution, even if the food and music are of middling quality. ***Note:*** Don't confuse this restaurant with **Hakodate Beer Hall** in the Kanemori Red Brick Warehouse, though that establishment offers a similar combination of local beer, Japanese pub grub, and hearty Western dishes; the difference is it doesn't have live music.

5–22 Ohtemachi. ✆ **0138-23-8000.** Sharing dishes ¥660–¥1,320; pizza ¥1,650; pasta ¥990–¥1,210. Daily 11am–3pm and 5pm–8:30pm (last orders). Station: Hakodate (6 min.).

Marutamagoya (まるたま小屋) ♥♥♥ RUSSIAN This LGBTQ cafe, overlooking the city from the foot of Mount Hakodate, serves Slavic dishes like borscht, piroshkies, *adjika* chicken stew, stuffed cabbage, curry stroganoff, and *shkmeruli*—a reminder that the north of Japan and Russia are close geographical neighbors. The food is delicious, reasonably priced, and wonderfully warming in winter. But it's the rustic, homely interior that really captures the heart. It feels like a little cabin in the woods that has slowly accumulated the memories of people passing through. Warmth is funneled in through portable heaters, diners look through the mullioned windows at snow thawing from the eaves of nearby buildings, and shelves are stacked with Russian recipe books, magnetic puzzles, old globes, Russian dolls, stuffed toys, biscuit packets, film cameras, vases, ceramics, and Ainu woodwork. Take some time here to relax with a beer or coffee, as it's not the sort of space that encourages you to leave in a hurry.

2–3 Motomachi. marutamasquare.wixsite.com/marutama. ✆ **0138-76-3749.** Set meals ¥1,100; main dishes ¥1,000–¥1,500. Thurs–Mon 11am–6pm. Streetcar: Jujigai (10 min.).

Tsutsuiken (ラーメン津つ井軒) ♥♥ RAMEN Diners huddle around the small tables in this mom n' pop ramen joint, slurping up the nuclear-hot broths to stave off the chill of winter. Miso ramen, often with corn and a lump of butter in the soup, is popular in Hokkaido and it's one of the menu's recommended items—order the one with spices and grilled green onions. The other *osusume,* or "recommendation," is a *shio* (salt-based) ramen with beansprouts; you'll hear lots of Japanese requesting this dish as they take their seats. *Gyoza* dumplings and bottled Sapporo beer are available on the side.

7–11 Wakamatsucho. ✆ **0138-83-5973.** Ramen ¥830–¥1,200. No credit cards. Tues–Sun noon–3pm and 5:30–10pm. Station: Hakodate (2 min.).

SAPPORO ♥♥♥

1,200km (746 miles) NE of Tokyo; 283km (177 miles) NE of Hakodate

Sapporo is one of Japan's newest cities. About 140 years ago, it was nothing more than a scattering of huts belonging to Ainu and Japanese families. With the dawning of the Meiji Period, however, the government decided to colonize the island, establishing the Colonization Commission in 1869. The area of Sapporo (the name comes from the Ainu word *satporopet,* meaning "big, dry river") was chosen as the new capital site, and in 1871, construction of the city began.

During the Meiji Period, Japan looked eagerly toward the West for technology, ideas, and education, and Hokkaido was no exception. Between 1871 and 1884, 76 foreign technicians and experts (including 46 Americans) were brought to this Japanese wilderness to aid in the island's development. Sapporo was laid out in a grid pattern of uniform blocks similar to that of an American city. In 1876, the Sapporo Agricultural College was founded to train youth in skills useful to Hokkaido's future growth.

The Sapporo of today, capital of Hokkaido Prefecture, has grown to 1.9 million residents, making it the largest city north of Tokyo (and the fifth largest in Japan). It's also one of the liveliest, with bars, restaurants, hostess clubs, and other entertainment establishments clustered around **Odori Park** and the gaudy, neon-suffused **Susukino** district. In 1972, Sapporo was introduced to the world when the Winter Olympics were held here, and its many fine ski slopes continue to attract winter vacationers, as does the Snow Festival, held every February (see "Japan Calendar of Events," in chapter 2). In August, when the rest of Japan is sweltering under uncomfortably high temperatures and humidity, Sapporo stays pleasantly cool.

Essentials

ARRIVING See p. 636 for flight details from Tokyo to **New Chitose Airport** (new-chitose-airport.jp; ✆ **0123-23-0111**), located about 43km (27 miles) southeast of Sapporo. It is connected to downtown by rapid trains (¥1,990) that carry passengers to Sapporo Station in under 40 minutes. **Trains** from Tohoku and other regions on Honshu arrive in Hakodate, where you'll transfer to a train departing every hour or so for Sapporo. The fare from Tokyo to Sapporo is ¥33,000; trips average 10 hours including transfers. Trains from Hakodate take about 3½ to 4 hours and cost ¥9,440 for a reserved seat (the LEX Hokuto and Super Hokuto have only reserved seats).

VISITOR INFORMATION In JR Sapporo Station, the excellent **Hokkaido-Sapporo Tourist Information Center** (sapporo.travel; ✆ **011-213-5088;** daily 8:30am–8pm), located opposite the west ticket gate, offers a wealth of information not only on Sapporo but all of Hokkaido. Here, too, is a JR information counter (daily 8:30am–7pm), where you can pick up JR train and bus schedules or get rail passes validated. (See p. 636 for information on JR Rail Passes in Hokkaido.) Next to the **Airport Express Bus Station** in Suskino (S4 W3, Chuo-ku; ✆ **0570-200-600**), there's a helpdesk with English-speaking staff that can recommend bars in the area or make reservations at nearby restaurants.

CITY LAYOUT After the jumble of most Japanese cities, Sapporo will come as a welcome surprise. Its streets are laid out in a grid pattern,

Sapporo

ATTRACTIONS
Ainu Museum **6**
Aurora Town **13**
Botanic Garden (Shokubutsu-en) **8**
Clock Tower (Tokeidai) **12**
Mount Moiwa **23**
Natural Science Museum **7**
Nopporo Forest Park **14**
Odori Koen (Park) Promenade **11**
Pole Town **17**
Sapporo Art Park **24**

HOTELS
Hotel Flourish 67 **22**
Hotel Gracery Sapporo **5**
Hotel Mercure Sapporo **19**
Hotel Monterey Edelhof **3**
JR Tower Hotel Nikko Sapporo **4**
Nakamuraya Ryokan **9**
Sapporo Grand Hotel **10**
Toyoko Inn Sapporo Nishi-Guchi-Hokudai-mae **1**

RESTAURANTS
Ganso Ramen Yokocho **21**
Hyosetsu-no-Mon **20**
Mikuni Sapporo **4**
Mochinoron **18**
Salt Moderate **15**
Sapporo Bier Garten **2**
Soup Curry Garaku **16**

Finding an Address in Sapporo

Addresses in Sapporo are generally given by block. **N1 W4,** for example, the address for the Sapporo Grand Hotel, means it's located in the first block north of Odori and 4 blocks west of West 1st Street. If you want to be more technical about it, the entire, formal address of the hotel would read N1-jo W4-chome. "Jo" refers to blocks north and south of Odori, while "chome" refers to blocks east and west of the river. Better yet, street signs in Sapporo are in English. Addresses below are written as they are given online (this will make them easier to find on mapping apps); the address of Sapporo Grand Hotel is rendered as 4 Kita 1 Jonishi, Chuo-ku.

making the city easy to navigate. Addresses in Sapporo refer to blocks that follow one another in logical, numerical order. **Sapporo Station** lies at the north end of the city, with downtown and many of its attractions, hotels, and restaurants spreading to the south. The center of Sapporo is **Odori** (**Main St.**), a tree-lined avenue south of Sapporo Station that runs east and west and bisects the city into north and south sections (i.e., North 1st Street refers to the street 1 block north of Odori, and so on). The other determinant landmark is the **Soseigawa River,** which marks addresses east and west—West 1st Street runs along the west bank of the Soseigawa River, while East 1st Street runs along the east bank.

GETTING AROUND Central Sapporo is easy to cover on foot. You can walk south from Sapporo Station to **Odori Park** in less than 10 minutes (overground or underground) and on to **Susukino,** Sapporo's nightlife district, in another 7 or 8 minutes. For longer distances, transportation in Sapporo is via **bus,** three **subway** lines (which interchange at **Odori Station**), and one **streetcar** line. Fares begin at ¥210 for buses and subways and ¥230 for streetcars. It's easiest to use prepaid cards, available in denominations beginning at ¥1,000 and valid for all conveyances. Short-term visitors may prefer to get a 1-day card for subways, which only costs ¥830, discounted to ¥520 on weekends and holidays. Children pay half fare. Cards can be purchased at subway stations and on buses and streetcars.

The blue- or orange-colored **Sapporo Walk Bus** (operating year-round) and the white-colored **Sapporo Sansaku Bus** (operating early July to mid-Oct only) travel in a loop to tourist sites around the city (unfortunately, neither goes to Nopporo Forest Park). Single fares are ¥210 for adults, half-price for children. A 1-day pass (¥750 adults, ¥380 children) allows you to get on and off as many times as you want between 9am and 7pm. Stops are announced in English and bus stops are clearly marked.

Exploring Sapporo

One of the first things you should do in Sapporo is walk around. Starting from **Sapporo Station** (which contains a chic shopping and restaurant complex) take the road leading directly south called **Eki-mae Dori** (which is also W. 4th St.). This is one of Sapporo's main thoroughfares, taking

The 19th-century Clock Tower is Sapporo's most iconic landmark.

you south through the heart of the city. Four blocks south of the station, you'll find Sapporo's most famous landmark, the **Clock Tower** (**Tokeidai; ✆ 011-231-0838**). This Western-style wooden building was built in 1878 as a drill hall for the Sapporo Agricultural College (now Hokkaido University). The large clock at the top was made in Boston and was installed in 1881. In summer, it attracts tourists even at night; they hang around the outside gates just to listen to the clock strike the hour. Inside the tower is a local-history museum, not worth the price of admission.

If you continue walking 1 block south of the Clock Tower, you'll reach **Odori Koen Promenade,** a 103m-wide (344-ft.) boulevard stretching almost 1.6km (1 mile) from east to west. In the middle of the boulevard is a wide median strip that has been turned into gracious **Odori Park** with trees, flower beds, and fountains, site of many outdoor celebrations throughout the year (see "Odori Park & Its Many Festivals," p. 648).

Rolling through the center of Sapporo, Odori Park is the site for outdoor festivals throughout the year.

From Odori Park, you can continue your walk either above or below ground. Appreciated especially during Hokkaido's long, cold winters are two underground shopping arcades, known collectively as Sapporo Chikagai, with about 140 shops open daily from 10am to 8pm. Underneath Odori Park, from the Odori subway station all the way to the TV tower in the east, is **Aurora Town,** with boutiques and restaurants. Even longer is the 390m (1,300-ft.) **Pole Town,** which extends from Odori station south all the way to **Susukino,** Sapporo's nightlife district, where you'll find many restaurants and pubs. Before reaching Susukino, however, you may want to emerge at **Sanchome**

ODORI PARK & ITS MANY festivals

In the heart of Sapporo, the long green strip of Odori Park is laid out perfectly for hosting urban gatherings. This is where much of the **Sapporo Snow Festival** is held in early February, when ice and packed snow are carved to form statues, palaces, and fantastical creatures. Begun in 1950 to add a bit of spice and life to the cold winter days, the Snow Festival now features up to 400 snow and ice sculptures and draws about 2.4 million visitors a year. One snow structure may require as much as 300 6-ton truckloads of snow, brought in from the surrounding mountains. The snow and ice carvings, depicting everything from anime characters and Japanese Castles to Salzburg Cathedral and the Taj Mahal, are done with so much attention to detail that it seems a crime they're doomed to melt (see "Japan Calendar of Events," in chapter 2).

Odori Park is also the scene of the **Sapporo Summer Festival,** with beer gardens set up the length of the park from late July to mid-August, open every day from noon on. Various Japanese beer companies sponsor booths and tables under the trees, while vendors put up stalls selling fried noodles, corn on the cob, and other goodies. Live bands serenade the beer drinkers under the stars. It all resembles the cheerful confusion of a German beer garden, which isn't surprising considering Munich is one of Sapporo's sister cities (Portland, Oregon, is another one).

In December, the park hosts a **Christmas Market** (probably Japan's best), featuring European vendors selling Christmas trinkets from Spain, Russian dolls, German beer, sausages, and pastries, and Dutch ceramics, as well as Japanese kiosks featuring Hokkaido venison, pretzels with sweet bean past and butter, and of course, Sapporo beer. The Sapporo Tower at its east end is lit up like a Christmas tree, making things all the more atmospheric.

Some of the other festivals held in Odori Park are the **Lilac Festival** in late May, heralding the arrival of summer, and **Bon-Odori** in mid-August with traditional dances to appease the souls of the dead.

(you'll see escalators going up), where you'll find more shopping at the 1km-long (½-mile) **Tanuki-koji** covered shopping arcade's 200 boutiques and traditional specialty shops.

Botanic Garden (Shokubutsu-en) ♥ GARDEN A lovely place for a summer picnic, just north of Odori Park, the 13-hectare (32-acre) Botanic Garden contains some virgin forest and more than 4,000 varieties of plants gathered from all over Hokkaido, arranged in marshland, herb, alpine, and other gardens. There's a particularly interesting section devoted to plants used by the Ainu, not only edible plants but also those with medicinal use and other properties (for example, organic poison used on arrows to kill bears and other game). Unfortunately, there's no English-language explanation of how the plant were used. Also on the grounds is Japan's oldest **natural science museum,** housed in a turn-of-the-20th-century Western-style building, which was founded in 1882 to document Hokkaido's wildlife. Be sure, too, to visit the small, one-room **Ainu Museum,** which displays some fine examples of Ainu artifacts, including traditional clothing, jewelry, farming tools, hunting traps, harpoons, a canoe, and bamboo mouth harps (played by women and children). A 13-minute video, filmed in 1935, shows the ritualistic killing of a brown bear, which included a ceremony to give thanks and send the bear's soul to the afterlife. You could easily spend an hour touring the garden and its museums.

N3-jo, W8-chome, Chuo-ku. hokudai.ac.jp. Apr 20–Nov 3 ¥420 adults, ¥300 children (includes museum admission); Tues–Sun 9am–4pm (closes 3:30pm Oct 1 onward). Nov 4–Apr 28 greenhouse only; ¥120 admission; Mon–Fri 10am–3pm, Sat 10am–noon.

Mount Moiwa ♥♥ VIEW/HIKE For panoramic views, take a trip west of the city to the summit of 531m (1,742-ft.) Mount Moiwa, where you can see just how far Sapporo sprawls across the Ishikari Plain, from the Sea of Japan to the mountains in the northwest and farmlands in the north and east. Hiking up the mountain is a historic pilgrimage of sorts: The old Ainu name for the mountain was *Inkarushibe,* meaning "the place we always climb up and look out from." There are five trails of varying lengths, enclosed by Yezo spruce, Mongolian oak, and Japanese linden trees, as well as species like Moiwa *bodaiju* and *mizunara* (which turn yellow in autumn), and many kinds of wildflower. The most accessible route starts at the Jikeikai Hospital (**Jikeikai Byoin Mae**) trailhead at 5–6 Ashigaoka, Chuo-ku, and gently meanders for around 2.6km (1.6 miles) to the observation deck. This should take 60 to 90 minutes, even for beginner hikers. To get to the trailhead, take the streetcar to Nishisen Juyojo then take a bus or walk for 20 minutes to Jikeikai Hospital. A slightly more challenging trail, 3km (1.85 miles) long, is the Moiwa-yama Asahiyama-Jikeikai Loop Hike, which takes around 90 minutes. To get to its starting point, the **Asahiyama Memorial Park Trailhead,** either walk 30 to 40 minutes or take a bus from Maryama Station, accessed by the subway Tozai Line. Note that underfoot conditions can become sludgy after heavy rain, and while you can hike in winter, it's best to be prepared for snow and freezing weather. For route maps see **hokkaidowilds.org** or enquire at the tourist information center. There is also a **ropeway,** especially popular with travelers and young couples hoping to catch romantic night views of the city or to dine at the fancy, glass-walled **The Jewels** restaurant (thejewels.jp; ✆ **011-518-6311**). Free shuttle buses run every 15 minutes from the Iriguchi streetcar stop to the ropeway station. The ropeway runs from 10:30am to 10pm daily (from 11am in winter) and costs ¥1,050 each way (¥530 children). As with Hakodate (p. 639), I don't advise using the ropeway unless you must, as it contributes to the congestion.

NOPPORO FOREST PARK (NOPPORO SHINRIN KOEN)

This rambling wooded park on Sapporo's eastern outskirts holds two very worthwhile attractions. It's about half an hour's travel by public transport. Take the **Hakodate Line train** to Shinrin Koen Station, then transfer to the **JR bus** no. 22, getting off at Hokkaido Hakubutsukan (fare: ¥580). Alternatively, take a **Rapid Airport** train 8 minutes to Shin-Sapporo Station (¥1,180), and then transfer to the no. 22 bus for a 20-minute ride to the last stop, Kaitakunomura (¥240), followed by a 10- to 15-minute walk.

Sapporo's open-air Kaitaku-no Mura (Historical Village) is an assemblage of historical buildings from around Hokkaido, like this Western-style government building from the 1870s.

Historical Village of Hokkaido (Kaitaku-no Mura) ♥♥ OPEN-AIR MUSEUM More than 50 historical Japanese- and Western-style buildings, dating mostly from the Meiji and Taisho eras, have been brought here from around Hokkaido—homes, farmhouses, a shrine, a church, a newspaper office, a post office, a police box (manned by a sword-wielding police officer), and many small businesses, including a blacksmith, brewery, barbershop, grocery, inn, and sleigh factory. Highlights include the Matsuhashi Family Residence, Hokkaido Middle School, the Aoyama fisherman's family complex, and the Hokuseikan Silkworm house. In summer, staff members dressed in Meiji-Era clothing are on hand to answer questions. For kids there's an old-fashioned playground; nearby is the Traditional Activities Room, where children can make crafts and play games. There are horse-drawn carriage rides in summer and horse-drawn sleighs in winter (extra fee charged). You can easily spend 2 hours here, wandering through a fishing village, farm village, mountain village, and town. ***Tip:*** Wear slip-on shoes, as they must be removed to enter many of the structures.

Konopporo 50–1, Atsubetsu-cho. kaitaku.or.jp. ✆ **011-898-2692.** ¥1,000; children and seniors free; free for high-school students on Sat and some national holidays. May–Sept daily 9am–5pm; Oct–Apr Tues–Sun 9am–4:30pm.

Hokkaido Museum ♥ MUSEUM This museum does a great job detailing Hokkaido's development from prehistoric to modern times, with lots of information in English. The section on the indigenous Ainu is especially good, with displays of clothing, a house, items used for trade with the Japanese, and other artifacts, along with descriptions of the Ainu's forced assimilation into Japanese culture (after the Meiji Restoration, Ainu were restricted from hunting and fishing on land they'd used for generations, and cultural markers like tattoos and earrings were prohibited; even today, there are ongoing legal battles to restore these rights to the Ainu people). You'll also learn about Hokkaido's early contacts with Russia and the lives of 19th-century Japanese pioneers, many of them former samurai dispossessed by the Meiji Restoration. The Living Experience Room provides hands-on experience with tools, including a hand loom, and interactive displays. If history's your thing, you can easily spend 2 hours here.
Konopporo, Atsubetsu-cho. hmh.pref.hokkaido.jp. ✆ **011-898-0456.** ¥800 adults, ¥300 college and high-school students, free for seniors and children. Tues–Sun 9:30am–5pm (until 4:30pm Oct–Apr). Closed some national holidays.

SAPPORO ART PARK & SCULPTURE GARDEN

On the southern fringes of the city, the **Sapporo Art Park** (artpark.or.jp; ✆ **011-592-5111**) makes a wonderful half-day excursion for anyone interested in art. To get here, take the **Namboku Line** train south from Sapporo Station to Makomanai, then switch to the **Takino Sen** bus to Geijutsu no Mori Iriguchi (50 min. total; ¥650).

With five to seven special exhibitions a year, the **Sapporo Art Museum** ♥ usually showcases the works of contemporary artists with some connection to Sapporo, but it has also displayed the works of European art masters, Japanese cartoonists, art collectives like teamLab, and well-known ceramicists. The museum is open 9:45am to 5pm (until 5:30pm in summer) during exhibitions periods; November through April it's closed Mondays. Admission varies but is usually around ¥1,500.

The main reason to come out here, though, is the extensive **sculpture garden** ♥♥, with 74 artworks (by 64 artists) of varying styles and themes set along undulating, leafy walking trails. Many of the works perfectly match their settings, like two Blackiston's fish owls standing sentinel in the forest or a waterfall feature tumbling over what looks like the remnants of a castle wall; others—an enraptured clown, a procession of bright yellow men sitting on each other's laps—are simply eye-catching, all the more delightful because they have no obvious rhyme nor reason. You'll find strange monoliths, a "meadow of clouds," landscaped spaces that encourage deeper investigation, and works by top domestic talents like Kyoko Asakura and Susumu Koshimizu. The garden is open the same hours as the museum, though it's closed in winter (though during this period, you can rent snowshoes from reception for ¥500 and walk through the park for free). Garden admission is ¥700 adults, ¥560 seniors, free children.

Outdoor Activities: Skiing

Skiing is big in Sapporo, host city for the 1972 Winter Olympics. There are even slopes within city limits, and more than a dozen skiing areas are less than 2 hours away, most open from early December to late April. On the west edge of town are **Okurayama Jump Hill** and **Miyanomori Jump Hill,** both sites for the 1972 Winter Olympics. Here, too, is the **Sapporo Bankei Ski Area** (✆ **011-641-0071**)—just 20 minutes from downtown Sapporo, it's popular for after-work and night skiing (it stays open to 10pm). You can reach them by subway to Maruyama Koen Station, followed by a 15-minute bus ride. Just 2.5km (1½ miles) south of Sapporo Station is **Nakajima Park** (station: Nakajima Koen), which offers free use of cross-country skis in winter.

Farther afield to the west, the **Sapporo Teine** ski areas (sapporo-teine.com; ✆ **011-682-6000**) were the sites of the alpine, bobsled, and toboggan events for the Olympics. A lift joins the two areas, creating Hokkaido's longest run (6km/3¾ miles). During the regular season, a 5-hour lift pass costs ¥6,000, a 1-day pass ¥8,200 (slight discounts if purchased online); ski equipment and snowboard gear is available from ¥8,000 in the day and ¥5,300 at night (discounted if outside the regular season). Take the **JR Ishikari Liner** train from Sapporo Station 20 minutes to Teine Station and then take **JR bus no. 70** another 15 minutes to Teine Olympia-mae.

Sapporo Teine ski slopes were sites for the 1972 Winter Olympics.

Once a quiet mountain village, **Niseko** (niseko.ne.jp), 90km (56 miles) and a 3-hour bus ride west of Sapporo, is now known as the best ski resort in Hokkaido for its fine powder, extensive night skiing, and hot-spring spas. It's comprised of four skiing regions (An'nupuri, Niseko Village, Grand Hirafu, and Hanazono), collectively called Niseko United and joined by a network of some 60 runs, 38 gondolas and lifts, and shuttle buses. It's very popular with Aussies wishing to ski in their off season, as well as hordes of skiers from other Western nations hoping to get a taste of the fabled *Japow*—the somewhat cheesy moniker for Japan's (arguably) unparalleled powdered snow. It's worth noting that this influx of foreigners has made prices skyrocket—subpar bowls of ramen go from more than ¥3,000 (triple what you'd pay in Tokyo)—and locals have been priced out; there's little sense you're actually in Japan when visiting here.

A 1-Day lift ticket costs ¥10,500, with rental prices comparable to those at Teine (prices vary from shop to shop). To get there, take the **JR Niseko Liner train** from Sapporo Station to Niseko (get off at Kutchan Station; 2 hr.; ¥2,100), followed by a shuttle bus. For more information on skiing around Sapporo, go to **snowjapan.com**.

Where to Stay in Sapporo

Sapporo has a large selection of fine hotels in various price categories. The busiest tourist seasons are summer and early February during the annual Snow Festival. If you plan to attend the festival, book your room at least 6 months in advance. At other times you should have no problem finding a room, but it's always wise to make a reservation in advance. In winter (excluding festival time), some upper- and medium-priced hotels lower their room rates, sometimes by as much as 40%; be sure to ask for a discount.

EXPENSIVE

Hotel Monterey Edelhof ♥♥ Although opened in 2000, this elegant hotel embraces the architectural exuberance of early 1900s Vienna, with lots of marble, stained-glass windows, Art Deco embellishments, and Otto Wagner–inspired designs. Even the elevators have old-fashioned floor dials, classical music plays in public spaces, and function rooms carry such names as Belvedere. Some may find the sepia-tinged color palette dated, but personally I love it, down to the antique furniture showing the wear of time—there's even an old writing bureau in each room with a sliding drawer containing a copy of the New Testament with Japanese translation. Located in downtown Sapporo, on the upper floors of an office building, the hotel offers small(ish) rooms, but the views and location make up for that in spades. The 14th-floor hotel spa, which uses hot springs tapped deep below ground, is a huge plus.

1–1–2 Kita Jonishi, Chuo-ku. hotelmonterey.co.jp. ✆ **011-242-7111.** 181 units. ¥10,000–¥20,000 single, ¥25,000–¥50,000 double (rates greatly reduced in winter outside festival time). Station: Sapporo (8 min.). **Amenities:** 2 restaurants; bar; lounge; hot-spring spa w/sauna and Jacuzzi; room service; free Wi-Fi.

JR Tower Hotel Nikko Sapporo ♥♥♥ Elegance and convenience—not to mention top-class restaurants, a deluxe spa (offering everything from reflexology to indoor/outdoor hot-spring baths), and spectacular views from all rooms—make this the best place to stay in Sapporo. Located above Sapporo Station and presided over by a walkie-talkie-toting staff who makes sure everything runs smoothly, it offers rooms (23rd–34th floors) with all the latest in hotel design, including desks with flip tops so they can double as mirrored vanities, separate tub/shower areas, and towels embroidered with different-colored insignia to take out the guessing game of which towel belongs to whom. ***A caveat:*** Train passengers are forced to undergo a roundabout hike to reach hotel elevators,

There are spectacular city views from all rooms at the JR Tower Hotel Nikko Sapporo.

though strategically placed signs help assure them they're on the right track.

5 Nishi 2, Kita 5, Chuo-ku, Sapporo. jrhotels.co.jp. ✆ **011-251-2222.** 350 units. ¥10,000–¥20,000 single; ¥30,000–¥60,000 double. 10% discount for Japan Rail Pass holders. **Amenities:** 4 restaurants; hot-spring spa w/sauna, Jacuzzi; room service; free Wi-Fi.

Sapporo Grand Hotel ♥ This dignified hotel, open since 1934 and one of Sapporo's old-timers, has a good downtown location near the Botanic Garden and Odori Park. An appealing choice of dining and drinking outlets (including those serving Hokkaido specialties) and a helpful English-speaking staff will make your stay enjoyable. The hotel occupies three buildings constructed at various times: Business travelers often go for the annex, which has mostly singles; company executives generally stay in the main building; and everyone else heads to the east building for its family rooms (with four beds) and so-called Comfort Rooms on top floors, with extra amenities like humidifiers, duvet-covered beds, and big-screen TVs. Most rooms are fairly large and nicely furnished but—a sign of the hotel's age—have small windows and small bathrooms. Note, too, that some of the cheapest rooms face another building.

4 Kita 1 Jonishi, Chuo-ku. grand1934.com. ✆ **011-261-3311.** 562 units. ¥10,000–¥20,000 single; ¥20,000–¥65,000 double. Station: Sapporo (8 min.). **Amenities:** 5 restaurants; 2 bars; lounge; room service; spa; free Wi-Fi.

MODERATE

Hotel Flourish 67 ♥♥ Not sure what this place has to do with flourishing (or the number 67, for that matter), but its unique offering is serviced apartments not far from the city center for as little as ¥15,000 per night (a minimum 2-night stay is required). Their design is fairly functional, yet clean and modern, and each unit is fitted with A/C, a dining area and kitchen (rice cooker, coffee pot, microwave, toaster, kettle, fridge), a TV lounge, and a private bathroom. Good for groups, families, longer stays, or workations.

7 Chome–3–5 Minami 6 Jonishi, Chuo-ku. Go to booking.com/hotel/jp/flourish-67.en-gb.html. No phone. 24 units. ¥15,000–¥25,000 per night (much higher during Snow Festival). Subway: Susukino (12 min.). **Amenities:** Free Wi-Fi.

Hotel Gracery Sapporo ♥♥ Its seventh-floor lobby, with massage chairs and free coffee, overlooks Sapporo station, with guest rooms rising above to the 16th floor. A no-contact key card allows you to enter your room with a simple wave, check out on departure day at lobby kiosks, and even buy beer. Rooms are small but stylish, especially the Ladies Rooms with special amenities such as humidifiers, window panels that close for complete darkness, and feminine decor.

4–1 Kita 4 Jonishi, Chuo-ku. gracery.com. ✆ **011-251-3211.** 440 units. ¥7,000–¥17,000 single, ¥11,000–¥25,000 double. Station: Sapporo (1 min.). **Amenities:** Restaurant; free Wi-Fi.

Hotel Mercure Sapporo ♥♥ One of the best options in the heart of Sapporo, this smart hotel is only a few minutes' walk from Susukino Station, and very reasonably priced given its offerings: a French restaurant, a wine and cocktail bar, a generous breakfast buffet, a gym and fitness center, and in the Privilege Queen rooms, beds so large and comfy you won't be in any rush to get out of them. As a chain hotel, the design is a little cut-and-paste and it doesn't have the atmosphere of the city's grand old hotels, but aside from those aesthetic shortcomings, most of its marks are in the plus column.

2–4 Minami 4 jonishi 2, Chuo-ku. all.accor.com. ✆ **011-513-1100.** 285 units. ¥10,000–¥30,000 single or double. Station: Susukino (3 min.). **Amenities:** Restaurant; buffet breakfast; bar; gym; free Wi-Fi.

Nakamuraya Ryokan ♥♥ If you want to stay in a ryokan, this modern and comfortable Japanese inn, just a stone's throw from the Botanic Garden (p. 648), is a good choice. First opened more than 110 years ago, it now occupies a nondescript 50-year-old building, where you'll find pleasant Japanese-style *tatami* rooms, some with a sitting area near the window. The hallways with eaves and slatted wooden doors to each room are a nice touch. Although rooms have their own tub, you might want to take advantage of the public baths here. If you order dinner, it will be served ryokan-style in your room by kimono-clad women.

Kita 3 jonishi 7, Chuo-ku. nakamura-ya.com. ✆ **011-241-2111.** 26 units. ¥6,000–¥10,000 single, ¥10,000–¥20,000 double. Station: Sapporo (10 min.). **Amenities:** Restaurant, public baths, free Wi-Fi.

INEXPENSIVE

Toyoko Inn Sapporo Nishi-Guchi Hokudai-mae ♥ This inexpensive business-hotel chain offers little extras such as semi-double- or double-size beds in the mostly single rooms (rooms are so small, a sign suggests stowing luggage under the bed). The twins are great for friends traveling together (or couples who wish they weren't)—the bathroom splits the room in halves, each containing its own bed, TV, mirror, hair dryer, and more. Because the hotel is located across from Hokkaido University, rooms are hard to come by during February entrance exams, but there are two other properties within walking distance of Sapporo Station, **Toyoko Inn Sapporo-eki Kita-Guchi,** a 2-minute walk northeast (✆ **011-728-1045**), and **Toyoko Inn Sapporo-eki Minami-Guchi,** a 5-minute walk southeast (✆ **011-222-1045**), as well as two properties in the Susukino nightlife district, the **Toyoko Inn Sapporo Susukino Minami** (✆ **011-551-1045**) and the **Toyoko Inn Sapporo Susukino Kosaten** (✆ **011-207-1045**).

4 Chome–22–7 Kita 8 Jonishi, Kita-ku. toyoko-inn.com. ✆ **011-717-1045.** 180 units. ¥7,000–¥11,000 single, ¥10,000–¥15,000 double. Rates include Japanese breakfast. Station: Sapporo (3 min.). **Amenities:** Free Wi-Fi.

Where to Eat in Sapporo

Hokkaido's specialties include crab, corn on the cob, potatoes, miso ramen, soup curry, *jingisukan* (Genghis Khan—a dish of mutton and vegetables that you grill yourself), *robatayaki* (meat and vegetables cooked over hot charcoal), and *Ishikari nabe* (a stew of salmon and other Hokkaido vegetables, also cooked at your table).

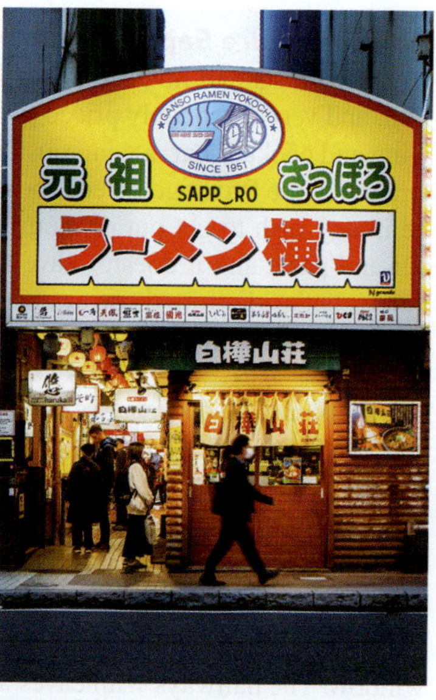

Sapporo's Ramen Alley is full of places to try the famed local miso ramen, including the long-established Ganso Ramen Yokocho.

EXPENSIVE

Hyosetsu-no-Mon ♥ KING CRAB In business more than 60 years in Sapporo's Susukino nightlife district, this well-known restaurant specializes in giant king crab caught in the Japan Sea north of Hokkaido. Its menu (in Japanese, but with photos) is easy enough—it consists almost entirely of king crab dishes. Set courses include cooked crab, sashimi, crab soup, crab tempura, and vegetables. Although dinners are expensive, lunches are more reasonably priced and there are usually seasonal specials available all day. Reservations recommended.

2–8–10 Minami 5 Jonishi, Chuo-ku. ✆ **011-521-3046.** Lunches ¥5,300–¥6,200, dinners ¥8,300–¥21,300. Mon–Fri 11am–3pm and 4:30–10pm (last order), Sat–Sun 11am–10pm (last order). Subway: Susukino (2 min.).

Mikuni Sapporo ♥♥ FRENCH The proprietor/chef of several Mikuni restaurants in Tokyo and elsewhere, Kiyomi Mikuni has a reputation as *the* Japanese authority on French food. Hokkaido-born Mikuni has now brought his expertise home to triumphant reviews. Located on the ninth floor of Stellar Place in Sapporo Station, in a setting that is less than stellar (and accessed by an elevator that is hard to find), the restaurant overcomes its drab and dated decor with great cuisine, available only as set meals. A seasonal autumn lunch, for example, may include cappuccino-style autumn mushrooms and chestnuts, then either pan-fried codfish with potatoes and lentils or braised pork garnished with French beans and sweet-potato purée, followed by dessert and coffee. As befits a French restaurant, there is an extensive wine list, with knowledgeable sommeliers to advise you. Stellar Place 9F, 2–5 Kita 5 Jonishi, Chuo-ku. ✆ **011-251-0392.** Set dinners ¥10,000–¥20,000; set lunches ¥3,800–¥13,000. Reservations recommended. Wed–Mon 11:30am–2pm and 5:30–8pm (last order). In Sapporo Station.

MODERATE

Mochinoron (炉端 酒 勿ノ論 / モチノロン) ♥♥♥ ROBATAYAKI This place is so dark it will take some time for your eyes to adjust, but once they do, chances are you'll like what you see. A U-shaped counter surrounds an open kitchen (you're so close, you're practically in it) with an industrial-sized meat slicer, a crackling charcoal pit, and a couple of chefs meticulously preparing food. A primal smell of charred meat wafts throughout as various cuts of lamb, pork, and chicken sizzle over the open flames—mercifully, a huge fan ensures you can eat your dinner without getting lungfuls of smoke. The QR code menu has some robatayaki classics: lamb in savory sauce, baked mushrooms with butter and garlic, chicken leg, pork-wrapped oysters (a must), and fillets of Hokkaido fish.

SLURPING NOODLES IN ramen alley

Hokkaido is famed for its miso ramen, and one of the best places to try is just 1 short block east of Susukino Station, in an alleyway of noodle shop after noodle shop, called **Ganso Ramen Yokocho** ♥♥♥. Thanks to much publicity in recent years, this place now gets frightfully busy (expect to wait in line), and while naysayers inevitably come with that sort of fame, the quality of food here is still par excellence. Usually served with sweetcorn and a lump of butter in it, the style of broth here is hefty, rich in umami, and warms diners to their cores—ideal in a city with bitterly cold winters. The origins of the dish are murky, but there are two popular theories: Either a sleep-deprived cook mixed up his pots, or better yet, a drunk customer demanded noodles be put in his miso soup—and voila! created this thriving northern soul food. It doesn't really matter which of the 17 shops here you choose—just look for an empty seat, if you can find one—though **Tokuichi Tomiya,** meaning "Special Fortune," is probably the most famous spot, having won multiple awards for its miso-butter-corn ramen. Each very small shop consists of a counter and some chairs, with photos of various dishes outside the front door. Most are open daily from 11:30am to 3am. Ramen generally begins at ¥800 or ¥900 for a steaming bowlful.

In the historic Sapporo Beer brewery, the Sapporo Beer Museum offers tasting sets and table-grilled jingisukan meals.

Some of the cold dishes, like octopus and chrysanthemum marinated in miso vinegar and lightly seared yellowtail steak, are also superb. 4–9 Minami 3 Jonishi (on the 7th floor), Chuo-ku. ✆ **011-1596-6230.** Dinner ¥3,000–¥5,000 per person. Daily 5pm–midnight. Subway: Susukino (2 min.).

Salt Moderate ♥♥ OYSTERS A strange name for sure, but there's nothing questionable about the quality of the food in this chic Susukino oyster bar. A menu showing "Today Oyster" includes set meals (usually between three and six pieces), or you can order a la carte options, like raw oysters with condiments, grilled oysters in herb butter, and "hollandaise" oysters with sea urchin and egg yolk cream. For the oyster-averse, there are also lobster and beef dishes, as well as Hawaiian fare, like oxtail soup and seafood pokes. 1–2–1 Minami 3 Jonishi, Chuo-ku. ✆ **011-215-1997.** Oyster meals ¥1,500–¥3,500; a la carte oysters around ¥500; other dishes ¥1,000–¥2,000. Daily 3–11pm (last order), closes 10pm Sun. Subway: Susukino (3 min.).

Sapporo Bier Garten ♥♥ JINGISUKAN Famous throughout the world, Sapporo beer was brewed in the handsome, ivy-covered brick buildings here from 1890 to 2003. Today they hold restaurants, shops, and the Sapporo Beer Museum (✆ **011-731-4368;** Tues–Sun 11am–6pm); displays are unfortunately in Japanese only (though English translation cards are available), but admission is free and you can purchase a tasting set of classic Sapporo brews for ¥1,000. This is also a good destination for a hearty meal, especially in the historic, cavernous Kessel Hall, where you dine underneath a huge 1912 mash tub in an atmosphere that's about the closest thing you'll find to Oktoberfest in Bavaria. The specialty here is *jingisukan,* which you cook yourself on a hot convex skillet at your table. The best deal in the house is the appropriately named King Viking, which for ¥5,280 gives you as much lamb, seasonal veg, and draft beer as you can consume in 100 minutes. It's a challenge most travelers enthusiastically accept. 9-2-10 Kita 7 Johigashi, Higashi-ku. sapporo-bier-garten.jp. ✆ **011-742-1531.** All-you-can-eat *jingisukan* ¥3,600 (¥5,280 with all-you-can-drink); discounts for children and teenagers. Kessel Hall daily 11:30am–9pm. No. 188 or 63 bus, 10-min. from Sapporo Station.

INEXPENSIVE

Soup Curry Garaku ♥♥ SOUP CURRY You can't visit Sapporo without eating soup curry, a dish that leaves little to the imagination: a runny curry-flavored broth filled with meat and/or vegetables, often served with a side of rice and melted cheese. Popular options here include a 15-vegetable soup curry, one with thin-sliced pork and seven kinds of forest mushroom, one with tender chicken leg and vegetables, and another with Frankfurter, bacon, and grilled cheese. After selecting your curry, choose your spice level (which goes all the way up to 40; heat levels on the English menu are color-coded), how much rice you want, and any additional toppings, like eggs, broccoli, eggplant, pumpkin, wood-ear or maitake mushrooms, camembert cheese fries or camembert spring rolls, and tender chicken leg. This place is a favorite among locals and travelers alike, but it doesn't accept reservations, so try to get down before the lunch or dinner opening hour to mitigate long waiting times. The entrance is on the ground floor, with stairs going down to the dining hall. Okumura Building B1, 2-6-1 Minami 2 Jonishi, Chuo-ku. s-garaku.com. ✆ **011-233-5568.** Soup curry ¥1,300–¥1,800. Daily 11:30am–3pm and 5–8:30pm (last order). Station: Susukino (5 min.).

Susukino Nightlife

Susukino is abuzz come nightfall, with lively izakaya, glittering karaoke parlors, drunken revelry, and fluorescent streets unfurling from the large Nikka Whiskey billboard at the heart of the district's main intersection. After Tokyo and Osaka, this is might be the best place to experience Japan's frenetic urban nightlife. Estimates put the number of bars here at more than 3,000 (try to find them all at your own peril), and they include everything from 500 bars (where all drinks cost ¥500) and Irish-style pubs to cocktail hideouts and clandestine host clubs. The following establishments are a taster of what you can expect to find. (Nonsmokers should note that many Susukino bars are cigarette-friendly.)

Jazz Café Bossa ♥♥♥ (✆ **011-271-5410**) is a venerable izakaya on the second floor of a building presiding over one of the busiest thoroughfares in the city. You wouldn't know it once you're inside, though, cocooned by shelves of old records, the enrapturing music of Chet Baker, Miles Davis, and Bill Evans, and a huge speaker system enshrined at one end of the bar. This place shows the wear of time—part of its charm, of course—and even if you're not a massive jazz fan, it's an easy place to relax with a beer, cocktail, or whisky (most of which cost ¥880), or a coffee and cake set at lunch (¥790).

Susukino offers one of Japan's most buzzing urban nightlife scenes.

The Long Bar ♥♥ (the-long-bar.com; ✆ **011-215-0677**) is an aptly named rectangular cocktail lounge (replete with tuxedo-clad staff) that attracts older salarymen and guests staying in the area's fancy hotels. Customers sip on creative cocktails made with fruit or inspired by desserts like tiramisu, or sample the range of international whiskies, starting at ¥1,200 per glass. Cigars are also available, as is a private karaoke room that can be rented for ¥4,000 per hour (¥6,000 Fri and Sat nights). It's open daily 7pm–3am; each customer also must pay an ¥800 cover charge. Just around the corner, **Bar Knight ♥♥** (✆ **011-205-0823**) is cut from the same cloth, with a stellar Japanese whisky collection. If you let loose in here, you could easily rack up a bill of ¥10,000 or more.

St John's Wood ♥♥ (sjw.k-ai.jp; ✆ **011-271-0085**) is not the most authentic Irish pub you'll find in Japan, but it's better than most, with a wood-paneled interior, bar stools and TVs for watching live sport, and decent pints of Guiness. It draws a lively crowd most nights of the week; it's a good spot to meet other foreigners and English-speaking locals, and it's open to 5am on weekends.

Students, English teachers, and young Aussies taking a break from the ski season are among the imbibers you'll find at **500 Bar ♥** (500bar-dining.gorp.jp; ✆ **050-5484-5261**). There's nothing fancy on the menu—at ¥500 per drink, how could there be?—but you'll still find shots, cocktails, wine, spirits, beer, and even food like edamame, fries, chicken, noodles, pasta, and pizza. This place gets rowdy, especially as the night wears on. It's open 5pm to 5am daily.

NOBORIBETSU SPA ♥♥ & SHIKOTSU-TOYA NATIONAL PARK ♥♥

The closest national park to Sapporo, and the first park you'll reach if you enter Hokkaido via train to Hakodate, **Shikotsu-Toya National Park** spreads over 987 sq. km (381 sq. miles), encompassing lakes, volcanoes,

ANOTHER ISLAND, ANOTHER PEOPLE: the ainu of hokkaido

Not much is known about the origins of the **Ainu,** the native inhabitants of Japan's northernmost island. They are clearly of different racial stock than the Japanese—many Ainu men, for example, are able to grow thick beards, unlike most Japanese, and do so as an indication of their heritage. It's thought the Ainu first arrived in Hokkaido, probably via land bridge from Siberia, 20,000 to 30,000 years ago, and a common Ainu culture formed around the 12th or 13th century. Because of Japan's successful efforts to assimilate the Ainu during the Meiji Period, however, most Ainu are now of mixed blood; self-identification has become an important part of reclaiming their ancient culture, which includes performing arts, folk crafts, rituals and festivals, traditional knowledge of plants and their uses, and a language of which there are believed to be no remaining native speakers.

Living in a harsh environment with few resources, the Ainu were skilled at using the plants and animals around them for everything from medicine to utensils. With no metal at their disposal, they carved arrows with wooden "knives" and then dipped them in poison to increase their efficiency. Clothes were fashioned from bark, wild rye, or even salmon skin. Traditionally, they lived as hunters and fishermen, using dogs to help in the hunt and setting up trip traps with arrows to catch wild animals. Animistic, they had gods for every object and phenomenon, whether sun, thunder, fire, or living creatures—Ussuri brown bears were known as *kimun kamuy,* gods of the mountains, and Blackiston's fish owls were seen as protectors of their villages. Most important to Ainu culture were bear cubs, kept in captivity before being killed, with elaborate ceremonies held to send the cub's spirit to the next life.

After Hokkaido was opened for development in the late 1800s, the Ainu were forcibly assimilated into Japanese society, and many died from smallpox, measles, cholera, and other newly introduced diseases. Like Native Americans, they were often discriminated against or treated as research objects, and their culture was largely destroyed. Hunting and fishing were prohibited, and male Ainu were taken from their families for forced labor. Eventually, the Ainu took Japanese names and adopted the Japanese language and clothing.

Today, there are an estimated 13,000 Ainu still living in Hokkaido (this figure, however, is basically guesswork, as some are unwilling to self-identify, and others are unaware of their heritage). Many of them earn their living from tourism, selling Ainu woodcarvings and other crafts, or performing traditional dances and songs. In 2008 the Ainu were formally acknowledged as an indigenous people of Japan, a watershed moment of sorts. But most Ainu scholars insist that until land rights, political representation, and even reparations are granted, the current fad for promoting Ainu culture is mostly lip service.

and the hot-spring resort of **Noboribetsu Onsen.** Famous for the variety of its hot-water springs ever since the first public bathhouse opened here in 1858, Noboribetsu Spa is one of Japan's best-known spa resorts and the most popular of Hokkaido's many onsen towns. It has 11 different types of hot water, each with a different mineral content, and gushes 10,000 tons a day. With temperatures ranging between 113°F (45°C) and 197°F (92°C), the waters contain all kinds of minerals, including sulfur, salt, iron, and gypsum, and are thought to help relieve high blood pressure, poor blood circulation, rheumatism, arthritis, eczema, and even constipation. Noboribetsu is also known for its seasonal beauty—it's an impressive sight in spring, when 2,000 cherry trees lining the road into the *onsen* are in full bloom, and in autumn thousands of Japanese maples burst into flame. In the nearby village of **Shiraoi** on Lake Poroto, a museum and village commemorate the native Ainu and their culture.

Essentials

ARRIVING By **car,** Noboribetsu Onsen is 3 hours from Hakodate (4 hr. if you avoid toll roads) or 1½ to 2 hours from Sapporo. **Noboribetsu Station,** in the nearby town of Noboribetsu, lies on the main **JR train** line between Hakodate and Sapporo (it's 2½ hr. from Hakodate, 1 hr., 10 min. from Sapporo). Fares for a reserved seat are ¥4,780 from Sapporo, ¥7,460 from Hakodate. From Noboribetsu Station it's only a 15-minute bus ride to Noboribetsu Onsen (¥350; departures two or more times an hour). There is also a **direct bus** (book through willer-travel.com/en/ or ✆ **050-5805-0383**) from Sapporo Station to Noboribetsu Onsen costing ¥2,140 for the 1¾-hour trip.

VISITOR INFORMATION The **Noboribetsu Tourist Association** (noboribetsu-spa.jp; ✆ **0143-84-3311;** daily 9am–6pm) is on Noboribetsu Onsen's main street, next to Yumoto Sagiriyu Onsen.

Exploring Around Noboribetsu Onsen

Although all the spa hotels and *ryokan* have their own taps into the spring water, almost everyone who comes to Noboribetsu Onsen makes a point of going to the most famous hotel bath in town, **Dai-ichi Takimotokan ♥♥** (takimotokan.co.jp; ✆ **0143-84-2111;** daily 9am–6pm; ¥2,250 adults, ¥1,100 children 3–12, ¥1,700 and ¥825 4–6pm), one of the first bathhouses to open at the hot springs. Now a huge, modern bathing hall with some 30 tubs and pools containing different mineral contents at various temperatures, it's an elaborate affair with hot-spring baths and Jacuzzis both indoors and out, saunas, steam rooms, and waterfall massage (you sit under the shooting water and let it pummel your neck and shoulders). Although the baths are separate for men and women, there's an indoor swimming pool for families with a slide and play area for children, so be sure to bring your swimsuit. If you're staying at the Dai-ichi Takimotokan or Takimoto Inn (see "Where to Stay," p. 666), you can use the baths for free at any time—in the evenings, don't miss bathing in the outdoor baths, where you can order drinks and enjoy the nice mountain scenery.

A short walk north from the main street lined with spa hotels, **Hell Valley (Jigokudani) ♥** is the town's most dramatic sight: a volcanic crater 446m (1,485 ft.) in diameter, full of bubbling, boiling water and rock formations of orange and brown. As you walk the concrete path that winds along the left side of the crater (called Hell Valley Promenade), keep an eye down below to the right for a tiny shrine dedicated to the deity that protects

A demon statue guarding Noboribetsu's Hell Valley.

eyes (those most in need are apt to miss it); local lore says that if you rub some of the protective water over ailing eyes, they'll be cured. Farther along, you'll soon reach a sign for OYUNUMA and a path leading uphill to the left through lush woods; if you follow it for about 10 minutes, you'll come to a lookout point over a large pond of hot bubbling water called **Oyunuma** (the lookout is across the road; it's another 5-min. walk to the pond). Return to the road and turn right (west) and then right again on the road leading downhill, where you will soon see a hiking path on the left that runs alongside the steaming Oyunuma River; halfway down is a natural foot bath. If you want to take a different route back, return to the road and the Oyunuma path but look for the Funamiyama (Mount Funami) Promenade to the right. It traces the backbone of several ridges, passing a number of small stone guardians before ending up back at Hell Valley.

IN NOBORIBETSU TOWN

Noboribetsu Date Jidai Mura ♥♥ ATTRACTION A visit to this reproduction of a Feudal-Era village is the closest you can get to taking a time machine back to the last days of the Edo Period. Shops, restaurants, theaters, the downtown, and a samurai district are built as they were of yore, staffed by people dressed in period clothing. See ninja warriors fighting in a trick mansion or outdoor theater, local merchants hawking their wares, Edo-Era tenements with life-size models, a ninja museum showing tricks of the trade, and courtesans performing in this Disney-esque recreation of how Japan might have looked when the shogun reigned. Although shows are in Japanese (the ninja shows are probably the only ones that would interest children), the various attractions are

Ninja warriors spar at the Noboribetsu Date Jidai Mura open-air village.

fun for the entire family. If you haven't seen another historical theme village elsewhere in Japan, this rather small one is worth a 2-hour visit. To commemorate the day, you can don a kimono, samurai, or ninja outfit and have your photo taken in front of a traditional backdrop for ¥3,500.

53–1 Naka-Noboribetsu-cho, Noboribetsu-shi. edo-trip.jp. ✆ **0143-83-3311.** ¥3,300 adults, seniors ¥2,600, ¥1,700 children, ¥600 toddlers. Apr–Oct daily 9am–5pm; Nov–Mar 9am–4pm (last entry 1 hr. before closing). Bus stop: Jidai Mura (fare: ¥350).

Noboribetsu Marine Park Nixe ♥ AQUARIUM Small children love this combination Danish theme park and aquarium, located near Noboribetsu Station. The aquarium, one of the largest in northern Japan, is in Castle Nixe, modeled after a Danish castle (its visible from the train station), where you'll see sharks (from an underwater tunnel), morays, salmon, sturgeon, king crab, giant octopus, and other sea creatures. More attractions include a touch pool; a reptile house; a king penguin parade; a game arcade; the ubiquitous souvenir shops (selling Danish and aquarium-related gifts); and a handful of kiddie rides (¥100 each). You can see everything in about 2 hours.

1–22 Noboribetsu Higashi-machi, Noboribetsu-shi. nixe.co.jp. ✆ **0143-83-3800.** ¥3,000 adults, ¥1,500 children. Daily 9am–5pm. Closed 5 days early Dec. Station: Noboribetsu (7 min.).

ELSEWHERE IN THE SHIKOKU-TOYA AREA

Around this part of Hokkaido, as you travel deeper into the hinterlands, that you begin to more signs of Ainu culture, in place names, traditional crafts, and museums and folk villages. or in the paucity of shrines, temples, cherry blossoms, and other touchstones of Japanese cultural life. The **Nibutani Ainu Culture Museum** and **Upopoy** both merit a visit if you want to dive deeper into this lost chapter of Japan's story. Both can be accessed via public transport, but the route to Nibutani is much more circuitous and is recommended only if you have a car.

Nibutani Ainu Culture Museum ♥♥ MUSEUM/PARK Farther east, on the banks of the Saru River, you'll another excellent museum and recreated village honoring Ainu culture and ways of life. The town's name, Nibutani, comes from the Ainu word *niputa,* meaning "a land where the trees grow thickly," and it's an apt description for this area surrounded by wetlands and wooded hills. When you arrive, you'll walk through the **Nibutani Kotan,** a few winding paths surrounded by *cise* (traditional homes) built with wood and reeds and topped by beautifully layered thatched roofs. You can enter these houses to watch demonstrations of carving and embroidery and get a little slice of old Ainu life. In the **Crafts Gallery,** a modern building on the edge of the kotan, you can purchase works made by active Ainu craftspeople, including wallets, purses, and scarves, as well as more traditional trinkets. You'll find some information pamphlets here and posters indicating upcoming events, like Ainu Art Week, taking place annually around late-November. The **museum,** with a modern facade that looks like a bird in flight or a dorsal fin protruding from the water, welcomes visitors with a sign saying *irankarapte,* an Ainu greeting that can be translated as "allow me to softly touch your heart." Inside is the largest repository of Ainu folkcraft artifacts in Japan, including woven jackets, rowing boats, hearths, cooking utensils, hunting equipment, musical instruments, wooden pacifiers called *tekokpe,* ceremonial drinking sticks known as *tukipasuy,* and fish-scale carvings, more than 900 of which have been designated as important tangible folk cultural properties.

Across the main road from the Nibutani Kotan, you may also want to visit the **Kayano Shigeru Nibutani Ainu Museum** (kayano-museum.com; ✆ **01457-2-3215**), named after Japan's first Ainu politician, whose personal collection of Ainu materials, including clothing, jewellery, metal tea bowls, animistic masks, and paintings, was amassed over 40 years. It's open the same hours as the culture museum, but can be visited only by advance reservations November 16 to April 15. Admission is ¥400 adults, ¥150 children; a combination ticket with the Nibutani Ainu Culture Museum is available (see below).

In Biratori. Biratori-ainu-culture.com. Grounds (including kotan) free, museum ¥400 adults, ¥150 children. Combination ticket w/ Kayano Shigeru museum ¥700 adults, ¥200 children. Daily 9am–4:30pm (closed Nov. 16–Dec 15 and Jan 16–Apr 15; Dec 16–Jan 15 open Tues–Sun only). By car, 1½–2 hr. from Noboribetsu, 2–2½ hr. Sapporo.

Upopoy (National Ainu Museum & Park) ♥♥ MUSEUM/PARK
Along the coast east from Noboribetsu, Shiraoi (an Ainu word meaning "Place of Many Horseflies") was settled by the Ainu long before Japanese arrived; today, it's a small town of some 20,000 inhabitants, including people of Ainu heritage. Upopoy (meaning "signing together in a large group") is considered one of the most important spaces for disseminating Ainu culture. Set on the small lake Poroto, it features a detailed museum, a replica native village, a native plant garden, a dance area, a theater, a research center, and a library. There's also a memorial site, but this has generated controversy as it holds the remains of Ainu people who were excavated in the early 20th century without the consent of the indigenous population; Ainu activists are trying to reclaim the remains for proper burial. Various events and exhibitions are held at Upopoy, some daily, including woodwork and embroidery workshops, language programs, and cooking and hunting experiences. Inside the modern concrete-and-glass **museum,** you'll find English-language descriptions of Ainu history, culture, society, and traditions, and excellent displays of utensils, clothing (such as salmon-skin boots), fishhooks (the Ainu excelled at fishing), jewelry, and other everyday artifacts. You'll also want to visit the Ainu ***kotan*** ("community") a cluster of traditionally built houses made from wood and reeds, where there are demonstrations of Ainu weaving techniques, woodworking, and other crafts, and where native dances and performances of the *mukkuri* (Ainu mouth harp) are performed by Ainu in traditional costume. In winter, when the huge lake is covered in a sheet of

ice, you can see old methods for preserving salmon, gutted and hanging on wooden racks to ensure a healthy source of protein when fishing became challenging and many woodland creatures went into hibernation. If you wish, you can lunch on dried salmon, potato cakes, *ohaw* (a stew of mountain vegetables, meat, and fish), and herb tea in one of three restaurants next to the museum.

2–3 Wakakusa-cho, Shiraoi-cho. ainu-upopoy.jp; ✆ **0144-82-3914.** ¥1,200 adults, ¥600 high-school students, children free. Tues–Sun 9am–8pm summer, until 5pm winter (check website, as closing time changes regularly). Express train from Noboribetsu Station (12 min.; fare: ¥1,290), then 10-min. walk. By car, 25 min. from Noboribetsu Onsen, 1¼ hr. from Sapporo.

Where to Stay in Noboribetsu Onsen

The busiest tourist seasons are July through September and during New Year's, which are when hotel rates are at their highest, particularly on weekends (avoid Golden Week, Obon in mid-Aug, and New Year's). October, when the leaves are changing, is also popular. Noboribetsu Onsen hotels charge a daily ¥150 hot-springs tax.

Dai-ichi Takimotokan ♥ This is Noboribetsu Onsen's best-known *ryokan,* thanks to its long history (opened in 1858) and its gigantic public baths. Today, however, it's a large, modern facility with little personality

In Noboribetsy Onsen, a public foot bath has been set up for passersby to take a quick soak in the steaming hot Oyunuma River.

and lots of noisy tour groups. The most compelling reasons to stay here are its location near Hell Valley (p. 662) and its famous hot-spring baths, which hotel guests are entitled to use free anytime, night or day. Most rooms are simple *tatami,* spread throughout four buildings. Oldest and cheapest are those in the East Building, without tubs or air-conditioning (but some with views of an enclosed garden), while rooms in the West Wing are a step up with private bathrooms. The South Building has Japanese-style rooms and eight Western-style rooms, but it's a hike to the hot-spring baths. Most luxurious are rooms in the Main Building, with top floors offering the best views. Most guests dine in a buffet restaurant offering Japanese, Chinese, and Western food (if staying consecutive nights, you'll be offered traditional Japanese meal items not on the normal menu), while those staying in tatami rooms in the Main building can opt for a Japanese dinner served in their rooms.

55 Noboribetsu Onsen-machi. takimotokan.co.jp. ✆ **0143-84-3322.** 399 units, 342 w/ private bath. ¥18,000–¥30,000 single, ¥30,000–¥60,000 double. Rates at higher end include 2 meals. Bus stop: Noboribetsu Onsen (5 min.). **Amenities:** 3 restaurants; lounge; 2 bars; indoor pool; 24-hr. indoor/outdoor hot-spring baths; free Wi-Fi.

Oyado Kiyomizu-ya ♥♥ Expect a royal welcome at this modern ryokan with traditional touches. You'll be ushered down a long corridor decorated with plants, stones, and paper lanterns to the elevator that will whisk you up to your room. Least expensive are average-looking Western-style rooms, making the simple but pleasant Japanese *tatami* rooms a better choice. For a splurge, combination rooms are actually two-room suites with a tatami room where you'll dine in a separate bedroom. The ryokan is beside a roaring river, the sounds of which will sing you to sleep as you snuggle against fur-lined futons and down covers. But it's the delicious seasonal *kaiseki* meals that assure the ryokan many repeat guests; the parade of beautifully prepared dishes includes local specialties. If you're looking for a place far from tour groups, souvenir shops, and impersonal service, you'll be happy here.

173 Noboribetsu Onsen-machi. kiyomizuya.co.jp. ✆ **0143-84-2145.** 42 units. ¥12,000–¥20,000 single; ¥20,000–¥40,000 double. Rates at higher end include 2 meals. Bus stop: Noboribetsu Onsen (10 min.). **Amenities:** Coffee shop; karaoke bar; indoor/outdoor hot-spring baths; free Wi-Fi.

OUTLYING AREA

Hotel Chupki (森のオーベルジュ三(みつ)) ♥♥♥ Drive out to this property for a secluded night in the forest that's decidedly luxurious, given its fairly reasonable rates. Look closely for the turnoff, down a thickly wooded lane that gives little suggestion as to the property lying beyond: a handsome wooden building with white half-curtains fluttering over the entrance, and modern design features like large windows emitting the warm glow of indoors. After being welcomed in the large *genkan* (entrance room), you'll walk, shoes off, along the corridors to one of the three spacious guest rooms. These also blend modernism with history;

wooden floorboards, deep stone tubs, shoji screens, transom panels, and soft lighting meet *huge* double beds, sound-proofed walls, a Bluetooth speaker in wood-latticed casings. Upholstery adds a small pop of color to the otherwise neutral palette. It can get eerily dark and quiet outside, but you won't mind when slumped in the steaming-hot bathtub or lounging on the sofa drinking herbal tea. Kaiseki is served in the tatami dining hall (sliding doors can be used as partitions for privacy) with advance reservation only, but you can also drive 5 minutes to the town of Atsuma (basically an anonymous stretch of straight road with a few houses, shops, and eateries) in search of a restaurant. **Shokukukan Yururi** (食空間ゆる**;** ✆ **0145-29-7344**), on the northern edge of the main street, does tasty *tonkatsu* sets for ¥1,500. You can also ask hotel staff for nearby dining recommendations. There's no onsen here, but if you want an al fresco dip, you'll get a free coupon for **Kobushi no Yu,** only a 10-minute drive away.

244–1 Toyosawa, Atsuma, Yufutsu District. hotelchupki.com. ✆ **0145-27-2081.** 3 units. ¥20,000–¥40,000 double (sometimes more with dinner reservation). By car, 90 min. from Noboribetsu; 45 min. from Nibutani; 30 min. from New Chitose Airport. **Amenities:** Dinner; onsen coupon; free Wi-Fi.

Where to Eat in Noboribetsu

Most visitors to Noboribetsu will eat their main meals—breakfast and dinner—in their hotels, especially given the paucity of good restaurants in the area. Below are a couple of options for lunch.

Ideyu Soba ♥♥ SOBA If you find yourself looking for a place for lunch, try this restaurant in the main building of Dai-ichi Takimotokan, which serves soba and tempura, as well as seafood like eel and sashimi, from an English-language menu with pictures. The classic *zaru soba* tempura meal, with the buckwheat noodles served on a bamboo tray, is a good deal at ¥1,320. If hungrier, order from the set menu which includes Hokkaido beef and crab, though these are a little pricier. Next to the soba shop is a ramen restaurant called **Takerokusuke** (たけろくらーめん), which might be preferable in winter.

55 Noboribetsu Onsen-machi. ✆ **0143-84-2205.** Soba ¥1,100–¥1,320; set meals ¥2,310–¥4,180. Daily 11:30am–1:45pm and 6–11:30pm (last order). Bus stop: Noborbetsu Onsen (5 min.).

Nobojin ♥♥ YAKINIKU Barbecued meat from animals reared in Hokkaido is the fare of choice in this lively counter-seat restaurant, where you can order pricey *yakiniku* (grilled meat) sets or beef hotpots called *shabu shabu* and *sukiyaki.* Cheaper are the *jingisukan* lamb and mutton, ordered a la carte and cooked in a savory sauce with cabbage, onion, beansprouts, and shiitake mushrooms. Sides like rice, noodles, pickles, and soups are also available.

2F, 76 Noboribetsu Onsencho. nobojin.com. ✆ **0143-83-6611.** Set meats ¥7,980–¥15,980; jingisukan around ¥4,000 per person. Daily 11–2:30pm and 5–8:30pm (last order). Irregular holidays. Bus stop: Noboribetsu Onsen (5 min.).

AKAN-MASHU NATIONAL PARK ♥♥♥

Spreading through the eastern end of Hokkaido, Akan-Mashu National Park features volcanic mountains, dense forests of subarctic primeval trees, and three caldera lakes, including Lake Akan. The best place to stay in the park is **Akanko Onsen,** a small hot-spring resort on the edge of Lake Akan. It makes a good base for active vacations ranging from fishing to hiking; from here you can explore both Akan-Mashu National Park and nearby Kushiro Marshland National Park, famous for its red-crested cranes. It also has a re-created Ainu village, with topnotch music and dance performances.

Essentials

ARRIVING A **JR train** from Sapporo takes about 4 hours to reach **Kushiro** (¥9,990); from JR Kushiro Station, buses depart two to five times a day for Akanko Onsen (2 hr.; ¥2,750 one-way). Alternatively, you can take a JR train 4½ hours to **Kitami** (via Asahikawa; ¥9,660); from Kitami, buses depart for Akanko twice a day (70 min.; ¥2,300). It's faster to get here **by car:** Akanko is 4 to 5 hours from Sapporo or Noboribetsu and 3½ to 4 hours from New Chitose Airport.

Because Akan-Mashu National Park lies at the eastern extremity of Hokkaido, you may wish to fly at least one-way between here and Tokyo. The closest airport is **Kushiro Airport** (KUH), which is generally a 1½-hour flight from Tokyo (¥15,000–¥25,000 one-way). From Kushiro Airport, buses travel to Akanko Onsen in about 1 hour for ¥2,190.

VISITOR INFORMATION Akanko Onsen's **Tourist Association** (en.kushiro-lakeakan.com; ✆ **0154-67-2254;** daily 9am–6pm) is located just a 3-minute walk from the Akanko Onsen bus terminal, in the direction of the lake and on the main street through town. For info on the park and its ecology, drop by the **Akankohan Eco Museum Center** (✆ **0154-67-2785;** Wed–Mon 9am–5pm), at the east end of the town's main street. Displays, in Japanese only, show off native flora and fauna, including the Hokkaido brown bear and sika deer (both stuffed), *marimo* (duckweed), and live freshwater fish such as white-spotted char and kokanee salmon. Admission is free.

Exploring Around Akan-Mashu National Park

AKANKO ONSEN

Akanko Onsen is small and easily covered on foot—it consists primarily of one main street that snakes along the lake, with ryokan and souvenir shops lining both sides. At the west end of the main street, you can visit the **Ainu Kotan Village** (akanainu.jp; ✆ **0154-67-2727;** ¥300 adults, ¥100 children). Although the Ainu originally lived near Kushiro, not Akan, this is now Hokkaido's largest Ainu community, numbering about

Hokkaido's largest Ainu community lives in Akanko Onsen, and the Ainu Kotan Village offers a window into its traditional culture.

130 individuals. The Ainu Kotan Village is just one street lined with shops (selling mostly woodcarvings), restaurants and cafes offering Ainu cuisine, and sculptures depicting creatures sacred in Ainu lore, as well as a thatched-roof dwelling showing the cultural touchstones of old Ainu life. Stop in the **Ainu Art Gallery** at the bottom of the hill, where you can admire the modern Ainu art pieces (some of which you can buy), watch a demonstration video showing Ainu hunting techniques and rituals, and pick up an English-language pamphlet with pictures explaining what takes place in each of the buildings. Atop the small village is ***Onne Cise*** (✆ **0154-67-2727**), meaning "the Big House," a lodge where you can view more artworks created by active Ainu artists. Admission to *Onne Cise* is ¥500 adults, ¥200 children; daily 9am to 5pm, only on weekends and holidays December through April.

Ainu Dance: An Offering to the Gods

If you've never seen a performance of traditional Ainu dance, don't miss the chance to take in a performance while in Akanko Onsen. This is the most professional Ainu production around, performing in a crescent-shaped auditorium at the **Akan Ainu Theater Ikor** (✆ **0154-67-2727**) in the Ainu Kotan Village. Even the space is large, with a capacity for 550 audience members (including standing tickets). The dances aren't the same as those performed at kotans in Shiraoi and Nibutani (see p. 665 and p. 664), so these are highly recommended even if you've already been to one of the others. Thirty-minute shows are performed three times a day in winter, six in summer. Admission is ¥1,500 to ¥2,200 for adults (depending on the show), ¥700 for children.

If you'd like a quick hike, start at the **Akankohan Eco Museum Center** (p. 669) at the east end of town, where you'll find an easy 30-minute footpath leading through a primeval forest of pines and ferns, past *bokke* (volcanic, bubbling mud), and along the lakeshore. It ends at the boat dock where cruises of Lake Akan depart (see below). To make this an hour's hike, take the steps to the right of the Eco Museum Center leading uphill at the orange *torii* gate to the Inari Shinto Shrine and follow the path through woodlands along a ridge before descending to the lake and joining the path described above.

AKAN-MASHU NATIONAL PARK

For Japanese visitors, one of the most popular activities in Akanko Onsen is a **boat cruise of Lake Akan,** which provides a close-up view of the mountains, islands, and shoreline, all stunningly beautiful. Lake Akan is famous for its very rare spherical green algae, a spongelike ball of duckweed called *marimo* that's been designated a Special Natural Monument. Found in only a few places in the world, marimo is formed when many separate and stringy pieces of algae at the bottom of the 43m-deep (144-ft.) lake roll around and eventually come together to form a ball, gradually growing larger and larger. It takes 150 to 200 years for marimo to grow to the size of a baseball; some in Lake Akan are as much as 29 centimeters (12 in.) in diameter—meaning they are very old indeed. Supposedly, when the sun shines, the marimo rise to the surface of the water, giving Lake Akan a wonderful green shimmer. On the **Akan Sightseeing Cruise** you'll make a 15-minute stop at Churui Islet to see the **Marimo Exhibition Center** with a few tanks of marimo. Ninety-minute cruises operate from mid-April to late November and cost ¥2,400 for adults and ¥1,240 for children (exhibition center admission included). Boats depart every hour or so, with the last boat departing at 4pm. For more information, visit the Akan Sightseeing Cruise Company office beside the pier, or call ✆ **011-5467-2511.**

Sightseeing cruise boat on Lake Aken.

North of Lake Akan, other highlights of the park include **Mashu,** a crater lake that was called "lake of the devil" by the Ainu because no water flows either into it or out of it. Mashu is considered one of Japan's most beautiful and least spoiled lakes, with steep 200m-high (660-ft.) rock walls making it largely inaccessible to humans (you can view it from an observation platform high above the water). **Kussharo** is one of Japan's largest

See Akan-Mashu in a Day Tour from Kushiro

If you're not renting a car, the best way to see Akan-Mashu National Park's wildlife and most arresting geographical features is aboard a **sightseeing bus** from Kushiro. These aren't perfect experiences: Frequent fog often eliminates scenic views, there are tacky souvenir shops at every stop, tours are in Japanese only, and they no longer operate in winter. But they're still worth taking if you've no other convenient way of seeing the park. The **Akan Piriko Gou** departs Kushiro Station daily in season (Apr 20–Oct 27) at 8am, returning by 5pm. It stops at several scenic spots along the way, including Mashu and Kussharo lakes, and at Akanko Onsen, where you have a couple hours to take the waters and have lunch. The day trip costs ¥5,600 (¥5,200 if getting off at Kushiro Airport; ¥4,000 if leaving the tour at Akanko Onsen); children pay half fare. For more information, visit the **Akan Bus Company** website (uu-nippon.com/hokkaido) or call an operator at ✆ **0154-37-2221.**

mountain lakes, but what makes it particularly intriguing is its hot-spring waters right on the beach. In some places rockpools have been constructed at the edges, tapping water from the springs, in which people sit and watch fog rolling across the lake or waterfowl skimming across its surface.

KUSHIRO MARSHLAND NATIONAL PARK

Red-crowned cranes, the official birds of Hokkaido, are regarded as both a good omen and a national symbol of Japan, and because they mate for life, they're considered a symbol of love. Their tremulous, dinosaur-esque squawk has even been designated as one of the 100 Soundscapes of Japan (the list also includes creaking drift ice in the sea of Okhotsk, the rushing waters of Aomori's Oirase River, and the croaking tree frogs of Tochigi Prefecture). Once threatened with extinction (at one point, only 40 remained in the wild), these graceful birds are still among the rarest cranes on earth but now lead protected lives in and around **Kushiro Marshland National Park (Kushiro Shitsugen)**, Japan's largest marshland. If you don't have a car, the best way to see the marshlands and catch a glimpse of the cranes in their natural habitat is via an organized tour. **Picchio** (shiretoko-picchio.com; ✆ **0152-26-7839**), which runs tours in rural Hokkaido, conducts private and group tours of the marshland between January 10 and March 20, when the cranes tend to flock towards feeding and mating sites in greater numbers. Four-hour tours start at 8:30am and 1:30pm daily (pick-up is in Kushiro at the airport, train station, or hotels) and include 30-minute stops at Tsurui Ito sanctuary and Tsurumi Dai observation spot (where the cranes gather in winter), a drive along Kushiro Marsh Road in search of other wildlife such as deer and eagles, and another observation deck from which you'll get sprawling views of the marshland. Tours cost ¥6,000 per person (a private tour for up to eight guests costs ¥45,000). Arrange pickup with the tour provider, though they should be able to accommodate most hotels in the area.

The Kushiro Marshlands protect the native habitat of endangered red-crowned cranes, a national symbol of Japan.

If you prefer sightseeing on your own, the best place to learn about cranes is at the excellent **Akan Kokusai Tsuru Center (Akan International Crane Center)** ♥♥, on National 240 northwest of Kushiro town (aiccgrus.wixsite.com/aiccgrus; ✆ **0154-66-4011;** daily 9am–5pm). In addition to a film showing their beautiful courtship dance and nesting habits, it has fun, interactive displays with lots of English-language explanations. You'll learn just about everything you'd ever want to know about red-crested cranes here, from why they fly to how much an egg weighs. Best of all, however, is adjacent **Tancho-no-Sato,** an excellent observatory on private land where 200 red-crested cranes live, court, and mate November through March. This is a top place to photograph the birds in action, and you'll be surprised at how large they are. Admission to both facilities is ¥480 for adults, ¥250 children. Plan on staying at least an hour in winter, less in summer when the birds have returned to their native marshlands. The International Crane Center is some 40 minutes from Akanko Onsen by bus; get off at the Tancho-no-Sato stop (fare: ¥1,650). The same bus can take you on to Kushiro Airport (30 min.) or Kushiro Station (1¼ hr.); buses are infrequent, however, so check the schedule beforehand.

In summer, your best bet for observing cranes outside the marshland is the **Japanese Crane Reserve (Tancho-Tsuru Koen; ✆ 0154-56-2219;** daily 9am–6pm, to 4pm mid-Oct to mid-Apr; ¥480 adults, ¥110 children), a marshy area set aside in 1958 for breeding and raising cranes. It now has some 20 cranes—some of them second and third generation—living in

Train Ride Through the Marshlands

Winding leisurely through the Kushiro Marsh, the **Kushiro Shitsugen Norokko** steam locomotive won't get you as close to the wetlands, but it will slow down at specific attractions and when wildlife comes into view. The train operates from April 27 to October 6, so it misses the red-crowned cranes' most active season, though train-lovers may not mind. The journey is about 45 minutes each way, with a 30-minute stop in Toro; tickets cost ¥1,480 for a reserved seat in an observation carriage (children pay half-fare). You can book tickets at Kushiro Station or use your JR Pass. For timetable enquiries, call JR Hokkaido at ✆ **011-222-7111.**

natural habitats behind high meshed fences. They are fed three times a day, at 9:30am and 1 and 4pm. Also on National Road 240 on the way to Kushiro airport and station, it's 1 hour by bus from Akanko Onsen (¥2,140); get off at the Tsuru-koen stop. If all you want is a quick look, note that one bus a day en route to the airport makes a 15-minute stop at this park, which is enough time to see some of the birds. Enquire at the Akanko ticket office for schedule.

Outdoor Activities

CANOEING To get a real feel for Lake Akan at duck and goose level, take a canoe trip in a two-person Canadian canoe, available May to October. The Adventure Course (¥6,000 adults, ¥4,000 children) gets you onto the lake for 2 hours; enquire with **Akan Nature Center** (✆ **0154-67-2801**) about that as well as shorter beginner excursions and an experienced canoer course to the uninhabited Yatai Island in the middle of the lake. You may see carp spawning, deer, or—if you are really lucky—a brown bear.

HIKING From Lake Akan, you can see two cone-shaped volcanoes: **Mount Oakan** (**Oakandake**) to the east and **Mount Meakan** (**Meakandake**) to the south. Both are surrounded by virgin forests and are popular daylong destinations for day hikers. **Mount Oakan** (called "male mountain" by the Ainu for its supposed manly features) is dormant, with a summit about a 4½-hour hike from Akanko Onsen. You can reach the trail entrance, Takiguchi, in 5 minutes via one of the buses going in the direction of Kushiro (get off at the Takiguchi stop). Plan about 6 hours for the ascent and descent. **Mount Meakan** (which the Ainu called "female mountain") is an active volcano, so check before you go. It's the highest mountain in the Akan area at 1,500m (4,900 ft.) above sea level and is covered with primeval forests of spruce and fir. There are three hiking trails up Mount Meakan. If you're hiking the entire distance, the trail access closest to Akanko is located at the west end of town; follow the Furebetsu Woodland Road, a former transport road, to an old sulfur mine for 3 hours to get to the trail entrance, from which it's another 3 hours to the peak, where you'll be rewarded with panoramic views.

A shorter hike, starting by the Ainu Kotan, follows a trail to **Mount Hakuto-zan,** from which you also have a good view of the town and lake. It takes about 20 minutes to reach Akan's skiing area and another 50 minutes to reach Mount Hakuto-zan observatory, a grassy and moss-covered knobby hill that remains slightly warm throughout the year because of thermal activity just below the surface. The woods of birch and pine here are beautiful, and what's more, you'll probably find yourself all alone.

WINTER ACTIVITIES In winter, Lake Akan freezes over and becomes a playland for winter sports. International marathon ice-skating races—200km (125 miles)—have brought attention to the area's natural riches. For downhill skiers, the **Kokusetsu Akan-kohan ski ground** (✆ **0154-67-2881**) is blessed with a magnificent view of Mount Oakan rising behind Lake Akan. The F.I.S.-certified slalom course attracts ski teams and individuals in training, while the intermediate and beginner slopes are popular with less demanding skiers. A day pass for lifts costs ¥3,100; ski-rental equipment costs around ¥4,000 per day.

In February, illuminated ice sculptures, traditional dance, nightly fireworks over the frozen lake, and stalls selling food make for a fun midwinter festival in Akanko Onsen. Contact the tourist office for more details.

Where to Stay Around Akanko

If you're staying in Kushiro to see the red-crowned cranes, consider **Toyoko Inn Kushiro Jujigai** (toyoko-inn.com; ✆ **0154-23-1045**), a reliable business hotel chain with rooms for as little as ¥6,000 per night, including breakfast.

(Akan) Yuku-no-Sato Tsuruga ♥♥♥ Cranes are the main motif throughout, but what makes this hotel in Akanko Onsen a standout are its fantasy-provoking hot-spring baths. One is designed as a village, spread on several levels and including a cavelike room and an outdoor bath beautifully landscaped with stones and pines overlooking the lake. The other includes a rooftop hot-spring bath with 360-degree panoramic views, and a recently installed domed-shaped observation sauna, which the hotel claims is the world's first. Even if you don't stay here, you can visit the baths (Mon–Fri 2–6pm; ¥2,500).

The rest of the hotel, with natural woods throughout, and large windows and lounge spaces in the rooms does not disappoint. Most rooms are Japanese style, the best (and most expensive) of which have lakeside views, spacious bathrooms (some with open-air tubs), bar areas for entertaining, and seating around an indoor hearth. There are also more than 50 combination rooms with *tatami* area and beds.

4–6–10 Akanko Onsen. ✆ **0154-67-2531.** tsuruga.com. 233 units. ¥40,000–¥120,000 double. Rates include 2 meals. Bus stop: Akano Onsen (10 min.). Free shuttle buses for guests (reservations required). **Amenities:** 2 restaurants; bars; lounge; indoor/outdoor hot-spring baths; free Wi-Fi.

Lamp no Yado Moritsubetsu ♥♥ This ryokan hotel is connected to Lake Kussharo by the winding Tsubetsu Pass. Enclosed by a forest and 20km from the nearest town, it's very secluded, literally in the middle of nowhere; you're just as likely to see foxes and deer on the road as other drivers. Most rooms are functional tatami-and-futon affairs (larger Japanese-Western style rooms can accommodate up to six people and are good for families), but it's worth staying here for the outdoor onsen, a large steamy rockpool surrounded by trees that feels like a scene from a Basho poem. A restaurant is on-site, serving Italian and Japanese fare for dinner as well as a Japanese-style buffet breakfast. And you'll want to make use of the lounge, with its Ainu-inspired wooden decor and seats that look towards the forest all lit up at night; you can watch deer grazing in the underbrush through floor-to-ceiling windows. ***Note:*** Standard Japanese rooms don't have private showers, so you'll have to use the public bath facilities. Also note, this hotel is difficult to access via public transport but is a great option for travelers driving to Shiretoko the next day.

738 Kamisato, Tsubetsu-cho, Abashiri-gun. moritsubetsu.com. ✆ **0152-76-3333.** 23 units. ¥10,000–¥20,000 single, ¥20,000–¥40,000 double (rates at higher end include 2 meals). By car, 30- to 40-min. from Lake Kussharo (1 hr. in winter when Tsubetsu Pass is closed), 1 hr. from Akanko Onsen. **Amenities:** Restaurant; souvenir shop; lounge; indoor/outdoor hot-spring baths; free Wi-Fi.

Where to Eat in Akanko

Dining options are limited in Akanko, so it's wise to include meal plans when booking your accommodation, or if driving, seek out places to buy a decent packed lunch—you could do worse than purchasing a few rice balls or sandwiches at a convenience store. Note that lots of restaurants are also closed or have irregular hours outside the main tourism seasons, while some seem to close entirely in winter. Google Maps and similar applications tend not to store reliable information on local restaurant opening times.

That said, **Marukibune ♥** (✆ **0154-67-2304**) in the Ainu Kotan Village in Akanko Onsen is worth visiting for a different kind of lunch. A log fire burns in one corner of a wood-paneled room decorated with Ainu carvings and lamp shades covered in symmetrical motifs. Take a seat at a table or on the tatami and order traditional Ainu dishes from the English-language menu. Items include venison and wild vegetables on rice, *parimono ruibe* (lake minnow sashimi from Lake Kussharo, frozen and sliced in the traditional style), a meat-and-veg soup called *ohaw; potche* (fermented potato cakes, a bit hard); and drinks such as *shikerebe* (bark tea). The food isn't amazing—in fact, there are other Ainu restaurants in the region serving *exactly* the same menu (down to the same pictures and fonts)—but it's nevertheless an interesting experience. It's open daily 11am to 9pm; dishes cost around ¥1,000 to ¥3,000.

SHIRETOKO NATIONAL PARK ♥♥♥

The word "unique" gets used a little too liberally in travel circles, but it's appropriate here, because there's nothing else in Japan quite like Shiretoko. Coming from the Ainu word *siretok,* meaning "the end of the earth," this long blade-shaped peninsula piercing the Sea of Okhotsk feels distant in every way, as though somehow out of time and place. As you approach the peninsula from eastern Hokkaido along arrow-straight highways, it becomes quickly apparent that you're leaving what remains of civilization behind; a land of wild deer, northern foxes, and the island's largest population of Ussuri brown bears; of frosty mountains (home to wildflowers in spring and summer) and virgin forests of beech, spruce, linden, birch, fir, and oak. From its northerly coast you can see Sakhalin in Russia and the disputed Kuril Islands, as well as Steller's sea eagles, cetacean species like whales, dolphins, and porpoises, and huge sheets of drift ice in winter,

The so-called Road to Heaven cuts an arrow-straight path across beautiful Hokkaido countryside to Shiretoko National Park.

stretching and creaking across the sea. Though the northern part of Shiretoko is practically untouched by human hands, adventurous travelers come to the 386-sq.-km (149-sq.-mile) **Shiretoko National Park,** a World Heritage Site since 2005, in summer and winter (spring and autumn are much quieter) to hike the mountain trails, strap on snowshoes to explore the sleeping forests, walk across the slowly drifting ice sheets, search for wildlife, and learn more about one of the world's richest integrated ecosystems, where marine and terrestrial animals interact with each other in interesting ways. For nature-focused travelers, the island of Hokkaido bears many gifts. But this, on Japan's northern tip, is undoubtedly its finest.

Essentials

ARRIVING JAL, ANA, and Air Do offer flights from Tokyo's Haneda Airport to **Memanbetsu Airport** (MMB), which take 1¾ hours and cost around ¥30,000 one-way. Two or three buses travel 2 hours daily from Memanbestu to the Shiretoko World Heritage Conservation Center (¥3,500) in **Utoro,** a small coastal town on the outskirts of the national park that's the best base for exploring Shiretoko.

A **JR train** from Kushiro Station (2½ hr.) goes to Shiretokoshari Station, where you can catch a 50-minute bus (four times a day) to Utoro for ¥1,650. Enquire at station ticketing offices, see **sharibus.co.jp** for winter and summer season bus timetables, or call ✆ **0152-23-0766.**

As you'd expect, traveling **by car** is much more convenient, and the drive is pretty epic, to boot. It's 2½ hours from Akanko Onsen, 3 hours from Kushiro, and 6 hours from Sapporo.

Driving the Road to Heaven

Aptly nicknamed "the Road to Heaven," the highway leading to Shiretoko National Park cuts a pencil-straight line across 18km (11 miles) of lovely Hokkaido countryside. As you approach Shiretoko from the southwest, cresting over hills on the highway, it creates an illusion that the road travels directly into the sky. It's at its most magnificent at dawn, when the early-morning sun glows over the Shari plains.

VISITOR INFORMATION The **Utoro tourist information center** is in the *Michi no Eki* ("roadside station"), a large modern building next to the conservation center (buses stop here). Be sure to pick up maps and pamphlets with information on Shiretoko National

Park; ask for English-language materials at the helpdesk. It also has QR codes that suggest driving routes, a souvenir shop, and a surprisingly good seafood restaurant (p. 682), which you'll be glad of during in spring and autumn when many restaurants shut or greatly reduce their hours. You can find more information on the national park at **shiretokotourist.com** and **env.go.jp/en/nature/nps/park/shiretoko**.

GETTING AROUND You can access various points of interest in Shiretoko by car, though to explore them properly, you'll need to disembark and walk. Many roads, however, are closed off in winter (when Shiretoko is at its most enchanting), and even with 4WD and snow tires, conditions can be tricky if you're not used to driving on icy roads. This is one of the reasons guides are recommended.

Exploring Shiretoko National Park

The first thing you should do is visit the **Shiretoko World Heritage Conservation Center** ♥♥ (policies.env.go.jp/park/shiretoko/whcc; ✆ **0152-24-3255**), which serves as an introduction to this aggressively beautiful, untamed stretch of wilderness. Excellent English-language displays explore the geography, geology, ecology, biodiversity, and climatology of this volcanic peninsula. The most southerly latitude where drift ice forms in the northern hemisphere, Shiretoko is a place where rivers plunge straight from the mountains into the sea, where towering cliff faces fringe the western coast and *banya* (fishermen's huts) line the gentle eastern shoreline, and where deer, bears, foxes, racoon dogs, whales, dolphins, owls, and otters have all made their habitat. (To get a sense of how alive Shiretoko is, play the electronic piano displayed at the center—every key

In Shiretoko National Park's Five Lakes region, an elevated boardwalk is open April through November for safely viewing the lakes and mountains.

emits the sound of a local natural phenomenon, from birdsong and snarling brown bears to the sound of drift ice and screeching northern cicadae.) The exhibits, though colored by nature and wildlife photography, are quite text-heavy, but don't miss the one detailing the Apical Region, the final unexplored frontier of Japan. Engulfing the northern tip of Shiretoko, it's completely undeveloped (though doubtless construction magnates have tried), with no roads no meaningful paths, extreme weather conditions on land and at sea, and a large brown bear population—dangerous to any explorers without high levels of orienteering skill, physical fitness, and mental judgement. The conservation center is located beside the bus terminal; it opens Wednesday to Monday 9am to 4:30pm in winter (late Oct to late Apr) and daily 8:30am to 5:30pm in summer.

Because Shiretoko is so isolated, has such an unpredictable climate, and hosts a healthy brown bear population (Japan's largest predators, contributing to a growing number of bear attacks nationwide), it's **highly recommended to travel with a guide.** Perhaps even more important is that guides can ensure that your excursions don't interfere with the delicate balance of this unique ecosystem. **Picchio** (info-shiretoko@m.picchio.co.jp; ✆ **0152-26-7839**) is one of the best private- and group-tour operators in Hokkaido and offers many engaging and affordable excursions in Shiretoko. Their bilingual guides have a genuine, infectious passion for the outdoors, and they'll pick you up from your accommodations in Utoro. **Alku** (alku-shiretoko.com) also offers a range of summer and winter tours, including forest walks, wildlife drives, and snowshoeing.

On snowshoeing tours, you'll trek through the **primeval forests** of the peninsula, home to herds of Ezo deer and northern foxes. When the forest ends, steep cliffs dive towards the sea, where drift ice forms and you're greeted with views of the final stretch of the land of Japan and the bristling waters beyond. You'll be given a pair of binoculars, which come in handy for spying on distant stags rubbing their antlers on trees or raptorial birds gliding in the empty skies. Listen out for winter songbirds, thriving in this hostile climate. This 3½-hour Picchio tour runs from December through March (discounts in early Dec and late Mar if there's not enough snow and hiking boots must be used). It costs ¥6,500 adults, ¥3,500 children, snowshoe and jacket rental included.

One of Picchio's most popular tours takes guests out to **walk on the drift ice** stretching across the Sea of Okhostk. For the 2-hour tour, you'll wear dry suits, in case you submerge in the water amid the blocks of ice, which is all too likely to happen as you struggle to get your bearing on the wobbly floating platforms underfoot. Keep an eye out for Stellar's sea eagles whirling in the sky, and on winter afternoons, the sun setting in the west. The tour usually only runs for about 6 or 7 weeks a year, when the drift ice conditions are suitable. Note that due to ice instability, guests cannot be taller than 190cm (6 ft., 2 in.) or heavier than 110kg (242 lb.). The tour costs ¥7,000 per person.

The Wonders of Shiretoko's Drift Ice

Why does drift ice form on the Sea of Okhostk, when seas at the same latitude across the globe don't have it? There are several reasons. Millions of metric tons of freshwater are dumped into the sea by Russia's Amur River, which lowers the sea's salinity, thus making it more liable to freeze. Add to that the cold winds from Siberia that whip across the surface, and you've got perfect conditions for freezing seawater. Most of the drift ice forms along the Siberian coastline, before seasonal winds and the East Sakhalin Current drag it towards northern Hokkaido and the Shiretoko Peninsula. Drift ice is prevalent in January and February, when temperatures are at their most unforgiving (as low as –20°C/–4°F).

From May through September, a variety of other outings are designed to get you close to Shiretoko's wildlife, including bears and whales, without the attendant risk to your personal safety. **Bear-spotting cruises** (¥12,200 adults, ¥6,700 children) travel to Rusha Bay, with an 80% chance of seeing wild brown bears fishing, foraging, or simply languishing along the coast of the Apical Region. **Whale-watching tours** (¥15,800 adults, ¥8,500 children) go from the peninsula's eastern side, near Rausu, where you may also see orcas, dolphins, and sea otters in their natural habitat. Each tour lasts around 8 hours and includes a trekking expedition, either through the peninsula's primeval forest or around the Shiretoko Five Lakes area, formed by the long-ago eruption of Mount Io. You can also add a night safari for an extra ¥4,200. ***Note:*** You have to arrange your own transportation to the cruise ports.

A 2-hour hike on the Sea of Okhostk's drift ice is one of the most memorable excursions in Shiretoko National Park.

HIKING MOUNT RAUSU

At 1,661m, Rausu is the tallest mountain on the Shiretoko Peninsula and is a rewarding hike if you're game for the challenge. A stratovolcano surrounded by elevated marshlands, mixed-leaf forests and alpine wildflowers, it has more bears, foxes, and deer than fellow humans. The Ainu knew it as *Chacha-Nupuri,* the "Father Mountain," and it was included in mountaineer and author Kyuya Fukada's 1964 book *100 Famous Japanese Mountains.* The slow trickle of people that followed the latter's publication carved

Steller's sea eagles are among the many rare species protected in Shiretoko National Park.

trails onto the slopes of the volcano, the most popular of which starts at a trailhead about 20 minutes' drive from Utoro, near **Kinoshita Hut** (kinoshitagoya.wordpress.com; ✆ **0152-24-2824**). As Rausu is an all-day hike (4–5 hr. up, 2–3 hr. to descend), staying somewhere else near the trailhead is recommended. (Kinoshita Hut charges ¥3,000 per night; no bedding or cooking utensils are supplied, but there is a hot-spring bath.) The trail is well marked, enclosed by dense tree cover in lower regions and scrubby vegetation and dwarf pines in the higher regions, before a final rocky ascent that requires you to scramble on all fours. Sprawling views of the peninsula, especially on a clear day, are just reward for your exertions. If you'd prefer to walk with a guide, search databases like **Activity Japan** (en.activityjapan.com) or enquire with **Picchio** (p. 679) about custom-made tours.

Where to Stay in Utoro

If you're here on a budget, **Shiretoko Village** (shiretoko-mura.jp; ✆ **0152-24-2124**) is a hostel-cum-guesthouse with basic Japanese-style rooms and dorms for ¥7,000 to ¥15,000 per person, most rates including two meals. There is a public bathhouse here; toilets and showers are shared.

Shiretoko Noble Hotel ♥♥ Coastal views, spacious rooms, and nearby restaurants are the main reasons to stay at this hotel on the Utoro seafront. It does lack character, but other pluses include a buffet breakfast, separate shower and toilets in guest bedrooms, and an option of Japanese- or Western-style bedding—if you've been hiking, your muscles will thank you for the latter. There's nothing too spectacular about the public outdoor bath and sauna, but those too will be vital to your recovery, especially if visiting here in winter.

3 Utorohigashi. ✆ **0152-22-5211.** shiretoko-noblehotel.com. 45 units. ¥10,000–¥20,000 per person. Bus stop: Utoro (5 min.). **Amenities:** Hot-spring baths; free Wi-Fi.

Yuhi no Ataruie (知床夕陽のあたる家) ♥♥♥ Many accommodations in Japan excel at blurring the line between hostel and hotel, and this property overlooking the town of Utoro is a classic example. Its kitchen-lounge area exudes the vibe of a cozy mountain lodge after a good spring cleaning, with a long U-shaped sofa draped in patterned upholstery and colorful pillows, and artworks depicting the deified animals—the brown bear, northern fox, and Yezo deer—that call this peninsula home. The spacious, modern rooms (most without a bathroom) are private, with both Western and Japanese bedding options available. The staff may vacate the property between 8pm and 7am, and again between 10am and 3pm (you'll be given a code to get in the front door), but when in attendance they're helpful, recommending attractions, guiding companies, and restaurants nearby. The onsen is particularly atmospheric when snow is falling, with an outdoor cold plunge pool that's not for the faint of heart in winter.

189 Utorokagawa. ✆ **0152-24-2764.** yuuhinoataruie.com. 24 units, most w/ shared bath. ¥12,000–¥30,000 per person. Bus stop: Utoro (25-min. walk, 5-min. drive). **Amenities:** Kitchen; hot-spring baths; free Wi-Fi.

Where to Eat in Utoro

14

Shiretoko National Park

HOKKAIDO

Lamb & Deer Jingisukan FOX (知床ジンギスカン・バーFOX) ♥♥ The name's a mouthful, but there's nothing better in winter than sliding open the wood-and-glass doors of a BBQ joint like this to be greeted by smoke hurtling up from the grills and the saliva-inducing smell of charred meat. The owner, who has a decent grasp of English, will let you know if anything is out of stock—this happens often as one season segues into the next—but menu staples include *wagyu* strips, lamb *jinguskan* (cooked on a hot skillet), venison, and local shellfish, like whelks and scallops. All the food is cooked at the table by diners; if you're unsure about timings, just ask. You can order from a QR code menu in English. Seafood *al ajillo* (cooked in hot oil) costs ¥1,380 to ¥1,750, meat cuts are around ¥1,500; all food is designed to be shared.

96–5 Utorohigashi. cafefox.jp/jingisukanfox.html. ✆ **0152-24-2680.** Dishes ¥4,000–¥5,000 per person. Daily 11:30–2:30pm and 4–10pm (hours may vary in off-season).

Shiretoko Michi-no-Eki ♥♥ SEAFOOD In Japan, *michi no eki,* or "roadside stations," often function as showreels for regional cuisine. Such is the case in Shiretoko's, where the sashimi bowls and grilled fish meals, using produce sourced in nearby waters, would pass muster in seafood restaurants throughout the country. Other options include pork *donburi,* Japanese curry rice, grilled mackerel or flounder, and venison cheeseburgers. Place your order at the vending machine, grab a seat in the large dining area, and wait for your number to be called (this will be in Japanese, so keep an eye on the screens). Food options may differ slightly from season to season, but even when other restaurants operate on reduced hours, this place opens daily.

8–186 Utoronishi. utopia-shiretoko.co.jp. ✆ **0152-22-5170.** Sashimi bowls ¥3,000–¥4,000; meat and curry bowls ¥1,000–¥2,000, grilled fish meals ¥1,500–¥2,000. Daily 10am–3pm.

15 PLANNING YOUR TRIP TO JAPAN

Many first-time visitors have two main worries about a trip to Japan: the language barrier and the high cost of living. To help alleviate fears about the first, I've provided the Japanese characters for establishments listed in this book that don't have English-language signs to help you recognize their names; made suggestions for ordering in restaurants without English-language menus; and given prices for everything from train rides to museums.

As for costs, in recent years, the Japanese yen has reached historic lows against other world currencies, which has made the country more affordable to foreign visitors than it had been for decades. Even travelers on modest middle-class incomes can spend 2 weeks traveling the country, staying in nice hotels, and gorging on exceptional food without much stress, especially in the off season (winter and June). That said, in light of tourists' increased purchasing power, as well as domestic economic insecurities and inflationary pressures, prices are no longer as static as the Japanese had become accustomed to. It's not unusual to see a bar increase the cost of a draft beer from ¥500 to ¥550 to ¥600 all within the space of 18 months, while some heavily touristed regions are floating the idea of a two-tiered pricing system, whereby inbound visitors pay two to three times as much as residents for museum tickets or entry to historical sights. And for much of 2024 and 2025, hotel room rates in Japan have been at record highs. So, while all prices in this book are accurate at the time of writing, they may be subject to change in the months ahead.

Japanese are a traditionally thrifty people, so the secret to seeing Japan on the cheap—or at least, to see it without breaking the bank—is to live and eat as the locals do. This book will help you do exactly that, with tips on how to save money on everything from transportation to sightseeing, plus descriptions of affordable eateries and Japanese-style inns or business hotels. While you may never find Japan as inexpensive as many other Asian countries, you will find it richly rewarding for all the reasons you chose Japan as a destination in the first place.

Furthermore, Japan remains one of the safest countries in the world; in general, you don't have to worry about muggers, pickpockets, or crooks. If anything, it's downright coddling. Everything runs like clockwork: Trains are on time, and the service—whether in hotels, restaurants, or department stores—ranks among the best in the world. And Japanese people are honest and extremely helpful toward foreign visitors. Indeed, it's the people themselves who make traveling in Japan such a delight.

 PREVIOUS PAGE: **Nidec Kyoto Tower in downtown Kyoto, next to Kyoto Station.**

GETTING THERE

By Plane

Many airports in Japan field international flights, but only around four or five are likely to be your entry or exit points for long-haul flights, even accounting for transits elsewhere. Outside Tokyo is **Narita International Airport** (**NRT;** narita-airport.jp; ✆ **0476-34-8000**), where you'll want to land if your main interest is in the capital or surrounding region. **Haneda Airport** (**HND;** haneda-airport.jp; ✆ **03-5757-8111**) is much closer to central Tokyo, but most international long-distance flights still land at Narita.

Outside Osaka, **Kansai International Airport** (**KIX;** kansai-airport.or.jp; ✆ **072-455-2500**) is convenient if you're heading to Osaka, Kyoto, or cities farther west. In between Narita and Kansai airports, outside Nagoya, **Central Japan International Airport** (**NGO;** centrair.jp; ✆ **0569-38-1195**), nicknamed Centrair, serves international flights mostly from Asia. **Fukuoka Airport** (**FUK;** fukuoka-airport.jp; ✆ **092-621-6059**), only 5 minutes from Fukuoka's city center, serves as a springboard for exploring the southern island of Kyushu, though its international flights come mostly from east Asia. **Sendai Airport** (**SDJ;** sendai-airport.co.jp; ✆ **022-382-0080**) is used by travelers heading further north into the depths of Tohoku, but currently the only international flights it handles are from China, Taiwan, and South Korea.

Japan also has dozens of regional airports, so you can make connecting flights without needing to check in again, particularly with the

Saving Money on Airfare

Book at the right time. It sounds odd, but you can often save a good amount by booking domestic international airfare 2 to 4 months in advance of departure. That figure comes from a 2023 study of 1 billion airfare transactions by an industry group called the Airlines Reporting Corporation. Book earlier than that, and you won't have access to the lowest-priced seats, as the airlines only release them when they have an idea of how the plane is selling. Book too close to departure, and the airline knows they've "got you" and will charge more. That same study found that those who purchased their tickets on a Sunday spent 13% less statistically—a decent savings.

Do a smart Web search. In a Frommers.com study conducted in early 2024, we found that sister sites Kayak and Momondo found the lowest airfares most consistently. Both search all the discount sites as well as the airline sites directly, so that you get a broader and more impartial search. They also show a chart of prices for 2 weeks around the day you search, which can be very helpful for flexible travelers.

Be anonymous in your search. Clear your cookies and engage the privacy setting on your browser, or better yet, use a different browser or computer than you usually do when searching for airfares. The airlines and airfare booking sites do track users (though they deny it) and are getting increasingly expert in serving up fares tailored to customers' past buying history. To see the actual lowest rates, you may have to cloak your identity.

country's main air carriers, **Japan Airlines** (**JAL;** jal.co.jp) and **All Nippon Airways** (**ANA;** ana.co.jp). Budget airlines also serve smaller airports. This can be a convenient, efficient, and cost-effective way to get around Japan; return flights on a budget airline are often cheaper than a one-way ticket on the Shinkansen, and when flying domestically, you're usually okay to arrive at the airport as late as 20 or 30 minutes before your flight.

GETTING AROUND

Japan has an extensive transport system, the most convenient segment of which is the nation's excellent **rail service. Buses** are useful for reaching places that trains don't go, like Shirakawa-go in the Japan Alps or Niyodo Gorge in Shikoku. The long-distance buses connecting major cities in western Honshu are cheaper alternatives than trains.

By Train

The most efficient way to travel around most of Japan is by train. Whether you're being whisked through the countryside aboard the famous Shinkansen bullet train or winding your way up a wooded mountainside in an electric tram, trains in Japan are punctual, comfortable, safe, and clean. And because train stations are usually located in the heart of the city, next to the main bus terminal or a subway station, arriving in a city by train usually is very convenient. Major train stations also have tourist offices, where you can pick up brochures and maps in English and often make reservations for local hotels or book tours at no extra charge. Most of Japan's passenger trains are run by the **Japan Railways** (**JR**) **Group,** made up of six regional passenger operators like JR East and JR West (plus a freight company) that together cover 20,000km (12,400 miles) and operate about more than 25,000 departures daily, including those of the Shinkansen. There are also private regional companies, like **Kintetsu** (**Kinki Nippon Railway**), operating around Osaka and Kyoto, and **Odakyu Electric Railway,** operating from Tokyo to Hakone.

SHINKANSEN (BULLET TRAIN) The Shinkansen is probably Japan's best-known train. With a front car that resembles a rocket, the Shinkansen hurtles along at a maximum speed of 320kmph (199 mph) through the countryside on its own special tracks. Most have seat-side electric plug-ins and Wi-Fi (though connection isn't always stellar).

In Honshu, the most widely used Shinkansen routes are the Tokaido and the Sanyo lines. The **Tokaido** Shinkansen runs from Tokyo, Shinagawa, and Yokohama stations west to Nagoya, Kyoto, Osaka (some go as far as Okayama),

Travel Tip

To help you reach the hotels, restaurants, and sights recommended in this book, I've included the nearest train or subway station or bus or streetcar stop, followed in parentheses by the approximate number of minutes it takes to walk from the station or bus stop to your destination.

while the **Sanyo** heads westward from Osaka to Himeji, Kurashiki, Hiroshima, and other cities before reaching its final destination on the island of Kyushu. Each stop is announced in English through a loudspeaker and on a digital signboard in each car. Different types of Shinkansen travel along these routes. The Nozomi Shinkansen, the fastest and most frequent train, is the only one that covers the entire 1,179km (730 miles) between Tokyo and Hakata in Kyushu; the Mizuho Shinkansen travels from Osaka farther into Kyushu. The Nozomi and the Mizuho trains are now covered by the Japan Rail Pass (see "Advantages of a Japan Rail Pass," p. 689), though pass-holders using these trains will be required to pay a supplemental fee. Japan Rail Pass holders pay nothing extra to take the Tokaido line's Hikari Shinkansen, which makes more stops than the Nozomi, or the Kodama, which stops at every station (if your destination is a smaller city on the Shinkansen line, make sure your train stops there). Rail-pass holders wishing to travel between Tokyo and Hiroshima must take the Hikari or Kodama and transfer in Osaka, Kobe, or Okayama to the Sakura Shinkansen on the Sanyo Line. On the other hand, if you're buying individual tickets, the price is not much different whether you're traveling by Nozomi or a slower Shinkansen. The **Hokuriku** Shinkansen ferries travelers between Tokyo and Kanazawa, with stops in Nagano and Joetsu-Myoko (both with good access to ski resorts). The **Tohoku** Shinkansen travels northward from Tokyo Station through Ueno (in north Tokyo), Omiya, Fukushima, Sendai, Morioka, and Hachinohe before culminating at Shin-Aomori Station. The **Hayabusa** Shinkansen goes on to Hakodate on the southern tip of Hokkaido.

REGULAR SERVICE In addition to bullet trains, there are two other types of long-distance trains that operate on regular tracks. The **limited-express trains,** or LEX (*Tokkyu*), branch off the Shinkansen system and are the fastest after the bullet trains, often traveling scenic routes; **express trains** (*Kyuko*) are slightly slower and make more stops. Slower still are **rapid express trains** (*Shin-Kaisoku*) and the even slower **rapid trains** (*Kaisoku*). To serve the everyday needs of Japan's commuting population, **local trains** (*Futsu*) stop at all stations.

INFORMATION For more on routes, transfers, fares, and timetables for trains in Japan **japantravel.navitime.com**. Google Maps is reliable, too, though less so in remote areas with limited transport networks.

In Japan, information on JR trains, fares, schedules, and routes is also available at **Travel Service Centers** at major stations. In Tokyo, the best place for personal consulting on routes and sightseeing is at the **JR East Travel Service Center** in Tokyo Station (p. 89), where you can also ask for timetables published in English and get schedules for the Shinkansen and limited express JR lines throughout Japan. **Tourist Information Centers** in downtown Tokyo or at the international airports in Narita or Osaka also carry timetables.

TRAIN FARES Ticket prices are based on the type of train (Shinkansen bullet trains are the most expensive), the distance traveled, whether your seat is reserved, and the season, with slightly higher prices (usually a ¥200–¥400 surcharge) during peak seasons (Golden Week, July 21–Aug 31, Dec 25–Jan 10, and spring break from Mar 21–Apr 5) and a ¥400 discount during low season. Children (ages 6–11) pay half-fare, while up to two children 5 and younger travel free if they do not require a separate seat. I've included train prices from Tokyo for many destinations covered in this book (see individual cities for more information). Unless stated otherwise, prices in this guide are for adults for **nonreserved seats** on the fastest train available during the regular season (some trains require seat reservations). Note, however, that you can save money by traveling on slower trains or purchasing a round-trip ticket for long distances. A round-trip ticket by train on distances exceeding 601km (373 miles) one-way costs 10% less than two one-way tickets. No matter which train you ride, be sure to hang onto your ticket—you'll be required to give it up at the end of your trip as you exit through the gate.

RESERVATIONS You can reserve seats for the Shinkansen, as well as for limited-express and express trains (but not for slower rapid or local trains, which are on a first-come, first-served basis) at any major JR station in Japan. You can also book tickets online at **smart-ex.jp/en/lp/app/**. Reserved seats cost slightly more than unreserved seats (often ¥500–¥1,000 for the Shinkansen and express trains). If you'll be traveling during peak times, it's a good idea to reserve seats for your entire trip as soon as you know your itinerary; however, you can only reserve 1 month in advance. If it's not peak season, you'll probably be okay using a more flexible approach to traveling—all JR trains also have nonreserved cars that fill up on a first-come, first-seated basis. You can also reserve seats on the day of travel up to departure time. Nonreserved seats (*jiyuuseki*) are located in cars at the front or back of Shinkansen trains. To determine where you should stand to board the train, look for the platform display showing a diagram of the train cars and which ones are reserved and nonreserved. Then look for signs—either on digital boards overhead or written on the platform itself—that shows the location for each car.

It's worth noting that Shinkansen fares are broken down by seat fee and the basic fare. So from Tokyo to Shin-Osaka, say, you may see the initial cost quoted as ¥8,910. This is the basic fare, but the seat fee (¥5,810 reserved or ¥4,960 nonreserved) will be added to generate the final price—that is, ¥13,780 for a nonreserved one-way ticket. Bear this in mind when using online search engines or ticketing machines at train stations. You wouldn't be the first to find it unnecessarily confusing.

SAVING MONEY WITH A RAIL PASS The Japan Rail (JR) Pass is without a doubt the most convenient way to travel around Japan. With the rail pass, you don't have to worry about buying individual tickets, you have unlimited travel on all JR trains throughout Japan including the Shinkansen

Advantages of a Japan Rail Pass

With a Japan Rail Pass, you can make seat reservations for free, which otherwise costs up to ¥1,000 per ride on the Shinkansen. Another advantage to a rail pass is that it offers a 10% discount or more off certain room rates at more than 50 JR Hotel Group hotels, including the Hotel Granvia in Kyoto, Osaka, and Hiroshima. A Japan Rail Pass booklet, which comes with your purchase of a rail pass, lists member hotels (or go to japanrailpass.net/en/special-offer/accommodation-privilege/). Note, however, that discounts are available only by booking directly with the hotel, at which time you should confirm the room type and rate (this may require a telephone call; discounts may not be available during peak seasons). Note, too, that regional rail passes do not qualify for the hotel discount.

(except regrettably, the Mizuho and Nozomi), and you can reserve your seats on all JR trains for free. That said, a whopping 69% price hike introduced in late 2023 may make you reconsider. The pass now costs ¥50,000 for 7 days, ¥80,000 for 14 days, or ¥100,000 for 21 days (or ¥70,000, ¥110,000, and ¥140,000 for access to the Green "Business" Class cars). To work out if a pass makes financial sense based on your itinerary, check Japan Rail's online fare calculator at **jrpass.com/farecalculator/**. More information on the JR Pass is available at **japanrailpass.net**, which also has links for purchasing it pass online.

The main thing to remember is that the Japan Rail Pass is available only to foreigners visiting Japan as tourists and in most cases *can be purchased only outside Japan.* It's available from most travel agents, including **JTB USA** (jtbusa.com). A full list of authorized travel agents, plus their addresses and contact information, is available at japanrailpass.net.

Upon purchasing your pass, you'll be issued a voucher (called an **Exchange Order**), which you'll then exchange for the real pass after your arrival in Japan. Note that once you receive your Exchange Order, you have 3 months until you must pick up the pass itself in Japan.

In Japan, you can exchange your voucher for a Japan Rail Pass at more than 40 JR stations that have Japan Rail Pass exchange offices, at which time you must present your passport and specify the date you wish to begin using the pass (it must be within 1 month of the date you pick it up). You'll find exchange offices at both Narita Airport (daily 6:30am–9:45pm) and Kansai International Airport (daily 5:30am–11pm); other exchange offices are located in JR train stations, including those at Tokyo, Ueno, Shinjuku, Ikebukuro, Shibuya, and Shinagawa stations in Tokyo; Kyoto Station; Shin-Osaka and Osaka stations; and Nara, Kanazawa, and Hiroshima stations. Stations and their open hours are listed in a pamphlet you'll receive with your voucher, as well as at japanrailpass.net.

REGIONAL PASSES FOR FOREIGN VISITORS In addition to the standard Japan Rail Pass above, regional JR rail passes for ordinary coach class are available (and convenient) for travel in western Honshu, among other places. These can be purchased before arriving in Japan from the same vendors that sell the standard pass but can also be reserved online or purchased inside Japan, usually only within the area covered by the pass (some passes can be purchased also at Narita Airport). These regional passes are available only to foreign visitors—you'll need to present your passport to verify your status as a "temporary visitor"; you may also be asked to show your plane ticket. Only one pass per region per visit to Japan is allowed. Children 6 to 11 years of age pay half-price for all passes; up to two children 5 years old and younger can travel free with a paying adult.

In the Tokyo area, the **JR Tokyo Wide Pass** (jreast.co.jp/multi/en/pass/tokyowidepass.html) is a 3-day pass for ¥15,000 that allows unlimited travel on JR trains, including Shinkansen bullet trains traveling north from Tokyo as far away as Utsunomiya (useful for trips to Nikko), Mount Fuji, Izu Peninsula, Narita (including the airport), and other areas. As for non-JR passes, the **Hakone Free Pass,** offered by Odakyu railways (odakyu.jp), includes round-trip transportation from Tokyo and unlimited travel in Hakone for a specific number of days (p. 237).

If you're arriving by plane at the Kansai Airport outside Osaka and intend to remain in western Honshu, consider buying one of several different **JR-West Passes** (westjr.co.jp/global/en/ticket/pass/), available at Kansai Airport, Osaka JR station, Kyoto Station, and other locations. You'll get a slight discount if you purchase it online in advance. The **Kansai Area Pass** can be used for travel between Osaka, Kyoto, Kobe, Nara, Himeji, and other destinations in the Kansai area; a 1-day pass costs ¥2,800, a 2-day pass ¥4,800, a 3-day pass ¥5,800, or a 4-day pass ¥7,000. Travel is restricted to JR rapid and local trains, as well as unreserved seating in the Kansai Airport Express Haruka operating between Kansai Airport, Shin-Osaka, and Kyoto (that is, Shinkansen are not included in the pass). Similar but covering a wider area, including all Shinkansen traveling between Shin-Osaka Station and Kurashiki stations (including Nozomi and Mizuho), is the **Kansai Wide Area Pass,** which costs ¥12,000 for 5 consecutive days. The 7-day **Sanyo-San'in Area Pass** covers a larger area still, including the Shinkansen from Shin-Osaka through Hiroshima all the way to Hakata (in the city of Fukuoka on Kyushu) and to Matsue for ¥23,000, while the 7-day Kansai-Hokuriku Area Pass includes the Kansai area, Okayama, and Kanazawa for ¥19,000.

Two other non-JR passes are available for Kansai. The **Kansai Railway Pass** (surutto.com/kansai_rw) is valid on city subways, private railways (*not* JR trains), and buses throughout the Kansai area, including Kansai Airport, Osaka, Kyoto, Nara, Kobe, Himeji, and Mount Koya, and provides slight discounts to hundreds of tourist facilities (usually ¥100 or 10%). Available only to tourists, it costs ¥5,600 for a 2-day pass and ¥7,000 for 3 days and can be used on non-consecutive days; it's sold at Kansai International Airport, Tourist Information Centers in Osaka and Nara, and the Kyoto Station Bus Information Center, among others, or can be purchased online.

TOP apps FOR TRAVELING AROUND JAPAN

Though Japan is still quite analog (despite its high-tech reputation), there are some apps you may find useful in getting around Japan.

Suica Mobile (jreast.co.jp/multi/en/wsmlp/), available only to iOS users—Android users need to have purchased the phone in Japan and have a compatible SIM—is a digital IC card (a prepaid card used for traveling on public transport), allowing you to tap onto buses and through train station barriers directly from your phone. You can also recharge the digital card through the app.

Uber is used in Japan, but for ride-sharing service, many locals prefer **GO** (go.goinc.jp/lp/inbound), which currently operates in 45 out of Japan's 47 prefectures.

Green-conscious travelers will be glad of **MyMizu** (mymizu.co/home-en), an app that pinpoints 200,000-plus locations where you can refill your water bottle for free. **Ramen Beast** (available on the Apple app store) and **Gourmet Navigator** (gurunavi.com) are worthwhile downloads for foodies.

By Bus

Buses often go where trains don't and thus may be the only way for you to get to the more remote areas of Japan. They are also low-cost alternatives to trains for long-distance travel.

Some intercity buses require that you make reservations or purchase your ticket in advance at the ticket counter at the bus terminal. For others (especially local buses), when you board a bus you'll generally find a ticket machine by the entry door. Take a ticket, which is number-coded with a digital board displayed at the front of the bus. The board shows the various fares, which increase with the distance traveled. You pay when you get off.

In addition to serving the remote areas of the country, **long-distance buses** (called *chokyori basu*) operate between all major cities in Japan and offer the cheapest mode of transportation. Private companies run the majority of buses. Some do not have English-language websites; those that do are listed on the **Nihon Bus Association** website (bus.or.jp), with links to companies around Japan. For routes and reservations, you should also check **kousokubus.net/JpnBus**. Otherwise, one of the largest national fleets is operated cooperatively by each of the six members of the **JR Group.** JR East (jrbuskanto.co.jp), for example, operates highway buses departing mostly from Tokyo Station and the Shinjuku Expressway Bus Terminal to Kanazawa, Kyoto, Osaka, and areas north of the city.

The company with the best English website, and the one that appears most frequently in this book, is **Willer Express** (willerexpress.com), which offers services from Tokyo, Kanazawa, Kyoto, Osaka, Nara, Kobe, Himeji, Okayama, Hiroshima, and other cities. It also sells tickets from other bus companies. Some buses travel during the night and offer reclining seats and toilets, thus saving passengers the price of a night's lodging;

STRATEGIES FOR hotel discounts

You have to be proactive nowadays to snag good prices on hotels in Japan. Here are some of our strategies:

1. **Make a reservation you can cancel.** As the date of the stay approaches, hotels start to play "chicken" with one another, dropping the price a bit one day to try to lure customers away from a nearby competitor. So search again the week you're traveling, and then within 48 hours of arrival. This strategy takes vigilance and persistence, but since your credit card won't usually be charged until 24 hours before check-in, little risk is involved, and it's paying off more often than ever before thanks to current conditions. These discounts are always better than the book-ahead discounts that require you to lock in a price.
2. **Bid for lodgings without knowing which hotel you'll get.** You can do so on **Priceline.com** and **Hotwire.com**, and both sites can be money-savers, particularly if you're booking within a week of travel (that's when the hotels resort to deep discounts to get beds filled according to a recent study of billions of hotels bookings). As these companies use only major chains, you can rest assured that you won't be put up in a dump. For Priceline, you can install the browser extension **Hotel Canary** for free on your computer, and it will tell you the name of the hotel Priceline is trying to hide from you. There's not as easy a hack for Hotwire, but if you search for it on Frommers.com you'll find a four-step method we figured out for correctly guessing which hotel you're being shown.
3. **Consider joining Room Steals, Travel + Leisure's Go, or one of the travel clubs associated with many professional organizations.** These clubs have access to the "fire sales"

double-decker buses may even have salons or bars on the first floor. Some buses are just for women, and many have a variety of seats to choose from. Long-distance buses between Tokyo and Kyoto cost ¥4,000–¥9,000, depending on the seat selected (reclining seats cost more), time of day (weekdays are generally cheaper), and season. Willer Express also offers a bus pass for foreign tourists good for any 3 days of travel for ¥12,800 or 5 days for ¥15,300 within a 2-month period (passes for traveling only Mon–Thurs are cheaper). To save more money, sign up for free Willer membership to collect points that can be used toward discount coupons.

By Car

Driving adds a freedom and spontaneity to your journey through Japan that public-transport users will simply never get, allowing you to pass through and visit the small towns, mountain villages, and hinterlands that bind the major cities together. If you're traveling in Hokkaido, Yakushima, or in Kochi Prefecture, say—some of the most scenic corners of Japan—driving is the only way to do it justice. That said, it does have its downsides: Driving is British-style (on the left side of the road), often a challenge for those not used to it; traffic can be horrendous in cities and major highways, of the hotel industry: room rates that are slashed to a level hotels would never want to surface on a Google search. These clubs work best for frequent travelers, as there are initial membership fees. Another alternative is **@Hotels** on Instagram, which unlocks the same types of discounts, but with no membership fee (it does have a slightly more cumbersome research and booking method, involving messaging @Hotels for access). But all these entities unlock wholesale prices that consistently shave 25% off the nightly rate at hotels, more for really pricey ones.

4. **Use loyalty points at a chain hotel.** The major cities of Japan, and many of the minor ones, are home to all of the multinational chain hotels, so look into whether you have enough points to score nights, or if there are other sorts of corporate discounts you can snag. I review the chain hotels with the best locations and the most character.
5. **Use the right hotel search engine.** They're not all equal, as we at Frommers.com learned in 2024 after putting the top 20 sites to the test in 20 cities around the globe. We discovered that HotelsCombined.com and Google/Hotels both listed the lowest rates for hotels in the city center 20 out of 20 times—the best record, by far, of all the sites we tested.
6. **Buy a money-saving package deal.** A travel package that combines your airfare and hotel stay may be the best bargain. In some cases, you'll get airfare, accommodations, transportation, and extras for less than the hotel alone would have cost. Check the airlines and the usual booking websites (Priceline, Expedia, etc.) to see if they offer good packages to the destinations you want to visit in Japan.

especially during rush hour; and it isn't necessarily economical to drive. Gas is expensive—about ¥175 per liter/¼ gallon, though basic rental cars tend to have good miles-to-the-gallon ratios. Free parking is hard to find, and garages are expensive. Moreover, all of Japan's expressways charge high tolls. The one-way toll from Tokyo to Kyoto, for example, is almost the same price as a ticket to Kyoto on the Shinkansen (and the Shinkansen makes the trip in only 3 hr., compared to about 8 hr. by car). For these reasons, it's best to leave your driving for remote areas only.

Major car-rental companies in Japan include **Toyota Rent-A-Car** (rent.toyota.co.jp), **Times Car Rental** (timescar-rental.com), **Nippon Rent-A-Car** (nipponrentacar.co.jp), and **Nissan Rent-A-Car** (nissan-rentacar.com). You'll need either an **International Driving Permit (IDP)** or a **Japanese driving license.** Although anyone 18 and older can drive in Japan, some rental companies may require a driver to have held a driving license at least 3 years.

Signs on all major highways are written in both Japanese and English, though some rental companies offer GPS with English voice guidance as well. It is against the law to drink alcohol and drive, all passengers must wear seat belts, and it's prohibited to use a mobile phone while driving.

BREAKDOWNS & ASSISTANCE The **Japan Automobile Federation (JAF;** jaf.or.jp) is one of several road service providers maintaining emergency telephone boxes along Japan's major arteries to assist drivers whose cars have broken down or who need help. Calls from these telephones are free and will connect you to JAF's operation center. English is spoken. The website also provides useful information on driving in Japan. Individual rental car providers will often supply toll-free contact numbers for you to reach English-speaking operators in the event of an accident or breakdown.

[Fast FACTS] JAPAN

Area Codes The country code for Japan is 81. All telephone area codes for Japanese cities begin with a zero (03 for Tokyo, 06 for Osaka, 075 for Kyoto), but drop the first zero if calling Japan from abroad. If you're calling a Japanese cellphone from overseas, which generally starts with **090, 080,** or **070,** drop the first zero and just dial **90** or **80** after the country code.

ATMs The best way to get cash is from an ATM (automated teller machine). Most bank ATMs in Japan accept only cards issued by Japanese banks, though you may find one in the corner of the bank accepting international cards. Your best bet for getting cash is the ubiquitous **7-Eleven, FamilyMart,** and **Lawson** convenience stores, most of which are open 24 hours and have ATMs that accept foreign bank cards. Note, however, that AMEX cards are often not accepted. I suggest traveling with at least two cards from different issuers.

You'll also find 30,000-some ATMs operated by the **Japan Post Bank** (jp-bank.japanpost.jp), mostly located in post offices all over Japan, with instructions in English. Major post offices, usually located near central train stations, often have long open hours for ATMs (generally 7am–11pm weekdays and 9am–7 or 9pm on weekends; some are open almost 24 hours a day). Small post offices may have limited ATM hours (closing around 6 or 7pm weekdays and 5pm weekends, for example). Increasingly, you'll also find Japan Post Bank and 7-Eleven ATMs outside of department stores, train stations, and shopping malls.

Banks Banks are generally open Monday through Friday 9am to 3pm, though foreign currency exchange hours usually don't begin until 10:30 or 11am (be prepared for a long wait; you'll be asked to sit down as your order is processed). All banks in Japan displaying an AUTHORIZED FOREIGN EXCHANGE sign can exchange currency and traveler's checks. Exchange rates are usually displayed at the foreign-exchange counter. ***Warning:*** We don't recommend using **Travelex** foreign-exchange kiosks, which you'll see in many tourist-heavy locales. They give a lousy exchange rate.

You can also exchange money at some hotels and **department stores,** which are often open until 7:30 or 8pm. Note, however, that hotels and department stores may charge a handling fee, offer a slightly less favorable exchange rate, and require a passport for all transactions. Some hotels and department stores now have money-changing machines, a welcome development.

Business Hours Banks are open Monday through Friday 9am–3pm. Neighborhood post offices are open Monday through Friday 9am–5pm; central post offices in large cities (usually located near major train stations) have longer hours and may even be open on weekends.

Keep in mind that museums, gardens, and attractions stop selling admission tickets at least 30 minutes before the actual closing time. Similarly, restaurants take their last orders at least 30 minutes before the posted closing time (even earlier for *kaiseki* restaurants).

Most national, prefectural, and city museums are closed on Monday; if Monday is a national holiday, however, they'll remain open and close on the following Tuesday instead. Privately owned museums usually close on holidays.

Lots of bars, izakaya, ramen shops, karaoke joints, and beef bowl joints stay open well after midnight and are sometimes open 24/7.

Customs

Visitors entering Japan must fill out a "Customs Declaration" form (handed out on incoming flights). If you're 20 or older, you can bring duty-free into Japan up to 400 cigarettes or 500 grams of tobacco or 100 cigars; three bottles (760cc each) of alcohol; and 2 ounces of perfume. You can also bring in goods for personal use that were purchased abroad if the total market value is under ¥200,000.

Japan has strict rules what medicines/chemicals are allowed into the country; even OTC medicines like Sudafed and Vicks inhalers are prohibited. If you require insulin or codeine-based painkillers, check what accompanying documents you need for declaration. For more information, check the **Ministry of Health, Labor, and Welfare's** website (mhlw.go.jp) for more information.

Disabled Travelers

For those with disabilities, traveling in Japan can be a nightmare, especially in Tokyo and other large metropolises. City sidewalks can be jam-packed, making it difficult to get around on crutches or in a wheelchair, and some busy thoroughfares can be crossed only via pedestrian bridges.

Toilets for the handicapped can be found across Japan, including in train stations (almost every station has at least one), department stores, and attractions.

Public transport can also be a challenge. Shinkansen and some limited express trains have spaces for wheelchairs and accessible toilets. Most major train and subway stations have elevators, but they can be hard to locate; smaller stations, especially in rural areas, may be accessible only by stairs or escalators, though in recent years some have been equipped with powered seat lifts. While some buses are no-step conveyances for easy access (including new ones being added in Tokyo), subway and train compartments are difficult for wheelchair travelers to navigate on their own, due to a gap or slight height difference between the coaches and platforms. In theory, you can ask a station attendant to help you board, though you might have to wait if they're busy; you can also request an attendant at your destination to help you disembark. City trains, subways, and buses do have seating for passengers with disabilities—called "Priority Seats"—but subways can be so crowded that there's barely room to move, and Priority Seats are almost always occupied by commuters. Unless you look visibly handicapped, no one is likely to offer you a seat.

As for **accommodations,** hotels with 50 or more rooms are required to offer one barrier-free room (called a "universal" room in Japan, used primarily by seniors). New hotels are also legally required to have a wheelchair accessible guestroom, but usually they only have one. A scant 1% of Japanese inns have such rooms. Lower-priced accommodations may also lack elevators.

Restaurants can also be difficult to navigate, with raised doorsills, crowded dining areas, and tiny bathrooms that cannot accommodate wheelchairs. Best bets for ramps and easily accessible bathrooms include restaurants in department stores and upper-end hotels. Even Japanese homes are not very accessible, since the main floor is always raised about a foot above the entrance-hall floor.

When it comes to **facilities for the blind,** Japan has an advanced system. At subway stations and on many major sidewalks in large cities, raised dots and lines on the ground guide blind people at intersections and to subway platforms (in fact, Japan pioneered the system). In some cities, streetlights chime a theme when the signal turns green east-west, and chime another for north-south. Even Japanese yen notes are identified by a slightly raised circle—the ¥1,000 note has one circle in a corner, while the ¥10,000 note has two.

For more information on accessibility in Japan, accessible-japan.com provides valuable tips on wheelchairs and accessibility for sights, neighborhoods, hotels, and more.

Doctors

Many first-class hotels offer medical facilities, an in-house doctor, or a doctor on call. Otherwise, your embassy or the **AMDA International Medical Information Center** (amdamedicalcenter.com; ✆ **03-6233-9266** in Tokyo; Mon–Fri 10am–4pm) can refer you to medical professionals who speak English.

Drinking Laws

The legal drinking age is 20. Beer, wine, and spirits are readily available in department stores, grocery stores, convenience stores, and liquor stores. Many bars, especially in nightlife districts such as Shinjuku and Roppongi, are open until dawn. If you intend to drive in Japan, however, you are not allowed even one drink. Drinking in public is usually fair game in Japan—cherry blossom season is a veritable outdoor party throughout the country—but some areas are tightening controls on this, like Shibuya in Tokyo.

Electricity

The electricity throughout Japan is 100 volts AC. That's close enough to the American system that you probably won't encounter any problems plugging in American electronics, including laptops and phone chargers. Leading hotels often have two outlets, one for 110 volts and one for 220 volts (with the appropriate plugs used in the U.S. and Europe), so you can use most American or European appliances during your stay. Note, too, that the flat, two-legged prongs used in Japan are the same size and fit as in North America, but three-pronged appliances are not accepted.

Emergencies

The national emergency numbers are ✆ **110** for **police** and ✆ **119** for **ambulance** and **fire** (ambulances are free in Japan unless you request a specific hospital). Be sure to speak slowly and precisely.

Health

It's safe to drink tap water and eat to your heart's content everywhere in Japan. Pregnant women, however, are advised to avoid eating raw fish and to avoid taking hot baths. To prevent the spread of flus and coronaviruses, all incoming passengers most international airports are monitored for fever; those with a higher-than-normal temperature may be quarantined.

You don't need any inoculations to enter Japan. Some physicians may offer a Japanese encephalitis jab if you're spending all your time in remote areas and islands, though fewer than 10 cases are reported each year. **Prescriptions** can be filled at Japanese pharmacies *only if they're issued by a Japanese doctor.* To avoid hassle, bring more prescription medications than you think you'll need, clearly labeled in their original containers, and be sure to pack them in your carry-on. Bring copies of your prescriptions with you, including generic names of medicines in case a local pharmacist is unfamiliar with the brand name. **Over-the-counter items** are easy to obtain, though name brands will be different from those back home, some ingredients may be forbidden in Japan, and prices may be higher. Japanese painkillers are weak; don't be deterred if the suggested dosage is four or more pills at a time, this is standard practice.

Internet & Wi-Fi

Narita International Airport, Haneda Airport, and Kansai International Airport all offer free **Wi-Fi** (wireless fidelity). Almost all accommodations provide free Wi-Fi in guest rooms and public spaces, except for some old inns (usually in order to preserve a relaxing atmosphere). In rural Japan connection may be iffy.

Many department stores, shopping centers, restaurants (including all McDonald's), cafes (including all Starbucks and Doutours), and bars offer free Wi-Fi, though you may have to ask for the password or register your email address. All but the smallest of towns now have free Wi-Fi hotspots, though time usage may be limited and reception can be spotty. Both JR East and JR West provide free Wi-Fi in many stations, including all JR stations and trains in Tokyo (Tokyo's subway stations also offer free Wi-Fi) and in major stations in the Kansai area.

Download the free Japan Connected Wi-Fi app (ntt-bp.net), which connects you to Wi-Fi hotspots around Japan and also offers offline maps.

Legal Aid Contact your embassy if you find yourself in legal trouble. Operated by three bar associations, the **Legal Counseling Center** (horitsu-sodan.jp) can provide legal counseling in English. The number of English-speaking law firms in Japan has grown in recent years; to find one, use a search database like **bestlawyers.com/Japan**.

LGBTQ Travelers Japan has no laws forbidding homosexual activity and there is no ban against homosexuality by either Buddhism or Shintoism. Indeed, same-sex relationships have been well-documented through the ages in Japanese literature and art. On the other hand, being openly gay in Japan can still lead to being ostracized. Although there are many gay and lesbian establishments in Tokyo (concentrated mostly in Shinjuku's Ni-chome district; see p. 215), the gay community in Japan is not a vocal one. That said, events such as **Kanamara Matsuri,** held the first Sunday of April just outside Tokyo, and **Tokyo Pride,** held over a weekend in June, have given gay communities more of a presence. A useful website for information on the gay scene in Japan, as well as gay and lesbian club listings, is **travelgay.com/destination/gay-japan**. Tokyo-based **Out Asia Travel** (outasiatravel.com) offers guided tours of gay nightlife districts in Tokyo, Kyoto, Osaka, and other towns, special-interest tours, individually oriented trips, and tours to other destinations in Japan and Asia.

Luggage & Lockers Coin-operated lockers are located at major train stations throughout the country, but lockers are generally not large enough to store huge pieces of luggage (and those that do are often taken). Lockers generally cost ¥300–¥1,000 per day depending on the size; if you leave them overnight, you'll have to pay the next-day's charge to retrieve them. Many major stations now also have check-in rooms or in-town delivery service for luggage (see individual city chapters). If your bag becomes too much to handle (for example, if you're riding a Shinkansen bullet train, which has limited luggage storage space), you can have it sent ahead to another destination via door-to-door service offered by companies like Yamato's **TA-Q-BIN** (kuronekoyamato.co.jp), available at homes, offices, upper- and mid-range hotels, and all convenience stores in Japan. At Narita and Kansai international airports, service counters will send luggage to your hotel the next day (or from your hotel to the airport) for about ¥2,000-plus per bag.

Mail & Postage Post offices in Japan are recognizable by the red logo of a capital T with a horizontal line over it. Mailboxes are bright orange-red. It costs ¥110 to airmail letters weighing up to 25 grams and ¥85 for postcards to Australia, North America, and Europe. Domestic mail costs ¥110 for letters up to 25 grams, and ¥85 for postcards. Post offices throughout Japan are also convenient for their ATMs (see "ATMs," above), which accept international credit cards for money exchange. All **post offices** are open Monday through Friday 9am–5pm; international post offices (often located close to the central train station) stay open often until 7pm or later on weekdays and are also open on weekends (in Tokyo and Kyoto, counters are open 24 hr.). If your hotel does not have a shipping service, you can mail packages abroad.only at these larger post offices that For more information, visit **post.japanpost.jp**.

Measurements Before the metric system came into use in Japan, the country had its own standards for measuring length and weight. Rooms are sometimes still measured by the number of *tatami* straw mats that will fit in them. A six-*tatami* room, for example, is the size of six *tatami* mats, with a *tatami* roughly .9m (3 ft.) wide and 1.8m (6 ft.) long.

Mobile Phones & SIMs

If you're mobile phone service provider doesn't offer plans for using data in Japan, you can **use your own mobile phone** and buy a prepaid SIM card in the arrival lobbies of Narita, Haneda, and Kansai airports from one of many companies like **Softbank.** In town, prepaid SIM cards are also available at Yodobashi Camera and Bic Camera shops. The cheapest SIM options are for data only, which means you can't make calls or send text messages.

THE VALUE OF THE YEN VS. OTHER POPULAR CURRENCIES

Yen¥	Aus$	Can$	Euro€	NZ$	UK£	US$
100	A$1.21	C$1.19	€0.79	NZ$1.32	£0.69	$0.91

Money & Costs

Frommer's lists exact prices in the local currency. The currency conversions quoted above were correct at press time. However, rates fluctuate, so before departing consult a currency exchange website such as **oanda.com/currency/converter** to check up-to-the-minute rates.

The **currency** in Japan is called the *yen,* symbolized by ¥. Coins come in denominations of ¥1, ¥5, ¥10, ¥50, ¥100, and ¥500. Bills come in denominations of ¥1,000, ¥2,000, ¥5,000, and ¥10,000, though ¥2,000 notes are rarely seen. In 2024 Japan updated its paper currency to immortalize different figures from its history on the new ¥1,000, ¥5,000, and ¥10,000 notes. The old notes are still in circulation, but they may not be accepted at vending machines or restaurant ordering machines, which have been recalibrated to fit the different size of the new notes.

Keep plenty of change handy for riding local transportation such as buses or streetcars. Although change machines are virtually everywhere (even on buses, where you can change larger coins and ¥1,000 bills), you'll find it faster to have the exact amount on hand (or buy an IC card like Suica; see p. 691).

Some people like to arrive in a foreign country with that country's currency already on hand, but I don't find it necessary for Japan. **Narita, Haneda,** and **Kansai** have ATMs and exchange counters for all incoming international flights that offer similar exchange rates to what you'd get abroad.

Most Japanese pay with either credit cards or cash for larger purchases, though digital payments like **LINE Pay** and **PayPay** are popular amongst the young. The most readily accepted cards are **MasterCard** and **Visa,** as well as the Japanese credit card **JCB** (Japan Credit Bank) and sometimes **AMEX.** You can use a credit card for the bulk of your expenses—hotels, train tickets, many restaurant meals, and major purchases. Shops and restaurants will usually post which cards they accept at the door or near the cash register.

Nevertheless, Japan is still largely a cash society. While many new restaurants, shops, and larger chains have begun to accept tap payments through apps and credit and debit cards, the vast majority of Japan's smaller businesses—noodle shops, fast-food joints, ma-and-pa establishments, and the cheapest accommodations—do not accept credit cards, and larger establishments may be reluctant to accept cards for small purchases and inexpensive meals. You'll want to have plenty of cash on hand, especially if you're traveling in rural areas where you might not have easy access to an ATM.

Newspapers & Magazines

Two English-language newspapers are published daily in Japan: the ***Japan Times*** (japantimes.co.jp), which comes distributed also with the *International New York Times,* and the ***Japan News*** (the-japan-news.com), published by *Yomiuri Shimbun.* In addition, the *Asahi Shimbun* has an English website, asahi.com/ajw/, with news on Japan, while the subscription-based ***Nikkei Asia*** (asia.nikkei.com), based in Tokyo, conducts reporting and publishes op-eds in Japanese and English.

You may also find English-language magazines in train stations, hotel lobbies, and cafes and restaurants, a good source for cultural news, travel recommendations, and calendars of events. These include **Tokyo Weekender** (tokyoweekender.com), **Metropolis** (metropolisjapan.com), and **TimeOut** (timeout.com/Tokyo), though they publish in print much less frequently than they used to.

Packing Tips

The first thing you'll want to do is select the smallest bag you can get away with and **pack as lightly as you can.** Storage space is limited on Japan's trains, including the Shinkansen bullet train, business hotels often lack closets, and you'll have to navigate multitudes of stairs and overhead and underground passageways in virtually every train station (though there are elevators and escalators in most).

The most important item is **a good pair of walking shoes,** well broken in, since you will probably be walking more than you do at home. Remember that you will have to remove shoes to enter Japanese homes, inns, shrines, temples, and even some restaurants, so bring a pair that's easy to slip on and off. As for **clothes,** you'll need a coat in winter and very light clothing for the hot and humid summer months. For sightseeing, casual wear is okay, including jeans, shorts, and sandals, but be aware that Japanese put more stock in how you dress and look than you may be accustomed to back home.

Because the sun rises early in summer (as early as 4am), you might also want to pack a pair of **eyeshades.** It's also good to carry a supply of **tissues,** as many bathrooms lack towels or a hand dryer. And note that many Japanese still wear **facemasks,** not only to protect against catching Covid, but to prevent spreading winter colds or keeping pollen at bay during hay fever season.

Pharmacies

Drugstores, called ***yakkyoku,*** are found readily in Japan. Note, however, that you cannot have a foreign prescription filled in Japan without first consulting a doctor in Japan, so be sure to bring an adequate supply of essential medicines with you. No drugstores in Japan stay open 24 hours, but basic stuff like cough drops and aspirin can be bought at all-night convenience stores.

Safety

The tragic 2011 Great East Japan Earthquake brought world-wide attention to the fact that Japan is earthquake-prone. In reality most earthquakes here are too small to detect (of the more than 100,000 earthquakes annually in Japan, only 1% are big enough to feel). In any case, Japan has the world's best early-warning systems for impending earthquakes and tsunamis. In the event of a warning or an earthquake, there are a few precautions you should take. If you're indoors, the three rules of thumb are Drop, Cover, and Hold On—you should drop to the ground, take cover under a sturdy piece of furniture or under a doorway, and then hold on until the shaking stops. Do not go outdoors—the greatest danger is from falling debris, collapsing walls, and flying glass. Never use elevators during a quake. If you are already outdoors, stay away from trees, power lines, streetlights, and the sides of buildings; if you're surrounded by tall buildings, seek cover in a doorway. If you're in a coastal area, move away from the beach. And expect aftershocks. Although secondary shockwaves are generally not as severe as the first one, they can damage weakened structures. They can occur in the first hours or days—and even months—after the first quake.

In case of major emergencies, there are emergency shelters throughout Japan, mostly schoolyards and other public facilities. Other precautions include noting emergency exits wherever you stay; all hotels supply flashlights, usually found attached to your bedside table. For more on what to do during earthquakes, evacuation shelters, updates on disasters and weather warnings and advisories, see the Japan government's **Disaster Prevention Portal** (mlit.go.jp/river/bousai/bousai-portal) and download the

NERV disaster prevention app (nerv.app).

As for crime, Japan has long been recognized as one of the safest countries in the world. If you lose something, say on a subway or in a park, chances are good that you'll get it back. To find out how, go to the nearest police station or contact the local tourist office. Pickpocketing and train groping are not entirely unheard of, however. As in any country, stay alert and be aware of your immediate surroundings. Be especially careful with cameras, purses, and wallets in congested areas like Narita airport, subways, department stores, or tourist attractions. Some Japanese caution women against walking through parks alone at night.

Smoking

The legal age for purchasing tobacco products and smoking in Japan is 20. Smoking is banned in most public areas, including in office buildings, trains and subways, and train stations (although some stations have a smoking room). In most cities, ordinances also ban smoking on sidewalks but allow it in marked areas, usually near train stations. Many restaurants have nonsmoking sections, though bars often do not. Legislation introduced in Tokyo in 2020 outlaws smoking inside most cafes and restaurants. Only old business hotels and the odd traditional inn have dedicated smoking floors or guestrooms, otherwise accommodations are pretty much smoke-free.

Taxes

A 10% tax is imposed on goods and services, including hotel rates and restaurant meals Hotels and restaurants are inconsistent about including the tax in their published rates, but will generally state on their tariff sheets and menus whether tax is included or will be added. Tokyo and Kyoto hotels also levy a separate accommodations tax (see chapters 4 and 7). In hot-spring resorts, a ¥150 *onsen* tax is added for each night of your stay (some areas are hiking this to ¥300 or more).

In addition, a 10%–15% **service charge** will be added to your bill in lieu of tipping at most high-end restaurants and at moderately priced and upper-end hotels; in *ryokan*, the service charge can be as high as 20%. Business hotels, *minshuku*, backpacker hostels, and inexpensive restaurants do not impose a service charge.

As for **shopping,** a consumption tax is also included in the price of most goods. Travelers from abroad are eligible for an exemption on goods taken out of the country within 6 months, although only department stores, designer boutiques, souvenir shops, and specialty stores seem equipped to deal with the procedures. General items such as clothing and household goods are eligible, as well as consumables (cosmetics, food, and drinks), as long as you don't consume them in Japan; they will be placed in a sealed bag. Stores will grant a refund on the consumption tax only if you've spent a total amount of ¥5,000 at the store; to obtain a refund immediately, have a sales clerk fill out a list of your purchases and then present the list to the tax-exemption counter of the department store (you must also show your passport). Note that stores are allowed to charge 1.1% commission on your refund. A Tax-free Proof of Purchase receipt will be attached to your passport to show when departing Japan; make sure to pack your purchases in your carry-on luggage. From November 2026, this will change to a "refund method," where tax will be returned on all applicable items at customs when leaving Japan. So be sure to keep records of what you buy.

Time

Japan is 9 hours ahead of Greenwich Mean Time, 14 hours ahead of New York, 15 hours ahead of Chicago, and 17 hours ahead of Los Angeles. Japan currently does not use **daylight saving time,** so subtract 1 hour from the above times in the months when daylight saving time is in effect elsewhere.

Because Japan is on the other side of the **international date line,** you lose a day when traveling from the United States to Asia. (If you depart the United States on Tues, you'll arrive on Wed.) Returning to North America, however, you gain a day, which means that you arrive on the same day you left.

Tipping

One of the delights of being in Japan is

that there's no tipping—not even to waitresses, taxi drivers, or bellhops. If you try to tip them, they'll probably be confused or may run after you with your change. Instead, a 10% to 15% service charge is added to your bill at higher-priced accommodations and restaurants.

Toilets If you need a restroom, your best bets are at train and subway stations, big hotels, department stores, convenience stores, and fast-food restaurants. Use of restrooms is free in Japan, and though public facilities supply toilet paper, it's a good idea to **carry a packet of tissues.** Many do not provide soap, so it's also wise to carry **hand sanitizer.** In parks and some restaurants in rural areas, don't be surprised if you go into a restroom and find men's urinals and private stalls in the same room. Women are supposed to walk past the urinals without noticing them.

Some toilets in Japan, especially in rural train stations or old family-run restaurants, are **Japanese-style toilets:** They're holes in the ground over which you squat, facing toward the end with a raised hood. Men stand and aim for the hole. Although these toilets may seem primitive, they're actually more sanitary because no part of your body touches anything.

Western-style toilets in Japan are famously high-tech. Called **Washlets,** these combination bidet/toilets have heated toilet seats, blow dryers, and buttons and knobs directing sprays of water to various body parts; they even have lids that raise automatically when you open the stall. Alas, instructions are often in Japanese only. Don't stand up until you've figured out how to turn the spray off—it's an awkward position to be in if you need to yell for assistance.

Visas For most foreign tourists, including Americans, Canadians, Australians, New Zealanders, and citizens of the United Kingdom, visas are not required for stays up to 90 days.

Visitor Information The **Japan National Tourism Organization (JNTO;** japan.travel) is one of the best sources for travel information on Japan. Although it is quite promotional, it's good for reading up on what's new or unique modes of transport, as well as for getting maps, current weather reports, and information on regional events. Consider signing up for JNTO's e-newsletter. The **japan-guide.com**, with links to many other websites, is also useful.

In Japan, your best bet for general or specific information is at JNTO's excellent **Tourist Information Centers (TIC)**. The **Tokyo Tourist Information Center** in the TMG Building (p. 89) has information on all 47 prefectures. There are locally run tourist offices in nearly every city and town throughout Japan, most of them conveniently located at or near the main train station. Look for the logo of a red question mark with the word INFORMATION written below.

Water The water is safe to drink anywhere in Japan. Bottled water is also readily available (usually ¥100–¥120) from the thousands of convenience stores and 4-million-plus vending machines throughout the country.

16

USEFUL JAPANESE PHRASES

Needless to say, it takes years to become fluent in Japanese, particularly in written Japanese, with its thousands of kanji, or Chinese characters, and its many hiragana and katakana characters. If you know even a few words of Japanese, however, they will not only be useful but will delight Japanese people you meet in the course of your trip.

Pronunciation

In pronouncing the following vocabulary, remember that there's very little stress on individual syllables (pronunciation of Japanese is often compared to Italian). Here's an approximation of some of the sounds of Japanese:

a	as in *father*
aa	held slightly longer than *a*
e	as in *pen*
i	as in *pick*
ii	held slightly longer than *i*
o	as in *oh*

oo	held slightly longer than *o*
u	as in *boo*
uu	held slightly longer than *u*
g	as in *gift* at the beginning of words; like *ng* in *sing* in the middle or at the end of words

Vowel sounds are almost always short unless they are pronounced doubled, in which case you hold the vowel a bit longer. *Okashi,* for example, means "a sweet," whereas *okashii* means "strange." As you can see, even slight mispronunciation of a word can result in confusion or hilarity. (Incidentally, jokes in Japanese are nearly always plays on words.) Similarly, double consonants are given more emphasis than only one consonant by itself.

Basic Terms

Yes **Hai**

No **Iie**

Good morning **Ohayo gozaimasu**

Good afternoon **Konnichiwa**

Good evening **Konbanwa**

Good night **Oyasuminasai**

Hello **Haro** (or **Konnichiwa**)

How are you? **Ogenki desu ka?**

How do you do? **Hajimemashite?**

Goodbye **Sayonara** (or **Bye-Bye**)

Excuse me/Pardon me/I'm sorry **Sumimasen**

Please (when offering something) **Doozo**

Please (when requesting something) **Kudasai**

Thank you **Domo arigato**

You're welcome **Doo-itashimashite**

Basic Questions & Expressions

I'm American **Amerikajin desu**

I'm Canadian **Canadajin desu**

I'm English **Igirisujin desu**

Sorry, I don't speak Japanese **Sumimasen, Nihongo wa hanasemasen**

Do you understand English? **Eigo wa wakarimasu ka?**

Do you understand? **Wakarimasu ka?**

I understand **Wakarimasu**

I don't understand **Wakarimasen**

Can I ask you a question? **Otazune shitaino desu ka?**

Just a minute, please **Chotto matte kudasai**

How much is it? **Ikura desu ka?**

It's expensive **Takai desu**

It's cheap **Yasui desu**

Where is it? **Doko desu ka?**

When is it? **Itsu desu ka?**

What is it? Kore-wa, nan-desu-ka?

I like it **Suki desu** (pronounced "ski")

Where is the toilet? **Toire wa, doko desu ka?**

My name is . . . [Your name] **to mooshimasu**

What is your name? O-namae wa, nan desu ka?

What time do you open/close? Nanji ni akimasuka? Nanjini shimarimasuka?

Credit card **Kurejitto kaado**

Do you accept credit cards? Kurejitto kādo wa tsukae masu ka?

Too expensive **Takasugimasu**

This one **Kore**

That one **Are**

Travel Expressions & Directionals

Where is . . . ? **Doko desu ka . . . ?**

Airport **Kuukoo**

I need a ride to the airport. **Kuukoo made notte iku hitsuyō ga arimasu.**

My flight was canceled. **Watashi no furaito wa kyanseru saremashita.**

Airplane **Hikooki**

Subway Chika-tetsu

Bus **Basu**

Taxi **Takushii**

Car rental agency **Rentakā gaisha**

Ferry **Ferii**

Train **Densha**

Bullet train **Shinkansen**

Limited express train (long distance) **Tokkyu**

Ordinary express train (doesn't stop at every station) **Kyukoo**

Rapid train **Kaisoku densha**

Local train (one that stops at every station) **Kakueki teisha** (or **futsu**)

Train station **Eki**

Where is the train station? **Eki wa, doko desu ka?**

I would like a reserved seat, please. **Shiteiseki o kudasai.**

I would like a seat in the nonsmoking car, please. **Kinensha no shiteiski o kudasai.**

Where should I transfer? **Norikae wa doko desu ka?**

Unreserved seat **Jiyuseki**

Platform **Platto-hoomu**

Ticket **Kippu**

Destination **Ikisaki**

One-way ticket Katamichi-kippu (or katamichiken)

Round-trip ticket **Oofuku-kippu** (or **oofukuken**)

I would like to buy a ticket. Kippu ichimai o kaitai no desu kedo.

I would like to buy two tickets. **Kippu nimai o kaitai no desu kedo.**

Exit **Deguchi**

Entrance **Iriguchi**

North **Kita**

South **Minami**

East **Higashi**

West **Nishi**

Left **Hidari**

Right **Migi**

Straight ahead **Massugu**

Is it far? **Tooi desu ka?**

Is it near? **Chikai desu ka?**

I'm lost. **Maigoni narimashita.**

I lost my passport. **Watashi wa pasupooto o nakushi mashita.**

I lost my wallet. **Watashi wa saifu o nakushi mashita.**

I lost my bag. **Watashi wa baggu o nakushi mashita.**

My bag was stolen. **Watashi no baggu ga nusumare mashita.**

Can I walk there? **Aruite ikemasu ka?**

Street **Dori** (or **michi**)

Tourist Information Office **Kanko annaijo** (or **kanko kyookai**)

Where is the tourist office? **Kanko annaijo wa, doko desu ka?**

May I have a map, please? **Chizu o kudasai?**

Where is the nearest public bathroom? **Koko kara ichiban chikai kooshuu toire wa doko ni arimasu ka.**

Police **Keisatsu**

Police box **Koban**

Post office **Yuubin-kyoku**

I'd like to buy a stamp. **Kitte o kaitai no desu kedo.**

Bank **Ginkoo**

Hospital **Byooin**

Drugstore **Yakkyoku**

Convenience store **Konbiniensu stoaa**

Embassy **Taishikan**

Department store **Depaato**

Downtown area **Hanka-gai**

Passport **Pasupooto**

I want to go to . . . **. . . e ikitai desu.**

I want to go to the station. **Eki e ikitai desu.**

What time does . . . leave? . . . **nanjini shuppatsu desu ka?**

Lodging Terms

Hotel **Hoteru**

Japanese-style inn **Ryokan**

Japanese-style lodging in a family home **Minshuku**

Youth hostel **Yuusu hosuteru**

Cotton kimono **Yukata**

Room **Heya**

Do you have a room available? **Heya ga arimasu ka?**

I'd like to confirm my reservation. **Yoyaku o kakunin shitai no desuga.**

Does that include meals? **Shokuji wa tsuite imasu ka?**

What time is breakfast? **Chooshoku wa nan ji desu ka.**

What time is check-out? **Chekku auto wa nan ji desu ka.**

Would you call me a taxi? **Takushii o yonde itadake masen ka.**

Do you have Internet access? **Intaanetto ni setsuzoku deki masu ka.**

Tax **Zei**

Service charge **Saabisu**

Key **Kagi**

Balcony **Beranda**

Hot-spring spa **Onsen**

Outdoor hot-spring bath **Rotenburo**

Bath **Ofuro**

Public bath **Sentoo**

Where is the nearest public bath? **Ichiban chikai sentoo wa, doko desu ka?**

I would like a room with one bed/two beds. **Singuru** (single bed), **Daberu** (double-size bed), **Tsuin** (twin beds) **no heya o onegaishimasu.**

Does it have a private bathroom? **Heya ni wa ofuro** (tub) **toire** (toilet) **ga tsuitemasuka?**

I'd like a private bathroom. Basu toile tsuki no heya o onegaishimasu.

Does the window open? **Kono mado wa akimasuka?**

Dining Terms & Phrases

Restaurant **Resutoran** (serves Western-style food)

Dining hall **Shokudoo** (usually serves Japanese food)

Coffee shop **Kissaten**

Japanese pub **Izakaya** or **Nomiya**

Western food **Yooshoku**

Japanese food **Washoku**

Breakfast **Chooshoku**

Lunch Ohiru/lanchi

Dinner **Yuushoku**

I'd like to make a reservation. **Yoyaku oneigaishimasu.**

May I see a menu? **Menyuu o misete itadake masen ka.**

I'd like to pay the bill. **Okanjyoo o oneigaishimasu.**

Menu **Menyu**

Japanese green tea **Ocha**

Black (Indian) tea **Koocha**

Coffee **Koohi**

Water **Mizu**

Lunch or daily special, set menu **Teishoku** (Japanese food)

Lunch or daily special, set menu **Coosu,** or **seto** (usually Western food)

What do you recommend to eat? **Nani ga osusume desu ka?**

This is delicious. **Oishii desu.**

Thank you for the meal. **Gochisoo-sama deshita.**

I would like a fork, please. **Fooku o kudasai.**

I would like a spoon, please. **Supuun o kudasai.**

I would like a knife, please. **Naifu o kudasai.**

May I have some more, please? (if you're asking for liquid, such as more coffee, or food) **Moo sukoshi kudasai?**

May I have some more, please? (if you're asking for another bottle—say, of soda or sake) **Moo ippon kudasai?**

May I have some more, please? (if asking for another cup—say, of coffee or tea) **Moo ippai kudasai?**

I would like sake, please. **Osake o kudasai.**

I would like a cup of coffee, please. **Koohi o ippai kudasai.**

I would like the set meal, please. **Seto o kudasai** or **Teishoku o kudasai.**

Soda **Tansan**

Salt **Shio**

Pepper **Koshoo**

Baked **Yaku**

Fried Ageru/furai

Not fried **Agemonode nai**

Broiled **Yaku**

Steamed **Musu**

Grilled **Yaki**

Well done **Yoku yaku**

Raw **Nama**

Rare **Reaa**

I'm a vegetarian. **Bejitarian desu.**

I can't eat meat/pork. **Oniku/butaniku ga taberemasen.**

I'm allergic to . . . **. . . no alelugii desu.**

Nuts **Nattsu/kinomi**

Milk **Gyuunyuu/miruku**

Shellfish **Kai**

Food

Anago Conger eel

Ayu A small river fish, or sweet fish; a delicacy of western Japan

Chu-hai Shochu Shochu (see below) mixed with soda water and flavored with syrup and lemon

Dengaku Lightly grilled tofu (see below) coated with a bean paste

Dojo Small, eel-like river fish, or loach

Fugu Pufferfish (also known as blowfish or globefish)

"Genghis Khan" or **Jingisu khan** Mutton and vegetables grilled at your table

Gohan Rice

Gyoza Chinese fried pork dumplings

Kaiseki Formal Japanese meal consisting of many courses and served originally during the tea ceremony

Kamameshi Rice casserole topped with seafood, meat, or vegetables

Kushiage (also **kushikatsu** or **kushiyaki**) Deep-fried skewers of chicken, beef, seafood, and vegetables

Maguro Tuna

Makizushi Sushi (see below), vegetables, and rice rolled inside dried seaweed

Miso Soybean paste, used as a seasoning in soups and sauces

Miso-shiru Miso soup

Mochi Japanese rice cake

Nabe A one-pot stew, usually cooked at the table

Nattoo Fermented soybeans

Nikujaga Stew of beef, potato, and carrot, flavored with sake (see below) and soy sauce; popular in winter

Oden Fish cakes, hard-boiled eggs, and vegetables, simmered in a light broth

Okonomiyaki Thick pancake filled with meat, fish, shredded cabbage, and vegetables or noodles, often cooked by diners at their table

Ramen Thick, yellow Chinese noodles, served in a hot soup

Sake (also **Nihon-shu**) Rice wine

Sansai Mountain vegetables, including bracken and flowering fern

Sashimi Raw seafood

Shabu-shabu Thinly sliced beef quickly dipped in boiling water and then dipped in a sauce

Shochu Japanese whiskey, made from rice, wheat, or potatoes

Shojin-ryori Japanese vegetarian food, served at Buddhist temples

Shooyu Soy sauce

Shuumai Steamed Chinese pork dumplings

Soba Buckwheat noodles

Soomen Fine white wheat vermicelli, eaten cold in summer

Sukiyaki Japanese fondue of thinly sliced beef cooked in a sweetened soy sauce with vegetables

Sushi (also **nigiri-zushi**) Raw seafood placed on top of vinegared rice

Tempura Deep-fried food coated in a batter of egg, water, and wheat flour

Teppanyaki Japanese-style steak, seafood, and vegetables cooked by a chef on a smooth, hot, tableside grill

Tofu Soft bean curd

Tonkatsu Deep-fried pork cutlets

Tonkotsu Pork that has been boiled for several hours in miso, shochu, and brown sugar

Udon Thick white wheat noodles

Unagi Grilled eel

Wasabi Japanese horseradish, served with sushi

Yakisoba Chinese fried noodles, served with sautéed vegetables

Yakitori Charcoal-grilled chicken, vegetables, and other specialties, served on bamboo skewers

Yudofu Tofu simmered in a pot at your table

Matters of Time

Now **Ima**

Later **Ato de**

Today **Kyoo**

Tomorrow **Ashita**

Day after tomorrow **Asatte**

Yesterday **Kinoo**

Which day? **Nan-nichi desu ka?**

What time is it? **Nan-ji desu ka?**

Daytime **Hiruma**

Morning **Asa**

Night **Yoru**

Afternoon **Gogo**

Holiday **Yasumi** (or **kyujitsu**)

Weekdays **Heijitsu**

1 hour **Ichijikan**

2 hours **Nijikan**

Days of the Week

Sunday **Nichiyoobi**

Monday **Getsuyoobi**

Tuesday **Kayoobi**

Wednesday **Suiyoobi**

Thursday **Mokuyoobi**

Friday **Kinyoobi**

Saturday **Doyoobi**

Months of the Year

January **Ichi-gatsu**

February **Ni-gatsu**

March **San-gatsu**

April **Shi-gatsu**

May **Go-gatsu**

June **Roku-gatsu**

July **Shichi-gatsu**

August **Hachi-gatsu**

September **Ku-gatsu**

October **Juu-gatsu**

November **Juuichi-gatsu**

December **Juuni-gatsu**

Numbers

one **Ichi**

two **Ni**

three **San**

four **Shi**

five **Go**

six **Roku**

seven **Shichi** (or **nana**)

eight **Hachi**

nine **Kyuu**

ten **Juu**

eleven **Juuichi**

twelve **Juuni**

twenty **Nijuu**

thirty **Sanjuu**

forty **Shijuu** (or **yonjuu**)

fifty **Gojuu**

sixty **Rokujuu**

seventy **Nanajuu**

eighty **Hachijuu**

ninety **Kyuuju**

one hundred **Hyaku**

one thousand **Sen**

ten thousand **Ichiman**

Other General Nouns

Fusuma Sliding paper doors

Gaijin Foreigner

Geta Wooden sandals

Haori Short kimono-like jackets (sometimes worn over a kimono), traditionally worn by men

Irori Open-hearth fireplace

Izakaya (or **Nomiya**) A Japanese-style bar or pub, with beer, sake, and Japanese food, generally open only from 5 or 6pm

Jinja Shinto shrine

Kotatsu Heating element placed under a low table (which is covered with a blanket) for keeping your legs warm

Nihonjin Japanese person

Noren Short curtains hung outside shops and restaurants to signify they are open

Tatami Rice mats

Tera (or **dera**) Temple

Tokonoma Small, recessed alcove in a Japanese room used to display a flower arrangement, scroll, or art object

Torii Entrance gate of a Shinto shrine, consisting usually of two poles topped with one or two crossbeams

Washlet Bidet toilet

Yukata Cotton kimono worn for sleeping

Zabuton Floor cushions

Index

L

M

Z

Accommodations

Restaurants

PHOTO CREDITS

p. i: © agustin.photo/Shutterstock; p. iii: © Blanscape/Shutterstock; p. 1: © Richie Chan/Shutterstock; p. 3, top: © Courtesy of Beppu SUGINOI HOTEL; p. 3, bottom: © Peera_stockfoto/Shutterstock; p. 4: © north-tail/Shutterstock; p. 5: © Takashi Images/Shutterstock; p. 6: © Sean Pavone/Shutterstock; p. 7: © Altug Galip/Shutterstock; p. 9: © Oscar Espinosa/Shutterstock; p. 11: © Obs70/Shutterstock; p. 12: © Guitar photographer/Shutterstock; p. 13: © Lee Yiu Tung/Shutterstock; p. 14: © Ung151/Shutterstock; p. 16: © Martin Voeller/Shutterstock; p. 17: © Mirko Kuzmanovic/Shutterstock; p. 19: © beeboys/Shutterstock; p. 20: © kuremo/Shutterstock; p. 22: © Jo Panuwat D/Shutterstock; p. 25: © ct_photo/Shutterstock; p. 27: © khuntapol/Shutterstock; p. 29: © Shawn.ccf/Shutterstock; p. 31: © AKKHARAT JARUSILAWONG/Shutterstock; p. 39: © Courtesy of Ryokan Kurashiki/Kenji Kudo; p. 47: © VTT Studio/Shutterstock; p. 49: © WildSnap/Shutterstock; p. 53: © Courtesy of Hoshino Resorts; p. 61: © Pinglabel/Shutterstock; p. 66: © korinnna/Shutterstock; p. 73: © Nigel Jarvis/Shutterstock; p. 75: © Luoxi/Shutterstock; p. 77: © Sergey_Bogomyako/Shutterstock; p. 78: © Yobab/Shutterstock; p. 79: © Nutchanunr/Shutterstock; p. 82: © Applepy/Shutterstock; p. 83: © nuu_jeed/Shutterstock; p. 85: © ItzaVU/Shutterstock; p. 91: © f11photo/Shutterstock ; p. 100: © FotoNova Shop/Shutterstock; p. 107: © Panwasin seemala/Shutterstock; p. 108: © posztos/Shutterstock; p. 110: © Pakpoom Phummee/Shutterstock; p. 112: © Danny Ye/Shutterstock; p. 113: © Tatiana SP/Shutterstock; p. 116, top: © Ned Snowman/Shutterstock; p. 116, bottom: © Sergio Delle Vedove/Shutterstock; p. 117: © Picturesque Japan/Shutterstock; p. 118: © ninabossley/Shutterstock; p. 120: © Jasmiennn/Shutterstock; p. 121: © ItzaVU/Shutterstock; p. 123: © cowardlion/Shutterstock; p. 124: © kino_250/Shutterstock; p. 126: © Takashi Images/Shuuterstock; p. 130: © Pabkov/Shutterstock; p. 132: © Malcolm Fairman/Shutterstock.; p. 136: © InfantryDavid/Shutterstock; p. 138: © KenSoftTH/Shutterstock; p. 139: © Kingmaya Studio/Shutterstock; p. 145: Courtesy of Hoshino Resorts; p. 146: Courtesy of Park Hotel Tokyo; p. 148: Courtesy of TSUKI Hotel; p. 150: Courtesy of Hoshino Resorts; p. 167: © Osugi/Shutterstock; p. 168: © Lecker Studio/Shutterstock; p. 171: © kuremo/Shutterstock.; p. 173: © Karl Panganiban/Shutterstock; p. 175: © Rizky Ade Jonathan/Shutterstock; p. 178: © Picturesque Japan/Shutterstock; p. 184: © Lewis Tse/Shutterstock; p. 187: © Caito/Shutterstock; p. 188: © aiyoshi597/Shutterstock; p. 190: © Ned Snowman/Shutterstock; p. 191: © Hiroshi-Mori-Stock/Shutterstock; p. 194: © Stockinasia/Shutterstock; p. 196: © Rileyjo/Shutterstock; p. 198: © Carolyne Parent/Shutterstock; p. 200: © kuremo/Shutterstock; p. 204: © Tammy95/Shutterstock; p. 205: © Naoto Shinkai/Shutterstock; p. 210: Courtesy of Park Hyatt Tokyo; p. 216: © Wirestock Creators/Shutterstock; p. 218: © Pakpoom Phummee/Shutterstock; p. 220: © Tang Yan Song/Shutterstock.; p. 223: © Guadalupe Polito/Shutterstock; p. 224: © yu_photo/Shutterstock; p. 226: © Bisual Photo/Shutterstock; p. 229: © SandraSWC/Shutterstock; p. 231: © Sanne Dost/Shutterstock; p. 235: © simpletun/Shutterstock; p. 236: © dowraik/Shutterstock; p. 240: © linegold/Shutterstock; p. 241: © Eduardo Firman/Shutterstock; p. 242: © Florian Augustin/Shutterstock; p. 249: © picture cells/Shutterstock; p. 250: © dekitateyo/Shutterstock; p. 252: © MasaPhoto/Shutterstock; p. 254: © Pierre Jean Durieu/Shutterstock; p. 256: © Sean Pavone/Shutterstock; p. 259: © Summit Art Creations/Shutterstock; p. 261: © DFLC Prints/Shutterstock; p. 264: © Phattana Stock/Shutterstock; p. 265: © Suthikait Teerawattanaphan/Shutterstock; p. 268: © Scirocco340/Shutterstock; p. 271: © Kit Leong/Shutterstock; p. 275: © Magdanatka/Shutterstock; p. 277: © Suthikait Teerawattanaphan/Shutterstock; p. 280, top: © DigitalPearls/Shutterstock.; p. 280, bottom: © MoreGallery/Shutterstock; p. 283: © BlueOrange Studio/Shutterstock; p. 286: © Daniele Aloisi/Shutterstock.; p. 288: © Cristi Croitoru/Shutterstock; p. 290: © pio3/Shutterstock; p. 299: © SNEHIT PHOTO/Shutterstock; p. 301: © FOTOGRIN/Shutterstock; p. 302: © Shawn.ccf/Shutterstock; p. 303: © cowardlion/Shutterstock; p. 304: © Photostravellers/Shutterstock; p. 306: © ItzaVU/Shutterstock; p. 307: © Jujumin Chu/Shutterstock; p. 315: © DigitalPearls/Shutterstock; p. 316: © Mistervlad/Shutterstock; p. 321: Courtesy of Garrya Nijo Castle Kyoto; p. 328: © marcobrivio.gallery/Shutterstock; p. 335: Courtesy of Ramen Nishiki; p. 337: © 18th Studio/Shutterstock; p. 340: © EvergreenPlanet/Shutterstock; p. 344: © Kristi Blokhin/Shutterstock; p. 347: © tvcuong8892/Shutterstock; p. 348: © Sean Pavone/Shutterstock; p. 353:

© Luca Brajato/Shutterstock; p. 356: © ItzaVU/Shutterstock; p. 359: © Phuong D. Nguyen/Shutterstock; p. 361: © Mirko Kuzmanovic/Shutterstock; p. 362: © Tupungato/Shutterstock; p. 366: © Mirko Kuzmanovic/Shutterstock; p. 370: © bonchan/Shutterstock; p. 371: © Nami Uchida/Shutterstock; p. 374: © iamlukyeee/Shutterstock; p. 376: © b-hide the scene/Shutterstock.; p. 378: © © MIKIMOTO PEARL ISLAND; p. 384: © CelTiArt/Shutterstock; p. 385: © mTaira/Shutterstock; p. 388: © MoreGallery/ Shutterstock; p. 389: © Pack-Shot/Shutterstock; p. 390: Courtesy of Korinkyo; p. 395: © TK Kurikawa/ Shutterstock; p. 399: © Neale Cousland/Shutterstock; p. 400: © Dmitry Morgan/Shutterstock; p. 402: © Sabino Parente/Shutterstock; p. 405: © Sean Pavone/Shutterstock; p. 407: © posztos/Shutterstock; p. 408: © Blanscape/Shutterstock; p. 411: © Shawn.ccf/Shutterstock; p. 413: Courtesy of Ryokan Kurashiki/Kenji Kudo; p. 419: © Alex_Mastro/Shutterstock; p. 421: © Koshiro K/Shutterstock; p. 426: © north-tail/Shutterstock; p. 434: © popcatter/Shutterstock; p. 435: © rweisswald/Shutterstock; p. 436: © Sean Pavone/Shutterstock; p. 443: © Sean Pavone/Shutterstock; p. 448: © Sean Pavone/ Shutterstock; p. 452: © Malcolm Fairman/Shutterstock; p. 458: © Luciano Mortula - LGM/Shutterstock; p. 461: © Lorevia/Shutterstock; p. 462: © Jellygoround/Shutterstock; p. 468: © SubstanceTproductions/ Shutterstock; p. 476: © beeboys/Shutterstock; p. 481: © Sean Pavone/Shutterstock; p. 483: © fukez84/ Shutterstock; p. 485: © Malcolm Fairman/Shutterstock; p. 487: © Florian Augustin/Shutterstock; p. 489: © Amehime/Shutterstock; p. 492: © Akio Miki JP/Shutterstock; p. 493: Courtesy of Nakanishi Chinshoen; p. 495: © show999/Shutterstock; p. 500: © YingHui Liu/Shutterstock; p. 501: © Mathias Berlin/Shutterstock; p. 502: © 365 Focus Photography/Shutterstock; p. 505: © Archcultures/ Shutterstock; p. 507: © lansa/Shutterstock; p. 510: © Alex_Mastro/Shutterstock; p. 512: © Attila JANDI/ Shutterstock; p. 513: © Sean Pavone/Shutterstock; p. 518: © goriyan/Shutterstock; p. 520: © Marlon Trottmann/Shutterstock; p. 522: © Jennifer M Piper/Shutterstock; p. 527: © since1827/Shutterstock; p. 531: © Blanscape/Shutterstock; p. 532: © byvalet/Shutterstock; p. 533: © cowardlion/Shutterstock.; p. 534: © Noa_80/Shutterstock; p. 536: © Pairoj R/Shutterstock; p. 537: © phinit/Shutterstock; p. 538: © cowardlion/Shutterstock; p. 545: © seaonweb/Shutterstock; p. 548: © Joshua Hawley/Shutterstock; p. 549: © cowardlion/Shutterstock; p. 554: © RUBEN M RAMOS/Shutterstock; p. 558: © Blanscape/ Shutterstock; p. 561: Courtesy of Unzen Kanko Hotel; p. 566: © Sean Pavone/Shutterstock; p. 567: © Windyboy/Shutterstock; p. 573: © RITSU MIYAMOTO/Shutterstock; p. 576: © aido/Shutterstock; p. 581: © iamlukyeee/Shutterstock; p. 584: © Vassamon Anansukkasem/Shutterstock; p. 585: Courtesy of Beppu SUGINOI HOTEL; p. 588: © dreamsky/Shutterstock; p. 590: © Vassamon Anansukkasem/ Shutterstock; p. 594: © Veerachart/Shutterstock; p. 595: © Athikhom Saengchai/Shutterstock; p. 596: © kazu8/Shutterstock; p. 598: © d3_plus/Shutterstock; p. 602: © PixHound/Shutterstock; p. 603: © Sean Pavone/Shutterstock; p. 605: © HIROSHI WATANABE/Shutterstock; p. 608: © Spyan/ Shutterstock; p. 609: © Kendo Nice/Shutterstock; p. 612: © Spyan/Shutterstock; p. 616: © Shawn.ccf/ Shutterstock; p. 618: © AndyLai/Shutterstock; p. 619: © Kanuman/Shutterstock; p. 621: © icosha/ Shutterstock; p. 623: © Piith Hant/Shutterstock; p. 624: © AthenaC/Shutterstock; p. 631: © Terence Toh Chin Eng/Shutterstock; p. 632: © yoshimi maeda/Shutterstock; p. 633: © Ricky Shen/Shutterstock; p. 635: © Korkusung/Shutterstock; p. 639: © Sean Pavone/Shutterstock; p. 640: © Richie Chan/ Shutterstock; p. 647, top: © HookeePui Lkb1235/Shutterstock; p. 647, bottom: © Niradj/Shutterstock.; p. 650: © tasch/Shutterstock; p. 652: © Pruchawal/Shutterstock; p. 654: Courtesy of JR Tower Hotel Nikko Sapporo; p. 656: © VTT Studio/Shutterstock; p. 658: © Pixel Wanderer/Shutterstock.; p. 660: © b-hide the scene/Shutterstock; p. 663, top: © Vassamon Anansukkasem/Shutterstock; p. 663, bottom: © SUJITRA CHAOWDEE/Shutterstock; p. 666: © Korkusung/Shutterstock; p. 670: © Warith82/ Shutterstock; p. 671: © AsiaTravel/Shutterstock; p. 673: © IamDoctorEgg/Shutterstock; p. 677: © Spyan/Shutterstock; p. 678: © rayints/Shutterstock; p. 680: © Tatsuo Nakamura/Shutterstock; p. 681: © YOSHI K/Shutterstock; p. 683: © Sean Pavone/Shutterstock